Teacher's Edition

Level B | Volume 1

Hampton-Brown

EDGE

Reading, Writing & Language

PROGRAM AUTHORS

David W. Moore

Deborah J. Short

Michael W. Smith

Alfred W. Tatum

Literature Consultant

René Saldaña, Jr.

NATIONAL GEOGRAPHIC LEARNING | CENGAGE Learning

NATIONAL GEOGRAPHIC LEARNING | CENGAGE Learning

Acknowledgments
Grateful acknowledgment is given to the authors, artists, photographers, museums, publishers, and agents for permission to reprint copyrighted material. Every effort has been made to secure the appropriate permission. If any omissions have been made or if corrections are required, please contact the Publisher.

Photographic Credits
Cover: Avian Island, the Pantanal, Mato Grosso, Brazil, Mike Bueno. Photograph © Mike Bueno/National Geographic Stock.

Acknowledgments continue on page Ack 1.

National Geographic Learning | Cengage Learning
1 Lower Ragsdale Drive
Building 1, Suite 200
Monterey, CA 93940

Cengage Learning is a leading provider of customized learning solutions with office locations around the globe, including Singapore, the United Kingdom, Australia, Mexico, Brazil, and Japan. Locate your local office at **www.cengage.com/global**.

Visit National Geographic Learning online at **ngl.cengage.com**
Visit our corporate website at **www.cengage.com**

Printed in the USA.
RR Donnelley, Menasha, WI

ISBN: 978-12854-39686

Printed in the United States of America
13 14 15 16 17 18 19 20 21 22
10 9 8 7 6 5 4 3 2 1

Contents at a Glance

Created by Leaders in Adolescent Literacy

Reviewers

We gratefully acknowledge the many contributions of the following dedicated educators in creating a program that is not only pedagogically sound, but also appealing to and motivating for high school students. We are greatful to the advice and support of the teachers who used prior versions of Edge who directed us in this copyright update.

Literature Consultant

Dr. René Saldaña, Jr., Ph.D.
Assistant Professor
Texas Tech University

Dr. Saldaña teaches English and education at the university level and is the author of *The Jumping Tree* (2001) and *Finding Our Way: Stories* (Random House/Wendy Lamb Books, 2003). More recently, several of his stories have appeared in anthologies such as *Face Relations, Guys Write for GUYS READ, Every Man for Himself,* and *Make Me Over,* and in magazines such as *Boy's Life* and *READ*.

Teacher Reviewers

Felisa Araujo-Rodriguez
English Teacher
Highlands HS
San Antonio, TX

Barbara Barbin
Former HS ESL Teacher
Aldine ISD
Houston, TX

Joseph Berkowitz
ESOL Chairperson
John A. Ferguson Sr. HS
Miami, FL

Dr. LaQuanda Brown-Avery
Instructional Assistant Principal
McNair MS
Decatur, GA

Troy Campbell
Teacher
Lifelong Education Charter
Los Angeles, CA

John Oliver Cox
English Language Development Teacher
Coronado USD
Coronado, CA

Clairin DeMartini
Reading Coordinator
Clark County SD
Las Vegas, NV

Lori Kite Eli
High School Reading Teacher
Pasadena HS
Pasadena, TX

Debra Elkins
ESOL Teamleader/Teacher
George Bush HS
Fort Bend, IN

Lisa Fretzin
Reading Consultant
Niles North HS
Skokie, IL

Karen H. Gouede
Asst. Principal, ESL
John Browne HS
Flushing, NY

Alison Hyde
ESOL Teacher
Morton Ranch HS
Katy, TX

Patricia James
Reading Specialist
Brevard County
Melbourne Beach, FL

Dr. Anna Leibovich
ESL Teacher
Forest Hills HS
New York, NY

Donna D. Mussulman
Teacher
Belleville West HS
Belleville, IL

Rohini A. Parikh
Educator
Seward Park School
New York, NY

Sally Nan Ruskin
English/Reading Teacher
Braddock SHS
Miami, FL

Pamela Sholly
Teacher
Oceanside USD
Oceanside, CA

Dilmit Singh
Teacher/EL Coordinator
Granada Hills Charter HS
Granada Hills, CA

Amanda E. Stewart
Reading Teacher
Winter Park High School
Winter Park, FL

Beverly Troiano
ESL Teacher
Chicago Discovery Academy
Chicago, IL

Dr. Varavarnee Vaddhanayana
ESOL Coordinator
Clarkston HS
Clarkston, GA

Donna Reese Wallace
Reading Coach
Alternative Education
Orange County
Orlando, FL

Bonnie Woelfel
Reading Specialist
Escondido HS
Escondido, CA

Pian Y. Wong
English Teacher
High School of American Studies
New York, NY

Izumi Yoshioka
English Teacher
Washington Irving HS
New York, NY

Student Reviewers

We also gratefully acknowledge the high school students who read and reviewed selections and tested some of the program's digital components.

Program Authors

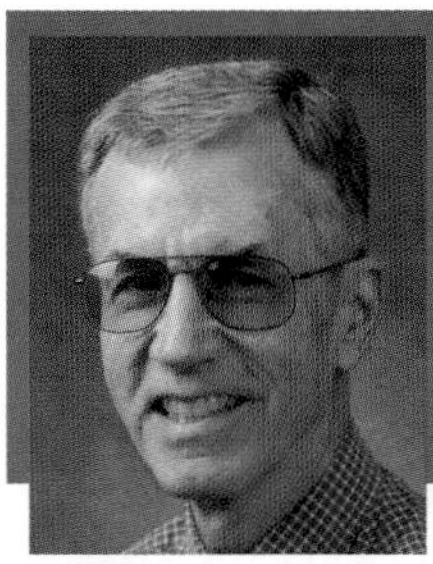

David W. Moore, Ph.D.
Arizona State University

Dr. Moore taught high school in Arizona public schools before becoming a professor of education. He co-chaired the International Reading Association's Commission on Adolescent Literacy and is actively involved with several professional associations. His thirty-year publication record balances research reports, professional articles, book chapter and books including *Developing Readers and Writers in the Content Areas, Teaching Adolescents Who Struggle with Reading, and Principled Practices for Adolescent Literacy.*

Deborah J. Short, Ph.D.
Center for Applied Linguistics

Dr. Short is a co-developer of the research-validated SIOP Model for sheltered instruction. She has directed scores of studies on English Language Learners and published scholarly articles in *TESOL Quarterly, The Journal of Educational Research, Language Teaching Research*, and many others. Dr. Short also co-wrote a policy report: *Double the Work: Challenges and Solutions to Acquiring Language and Academic Literacy for Adolescent English Language Learners.* She has conducted extensive research on secondary level newcomers programs and on long term English language learners.

Michael W. Smith, Ph.D.
Temple University

Dr. Michael Smith joined the ranks of college teachers after eleven years teaching high school English. He has won awards for his teaching both at the high school and college level. He contributed to the Common Core State Standards initiative by serving on the Aspects of Text Complexity working group. His research focuses on how readers read and talk about texts and what motivates adolescents' reading and writing both in and out of school. His books include *"Reading Don't Fix No Chevys": Literacy in the Lives of Young Men, Fresh Takes on Teaching Literary Elements: How to Teach What Really Matters About Character, Setting, Point of View, and Theme,* and *Oh, Yeah?! Putting Argument to Work Both in School and Out.*

Alfred W. Tatum, Ph.D.
University of Illinois at Chicago

Dr. Tatum began his career as an eighth-grade teacher and reading specialist. He conducts research on the power of texts and literacy to reshape the life outcomes of striving readers. His research focuses on the literacy development of African American adolescent males. He has served on the National Advisory Reading Committee of the National Assessment of Educational Progress (NAEP). Dr. Tatum's books include *Reading for Their Life: (Re)Building the Textual Lineages of African American Adolescent Males* and *Teaching Reading to Black Adolescent Males: Closing the Achievement Gap.*

Hampton-Brown
EDGE
Prepare all students for college and career success with dynamic National Geographic content and authentic, multicultural literature.
Access relevant and motivating content with print or digital options
Prepare students for Common Core State Standard success
Utilize systematic and focused teaching materials

Build Reading and Writing Power

Level A

Level B

Level C

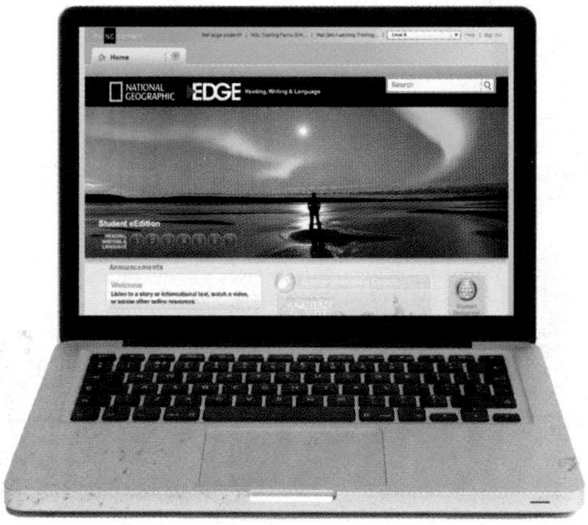

myNGconnect.com

Learn the Fundamentals

NEWCOMER
Inside the USA

Inside Phonics

Fundamentals

Digital and Print Student Resources

Meet the full range of student needs with an abundance of resources.

Student Materials

Student Edition

Interactive Practice Book

Grammar and Writing Practice Book

Selection Readings, Close Readings, and Fluency Models on CD and in MP3 format

Award-winning titles with built-in support

Leveled Library

InZone Library

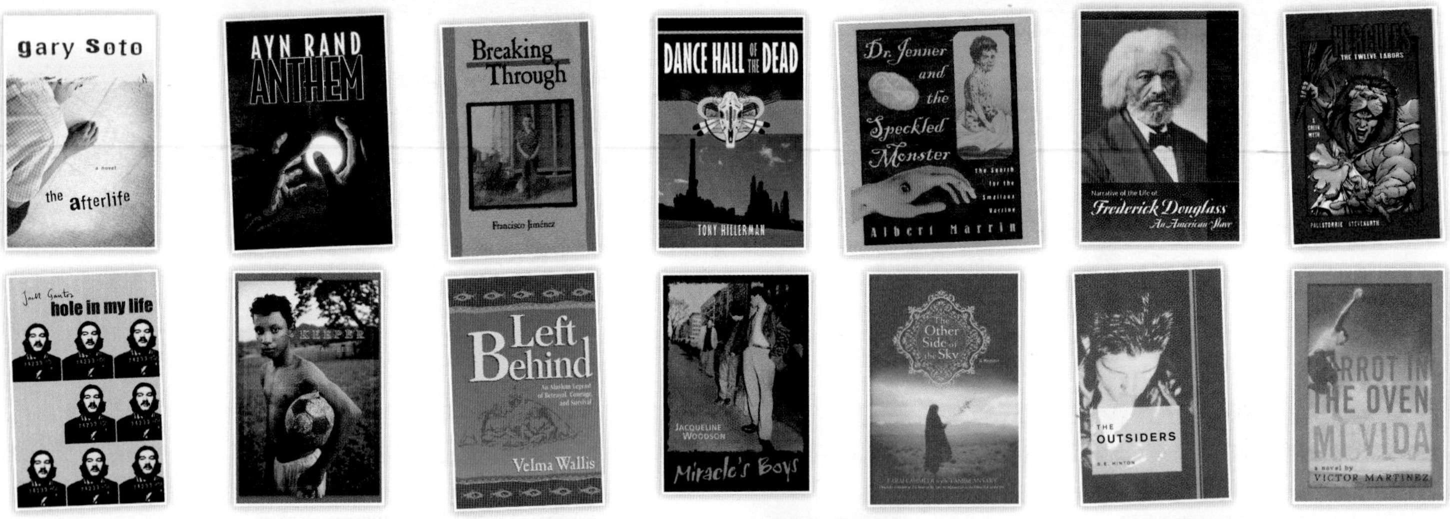

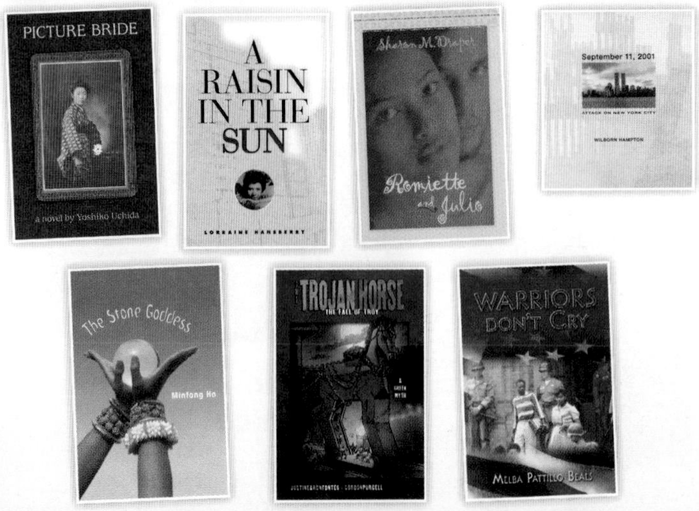

Also available

Complex Text Library

Informational texts at grade-level complexity include video and audio support.

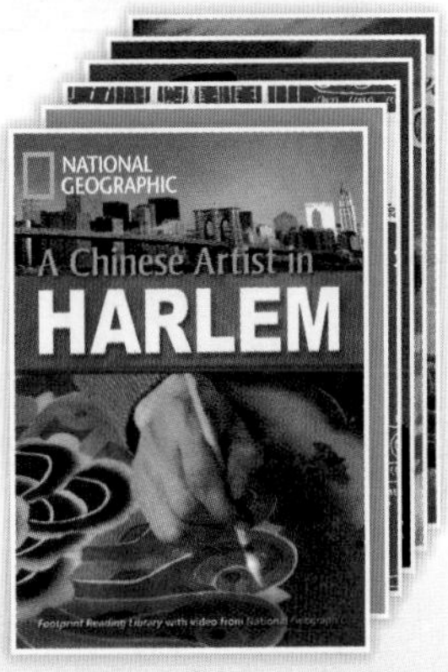

Also available

eBooks for mobile devices

Experience interactive text with embedded:

- Audio
- Highlighting
- Note-taking

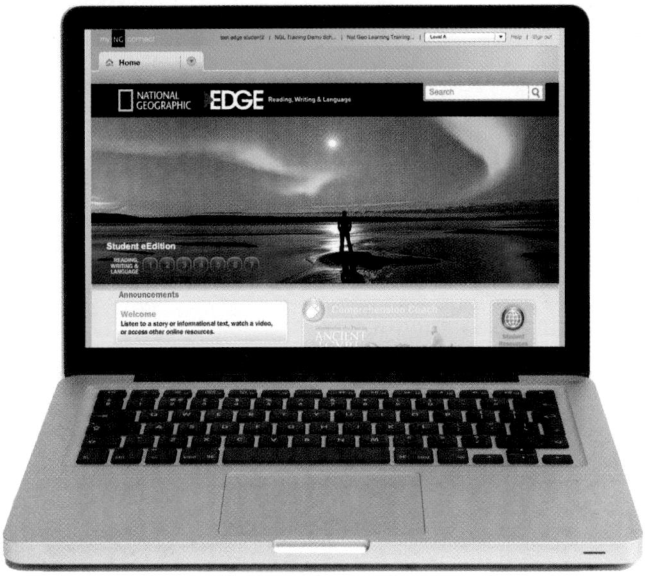

myNGconnect.com for Students

- Student eEdition
- My Assignments
- Digital Library
- Comprehension Coach
- Selection Recordings, Fluency Models, and Close Readings
- Language MP3s
- Links to Online Resources
- Glossaries in multiple languages

Comprehension Coach

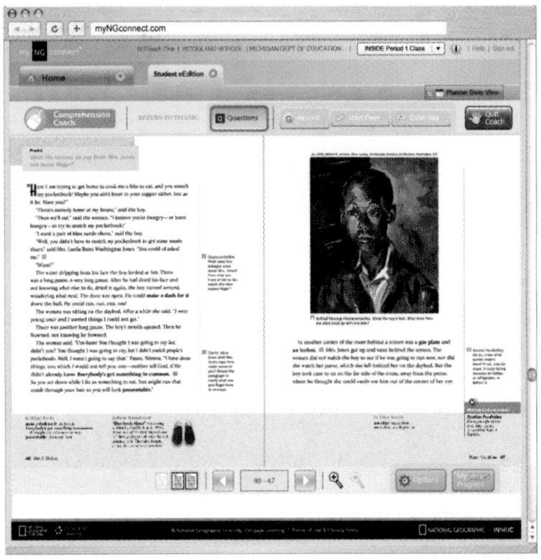

Practice and assess fluency with built-in voice recognition and automatic WCPM scoring

Digital Library Viewer

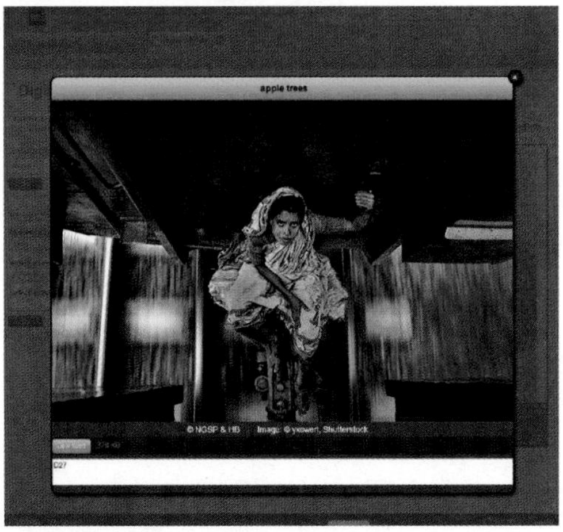

Projection-ready images to spark discussion about Essential Questions.

Digital and Print Teacher Resources

Help all students become college and career ready with systematic and focused teacher resources.

Teacher Materials

Teacher's Edition

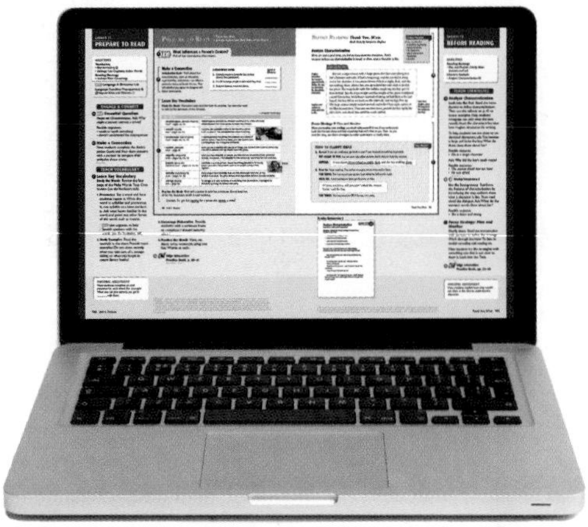

Teacher's eEdition

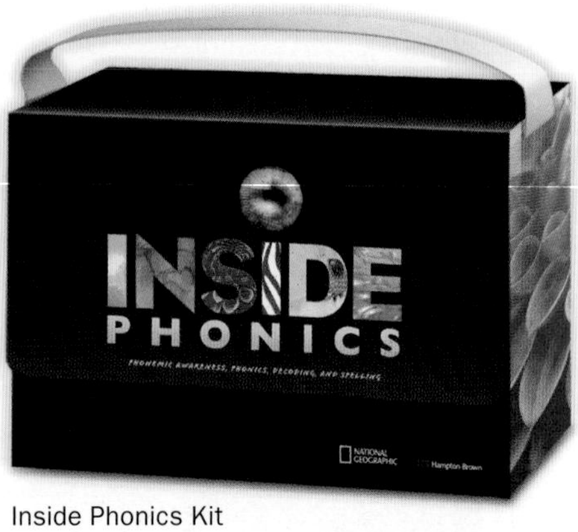

Inside Phonics Kit

Language & Grammar Lab

Language & Grammar Lab Teacher's Edition

Interactive Practice Book Teacher's Annotated Edition

Grammar and Writing Practice Book Teacher's Annotated Edition

Online Transparencies

- Reading
- Writing
- Grammar
- Language Functions
- Language Transfer

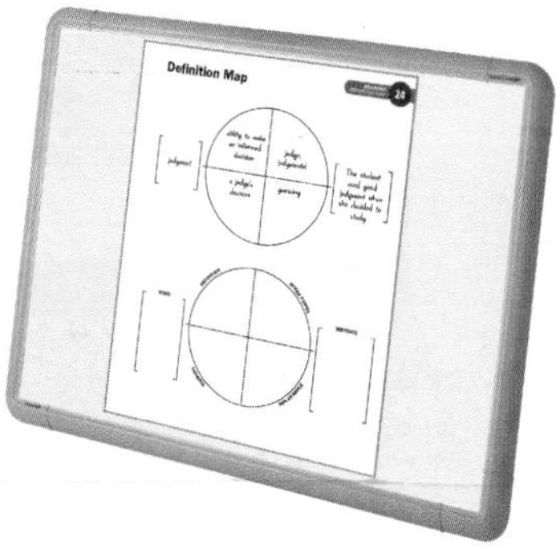

Assessments

Assessments Handbook

Unit Test Booklet and Teacher's Manual

Test Preparation for PARCC and Smarter Balanced Assessments

Level Tests

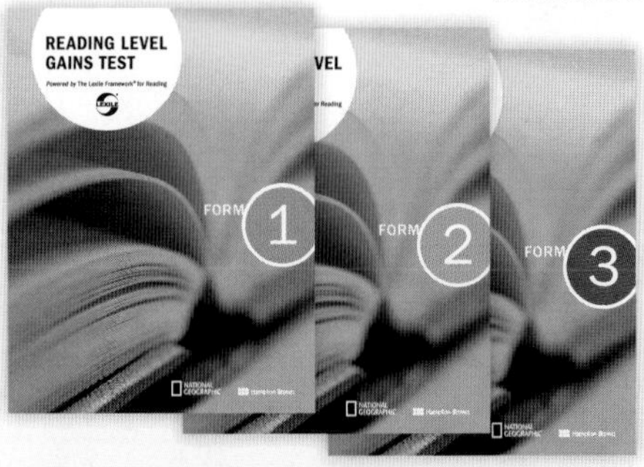

Reading Level Gains Tests

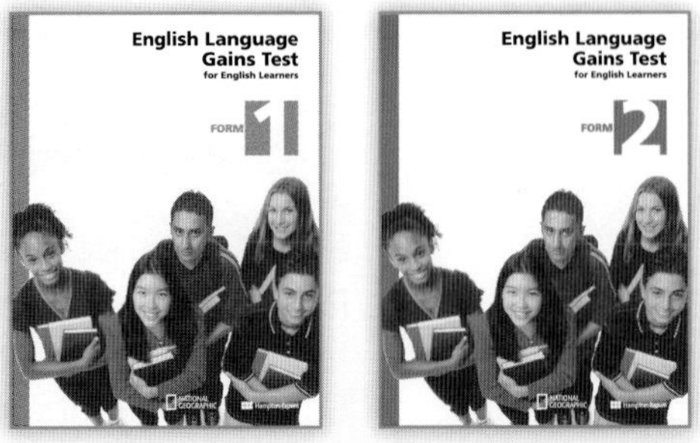

English Language Gains Tests

myNGconnect.com for Teachers

- eAssessment and progress reports
- Teacher's eEdition
- Transparencies
- PDFs of teaching and learning resources
- Family Newsletters in multiple languages
- Online Lesson Planner
- Online professional development

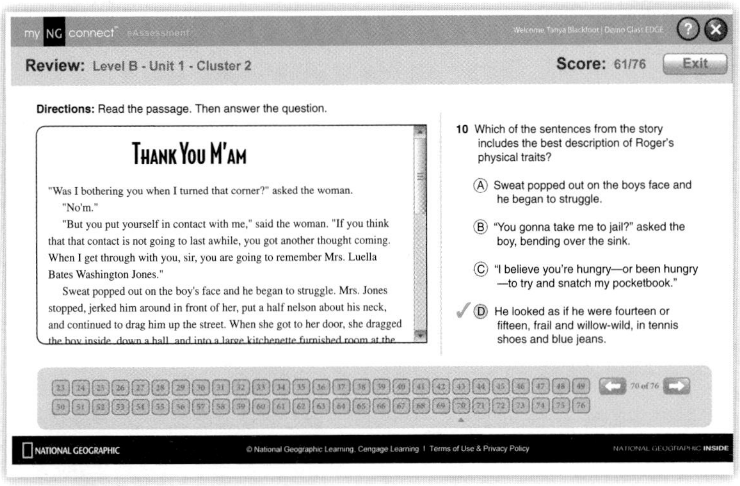

Online testing

Reports & Grading, with individualized reteaching prescriptions

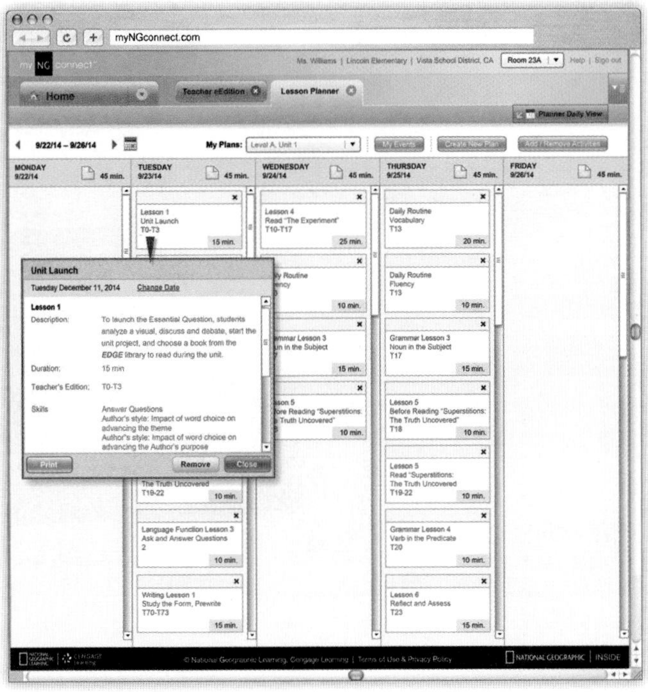

Online Lesson Planner

Also available

Complex Text Read Alouds

National Geographic articles aligned with Essential Questions

Compelling Content

Engage students with a balance of informational text and literature.

Informational Texts

- National Geographic articles
- Narrative nonfiction
- Expository texts
- Digital genres
- Arguments

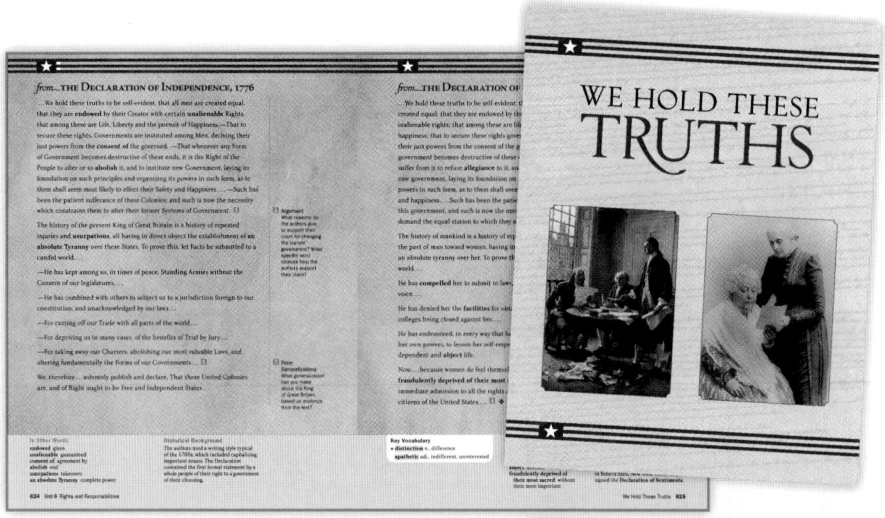

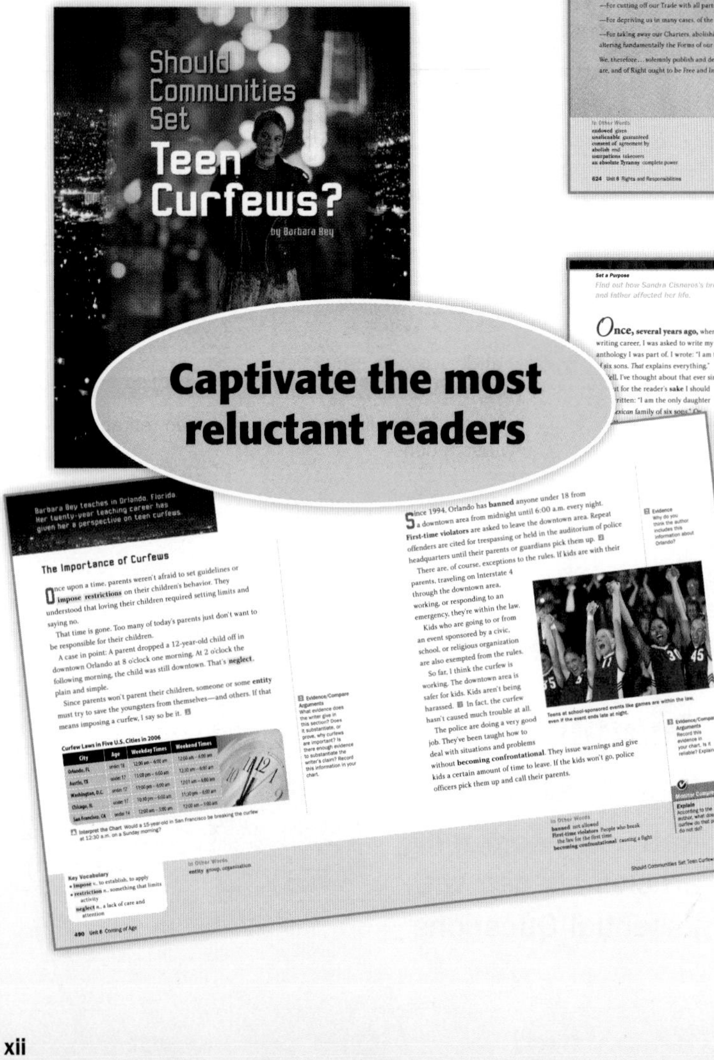

Captivate the most reluctant readers

Literature

- Common Core Exemplars
- Multicultural authors and characters
- Contemporary literature
- Poems and plays
- Classics

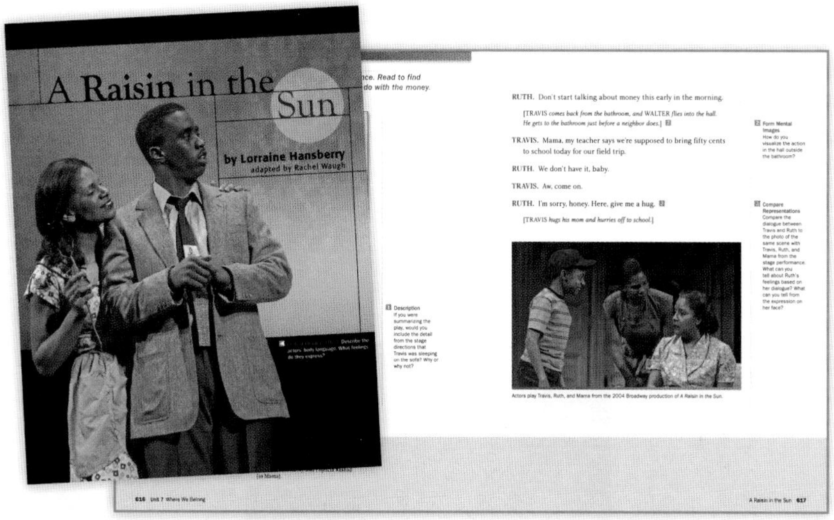

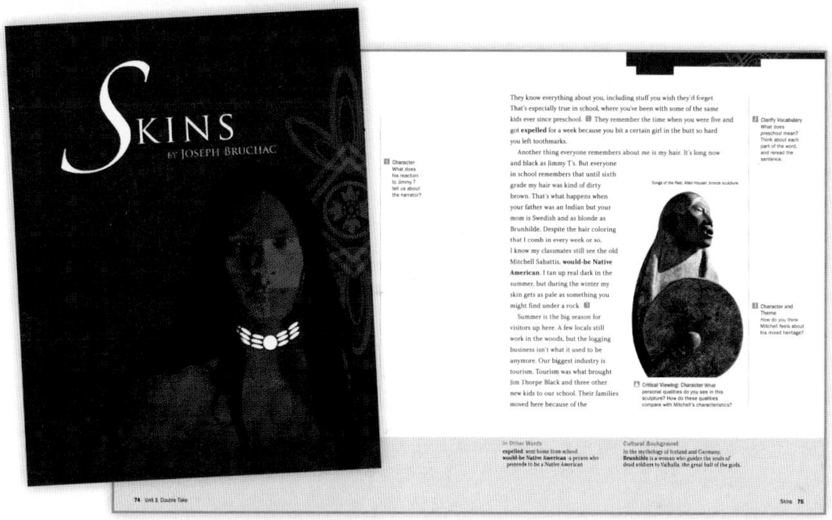

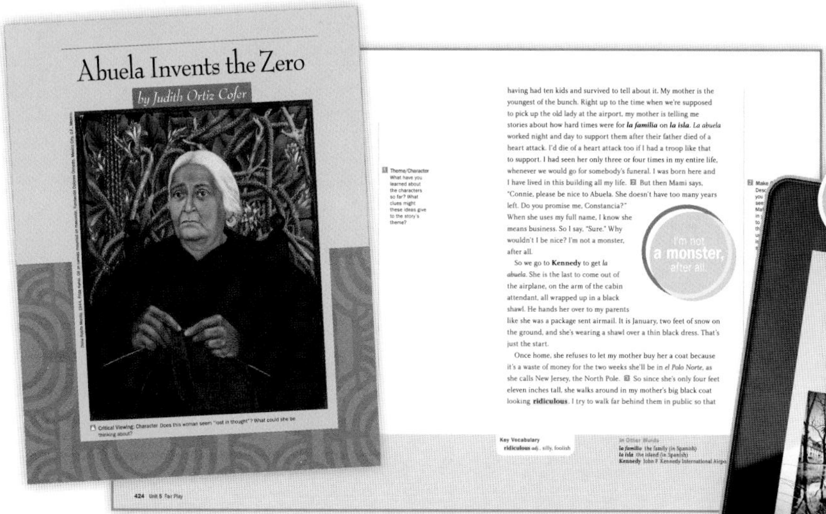

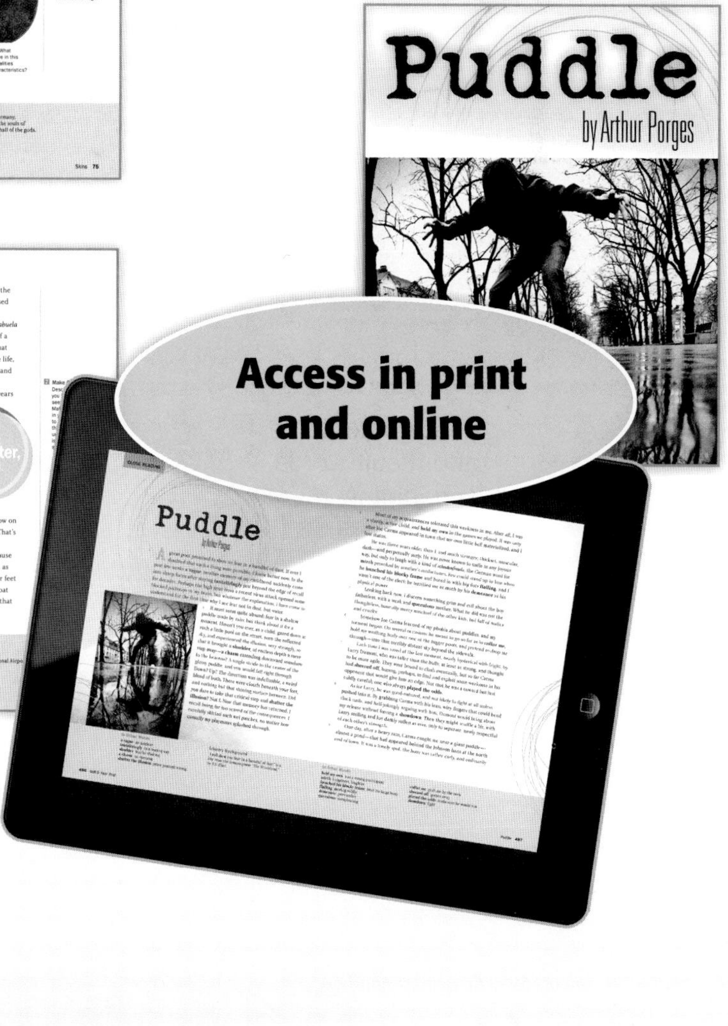

Reading for All Levels

Support all students to become college and career ready.

Build language and literacy with robust instruction and accessible instructional selections.

Selections are divided into manageable chunks

Text-dependent questions

Critical Viewing questions for analysis across artistic mediums

Predict
What life lessons do you think Mrs. Jones will teach Roger?

"Here I am trying to get home to cook me a bite to eat, and you snatch my pocketbook! Maybe you ain't been to your supper either, late as it be. Have you?"

"There's nobody home at my house," said the boy.

"Then we'll eat," said the woman. "I believe you're hungry—or been hungry—to try to snatch my pocketbook!"

"I want a pair of blue suede shoes," said the boy.

"Well, you didn't have to snatch *my* pocketbook to get some suede shoes," said Mrs. Luella Bates Washington Jones. "You could of asked me." 6

"M'am?"

The water dripping from his face the boy looked at her. There was a long pause. A very long pause. After he had dried his face and not knowing what else to do, dried it again, the boy turned around, wondering what next. The door was open. He could **make a dash for it** down the hall. He could run, run, run, *run!*

The woman was sitting on the daybed. After a while she said, "I were young once and I wanted things I could not get."

There was another long pause. The boy's mouth opened. Then he frowned, not knowing he frowned.

The woman said, "Um-hum! You thought I was going to say *but*, didn't you? You thought I was going to say, *but I didn't snatch people's pocketbooks*. Well, I wasn't going to say that." Pause. Silence. "I have done things, too, which I would not tell you, son—neither tell God, if He didn't already know. **Everybody's got something in common.** 7 So you set down while I fix us something to eat. You might run that comb through your hair so you will look **presentable**."

6 Characterization What does this dialogue show about Mrs. Jones? From what you know of her so far, would she have helped Roger?

7 Clarify Ideas Does what Mrs. Jones says here make sense to you? Reread the paragraph to clarify what she and Roger have in common.

Jim, 1930, William H. Johnson. Oil on canvas, Smithsonian American Art Museum, Washington, D.C.

A Critical Viewing: Characterization Study the boy's look. What lines from the story could go with this look?

In another corner of the room behind a screen was a **gas plate** and **an icebox.** 8 Mrs. Jones got up and went behind the screen. The woman did not watch the boy to see if he was going to run now, nor did she watch her purse, which she left behind her on the daybed. But the boy took care to sit on the far side of the room, away from the purse, where he thought she could easily see him out of the corner of her eye

8 Access Vocabulary Do you know what *screen* means here? If not, look for clues. It must be big because an icebox, or refrigerator, is behind it.

Monitor Comprehension
Confirm Prediction Were you right about what Mrs. Jones is teaching Roger? Explain.

In Other Words
make a dash for it try to run
Everybody's got something in common. All people are alike in some way.
presentable clean and neat

Cultural Background
"Blue Suede Shoes" was a song written by Carl Perkins in 1955. It was one of the first big rock and roll hits, and teens all over the U.S. listened to it. They also bought shoes like the ones shown here.

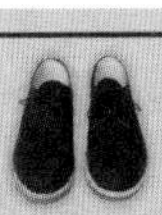

In Other Words
gas plate small stove
an icebox a refrigerator

48 Unit 1 Choices

Thank You, M'am 49

Student Edition

Restatements of difficult words and idioms

Background building

Frequent comprehension checks

Selection recordings and fluency models are available in CD and online in MP3 format

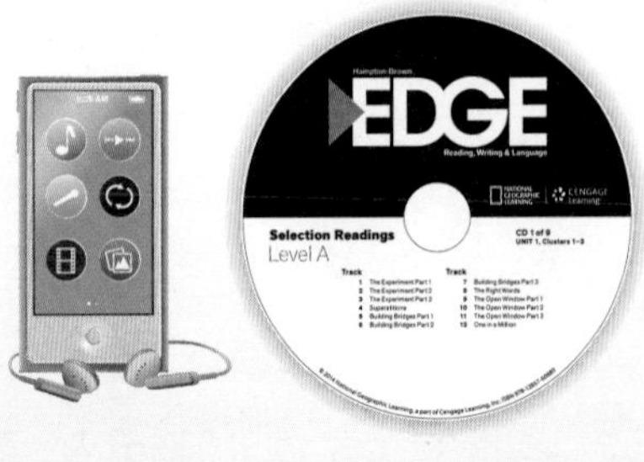

CCSS **Instructional Texts**
Complex Texts
Independent Reading

Apply reading skills and strategies with complex texts.

CLOSE READING

Common Core Exemplars and other grade-level complex texts

Paragraph numbers to support students in citing text evidence

CLOSE READING

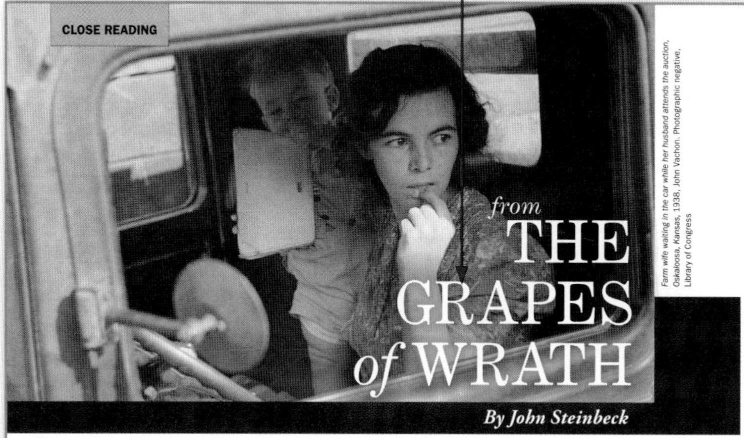

Farm wife waiting in the car while her husband attends the auction, Oskaloosa, Kansas, 1938, John Vachon. Photographic negative, Library of Congress

Critical Viewing: Mood What is the mood, or feeling, of this photograph? How did the photographer achieve the mood?

1 "...the road is full a them families goin' west. Never seen so many. Gets worse all a time. Wonder where the hell they all come from?"

2 "Wonder where they all go to," said Mae. "Come here for gas sometimes, but they don't hardly never buy nothin' else. People says they steal. We **ain't got nothin' layin'** around. They never stole nothin' from us."

3 Big Bill, munching his pie, looked up the road through the screened window. "Better tie your stuff down. I think you got some of 'em comin' now."

4 A 1926 Nash **sedan** pulled wearily off the highway. The back seat was piled nearly to the ceiling with sacks, with pots and pans, and on the very top, right up against the ceiling, two boys rode. On the top of the car, a mattress and a folded tent; tent poles tied along the running board. The car pulled up to the gas pumps. A dark-haired, hatchet-faced man got slowly out. And the two boys slid down from the load and hit the ground.

5 Mae walked around the counter and stood in the door. The man was dressed in gray wool trousers and a blue shirt, dark blue with sweat on the back and under the arms. The boys in overalls and nothing else, ragged patched overalls. Their hair was light, and it stood up evenly all over their heads, for it had been **roached**. Their faces were streaked with dust. They went directly to the mud puddle under the hose and dug their toes into the mud.

6 The man asked, "Can we **git** some water, ma'am?"

7 A look of annoyance crossed Mae's face. "Sure, go ahead." She said softly over her shoulder, "I'll keep my eye on the hose." She watched while the man slowly unscrewed the radiator cap and ran the hose in.

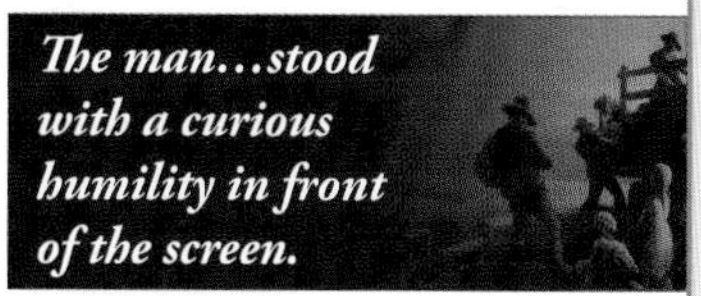

8 A woman in the car, a flaxen-haired woman, said, "See if you can't git it here."

9 The man turned off the hose and screwed on the cap again. The little boys took the hose from him and they upended it and drank thirstily. The man took off his dark, stained hat and stood with a curious **humility** in front of the screen. "**Could you see your way to** sell us a loaf of bread, ma'am?"

10 Mae said, "This ain't a grocery store. We got bread to make **san'widges**."

11 "I know, ma'am." His humility was **insistent**. "We need bread and there **ain't nothin' for quite a piece**, they say."

12 " 'F we sell bread we gonna run out." Mae's tone was **faltering**.

13 "We're hungry," the man said.

14 "**Whyn't** you buy a san'widge? We got nice san'widges, hamburgs."

15 "We'd sure **admire** to do that, ma'am. But we can't. We got to make a dime do all of us." And he said embarrassedly, "We **ain't got but** a little."

16 Mae said, "You can't get no loaf a bread for a dime. We only got fifteen-cent loafs."

17 From behind her Al growled, "God Almighty, Mae, give 'em bread."

18 "We'll run out 'fore the bread truck comes."

In Other Words
a them families goin' of those families going
ain't got nothin' layin' don't have anything lying
sedan medium-sized car

Historical Background
In the early 1930s, a drought hit the midwestern U.S. and farmers in the area lost all their crops. This area became known as the **Dust Bowl** because of the wind storms that swept dust over everything. Many families packed what little they had left and drove west to work in the fields of California.

In Other Words
roached brushed to stand upright
git get
humility modesty, lack of pride
Could you see your way to Would you
san'widges sandwiches
insistent demanding, persistent
ain't nothin' for quite a piece isn't anything for quite a while
faltering uncertain, hesitating
Whyn't Why don't
admire like
ain't got but only have

90 Unit 1 Choices

Student Edition

Short, high-quality, authentic texts that merit reading and rereading

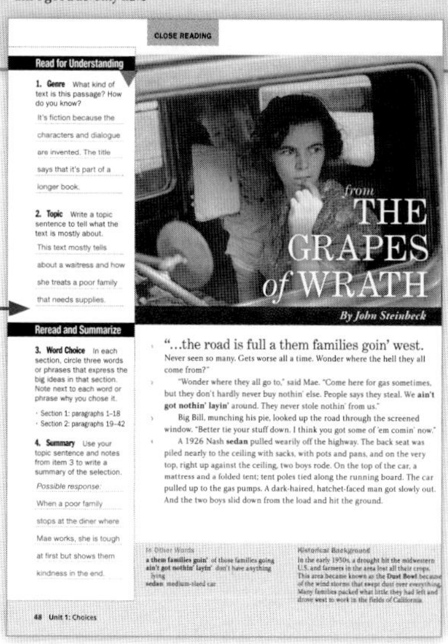
CLOSE READING

Read for Understanding

1. Genre What kind of text is this passage? How do you know?
It's fiction because the characters and dialogue are invented. The title says that it's part of a longer book.

2. Topic Write a topic sentence to tell what the text is mostly about.
This text mostly tells about a waitress and how she treats a poor family that needs supplies.

Reread and Summarize

3. Word Choice In each section, circle three words or phrases that express the big ideas in that section. Note next to each word or phrase why you chose it.
· Section 1: paragraphs 1–18
· Section 2: paragraphs 19–42

4. Summary Use your topic sentence and notes from item 3 to write a summary of the selection.
Possible response: When a poor family stops at the diner where Mae works, she is tough at first but shows them kindness in the end.

from THE GRAPES of WRATH
By John Steinbeck

"...the road is full a them families goin' west. Never seen so many. Gets worse all a time. Wonder where the hell they all come from?"

"Wonder where they all go to," said Mae. "Come here for gas sometimes, but they don't hardly never buy nothin' else. People says they steal. We **ain't got nothin' layin'** around. They never stole nothin' from us."

Big Bill, munching his pie, looked up the road through the screened window. "Better tie your stuff down. I think you got some of 'em comin' now."

A 1926 Nash **sedan** pulled wearily off the highway. The back seat was piled nearly to the ceiling with sacks, with pots and pans, and on the very top, right up against the ceiling, two boys rode. On the top of the car, a mattress and a folded tent; tent poles tied along the running board. The car pulled up to the gas pumps. A dark-haired, hatchet-faced man got slowly out. And the two boys slid down from the load and hit the ground.

In Other Words
a them families goin' of those families going
ain't got nothin' layin' don't have anything lying
sedan medium-sized car

Historical Background
In the early 1930s, a drought hit the midwestern U.S. and farmers in the area lost all their crops. This area became known as the **Dust Bowl** because of the wind storms that swept dust over everything. Many families packed what little they had left and drove west to work in the fields of California.

48 Unit 1: Choices

Interactive versions of texts support note-taking

Interactive Practice Book

Apply skills in independent reading.

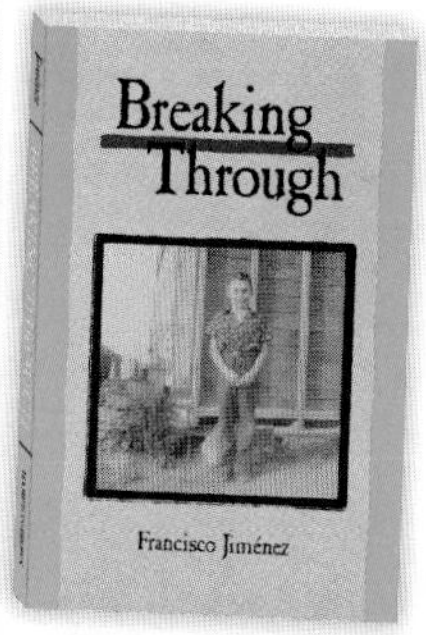

Leveled Library

Systematic and Focused Teacher Support

Meet the Common Core with coordinated lessons that put texts at the center of instruction.

Essential Questions promote argumentation

Clear objectives

Step-by-step lessons provide systematic, explicit instruction

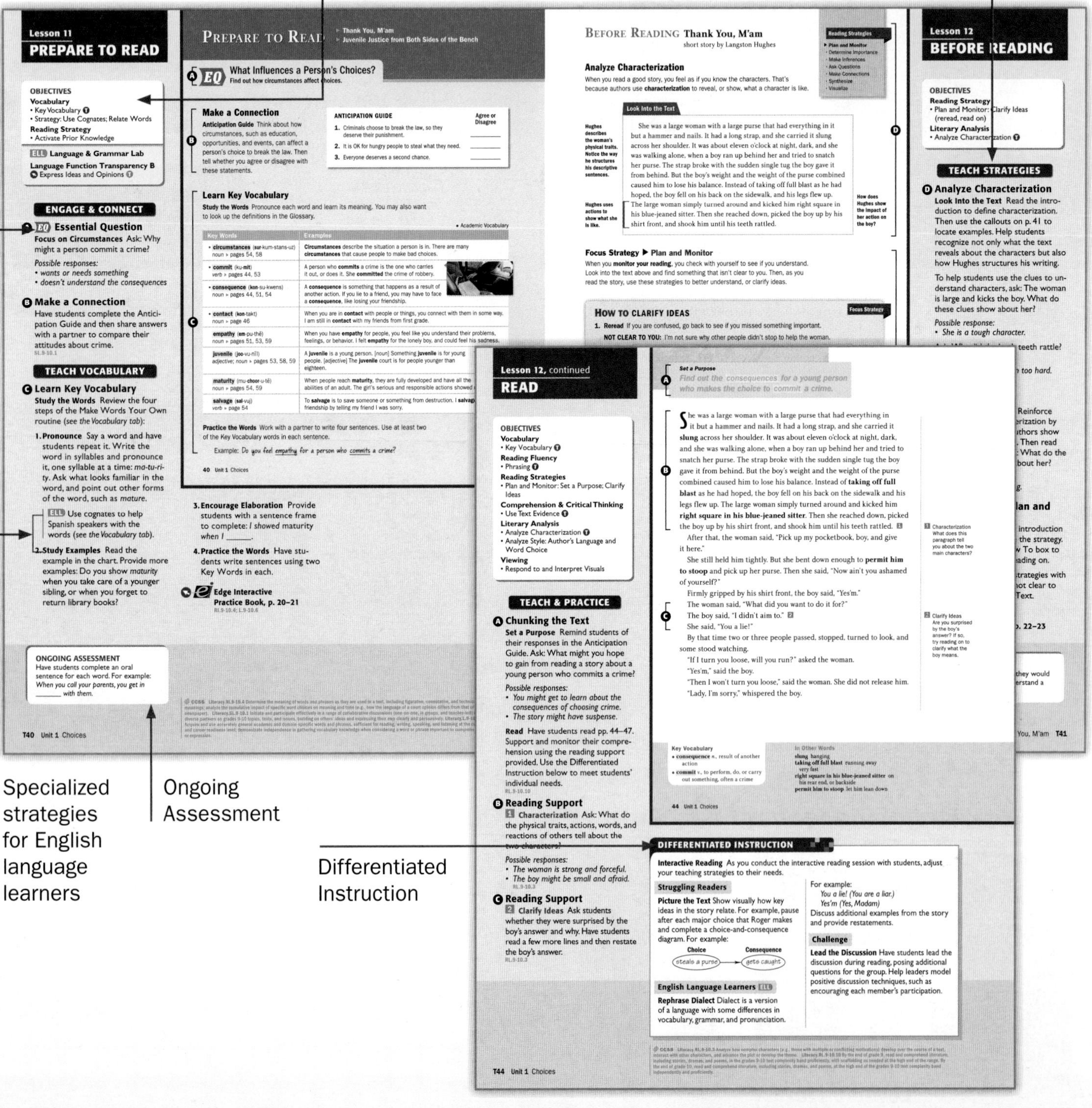

Specialized strategies for English language learners

Ongoing Assessment

Differentiated Instruction

Online Lesson Planner

myNGconnect.com

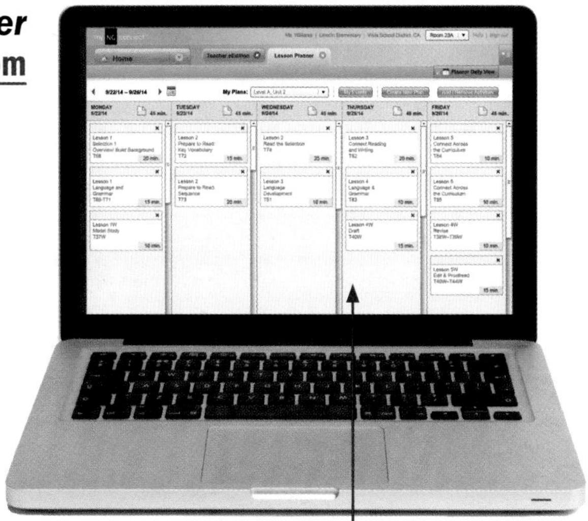

Access digital resources for planning and teaching

Analysis of author's word choice and syntax

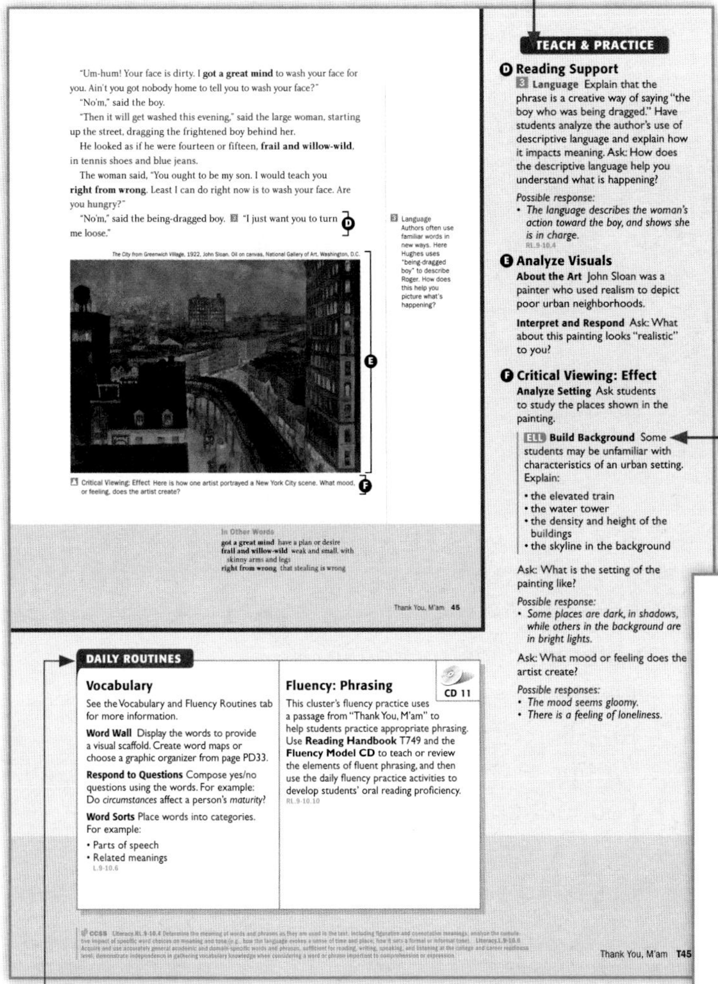
"Um-hum! Your face is dirty. I **got a great mind** to wash your face for you. Ain't you got nobody home to tell you to wash your face?"

"No'm," said the boy.

"Then it will get washed this evening," said the large woman, starting up the street, dragging the frightened boy behind her.

He looked as if he were fourteen or fifteen, **frail and willow-wild**, in tennis shoes and blue jeans.

The woman said, "You ought to be my son. I would teach you **right from wrong**. Least I can do right now is to wash your face. Are you hungry?"

"No'm," said the being-dragged boy. "I just want you to turn me loose."

Language Authors often use familiar words in new ways. Here Hughes uses "being-dragged boy" to describe Roger. How does this help you picture what's happening?

The City from Greenwich Village, 1922, John Sloan. Oil on canvas. National Gallery of Art, Washington, D.C.

Critical Viewing: Effect Here is how one artist portrayed a New York City scene. What mood, or feeling, does the artist create?

In Other Words
got a great mind have a plan or desire
frail and willow-wild weak and small, with skinny arms and legs
right from wrong that stealing is wrong

Thank You, M'am 45

TEACH & PRACTICE

D Reading Support
Language Explain that the phrase is a creative way of saying "the boy who was being dragged." Have students analyze the author's use of descriptive language and explain how it impacts meaning. Ask: How does the descriptive language help you understand what is happening?
Possible response:
- *The language describes the woman's action toward the boy, and shows she is in charge.*

RL.9-10.4

E Analyze Visuals
About the Art John Sloan was a painter who used realism to depict poor urban neighborhoods.
Interpret and Respond Ask: What about this painting looks "realistic" to you?

F Critical Viewing: Effect
Analyze Setting Ask students to study the places shown in the painting.

ELL Build Background Some students may be unfamiliar with characteristics of an urban setting. Explain:
- the elevated train
- the water tower
- the density and height of the buildings
- the skyline in the background

Ask: What is the setting of the painting like?
Possible response:
- *Some places are dark, in shadows, while others in the background are in bright lights.*

Ask: What mood or feeling does the artist create?
Possible responses:
- *The mood seems gloomy.*
- *There is a feeling of loneliness.*

DAILY ROUTINES

Vocabulary
See the Vocabulary and Fluency Routines tab for more information.
Word Wall Display the words to provide a visual scaffold. Create word maps or choose a graphic organizer from page PD33.
Respond to Questions Compose yes/no questions using the words. For example: Do *circumstances* affect a person's *maturity*?
Word Sorts Place words into categories. For example:
- Parts of speech
- Related meanings

L.9-10.6

Fluency: Phrasing CD 11
This cluster's fluency practice uses a passage from "Thank You, M'am" to help students practice appropriate phrasing. Use **Reading Handbook** T749 and the **Fluency Model CD** to teach or review the elements of fluent phrasing, and then use the daily fluency practice activities to develop students' oral reading proficiency.
RL.9-10.10

Thank You, M'am T45

Scaffolding at point-of-use

Teacher-friendly instructional routines

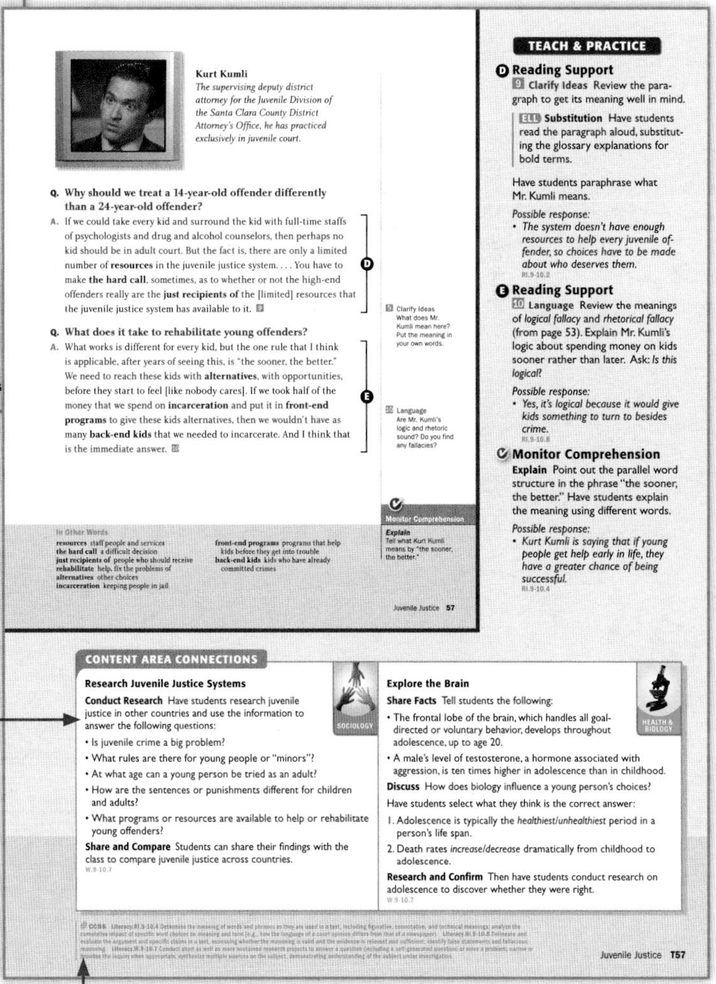
Kurt Kumli
The supervising deputy district attorney for the Juvenile Division of the Santa Clara County District Attorney's Office, he has practiced exclusively in juvenile court.

Q. Why should we treat a 14-year-old offender differently than a 24-year-old offender?

A. If we could take every kid and surround the kid with full-time staffs of psychologists and drug and alcohol counselors, then perhaps no kid should be in adult court. But the fact is, there are only a limited number of **resources** in the juvenile justice system. . . . You have to make **the hard call**, sometimes, as to whether or not the high-end offenders really are the **just recipients of** the [limited] resources that the juvenile justice system has available to it.

Q. What does it take to rehabilitate young offenders?

A. What works is different for every kid, but the one rule that I think is applicable, after years of seeing this, is "the sooner, the better." We need to reach these kids with **alternatives**, with opportunities, before they start to feel [like nobody cares]. If we took half of the money that we spend on **incarceration** and put it in **front-end programs** to give these kids alternatives, then we wouldn't have as many **back-end kids** that we needed to incarcerate. And I think that is the immediate answer.

Clarify Ideas What does Mr. Kumli mean here? Put the meaning in your own words.

Language Are Mr. Kumli's logic and rhetoric sound? Do you find any fallacies?

Monitor Comprehension
Explain Tell what Kurt Kumli means by "the sooner, the better."

In Other Words
resources staff people and services
the hard call a difficult decision
just recipients of people who should receive
rehabilitate help. fix the problems of
alternatives other choices
incarceration keeping people in jail
front-end programs programs that help kids before they get into trouble
back-end kids kids who have already committed crimes

Juvenile Justice 57

TEACH & PRACTICE

D Reading Support
Clarify Ideas Review the paragraph to get its meaning well in mind.

ELL Substitution Have students read the paragraph aloud, substituting the glossary explanations for bold terms.

Have students paraphrase what Mr. Kumli means.
Possible response:
- *The system doesn't have enough resources to help every juvenile offender, so choices have to be made about who deserves them.*

RL.9-10.2

E Reading Support
Language Review the meanings of *logical fallacy* and *rhetorical fallacy* (from page 53). Explain Mr. Kumli's logic about spending money on kids sooner rather than later. Ask: *Is this logical?*
Possible response:
- *Yes, it's logical because it would give kids something to turn to besides crime.*

RI.9-10.8

Monitor Comprehension
Explain Point out the parallel word structure in the phrase "the sooner, the better." Have students explain the meaning using different words.
Possible response:
- *Kurt Kumli is saying that if young people get help early in life, they have a greater chance of being successful.*

RI.9-10.4

CONTENT AREA CONNECTIONS

Research Juvenile Justice Systems SOCIOLOGY
Conduct Research Have students research juvenile justice in other countries and use the information to answer the following questions:
- Is juvenile crime a big problem?
- What rules are there for young people or "minors"?
- At what age can a young person be tried as an adult?
- How are the sentences or punishments different for children and adults?
- What programs or resources are available to help or rehabilitate young offenders?

Share and Compare Students can share their findings with the class to compare juvenile justice across countries.
W.9-10.7

Explore the Brain HEALTH & BIOLOGY
Share Facts Tell students the following:
- The frontal lobe of the brain, which handles all goal-directed or voluntary behavior, develops throughout adolescence, up to age 20.
- A male's level of testosterone, a hormone associated with aggression, is ten times higher in adolescence than in childhood.

Discuss How does biology influence a young person's choices?
Have students select what they think is the correct answer:
1. Adolescence is typically the *healthiest/unhealthiest* period in a person's life span.
2. Death rates *increase/decrease* dramatically from childhood to adolescence.

Research and Confirm Then have students conduct research on adolescence to discover whether they were right.
W.9-10.7

Juvenile Justice T57

Short research projects

Common Core State Standards

Resources for foundational reading skills

Frequent and Varied Assessments

Use multiple measures to assess learning outcomes.

Assess & Place

- Assess foundational reading skills
- Determine reading level (Lexile®)
- Place into the appropriate program level

Instruct

Develop language and provide explicit and systematic instruction in:

- Vocabulary
- Comprehension and Critical Thinking
- Grammar and Sentence Structure
- Literary Analysis
- Listening and Speaking
- Reading Strategies
- Writing
- Foundational Reading Skills

Assess to Monitor Progress

- **Cluster Tests** for timely information as you deliver instruction
- **Unit Tests** to measure skills mastery and monitor progress

Reteach

Reteaching prescriptions for tested skills

Show Success!

Use these measures to move students to the next program level or to exit them from the program

- **Summative Assessments** demonstrate achievement with Level Tests aligned with the Common Core State Standards
- **Reading Lexile® Gains Test** shows increase in reading level
- **Reading Fluency Measures** show increase in words read correct per minute

Also available

eAssessment

- Online tests
- Reports
- Individualized reteaching prescriptions

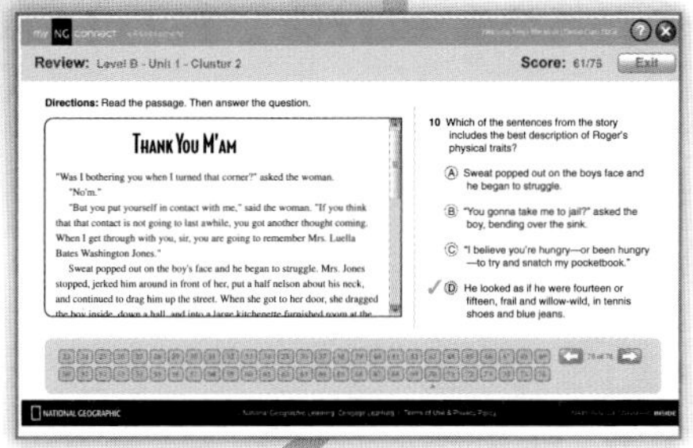

Assessment Purpose	Test Type	Format: Print	Format: eAssessment
Placement & Gains	**Reading Placement and Gains Test** Places students into the appropriate level of the program by reading level. Three parallel forms report Lexile® text measures. Foundational skills are measured to determine placement and identify targeted intervention needs.	✔	✔
	Language Placement and Gains Test Places students into the appropriate level of the program by language proficiency level. Three parallel forms report out Beginning, Intermediate, or Advanced proficiency level.	✔	✔
Progress Monitoring	**Cluster Tests** These weekly tests allow you to provide immediate feedback and reteaching of the week's instruction in reading, literary analysis, vocabulary, and comprehension & critical thinking. Each test includes a Reader Reflection form that provides input from students on their own progress.	✔	✔
	Oral Reading Fluency Measures students' progress toward their words correct per minute goal (wcpm) and includes self-evaluation for prosody skills including intonation, expression, and phrasing.	✔	Comprehension Coach
Performance Assessment	**Language Acquisition Rubrics** Assess the movement of English learners through the stages of language acquisition.	✔	
	Unit Project Rubrics Holistic assessment of students' performance on the unit project, including key unit skills.	✔	
Summative & Metacognitive Assessments	**Unit Reading and Literary Analysis Tests** Constructed-response and selected-response items measure students' performance in the targeted unit skills: vocabulary strategies, key vocabulary, reading strategies, literary analysis, and comprehension & critical thinking.	✔	✔
	Unit Grammar and Writing Tests Constructed-response and selected-response items measure students' performance in the targeted unit skills: grammar, traits of good writing, revising and editing for written conventions, and written composition.	✔	✔
Reteaching	**Reteaching Prescriptions** Include suggestions for re-presenting the skill (from Cluster and Unit Tests), guided practice, and application.		✔
Affective Measures	**Surveys, Reflection Forms, Self- and Peer-Assessments** Help students make personal connections and get committed to their own learning through reflection and metacognition.	✔	

UNIT 1

Genre Focus
Short Stories

Focus Strategy
Plan and Monitor

CHOICES

EQ ESSENTIAL QUESTION:
What Influences a Person's Choices?

Unsafe Journey, near Dhaka, Bangladesh, Amy Helene Johansson. Photograph ©Amy Helene Johansson.

Writing Project

Good Writing Trait
Focus and Unity

UNIT 2

Genre Focus
Nonfiction

Focus Strategy
Determine Importance

THE ART OF EXPRESSION

EQ **ESSENTIAL QUESTION:**
Does Creativity Matter?

A Boy Plays the Violin at Sulaimaniya Music Institute, Sulaimaniya, Iraq, 2009, Julie Adnan. Photograph ©REUTERS/Julie Adnan.

Writing Project

Good Writing Trait
Focus and Unity

UNIT 3

Genre Focus
Short Stories

Focus Strategy
Make Inferences

THE HERO WITHIN

EQ **ESSENTIAL QUESTION:**
What Makes a Hero?

A Rescuer Helps Airlift an Injured Hiker, Cumbria, England, 2005, Ashley Cooper. Photograph ©Ashley Cooper/Corbis.

UNIT 4

Genre Focus
Nonfiction

Focus Strategy
Ask Questions

OPENING DOORS

EQ **ESSENTIAL QUESTION:**
How Can Knowledge Open Doors?

A Buddhist Monk at the Angkor Wat Temple Complex, Siem Reap, Cambodia, Tino Soriano. Photograph ©Tino Soriano/National Geographic Stock.

Writing Project

Good Writing Trait
Development of Ideas

[redacted]

Focus Strategy
Make Connections

FEAR THIS!

EQ **ESSENTIAL QUESTION:**
What Makes Something Frightening?

An Oceanic Whitetip Shark Swims Past a Diver, The Bahamas, Brian J. Skerry. Photograph ©Brian Skerry/National Geographic Stock.

Writing Project

Good Writing Trait
Organization

UNIT 6

Genre Focus
Nonfiction

Focus Strategy
Synthesize

ARE YOU BUYING IT?

EQ **ESSENTIAL QUESTION:**
How Do the Media Shape the Way People Think?

Young Woman in Front of Soft Drink Advertising Sign, Ho Chi Minh City, Vietnam, Stu Smucker. Photograph ©Stu Smucker/Lonely Planet Images/Getty Images.

UNIT 7

Genre Focus
Drama and Poetry

Focus Strategy
Visualize

WHERE WE BELONG

EQ **ESSENTIAL QUESTION:**

What Holds Us Together? What Keeps Us Apart?

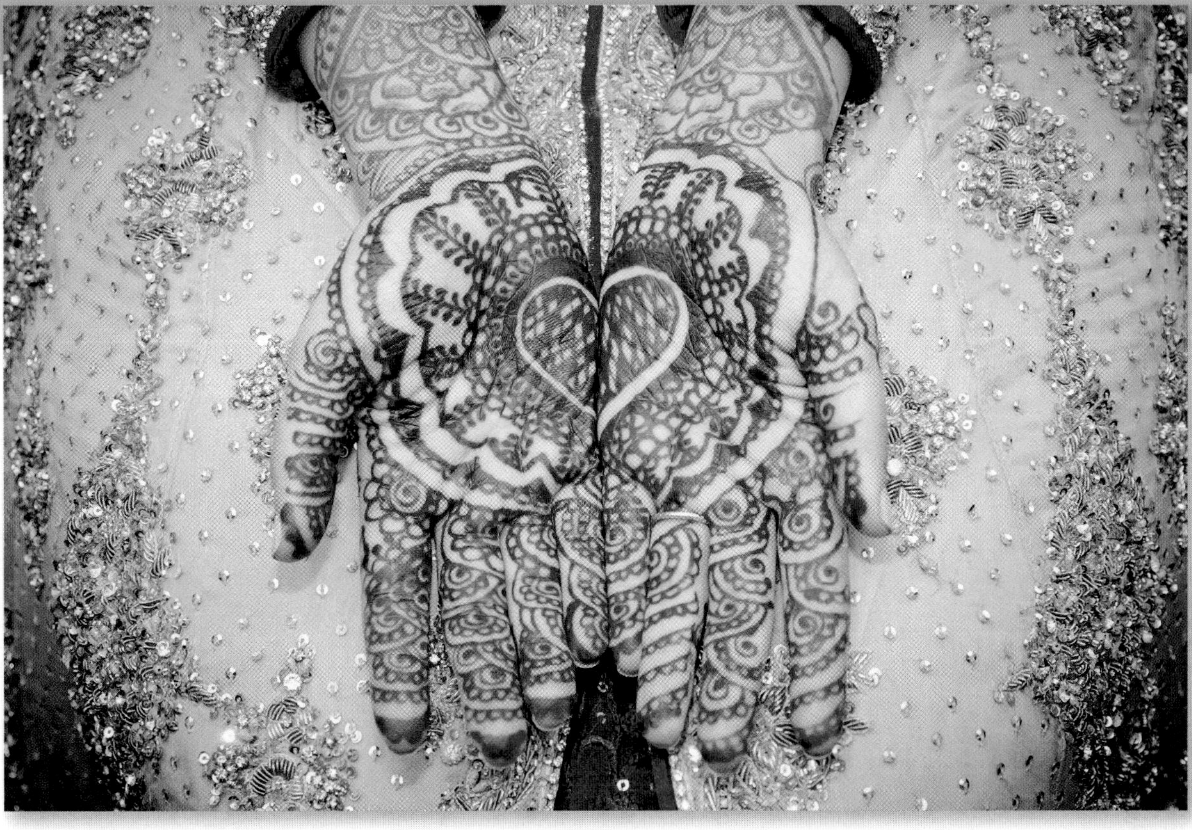

Design Within Reach, Heather Liebensohn. Photograph ©Heather Liebensohn.

RESOURCES

Language and Learning Handbook

Language, Learning, Communication

Reading Handbook

Reading, Fluency, Vocabulary

Writing Handbook

Writing Process, Traits, Conventions

LITERATURE

Bicultural Tablesetting, 1998, Rolando Briseño. Serigraph, private collection.

A Refugee Near the Pakistani Border, Afghanistan, 1983, Reza Deghati. Photograph ©Reza.

Best Practices & Research Base

Best Practices & Research Base

Hampton-Brown Edge has been designed and updated by experts in the fields of reading, writing, and language learning. In this section, program authors present the best practices for teaching—practices that are grounded in the current research and reflect the Common Core State Standards. These practices are built into the resources and instruction included in the program.

BEST PRACTICES

RESEARCH BASE

Giving Students an Edge: Shaping Equitable Pathways

by Dr. Alfred W. Tatum

The adoption of the Common Core State Standards (CCSS) is shifting the instructional focus for high school students in the United States. Literacy demands have increased for all students, including those who struggle with reading and writing. According to national assessment data, only thirty-eight percent of twelfth-graders performed at or above a proficient level in reading in 2009 (NCES, 2010). Therefore, it is imperative that educators shape equitable pathways to protect the literacy rights of high school students to prepare them for a wide range of post-secondary options.

Broaden the Lens of Reading, Writing, and Language Instruction

Instruction for high school students must be conceptualized to align to the broader contexts that inform their lives. Often, high school students live on the outside of literacy instruction. Many will remain there unless instructional practices are planned and educational contexts are shaped to meet their specific language and literacy needs to bring them in from the margins. Literacy-related difficulties are often exacerbated for students who lack the English proficiency needed to handle the academic language, vocabulary, and content found in the texts that they must read from high school on.

"Instruction for high school students must be conceptualized to align to the broader contexts that inform their lives."

Narrow approaches to literacy instruction that have simply focused on skill and strategy development without regard to students' intellectual development have only yielded small upticks in reading achievement over the past four decades (NCES, 2010). A broader frame of literacy instruction as outlined by the CCSS brings attention to the intersection of reading, writing, language, and knowledge development that should benefit high school struggling readers who have been traditionally underserved by schools. Educators must safeguard this intersection to counter inequitable literacy pathways to ensure that a significant proportion of high school students receive the instruction they need and deserve. Educators must balance a focus on complex texts as called for by the CCSS while honoring the complexity of high school students' lives and their need for academic, cultural, emotional, and personal development.

Shaping Equitable Pathways

Advancing the literacy needs and shaping equitable pathways for high school students will involve, at minimum, nurturing students' resilience and increasing their experiences with more cognitively demanding texts, including disciplinary texts (Shanahan & Shanahan, 2008). High school students are more likely to become resilient if they feel secure in the presence of adults who clearly communicate high expectations along with realistic goals, and who support the students' active participation in authentic tasks and "real-world" dialogue (Henderson & Milstein, 2003; Stanton-Salazar & Spina, 2000). During reading instruction, educators can help nurture student resilience by modeling specific reading and writing strategies that students can use independently, while simultaneously engaging students with a wide range of fiction and nonfiction texts. These actions are particularly effective for students who often feel disconnected from literacy instruction (Ivey, 1999; Miller, 2006). Building these contexts and relationships helps to construct students' literacy identities (Triplett, 2004).

Literacy classrooms and instructional practices that invite students in from the margins and shape equitable pathways are characteristically non-threatening. Students engage in conversations with teachers and classmates about the multiple literacies in their lives and feel supported and valued. Educators who structure such classroom environments and instructional practices have the potential to promote more active student participation in literacy-related tasks and to increase student motivation, leading to improved academic outcomes (Guthrie & McRae, 2011). For too long, policies and practices have inadvertently authorized failure in high school (Tatum & Muhammad, 2012).

Educators should keep in mind the following as they move to authorize a different set of instructional practices to shape equitable pathways for high school students:

Adolescent Readers, continued

1. Conceptualize reading, writing, and language as tools of protection for high school students. Instruction in high school can shape the trajectory for post-seconary options.

2. Focus on the intersection of reading, writing, and intellectual development. Require students to demonstrate their comprehension through reading, writing, and discussion. Develop a writing routine that requires students to demonstrate their new understandings that emerge from the texts.

3. Increase students' exposure to academic words and language in the high school. Use rich language while speaking. Share examples of your own writing that model how you use rich language.

4. Move beyond texts during instruction that are "cultural and linguistic feel goods" in favor of texts that advance students' cognitive and social development.

5. Become better arbiters of the texts you use with students or change how you plan to use the texts. Establish a litmus test for your text selections that moves beyond mandated materials.

6. Provide direct and explicit strategy instruction.

7. Recognize that young adolescents are developing a sense of self, and that they draw on cultural, linguistic, gender, and personal identities to define that self.

8. Honor cultural and linguistic diversity during instruction while holding all students to standards of excellence.

9. Provide adequate language supports before, during, and after instruction.

10. Select and discuss texts in ways that engage students.

11. Use appropriate pacing during instruction.

12. Involve students in the assessment process and develop an assessment plan that pays attention to students' cognitive and affective needs.

13. Do not reject complex texts for struggling readers and writers based on perceived notions of ability or capacity to handle complex texts across a wide range of subjects. Be patient and steadfast.

As this list indicates, there are multiple ways to shape equitable pathways for high school students. It is important for teachers to be flexible in finding the ways that work best with their students, and to avoid approaching literacy instruction with a single technique or method.

Powerful Texts

It is prudent to use a combination of powerful texts, in tandem with powerful reading instruction, to influence the literacy development and lives of adolescents. Texts are the center of instruction and must be selected with a clearer audit of the struggling adolescent reader, many of whom are suffering from an underexposure to text that they find meaningful. These students need exposure to *enabling* texts (Tatum, 2009). An enabling text is one that moves beyond a sole cognitive focus—such as skill and strategy development—to include an academic, cultural, emotional, and social focus that moves students closer to examining issues they find relevant to their lives. For example, texts can be used to help high school students wrestling with the question, What am I going to do with the rest of my life? This is a question most adolescents find essential as they engage in shaping their identities.

The texts selected for ***Hampton-Brown Edge*** are enabling texts. First, they serve as the vehicle for exploring Essential Questions, but secondly, the texts are diverse—from classics that have inspired readers for decades (Shakespeare, Frost, St. Vincent Millay, Saki, de Maupassant, Poe, et al.) to contemporary fiction that reflects the diversity of the U.S. (Allende, Alvarez, Angelou, Bruchac, Cisneros, Ortiz Cofer, Soto, Tan, et al.).

Teens develop eco-friendly cars.

"My English" reflects on the immigrant experience.

Art has the power to build bridges.

The texts are also diverse in subject matter and genre, exploring issues of personal identity as well as cultural and social movements. Here are just a few examples of selections in ***Edge*** that deal with personal identity:

- "Who We Really Are"—being a foster child
- "Curtis Aikens and the American Dream"—overcoming illiteracy
- "Nicole"—being biracial
- "My English," "Voices of America," "La Vida Robot"—being an immigrant to the U.S.

And here are just a few examples of selections dealing with social and cultural issues:

- "Long Walk to Freedom"—overthrowing apartheid
- "Hip-Hop as Culture" and "Slam: Performance Poetry Lives On"—the power of art to build bridges and shape culture
- "Violence Hits Home"—how young people are working to stop gang violence
- "The Fast and the Fuel Efficient"—how teens are developing eco-friendly cars.

Unfortunately, many high school students who struggle with reading are encountering texts that are characteristically *disabling.* A disabling text reinforces a student's perception of being a struggling reader. A disabling text also ignores students' local contexts and their desire as adolescents for self-definition. Disabling texts do not move in the direction of closing the reading achievement gap in a class-based, language-based, and race-based society in which many adolescents are underserved by low-quality literacy instruction.

It is important to note that meaningful texts, although important, are not sufficient to improve literacy instruction. High school students who struggle with reading and lack the skills and strategies to handle text independently need support to become engaged with the text.

Powerful Instruction

One of the most powerful techniques is to *use the text* to teach the text. This is a productive approach to help struggling readers become engaged. It simply means that the teacher presents a short excerpt of the upcoming reading selection—before reading—and then models skills or strategies with that text. For example, if the instructional goal is to have students understand how an author uses characterization, the teacher could use an excerpt of the text to introduce the concept.

There are several pedagogical and student benefits associated with using the text to teach the text, namely nurturing fluency and building background knowledge. Because students are asked to examine an excerpt of a text they will see again later as they read independently, rereading has been embedded. Rereadings are effective for nurturing fluency for students who struggle with decoding and for English language learners. Secondly, the students are introduced to aspects of Langston Hughes; writing that will potentially shape their reading of the text. Having background knowledge improves reading comprehension. Using the text to teach the text provides a strategic advantage for struggling readers while allowing teachers to introduce the text and strategies together. It is a win-win situation for both teacher and student.

Conclusion

It is difficult for many teachers to engage struggling adolescent readers with text. I hear the common refrain, "These kids just don't want to read." There are several reasons adolescents refuse to read. Primary among them are a lack of interest in the texts and a lack of requisite skills and strategies for handling the text independently.

It is imperative to identify and engage students with texts that pay attention to their multiple identities. It is equally imperative to grant them entry into the texts by providing explicit skill and strategy instruction. The texts should be as diverse as the students being taught. The texts should also challenge students to wrestle with questions they find significant. This combination optimizes shaping students' literacies along with shaping their lives, an optimization that informs ***Edge***.

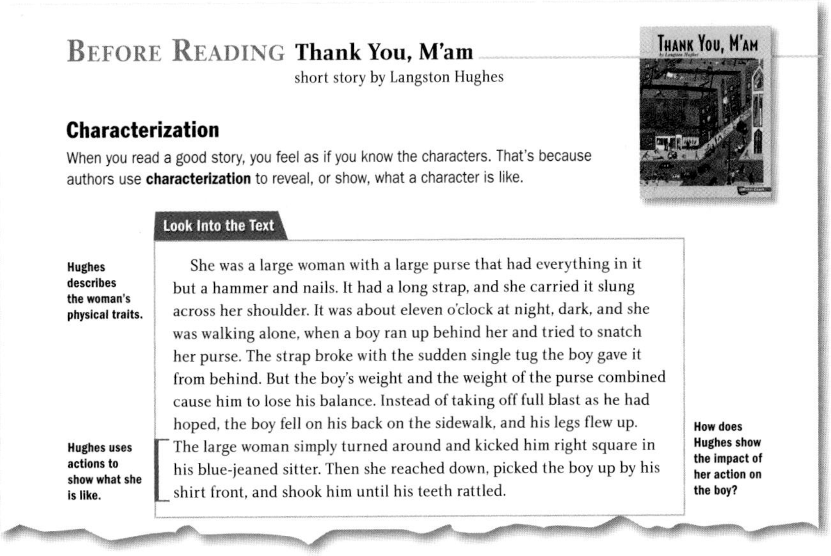
BEFORE READING **Thank You, M'am**
short story by Langston Hughes

Characterization

When you read a good story, you feel as if you know the characters. That's because authors use **characterization** to reveal, or show, what a character is like.

Look Into the Text

Hughes describes the woman's physical traits.

She was a large woman with a large purse that had everything in it but a hammer and nails. It had a long strap, and she carried it slung across her shoulder. It was about eleven o'clock at night, dark, and she was walking alone, when a boy ran up behind her and tried to snatch her purse. The strap broke with the sudden single tug the boy gave it from behind. But the boy's weight and the weight of the purse combined cause him to lose his balance. Instead of taking off full blast as he had hoped, the boy fell on his back on the sidewalk, and his legs flew up. The large woman simply turned around and kicked him right square in his blue-jeaned sitter. Then she reached down, picked the boy up by his shirt front, and shook him until his teeth rattled.

Hughes uses actions to show what she is like.

How does Hughes show the impact of her action on the boy?

An example of using the text to teach the text before reading – a powerful instructional technique that keeps the text at the center of instruction.

Meeting the Common Core State Standards

by Dr. Michael W. Smith

The Common Core State Standards (CCSS) are designed to "ensure that all students are college and career ready in literacy no later than the end of high school." (National Governors Association Center for Best Practices, Council of Chief State School Officers, 2010) A recent analysis (Porter, McMaken, Hwang, Yang, 2011) of the standards establishes that the CCSS will "shift content . . . toward higher levels of cognitive demand" (p. 106). But the CCSS are about more than rigor. They also pose new challenges for what and how we teach. Let's explore how ***Hampton-Brown Edge*** meets those challenges.

Challenge 1: An Increased Emphasis on Informational Texts

The CCSS push for an increased emphasis on informational texts is absolutely clear:

> Part of the motivation behind the interdisciplinary approach to literacy promulgated by the Standards is extensive research establishing the need for college and career ready students to be proficient in reading complex informational text independently in a variety of content areas. (p. 4).

Indeed, the Standards call for 70 percent of the reading that secondary students do to be informational, although they stress that "teachers of senior English classes, for example, are not required to devote 70 percent of reading to informational texts. Rather, 70 percent of student reading across the grade [i.e. across all of their subjects] should be informational" (p. 5). Despite this caveat, there's sufficient concern about this changing emphasis that *Washington Post* columnist Jay Matthews published an article entitled "Fiction vs. Nonfiction Smackdown."

"Rather than seeing fiction and nonfiction as being in competition, Edge sees them as complementary."

Rather than seeing fiction and nonfiction as being in competition, ***Edge*** sees them as complementary. All of our units are built around Essential Questions. These questions are so interestingly complex that they have been taken up by a variety of disciplines. If we want our students to think about them, they have to read literature, to be sure, but they also have to read a wide range of informational texts as well. Reading fiction and nonfiction together in service of thinking about those questions invigorates both types of texts. And perhaps more importantly, it makes it clear to kids that what they read matters in the here and now (cf., Smith & Wilhelm, 2002).

Challenge 2: An Increased Emphasis on Text Complexity

The CCSS "emphasize increasing the complexity of texts students read as a key element in improving reading comprehension." In fact, Cunningham (in press) argues that "the most widely discussed reading instructional change called for by the CCSS is a significant increase in text complexity." Indeed, he continues, "those who have not read the standards and only listened to the chatter about them may well have concluded that this is the only major change in reading instruction the CCSS entails."

Text complexity is itself a complex matter. As the Supplemental Information for Appendix A of the Common Core State Standards for English Language Arts and Literacy indicates assessing text complexity involves the consideration of three dimensions—qualitative, quantitative, and reading and task.

Edge is designed for striving readers and English language learners. These students need instructional-level texts. So the CCSS's emphasis on the reading of complex text provided a significant challenge. We met that challenge by including instructional-level texts accessible reading levels and complex texts that stretch students' ability. In selecting those texts we drew on both the quantitative dimension of complexity (Lexile ratings) and the qualitative dimension of complexity (our analyses of the complexity of the text's structure, language, knowledge demands, and levels of meaning).

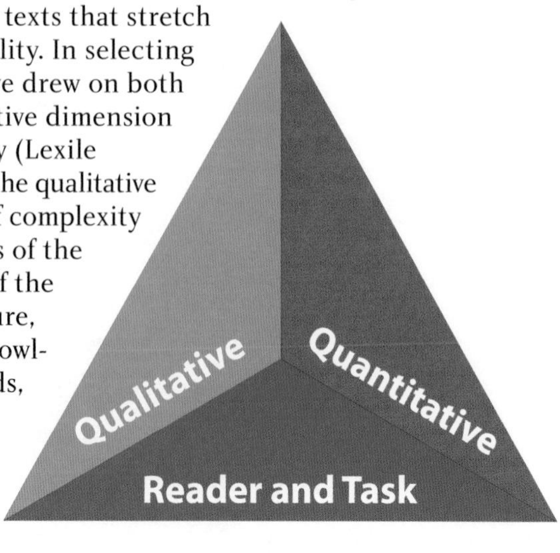

Although the CCSS require all students to read complex texts, they explicitly state that they do not define the intervention methods or materials necessary to support students who are well below or well above grade-level expectations. Therefore, once we selected the texts, we had to draw on our understanding of reader and task considerations to help students grapple with those texts. The very structure of our books is designed to help students do the stretching we ask them to do. In the first place, we provide instruction designed to help them have meaningful transactions with the texts we ask them to read. (More on that in the next section.) In addition, because our units are built around Essential Questions, they involve extended reading, writing, and discussion about texts that address a similar issue. As a consequence, all of the reading, writing, and talking that students do acts as a kind of frontloading (Wilhelm, Baker, & Dube-Hackett, 2001) for Close Readings, the "stretch" texts that close each unit. Moreover, because our units are built around questions that address issues that are important in adolescents' lives, students can draw on their prior knowledge and experiences outside of school as a source of implication. This background knowledge will help students understand the content of the texts, freeing up mental resources to cope with more sophisticated syntax. Moreover, the feelings of competence that our instruction and unit organization develop coupled with the meaningful social work we ask students to do will increase their motivation (cf. Smith & Wilhelm, 2002). And as the Supplemental Information for Appendix A of the Common Core State Standards for English Language Arts and Literacy explains, "Students who have a great deal of interest or motivation in the content are ... likely to handle more complex texts" (p. 6).

Challenge 3: Close Reading of Particular Texts

Without question, the CCSS emphasize developing deep understanding of particular texts. Here are the first three anchor reading standards:

1. Read closely to determine what the text says explicitly and to make logical inferences from it; cite specific textual evidence when writing or speaking to support conclusions drawn from the text.

2. Determine central ideas or themes of a text and analyze their development; summarize the key supporting details and ideas.

3. Analyze how and why individuals, events, and ideas develop and interact over the course of a text.

However, although these standards focus on learning from individual texts they do so in a way very much in line with the strategy instruction we provide. We focus on making inferences (Standard 1). We focus on determining importance (Standard 2). We focus on synthesizing (Standard 3).

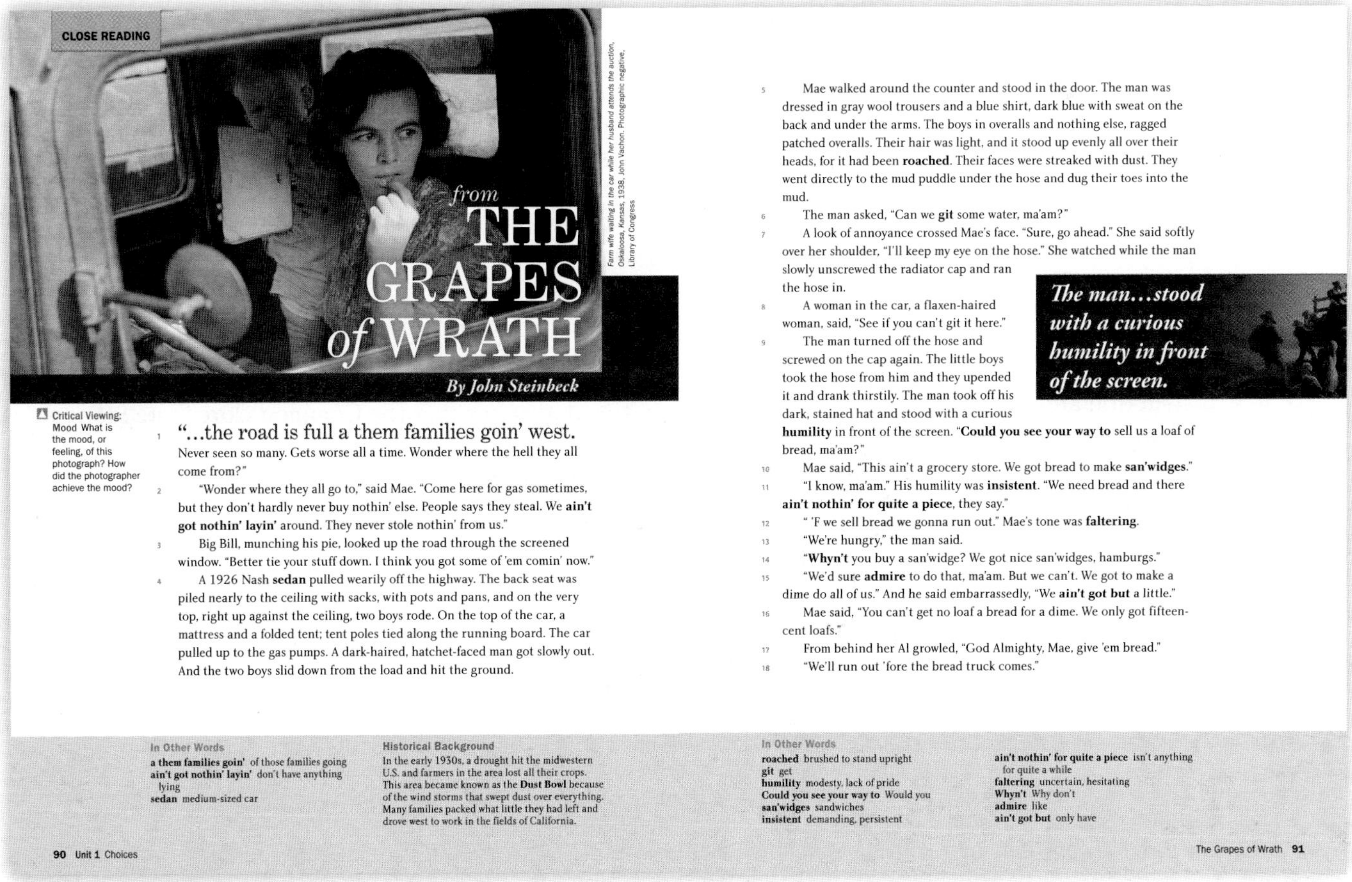

CLOSE READING

from THE GRAPES *of* WRATH

By John Steinbeck

Farm wife waiting in the car while her husband attends the auction, Oskaloosa, Kansas, 1938, John Vachon. Photographic negative, Library of Congress

Critical Viewing: Mood What is the mood, or feeling, of this photograph? How did the photographer achieve the mood?

1 "...the road is full a them families goin' west. Never seen so many. Gets worse all a time. Wonder where the hell they all come from?"

2 "Wonder where they all go to," said Mae. "Come here for gas sometimes, but they don't hardly never buy nothin' else. People says they steal. We **ain't got nothin' layin'** around. They never stole nothin' from us."

3 Big Bill, munching his pie, looked up the road through the screened window. "Better tie your stuff down. I think you got some of 'em comin' now."

4 A 1926 Nash **sedan** pulled wearily off the highway. The back seat was piled nearly to the ceiling with sacks, with pots and pans, and on the very top, right up against the ceiling, two boys rode. On the top of the car, a mattress and a folded tent; tent poles tied along the running board. The car pulled up to the gas pumps. A dark-haired, hatchet-faced man got slowly out. And the two boys slid down from the load and hit the ground.

5 Mae walked around the counter and stood in the door. The man was dressed in gray wool trousers and a blue shirt, dark blue with sweat on the back and under the arms. The boys in overalls and nothing else, ragged patched overalls. Their hair was light, and it stood up evenly all over their heads, for it had been **roached**. Their faces were streaked with dust. They went directly to the mud puddle under the hose and dug their toes into the mud.

6 The man asked, "Can we **git** some water, ma'am?"

7 A look of annoyance crossed Mae's face. "Sure, go ahead." She said softly over her shoulder, "I'll keep my eye on the hose." She watched while the man slowly unscrewed the radiator cap and ran the hose in.

8 A woman in the car, a flaxen-haired woman, said, "See if you can't git it here."

9 The man turned off the hose and screwed on the cap again. The little boys took the hose from him and they upended it and drank thirstily. The man took off his dark, stained hat and stood with a curious **humility** in front of the screen. "**Could you see your way to** sell us a loaf of bread, ma'am?"

The man...stood with a curious humility in front of the screen.

10 Mae said, "This ain't a grocery store. We got bread to make **san'widges**."

11 "I know, ma'am." His humility was **insistent**. "We need bread and there **ain't nothin' for quite a piece**, they say."

12 " 'F we sell bread we gonna run out." Mae's tone was **faltering**.

13 "We're hungry," the man said.

14 "**Whyn't** you buy a san'widge? We got nice san'widges, hamburgs."

15 "We'd sure **admire** to do that, ma'am. But we can't. We got to make a dime do all of us." And he said embarrassedly, "We **ain't got but** a little."

16 Mae said, "You can't get no loaf a bread for a dime. We only got fifteen-cent loafs."

17 From behind her Al growled, "God Almighty, Mae, give 'em bread."

18 "We'll run out 'fore the bread truck comes."

In Other Words
a them families goin' of those families going
ain't got nothin' layin' don't have anything lying
sedan medium-sized car

Historical Background
In the early 1930s, a drought hit the midwestern U.S. and farmers in the area lost all their crops. This area became known as the **Dust Bowl** because of the wind storms that swept dust over everything. Many families packed what little they had left and drove west to work in the fields of California.

In Other Words
roached brushed to stand upright
git get
humility modesty, lack of pride
Could you see your way to Would you
san'widges sandwiches
insistent demanding, persistent
ain't nothin' for quite a piece isn't anything for quite a while
faltering uncertain, hesitating
Whyn't Why don't
admire like
ain't got but only have

90 Unit 1 Choices

The Grapes of Wrath 91

Close Reading passages provide opportunities for reading and rereading short, more complex texts.

In fact, in a guide for publishers seeking to develop materials consistent with the CCSS, two of the lead authors of the standards (Coleman and Pimentel, 2012) suggest that strategy instruction can support the learning from text goal the CCSS articulate:

> Close reading and gathering knowledge from specific texts should be at the heart of classroom activities … Reading strategies should work in the service of reading comprehension (rather than an end unto themselves) and assist students in building knowledge and insight from specific texts. (p. 9)

That's just what ***Edge*** does. It teaches students strategies so that they can independently apply them to understand the specific reading we ask them to do. We avoid the "cookie-cutter" strategy-based questions that Coleman and Pimental critique. The Look Into the Text feature is a salient example of embedding strategy instruction in rich, textual context. In short, we connect text-dependent questions and strategic instruction. As a consequence, we support students' "gathering evidence, knowledge, and insight from [the specific text] they read" even as we are teaching strategies that they can apply in new textual contexts.

In his comprehensive review of research on transfer, Haskell (2000) points out that "Despite the importance of transfer of learning, research findings over the past nine decades clearly show that as individuals, and as educational institutions, we have failed to achieve transfer of learning on any significant level (p. xiii)." Despite this finding, Perkins and Salomon (1988) argue that teachers are too sanguine about the likelihood of transfer, relying on what Perkins and Salomon call the Little Bo Peep view of transfer; that is, if we "leave them alone" they come to a new task and naturally transfer relevant knowledge and skills. But that transfer doesn't happen. Perkins and Solomon note that "a great deal of the knowledge students acquire is 'inert'" (p. 23), meaning that students don't apply it in new problem-solving situations. As a consequence, Perkins and Salomon (1988) argue that teachers must work hard and quite consciously to cultivate transfer. They explain cultivating a "mindful abstraction" of a strategy allows it to be moved from "one context to another" (p. 25). That's why we provide explicit strategy instruction and provide multiple opportunities for students to apply their understanding.

We want students to grapple with the texts that they read so they can learn from them and use them to think about the Essential Questions that organize our units. Strategy instruction coupled with repeated opportunities to apply those strategies in meaningful ways in a range of textual contexts is the way to do just that.

Challenge 4: An Emphasis on Argumentation

The prominence of argumentation in the CCSS is undeniable: "[T]he Standards put particular emphasis on students' ability to write sound arguments on substantive topics and issues, as this ability is critical to college and career readiness." We respond to that increased emphasis in two ways. The first is by working to create a culture of argumentation in the classroom through the use of Essential Questions, questions that have no definite answers. Structuring units around such questions signals to students that they'll need to think critically and make the kind of sound arguments that the CCSS are calling for if their ideas about the Essential Questions are to carry the day.

This emphasis on argumentation stands in stark contrast to the patterns of discourse that prevail in schools. Indeed Applebee, Langer, Nystrand, and Gamoran's (2003) analysis of twenty 7-12 grade classrooms reveals that what they call open-discussion, defined as "more than 30 seconds of free exchange of ideas among students or between at least three participants" which "usually begins in response to an open-ended question about which students can legitimately disagree" (p. 707) averaged 1.7 minutes per 60 minutes of class time. This is a pretty depressing finding, but one that we work to overcome by the very structure of ***Edge***.

The second response to argument is to provide explicit instruction on how to read and write arguments. We teach students how to understand and employ Toulmin's (1958) model of argumentation, a model of argumentation that allows students to draw on their ability to make effective oral arguments, analyze arguments, and craft effective written ones (cf., Smith, Wilhelm, & Fredrickson). Just as providing explicit strategy instruction with plenty of opportunities for applying that instruction in specific textual situations fosters transfer of learning in reading, so too does providing explicit instruction in the elements of argumentation along with plenty of opportunities to practice applying those elements foster transfer of learning in writing.

We want the struggling readers that our books are designed to serve to be college and career ready by the time they graduate from high school. That's why we have embraced the challenges that the Common Core State Standards pose.

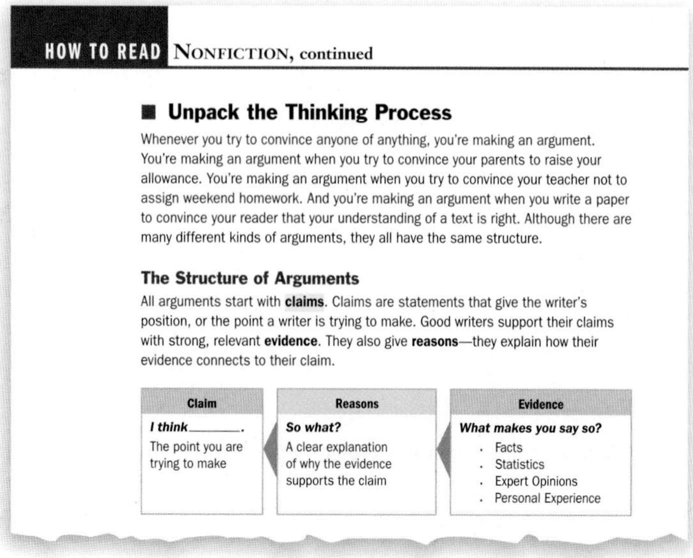

HOW TO READ NONFICTION, continued

Unpack the Thinking Process

Whenever you try to convince anyone of anything, you're making an argument. You're making an argument when you try to convince your parents to raise your allowance. You're making an argument when you try to convince your teacher not to assign weekend homework. And you're making an argument when you write a paper to convince your reader that your understanding of a text is right. Although there are many different kinds of arguments, they all have the same structure.

The Structure of Arguments

All arguments start with **claims**. Claims are statements that give the writer's position, or the point a writer is trying to make. Good writers support their claims with strong, relevant **evidence**. They also give **reasons**—they explain how their evidence connects to their claim.

Claim	Reasons	Evidence
I think_______. The point you are trying to make	***So what?*** A clear explanation of why the evidence supports the claim	***What makes you say so?*** · Facts · Statistics · Expert Opinions · Personal Experience

We teach students to understand and apply Toulmin's model of argumentation.

Robust Vocabulary Instruction

by Dr. David W. Moore

Instruction that helps high school students develop broad and deep vocabulary knowledge is crucial for their literate, academic, and occupational success. For striving readers and students who are learning English, such instruction is imperative (Cummins, 2003; Nation, 2001; Torgeson et al., 2007). According to the Common Core State Standards (CCSS) (National Governors Association Center for Best Practices, Council of Chief State School Officers, 2010):

> To be college and career ready in language, students must have extensive vocabularies, built through reading and study, enabling them to comprehend complex texts and engage in purposeful writing about and conversations around content. They need to become skilled in determining or clarifying the meaning of words and phrases they encounter, choosing flexibly from an array of strategies to aid them. (p. 51)

Research in promoting high school English learners and striving readers' vocabularies (Blachowicz, Fisher, Ogle, & Watts-Taffe, 2006; Graves, August, & Mancilla-Martinez, 2013; Harmon, Wood, & Medina, 2009; Kame'enui & Baumann, 2012; Lesaux, Kieffer, Fuller, & Kelley, 2010) indicates that effective instruction includes four components— rich and varied language experiences, direct teaching of specific words, instruction in word-learning strategies, and fostering word consciousness.

Rich and Varied Language Experiences

Most word learning occurs through meaningful oral language and wide reading of diverse materials (National Reading Panel, 2000). The oral language that young children hear and participate in at home is their major source of word learning. Once children begin school, the ways in which they use language to interact with teachers and classmates become especially important contributors to vocabulary growth. Teachers increase this growth when they support students' oral language centered on academic purposes, structures, and terminology.

Rich oral language experiences are essential to students' vocabulary growth; however, as students move through school, reading becomes a principal source of new words (Cunningham & Stanovich, 1998). Indeed, some researchers consider the amount of reading that students do to be the most powerful influence on their vocabulary development (Anderson & Nagy, 1992). When students read a range of print materials—trade books, textbooks, reference sources, periodicals, web sites, and multimedia presentations—they gain access to the meanings of unfamiliar words along with information about how familiar words are used in different ways in different contexts.

To make new words their own, students benefit from frequent and varied activities that allow them to use the words as they read, write, speak, and listen (Marzano, 2004). Engaging students in collaborative content-rich tasks, regularly prompting them to elaborate their ideas, and supporting their efforts are all rich language experiences associated with vocabulary growth.

Hampton-Brown Edge provides informative nonfiction and fiction selections that present new words through a range of oral and written language experiences. The selections shed light on many fascinating topics and are grouped in thematic units so that students encounter ideas and information that relate to and build on each other. The selections also grow in difficulty, which allows students to encounter words in a logical sequence. Instruction related to the selections leads students to interact with the materials meaningfully throughout each unit.

Direct Teaching of Specific Words

Complementing rich and varied language experiences with the direct teaching of specific words is important. Direct teaching of specific words helps students develop in-depth knowledge (Beck, McKeown, & Kucan, 2008; Graves, 2009). Such instruction is especially valuable for students who do not read or understand English well enough to acquire vocabulary through reading and listening alone.

"Complementing rich and varied language experiences with the direct teaching of specific words is important."

Directly teaching specific words well requires choosing particular words for instruction, then bringing them to life in ways that allow students to gain permanent ownership of them. It means explaining word meanings so that students form connections with what they already know, detecting relationships as well as distinctions among known words.

It means modeling correct usage of the words and providing numerous opportunities for students to see and use the words in active meaningful contexts.

Key Vocabulary The program directly teaches specific words before each major reading selection. Key Vocabulary contains words that are essential to understanding a unit concept, central to comprehension of a selection, valuable for students in classroom discussions, and highly useful for future academic studies. Directly teaching these words helps students unlock meanings of both the words and of related words they will encounter in the future.

Introductions to each word follow a consistent pattern that calls for students to assess their knowledge of the word, pronounce and spell it, study its meaning, and connect it to known words. Student-friendly definitions and interactive practice activities support vocabulary development.

Academic Vocabulary Along with Key Vocabulary, ***Edge*** focuses on academic vocabulary, words such as *function* and *transform* that make up the distinctive language of school (Coxhead, 2000; Nagy & Townsend, 2012). Academic terminology typically is bundled together more densely in the materials students read inside school than outside of school, and it typically is more abstract. Despite differences between academic and general vocabulary, shared principles of instruction apply to both. For instance, students benefit from rich and varied language experiences along with direct and meaningful teaching of academic and general vocabulary.

Learn Key Vocabulary

Study the Words Pronounce each word and learn its meaning. You may also want to look up the definitions in the Glossary.

• Academic Vocabulary

Key Words	Examples
• **achieve** (u-**chēv**) *verb* ▸ pages 143, 147	To **achieve** means to succeed or do well. If you work hard, you can **achieve** your goals.
assert (u-**surt**) *verb* ▸ page 139	When you **assert** something, you insist on having your opinions and ideas heard. The song lyrics **assert** the band's ideas about the power of music.
• **culture** (**kul**-chur) *noun* ▸ pages 136, 143	**Culture** includes the beliefs, attitudes, and behaviors that are shared by a group of people. Young people have a **culture** that appreciates creativity and independence.
evolve (ē-**valv**) *verb* ▸ page 138	When something **evolves**, it changes over time. My taste in music has **evolved** over the years.
heritage (**her**-u-tij) *noun* ▸ page 146	Your **heritage** is your background. **Heritage** includes the traditions and beliefs given to you by your family, culture, and society.
innovator (in-nu-**vā**-tur) *noun* ▸ page 138	An **innovator** is someone who introduces something new. The new styles and sounds the musician uses make her an **innovator** of music.
• **perspective** (pur-**spek**-tiv) *noun* ▸ page 136	Your **perspective** is your point of view. Our teacher's background in classical music gives him a unique **perspective** when he hears our music.
self-esteem (**self** es-**tēm**) *noun* ▸ pages 147, 148	**Self-esteem** is the feeling that you are valuable. The confident girl has high **self-esteem**. *Synonyms*: confidence, self-respect

Practice the Words Complete a **Word Square** for each Key Vocabulary word.

Word Square

Definition: beliefs, attitudes, and behaviors shared by a group	**Important Characteristics:** large group of people
Examples: trick or treating for Halloween	**Non-Examples:** painting

culture

132 Unit 2 The Art of Expression

Student-friendly definitions and interactive practice activities support vocabulary development.

Vocabulary Routines Throughout the ***Edge*** units, instructional routines offer extended opportunities to engage students in word study. Students gain control of specific words through actions such as graphically organizing them, comparing them with synonyms and antonyms, and using them orally and in writing. Students connect the words to their lives and to the selections' and units' topics. Vocabulary routines are featured in the Teacher Editions and used throughout the levels. Regular use of these routines helps students internalize the habits of thinking about, exploring, and connecting words. Additionally, students' knowledge of the words directly taught is assessed regularly throughout the program to inform instructional decisions.

Instruction in Word-Learning Strategies

Proficient readers apply independent strategies to figure out the meanings of unfamiliar words (Anderson & Nagy, 1992). As the CCSS make clear, college and career ready students independently determine the meanings of unfamiliar words through contextual analysis, morphemic analysis, and the use of specialized reference materials.

Contextual Analysis Analyzing the context of an unfamiliar word to clarify its meaning involves actively using the text and illustrations that surround the word (Baumann, Edwards, Boland, & Font, 2012; Stahl & Nagy, 2006). Proficient readers use contextual analysis when they determine that they do not know a word (e.g., "I don't understand *hitched* in 'They got hitched.'"). They then look back in the selection, rereading for clues to the word's meaning they might have missed, and they look forward, reading on for new information that might help. They search the surrounding words for particular types of clues, such as definitions, examples, and restatements that clarify word meanings. They adjust their rates of reading, slowing down or speeding up, to find clarifying information.

Morphemic Analysis Analyzing an unfamiliar word's morphemes—its meaningful parts such as prefixes, bases, roots, and suffixes—plays a valuable role in word learning (Bowers, Kirby, Deacon, 2010; Carlisle, 2010). Proficient readers use morphemic analysis by first noting an unfamiliar word's use in context ("Distances among the stars are just *incredible!*"). They break the word into parts (*in* + *cred* + *ible*) and assign meaning to each part (*in* = not, *cred* = believe, *ible* = can be done). Then they combine the word-part meanings ("cannot be believed") and see if this combination makes sense in the selection.

Proficient readers also use morphemic analysis to identify words that are derived from a common base word (e.g., *night* as in midnight, nightly, nightshirt) or root (e.g., *cred* as in credit, credible, credence) to determine word meanings. Second-language learners who are proficient readers in their first language use morphemic analysis to identify morphemes in words that have first-language cognates in English (e.g., English-Spanish pairs: continent/continente, history/historia) (August & Shanahan, 2006).

Specialized Reference Materials Information about words and their meanings is available in numerous references. Students can consult print and digital dictionaries, glossaries, and thesauruses; personal productivity software and knowledgeable people are other possible references. Students who meet an unfamiliar word that is difficult to figure out through its context or morphemes do well to look it up in a word meaning reference and confirm its proper meaning.

Edge teaches multiple aspects of independent word-learning strategies. Each unit includes a Vocabulary Workshop that explicitly teaches a word-learning strategy and how to use it. The strategy is then carried through the unit in a scaffolded instructional plan. In each selection teachers first model the strategy explicitly, guide students in using it, then provide opportunities for students to apply the strategy on their own.

Fostering Word Consciousness

Students who are conscious of words habitually examine their meanings and uses (Graves & Watts-Taffe, 2002; Scott & Nagy, 2004). In line with the CCSS, these students interpret figurative language, analyze word choice, and note word relationships.

Figurative Language Students who interpret figurative language make sense of word meanings that go beyond literal definitions. They understand figures of speech such as allusions (*self evident truths*), idioms (*make ends meet*), metaphors (*Life is a rollercoaster.*), and personification (*The wind screamed.*). Students interpret such figurative language in context, and they grasp its role in shaping the meanings of texts.

Word Choice Analyzing word choice involves nuances in words' literal meanings. For example, students notice how particular words' connotations (*steady, monotonous*) affect texts' messages. They appreciate particularly striking word usage (*Parting is such sweet sorrow*). They realize that technical words in different disciplines often convey different meanings (*positive electrical charge, positive emotional appeal*). In general, they follow the impact of a text's specific wording on its cumulative meaning and tone.

Word Relationships Word relationships are meaningful connections among words that students can use to understand and remember each word. To cement their word knowledge, students draw on relationships such as antonyms (*remember, forget*), examples (*empire, Roman*), semantic family members (*nature, natural*), and synonyms (*shy, bashful*). They also make use of terminology that signals such relationships in texts (including, similarly).

Students are encouraged throughout ***Edge*** to explore and become excited about words, to notice their shades of meaning, and to use them with increasing skill. Structured discussions of authors' word choices regularly draw attention to figurative and connotative word meanings and guide students' judgments about how well certain words fit particular contexts. Inquiries guided by Essential Questions (*What makes a hero? How can knowledge open doors?*) focus students on the ways different authors refine the meanings of significant terms. Vocabulary routines involving notebooks, study cards, word maps, and word sorts highlight word relationships.

Students also are encouraged to respect and value the word knowledge they bring with them from outside school. They are led to connect new word meanings with what they already know. Literature selections include many examples of young people valuing their linguistic heritages. All of these instructional supports help striving readers and English learners develop their awareness of and interest in words.

Conclusion

Edge's vocabulary instruction consists of interactive components that support one another. Engaging high school English learners and striving readers in rich and varied language experiences, direct teaching of specific words, instruction in independent word learning strategies, and word consciousness encouragement lead to them becoming college and career ready.

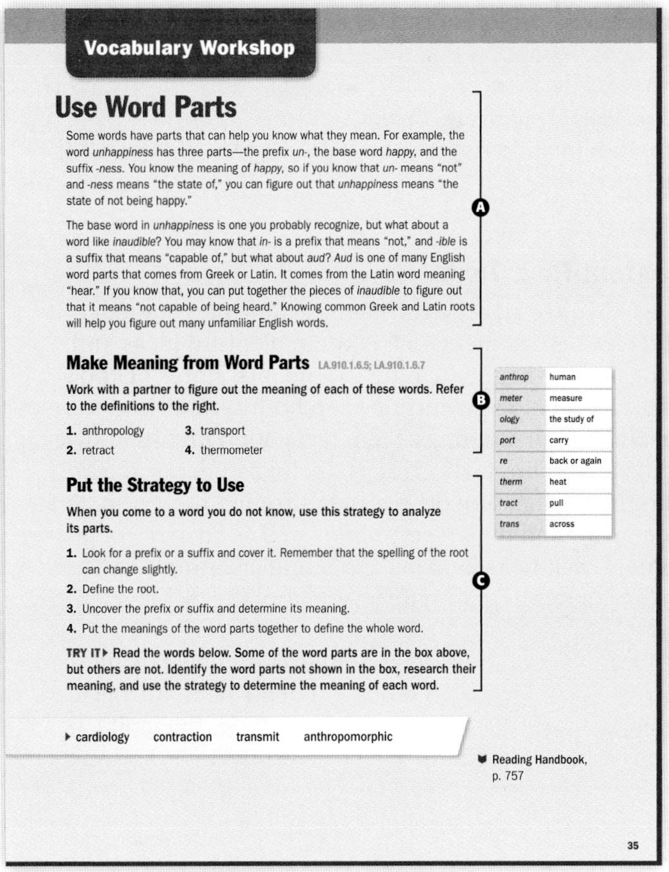

Vocabulary Workshop

Use Word Parts

Some words have parts that can help you know what they mean. For example, the word *unhappiness* has three parts—the prefix *un-*, the base word *happy*, and the suffix *-ness*. You know the meaning of *happy*, so if you know that *un-* means "not" and *-ness* means "the state of," you can figure out that *unhappiness* means "the state of not being happy."

The base word in *unhappiness* is one you probably recognize, but what about a word like *inaudible*? You may know that *in-* is a prefix that means "not," and *-ible* is a suffix that means "capable of," but what about *aud*? *Aud* is one of many English word parts that comes from Greek or Latin. It comes from the Latin word meaning "hear." If you know that, you can put together the pieces of *inaudible* to figure out that it means "not capable of being heard." Knowing common Greek and Latin roots will help you figure out many unfamiliar English words.

A

Make Meaning from Word Parts LA.910.1.6.5; LA.910.1.6.7

Work with a partner to figure out the meaning of each of these words. Refer to the definitions to the right.

1. anthropology **3.** transport
2. retract **4.** thermometer

B

anthrop	human
meter	measure
ology	the study of
port	carry
re	back or again
therm	heat
tract	pull
trans	across

Put the Strategy to Use

When you come to a word you do not know, use this strategy to analyze its parts.

1. Look for a prefix or a suffix and cover it. Remember that the spelling of the root can change slightly.
2. Define the root.
3. Uncover the prefix or suffix and determine its meaning.
4. Put the meanings of the word parts together to define the whole word.

TRY IT▸ Read the words below. Some of the word parts are in the box above, but others are not. Identify the word parts not shown in the box, research their meaning, and use the strategy to determine the meaning of each word.

C

▸ cardiology contraction transmit anthropomorphic

Reading Handbook, p. 757

35

Each unit includes a Vocabulary Workshop that explicitly teaches how to use a word-learning strategy.

Developing Comprehension

by Dr. David W. Moore

The Common Core State Standards (CCSS) portray readers who are prepared to successfully enter college and careers as independent builders of strong content knowledge (National Governors Association Center for Best Practices, Council of Chief State School Officers, 2010). These readers understand and critique complex texts from different genres and disciplines. They value evidence when interpreting authors' messages. As participants in the twenty-first century's global society and economy, they engage with diverse media, ideas, and perspectives.

Hampton-Brown Edge is designed to help high school English learners and striving readers meet and exceed the rigorous CCSS expectations for reading. The program promotes the knowledge, skills, and mindsets required by the standards, and it is informed by major reviews of reading comprehension research (Duke, Pearson, Strachan, & Billman, 2011; Edmonds, Vaughn, Wexler, Reutebuch, Cable, Tackett, et al., 2009; RAND Reading Study Group, 2002; Short & Fitzsimmons, 2007; Torgesen et al., 2007). Central elements of the program include its texts, activities, and instruction.

"Texts that are content-rich contain plentiful ideas and information that contribute to students' stores of knowledge."

Content-Rich Texts

The CCSS are all about students acquiring knowledge. Texts that are content-rich contain plentiful ideas and information that contribute to students' stores of knowledge. They help students develop both general and subject-specific understandings. Such texts often highlight diverse cultural and linguistic groups, fueling students' insights into the heritages of others and affirming their own. Drawn from print and digital settings as well as an array of genres, content-rich texts help make reading meaningful and relevant (McKenna, Conradi, Lawrence, Jang, & Meyer, 2012).

As CCSS expectations to read informational texts increase across the grades, high school students benefit from a range of materials such as essays, histories, memoirs, news features, proclamations, scientific expositions, and speeches that are well crafted and memorable. Engaging students with such content-rich literary nonfiction goes far in building content knowledge (Pearson, in press).

Viewing fiction and nonfiction as complementary, each unit of ***Edge*** includes a wealth of content-rich selections from both genres. Informational texts make up a significant portion of the reading materials. Selections explore science and social studies topics, and they examine personal identity, loyalty, and other life issues. In addition, selections by authors such as Isabelle Allende, Maya Angelou, Sandra Cisneros, Gary Soto, Amy Tan, and Joseph Bruchac permit students to learn about other people and cultures as well as to identify with recognizable characters and settings.

Complex Texts

The CCSS expect all students to comprehend complex texts independently and proficiently. Raising the text complexity bar for English learners and striving readers is meant to enable them to gain mature insights into the human condition, develop advanced knowledge, and increase capacity with similar challenges.

At the end of each unit, ***Edge*** provides a complex reading passage that extends the materials students just read. These texts are designed to stretch students' abilities. They meet CCSS quantitative guidelines for complexity based on Lexile® ratings as well as qualitative guidelines based on levels of meaning, structure, language, and knowledge demands.

Engaging vulnerable readers with complex texts involves more than just making them available. It means helping students bridge the gap between their current abilities and the challenges posed by the texts. It means supporting students' efforts to navigate sophisticated linguistic and conceptual structures as well as accomplish rigorous academic work. Consistent with research (Moje, 2007), the CCSS call for scaffolding learners' comprehension as needed.

Edge includes a wealth of instructional-level texts and texts for independent reading in addition to complex texts. There are scaffolds for English learners and striving readers to succeed with all types of texts. The instructional-level content-rich selections provided in each unit give students a running start to prepare them for the complex texts that end each unit. Students are prepared for the especially challenging selections through the opportunities they have early on to develop needed background knowledge, language, motivation, and confidence.

Other comprehension scaffolds include leveled library books, that offer challenging but not defeating levels of text complexity. Preparation to read includes quickwrites, graphic organizers, and read-alouds. Glosses of unfamiliar words, text-dependent questions for students to think through what they have read before moving on, and post-reading discussion prompts support comprehension. Independent reading in the ***Edge*** library comes with complete online lesson plans and blackline masters for Student Journals are provided for ***Edge*** Library books.

Purposeful Activities

According to the CCSS, college and career ready students read purposefully. Purposeful activities, academic engagements that are relevant and interesting, encourage youth to seek meaning vigorously. Purposeful activities emphasize attention to conceptual networks and keeps texts at the center of instruction. They promote students' views of facts and ideas as facts-in-action and ideas-in-action. When purposes for reading are unclear to students, or when they cannot see the relevance of the reading, their comprehension suffers (Guthrie, 2007). This can also be the case when reading purposes do not take into consideration—or are insensitive to—students' social and cultural backgrounds.

Purposeful activities permeate ***Edge***. Each unit contains selections unified by a common theme such as the role of media or the importance of creativity to promote coherent inquiries. Each unit begins with an Essential Question like "Do People Get What They Deserve?" or "What Influences a Person's Choices?" Such questions have no single, simple, or predetermined answers; they allow verbal, artistic, and dramatic responses (Langer, 2002). The program's emphasis on inquiry helps students see authentic purposes for reading and provokes active thinking.

Edge also consistently sets up discussions to encourage purposeful reading. Combining individual reading with student-led, small-group discussion contributes substantially to learning to understand the texts they read and think critically about (Nystrand, 2006; Soter, Wilkinson, Murphy, Rudge, Reninger, & Edwards, 2008). The program offers students opportunities to talk with partners, in groups, and as a whole class. Knowing they soon will talk with their peers about what they have read provides high school students an audience and a meaningful reason to read. During these exchanges, students explain and justify their interpretations while noting features of others' interpretations that they might take up for themselves. Such talk helps students clarify and organize their thinking about selections, promotes metacognition, and develops argumentation skills.

Close Reading

The CCSS place close reading "at the heart of understanding and enjoying complex works of literature" (p. 3). Because good books don't give up all their secrets at once (King, n.d.), close reading is a sensible part of readers' repertoires. Readers benefit from strategically reading and rereading selected instructional-level selections and complex texts closely and attentively. The practice of close reading includes four fundamental characteristics (Adler & Van Doren, 1972; Beers & Probst, 2012; Hinchman & Moore, in press):

- rigor,
- multiple readings of the target text,
- academic discussion, and
- focus on text evidence.

When applied to close reading, rigor is a term that links features of the passage with how the reader interacts with the passage (Beers & Probst, 2012). Close reading rigor is determined by the complexity of texts as well as by the levels of engagement and commitment readers put into making sense of them. To read rigorously is to examine complex texts in a disciplined, dedicated, and thorough manner.

At the end of each unit, ***Edge*** provides texts and tasks for close reading that meet CCSS guidelines for grade-level complexity. They draw students into deep and thoughtful readings and rereadings. They are interesting and meaningful, contributing to rigorous study.

The program leads students through multiple readings of the target text by means of a Close Reading Routine. This routine involves a four-part spiraling analysis that is based on the CCSS for Reading strands, Key Ideas and Details, Craft and Structure, and Integration of Knowledge and Ideas. Readers are led to read and reread successively in order to:

- form initial understandings of the text,
- summarize the text,
- deepen their understandings while examining the author's use of text elements to shape understandings, and
- build knowledge.

Academic discussion permeates the program's Close Reading Routine. In preparation for summarizing selections, students compare the topic statements they compose and the important words they select. When time permits, they share and compare their summaries. As a class they synthesize the ways particular text elements shape the meaning of selections. Finally, they discuss the new ideas they generated while reading, and apply those ideas to the units' Essential Questions.

Focusing on text evidence is a key aspect of ***Edge***. Of necessity readers use their knowledge and experience to make sense of authors' meanings (Pearson, 2012), but misunderstandings can arise when readers rely too much on what they bring to the text and substitute it for what authors actually presented. Consequently, the program consistently prompts students to ground their interpretations with wording from the text. All the reading selections in the program, including the ones for close reading, are accompanied by text-dependent questions that prompt students to directly engage authors' ideas and cite the evidence that supports their responses to the ideas.

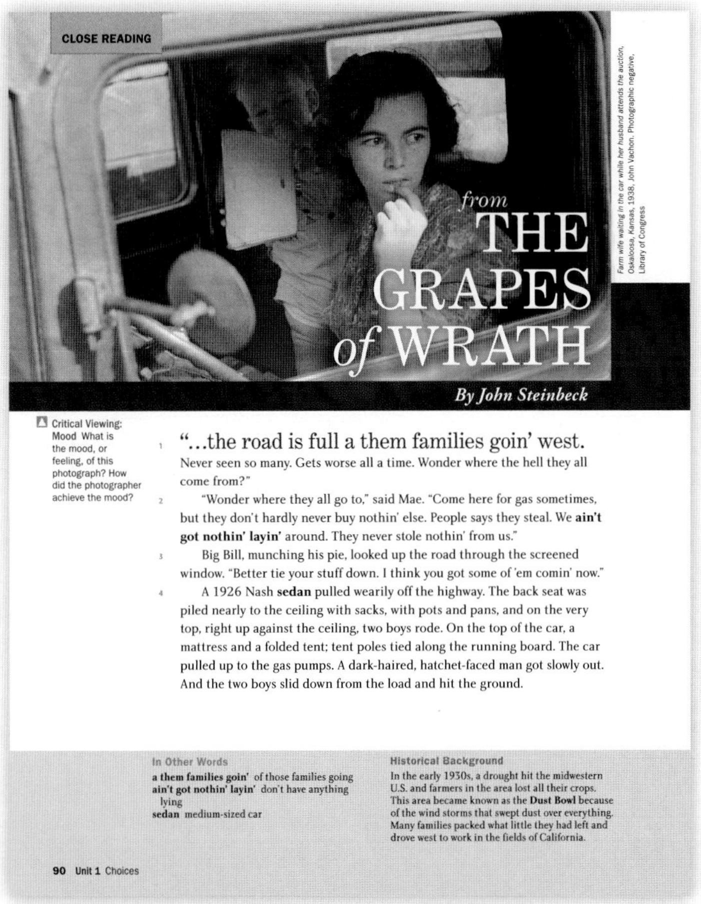
CLOSE READING

from THE GRAPES of WRATH

By John Steinbeck

Farm wife waiting in the car while her husband attends the auction, Oskaloosa, Kansas, 1938, John Vachon. Photographic negative, Library of Congress

Critical Viewing: Mood What is the mood, or feeling, of this photograph? How did the photographer achieve the mood?

1 "...the road is full a them families goin' west. Never seen so many. Gets worse all a time. Wonder where the hell they all come from?"

2 "Wonder where they all go to," said Mae. "Come here for gas sometimes, but they don't hardly never buy nothin' else. People says they steal. We **ain't got nothin' layin'** around. They never stole nothin' from us."

3 Big Bill, munching his pie, looked up the road through the screened window. "Better tie your stuff down. I think you got some of 'em comin' now."

4 A 1926 Nash **sedan** pulled wearily off the highway. The back seat was piled nearly to the ceiling with sacks, with pots and pans, and on the very top, right up against the ceiling, two boys rode. On the top of the car, a mattress and a folded tent; tent poles tied along the running board. The car pulled up to the gas pumps. A dark-haired, hatchet-faced man got slowly out. And the two boys slid down from the load and hit the ground.

In Other Words

a them families goin' of those families going
ain't got nothin' layin' don't have anything lying
sedan medium-sized car

Historical Background

In the early 1930s, a drought hit the midwestern U.S. and farmers in the area lost all their crops. This area became known as the **Dust Bowl** because of the wind storms that swept dust over everything. Many families packed what little they had left and drove west to work in the fields of California.

90 Unit 1 Choices

Students annotate passages as they respond to text-dependent questions and discuss selections.

Strategy Instruction

As the CCSS put it, a full range of strategies may be needed for students to monitor and direct their comprehension. Whether they are reading to acquire new knowledge, to perform a task, or for pleasure, independent readers are strategic (McNamara, 2007). They take charge of what they read, adopting strategies that fit their selections and their reasons for reading. If something in a text is puzzling or confusing, independent readers realize this immediately, shift mental gears, and apply strategies to repair their understanding. Convincing research of effective secondary-school literacy programs confirms the need to teach students comprehension strategies (Langer, 2002).

Edge presents the following eight strategies known to promote students' reading comprehension:

- Plan: Preview, set a purpose, and predict what you will meet in the text before reading it more carefully.
- Monitor: Notice confusing parts in the text then reread and make them clear.
- Determine Importance: Focus attention on the author's most significant ideas and information.
- Ask Questions: Think actively by asking and answering questions about the text.
- Visualize: Imagine the sight, sound, smell, taste, and touch of what the author is telling.
- Make Connections: Combine your knowledge and experiences with the author's ideas and information.
- Make Inferences: Use what you know to figure out what the author means but doesn't say directly.
- Synthesize: Bring together ideas gained from texts and blend them into a new understanding.

Following the National Reading Panel's (2000) findings, the program's introductory lessons teach students to flexibly apply this set of eight strategies. The lessons focus students on orchestrating this repertoire, deliberately using multiple strategies to foster their understandings of texts. Each unit in the program then supplements this introduction by concentrating attention on a single strategy, an intervention that develops expertise and improves transfer across genres (Nokes & Dole, 2004).

Along with the eight comprehension strategies that fit all selections, ***Edge*** includes instruction in analyzing literary devices, text structures, and genres. These strategies enable readers to analyze authors' organization of ideas (e.g., sequence, topic-detail, compare-contrast), purpose for writing (e.g., to tell a story, to explain, to convince), and genre-specific features (e.g., foreshadowing, symbolism, visual representations, testimonials). Text structure and genre strategies are especially important to teach because the ability to navigate textual arrangements as an aid to understanding and remembering is a robust characteristic of independent readers (Meyer, Wijekumar, Middlemiss, Higley, Lei, Meier, & Spielvogel, 2010; Kamil, 2012).

Conclusion

The reading comprehension instruction in ***Edge*** is best seen as a set of interactive elements that support one another. Engaging high school English learners and striving readers with content-rich texts at varying levels (independent, instructional, and complex) along with purposeful activities balances scaffolds and rigor to accelerate achievement and build resilient, engaged, literate graduates that can leverage literacy skills in school and beyond.

Increasing Reading Fluency

by Dr. Alfred W. Tatum

Efforts to develop instruction that more effectively addresses the reading and language needs of adolescent students must include attention to increasing their reading fluency. When proficient readers read, they achieve comprehension by applying what they know about how to maneuver the challenges in a text, such as word meanings and language structures and concepts that are new or unusual. They can call on a store of skills and strategies to negotiate these challenges to understanding. Readers who lack these skills and strategies are stuck, striving to make it though a text, and growing increasingly frustrated with their inability to understand what they read. Improving reading fluency is one way to help these readers move through text the way that proficient readers do and so reduce the frustration that often leads them to give up on reading altogether. Indeed, research analyses identify reading fluency as one of the five key components of effective reading instruction (National Reading Panel, 2000). More specifically, the research shows that increased reading fluency is related strongly and positively to increased reading comprehension (Samuels & Farstrup, 2006). Reading fluency is a critical component of effective reading instruction and most be considered as highly as decoding, vocabulary and comprehension instruction (Rasinski, Reutzel, Chard, & Linan-Thompson, 2011). Still, instructional intensity around fluent reading at the secondary level is less than adequate to create fluent readers (Paige, 2012).

"Research shows that increased reading fluency is related strongly and positively to increased reading comprehension."

What Is Reading Fluency?

Researchers offer varying definitions of fluency, but most agree that, in broad terms, reading fluency refers to the ability of readers to recognize and decode words and comprehend at the same time. As Pikulski and Chard (2005, p. 510) explain, fluency is a developmental process that is "manifested in accurate, rapid, expressive oral reading and is applied during, and makes possible, silent reading comprehension."

Oral reading with speed, accuracy, and expression are indicators of the ability to decode. For students to comprehend what they read, however, they must possess more than well-developed decoding skills. Suppose, for example, that students are given the following paragraph to read:

> The national debate over the impoverishment of inner-city populations and the presumed failure of New Deal initiatives such as Aid to Families with Dependent Children and public housing have, for the most part, been structured by a group of theoretical perspectives and empirical assumptions emphasizing individual responsibility for a variety of social ills such as economic dependency, family disorder, and crime (Bennett, Smith, & Wright, 2006, p. 9).

Some students may be able to accurately decode each word of the paragraph, and with a speed that is characteristic of a moderately fluent reader. However, these students may still be unfamiliar with the words impoverishment, initiatives, and empirical, and with concepts such as New Deal or inner-city. Therefore, even though they read with speed and accuracy, these students do not read with comprehension. For comprehension to take place, readers must have sufficient vocabulary and background knowledge to access the information in the text.

Effective fluency instruction recognizes that limited vocabulary and background knowledge are major barriers to comprehension, particularly for striving readers and English learners, and takes care to address both vocabulary and cognitive development (Pressley, Gaskins, & Fingeret, 2006).

For English learners (ELs), the English vocabulary and language structures in their content area reading materials pose a special challenge to fluency. As Palumbo and Willicutt (2006, p. 161) explain, even when these students determine the meaning of a new word in a text, they must "have a place to fit the meaning within a mental framework, or schema for representing that meaning with associated concepts . . . . English words they decode may not yield meaning for them."

Palumbo and Willicutt conclude that if instruction is to help ELs to decode and comprehend at a productive pace, it must increase both their store of English words and their familiarity with English story grammars, text structure, and, perhaps, new concepts. Research shows that ELs benefit when vocabulary support is incorporated into texts; when students are afforded opportunities to read multiple texts on the same subject; and when they receive explicit instruction about how to apply their own, culturally familiar experiences to achieve understanding.

In addition to improving vocabulary and comprehension strategies, many striving readers also need practice routines to develop their reading fluency. They may need practice with intonation, phrasing, and expression. Striving readers often benefit from repeated readings of familiar text in which they gradually improve phrasing and intonation and also record improvements in reading rate measured in words correct per minute (WCPM). Readers enhance textual meaning by reading with appropriate fluency (Paige, Rasinski, Magpuri-Lavell, 2012).

Effective Fluency Instruction

Scientifically based research findings converge on several practices that are essential for effective fluency instruction. These practices include the following:

- Identifying students in need of foundational skill development and providing age-appropriate, systematic, explicit instruction for those students.
- Selecting appropriate texts that are engaging and age-appropriate.
- Building vocabulary and background knowledge so students can access new and unfamiliar texts.
- Helping students become familiar with the syntax or language structures of different text genres.
- Teaching students specific comprehension strategies that allow them to read successfully and independently.
- Engage students in deep and wide reading.
- Allowing students to sometimes choose materials to read that they find interesting.
- Teaching routines that combine teacher modeling with guided and independent student practice, along with constant encouragement and feedback.
- Practice routines to develop automaticity and fluency at the word level and in reading connected text.
- Encouraging students to monitor and improve their fluent reading rates.

Applying the Research: *Hampton-Brown Edge*

Edge provides robust support for fluency development, including all of the research-based practices cited above. Explicit, systematic instruction in foundational reading skills is provided through ***Inside Phonics***. The ***Edge*** anthologies build fluency and vocabulary and the Language and Grammar Lab addresses foundational and grade level syntax and grammar skills.

Engaging Literature Student literature includes a wide variety of selections on engaging, challenging, and age-appropriate topics. Students are further motivated to read through lessons that connect to their own experience and generate curiosity about selection content. Narratives that have a strong voice and that are useful for fluency instruction are included. While students are consistently and systematically exposed to more complex grade-level texts, fluency practice focuses on short passages that are accessible.

Vocabulary, Language, and Comprehension The instructional plan includes extensive exploration and development of vocabulary, genre understanding, and language structures. Comprehension lessons provide scaffolded direct instruction support to help students understand and internalize the comprehension strategies that proficient readers use habitually.

Fluency Practice Routines ***Edge*** also provides daily practice routines for developing reading accuracy, intonation, phrasing, expression, and rate. Fluency practice passages are included for each week of instruction, with teaching support that includes modeling of the target skill (for example, phrasing), and a five-day plan for improving the skill through choral reading, collaborative reading, recorded reading, reading and marking the text, and reading to assess. Assessment includes a timed reading of the passage and reading rate in words correct per minute (WCPM). Students are encouraged to graph their reading rate over time so they can monitor their improvement.

Comprehension Coach

The Comprehension Coach interactive software at Levels C–E provides a risk-free and private environment where striving readers and ELs can develop their reading power and fluency. All student literature selections are included with comprehension and vocabulary supports. Students can read silently or listen to a model of the selection being read fluently. They can also record and listen to their own reading of the selection. After a recording, the software automatically calculates and graphs their reading rate in WCPM.

Conclusion

Edge provides the full range of research-based support that striving readers and English learners need to become fluent, proficient, and confident readers.

Talking the Talk: Meeting the Standards for Speaking and Listening

by Dr. Deborah J. Short and Dr. Michael W. Smith

Among the less noticed aspects of the Common Core State Standards is their emphasis on the importance of speaking and listening. As the standards document states, "To become college and career ready, students must have ample opportunities to take part in a variety of rich, structured conversations—as part of a whole class, in small groups, and with a partner." (National Governors Association Center for Best Practices, Council of Chief State School Officers, 2010)

The Problem

Unfortunately, a wealth of research demonstrates that students seldom have opportunities to take part in rich conversations. Goodlad's (1984) classic study of over a thousand classrooms led him to this conclusion:

> The data from our observation in more than a thousand classrooms support the popular image of a teacher standing or sitting in front of a class imparting knowledge to a group of students. Explaining and lecturing constituted the most frequent teaching activities, according to teachers, students, and our observations. Teachers also spent a substantial amount of time observing students at work or monitoring their seatwork. (p. 105).

"...research demonstrates that students seldom have opportunities to take part in rich conversations."

More recently, Applebee, Langer, Nystrand, and Gamoran's (2003) analysis of twenty seventh- to twelfth-grade classrooms found that what they call open-discussion, defined as "more than 30 seconds of free exchange of ideas among students or between at least three participants" which "usually begins in response to an open-ended question about which students can legitimately disagree" (p. 707) averaged 1.7 minutes per 60 minutes of class time. As depressing as that finding is, it is even more depressing when you consider that Applebee and his colleagues found that lower-track students, the students we are targeting in ***Hampton-Brown Edge***, are much less likely to have the opportunity to participate in such discussions.

The dearth of discussion is especially troubling because when it does occur it has dynamic effects. In Langer's (2001) study of schools that beat the odds, those "whose students perform higher [on high-stakes tests] than demographically comparable schools" (p. 837), she found that "in the most successful schools, there was always a belief in students' abilities to be able and enthusiastic learners; they believed all students can learn and that they, as teachers, could make a difference. They therefore took on the hard job of providing rich and challenging instructional contexts in which important discussions about English, language, literature, and writing in all its forms could take place." (p. 876). Moreover, Applebee and his colleagues (2003) found that these benefits accrue to all students, regardless of track.

Little wonder. In their study of the literate lives of young men both in and out of school, Smith and Wilhelm (2006) found that their participants "wanted to solve problems, debate, and argue in ways through which they could stake their identity and develop both ideas and functional tools that they could share and use with others in very immediate ways" (p. 57). This finding resonates with research that looked more specifically at struggling readers. Roberts and his colleagues (2008) found that struggling readers' motivation increases when they have the opportunity for interaction, and Faggella-Luby and Deshler (2008) found that collaborative learning tasks increase student ownership of their literacy learning, generate rich thinking, and can be expected to improve reading achievement. These findings apply to English language learners as well, but in their case besides being relevant and meaningful, the interactions must be carefully planned to yield gains in oral language development (Saunders & Goldenberg, 2010; Torgesen et al., 2007).

So What Do We Do?

Why do classroom discussions remain closed in light of such findings? Why is it so hard to break the pattern of discourse that typifies discussions of texts, even for teachers who strive to do so (cf. Marshall, Smagorinsky, & Smith, 1995)? Rabinowitz (Rabinowitz & Smith, 1998) provides one possible explanation when he notes that teachers typically teach texts that they have read many times to kids who are reading them for the first time. As a consequence, they've settled in their own minds at least many of the potential questions they could ask. And when they have, they understandably want to share their thinking with our students.

In *Edge* we do something that necessitates breaking the mold: We embed our reading and instruction in units that focus on Essential Questions. Our Essential Questions are designed to foster substantial talk about important issues that really matter. Take a look at a question from Level B: "What influences a person's choices?" The question is deceptively simple but has a wide range of possible answers. Cluster 1 selections and activities focus on how family and friends influence choices. Cluster 2 explores how circumstances impact choices. And Cluster 3 considers the impact of the broader society on our choices. The point is that the multiple possibilities for responses lead to multiple opportunities for rigorous discussion. Students must take a position and make a claim. They then must use relevant text information as evidence to support their claim. Our units make it clear right from the start that they are designed to foster rich collaborative exchanges.

Posing compelling questions isn't enough, however. It's also important that the academic talk those questions foster takes a variety of forms to meet the expectations of the new standards. ***Edge*** includes an array of whole-class discussions, small-group discussions, and paired discussions. Some are spontaneous and others are more formal. But all of them occur only after we have prepared students to engage in them in a meaningful way. For English language learners (ELLs) this is particularly important. First, we help negotiate the dynamics of a class discussion (how to get a turn, how to build on a peer's idea) and second, we provide teachers with language frames aligned with the Common Core State Standards to help ELLs organize and state their ideas or opinions clearly.

Another benefit of building units around Essential Questions is that students have the opportunity to tap into and develop their background knowledge, something that is important for all students but is especially crucial for English language learners (Short & Fitzsimmons, 2007). No one perspective is privileged with Essential Questions; rather, different cultural and personal viewpoints are welcome to inform the dialogue among the students. In short, we offer students important issues to talk about and provide the texts and the contexts they need to make that talk as rewarding as possible.

1 Plan a Project

Press Conference

In this unit, you'll be holding a press conference, or a gathering of reporters to interview a famous person about issues that address the Essential Question. To get started, watch a few different press conferences on TV or on the Internet. Look for

- what types of questions the reporters ask
- how the famous person answers the questions
- how much time the press conference takes.

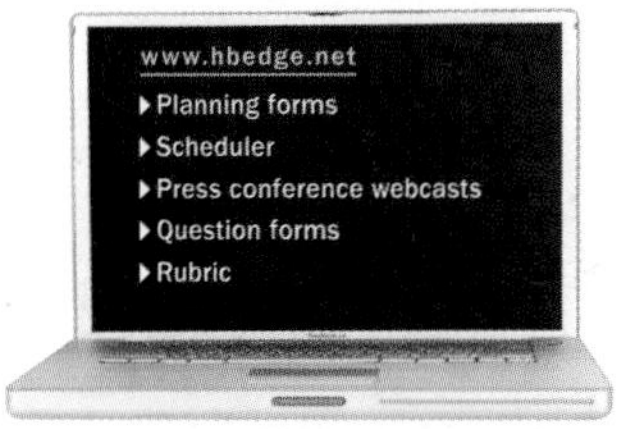

Study Skills Start planning your press conference. Use the forms on hbedge.net to plan your time and to prepare the content.

Throughout each unit, as students read texts, they generate questions and conduct research relating to the Essential Question, culminating in the presentation of a Unit Project.

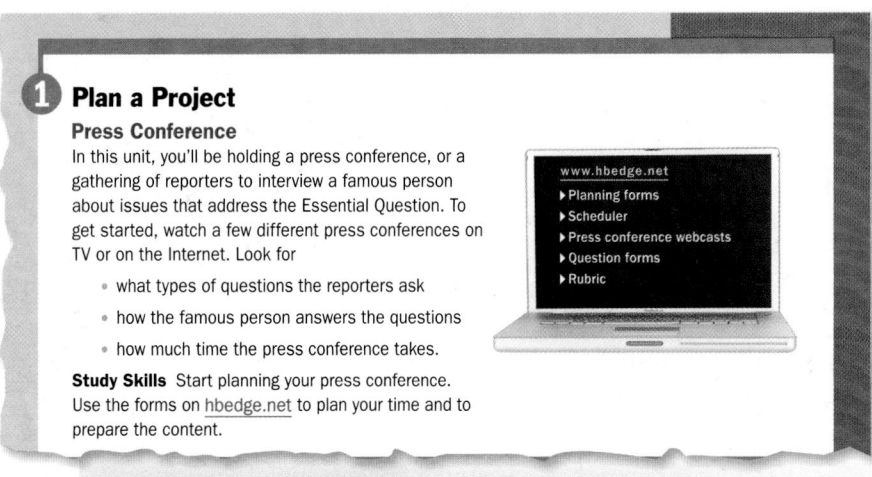

Developing Academic Literacy in Adolescent English Language Learners

by Dr. Deborah J. Short

Educators of English learners (ELs) should have two goals: to accelerate their development of academic English and to strengthen their content knowledge. Research has shown that ELs improve their academic English skills and learn more of the content of school subjects through an integrated instructional approach (Echevarria, Richards-Tutor, Canges, & Francis, 2011; Lindholm-Leary & Borsato, 2006; Short, Fidelman & Louguit, 2012). This integrated approach provides the means for English learners to achieve rigorous standards such as the Common Core when they receive systematic content and language instruction and assessment along with a solid, research-based curriculum. Through this type of program, they advance their academic language and literacy skills and thus are better prepared for college and careers.

Understanding English Learners in High School

Most English learners in high school are already on the path to academic literacy. They have not stalled; rather, they are making steady progress, but perhaps at different rates. Second-language acquisition takes time and requires understanding of what English learners bring to our classrooms.

"Second-language acquisition takes time and requires understanding of what English learners bring to our classrooms."

Some English learners arrive in the United States without literacy in their native language. Yet many are placed in classrooms with teachers who are unprepared to teach basic literacy skills to adolescents (McGraner & Saenz, 2009). These newcomers need a developmental program of language and literacy with direct instruction in phonics, vocabulary, grammar, and the fundamentals of reading and writing. This is important to note because standards such as the Common Core do not plan for students at Grade 6 or higher who need basic instruction in phonics and grammar.

Other ELs have grown up in the U.S., but for reasons such as family mobility, intermittent school attendance, or limited access to ESL or bilingual instruction, they have not developed the degree of academic literacy required for reading and understanding high school texts or for interacting productively in instruction with teachers and classmates. Some of these students may need a targeted intervention.

Still other ELs enter high school with native-language literacy. They have a strong foundation that can facilitate their academic English growth. Their prior knowledge and some literacy skills can transfer from the native language to their new one. They may have already mastered some of the literacy expectations called for in the Common Core and other standards but they need to learn and apply academic English.

What, then, do ELs from all these different backgrounds need as they move through the high school years?

Explicit Instruction in English Vocabulary and Structures

We know that the connections between language, literacy, and academic achievement grow stronger as students progress through the grades (Anstrom et al., 2010), and that the development of proficiency in academic English is a complex process for adolescent ELs. The Common Core has increased the rigor of instruction. High school ELs must develop literacy skills for each content area in their second language as they simultaneously try to comprehend and apply content area concepts through that second language (García & Godina, 2004; Genesee, Lindholm-Leary, Saunders, & Christian, 2006). Therefore, even while we focus on developing literacy and bolstering content area knowledge, we must provide explicit instruction in English semantics, syntax, phonology, pragmatics, and discourse levels of the language as they are applied in school (Bailey, 2007; Schleppegrell, 2004).

Personal Connections to Learning The complexity of second language acquisition is not the only variable in becoming literate in English. Identity, engagement, motivation, and life outside school are other important factors (Moje, 2006; Moje et al., 2004; Tatum, 2005, 2007). Adolescents engage more with texts that they have chosen themselves, and they read material above their level if it is of interest. Engagement and motivation increase when students can see themselves in the characters, events, and settings of the materials. That is why multicultural literature and expository text on numerous topics should be part of the curriculum. Moreover, teachers must also push students beyond their comfort zone and ensure they engage with complex text and a variety of genres at their current reading level and above.

Self-perceptions (e.g., strong vs. weak reader), personal goals, and opportunities to participate in collaborative literacy activities with classmates also influence motivation. Out-of-school experiences and literacies play an important role too. Stressors outside of school—hectic home lives, work, lack of study space, peer pressures—may diminish students' interest in and ability to develop English literacy. Positive out-of-school interactions with English literacy (e.g., the Internet, music, work), however, may strengthen their engagement with literacy practices in the classroom.

Promoting English Literacy Development

A number of research reports have examined more than two decades of rigorous studies of English second language development (e.g., August & Shanahan, 2006; Genesee et al., 2006; Short & Fitzsimmons, 2007). These reports provide a great deal of valuable information about adolescent ELs and the curricular content and instructional practices that work best to promote their academic language and literacy skills. The following are among the key findings:

1. **Transfer of Skills** Certain native-language skills often transfer to English literacy, including phonemic awareness, comprehension, language-learning strategies, and knowledge learned through oral interaction. If students have opportunities to learn and maintain their native language literacy, they may acquire English more quickly. Concepts that students learn in their native language often transfer to English. ELs may require assistance to articulate prior knowledge gained in their native-language instruction in English, but they do not have to relearn it. Transfering knowledge from one language to another, however, is not automatic (Gersten, Brengelman, & Jiménez, 1994). It requires teachers to make explicit links to students' prior knowledge and to prompt students to make connections.

2. **Native Language Literacy** Academic literacy in the native language facilitates the development of academic literacy in English. For example, once students have enough English proficiency (e.g., vocabulary, sense of sentence structure) to engage with text, those who have learned comprehension strategies (e.g., finding the main idea, making inferences) in their native language have the cognitive background to use those strategies in their new language (August & Shanahan, 2006). Similarly if they are able to make a claim and counter-argument in their native language, they understand cognitively how to do so in English.

3. **Academic English** Teaching the five components of proficient reading—phonemic awareness, phonics, vocabulary, fluency, and comprehension (National Reading Panel, 2000)—to English learners is necessary but not sufficient for developing their academic literacy. ELs need to develop oral language proficiency, language functions, and academic discourse patterns. In this way students can participate in classroom talk, such as evaluating a historical perspective or presenting evidence for a scientific claim, and therefore meet the speaking and listening standards defined in the Common Core. As a corollary to this point, students benefit from the integration of reading, writing, listening, and speaking in lessons. As they develop knowledge in one language domain, they reinforce their learning in other domains.

4. **Instructional Accommodations** High-quality instruction for English learners is similar to high-quality instruction for native English-speaking students. However, beginning- and intermediate-level ELs need frequent instructional and linguistic supports to help them access core content (Saunders & Goldenberg, 2010). Even advanced students need accommodations on occasion.

5. **Enhanced and Explicit Vocabulary Development** English learners need enhanced vocabulary development. Direct teaching of specific words can facilitate vocabulary growth and lead to increased reading comprehension for English language learners (Carlo et al., 2004). However, many high school ELs need to learn many more vocabulary words than teachers have time to teach. As a result, specific-word instruction must be supplemented with explicit instruction in strategies for word learning, such as contextual and word part analysis and use of native-language cognates. Helping ELs develop knowledge of words, roots, affixes, and word relationships is crucial if they are to understand topics in the content areas well enough to increase both their academic knowledge and reading comprehension (Graves, 2006).

Designing Appropriate Curricula for ELs

Comprehensive literacy instruction programs for English learners must incorporate and provide extensive practice in the following elements:

- lesson objectives based on state content and language standards, such as the Common Core and WIDA, CELD, ELDA21, or ELPS
- explicit attention to general academic and cross-curricular vocabulary, domain-specific terminology, word parts (roots and affixes), and word relationships
- developmental reading instruction tied to a wide range of expository and narrative text genres that increase in complexity over time
- explicit writing instruction for all other content areas
- instruction for listening, speaking, and discourse level interaction
- grammar instruction
- teaching practices that tap students' prior knowledge and build background for new topics
- explicit instruction in learning strategies and cognitive processing skills
- instruction in typical subject matter tasks
- comprehension checks and opportunities for review

In effective programs, teachers use specific techniques, such as those in the SIOP Model for sheltered instruction (Echevarria, Vogt, & Short, 2013), to make the presentation of new content comprehensible for English learners and to advance their academic language development. For example:

- Teachers make the standards-based lesson objectives explicit to the students and connect objectives to Essential Questions and unit themes.
- Before a reading or a writing activity, teachers activate students' prior knowledge and link to past learning. They preteach vocabulary and build background appropriate to the content and task at hand.
- Teachers chunk the presentation of information according to students' proficiency levels; utilize realia, pictures, and demonstrations; teach note-taking skills with specific organizers; and include time for review and reflection.
- To differentiate instruction as well as build competence and the ability to work independently, teachers scaffold subject matter tasks and classroom routines by using, for example, sentence and paragraph frames graduated to students' proficiency levels or graphic organizers to record and organize information.
- Language skills are sequenced and taught explicitly as well as integrated into lessons on other skills so that students have every opportunity to grow their academic English. Students practice using language functions, for example, with sentence starters while interacting with classmates.
- To ensure that learning is taking place and students are making expected progress, teachers check ELs' comprehension frequently during instruction. They use multiple measures to monitor progress on a more formal basis, with assessments that accommodate the students' developing language skills and lead to timely reteaching.

Applying the Research

Edge provides all these elements of successful instruction for English learners. The program uses Common Core State Standards for language, literacy, and content as the foundation for the lesson objectives and to inform each unit's Essential Question (on topical issues like "What tests a person's loyalty?" and "Do we find or create our true selves?" These Essential Questions engage and motivate students to share possible answers as they read. They also offer students opportunities to build vocabulary, listening, and speaking skills in context over time and to respond more thoughtfully as they gain new perspectives, information, and data.

To promote growth in vocabulary, the program teaches key content-specific words from the texts and important academic words (e.g., conflict, sequence, however) that students can apply across content areas. English learners also engage in a wide range of vocabulary-building activities with multiple opportunities to practice new words and determine word meanings. Daily vocabulary routines help students use independent word-learning strategies.

Furthermore, ***Edge*** makes strategic use of native language. Resources are provided in multiple languages. Particular attention is paid to helping students recognize cognates and false cognates.

Lesson plans are built around techniques that are appropriate for English learners. The How to Read features at the start of each unit prepare students for the types of text they will encounter during instruction. Make a Connection activities are provided in each cluster and provide anticipatory tasks that activate and build prior knowledge. Academic discussions of what was read involve collaborative learning tasks with pairs and small groups to promote the use of oral language. Readings are linked to writing lessons so students learn to persuade, defend claims, and conduct research.

Additionally, the Look into the Text feature use the text to teach skills critical to the Common Core state standards and to literacy development. This not only provides text-based context, it gives ELs background and context critical to a selection. Using the text to teach the text helps ELs learn about features of genres (e.g. use of captions and illustrations in nonficiton articles, the role of character and setting in short stories), but they become familiar with a portion of the text as they do so.

Edge also includes instructional resources dedicated to systematic language development. The ***Edge*** Language and Grammar Lab includes a Teacher's Guide with lessons that address language functions, grammar, and language transfer. Language and Grammar Lab resources are thematically aligned with ***Edge*** units to provide a common schema for language learning and literacy development.

Finally, the lessons offer techniques to adapt instruction for students at different levels of language proficiency access to the text and to support their participation in academic tasks.

Conclusion

Effective instruction for English learners requires both high expectations and specialized strategies to ensure success. The standards base of ***Edge***, along with its structured language supports and scaffolding techniques, allows English learners to accelerate their growth in academic language and literacy.

Teaching Writing to Adolescents

by Dr. Michael W. Smith

The Common Core State Standards (CCSS) have to be regarded as good news for teachers who care about writing. The CCSS emphasize writing clear and convincing arguments drawing on multiple sources, informational papers that do meaningful work, and compelling narratives that foster an understanding of oneself and/or others (National Governors Association Center for Best Practices, Council of Chief State School Officers, 2010). This is a far cry from the "formulaic writing and… thinking" that, according to Hillocks (2002, p. 200), is rewarded by so many current standards and standards-based assessments. But, as I've argued elsewhere (Fredricksen, Wilhelm, & Smith, 2012; Smith, Wilhelm, & Fredricksen, 2012; Wilhelm, Smith, & Fredricksen, 2012), with this good news comes a challenge: Traditional approaches to teaching writing aren't enough to meet these new standards.

"Traditional approaches to teaching writing aren't enough to meet these new standards."

Langer's (2001) study of schools that beat the odds, that is, schools whose students did better on high-stakes assessments than demographically comparable schools, provided far more compelling instruction than what is traditional. She puts it this way:

> In the most successful schools, there was always a belief in students' abilities to be able and enthusiastic learners; they believed all students can learn and that they, as teachers, could make a difference. They therefore took on the hard job of providing rich and challenging instructional contexts in which important discussions about English, language, literature, and writing in all its forms could take place, while using both the direct instruction and contextualized experiences their students needed for skills and knowledge development. Weaving a web of integrated and interconnected experiences, they ensured that their students would develop the pervasive as well as internalized learning of knowledge, skills, and strategies to use on their own as more mature and more highly literate individuals at school, as well as at home and in their future work. (p. 876)

Langer's analysis suggests two major dimensions of the teaching done in the successful schools: They created integrated and motivating contexts and they provided powerful instruction. Let's take each of these in turn.

Provide Integrated and Motivating Contexts

All of the writing we ask students to do in ***Hampton-Brown Edge*** is embedded in units built around authentic Essential Questions that matter in the here and now. When Jeff Wilhelm and I did our study of the literate lives of boys both in and out of school (Smith & Wilhelm, 2002; 2006) one of our participants said something in an interview that haunts us to this day:

> English is about NOTHING! It doesn't help you DO anything. English is about reading poems and telling about rhythm. It's about commas and crap like that for God's sake. What does that have to DO with DOING anything? It's about NOTHING!

His contention was echoed in one way or another by many of the other boys. Little wonder that so many of them rejected the reading and writing they were given to do in school.

But they didn't reject reading and writing outside school. Every one of the young men in our study had an active literate life. One of the foundational principles of ***Edge*** is that we wanted the series to make it clear that English is about something important. That's why we built our units around Essential Questions, the deep and abiding questions we all face as we think about our lives.

Here's another haunting response from one of our young men: "I can't stand writing if I've been put on a line and if I walk outside of it something happens. I like to be able to just kind of go off in my own little rampage of self-expression." The writing projects and shorter writing activities we ask students to do don't ask kids to walk a line. Instead each unit casts students in the role of authors who have a contribution to make to the ongoing classroom conversation about those deep and abiding questions. In short, our units provide the "rich and challenging" writing contexts that Langer calls for.

But the ***Edge*** unit structure does more than that. Because our units are integrated, they engage students in an extended consideration of the Essential Questions by bringing a variety of different kinds of texts into meaningful conversation. This structure facilitates writing to sources. The extended consideration alone helps students to develop the topic knowledge they need to write. The other payoff for our unit structure is that it allows students to draw on multiple sources in their own writing, something that assessments from both the Partnership for Assessment of Readiness for College and Careers (PARCC) and the Smarter Balanced Assessment Consortia (SBAC) call for. PARCC, for example, requires "writing to sources rather than writing to decontextualized expository prompts" (Partnership for Assessment of Readiness for College and Careers) and encourages the comparison and synthesis of ideas across a range of informational sources. So does ***Edge***. Frequent shorter and longer writing activities build writing fluency in authentic and meaningful contexts.

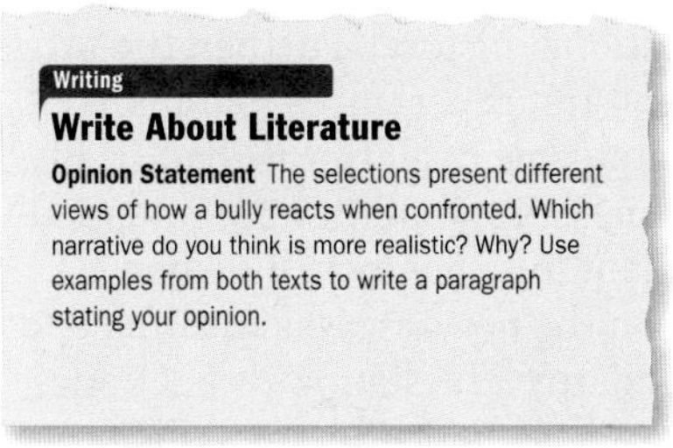
Writing

Write About Literature

Opinion Statement The selections present different views of how a bully reacts when confronted. Which narrative do you think is more realistic? Why? Use examples from both texts to write a paragraph stating your opinion.

Writing activities require synthesis of ideas across a range of texts.

Provide Powerful Instruction

In ***Edge***, we ask students to do compelling writing. But we do far more than that. We teach them how to do that writing. And through the course of our books we provide lots and lots of opportunities for students to practice what we've taught them as they write in response to reading, write to learn, and write to sources. In each unit we help students analyze a model of the target text. Then we help them learn how to successfully write their own text. The CCSS emphasize the importance of evidence, so for each of our major texts we ask students to return to the text to reread and then write. And remember, because that writing is about an authentic question, students have to select the best possible evidence. The classroom conversations that follow their writing provide clear and immediate feedback on the quality of their work. But that's not all. We provide planning heuristics to help them develop and organize their writing. We provide sentence frames to help them develop the syntactic skills they need. We also engage them in assessing and revising their own work and provide supports for their collaboration with other student writers.

In addition, because we engage them in writing that matters, we create a context in which they will be motivated to learn the grammar and usage conventions they need. Study after study after study has clearly established that teaching grammar and usage through skill and drill approaches that are isolated from students' writing is ineffective (cf. Hillocks, 1986, Hillocks & Smith, 2003; Smith, Cheville, & Hillocks, 2005; Smith & Wilhelm, 2007). Such isolated grammatical instruction not only doesn't help students, it actually hurts them. It takes instructional time away from more effective instructional approaches and it sours their attitude toward their English classes.

Edge embeds instruction in correctness into the work that students are doing on their own writing. Each writing project has several focal correctness areas. For example, the instruction on autobiographical narratives includes instruction on capitalization, punctuating quotations, homonym confusion, and sentence completion. Students are given instruction and practice and then provided an immediate opportunity to apply what they learned to their own writing.

Think about the students for whom this series is intended. Many of them will be plagued by a wide variety of correctness problems. And these problems will have persisted despite the fact that those students have been in school for years. A scattershot approach that tries to focus on every error in every paper is sure to be frustrating both to teachers and to students. It won't improve writing, but, as research on writing apprehension (cf. Hillocks, 1986) suggests, it might shut students' writing down. Marrying meaning with mechanics is sure to be more effective.

In short, the ***Edge*** series provides instruction that will help students become more competent and compelling writers, abilities that are crucially important both in and out of school.

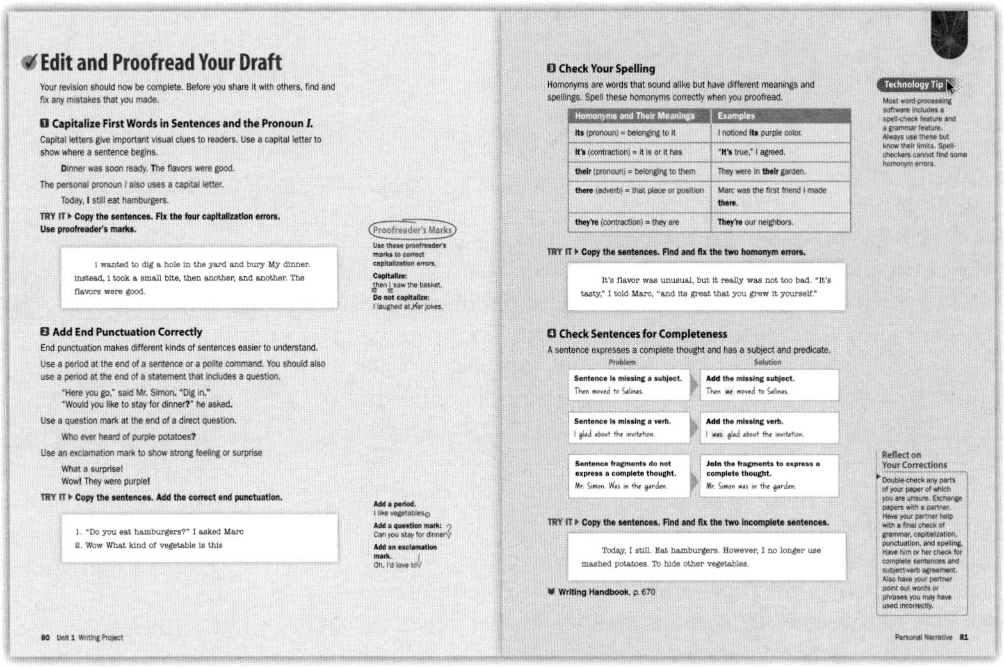
Edit and Proofread Your Draft

Your revision should now be complete. Before you share it with others, find and fix any mistakes that you made.

1 Capitalize First Words in Sentences and the Pronoun *I*.

Capital letters give important visual clues to readers. Use a capital letter to show where a sentence begins.

Dinner was soon ready. The flavors were good.

The personal pronoun *I* also uses a capital letter.

Today, I still eat hamburgers.

TRY IT ▸ Copy the sentences. Fix the four capitalization errors. Use proofreader's marks.

i wanted to dig a hole in the yard and bury My dinner. instead, i took a small bite, then another, and another. The flavors were good.

Proofreader's Marks

Use these proofreader's marks to correct capitalization errors.

Capitalize: then i saw the basket.

Do not capitalize: I laughed at Her jokes.

2 Add End Punctuation Correctly

End punctuation makes different kinds of sentences easier to understand.

Use a period at the end of a sentence or a polite command. You should also use a period at the end of a statement that includes a question.

"Here you go," said Mr. Simon. "Dig in."
"Would you like to stay for dinner?" he asked.

Use a question mark at the end of a direct question.

Who ever heard of purple potatoes?

Use an exclamation mark to show strong feeling or surprise

What a surprise!
Wow! They were purple!

TRY IT ▸ Copy the sentences. Add the correct end punctuation.

1. "Do you eat hamburgers?" I asked Marc
2. Wow What kind of vegetable is this

Add a period. I like vegetables

Add a question mark: Can you stay for dinner

Add an exclamation mark. Oh, I'd love to

80 Unit 1 Writing Project

3 Check Your Spelling

Homonyms are words that sound alike but have different meanings and spellings. Spell these homonyms correctly when you proofread.

Homonyms and Their Meanings	Examples
its (pronoun) = belonging to it	I noticed **its** purple color.
it's (contraction) = it is or it has	"**It's** true," I agreed.
their (pronoun) = belonging to them	They were in **their** garden.
there (adverb) = that place or position	Marc was the first friend I made **there**.
they're (contraction) = they are	**They're** our neighbors.

Technology Tip

Most word-processing software includes a spell-check feature and a grammar feature. Always use these but know their limits. Spell-checkers cannot find some homonym errors.

TRY IT ▸ Copy the sentences. Find and fix the two homonym errors.

It's flavor was unusual, but it really was not too bad. "It's tasty," I told Marc, "and its great that you grew it yourself."

4 Check Sentences for Completeness

A sentence expresses a complete thought and has a subject and predicate.

Problem	Solution
Sentence is missing a subject. Then moved to Salinas.	**Add the missing subject.** Then we moved to Salinas.
Sentence is missing a verb. I glad about the invitation.	**Add the missing verb.** I was glad about the invitation.
Sentence fragments do not express a complete thought. Mr. Simon. Was in the garden.	**Join the fragments to express a complete thought.** Mr. Simon was in the garden.

TRY IT ▸ Copy the sentences. Find and fix the two incomplete sentences.

Today, I still. Eat hamburgers. However, I no longer use mashed potatoes. To hide other vegetables.

Writing Handbook, p. 670

Reflect on Your Corrections

Double-check any parts of your paper of which you are unsure. Exchange papers with a partner. Have your partner help with a final check of grammar, capitalization, punctuation, and spelling. Have him or her check for complete sentences and subject-verb agreement. Also have your partner point out words or phrases you may have used incorrectly.

Personal Narrative 81

Instruction to improve writing accuracy is integrated into writing projects.

Comprehensive and Responsive Assessment

by Dr. Deborah J. Short and Dr. Alfred W. Tatum

The growing concern about students' readiness for college and careers among governors, chief state school officers, business leaders, college faculty, and teachers has led to a demand for more rigorous instruction for the nation's children (Grossman, Reyna, & Shipton, 2011). The concerns have engendered two major shifts in K-12 education:

1. the implementation of the Common Core State Standards, and

2. the development of assessments that align with these new state standards.

Descriptive data of student performance indicate our students are not performing as well as we would like. For instance, only 38 percent of U.S. 12th graders performed at or above proficiency in reading according to 2009 NAEP data, and only 25 percent of high school graduates in 2011 scored at a level on the ACT that indicates readiness for entry-level, credit-bearing college coursework. We can reverse this long-standing trend of underperformance on reading assessments by a large number of U.S. students with responsive instruction to improve high school students' reading abilities. Assessments are critical in planning responsive instruction for students who struggle with reading and writing.

"Assessments are critical in planning responsive instruction for students who struggle with reading and writing."

Reading and writing assessments help teachers construct an understanding of how students are developing, and thus provide critical information that allows them to make important instructional decisions (Afflerbach, 2007). Afflerbach notes that responsive teachers need to examine the consequences, usefulness, roles, and responsibilities related to assessments, as well as the reliability and validity of the assessments.

This point is particularly important for the assessment of students who are English learners (ELs). Standardized tests that aim to measure knowledge of academic content (e.g., science, math) generally are not sensitive to second-language literacy development. As a consequence, some educators may incorrectly interpret data from these measures as evidence that students lack content mastery. A closer look might show, however, that the students performed at the normal pace of the second-language acquisition process (IRA & NICHD, 2007; Solano-Flores & Trumbull, 2003). Tests results also are confounded by aspects of EL students' diversity (e.g., native-language literacy, educational history). Further, the tests may require knowledge of cultural experiences that many EL students have not had. The outcome of all this is that for EL students, many tests do not measure what they are intended to measure. It will be important to remember this when interpreting results for ELs on the new assessments linked to the Common Core state standards. The standards at Grades 6 and higher assume students have basic literacy skills, which may not be the case for newcomer and beginning level English learners.

Using Assessments to Plan Instruction

To plan responsive instruction, assessment must be ongoing. The assessment plan must include both formal and informal measures to gauge student progress and determine the effectiveness of instructional programs and their impact on students. All students can benefit from a diagnostic assessment at the start of the school year. Instruction in reading, writing, language, listening, and speaking can be more carefully tailored to the students' needs when teachers know, for example, that students have strong decoding skills but lack understanding of specific comprehension strategies, such as determining importance or making inferences.

EL students also benefit when teachers know the extent of their native-language literacy skills, because many of these skills transfer to English literacy acquisition (Genesee, Lindholm-Leary, Saunders, & Christian, 2006). In addition, EL students who have strong home-literacy experiences and opportunities generally achieve better English literacy outcomes than do those without such experiences (Goldenberg, Rueda, & August, 2006). Therefore, effective assessment practices include the initial testing of students' native-language literacy as well as their English literacy.

To capture students' varied reading, writing, and linguistic abilities and interests, assessment plans must endeavor to create comprehensive student profiles that measure the full range of student performance. This may include:

1. Ascertaining students' concept of reading and writing
2. Identifying students' strengths and weaknesses at both the word level and text level
3. Assessing students' acumen for reading increasingly complex narrative and expository texts over time
4. Assessing students' acumen for applying the knowledge of language and conventions when writing.
5. Gauging students' affective responses to reading and writing activities
6. Involving students in the assessment process and using their voices to adjust instructional practice and assessment practices, if necessary.
7. Having students cite evidence for arguments and inferences based on close readings of text

Using these seven dimensions to develop comprehensive profiles increases the likelihood that assessment practices will be of maximum benefit to students. Comprehensive and timely profiles allow teachers to focus attention on whether students view reading as a word-calling task, or on whether they strive actively to construct meaning as they read. The profiles give teachers ways to become aware of students' reading fluency, observe their reading for miscues, and assess their comprehension-monitoring strategies. Additionally, the profiles guide teachers in examining the texts students read, determining whether the content engages their interest. Regular use of eAssessments or other online assessments can help facilitate timely snapshots of students' skills to inform instruction and improve accommodations for students who struggle with reading and writing. Additionally, using constructed responses gives a more comprehensive view of students' strengths and weakness in writing and in citing text evidence.

Responsive instruction for ELs may be more complicated than for native English speakers. In general, EL students attain word-level skills, such as decoding, word recognition, and spelling, in a way similar to their English-speaking peers. For text-level skills, such as reading comprehension and writing, however, the situation differs because of EL students' more limited oral English proficiency and knowledge of English vocabulary and syntax. Given the important roles that well-developed listening and speaking and extensive vocabulary knowledge play in English reading and writing success, not to mention background schema, literacy instruction for EL students must incorporate extensive opportunities for language and vocabulary development. In particular, language and writing skills must be taught directly and explicitly. Students' writing, for example, can improve when teachers model a range of writing forms and techniques, and review writing samples with students to help students expand their English usage. Writing can also improve when teachers have beginning-level students copy words and text until they gain more proficiency (Graham & Perin, 2007). Discussion and repeated practice with words and sentence patterns familiarizes EL students with English language conventions, such as how words and sentences are arranged in oral and written discourse (Garcia & Beltran, 2003).

Applying the Research:

Hampton-Brown Edge provides a robust array of tools for both formal and informal assessments aligned with instructional materials to support teachers in understanding their students' needs and monitoring their progress. The assessment also identifies which students are in need of basic or advanced phonics, phonological awareness, decoding, and spelling instruction, provided in the Inside Phonics Kit.

Diagnostic and Placement Assessments Students entering the program can take a Phonics Test and a Lexile® Placement Test. This assessment provides a recommended placement in the appropriate level of ***Edge***—Fundamentals, Level A, Level B, or Level C.

In addition to these placement tools, the program includes recommendations for further diagnostic assessment with standardized instruments from a number of test publishers. Such measures can give additional information on students' strengths and instructional needs in phonics, decoding, vocabulary, comprehension, fluency, grammar, and writing. The instructional plan also provides consistent support for informal diagnosis of student needs. Lessons include frequent checks for understanding and many opportunities for students to demonstrate their skills through a variety of oral and written responses. Ongoing progress monitoring enables teachers to gauge which students in levels A–C may need intervention on targeted basic or advanced-level phonics skills or more extensive systematic and explicit instruction in reading foundational skills. As they observe and evaluate these steps of the plan, teachers engage in continuing diagnosis of students' needs and progress in all areas of literacy and language development.

Formal Progress Monitoring The main formal assessment of student progress in ***Edge*** is tailored to the language and reading proficiency level of the student. Unit Tests include unique reading passages, and context-rich opportunities to assess language and grammar, and prompts for writing composition. A balance of selected response and constructed response items help students gain comfort with the question types they will encounter on high-stakes tests.

Informal Progress Monitoring The program provides a wealth of resources and daily support to help teachers monitor student progress informally. and provide immediate scaffolding or feedback. Lessons include an Ongoing Assessment step to assist teachers in quickly determining if students understand the skill. In addition, lessons are constructed so that at each step of the learning process, all students respond in ways that demonstrate how successfully they are learning the strategy or content objectives. Students respond in a variety of ways, through graphic organizers, language frames and sentence frames, choral responses, written responses, gestures, and more. This interactive lesson structure gives teachers continual opportunities to note students' successes and areas of need. When students have difficulty with a strategy or concept, lessons provide specific suggestions for corrective feedback, addressing student needs immediately.

Affective and Metacognitive Measures Responsive assessment examines students' attitudes toward reading and writing and their self-assessments of achievement. ***Edge*** includes interest surveys, inventories related to the behaviors of reading and writing, metacognitive measures in which students can share the strategies they are using to determine the meaning of words and comprehend selections, and student self-assessments that lead to goal-setting.

Summative Assessments The program also includes two Level Tests that measure achievement on the standards taught in the program that are typically assessed on high-stakes tests. Two forms are provided.

Reteaching and Review The program includes flexible reteaching prescriptions for the informal and formal progress-monitoring tests and for the summative assessments so that teachers meet the learning needs of the students who were assessed. Review activities and resources aid retention and help students integrate knowledge.

Fluency Assessment Each week students can practice fluency with a passage, excerpted from the reading selection. This same passage can be used for a timed reading in which the words-correct-per-minute (WCPM) fluency rate is calculated. Students are encouraged to graph their fluency rates over time so they can see the evidence of their improvement. Fluency development in the core materials is supported by daily fluency activities including listening, choral reading, partner reading, and recording, with emphasis on intonation, phrasing, and expression. Additional technology support for fluency practice and assessment of WCPM rates is provided in the Comprehension Coach at levels A–C.

Preparation for Common Core Assessments

To provide our learners with the best opportunities to demonstrate their knowledge on the new Common Core aligned assessments, we have incorporated the best instructional practices for striving readers and writers and English learners in our program. In addition, we have a range of measures to help teachers monitor student progress and prepare for these high-stakes tests, including interim measures. Our writing and language rubrics and our Unit Tests can help teachers determine where gaps in understanding occur as well as where language acquisition may interfere with demonstrating content knowledge. The passages and content in the Level Tests are calibrated so students have a chance to demonstrate their knowledge with texts written at accessible reading levels and the English Language Gains Test helps teachers determine language growth.

To help students practice for these new, computer-based standardized assessments, ***Edge*** includes online testing to help students become familiar with the particular skills and logistics required for computer-based testing. In addition to the frequent opportunities for students to practice taking tests online, eAssessment provides reports that identify target skills for reteaching and align performance to standards.

Conclusion

Edge provides a full range of tools for formal and informal assessment that supports teachers in diagnosing their students' interest and needs and using assessment to continually monitor students' progress in order to provide striving readers and English learners with responsive instruction that optimizes growth and fosters success.

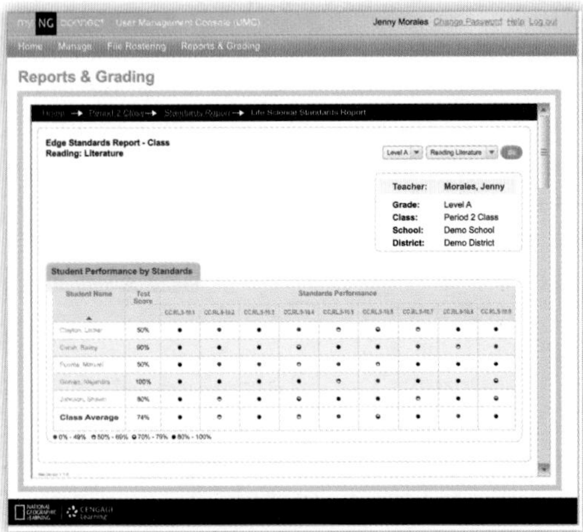

Reports help gauge student progress on Common Core State Standards and identify opportunities for intervention and reteaching.

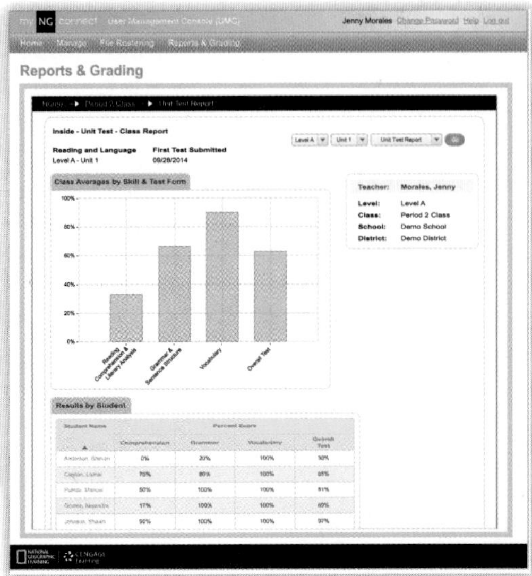

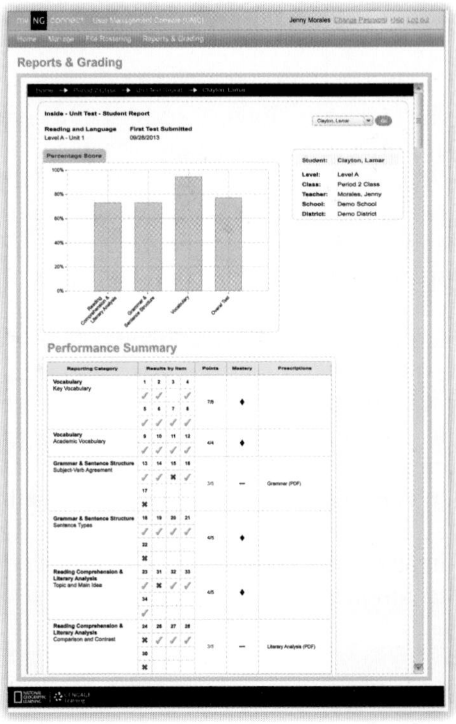

Research Base and Bibliography for *Hampton-Brown Edge*

Reading/Adolescent Literacy

Applebee, A. N., Langer, J. A., Nystrand, M., Gamoran, A. (2003). Discussion-based approaches to developing understanding: Classroom instruction and student performance in middle and high school English. *American Educational Research Journal, 40,* pp. 685–730.

Adler, M. J., & Van Doren, C. (1972). *How to read a book.* New York, NY: Touchstone. (Original work published 1940)

Afflerbach, P. (2007). *Understanding and Using Assessments.* Newark, DE: International Reading Association.

Alexander, P. A., & Jetton, T. L. (2000). Learning from text: A multidimensional and developmental perspective. In M.L Kamil, P. B. Mosenthal, P. D. Pearson, & R. Barr (Eds.), *Handbook of reading research* (Vol. 3; pp. 285–310). Mahwah, NJ: Erlbaum.

Allington, R. L., & Baker, K. (2007). In L. B. Gambrell, L. M. Morrow, & M. Pressley (Eds.), *Best practices in literacy instruction* (pp. 83–103). New York: The Guilford Press.

Alvermann, D., Hinchman, K., Moore, D., Phelps, S., & Waff, D. (2006). *Reconceptualizing the literacies in adolescents' lives* (2nd ed.). Mahwah, NJ: Lawrence Erlbaum Associates.

Applebee, A. N., Langer, J. A., Nystrand, M. & Gamoran, A. (2003). Discussion-based approaches to developing understanding: Classroom instruction and student performance in middle and high school English. *American Educational Research Journal, 40,* 685–730.

Bauerein, M., & Stotsky, S. (2012). *How Common Core's ELA standards place college readiness at risk: A Pioneer Institute white paper.* Retrieved from http://pioneerinstitute.org/pdf/120917_CommonCoreELAStandards.pdf

Beers, K., & Probst, R. (2012). *Notice and note: Strategies for close reading.* Portsmouth, NH: Heinemann.

Biancarosa, C., & Snow, C. (2006). *Reading next—A vision for action and research in middle and high school literacy: A report to the Carnegie Corporation of New York* (2nd ed.). Washington, DC: Alliance for Excellent Education.

Calfee, R. C., Lindamood, P. E., & Lindamood, C. H. (1973). Acoustic-phonetic skills and reading—kindergarten through 12th grade. *Journal of Educational Psychology,* 64, 293–298.

Coleman D. (2011). *Bringing the Common Core to life.* Retrieved from usny.nysed.gov/rttt/resources/bringing-the-common-core-to-life.html

Cunningham, J. W. (in press). Research on text complexity: The Common Core State Standards as catalyst. In S.B. Neuman & L.B. Cambred (Eds.), *Reading instruction in the age of Common Core State Standards.* Newark, DE: International Reading Association.

Cunningham, P. M. (2007). Best practices in teaching phonological awareness and phonics. In L. B. Gambrell, L. M. Morrow, & M. Pressley (Eds.), *Best practices in literacy instruction* (pp. 159–177). New York: The Guilford Press.

Duke, N. K., Pearson, P. D., Strachan, S. L., & Billman, A. K. (2011). Essential elements of fostering and teaching reading comprehension. In S. J. Samuels & A. E. Farstrup (Eds.), *What research has to say about reading instruction* (4th ed., pp. 51–93). Newark, DE: International Reading Association.

Edmonds, M. S., Vaughn, S., Wexler, J., Reutebuch, C., Cable, A., Tackett, K. K., et al. (2009). A synthesis of reading interventions and effects on reading comprehension outcomes for older struggling readers. *Review of Educational Research, 79,* 262–300.

Fagella-Luby, M. N., & Deshler, D. D. (2008). Reading comprehension in adolescents with LD: What we know; what we need to learn. *Learning Disabilities Research and Practice,* 23(2), 70–78.

Farstrup, A. E., & Samuels, S. J. (Eds.) (2002). *What research has to say about reading instruction.* Newark, DE: International Reading Association.

Fisher, D., Frey, N., & Lapp D. (2012). *Text Complexity: Raising the Rigor in Reading.* Newark, DE: International Reading Association.

Franzak, J. (2006). Zoom: A review of the literature on marginalized adolescent readers, literacy theory, and policy implications. *Review of Educational Research,* 76(2), 209–248.

Gambrell, L. B., Morrow, L. M., & Pressley, M. (Eds.). (2007). *Best practices in literacy instruction.* New York: The Guilford Press.

Grossman, T., Reyna, R., & Shipton, S. (2011). *Realizing their potential: How governors can lead effective implementation of the common core state standards.* Washington, D.C.: National Governors Association.

Guthrie, J., & McRae, A. (2011). Reading engagement among African American and European American students. In. S. Samuels & A. Farstrup (Eds.), *What research has to say about reading instruction, 4th,* (pp. 115–142). Newark: DE: International Reading Association.

Guthrie, J. T. (Ed.) (2007). *Engaging adolescents in reading.* Thousand Oaks, CA: Corwin. *Transfer of learning: Cognition, instruction, and reasoning.* San Diego: Academic Press

Haskell, R. (2000). *Transfer of learning: Cognition, instruction, and reasoning.* San Diego: Academic Press

Henderson, N., & Milstein, M. (2003). Resiliency in schools: Making it happen for students and educators. Thousand Oaks, CA: Corwin Press.

Hinchman, K. A., & Moore, D. W. (in press). Close reading: A cautionary interpretation. *Journal of Adolescent and Adult Literacy.*

Hinchman, K., Alvermann, D., Boyd, F., Brozo, W. G., & Vacca, R. (2003/04). Supporting older students' in- and out-of-school literacies. *Journal of Adolescent & Adult Literacy,* 47, 304–310.

Ivey, G. (1999). A multicase study in the middle school: Complexities among young adolescent readers. *Reading Research Quarterly,* 34(2), 172–192.

Research Base and Bibliography, continued

Ivey, G., & Broaddus, K. (2001). Just plain reading: A survey of what makes students want to read in middle schools. *Reading Research Quarterly,* 36, 350–377.

Kamil, M. (2012). Current and historical perspectives on reading research and instruction. In Harris, K. R., Graham, S., & Urdan, T. (Eds.), *APA educational psychology handbook* (Vol. 3, Application to teaching and learning; pp. 161–188). Washington, DC: American Psychological Association.

King, S. (n.d.). *Stephen King quotes.* Retrieved from http://www.goodreads.com/author/quotes/3389.Stephen_King

Langer. J. A. (2001) Beating the odds: Teaching middle and high school students to read and write well. *American Educational Research Journal,* 38, 837–880.

Langer, J. A. (2002). *Effective literacy instruction: Building successful reading and writing programs.* Urbana, IL: National Council of Teachers of English.

Lapp D., Moss, B., Johnson, K., Grant, M. (2012). "Teaching Students to Closely Read Texts: How and When?" *Rigorous Real-World Teaching and Learning.* Newark, DE: International Reading Association.

Learned, J. E., Stockdill, D., & Moje, E. B. (2011). Integrating reading strategies and knowledge building in adolescent literacy instruction. In S. J. Samuels & A. E. Farstrup (Eds.), *What research has to say about reading instruction* (4th ed., pp. 159–185). Newark, DE: International Reading Association.

Marshall, J. D., Smagorinsky, P., & Smith, M. W. (1995). *The language of interpretation: Patterns of discourse in discussions of literature.* Urbana, IL: NCTE.

McKenna, M. C., Conradi, K., Lawrence, C., Jang, B. G., & Meyer, J. P. (2012). Reading attitudes of middle school students: Results of a U.S. survey. *Reading Research Quarterly,* 47, 283–306.

McNamara, D. S. (Ed.). (2007). *Reading comprehension strategies: Theory, interventions, and technologies.* Mahwah, NJ: Erlbaum.

Meyer, B. J. F., Wijekumar, K., Middlemiss, W., Higley, K., Lei, P-W, Meier, C., & Spielvogel, J. (2010). Web-based tutoring of the structure strategy with or without elaborated feedback or choice for fifth- and seventh-grade readers. *Reading Research Quarterly,* 45, 62–92.

Miller, M. (2006). Where they are: Working with marginalized students. *Educational Leadership,* 63(5), 50–54.

Moats, L. C. (2000). *Speech to print: Language essentials for teachers.* Baltimore, MD: Paul H. Brookes Publishing.

Moje, E. B. (2007). Developing socially just subject-matter instruction—A review of the literature on disciplinary literacy teaching. *Review of Research in Education,* 31(1), 1–44.

Moje, E. B. (2006). Motivating texts, motivating contexts, motivating adolescents: An examination of the role of motivation in adolesent literacy practices and development. *Perspectives,* 32(3), 10–14.

Moje, E. B., McIntosh Ciechanowski, K., Kramer, K., Ellis, L., Carrillo, R., & Collazo, T. (2004). Working toward third space in content area literacy: An Examination of everday funds of knowledge and discourse. *Reading Research Quarterly,* 39(1), 38–71.

Moore, D. W., Bean, T. W., Birdyshaw, D., & Rycik, J. A. for the Commission on Adolescent Literacy of the International Reading Association (1999). *Adolescent literacy: A position statement.* Newark, DE: International Reading Association. Retrieved March 18, 2006 from the IRA site: [online: www.reading.org/resources/issues/positions_adolescent.html]

National Center for Education Statistics. (2010). *The nation's report card: Grade 12 reading and mathematics 2009 national and pilot state results* (NCES 2011-455). National Center for Education Statistics, Institute of Education Sciences, U.S. Department of Education, Washington, D.C.

National Governors Association Center for Best Practices, Council of Chief State School Officers. (2010). *Common Core State Standards for English language arts & literacy in history/social studies, science, and technical subjects.* Washington, DC: Author. Retrieved from http://www.corestandards.org/the-standards

National Governors Association Center for Best Practices (2005). *Reading to achieve: A governor's guide to adolescent literacy.* Washington, DC: Author.

National Reading Panel. (2000). *Teaching children to read: An evidence-based assessment of the scientific research literature on reading and its implications for reading instruction: Reports of the subgroups.* Bethesda, MD: National Institute of Child Health and Human Development, National Institutes of Health.

Nokes, J. D. & Dole, J. A. (2004). Helping adolescent readers through explicit strategy instruction. In T. L. Jetton & J.A. Dole (Eds.). *Adolescent literacy research and practice* (pp. 162–182). New York: The Guilford Press.

Nystrand, M. (2006). Research on the role of discussion as it affects reading comprehension. *Research in the Teaching of English,* 40 (4), 392–412.

Paige, D. (2012). The importance of adolescent fluency. In. T. Rasinky, C. Blachowitz, & K. Lems (Eds.), *Fluency instruction: Research-based best practices,* 2nd Ed. (pp. 55–71). New York: Guilford.

Paige, D., Rasinski, T., Magpuri,-Lavell, T. (2012). Is fluent, expressive reading important for high school readers? *Journal of Adolescent & Adult Literacy,* 56(1), 67–76.

Pearson, P. D. (in press). Research foundations for the Common Core State Standards in English language arts. In S. Neuman and L. Gambrell (Eds.), *Reading instruction in the age of Common Core State Standards.* Newark, DE: International Reading Association.

Pearson, P. D., & Camperell, K. (1994). Comprehension of text structures. In R. B. Ruddell, M. R. Ruddell, & H. Singer (Eds.), *Theoretical models and processes of reading* (4th ed.; pp. 448–468). Newark, DE: International Reading Association.

Pearson, P. D., Roehler, L. R., Dole, J. A., & Duffy, G. G. (1992). Developing expertise in reading comprehension. In S. J. Samuels & A. E. Farstrup (Eds.), *What research has to say about reading instruction* (2nd ed., pp. 145–199). Newark, DE: International Reading Association.

Perkins, D. N., & Salomon, G. (1988). Teaching for transfer. *Educational Leadership,* 46(1), 22–32.

Porter, A., McMaken, J., Hwang, J. Yang, R. (2011). Common Core Standards: The new U.S. intended curriculum. *Educational Researcher,* 40, 103–116.

Pressley, M., & Afflerbach, P. (1995). *Verbal protocols of reading: The nature of constructively responsive reading.* Hillsdale, NJ: Erlbaum.

Rabinowitz, P., & Smith, M. W. (1998). *Authorizing readers: Resistance and respect in the teaching of literature.* New York: Teachers College Press.

RAND Reading Study Group. (2002). *Reading for understanding: Toward an R&D program in reading comprehension.* Santa Monica, CA: Science and Technology Policy Institute, RAND Education.

Rasinski, T., Blachowicz, C., & Lems, K. (Eds.). (2012). *Fluency instruction: Research-based best practices,* 2nd Ed. New York: Guilford.

Rasinski, T.V., Reutzel, R., Chard, D., & Linan-Thompson, S. (2011). Reading fluency. In M. L. Kamil, P.D. Pearson, E. Moje, & P. Afflerbach (Eds.), *Handbook of reading research* (vol. IV, pp. 286–319). New York: Routledge.

Roberts, G., Torgesen, J. K., Boardman, A, & Scammacca, N. (2008). Evidence-based strategies for reading instruction of older students with learning disabilities. *Learning Disabilities Research and Practice,* 23(2), 63–69.

Rosenshine, B. & Meister, C. (1992). The use of scaffolds for teaching higher-level cognitive strategies. *Educational Leadership,* 50, 26–33.

Schoenbach, R., Greenleaf, C., Cziko, C., Hurwitz, L. (1999). *Reading for understanding.* San Francisco: Jossey-Bass.

Shanahan, T., and Shanahan, C. (2008). Teaching disciplinary literacy to adolescents: Rethinking content-area literacy. Harvard Educational Review, 38, 40–59.

Smith, M. W. & Wilhelm, J. (2006). *Going with the flow: How to engage boys (and girls) in their literacy learning.* Portsmouth, NH: Heinemann.

Smith, M. W., & Wilhelm. J. (2002).*"Reading don't fix no Chevys": Literacy in the lives of young men*. Portsmouth, NH: Heinemann.

Snow, C. E., Burns, M. S., & Griffin, P. (1998). *Preventing reading difficulties in young children. Report of the National Reading Council.* Washington, DC: National Academy Press.

Soter, A. O., Wilkinson, I. A., Murphy. P. K., Rudge, L., Reninger. K., & Edwards, M. (2008). What the discourse tells us: Talk and indicators of high-level comprehension. *International Journal of Educational Research,* 47, 372–391.

Stanton-Salazar, R., & Spina, S. (2000). The network orientations of highly resilient urban minority youth: A network-analytic account of minority socialization and its educational implications. *Urban Review,* 32(3), 227.

Tatum, A.W. & Muhammad, G. (2012). African American males and literacy development in contexts that are characteristically urban. *Urban Education,* 47(2), 434–463.

Tatum, A. W. (2007). Building the textual lineages of African American adolescent males. In K. Beers, R. Probst, & L. Reif (Eds.), *Adolescent literacy: Turning promise into practice.* Portsmouth, NH: Heinemann.

Tatum, A. W. (2005). *Teaching reading to black adolescent males: Closing the achievement gap***.** Portland, ME: Stenhouse Publishers.

Torgesen, J. K., Houston, D. D., Rissman, L. M., Decker, S. M., Roberts, G., Vaughn, S., Wexler, J., Francis, D. J., Rivera, M. O., & Lesaux, N. (2007). *Academic literacy instruction for adolescents: A guidance document from the Center on Instruction* (p. 3). Portsmouth, NH: RMC Research Corporation, Center on Instruction. Retrieved May 3, 2007 from [online: www.centeroninstruction.org]

Toulmin, S. (1958). *The uses of argument.* New York: Cambridge University Press.

Tovani, C. (2000). *I read it, but I don't get it.* Portland, ME: Stenhouse.

Triplett, C. (2004). Looking for a struggle: Exploring the emotions of a middle school reader. *Journal of Adolescent & Adult Literacy,* 48(3), 214–222.

Vygotsky, L. S. (1978). *Mind in society: The development of higher psychological processes.* Cambridge, MA: Harvard University Press.

Walker, B.J. (2008). *Diagnostic Teaching of Reading: Techniques for Instruction and Assessment* (7th ed.). Columbus, OH: Merrill.

Wilhelm, J.D., Baker, T., & Dube-Hackett, J. (2001). *Strategic reading: Guiding adolescents to lifelong literacy.* Portsmouth, NH: Heinemann.

Vocabulary

Anderson, R. C., & Nagy, W. E. (1992). The vocabulary conundrum. *American Educator, 16* (4), 14–18, 44–47.

August, D., & Shanahan, T. (2006). *Developing literacy in second-language learners: Report of the National Literacy Panel on Language-Minority Children and Youth*. Mahwah, NJ: Lawrence Erlbaum Associates.

Baumann, J. K., & Kame'enui, E. J. (Eds.) (2004). *Vocabulary instruction: Research to practice*. New York: The Guilford Press.

Beck, I. L., McKeown, M. G., & Kucan, L. (2008). *Robust vocabulary: Frequently asked questions and extended examples.* New York: Guilford.

Beck, I. L., McKeown, M. G., & Kucan, L. (2002). *Bringing words to life: Robust vocabulary instruction*. New York: The Guilford Press.

Blachowicz, C. L. Z., Fisher, P. J. L., Ogle, D., & Watts-Taffe, S. (2006). Vocabulary: Questions from the classroom. *Reading Research Quarterly,* 41, 524–539.

Blachowicz, C. L. Z., & Fisher, P. J. L. (2000). Vocabulary instruction. In M.J. Kamil, P.B. Mosenthal, P.D. Pearson, & R. Barr (Eds.), *Handbook of reading research* (vol. 3) (pp. 503–523). Mahwah, NJ: Lawrence Erlbaum Associates.

Bowers, P. N., Kirby, J. R., & Deacon, S. H. (2010). The effects of morphological instruction on literacy skills: A systematic review of the literature. *Review of Educational Research,* 80, 144–179.

Carlisle, J. F. (2010). Effects of instruction in morphological awareness on literacy achievement: An integrative review. *Reading Research Quarterly,* 45, 464–487.

Coxhead, A. (2000). A new academic word list. *TESOL Quarterly,* 34, 213–238.

Cummins, J. (2003). Reading and the bilingual student: Fact and fiction. In G. G. Garcia (Ed.), *English learners: Reaching the highest level of English literacy.* Newark, DE: International Reading Association.

Cunningham, A. E., & Stanovich, K. (1998). What reading does to the mind. *American Educator, 22*(1), 8–15.

Cunningham, J. W., & Moore, D. W. (1993). The contribution of understanding academic vocabulary to answering comprehension questions. *Journal of Reading Behavior, 25,* 171–180.

Edwards, E. C., Font, G., Baumann, J. F., & Boland, E. (2004). Unlocking word meanings: Strategies and guidelines for teaching morphemic and contextual analysis. In J. F. Baumann & E. J. Kame'enui (Eds.), *Vocabulary instruction: Research to practice* (pp. 159–176). New York: The Guilford Press.

Graves. (2009). *Teaching individual words: One size does not fit all.* New York: Teachers College Press and International Reading Association.

Graves, M. (2000). A vocabulary program to complement and bolster a middle-grade comprehension program. In B. M. Taylor, M. F. Graves, & P. van den Broek (Eds.). *Reading for meaning: Fostering comprehension in the middle grades* (pp. 116–135). Newark, DE: International Reading Association.

Graves, M. F. (2006). *The vocabulary book: Learning and instruction.* New York: Teachers College Press.

Graves, M. F., & Watts-Taffe, S. M. (2002). The place of word consciousness in a research-based vocabulary program. In A.E. Farstrup & S.J. Samuels (Eds.), *What research has to say about reading instruction* (3rd ed., pp. 140–165). Newark, DE: International Reading Association.

Harmon, J. S., Wood, K. D., & Medina, A. L. (2009). Vocabulary learning in the content areas: Research-based practices for middle and secondary school classrooms. In K. D. Wood & W. E. Blanton (Eds.), *Literacy instruction for adolescents: Research-based practice* (pp. 344–367). New York: Guilford.

Hyland, K., & Tse, P. (2007). Is there an academic vocabulary? *TESOL Quarterly, 41,* 235–253.

Kame'enui, E. J., & Baumann, J. F. (Eds.) (2012). *Vocabulary instruction: Research to practice (2nd ed.).* New York: Guilford.

Lesaux, N. K., Kieffer, M. J., Fuller, S. E., & Kelley, J. G. (2010). The effectiveness and ease of implementation of an academic vocabulary intervention for linguistically diverse students in urban middle schools. *Reading Research Quarterly,* 45, 196–228.

Lubliner, S., & Smetana, L. (2005). The effects of comprehensive vocabulary instruction on Title I students' metacognitive word-learning skills and reading comprehension. *Journal of Literacy Research, 37* (2), 163–200.

Marzano, R. J. (2004). *Building background knowledge for academic achievement: Research on what works in schools.* Alexandria, VA: Association for Supervision and Curriculum Development.

Nagy, W., & Townsend, D. (2012). Words as tools: Learning academic vocabulary as language acquisition. *Reading Research Quarterly, 47,* 91–108.

Nagy, W. E., Berninger, V. W., & Abbott, R. D. (2006). Contribution of morphology beyond phonology to literacy outcomes of upper elementary and middle-school students. *Journal of Educational Psychology, 98,* 134–147.

Nagy, W. E., & Scott, J. A. (2000). Vocabulary processes. In M. J. Kamil, P. B. Mosenthal, P. D. Pearson, & R. Barr (Eds.), *Handbook of reading research* (v. III; pp. 269–284). Mahwah, NJ: Lawrence Erlbaum Associates.

Scott, J. A., & Nagy, W. E. (2004). Developing word consciousness. In J.F. Baumann & E.J. Kame'enui (Eds.), *Vocabulary instruction: Research to practice* (pp. 201–217). New York: The Guilford Press.

Stahl, S. A., Nagy, W. E. (2006). *Teaching word meanings.* Mahwah, NJ: L. Erlbaum Associates.

Torgesen, J. K., Houston, D. D., Rissman, L. M., Decker, S. M., Roberts, G., Vaughn, S., Wexler, J., Francis, D. J., Rivera, M. O., & Lesaux, N. (2007). *Academic literacy instruction for adolescents: A guidance document from the Center on Instruction* (p. 3). Portsmouth, NH: RMC Research Corporation, Center on Instruction. Retrieved May 3, 2007 from [online: www.centeroninstruction.org]

Fluency

Bennett, L., Smith, J., & Wright, P. (2006). *Where are poor people to live? Transforming public housing communities.* New York: M. E. Sharpe.

Kuhn, M. R. (2005). Helping students become accurate, expressive readers: Fluency instruction for small groups. *The Reading Teacher, 58,* 338–344.

Palumbo, T., & Willcutt, J. (2006). Perspectives on fluency: English-language learners and students with dyslexia. In S. J. Samuels & A. E. Farstrup (Eds.), *What research has to say about fluency instruction* (pp. 159–178). Newark, DE: International Reading Association.

Pikulski, J., & Chard, D. (2005). Fluency: The bridge between decoding and reading comprehension. *The Reading Teacher, 58,* 510–521.

Pressley, M., Gaskins, I. W., & Fingeret, L. (2006). Instruction and development of reading fluency in striving readers. In S. J. Samuels & A. E. Farstrup (Eds.), *What research has to say about fluency instruction* (pp. 47–69). Newark, DE: International Reading Association.

Samuels, S. J. (2002). Reading fluency: Its development and assessment. In A. E. Farstrup & S. J. Samuels (Eds.), *What research has to say about reading instruction* (3rd ed., pp. 166–183). Newark, DE: International Reading Association.

Samuels, S. J., & Farstrup, A. E. (2006). *What research has to say about fluency instruction.* Newark, DE: International Reading Association.

Writing

Atwell, N. (1998). *In the Middle: New understandings about writing, reading and learning.* Portsmouth, NH: Heinemann.

Cunningham, P., & Allington, R. (2003). *Classrooms that work.* New York: Pearson Education, Inc.

Elbow, P. (1973). *Writing without teachers.* London: Oxford University Press.

Fredrickson, J., Wilhelm, J., & Smith, M. W. (2012). *So, what's the story?: Teaching narrative to understand ourselves, others, and the world.* Portsmouth, NH: Heinemann.

Graham, S., & Perin, D. (2007). *Writing next: Effective strategies to improve writing of adolescents in middle and high schools—A report to the Carnegie Corporation of New York.* Washington, DC: Alliance for Excellent Education.

Hillocks, G., Jr. (1986). *Research on written composition: New directions for teaching.* Urbana, IL: ERIC and National Conference for Research in English.

Hillocks, G., Jr., & Smith, M. W. (2003). Grammars and literacy learning. In J. Flood, J. Jensen, D. Lapp, & J. Squire (Eds.), *Handbook of research on teaching the English language arts* (2nd. ed., pp. 721-737). Mahwah, NJ: Erlbaum.

Kirby, D., Kirby D. L., & Liner, T. (2004). *Inside out: Strategies for teaching writing.* Portsmouth, NH: Heinemann.

Kohn, A. (2006). *The homework myth.* Cambridge, MA: DaCapo Lifelong Books.

Lane, B. (1993). *After the end: Teaching and learning creative revision.* Portsmouth, NH: Heinemann.

Langer, J. (2000). *Guidelines for teaching middle and high school students to read and write well.* Albany, NY: Center on English Learning & Achievement.

Moffett, J. (1983). *Teaching the universe of discourse.* Portsmouth, NH: Heinemann.

Murray, D. M. (1990). *Shoptalk: Learning to write with writers.* Portsmouth, NH: Heinemann.

Newkirk, T. (2005). *The school essay manifesto.* Shoreham, VT: Discover Writing Press.

Newkirk, T. (2002). *Misreading masculinity.* Portsmouth, NH: Heinemann.

Noden, H. (1999). *Image grammar: Using grammatical structures to teach writing.* Portsmouth, NH: Heinemann.

Partnership for Assessment of Readiness for College and Careers "Item and Task Prototypes." *Partnership for Assessment of Readiness for College and Careers.* Partnership for Assessment of Readiness for College and Careers, 18 Aug. 2012. Web. 28 Jan. 2013. <http://www.parcconline.org/samples/item-task-prototypes>.

Ray, K. W. (2002). *What you know by heart.* Portsmouth, NH: Heinemann.

Rief, L. (1992). *Seeking diversity: Language arts with adolescents.* Portsmouth, NH: Heinemann.

Romano, T. (2004). *Crafting authentic voice.* Portsmouth, NH: Heinemann.

Shaughnessy, M. (1977). *Errors and expectations.* London: Oxford University Press.

Smith, F. (1998). *The book of learning and forgetting.* New York: Teachers College Press.

Smith, M. (2007). Boys and writing. In Newkirk, T., & Kent, R. (Eds.), *Teaching the neglected "r": Rethinking writing instruction in secondary classrooms* (pp. 243–253). Portsmouth, NH: Heinemann Boynton/Cook.

Smith, M., Cheville, J., & Hillocks, G., Jr. (2006). "I guess I'd better watch my English": Grammar and the teaching of English language arts. In C. MacArthur, S. Graham, & J. Fitzgerald (Eds.), *Handbook on writing research* (pp. 263-274). New York: Guilford Press.

Smith, M. W. & Wilhelm, J. (2007). *Getting it right: Fresh approaches to teaching grammar, usage, and correctness.* New York: Scholastic.

Smith, M. W. & Wilhelm, J. (2006). *Going with the flow: How to engage boys (and girls) in their literacy learning.* Portsmouth, NH: Heinemann.

Smith, M. W., & Wilhelm. J. (2002) *"Reading don't fix no Chevys": Literacy in the lives of young men.* Portsmouth, NH: Heinemann.

Smith, M. W., Wilhelm, J., Fredrickson, J. (2012). *O, yeah?!: Putting argument to work both in school and out.* Portsmouth, NH: Heinemann.

Strong, W. (2001). *Coaching writing: The power of guided practice.* Portsmouth, NH: Heinemann-Boynton/Cook.

Vygotsky, L. S. (1978). *Mind and society: The development of higher psychological processes.* Cambridge, MA: Harvard University Press.

Weaver, C. (1996). *Teaching grammar in context.* Portsmouth, NH: Heinemann.

Wilhelm, J., Smith, M. W., & Fredrickson, J. (2012). *Get it done!: Writing and analyzing informational text to make things happen.* Portsmouth, NH: Heinemann.

Language & Literacy for ELLs

Anstrom, K., DiCerbo, P., Butler, F., Katz, A., Millet, J., & Rivera, C. (2010). A review of the literature on academic English: Implications for K–12 English language learners. Arlington, VA: The George Washington University Center for Equity and Excellence in Education.

August, D., & Shanahan, T. (Eds.). (2006). *Developing literacy in second-language learners: A report of the National Literacy Panel on language-minority children and youth.* Mahwah, NJ: Lawrence Erlbaum Associates.

Bailey, A. (Ed.). (2007). *The language demands of school: Putting academic English to the test.* New Haven, CT: Yale University Press.

Beck, I. L., Perfetti, C., & McKeown, M. G. (1982). Effects of long-term vocabulary instruction on lexical access and reading comprehension. *Journal of Educational Psychology, 74*, 506–521.

Biancarosa, G., & Snow, C. (2004). *Reading next: A vision for action and research in middle and high school literacy.* Report to the Carnegie Corporation of New York. Washington, DC: Alliance for Excellent Education.

Carlo, M. S., August, D., McLaughlin, B., Snow, C. E., Dressler, C., Lippman, D., Lively, T., & White, C. E. (2004). Closing the gap: Addressing the vocabulary needs of English language learners in bilingual and mainstream classrooms. *Reading Research Quarterly, 39*(2), 188–215.

Dutro, S., & Kinsella, K. (2010). English language development: Issues and implementation at grades 6–12. In California Department of Education (Ed.), *Improving education for English learners: Research-based approaches* (pp. 151–207). Sacramento: California Department of Education.

Echevarría, J., Richards-Tutor, C., Canges, R., & Francis, D. (2011). Using the SIOP® Model to promote the acquisition of language and science concepts with English learners. *Bilingual Research Journal,* 34, 1–18.

Echevarría, J., Vogt, M. E., & Short, D. (2013). *Making content comprehensible for English learners: The SIOP® Model.* 4th ed. Boston: Pearson Allyn & Bacon.

Echevarria, J., Vogt, M.E., & Short, D. (2008). *Making content comprehensible for English learners: The SIOP® model* (3rd ed.). Boston: Pearson/Allyn & Bacon.

Gándara, P., Maxwell-Jolly, J., & Driscoll, A. (2005). *Listening to teachers of English language learners: A survey of California teachers' challenges, experiences, and professional development needs.* Santa Cruz, CA: Center for the Future of Teaching and Learning.

Garcia, G. & Beltran, D. (2003). Revisioning the blueprint: Building for the academic success of English learners. In G. Garcia (Ed.), *English learners: Reaching the highest levels of English literacy.* Newark, DE: International Reading Association.

García, G. E., & Godina, H. (2004). Addressing the literacy needs of adolescent English language learners. In T. Jetton & J. Dole (Eds.), *Adolescent literacy: Research and practice* (pp. 304–320). New York: The Guilford Press.

Genesee, F., Lindholm-Leary, K., Saunders, W., & Christian, D. (2006). *Educating English language learners: A synthesis of research evidence.* New York: Cambridge University Press.**Goldenberg, C.** (2006). Improving achievement for English learners: What research tells us. *Education Week,* July 26, 2006

Graves, M. F., August, E., & Mancilla-Martinez, J. (2013). *Teaching vocabulary to English Language Learners.* New York: Teachers College Press.

Graves, M. (2006). *The vocabulary book: Learning & instruction.* New York: Teachers College Press.

IRA & NICHD. (2007). *Key issues and questions in English language learners literacy research.* Washington, DC: International Reading Association and National Institute of Child Health and Human Development. Retrieved from http://www.reading.org/downloads/resources/ELL_paper_071022.pdf

Lindholm-Leary, K., & Borsato, G. (2006). Academic achievement. In F. Genesee, K. Lindholm-Leary, W. Saunders, & D. Christian (Eds.), *Educating English language learners: A synthesis of research evidence* (pp. 176–222). New York: Cambridge University Press.

McGraner, K., & Saenz, L. (2009). *Preparing teachers of English*

language learners. Washington DC: National Comprehensive Center for Teacher Quality.

Nation, I. S. P. (2001). *Learning vocabulary in another language.* New York: Cambridge University Press.

Saunders, W., & Goldenberg, C. (2010). Research to guide English language development instruction. In California Department of Education (Ed.), *Improving education for English learners: Research-based approaches* (pp. 21–81). Sacramento, CA: CDE Press.

Schleppegrell, M. (2004). *The language of schooling: A functional linguistic perspective.* Mahwah, NJ: Lawrence Erlbaum Associates.

Short, D., Fidelman, C., & Louguit, M. (2012). Developing academic language in English language learners through sheltered instruction. *TESOL Quarterly 46*(2), 333–360.

Short, D., & Fitzsimmons, S. (2007). *Double the work: Challenges and solutions to acquiring language and academic literacy for adolescent English language learners.* Report to Carnegie Corporation of New York. Washington, DC: Alliance for Excellent Education.

Slavin, R. E., & Cheung, A. (2003). *Effective programs for English language learners: A best-evidence synthesis.* Baltimore, MD: Johns Hopkins University, CRESPAR.

Wong Fillmore, L. & Fillmore, C. (2012). *What does text complexity mean for English learners and language minority students?* Paper presented at the Understanding Language Conference, Stanford, CA.

Teaching Routines & Strategies

Teaching Routines & Strategies

To bring best practices into your classroom, use the following routines and instructional strategies.

Vocabulary Routines

Reading Routines

Make Words Your Own

Vocabulary Routine 1

Decades of research have confirmed the important role that vocabulary plays in reading comprehension and in students' overall academic success (Hiebert & Kamil, 2005). Immersing students in rich and varied language experiences permits them to learn words through listening, speaking, reading, and writing. In this new view of robust, explicit instruction, vocabulary is introduced using a consistent, predictable routine (Beck et al., 2002). Follow these steps to help students make words fully their own, so that vocabulary can be accessed at will in a variety of situations.

1. **Pronounce** Guide students in correctly pronouncing the word (by syllables and as a whole). Have students repeat the word after you multiple times; you may want to have ELLs repeat syllable-by-syllable before building up to the whole word. Point out spelling patterns. For higher-level students, point out if the word is a compound word, includes prefixes or suffixes, or has Latin or Greek roots. For example: *The word* **structure** *includes the Latin root* -struct, *which means "to build." Knowing that, what do you think the word* destruction *means?*
2. **Explain** Refer to the examples in **Prepare to Read** to provide a clear, student-friendly explanation of the word's meaning. Provide any synonyms and/or antonyms that students may be familiar with. For example: *The word* **opponent** *means the person or team who is against you. A synonym is* rival, *and an antonym is* teammate. *Our opponents in next week's basketball game are the varsity team from Middletown High.*
3. **Study Examples** Encourage students to think about how and why words are being used in example sentences. Systematic use of tools such as word squares, definition maps, and vocabulary study cards provides students with the opportunity to study words in various contexts.
4. **Encourage Elaboration** Students elaborate word meanings by generating their own examples and through practice. Choose from these techniques:
   - Role-play, drama, or pantomime
   - Create a drawing or visual representation
   - Generate more examples. Build schema by creating a list of examples within a specific category. For example: *A* **mammal** *is a warm-blooded animal that feeds its young with milk. Human beings are mammals. What other animals are mammals?* (cat, dog, whale, elephant, cow, etc.)
   - Prompt a discussion by asking open-ended questions. For example: *Talk about* **standards** *that you have chosen for yourself and your own life.*
5. **Assess** Check student understanding through both informal, ongoing assessment and summative evaluations. In all cases, assessments should go beyond simple memorization or matching, requiring students to demonstrate a deeper level of thinking and understanding. The following are examples of assessment types that require deep thinking:
   - Students complete a sentence that requires giving an example or explaining the word. For example: *The workers* **struggled** *to* ____________. (lift the heavy boxes, move the large sofa, etc.)
   - Students complete a sentence with the target word. For example: *Because I didn't want to be late to class, I took the* ____________ *of setting my clock ten minutes ahead.* (precaution)
   - Ask students to identify appropriate use in a sentence. For example: *Which sentence makes sense? It is an American tradition to celebrate July 4th with fireworks. OR It is an American tradition to play soccer on Labor Day.*

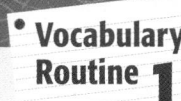

Vocabulary Notebook

Vocabulary Routine 2

Materials: dedicated section of three-ring binder or spiral-bound notebook; print or online student dictionary

1. Before explicitly teaching key words, have students conduct a self-assessment by completing a **knowledge-rating scale** for each word. (After students work with the word in multiple vocabulary routines, ask them to re-rate their word knowledge.)
2. Model how to trap information for each key word, including **a student-generated example and a definition**. Students can develop the information individually or with a partner. Although students can consult a dictionary for help, discourage them from directly copying definitions as this requires little thought or understanding.
3. In addition to the example and definition, encourage students to include other helpful information. For example, a **phonetic respelling** may help them remember how to pronounce the word. Sometimes, a **common opposite** or **a common prefix, root, or suffix** will help jog the students' memory of the word's meaning. For some words, students may draw a picture, diagram, or cartoon.
4. As extra support for English language learners, suggest they include **a translation of each key word** and examples in English of multiple meanings for the word.
5. To foster word consciousness, encourage students to **add to the notebook** interesting words that they come across in other sources: outside reading, conversations, the Internet, music, etc.

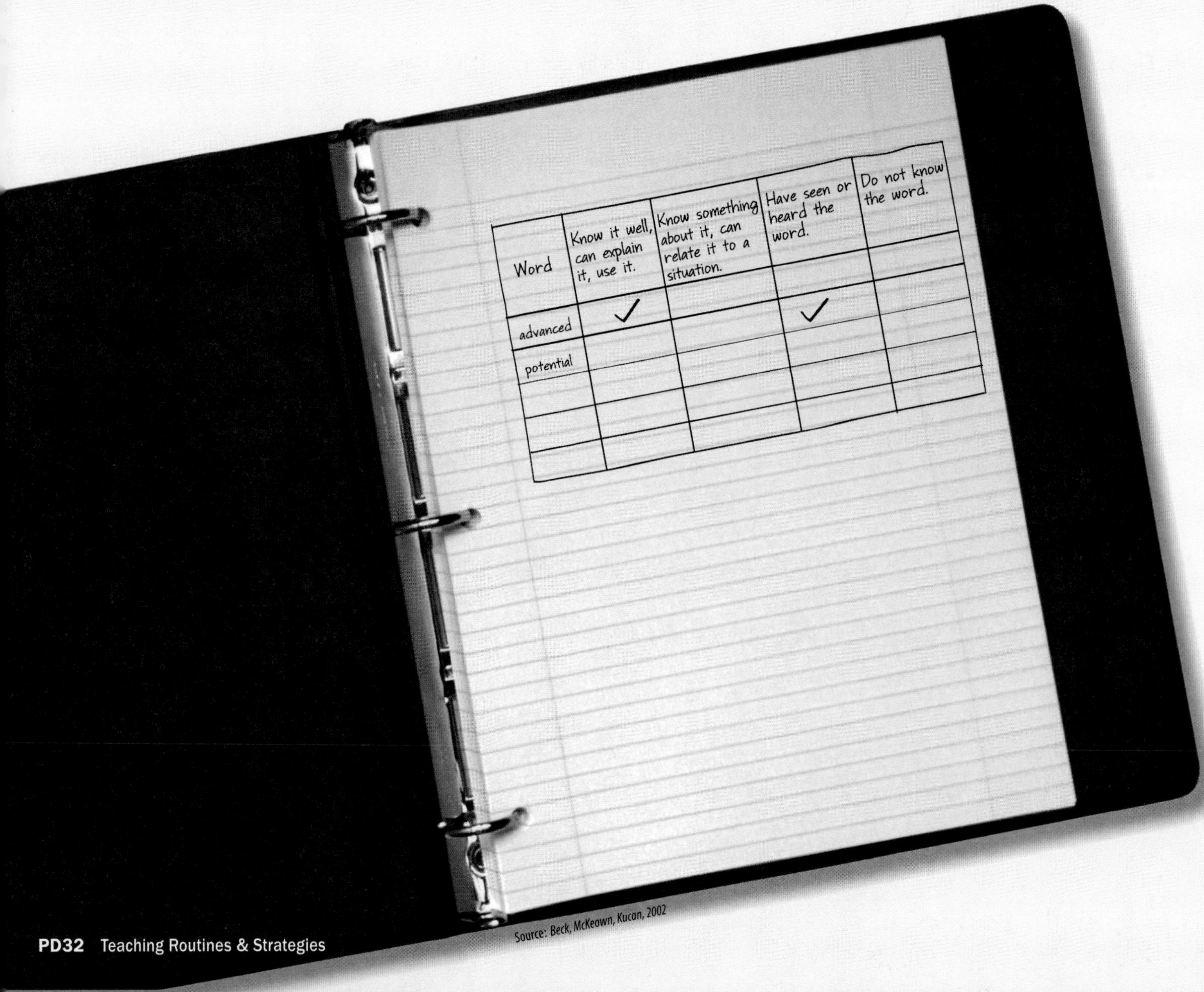

Word
Know it well, can explain it, use it.
Know something about it, can relate it to a situation.
Have seen or heard the word.
Do not know the word.
advanced
potential

Source: Beck, McKeown, Kucan, 2002

Vocabulary Study Cards

Vocabulary Routine 3

Materials: 3" x 5" index cards; thesaurus and pronunciation guide (optional)

Have students create a **study card** for each key word they wish to learn. They may want to keep the cards in their vocabulary notebooks for quick reference.

1. Demonstrate how to draw the **word map** with the labels and four cells. Then model adding the information to the map by writing the word in the center, a student-generated definition at the top, and an example and non-example in the two bottom cells. Encourage the student to draw on prior knowledge to come up with examples and non-examples from his or her own life.
2. Turn the card over and model how to note additional information about the word's pronunciation, synonyms and antonyms, connotation, word family, and a sample sentence.
3. Suggest that students use these study cards for periodic cumulative review and to prepare for vocabulary tests.

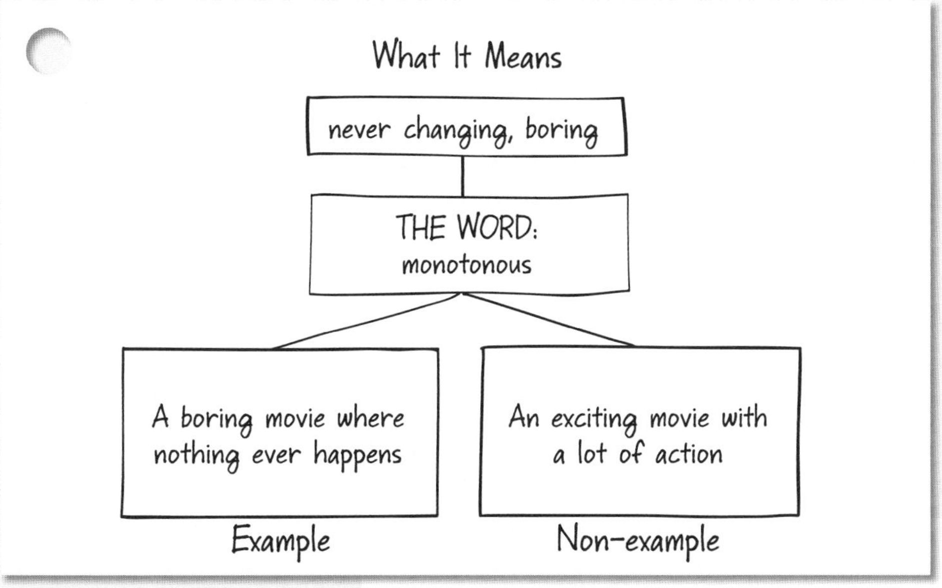

Pronunciation	mu•not•u•nus
Synonyms	unchanging, boring
Antonyms	changing, exciting
Connotation	negative
Word Family	monotony, monotone
Sentence	The movie was so monotonous, I almost fell asleep.

Wordbench

Vocabulary Routine 4

Materials: overhead projector or board

Use a Wordbench to provide explicit instruction in spelling, morphemic analysis, word families, and cognates. Wordbench helps connect basic and advanced phonics knowledge with more complex vocabulary learning.

1. Display these two questions in a prominent place in the classroom:
   Do I know any other words that look like this word?
   Are the meanings of the look-alike words related?
2. Use these questions to examine new vocabulary with students. **Display a word** and explain that this is like a carpenter's workbench, where you can take a word apart and put it back together.
3. Have students **pronounce the word** and **divide it into syllables**. Then ask them to name other words that look like it. List the words and invite students to underline and "spell out" the letters that make up the common parts.
4. Next, **focus on meaning** by asking students what each familiar word means. Refer students back to the passage where the new word appears. The more examples of its use that you can provide, the better. Then ask: *Does the meaning of the word you know relate in some way to this new word? If so, how?*
5. If the two words are related in meaning, lead students in exploring why the words are in the **same word family** or are **cognates**. Discuss their common roots, affixes, and word origins. Then point out the differences between the words—spelling, pronunciation, affixes, etc.
6. Encourage students to add insights from the Wordbench to their **Vocabulary Notebooks** and **Vocabulary Study Cards**. Remind them that they can draw on their knowledge of word families and cognates to figure out the meanings of new words during reading.

Wordbench

judicial
ju-di-cial
judge judgment
justice justify
jud=law
-ial=relating to
Meaning: having to do with laws and courts

Text Talk Read-Aloud Method

Vocabulary Routine 5

The Text Talk method (Beck, et al., 2002) teaches text-specific vocabulary after a story or passage has been read aloud to students.

1. **Read Aloud** Read aloud the text or excerpt; as you are reading, pause to provide a short explanation of each target word as you reach it in the text, as well as any other words that may affect comprehension. Don't let your explanations break the flow of your reading; you will be explaining the target words more fully after reading the story or passage. If your target words were *tradition*, *celebrate*, *purpose*, and *freedom*, you would do the following:
   - For the target word *tradition*, pause and say: *A tradition is a belief or way of doing things.*
   - For the target word *celebrate*, pause and say: *To celebrate is to have a party or other special activities to show that an event is important.*
   - For the target word *purpose*, pause and say: *A purpose is a reason for something.*
   - For the target word *freedom*, pause and say: *Freedom is the power to do, say, or be whatever you want.*
2. **After Reading** After reading the story or passage, explain the meanings of the target words more fully. Use the **Make Words Your Own** routine (p. PD27), which includes these steps: Pronounce, Explain, Study Examples, Encourage Elaboration, and Assess.
3. **Bring the Target Words Together** After you introduce the target words one at a time, give students opportunities to use the words together.
   - **One Question** Using all the target words, create one thoughtful question and ask students to answer it. For example if your target words were *tradition*, *celebrate*, *purpose*, and *freedom*, you could ask: *Which U.S. tradition has the purpose of celebrating people's freedom?*
   - **Questions: Two Choices** Form a question that requires that students choose the best target word between two options. For example, ask: *If a group of people always wears the color red to celebrate a holiday, is it a tradition or a purpose?* (tradition)
   - **Questions: One Context** Form a question for each of the target words, keeping all questions within a single context. Ask students to answer the question set. For example, if the single context is learning about Thai culture, you could ask: *What tradition do Thai farmers have after the January rice harvest? How do Thai families celebrate the New Year? What is the purpose of the* wai *gesture? Why is freedom important to Thai people?*
   - **Questions: Same Format** Use a consistent format to form a question for each target word. Encourage students to explain their answers. For example, ask: *When you follow a tradition, are you doing something original or something many people do? When you have a celebration, are you excited or bored?*
   - **Prompts** Create a discussion prompt for each of the words. Be sure your prompts are open-ended, and encourage students to answer creatively. For example, ask: *How could you and your classmates create new traditions? If you wanted to celebrate your friend's birthday, what would you do?*
4. **Extend Word Use Beyond the Classroom** In order to develop a rich, deep, and lasting understanding of new vocabulary, students require multiple exposures to target words, in more than one context. Encourage students to think about and use target words beyond the classroom as often as they can.

Word Sorts

Vocabulary Routine 6

Materials: 3" x 5" index cards or narrow paper strips

Students explore word relationships by sorting, or categorizing, words into groups.

1. Have students **write a word on each card or paper strip**. You can have students do a **closed sort** by providing the categories of how the cards should be sorted. Choose closed sorts when progress monitoring indicates that students need additional review, reinforcement, or practice with particular skills.

When students need to apply spelling and structural analysis for more advanced vocabulary development, use the following sorts for **spelling patterns:**

- **number of syllables**
- **common affixes**
- **derived vs. non-derived forms**

When students struggle with grammar and syntax, use the following sorts:

- **Part of speech**
- **Formal and informal language**
- **Words with cognates (for English learners)**

When students are learning to synthesize ideas or analyze word choice, use the following sorts:

- **Related meanings or concepts**
- **Multiple meanings**
- **Positive or negative connotations**

Another option is an **open sort** where you provide students with a list of words only. Then students work together to identify the common patterns and attributes of the words on their own. Open word sorts foster creativity, support student independence, motivate students, and foster word consciousness.

2. When students have sorted the cards, ask students to **explain their sorts**. Then have them create a chart or web to record the word relationships.

3. Finally, encourage students to **sort the words again using different categories** and to once again record the information in a graphic organizer.

4. **List-Group-Label** is a more sophisticated version of a word sort.

- Students brainstorm words associated with a topic.
- Students look at the word list and group words into different categories.
- Then students label the categories.

When students are sorting words, supply a "parking lot" category for words that might not fit existing groups. Additionally, allow students to assign one word to more than one category when appropriate.

Parts of Speech Sort

Nouns	Verbs	Adverbs
abstract (n.)	adhere (v.)	ethically (adv.)
dilemma (n.)	advocate (v.)	desolately (adv.)
	reinforce (v.)	deliberately (adv.)

Number of Syllables Sort

2	3	4	5
ab-stract	ad-vo-cate	des-o-late-ly	de-lib-er-ate-l
ad-here	di-lem-ma		
	e-thi-cal		
	re-in-force		

List-Group-Label Sort

Topic: War

general	planes	courage
soldier	weapons	uniform
plan	fear	spy

People	Tools	Feelings	Actions
general	planes	fear	plan
soldier	weapons	courage	spy
	uniforms		

Graphic Organizers

Vocabulary Routine 7

Materials: overhead projector; models of completed graphic organizers (optional)

Students can use graphic organizers to visually represent dimensions of word meanings and build connections between groups of semantically connected words. There are many different types of graphic organizers that you can choose from:

1. Word Web A **word web** shows the meaning(s) and examples of a key word. The key word is written in a central oval, with spokes connecting it to its various meanings and examples. The web can be further extended by adding other words that are related to each of the meanings. A word web is ideal for the study of polysemous (multiple-meaning) words and their synonyms.

2. Semantic Map In a **semantic map**, students group words related to a predetermined concept. For example, in a unit on extreme sports, they might group together the following terms under the topic of Cave Exploration: spelunking, stalactite, crevasse, mineral. Semantic maps are adaptable to a number of different topics and contexts. You may want to develop an initial semantic map based on a preview of a reading selection, and then revise and expand it after students have finished reading the text.

To gain the most out of semantic mapping, actively engage students in a discussion using **questions that contain the target words**. For example, *What is the difference between* a cave *and* a cavern? *Would you like to go* spelunking? *Why, or why not?* Use yes/no questions for students with limited oral English.

3. Matrix Grid A **matrix grid** is a good way to quickly compare things in a category. Students write the category at the top of the first column. Below it, they list examples of items in the category. Across the top they list the attributes or key features of things in the category. Then they go through each example, deciding whether or not it has each feature they listed. A plus sign (+) indicates that it does; a minus sign (-) means that it does not. When the grid is complete, students can see at a glance how the items are similar and what makes each one unique.

5. Denotation and Connotation Chart In a **Denotation and Connotation Chart**, students determine the feeling that the word suggests. This can help students choose the best word when they are trying to describe something.

Word Web

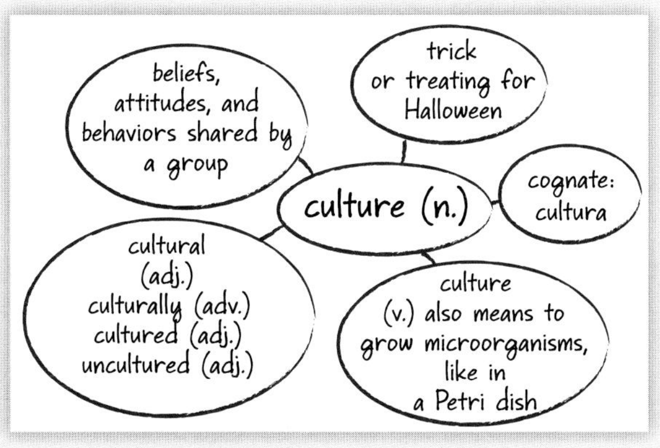

Semantic Map

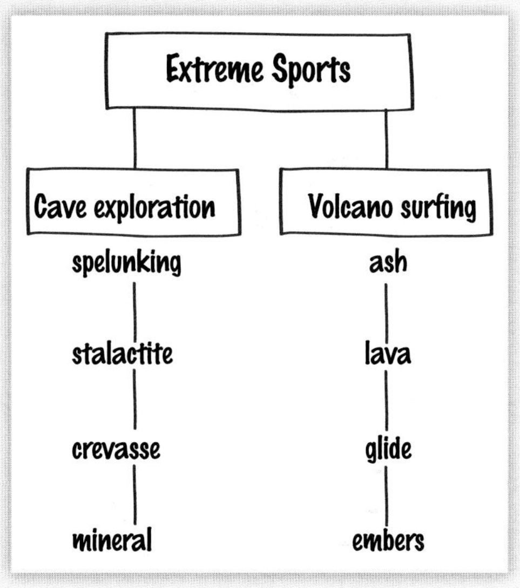

Matrix Grid

Instruments	wood body	metal body	strings	pedals
piano	+	–	+	+
guitar	+	–	+	–
vibraphone	–	+	–	+
marimba	+	–	–	–
saxophone	–	+	–	–

Denotation and Connotation Chart

Word	Denotation	Example from My Life	Connotation
steady	"not changing, constant"	when the beat in a song stays the same	◇positive ✓neutral ◇negative
monotonous	"not changing; repetitious and dull"	when the beat in a song is boring	◇positive ◇neutral ✓negative

Discuss Author's Word Choice

Vocabulary Routine 8

Structured discussions about an author's word choices provide students opportunities to extend their knowledge of known words, learn new words, and realize how specific words shape the meanings of texts.

1. To introduce word choice discussions to your students, first select 2 or 3 words or phrases from a passage that are especially effective in shaping meaning and tone, engaging feelings, or triggering sensory images. These terms often have strong connotative or figurative meanings.
2. After students read the passage, use the **eEdition** to display a page containing the words or phrases that you selected. Briefly describe word choice by explaining: Authors choose words to grab your attention and influence your thinking. These words suggest important ideas, positive or negative feelings, and sensory images. Identifying these words and talking about them adds to your understanding of the word and of the text that you're reading.
3. Then model how to analyze an author's choice of words. For instance, for "The Grapes of Wrath," say:

   John Steinbeck writes "A 1926 Nash sedan pulled wearily off the highway." The phrase *pulled wearily* grabbed my attention. This phrase means the car was tired. The car doesn't have feelings, of course. But the phrase makes me think the car and passengers have come a long way and they're very tired. I imagine an old, creaky car rolling slowly to the side of the road. If Steinbeck had used the words *zipped quickly* then I would expect the car and the car's passengers to be in a hurry and full of energy.
4. Display the page containing other words you identified, and have students chorally read the sentences in which they appear. Then collaboratively discuss with your students the author's choices of the particular words or phrases. Use the following questions to generate discussions about word choice:
   - Why do you think the word(s) ________ is/are important?
   - How does/do the word(s) ________ make you feel?
   - What images does/do the word(s) ________ create for you as a reader?
5. Have pairs or small groups of students identify 2 or 3 additional noteworthy words or phrases. Then invite the pairs or groups to compare the words they identified. Display language frames to support English language learners.
6. Have students add the new words to their Vocabulary Notebooks using to Step 5 in **Vocabulary Routine 2** (PD 32). Encourage students to record the following details in their notebook entries:
   - The context for the word and citation of the passage
   - Why the word is important
   - The feeling or image the word creates
7. Gradually release responsibility for discussing word choices. Before reading a new passage, remind students to be prepared to talk about noteworthy words. After reading, have students discuss the author's use of noteworthy terms and encourage students to add them to their Vocabulary Notebooks. Use additional language frames to promote academic discussions. Fade out the use of prompts and language frames gradually so your students independently discuss the words that authors choose.

Language Frames

Identify Words or Phrases

- I think the word(s) ________ is/are important because ________ .
- The word(s) ________ makes/make me feel ________ .
- The words ________ create images of ________ .

Language Frames

Discuss Word Choice

- *The author probably chose the words ________ to make me think ________ .*
- *The words ________ tell me that ________ .*
- *The author used the words ________ because ________ .*
- *The words ________ made me feel positive/negative about ________ because ________ .*
- *The words ________ made me use my senses to ________ .*
- *If the author had used the word ________ instead of ________ , I would think ________ .*
- *The word ________ seemed like it didn't belong in the text, but it does belong because ________ .*

Games and Drama

Vocabulary Routine 9

Games motivate students to be word conscious while actively manipulating and using language. Drama activities allow students to explore word meanings through a total physical response. Games are especially beneficial for English language learners since they create an authentic context for social interaction and build listening and speaking skills; pantomime and charades are ideal for students who have limited oral vocabularies. In addition to the time-honored **20 questions**, **classroom baseball**, **concentration**, and **Pictionary®**, make the following games and drama activities part of your daily vocabulary routines:

1. **Stump the Expert** Designate an expert. A stumper presents a definition and the expert has 10 seconds to produce the term. If the expert responds accurately, the next stumper offers a challenge. This continues until the expert is stumped, or until the expert answers a set number of challenges and earns applause or a prize. The person who stumps the expert becomes the next expert.
2. **Around the World** A student designated as the traveler moves from his or her seat and stands by a student in the next seat. Give the traveler and the challenger a definition; whoever correctly identifies the word first is the traveler and stands by the student in the next seat. A traveler who continues responding first and returns to his or her seat has successfully gone "Around the World."
3. **Whatta' Ya' Know** Pose *yes/no* questions using two key vocabulary words. You or your students can make up the questions. The responses can be written or stated orally, and hands can be raised for *yes* and then for *no*. For instance, the following questions might be asked about words associated with volcanoes: Are **volcanoes** made of **lava**? Do **igneous** rocks come from **magma**?
4. **Multiple Key Word Skit** Groups can work together to create and act out a skit with dialogue that includes at least five of the key words. Allow groups a few minutes of preparation time to brainstorm ways that the words relate to each other. You may wish to award points for the most original skit, the most humorous, or the most accurate use of the words' meanings.
5. **Charades** Students can play Charades to pantomime an action or emotion associated with a key word or phrase.
   - Write out words or phrases on index cards and place them in a stack.
   - Divide students into teams; one member of a team takes a card and acts out each word or syllable of a word using only physical signals. His or her teammates must guess the word or phrase being acted out.
   - A time-keeper from the other team monitors the time, and the team with the lowest time score after a full round wins.
6. **Synonym Strings** Have teams compete to form synonym strings. Divide the class into two teams, and assign a starter word, such as *talk*, to each team. Teams then work to come up with as many synonyms as they can, and act out the meaning of each one. For example, for the starter word *talk*, students might come up with *babble*, *blab*, *chat*, *drawl*, *intone*, *squeal*, *yell*, etc. Synonyms can be checked in a thesaurus, or against a teacher-generated list. Building synonym strings leads to distinguishing denotations / connotations and shades of meaning.

Word Wall

Vocabulary Routine 10

Materials: bulletin board; word cards or butcher paper; photographs and diagrams

Word walls present a **visual reminder** of key vocabulary throughout a unit of study. Reserve a bulletin board to display important words. The words can be shown in graphic organizers, by themselves, or with photos or diagrams that help clarify their meanings.

- Some teachers create a complete display of all the key vocabulary and refer to it throughout the unit. Other teachers prefer to add words gradually, as they come up in reading or class discussion. In either case, do some culminating activities asking students what they learned about each word.
- Many new meanings that students must learn are words that represent concrete, real things. You can create word/picture boards around certain themes and areas of study. For example, a music board might display the symbols for *sharp*, *flat*, *note*, *repeat*, and so forth, along with the words for which they stand.
- Cover a bulletin board or display a banner with acronyms that occur in your study. List the acronym and the words for which it stands. Invite volunteers to draw something that symbolizes each one. Examples of common acronyms include:

ASAP	As soon as possible
ATM	Automatic teller machine
BTW	By the way
DVD	Digital Video Disk
FYI	For your information
GPA	Grade Point Average
ID	Identification
LASER	Light Amplification by Stimulated Emission of Radiation
MC	Master of Ceremonies
MLB	Major League Baseball
NASCAR	National Association for Stock Car Auto Racing
NFL	National Football League
PS	Postscript
Q&A	Question and Answer
SCUBA	Self-Contained Underwater Breathing Apparatus
VIP	Very Important Person
WWW	World Wide Web

Synonym Word Wall

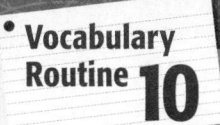

Academic Vocabulary

For many students, reading in the content areas is particularly challenging due to the academic vocabulary used by writers in these disciplines. Even native speakers of English are rarely exposed to academic English in either daily conversation or popular video and print media. Yet it is words such as *achieve*, *motivate*, and *vary* that carry much of the meaning in written texts. The Academic Word List (Coxhead, 2000) is an excellent resource for building students' academic vocabulary. It is a research-based corpus of 570 word families that appear in many academic texts across various domains. In ***Edge***, students have the opportunity to read these words in context and to reinforce their understanding through a variety of repeated, rich language experiences. Academic vocabulary is marked with a red dot in all Prepare to Read and on-page definitions.

AV Word	Related Words	Definitions
access (*n., v.*) pp. 562, 566, 573, 583	accessibility (*n.*) accessible (*adj.*) inaccessible (*adj.*)	**General:** *noun* the way of reaching a place or person, or the right to use or look at something *verb* to reach something or someone **Computer Science:** *verb* to open a computer file in order to look at or change the information in it
achieve (*v.*) pp. 138, 149, 153	achievement (*n.*) achievable (*adj.*)	**General:** *verb* to succeed in finishing something or accomplishing a goal, especially after a lot of work or effort
affect (*v., n.*) pp. 10, 19, 25, 35	affected (*adj.*) affectation (*n.*) affection (*n.*) affectionate (*adj.*) affective (*adj.*)	**General:** *verb* to influence someone or something; to cause someone or something to change *verb* (formal) to pretend to feel or think something **Psychology:** *noun* emotion or feeling
alternative (*adj.*) pp. 542, 550	alternate (*v.*) alternative (*n.*) alternatively (*adv.*)	**General:** *noun* something that is different from something else, especially from what is usual, and offering the possibility of choice *adjective* allowing or requiring a choice between two or more things **alternative energy:** *noun* energy from moving water, wind, the sun, and gas from animal waste **alternative medicine:** *noun* different treatments for medical conditions that people use instead of, or with western medicine
aspect (*n.*) p. 621	n/a	**General:** *noun* one feature or part of a situation, problem, subject, etc. **Mathematics:** *noun* the side or surface facing a given direction
assemble (*v.*) pp. 362, 371, 380, 387	assembly (*n.*) assembled (*adj.*)	**General:** *verb* to put something together; to gather a group of people
assume (*v.*) pp. 340, 346	assumption (*n.*) unassuming (*adj.*)	**General:** *verb* to accept that something is true without question or proof; to pretend to be someone you are not; to take responsibility for or control of something
authority (*n.*) pp. 262, 282, 285, 287	authoritative (*adj.*)	**General:** *noun* the right or ability to control, command, or decide; a person or institution that has this right or ability
bias (*n.*) pp. 562, 572, 575, 578	biased (*adj.*)	**General:** *noun* an opinion or mindset that prevents objective judgment; partiality **Design:** *noun* a diagonal line of direction, especially across a woven fabric
bond (*n.*) pp. 612, 635, 640, 641	bond (*v.*) bonded (*adj.*)	**General:** *noun* a close connection joining two or more people; a cord, rope, or band **Chemistry:** *noun* the attraction between atoms in a molecule or crystalline structure **Economics:** *noun* an official paper issued by the government or a company to show that you have lent money that they will pay back at a fixed interest rate **Law:** *noun* money that is paid to officially promise that someone accused of a crime and being kept in jail will appear for trial if released

AV Word	Related Words	Definitions
capable *(adj.)* pp. 436, 448, 456, 459	capability *(n.)* capably *(adj.)* incapable *(adj.)*	**General**: *adjective* able to do something; efficient, competent
categorize *(v.)* p. 411	categorizable *(adj.)* category *(n.)* categorization *(n.)*	**General:** *verb* to put people or things into groups with the same features *noun* any group of things which have some shared features; a class, a type, or a set **Mathematics:** *noun* a type of mathematical object, as a set, group, or metric space, together with a set of mappings from such an object to other objects of the same type
cease *(v.)* pp. 462, 475	ceaseless *(adj.)* cessation *(n.)* unceasing *(adj.)*	**General:** *verb (slightly formal)* to stop or come to an end
circumstance(s) *(n.)* pp. 40, 54, 58	circumstantial *(adj.)*	**General:** *noun (usually plural)* a fact or event that makes a situation the way it is **Economics:** *plural noun* how much money someone has **Law: circumstantial** *adjective* containing information, especially about a crime, which makes you think something is true but does not prove it
clarify *(v.)* pp. 9, 313	clarity *(n.)* clarification *(n.)*	**General:** *verb* to make something clear or easier to understand by giving more details or a simpler explanation **Cooking:** *verb* to purify and remove water from fat, such as butter, by heating it
collapse *(v.)* pp. 612, 628	collapse *(n.)* collapsible *(adj.)*	**General:** *verb* to fall down or inward suddenly; to fold compactly; (of people and business) to suffer the sudden inability to continue or work correctly **Medicine:** *verb* to sink into extreme weakness; (of lungs or blood vessels) to become flattened
commit *(v.)* pp. 40, 44, 53, 118, 123	committal *(n.)* commitment *(n.)* committed *(adj.)*	**General:** *verb* to do, perform, or perpetrate; to promise or give your loyalty, time, or money to a particular principle, person, or plan of action *noun* a pledge or promise; obligation **Law:** *verb* to send someone officially to a prison or hospital
conflict *(n.)* pp. 10, 14, 25	conflict *(v.)* conflicting *(adj.)*	**General :** *noun* a disagreement between people with opposing opinions or principles; fighting
consequence(s) *(n.)* pp. 40, 44, 51, 54	consequential *(adj.)* consequently *(adj.)*	**General:** *noun* an often bad or inconvenient result of a particular action or situation *adjective* happening as a result of something
constant (adj.) pp. 340, 355, 356	constancy *(n.)* constantly *(adv.)* inconstancy *(n.)*	**General:** *adjective* staying the same, or not getting less or more **Mathematics:** *noun* a particular number or amount that never changes
consumer *(n.)* pp. 514, 520, 537	consumables *(n. pl.)* consume *(v.)* consumption *(n.)*	**General:** *noun* a person who buys goods or services for their own use
contribute *(v.)* pp. 10, 30	contributing *(adj.)* contribution *(n.)* contributory *(adj.)*	**General:** *verb* to give something, especially money, together with other people; to write articles for a newspaper, magazine, or book
convince *(v.)* pp. 514, 518, 537	convinced *(adj.)* convincing *(adj.)* convincingly *(adv.)*	**General:** *verb* to persuade someone or make them certain
culture *(n.)* pp. 138, 149	cultural *(adj.)* culturally *(adv.)* cultured *(adj.)* uncultured *(adj.)*	**General:** *noun* the way of life, especially the general customs and beliefs, of a particular group of people at a particular time; music, art, theatre, literature, etc. **Biology:** *noun* cells, tissues, organs or organisms grown for scientific purposes, or breeding and keeping certain living things in order to get substances they produce
detect *(v.)* pp. 562, 575	detectable *(adj.)* detection *(n.)* detective *(n.)*	**General:** *verb* to notice something that is partly hidden or not clear or to discover something, especially using a special method; to discover something, usually using special equipment

AV Word	Related Words	Definitions
device *(n.)* pp. 362, 378, 380, 382	devise *(v.)*	**General:** *noun* an object or machine which has been invented to fulfill a particular purpose; a method which is used to produce a desired effect, such as a literary device; a bomb or other explosive
devotion *(n.)* pp. 646, 667, 673	devote *(v.)* devoted *(adj.)*	**General:** *noun* loyalty and love or care for someone or something; religious worship
discriminate *(v.)* pp. 262, 266, 284, 285	discriminating *(adj.)* discrimination *(n.)*	**General:** *verb* to treat a person or particular group of people differently, especially in a worse way, because of their race, religion, gender, etc.; to be able to see the difference between two things or people *noun* treating a person or particular group of people differently, especially in a worse way, because of their race, religion, gender, etc.
distorted *(adj.)* pp. 562, 570	distort *(v.)* distortion *(n.)*	**General:** *adjective* changed from the usual, original, natural or intended meaning, condition, or shape
emphasis *(n.)* p. 115	emphasizing *(adj.)* emphasize *(v.)* emphatic *(adj.)* emphatically *(n.)*	**General:** *noun* the particular importance or attention that you give to something *verb* to show or state that something is particularly important or worth giving attention to; to make something more obvious **Linguistics:** *noun* the extra force that you give to a word or part of a word
environment *(n.)* pp. 362, 368	environmental *(adj.)* environmentalist *(n.)* environmentally *(adv.)*	**General:** *noun* the conditions that you live or work in and the way that they influence how you feel or how effectively you can work; the air, water, and land in or on which people, animals, and plants live
evaluate *(v.)* pp. 118, 131	evaluative *(adj.)* evaluation *(n.)* re-evaluate *(v.)* re-evaluation *(n.)*	**General:** *verb* to judge or calculate the quality, importance, amount, or value of something *noun* judgment or calculation
evidence *(n.)* pp. 208, 221, 226, 230, 512	evidential *(adj.)* evident *(adj.)* evidently (adv.)	**General:** *noun* one or more reasons for believing that something is or is not true *adjective* easily seen or understood; obvious **Law: state's evidence** *noun* evidence from someone who has been accused of committing a crime, given in order to have their own punishment reduced
expand *(v.)* pp. 542, 551, 585	expansion *(n.)* expansive *(adj.)*	**General:** *verb* to increase in size, number, or importance, or to make something increase in this way
feature *(n.)* pp. 678, 686	feature *(v.)* featuring *(adj.)*	**General:** *noun* a typical quality or an important part of something; one of the parts of someone's face that you notice when you look at them **Journalism:** *noun* a special article in a newspaper or magazine, or a part of a television or radio broadcast, that deals with a particular subject
generation *(n.)* pp. 10, 31, 33, 35	generate *(v.)*	**General :** *noun* all the people of about the same age within a society or family; a group of devices which are all at the same stage of development **Biology:** *noun* one complete life cycle; one of the alternate phases that complete a life cycle having more than one phase (for example, the gametophyte generation) **Mathematics:** *noun* the production of a geometrical figure by motion of another one **Physics:** *noun* one of the successive sets of nuclei produced in a chain reaction
grant *(v.)* pp. 412, 416	granted *(adj.)* granting *(adj.)*	**General:** *verb* to give or allow someone something, usually in an official way; to accept that something is true, often before expressing an opposite opinion **Government:** *noun* a sum of money given, especially by the government, to a person or organization for a special purpose
guarantee *(n.)* p. 409	guarantee *(v.)* guaranteed *(adj.)*	**General:** *noun* a promise that something will be done or will happen, especially a written promise by a company; a formal acceptance of responsibility for something, such as the payment of someone else's debt

AV Word	Related Words	Definitions
image *(n.)* p. 607	image *(v.)* imagery *(n.)*	**General:** *noun* a picture in your mind or an idea of how someone or something is; the way that something or someone is thought of by other people **Literature:** *noun* a mental picture or idea which forms in a reader's or listener's mind from the words that they read or hear **Mathematics:** *noun* the point or set of points in the range corresponding to a designated point in the domain of a given function
impact *(n.)* pp. 514, 521, 531	impact *(v.)* impacted *(adj.)*	**General:** *noun* the force or action of one object hitting another; a powerful effect that something, especially something new, has on a situation or person
infer *(v.)* p. 205	inferential *(adj.)* inference *(n.)* inferentially (adv.)	**General:** *verb* to form an opinion or guess that something is true because of the information that you have *noun* an opinion or guess based on information that you have
inherent *(adj.)* pp. 236, 255, 256, 257	inherently *(adv.)*	**General:** *adjective* existing as a natural or basic part of something **Grammar**: *adjective* standing before a noun
inhibit (v.) pp. 236, 255, 257	inhibited *(adj.)* inhibiting *(adj.)* inhibition *(n.)*	**General:** *verb* to prevent someone from doing something, or to slow down a processor the growth of something **Biology:** *noun* the condition in which or the process by which an enzyme, for example, is inhibited **Chemistry:** *noun* a condition or process which inhibits a reaction **Psychology:** *noun* conscious or unconscious restraint of certain behavior
insight *(n.)* pp. 118, 129, 133, 182	insightful *(adj.)*	**General:** *noun* (the ability to have) a clear, deep, and sometimes sudden understanding of a complicated problem or situation **Psychology:** *noun* an understanding of relationships that on or helps solve a problem
inspire *(v.)* pp. 64, 84, 86, 87	inspiration *(n.)* inspirational *(adj.)*	**General:** *verb* to make someone feel that they want to do something and can do it; to make someone have a strong feeling or reaction; to give someone an idea for a book, film, product, etc.
integrity *(n.)* pp. 612, 630, 641	n/a	**General:** *noun* the quality of being honest and having strong moral principles that you refuse to change; the quality of being whole and complete
interactive *(adj.)* p. 608	interaction *(n.)* interactively *(adv.)*	**General:** *verb* to communicate with or react to *adjective* involving communication between people **Technology:** *adjective* describes a system or computer program which is designed to involve the user in the exchange of information
interpret *(v.)* **interpretation** *(n.)* pp. 609, 678, 686	interpretive *(adj.)* interpreter *(n.)* misinterpret *(v.)* misinterpretation *(n.)* reinterpret *(v.)* reinterpretation *(n.)*	**General:** *verb* to decide what the intended meaning of something is; to change what someone is saying into another language *noun* an explanation or opinion of what something means; a performance **Performing Arts:** *verb* to express your own ideas about the intended meaning of a play or a piece of music when performing it
invest *(v.)* pp. 612, 618	investment *(n.)* investor *(n.)* reinvest *(v.)*	**General:** *verb* to put money, effort, time, etc. into something to make a profit or get a advantage; to buy something because you think it will be useful, even if you think it is expensive
investigation *(n.)* pp. 208, 227	investigate *(v.)* investigative *(adj.)* investigator *(n.)*	**General:** *noun* to examine a crime, problem, statement, etc. carefully, especially to discover the truth
issue *(n.)* pp. 646, 665, 667, 673	issue *(v.)*	**General:** *noun* a subject or problem which people are thinking and talking about; (*informal*) a personal problem or emotional disorder *verb* to produce or provide something official **Finance:** *noun* an issue of shares is when a company gives people the chance to buy part of it or gives extra shares to people who already own some **Media:** *noun* a set of newspapers or magazines published at the same time or a single copy of a newspaper or magazine

AV Word	Related Words	Definitions
major (*adj. n.*) pp. 678, 693	majority (*n.*)	**General:** *adjective* more important, bigger, or more serious than others **Education:** *noun* the most important subject a college or university student studies **Military:** *noun* an officer of middle rank in the British, U.S., and many other armed forces, such as the U.S. Air Force **Music:** *adjective* based on a scale in which there is a whole tone between the second and third notes and a half tone between the third and fourth notes
manipulate (*v.*) pp. 514, 524, 537	manipulated (*adj.*) manipulation (*n.*) manipulative (*adj.*)	**General:** *verb* to control something using the hands; (*usually negative*) to control something or someone to your advantage, often unfairly or dishonestly **Medicine:** *verb* to handle and move in an examination or for therapeutic purposes
media (*n.*) pp. 542, 546, 551, 553, 557, 583	n/a	**General:** *group noun* a type of mass communication, such as newspapers, magazines, radio and television, usually considered as a group **medium** *noun* a method or way of expressing something **Art: medium** *noun* a liquid with which pigments are mixed; the material or technique with which an artist works, such as oil or watercolor paint **Biology: medium** *noun* the substance in which a specific organism lives and thrives **Chemistry: medium** *noun* a filtering substance, such as filter paper **Technology: medium** *noun* an object or device on which data is stored
mental (*adj.*) p. 607	mentality (*n.*) mentally (*adv.*)	**General:** *adjective* relating to the mind, or involving the process of thinking
minor (*adj.*) pp. 678, 693	minority (*n.*)	**General:** *adjective* having little importance, influence or effect, especially when compared with other things of the same type **Education:** *noun* a less important subject studied by a student (see *major*) **Law:** *noun* someone who is too young to have the legal responsibilities of an adult **Music:** *adjective* belonging or relating to a type of musical scale that generally has a sad sound, typically having a half tone between the second and third and between the fifth and sixth notes, and a whole tone between each of the others
monitor (*v.*) p. 7	monitor (*n.*) monitored (*adj.*) unmonitored (*adj.*)	**General:** *verb* to watch and check a situation carefully for a period of time in order to discover something about it **Technology:** *noun* a device with a screen on which words or pictures can be shown
motivate (*v.*) pp. 10, 29, 35	motivator (*n.*) motivated (*adj.*) motivation (*n.*) unmotivated (*adj.*)	**General:** *verb* to cause someone to behave in a particular way; to make someone want to do something well *adjective* given a reason for action; enthusiastic *noun* enthusiasm for doing something; the need or reason for doing something
objectivity (*n.*) pp. 562, 575, 578, 579	objective (*adj., n.*) objectively (*adv.*)	**General:** *noun* judgment based on observable phenomena and uninfluenced by emotions or personal prejudices **Technology: objective** *noun* the lens or lens system in a microscope or other optical instrument that first receives light rays from the object and forms the image
obvious (*adj.*) pp. 318, 418	obviously (*adv.*)	**General:** *adjective* clear; easy to see, recognize, or understand

AV Word	Related Words	Definitions
orient (*v.*) p. 313	oriented (*adj.*) orientation (*n.*) orienting (*adj.*) reorient (*v.*) reorientation (*n.*)	**General:** *verb* to aim something at someone or something, or make something suitable for a particular group of people **orientation** *noun* the particular interests, activities, or aims that someone or something has; an introduction, as to guide one in adjusting to new surroundings, employment, activity, or the like (for example, freshman orientation); location or position relative to the points of the compass (for example, an easterly orientation) **Chemistry:** *noun* the relative positions of certain atoms or groups, especially in aromatic compounds **Mathematics:** *verb* to assign a constant, outward direction at each point
perceive (*v.*) pp. 64, 79, 86, 206	perceived (*adj.*) perception (*n.*) perceiving (*adj.*)	**General:** *verb* to see something or someone, or to become aware of something that is obvious; to come to an opinion or have a belief about something *noun* an awareness of things through the physical senses, especially sight; someone's ability to notice and understand things that are not obvious to other people; a belief or opinion, often held by many people and based on appearances **Psychology:** *noun* recognition and interpretation of sensory stimuli
persistent (*adj.*) pp. 262, 282	persist (*v.*) persistence (*n.*) persistently (*adv.*)	**General:** *adjective* lasting for a long time or difficult to get rid of **Biology:** *adjective* continuing or permanent; having continuity of phylogenetic characteristics
perspective (*n.*) pp. 138, 142, 182, 207	n/a	**General:** *noun* a particular way of thinking about something; a point of view **Art:** *noun* the way that objects appear smaller when they are further away and the way parallel lines appear to meet each other at a point in the distance
phenomenon (*n.*) pp. 160, 171, 173, 177, 181	phenomena (*n. pl.*) phenomenal (*adj.*)	**General:** *noun* someone or something extremely successful, often because of special qualities or abilities; something that exists and can be seen, felt, tasted, etc., especially something which is unusual or interesting **Physics:** *noun* an observable event
precision (*n.*) pp. 436, 442, 459	precise (*adj.*) precisely (*adv.*) imprecise (*adj.*)	**General:** *noun* the quality of being exact; (usually positive) the qualities of being careful and accurate **Mathematics:** *noun* the degree to which the correctness of a quantity is expressed **Chemistry, Physics:** *noun* the extent to which a given set of measurements of the same sample agree with their mean
predict (*v.*) p. 7	prediction (*n.*) predictable (*adj.*) predictably (*adv.*) unpredictable (*adj.*)	**General:** *verb* to say that an event or action will happen in the future, especially as a result of knowledge or experience *noun* when you say what will happen in the future
priority (*n.*) pp. 562, 569	prioritize (*v.*) prioritization (*n.*)	**General:** *noun* something that is very important and must be dealt with before other things; a preceding or coming earlier in time
profession (*n.*) pp. 314, 332, 334	professional (*adj., n.*) professionally (*adv.*) professionalism (*n.*)	**General:** *noun* any type of work which needs special training or a particular skill, often one which is respected because it involves a high level of education; the people who do a type of work, considered as a group
release (*v.*) pp. 318, 417	release (*n.*)	**General:** *verb* to give freedom or free movement to someone or something; to move a device from a fixed position to allow it to move freely; to allow something to be shown in public or to be available for use **Law:** *noun* the surrender of a right or the like to another
relevance (*n.*) pp. 462, 473, 477, 481, 483	relevant (*adj.*) irrelevance (*n.*) irrelevant (*adj.*)	**General:** *noun* the degree to which something is related or useful to what is happening or being talked about
rely (*v.*) pp. 205, 436, 442, 457, 459	reliability (*n.*) reliable (*adj.*) reliably (*adv.*)	**General:** *verb* to need a particular thing or the help and support of someone or something in order to continue, to work correctly, or to succeed; to trust someone or something or to expect them to behave in a particular way

AV Word	Related Words	Definitions
restore (*v.*) pp. 646, 670	restoration (*n.*) restorative (*adj.*) restorer (*n.*)	**General:** *verb* to return something or someone to an earlier good condition or position; to bring back into use something that has been absent for a period of time **Dentistry:** *verb* to bring teeth or parts of teeth back to a former or original state **History: the Restoration** *noun* the reestablishment of the monarchy in England with the return of Charles II in 1660
sequence (*n.*) p. 311	sequence (*v.*) sequential (*adj.*) sequencing (*n.*) sequentially (*adv.*)	**General:** *noun* a series of related things or events, or the order in which they follow each other *adjective (formal)* following a particular order **Biochemistry:** *noun* the order of constituents in a polymer, especially the order of nucleotides in a nucleic acid or of the amino acids in a protein **Mathematics:** *noun* an ordered set of quantities, such as x, 2x2, 3x3, 4x4
structure (*n.*) pp. 160, 166, 174, 175, 611	structure (*v.*) structural (*adj.*) structurally (*adv.*) structuralism (*n.*) structuralist (*n.*) restructure (*v.*) restructuring (*n.*) unstructured (*adj.*)	**General:** *noun* the way in which the parts of a system or object are arranged or organized, or a system arranged in this way; something which has been made or built from parts, especially a large building **Biology:** *noun* the arrangement or formation of the tissues, organs, or other parts of an organism; an organ or other part of an organism **Chemistry:** *noun* the manner in which atoms in a molecule are joined to each other **Geology:** *noun* the attitude of a bed or stratum or of beds or strata of sedimentary rocks, as indicated by the dip and strike
summarize (*v.*) pp. 117	summarization (*n.*) summary (*n.*) summary (*adj.*)	**General:** *verb* to express the most important facts or ideas about something or someone in a short and clear form *noun* a short clear description that gives the main facts or ideas about something
survive (*v.*) pp. 236, 253	survival (*n.*) survivor (*n.*)	**General:** *verb* to continue to live or exist, especially after coming close to dying or being destroyed or after being in a difficult or threatening situation *noun* a person who continues to live, despite nearly dying; a person who is able to continue living their life successfully despite experiencing difficulties **Law:** *verb* to live longer than someone you are related to noun the members of a person's family who continue to live after he or she has died
symbol (*n.*) pp. 64, 73, 87	symbolically (*adv.*) symbolism (*n.*) symbolize (*v.*)	**General:** *noun* a sign, shape or object which is used to represent something else; something that is used to represent a quality or idea; a number, letter or sign used in mathematics, music, science, etc. **Psychology:** *noun* an object or image that an individual unconsciously uses to represent repressed thoughts, feelings, or impulses
technology (*n.*) pp. 362, 374, 377, 380, 381, 387	technological (*adj.*) technologically (adv.)	**General:** noun (the study and knowledge of) the practical, especially industrial, use of scientific discoveries **Computer Science: information technology** *noun* the science and activity of using computers and other electronic equipment to store and send information (often abbreviated as IT)
trace (*n.*) pp. 436, 455, 456	trace (*v.*) tracing (*n.*) traceable (*adj.*)	**General:** *noun* a very slight amount **Mathematics:** *noun* the point at which a line, or the curve in which a surface, intersects a coordinate plane
transform (*v.*) pp. 118, 125	transformation (*n.*) transformational (*adj.*)	**General:** *verb* to change completely the appearance or character of something or someone, especially so that they are improved **Mathematics:** *verb* to change the form of (a figure, expression, etc.) without in general changing the value **Physics:** *verb* to change into another form of energy

Spanish-English Cognates

Cognates are words in two languages that share a similar spelling, pronunciation, and meaning. Due to common Latin and Greek roots, English and Spanish share a large number of cognate pairs. In fact, researchers estimate that from 20% to over 30% of English words have Spanish cognates (Kamil and Bernhardt, 2004). English language learners can draw on their knowledge of cognates as a powerful tool for building English word knowledge and boosting reading comprehension. However, it's been found that second-language learners do not automatically recognize or make use of cognates. Therefore, it is important to build students' awareness of the strategy and to explicitly identify the words in reading selections that have cognates in their home languages (Nagy et al.; 1993; Bravo, Hiebert, and Pearson, 2005).

Key:
afectar: Spanish cognate
not *salvaje*, but *salvar*: false cognate with correct Spanish translation

Unit 1

T10: The Good Samaritan and The World Is in Their Hands

affect (*v.*)	*afectar*	pages 10, 19, 25, 35
conflict (*n.*)	*conflicto*	pages 10, 14, 25
contribute (*v.*)	*contribuir*	pages 10, 30
generation (*n.*)	*generación*	pages 10, 31, 33, 35
motivation (*n.*)	*motivación*	pages 10, 29, 35
privilege (*n.*)	*privilegio*	pages 10, 19
responsible (*adj.*)	*responsable*	pages 10, 18, 35

T40: Thank You, M'am and Juvenile Justice from Both Sides of the Bench

circumstances (*n.*)	*circunstancias*	pages 40, 54, 58
commit (*v.*)	*cometer*	pages 40, 44, 53
consequence (*n.*)	*consecuencia*	pages 40, 44, 51, 54
contact (*n.*)	*contacto*	pages 40, 46
empathy (*n.*)	*empatía*	pages 40, 51, 53, 59, 61
juvenile (*adj.*)	*juvenil*	pages 40, 53, 58, 59
maturity (*n.*)	*madurez*	pages 40, 54, 59
salvage (*v.*)	not *salvaje*, but *salvar*	pages 40, 54

T64: The Necklace and The Fashion Show

humiliating (*adj.*)	*humillante*	pages 64, 71
imitation (*n.*)	*imitación*	pages 64, 79
inspire (*v.*)	*inspirar*	pages 64, 84, 86, 87
luxury (*n.*)	*lujo*	pages 64, 68
perceive (*v.*)	*percibir*	pages 64, 79, 86
poverty (*n.*)	*pobreza*	pages 64, 76
symbol (*n.*)	*símbolo*	pages 64, 73, 87
value (*v.*)	*valorar*	pages 64, 79, 85

Unit 2

T118: Creativity at Work and The Hidden Secrets of the Creative Mind

career (*n.*)	*carrera*	pages 118, 122
collaborate (v.)	*colaborar*	pages 118, 122, 133
commitment (*n.*)	not *cometido*, but *compromiso*	pages 118, 123
evaluate (v.)	*evaluar*	pages 118, 131
expectation (*n.*)	*expectativa*	pages 118, 122, 127
talent (*n.*)	*talento*	pages 118, 124
transform (v.)	*transformar*	pages 118, 125

T138: Hip-Hop as Culture, I Am Somebody, and The Creativity Crisis

assert (*v.*)	*asertar*	pages 138, 145
culture (*n.*)	*cultura*	pages 138, 142, 149
evolve (*v.*)	*evolucionar*	pages 138, 144
heritage (*n.*)	*herencia*	pages 138, 152
innovator (*n.*)	*innovador*	pages 138, 144
perspective (*n.*)	*perspectiva*	pages 138, 142, 182

T160: Slam: Performance Poetry Lives On, Euphoria, and The Creativity Crisis

compose (*v.*)	*componer*	pages 160, 167, 177
euphoria (*adj.*)	*euphoria*	pages 160, 175, 176
expression (*n.*)	*expresión*	pages 160, 166, 176
improvisation (*n.*)	*improvisación*	pages 160, 171
phenomenon (*n.*)	*fenómeno*	pages 160, 171, 173, 177, 181
recitation (*n.*)	*recitación*	pages 160, 164
structure (*n.*)	*estructura*	pages 160, 166, 174, 175
transcend (*v.*)	*trascender*	pages 160, 166

Unit 3

T208: The Sword and the Stone and Was There a Real King Arthur?

conscientiously (*adv.*)	*concienzudamente*	pages 208, 213
endure (*v.*)	not *endurecer*, but *aguantar*	pages 208, 223, 230, 233
evidence (*n.*)	*evidencia*	pages 208, 221, 226, 230
genuine (*adj.*)	*genuino*	pages 208, 228, 231
historian (*n.*)	*historiador*	pages 208, 223, 230
investigation (*n.*)	*investigación*	pages 208, 227
just (*adj.*)	*justo*	pages 208, 219, 221
skeptic (*n.*)	*escéptico*	pages 208, 229

T236: A Job for Valentín, In the Heart of a Hero, and The American Promise

anxiety (*n.*)	*ansiedad*	pages 236, 246, 250, 257
distracted (*adj.*)	*distraído*	pages 236, 241
inherent (*adj.*)	*inherente*	pages 236, 255, 256, 257
inhibit (*v.*)	*inhibir*	pages 236, 255, 257
protest (*v.*)	*protestar*	pages 236, 242, 288
survivor (*n.*)	*sobreviviente*	pages 236, 253
tragedy (*n.*)	*tragedia*	pages 236, 253

T262: The Woman in the Snow, Rosa Parks, and The American Promise

authority (*n.*)	*autoridad*	pages 262, 282, 285, 287, 288
compassion (*n.*)	*compasión*	pages 262, 274, 277
desperately (*adv.*)	*desesperadamente*	pages 262, 270
discrimination (*n.*)	*discriminación*	pages 262, 266, 284, 285
persistent (*adj.*)	*persistente*	pages 262, 282, 289
provoke (*v.*)	*provocar*	pages 262, 283
segregation (*n.*)	*segregación*	pages 262, 280

Unit 4

T314: Curtis Aikens and the American Dream and Go For It!

ambitious (*adj.*)	*ambicioso*	pages 314, 332
cause (*n.*)	*causa*	pages 314, 327
confession (*n.*)	*confesión*	pages 314, 326, 328
profession (*n.*)	*profesión*	pages 314, 332, 334
reputation (*n.*)	*reputación*	pages 314, 321, 335

T340: Superman and Me and A Smart Cookie/It's Our Story, Too

arrogant (*adj.*)	*arrogante*	pages 340, 347, 357
assume (*v.*)	not *asumir,* but *suponer*	pages 340, 346
constant (*adj.*)	*constante*	pages 340, 355, 356
prodigy (*n.*)	*prodigio*	pages 340, 346

T362: The Fast and the Fuel-Efficient, Teens Open Doors, and The Sky Is Not the Limit

aggressive (*adj.*)	*agresivo*	pages 362, 374
efficient (*adj.*)	*eficiente*	pages 362, 366, 374, 381
obstacle (*n.*)	*obstáculo*	pages 362, 368, 374, 380, 381
solution (*n.*)	*solución*	pages 362, 363, 366, 380, 381, 383
technology (*n.*)	*tecnología*	pages 362, 374, 377, 380, 381, 387

Unit 5

T412: The Interlopers and An Interview with the King of Terror

identification (*n.*)	*identificación*	pages 412, 427, 430
obvious (*adj.*)	*obvio*	pages 412, 418
reconciliation (*n.*)	*reconciliación*	pages 412, 422
terror (*n.*)	*terror*	pages 412, 423, 425, 430, 431

T436: The Baby-Sitter and Beware: Do Not Read This Poem

capable (*adj.*)	*capaz*	pages 436, 448, 456, 459
precision (*n.*)	*precision*	pages 436, 442, 459
resist (*v.*)	*resistir*	pages 436, 455, 457, 459
ritual (*n.*)	*rito*	pages 436, 440, 450, 457
trace (*n.*)	not *trazo,* but *rastro*	pages 436, 455, 456
vulnerable (*adj.*)	*vulnerable*	pages 436, 445, 450

T462: The Tell-Tale Heart, The Raven, and Puddle

cease (*v.*)	*cesar*	pages 462, 475, 485
prophet (*n.*)	*profeta*	pages 462, 480, 481, 485
relevance (*n.*)	*relevancia*	pages 462, 473, 477, 481, 483
suspect (*v.*)	*sospechar*	pages 462, 466, 485, 488

Unit 6

T514: Ad Power and What's Wrong with Advertising?

advertising (*n.*)	not *advertencia,* but *publicidad*	pages 514, 518, 526, 531
appeal (*v.*)	*apelar*	pages 514, 521, 531
consumer (*n.*)	*consumidor*	pages 514, 520, 526, 537
convince (*v.*)	*convencer*	pages 514, 518, 526, 537
impact (*v.*)	*impacto*	pages 514, 521, 531
manipulate (*v.*)	*manipular*	pages 514, 524, 537
persuasive (*adj.*)	*persuasivo*	pages 514, 518, 526, 531, 537

T542: A Long Way to Go: Minorities and the Media, Reza: Warrior of Peace, and Is Google Making Us Stupid?

alternative (*adj.*)	*alternativa*	pages 542, 550
influence (*v.*)	*influencia*	pages 542, 547, 551, 552, 553
media (*n.*)	*medios [de comunicación]*	pages 542, 546, 551, 552, 553, 583
minority (*n., adj.*)	*minoría*	pages 542, 547, 551
racism (*n.*)	racismo	pages 542, 556
stereotype (*n.*)	estereotipo	pages 542, 546, 551

T562: What Is News? How to Detect Bias in the News, and Is Google Making Us Stupid?

access (*n.*)	*acceso*	pages 562, 566, 573, 583
deliberate (*adj.*)	*deliberar*	pages 562, 573
detect (*v.*)	*detectar*	pages 562, 575
distorted (*adj.*)	*distorcionado*	pages 562, 570
objectivity (*n.*)	*objetividad*	pages 562, 575, 578, 579
priority (*n.*)	*prioridad*	pages 562, 569

Unit 7

T612: A Raisin in the Sun and Family Bonds

bond (*n.*)	not *bondad,* but *vínculo*	pages 612, 635, 640, 641
integrity (*n.*)	*integridad*	pages 612, 630, 641
invest (*v.*)	*invertir*	pages 612, 618
loyalty (*n.*)	*lealtad*	pages 612, 630, 641
provider (*n.*)	*proveedor*	pages 612, 637, 641

T646: The Outsiders and Standing Together

conquer (*v.*)	*conquistar*	pages 646, 668, 672, 673
devotion (*n.*)	*devoción*	pages 646, 667, 673
refuge (*n.*)	*refugio*	pages 646, 657, 665
restore (*v.*)	*restaurar*	pages 646, 657, 670
territory (*n.*)	*territorio*	pages 646, 659, 675

T678: Voices of America and Human Family

interpret (*v.*)	*interpretar*	pages 678, 686
major (*adj.*)	*mayor*	pages 678, 693, 694
melodious (*adj.*)	*melodioso*	pages 678, 682
minor (*adj.*)	*menor*	pages 678, 693, 694
variety (*n.*)	*variedad*	pages 678, 692

The Cooperative Classroom

Cooperative learning strategies transform today's classroom diversity into a vital resource for promoting students' acquisition of both challenging academic content and language. These strategies promote active engagement and social motivation for all students, but for English language learners, they create opportunities for purposeful communication. Regular use of such strategies has been shown to be effective (Johnson & Johnson, 1986; Kagan, 1986; Slavin, 1988). The following cooperative learning strategies are built into the lessons in the Teacher's Editions.

STRUCTURE & GRAPHIC	DESCRIPTION	BENEFITS & PURPOSE
CORNERS 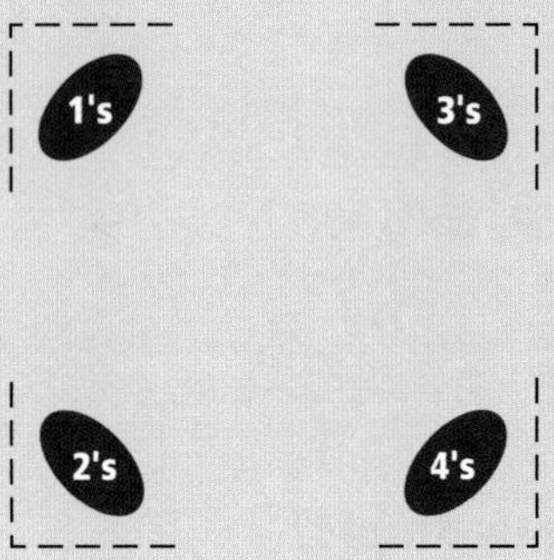	• Corners of the classroom are designated for focused discussion of four aspects of a topic. • Students individually think and write about the topic for a short time. • Students group into the corner of their choice and discuss the topic. • At least one student from each corner shares about the corner discussion.	• By "voting" with their feet, students literally take a position about a topic. • Focused discussion develops deeper thought about a topic. • Students experience many valid points of view about a topic.
FISHBOWL 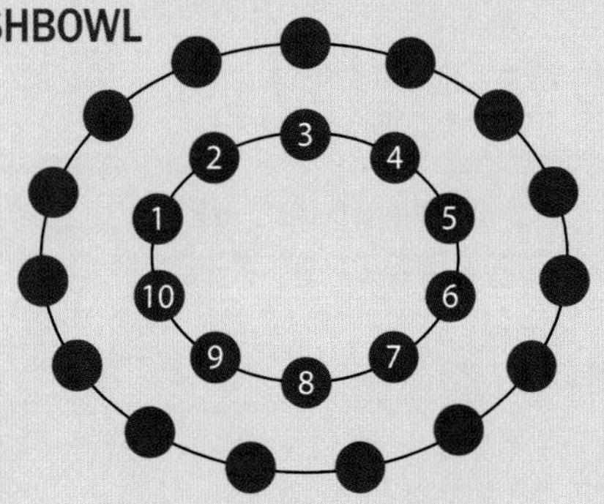	• Part of the class sits in a close circle, facing inward; the other part of the class sits in a larger circle around them. • Students on the inside discuss a topic while those outside listen for new information and/or evaluate the discussion according to pre-established criteria. • Groups reverse positions.	• Focused listening enhances knowledge acquisition and listening skills. • Peer evaluation supports development of specific discussion skills. • Identification of criteria for evaluation promotes self-monitoring.
INSIDE-OUTSIDE CIRCLE 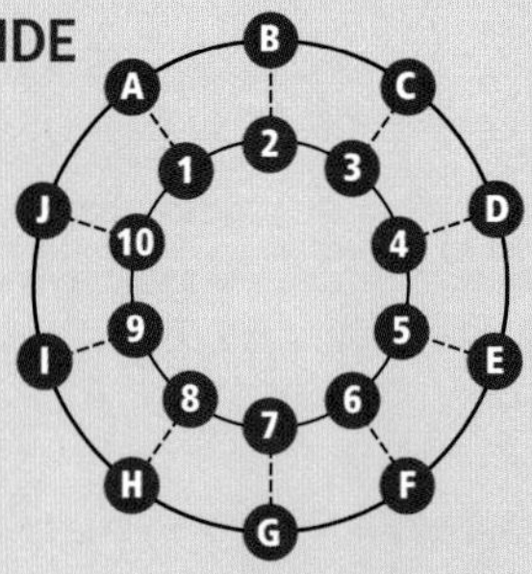	• Students stand in concentric circles facing each other. • Students in the outside circle ask questions; those inside answer. • On a signal, students rotate to create new partnerships. • On another signal, students trade inside/outside roles.	• Talking one-on-one with a variety of partners gives risk-free practice in speaking skills. • Interactions can be structured to focus on specific speaking skills. • Students practice both speaking and active listening.
JIGSAW 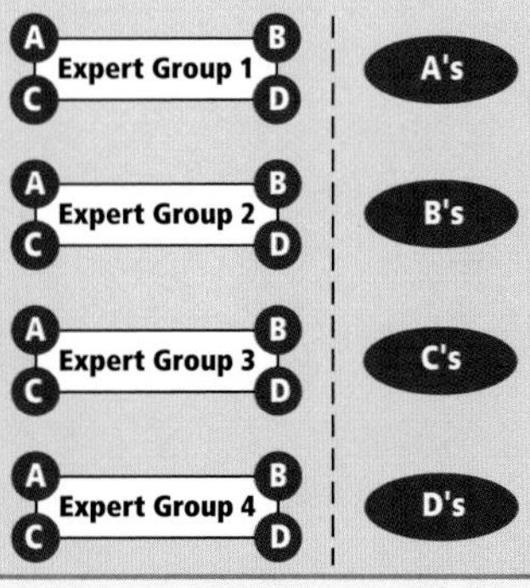	• Group students evenly into "expert" groups. • Expert groups study one topic or aspect of a topic in depth. • Regroup students so that each new group has at least one member from each expert group. • Experts report on their study. Other students learn from the experts.	• Becoming an expert provides in-depth understanding in one aspect of study. • Learning from peers provides breadth of understanding of over-arching concepts.

STRUCTURE & GRAPHIC	DESCRIPTION	BENEFITS & PURPOSE
NUMBERED HEADS 	• Students number off within each group. • Teacher prompts or gives a directive. • Students think individually about the topic. • Groups discuss the topic so that any member of the group can report for the group. • Teacher calls a number and the student from each group with that number reports for the group.	• Group discussion of topics provides each student with language and concept understanding. • Random recitation provides an opportunity for evaluation of both individual and group progress.
ROUNDTABLE 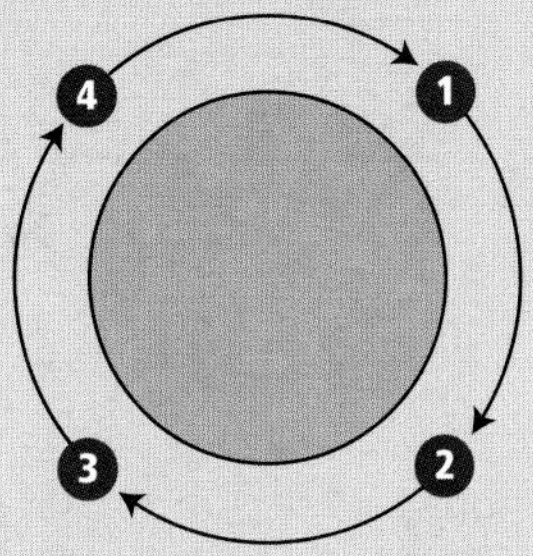	• Seat students around a table in groups of four. • Teacher asks a question with many possible answers. • Each student around the table answers the question a different way.	• Encouraging elaboration creates appreciation for diversity of opinion and thought. • Eliciting multiple answers enhances language fluency.
TEAM WORD WEBBING 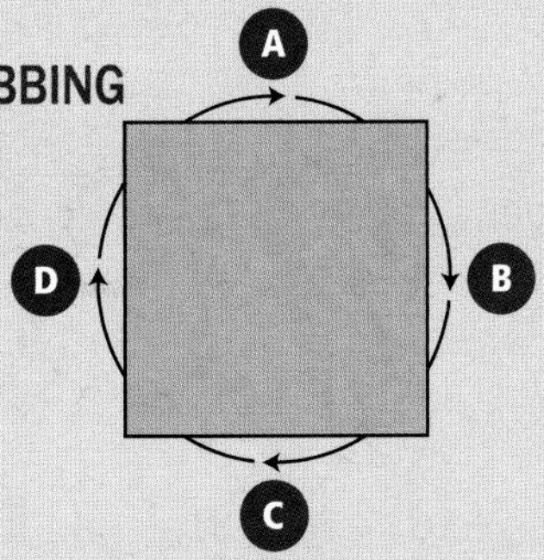	• Provide each team with a single large piece of paper. Give each student a different colored marker. • Teacher assigns a topic for a word web. • Each student adds to the part of the web nearest to him/her. • On a signal, students rotate the paper and each student adds to the nearest part again.	• Individual input to a group product ensures participation by all students. • Shifting point of view support both broad and in-depth understanding of concepts.
THINK, PAIR, SHARE 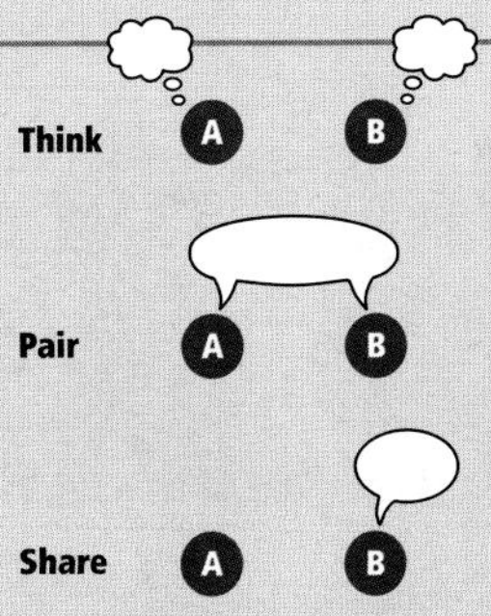	• Students think about a topic suggested by the teacher. • Pairs discuss the topic. • Students individually share information with the class.	• The opportunity for self-talk during the individual think time allows the student to formulate thoughts before speaking. • Discussion with a partner reduces performance anxiety and enhances understanding.
THREE-STEP INTERVIEW 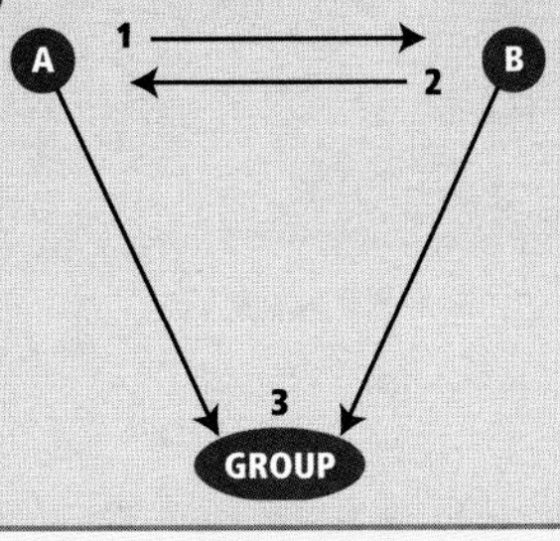	• Students form pairs. • Student A interviews student B about a topic. • Partners reverse roles. • Student A shares with the class information form student B; then B shares information from student A.	• Interviewing supports language acquisition by providing scripts for expression. • Responding provides opportunities for structured self-expression.

Oral Reading Fluency Routines

Research has shown that **repeated reading** (3–4 readings) of texts at an appropriate instructional level can increase reading fluency for students who struggle with reading (Chard, Vaughn, & Tyler, 2002; Dowhower, 1987; Kuhn & Stahl, 2003; O'Shea, Sindelar, & O'Shea, 1985; Samuels, 1979), and that it can enhance comprehension (Daly & Martens, 1994; Dowhower, 1987; Freeland, Skinner, Jackson, McDaniel, & Smith, 2000). In addition, **listening while reading** has been shown to enhance comprehension in students (McDaniel et al., 2001).

So, in addition to practicing vocabulary phonics, grammar, and structured response—via the preceding routines—it's also beneficial to establish daily fluency routines, allotting several minutes for students to practice. Use a variety of routines in order to keep the practice fresh.

When working on fluency, keep the passages short and use a variety: narrative, expository, poems, songs, even student writing. The key is to choose text that is motivating to the student and to provide immediate corrective feedback.

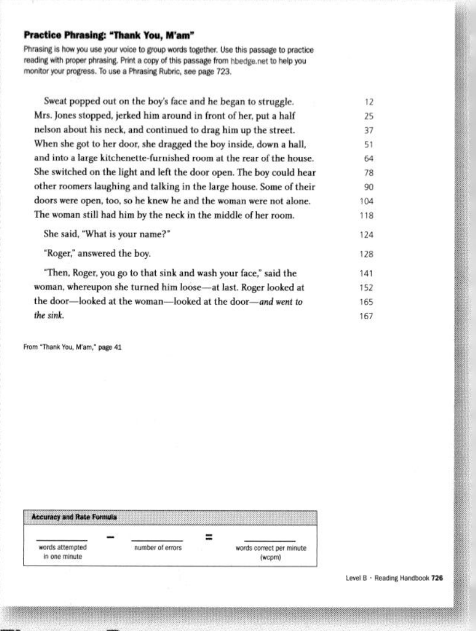

Practice Phrasing: "Thank You, M'am"

Phrasing is how you use your voice to group words together. Use this passage to practice reading with proper phrasing. Print a copy of this passage from hbedge.net to help you monitor your progress. To use a Phrasing Rubric, see page 723.

Sweat popped out on the boy's face and he began to struggle. 12
Mrs. Jones stopped, jerked him around in front of her, put a half 25
nelson about his neck, and continued to drag him up the street. 37
When she got to her door, she dragged the boy inside, down a hall, 51
and into a large kitchenette-furnished room at the rear of the house. 64
She switched on the light and left the door open. The boy could hear 78
other roomers laughing and talking in the large house. Some of their 90
doors were open, too, so he knew he and the woman were not alone. 104
The woman still had him by the neck in the middle of her room. 118

She said, "What is your name?" 124

"Roger," answered the boy. 128

"Then, Roger, you go to that sink and wash your face," said the 141
woman, whereupon she turned him loose—at last. Roger looked at 152
the door—looked at the woman—looked at the door—*and went to* 165
the sink. 167

From "Thank You, M'am," page 41

Accuracy and Rate Formula				
______ words attempted in one minute	–	______ number of errors	=	______ words correct per minute (wcpm)

Level B · Reading Handbook **726**

Fluency Passage

1. **Choral or Echo Reading / Marking the Text** Use in a teacher-directed instructional setting and for purposes of developing **phrasing** and **intonation**. First, provide a model for students to listen to. Have them mark the reader's phrasing (/ for a short pause; // for a longer pause) or intonation (rising and falling inflections) on a copy of the text. Then have students echo or choral read with you. Finally, have partners practice reading the same text in its unmarked version until they can read it fluently.
2. **Collaborative (Paired) Reading** Use with a selection that contains strong emotions in a peer-to-peer grouping or a student-adult grouping. Note that performance tends to be better when students read aloud to an adult as opposed to a peer. This technique can be used to practice **prosody** (phrasing, expression, and intonation). Partners alternate reading sentences, checking each other's readings as they go.
3. **Recording** Students can use the **Comprehension Coach** to record, analyze, and repeat their readings until they are satisfied with their **accuracy** and **rate**, which are the attributes measured by the **Comprehension Coach**. Students can also use tablets, computers, or other recording devices to capture oral readings.
4. **Listening While Reading** Use this technique when you want students to pay attention to **intonation** and **expression**. Have students listen to a fluent reading (using the **Selection Recordings and Fluency Models CD, MP3s** or the **Comprehension Coach**) several times until they have internalized the reader's interpretation.
5. **Timed Repeated Readings** Use this technique to help students develop an appropriate **reading rate** with good **accuracy**. Research says this technique is very motivational if students have a clear target (words read correct per minute, or WCPM) and then chart their progress. The most efficient way to implement this technique is by using the **Comprehension Coach**. The **Comprehension Coach** encourages students to read carefully and thoughtfully, repairing miscues, thinking about vocabulary, and actively comprehending as they read. Consequently, the WCPM goal at all levels of the **Comprehension Coach** has been set at a comfortable (not too fast), fluent rate of between 125 WCPM and 140 WCPM.

Close Reading Routine

Edge provides opportunities for students to engage with complex texts as Read Alouds and Close Readings. One of the Common Core State Standards' goals is to enable students to "undertake the close, attentive reading that is at the heart of understanding and enjoying complex works of literature" (CCSS, 2010, p. 3). The practice of close reading includes four fundamental characteristics (Beers & Probst, 2012; Coleman, 2011; Frey et al., 2012; Hinchman & Moore, in press; Lapp et al., 2012)— short, rigorous texts, multiple readings, academic discussion, and a focus on text evidence. This routine combines the three strands of the CCSS—Key Ideas and Details, Craft and Structure, and Integration of Knowledge and Ideas.

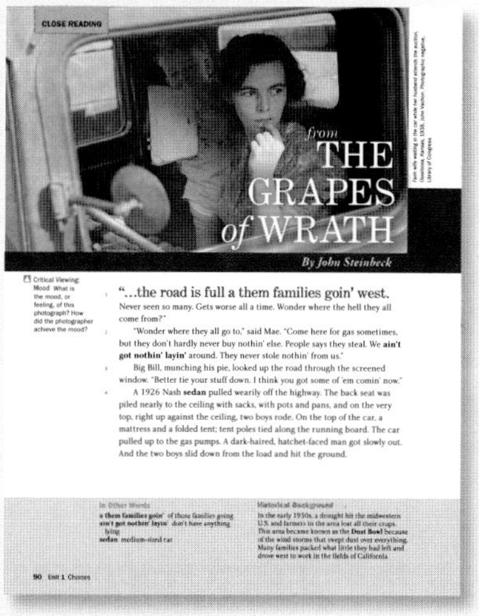

Student Book

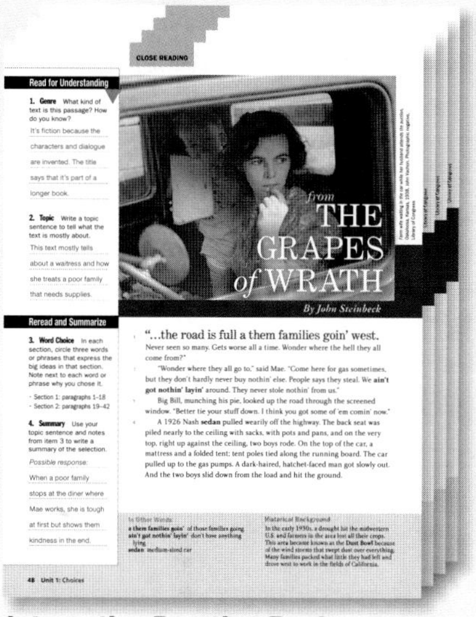

Interactive Practice Book

1. **Read for Understanding** To begin, display the **Student eEdition** for the class. The purpose of the first reading is to help students form initial understandings of the text by determining a text's genre and topic.
   - Read the entire selection aloud and help students examine its purpose, structural patterns, and features to determine its genre. Have students respond to two basic questions: What kind of text is this? and How do you know? Have partners enrich their responses by identifying relevant elements of the text, reading illustrative sections aloud, and comparing the text to others in the **Student Book**.
   - Help students compose a topic statement by leading them through two steps: (1) Identify the topic: This text mostly tells about . . . and; (2) Compose a topic-plus-comment: This text mostly tells about . . . (insert the key word) . . . and . . . (supply a phrase stating what the text mostly tells about the key word) . . .
2. **Reread and Summarize** The purpose of the second reading is to help students deepen understandings of the author's key ideas and details.
   - Direct students to reread the text in order to summarize it. For students who need extra support, read chorally or have students take turns reading aloud with a partner. Students may also read along with the audio recordings provided in CD and MP3 formats.
   - Have students identify the 3–5 most important words in each section of the text.
   - Have partners compare their topic statements and important words in preparation for summarizing the selection. Then have students individually compose their summaries. When time permits, lead them to share, compare, and revise their summaries.
3. **Reread and Analyze** In the third reading, students deepen understandings of (a) the author's meaning, and (b) the author's use of craft and structure. Model how to analyze a text element such as word choice, descriptive language, text structure, or point of view. Point out an example in the text. Then have students explain how it helps shape the meaning of the selection. Invite students to examine how the element affects meaning in other segments of the text. Have students use the **Interactive Practice Book** to mark and explain text evidence.
4. **Discuss** The purpose of this step is to help students integrate their knowledge and ideas to build new understandings that they can apply to other readings. Begin a whole-class discussion that leads students to develop ideas and form general statements about how authors craft their texts. Ask questions about relating, applying, and evaluating texts.
5. **Connect to the Guiding Question** Finally, help students connect the text to the unit topic and build new understandings of the world. Support students as they apply the ideas in the text to the unit's **Essential Question**. Conduct a discussion and have students generate questions to use for short research projects.

Academic Discussion Strategies

Discuss Texts and Essential Questions

Units are built around **Essential Questions**, content-rich questions that do not have a single definitive answer. Analyzing these questions is like conducting a scientific inquiry. These questions provide the occasion for the substantive and interactive classroom conversations that motivate students to read, keep them focused on text evidence, and increase their comprehension. To take full advantage of the **Essential Questions**, keep the following principles in mind:

1. **Highlight the question's authenticity.** All true **Essential Questions** are debatable. When introducing a question, note that people have taken different positions on them over the years. Tell students that they will have to formulate their own hypotheses and then cite text evidence to defend a position.
2. **Let student responses dictate the direction of the discussion.** Sometimes teachers preempt student thinking by asking yes/no or fill-in-the blank questions. This slots students' responses in the teacher's interpretation. Promote creativity and originality. Make sure that students are the ones who are doing the higher-order thinking. Discussions can be unpredictable. If a student's response takes the discussion in a new direction, go with it. Recognizing student-generated ideas propels discussion. Identify and credit the idea by writing responses on a board or display device. Follow up to invest them with authorship and reinforce authenticity. For example, say: Does what I wrote down reflect what you were saying?
3. **Establish routines for argumentation.** Promote argumentation using consistent series of questions that focus students on citing evidence and explaining reasons. Model and provide practice in turning a question upside down or inside out.
   - After students make a claim, ask: What makes you say so? This cues them to produce evidence. Remind students to mine the text for evidence.
   - After they cite evidence, ask: So what? This cues students to connect the evidence and the claim and help them discriminate between relevant and irrelevant evidence.
   - Ask: What would someone who disagrees say? and How would you respond? This cues students to anticipate and respond to counter-arguments.

   Extend discussion with follow-up prompts. In addition to the phrases supporting the argumentation routine, encourage elaboration in more general ways.
   - To help students complete ideas or elaborate, ask: Can you tell me more about that?
   - To help students connect ideas, ask: How does what you just said connect to what _________ said?
4. **Create Student-to-Student Interactions.** In addition to the **Cooperative Learning Structures** (PD52-PD53), make frequent use of small-group and partner discussions to engage more individuals in active participation and support the development of multiple perspectives. In whole-class discussions encourage students to summarize the previous speaker's points before making their own.
5. **Provide Time to think.** Silence can be daunting but it is important to create an environment time for reviewing the text and where silent thinking time is allowed and supported. Acknowledge silence as a part of the thinking and learning process. Say: I'm glad you're taking time to think that through, let's come back to that topic in a minute or two. Or stop the discussion and say: Let's take a minute to review the text and collect our thoughts. Everyone write what you're thinking about.

Student Edition
Units 1–4

STUDENT EDITION
UNITS 1–4

myNGconnect.com

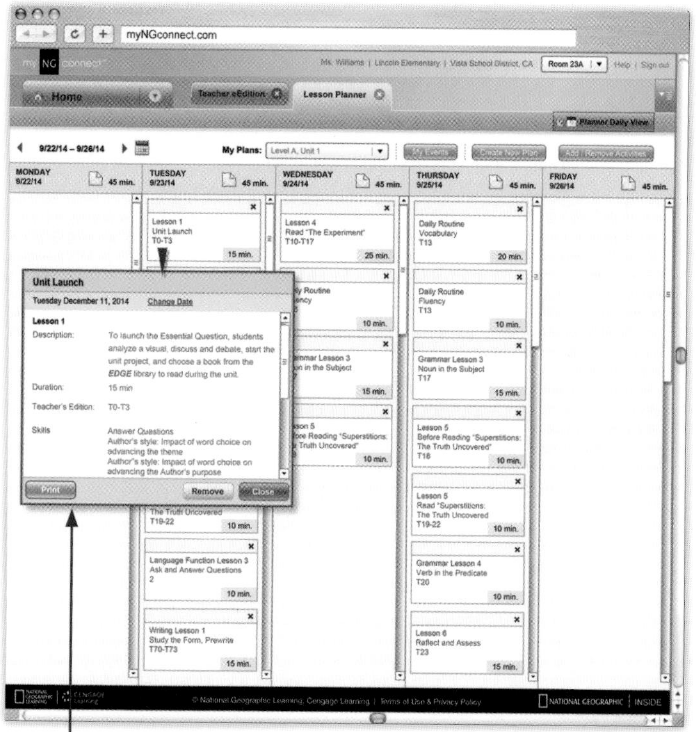

Online Planner

- Ready-made and customizable lesson plans
- Correlations to Common Core State Standards

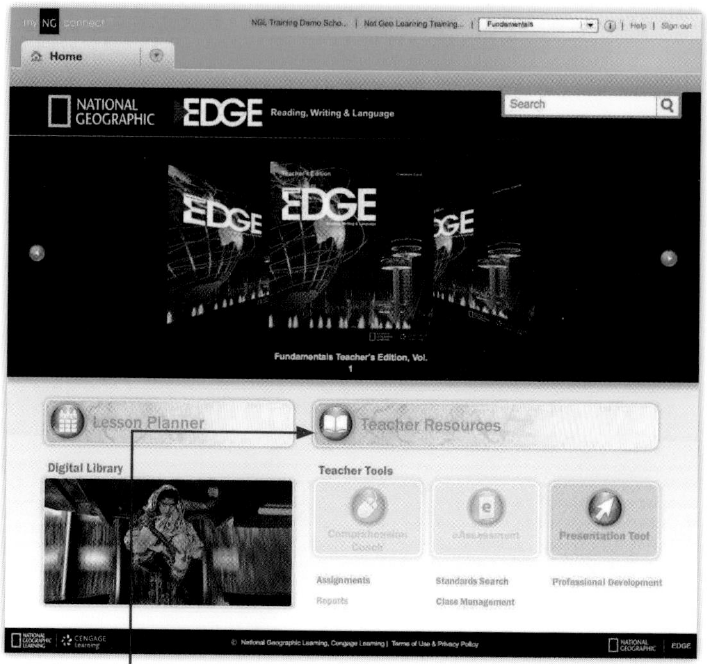

Resource Directory

- PDFs for all instructional resources and assessments
- Lessons and student resources for the Leveled Library
- Projection-ready digital transparencies
- Downloadable MP3 files for all audio resources

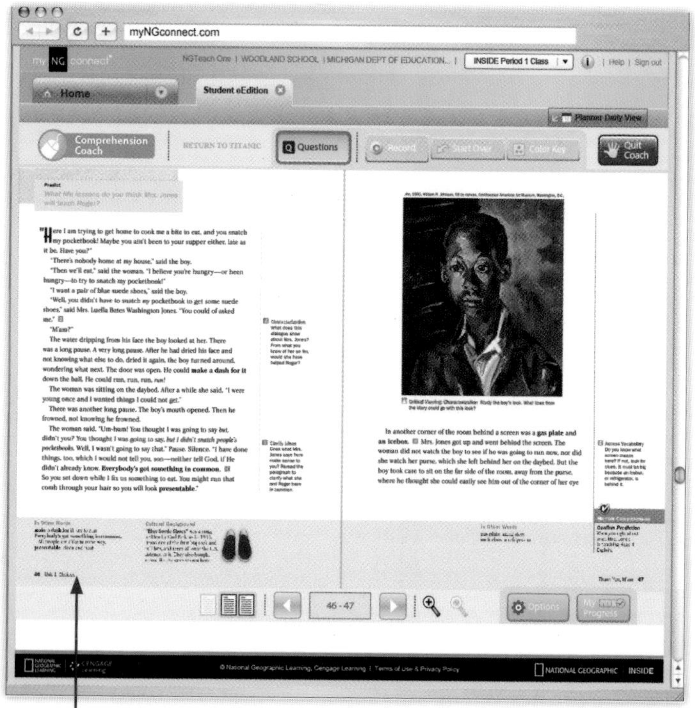

Comprehension Coach

- Oral reading fluency practice and assessment
- Text-dependent comprehension questions with scaffolded feedback that directs rereading and analysis

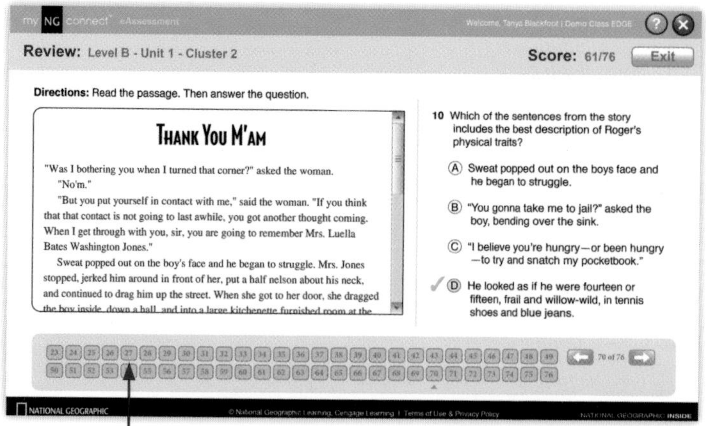

eAssessment

- Online testing
- Reports for progress monitoring
- Personalized reteaching prescriptions

UNITS 1–4

Student Edition

UNIT	Essential Question	Genre Focus	Focus Strategy	Grammar	Writing
1 Choices page T1A	What Influences a Person's Choices?	Short Stories: Plot, Characterization, Setting	Plan and Monitor	Sentences Subjects and Predicates Subject-Verb Agreement	Autobiographical Narrative
2 The Art of Expression page T109A	Does Creativity Matter?	Nonfiction: Author's Purpose	Determine Importance	Subject Pronouns Present Tense Verbs Subject-Verb Agreement	Position Paper
3 The Hero Within page T199A	What Makes a Hero?	Short Stories: Viewpoint	Make Inferences	Present, Past, and Future Tense Subject and Object Pronouns	Response to Literature
4 Opening Doors page T305A	How Can Knowledge Open Doors?	Nonfiction: Text Structure	Ask Questions	Possessive Words Prepositions Pronoun Agreement	Research Report

UNIT 1 **SHORT STORIES**

CHOICES

EQ ESSENTIAL QUESTION:

What Influences How You Act?

CLUSTER 1

Explore the effect of family and friends on choices.

Short Story

The Good Samaritan
by René Saldaña, Jr.

Poem

Don't Go Gentle Into That Good Expressway
by Luis J. Rodriquez

Informational Text

The World Is in Their Hands
by Eric Feil

PROJECTS

Writing Project
Autobiographical Narrative

Unit Project
TV Talk Show

WORKSHOPS

Workplace
Inside a Law Office

Vocabulary
Use Word Parts

Listening and Speaking
Oral Response to Literature

CLUSTER 2

Find out how circum-stances affect choices.

Short Story

Thank You, M'am
by Langston Hughes

Interviews

Juvenile Justice from Both Sides of the Bench
by Janet Tobias and Michael Martin

CLUSTER 3

Discover how society influences choices.

Short Story

The Necklace
by Guy de Maupassant

Memoir

The Fashion Show
by Farah Ahmedi

CLOSE READING

Consider what causes people to change their minds.

Novel Excerpt

The Grapes of Wrath
by John Steinbeck

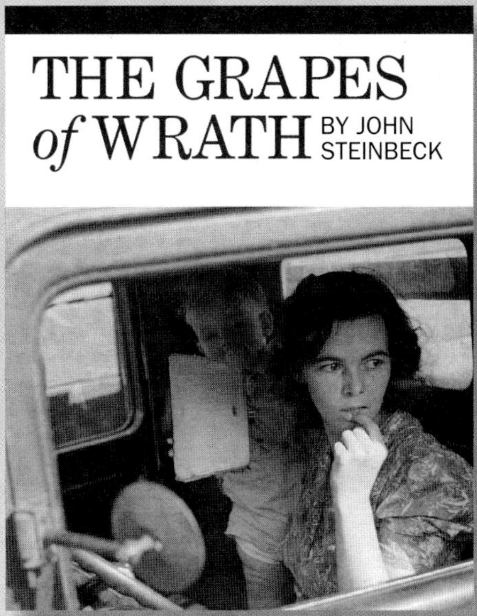

EDGE LIBRARY

The Trojan Horse ●
by Justine and Ron Fontes

Lexile® 550L

Genre/Length:
Graphic Novel; 53 pages

Miracle's Boys ●●
by Jacqueline Woodson

Lexile® 660L

Genre/Length:
Contemporary Fiction; 152 pages

Breaking Through ●●●
by Francisco Jiménez

Lexile® 750L

Genre/Length:
Autobiography; 216 pages

UNIT 1 Edge Library

The **EDGE LIBRARY** provides an opportunity for student choice. Students self-select literature based on their interests and reading ability. Books support exploration of the **Essential Question**, forming an integral part of instruction.

1 Select

- Select a variety of appropriate materials to read

Self-Select Have students choose a book according to their interests and reading level.

The Trojan Horse

by Justine and Ron Fontes

When is a risk worth taking?

This graphic novel tells the story of the Trojan War, the Greeks' ultimate victory, and the destruction of the city of Troy. Students who read this adventure story will also learn about Greek mythology and the role of Greek gods and goddesses in the lives of mortals.

2 Read

- Read to develop and evaluate personal preferences

Download the **Teacher's Guide** and **Student Journals**. Have students read their chosen book independently or in small groups. Use the planner on **Student Journal, page 1** to establish a reading schedule. RL.9-10.10; RI.9-10.10

myNGconnect.com

- **Unit 1 Resources**
- **Teacher's Guide**
- **Student Journal**

- **Reading Level** Lexile® 550L
  Genre: Graphic Novel
  Length: 53 pages

3 Use Strategies

- Identify, assess, and apply effective personal reading strategies

Have students identify the strategies they selected to use during reading. Use the prompts at the right to elicit student analysis and discussions.

Plan and Monitor

- What did you do when you came to a word or phrase that was confusing?

Determine Importance

- What was the main reason for the Trojan War? Why is that information important?

Make Connections

- Were you reminded of other conflicts or characters as you read? How did making that connection help you understand this text?

4 Discuss

- Exchange and extend ideas

EQ What Influences a Person's Choices?

Engage students in a discussion comparing how the texts address the **Essential Question**.

Explore the effect of family and friends on choices. Achilles's son is driven by revenge for his father's death.

Find out how circumstances affect choices. Paris and Helen are in love. The characters are engaged in a war.

Discover how society influences choices. Citizens had great loyalty to their country and kings. Men were expected to be warriors.

CCSS Literacy.RL.9-10.10 By the end of grade 9, read and comprehend literature, including stories, dramas, and poems, in the grades 9–10 text complexity band proficiently, with scaffolding as needed at the high end of the range. By the end of grade 10, read and comprehend literature, including stories, dramas, and poems, at the high end of the grades 9–10 text complexity band independently and proficiently. **Literacy.RI.9-10.10** By the end of grade 9, read and comprehend literary nonfiction in the grades 9–10 text complexity band proficiently, with scaffolding as needed at the high end of the range. By the end of grade 10, read and comprehend literary nonfiction at the high end of the grades 9–10 text complexity band independently and proficiently.

READ ALOUD

Miracle's Boys Read aloud the introduction to engage students' interest in the book. Provide support for the highlighted key vocabulary. Use the feature on legal guardianship to explain the concept to students. Then model fluency by reading aloud pages 11–13.

Miracle's Boys

by Jacqueline Woodson

Do we choose our path in life?

Set in contemporary Harlem, *Miracle's Boys* is told through the eyes of the youngest of three brothers, Lafayette, who speaks with strong emotion about the death of both his parents and his feelings toward his brothers.

● ● **Reading Level** Lexile® 660L

Genre: Contemporary Fiction

Length: 152 pages

Awards: Coretta Scott King Award 2001, Los Angeles Times Book Prize Winner 2000

Plan and Monitor

- Could you tell which events were in the past and which were in the present?

Make Inferences

- Did you figure out why it was so hard for Lafayette and Charlie to get along? How did you do it?

Ask Questions

- What questions did you ask as you read? How did you get the answers?

Explore the effect of family and friends on choices. Ty'ree chooses his family over school, and is motivated to keep his family together. The boys' choices are in response to the death of their mother.

Find out how circumstances affect choices. The boys are without parents. They have little money. Their choices are driven by economic necessity.

Discover how society influences choices. The boys must stay out of trouble or they will be separated.

Breaking Through

by Francisco Jiménez

True or False? The most difficult choices have the best results.

Breaking Through is Francisco Jiménez's account of his experiences as an illegal immigrant, a migrant worker, and a determined student. Students who read this book will learn about the struggle of illegal immigrants to make dreams come true despite poverty and other obstacles.

● ● ● **Reading Level** Lexile® 750L

Genre: Autobiography

Length: 216 pages

Awards: Americas Award for Children's and Young Adult Literature 2001, Pura Belpré Award, Tomás Rivera Mexican American Children's Book Award Winner 2001

Plan and Monitor

- Tell about a prediction you made. For example, did you predict what would happen because Francisco was an illegal immigrant? Did you confirm or change your prediction? How?

Synthesize

- Describe the relationship between obstacles, hard work, and success.

Visualize

- Did you picture the army barracks where the family lived or the fields where they worked? Describe them.

Explore the effect of family and friends on choices. Francisco's choices must reflect respect for his father and duty toward his family.

Find out how circumstances affect choices. The family lived in poverty and had to work hard to make ends meet. Francisco had a personal goal to become a teacher.

Discover how society influences choices. Francisco was in the country illegally, so some of his choices were limited. The family encountered prejudice against Mexicans.

UNIT 1 Instructional Focus

EQ ESSENTIAL QUESTION:
What Influences a Person's Choices?

	UNIT LAUNCH How to Read Short Stories	CLUSTER 1 The Good Samaritan The World Is in Their Hands
Reading		
Analyze Text Genre Focus **Short Stories**	T **Analyze Characterization, Setting, and Plot** RL.9-10.3	T **Analyze Plot** RL.9-10.5 T **Analyze Text Features: Article** RI.9-10.7 T **Analyze Theme** RL.9-10.2 T **Use Text Evidence** RL.9-10.1
Build Vocabulary	**Academic Vocabulary** L.9-10.6 • clarify • predict • monitor	T **Key Vocabulary** L.9-10.6 • affect • conflict • contribute disrespect • generation • motivation privilege responsible T **Vocabulary Strategy** L.9-10.4.c; L.9-10.4.d • Prefixes T **Reading Fluency** RL.9-10.10 Comprehension Coach
Writing		
Respond to Literature		T **Written Composition** L.9-10.6, W.9-10.2; W.9-10.2.a; W.9-10.2.b; W.9-10.2.f • Write a Definition Paragraph
Writing Project		T **Writing Project** W.9-10.3.a-e; W.9-10.4-6; W.9-10.10 • Writing Trait: Focus and Unity
Language		
ELL **Develop Language**		T **Ask and Answer Questions** SL.9-10.1.b
Use Grammar Grammar Focus **Complete Sentences**		T **Subjects and Predicates** L.9-10.1.b T **Complete Sentences** L.9-10.1.b
Build Listening and Speaking Skills	**Unit Project** T **Discuss the EQ** SL.9-10.1.c; SL.9-10.6 • Plan Your Project: TV Talk Show	

• **Academic Vocabulary** T = Tested on Cluster and/or Unit Reading and Literary Analysis Test T = Tested on Unit Writing Test

UNIT SUMMARY

Students explore the Essential Question "What Influences a Person's Choices?" through reading, writing, and discussion. Each cluster focuses on a specific aspect of the larger question:

Cluster 1: Explore the effect of family and friends on choices.
Cluster 2: Find out how circumstances affect choices.
Cluster 3: Discover how society influences choices.
Close Reading: Consider what causes people to change their minds.

CLUSTER 2 **Thank You, M'am** Juvenile Justice from Both Sides of the Bench	CLUSTER 3 **The Necklace** The Fashion Show	CLOSE READING **The Grapes of Wrath**
Analyze Characterization RL.9-10.3 **Analyze Text Features: Interview** RL.9-10.3 **Use Text Evidence** RL.9-10.1	**Analyze Setting** RL.9-10.3 **Determine Viewpoint** RL.9-10.6 **Analyze Setting and Theme** RL.9-10.2 **Use Text Evidence** RL.9-10.1	**Analyze Characterization** RI.9-10.3
Key Vocabulary L.9-10.6 • circumstances • commit • consequence • contact empathy juvenile maturity salvage **Vocabulary Strategy** L.9-10.4.c • Word Roots **Reading Fluency** RI.9-10.10 Comprehension Coach	**Key Vocabulary** L.9-10.6 humiliating imitation • inspire luxury • perceive poverty • symbol value **Vocabulary Strategy** L.9-10.4.b • Suffixes **Reading Fluency** RL.9-10.10 Comprehension Coach	**Academic Vocabulary** L.9-10.6 • perceive 
Writing on Demand RL.9-10.2; W.9-10.2; • Write a Short Comparison Essay W.9-10.2.a; W.9-10.2.b; W.9-10.2.c; W.9-10.2.f; W.9-10.9.a	**Writing Trait** W.9-10.5 • Focus and Unity: Thesis or Central Idea	
Writing Project W.9-10.3.a-e; W.9-10.4-6; • Writing Trait: Focus and Unity W.9-10.10	**Writing Project** W.9-10.3.a-e; W.9-10.4-6; • Writing Trait: Focus and Unity W.9-10.10	
Express Ideas and Opinions SL9-10.1.a	**Express Feelings and Intentions** SL.9-10.4	
S-V Agreement: Forms of *Be* L.9-10.1 **S-V Agreement: Action Verbs** L.9-10.1 **Verbs With Compound Subjects** L.9-10.1 **Review: S-V Agreement** L.9-10.1	**Sentence Fragments** L.9-10.1 **Fix Fragments: Add a Subject** L.9-10.1 **Fix Fragments: Add a Verb** L.9-10.1 **Fix Fragments: Combine Sentences** L.9-10.1 **Review: Sentence Fragments** L.9-10.1	**UNIT WRAP-UP**
Oral Response to Literature SL.9-10.1.a; SL.9-10.4; L.9-10.3		**Unit Project** **Respond to the EQ** SL.9-10.1.c; SL.9-10.6 • Present Your Project: TV Talk Show

T = Tested on Language Acquisition Assessment   T = Assessed with a Rubric

UNIT 1 Resource Manager

Edge resources include practical, easy-to-use teaching tools for comprehensive instruction, practice, assessment, and reteaching.

Reading & Writing

Reading Resources

UNIT LAUNCH

Edge Library

Trojan Horse

Miracle's Boys

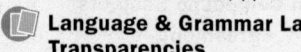

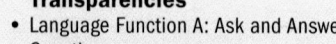

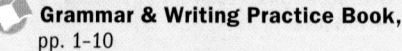

Breaking Through

Edge Library Resources
- Student Journals
- Teacher's Guides

CLUSTER 1
The Good Samaritan
The World Is in Their Hands

Cluster 1 Resources
- Learn more about René Saldaña, Jr.
- Selection summaries in eight languages
- Workplace Workshop resources

Comprehension Coach
- The Good Samaritan
- The World Is in Their Hands

Reading and Writing Transparencies
- Reading Transparency 1: Analyze Plot

Selection CD and MP3s
- The Good Samaritan, CD 1 Tracks 1–3
- The Good Samaritan: Fluency Passage, CD 11 Track 1
- The World Is in Their Hands, CD 1 Track 4

Edge Interactive Practice Book
- The Good Samaritan, pp. 6–10
- The World is in Their Hands, pp. 11–16
- Further Practice, pp. 17–19

Assessments Handbook
- Reader Reflection, p. 1b
- Cluster 1 Test, pp. 1c–1e

Reteaching Activities

Writing Project

CLUSTER 1

Writing Project Tools
- Student Samples
- Scheduler
- Rubric

Reading and Writing Transparencies
- Writing Transparencies 1-4: Autobiographical Narrative

Language & Grammar

UNIT LAUNCH

Unit Project Tools
- Planning Forms
- Scheduler
- Talk Show Sites
- Interview Forms
- Rubric

CLUSTER 1

Language & Grammar Lab Teacher's Edition, pp. 2-7

Language & Grammar Lab Transparencies
- Language Function A: Ask and Answer Questions
- Grammar Transparencies 1-5: Complete Sentences

Grammar & Writing Practice Book, pp. 1-10

Language CD and MP3
- Ask and Answer Questions, Track 1

Assessments Handbook
- Language Acquisition Rubric p. 1o

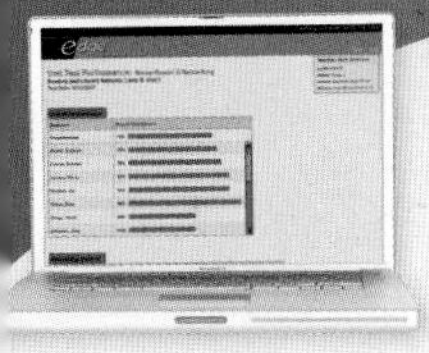

All Edge resources can be found online. Use the Online Lesson Tool, and all the relevant resources will automatically load into My Presentation Tool on myNGconnect.com.

CLUSTER 2

Thank You, M'am
Juvenile Justice from Both Sides of the Bench

Cluster 2 Resources
- Learn more about Langston Hughes
- Selection summaries in eight languages

Comprehension Coach
- Thank You, M'am
- Juvenile Justice from Both Sides of the Bench

Reading and Writing Transparencies
- Reading Transparency 2: Analyze Characterization

Selection CD and MP3s
- Thank You, M'am, CD1 Tracks 5-6
- Thank You, M'am: Fluency Passage, CD 11 Track 2
- Juvenile Justice, CD 1 Track 7

Edge Interactive Practice Book
- Thank You, M'am, pp. 20-14
- Juvenile Justice, pp. 25-30
- Further Practice, pp. 31-33

Assessments Handbook
- Reader Reflection, p. 1f
- Cluster 2 Test, pp. 1g-1i

Reteaching Activities

Writing Project Tools
- Student Samples
- Scheduler
- Rubric

Reading and Writing Transparencies
- Writing Transparencies 1-4: Autobiographical Narrative

Language & Grammar Lab Teacher's Edition, pp. 8-13

Language & Grammar Lab Transparencies
- Language Function B: Express Ideas and Opinions
- Grammar Transparencies 6-10: Subject-Verb Agreement

Grammar & Writing Practice Book, pp. 11-20

Language CD and MP3
- Express Ideas and Opinions, Track 2

Assessments Handbook
- Language Acquisition Rubric p. 1o

Oral Response Rubric

CLUSTER 3

The Necklace
The Fashion Show

Cluster 3 Resources
- Learn more about Guy de Maupassant
- Selection summaries in eight languages

Comprehension Coach
- The Necklace
- The Fashion Show

Reading and Writing Transparencies
- Reading Transparency 3: Key Vocabulary Chart
- Reading Transparency 4: Analyze Setting

Selection CD and MP3s
- The Necklace, CD 2 Tracks 1-3
- The Fashion Show, CD 2 Track 4
- The Fashion Show: Fluency Passage, CD 11 Track 3

Edge Interactive Practice Book
- The Necklace, pp. 34-38
- The Fashion Show, pp. 39-44
- Further Practice, pp. 45-47

Assessments Handbook
- Reader Reflection, p. 1j
- Cluster 3 Test, pp. 1k-1m

Reteaching Activities

Writing Project Tools
- Student Samples
- Scheduler
- Rubric

Reading and Writing Transparencies
- Writing Transparencies 1-4: Autobiographical Narrative

Language & Grammar Lab Teacher's Edition, pp. 14-19

Language & Grammar Lab Transparencies
- Language Function C: Express Feelings and Intentions
- Grammar Transparencies 11-15: Sentence Fragments

Grammar & Writing Practice Book, pp. 21-30

Language CD and MP3
- Express Feelings and Intentions, Track 3

Assessments Handbook
- Language Acquisition Rubric p. 1o

CLOSE READING

from The Grapes of Wrath

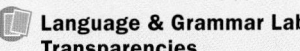

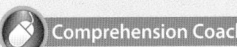

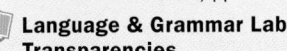

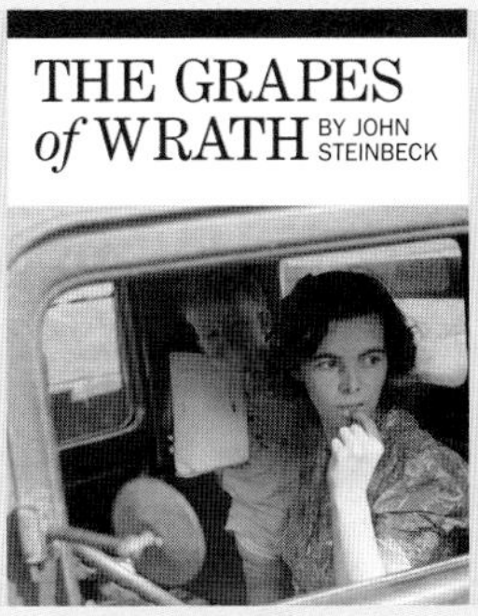

Selection CD and MP3s
- The Grapes of Wrath, CD 11 Track 1

Edge Interactive Practice Book
- The Grapes of Wrath, pp. 48-53

UNIT WRAP-UP

Unit Project
- Rubric

Assessments Handbook
- Reading and Literary Analysis, pp. 2-9
- Grammar and Writing, pp. 10-14
- Affective and Metacognitive Measures, pp. 105-119
- Self-Assessment: Written Composition, p. 133
- Peer Assessment: Written Composition, p. 134

Reteaching Activities

Lesson 1

UNIT LAUNCH

OBJECTIVES

Listening and Speaking
- Classroom Discussion
- Evaluate a Speaker's Message

Viewing
- Respond to and Interpret Visuals

Cultural Perspectives
- Compare Cultures: Customs

ENGAGE & DISCUSS

A EQ Essential Question

Brainstorm and Map Ask students to share one choice they made and chart influences on that choice.
SL.9-10.1

B Discuss the Quotations

Access Meaning Help students identify the most important words in each quotation: *determined, control, experience, choice.*

ELL Rephrase Language and Demonstrate Give synonyms for *determined* (*set, already decided*) and *control* (*power, choice*).

Demonstrate painting a canvas, and explain "thought by thought, choice by choice": Each thought you have and each choice you make changes the painting.

Evaluate a Speaker's Message Ask: What is the difference between the two quotations?

Possible response:
- *Einstein says people do not control their own lives; Winfrey says they do.*

Use the cooperative learning activity to explore different perspectives.
SL.9-10.1.b; SL.9-10.3

COOPERATIVE LEARNING

Four Corners

UNIT 1 SHORT STORIES

A EQ ESSENTIAL QUESTION:

What Influences a Person's Choices?

Everything is determined, the beginning as well as the end, by forces over which we have no control.
—ALBERT EINSTEIN

B With every experience, you alone are painting your own canvas, thought by thought, choice by choice.
—OPRAH WINFREY

C Critical Viewing
A woman balances between the cars of a moving train in Bangladesh, Asia, on the day before an important religious holiday. What may have influenced her choice to take this life-threatening risk?

LISTENING AND SPEAKING

Evaluate a Speaker's Message

Use the Four Corners cooperative learning technique (*see the Best Practices tab*) to explore the quotations.

Discuss Assign one corner of the room to each of the following positions:

1. Agree strongly with Albert Einstein.
2. Mostly agree with Albert Einstein.
3. Agree strongly with Oprah Winfrey.
4. Mostly agree with Oprah Winfrey.

Students group into the appropriate corner and discuss the various reasons for their response. One person from each corner shares the group's thinking while the listeners evaluate.

Debrief Discuss as a class:
- Was it difficult to choose one position? Why?
- Evaluate reasons for each position. Which were the strongest?
- Did the discussion change students' positions?

Remind students to keep thinking about the influences on choices as they read the selections in this unit.

CCSS **Literacy SL.9-10.1** Initiate and participate effectively in a range of collaborative discussions (one-on-one, in groups, and teacher-led) with diverse partners on grades 9–10 topics, texts, and issues, building on others' ideas and expressing their own clearly and persuasively. **Literacy SL.9-10.1.*b*** Work with peers to set rules for collegial discussions and decision-making (e.g., informal consensus, taking votes on key issues, presentation of alternate views), clear goals and deadlines, and individual roles as needed. **Literacy SL.9-10.3** Evaluate a speaker's point of view, reasoning, and use of evidence and rhetoric, identifying any fallacious reasoning or exaggerated or distorted evidence.

Unit Launch 1

ENGAGE & INTERPRET

C Critical Viewing

Observe Details Have students study the photograph. Ask:

- What does the woman's body language tell you about how she feels about her choice?
- What does her expression show?
- What does the blurriness below the train show?

Interpret and Respond Explain that there are many things that cannot be known about the woman in the photo without understanding more about her country and culture.

Ask: What information in the caption might help you understand what influenced the woman's choice?

Possible response:

- *The photo was taken the day before a holiday. Perhaps the woman was influenced by a desire to celebrate the holiday.*

D About the Photograph

This photograph was taken on the day before the last Friday of Ramadan, one of the most important holidays in the Islamic religion. Each year, tens of thousands of Bangladeshis leave their capital city and travel to their home villages to celebrate the end of the holiday with their families. Trains leaving the city fill up quickly, and people who are too late or cannot afford tickets often force their way onto them. People squeeze through train windows, sneak onto rooftops, or balance between the cars, like the woman in the photo.

Interpret and Respond Have students think about if their understanding of the situation has changed their perspective.

Ask: Does knowing that others take a risk make the risk seem less dangerous? Do you think that is why the woman would risk her life by sitting on the train like this?

Possible response:

- *People might feel safer when others are doing something. However, the woman might have no other choice.*

CULTURAL PERSPECTIVES

Beliefs About Choices

Explore how different cultures view what does or should influence choices.

Collect Ideas Have students complete the following sentence frames:

In [name a culture to explore] . . .

- people are free to make choices about ______.
- some choices are made for people, such as ______.
- ______ is a strong influence on people's choices. For example, ______.
- young people are allowed to choose ______.
- young people are not allowed to choose ______.

Compare Perspectives As a class, discuss the similarities and differences among the cultural perspectives. Be sure to discuss the concepts of circumstances and consequences.

Lesson 1, continued

UNIT LAUNCH

OBJECTIVES

Comprehension & Critical Thinking
- Read and Interpret a Table

Listening and Speaking
- Debate

ENGAGE & DEBATE

EQ Essential Question

Students analyze teen choices and debate the influences on these choices.

A Study the Facts

If students need help interpreting charts, preteach the Research Skills activity below. Then examine the first fact with students. Ask:

- Which gender participates more in sports? Are you surprised?
- What might influence a teen's choice to participate in sports?

Have students read through the rest of the statistics in the chart. Ask:

- Which fact about teen choices surprised you? Why?

B Analyze and Debate

Have students respond in writing to the two questions.

ELL Sentence Frames Provide frames to help ELLs respond:

1. Some young men/women make their choices based on ______. Some examples are ______.
2. I think a person's choices are influenced most by ______. I think this because ______.

Then debate the questions in small groups. Have students share some examples, supporting their ideas with evidence from the research and their own experiences.
SL.9-10.4

ONGOING ASSESSMENT

Have students complete an "exit slip":

- Choices can be influenced by _______.
- Today I learned that choices _______.
- One thing about choices that is still on my mind is _______.

UNIT 1

EQ ESSENTIAL QUESTION: What Influences a Person's Choices?

Study the Facts

People make choices every day. What causes some people to make good choices? What influences others to make poor choices or harmful choices? Look at these facts:

A

Teen Choices	FEMALE	MALE
High school students who participate in sports**	32%	45%
High school students who said they had carried a weapon in the past 30 days**	7%	27%
High school students who said they had registered and voted*	21%	27%
High school students who said they had driven after drinking alcohol in the past 30 days**	9%	15%
High school students who said they had taken part in a physical fight in the past 12 months**	25%	41%
High school seniors who participated each month in community affairs or volunteer work***	39%	28%

* Data for 2002 ** Data for 2003 *** Data for 2004 Source: U.S. Dept. of Education, National Center for Education Statistics: *Youth Indicators 2005.*

Analyze and Debate

B

1. According to the data, young men and young women seem to be making different choices. What general statements can you make about these differences? What might influence a young man to behave differently from a young woman?
2. Which is the greatest influence on a person's choices—family, friends, culture, money, or wealth?

Talk with a group. Explain your opinions and support your ideas with evidence from your own experience.

EQ ESSENTIAL QUESTION

In this unit, you will explore the **Essential Question** in class through reading, discussion, research, and writing. Keep thinking about the question outside of school, too.

2 Unit 1 Choices

RESEARCH SKILLS

Reading and Interpreting Charts

Teach/Model Explain that a chart is a useful tool to show data for comparing and contrasting. Point to each feature of the chart: the headings, the columns, the rows. Use the first row as an example:

- The first column in the row describes a teen choice: to participate in sports.
- The second column shows how many female teens make this choice: 32%.
- The third column shows how many male teens make this choice: 45%.

Practice Read through the rest of the choices in the chart. For each one, ask:

- Which gender makes this choice more often, females or males?

Apply Ask these questions about the chart:

1. Which of the following choices is made by a higher percentage of males than females?
   - carrying a weapon in the past 30 days *(males)*
   - registering and voting *(males)*
   - taking part in a physical fight in the past 12 months *(males)*
2. Which choice is made by a greater percentage of female teens than male teens? How can you tell? *(participating in volunteer work; compare the percentages in the last two columns)*

CCSS Literacy.SL.9-10.4 Present information, findings, and supporting evidence clearly, concisely, and logically such that listeners can follow the line of reasoning and the organization, development, substance, and style are appropriate to purpose, audience, and task.

1 Plan a Project

TV Talk Show

In this unit, you'll be producing a TV talk show about the Essential Question. Choose the kind of show, host, guests, and set to produce. To get started, watch a few different TV talk shows. When listening to a partner read, notice if you can understand the sound of each word. Then listen again to hear how your partner's intonation changes. Look for

- how the interviewer introduces each guest
- whether the interviewer reads from notes, talks from memory, or takes notes
- whether the guest and interviewer look directly at each other
- how the parts of the show relate to the topic.

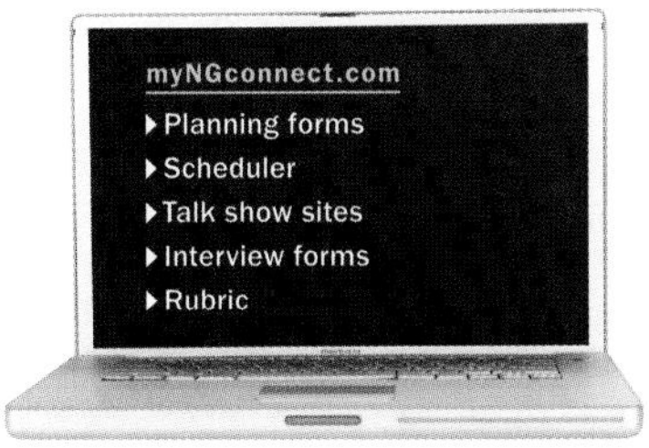

Study Skills Start planning your talk show. Use the forms on myNGconnect.com.

2 Choose More to Read

These readings provide different answers to the Essential Question. Choose a book and online selections to read during the unit.

Breaking Through
by Francisco Jiménez

Francisco "Panchito" Jiménez and his family worked day after day as migrant farm workers. Panchito was a good student and he wanted a better life. But his father wanted him to stay and help his family. How could Panchito please his father without giving up his future?

▸ NONFICTION

The Trojan Horse
by Justine and Ron Fontes

The beautiful Helen is married to the King of Sparta. When Helen runs away with a Trojan prince, her husband declares war on Troy! After ten years, the battle seems to have no end. But the Greek soldier Odysseus has a secret plan to defeat the Trojans. Will it work?

▸ GRAPHIC CLASSIC

Miracle's Boys
by Jacqueline Woodson

Ty'ree, Charlie, and Lafayette are Miracle's sons. When Miracle dies, the boys have to keep their family together. Staying together isn't easy. Charlie goes to jail, and Ty'ree has to work full-time to support them. How can Miracle's boys survive when so much is against them?

▸ NOVEL

myNGconnect.com

- **Read biographies of celebrities and teens who have made difficult choices.**
- **Take a personality test to find out what traits and talents might influence your choices.**
- **Play a game to explore the consequences of different choices.**

UNIT PROJECT & MORE TO READ

OBJECTIVES

Reading Behaviors
- Read Independently

Study Skill
- Complete Tasks on Schedule

Media
- Create and Deliver a Media Presentation (TV talk show)

1 Plan a Project

TV Talk Show To help students view the talk shows, guide them to use contextual, linguistic, and visual support to help them understand the language, ideas, and details they hear. Ask:

- What is a typical format of a TV talk show?
- What topics are discussed?
- What is the tone, or mood?

Assign project groups and review the Unit Project Evaluation Rubric and other Project Tools (*available online*). Have groups follow these steps:

1. Decide on a topic and a tone for the show.
2. Choose roles: host, guests.
3. Compose a script.

Project Support Teach the Study Skills lesson below.
SL.9-10.1.b

2 Choose More to Read

Guide students toward an independent reading choice from the **Edge Library**.

- ***The Trojan Horse*** Lexile® 550L
- ***Breaking Through*** Lexile® 750L
- ***Miracle's Boys*** Lexile® 660L

(Some titles may contain mature themes. Preview the books before assigning them.)
RL.9-10.10; RI.9-10.10

Distribute **Student Journals** and have students complete the time-management planning form on p. 1.

myNGconnect.com

- **Unit Project Planning Tools**
- **Unit Project Evaluation Rubric**
- **Edge Library Student Journals and Teacher's Guides**

STUDY SKILLS

Time Management

Help students create a schedule for completing the Unit Project. Have them start by listing the key steps:

1. Decide on the topic and the format for the show.
2. Choose roles for each group member.
3. Complete a script or outline.
4. Rehearse the show.
5. Perform the show.

Point out that some steps will take longer than others. For example, steps 1 and 2 could be completed in the same group meeting. Step 3 might require several group meetings to complete.

Inform students of the date the Unit Project will be due. Help them work backwards from that date to create their schedule. Have students check off each step as it is completed to be sure they stay on schedule.

CCSS **Literacy.RL.9-10.10** By the end of grade 9, read and comprehend literature, including stories, dramas, and poems, in the grades 9–10 text complexity band proficiently, with scaffolding as needed at the high end of the range. By the end of grade 10, read and comprehend literature, including stories, dramas, and poems, at the high end of the grades 9–10 text complexity band independently and proficiently. **Literacy.RI.9-10.10** By the end of grade 9, read and comprehend literary nonfiction in the grades 9–10 text complexity band proficiently, with scaffolding as needed at the high end of the range. By the end of grade 10, read and comprehend literary nonfiction at the high end of the grades 9–10 text complexity band independently and proficiently. **Literacy SL.9-10.1.b** Work with peers to set rules for collegial discussions and decision-making (e.g., informal consensus, taking votes on key issues, presentation of alternate views), clear goals and deadlines, and individual roles as needed.

Lesson 2
HOW TO READ

OBJECTIVES

Vocabulary
- Academic Vocabulary

Reading Strategy
- Plan and Monitor
- Visualize
- Make Inferences
- Ask Questions
- Synthesize
- Make Connections
- Determine Importance

ENGAGE & CONNECT

Reading Strategies

In this lesson, students examine reading strategies they can use to help fully understand the text. Explain that each unit in the program includes a focus strategy, but students will apply all reading strategies each time they read.

A Introduce Strategies

Teach the Academic Vocabulary word. Read the top half of the page with students. Ask:

- What do you do if you are having trouble understanding something you are reading? For example, what do you do if you don't understand an idea in the text?

B Focus on Demo Text

Plan Before you read the Demo Text, read the first callout. Use the title and headings to help preview the selection and predict what it will be about.

Read Have students follow along as you read "Healthy Choices, Healthy Teens" aloud.

ELL **Access Text** Restate and demonstrate actions to explain difficult words.

- Restate: *valedictorian* (person with the best grades in the class), *word was out* (everyone was talking about), *eating disorder* (not eating normally); *body mass index* (the size of people's bodies)
- Demonstrate: *collapse*

HOW TO READ

USING READING STRATEGIES

Reading Strategy

When you read fiction or nonfiction, you can use strategies to understand different parts of the text. Reading strategies are tools for thinking that help you interact with the text and take control of your reading comprehension.

A

Reading Strategies

Plan and Monitor	Set a purpose before you read. Make predictions and then read on to confirm them. Figure out confusing text by rereading or reading on.
Visualize	Picture sensory details in your mind.
Make Inferences	Combine what you read with what you know to figure out what the author doesn't say directly.
Ask Questions	Ask about things you don't know. Look for clues in the text.
Synthesize	Bring several ideas together to understand something new.
Make Connections	Connect what you read with what you have read or experienced.
Determine Importance	Identify and summarize the most important ideas.

Reading Handbook, page 707

B

Now read how one student applied reading strategies with this selection. As you read, pay attention to the reading strategies you use.

DEMO TEXT

HEALTHY CHOICES, HEALTHY TEENS

by Alicia Ramos

What Happened to Nina?

During PE today, a guest speaker discussed "Healthy Choices, Healthy Teens." Everyone usually messes around during health talks, but a lot more people paid attention this time. I think it's because of what happened to Nina.

Nina Kim is our school valedictorian, varsity softball player, and homecoming princess. In other words, she's smart, sporty, and gorgeous. Her life has always seemed so perfect. Then everything changed. Last week, Nina collapsed in the middle of the crowded girls' locker room. By the next morning, word was out: she was in the Intensive Care Unit being treated for an eating disorder and related health problems.

Before I read, I can ***plan and monitor****. I preview the title and headings. I predict the text will be about "peer pressure."*

I can use details to ***visualize****, or picture, what Nina is like.*

ACADEMIC VOCABULARY

Make Word Maps Present the Academic Vocabulary words. Have students make a Word Map for each.

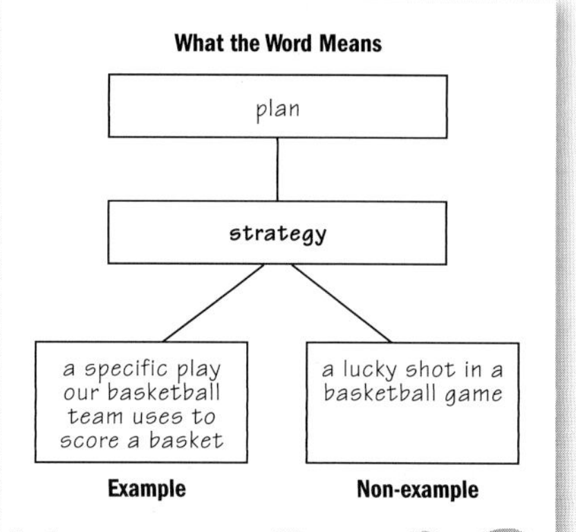

1. Write the word in the center. Write what it means in the top box. Give an example and a non-example in the boxes below.
2. Use a dictionary to check the information in your map.
3. Keep your word maps in a vocabulary notebook.

L.9-10.6

CCSS Literacy.L.9-10.6 Acquire and use accurately general academic and domain-specific words and phrases, sufficient for reading, writing, speaking, and listening at the college and career readiness level; demonstrate independence in gathering vocabulary knowledge when considering a word or phrase important to comprehension or expression.

"They said she might die," my friend Ben said. "Is that true?"

I didn't know for sure. I also didn't know how someone with the perfect life could have made so many horrible choices.

Under the Influence

According to the speaker today, teens don't make important choices on their own. Whether they know it or not, many of their decisions—including how they look at themselves—are influenced by a variety of people and things, including family, friends, and the media.

Parents complain that kids never listen, but this is far from true. From a young age, children pick up signals from relatives about weight, appearance, and what makes someone attractive. They see how adults view their own bodies and hear the positive and negative comments they make about others. As a result, kids often make decisions about diet and appearance based on the qualities their own parents value.

Peers are another powerful force that affects teen decisions. According to statistics, 40–60% of teenage girls diet whether they are overweight or not. The everyday choices they make about food and exercise affect how their friends think and act. Even if peer pressure is not verbal, or spoken aloud, teens are influenced just by looking at the people around them. According to the Journal of Health and Social Behavior, teens in schools where the majority of students have a high body mass index do not feel a strong pressure to diet. But if the average body mass index of students at a school is low, kids are much more likely to diet.

Another major influence on teens is the media, including TV, movies, magazines, music, and blogs. The average teen watches 30 hours of TV a week. After spending 1560 hours a year watching unrealistic images of super-beautiful celebrities on TV, many teens are not satisfied by their own reflection in the mirror. More than 90% of girls 15–17 want to change at least one part of their appearance—usually their weight. For up to 11 million young people like Nina, this distorted image of beauty can lead to serious eating disorders.

Making Your Own Choices

The thought of so many outside influences on teens can be intimidating—but it doesn't have to be. Instead of accepting what the media has to say about beauty and self-worth, consider the qualities you value and find attractive. Have discussions with friends and family about how their attitudes affect your decisions. Most of all, use your own influence to encourage others to make healthy choices. Peer pressure isn't always negative. If more teens speak up, kids like Nina Kim might find the support they need to feel good about themselves—inside and out.

*Based on what I read and know, I can make an **inference** that the writer had looked up to Nina.*

*I can **ask questions** about words or ideas. Clues in the text help me figure out what they mean.*

C

*I can **synthesize** the facts here and conclude that teens feel pressured to look like the people they see.*

*Sometimes, I wish I looked like people on T.V. I can **make a connection** to how many teens feel about themselves.*

*I can **determine importance** by finding the main idea: people should stand up to peer pressure.*

TEACH & PRACTICE

C Analyze Examples

Explain that all readers encounter text that they need help understanding. As you read, discuss each callout. Then have students share another place in the text where they used the reading strategy.

RI.9-10.10

Monitor As you read, monitor your understanding of the text to clarify ideas and to confirm or adjust any predictions you have made.

Visualize Look for words that tell how things look, sound, smell, taste, and feel. Form a mental picture to understand what the author is describing.

Make Inferences Sometimes the text doesn't tell you everything and you need to make an educated guess about the content

Ask Questions You can ask yourself questions or even question the author. To answer your questions, look in the text or think about what you know.

Synthesize When you synthesize, you put ideas together and draw conclusions, make generalizations, or compare new information to information you have read in other texts.

Make Connections You can make connections to other texts you have read, things you have experienced, or events you know about. Thinking about what you know helps you understand the text better.

Determine Importance What is the most important idea in a text? Put the ideas in your own words to summarize them.

DIFFERENTIATED INSTRUCTION

English Language Learners ELL

Provide Language Frames to help students as they use reading strategies.

Plan and Monitor

- I read _______. I see _______.
- I predict _______.
- What does _______ mean? It means _______.

Visualize

- I read _______. I picture _______. I feel _______.

Make Inferences

- I read _______. I know _______. And so _______.

Ask Questions

- I wonder _______.
- I read _______.

Synthesize

- I read _______ and I know _______. I think that most _______.
- I conclude _______.

Make Connections

- _______ reminds me of _______. Now I understand _______.

Determine Importance

- The text is mostly about _______. The details are _______.
- The main idea is _______.

CCSS Literacy.RI.9-10.10 By the end of grade 9, read and comprehend literature, including stories, dramas, and poems, in the grades 9-10 text complexity band proficiently, with scaffolding as needed at the high end of the range. By the end of grade 10, read and comprehend literature, including stories, dramas, and poems, at the high end of the grades 9-10 text complexity band independently and proficiently.

OBJECTIVES

Vocabulary
- Academic Vocabulary

Reading Strategy
- Plan and Monitor: Predict; Review Strategies

Literary Analysis
- Recognize Genre: Short Stories
- Analyze Characterization, Setting, and Plot (T)

Media
- Compare Across Media

ENGAGE & CONNECT

Short Stories

In this lesson, students experience how the elements of a short story work together. After reading a sample story, students predict plot events based on the characters and setting.

Introduce Genre

Engage students in talking about stories they like. Ask:

- What is your favorite story? Why?
- Do you think stories are important in a person's life? Why?

Encourage students to share examples of the things they like about the stories they know.

(A) Focus on Demo Text

Preview and Predict Use the title to identify the setting. Have students predict what might happen.

Read Students read "On the Bus."

ELL Rephrase Language and Demonstrate Text Read the Demo Text aloud, rephrasing difficult words and demonstrating actions.

- Rephrase: *draw attention* (make people notice), *church fundraiser* (event to raise money for a church), *threatening voice* (voice that suggests danger)
- Demonstrate: *waltzed, shot quick looks, playing air guitar*

Now let's learn about short stories. One way to find out how stories work is to think about how you make sense of a little story like this one. Read "On the Bus."

DEMO TEXT (A)

On the Bus

The first week of school was always a tough one for ninth-graders, at least for most ninth-graders. But not, it seemed, for James. From the first day of school he waltzed right to the back of the bus, a spot usually reserved for juniors and seniors. He talked with everyone and made fun of the other ninth-graders who shot quick looks to the back of the bus and then sank quietly into their seats up front.

Catherine had always admired James a little. She'd always been so shy that anybody who would draw attention to himself or herself would earn a little of Catherine's admiration. Because this was her first year at public school after having gone to a small church school all the way through eighth grade, she felt especially afraid to speak out.

Catherine didn't really like James, though. They'd lived in the same neighborhood for years, yet he hardly seemed to recognize her. And when he did, it was for all the wrong reasons. Once in eighth grade he saw her washing cars for a church fundraiser. He was walking past her church with a group of friends and he shouted, "Hey, everybody, look. It's little Miss Missionary." Catherine didn't mind people's knowing that she was really religious because church was the most important thing in her life. It was just the way he had said it.

One day that first week James was doing more bragging than usual. He had just gotten the hottest new digital audio player. He came on the bus doing exaggerated dances and playing air guitar to songs he must have been hearing. Even the seniors in the back were impressed, or at least they pretended to be. Stefone, a kid who had a reputation as being a tough guy, asked James if he could hear a song. James handed him his player. Stefone listened, nodded his head, and looked hard at James. "This thing is great. I'm glad I got one. Too bad you lost yours. You understand what I'm saying? Too bad you lost yours." James slumped down in his seat.

Catherine saw the whole thing and felt queasy, or sick to her stomach. She looked at James and then at Stefone. Stefone stared hard at her and said in a threatening voice, "The poor kid lost his new toy. Don't worry about it, little girl. You wouldn't want to lose anything of yours, would you?"

OUT-OF-SCHOOL LITERACY

Media Literacies

Ask students about other ways they "read" stories: via audio, on Web sites, and in graphic or visual form. Ask: How are they similar to stories you read in print? Are there characters, setting, and plot?

Work with students to identify the ways that short story elements are expressed in other formats. Consider these features:

Audio
- A reader's pitch or accent can indicate different characters.
- Tone of voice can show a mood or atmosphere in the setting.
- Changes in volume or rate can show development of plot events.

Web Sites
- The plot usually unfolds Web page by Web page, in images and words.
- Information on characters may be links to separate pages.
- Setting can be shown through color and graphics, as well as text.

Visual (graphic novel)
- Plot moves through panels, usually left to right and down the page.
- Characters' facial expressions and postures can show their attitudes.
- Setting is shown with graphics.

Have students bring in examples of stories they have read in different forms.

CCSS Literacy.L.9-10.6 Acquire and use accurately general academic and domain-specific words and phrases, sufficient for reading, writing, speaking, and listening at the college and career readiness level; demonstrate independence in gathering vocabulary knowledge when considering a word or phrase important to comprehension or expression.

■ Connect Reading to Your Life

What will Catherine do? First, think of all the possible choices she could make.

I think she's going to try to get Stefone to give it back.
I don't think so. I think she won't do anything, just like he said.

Reading Strategies
- ▶ **Plan and Monitor**
- Determine Importance
- Make Inferences
- Ask Questions
- Make Connections
- Synthesize
- Visualize

1. Catherine could ______________________________
2. Or ______________________________
3. Or ______________________________

Now that you have thought about the alternatives, which one do you **predict** she will do? Explain your answer. Also tell what you want to know about Catherine that would give you more confidence in your prediction.

Focus Strategy ▶ Plan and Monitor

The kind of educated guesses you just made about Catherine and James are called **predictions**. In your life, you make predictions all the time. You predict how your teacher will react if you are late to class. You predict how a friend will like the gift you gave. You do this by thinking about what people are like, what they have done before, and what the current situation is like. Sometimes people surprise you, so you need to revise, or change, your predictions.

Making predictions is a key part of **monitoring**—or checking—your understanding as you read.

■ Your Job as a Reader

When you read, you first figure out what it is you are reading. You look at the title, a little of the text, and maybe the illustrations to figure out that you're reading a story. Then you pay attention to the characters, setting, and plot. For example, you had to learn as much as you could about Catherine in order to predict what she would do. If there were more to this little story, you would then read to find out whether your predictions were accurate.

Academic Vocabulary
- **predict** *v.*, to tell in advance; **prediction** *n.*, a statement of what someone thinks will happen
- **monitor** *v.*, to keep track of, to check

ENGAGE & CONNECT

B Connect Reading to Your Life

Help students connect the story and the strategy to their own lives by considering what they would do in Catherine's situation. Ask: Do you know anyone like Catherine? What might that person do?

Have students work in pairs to complete the three statements in the box and identify which choice Catherine is most likely to make. Encourage them to use information from their own experience and from the story to explain their predictions.

Focus Strategy: Plan and Monitor Read this section with students. Use the activity below to teach the Academic Vocabulary in this unit. Ask:

- What do you predict I would do if you were late to class? Why do you think so?
- How can you tell whether a friend will like a gift you give?

Review Strategies Remind students that they use a variety of strategies as they read the text. Have students share a strategy they used when they read "On the Bus."

Possible responses:
- *While reading "On the Bus," I wondered what was tough about the first week of school. Then I made a connection to my first week in ninth grade and remembered how hard it was to be in a new school with so many new people. This helped me understand how Catherine must have felt.*

RL.9-10.10

TEACH STRATEGIES

C Your Job as a Reader

Explain that good readers monitor their reading all the time to be sure they understand. Tell students they have already begun practicing this strategy by making predictions, and they will continue to do so during this unit.

ACADEMIC VOCABULARY

Make Word Maps Present the Academic Vocabulary words. Have students make a Word Map for each.

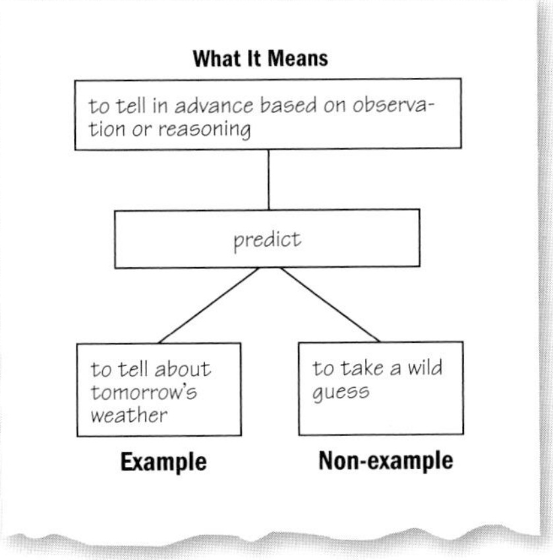

to tell about tomorrow's weather
to take a wild guess

1. Write the word in the center. Write what it means in the top box. Give an example and a non-example in the boxes below.
2. Use a dictionary to check the information in your map.
3. Keep your Word Maps in a vocabulary notebook.

L.9-10.6

CCSS Literacy.RL.9-10.10 By the end of grade 9, read and comprehend literature, including stories, dramas, and poems, in the grades 9–10 text complexity band proficiently, with scaffolding as needed at the high end of the range. By the end of grade 10, read and comprehend literature, including stories, dramas, and poems, at the high end of the grades 9–10 text complexity band independently and proficiently.

TEACH STRATEGIES

A Unpack the Thinking Process

Read through and discuss each of the short story elements and the reading strategy.

Characterization Help students identify what they know about Catherine: description, dialogue, actions, reactions of others.

Setting Have students describe the setting by telling where and when the story takes place. Ask: How do you think a character like Catherine feels in this setting?

Plot Help students identify choices the characters make.

Explain that the elements—character, setting, plot—are all connected. Setting can often determine a character's actions and choices.

SETTING: A bus during Catherine's first week at a new school

Character and Plot: Catherine acts the way she does because of the setting she is in. Her actions and choices move the plot along.

■ Unpack the Thinking Process

Characterization

Authors leave clues to let readers know what their characters are like. This is called **characterization**. For example, an author may include:

- **describing words** to tell what a character looks like
- **dialogue** to show how characters express themselves
- **actions** to show just what a character does
- **reactions** of other characters to show the impact of a character's actions.

A Setting

Characters make choices because of who they are and the situations they are in. That's why the **setting**—where and when a story takes place—is so important. "On the Bus" is set during Catherine's first week at a public high school. You know that she is likely to act differently during her first week than in her senior year. If you notice the setting and use what you know, you can predict what she is likely to do.

Plot

The choices characters make determine the action in many stories. The way that authors select and arrange the choices and action is called the **plot**. These choices are affected by what the characters are like as well as when and where they live.

Plan and Monitor

Use the elements of short stories—character, setting, and plot—to plan and monitor your reading of short stories. Here's a way to do that:

B

Prediction Chart

I Notice	I Know	I Predict	Prediction Confirmed?
The title "On the Bus" The first sentence: "The first week of school. . ."	This sounds like a back-to-school story.	I think there will be some problem related to starting school.	[ ] yes [ ] no
Catherine is new to public school. She used to go to a small church school.	Public high schools are very different than small private schools.	Catherine will have a hard time adjusting.	[ ] yes [ ] no

Elements of Literature

characterization *n.*, the techniques an author uses to show what the characters are like

setting *n.*, the time and place of a story

plot *n.*, the series of events that make up a story

As you read, keep track of your predictions. Good readers actively keep track of their thinking while they read. Think about whether your predictions are confirmed, or whether you need to revise them based on new information. If you find that you're lost, take time to **clarify**, or get clear, so that you can keep reading. Here are just a few ways that you can get back on track: **B**

- **reread** (or keep reading—sometimes you just need to read a bit more to know what's happening)
- **slow down** and read closely (or read faster—sometimes that helps)
- **paraphrase**, or say what's happening in your own words.

Try an Experiment

Pretend that the first part of the story is written like this:

DEMO TEXT *Take 2*

On the Bus

The first week of school was always a tough one for ninth-graders, at least for most ninth-graders. But not, it seemed, for James. From the first day of school he waltzed right to the back of the bus, a spot usually reserved for juniors and seniors. He talked with everyone and made fun of the other ninth-graders who shot quick looks to the back of the bus and then sank quietly into their seats up front.

Catherine had always admired James. People seemed to notice him. She wondered if they noticed her. She hoped so. After all, she had spent most of her savings to buy the trendiest new clothes she could find. This was her first year at public school after having gone to a small church school through eighth grade, and she wanted the new kids to think she was cool.

Think, Pair, Share Answer these questions with a partner. **C**

1. What details about Catherine have changed? What do those new details tell you about the kind of person she is? Explain your answer.
2. Look back at your list of possible choices Catherine could make. Which one do you predict she will choose now? How do you expect the story to change if she does that?

Academic Vocabulary
- **clarify** *v.*, to make clear and understandable, to get rid of confusion

Monitor Comprehension

Characterization What clues do authors give to help you understand characters? How do these help you make predictions?

TEACH STRATEGIES

B Plan and Monitor

Explain Predictions Say: When you make a prediction, you guess what will happen next. To plan how you will read a story, try making a prediction. Then read to see if your prediction comes true.

Read through the predictions in the chart and ask students whether they were confirmed by reading.

Explain Monitoring Rereading, reading on, and paraphrasing are strategies for clarifying ideas and monitoring comprehension during reading. Tell students they will learn and practice these strategies during this unit.

APPLY

C Try an Experiment

Have students read the revised opening of the story.

Think, Pair, Share Students work in pairs to discuss and respond to the questions.

Discuss the questions as a class.

Possible responses:

1. *Catherine wants to be noticed. She might choose to do something because it is cool.*
2. *Catherine in the new story might join in with Stefone. If she did this, it might show her character is not shy.* RL.9-10.3

Monitor Comprehension

Possible responses:

- *Describing words, dialogue, actions, and reactions of other characters can help to understand characters.*
- *Understanding characters will help you predict what they will do.*

DIFFERENTIATED INSTRUCTION

Teach Literary Elements As you teach the selections in this unit, use these strategies to meet students' individual needs.

Struggling Readers

Visualize Draw a stick figure for each character in the selection. Ask:

- What is the character wearing? *(fancy dress, work boots, etc.)*
- What objects are around the character? *(basketball, purse, necklace, etc.)*
- What action or posture might the character show? *(dancing, weariness, anger)*

Add these details to the stick figures to help students visualize each character.

English Language Learners ELL

Use Realia Show objects and pictures that connect to character, setting, and plot in the selections. For example:

- "The Good Samaritan": gardening tools, photos of flat tires
- "Thank You, M'am": a large purse, photos of Harlem
- "The Necklace": costume jewelry, photos of Paris

Challenge

Make Analogies Provide a sentence frame for making analogies about characters:

- This character is like (movie star/historical figure/someone students know) because _______.

ONGOING ASSESSMENT

Have students work in small groups to create a test item about reading short stories. Have students turn in the items as "exit slips."

CCSS Literacy.RL.9-10.3 Analyze how complex characters (e.g., those with multiple or conflicting motivations) develop over the course of a text, interact with other characters, and advance the plot or develop the theme.

UNIT 1 Cluster 1 Planner

EQ ESSENTIAL QUESTION:

What Influences a Person's Choices?

Find out how circumstances affect choices.

Online Planner
myNGconnect.com

	LESSON 3 Prepare to Read	LESSON 4 The Experiment Main Selection
Reading		
Reading Strategies Focus Strategy **Plan and Monitor**	**Activate Prior Knowledge** SL.9-10.1 • Make a Connection: Ranking Chart *T10*	**Plan and Monitor** RI.9-10.10 • Make and Confirm Predictions *T11, T14–T25* • Set a Purpose *T14* • Monitor Comprehension *T17, T20*
Literary Analysis Genre Focus **Short Stories**		T **Analyze Plot** RL.9-10.5 *T11, T14–T25* **Compare Literature** • Parables *T12*
Vocabulary	T **Key Vocabulary** RI.9-10.4; L.9-10.6 • Introduce *T10* • affect • generation • conflict • motivation • contribute privilege disrespect responsible	T **Key Vocabulary** L.9-10.6 • Daily Routines *T15* • Link to Essential Question *T17* • Selection Reading *T14–T25* • affect disrespect responsible • conflict privilege
Fluency		T **Expression** RL.9-10.10 • Daily Routines *T15* T **Accuracy and Rate** RL.9-10.10 Comprehension Coach *T13*
Writing		
Response to Literature		**Return to the Text** W.9-10.9.a; W.9-10.10 • **Reread and Write** How does Rey's father affect Rey's decision to help Mr. Sánchez? *T25*
Writing Across the Curriculum		**Research and Writing** SL.9-10.1.a • **Language and Culture Connection** *T24*
Language		
ELL **Language Development**	T **Ask and Answer Questions** SL.9-10.1.b • Language and Grammar Lab, Transparency A *LAB TE p. 2*	T **Ask and Answer Questions** SL.9-10.1.b • Daily Routines *LAB TE p. 2*
Grammar Grammar Focus **Complete Sentences**		**Kinds of Sentences** *T16* L.9-10.1; L.9-10.2 T **Subjects and Predicates** *T18* L.9-10.1.b **Noun in the Subject** *T22* L.9-10.1.b
Listening and Speaking	**Partner Talk** SL.9-10.1 • Reasons for Helping Others *T10*	**Listen to a Selection** Comprehension Coach *T13* *CD 1, Tracks 1–3* **Out-of-School Literacy** SL.9-10.1.a • Interpreting a Television Show or Movie *T23*

T = Tested on Cluster and/or Unit Reading and Literary Analysis Test
T = Tested on Language Acquisition Assessment
T = Tested on Unit Writing Test
T = Assessed with a Rubric
• **Academic Vocabulary**

The Good Samaritan

Genre: Short Story Lexile® 730L

Rey feels betrayed by his neighbor, Mr. Sánchez, who often takes advantage of Rey's help. When Rey sees Mr. Sánchez stranded on the side of the road, he must decide whether to help him. A vision of his own father in need of help inspires Rey to do the right thing.

The World Is in Their Hands

Genre: Newspaper Article Lexile® 1090L

Volunteer advocate Eric Feil surveys teen volunteerism in the United States. Using graphs, charts, statistics, and testimonials, Feil argues that teen volunteerism is the strongest it has ever been, and that the current teen generation is the greatest, most tolerant generation in history.

LESSON 5 **The World Is in Their Hands** Second Selection	LESSON 6 **Reflect and Assess**	LESSONS 7 & 8 **Integrate the Language Arts**	LESSONS 9 & 10 **Workshops**
Plan and Monitor RI.9-10.10 • Preview and Set a Purpose *T28, T29–T33* • Monitor Comprehension *T31*	**Comprehension and Critical Thinking** *T35* RI.9-10.1; RI.9-10.3 • Compare Across Texts • Analyze, Interpret, Compare, Speculate, Judge, Synthesize		
Analyze Text Features: Article *T28, T29–T33* RI.9-10.3	**Interpret and Evaluate Literature** RL.9-10.10 (T) **Use Text Evidence** *T35* RI.9-10.1	(T) **Analyze Theme** *T36* RL.9-10.2	
(T) **Key Vocabulary** L.9-10.6 • Link to Essential Question *T30* • Selection Reading *T29–T33* • **contribute** • **motivation** • **generation**	(T) **Key Vocabulary** L.9-10.6 • Review *T35* • **affect** • **generation** • **conflict** • **motivation** • **contribute** **privilege** **disrespect** **responsible**	(T) **Vocabulary Strategy** L.9-10.4.c • Use Structural Clues: Prefixes *T37*	**Vocabulary Workshop: Use Word Parts** L.9-10.4; L.9-10.4.b; L.9-10.4.c; L.9-10.4.d (T) **Vocabulary Strategy** • Use Structural Clues: Word Parts *T39*
(T) **Expression** RL.9-10.10 • Daily Routines *T15* (T) **Accuracy and Rate** RI.9-10.10 Comprehension Coach *T29*	(T) **Expression** RL.9-10.10 • Peer Assessment *T35*		
Return to the Text RI.9-10.1; W.9-10.9.b • **Reread and Write** Are today's youth the "greatest generation . . . we've ever seen in this country"? *T33*	**Write About Literature** W.9-10.1 • **Order-of-Importance Paragraph** Why should teens help others? Give three or four reasons in order of importance. *T35*	(T) **Writing Form** W.9-10.2 • **Definition Paragraph** *T37*	
Research and Writing W.9-10.7 • **Sociology Connection** *T31*			**Workplace Workshop: Inside a Law Office** **Research and Writing** W.9-10.7; W.9-10.10 • Conduct an Informational Interview *T38*
(T) **Ask and Answer Questions** SL.9-10.1.b • Daily Routines *LAB TE p. 2*		(T) **Ask and Answer Questions** SL.9-10.1.b • Role Play *T36*	
Verb in the Predicate L.9-10.1.b *T32*		(T) **Complete Sentences** *T36* L-9-10.1.b	
Listen to a Selection RL.9-10.10 Comprehension Coach *T29* *CD 1, Track 4*	**Participate in a Discussion** *T35* SL.9-10.1	**Oral Report** *T37* W.9-10.7; SL.9-10.4	

EDGE LIBRARY

Trojan Horse •
by Justine and Ron Fontes

Miracle's Boys • •
by Jacqueline Woodson

Breaking Through • • •
by Francisco Jiménez

Lesson 3

PREPARE TO READ

OBJECTIVES

Vocabulary
- Key Vocabulary T
- Strategy: Use Cognates; Relate Words

Reading Strategy
- Activate Prior Knowledge

ELL Language & Grammar Lab

Language Function Transparency A
Ask and Answer Questions T

ENGAGE & CONNECT

A EQ Essential Question

Focus on Family and Friends Why might a young person choose to help an older neighbor?

Possible responses:
- *to get something from him or her*
- *to be a kind person*
- *because your family expects it*

B Make a Connection

Have students complete the ranking activity and share responses with a partner to compare their thoughts on helping others.
SL.9-10.1

TEACH VOCABULARY

C Learn Key Vocabulary

Study the Words Review the four steps of the Make Words Your Own routine (*see the Vocabulary tab*):

1. **Pronounce** Say a word and have students repeat it. Write the word in syllables, and point to each one as you pronounce it: *mo-ti-va-tion*. Ask what looks familiar in the word, and point out other forms of the word, like *motivate*.

   ELL Use cognates to help Spanish speakers with the words (*see the Vocabulary tab*).

2. **Study Examples** Read the example in the chart. Ask an either/or question: Is *motivation* a reason for doing something or the way you do it?

ONGOING ASSESSMENT
Have students complete an oral sentence for each word. For example: *When you are upset with someone, you are in _______ with that person.*

PREPARE TO READ

- The Good Samaritan
- Don't Go Gentle Into That Good Expressway
- The World Is in Their Hands

A EQ What Influences a Person's Choices?

Explore the effect of family and friends on choices.

B Make a Connection

Rank Reasons Often our families, friends, and values or beliefs direct our actions. Read the **Ranking Chart** to see a list of reasons people help others. Rank each reason from 1 to 5 (1 means you agree with that reason the most). Then discuss these questions with a partner: Which reasons ranked highest? How did you rank your friends and family?

RANKING CHART Reasons for Helping Others	Rank (1 to 5)
"My parents taught me to do it."	_______
"My friends will respect me more."	_______
"Good works look good on a résumé or college application."	_______
"Changing the world starts with me."	_______

C Learn Key Vocabulary

Study the Words Pronounce each word and learn its meaning. You may also want to look up the definitions in the Glossary.

• Academic Vocabulary

Key Words	Examples
• **affect** (u-**fekt**) *verb* ▸ pages 19, 35	When you **affect** something, you change it in some way. You can **affect** the environment by using more or less water.
• **conflict** (**kon**-flikt) *noun* ▸ pages 14, 25	When people or things are in **conflict**, they do not agree. A story's **conflict** is the main problem.
• **contribute** (kun-**tri**-byūt) *verb* ▸ page 30	When you **contribute**, you give something with others. Students **contribute** ideas to a group discussion. *Synonym*: give; *Antonym*: take
disrespect (dis-ri-**spekt**) *noun* ▸ pages 19, 25	When you are rude to someone, you show them **disrespect**. When children yell at their parents, they show **disrespect**. *Synonym*: rudeness; *Antonyms*: courtesy, respect
• **generation** (je-nu-**rā**-shun) *noun* ▸ pages 31, 33, 35	People who are about the same age belong to the same **generation**. We can learn a lot from our parents' **generation**.
• **motivation** (mō-tu-**vā**-shun) *noun* ▸ pages 29, 35	**Motivation** is the reason you act or think in a certain way. My **motivation** for volunteering is to help my neighbors. *Synonyms*: reason, drive
privilege (**pri**-vu-lij) *noun* ▸ page 19	A **privilege** is something special that someone is allowed to have, be, or do. The football team gets the **privilege** of leaving school early on game days. *Synonym*: favor
responsible (ri-**spon**-su-bul) *adjective* ▸ pages 18, 35	When you are **responsible** for something, it is your duty to take care of it. If you borrow a pen, you are **responsible** for returning it when you are done.

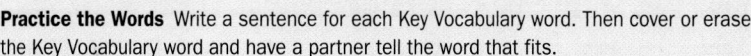

Practice the Words Write a sentence for each Key Vocabulary word. Then cover or erase the Key Vocabulary word and have a partner tell the word that fits.

Example: *Freedom of speech is a right, but driving a car is a privilege.*

3. **Encourage Elaboration** Read the example in the chart, and have students answer questions. Ask: What is your *motivation* for studying?

4. **Practice the Words** Have students write a cloze sentence for each Key Vocabulary word and ask a partner to write the word that fits.

Edge Interactive
Practice Book, p. 6–7
RL.9-10.4; L.9-10.6

CCSS **Literacy.RL.9-10.4** Determine the meaning of words and phrases as they are used in the text, including figurative and connotative meanings; analyze the cumulative impact of specific word choices on meaning and tone (e.g., how the language evokes a sense of time and place; how it sets a formal or informal tone). **Literacy.L.9-10.6** Acquire and use accurately general academic and domain-specific words and phrases, sufficient for reading, writing, speaking, and listening at the college and career readiness level; demonstrate independence in gathering vocabulary knowledge when considering a word or phrase important to comprehension or expression. **Literacy.SL.9-10.1** Initiate and participate effectively in a range of collaborative discussions (one-on-one, in groups, and teacher-led) with diverse partners on grades 9–10 topics, texts, and issues, building on others' ideas and expressing their own clearly and persuasively.

BEFORE READING The Good Samaritan

short story by René Saldaña, Jr.

Reading Strategies

- ▶ **Plan and Monitor**
- Determine Importance
- Make Inferences
- Ask Questions
- Make Connections
- Sythesize
- Visualize

Analyze Plot

Plot is the sequence of events in a story. The story begins with the **exposition**, which introduces the characters and setting. Most plots have these parts:

- The **conflict** is the main problem that the characters face.
- **Complications** are events that make the conflict worse and lead to the climax.
- The **climax** is the turning point, or the most important event.
- The **resolution** is how the story ends and the problem is solved.

Look Into the Text

The characters make an agreement.

Mr. Sánchez told us, "If you help clean up the yard, you boys can use the pool any time you want so long as one of us is here." . . . After a hard day's work cleaning his yard, I so looked forward to taking a dip. I'd even worn my trunks under my work clothes. Then Mr. Sánchez said, "Come by tomorrow. I don't want you fellas to track all this dirt into the pool."

How might this statement lead to a conflict between the characters?

Focus Strategy ▶ Plan and Monitor

Most stories include characters who have a conflict that will be resolved in some way. Events almost always lead to a climax. Use this information to **plan your reading**. Then as you read, make predictions, or guesses, about what will happen later in the story's plot.

Focus Strategy

HOW TO MAKE AND CONFIRM PREDICTIONS

Before you read a story:

1. **Read the story's title.** Also, look at any section introductions. You might find clues about the story's plot and characters.
2. **Look at art and quotations in large type.** They might contain clues about story events.
3. **Make predictions.** Put the clues together and predict what will happen next and what the characters will do, or how they will change.
4. **Confirm or change predictions.** As you read, notice details that either confirm your prediction or make you change your mind.

Prediction Chart

My Predictions	Confirmed or Changed Predictions
I think the story is about a basketball player and a man that he often helps.	I now think this story is about a conflict between a teenager and an older man.

Reading Transparency 1

READING PLOT 1

Analyze Plot

How can you recognize the plot of a story?

Introduce The plot is a series of related events in a story. Most plots include these parts:

Exposition

The exposition introduces the story's setting and characters. It sets the scene for the story's conflict, or main problem.

Rising Action

The rising action adds complications, or events that make the conflict or problem build.

Climax

The climax is the highest point of interest in the story. It is the turning point or the most important event.

Falling Action and Resolution

The falling action is what happens after the conflict or climax. In the resolution, the conflict ends or the problem is solved.

Lesson 4

BEFORE READING

OBJECTIVES

Reading Strategy

- Plan and Monitor: Make and Confirm Predictions

Literary Analysis

- Analyze Plot T

TEACH STRATEGIES

D Plot

Look Into the Text Read the introduction to define plot and its parts. Read aloud the text passage. Use the callouts to discuss plot elements. Ask: What agreement do the characters make?

Possible response:

- *The boys can use Mr. Sánchez's pool if they clean his yard.*

Then ask: What happens that might lead to a conflict?

Possible response:

- *Mr. Sánchez tells the boys to come back tomorrow.*

Reading Transparency 1

Use the Transparency Reinforce plot elements and show how they connect. Ask: Which part of the plot includes the story's setting and introduces the characters?

Possible response:

- *the exposition*

RL.9-10.5

E Focus Strategy: Plan and Monitor

Make and Confirm Predictions Review that students use a variety of strategies as they read. Then read the introduction with students. Work through the How To box and model how to use text features to make and confirm complex predictions of selection content.

Have students flip through pp. 11–26 and record a few of their own predictions to monitor and confirm as they read.

RL.9-10.10

Edge Interactive
Practice Book, pp. 8–9

ONGOING ASSESSMENT

Ask: What is the most important event in the plot? What event comes next?

CCSS **Literacy RL.9-10.5** Analyze how an author's choices concerning how to structure a text, order events within it (e.g., parallel plots), and manipulate time (e.g., pacing, flashbacks) create such effects as mystery, tension, or surprise. **Literacy RL.9-10.10** By the end of grade 9, read and comprehend literature, including stories, dramas, and poems, in the grades 9-10 text complexity band proficiently, with scaffolding as needed at the high end of the range. By the end of grade 10, read and comprehend literature, including stories, dramas, and poems, in the grades 9-10 text complexity band proficiently, with scaffolding as needed at the high end of the range.

OBJECTIVES

Literary Analysis
- Compare Literature

Viewing
- Respond to and Interpret Visuals

BUILD BACKGROUND

A The Writer and His Beliefs

Have students read the biography of René Saldaña, Jr.

Connect with Author's Life Help students connect with the author. Ask: Why do you think René Saldaña, Jr. "hated literature" in school?

Possible responses:
- *He might not have been mature enough to enjoy what he read.*
- *He might have had other interests.*

Then ask: What might have made Saldaña change his mind about literature in college?

Possible responses:
- *He was influenced by his friends.*
- *He found books that had a special meaning for him.*

Connect Across Texts Read the title of the selection and share this information with students:

This story's title is shared by a well-known parable, or story that teaches a lesson. In this Bible parable, a man lay injured near the road. Several people passed him by, but one person stopped to help him. This person was a Samaritan by ethnicity, while the injured man was a Jew. Their countries were enemies, but this did not influence the Samaritan's decision to help him. Today, the term *good Samaritan* is used to describe a person who helps another regardless of status, age, race, or gender.

myNGconnect.com

Selection Summaries in eight languages

The Writer and His Beliefs

René Saldaña, Jr.

(1968–)

Students teach me new things about my stories all the time. They have amazing insights.

As a teenager, **René Saldaña, Jr.**, never guessed that he would become a writer. "In school, I hated literature!" It wasn't until college **A** that Saldaña began to appreciate literature. "My friends taught me. They introduced me to books like *The Great Gatsby* and *The House on Mango Street*. But they weren't just reading; they were writing, too."

Still, Saldaña didn't begin writing until he became an English teacher. "I wanted my students to know that they could be writers. But they needed examples of writing that they could relate to, so I began to tell them my own stories." These stories grew into Saldaña's first novel, *The Jumping Tree*. The book is about a teenage boy struggling with what it means to be a real man. "The Good Samaritan" is about that same boy becoming an adult. "He is learning his own place in the world. He is realizing that he is part of a community."

Today, as a college professor, Dr. Saldaña continues to inspire students to write about their lives. "One of my favorite writers once said that wherever there is a group of people, there is a group of writers. I've always believed that."

René Saldaña, Jr.

myNGconnect.com

Read an excerpt from *The Jumping Tree*.

Learn more about *The Great Gatsby* and *The House on Mango Street*.

12 Unit 1 Choices

DIFFERENTIATED INSTRUCTION

English Language Learners ELL

Preview the selection:
- Introduce the characters: *The main character is Rey. His neighbor is Mr. Sánchez.*
- Point to bolded words in Spanish at the bottom of p. 14: *The characters speak Spanish and English.*
- Point out the visual on p. 15 and pantomime raking. Explain: *Rey and his friends rake leaves for Mr. Sánchez. Why might they do this?* Confirm: *Mr. Sánchez promises the boys rewards for their help.*
- Describe the picture of the basketball on p. 17: *The boys are excited to play basketball at the Sánchez house.*

Read Aloud to provide a supported listening experience:
- Play the **Selection Recording** as students track text in their books. **CD 1**
- Have students use the Listen feature in the **Comprehension Coach** where they see the text as it is read aloud.
- Read the selection aloud to students as you provide comprehensible input. For example, reenact dialogue between characters to show how they feel about each other and to demonstrate conflict, complications, and resolution.

CCSS Literacy.RL.9-10.10 By the end of grade 9, read and comprehend literature, including stories, dramas, and poems, in the grades 9–10 text complexity band proficiently, with scaffolding as needed at the high end of the range. By the end of grade 10, read and comprehend literature, including stories, dramas, and poems, at the high end of the grades 9–10 text complexity band independently and proficiently.

The Good Samaritan

by René Saldaña, Jr.

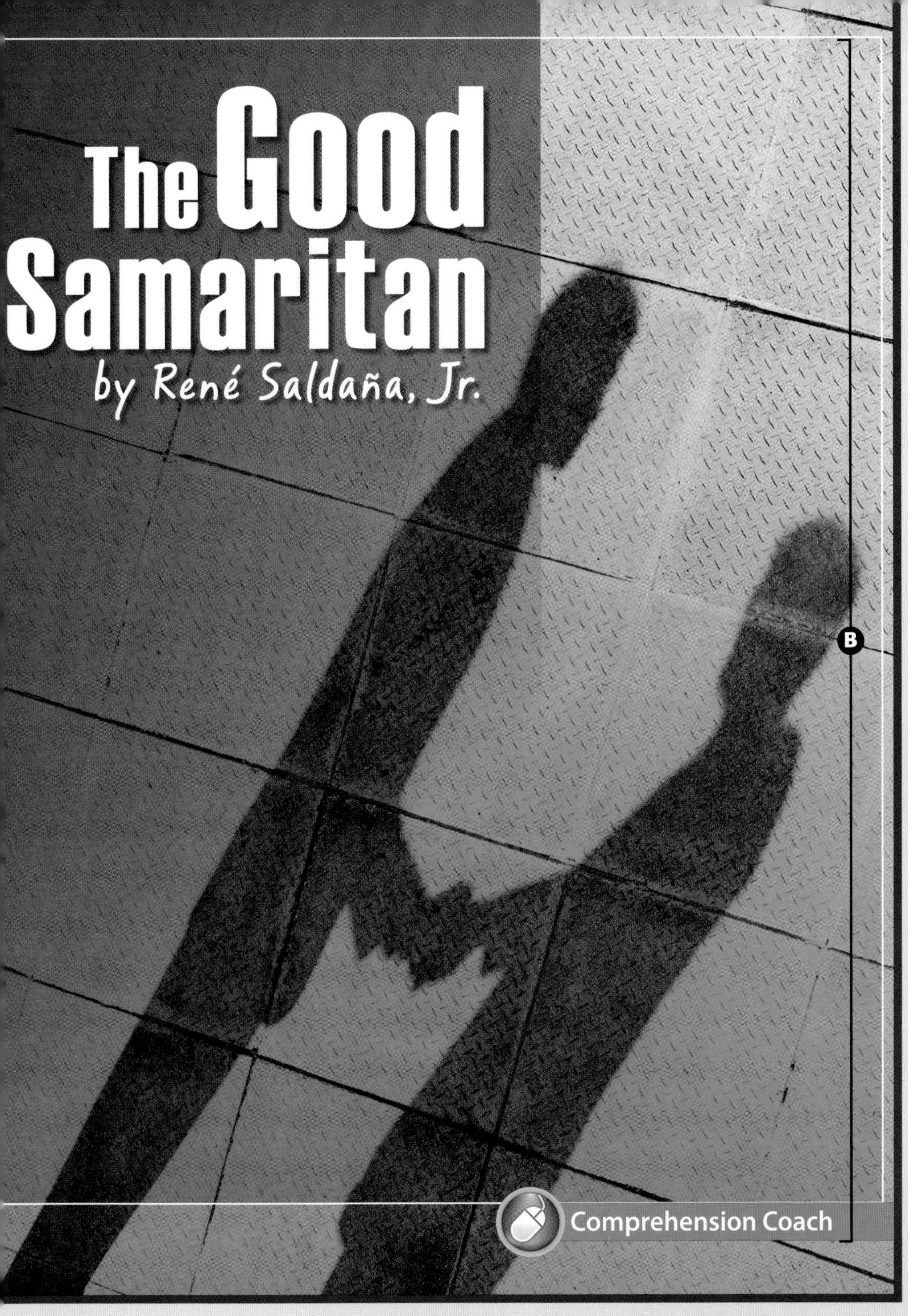

Comprehension Coach

TEACH & PRACTICE

B Analyze Visuals

About the Visuals The visuals in a story can help you understand the events of the story. The designer chose to accompany this story with photographic images that show different actions.

Interpret and Respond To create the art on p. 12, the artist combined a photographic image, a pattern, and color. Ask: What do you notice about the way the art is created? What shapes do you see? What mood or feeling does the combination of texture and color give you?

> ELL **List Vocabulary** Write a list of possible reactions or emotions, including *hot*, *nervous*, *uncomfortable*, and *serious*. Encourage students to use the words during the discussion.

Possible responses:

- *You can't see the men's faces, and their shadows aren't straight. The background has a lot of squares and a pattern of arrow shapes.*
- *The warm color and rough texture give the image a hot, nervous mood.*

RL.9-10.4; L.9-10.6

Comprehension Coach

Build Reading Power

Assign students to use the software, based on their instructional needs.

Read Silently
- Comprehension questions with immediate feedback
- Glossary support
- Review text evidence

RL.9-10.10

Listen
- Professional model of fluent reading

Record
- Oral reading fluency practice
- Ongoing fluency assessment with immediate feedback

CCSS Literacy.RL.9-10.4 Determine the meaning of words and phrases as they are used in the text, including figurative and connotative meanings; analyze the cumulative impact of specific word choices on meaning and tone (e.g., how the language evokes a sense of time and place; how it sets a formal or informal tone). Literacy.L.9-10.6 Acquire and use accurately general academic and domain-specific words and phrases, sufficient for reading, writing, speaking, and listening at the college and career readiness level; demonstrate independence in gathering vocabulary knowledge when considering a word or phrase important to comprehension or expression.

READ

OBJECTIVES

Vocabulary
- Key Vocabulary Ⓣ

Reading Fluency
- Expression Ⓣ

Reading Strategies
- Plan and Monitor: Make Predictions; Set a Purpose
- Visualize

Comprehension & Critical Thinking
- Use Text Evidence Ⓣ

Literary Analysis
- Analyze Plot Ⓣ

Viewing
- Respond to and Interpret Visuals

TEACH & PRACTICE

Ⓐ Chunking the Text

Set a Purpose Have students discuss why people help neighbors to frame their purpose for reading. Ask: Why is it important to have a good relationship with your neighbors? What can you learn by reading a story about a young man and his neighbors?

Possible response:
- *Reading this story might show you how to treat your neighbors.*

Read Have students read pp. 14–17. Support and monitor their comprehension using the reading support provided. Use the Differentiated Instruction below to meet students' individual needs.
RL.9-10.10

Ⓑ Reading Support

1 Plot/Predict Review the elements of text structure, or plot. Have students use their knowledge of text structure in a short story to make a complex prediction about the conflict. Ask: Based on the exposition, which characters do you think will have a conflict, and why?

Possible response:
- *Rey might have a conflict with someone in the Sánchez family. In an earlier event, they said Rey could use their pool, but now they are saying he can't.*

RL.9-10.5; RL.9-10.10

Set a Purpose

Ⓐ *Find out how Rey feels about his neighbors, the Sánchezes.*

I know he's in there, I thought. I saw the curtains of his bedroom move, only a little, yes, but they moved.

Yesterday Orlie told me, "Come over tomorrow afternoon. We'll **hang out** by the pool."

I rang the doorbell again. Then I knocked.

The door creaked open. The afternoon light crept into the dark living room inch by slow inch. Mrs. Sánchez, Orlie's mom, stuck her head through the narrow opening, her body hidden behind the door. "Hi, Rey, how can I help you?"

Ⓑ "Ah, Mrs. Sánchez, is Orlando here?" I tried looking past her but only saw a few pictures hanging on the wall. One of the Sánchez family all dressed up fancy and smiling, standing in front of a gray marble background.

"No, he's not. He went with his father to **Mission**."

"Oh, because Orlando said he would be here, and told me to come over."

"They won't be back until later tonight," she said. "You can come by tomorrow and see if he's here. You know how it is in the summer. He and his dad are always doing work here and there. Come back tomorrow, but call first."

"It's just that he said I could come by and swim in your pool. ***Dijo***, 'Tomorrow, come over. I'll be here. We'll go swimming.' "

"I'm sorry he told you that, but without him or my husband here, you won't be able to use the pool," ***me dijo Mrs. Sánchez***.

"Okay," I said.

"Maybe tomorrow?"

"Yeah, maybe." 1

1 Plot/Predict Based on what you've read so far, which characters do you predict might become involved in a **conflict**? Add this to your Prediction Chart.

Key Vocabulary
- **conflict** *n.*, disagreement or argument

In Other Words
hang out relax together
Mission a city at the southern tip of Texas
Dijo He said (in Spanish)
me dijo Mrs. Sánchez Mrs. Sánchez told me (in Spanish)

DIFFERENTIATED INSTRUCTION

Interactive Reading As you conduct the interactive reading session with students, adjust your teaching strategies to their needs.

Struggling Readers

Sequence Events Show plot events visually, using a time line. Pay particular attention to those events told in flashback and those in the present. For example, the events described on p. 15 occur before the opening event of the story.

English Language Learners ELL

Role-Play Have students work in small groups to act out the scenes during the reading. Ask each group to show one scene and other groups to identify what is happening.

Challenge

Character Motivation Pause in reading to have students identify the motivation behind the characters' choices. For example, ask: Why does Rey agree to help Mr. Sánchez at first? What is the motivation for Rey's choice at the end?

CCSS **Literacy.RL.9-10.5** Analyze how an author's choices concerning how to structure a text, order events within it (e.g., parallel plots), and manipulate time (e.g., pacing, flashbacks) create such effects as mystery, tension, or surprise. **Literacy.RL.9-10.10** By the end of grade 9, read and comprehend literature, including stories, dramas, and poems, in the grades 9-10 text complexity band proficiently, with scaffolding as needed at the high end of the range. By the end of grade 10, read and comprehend literature, including stories, dramas, and poems, in the grades 9-10 text complexity band proficiently, with scaffolding as needed at the high end of the range.

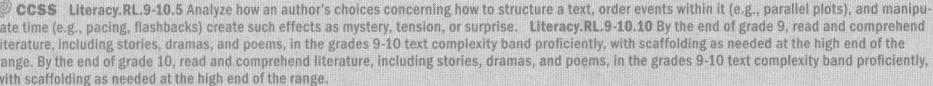

But there was no maybe about it. I wouldn't be coming back. Because I knew that Orlando was in the house, he just didn't want to hang out. ***Bien codo con su pool.*** **Plain stingy.** And tricky. This guy invited me and a few others over all summer to help his dad with some yard work because Mr. Sánchez told us, "If you help clean up the yard, you boys can use the pool any time you want so long as one of us is here." And we cleaned up his yard. On that hot day the water that smelled of chlorine looked delicious to me. And after a hard day's work cleaning his yard, I so looked forward to **taking a dip**. I'd even worn my trunks under my work clothes. Then Mr. Sánchez said, "Come by tomorrow. I don't want you fellas to track all this dirt into the pool." 2

C

2 Language
Authors use language in ways that help us picture words. What does this paragraph help you see, hear, smell, taste, or touch?

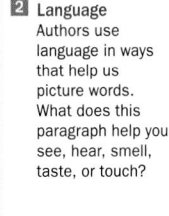

D

Critical Viewing: Design
The two shadows in this photo appear to be tilted. What does this **composition** make you think about the relationship between the two people who cast the shadows?

In Other Words
Bien codo con su pool. He's selfish about his pool. (Spanish slang)
Plain stingy. Not generous at all.
taking a dip going swimming
composition combination of images and ideas

TEACH & PRACTICE

C Reading Support

2 Language Post the word *imagery* and model how to analyze and evaluate an author's use of descriptive language. Explain that imagery helps readers use their senses to connect to the story. Read the paragraph aloud and ask: What words or phrases help you see, smell, feel, or hear after reading these words?

Possible responses:
- *hot day, chlorine, delicious*

Then ask: How does the author's use of descriptive language impact the meaning in this paragraph?

Possible response:
- *The descriptive language shows how much the boys want to go swimming.*

RL.9-10.4

D Critical Viewing: Design

Composition Have students describe the figures in the photograph, and the way they are arranged.

ELL Questioning Include less proficient students by asking yes/no questions or giving them a choice:

- Are the figures close or far apart?
- Do the figures look like friends?

To justify their responses, allow them to point to evidence in the picture or explain it.

Ask: What does the composition show about the relationship between the two people?

Possible responses:
- *Their relationship might not be good.*
- *They are ignoring each other.*

DAILY ROUTINES

Vocabulary

See the Vocabulary and Fluency Routines tab for more information.

Word Wall Display the words in a prominent place to provide a visual scaffold. Have students act out a skit that features the Key Words, such as *conflict*, *contribute*, and *disrespect*.

Short Questions Ask short questions that can be answered with vocabulary words. Have students hold up cards with the written words to respond. For example, ask: Which word means *problem*?

Pair Practice Have students work in pairs to quiz each other. One partner should say the definition, and the other should name the corresponding vocabulary word.

L.9-10.6

Fluency: Expression

CD 11

This cluster's fluency practice uses a passage from "The Good Samaritan" to help students practice appropriate expression. Use **Reading Handbook** T733 and the **Fluency Model CD** to teach or review the elements of fluent expression, and then use the daily fluency practice activities to develop students' oral reading proficiency.

RL.9-10.10

CCSS Literacy.RL.9-10.4 Determine the meaning of words and phrases as they are used in the text, including figurative and connotative meanings; analyze the cumulative impact of specific word choices on meaning and tone (e.g., how the language evokes a sense of time and place; how it sets a formal or informal tone). Literacy.L.9-10.6 Acquire and use accurately general academic and domain-specific words and phrases, sufficient for reading, writing, speaking, and listening at the college and career readiness level; demonstrate independence in gathering vocabulary knowledge when considering a word or phrase important to comprehension or expression.

OBJECTIVES

Reading Strategy
- Plan and Monitor: Make and Confirm Predictions; Review Strategies

Comprehension & Critical Thinking
- Use Text Evidence Ⓣ

Literary Analysis
- Analyze Plot Ⓣ

Grammar
- Kinds of Sentences

TEACH & PRACTICE

Ⓐ Reading Support

3 Language Point out the bolded Spanish phrases in the text. Ask: What does this tell you about the community where Rey and the Sánchez family live?

Possible response:
- *Rey and the Sánchezes live in a bilingual community.*

L.9-10.3

Ⓑ Reading Support

4 Plot/Confirm Prediction Review the elements of text structure, or plot, of a short story. Have students use information from plot complications to revise their earlier predictions about the conflict.

ELL Rephrase Language Discuss the phrase that explains the conflict: *twice before he had gypped us*. Check comprehension by asking: Who said this? About whom was he speaking?

Confirm and summarize the answers.

Ask: What did you find out in this section? Is your prediction still the same, or do you need to change it based on plot complications?

Possible response:
- *The conflict is between the boys and Mr. Sánchez. Mr. Sánchez does not keep his promises to them.*

RL.9-10.5

Ⓐ "We can go home and shower and be back," said Hernando.

"No, ***mejor que regresen mañana***. I'll be here tomorrow and we can swim. After lunch, okay. For sure we'll do it tomorrow," said Mr. Sánchez. 3

Ⓑ The following day he was there, but he was headed out right after lunch and he didn't feel safe leaving us behind without supervision. "If one of you drowns, your parents will be angry at me and . . ." He didn't say it, but he didn't need to. One of our parents could sue him. And he needed that like I needed another F in my Geometry I class! Or, we figured out later, he could have just said, "I used you **saps** to do my dirty work. And I lied about the pool, suckers!"

I don't know why we hadn't learned our lesson. Twice before he had **gypped** us this way of our time and effort. Always **dangling the carrot in front of our eyes**, then snatching it away last second. 4

One of those times he promised us soft drinks and snacks if we helped clean up a yard across the street from his house. It wasn't his yard to worry about, but I guess he just didn't like to see the weeds growing as tall as dogs. What if he had company? What would they think? And he was **angling for** a position on the school board. How could a ***político*** live in such filth!

3 Language Some of the characters switch between English and Spanish. What can you guess about their community?

4 Plot/Confirm Prediction Which characters will have a conflict? Do you want to change your prediction?

In Other Words

mejor que regresen mañana it's better if you come back tomorrow
saps foolish kids
gypped cheated, robbed (slang)
dangling the carrot in front of our eyes getting us to work by promising a reward
angling for making plans to get
político politician (in Spanish)

GRAMMAR

Kinds of Sentences

Teach/Model Display the transparency. Remind students that a sentence tells a complete thought. As you explain the four kinds of sentences, point out capitalization and end punctuation for each sentence.

Practice A. Have volunteers read each sentence and identify the kind of sentence. Elicit reasons for their choice. Help students change each sentence to a different kind.

B. After partners write their sentences about promises, have each student read a favorite aloud. Record a few, and ask the group to identify the kind of sentence and punctuation.

L.9-10.1; L.9-10.2

Grammar & Writing Practice Book, pp. 1–2

Grammar Transparency 1

Are All Sentences the Same? GRAMMAR KINDS OF SENTENCES 1

No. They Have Different Purposes.

Four Kinds of Sentences

1. Make a **statement** to tell something. End with a period.
   I ring the doorbell. The door opens. Orlie's mother answers.
2. Ask a **question** to find out something. End with a question mark.
   Is Orlie at home? Where is he? Why is he gone?
3. Use an **exclamation** to express a strong feeling. End with an exclamation point.
   It is so hot! That pool is wonderful! I hate being tricked!
4. Give a **command** to tell someone what to do. How do commands end?
   Clean up the yard. Come back tomorrow. Leave right now!

Start every sentence with a capital letter.

Try It

A. Say each sentence aloud. Tell if it is a statement, a question, an exclamation, or a command. Then change it to another kind of sentence.

1. The friends work hard. statement
2. Where is the pool? question
3. We want to swim. statement
4. Show us the pool. command
5. You promised to let us use the pool! exclamation

B. Now tell a partner about a time you made or kept a promise. From your conversation, write three different kinds of sentences.
Sentences will vary.

GRAMMAR SKILLS PATH
1 Kinds of Sentences — ELL Language & Grammar Lab
2 Subjects and Predicates
3 Noun in the Subject
4 Verb in the Predicate
5 Review: Complete Sentences

CCSS **Literacy.RL.9-10.5** Analyze how an author's choices concerning how to structure a text, order events within it (e.g., parallel plots), and manipulate time (e.g., pacing, flashbacks) create such effects as mystery, tension, or surprise. **Literacy.L.9-10.3** Apply knowledge of language to understand how language functions in different contexts, to make effective choices for meaning and style, and to comprehend more fully when reading or listening. **Literacy.L.9-10.1** Demonstrate command of the conventions of standard English grammar and usage when writing or speaking. **Literacy.L.9-10.2** Demonstrate command of the conventions of standard English capitalization, punctuation, and spelling when writing.

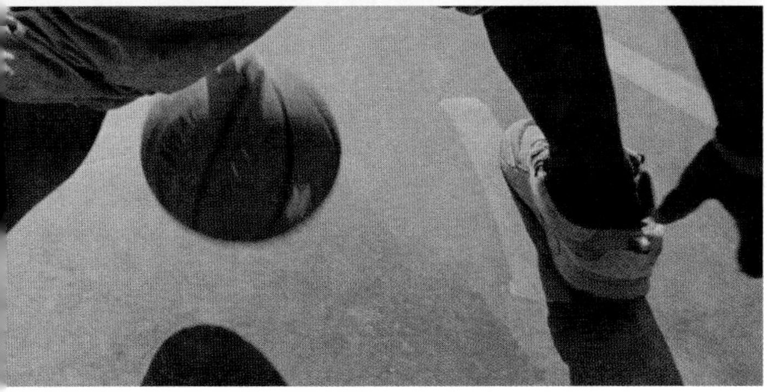

Well, we did get a soft drink and chips, only it was one two-liter bottle of Coke and one bag of chips for close to ten of us. We had no cups, and the older, stronger boys **got dibs on** most of the eats. "I didn't know there'd be so many of you," he said. "Well, share. And thanks. You all are good, strong boys."

The next time was real hard labor. He said, "Help me dig these holes here, then we can put up some basketball rims. Once the cement dries on the court itself, you all can come over and play anytime since it's kind of your court too. That is, if you help me dig the holes."

"I didn't know there'd be so many of you," he said. "Well, share."

And we did. We dug and dug and dug for close to six hours straight until we got done, passing on the shovel from one of us to the next. But we got it done. We had our court. Mr. Sánchez **kept his word**. He reminded us we could come over to play anytime, and we took special care not to **dunk** and grab hold of the rim. Even the shortest kid could practically dunk it because the baskets were so low. But we'd seen the rims all bent down at the different yards at school. And we didn't want that for *our* court. 5

C

5 Plot/Predict
Mr. Sánchez keeps his promise. Do you think his relationship with Rey will change? Explain.

Monitor Comprehension

Summarize
How have Rey's feelings about Mr. Sánchez changed over time?

In Other Words

got dibs on had the first choice of
kept his word did what he had promised
dunk slam the basketball into the hoop

TEACH & PRACTICE

Reading Support

Review major features of a report. Students should keep in mind that the meaning of their report could be affected if the conventions of the genre are not addressed.

C Reading Support

5 Plot/Predict Guide students in reviewing Mr. Sánchez's actions up to now. Ask: Do you think his relationship with Rey will now be different than before? Why or why not?

Possible responses:

- *It will change, because he finally kept his promise.*
- *Maybe he keeps this promise, but Mr. Sánchez has not changed. He will do something else to make Rey angry.*

RL.9-10.10

Review Strategies Have partners say what other strategies they used as they read the text.

Possible response:

- *I read that Mr. Sánchez had let the boys down two other times. I know that if people let me down, I don't trust them anymore. So I made the inference that Mr Sánchez is not a trustworthy person. This helped me to understand why it was important to Rey that Mr. Sánchez "kept his word" about the basketball court.*

RL.9-10.1

Monitor Comprehension

Summarize Remind students that *summarize* means "briefly retell the main idea or events of a story." Have them use one sentence to explain the change in Rey's feelings. Provide a sentence frame: *Rey used to feel* _______. *Now, Rey feels* _______ *because* _______.

RL.9-10.2

CCSS **Literacy.RL.9-10.1** Cite strong and thorough textual evidence to support analysis of what the text says explicitly as well as inferences drawn from the text. **Literacy. RL.9-10.2** Determine a theme or central idea of a text and analyze in detail its development over the course of a text, including how it emerges and is shaped and refined by specific details; provide an objective summary of the text. **Literacy.RL.9-10.5** Analyze how an author's choices concerning how to structure a text, order events within it (e.g., parallel plots), and manipulate time (e.g., pacing, flashbacks) create such effects as mystery, tension, or surprise. **Literacy.RL.9-10.10** By the end of grade 9, read and comprehend literature, including stories, dramas, and poems, in the grades 9–10 text complexity band proficiently, with scaffolding as needed at the high end of the range. By the end of grade 10, read and comprehend literature, including stories, dramas, and poems, at the high end of the grades 9–10 text complexity band independently and proficiently.

READ

OBJECTIVES

Vocabulary
- Key Vocabulary (T)

Reading Strategy
- Plan and Monitor: Make Predictions

Comprehension & Critical Thinking
- Use Text Evidence (T)

Literary Analysis
- Analyze Plot (T)

Grammar
- Subjects and Predicates (T)

TEACH & PRACTICE

(A) Chunking the Text

Predict Have students use the visuals and text features on upcoming pages, as well as their knowledge about the story, to predict what will happen.

ELL Rephrase Language Write and explain the idiom "keep his word." Below it write the similar phrase *keep his promise*. Then read the question and rephrase it: Will Mr. Sánchez *keep his word* to the boys? Will he let the boys use the court as he promised?

Ask: What do you predict Mr. Sánchez will do and why?

Read Have students read pp. 18–21. Support and monitor their comprehension using the reading support provided.
RL.9-10.10

(B) Reading Support

6 Plot Explain the conflict in simple terms: Mr. Sánchez does not keep his word after the boys work hard for him. Then ask what event in the plot just complicated the conflict.

Possible responses:
- *Mr. Sánchez gets angry with the boys for using his court when he is not home.*
- *Mr. Sánchez breaks a promise again.*

RL.9-10.5

(A) ***Predict***
Will Mr. Sánchez keep his word to the boys who helped him?

(B) One day, we wanted to play a **little three on three**. After knocking on the different doors several times and getting no answer, we figured the Sánchez family had gone out. We decided that it'd be okay to play. We weren't going to do anything wrong. The court was far enough from the house that we couldn't possibly break a window. And Mr. Sánchez had said we could come over any time we wanted. It was *our* court, after all. Those were his words exactly.

A little later in the afternoon, Mr. Sánchez drove up in his truck, honking and honking at us. "Here they come. Maybe Orlando and Marty can play with us," someone said.

Pues, it was not to be. The truck had just **come to a standstill** when Mr. Sánchez **shot out of** the driver's side. He ran up to us, waving his hands in the air like a crazy man, first saying, then screaming, "What are you guys doing here? You all can't be here when I'm not here." 6

"But you told us we could come over anytime. And we knocked and knocked, and we were being very careful."

"It doesn't matter. You all shouldn't be here when I'm not home. What if you had broken something?" he said.

"But we didn't," I said.

"But if you had, then who would have been **responsible** for paying to replace it? I'm sure every one of you would have denied breaking anything."

"***Este vato!***" said Hernando.

"*Vato*? Is that what you called me? I'm no street punk, no hoodlum. I'll have you know, I've worked my whole life, and I won't be called a *vato*. It's Mr. Sánchez. Got that? And you boys know what—from now on, you are not allowed to come here whether I'm home or not! You all

6 Plot
An event that makes the conflict worse is called a complication. What complication happens here?

Key Vocabulary
responsible *adj.*, have the duty of taking care of

In Other Words
little three on three small game of basketball with three players on each team
Pues Well (in Spanish)
come to a standstill stopped
shot out of jumped quickly from
Este vato! This dude! This guy! (Spanish slang)

GRAMMAR

Subjects and Predicates

Teach/Model Display the transparency. Explain how to ask questions to find the subject and the predicate. Use the chart to practice asking questions. Record answers to the questions in the chart, and show how subjects and predicates combine to make a complete thought.

Practice A. Ask students to form a complete sentence and read it aloud. Draw connecting lines to join the sentence parts. **B.** After partners write sentences about chores, have each student read one sentence aloud, and ask the group to identify the subject and predicate.
L.9-10.1.b

Grammar & Writing Practice Book, pp. 3–4

GRAMMAR SKILLS PATH

1 Kinds of Sentences
2 Subjects and Predicates
ELL Language & Grammar Lab
3 Noun in the Subject
4 Verb in the Predicate
5 Review: Complete Sentences

Grammar Transparency 2

GRAMMAR SUBJECTS AND PREDICATES 2

What Do You Need for a Sentence?
A Subject and a Predicate

A complete sentence has two parts: the **subject** and the **predicate**.

subject **predicate**
Mr. Sánchez asks for help.

To find the parts, in most sentences, ask yourself:

1. Whom or what is the sentence about? Your answer is the **subject**. It may be one word or more than one word.
2. What does the subject do? Your answer is the **predicate**. Like the subject, the predicate may be one word or more than one.

Sentence	Whom or What?	What Does the Subject Do?
The friends clean the yard.	The friends	clean the yard
A truck arrives.	A truck	arrives

Try It

A. Match each subject to a predicate. Say the new sentence.

1. Rey and his friends	help Mr. Sánchez.
2. The boys	runs to the basket.
3. The truck	knock on several doors.
4. Mr. Sánchez	yells.
5. Hernando	stops in the driveway.

B. Now tell a partner about a chore you do at home. Write your three best sentences. Include a subject and a predicate in each.
Sentences will vary.

CCSS **Literacy RL.9-10.5** Analyze how an author's choices concerning how to structure a text, order events within it (e.g., parallel plots), and manipulate time (e.g., pacing, flashbacks) create such effects as mystery, tension, or surprise. **Literacy.RL.9-10.10** By the end of grade 9, read and comprehend literature, including stories, dramas, and poems, in the grades 9–10 text complexity band proficiently, with scaffolding as needed at the high end of the range. By the end of grade 10, read and comprehend literature, including stories, dramas, and poems, at the high end of the grades 9–10 text complexity band independently and proficiently. **Literacy.L.9-10.1.b** Use various types of phrases (noun, verb, adjectival, adverbial, participial, prepositional, absolute) and clauses (independent, dependent; noun, relative, adverbial) to convey specific meanings and add variety and interest to writing or presentations.

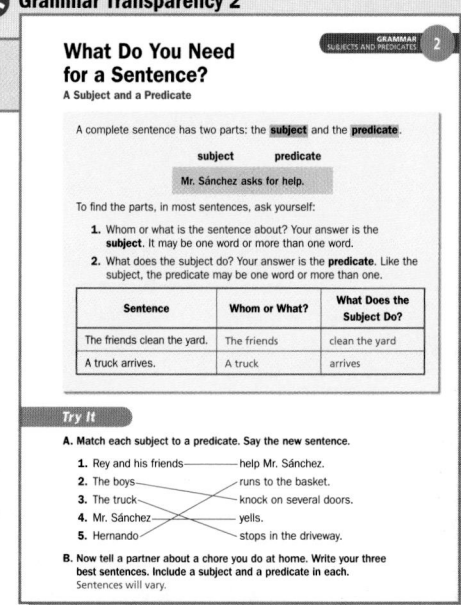

messed it up for yourselves. You've shown me so much **disrespect** today you don't deserve to play on my court. It was a **privilege** and not **a right**, and you messed it up. Now leave!" 7 **C**

Hernando, who was **fuming**, said, "***Orale***, guys, let's go." He took the ball from one of the smaller boys and began to run toward the nearest basket. He slowed down the closer he came to the basket and leapt in the air. I'd never seen him jump with such grace. He floated from the foul line, his long hair like wings, all the way to the basket. He grabbed the ball in both his hands and let go of it at the last moment. Instead of dunking the ball, he let it shoot up to the sky; then he wrapped his fingers around the rim and pulled down as hard as he could, hanging on for a few seconds. Then the rest of us walked after him, **dejected**. He hadn't bent the rim even a millimeter. 8 **D** Eventually Orlie talked us into going back when his dad wasn't home. His baby brother, Marty, was small and slow, and Orlie wanted some competition on the court.

7 Plot
Mr. Sánchez thinks the boys have shown him disrespect. How do you think the boys feel about this?

8 Plot
How does Hernando's reaction to Mr. Sánchez **affect** the conflict in the story?

Key Vocabulary
disrespect *n.*, rudeness
privilege *n.*, something special that someone can have, be, or do
• **affect** *v.*, to change or influence

In Other Words
a right something you were allowed to do without questions or conditions
fuming very angry, furious
Orale Come on (Spanish slang)
dejected feeling sad and disappointed

TEACH & PRACTICE

C Reading Support

7 Plot Review the boys' actions. Ask: Why does Mr. Sánchez believe the boys showed disrespect? How do you think the boys feel about Mr. Sánchez?

Possible responses:
- *The boys played on the court without supervision. They also refer to Mr. Sánchez as a vato (or dude).*
- *The boys feel Mr. Sánchez has disrespected them by not keeping his word to them.*

RL.9-10.3

D Reading Support

8 Plot Review what Hernando did and why. Ask students how Hernando's actions affect the plot. Scaffold with more specific questions. Ask: Does his action solve the conflict? Does it complicate the conflict?

Possible responses:
- *Hernando complicated the plot again, because he shows more disrespect to Mr. Sánchez.*
- *His actions do not solve the conflict.*

RL.9-10.3

VOCABULARY

Link Vocabulary and Concepts

Ask questions to link Key Vocabulary with the Essential Question.

EQ ESSENTIAL QUESTION:
What influences a person's choices?

Some possible questions:
- *How does the possibility of earning* **privileges** *influence the boys' decisions?*
- *Give examples of* **disrespect** *in the story. How does disrespect influence the characters?*
- *What was Mr. Sánchez's* **motivation** *to tell the boys they could not play on the court anymore?*
- *If something on the basketball court had broken, who do you think would have been* **responsible** *for paying for it?*
- *How did Hernando* **contribute** *to the conflict of the story?*

Have students use Key Vocabulary words in their responses.
L.9-10.6

CCSS Literacy RL.9-10.3 Analyze how complex characters (e.g., those with multiple or conflicting motivations) develop over the course of a text, interact with other characters, and advance the plot or develop the theme. **Literacy.L.9-10.6** Acquire and use accurately general academic and domain-specific words and phrases, sufficient for reading, writing, speaking, and listening at the college and career readiness level; demonstrate independence in gathering vocabulary knowledge when considering a word or phrase important to comprehension or expression.

READ

OBJECTIVES

Vocabulary
- Content Area Vocabulary: Driving

Reading Strategy
- Plan and Monitor: Make and Confirm Predictions

Comprehension & Critical Thinking
- Use Text Evidence (T)

Literary Analysis
- Analyze Plot (T)

TEACH & PRACTICE

(A) Reading Support

9 **Plot/Predict** Ask: What has happened in the story so far that can help you predict whether Rey will ever go back to the Sánchezes' house?

Possible responses:
- *Rey has already been fooled twice by Mr. Sánchez, so he probably won't help him again.*
- *Mr. Sánchez is Rey's neighbor, so he might think he has to help him.*

RL.9-10.5; RL.9-10.10

Monitor Comprehension

Confirm Prediction Have students review the predictions they made on page 18 and discuss whether or not they correctly predicted what Mr. Sánchez would do. Have students share what led them to their predictions.

MODEL Say:
- *So far Mr. Sánchez has failed to keep his promises to the boys.*
- *I predicted that Mr. Sánchez would keep disappointing the boys because he has never kept his promises in the past.*
- *I predict that the boys won't agree to help him anymore in the future.*

RL.9-10.10

(A) Today was it for me, though. I made up my mind never to go back to the Sánchezes'. 9 I walked to the little store for a Fanta Orange. That and a grape Popsicle would cool me down. I sat on the bench outside, finished off the drink, returned the bottle for my nickel refund, and headed for home.

9 **Plot/Predict** Do you think Rey will keep this promise to himself? What evidence in the text makes you think so?

Monitor Comprehensi

Confirm Prediction Was your prediction accurate? If not, why? What happened that you did not expect?

CCSS Literacy.RL.9-10.5 Analyze how an author's choices concerning how to structure a text, order events within it (e.g., parallel plots), and manipulate time (e.g., pacing, flashbacks) create such effects as mystery, tension, or surprise. Literacy.RL.9-10.10 By the end of grade 9, read and comprehend literature, including stories, dramas, and poems, in the grades 9–10 text complexity band proficiently, with scaffolding as needed at the high end of the range. By the end of grade 10, read and comprehend literature, including stories, dramas, and poems, at the high end of the grades 9–10 text complexity band independently and proficiently.

Predict

Mr. Sánchez needs help again. What will Rey do? **B**

As soon as I walked through our front door, my mother said, "***Mi'jo***, you need to go pick up your brother at summer school. He missed the bus."

"Again? He probably missed it on purpose, ***'Amá***. He's always walking over to Leo's Grocery to talk to his little girlfriends, then he calls when he needs a ride." I turned toward the bedroom.

"Come back here," she said. So I turned and took a seat at the table. "Have you forgotten the times we had to go pick you up? Your brother always went with us, no matter what time it was." **C**

"Yeah, but I was doing school stuff. Football, band. He's in summer school just **piddling his time away**!"

She looked at me as she brushed sweat away from her face with the back of her hand and said, "Just go pick him up, and hurry home. On the way back, stop at Circle Seven and buy some tortillas. There's money on the table."

I shook my head **in disgust**. Here I was, already a senior, having to be my baby brother's **chauffeur**. 10

I'd driven halfway to Leo's Grocery when I saw Mr. Sánchez's truck up ahead by the side of the road. I could **just make him out** sitting under the shade of his truck. Every time he heard a car coming his way, he'd raise his head slightly, try to catch the driver's attention by staring at him, then he'd hang his head again when the car didn't stop.

I slowed down as I approached. Could he tell it was me driving? When he looked up at my car, I could swear he almost smiled, thinking he had been saved. 11 He had been leaning his head between his bent knees, and I could tell he was tired; his white shirt stuck to him because of all the sweat. His sock on one leg was bunched up at his ankle like a **D**

10 **Plot**
What do Rey's comments and thoughts tell you about how he feels about helping his brother? How is this similar to his feelings about helping Mr. Sánchez?

11 **Predict**
Do you think Rey will stop the car? Add this to your Chart.

In Other Words

Mi'jo My son (in Spanish)
'Amá Mom (in Spanish)
piddling his time away wasting his time
in disgust feeling angry and irritated
chauffeur paid driver
just make him out see him a little

TEACH & PRACTICE

B Chunking the Text

Predict Remind students about how Rey has felt about Mr. Sánchez throughout the story.

ELL **Rephrase Language** Reread p. 21 and explain idiomatic language that describes Rey's emotions:

- *Today was it for me, though*: I was finished believing Mr. Sánchez.
- *made up my mind*: was sure about my decision
- *cool me down*: make me less angry

Ask: Does Rey sound as if he will give Mr. Sánchez another chance?

Ask: Considering this evidence from the text, what do you predict Rey will decide to do?

Possible response:

- *He will decide not to help Mr. Sánchez.*

Support and monitor their comprehension using the reading support provided.
RL.9-10.10

C Reading Support

Access Vocabulary Point out that *chauffeur* is a word from French that is commonly used in English. Ask: Does the writer's use of the word *chauffeur* suggest a positive or a negative connotation? How can you tell?

Possible response:

- *The usage here suggests something negative. Rey uses it after he shakes his head "in disgust."*

10 **Plot** Guide students in understanding Rey's attitude about picking up his brother. Then ask: What does it have in common with his attitude toward Mr. Sanchez?

Possible response:

- *Rey doesn't think his brother or Mr. Sanchez deserve his help.*
RL.9-10.3

D Reading Support

11 **Predict** Have students picture the scene in their minds. Ask: What might cause Rey to stop the car?

Possible response:

- *Mr. Sanchez looks hot and tired. Rey might feel sorry for him.*
RL.9-10.10

VOCABULARY

SOCIOLOGY

Content Area Vocabulary: Driving

Build vocabulary related to driving a car.

Teach/Model Use the Make Words Your Own routine (see *the Vocabulary tab*) and the sample sentences below to introduce these words from the selection. Have students use digital tools, such as online audio, to determine pronunciations.

chauffeur (**shō**-fur) ▸ p. 21

A **chauffeur** *is a person who drives someone else.*

lug nut (lug nut) ▸ p. 22

A **lug nut** *is a special part made to hold large bolts in place on wheels of cars.*

crowbar (**krō**-bar) ▸ p. 22

A **crowbar** *is a metal bar used to pull a tire from a car.*

flat tire (flat tīr) ▸ p. 22

A **flat tire** *is one that has little air inside.*

U-turn (**yū**-turn) ▸ p. 24

I noticed I forgot my wallet and did a **U-turn** *in the road to head right back home.*

Practice Have students use the words to make new sentences.

Apply Tell students to ask each other questions using the words. For example: Do you know how to fix a **flat tire**?
L.9-10.6

CCSS **Literacy.RL.9-10.3** Analyze how complex characters (e.g., those with multiple or conflicting motivations) develop over the course of a text, interact with other characters, and advance the plot or develop the theme. **Literacy.L.9-10.6** Acquire and use accurately general academic and domain-specific words and phrases, sufficient for reading, writing, speaking, and listening at the college and career readiness level; demonstrate independence in gathering vocabulary knowledge when considering a word or phrase important to comprehension or expression.

OBJECTIVES

Reading Strategy
- Plan and Monitor: Make Predictions

Comprehension & Critical Thinking
- Use Text Evidence Ⓣ

Literary Analysis
- Analyze Plot Ⓣ

Grammar
- Noun in the Subject

TEACH & PRACTICE

Ⓐ Reading Support

12 Plot Ask: Do you think this situation will resolve the conflict between Rey and Mr. Sánchez or make it worse?

Possible responses:
- *It will resolve the conflict, because Rey feels sorry for Mr. Sánchez.*
- *It will make the conflict worse, because it reminds Rey of promises Mr. Sánchez did not keep.*

RL.9-10.5

Ⓑ Reading Support

13 Plot/Character Ask: In this daydream, what does Rey's father want him to do? How does this imagined scene add to Rey's conflict?

Possible responses:
- *Rey's father wants Rey to explain to Mr. Sánchez why he didn't help him.*
- *Rey feels obligated to do what his father would expect him to.*

RL.9-10.5

carnation. He had the whitest legs I'd ever seen on a Mexican. Whiter than even my dad's. I kept on looking straight; that is, I **made like** I was looking ahead, not a care in the world, but out of the corner of my eye I saw that he had a flat tire, that he had gotten two of the lug nuts off but hadn't gotten to the others, that the crowbar lay half on his other foot and half on the ground beside him, that his hair was matted by sweat to his forehead. 12

I knew that look. I'd probably looked just like that digging those holes for *our* basketball court, cleaning up his yard and the one across the street from his house. I wondered if he could use a cold two-liter Coke right about now! If he was dreaming of taking a dip in his pool!

I drove on. No way was I going to help him out again! Let him do his own dirty work for once. He could stay out there and melt in this heat for all I cared. And besides, someone else will stop, I thought. Someone who doesn't know him like I do.

No way was I going to help him out again!

And I knew that when Mr. Sánchez got home, he'd stop at my house on his walk around the ***barrio***. My dad would be watering the plants, **his evening ritual** to relax from a hard day at work, and Mr. Sánchez would **mention in passing** that I had probably not seen him by the side of the road so I hadn't stopped to help him out; "Kids today," he would say to my dad, "not a care in the world, their heads up in the clouds somewhere." My dad would call me out and ask me to tell him and Mr. Sánchez why I hadn't helped out a neighbor when he needed it most. 13 I'd say, to both of them, "That was you? I thought you and Orlie were in Mission taking care of some business, so it never occurred to me to stop to help a neighbor. Geez, I'm so sorry." Or I could say, "You know, I was in

12 Plot
Mr. Sánchez needs help again. How does this situation add to the conflict between Rey and him?

13 Plot/Character
What does Rey imagine about his dad? How does this add to the conflict he feels?

In Other Words

carnation folded-looking flower
made like pretended
barrio neighborhood (in Spanish)
his evening ritual the same thing he did every night
mention in passing say in a way that seemed unimportant

GRAMMAR

Noun in the Subject

Teach/Model Display the transparency. Remind students that the subject is one part of a complete sentence. Ask a volunteer to read the first sentence. Then ask: Is the sentence about a person, place, thing, or idea? Write the answer on the chart next to *Thing*. (*truck*) Continue to ask questions and fill in the chart with the subject nouns.

Practice A. Have students suggest subjects. Choose one to write. **B.** After students complete the sentences, ask them to share their work and identify subjects.

L.9-10.1.b

Grammar & Writing Practice Book, pp. 5–6

GRAMMAR SKILLS PATH

1 Kinds of Sentences
2 Subjects and Predicates
▶ 3 Noun in the Subject
   ELL Language & Grammar Lab
4 Verb in the Predicate
5 Review: Complete Sentences

Grammar Transparency 3

What Is a Sentence About?

GRAMMAR NOUN IN THE SUBJECT 3

The Subject

The **complete subject** can be one word or a phrase of several words. Zoom in on the most important word. Is it a noun? A **noun** is the name of a person, place, thing, or idea.

1. Mr. Sánchez's **truck** has a flat tire.
2. The hot, tired **man** sits in the shade.
3. **Rey** drives past.
4. Every **driver** passes by.
5. The **highway** is a lonely place.
6. **Help** is nowhere in sight.

Nouns in the Subject	
Person	Rey man driver
Place	highway
Thing	truck
Idea	help

Try It

A. Tell what happens in the story. Add a noun to complete the subject of the sentence. Possible answers:

1. The young __driver__ sees Mr. Sánchez.
2. Mr. Sánchez's __shirt__ is wet with sweat.
3. The __tire__ on the truck is completely flat.
4. The __sadness__ on Mr. Sánchez's face reminds Rey of his own father.
5. __Rey__ decides to help Mr. Sánchez.

B. Now tell a friend what happened in the story. Write three more sentences about "The Good Samaritan." Circle the most important word in the subject. Sentences will vary.

Rey changes his mind.

CCSS **Literacy.RL.9-10.5** Analyze how an author's choices concerning how to structure a text, order events within it (e.g., parallel plots), and manipulate time (e.g., pacing, flashbacks) create such effects as mystery, tension, or surprise. **Literacy.L.9-10.1.b** Use various types of phrases (noun, verb, adjectival, adverbial, participial, prepositional, absolute) and clauses (independent, dependent, noun, relative, adverbial) to convey specific meanings and add variety and interest to writing or presentations.

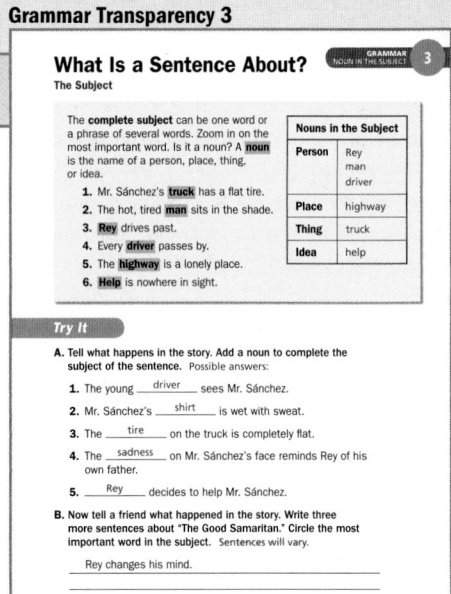

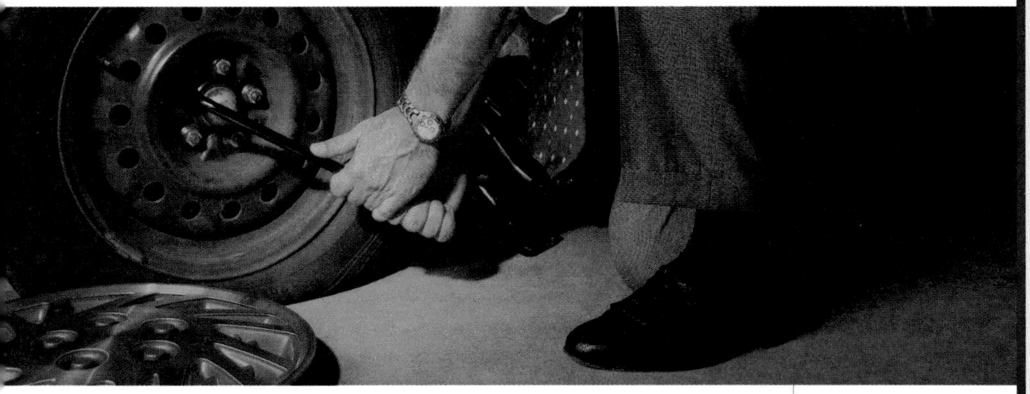

such a hurry to pick up my brother in La Joya that I didn't even notice you by the side of the road." 14

I'd be off the hook. Anyways, why should I be the one to **extend a helping hand** when he's done every one of us in the barrio wrong in one way or another! He deserves to sweat a little. A taste of his own bad medicine. Maybe he'll learn a lesson.

But I remembered the look in his eyes as I drove past him. That same tired look my father had when he'd get home from work and he didn't have the strength to take off his boots. My father always looked like he'd been working for centuries without any rest. He'd sit there in front of the television on his favorite green vinyl sofa chair and stare at whatever was on TV. He'd sit there for an hour before he could move, before he could eat his supper and take his shower, that same look on his face Mr. Sánchez had just now.

What if this were my dad **stranded** on the side of the road? I'd want someone to stop for him.

"My one **good deed** for today," I told myself. "And I'm doing it for my dad really, not for Mr. Sánchez."

C

14 **Plot/Predict** Do you think the scene Rey is imagining will really take place? Explain.

In Other Words

I'd be off the hook. No one could blame me.
extend a helping hand help him
stranded left alone without help
good deed helpful act

TEACH & PRACTICE

C Reading Support

14 **Plot/Predict** Remind students that Rey's conversation with his father is imagined.

> **ELL Comprehensible Input**
> Help students differentiate between actual and imagined events in the scene. Write the headings *Real* and *Imagined*. Under *Real*, write *Rey drives*. Under *Imagined*, write *Rey's father asks him a question.*
>
> Explain that the word *would* is often a signal for imagined events.

Ask: Do you think this scene will happen? Why or why not?

Possible response:

- *This scene might not happen if Rey decides to do what his father expects of him.*

RL.9-10.5; RL.9-10.10

OUT-OF-SCHOOL LITERACY

Interpreting a Television Show or Movie

Have students apply what they have learned about conflict and plot by asking if they have seen a television show or movie in which a character had to make a decision similar to the one Rey had to make.

Have students record answers to questions about this show or movie:

- **What** was the name of the movie or television show?
- **Who** was the main character?
- **Why** was the character's decision similar to Rey's?
- **How** did the character resolve his or her conflict? In other words, what did he or she decide?
- **In your opinion**, did the character make the right decision? What about Rey?

SL.9-10.1.a

CCSS **Literacy.RL.9-10.10** By the end of grade 9, read and comprehend literature, including stories, dramas, and poems, in the grades 9–10 text complexity band proficiently, with scaffolding as needed at the high end of the range. By the end of grade 10, read and comprehend literature, including stories, dramas, and poems, at the high end of the grades 9–10 text complexity band independently and proficiently. **Literacy.SL.9-10.1.a** Come to discussions prepared, having read and researched material under study; explicitly draw on that preparation by referring to evidence from texts and other research on the topic or issue to stimulate a thoughtful, well-reasoned exchange of ideas.

READ

OBJECTIVES

Reading Strategy
- Plan and Monitor: Make and Confirm Predictions

Comprehension & Critical Thinking
- Use Text Evidence Ⓣ

Literary Analysis
- Analyze Plot Ⓣ

Research Skills
- Formulate Research Questions
- Convert Data into Graphic Aids

Writing
- Response to Literature

TEACH & PRACTICE

Ⓐ Reading Support

15 Plot Tell students that in this part they will read the climax, or turning point, of the story. Review the thoughts Rey has before he decides to make a U-turn.

ELL Comprehensible Input Look back at Rey's thoughts on p. 23 and clarify the pronoun references. Read aloud the second paragraph. Ask: Who does the *he* refer to? *(Mr. Sánchez)*

Read the third paragraph, sentence by sentence:

- In the first sentence, the pronoun *his* still refers to Mr. Sánchez.
- In the second sentence, Rey begins talking about his father.
- All the pronouns after the second sentence refer to Rey's father.

Ask: How does Rey's vision of his father help you understand Rey's decision to help Mr. Sánchez?

Ask: Why does Rey decide to help Mr. Sánchez?

Possible responses:
- *Rey helps Mr. Sánchez because he knows his father would expect him to do that.*
- *Rey helps Mr. Sánchez because he would want someone to do the same for his father.*

RL.9-10.5

Ⓐ I **made a U-turn**, drove back to where he was still sitting, turned around again, and pulled up behind him. 15

"I thought that was you, Rey," he said. He wiped at his forehead with his shirtsleeve. "And when you drove past, I thought you hadn't seen me. Thank goodness you stopped. I've been here for close to forty-five minutes and nobody's stopped to help. Thank goodness you did. I just can't get the tire off."

Thank my father, I thought. If it weren't for my father, you'd still be out here.

I had that tire changed in no time. All the while Mr. Sánchez stood behind me and a bit to my left saying, "Yes, thank God you came by. Boy, it's hot out here. You're a good boy, Rey. You'll make a good man. How about some help there?"

15 Plot
Why does Rey make his decision?

In Other Words
made a U-turn turned the car around

CONTENT AREA CONNECTIONS

SOCIOLOGY

Bilingualism

Interview Have students interview a bilingual person about how bilingualism has helped that person. Have students form questions they plan to ask. Provide suggestions:

- What is your first language?
- What other languages do you speak fluently, and how did you learn them?
- Was it difficult for you to learn other languages?
- Has knowing a language helped you in your career?
- Does knowing more than one language help people make more friends or feel more confident? Why?
- In what other ways has being bilingual helped you?

Present Have students design a poster with images and words that reflect the answers they were given. Have students review posters and note various ways bilingualism has helped others.

SL.9-10.1.a

CCSS Literacy.RL.9-10.5 Analyze how an author's choices concerning how to structure a text, order events within it (e.g., parallel plots), and manipulate time (e.g., pacing, flashbacks) create such effects as mystery, tension, or surprise. Literacy.SL.9-10.1.a Come to discussions prepared, having read and researched material under study; explicitly draw on that preparation by referring to evidence from texts and other research on the topic or issue to stimulate a thoughtful, well-reasoned exchange of ideas.

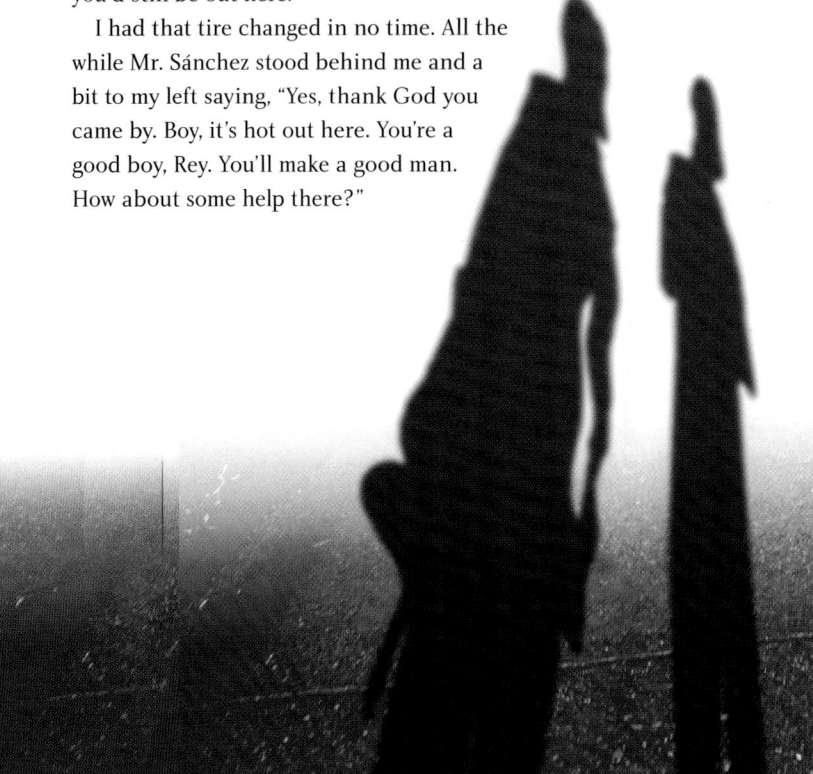

"No, I've got it," I answered. "I'm almost done."

"***Oyes***, Rey, what if you come over tomorrow night to my house? I'm having a little barbecue for some important people here in town. You should come over. We're even going to do some swimming. What do you say?"

I tightened the last of the nuts, replaced the jack, the flat tire, and the crowbar in the bed of his truck, looked at him, and said, "Thanks. But I'll be playing football with the *vatos*." 16 ❖

B

16 Plot/Character Why does Rey refuse Mr. Sánchez's invitation?

ANALYZE The Good Samaritan

1. **Recall and Interpret** What does Rey do when Mr. Sánchez needs help at the end of the story? Were you surprised by Rey's response? Explain.
2. **Vocabulary** Do any characters show **disrespect** in the story? Explain.
3. **Analyze Plot** With a partner, create a map of the events in the story. Use a **Story Map** to describe the major events that lead to the main **conflict**.

Story Map

Rey does yard work for Mr. Sánchez.	The Sánchezes don't keep their promise.	

4. **Focus Strategy Make and Confirm Predictions** Reread the **Prediction Chart** that you began on page 11. Show a partner the details in the story that confirmed your predictions or made you change them.

C

Return to the Text

Reread and Write How does Saldāna draw on the parable of the Good Samaritan for this story? Support your answer with evidence from the text.

D

In Other Words
Oyes Listen (in Spanish)

TEACH & PRACTICE

B Reading Support

16 **Plot/Character** Ask: Why does Rey choose to resolve the conflict in this way?

Possible response:

- *Rey did the right thing, so he is satisfied. But he doesn't expect anything from Mr. Sánchez.*

RL.9-10.5

APPLY

C ANALYZE

1. **Recall and Interpret** Rey helps Mr. Sánchez. I was not surprised, because he seemed to feel guilty when he thought about his father.
2. **Vocabulary** Mr. Sánchez shows disrespect to the boys by asking them for help but then not giving them what he promises. Hernando shows disrespect by calling Mr. Sánchez a *vato*.
L.9-10.6
3. **Analyze Plot** After partners complete their map, have them use it to discuss the plot.
RL.9-10.5
4. **Focus Strategy: Make and Confirm Predictions** Have partners share one prediction they found that was the same and one that was different.
RL.9-10.10

D Return to the Text

Review the biblical parable on page T12. Ask how the author draws on and transforms the source material to create his own story about a good Samaritan.

Possible response:

- *In the parable, the Samaritan helps the injured man, even though they are supposed to be enemies. In the story, Rey helps Mr. Sánchez, even though he does not like or trust the older man.*

W.9-10.9.a; W.9-10.10

Edge Interactive Practice Book, p. 10

CCSS **Literacy.RL.9-10.5** Analyze how an author's choices concerning how to structure a text, order events within it (e.g., parallel plots), and manipulate time (e.g., pacing, flashbacks) create such effects as mystery, tension, or surprise. **Literacy.RL.9-10.10** By the end of grade 9, read and comprehend literature, including stories, dramas, and poems, in the grades 9–10 text complexity band proficiently, with scaffolding as needed at the high end of the range. By the end of grade 10, read and comprehend literature, including stories, dramas, and poems, at the high end of the grades 9–10 text complexity band independently and proficiently. **Literacy.W.9-10.9.a** Apply grades 9–10 Reading standards to literature (e.g., "Analyze how an author draws on and transforms source material in a specific work [e.g., how Shakespeare treats a theme or topic from Ovid or the Bible or how a later author draws on a play by Shakespeare]"). **Literacy.W.9-10.10** Write routinely over extended time frames (time for research, reflection, and revision) and shorter time frames (a single sitting or a day or two) for a range of tasks, purposes, and audiences. **Literacy.L.9-10.6** Acquire and use accurately general academic and domain-specific words and phrases, sufficient for reading, writing, speaking, and listening at the college and career readiness level; demonstrate independence in gathering vocabulary knowledge when considering a word or phrase important to comprehension or expression.

READ

OBJECTIVES

Literary Analysis
- Evaluate Literature: Poet's Purpose
- Connect Across Texts

Listening and Speaking
- Listen Actively
- Respond to Literature

TEACH & PRACTICE

Read the Poem Aloud

Active Listening Have students listen to and read text to prepare for discussion. Read aloud a few lines in the poem at a time. Pause to explain phrases and idioms students may not know.

ELL **Role-Play** After reading the line that contains "rip into you," explain that it means "treat you unkindly." Then act out one person asking for the time and another yelling back "How would I know?!" Repeat for other idioms:

- "back-street mugging" (robbery in an alley)
- "People were upfront" (People were honest)
- "showed me some heart" (proved it was kind)

Then read the entire poem aloud again. Partners can then take turns reading the poem a third time.
SL.9-10.1; L.9-10.4

Don't Go Gentle Into That Good Expressway

by Luis J. Rodríguez

They say people in New York City are cold,
that they enter like the blackness of night
and rip into you when you shine with the
weakness of a smile. They say, you can't smile
in New York City because it could be
a death warrant. A kind word is a likely
ticket to a back-street mugging. Nobody
cares in New York City.

But I don't know . . . the city seemed refreshing
to me. People were upfront. They yelled,
they laughed, they had no qualms about your worth.
I could walk these streets and face anyone and be
crazier than the craziest dude
and ride the subways looking untouchable
and nobody knew whether to talk to me
or walk away. In most cities
madness seethes below the skin.
In New York City, it storms through the eyes.

And, at least once, New York City
showed me some heart.

In Other Words

be a death warrant invite someone to hurt you
upfront honest and real
had no qualms about did not worry about
seethes grows stronger, starts to boil
bobtail truck a small delivery truck
summon call for
getting sued being blamed if he got hurt
reasoned thought out loud

CCSS Literacy.SL.9-10.1 Initiate and participate effectively in a range of collaborative discussions (one-on-one, in groups, and teacher-led) with diverse partners on grades 9–10 topics, texts, and issues, building on others' ideas and expressing their own clearly and persuasively. Literacy.L.9-10.4 Determine or clarify the meaning of unknown and multiple-meaning words and phrases based on grades 9–10 reading and content, choosing flexibly from a range of strategies.

I had entered a packed expressway when a bobtail
truck in front of me rammed into a stalled car.
Fire then flared out of the truck's hood.
The truck driver dove out the side window
onto the asphalt and struck his head.
As he lay unconscious, we all got out
of our cars; somebody ran to an emergency phone
to summon help.
The rest of us rushed over to the driver.
We looked at each other and figured if we
didn't move him, the truck could explode
and break up over his body. But to move him
meant the risk of getting sued,
a New Yorker reasoned next to me.

In the seconds that followed,
we decided that everyone there
would take a hold of the guy.
Somebody got an arm, another a leg . . .
one guy just placed a hand on the dude's chest.

We carried the truck driver to the side
of the road. An ambulance finally came.
We continued to stand by the dude
until they laid him on a stretcher
and the truck in the distance
burst into a blaze.

About the Poet

Luis J. Rodríguez (1954–) is an award-winning poet, author, and journalist. He captured the life of a gang member in his memoir *Always Running: La Vida Loca—Gang Days in L.A.* He now commits his life to helping kids stay out of gangs and empowering the local Latino community through his cultural center in Los Angeles.

TEACH & PRACTICE

Connect Across Texts

Themes Across Genres The drivers in the poem have to make a difficult choice. In the short story, Rey had to make a choice about helping Mr. Sánchez. Ask: How is the theme of choices shown or treated differently in the short story and the poem?

Possible response:

- *The short story tells mostly about the events that lead up to Rey's choice. The poem focuses on one event and has more descriptive detail.*

RL.9-10.2

Sensory Words

Explain that sensory words are words that help us use our senses of sight, hearing, smell, taste, and touch to understand texts. Say: Sensory words help us imagine the setting and events taking place.

Ask: Can you find a sensory word in the first line of the poem? Confirm that the word *cold* helps readers imagine how the scene feels. Ask: Can you find a sensory word in the second line? What sense does it appeal to?

Possible response:

- Blackness *helps me see what the scene looks like.*

L.9-10.5

ONGOING ASSESSMENT
Have students draw a scene from the poem and label it with sensory words from the poem.

CCSS **Literacy.RL.9-10.2** Determine a theme or central idea of a text and analyze in detail its development over the course of the text, including how it emerges and is shaped and refined by specific details; provide an objective summary of the text. **Literacy.L.9-10.5** Demonstrate understanding of figurative language, word relationships, and nuances in word meanings.

Lesson 5

BEFORE READING

OBJECTIVES

Reading Strategy
- Plan and Monitor: Preview and Set a Purpose; Review Strategies

Literary Analysis
- Analyze Text Features: Article T

TEACH STRATEGIES

A Analyze Text Features: Article

Charts and Graphics Explain how text features visually explain information in nonfiction texts.

Look Into the Text Use the callouts on p. 28 to teach the text features. Point out how words, charts, and graphics work together. Read the first callout and the highlighted sentence. Ask: How does the graphic support the text?

Possible response:
- *The graphic shows that youths volunteer almost twice as much as adults.* RI.9-10.7

B Focus Strategy: Plan and Monitor

Preview and Set a Purpose Read aloud the introduction. Have small groups generate questions they want to answer in the 5W/How Chart.

> **ELL Questioning** Post question starters with *who, what, when, where,* and *why* to help students form purpose-setting questions.

Have students try to answer their questions during the reading. RI.9-10.10

Review Strategies Have students tell which other reading strategy they used as they read the article.

Possible response:
- *The longest paragraph has a lot of facts, so I determined that the main idea is that "youth activism levels are at an all-time high." I can see how the other sentences in this paragraph support the idea.* RI.9-10.2

ONGOING ASSESSMENT
Ask students to explain how charts and graphs can help visualize information.

BEFORE READING The World Is in Their Hands

newspaper article by Eric Feil

Reading Strategies
- ▶ **Plan and Monitor**
- Determine Importance
- Make Inferences
- Ask Questions
- Make Connections
- Synthesize
- Visualize

Analyze Text Features: Article

Newspaper articles often use a combination of words and graphics to get a message across. Charts and other graphics can provide additional useful information. They can also restate or summarize what is in the text.

A

Look into the Text

Written text provides a main idea.

Youth activism levels are at all-time highs. Nearly three-quarters of young adults say they have donated money, clothes, or food to a community or church organization over the past few years.

Graphics provide details that support the main idea.

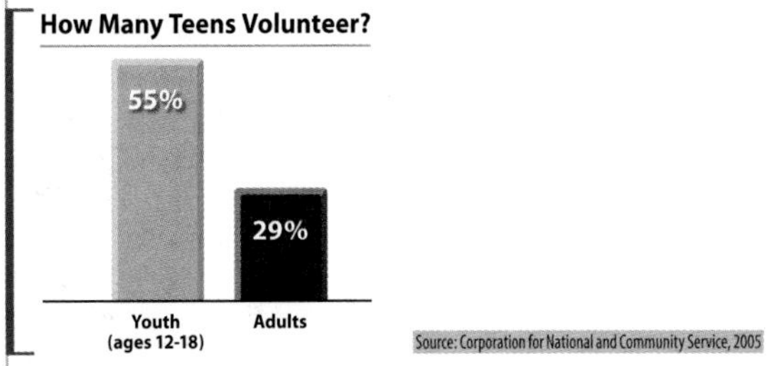

The source for the information helps you decide if the data is reliable.

Focus Strategy ▶ Plan and Monitor

Reading nonfiction is different from reading a short story. Depending on your purpose, or reason, for reading, you may need to read slowly to understand all of the facts, numbers, and examples. Or you may read quickly if your purpose is to scan for one piece of information.

B

Focus Strategy

HOW TO PREVIEW AND SET A PURPOSE

1. **Look for clues about the text.** As you look over, or preview, a text, use visual clues to determine the type of text and its topic.
   - Title and headings show the text's main ideas.
   - Graphics show what subject the text deals with.
   - Photos can show whether the text discusses history or the present day.
   - The overall layout may give clues about the type of text.
2. **Set your purpose.** Think of the questions you want to answer and write them in a **5W/How Chart**. Then read the selection to find the answers. This is your purpose, or reason, for reading.

5W/How Chart

As I read, I want to find out
who ...
what ... kind of youth volunteer?
when ...
where ...
why ... do they volunteer?
how ...

CCSS **Literacy.RI.9-10.2** Determine a central idea of a text and analyze its development over the course of the text, including how it emerges and is shaped and refined by specific details; provide an objective summary of the text. **Literacy.RI.9-10.7** Analyze various accounts of a subject told in different mediums (e.g., a person's life story in both print and multimedia), determining which details are emphasized in each account. **RI.9-10.10** By the end of grade 9, read and comprehend literary nonfiction in the grades 9–10 text complexity band proficiently, with scaffolding as needed at the high end of the range. By the end of grade 10, read and comprehend literary nonfiction at the high end of the grades 9–10 text complexity band independently and proficiently.

NEWSPAPER ARTICLE

The World Is in Their Hands

by Eric Feil

C

Connect Across Texts

In "The Good Samaritan," Rey must decide whether to help a neighbor. What makes people choose to help others?

D

Changing the World

With sincere apologies to that old song, the children are not the future.

They are the present.

They are not going to lead the way one day.

They are leading it right now.

E **Youth activism levels** are at all-time highs. Nearly three-quarters of young adults say they have **donated** money, clothes, or food to a community or church organization over the past few years. They **get involved** at national and local levels, and their numbers are growing. Doing good, not **gaining recognition**, is their **motivation**. 1

"We've seen a huge demand from young people who want their voices

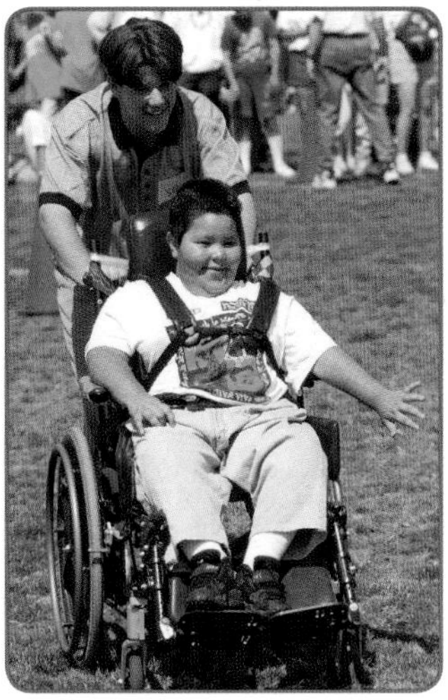

A volunteer helps out at an event for youth with special needs.

1 Text Features
What is the main idea of this paragraph?

Key Vocabulary

- **motivation** *n.*, reason for doing something or thinking a certain way

In Other Words

Youth activism levels The numbers of young people who help others
donated given
get involved join, offer to help
gaining recognition getting attention

Comprehension Coach

Build Reading Power

Assign students to use the software, based on their instructional needs.

Read Silently
- Comprehension questions with immediate feedback
- Glossary support
- Review text evidence

RI.9-10.10

Listen
- Professional model of fluent reading

Record
- Oral reading fluency practice
- Ongoing fluency assessment with immediate feedback

OBJECTIVES

Vocabulary
- Key Vocabulary T

Comprehension & Critical Thinking
- Use Text Evidence T

Literary Analysis
- Analyze Text Features: Article T

BUILD BACKGROUND

C Youth Who Volunteer

Read the title, examine the photograph, and read the caption.

ELL Use Visuals Use the photograph to explain the term *volunteer.* Point to the young man assisting the child. Say: This is a volunteer. He is helping the child. Volunteers help others without getting paid.

Ask: What are some reasons you think young people decide to volunteer?

RI.9-10.5

D Connect Across Texts

Ask students what volunteers have in common with Rey in "The Good Samaritan."

Possible response:
- *At the end of the story, Rey helped Mr. Sánchez without expecting anything in return. This is what volunteers do.*

TEACH & PRACTICE

E Reading Support

1 Text Features Remind students that the first few sentences of a paragraph in a news article are usually the most important. Ask: What is the main idea?

Possible response:
- *More young adults are volunteering now than before.*

RI.9-10.2

CCSS **Literacy.RI.9-10.2** Determine a central idea of a text and analyze its development over the course of the text, including how it emerges and is shaped and refined by specific details; provide an objective summary of the text. **Literacy.RI.9-10.5** Analyze in detail how an author's ideas or claims are developed and refined by particular sentences, paragraphs, or larger portions of a text (e.g., a section or chapter). **Literacy.RI.9-10.10** By the end of grade 9, read and comprehend literary nonfiction in the grades 9–10 text complexity band proficiently, with scaffolding as needed at the high end of the range. By the end of grade 10, read and comprehend literary nonfiction at the high end of the grades 9–10 text complexity band independently and proficiently.

OBJECTIVES

Vocabulary
- Key Vocabulary (T)

Comprehension & Critical Thinking
- Read and Interpret Visuals
- Use Text Evidence (T)

Literary Analysis
- Analyze Text Features: Article (T)

Research Skill
- Formulate Research Questions

TEACH & PRACTICE

(A) Reading Support

2 Text Features Have students use the question above each graph to find out the information shown in each. Ask: What are some ways that young people volunteer?

Possible response:
- *Young people volunteer through religious organizations, school groups, and leadership groups.*

Then ask: What other information do the graphics provide?

Possible response:
- *The graphs also show how many teens volunteer and their reasons for volunteering.*

RI.9-10.7

(B) Analyze Visuals

Interpret the Data Have students identify reasons teens volunteer, as shown in the graph. Ask: Who might ask a teen to volunteer?

Possible responses:
- *a parent, a teacher, a coach, a religious leader*

Reading Support

Monitor Reading Remind students of their purpose for reading. After reading the page and examining the graphics, pause to have students record the answers to any questions on their 5W/How Charts.

RI.9-10.10

heard and who feel they've got something to **contribute** to society," says **Youth Service America** president and CEO Steve Culbertson. "And they're not going to wait until they grow up to do it."

Clearly. Millions of youth volunteers will be out in force again this year, from five-year-olds visiting and decorating senior citizen homes to high school kids tutoring **peers**. Distributing HIV/AIDS educational materials, cleaning up the environment, **registering voters**—the list of projects is almost as limitless as the **enthusiasm** and energy of the people engaged in them. Young people are making a difference in their

(A)

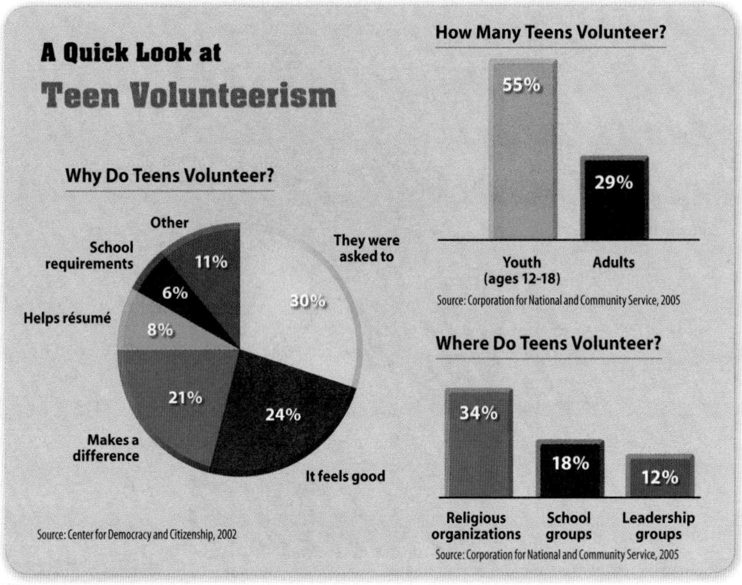

(B) **Interpret the Data** The pie graph says 30% of teens volunteer because they were asked to. Who might have asked them? 2

2 Text Features What are some of the ways people volunteer? What additional information do the graphs provide?

Key Vocabulary
- **contribute** *v.*, to give with others

In Other Words
Youth Service America youth volunteer organization
peers people who are the same age
registering voters signing people up to vote
enthusiasm excitement, eagerness
Data Facts, Information

VOCABULARY

Link Vocabulary and Concepts

Ask questions to link Key Vocabulary with the Essential Question.

EQ **ESSENTIAL QUESTION:**
What influences a person's choices?

Some possible questions:
- *Why might youth today volunteer more than those from other* **generations***?*
- *What is the most common* **motivation** *to volunteer?*
- *How many youth have* **contributed** *money, clothes, or food to church or community groups in recent years?*
- *How does the work of volunteers* **affect** *the community and lives of people they help?*

Have students use the Key Vocabulary words in their responses.

L.9-10.6

CCSS Literacy.RI.9-10.7 Analyze various accounts of a subject told in different mediums (e.g., a person's life story in both print and multimedia), determining which details are emphasized in each account. **Literacy.RI.9-10.10** By the end of grade 9, read and comprehend literary nonfiction in the grades 9–10 text complexity band proficiently, with scaffolding as needed at the high end of the range. By the end of grade 10, read and comprehend literary nonfiction at the high end of the grades 9–10 text complexity band independently and proficiently. **Literacy.L.9-10.6** Acquire and use accurately general academic and domain-specific words and phrases, sufficient for reading, writing, speaking, and listening at the college and career readiness level; demonstrate independence in gathering vocabulary knowledge when considering a word or phrase important to comprehension or expression.

Text Features A volunteer paints a mural to celebrate Youth Service Day. 3

3 Text Features What does the photo lead you to think about volunteering?

communities. These volunteers also learn such life skills as planning events, raising funds, and holding leadership roles and responsibilities.

"Young people **have gotten sort of a negative rap**, when the majority of young people really are involved in their communities in very positive ways," says Carl Nelson. His company, State Farm, was the **Presenting Sponsor of** National Youth Service Day (NYSD) 2005, "a celebration of community service and service learning that goes on year-round."

Today's youth are building a unique background in **altruism**. And they are not going to leave their service history behind them when they enter the workforce. "We know that the one key predictor to lifetime service is whether you did it as a child," Culbertson states. "There's a whole **generation** of young people that have grown up giving back and

Key Vocabulary
- **generation** *n.*, people who are about the same age

In Other Words
have gotten sort of a negative rap are talked about in a bad way
Presenting Sponsor of company that paid for
altruism caring about the well-being of others

Monitor Comprehension
Summarize
On pages 29-31, what is the most important point the author makes about young volunteers in the U.S. today?

TEACH & PRACTICE

C Reading Support

3 Text Features Read the caption and discuss the photograph. Have students describe the actions and attitude of the girl in the photo. Ask: What does this photograph say about volunteering?

Possible responses:
- *Volunteering is fun.*
- *Volunteering involves lots of different types of activities.*

RI.9-10.7

Monitor Comprehension

Summarize Remind students that summarizing requires telling a main idea, not a detail. Suggest that students reread the first sentences of paragraphs, since these sentences usually contain the main ideas.

Possible response:
- *The author's main idea is that large numbers of youths are making a difference by volunteering.*

RI.9-10.2

CONTENT AREA CONNECTIONS

SOCIOLOGY

Research Service Organizations

Conduct Research Provide materials such as brochures, pamphlets, and Web links to well-known service organizations. Have students formulate research questions to explore. For example:

- In what countries do service organizations operate?
- What kinds of services do they provide?
- What projects do service organizations do?
- What are the benefits of being a volunteer?
- What kinds of activities can people volunteer to do?
- How does volunteerism help individuals and communities?

Share Information Students can share their research findings with the class.

W.9-10.7

CCSS Literacy.RI.9-10.2 Determine a central idea of a text and analyze its development over the course of the text, including how it emerges and is shaped and refined by specific details; provide an objective summary of the text. Literacy.RI.9-10.7 Analyze various accounts of a subject told in different mediums (e.g., a person's life story in both print and multimedia), determining which details are emphasized in each account. Literacy.W.9-10.7 Conduct short as well as more sustained research projects to answer a question (including a self-generated question) or solve a problem; narrow or broaden the inquiry when appropriate; synthesize multiple sources on the subject, demonstrating understanding of the subject under investigation.

Lesson 5, continued

READ

OBJECTIVES

Vocabulary
- Key Vocabulary Ⓣ

Reading Strategies
- Plan and Monitor: Use Nonfiction Text Features; Confirm Purpose

Comprehension & Critical Thinking
- Use Text Evidence Ⓣ

Literary Analysis
- Analyze Text Features: Article Ⓣ

Viewing
- Respond to and Interpret Visuals

Writing
- Response to Literature

Grammar
- Verb in the Predicate

TEACH & PRACTICE

A Reading Support

4 Text Features Have students study the data presented in the boxed feature.

ELL Use Visuals Help students identify important information in the boxed feature.

- Write 2.4 billion and 34.3 billion as numbers.
- Use two pie graphs to show the increase in college freshman volunteers.
- Show 3,663% as a fraction.

Then ask: How do the photograph and caption support this information?

Possible response:
- *It shows a real person doing what is described by the data in the boxed feature.*

RI.9-10.7

B Analyze Visuals

Interpret the Data Ask: How does the data support the main ideas in the article?

Possible response:
- *The data proves that volunteerism among young people is increasing.*

RI.9-10.2

making that a **fundamental** part of their lives and it's not something you give up."

Not when they are so **engaged**, so passionate. Not where events like NYSD show them that there is a **diverse** group of peers striving for a common goal: a better world for everyone. "They're the most **tolerant** generation we've ever seen in history," Culbertson says. "They can't imagine that somebody should be left out of society simply because they're black or they're gay or they have a disability or they come from an ethnic background that's unusual. They just don't look at those differences as anything more than just part of what it means to be a

A

Volunteer Work:
By the Numbers

Teenagers volunteer 2.4 billion hours annually — worth $34.3 billion to the U.S. economy.
Source: Independent Sector/Gallup, 1996, and 1999 hourly value

82.6% of incoming college freshmen did volunteer work, compared to 66% in 1989.
Source: UCLA/Higher Education Research Institute Annual Freshmen Survey, 2001

The number of high school students involved in service learning increased 3,663% in the past decade from 81,000 to 2,967,000.
Source: U.S. Department of Education, 1999

A library volunteer keeps his audience's attention. 4

B **Interpret the Data** How do the numbers in this boxed feature support the main ideas of this article?

4 Text Features How do the picture and caption support the data in the boxed feature?

In Other Words
fundamental basic and important
engaged interested
diverse mixed
tolerant accepting, open-minded

32 Unit 1 Choices

GRAMMAR

Verb in the Predicate

Teach/Model Display the transparency. Remind students that the predicate is one part of a complete sentence. Use the example sentences to show the three different functions of the predicate.

Practice A. Guide students in identifying the subject of the sentence as they decide on a verb that fits with it and with the rest of the predicate. Choose some of their suggestions to write on the transparency. **B.** After partners talk and write about a volunteer experience, have each student read a favorite sentence aloud and ask the group to identify the predicate.
L.9-10.1.b

Grammar & Writing Practice Book, pp. 7–8

GRAMMAR SKILLS PATH

1	Kinds of Sentences
2	Subjects and Predicates
3	Noun in the Subject
4	Verb in the Predicate ELL Language & Grammar Lab
5	Review: Complete Sentences

Grammar Transparency 4

What's the Most Important Word in the Predicate?
The Verb

GRAMMAR VERB IN THE PREDICATE 4

- The **complete predicate** in a sentence often tells what the subject does. It can be one word or several words. The **verb** shows the action.
  Volunteers **spend** time with others.
- Sometimes the predicate tells what the subject has. It uses these **verbs**:
  Our club **has** ideas for many projects.
  We **have** a special interest in our neighborhood.
- Other times, the predicate tells what the subject is or is like. The **verb** is a form of **be**.
  Each project **is** helpful.
  We **are** great volunteers.
  I **am** president of the club.

Try It

A. Complete each predicate with a verb. Possible answers:
1. Our neighborhood ___has___ a new project.
2. Volunteers ___paint___ the houses.
3. They ___fix___ broken windows.
4. The project ___builds___ lasting friendships.
5. Our neighborhood ___is___ a better place now.

B. Tell a partner about a time when you were a volunteer. Write three sentences. Use verbs such as help, work, am, is, are, has, and have. Sentences will vary.

CCSS Literacy RI.9-10.2 Determine a central idea of a text and analyze its development over the course of the text, including how it emerges and is shaped and refined by specific details; provide an objective summary of the text. Literacy.RI.9-10.7 Analyze various accounts of a subject told in different mediums (e.g., a person's life story in both print and multimedia), determining which details are emphasized in each account. Literacy.L.9-10.1.b Use various types of phrases (noun, verb, adjectival, adverbial, participial, prepositional, absolute) and clauses (independent, dependent, noun, relative, adverbial) to convey specific meanings and add variety and interest to writing or presentations.

human. They don't let those differences get in the way of progress. That's what makes this the greatest generation I think we've ever seen in this country, and nobody knows it." **C**

They do now. ❖

ANALYZE The World Is in Their Hands

1. **Recall and Interpret** According to Steve Culbertson, why are more young people volunteering? Do the graphics support his idea? Explain.
2. **Vocabulary** What does the graph on page 30 say about the percentage of volunteers in the teen **generation** compared with adults?
3. **Analyze Text Features: Article** Which graphic gave you the most useful information about the article's topic? Why? Compare your choice with a partner's.
4. **Focus Strategy Preview and Set a Purpose** Reread the **5W/How Chart** you began on page 28. Did you find answers to all of your questions? Share your questions and answers with a partner. **D**

Return to the Text

Reread and Write Steve Culbertson says that today's youth are the "greatest generation I think we've ever seen in this country." Find two examples in the text that support his opinion. Do you agree? Support your opinion. **E**

TEACH & PRACTICE

C Reading Support

Confirm Purpose After students read the last sentence, have them review the questions in their 5W/How charts. Tell them to record new answers they found while reading the last section. Then suggest that students scan the reading for any questions that remain unanswered. Ask them to work in pairs or small groups to share what they have learned.

APPLY

D ANALYZE

1. **Recall and Interpret** More youth volunteer because they want to make a difference. The graphics support his idea—they show how many young people volunteer and why they do it. The photos show teens volunteering.
RI.9-10.7
2. **Vocabulary** The graph on p. 30 says that the teen generation volunteers more than adults.
L.9-10.6
3. **Analyze Text Features: Article** The pie graph gives the most useful information on the article's topic, because it tells why youths volunteer.
RI.9-10.7
4. **Focus Strategy: Preview and Set a Purpose** Have partners share and compare answers, adding to and revising their charts as needed.
RI.9-10.10

E Return to the Text

Discuss what types of facts students should look for. For example, six percent of youth volunteered because their school required it. Ask: Does this support Mr. Culbertson's opinion?
RI.9-10.1; W.9-10.9.b

Unit Project

Progress Check Allow time for students to work on their unit projects. Meet with individuals and/or groups to provide guidance and check on their progress.

myNGconnect.com

- **Unit Project Planning Tools**
- **Unit Project Evaluation Rubric**

Interactive Reading

Have students reread and mark "The World Is in Their Hands" within the Edge Interactive Practice Book to apply their knowledge of nonfiction text features and to practice the Focus Strategy—Plan and Monitor: Preview and Set a Purpose.

Edge Interactive Practice Book, pp. 11–16

CCSS **Literacy.RI.9-10.1** Cite strong and thorough textual evidence to support analysis of what the text says explicitly as well as inferences drawn from the text. **Literacy.RI.9-10.7** Analyze various accounts of a subject told in different mediums (e.g., a person's life story in both print and multimedia), determining which details are emphasized in each account. **Literacy.RI.9-10.10** By the end of grade 9, read and comprehend literary nonfiction in the grades 9–10 text complexity band proficiently, with scaffolding as needed at the high end of the range. By the end of grade 10, read and comprehend literary nonfiction at the high end of the grades 9–10 text complexity band independently and proficiently. **Literacy.W.9-10.9.b** Apply grades 9–10 Reading standards to literary nonfiction (e.g., "Delineate and evaluate the argument and specific claims in a text, assessing whether the reasoning is valid and the evidence is relevant and sufficient; identify false statements and fallacious reasoning"). **Literacy.L.9-10.6** Acquire and use accurately general academic and domain-specific words and phrases, sufficient for reading, writing, speaking, and listening at the college and career readiness level; demonstrate independence in gathering vocabulary knowledge when considering a word or phrase important to comprehension or expression.

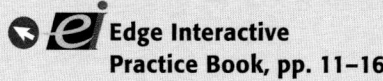

READ

OBJECTIVES

Reading Strategy
- Plan and Monitor: Preview and Predict

Comprehension & Critical Thinking
- Use Text Evidence Ⓣ

Literary Analysis
- Analyze Text Features: Article Ⓣ
- Compare Literature: Graphics

TEACH & PRACTICE

Preview and Predict Have students use text features to preview and make predictions about the article:

- Based on the title and subtitles, what might the article be about?
- Look at the map and the photograph. What types of places do you think will be described in this article?

RI.9-10.7; RI.9-10.10

Read and Check Comprehension Read the two features about volunteerism. When students are finished, ask a comprehension question: How did the youths described in this article make a difference?

Possible responses:
- *Christina and Danny helped raise money to build schools for Maya Indian children in Mexico.*
- *Shawn started an organization that improves New York City neighborhoods.*

RI.9-10.2

Connect Across Texts Review the graphics in this article and in "The World Is in Their Hands." Have students describe the similarities and differences between the graphics in the two selections.

RI.9-10.7

Making a Difference

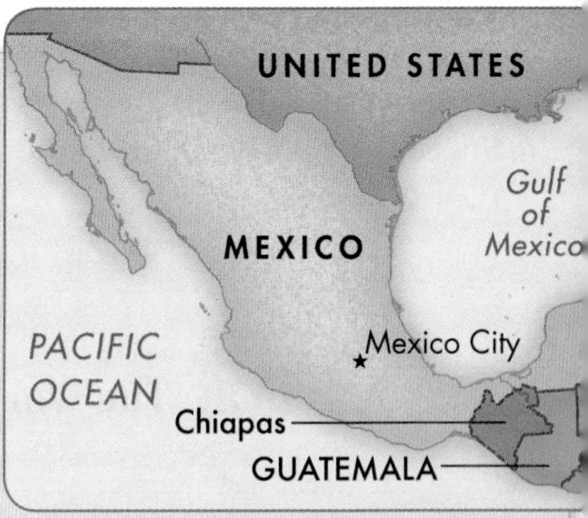

Schools for Indigenous Children

Chiapas, Mexico

Christina Fletes and Danny Acosta

In Chiapas, Mexico, on the border with Guatemala, thousands of Maya Indian children do not have easy **access** to schools. To get a formal education, children must walk miles. They are often **ridiculed** by teachers and classmates once they arrive. **In partnership with** the group Schools for Chiapas, Danny Acosta and Christina Fletes organized their high school to raise money to help build schools for these children. They feel **connected to** this issue, as their families are from Mexico and Central America. Through their work, they have created new educational opportunities for indigenous children.

Garden Angels

Brooklyn, New York

Planting the seeds of a better tomorrow is the perfect **metaphor for** youth volunteers. Shawn Henry **took it literally**. Today, neighborhoods throughout his hometown of Brooklyn are reaping the benefits of his Garden Angels project. Founded in 2002, Garden Angels is a group of 50 core members and some 200 other youths who are dedicated to improving life in New York. But Shawn wants to get even more young people involved in **civic activities**. He helps plan workshops and events for other students in NYC so that they too can build the skills to plant their own seeds for a better city.

Shawn Henry

In Other Words

Indigenous Native
access ways to get
ridiculed teased, made fun of
In partnership with Working together with
connected to felt especially close to
metaphor for way to describe
took it literally actually did it
civic activities things to help the community

CCSS **Literacy.RI.9-10.2** Determine a central idea of a text and analyze its development over the course of the text, including how it emerges and is shaped and refined by specific details; provide an objective summary of the text. **Literacy.RI.9-10.7** Analyze various accounts of a subject told in different mediums (e.g., a person's life story in both print and multimedia), determining which details are emphasized in each account. **RI.9-10.10** By the end of grade 9, read and comprehend literary nonfiction in the grades 9–10 text complexity band proficiently, with scaffolding as needed at the high end of the range. By the end of grade 10, read and comprehend literary nonfiction at the high end of the grades 9–10 text complexity band independently and proficiently.

Reflect and Assess

- The Good Samaritan
- Don't Go Gentle Into That Good Expressway
- The World Is in Their Hands

EQ What Influences a Person's Choices?

Reading

Critical Thinking

1. **Analyze** Review the **Ranking Chart** on page 10. Then talk with a partner about how the statements relate to characters like Rey and the real-life volunteers in "The World Is in Their Hands."
2. **Interpret** Steve Culbertson says, "There's a whole **generation** of young people that have grown up giving back and making that a fundamental part of their lives." What does he mean? Explain whether this statement is true for Rey in "The Good Samaritan."
3. **Compare** What **affects** Rey's decision to help Mr. Sánchez clean a neighbor's yard? How does this compare with Shawn Henry's **motivation** to clean up his own neighborhood?
4. **Speculate** What would Mr. Sánchez say about the young people in his neighborhood? What do you think Steve Culbertson would say to Mr. Sánchez if he could?
5. **Judge** Is there ever a bad motivation for choosing to help others who are in need? Support your opinion with examples from the selections and your own experience.
6. **Synthesize** What do you think is the motivation for most people to do good deeds? Explain, using examples from both selections.

Writing

Write About Literature

Order-of-Importance Paragraph Brainstorm three or four reasons that teens choose to help others. Write a paragraph presenting these reasons in order of importance, ending with the reason that you think is most important. Use examples from both selections to support your ideas.

Vocabulary

Key Vocabulary Review

Oral Review Work with a partner. Use these words to complete the paragraph.

affect	**disrespect**	**privilege**
conflicts	**generation**	**responsible**
contribute	**motivations**	

Young people of today's __(1)__ are finding ways to give back or __(2)__ to their communities. The __(3)__ for volunteering are varied. Some may feel they enjoy more than their share of security and special __(4)__ in a world filled with violent __(5)__. Other youths volunteer because of values learned from their parents and grandparents. To avoid volunteering would seem like __(6)__ or rudeness for their families. Whatever makes them feel __(7)__ for helping others, "good samaritans" everywhere __(8)__ their communities in positive ways.

Writing Application Write your ideas about how teenagers can be **responsible**. Use at least five Key Vocabulary words.

Fluency

Read with Ease: Expression

Assess your reading fluency with the passage in the Reading Handbook, p. 751. Then complete the self-check below.

1. My expression did/did not sound natural.
2. My words correct per minute: ________

Writing

Write About Literature

Edge Interactive Practice Book, p. 17

Order-of-Importance Paragraph
Remind students that their paragraphs should begin with reasons that young people do good deeds, and the next sentences should explain the reasons. Point out that they should also include words such as *first*, *second*, and *last*.
W.9-10.1

Vocabulary

Key Vocabulary Review

1. *generation* 2. *contribute*
3. *motivations* 4. *privilege*
5. *conflicts* 6. *disrespect*
7. *responsible* 8. *affect*
L.9-10.6

Fluency

Read with Ease: Expression

Ensure that students complete the self-check.
RL.9-10.10

Lesson 6

REFLECT AND ASSESS

OBJECTIVES

Vocabulary
- Key Vocabulary T

Reading Fluency
- Expression T

Comprehension & Critical Thinking
- Compare Across Texts
- Use Text Evidence T

Literary Analysis
- Evaluate Literature

Writing
- Form: Paragraph

Reading

Critical Thinking

1. **Analyze** Have students recall their responses to the ranking activity and discuss how the statements relate to what they have read.
2. **Interpret** Today's teens choose to volunteer because they believe it is the right thing to do. Rey makes a similar decision to help his neighbor.
3. **Compare** Rey cleans the yard for a reward. Shawn Henry's motivation is to clean up his neighborhood so it is cleaner and safer.
RL.9-10.3
4. **Speculate** Mr. Sánchez might say the youth in his neighborhood help some, but they show disrespect. Mr. Culbertson might point out that the youth today help much more than other generations.
5. **Judge** Students may point out that the characters and people in these selections are motivated to help because it is the right thing to do.
RL.9-10.1
6. **Synthesize**
   - The boys help Mr. Sánchez for rewards. However, Rey helped Mr. Sánchez because of his father.
   - Many youths volunteer because it feels good to help or to improve their résumé.

   RL.9-10.1

ASSESS & RETEACH

Assessments Handbook, pp. 1b–1e

Have students complete the **Reader Reflection**. Then give students the **Cluster Test** to measure their progress. Group students as needed for reteaching.

CCSS **Literacy.RL.9-10.1** Cite strong and thorough textual evidence to support analysis of what the text says explicitly as well as inferences drawn from the text. **Literacy.RL.9-10.3** Analyze how complex characters (e.g., those with multiple or conflicting motivations) develop over the course of a text, interact with other characters, and advance the plot or develop the theme. **Literacy.RL.9-10.10** By the end of grade 9, read and comprehend literature, including stories, dramas, and poems, in the grades 9–10 text complexity band proficiently, with scaffolding as needed at the high end of the range. By the end of grade 10, read and comprehend literature, including stories, dramas, and poems, at the high end of the grades 9–10 text complexity band independently and proficiently. **Literacy.W.9-10.1** Write arguments to support claims in an analysis of substantive topics or texts, using valid reasoning and relevant and sufficient evidence. **Literacy.L.9-10.6** Acquire and use accurately general academic and domain-specific words and phrases, sufficient for reading, writing, speaking, and listening at the college and career readiness level; demonstrate independence in gathering vocabulary knowledge when considering a word or phrase important to comprehension or expression.

Lesson 7

INTEGRATE THE LANGUAGE ARTS

OBJECTIVES

Language Function
- Ask and Answer Questions

Literary Analysis
- Analyze Theme

Grammar
- Complete Sentences

Grammar

Write Complete Sentences

Grammar Transparency 5

Review Use the transparency to review complete sentences. Then conduct the activity on p. 36. Review that both the subject and the predicate may be one word or a phrase and that a phrase is a group of related words.

Oral Practice Make sure students identify the correct subject and predicate.

Written Practice Rey knocks on the door. Mrs. Sánchez opens the door. Rey wants to swim. Mr. Sánchez …
L.9-10.1.b

Language Development

Ask and Answer Questions

Evaluate with the Language Acquisition Rubric.

Assessments Handbook, p. lo

Give and Follow Instructions

Confirm that students' oral instructions are correct and complete.
SL.9-10.1.b

Literary Analysis

Analyze Theme

Encourage students to consider the unit theme—choices. Be sure students provide evidence from the selection to support their themes.
RL.9-10.2

Edge Interactive Practice Book, p. 18

GRAMMAR SKILLS PATH
1 Kinds of Sentences
2 Subjects and Predicates
3 Noun in the Subject
4 Verb in the Predicate
▶ 5 Review: Complete Sentences ELL Language & Grammar Lab

INTEGRATE THE LANGUAGE ARTS

Grammar

Write Complete Sentences

Sentences are the building blocks for most writing. In formal English, a sentence expresses a complete idea.

The boy helps his neighbor.

A sentence is complete if it has two parts. The part called the **subject** tells whom or what the sentence is about. The complete subject may be one word or several words.

The boy helps his neighbor.
Mr. Sánchez needs help.

The part called the **predicate** tells what the subject *does*, *has*, or *is*. The complete predicate may be one word or several words.

The boy **works for a reward**.
He **is disappointed**.

Oral Practice (1–5) Find five complete sentences in the selections you just read. Tell a partner what the subject and predicate are in each sentence.

Written Practice (6–10) On your paper, use these phrases in complete sentences.

6. knocks on the door
7. Mrs. Sánchez
8. wants to swim
9. makes a promise
10. the friends

Language Development

Ask and Answer Questions

Role-Play Work with a partner to act out an interview with one of the people in the selections you read. Take turns asking the person questions that start with one of these words: *Who*, *What*, *When*, *Where*, *How*, *Why*. Listen to the person's answers. Then switch roles.

Literary Analysis

Analyze Theme

A **theme** is the central idea or message of a selection. The theme is a general statement that the author makes about people or life.

In some works, the theme is **stated** directly. But in most cases, the theme is **implied**, or hinted at, in the selection. The reader must infer what the truth or message is from what the writer provides. To discover the implied theme, look for clues in the events, characters, and dialogue.

Study the following details from "The Good Samaritan."

Event:	Character:	Dialogue:
Rey imagines what his dad will say if he doesn't help Mr. Sánchez.	Rey loves and respects his father.	Rey says: "I'm doing it for my dad really, not for Mr. Sánchez."

Theme:

With a partner, identify the central theme of "The Good Samaritan." Add more evidence from the story that supports this theme. Share ideas with the class.

Language Development

Give and Follow Instructions

Pair Talk Think of something you have done to help someone. Give your partner instructions that tell how to do the same thing. Have your partner pantomime following your instructions. Then have your partner describe how he or she solved a similar problem. Listen and repeat as your partner gives instructions.

GRAMMAR

Review: Complete Sentences

Review Display the transparency. Read each example sentence, and ask the group to find the most important word in the complete subject. Circle it. Review that verbs tell what the subject *does, is,* or *has*. Have students find the verb and tell what it shows.

A. Oral Practice Model how to complete the first sentence. Then have students suggest a noun or a verb for the remaining sentences.

B. Written Practice Work through the example. Explain that some sentences have no errors. Have the group tell you how to edit the paragraph. Ask a volunteer to read the corrected paragraph aloud.
L.9-10.1.b

Grammar & Writing Practice Book, pp. 1–2

Grammar Transparency 5

Write Complete Sentences

GRAMMAR REVIEW: COMPLETE SENTENCES 5

Remember: You need a **subject** and a **predicate** to make a complete sentence. Often, the most important word in the subject is a **noun**. Every predicate needs a **verb**.

Let's circle the most important word in each subject.
Let's underline each verb.

Subject	Predicate
Our community	depends on volunteers.
Some people	have more than others.
Kids from the high school	clean the park on weekends.
The volunteers	are a big help.

Try It

A. Add a subject, a verb, or a predicate. Say the complete sentence.
Possible responses:
1. Volunteers __make__ many kinds of choices.
2. Sometimes a choice __is hard__.
3. __Ellie__ chooses to give up her Saturdays.
4. She __volunteers at a nursing home__.
5. __Ellie__ helps people. They __have__ respect for her.

B. Edit the paragraph. Fix five mistakes. The first is done for you.

A neighbor once broke a promise to you. Now the neighbor ^needs your help. You ^choose to help the neighbor anyway. ~~Remembers~~ The person remembers your good deed. Do your choices make a difference? ^Choices influence others. Next time, that person ^makes a better choice. He helps someone else.

CCSS **Literacy RL.9-10.2** Determine a theme or central idea of a text and analyze in detail its development over the course of the text, including how it emerges and is shaped and refined by specific details; provide an objective summary of the text. **Literacy.SL.9-10.1.b** Work with peers to set rules for collegial discussions and decision-making (e.g., informal consensus, taking votes on key issues, presentation of alternate views), clear goals and deadlines, and individual roles as needed. **Literacy.L.9-10.1.b** Use various types of phrases (noun, verb, adjectival, adverbial, participial, prepositional, absolute) and clauses (independent, dependent; noun, relative, adverbial) to convey specific meanings and add variety and interest to writing or presentations.

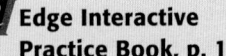

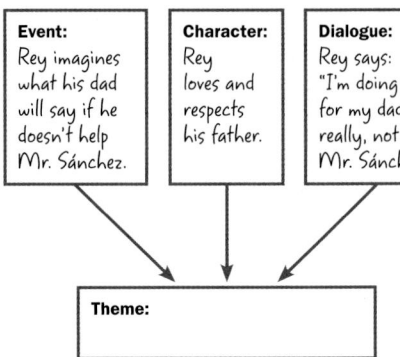

Lesson 8

INTEGRATE THE LANGUAGE ARTS

Vocabulary Study

Prefixes

A **prefix** is a word part added to the beginning of a word. The prefix *pre-* means "before," so *preview* means "look *before*." Here are more prefixes:

PREFIX	ORIGIN	MEANING
auto-	Greek	self
inter-	Latin	between
off-	Middle-English	from

Write the meaning of each word below. Check your definitions using a print or online dictionary. Then add entries for each prefix to a Prefix Chart.

1. intersect **2.** autocracy **3.** offspring

Research / Speaking

Oral Report

Social Studies: Good Samaritan Laws Find out what "Good Samaritan" laws are and the problems they are written to solve. Come up with a question you have about them. Then investigate these online sources:

myNGconnect.com

- **Search online for The Emerson Good Samaritan Food Donation Act.**
- **Check out the topic on the American Medical Association's Web site.**

Write a definition of Good Samaritan laws, including examples of how they work. Then present your findings in an oral report to the class.

Language and Learning Handbook, page 702

Writing

Write a Definition Paragraph

In a **definition paragraph**, you explain the meaning of a big concept. You restate the word's dictionary meaning and give examples that show what the word means to you. Write a definition paragraph for *responsibility*, *duty*, or a similar "big idea."

1. **Prewrite** Brainstorm a list of ideas about what the word means. Include examples from your life.
2. **Draft** Organize your ideas in a chart.

Word: duty	
Dictionary Definition: what a person is required or expected to do (by law, family, friends, society)	
Synonyms: responsibility, job, task, assignment	
Example 1: taking care of my little brother	
Example 2: staying in school	
My Definition: doing what you have to do	

3. **Revise** Think about whether your examples support your main definition. Add, move, or replace examples to make your definition clearer.
4. **Edit and Proofread** Work with a partner to correct spelling and grammar mistakes.
5. **Publish** Publish your definition paragraph by creating a class dictionary of terms.

Definition Paragraph Model

Duty

The dictionary says, "A duty is something you are required to do by law, family, friends, or society." [dictionary definition] I think duty also means doing something because it is right. For example, no one tells me that I have to look out for my little brother, but I still do it because I care about him. [example 1] Also, the law says I have to go to school until I'm older, but I feel like staying in school is my duty if I want a good education. [example 2] So, to me, duty is more than what others require of you. It's what you require of yourself. [conclusion with your definition]

(Labels: word; dictionary definition; example 1; example 2; conclusion with your definition)

Writing Handbook, page 784

OBJECTIVES

Vocabulary
- Prefixes Ⓣ

Research Skills
- Formulate Research Questions
- Gather Information

Speaking
- Oral Report

Writing
- Writing Process
- Form: Definition Paragraph Ⓣ

Vocabulary Study

Prefixes

1. intersect; crossing of two lines

2. autocracy; government ruled by one person

3. offspring; an animal's babies

Have students make a list of words with the Greek, Latin, and Middle English prefixes in the chart.
L.9-10.4.c

Edge Interactive Practice Book, p. 19

Research/Speaking

Oral Report

Social Studies: Good Samaritan Laws These laws protect people who help others in an emergency.

See **Language and Learning Handbook** p. 726 for further instruction.
W.9-10.7; SL.9-10.4

Writing

Writing a Definition Paragraph

1. **Prewrite** Have students list their responsibilities at home and school.
2. **Draft** Model completing the chart.
3. **Revise** Model revising the definition by making examples more clear.
4. **Edit and Proofread** Have students work with a partner to correct spelling and grammar errors.
5. **Publish** Assemble finished papers into a dictionary of terms.

See **Writing Handbook** p. 784 for further instruction.
W.9-10.2

Writing Rubric **Definition Paragraph**

Exceptional	• Paragraph addresses topic by showing a clear definition. • Examples are detailed and relevant to the topic. • Sentences are complete.
Competent	• Paragraph pertains to topic. • Examples are adequate. • Sentences are complete with no more than one sentence error.
Developing	• Paragraph may stray from topic. • Examples are loosely connected to topic. • Sentences are sometimes incomplete.
Beginning	• Paragraph does not address topic. • Examples are not clearly connected to topic. • Sentences are often incomplete.

CCSS **Literacy.W.9-10.2** Write informative/explanatory texts to examine and convey complex ideas, concepts, and information clearly and accurately through the effective selection, organization, and analysis of content. **Literacy.W.9-10.7** Conduct short as well as more sustained research projects to answer a question (including a self-generated question) or solve a problem; narrow or broaden the inquiry when appropriate; synthesize multiple sources on the subject, demonstrating understanding of the subject under investigation. **Literacy.SL.9-10.4** Present information, findings, and supporting evidence clearly, concisely, and logically such that listeners can follow the line of reasoning and the organization, development, substance, and style are appropriate to purpose, audience, and task. **Literacy.L.9-10.4.c** Consult general and specialized reference materials (e.g., dictionaries, glossaries, thesauruses), both print and digital, to find the pronunciation of a word or determine or clarify its precise meaning, its part of speech, or its etymology.

Lesson 9

WORKPLACE WORKSHOP

OBJECTIVES

Vocabulary
- Content Area Vocabulary: Legal Profession

Research and Writing
- Conduct an Informational Interview

ENGAGE & CONNECT

A Activate Prior Knowledge

Introduce Ask students what they know about lawyers, judges, and courts. Then read the introduction.

TEACH & PRACTICE

B Jobs in the Legal Profession

Use the Chart Compare jobs in the legal profession. Discuss which career would be best for a person with each of these skills:

- strong organizational skills
- good research skills
- good public speaking skills

C Conduct an Informational Interview

Brainstorm Questions Ask: What do you want to know about the work done inside a law office?

Possible responses:
- *What are the responsibilities?*
- *What is a typical day like?*
- *What tasks are the most challenging?*

Telephone Skills Model how to make a business call:

1. Identify yourself and explain your purpose for calling.
2. Ask if there is someone who would be willing to speak with you about his or her work.
3. Find out when it is convenient for that person to speak with you. Make an appointment and thank the person.

W.9-10.7

ONGOING ASSESSMENT

Have students role-play conducting the informational interview. Did they follow the interview guidelines?

SL.9-10.1

Workplace Workshop

Inside a Law Office

A People in the legal profession work to apply local, state, or federal laws to protec people, businesses, and even ideas. Some people in this profession argue cases in a courtroom. Others do their work entirely in an office, preparing cases that ar settled without a courtroom trial.

Jobs in the Legal Profession

B To be successful, a law office needs people to do a variety of jobs. Each job requires specific training, education, and work experience.

Job	Responsibilities	Education/Training Required
Legal Secretary 1	• Types and files legal documents • Answers the telephone • Updates lawyers' calendars • Assists in legal research	• High school diploma • Computer training • On-the-job training
Paralegal 2	• Interviews witnesses • Investigates facts • Does legal research • Helps lawyers prepare agreements and get ready for court	• Associate's degree in paralegal studies *or* • College degree plus certificate of paralegal studies
Lawyer 3	• Writes legal contracts • May argue cases in court • Helps people and companies reach agreements	• College degree • Law school degree • Pass a state bar exam

Conduct an Informational Interview

C Find out what a job in the legal profession would be like.

1. From the chart above, choose the job that interests you most. Then prepare five interview questions about the job you chose.
2. Call a law firm. You can find one under "Attorneys" in the yellow pages of your local telephone book, or search for local attorneys on the Internet.
3. Explain that you are a student interested in learning about a career in the lega profession. Ask if someone in that career would be willing to talk with you for a few minutes about his or her work.
4. Interview the person. Take notes and share what you learned with other students interested in the same career. Save the information in a professiona career portfolio.

myNGconnect.com
- **Learn more about the legal profession.**
- **Download a form to evaluate whether you would like to work in this field.**
- **Download an interview form.**

Language and Learning Handbc page 702

VOCABULARY

Content Area Vocabulary: Legal Profession

Build vocabulary related to the content area of law.

POLITICAL SCIENCE

Teach/Model Use the Make Words Your Own routine (*see the Vocabulary tab*) and the sample sentences below to introduce these words from the workshop.

court (kort)

*Criminal trials are held in **court**.*

• **evidence** (e-vu-duns)

*A lawyer uses **evidence** to prove the facts of a case.*

witness (**wit**-nis)

*The **witness** saw the crime being committed and will appear in court to testify.*

judge (juj)

*A **judge** makes decisions in a court of law.*

Practice Have students use the words to describe a television show, movie, or news story they have seen recently. Help them identify the different legal professions that were shown in the story.

Apply Set up a law office scenario and have students role-play the various professions. Students can work in groups of three: a legal secretary, a paralegal, and a lawyer.

L.9-10.6

• Academic Vocabulary

CCSS **Literacy.W.9-10.7** Conduct short as well as more sustained research projects to answer a question (including a self-generated question) or solve a problem; narrow or broaden the inquiry when appropriate; synthesize multiple sources on the subject, demonstrating understanding of the subject under investigation. **Literacy.SL.9-10.1** Initiate and participate effectively in a range of collaborative discussions (one-on-one, in groups, and teacher-led) with diverse partners on grades 9–10 topics, texts, and issues, building on others' ideas and expressing their own clearly and persuasively. **Literacy.L.9-10.6** Acquire and use accurately general academic and domain-specific words and phrases, sufficient for reading, writing, speaking, and listening at the college and career readiness level; demonstrate independence in gathering vocabulary knowledge when considering a word or phrase important to comprehension or expression.

Use Word Parts

A

Bakers often prepare a big batch of basic dough. They can add sugar to the dough to change it into coffee cakes or other sweet pastries.

Many base words are like the basic dough. When you add an affix to the base word, you change its meaning. A prefix is an affix added to the beginning of the base word. A suffix is an affix added to the end. If you know what each part of the new word means, you can often figure out its meaning.

Make Meaning from Word Parts

B

Work with a partner to learn the meaning of some base words, prefixes, and suffixes.

1. Write each base word, prefix, and suffix on a separate card.
2. Mix and match cards to make a new word. Check a dictionary to confirm that you made a real word.
3. Have your partner give the meanings of the parts and the whole word.
4. Check the meaning in a print or online dictionary.
5. Switch roles. Continue until you cannot make any more words.

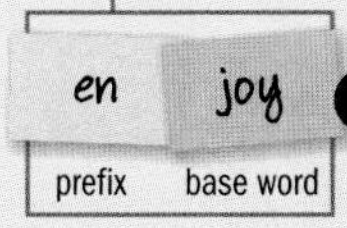

Base Word	Meaning
caution	care
connected	linked
history	past
joy	happiness
pay	give money

Prefix	Meaning
en-, em- (Latin)	to be in *or* to put in a certain way
inter- (Latin)	between
non- (Latin)	not
pre- (Latin)	before

Suffix	Meaning
-ic (Greek)	relating to
-ful (Old English)	full of
-ment (Latin)	action *or* result
-less (Old English)	free from

Put the Strategy to Use

C

When you come to a word you do not know, use this strategy to check its parts.

1. Look for a prefix or suffix and cover it.
2. Define the base word.
3. Uncover the prefix or suffix and determine its meaning.
4. Put the meanings of the word parts together to define the whole word.

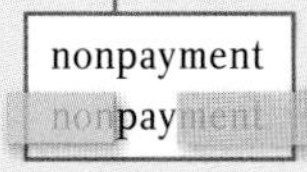

TRY IT ▸ Read the following sentences. Use the strategy described above to write the meaning of the words printed in blue.

1. Dinosaurs are prehistoric.
2. The robin in the poem is symbolic of spring.
3. Coral and algae have an interdependent relationship.
4. Natural gas, coal, and oil are nonrenewable resources.
5. There is no such thing as a frictionless surface.

Reading Handbook, page 733

Lesson 10

VOCABULARY WORKSHOP

OBJECTIVES

Vocabulary

- Strategy: Use Structural Analysis (affixes) T

ENGAGE & CONNECT

A Build Background

Connect Explain: Adding ingredients to basic bread dough changes the dough. Similarly, adding affixes to a base word changes the word's meaning.

TEACH & PRACTICE

B Make Meaning from Word Parts

Use Word Cards Have students use cards to make words. Explain that not all combinations of base words, prefixes, and suffixes make a real word. Have students check the meaning of their words in a dictionary, glossary, or thesaurus.

ELL Rephrase and Demonstrate Demonstrate mixing the prefix card *inter-* with the base word card *pay.* Say: *Interpay* is not a real word.

Also explain that sometimes when a suffix is added, the spelling of the base word changes slightly. For example: *history* + *ic* = *historic.*

Possible responses:

- *precaution, interconnected, historic, enjoy, joyful, prepay, payment, nonpayment*

C Put the Strategy to Use

Try It Tell students they need to decode words before figuring out their meanings. Model decoding a word using sound-letter relationships, affixes, and/or root words. Remind students to revisit the four steps of the strategy as they define the words.

L.9-10.4; L.9-10.4.b; L.9-10.4.c; L.9-10.4.d

ONGOING ASSESSMENT

Have students write sentences using each of the base words in the chart with a prefix or suffix.

DIFFERENTIATED INSTRUCTION

Additional Vocabulary Practice

Use these strategies to help students practice structural analysis.

Struggling Readers

Combine Word Parts Work with students to make word cards for the following base words: *arrange, commit, verbal, trust.* Have students use the prefixes and suffixes from the workshop to create words: *prearrange, commitment, nonverbal, entrust.* Have students use the words in sentences.

English Language Learners ELL

Identify Word Parts Provide students with the following word cards: *successful, premade, enclose,* and *advancement.* Work with students to identify the base word and the prefix or suffix. Have students remove the prefix or suffix from the word to clarify that they are word parts. Then have students put the words back together. Help students define the words using the chart from the workshop.

Challenge

Mix and Match Word Parts Have students create word cards for the affixes *re-, dis-,* and *-less,* and the base words *agree, attach, comfort, name, adjust,* and *blame.* Have students mix and match cards to generate words such as *reattach, disagree, blameless, nameless, readjust,* and *discomfort.*

CCSS **Literacy.L.9-10.4** Determine or clarify the meaning of unknown and multiple-meaning words and phrases based on grades 9–10 reading and content, choosing flexibly from a range of strategies. **Literacy.L.9-10.4.b** Identify and correctly use patterns of word changes that indicate different meanings or parts of speech (e.g., analyze, analysis, analytical; advocate, advocacy). **Literacy.L.9-10.4.c** Consult general and specialized reference materials (e.g., dictionaries, glossaries, thesauruses), both print and digital, to find the pronunciation of a word or determine or clarify its precise meaning, its part of speech, or its etymology. **Literacy.L.9-10.4.d** Verify the preliminary determination of the meaning of a word or phrase (e.g., by checking the inferred meaning in context or in a dictionary).

UNIT 1 Cluster 2 Planner

EQ ESSENTIAL QUESTION:
What Influences a Person's Choices?
Find out how circumstances affect choices.

Online Planner
myNGconnect.com

	LESSON 11 **Prepare to Read**	LESSON 12 **Thank You, M'am** Main Selection
Reading		
Reading Strategies Focus Strategy **Plan and Monitor**	**Activate Prior Knowledge** SL.9-10.1 • Make a Connection: Anticipation Guide *T40*	**Plan and Monitor** RL.9-10.2 • Clarify Ideas (reread; read on) *T41, T44–T51* • Set a Purpose *T44* • Make and Confirm Predictions *T48–T49* • Monitor Comprehension *T46, T49*
Literary Analysis Genre Focus **Short Stories**		Ⓣ **Analyze Characterization** RL.9-10.3 *T41, T44–T51* **Identify Literary Movements** • Harlem Renaissance *T42*
Vocabulary	Ⓣ **Key Vocabulary** RI.9-10.4; L.9-10.6 • Introduce *T40* • **circumstances** empathy • **commit** juvenile • **consequence** maturity • **contact** salvage	Ⓣ **Key Vocabulary** L.9-10.6 • Daily Routines *T45* • Link to Essential Question *T47* • Selection Reading *T44–T51* • **commit** • **contact** • **consequence** empathy
Fluency		Ⓣ **Phrasing** RL.9-10.10 • Daily Routines *T45* Ⓣ **Accuracy and Rate** RL.9-10.10 Comprehension Coach *T43*
Writing		
Response to Literature		**Return to the Text** W.9-10.9 • **Reread and Write** What do you think influenced Roger's choices? *T51*
Writing Across the Curriculum		
Language		
ELL **Language Development**	Ⓣ **Express Ideas and Opinions** SL.9-10.1.a • Language and Grammar Lab, Transparency B *LAB TE p. 8*	Ⓣ **Express Ideas and Opinions** SL.9-10.1.a • Daily Routines *LAB TE p. 8*
Grammar Grammar Focus **Subject-Verb Agreement**		**Plural Nouns** *T46* L.9-10.1; L.9-10.2.c Ⓣ **Subject-Verb Agreement** L.9-10.1 *T48* Ⓣ **Subject-Verb Agreement** *T50* L.9-10.1
Listening and Speaking	**Partner Talk** SL.9-10.1 • Attitudes About Crime *T40*	**Listen to a Selection** Comprehension Coach *T43* • CD 1, Tracks 5–6 **Out-of-School Literacy** SL.9-10.1.a • Interpreting Television Shows *T49*

Ⓣ = Tested on Cluster and/or Unit Reading and Literary Analysis Test
Ⓣ = Tested on Language Acquisition Assessment
Ⓣ = Tested on Unit Writing Test
Ⓣ = Assessed with a Rubric
• **Academic Vocabulary**

SELECTION SUMMARIES

Thank You, M'am

Genre: Short Story **Lexile® 840L**

A young man attempts to steal a woman's purse but fails. In the end, the woman gives the young man the money he was trying to steal so he can buy what he desires. More important, though, she teaches him a valuable lesson about how to make the right choices.

Juvenile Justice

Genre: Television Interview **Lexile® 990L**

Judges and attorneys discuss various aspects of the juvenile justice system. Topics include the differences between juvenile and adult offenders, the implications of trying young offenders as adults, and rehabilitation.

LESSON 13 **Juvenile Justice** Second Selection	LESSON 14 **Reflect and Assess**	LESSONS 15 & 16 **Integrate the Language Arts**	LESSON 17 **Workshop**
Plan and Monitor RI.9-10.2 • Clarify Ideas (paraphrase) *T52, T53–T58* • Monitor Comprehension *T55, T57*	**Comprehension and Critical Thinking** *T59* RL.9-10.1; RI.9-10.1 • Compare Across Texts • Analyze, Compare, Interpret, Speculate, Draw Conclusions		
(T) **Analyze Text Features: Interview** RI.9-10.3 *T52, T53–T58*	**Interpret and Evaluate Literature** RI.9-10.10 (T) **Use Text Evidence** RI.9-10.1 *T59*	**Analyze Dialogue in Short Stories** *T60* L.9-10.3.a	
(T) **Key Vocabulary** L.9-10.6 • Selection Reading *T53-T58* • **circumstances** **juvenile** • **commit** **maturity** • **consequence** **salvage** **empathy**	(T) **Key Vocabulary** L.9-10.6 • Review *T59* • **circumstances** **empathy** • **commit** **juvenile** • **consequence** **maturity** • **contact** **salvage**	**Vocabulary Strategy** L.9-10.4.c • Use Structural Clues: Word Roots *T61*	
(T) **Phrasing** RL.9-10.10 • Daily Routines *T45* (T) **Accuracy and Rate** RI.9-10.10 Comprehension Coach *T53*	(T) **Phrasing** RL.9-10.10 • Peer Assessment *T59*		
Return to the Text W.9-10.9 • **Reread and Write** Which interviewee's ideas are closest to your own? *T58*	**Write About Literature** W.9-10.1 • **Interpretive Response** Why should we treat a 14-year-old offender differently than a 24-year-old offender? *T59*	(T) **Writing on Demand for Tests** W.9-10.2; W.9-10.2.a; W.9-10.2.b; W.9-10.2.c; W.9-10.2.f; W.9-10.9.a • **Short Comparison Essay** *T61*	
Research and Writing SL.9-10.1; SL.9-10.1.a • **Government Connection** *T57* • **Biology Connection** *T57*			
(T) **Express Ideas and Opinions** SL.9-10.1.a • Daily Routines *LAB TE p. 8*		(T) **Express Ideas and Opinions** SL.9.10.1.a • Group Talk *T60*	
(T) **Verbs with Compound Subjects** *T56* L.9-10.1		(T) **Subject-Verb Agreement** *T60* L.9-10.1	
Listen to a Selection RI.9-10.10 Comprehension Coach *T53* *CD 1, Track 7*	**Participate in a Discussion** *T59* SL.9-10.1	**Interview** *T61* SL.9-10.4	**Listening and Speaking Workshop** SL.9-10.1.a; SL.9-10.4; L.9-10.3 **Oral Response to Literature** • Plan, Practice, Present, and Evaluate an Oral Response *T62–T63*

EDGE LIBRARY

Trojan Horse •
by Justine and Ron Fontes

Miracle's Boys • •
by Jacqueline Woodson

Breaking Through • • •
by Francisco Jiménez

Lesson 11
PREPARE TO READ

OBJECTIVES
Vocabulary
- Key Vocabulary
- Strategy: Use Cognates; Relate Words

Reading Strategy
- Activate Prior Knowledge

ELL Language & Grammar Lab
Language Function Transparency B
Express Ideas and Opinions

ENGAGE & CONNECT

A EQ Essential Question

Focus on Circumstances Ask: Why might a person commit a crime?

Possible responses:
- *wants or needs something*
- *doesn't understand the consequences*

B Make a Connection

Have students complete the Anticipation Guide and then share answers with a partner to compare their attitudes about crime.
SL.9-10.1

TEACH VOCABULARY

C Learn Key Vocabulary

Study the Words Review the four steps of the Make Words Your Own routine (*see the Vocabulary tab*):

1. **Pronounce** Say a word and have students repeat it. Write the word in syllables and pronounce it, one syllable at a time: *ma-tu-ri-ty*. Ask what looks familiar in the word, and point out other forms of the word, such as *mature*.

   ELL Use cognates to help Spanish speakers with the words (*see the Vocabulary tab*).

2. **Study Examples** Read the example in the chart. Provide more examples: Do you show *maturity* when you take care of a younger sibling, or when you forget to return library books?

3. **Encourage Elaboration** Provide students with a sentence frame to complete: *I showed* maturity *when I* ______.

4. **Practice the Words** Have students write sentences using two Key Words in each.

Edge Interactive
Practice Book, p. 20–21
RI.9-10.4; L.9-10.6

PREPARE TO READ

- Thank You, M'am
- Juvenile Justice from Both Sides of the Bench

A EQ What Influences a Person's Choices?

Find out how circumstances affect choices.

B Make a Connection

Anticipation Guide Think about how circumstances, such as education, opportunities, and events, can affect a person's choice to break the law. Then tell whether you agree or disagree with these statements.

ANTICIPATION GUIDE	Agree or Disagree
1. Criminals choose to break the law, so they deserve their punishment.	______
2. It is OK for hungry people to steal what they need.	______
3. Everyone deserves a second chance.	______

C Learn Key Vocabulary

Study the Words Pronounce each word and learn its meaning. You may also want to look up the definitions in the Glossary.

• Academic Vocabulary

Key Words	Examples
• **circumstances** (**sur**-kum-stans-uz) *noun* ▸ pages 54, 58	**Circumstances** describe the situation a person is in. There are many **circumstances** that cause people to make bad choices.
• **commit** (ku-**mit**) *verb* ▸ pages 44, 53	A person who **commits** a crime is the one who carries it out, or does it. She **committed** the crime of robbery.
• **consequence** (**kon**-su-kwens) *noun* ▸ pages 44, 51, 54	A **consequence** is something that happens as a result of another action. If you lie to a friend, you may have to face a **consequence**, like losing your friendship.
• **contact** (**kon**-takt) *noun* ▸ page 46	When you are in **contact** with people or things, you connect with them in some way. I am still in **contact** with my friends from first grade.
empathy (**em**-pu-thē) *noun* ▸ pages 51, 53, 59	When you have **empathy** for people, you feel like you understand their problems, feelings, or behavior. I felt **empathy** for the lonely boy, and could feel his sadness.
juvenile (**joo**-vu-nīl) *adjective; noun* ▸ pages 53, 58, 59	A **juvenile** is a young person. [*noun*] Something **juvenile** is for young people. [*adjective*] The **juvenile** court is for people younger than eighteen.
maturity (mu-**choor**-u-tē) *noun* ▸ pages 54, 59	When people reach **maturity**, they are fully developed and have all the abilities of an adult. The girl's serious and responsible actions showed **maturity**.
salvage (**sal**-vuj) *verb* ▸ page 54	To **salvage** is to save someone or something from destruction. I **salvaged** my friendship by telling my friend I was sorry.

Practice the Words Work with a partner to write four sentences. Use at least two of the Key Vocabulary words in each sentence.

Example: *Do you feel empathy for a person who commits a crime?*

40 Unit 1 Choices

ONGOING ASSESSMENT
Have students complete an oral sentence for each word. For example: *When you call your parents, you get in* _______ *with them.*

CCSS **Literacy.RI.9-10.4** Determine the meaning of words and phrases as they are used in a text, including figurative, connotative, and technical meanings; analyze the cumulative impact of specific word choices on meaning and tone (e.g., how the language of a court opinion differs from that of a newspaper). **Literacy.SL.9-10.1** Initiate and participate effectively in a range of collaborative discussions (one-on-one, in groups, and teacher-led) with diverse partners on grades 9-10 topics, texts, and issues, building on others' ideas and expressing their own clearly and persuasively. **Literacy.L.9-10.6** Acquire and use accurately general academic and domain-specific words and phrases, sufficient for reading, writing, speaking, and listening at the college and career readiness level; demonstrate independence in gathering vocabulary knowledge when considering a word or phrase important to comprehension or expression.

BEFORE READING Thank You, M'am

short story by Langston Hughes

Reading Strategies

- ▶ **Plan and Monitor**
- Determine Importance
- Make Inferences
- Ask Questions
- Make Connections
- Synthesize
- Visualize

Analyze Characterization

When you read a good story, you feel as if you know the characters. That's because authors use **characterization** to reveal, or show, what a character is like.

Look Into the Text

Hughes describes the woman's physical traits. Notice the way he structures his descriptive sentences.

She was a large woman with a large purse that had everything in it but a hammer and nails. It had a long strap, and she carried it slung across her shoulder. It was about eleven o'clock at night, dark, and she was walking alone, when a boy ran up behind her and tried to snatch her purse. The strap broke with the sudden single tug the boy gave it from behind. But the boy's weight and the weight of the purse combined caused him to lose his balance. Instead of taking off full blast as he had hoped, the boy fell on his back on the sidewalk, and his legs flew up. The large woman simply turned around and kicked him right square in his blue-jeaned sitter. Then she reached down, picked the boy up by his shirt front, and shook him until his teeth rattled.

Hughes uses actions to show what she is like.

How does Hughes show the impact of her action on the boy?

D

Focus Strategy ▶ Plan and Monitor

When you **monitor your reading**, you check with yourself to see if you understand. Look into the text above and find something that isn't clear to you. Then, as you read the story, use these strategies to better understand, or clarify ideas.

Focus Strategy

HOW TO CLARIFY IDEAS

1. **Reread** If you are confused, go back to see if you missed something important.

   NOT CLEAR TO YOU: I'm not sure why other people didn't stop to help the woman.

   REREAD: It was about eleven o'clock at night, dark, and she was walking alone.

2. **Read On** Keep reading. The author may give more information later.

   YOU THINK: The boy must have gotten hurt when he fell on his back.

   READ ON: A few sentences later you'll come to this:

   "If I turn you loose, will you run?" asked the woman.
   "Yes'm," said the boy.

   YOU THINK: The boy must be OK if he can run away.

E

Reading Transparency 2

Analyze Characterization

READING CHARACTERIZATION 2

How does an author create characters?

Introduce Authors use several techniques to show what a character is like. They:

- tell the character's physical traits.
- describe the character's actions.
- show how other characters react.
- show what a character says or thinks.

The exact words a character speaks are called **dialogue**. Quotation marks show where the exact words begin and end.

After that, the woman said, "Pick up my pocketbook, boy, and give it here."

"If I turn you loose, will you run?" asked the woman.
"Yes'm," said the boy.
"Then I won't turn you loose," said the woman. She did not release him.
"Lady, I'm sorry," whispered the boy.

The woman said, "You ought to be my son. I would teach you right from wrong. Least I can do right now is to wash your face. Are you hungry?"

Lesson 12
BEFORE READING

OBJECTIVES

Reading Strategy
- Plan and Monitor: Clarify Ideas (reread, read on)

Literary Analysis
- Analyze Characterization T

TEACH STRATEGIES

D Analyze Characterization

Look Into the Text Read the introduction to define characterization. Then use the callouts on p. 41 to locate examples. Help students recognize not only what the text reveals about the characters but also how Hughes structures his writing.

To help students use the clues to understand characters, ask: The woman is large and kicks the boy. What do these clues show about her?

Possible response:
- *She is a tough character.*

Ask: Why did the boy's teeth rattle?

Possible responses:
- *The woman shook him too hard.*
- *He was afraid.*

RL.9-10.3

Reading Transparency 2

Use the Transparency Reinforce the features of characterization by introducing the ways authors show what a character is like. Then read aloud the dialogue. Ask: What do the woman's words show about her?

Possible response:
- *She is bossy and strong.*

E Focus Strategy: Plan and Monitor

Clarify Ideas Read the introduction with students to define the strategy. Work through the How To box to model rereading and reading on.

Have students try the strategies with something else that is not clear to them in Look Into the Text.

RL.9-10.2

Edge Interactive Practice Book, pp. 22–23

ONGOING ASSESSMENT

Have students explain how they would use clues in the text to understand a character.

CCSS **Literacy.RL.9-10.2** Determine a theme or central idea of a text and analyze in detail its development over the course of the text, including how it emerges and is shaped and refined by specific details; provide an objective summary of the text. **Literacy.RL.9-10.3** Analyze how complex characters (e.g., those with multiple or conflicting motivations) develop over the course of a text, interact with other characters, and advance the plot or develop the theme.

OBJECTIVES

Literary Analysis
- Identify Literary Movements

Viewing
- Respond to and Interpret Visuals

BUILD BACKGROUND

A The Writer and His Times

Have students read the article on Langston Hughes.

Literary Movement Share this information to place Langston Hughes and his work in historical context:

The Harlem Renaissance took place in the 1920s and 1930s. The movement gave African Americans a voice in the arts and a sense of racial pride. It even helped to build the foundation of the civil rights movement that would begin in the 1950s and 1960s. "Thank You, M'am" was published in 1958. The setting and characters are consistent with Hughes's writing about the experience of being African American during the middle part of the century.

Historical Context Help students interpret the possible influences of the Harlem Renaissance on Hughes's work. Ask: How might Hughes's work have been influenced by the growing presence of African American artists?

Possible response:
- *It might have inspired him to focus his themes on the voice and struggles of African Americans.*

Connect with Author's Life Ask: How do you think belonging to a group of artists helped Langston Hughes? Do you think it is important to belong to a group?

Possible responses:
- *The artists might have encouraged each other.*

myNGconnect.com
- **Selection Summaries in eight languages**

The Writer and His Times

Langston Hughes
(1902–1967)

Langston Hughes believed in equal opportunities for all Americans.

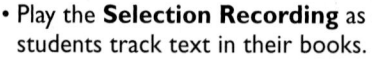

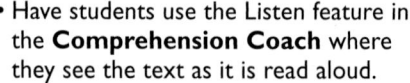

A **Langston Hughes** wrote about the experience of being an African American in the early and middle 20th century. He was one of the most famous members of the "Harlem Renaissance," a group of writers, musicians, and artists who lived and worked in the Harlem neighborhood in New York City. Harlem became the setting, or location, for many of Hughes's works, including "Thank You, M'am."

When he was growing up, Hughes moved a lot. He lived in Missouri, Kansas, Illinois, Ohio, and Mexico. His parents were divorced, and he also spent time living with his grandmother and other relatives. In one essay, Hughes said that during these years he slept in "ten thousand beds."

Even though his home changed often, the one thing that never changed was his love of books and writing. Hughes wrote his first poem in the eighth grade, and he was named class poet. The *Central High School Monthly* in Cleveland, Ohio, was the first magazine to publish one of his poems.

Hughes went on to write three novels, nineteen books of poetry and short stories, twenty plays, and many newspaper articles and essays. Many of his poems were also set to music by the jazz musicians of his time.

myNGconnect.com
- **Listen to a jazz song with lyrics by Hughes.**
- **Hear Hughes read and discuss his work.**

DIFFERENTIATED INSTRUCTION

English Language Learners ELL

Preview the selection:
- Show the art on p. 43: *The story takes place in a neighborhood like this, at night.*
- Show the portraits on pp. 47 and 49: *Two people who might look like this come in contact with each other in the story.*
- Demonstrate stealing a purse and explain: *The story gets started when the boy tries to steal a woman's purse.*
- Make an angry face and explain: *The woman gets angry. Listen to her words.* Read the quote in paragraph 3 on p. 46.

Read Aloud to provide a supported listening experience:
- Play the **Selection Recording** as students track text in their books. **CD 1**
- Have students use the Listen feature in the **Comprehension Coach** where they see the text as it is read aloud.
- Read the selection aloud to students as you provide comprehensible input. For example, you can pantomime a number of the actions, such as losing balance or taking off full blast on p. 44.

THANK YOU, M'AM

by Langston Hughes

Harlem Street Scene, 1942, Jacob Lawrence. Gouache on paper, private collection.

B

▲ Critical Viewing: Setting What is this neighborhood like? How would the scene change late at night? C

Comprehension Coach

TEACH & PRACTICE

B Analyze Visuals

About the Art Jacob Lawrence, like Hughes, lived in Harlem during the Harlem Renaissance.

Interpret and Respond Ask students: If you painted your own neighborhood, what would you show?

C Critical Viewing: Setting

Observe Daytime Details Ask: What is this neighborhood like?

ELL **Questioning** For less proficient students, ask yes/no questions or questions with embedded answer choices:

- Is there a place for children to play?
- Is this neighborhood a quiet place or a busy place? How can you tell?

For more proficient students, ask open-ended questions:

- What kinds of work are people doing? How are they having fun?

Have students point out the parts of the image that support their observations.

Possible responses:

- *Children have to play on sidewalks.*
- *It is very busy. People are working and playing.*
- *For work: A vendor is selling food. Some men are moving furniture. For fun: Children are jumping rope.*

Visualize the Night Scene Ask: How would the scene change late at night?

Possible response:

- *At night, there may be fewer people on the streets. Young people might be hanging around together.*

Comprehension Coach

Build Reading Power

Assign students to use the software, based on their instructional needs.

Read Silently

- Comprehension questions with immediate feedback
- Glossary support
- Review text evidence

RL.9-10.10

Listen

- Professional model of fluent reading

Record

- Oral reading fluency practice
- Ongoing fluency assessment with immediate feedback

CCSS **Literacy.RI.9-10.10** By the end of grade 9, read and comprehend literary nonfiction in the grades 9–10 text complexity band proficiently, with scaffolding as needed at the high end of the range. By the end of grade 10, read and comprehend literary nonfiction at the high end of the grades 9–10 text complexity band independently and proficiently.

READ

OBJECTIVES

Vocabulary
- Key Vocabulary Ⓣ

Reading Fluency
- Phrasing Ⓣ

Reading Strategies
- Plan and Monitor: Set a Purpose; Clarify Ideas

Comprehension & Critical Thinking
- Use Text Evidence Ⓣ

Literary Analysis
- Analyze Characterization Ⓣ
- Analyze Style: Author's Language and Word Choice

Viewing
- Respond to and Interpret Visuals

TEACH & PRACTICE

Ⓐ Chunking the Text

Set a Purpose Remind students of their responses in the Anticipation Guide. Ask: What might you hope to gain from reading a story about a young person who commits a crime?

Possible responses:
- *You might get to learn about the consequences of choosing crime.*
- *The story might have suspense.*

Read Have students read pp. 44–47. Support and monitor their comprehension using the reading support provided. Use the Differentiated Instruction below to meet students' individual needs.
RL.9-10.10

Ⓑ Reading Support

1 Characterization Ask: What do the physical traits, actions, words, and reactions of others tell about the two characters?

Possible responses:
- *The woman is strong and forceful.*
- *The boy might be small and afraid.*

RL.9-10.3

Ⓒ Reading Support

2 Clarify Ideas Ask students whether they were surprised by the boy's answer and why. Have students read a few more lines and then restate the boy's answer.
RL.9-10.3

Ⓐ ***Set a Purpose***
Find out the consequences for a young person who makes the choice to commit a crime.

Ⓑ She was a large woman with a large purse that had everything in it but a hammer and nails. It had a long strap, and she carried it **slung** across her shoulder. It was about eleven o'clock at night, dark, and she was walking alone, when a boy ran up behind her and tried to snatch her purse. The strap broke with the sudden single tug the boy gave it from behind. But the boy's weight and the weight of the purse combined caused him to lose his balance. Instead of **taking off full blast** as he had hoped, the boy fell on his back on the sidewalk and his legs flew up. The large woman simply turned around and kicked him **right square in his blue-jeaned sitter**. Then she reached down, picked the boy up by his shirt front, and shook him until his teeth rattled. 1

After that, the woman said, "Pick up my pocketbook, boy, and give it here."

She still held him tightly. But she bent down enough to **permit him to stoop** and pick up her purse. Then she said, "Now ain't you ashamed of yourself?"

Firmly gripped by his shirt front, the boy said, "Yes'm."

Ⓒ The woman said, "What did you want to do it for?"

The boy said, "I didn't aim to." 2

She said, "You a lie!"

By that time two or three people passed, stopped, turned to look, and some stood watching.

"If I turn you loose, will you run?" asked the woman.

"Yes'm," said the boy.

"Then I won't turn you loose," said the woman. She did not release him.

"Lady, I'm sorry," whispered the boy.

1 Characterization What does this paragraph tell you about the two main characters?

2 Clarify Ideas Are you surprised by the boy's answer? If so, try reading on to clarify what the boy means.

Key Vocabulary
- **consequence** *n.*, result of another action
- **commit** *v.*, to perform, do, or carry out something, often a crime

In Other Words
slung hanging
taking off full blast running away very fast
right square in his blue-jeaned sitter on his rear end, or backside
permit him to stoop let him lean down

DIFFERENTIATED INSTRUCTION

Interactive Reading As you conduct the interactive reading session with students, adjust your teaching strategies to their needs.

Struggling Readers

Picture the Text Show visually how key ideas in the story relate. For example, pause after each major choice that Roger makes and complete a choice-and-consequence diagram. For example:

Choice		Consequence
steals a purse	→	gets caught

English Language Learners ELL

Rephrase Dialect Dialect is a version of a language with some differences in vocabulary, grammar, and pronunciation. For example:

You a lie! (You are a liar.)
Yes'm (Yes, Madam)

Discuss additional examples from the story and provide restatements.

Challenge

Lead the Discussion Have students lead the discussion during reading, posing additional questions for the group. Help leaders model positive discussion techniques, such as encouraging each member's participation.

CCSS **Literacy.RL.9-10.3** Analyze how complex characters (e.g., those with multiple or conflicting motivations) develop over the course of a text, interact with other characters, and advance the plot or develop the theme. **Literacy.RL.9-10.10** By the end of grade 9, read and comprehend literature, including stories, dramas, and poems, in the grades 9-10 text complexity band proficiently, with scaffolding as needed at the high end of the range. By the end of grade 10, read and comprehend literature, including stories, dramas, and poems, at the high end of the grades 9-10 text complexity band independently and proficiently.

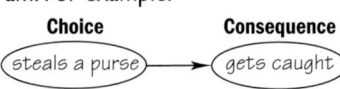

"Um-hum! Your face is dirty. I **got a great mind** to wash your face for you. Ain't you got nobody home to tell you to wash your face?"

"No'm," said the boy.

"Then it will get washed this evening," said the large woman, starting up the street, dragging the frightened boy behind her.

He looked as if he were fourteen or fifteen, **frail and willow-wild**, in tennis shoes and blue jeans.

The woman said, "You ought to be my son. I would teach you **right from wrong**. Least I can do right now is to wash your face. Are you hungry?"

"No'm," said the being-dragged boy. 3 "I just want you to turn me loose." D

3 Language Authors often use familiar words in new ways. Here Hughes uses "being-dragged boy" to describe Roger. How does this help you picture what's happening?

The City from Greenwich Village, 1922, John Sloan. Oil on canvas, National Gallery of Art, Washington, D.C.

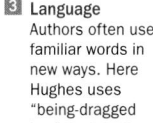

E

Critical Viewing: Effect Here is how one artist portrayed a New York City scene. What mood, or feeling, does the artist create? F

In Other Words

got a great mind have a plan or desire
frail and willow-wild weak and small, with skinny arms and legs
right from wrong that stealing is wrong

TEACH & PRACTICE

D Reading Support

3 Language Explain that the phrase is a creative way of saying "the boy who was being dragged." Have students analyze the author's use of descriptive language and explain how it impacts meaning. Ask: How does the descriptive language help you understand what is happening?

Possible response:

- *The language describes the woman's action toward the boy, and shows she is in charge.*

RL.9-10.4

E Analyze Visuals

About the Art John Sloan was a painter who used realism to depict poor urban neighborhoods.

Interpret and Respond Ask: What about this painting looks "realistic" to you?

F Critical Viewing: Effect

Analyze Setting Ask students to study the places shown in the painting.

ELL Build Background Some students may be unfamiliar with characteristics of an urban setting. Explain:

- the elevated train
- the water tower
- the density and height of the buildings
- the skyline in the background

Ask: What is the setting of the painting like?

Possible response:

- *Some places are dark, in shadows, while others in the background are in bright lights.*

Ask: What mood or feeling does the artist create?

Possible responses:

- *The mood seems gloomy.*
- *There is a feeling of loneliness.*

DAILY ROUTINES

Vocabulary

See the Vocabulary and Fluency Routines tab for more information.

Word Wall Display the words to provide a visual scaffold. Create word maps or choose a graphic organizer from page PD33.

Respond to Questions Compose yes/no questions using the words. For example: Do *circumstances* affect a person's *maturity*?

Word Sorts Place words into categories. For example:

- Parts of speech
- Related meanings

L.9-10.6

Fluency: Phrasing

CD 11

This cluster's fluency practice uses a passage from "Thank You, M'am" to help students practice appropriate phrasing. Use **Reading Handbook** T749 and the **Fluency Model CD** to teach or review the elements of fluent phrasing, and then use the daily fluency practice activities to develop students' oral reading proficiency.

RL.9-10.10

CCSS Literacy.RL.9-10.4 Determine the meaning of words and phrases as they are used in the text, including figurative and connotative meanings; analyze the cumulative impact of specific word choices on meaning and tone (e.g., how the language evokes a sense of time and place; how it sets a formal or informal tone). **Literacy.L.9-10.6** Acquire and use accurately general academic and domain-specific words and phrases, sufficient for reading, writing, speaking, and listening at the college and career readiness level; demonstrate independence in gathering vocabulary knowledge when considering a word or phrase important to comprehension or expression.

READ

OBJECTIVES

Vocabulary
- Key Vocabulary Ⓣ

Reading Strategy
- Plan and Monitor: Adjust Purpose for Reading

Comprehension & Critical Thinking
- Use Text Evidence Ⓣ

Literary Analysis
- Analyze Characterization Ⓣ

Viewing
- Respond to and Interpret Visuals

Grammar
- Plural Nouns Ⓣ

TEACH & PRACTICE

Ⓐ Reading Support

4 Characterization Ask what type of person might talk like this.

Possible response:
- *Mrs. Jones sounds like a teacher, parent, or very confident person.*

RL.9-10.3

Ⓑ Reading Support

5 Characterization Ask why Roger's action is so important here.

Possible response:
- *Roger wants to do the right thing, and he knows she is trying to help.*

RL.9-10.3

Monitor Comprehension

Explain Have students think aloud to explain if they have found out the consequences Roger faces.

MODEL Say:
- *So far Roger has been dragged to the woman's house and had his face washed.*
- *We don't know yet what else Mrs. Jones might do. Roger still may have to face more consequences.*
- *My purpose for reading will probably not be completely met until the end of the story.*

Ask if students had any other purposes for reading the story. Have them think aloud how other purposes have been met so far.

RL.9-10.2

Ⓐ

"Was I bothering *you* when I turned that corner?" asked the woman.

"No'm."

"But you put yourself in **contact** with *me*," said the woman. "If you think that that contact is not going to last awhile, **you got another thought coming**. When I get through with you, sir, you are going to remember Mrs. Luella Bates Washington Jones." 4

Sweat popped out on the boy's face and he began to struggle. Mrs. Jones stopped, jerked him around in front of her, put **a half nelson about** his neck, and continued to drag him up the street. When she got to her door, she dragged the boy inside, down a hall, and into a large **kitchenette-furnished room** at the rear of the house. She switched on the light and left the door open. The boy could hear other **roomers** laughing and talking in the large house. Some of their doors were open, too, so he knew he and the woman were not alone. The woman still had him by the neck in the middle of her room.

> **When I get through with you, sir, you are going to remember Mrs. Luella Bates Washington Jones.**

Ⓑ

She said, "What is your name?"

"Roger," answered the boy.

"Then, Roger, you go to that sink and wash your face," said the woman, **whereupon** she turned him loose—at last. Roger looked at the door—looked at the woman—looked at the door—*and went to the sink.* 5

"Let the water run until it gets warm," she said. "Here's a clean towel."

"You gonna take me to jail?" asked the boy, bending over the sink.

"Not with that face, I would not take you nowhere," said the woman.

4 Characterization Have you ever known a person who talks in a tough, bossy way like this? What does her language tell you about the character of Mrs. Jones?

5 Characterization Hughes uses italics to draw your attention to what Roger did. What does this choice tell you about Roger?

Monitor Comprehension

Explain What consequences has Roger faced so far?

Key Vocabulary
- **contact** *n.*, connection

In Other Words

you got another thought coming think again
a half nelson about a strong hold around
kitchenette-furnished room room with a small kitchen
roomers boarders, people who lived there
whereupon and then

46 Unit 1 Choices

GRAMMAR

Plural Nouns

Teach/Model Display the transparency. Remind students that a noun names a person, place, thing, or idea. Explain the definitions and spelling rules, writing the plural nouns on the transparency as you work through the chart.

Practice A. Have students collect the nouns and tell if they are singular or plural. Write some in the chart and ask students to fill in the corresponding form—singular or plural. **B.** After partners talk and write sentences, have each student read his or her favorite sentence aloud. Ask the group to identify the plural.

L.9-10.1; L.9-10.2.c

Grammar & Writing Practice Book, pp. 11–12

Grammar Transparency 6

GRAMMAR PLURAL NOUNS 6

What's a Plural Noun?

A Word That Names More Than One Thing

One	More Than One
A **singular noun** names one thing.	A **plural noun** names more than one thing.

Use these spelling rules for forming plural nouns.

1. To make most nouns plural, just add **-s**.
2. If the noun ends in **s, z, sh, ch,** or **x,** add **-es**.
3. If the noun ends in **y** after the consonant, change the **y** to **i** and add **-es**.
4. Some nouns have special plural forms.

One	More Than One
dollar	**dollars**
dish	dishes
baby	babies
lady	ladies
child	children
man	men
woman	women

Try It

A. Look back at "Thank You, M'am." Find a noun. Is it singular or plural? Put it in the correct column. Then add its other form.
Possible answers:

Singular Nouns (one)	Plural Nouns (more than one)
purse	purses
hammer	hammers
tooth	teeth
door	doors
shoe	shoes
towel	towels

B. Now tell a partner something about "Thank You, M'am" using nouns from the chart. Write your three best sentences with plural nouns.
Sentences will vary.

GRAMMAR SKILLS PATH

- ▶ **6 Plural Nouns** — ELL Language & Grammar Lab
- **7 Subject-Verb Agreement: Forms of Be**
- **8 Subject-Verb Agreement: Action Verbs**
- **9 Verbs with Compound Subjects**
- **10 Review: Subject-Verb Agreement**

CCSS **Literacy.RL.9-10.2** Determine a theme or central idea of a text and analyze in detail its development over the course of the text, including how it emerges and is shaped and refined by specific details; provide an objective summary of the text. **Literacy.RL.9-10.3** Analyze how complex characters (e.g., those with multiple or conflicting motivations) develop over the course of a text, interact with other characters, and advance the plot or develop the theme. **Literacy.L.9-10.1** Demonstrate command of the conventions of standard English grammar and usage when writing or speaking. **Literacy.L.9-10.2.c** Spell correctly.

The Window, 1970, Bernard Safran. Oil on masonite, private collection.

C

Critical Viewing: Characterization How does this picture compare to the picture you have in your mind of Mrs. Jones? D

TEACH & PRACTICE

C Analyze Visuals

About the Art At the time this story was written, Bernard Safran was painting portraits of world leaders and other important figures for the cover of *Time* magazine. After leaving *Time*, Safran turned his attention to painting images of daily life in his native New York City.

Interpret and Respond Ask:

- If you saw this image on the cover of *Time*, what would you predict the feature story might be about?
- If you were an artist, which would you prefer as your subject: famous or regular people? Why?

D Critical Viewing: Characterization

Analyze Character Ask students to identify details that show what the woman in the painting is like.

ELL **Use Graphic Organizer** List the details students notice and use a graphic to show how details lead to conclusions.

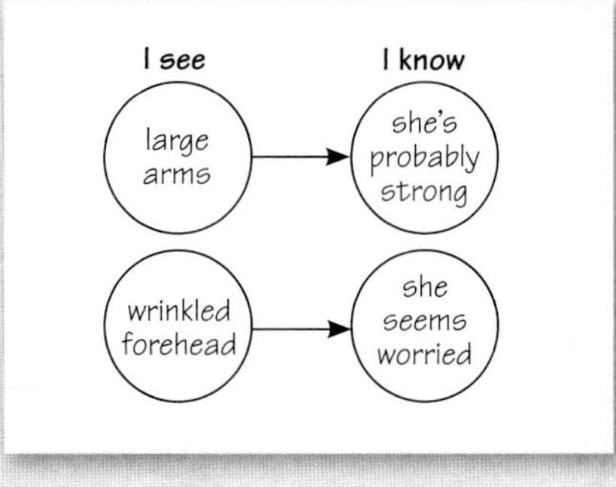

Ask: What is your impression of the woman?

Have students compare the woman in the picture to how they see Mrs. Jones.

Possible responses:

- *Both are large.*
- *Neither is wealthy.*
- *Mrs. Jones doesn't seem worried like the woman in the painting.*

RL.9-10.7

VOCABULARY

Link Vocabulary and Concepts

Ask questions to link Key Vocabulary with the Essential Question.

EQ **ESSENTIAL QUESTION:**
What Influences a Person's Choices?

Some possible questions:

- *What* **circumstances** *might have led the boy to make the choice to steal?*
- *Why did the boy choose to* **commit** *this crime?*
- *Do you think the boy considered the* **consequences** *of his choice?*
- *The boy is a* **juvenile***. Would an adult have made the same choice?*
- *What can be done to* **salvage** *the boy's future and stop him from choosing crime?*
- *Does the boy's choice show* **maturity***?*

Have students use the Key Vocabulary words in their responses.

L.9-10.6

CCSS **Literacy.RL.9-10.7** Analyze the representation of a subject or a key scene in two different artistic mediums, including what is emphasized or absent in each treatment (e.g., Auden's "Musée des Beaux Arts" and Breughel's Landscape with the Fall of Icarus). **Literacy.L.9-10.6** Acquire and use accurately general academic and domain-specific words and phrases, sufficient for reading, writing, speaking, and listening at the college and career readiness level; demonstrate independence in gathering vocabulary knowledge when considering a word or phrase important to comprehension or expression.

READ

OBJECTIVES

Vocabulary
- Strategy: Use Contextual Analysis

Reading Strategies
- Plan and Monitor: Predict; Clarify Ideas; Confirm Prediction
- Review Strategies

Comprehension & Critical Thinking
- Use Text Evidence (T)

Literary Analysis
- Analyze Characterization (T)

Viewing
- Respond to and Interpret Visuals

Grammar
- Subject-Verb Agreement (*be*) (T)

TEACH & PRACTICE

(A) Chunking the Text

Predict Have students discuss and generate questions about Mrs. Jones to make a complex prediction about what she will teach Roger.

ELL Rephrase Language Explain that in this phrase, *life* is used as an adjective: "life lessons" are lessons one learns about life. Ask students for other ways they might explain "life lessons."

Read Have students read pp. 48–51. Support and monitor their comprehension using the reading support.
RL.9-10.10

(B) Reading Support

6 Characterization Have volunteers role-play this dialogue. Ask: How do Mrs. Jones's words show whether she means to help Roger?

Possible response:
- *Mrs. Jones's words are angry, but she offers Roger dinner.*
RL.9-10.3

(C) Reading Support

7 Clarify Ideas Reread the paragraph aloud. Ask what Mrs. Jones might have in common with Roger.

Possible response:
- *Mrs. Jones might have grown up without anyone taking care of her.*
RL.9-10.2

GRAMMAR SKILLS PATH

6 Plural Nouns
▶ 7 Subject-Verb Agreement: Forms of *Be* — ELL Language & Grammar Lab
8 Subject-Verb Agreement: Action Verbs
9 Verbs with Compound Subjects
10 Review: Subject-Verb Agreement

(A) ***Predict***
What life lessons do you think Mrs. Jones will teach Roger?

(B) "Here I am trying to get home to cook me a bite to eat, and you snatch my pocketbook! Maybe you ain't been to your supper either, late as it be. Have you?"

"There's nobody home at my house," said the boy.

"Then we'll eat," said the woman. "I believe you're hungry—or been hungry—to try to snatch my pocketbook!"

"I want a pair of blue suede shoes," said the boy.

"Well, you didn't have to snatch *my* pocketbook to get some suede shoes," said Mrs. Luella Bates Washington Jones. "You could of asked me." 6

"M'am?"

The water dripping from his face the boy looked at her. There was a long pause. A very long pause. After he had dried his face and not knowing what else to do, dried it again, the boy turned around, wondering what next. The door was open. He could **make a dash for it** down the hall. He could run, run, run, *run!*

The woman was sitting on the daybed. After a while she said, "I were young once and I wanted things I could not get."

There was another long pause. The boy's mouth opened. Then he frowned, not knowing he frowned.

(C) The woman said, "Um-hum! You thought I was going to say *but*, didn't you? You thought I was going to say, *but I didn't snatch people's pocketbooks*. Well, I wasn't going to say that." Pause. Silence. "I have done things, too, which I would not tell you, son—neither tell God, if He didn't already know. **Everybody's got something in common.** 7 So you set down while I fix us something to eat. You might run that comb through your hair so you will look **presentable**."

6 Characterization What does this dialogue show about Mrs. Jones? From what you know of her so far, would she have helped Roger?

7 Clarify Ideas Does what Mrs. Jones says here make sense to you? Reread the paragraph to clarify what she and Roger have in common.

In Other Words
make a dash for it try to run
Everybody's got something in common. All people are alike in some way.
presentable clean and neat

Cultural Background
"Blue Suede Shoes" was a song written by Carl Perkins in 1955. It was one of the first big rock and roll hits, and teens all over the U.S. listened to it. They also bought shoes like the ones shown here.

GRAMMAR

Subject-Verb Agreement: Forms of *Be*

Teach/Model Display the transparency. Review the present tense forms of the verb *be*: *am*, *is*, and *are*. Use the examples on the transparency to explain how the verb you choose depends on the subject.

Practice A. Have students complete sentences about the characters. Point out each subject as you read the paragraph aloud. Ask students to look back at the examples to verify which verb to use. **B.** After the class starts the reaction paragraph, ask students to write two more sentences and share one sentence aloud.
L.9-10.1

Grammar & Writing Practice Book, pp. 13–14

Grammar Transparency 7

GRAMMAR SUBJECT-VERB AGREEMENT: FORMS OF *BE* 7

How Do You Know What Verb to Use?
Match It to the Subject.

- Use **I** with **am**.
  I am surprised at Roger.
- Use **he**, **she**, or **it** with **is**.
  Roger grabs a woman's purse. Now **it is** on the ground.
  Roger looks up. **He is** scared.
  Mrs. Jones shakes him. **She is** angry.
- Use **we**, **you**, or **they** with **are**.
  We are also surprised at Mrs. Jones.
  Are you?
  Mrs. Jones and Roger leave. **They are** on their way to her apartment.
  They are both very upset.

Forms of *Be*
I **am**
he, she, or it **is**
we, you, or they **are**

Try It

A. Tell what happens at the start of the story. Use is or are.

Late at night, Mrs. Jones __is__ on a dark street. Roger __is__ behind her, and he tries to steal her purse. She __is__ angry, and he __is__ afraid. They __are__ both very upset.

B. Now let's write a reaction to the story. Use am, is, or are in these sentences. Then add two more sentences. Sentences will vary.

At first, I __am__ surprised that Mrs. Jones didn't call the police. Instead, she helps Roger. She __is__ his friend. I think they __are more comfortable now. They are both curious about what will happen next.__

CCSS **Literacy.RL.9-10.2** Determine a theme or central idea of a text and analyze in detail its development over the course of the text, including how it emerges and is shaped and refined by specific details; provide an objective summary of the text. **Literacy.RL.9-10.3** Analyze how complex characters (e.g., those with multiple or conflicting motivations) develop over the course of a text, interact with other characters, and advance the plot or develop the theme. **Literacy.RL.9-10.10** By the end of grade 9, read and comprehend literature, including stories, dramas, and poems, in the grades 9–10 text complexity band proficiently, with scaffolding as needed at the high end of the range. By the end of grade 10, read and comprehend literature, including stories, dramas, and poems, at the high end of the grades 9–10 text complexity band independently and proficiently. **Literacy.L.9-10.1** Demonstrate command of the conventions of standard English grammar and usage when writing or speaking.

Jim, 1930, William H. Johnson. Oil on canvas, Smithsonian American Art Museum, Washington, D.C.

Critical Viewing: Characterization Study the boy's look. What lines from the story could go with this look?

In another corner of the room behind a screen was a **gas plate** and **an icebox**. 8 Mrs. Jones got up and went behind the screen. The woman did not watch the boy to see if he was going to run now, nor did she watch her purse, which she left behind her on the daybed. But the boy took care to sit on the far side of the room, away from the purse, where he thought she could easily see him out of the corner of her eye

8 Access Vocabulary Do you know what *screen* means here? If not, look for clues. It must be big because an icebox, or refrigerator, is behind it.

Monitor Comprehension

Confirm Prediction Were you right about what Mrs. Jones is teaching Roger? Explain.

In Other Words
gas plate small stove
an icebox a refrigerator

TEACH & PRACTICE

D Analyze Visuals

About the Art William H. Johnson was an accomplished painter during and after the Harlem Renaissance.

Interpret and Respond Ask: Do you think the painting is realistic? Explain.

E Critical Viewing: Characterization

Analyze Character Ask students to study the boy's eyes and facial expression.

Ask: What is your impression of the boy?

Have students scan p. 48 for lines from the story that go with this look.

Possible response:

- *Roger may have looked uncertain like this when he was deciding if he should run out of Mrs. Jones's kitchen.*

RL.9-10.7

F Reading Support

8 Access Vocabulary Ask students where they have heard the word *screen*. For example: *movie/tv screen, screen door, sunscreen*. Have them identify what these have in common.

Possible response:

- *A shield or barrier, a flat surface, something you can almost see through.*

RL.9-10.4

Review Strategies Have students tell which other reading strategy they used as they read the story.

Possible response:

- *I read that Mrs. Jones left her purse near the boy. I know that she's a smart, careful woman. I made an inference that she left the purse there on purpose to show the boy that she trusts him. This helps me understand more about what Mrs. Jones is like.*

RL.9-10.1

Monitor Comprehension

Confirm Prediction Have students match their predictions with what Mrs. Jones teaches Roger. Discuss the accuracy of their predictions.

RL.9-10.10

OUT-OF-SCHOOL LITERACY

MEDIA & TECHNOLOGY

Interpreting Television Shows

Help students see how much prior knowledge they bring to the text by connecting the selection to students' experience with watching television crime shows.

- What crime or police shows have you seen recently on television?
- What are some reasons that people in these shows **commit** crimes?
- What **circumstances** might lead someone to choose crime?
- What **consequences** did the people in the shows have to face when they made bad choices?
- Do you have **empathy** for people who make bad choices? Why or why not?

As students answer, encourage the use of the highlighted Key Vocabulary.

SL.9-10.1.a

CCSS **Literacy.RL.9-10.1** Cite strong and thorough textual evidence to support analysis of what the text says explicitly as well as inferences drawn from the text. **Literacy.RL.9-10.4** Determine the meaning of words and phrases as they are used in the text, including figurative and connotative meanings; analyze the cumulative impact of specific word choices on meaning and tone (e.g., how the language evokes a sense of time and place; how it sets a formal or informal tone). **Literacy.RL.9-10.7** Analyze the representation of a subject or a key scene in two different artistic mediums, including what is emphasized or absent in each treatment (e.g., Auden's "Musée des Beaux Arts" and Breughel's Landscape with the Fall of Icarus). **Literacy.SL.9-10.1.a** Come to discussions prepared, having read and researched material under study; explicitly draw on that preparation by referring to evidence from texts and other research on the topic or issue to stimulate a thoughtful, well-reasoned exchange of ideas.

READ

OBJECTIVES

Vocabulary
- Key Vocabulary Ⓣ

Reading Strategy
- Plan and Monitor: Clarify Ideas

Comprehension & Critical Thinking
- Use Text Evidence Ⓣ

Literary Analysis
- Analyze Characterization Ⓣ

Writing
- Form: Response to Literature

Grammar
- Subject-Verb Agreement (action verbs) Ⓣ

TEACH & PRACTICE

A Reading Support

9 Characterization Ask students to recall Roger's words and actions earlier in the story. Have them contrast them with what he says at the top of p. 50.

Point out that Roger offers to go to the store. Ask: How is Roger feeling at this point in the story?

Possible responses:
- *Roger might be feeling like he wants to do something for Mrs. Jones because he knows she is trying to help him. He also might feel bad about trying to steal from her, so he is trying to make it up to her.*
- *Roger might want a polite way to escape.*

RL.9-10.3

B Reading Support

10 Clarify Ideas Have students reread the paragraph to identify the reason Mrs. Jones doesn't ask Roger about himself. Ask: If Mrs. Jones doesn't ask Roger about himself, why does she tell him so much about herself and her work?

Possible response:
- *She wants to make Roger feel comfortable rather than ashamed. She is treating him like a friend.*

RL.9-10.2

---

if she wanted to. He did not trust the woman *not* to trust him. And he did not want **to be mistrusted** now.

A "Do you need somebody to go to the store," asked the boy, "maybe to get some milk or something?" 9

"Don't believe I do," said the woman, "unless you just want sweet milk yourself. I was going to make cocoa out of this canned milk I got here."

"That will be fine," said the boy.

B She heated some lima beans and ham she had in the icebox, made the cocoa, and set the table. The woman did not ask the boy anything about where he lived, or his folks, or anything else that would embarrass him. Instead, as they ate, she told him about her job in a hotel beauty shop that stayed open late, what the work was like, and how all kinds of women came in and out, blondes, redheads, and Spanish. Then she cut him a half of her ten-cent cake. 10

> HE DID NOT TRUST THE WOMAN *NOT* TO TRUST HIM. AND HE DID NOT WANT TO BE MISTRUSTED NOW.

"Eat some more, son," she said.

When they were finished eating, she got up and said, "Now here, take this ten dollars and buy yourself some blue suede shoes. And next time, do not make the mistake of **latching onto** *my* pocketbook *nor nobody else's*—because shoes got by **devilish ways** will burn your feet. I got to get my rest now. But from here on in, son, I hope you will **behave yourself**."

She led him down the hall to the front door and opened it. "Good night! Behave yourself, boy!" she said, looking out into the street as he went down the steps.

9 Characterization What do Roger's words tell about how he's feeling at this point in the story?

10 Clarify Ideas Why does Mrs. Jones tell Roger so much about herself, instead of asking him questions? Reread the paragraph to find clues to her reason.

In Other Words
to be mistrusted her to stop trusting him
latching onto grabbing, taking
devilish ways bad behavior, wrong actions
behave yourself do the right thing, follow the rules

GRAMMAR

Subject-Verb Agreement: Action Verbs

Teach/Model Display the transparency. Compare the action verbs in each pair, and ask students why the verb in each even-numbered sentence ends in -s.

Practice A. Have students recall events in the story to generate sentence endings. For numbers 1–4, ask students to identify the subject in the sentence and to tell you how the verb for each subject should end. **B.** Have students write three sentences to tell about the characters. Have volunteers find the verbs and explain why some end in -s.

L.9-10.1

Grammar & Writing Practice Book, pp. 15–16

GRAMMAR SKILLS PATH

6 Plural Nouns
7 Subject-Verb Agreement: Forms of *Be*
▶ 8 Subject-Verb Agreement: Action Verbs — ELL Language & Grammar Lab
9 Verbs with Compound Subjects
10 Review: Subject-Verb Agreement

Grammar Transparency 8

GRAMMAR SUBJECT-VERB AGREEMENT: ACTION VERBS 8

How Do You Know What Action Verb to Use?

Match It to the Subject.

- **Action verbs** tell when a subject does something, like **call**, **hide**, or **get**. If the sentence is about one other person, place, or thing, add -s to the action verb.

1. I **see** a bank robbery.	2. My friend Tom **sees** the robbery, too.
3. You **call** the police.	4. He **calls** 911.
5. We **hide** behind a car.	6. A girl is scared. She **hides** with us.
7. The robbers **get** in a car.	8. It **gets** out of the parking lot fast!

- If there is more than one action verb in a sentence, all verbs must agree with the subject:

  The robber **breaks** into the bank, **takes** the money, and **drives** away in a car.

Try It

A. What do the characters from "Thank You, M'am" do? Finish the sentences. Use action verbs. Possible responses:

1. Mrs. Jones heats beans and ham.
2. Roger sits far away from the purse.
3. The two characters eat at the table.
4. The woman talks to Roger, cuts the cake, and gives him ten dollars.

B. Write three sentences to tell more about what Mrs. Jones does in the story. Sentences will vary.

CCSS **Literacy.RL.9-10.2** Determine a theme or central idea of a text and analyze in detail its development over the course of the text, including how it emerges and is shaped and refined by specific details; provide an objective summary of the text. **Literacy.RL.9-10.3** Analyze how complex characters (e.g., those with multiple or conflicting motivations) develop over the course of a text, interact with other characters, and advance the plot or develop the theme. **Literacy.L.9-10.1** Demonstrate command of the conventions of standard English grammar and usage when writing or speaking.

The boy wanted to say something other than, "Thank you, m'am," to Mrs. Luella Bates Washington Jones, but although his lips moved, he couldn't even say that as he turned at the foot of the **barren stoop** and looked up at the large woman in the door. Then she shut the door. ❖

ANALYZE Thank You, M'am

1. **Explain** Using details from the story, explain why Mrs. Jones wants Roger to learn the lessons she is teaching him. What might be the **consequences** of ignoring these lessons?
2. **Vocabulary** How does Mrs. Jones show that she has **empathy** for Roger?
3. **Analyze Characterization** Collect examples of characterization in a chart. Tell a partner what each character is like.

Type of Clue	Mrs. Jones	Roger
physical traits	large woman	frail, willow-wild
thoughts		wants to run
words		
actions		
reactions of others		

4. **Focus Strategy Clarify Ideas** As you read, the author may provide information that clarifies your ideas. Talk with a partner about a time when your ideas about the events or characters changed as you read on.

Return to the Text

Reread and Write What do you think influenced Roger's choices? Reread to form an opinion and gather at least two pieces of evidence from the text. Then write your opinion. When you are finished, write a response in which you give your opinion of how Mrs. Jones treated Roger.

Key Vocabulary
empathy *n.*, understanding someone else's problems, feelings, or behavior

In Other Words
barren stoop empty staricase that led to her door

APPLY

C ANALYZE

1. **Explain** She has made mistakes in the past and wants him to be a good person and avoid the kinds of problems she had. If he ignores her lessons, he could continue to make poor choices.
RL.9-10.1; L.9-10.6
2. **Vocabulary** Mrs. Jones did have empathy for Roger because she had done some bad things herself.
L.9-10.6
3. **Analyze Literature: Characterization** After partners complete their chart, have them use it to describe the characters.
RL.9-10.3

Character Chart

Clue	Mrs. Jones	Roger
physical traits	large woman	frail, willow-wild
thoughts	things you get by stealing can harm you	wants to run wants to be trusted
words	"I have done things, too, which I would not tell you, son—neither tell God, if He didn't already know."	"Lady, I'm sorry." "You gonna take me to jail?
actions	makes dinner for the boy	tries to steal does what he is told
reactions of others	Roger does what she says	Mrs. Jones tries to teach him a lesson

4. **Focus Strategy: Clarify Ideas** Have volunteers share their partner's passage and strategy with the class. Make sure students include examples of changes in their thinking.
RL.9-10.2

D Return to the Text

Students' opinions might reflect these influences and evidence:

- *Roger wants shoes but has no money.*
- *Mrs. Jones catches him but is kind to him.*

Students' responses should extend beyond a summary and literal analysis to clearly support their opinions with details from the story.
W.9-10.9

Edge Interactive Practice Book, p. 24

CCSS **Literacy.RL.9-10.1** Cite strong and thorough textual evidence to support analysis of what the text says explicitly as well as inferences drawn from the text. **Literacy.RL.9-10.2** Determine a theme or central idea of a text and analyze in detail its development over the course of the text, including how it emerges and is shaped and refined by specific details; provide an objective summary of the text. **Literacy.RL.9-10.3** Analyze how complex characters (e.g., those with multiple or conflicting motivations) develop over the course of a text, interact with other characters, and advance the plot or develop the theme. **Literacy.W.9-10.9** Draw evidence from literary or informational texts to support analysis, reflection, and research. **Literacy.L.9-10.6** Acquire and use accurately general academic and domain-specific words and phrases, sufficient for reading, writing, speaking, and listening at the college and career rediness level; demonstrate independence in gathering vocabulary knowledge when considering a word or phrase important to comprehension or expression.

OBJECTIVES

Reading Strategy
- Plan and Monitor: Clarify Ideas (paraphrase)

Literary Analysis
- Analyze Text Features: Interview Ⓣ

TEACH STRATEGIES

Ⓐ Analyze Text Features: Interview

Introduce Read the introduction under Analyze Text Features and ask students what they already know about how interviews work. Present any points that the students didn't mention; such as quoting what was said and showing where it was changed.

Look Into the Text Use the callouts on p. 52 to teach the text features of an interview. Ask: Why would text that shows background information look different?

Possible response:
- *It is not part of the actual interview.*

Guide students to analyze and evaluate information from text features, such as italicized text, brackets, and ellipses. Then ask: What is the purpose of brackets and ellipses?

Possible response:
- *They show where the text is changed.*

RI.9-10.3

Ⓑ Focus Strategy: Plan and Monitor

Clarify Ideas Review that students use a variety of strategies as they read. Then define this strategy and work through the How To box.

Then have partners paraphrase the last sentence in Look Into the Text.

Possible response:
- *There are not a lot of young offenders who belong in adult court, but there are some.*

RI.9-10.2

ONGOING ASSESSMENT

Ask: What are two special text features that might be used to show information is important?

BEFORE READING Juvenile Justice

interviews by Janet Tobias and Michael Martin

Reading Strategies
- ▶ **Plan and Monitor**
- Determine Importance
- Make Inferences
- Ask Questions
- Make Connections
- Synthesize
- Visualize

Ⓐ

Analyze Text Features: Interview

You're about to read an excerpt from a TV show in which a number of people are interviewed. In an **interview**, one person asks questions for another person to answer. Interviews have specific kinds of features.

Look Into the Text

Judge LaDoris Cordell

A state court trial judge since 1982, until recently she served on the Superior Court of Santa Clara County, where she heard both juvenile and adult cases.

Background information often appears in italics at the beginning of an article or interview.

Q. Do you think any kid ever belongs in adult court?

A. Yes. ... I have come across some young people who are so sophisticated and who have committed such heinous crimes that the adult system is the place for them to be. I haven't come across a lot, but there have been some. ... It can happen, and it does [happen].

Questions and answers make up the interview.

Brackets show that a word has been changed or added.

Ellipses show where the speaker's words have been left out.

Ⓑ

Focus Strategy ▶ Plan and Monitor

As you read, notice when you need to clarify ideas. One way to clarify is to **paraphrase** the text, or restate what's happening in your own words.

HOW TO CLARIFY IDEAS

Focus Strategy

1. Read Judge Cordell's answer above.
2. Identify the main points in the text.
3. Paraphrase the text by putting those main points into your own words.
4. Try it with a partner. Pick a new paragraph and compare your paraphrases.

The Text:

A. Yes. ... I have come across some young people who are so sophisticated and who have committed such heinous crimes that the adult system is the place for them to be.

My Words:

Judge Cordell says that some kids act like adults, so they belong in adult court.

CCSS **Literacy.RI.9-10.2** Determine a central idea of a text and analyze its development over the course of the text, including how it emerges and is shaped and refined by specific details; provide an objective summary of the text. **Literacy. RI.9-10.3** Analyze how the author unfolds an analysis or series of ideas or events, including the order in which the points are made, how they are introduced and developed, and the connections that are drawn between them.

INTERVIEWS

Juvenile Justice from Both Sides of the Bench

by Janet Tobias and Michael Martin

Connect Across Texts

In "Thank You, M'am," Mrs. Jones shows ***empathy*** *for Roger despite what he does. In these interviews, read how real-life judges and attorneys deal with teens who* ***commit*** *crimes.*

Recent legislation in many U.S. states makes it easier to try, or judge, **juvenile** offenders in adult criminal court and not in juvenile court. As a result, more and more teen offenders are **doing time** alongside adults in prison. 1

Teens who are tried as adults can also receive longer sentences, or periods of punishment. Many people believe such punishment is a better fit for more serious crimes. They see this as more important than how old the person is.

Public opinion has changed over the last hundred years. In 1899, the first juvenile court was set up in Illinois. Then, most people believed juveniles were not as responsible for their actions as adults. Illinois wanted to protect each young person, even while it protected the public from crime. The goal of juvenile court was to help offenders make better choices about the future.

Today, however, many people believe that harsh punishment is the better way to stop teens from committing crimes in the future. To explore this topic, the Public Broadcasting System's *Frontline* TV news team interviewed **people from both sides of "the bench."**

1 Clarify Ideas
This paragraph has many difficult ideas and terms. Check **In Other Words**. Then tell the meaning of this paragraph in your own words.

Key Vocabulary
empathy *n.*, the understanding of someone else's problems, feelings, or behavior
• **commit** *v.*, to perform, do, or carry out something, often a crime
juvenile *adj.*, young; *n.*, young person

In Other Words
Recent legislation New laws
doing time being punished
people from both sides of "the bench" judges, who sit on one side of the bench, or desk, and lawyers, who stand on the other side

READ

OBJECTIVES

Vocabulary
• Key Vocabulary T

Reading Strategy
• Plan and Monitor: Clarify Ideas (paraphrase)

Comprehension & Critical Thinking
• Use Text Evidence T

Cultural Perspectives
• U.S. Culture: Symbols

BUILD BACKGROUND

C The Judicial System

Have students study the image. Read the title and introduction.

ELL Explain Symbols Tell students that Lady Justice:

- comes from Greek mythology
- often appears as a statue in front of courthouses
- carries scales to measure the sides in an argument

Ask: Why is Lady Justice blindfolded?

Possible response:
- *justice treats everyone fairly*

D Connect Across Texts

Ask students to predict what might have happened to Roger if Mrs. Jones had called the police.

Possible response:
- *He might have been arrested.*

Read Have students read pp. 53–58. Support and monitor their comprehension using the reading support provided.
RL.9-10.10

TEACH & PRACTICE

E Reading Support

1 Clarify Ideas Provide this sentence prompt: In this paragraph, the writer says that young offenders…

Possible response:
- *are in the same courts as adults, so they go to jail with adults.*

RI.9-10.2

Comprehension Coach

Build Reading Power

Assign students to use the software, based on their instructional needs.

Read Silently
- Comprehension questions with immediate feedback
- Glossary support
- Review text evidence

RL.9-10.10

Listen
- Professional model of fluent reading

Record
- Oral reading fluency practice
- Ongoing fluency assessment with immediate feedback

CCSS Literacy.RI.9-10.10 By the end of grade 9, read and comprehend literary nonfiction in the grades 9–10 text complexity band proficiently, with scaffolding as needed at the high end of the range. By the end of grade 10, read and comprehend literary nonfiction at the high end of the grades 9–10 text complexity band independently and proficiently.

READ

OBJECTIVES

Vocabulary
- Key Vocabulary Ⓣ
- Content Area Vocabulary: Government
- Strategy: Use Contextual Analysis (idioms)

Reading Strategy
- Plan and Monitor: Clarify Ideas (paraphrase)
- Analyze Idioms

Comprehension & Critical Thinking
- Use Text Evidence Ⓣ

Literary Analysis
- Analyze Text Features: Interview Ⓣ

TEACH & PRACTICE

Ⓐ Reading Support

2 Text Features Explain that italics make statements in a text stand out. Ask students to identify the information given in italics.

Possible response:
- *The section in italics introduces the person who is being interviewed. It describes the person's job and his or her experience with juvenile offenders in the court system.*

RI.9-10.3

Ⓑ Reading Support

Analyze Idioms Help students interpret the speaker's use of idioms and how it impacts meaning. Explain that people might use idioms when speaking or writing informally.

Paraphrase this part of a sentence from the interview:

I think we have a real shot at trying to straighten out the 14-year-old, and even the people who are a little bit hard-nosed in the system.

real shot = good chance

straighten out = help

hard-nosed = unwilling to change

Ask: What effect does Judge Edwards's use of idioms have on your understanding?

Possible response:
- *The idioms help readers relate to his ideas.*

RI.9-10.4

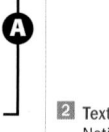

Judge Thomas Edwards
Until recently he was the presiding judge of the Juvenile Court of Santa Clara County, a division of the California Superior Court. He heard between 300 and 350 cases a month. 2 Ⓐ

2 Text Features Notice the italicized words. What information is given here?

Q. Why should we treat a 14-year-old offender differently than a 24-year-old offender?

A. It depends on many, many **circumstances**. But very generally, the 14-year-old does not have the level of **maturity**, thought process, decision-making, experience, or wisdom that a 24-year-old presumably has.

Secondly, a 14-year-old is still growing, may not appreciate the **consequences** of that type of behavior, and **is susceptible to** change, at least to a higher degree than a 24-year-old is. . . . I think we have a real shot at trying to straighten out the 14-year-old, and even the people who are a little bit hard-nosed in the system, such as your average **prosecutor**, will sometimes grudgingly admit that, with a 14-year-old, given the proper level of accountability and the proper types of programs to change their behavior, we have a chance at **salvaging** these kids. Ⓑ

Q. Are there kids who don't belong in juvenile court?

A. Oh, sure. Yes. I've had **sociopaths** in court here. I've had only a few of them, and I've been doing this for a long time. I can only really count maybe a half a dozen, and only two in particular that I would be very frightened to see on the street. But I see them from time to time.

Key Vocabulary
- **circumstances** *n.*, situation
- **maturity** *n.*, the time when a person has all the abilities of an adult
- **consequence** *n.*, result
- **salvage** *v.*, to save or rescue

In Other Words
- **is susceptible to** probably will
- **prosecutor** lawyer whose job is to get punishment for criminals
- **sociopaths** people who do not know right from wrong

VOCABULARY

GOVERNMENT

Content Area Vocabulary: Government

Build vocabulary related to the content area of government.

Teach/Model Use the Make Words Your Own routine (*see the Vocabulary tab*) and the sample sentences below to introduce these words from the selection.

legislation (le-jis-**lā**-shun) ▸ p. 53

The city council passed **legislation** *making cell phone use illegal in schools.*

lawyer (**loi**-yur) ▸ p. 53

To become a **lawyer**, *you have to study the law.*

attorney (u-**tur**-nē) ▸ pp. 53, 57

If you are arrested, you may need to hire an attorney. An **attorney**, *or lawyer, can help sort out your problems with the law.*

offender (u-**fend**-ur) ▸ pp. 53, 54, 55, 56, 57, 58

In a court of law, the **offender** *is the one accused of the crime.*

Practice Have students use the words to describe a television show, movie, or news story they've seen recently.

Apply Set up a courtroom scenario and have students role-play the participants in a trial.

L.9-10.6

CCSS **Literacy.RI.9-10.4** Determine the meaning of words and phrases as they are used in a text, including figurative, connotative, and technical meanings; analyze the cumulative impact of specific word choices on meaning and tone (e.g., how the language of a court opinion differs from that of a newspaper). **Literacy.L.9-10.6** Acquire and use accurately general academic and domain-specific words and phrases, sufficient for reading, writing, speaking, and listening at the college and career readiness level; demonstrate independence in gathering vocabulary knowledge when considering a word or phrase important to comprehension or expression.

Judge LaDoris Cordell

A state court trial judge since 1982, until recently she served on the Superior Court of Santa Clara County, where she heard both juvenile and adult cases.

Q. Why should we treat a 14-year-old offender differently than a 24-year-old offender? 3

A. The problem is that we're taking 14-year-olds, 15-year-olds, 16-year-olds, and we're giving up on them. We're saying, "You've committed a crime, and we're just going to give up on you. You're out of here; society has no use for you." We're throwing away these kids. And I have found, in my own experience, that there are salvageable young people. They have committed some very horrible kinds of crimes, but they are able to get their lives together and **be productive members of society**. I think it is a mistake to just . . . give up on these young people. There is so much more that goes into why that person got there at that point in time so young in their lives. 4

Q. Do you think any kid ever belongs in adult court?

A. Yes. . . . I have come across some young people who are so **sophisticated** and who have committed such **heinous** crimes that the adult system is the place for them to be. I haven't come across a lot, but there have been some. . . . It can happen, and it does [happen]. 5

3 Text Features
The interviews repeat the same question for each person. How is this a good way to get information?

4 Clarify Ideas
What has the judge's experience shown her about how to treat most young offenders?

5 Language
A *logical fallacy* is an error in reasoning. A *rhetorical fallacy* is a way of persuading people with emotion or authority instead of with logic. Do you notice either type of fallacy in Judge Cordell's argument?

In Other Words

be productive members of society work and be responsible like other people
sophisticated clever in a grown-up way
heinous horrible, evil

Monitor Comprehension

Summarize
According to these judges, why should teens be treated differently than adults in court?

TEACH & PRACTICE

C Reading Support

3 Text Features
Rephrase the question: What can you learn when you ask different people the same question?

Possible response:
- *You can hear different viewpoints on the same topic.*

RI.9-10.3

D Reading Support

4 Clarify Ideas Have students reread the paragraph before they answer the question.

ELL Rephrase Language Help students focus in on the key concepts in the paragraph and then rephrase difficult vocabulary. For example:
- Key concept: *The problem is that … we're giving up on them.* Restatement: *We no longer help them; we do not try and save them.*
- Key concept: *I have found … that there are salvageable young people.* Restatement: *Some young people can be saved.*

Ask: What does the judge think about how to treat young offenders?

Possible response:
- *The judge believes young offenders should be treated as though they still have a chance to turn their lives around.*

RI.9-10.2

E 5 Language Explain that logical or rhetorical fallacies distract the reader from sound reasoning. Ask: *Does Judge Cordell use any distracting reason?*

Possible response:
- *She says we are throwing kids away, but then says some belong in the adult system.*

RI.9-10.8

Monitor Comprehension

Summarize Have students review the selection. Then ask: What are reasons stated in the interviews that teen offenders should be treated differently than adult offenders?

Possible responses:
- *Juvenile offenders still have a chance to change.*
- *Juvenile offenders might not have the maturity to make good choices.*

RI.9-10.2

CCSS Literacy.RI.9-10.2 Determine a central idea of a text and analyze its development over the course of the text, including how it emerges and is shaped and refined by specific details; provide an objective summary of the text. Literacy.RI.9-10.3 Analyze how the author unfolds an analysis or series of ideas or events, including the order in which the points are made, how they are introduced and developed, and the connections that are drawn between them. Literacy.RI.9-10.8 Delineate and evaluate the argument and specific claims in a text, assessing whether the reasoning is valid and the evidence is relevant and sufficient; identify false statements and fallacious reasoning.

OBJECTIVES

Reading Strategy
- Plan and Monitor: Clarify Ideas (paraphrase)

Comprehension & Critical Thinking
- Use Text Evidence Ⓣ

Literary Analysis
- Analyze Text Features: Interview Ⓣ

Research Skill
- Gather Information

Grammar
- Verbs with Compound Subjects Ⓣ

Cultural Perspectives
- Compare Cultures

TEACH & PRACTICE

Ⓐ Reading Support

6 Clarify Ideas Have students reread the paragraph and identify essential words and phrases.

Possible responses:
- *person had been maimed, young person, shot him, graduate from college, graduate from prison*

Then have students paraphrase the paragraph into their own words.

Possible response:
- *One victim of a crime committed by a youth would rather have him go to school than to jail.*

RI.9-10.2

Ⓑ Reading Support

7 Content Area Connections See the Health & Biology activity on T57.

RI.9-10.8

Ⓒ Reading Support

8 Text Features Explain that when a text is an exact record of what was said, anything that is changed must be shown clearly. Sometimes words are added or changed to help the reader understand what is being said. Ask students what the brackets might show.

Possible response:
- *The brackets show words that are added or changed to make the sentence make sense.*

RI.9-10.3

GRAMMAR SKILLS PATH
6 Plural Nouns
7 Subject-Verb Agreement: Forms of *Be*
8 Subject-Verb Agreement: Action Verbs
▶ 9 Verbs with Compound Subjects — ELL Language & Grammar Lab
10 Review: Subject-Verb Agreement

Bridgett Jones
Former supervisor of the Juvenile Division of the Santa Clara County Public Defender's Office

Q. Why should we treat a 14-year-old offender differently than a 24-year-old offender?

A. I think the community understands, or should understand, that the younger a person is, the more likely it is that they can change. And the best way I've heard it put is from a **victim** in a very serious case.

Ⓐ This person had been **maimed** for life. He had **indicated to** the young person who shot him, or was **alleged** to have shot him, that he would rather meet up with this person ten years down the road as a graduate from a college versus a graduate from [prison]. 6

He [understood] that this person was eventually going to get back out and be in our community. They don't go away. They come back. And the younger they are, the more likely it is that they are going to come back into our community. So I guess as a community we have to decide what is it we're willing to get back in the long run.

Ⓑ Children are not little adults. They think differently. They respond and react to things differently than adults do. . . . So why should the consequences be the same as for an adult? 7

Ⓒ The only thing that's going to work with kids like [these] is a willingness of the community to **redeem** them and saying, "Look, your life's not over, there's still hope for you." 8

6 **Clarify Ideas** What does the judge's story show? Put the meaning in your own words.

7 **Content Area Connections** The teen brain is biologically different than the adult brain. How does this fact support the judge's argument?

8 **Text Features** What do the brackets mean in this sentence?

In Other Words
victim person hurt by a crime
maimed physically hurt, wounded
indicated to told or shown
alleged suspected
redeem help and forgive

Social Studies Background
A district attorney prosecutes, or seeks punishment for, someone charged with a crime. If the person cannot afford a lawyer, a public defender has the job of advising and representing the person.

GRAMMAR

Verbs with Compound Subjects

Teach/Model Display the transparency. Explain the definition of a compound subject. Point out the conjunctions that signal two subjects as you work through the examples. Explain the rules for compound subjects and verbs. Show how the sentences above fit the rules.

Practice A. Have students locate conjunctions in numbers 2–5 to help them choose the correct verb. **B.** After students write new sentences, have volunteers share their sentences and name the compound subjects.

L.9-10.1

Grammar & Writing Practice Book, pp. 17–18

Grammar Transparency 9

GRAMMAR VERBS WITH COMPOUND SUBJECTS 9

What's a Compound Subject?

It's a Subject with Two or More Nouns.

When a subject has two or more nouns joined by **and** or **or**, it is called a **compound subject**.

1. **Judges and lawyers** make decisions in juvenile courts.
2. A **juvenile and** an **adult** are different.
3. A **counselor or** a **psychologist** helps young people.
4. The **parents or** the **school** needs to help.
5. The **school or** the **parents** need to help.

How do you know what verb to use with a compound subject?
- If you see **and**, use a plural verb like **make** or **are**.
- If you see **or**, look at the last noun in the subject. Is it singular? Then use a singular verb. Is it plural? Then use a plural verb.

Try It

A. Say the sentences with the correct form of the verb.

1. A juvenile offender **(is / are)** a young person who commits a crime.
2. A judge and lawyers **(is / are)** involved in these cases.
3. Many judges and lawyers **(believe / believes)** that these young people deserve help.
4. Counselors or the psychologist **(help / helps)** a young offender make better decisions.
5. The judge and the other professionals **(want / wants)** young offenders to get the help they need.

B. Now write two more sentences about judges and lawyers. Use a compound subject. Sentences will vary.

CCSS **Literacy.RI.9-10.2** Determine a central idea of a text and analyze its development over the course of the text, including how it emerges and is shaped and refined by specific details; provide an objective summary of the text. **Literacy.RI.9-10.3** Analyze how the author unfolds an analysis or series of ideas or events, including the order in which the points are made, how they are introduced and developed, and the connections that are drawn between them. **Literacy.L.9-10.1** Demonstrate command of the conventions of standard English grammar and usage when writing or speaking. **Literacy.SL.9-10.1.a** Come to discussions prepared, having read and researched material under study; explicitly draw on that preparation by referring to evidence from texts and other research on the topic or issue to stimulate a thoughtful, well-reasoned exchange of ideas.

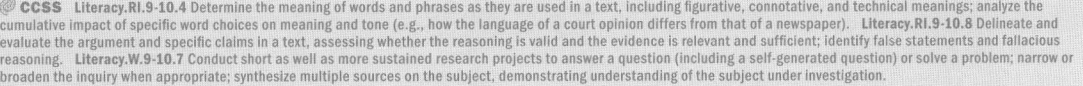

Kurt Kumli
The supervising deputy district attorney for the Juvenile Division of the Santa Clara County District Attorney's Office, he has practiced exclusively in juvenile court.

Q. Why should we treat a 14-year-old offender differently than a 24-year-old offender?

A. If we could take every kid and surround the kid with full-time staffs of psychologists and drug and alcohol counselors, then perhaps no kid should be in adult court. But the fact is, there are only a limited number of **resources** in the juvenile justice system. . . . You have to make **the hard call**, sometimes, as to whether or not the high-end offenders really are the **just recipients of** the [limited] resources that the juvenile justice system has available to it. 9 **D**

Q. What does it take to rehabilitate young offenders?

A. What works is different for every kid, but the one rule that I think is applicable, after years of seeing this, is "the sooner, the better." We need to reach these kids with **alternatives**, with opportunities, before they start to feel [like nobody cares]. If we took half of the money that we spend on **incarceration** and put it in **front-end programs** to give these kids alternatives, then we wouldn't have as many **back-end kids** that we needed to incarcerate. And I think that is the immediate answer. 10 **E**

9 **Clarify Ideas**
What does Mr. Kumli mean here? Put the meaning in your own words.

10 **Language**
Are Mr. Kumli's logic and rhetoric sound? Do you find any fallacies?

Monitor Comprehension
Explain
Tell what Kurt Kumli means by "the sooner, the better."

In Other Words
resources staff people and services
the hard call a difficult decision
just recipients of people who should receive
rehabilitate help, fix the problems of
alternatives other choices
incarceration keeping people in jail
front-end programs programs that help kids before they get into trouble
back-end kids kids who have already committed crimes

TEACH & PRACTICE

D Reading Support

9 **Clarify Ideas** Review the paragraph to get its meaning well in mind.

ELL Substitution Have students read the paragraph aloud, substituting the glossary explanations for bold terms.

Have students paraphrase what Mr. Kumli means.

Possible response:
- *The system doesn't have enough resources to help every juvenile offender, so choices have to be made about who deserves them.*

RI.9-10.2

E Reading Support

10 **Language** Review the meanings of *logical fallacy* and *rhetorical fallacy* (from page 53). Explain Mr. Kumli's logic about spending money on kids sooner rather than later. Ask: *Is this logical?*

Possible response:
- *Yes, it's logical because it would give kids something to turn to besides crime.*

RI.9-10.8

Monitor Comprehension

Explain Point out the parallel word structure in the phrase "the sooner, the better." Have students explain the meaning using different words.

Possible response:
- *Kurt Kumli is saying that if young people get help early in life, they have a greater chance of being successful.*

RI.9-10.4

CONTENT AREA CONNECTIONS

Research Juvenile Justice Systems

SOCIOLOGY

Conduct Research Have students research juvenile justice in other countries and use the information to answer the following questions:

- Is juvenile crime a big problem?
- What rules are there for young people or "minors"?
- At what age can a young person be tried as an adult?
- How are the sentences or punishments different for children and adults?
- What programs or resources are available to help or rehabilitate young offenders?

Share and Compare Students can share their findings with the class to compare juvenile justice across countries.
W.9-10.7

Explore the Brain

HEALTH & BIOLOGY

Share Facts Tell students the following:

- The frontal lobe of the brain, which handles all goal-directed or voluntary behavior, develops throughout adolescence, up to age 20.
- A male's level of testosterone, a hormone associated with aggression, is ten times higher in adolescence than in childhood.

Discuss How does biology influence a young person's choices?

Have students select what they think is the correct answer:

1. Adolescence is typically the *healthiest/unhealthiest* period in a person's life span.
2. Death rates *increase/decrease* dramatically from childhood to adolescence.

Research and Confirm Then have students conduct research on adolescence to discover whether they were right.
W.9-10.7

CCSS **Literacy.RI.9-10.4** Determine the meaning of words and phrases as they are used in a text, including figurative, connotative, and technical meanings; analyze the cumulative impact of specific word choices on meaning and tone (e.g., how the language of a court opinion differs from that of a newspaper). **Literacy.RI.9-10.8** Delineate and evaluate the argument and specific claims in a text, assessing whether the reasoning is valid and the evidence is relevant and sufficient; identify false statements and fallacious reasoning. **Literacy.W.9-10.7** Conduct short as well as more sustained research projects to answer a question (including a self-generated question) or solve a problem; narrow or broaden the inquiry when appropriate; synthesize multiple sources on the subject, demonstrating understanding of the subject under investigation.

READ

OBJECTIVES

Reading Strategy
- Plan and Monitor: Clarify Ideas (paraphrase)

Comprehension & Critical Thinking
- Use Text Evidence Ⓣ

Literary Analysis
- Analyze Text Features: Interview Ⓣ

Writing
- Form: Response to Literature

APPLY

Ⓐ ANALYZE

1. **Recall and Interpret** Teen offenders tried in adult court might receive longer sentences and serve their time along with adult criminals.
   One rhetorical fallacy is the argument that if an offender is a sociopath, he or she automatically belongs in adult court ("Are there kids who don't belong in juvenile court? Oh, sure. Yes. I've had sociopaths in court here." p. 54).
   RI.9-10.1; RI.9-10.8; L.9-10.6
2. **Vocabulary** Young people should be tried as adults when they commit violent crimes or seem like adults.
   L.9-10.6
3. **Analyze Text Features: Interview** The Q. and A. labels show that this article is an interview. The brackets show words that were changed or added. Ellipses show where words were left out.
   RI.9-10.3
4. **Focus Strategy: Clarify Ideas** Young offenders might not understand the effects of their actions. They can often be taught to change their bad behavior.
   RI.9-10.2

Ⓑ Return to the Text

Before they begin writing, encourage students to express their own thoughts about juvenile justice. After reading each interview, students can make note of which statements in the interview match with their own.
W.9-10.9

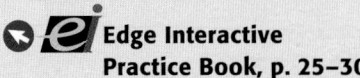

Judge Nancy Hoffman
Judge Hoffman served on the Superior Court of Santa Clara County, where she handled both juvenile and adult cases. She is currently retired.

Q. What does it take to rehabilitate young offenders?

A. I would like to see groups . . . working with troubled families and youth, before they get to middle school and . . . high school. Something is causing the **minor** to do things like not go to school, stay out till three o'clock in the morning . . . We **intervene** with a minor, but there's very little done with the family, and we're sending the minor right back in that situation. ❖

ANALYZE Juvenile Justice

Ⓐ

1. **Recall and Interpret** What are some of the reasons that judges and attorneys decide not to try **juveniles** as adults? Are there any fallacies in the debate? Support your answer with text evidence.
2. **Vocabulary** According to Judge Cordell, under what **circumstances** should juveniles be tried as adults?
3. **Analyze Text Features: Interview** What text features in this selection show that it includes interviews? Why is this a good way to present the information?
4. **Focus Strategy Clarify Ideas** Paraphrase Judge Edwards's thoughts about how to treat teen offenders.

Ⓑ

Return to the Text

Reread and Write Which person's ideas are closest to your own? Reread to confirm. Write a paragraph to tell why.

In Other Words
minor person under the age of 18
intervene get involved to prevent or solve problems

Interactive Reading

Have students reread and mark "Juvenile Justice" within the Edge Interactive Practice Book to apply their knowledge of text features and to practice the Focus Strategy—Plan and Monitor: Clarify Ideas.

Edge Interactive Practice Book, p. 25–30

Unit Project

Progress Check Allow time for students to work on their unit projects. Meet with individuals and/or groups to provide guidance and check on their progress.

myNGconnect.com
- **Unit Planning Tools**
- **Unit Project Evaluation Rubric**

CCSS **Literacy.RI.9-10.1** Cite strong and thorough textual evidence to support analysis of what the text says explicitly as well as inferences drawn from the text. **Literacy.RI.9-10.3** Analyze how the author unfolds an analysis or series of ideas or events, including the order in which the points are made, how they are introduced and developed, and the connections that are drawn between them. **Literacy.RI.9-10.8** Delineate and evaluate the argument and specific claims in a text, assessing whether the reasoning is valid and the evidence is relevant and sufficient; identify false statements and fallacious reasoning. **Literacy.W.9-10.9** Draw evidence from literary or informational texts to support analysis, reflection, and research. **Literacy.L.9-10.6** Acquire and use accurately general academic and domain-specific words and phrases, sufficient for reading, writing, speaking, and listening at the college and career readiness level; demonstrate independence in gathering vocabulary knowledge when considering a word or phrase important to comprehension or expression.

EQ What Influences a Person's Choices?

Reading

Critical Thinking

1. **Analyze** Complete the **Anticipation Guide** on page 40 again as if you were a character or person interviewed in the text. Defend your answers using ideas and quotations from the selections.
2. **Compare** How would Roger's treatment by today's court system be similar to how Mrs. Jones treats him? How would it be different?
3. **Interpret** Mrs. Jones tells Roger, "I have done things, too." Describe what she might have done in the past that helped her have **empathy** with Roger.
4. **Speculate** Imagine that Roger goes home that night and writes Mrs. Jones a letter. What does he say?
5. **Draw Conclusions** What things influence people's choices as **juveniles**? As adults? Give examples from both texts.

Writing

Write About Literature

Interpretive Response Why should we treat a 14-year-old offender differently than a 24-year-old offender? Identify the strongest reasons, and support them with examples and quotations from both texts. Embed the quotations in your writing. Gather text evidence in a T chart:

Thank You, M'am	Juvenile Justice

Vocabulary

Key Vocabulary Review

Oral Review Work with a partner. Use these words to complete the paragraph.

circumstances	**contact**	**maturity**
commit	**empathy**	**salvage**
consequences	**juvenile**	

Some young people grow up in difficult __(1)__ that influence the choices they make. Like Roger in "Thank You, M'am," some teens break the law, __(2)__ crimes, and come in __(3)__ with the law. They do not have the wisdom or __(4)__ to make different choices. Some do not understand the __(5)__ that result from breaking the law. They usually end up in the __(6)__ justice system for young people. Many judges and lawyers, however, have __(7)__ for troubled teens and understand their problems. They believe that they can __(8)__, or save, teens. These adults trust that teens can change their lives for the better.

Writing Application Recall a time when you or a friend showed **maturity** in a difficult situation. Write a paragraph that uses at least four Key Vocabulary words.

Fluency

Read with Ease: Phrasing

Assess your reading fluency with the passage in the Reading Handbook, p. 752. Then complete the self-check below.

1. I did/did not pause appropriately for punctuation and phrases.
2. My words correct per minute: ____

Writing

Write About Literature

Edge Interactive Practice Book, p. 31

Interpretive Response Have students use the graphic organizer to plan and write the response. Help students identify important quotations and embed them within the response. Invite volunteers to share their responses. Chart the supporting reasons and have the group vote to choose the strongest argument.
RI.9-10.1; W.9-10.1

Vocabulary

Key Vocabulary Review

1. *circumstances* **2.** *commit* **3.** *contact* **4.** *maturity* **5.** *consequences* **6.** *juvenile* **7.** *empathy* **8.** *salvage*
L.9-10.6

Fluency

Read with Ease: Phrasing

Ensure that students complete the self-check.
RI.9-10.10

Lessson 14

REFLECT AND ASSESS

OBJECTIVES

Vocabulary
- Key Vocabulary Ⓣ

Comprehension & Critical Thinking
- Compare Across Texts
- Use Text Evidence Ⓣ

Reading Fluency
- Phrasing Ⓣ

Literary Analysis
- Evaluate Literature

Writing
- Form: Analysis of an Issue
- Form: Paragraph

Reading

Critical Thinking

1. **Analyze** Model completing the Anticipation Guide as if you are Mrs. Jones. Have students complete the activity and defend their answers.
RL.9-10.1; RI.9-10.1
2. **Compare** Some judges in today's court system might want to help Roger in a similar way to Mrs. Jones during the 1950s. However, other judges might not want to help him. Unlike Mrs. Jones, judges would also not be able to give Roger food or money.
3. **Interpret** Mrs. Jones might have stolen or tried to steal.
4. **Speculate** Roger may thank Mrs. Jones for giving him a second chance. Because she is so nice to him, he probably feels remorse.
5. **Draw Conclusions** Juveniles may make choices that are influenced by what they want, as Roger shows when he steals to get money to buy the shoes. Adults may make choices to protect children, as Mrs. Jones does when she takes Roger home and tries to help him.
   - Roger needs money; teens do not have the maturity or experience of adults.
   - Mrs. Jones has empathy for Roger; many adults don't want to give up on teen offenders.

RL.9-10.1; RI.9-10.1

ASSESS & RETEACH

Assessments Handbook, pp. 1f–1i

Have students complete the **Reader Reflection**. Then give students the **Cluster Test** to measure their progress. Group students as needed for reteaching.

CCSS **Literacy.RL.9-10.1** Cite strong and thorough textual evidence to support analysis of what the text says explicitly as well as inferences drawn from the text. **Literacy. RI.9-10.1** Cite strong and thorough textual evidence to support analysis of what the text says explicitly as well as inferences drawn from the text. **Literacy.RI.9-10.10** By the end of grade 9, read and comprehend literary nonfiction in the grades 9-10 text complexity band proficiently, with scaffolding as needed at the high end of the range. By the end of grade 10, read and comprehend literary nonfiction at the high end of the grades 9-10 text complexity band independently and proficiently. **Literacy.W.9-10.1** Write arguments to support claims in an analysis of substantive topics or texts, using valid reasoning and relevant and sufficient evidence. **Literacy.L.9-10.6** Acquire and use accurately general academic and domain-specific words and phrases, sufficient for reading, writing, speaking, and listening at the college and career readiness level; demonstrate independence in gathering vocabulary knowledge when considering a word or phrase important to comprehension or expression.

Lesson 15

INTEGRATE THE LANGUAGE ARTS

OBJECTIVES

Language Function
- Express Ideas and Opinions

Literary Analysis
- Analyze Dialogue

Grammar
- Subject-Verb Agreement

Grammar

Make Subjects and Verbs Agree

Grammar Transparency 10

Review Use the transparency to review subject-verb agreement. Then conduct the activity on p. 60.

Oral Practice Make sure the subject and verb agree in students' sentences.

Written Practice Mrs. Jones *takes* Roger home. He *is* scared and hungry. Mrs. Jones *decides* to make dinner for Roger.
L.9-10.1

Language Development

Express Ideas and Opinions

Evaluate students' acquisition of this language function with the Language Acquisition Rubric.
SL.9-10.1.a

Assessments Handbook, p. 1o

Literary Analysis

Analyze Dialogue

1. "I want a pair of blue suede shoes," Roger said.
2. Mrs. Jones said, "Don't you dare steal again!"
3. "Wash your face, boy!" Mrs. Jones demanded.
4. "There is no one home at my house," Roger told her.

L.9-10.3.a

Edge Interactive Practice Book, p. 32

Grammar

Make Subjects and Verbs Agree

The verb you use depends on your subject. These subjects and verbs go together. All the verbs are **forms of be**.

I **am**	We **are**
You **are**	You **are**
He, She, or It **is**	They **are**

Action verbs have two forms in the present:

I **work** a lot. Mrs. Jones **works** every day.

Add **-s** to the action verb only when you talk about one other person, place, or thing. Find the subject in each sentence. How does the verb end?

Roger **pulls** at the pocketbook.
The strap **breaks**. The pocketbook **falls**.
Mrs. Jones **sees** Roger. She **shakes** him.

Oral Practice (1–5) Choose from each column to make five sentences. **Example:** Roger is hungry.

Roger	work	at home.
They	is	every day.
Mrs. Jones	are	respect.
The neighbors	eats	young.
Young people	need	hungry.

Written Practice (6–15) Write ten sentences to tell what happens when Mrs. Jones makes dinner for Roger. Start with these sentences and choose the correct verb. Then tell what else happens.

Mrs. Jones (take/takes) Roger home. He (is/are) scared and hungry. Mrs. Jones (decide/decides) to make dinner for Roger.

Language Development

Express Ideas and Opinions

Group Talk What do you think happened to Roger after he left Mrs. Jones's apartment? Tell your ideas. Then tell what you think about Roger, Mrs. Jones, and all that happened.

Literary Analysis

Analyze Dialogue

An important part of characterization is how the characters talk, or their **dialogue**. A writer shows dialogue in several ways:

- Quotation marks are set at the beginning and end of the character's spoken words.
- Every time a different character speaks, a new paragraph starts.
- Speaker words such as *she said, he asked,* or *whispered the boy* tell who said the words and sometimes how the words were spoken.

Dialogue makes the characters seem real by revealing their thoughts, responses, and feelings. For example, in "Thank You, M'am," Mrs. Jones says, "You a lie!" Hughes could have written: "Mrs. Jones called the boy a liar." Her spoken words show more about her character than a simple description.

With a partner, rewrite these sentences as dialogue. Use quotation marks and add speaker words that tell how the words were spoken.

1. Roger said he wanted some blue suede shoes.
2. Mrs. Jones told Roger not to steal again.
3. Mrs. Jones told Roger to wash his face.
4. Roger explained that there was nobody home at his house.

GRAMMAR

Review: Subject-Verb Agreement

Review Display the transparency. Remind students that the verb they use depends on the subject. Use the charts to review the forms of *be* and action verbs.

A. Oral Practice As students choose the correct verb form, underline and have them say the sentence aloud. Use the charts to offer immediate corrective feedback.

B. Written Practice Work through the example. Explain that some sentences have no errors. Have the group tell you how to edit the paragraph. Ask a volunteer to read the corrected paragraph to the class.
L.9-10.1

Grammar & Writing Practice Book, pp. 19–20

GRAMMAR SKILLS PATH
6 Plural Nouns
7 Subject-Verb Agreement: Forms of Be
8 Subject-Verb Agreement: Action Verbs
9 Verbs with Compound Subjects
10 Review: Subject-Verb Agreement ELL Language & Grammar Lab

Grammar Transparency 10

GRAMMAR REVIEW: SUBJECT-VERB AGREEMENT 10

Make Subjects and Verbs Agree

Remember: The verb you use depends on your subject. These subjects and verbs go together:

Forms of *Be*	Action Verbs
I **am** here.	I **make** choices.
You **are** here.	You **make** choices.
He, she, or it **is** here.	He, she, or it **makes** choices.
We, you, or they **are** here.	We, you, or they **make** choices.
My friends **are** here.	Teenagers **make** choices.
My friends and I **are** here.	My friends and I **make** choices.

Try It

A. Say each sentence with the correct verb form.

1. I **(make / makes)** choices every day.
2. I **(am / are)** sure my choices affect my future.
3. My best friend **(is / are)** an influence on my choices.
4. She **(help / helps)** me make responsible choices.
5. I think a teenager **(is / are)** mature enough to make many choices.

B. Edit the paragraph. Fix five mistakes. The first is done for you.

Maria ~~am~~ is a teenager. She ~~make~~ makes choices every day. Her parents help her. They think a teenager ~~need~~ needs guidance. Maria and her friend ~~makes~~ make some choices together. They think it's important to have help. Either their parents or their friends ~~helps~~ help them.

CCSS **Literacy.SL.9-10.1.a** Come to discussions prepared, having read and researched material under study; explicitly draw on that preparation by referring to evidence from texts and other research on the topic or issue to stimulate a thoughtful, well-reasoned exchange of ideas. **Literacy.L.9-10.1** Demonstrate command of the conventions of standard English grammar and usage when writing or speaking. **Literacy.L.9-10.3.a** Write and edit work so that it conforms to the guidelines in a style manual (e.g., MLA Handbook, Turabian's Manual for Writers) appropriate for the discipline and writing type.

Vocabulary Study

Word Roots

Many English words come from other languages. This chart shows some common roots.

ROOT	MEANING	ORIGIN
circum	around	Latin
dem	people	Greek
swer	proclaim	Anglo-Saxon

Knowing these roots can help you learn more words in various content areas in English. Find the root in each word, guess the word's meaning, and confirm your guess in a print or an online dictionary.

1. answer **2.** democracy **3.** circumference

Listening / Speaking

Interview

History: Choices Interview a teacher about a person in history who made an important choice.

1. **Prepare for the Interview** Think about what you want to know. Then write a list of open-ended questions you will ask, such as "Why do you think the person made that choice?"
2. **Conduct the Interview** Ask your questions and listen respectfully to the answers. Make sure you understand the main ideas and details as well as the language your teacher uses. Ask clarifying questions, if necessary.
3. **Share What You Learned** Tell the class about the highlights of your interview.

Language and Learning Handbook, page 702

Writing on Demand

Write a Short Comparison Essay

A test may ask you to write a response to literature. The prompt often names the selection and asks you to think about some aspect of it.

1. **Unpack the Prompt** Read the prompt and underline the key words.

> **Writing Prompt**
> In "Thank You, M'am," Roger learned an important lesson. Think about a lesson you have learned. Write an essay to compare the lessons. Use examples from the story and your life for support.

2. **Plan Your Response** Choose a life lesson to write about. Then compare it to Roger's. Use a Venn diagram to help you plan.

Venn Diagram

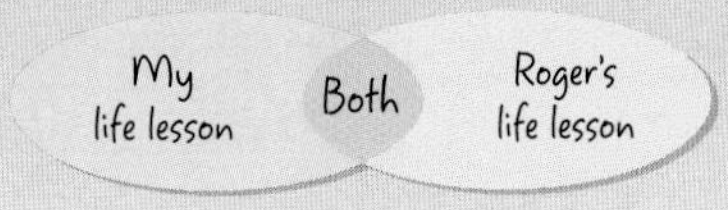

3. **Draft** Organize your essay like this.

Essay Organizer

> In "Thank You, M'am," Roger learned [tell what his lesson was]. In my life, I have learned [tell what my lesson was].
> Our life lessons are alike because [tell how they are alike]. For example, in the story Roger [give an example from the story]. I also [give an example from my own life that is similar].
> However, our life lessons are different because [tell how they differ]. [give an example from the story], but [give an example from my own life that is different]. In conclusion, [summarize the comparison].

4. **Check Your Work** Reread your essay. Ask:
   - Does my essay address the writing prompt?
   - Did I give examples to support my ideas?
   - Are all my sentences complete?

Writing Handbook, page 784

Lesson 16

INTEGRATE THE LANGUAGE ARTS

OBJECTIVES

Vocabulary
- Word Roots Ⓣ

Listening and Speaking
- Interview

Writing
- Writing Process
- Form: Comparison Essay Ⓣ

Vocabulary Study

Word Roots

1. swer; a reply to a question
2. dem; government by the people
3. circum; the distance around a circle

Introduce several new roots and brainstorm other content-area words: *kno* (Anglo-Saxon); *knowledge, chron* (Greek); *chronological; port* (Latin); *export.*
L.9-10.4.c

Edge Interactive Practice Book, pp. 33

Listening / Speaking

Interview

History: Choices Brainstorm famous people and some important life choices they made. For example:

César Chávez	to fight for migrant workers
Rosa Parks	not to sit in the back of the bus

Remind students to listen carefully and to ask questions for clarification so they can summarize the information correctly.
SL.9-10.1.a; SL.9-10.4

See **Language and Learning Handbook** p. 726 for further instruction.

Writing on Demand

Comparison Essay

1. **Unpack the Prompt** Help students identify the key words.
2. **Plan Your Response** Model the completion of a Venn Diagram.
3. **Draft** Have students use the essay organizer as a model.
4. **Check Your Work** Have students use the Writing Rubric.

See **Writing Handbook** p. 784.
W.9-10.2; W.9-10.9.a

Writing Rubric Comparison Essay

Exceptional	• Essay addresses topic by showing clear comparisons. • Examples are detailed and relevant to topic. • Sentences are complete.
Competent	• Essay pertains to topic. • Examples are adequate. • Sentences are complete with no more than one sentence error.
Developing	• Essay may stray from topic. • Examples are loosely connected to topic. • Sentences are sometimes incomplete.
Beginning	• Essay does not address topic. • Examples are not clearly connected to topic. • Sentences are often incomplete.

CCSS **Literacy.W.9-10.2** Write informative/explanatory texts to examine and convey complex ideas, concepts, and information clearly and accurately through the effective selection, organization, and analysis of content. **Literacy.W.9-10.9.a** Apply grades 9-10 Reading standards to literature (e.g., "Analyze how an author draws on and transforms source material in a specific work [e.g., how Shakespeare treats a theme or topic from Ovid or the Bible or how a later author draws on a play by Shakespeare]"). **Literacy.SL.9-10.4** Present information, findings, and supporting evidence clearly, concisely, and logically such that listeners can follow the line of reasoning and the organization, development, substance, and style are appropriate to purpose, audience, and task. **Literacy.L.9-10.4.c** Consult general and specialized reference materials (e.g., dictionaries, glossaries, thesauruses), both print and digital, to find the pronunciation of a word or determine or clarify its precise meaning, its part of speech, or its etymology.

Lesson 17

LISTENING AND SPEAKING WORKSHOP

OBJECTIVES

Listening and Speaking
- Respond to Literature
- Oral Response Ⓣ
- Use a Rubric

BUILD BACKGROUND

Ⓐ Oral Response to Literature

Introduce Explain that in a response to literature, the reader describes his or her thoughts about a selection.

Oral Response Responding to literature orally requires different skills from a written response.

TEACH & PRACTICE

Ⓑ Plan Your Oral Response

Brainstorm Have each student choose a selection. List and discuss the elements students should incorporate into their responses:

- **Characters:** Were they believable? Did you connect with them?
- **Setting:** Did it seem real? What details made it real?
- **Plot:** What was the conflict? Did the resolution make sense?
- **Feeling:** How did the selection make you feel?

ELL Use Visuals Encourage students to look through the selection and use the images to help them think about the characters, setting, and plot events.

If students recognize literary or mythological allusions in the selection they are considering, ask them to discuss whether the listening audience would understand the allusions.

Listening and Speaking Workshop

Oral Response to Literature

Ⓐ **You've just finished reading a selection. Did you like it? Did you think it was boring? Did you identify with a character's point of view? Tell everyone what you think and why. Share your response to one of the selections in this unit with your classmates. Here is how to do it.**

1. Plan Your Oral Response

Ⓑ **Choose the selection about which you will present your oral response. Then do the following:**

- Read the selection several times. Get to know it well.
- Think about how you feel about the selection. Did it move you, teach you something, or entertain you? What do you think it means?
- Look at the individual parts of the selection—the plot, the characters, and the setting. Decide what you like the most.
- Write down some notes about your response to the selection.

2. Practice Your Oral Response

Ⓒ **Practice your oral response for another person who knows the selection.**

- Begin by telling what you liked or disliked about the selection and why.
- Be sure to include a few examples from the selection to support your ideas.
- Make sure you give your response within the time limit.
- Get helpful suggestions from your listener.
- Edit your presentation by incorporating the listener's comments.

3. Present Your Oral Response

Ⓓ **Keep your oral response focused and clear by doing the following:**

- Clearly state your main points.
- Let your feelings about the selection show in your words, tone of voice, facial expressions, and body language.
- Establish eye contact with your audience.
- Look at your notes occasionally, but not too often.
- Speak clearly and loudly so that the audience can understand everything you say.

myNGconnect.com
Download the rubric.

62 Unit 1 Listening and Speaking Workshop

4. Discuss and Rate the Oral Responses

Use the rubric to discuss and rate the oral responses, including your own.

Oral Response Rubric

Scale	Content of Oral Report	Student's Preparation	Student's Delivery
3 Great	• Expressed a clear, well-focused response to the selection • Was interesting and held my attention throughout	• Seemed to understand the selection very well • Included good support from the selection to develop the response	• Expressed feelings well and made eye contact • Spoke clearly and loudly
2 Good	• Expressed a fairly clear response to the selection • Held my interest much of the time	• Seemed to understand the selection fairly well • Included some support to develop the response	• Expressed feelings and made eye contact most of the time • Could be heard most of the time
1 Needs Work	• Didn't express a clear response to the selection • Was not very interesting	• Did not seem to understand the selection • Did not include support for the response	• Was stiff, not convincing, and did not make eye contact • Could not be heard or understood well

E

DO IT ▸ When you are finished preparing, present your oral response, and share your views with your audience.

Language and Learning Handbook, page 702

Which aspects of a good oral presentation is this speaker demonstrating?

C Practice Your Oral Response

Model Model a short oral response for students.

- Tell students why you liked a book you have recently read, and why.
- Give examples from the book to support your reasons.
- Make eye contact, speak clearly and loudly, and express your feelings.
- Only glance at your notes occasionally.

Prepare Have students write an outline of their response. Remind them to include examples from the text to support their thoughts about the selection.

Use a Rubric Review the Oral Response Rubric. Have partners practice their responses together and use the rubric to offer feedback. Remind students to incorporate any feedback from their partner into their responses.
SL.9-10.1.a

myNGconnect.com

Oral Response Rubric

APPLY

D Present Your Oral Response

Present Have students review the presentation tips and present their oral responses. Have students take notes while listening in order to summarize the speaker's ideas and help with feedback. Conclude by having students ask the presenter questions for clarification and elaboration.
SL.9-10.4; L.9-10.3

E Discuss and Rate the Oral Responses

Give Feedback Have students give written or oral feedback to the presenter. Reviewers should rate the presenter with a 1, 2, or 3 and support their rating with comments about the content, preparation, and delivery. Students should also rate themselves.
SL.9-10.3

ONGOING ASSESSMENT
Have students incorporate peer feedback into their responses and explain how the feedback helped.

DIFFERENTIATED INSTRUCTION

As you conduct the workshop with students, adjust your teaching strategies to their needs.

Struggling Readers

Graphic Organizer Help students complete a chart to help organize their notes about the selection.

Characters	Setting	Main Plot Events	Reactions

Have students work with a partner to share their ideas or present their responses together.

English Language Learners ELL

Use Visuals Have students respond to the literature by drawing a picture, or using a graphic organizer or other visuals to help with their response.

Challenge

Lead the Activity Have students prepare their oral response and model it as an example for the group. Then students can help the group as they prepare to present.

CCSS **Literacy.SL.9-10.1.a** Come to discussions prepared, having read and researched material under study; explicitly draw on that preparation by referring to evidence from texts and other research on the topic or issue to stimulate a thoughtful, well-reasoned exchange of ideas. **Literacy.SL.9-10.3** Evaluate a speaker's point of view, reasoning, and use of evidence and rhetoric, identifying any fallacious reasoning or exaggerated or distorted evidence. **Literacy.SL.9-10.4** Present information, findings, and supporting evidence clearly, concisely, and logically such that listeners can follow the line of reasoning and the organization, development, substance, and style are appropriate to purpose, audience, and task. **Literacy.L.9-10.3** Apply knowledge of language to understand how language functions in different contexts, to make effective choices for meaning or style, and to comprehend more fully when reading or listening.

UNIT 1 Cluster 3 Planner

EQ ESSENTIAL QUESTION:

What Influences a Person's Choices?

Find out how circumstances affect choices.

Online Planner
myNGconnect.com

	LESSON 18 **Prepare to Read**	LESSON 19 **The Necklace** Main Selection
Reading		
Reading Strategies Focus Strategy **Plan and Monitor**	**Activate Prior Knowledge** SL.9-10.1 • Make a Connection: Quickwrite *T64*	**Plan and Monitor** RL.9-10.4; L.9-10.4.a • Clarify Vocabulary *T65, T68–T79* • Set a Purpose *T68* • Make and Confirm Predictions *T74, T75, T76* • Monitor Comprehension *T73, T75*
Literary Analysis Genre Focus **Short Stories**		T **Analyze Setting** *T65, T68–T79* RL.9-10.3 **Identify Literary Movements** • Realism: French Writers in the 1800s *T66*
Vocabulary	T **Key Vocabulary** RL.9-10.4; L.9-10.6 • Introduce *T64* **humiliating** **imitation** • **inspire** **luxury** • **perceive** **poverty** • **symbol** **value**	T **Key Vocabulary** L.9-10.6 • Daily Routines *T69* • Link to Essential Question *T71, T78* • Selection Reading *T68–T79* **humiliating** **imitation** **luxury** • **perceive** **poverty** • **symbol** **value**
Fluency		T **Intonation** RL.9-10.10 • Daily Routines *T69* T **Accuracy and Rate** RL.9-10.10 Comprehension Coach *T67*
Writing		
Response to Literature		**Return to the Text** W.9-10.9 • **Reread and Write** Madame Loisel's choices are influenced by what she values in life. Does her attitude toward these things change by the end of the story? *T79*
		Research and Writing W.9-10.7 • **Geography Connection** *T73*
Language		
ELL **Language Development**	T **Express Feelings and Intentions** SL.9-10.4 • Language and Grammar Lab, Transparency C *LAB TE p. 14*	T **Express Feelings and Intentions** SL.9-10.4 • Daily Routines *LAB TE p. 14*
Grammar Grammar Focus **Sentence Fragments**		T **Sentence Fragments** *T70* L.9-10.1 T **Fixing a Fragment: Add the Subject/Verb** *T74, T76* L.9-10.1
Listening and Speaking	**Partner Talk** SL.9-10.1 • Ideas About Conforming *T64*	**Listen to a Selection** Comprehension Coach *T67* *CD 2, Tracks 1–3*

T = Tested on Cluster and/or Unit Reading and Literary Analysis Test
T = Tested on Language Acquisition Assessment
T = Tested on Unit Writing Test
T = Assessed with a Rubric
• **Academic Vocabulary**

The Necklace

Genre: Short Story **Lexile® 750L**

Madame Loisel loses a necklace that she borrowed from a wealthy friend. She goes into debt to replace the necklace. After ten years of working hard to pay her debt, Madame Loisel discovers that she bought an expensive necklace to replace an imitation.

The Fashion Show

Genre: Memoir **Lexile® 810L**

Farah Ahmedi fears modeling in her high school's fashion show because she had lost her leg in a land mine accident in Afghanistan. Farah's friend Alyce convinces her not to give up. Farah participates in the fashion show with pride and confidence.

LESSON 20 **The Fashion Show** Second Selection	LESSON 21 **Reflect and Assess**	LESSONS 22 & 23 **Integrate the Language Arts**	LESSON 24 **The Grapes of Wrath** Close Reading
Plan and Monitor RI.9-10.4; L.9-10.4.a • Clarify Vocabulary *T80, T82–T86* • Monitor Comprehension *T83, T85*	**Comprehension and Critical Thinking** *T87* RL.9-10.2; RL.9-10.3; RI.9-10.2; • Compare Across Texts RL.9-10.6 • Interpret, Compare, Analyze, Speculate, Evaluate		
Determine Viewpoint RI.9-10.6 *T80, T82–T86*	**Interpret and Evaluate Literature** RI.9-10.10 **Use Text Evidence** *T87* RI.9-10.1	**Analyze Setting and Theme** *T88* RL.9-10.2	**Analyze Characterization** RL.9-10.3; L.9-10.3
Key Vocabulary L.9-10.6 • Selection Reading *T82–T86* • **inspire** **value** • **perceive**	**Key Vocabulary** L.9-10.6 • Review *T87* **humiliating** • **perceive** **imitation** **poverty** • **inspire** • **symbol** **luxury** **value**	**Vocabulary Strategy** L.9-10.4.b • Use Structural Clues: Suffixes *T89*	**Academic Vocabulary** L.9-10.3; L.9-10.6 • Review *T88* • **clarify**
Intonation RI.9-10.10 • Daily Routines *T69* **Accuracy and Rate** RI.9-10.10 Comprehension Coach *T81*	**Intonation** RI.9-10.10 • Peer Assessment *T87*		
Return to the Text W.9-10.10 • **Reread and Write** Who inspires Ahmedi more—Alyce or the girl who picks on her? *T86*	**Write About Literature** W.9-10.3 • **Response Log** Write about a time when a choice you made had surprising consequences. *T87*	**Writing Trait** W.9-10.5 • **Focus and Unity: Thesis or Central Idea** *T89*	**The Grapes of Wrath** **Genre:** Novel Excerpt **Lexile® 690L** *CD 12, Track 1*
Research and Writing W.9-10.7 • **History Connection** *T85*		**Research and Writing** W.9-10.2; W.9-10.7; W.9-10.8 • **Brochure on Peer Pressure** *T89*	
Express Feelings and Intentions SL.9-10.4 • Daily Routines *LAB TE p. 14*		**Express Feelings and Intentions** SL.9-10.4 • Role Play *T88*	LESSON 25 **UNIT WRAP-UP**
Fixing a Fragment: Combine Sentences *T82* L.9-10.1		**Fix Sentence Fragments** *T88* L.9-10.1	**Unit Project** SL.9-10.1.c; SL.9-10.6; L.9-10.1 • Present a TV Talk Show *T94*
Listen to a Selection Comprehension Coach *T81* *CD 2, Track 4* **Out-of-School Literacy** SL.9-10.1.a • Sharing World Cultures *T84*	**Participate in a Discussion** *T87* SL.9-10.1		

EDGE LIBRARY

Trojan Horse • *by Justine and Ron Fontes*

Miracle's Boys • • *by Jacqueline Woodson*

Breaking Through • • • *by Francisco Jiménez*

Lesson 18

PREPARE TO READ

OBJECTIVES

Vocabulary
- Key Vocabulary T
- Strategy: Use Cognates; Relate Words

Reading Strategy
- Activate Prior Knowledge

ELL Language & Grammar Lab

Language Function Transparency C
Express Feelings and Intentions T

ENGAGE & CONNECT

A EQ Essential Question

Focus on Society Explain that *society* refers to the people in a community or country. Ask: How can society's opinions affect a person's choices?

Possible responses:
- *He or she might want to be like the others.*
- *He or she could decide to be different.*

B Make a Connection

Have students complete the Quickwrite and compare their thoughts with a partner about making a major change in order to belong.
SL.9-10.1

TEACH VOCABULARY

C Learn Key Vocabulary

Study the Words Review the four steps of the Make Words Your Own routine (see *the Vocabulary tab*):

1. **Pronounce** Say one word and have students repeat it. Write the word in syllables and pronounce it, one syllable at a time: *im-i-ta-tion*. Ask what looks familiar in the word, and point out other forms of the word, such as *imitate*.

   ELL Use cognates to help Spanish speakers with the words (see *the Vocabulary tab*).

2. **Study Examples** Read the example in the chart. Provide more examples: This cheap watch is an *imitation* of an expensive one.

ONGOING ASSESSMENT
Have students complete an oral sentence for each word. For example: *Falling down the stairs is such a _______ experience.*

PREPARE TO READ
- The Necklace
- The Fashion Show

A EQ What Influences a Person's Choices?
Discover how society influences choices.

B Make a Connection

Quickwrite Imagine there is a club that you want to join. However, joining calls for a major change. Maybe you have to buy an expensive jacket or cut your hair very short. What would you do? Record your thoughts.

C Learn Key Vocabulary

Study the Words Pronounce each word and learn its meaning. You may also want to look up definitions in the Glossary.

• Academic Vocabulary

Key Words	Examples
humiliating (hyū-**mi**-lē-ā-ting) *adjective* ▸ page 71	When someone teases you, it feels **humiliating**. A **humiliating** experience hurts your pride.
imitation (im-u-**tā**-shun) *noun* ▸ page 79	An **imitation** is something that looks or acts like something else. *Synonym*: fake; *Antonym*: real, genuine
inspire (in-**spīr**) *verb* ▸ pages 84, 86, 87	When something **inspires** you, it motivates you to do something. A movie about an Olympic athlete **inspired** me to start exercising.
luxury (**luk**-shu-rē) *noun* ▸ page 68	A **luxury** is something expensive that is nice to have, but not necessary. Is it a **luxury** to have two pairs of dress shoes?
• **perceive** (per-**sēv**) *verb* ▸ pages 79, 86	When you **perceive** something, you see it in a certain way. People with different points of view **perceive** things differently. *Synonym*: see; *Antonym*: ignore
poverty (**pov**-er-tē) *noun* ▸ page 76	**Poverty** is being very poor. People without enough money for food, shelter, or clothing live in **poverty**. *Synonym*: need; *Antonym*: wealth
• **symbol** (**sim**-bul) *noun* ▸ pages 73, 87	A **symbol** is something that represents, or stands for, something else. An eagle is a **symbol** of the United States. A dove is a **symbol** of peace.
value (**val**-ū) *verb* ▸ pages 79, 85	When you **value** something, you think it is important or useful. I **value** friends more than money.

Practice the Words Take notes about each Key Vocabulary word in a chart. Then quiz a partner about the words. For example:

Q: What is a synonym for *humiliating*?
A: embarrassing

Key Vocabulary Chart

Word	Synonym(s)	Definition	Sentence or Picture
humiliating	embarrassing	hurting your pride	Spilling my backpack at school was humiliating.
imitation			

3. **Encourage Elaboration** Have students complete a sentence with an antonym for *imitation*: *The jacket costs so much because it is made from _______ leather.* (genuine, real)

Reading Transparency 3

4. **Practice the Words** Use the transparency to model completing a Note-Taking Chart. Have students fill in the chart for each Key Word.

Edge Interactive Practice Book, p. 34–35
RL.9-10.4; L.9-10.6

Reading Transparency 3

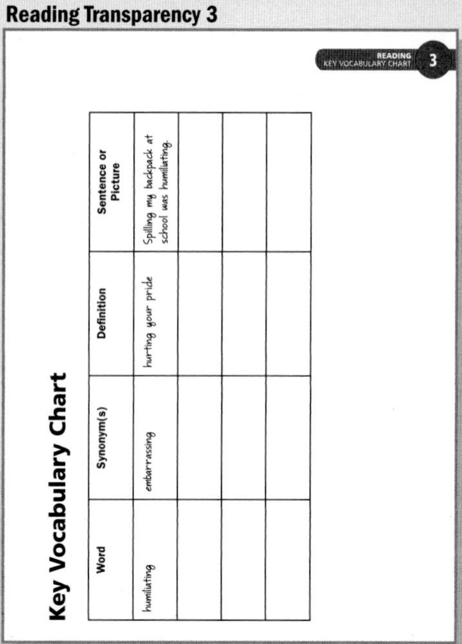

READING KEY VOCABULARY CHART 3

Key Vocabulary Chart

Word	Synonym(s)	Definition	Sentence or Picture
humiliating	embarrassing	hurting your pride	Spilling my backpack at school was humiliating.

CCSS **Literacy.RL.9-10.4** Determine the meaning of words and phrases as they are used in the text, including figurative and connotative meanings; analyze the cumulative impact of specific word choices on meaning and tone (e.g., how the language evokes a sense of time and place; how it sets a formal or informal tone). **Literacy.SL.9-10.1** Initiate and participate effectively in a range of collaborative discussions (one-on-one, in groups, and teacher-led) with diverse partners on grades 9-10 topics, texts, and issues, building on others' ideas and expressing their own clearly and persuasively. **Literacy.L.9-10.6** Acquire and use accurately general academic and domain-specific words and phrases, sufficient for reading, writing, speaking, and listening at the college and career readiness level; demonstrate independence in gathering vocabulary knowledge when considering a word or phrase important to comprehension or expression.

Before Reading The Necklace

short story by Guy de Maupassant

Reading Strategies
- ▶ **Plan and Monitor**
- Determine Importance
- Make Inferences
- Ask Questions
- Make Connections
- Synthesize
- Visualize

Analyze Setting

The **setting** of a story includes the time and place in which the events happen and the circumstances of the characters' lives. The main setting of "The Necklace" is Paris, France, during the late 1800s. It is a time when wealthy people live in fancy homes and throw expensive parties. Within this main setting, there are other scenes, such as a shabby apartment and an elegant party. As you read, consider how the setting affects the characters and the choices they make.

Look Into the Text

The setting tells when and where this scene takes place.

Then one evening, her husband came home and proudly handed her a large envelope . . .

She . . . threw the invitation onto the table and murmured, "What do you want me to do with that?"

"But, my dear, I thought you would be so pleased. This is a big event! I had a lot of trouble getting this invitation. All the clerks at the Ministry want to go, but there are only a few invitations reserved for workers. You will meet all the most important people there."

Is this party only for rich, important people? How can you tell?

She gave him an irritated look and said, impatiently, "I do not have anything I could wear. How could I go?"

She acts this way at home. How would she act in a setting like the party?

Focus Strategy ▶ Plan and Monitor

When you come to a word that you don't know, ask yourself, "What could this mean?" Sometimes the context of the sentence will give you a clue. Some words are used regularly in different subjects. For example, *important* might be used in social studies, science, and math.

Focus Strategy

How to Clarify Vocabulary

1. **Look for context clues.** These words or phrases can give hints about the word's meaning.

   Unknown word: important
   Context clues: She did not even have a chance of meeting and marrying a rich, **important** man. Instead, she married a lowly clerk.

2. **Try to figure out what the word means.** Sometimes context clues will also tell you what the word *doesn't* mean.

   You think: A clerk is someone who is not rich or worth talking about. He must be poor.

3. **Try out the meaning.** See if the meaning makes sense in the sentence.

   New sentence: She did not even have a chance of meeting and marrying a rich man **of value, worth talking about**. Instead she married a lowly clerk.

Reading Transparency 4

Analyze Setting

READING SETTING 4

What does the setting describe?

Introduce When authors describe the setting, they:

- tell **when** the story takes place. They can name a day, month, year, time of day, or a period of time.
- describe **where** the story takes place. They can name a country, city, town, or even a different world. In some stories, the setting is specific; for example, a palace or a café.
- describe **how** the characters live. The characters might live in great poverty or wealth, for example.

The setting and events of a story affect the characters and their choices.

Setting	Events	Character's Reaction/ Choices
evening; 1800s; Paris; shabby apartment	A working-class husband gives his wife an invitation to a party with important people.	She does not want to go to the fancy party because she is poor.

Lesson 19

BEFORE READING

OBJECTIVES

Reading Strategy
- Plan and Monitor: Clarify Vocabulary

Literary Analysis
- Analyze Setting T

TEACH STRATEGIES

D Analyze Setting

Look Into the Text Read the introduction to define setting and describe the setting of "The Necklace."

Read the text passage aloud. Ask: How can you tell the party will be elegant and fashionable?

Possible responses:
- *Only important people are invited.*
- *The wife is upset because she has nothing to wear.*

Then ask: How might her behavior be different in a more elegant setting?

Possible response:
- *She might act more sophisticated and show good manners.*

RL.9-10.3

Reading Transparency 4

Use the Transparency Reinforce the features of setting. Use the example in the chart to show how setting affects characters and their choices. Ask students to describe the classroom setting to a partner. Encourage them to use descriptive language when doing so.

E Focus Strategy: Plan and Monitor

Clarify Vocabulary Review that students use a variety of strategies as they read. Then read the introduction with students. Work through the steps in the How To box to model looking for context clues.

Have students try the strategies to clarify the meaning of unfamiliar words in Look Into the Text.

RL.9-10.4; L.9-10.4.a

Edge Interactive Practice Book, pp. 36–37

ONGOING ASSESSMENT

Have students explain to a partner how a particular setting might affect a character and his or her choices.

CCSS **Literacy.RL.9-10.3** Analyze how complex characters (e.g., those with multiple or conflicting motivations) develop over the course of a text, interact with other characters, and advance the plot or develop the theme. **Literacy.RL.9-10.4** Determine the meaning of words and phrases as they are used in the text, including figurative and connotative meanings; analyze the cumulative impact of specific word choices on meaning and tone (e.g., how the language evokes a sense of time and place; how it sets a formal or informal tone). **Literacy.L.9-10.4.a** Use context (e.g., the overall meaning of a sentence, paragraph, or text; a word's position or function in a sentence) as a clue to the meaning of a word or phrase.

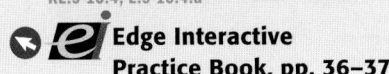

READ

OBJECTIVES

Literary Analysis
- Identify Literary Movements

Viewing
- Respond to and Interpret Visuals

BUILD BACKGROUND

A The Writer and His Times

Have students read the biography of Guy de Maupassant.

Literary Movement Share this additional information to place Maupassant and his work in historical context:

Maupassant was among a group of French writers in the 1800s who wrote literature described as *realism.* Their stories describe the real lives of ordinary men and women in realistic situations. Although Maupassant spent time with very successful, rich, and sophisticated people, he wrote about the upper, middle, and lower classes. His characters often show the negative power of jealousy, lies, and greed.

Connect with Author's Life Guide students to make connections with the author's life.

Ask: What effect do you think Maupassant's place in society had on what he chose to write about?

Possible response:
- *He may have wanted to show what it was really like to be part of the upper, middle, or lower class in French society.*

Then ask: What effect do jealousy, lies, and greed have on the way people choose to behave?

Possible responses:
- *They cause conflict and divisions between people.*
- *They cause people to make bad choices.*

myNGconnect.com
- Selection Summaries in eight languages

The Writer and His Times

Guy de Maupassant
(1850–1893)

Guy de Maupassant wrote his first short stories as a teenager.

A **Guy de Maupassant** (gē du mō-pa-sahn) lived in France in the late 1800s. When he was a teenager, he worked with Gustave Flaubert, a famous novelist. Flaubert coached Maupassant in his writing and acted as a father figure to him. Flaubert also introduced him to other important writers of the day, including Emile Zola. In 1880, Zola helped Maupassant publish his story "Boule de Suif" ("Ball of Fat"). The story was so well received that Maupassant became an instant success.

During the next ten years, Maupassant published almost 300 short stories and six novels. He wrote about the Franco-German War (1870–1871) and about all kinds of people—rich and poor. Readers loved his stories for their realistic portrayal of French life.

Because of his success, Maupassant could afford the wealthy lifestyle that he wrote about in "The Necklace" and many of his other stories. He owned yachts and several homes throughout France, and he loved to travel.

Although Maupassant died more than one hundred years ago, he is still remembered as one of the greatest short story writers of all time.

myNGconnect.com
- See photographs of Paris in the 1800s.
- Read other stories by Guy de Maupassant.

DIFFERENTIATED INSTRUCTION

English Language Learners ELL

Preview the selection:
- Show the art on pp. 67 and 69: *The story begins with an invitation to a fancy party with rich people.*
- Point to the image of the necklace on p. 67: *A necklace like this one causes a problem in the story.*
- Show the art on pp. 75 and 78: *The man and woman who get invited to the party are not rich.*
- Make a sad face and explain: *The woman is very unhappy. She thinks her life is not good enough. She wants to be rich.* Ask: Why does someone want to be rich?

Read Aloud to provide a supp
listening experience:
- Play the **Selection Record**
students track text in their
- Have students use the Liste
the **Comprehension Coa**
they see the text as it is rea
- Read the selection aloud to
as you provide comprehens
For example, you can use b
and facial expressions to de
behavior, such as in the con
between the husband and w

The Necklace

by Guy de Maupassant

Margherita Goldsmid, later Mrs Raphael, John Singer Sargent (1856-1925). Oil on canvas, private collection. The Bridgeman Art Library.

Critical Viewing: Design This painting is a realistic portrait of a woman in the past. How does the artist use color, light, and texture to tell you more about the woman?

Comprehension Coach

TEACH & PRACTICE

B Analyze Visuals

About the Art John Singer Sargent, like Maupassant, lived in the 1800s in Europe. Sargent became famous for painting the wealthy and stylish people of his time.

Point out details in the painting, such as the elegant dress, that let viewers know that this is a wealthy and fashionable woman.

Interpret and Respond Ask: If you painted a wealthy and stylish person living today, what details would you paint to show his or her place in society?

C Critical Viewing: Design

Observe Artist's Technique Tell students to think about color, light, and texture in the painting.

ELL Questioning For less proficient students, ask yes/no questions or questions with embedded answer choices:

- Is the woman sitting in the dark or in the light?
- Is the woman's dress made of a nice material? Is it soft or rough?

For more proficient students, ask open-ended questions.

- What is this woman sitting on?
- What is on the table next to her?

Ask: What do the details tell you about the woman?

Possible responses:

- *Her dress is made of a fine material. It is probably silky and expensive.*
- *The details, such as the furniture and jewelry, tell you she is wealthy.*

Comprehension Coach

Build Reading Power

Assign students to use the software, based on their instructional needs.

Read Silently

- Comprehension questions with immediate feedback
- Glossary support
- Review text evidence

RL.9-10.10

Listen

- Professional model of fluent reading

Record

- Oral reading fluency practice
- Ongoing fluency assessment with immediate feedback

CCSS Literacy.RL.9-10.10 By the end of grade 9, read and comprehend literature, including stories, dramas, and poems, in the grades 9–10 text complexity band proficiently, with scaffolding as needed at the high end of the range. By the end of grade 10, read and comprehend literature, including stories, dramas, and poems, at the high end of the grades 9–10 text complexity band independently and proficiently.

OBJECTIVES

Vocabulary
- Key Vocabulary Ⓣ

Reading Fluency
- Intonation Ⓣ

Reading Strategy
- Plan and Monitor: Set a Purpose

Comprehension & Critical Thinking
- Use Text Evidence Ⓣ

Literary Analysis
- Analyze Setting Ⓣ

Viewing
- Respond to and Interpret Visuals

TEACH & PRACTICE

Ⓐ Chunking the Text

Set a Purpose Remind students of their Quickwrite responses. As they read, tell them to look for clues about what Madame Loisel wants in her life.

Read Have students read pp. 68–73. Support and monitor their comprehension using the reading support provided. Use the Differentiated Instruction below to meet students' individual needs.
RL.9-10.10

Ⓑ Reading Support

1 Setting Ask: What does Madame Loisel's apartment look like, and how does it make her feel?

Possible response:
- *It is old and worn, and it makes her feel like she is not important.*

RL.9-10.3

Ⓒ Reading Support

2 Setting Reread the last paragraph. Ask: What words tell what Madame Loisel *does not* have?

Possible responses:
- *no fancy clothes, no jewels, nothing*

Ask: What is the difference between what Madame Loisel has and what she wants?

Possible response:
- *She has a shabby apartment and plain clothes. She wants jewelry, stylish clothes, and a fancy home.*

RL.9-10.3

She was one of those beautiful, charming women who are born, as if by accident, into a lower-class family. Because of this, she did not have even a chance of meeting and marrying a rich, important man. Instead, she married a lowly **clerk** from the Ministry of Education.

She had to dress plainly because she could not afford fine clothes or jewelry. This made her feel like someone of little **worth**. She thought that if she could dress well, other people might consider her more important.

Ⓑ She was miserable, feeling that she deserved a life of wealth and **luxury**. Her shabby apartment, with its dingy walls, worn furniture, and ugly upholstery was an embarrassment to her. Any other woman in her class would not have noticed these things, but for her they were a mark of her worthlessness. 1

Ⓒ She dreamed of big rooms with thick carpets, bronze lamps, and fancy tapestries. She imagined two butlers napping in large, overstuffed chairs by a fire. She pictured silk draped from the walls, and priceless **knickknacks** cluttering delicate tables. She dreamed of tea with close friends and handsome men in stylish sitting rooms.

At dinner, she watched her husband lift the lid of the soup tureen and exclaim, with delight, "Ah! A good stew! There's nothing I like better. . . ." She imagined elegant dinner parties, shining silverware, dining rooms covered with tapestries of knights, ladies, and magical birds from fairy tales. She dreamed of delicious food served on expensive dishes and of **flattery** whispered and listened to with mysterious smiles.

But she had no fancy clothes, no jewels, nothing. Those were the things she loved; she felt she was made for them. She wanted to please, to **be envied**, to be admired, and to be popular. 2

1 Setting Picture Madame Loisel in her apartment. How does this setting make her feel?

2 Setting Compare Madame Loisel's daydreams with her real surroundings. What kind of life does she want?

Key Vocabulary
luxury *n.*, expensive thing that you do not really need

In Other Words
clerk office worker
worth importance
knickknacks little decorations
flattery compliments to make her feel special
be envied make other people wish they had what she had

DIFFERENTIATED INSTRUCTION

Interactive Reading As you conduct the interactive reading with students, adjust your teaching strategies to their needs.

Struggling Readers

Picture the Text Show visually the difference between what Madame Loisel has and what she wants. For example, each time she expresses dissatisfaction, add to a chart like this one:

Has	Wants
shabby apartment	fancy house
plain clothes	fine clothes
no jewelry	jewels
stew	delicious meals

English Language Learners ELL

Sentence Frames Provide sentence frames for understanding setting and character.
- The setting around Madame Loisel is ______, and it makes her feel ______.
- Madame Loisel wants ______ so that she will feel ______.

Challenge

Compare Characters Have students compare Madame Loisel to other characters in the story, such as her husband and Madame Forestier. How are their desires similar or different?

CCSS Literacy.RL.9-10.3 Analyze how complex characters (e.g., those with multiple or conflicting motivations) develop over the course of a text, interact with other characters, and advance the plot or develop the theme. Literacy.RL.9-10.10 By the end of grade 9, read and comprehend literature, including stories, dramas, and poems, in the grades 9-10 text complexity band proficiently, with scaffolding as needed at the high end of the range. By the end of grade 10, read and comprehend literature, including stories, dramas, and poems, at the high end of the grades 9-10 text complexity band independently and proficiently.

The Salon of Princess Mathilde (1820–1904), 1883, Giuseppe or Joseph de Nittis. Oil on canvas, Museo Civico, Barletta, Italy, The Bridgeman Art Library.

D

▲ Critical Viewing: Setting How does this scene represent what Mathilde wants from life? E

TEACH & PRACTICE

D Analyze Visuals

About the Art Giuseppe, or Joseph, de Nittis was an Italian painter who liked to experiment with different ways to show light in his work.

Interpret and Respond Ask: Which parts of this scene are bright? Which are darker? How does this affect what you see?

E Critical Viewing: Setting

Analyze Setting Have students identify details of the setting shown in the painting.

ELL List Vocabulary Use the art on this page to help students build vocabulary by identifying some elements of the setting. Point out *stylish sitting room, thick carpets, tapestries, overstuffed chairs,* and *knickknacks* in the art as you say the words, and have students repeat.

Ask: How is this scene similar to what Madame Loisel dreams of?

Possible response:

- *It is a stylish room with thick carpets, tapestries, overstuffed chairs, and knickknacks.*

RL.9-10.3; RL.9-10.7

DAILY ROUTINES

Vocabulary

See the Vocabulary and Fluency Routines tab for more information.

Respond to Questions Compose yes/no questions. You can use more than one word in a sentence. For example: Is an eagle a *symbol* of something people *value*?

Word Sorts Have students write each word on an index card. On the reverse side of each card, tell students to write the definition. Encourage students to work with a partner to organize the word cards into verbs, nouns, and adjectives.

Drama Have students pantomime the action associated with a Key Word, such as *humiliating* or *luxury*.

L.9-10.6

Fluency: Intonation

CD 11

This cluster's fluency practice uses a passage from "The Fashion Show" to help students practice appropriate intonation. Use **Reading Handbook** T748 and the **Fluency Model CD** to teach or review the elements of fluent intonation, and then use the daily fluency practice activities to develop students' oral reading proficiency.

RI.9-10.10

CCSS **Literacy.RL.9-10.7** Analyze the representation of a subject or a key scene in two different artistic mediums, including what is emphasized or absent in each treatment (e.g., Auden's "Musée des Beaux Arts" and Breughel's Landscape with the Fall of Icarus). **Literacy.RI.9-10.10** By the end of grade 9, read and comprehend literary nonfiction in the grades 9–10 text complexity band proficiently, with scaffolding as needed at the high end of the range. By the end of grade 10, read and comprehend literary nonfiction at the high end of the grades 9–10 text complexity band independently and proficiently. **Literacy.L.9-10.6** Acquire and use accurately general academic and domain-specific words and phrases, sufficient for reading, writing, speaking, and listening at the college and career readiness level; demonstrate independence in gathering vocabulary knowledge when considering a word or phrase important to comprehension or expression.

READ

OBJECTIVES

Vocabulary
- Key Vocabulary Ⓣ
- Strategy: Use Contextual Analysis

Reading Strategy
- Plan and Monitor: Clarify Vocabulary

Comprehension & Critical Thinking
- Use Text Evidence Ⓣ

Literary Analysis
- Analyze Setting Ⓣ
- Analyze Style: Language and Word Choice

Grammar
- Sentence Fragments Ⓣ

TEACH & PRACTICE

Ⓐ Reading Support

3 Setting Read aloud the passage beginning with "She excitedly tore" through "How could I go?"

ELL Rephrase Language Explain that in Europe during the 1800s when this story is set, the title of *Minister* is used for government workers with very important jobs. *Clerks* are workers who have less important jobs. *Monsieur* and *Madame* are French words that mean "Mr." and "Mrs."

Ask: Who is the invitation from? What kind of place do you think the party will be in?

Possible response:
- *The invitation is from a Minister and his wife. The party will probably be in a fancy home.*

Ask: Which details in the text suggest that the party is important in Madame Loisel's culture?

Possible response:
- *According to Monsieur Loisel, the party is such "a big" event," that it is hard to get an invitation. Only "important people" in society can attend.*

RL.9-10.3; RL.9-10.6

She had a rich friend from school, but she did not like to visit this friend. It made her so miserable. When she returned home, she would weep for days, feeling sad and hopeless about her own life.

Then one evening, her husband came home and proudly handed her a large envelope.

"Look," he said. "I have something for you."

She excitedly tore open the envelope. Inside was a printed card that said: "The Minister of Education and Madame Georges Ramponneau invite Monsieur and Madame Loisel to an evening **reception** on Monday, January 18th."

She was not delighted, as her husband had hoped. Instead, she threw the invitation onto the table and **murmured**, "What do you want me to do with that?"

Ⓐ "But, my dear, I thought you would be so pleased. This is a big event! I had a lot of trouble getting this invitation. All the clerks at the Ministry want to go, but there are only a few invitations reserved for workers. You will meet all the most important people there."

She gave him an **irritated** look and said, impatiently, "I do not have anything I could wear. How could I go?" 3

He had not thought about this. He stammered, "But what about the dress you wear to the theater? I think it looks quite nice."

He was amazed to see that his wife was sobbing. "What is it?" he gasped. "What is the matter?"

With great effort, she stopped crying. Wiping her wet cheeks, she replied, "It's nothing. I just don't have **an evening gown**, so I cannot go to the party. Give the

3 **Setting** What does the invitation tell you about the kind of place where the party will be held? Why does Madame Loisel refuse to go?

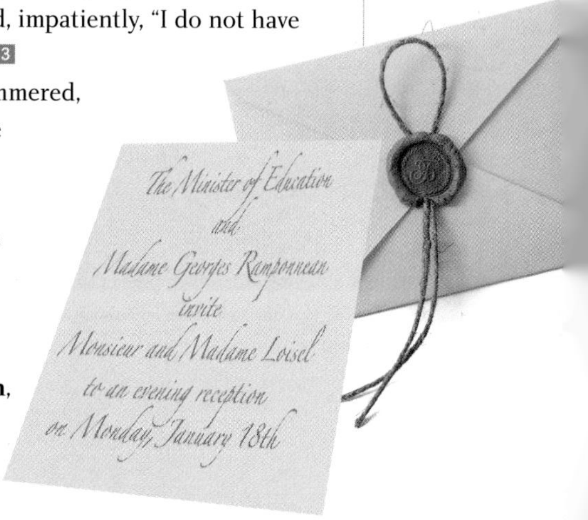

In Other Words

reception party
murmured said very quietly
irritated angry, annoyed
an evening gown a long, expensive dress to wear to fancy parties

Historical Background

At the time of the story, the average French worker earned about 900 *francs* a year. It would be difficult for a clerk to afford expensive luxuries.

GRAMMAR

Sentence Fragments

Teach/Model Display the transparency. Explain what a fragment is, stressing that a fragment does not express a complete thought. Read each fragment and ask: What is missing? Then read the complete sentence.

Practice A. Have students say if each item expresses a complete thought or if it is a fragment. Label each item. For the fragments, ask if the subject or the verb is missing before students provide a complete sentence.
B. Have students write their sentences and read one aloud. Choose some to write on the transparency. Have the group identify the subject and the verb.
L.9-10.1

Grammar & Writing Practice Book, pp. 21–22

Grammar Transparency 11

What Is a Fragment?
It's an Incomplete Sentence.

GRAMMAR SENTENCE FRAGMENTS 11

A **fragment** is a group of words that begins with a capital letter and ends with a period. It looks like a sentence, but it is not complete. A subject or a verb may be missing.

Fragments	Sentences
1. Marries a clerk.	The charming woman marries a clerk.
2. The apartment.	The apartment looks shabby.
3. The stew in the pot.	The stew simmers in the pot.
4. Loves jewelry.	The woman loves jewelry.

Try It

A. Tell if each group of words is a fragment or a sentence. If it is a fragment, add a subject or a verb. Say the sentence.
Possible answers:
1. Dresses plainly. fragment; Mathilde dresses plainly.
2. Mathilde and her husband eat stew for dinner. sentence
3. Mathilde elegant dinner parties. fragment; Mathilde imagines elegant dinner parties.
4. Finally get invited to a party. fragment; Mathilde and her husband finally get invited to a party.
5. Her husband worked hard for the invitation. sentence

B. Now write three complete sentences to tell more about the husband and the wife in "The Necklace." Sentences will vary. Mathilde reads the invitation. She looks unhappy. Her husband feels disappointed.

GRAMMAR SKILLS PATH

- 11 Sentence Fragments
  ELL Language & Grammar Lab
- 12 Fixing a Fragment: Add the Subject
- 13 Fixing a Fragment: Add the Verb
- 14 Fixing a Fragment: Combine Sentences
- 15 Review: Fix Sentence Fragments

CCSS **Literacy.RL.9-10.3** Analyze how complex characters (e.g., those with multiple or conflicting motivations) develop over the course of a text, interact with other characters, and advance the plot or develop the theme. **Literacy.RL.9-10.6** Analyze a particular point of view or cultural experience reflected in a work of literature from outside the United States, drawing on a wide reading of world literature. **Literacy.L.9-10.1** Demonstrate command of the conventions of standard English grammar and usage when writing or speaking.

invitation to a friend at the office whose wife can dress better than I can."

He was stunned and said, "Mathilde, how much would it cost for a **suitable** dress that you could wear again?"

She thought for several seconds, wondering how much she could ask for without a shocked refusal from her **thrifty husband**.

Finally, she answered, "I am not sure exactly, but I think I could manage with four hundred *francs*." **B**

His face turned pale because that was exactly the amount of money he had saved to buy a new rifle. He wanted to go hunting in Nanterre the next summer with some of his friends.

However, he said, "All right. I'll give you four hundred *francs*, but try to find a beautiful dress."

The day of the party approached. Madame Loisel's gown was ready, but she still seemed depressed and anxious. 4 **C**

One evening, her husband asked, "What is wrong? You have been acting strangely for the past three days."

She answered, "I do not have a single jewel to wear. I will look like a **pauper**! I would rather not go to the party at all."

He replied, "You can wear some fresh flowers. They are very **fashionable** this season. For ten *francs*, you can buy two or three gorgeous roses."

She did not like his suggestion at all. "No . . . there is nothing more **humiliating** than to look poor among a lot of rich women." 5 **D**

Then her husband exclaimed, "I know! Go see your friend Madame Forestier and ask her to lend you some jewelry. You two know each other well enough to do that."

She gave a cry of joy. "Yes! That did not occur to me!"

The next day, she went to visit her friend and told her about the

4 Clarify Vocabulary
What does *anxious* mean in this sentence? What surrounding words, or context clues, help you figure it out? What might Madame Loisel be anxious about?

5 Language
Mathilde thinks that looking poor is "humiliating." What other negative words on pages 68–70 does she use to describe being poor?

Key Vocabulary
humiliating *adj.*, very embarrassing

In Other Words
suitable nice enough, appropriate
thrifty husband husband who liked to save money
pauper person who is very poor
fashionable popular, stylish

TEACH & PRACTICE

B Reading Support

Build Background Explain that the *franc* was the currency used in France until 2002, when it was replaced by the euro. In 2001, 500 francs was equivalent to one hundred U.S. dollars.

C Reading Support

4 **Clarify Vocabulary** Ask students to find context clues that help them understand the meaning of *anxious*. Then have students tell you why Madame Loisel is anxious.

Possible response:

- *The word* depressed *shows that Madame Loisel is unhappy. She is still worried about going to the party.*

RL.9-10.4; L.9-10.4.a

D Reading Support

5 **Language** Explain that Madame Loisel describes many things that she feels humiliated about that are all related to being poor.

Ask: What negative words does Madame Loisel use on pages 68–70 that relate to being poor?

Possible responses:

- *lowly; little worth; miserable; sad; hopeless; pauper*

L.9-10.5.b; L.9-10.6

Reading Support

Analyze Character Ask students to identify details in the story that reveal what kind of person Madame Loisel is.

ELL **Use Graphic Organizer** In a chart, list the details students offer and what they indicate about Madame Loisel's character.

Character	What the Character Does	What This Shows About the Character
Madame Loisel	doesn't like to visit her rich friend	jealous

Ask: Do you think Madame Loisel's choices are influenced by other people's opinions?
RL.9-10.3

VOCABULARY

Link Vocabulary and Concepts

Ask questions to link Key Vocabulary with the Essential Question.

EQ **ESSENTIAL QUESTION:**
What influences a person's choices?

Some possible questions:

- *Why does Madame Loisel desire a life of* **luxury** *over a life of* **poverty**?
- *Monsieur Loisel thinks his wife should choose to wear her theater dress. Why does his wife think this is* **humiliating**?
- *What does Madame Loisel* **value**? *What things would she want to have if she could have her choice?*
- *Is having a beautiful dress a* **symbol** *of wealth to Madame Loisel?*

Have students use the Key Vocabulary words in their responses.
L.9-10.6

CCSS **Literacy.RL.9-10.4** Determine the meaning of words and phrases as they are used in the text, including figurative and connotative meanings; analyze the cumulative impact of specific word choices on meaning and tone (e.g., how the language evokes a sense of time and place; how it sets a formal or informal tone). **Literacy.L.9-10.4.a** Use context (e.g., the overall meaning of a sentence, paragraph, or text; a word's position or function in a sentence) as a clue to the meaning of a word or phrase. **Literacy.L.9-10.5.b** Analyze nuances in the meaning of words with similar denotations. **Literacy.L.9-10.6** Acquire and use accurately general academic and domain-specific words and phrases, sufficient for reading, writing, speaking, and listening at the college and career readiness level; demonstrate independence in gathering vocabulary knowledge when considering a word or phrase important to comprehension or expression.

READ

OBJECTIVES

Vocabulary
- Key Vocabulary Ⓣ
- Strategy: Use Contextual Analysis

Reading Strategy
- Plan and Monitor: Clarify Vocabulary
- Summarize

Comprehension & Critical Thinking
- Use Text Evidence Ⓣ

Literary Analysis
- Analyze Setting Ⓣ

Research Skills
- Gather Information; Create a Graphic Aid

TEACH & PRACTICE

Ⓐ Reading Support

6 **Setting** Ask students to identify details about Madame Forestier's apartment and jewelry. Ask: Based on what you know about her character, how would Madame Loisel describe her friend's home and jewels?

Possible responses:
- *fancy and stylish*
- *big and important*

Ask: How does Madame Loisel's opinion about her friend's home influence what jewelry she chooses?

Possible response:
- *Because she is in a big, fancy home, she chooses what appears to be the most valuable piece of jewelry.*

RL.9-10.3

Ⓑ Reading Support

7 **Setting** Have students reread the paragraph to find words that describe how Madame Loisel feels at the party.

ELL **Restate Language** Explain that the phrase "floated in a happy cloud" means that Madame Loisel was completely happy.

Ⓐ problem. Madame Forestier went to her large closet with mirrored doors, took out a big jewelry box, brought it to Madame Loisel, opened it, and said, "Choose whatever you like, my dear."

Her eyes wandered over some bracelets, then a pearl necklace, then a gold Venetian cross set with stones. She tried on the jewelry in front of the mirror, but she could not decide what to choose.

Suddenly she discovered a superb diamond necklace in a black satin case. Her heart started beating faster, and her hands trembled as she picked it up. She fastened it around her neck and stood there, gazing at herself in **ecstasy**.

Her voice was hesitant and filled with **agony** when she asked, "Could you lend me this one—just this and nothing else?"

"Yes, of course."

She threw her arms around her friend, kissed her cheek, and then fled with her treasure. 6

"Choose whatever you like, my dear."

Ⓑ The day of the party arrived. Madame Loisel was a great success. She was the prettiest woman there. She was elegant, fashionable, and gracious, and she was beaming with happiness. All the men looked at her, asked who she was, and begged to be introduced. All the **Cabinet officials** wanted to **waltz** with her. Even the Minister noticed her.

She danced **madly**, thinking of nothing but her beauty and success. She was dazed by all the admiration and floated in a happy cloud brought on by all her awakened desires. She felt the complete victory that is so sweet to a woman's heart. 7

She went to find her husband around four o'clock in the morning. Since midnight, he had been napping in a small sitting room along with

6 **Setting** How would Madame Loisel describe her friend's home and jewels? How does being in this new setting influence her choice?

7 **Setting** How does Madame Loisel change in this setting? What does this tell you about her?

In Other Words
ecstasy extreme happiness
agony deep pain and sadness
Cabinet officials men who held important jobs in the government
waltz dance
madly wildly

Ask: How does Madame Loisel change at the party? Why does she feel this way?

Possible response:
- *Madame Loisel is very happy because it is important to her to feel she is beautiful and to be admired by important people in an elegant home.*

RL.9-10.3

CCSS Literacy.RL.9-10.3 Analyze how complex characters (e.g., those with multiple or conflicting motivations) develop over the course of a text, interact with other characters, and advance the plot or develop the theme.

three other gentlemen whose wives were having a wonderful time.

He covered her shoulders with her wraps. They were plain, from her everyday life, and their shabbiness clashed with the elegance of her evening gown. **C** 8 She felt this and longed to escape quickly so that the other women, who were covered in expensive furs, would not see her.

Loisel held her back.

"Wait, you'll catch cold outside. I'll go for a cab."

But she wouldn't listen to him and went quickly down the stairs. When they reached the street, they did not see a carriage. They set out to find one, waving at the drivers they saw in the distance.

D They walked toward **the *Seine***, desperate and shivering. Finally, they found a cab on the wharf. It was one of those old carriages that are only seen at night in Paris, as if they are too **ashamed** to show their shabbiness during the daylight.

It took them to their door in the ***Rue des Martyrs***, and they climbed sadly up to their apartment. For her, it was all over. He was thinking that he had to be at the Ministry at ten o'clock. 9

She took off her wraps in front of the mirror, so that she could see herself once again **in all her glory**. Suddenly, she cried out. There was nothing around her neck. The necklace was gone!

Her husband, who was already half undressed, asked, "What's the matter?"

She turned toward him in a panic. "I . . . I . . . I don't have Madame Forestier's necklace."

"What? That's impossible!"

8 **Clarify Vocabulary**
What words and phrases in this sentence give clues about the meaning of the word *elegance*?

9 **Content Area Connections**
Use a map of Paris to locate the places mentioned in the story.

Monitor Comprehension

Summarize
Explain what Mathilde wants in her life. How is the necklace a **symbol** of what she wants?

Key Vocabulary

- **symbol** *n.*, something that represents, or stands for, something else

In Other Words

the *Seine* the main river in Paris
ashamed embarrassed
Rue des Martyrs Street of the Martyrs (in French)
in all her glory looking so beautiful

TEACH & PRACTICE

C Reading Support

8 Clarify Vocabulary Read the first paragraph aloud to students. Ask: What context clues can you use to clarify the meaning of *elegance*? What does *elegance* mean?

Possible response:

- *The word* clashed *and the words* plain, everyday, *and* shabbiness *suggest that* elegance *means "stylishness."*

RL.9-10.4; L.9-10.4.a

D Reading Support

9 Content Area Connections Refer to the activity below for further connections to geography.

W.9-10.7

Monitor Comprehension

Summarize Have students think aloud to summarize what Madame Loisel wants in her life and why the necklace is a symbol of what she wants.

MODEL Have students supply important ideas as you think aloud. Say:

- *Madame Loisel is not happy with ______ [her life]. She wants a life of ______ [wealth and luxury]. She wants a ______ [fancy home] and ______ [fine clothes] and ______ [jewels].*
- *Madame Loisel chooses the ______ [diamond necklace] because it is ______ [the most elegant and expensive] of her friend's jewelry. It is a symbol of ______ [the kind of life she wants]. She hopes it will ______ [make her look as wealthy and important as she wants to be].*

RL.9-10.2

CONTENT AREA CONNECTIONS

GEOGRAPHY

Research Paris

Conduct Research Have students research Paris and use articles, maps, and photos to answer the following questions.

- What are the most important places to see in Paris? What is the Champs Elysées? What is the Palais Royal? What is the Louvre? What is the Eiffel Tower? Where are these places located within the city?
- How did people travel in Paris in the mid-1800s? How do they travel today?
- Why is the Seine important to Paris today? How do people travel across it?
- Where is the *Rue des Martyrs*? Is it near the Seine?

Share and Compare Have students choose two places they would like to visit in Paris and work in small groups to write detailed travel directions from one destination to another. Groups should design a graphic to accompany written directions that shows compass directions, street names, and distances.

W.9-10.7

CCSS Literacy.RL.9-10.2 Determine a theme or central idea of a text and analyze in detail its development over the course of the text, including how it emerges and is shaped and refined by specific details; provide an objective summary of the text. **Literacy.RL.9-10.4** Determine the meaning of words and phrases as they are used in the text, including figurative and connotative meanings; analyze the cumulative impact of specific word choices on meaning and tone (e.g., how the language evokes a sense of time and place; how it sets a formal or informal tone). **Literacy.W.9-10.7** Conduct short as well as more sustained research projects to answer a question (including a self-generated question) or solve a problem; narrow or broaden the inquiry when appropriate; synthesize multiple sources on the subject, demonstrating understanding of the subject under investigation. **Literacy.L.9-10.4.a** Use context (e.g., the overall meaning of a sentence, paragraph, or text; a word's position or function in a sentence) as a clue to the meaning of a word or phrase.

OBJECTIVES

Vocabulary
- Strategy: Use Contextual Analysis

Reading Strategies
- Plan and Monitor: Make and Confirm Predictions; Clarify Vocabulary

Comprehension & Critical Thinking
- Use Text Evidence (T)

Literary Analysis
- Analyze Style: Language and Word Choice

Viewing
- Respond to and Interpret Visuals

Grammar
- Missing Subject (T)

TEACH & PRACTICE

(A) Chunking the Text

Predict Have students use their knowledge of text structure to review plot events, to help them predict what the Loisels will do.

Ask: What do you think the Loisels will do to solve their problem?

Possible response:
- *They might go back to all the places they were to try to find the necklace.*

Read Have students read pp. 74–75. Support and monitor their comprehension using the reading support.
RL.9-10.10

(B) Reading Support

10 Language Work with students to interpret the idioms "her mind a blank" and "lost all hope." Ask: How do the phrases help you understand how the Loisels feel?

Possible response:
- *The words show how upset they are.*

RL.9-10.4; L.9-10.5.a

(C) Reading Support

Literature Background Review the plot of *The Trojan Horse* with students. Point out that Helen's escape to Troy lead to war and the fall of Troy. Similarly, Madame Loisel's loss of the necklace lead to her husband's life of debt.

They searched in the folds of her dress, in the folds of her wraps, in the pockets, everywhere. They found nothing.

He asked, "Are you sure you still had it when we left the ball?"

"Yes. I felt it in the hallway of the Ministry."

"But if you had lost it in the street, we would have heard it fall. It must be in the cab."

"Yes, most likely. Did you get its number?"

"No. What about you?"

"No."

They looked at each other in shock. Finally, Loisel got dressed again. "I'm going to retrace our steps on foot to see if I can find it," he said.

(B) And he left the house. She slumped in her chair in the cold room, her mind a blank.

Her husband returned around seven o'clock. He had found nothing.

The next day he went to the police station, to the cab companies, and anywhere there was the slightest hope of finding it. He placed an advertisement in the paper offering a reward.

She spent the whole day waiting, feeling completely hopeless **in the face of** such an awful disaster.

When Loisel returned that evening, his face was pale and lined. He had learned nothing. "You must write to your friend," he said. "Tell her that you broke the **clasp** of the necklace and that you are having it repaired. That will give us time to think."

She wrote the letter **at his dictation**.

By the end of the week, they had lost all hope. 10

Loisel, who looked like he had aged five years, declared, "We must replace the necklace." The next day, they went to the jeweler whose

10 Language
The story includes phrases such as "her mind a blank" and "they had lost all hope." How do they add to your understanding of the characters' feelings?

(C) **Literature Background**
A familiar archetype is the character whose actions lead to the downfall of another. Helen of Troy, from *The Trojan Horse*, is one example from classical literature. Madame Loisel is an example from 19th-century literature. Analyze how each character represents this archetype.

In Other Words
in the face of because she was thinking about
clasp hook, fastener
at his dictation with the words he told her to write

GRAMMAR

Fixing a Fragment: Add the Subject

Teach/Model Display the transparency. Remind students that a fragment is not a complete thought. Read each group of words in the chart aloud and ask: Whom or what is the sentence about? Have students suggest a missing subject for each fragment. Write the complete sentence in the chart. Circle each subject.

Practice A. Have students tell you how to fix the fragments. Mark their answers as edits. **B.** Have students write their sentences and read one aloud. Then ask the group to identify each subject.
L.9-10.1

Grammar & Writing Practice Book, pp. 23–24

GRAMMAR SKILLS PATH

11 Sentence Fragments
▶ 12 Fixing a Fragment: Add the Subject ELL Language & Grammar Lab
13 Fixing a Fragment: Add the Verb
14 Fixing a Fragment: Combine Sentences
15 Review: Fix Sentence Fragments

Grammar Transparency 12

GRAMMAR FIXING A FRAGMENT: ADD THE SUBJECT 12

What's One Way to Fix a Fragment?

Add a Subject.

- A complete sentence has a **subject** and a **predicate**.
- To check for a subject, ask yourself:
  Whom or what is the sentence about?

Which of these are fragments?	Fix them.
1. Gets an invitation.	Mr. Loisel gets an invitation.
2. Buys a new dress for the party.	Mathilde buys a new dress for the party.
3. Mathilde looks beautiful.	(correct)
4. Dance around the room.	Mr. Loisel and his wife dance around the room.

Try It

A. Find five fragments. Add a subject to turn each fragment into a complete sentence. The first is done for you.

Mathilde wants to go to the party. She dresses her best. [She] Wears a beautiful necklace. [It] Belongs to Madame Forestier. [Mathilde] Loses the necklace. Mathilde and her husband are both very upset. [They] Look everywhere for the necklace. [They] Wonder what to do next.

B. Now tell a friend about the story. Write three complete sentences. Include a subject in each sentence. Sentences will vary.

CCSS **Literacy.RL.9-10.4** Determine the meaning of words and phrases as they are used in the text, including figurative and connotative meanings; analyze the cumulative impact of specific word choices on meaning and tone (e.g., how the language evokes a sense of time and place; how it sets a formal or informal tone). **Literacy.L.9-10.1** Demonstrate command of the conventions of standard English grammar and usage when writing or speaking. **Literacy.L.9-10.5.a** Interpret figures of speech (e.g., euphemism, oxymoron) in context and analyze their role in the text.

name they found inside the case. He looked through his **records**.

"I did not sell this necklace, madame," he said. "I only supplied the case."

Then they went from one jeweler to the next, trying to find a similar necklace. Both of them felt sick with worry and **anguish**.

In a shop in **the *Palais Royal***, they found a string of diamonds which looked exactly like the one they were seeking. It was worth 40,000 *francs*. They could have it for 36,000.

The Poor, 1896, Andre Collin. Oil on canvas, Musee des Beaux-Arts, Tournai, Belgium.

They begged the jeweler to hold it for them for three days. He agreed to take it back for 34,000 *francs* if they found the other necklace before the end of February.

Loisel had 18,000 *francs* that his father had left him. He would borrow the rest.

He borrowed, asking a thousand *francs* from one man, five hundred from another, a hundred here, fifty there. He signed **promissory notes** and made deals that could ruin him with all kinds of people. He compromised the rest of his life, agreeing to pay back money even when he wasn't sure that he would be able to do it. Then, terrified by a future of **anxiety and black misery**, he went to get the new necklace and placed 36,000 *francs* on the jeweler's counter. 11

When Madame Loisel took the necklace back, Madame Forestier said, coldly, "You could have brought it back sooner! I might have needed it."

She did not open the case, as her friend had feared. If she had noticed the substitution, what would she have thought? What would she have said? Wouldn't she have thought Madame Loisel was a thief?

Critical Viewing: Effect How does use of shadow affect the feeling of this painting? How does the painting's feeling match the mood of the Loisel's home?

11 Clarify Vocabulary What context clues in this paragraph help you understand what *compromised* means?

Monitor Comprehension

Confirm Prediction Is your prediction correct, or is it still too soon to tell? Explain.

In Other Words

records papers that showed what he had sold and who he had sold it to
anguish suffering
the *Palais Royal* a building lined with shops
promissory notes papers that promised he would pay back the money he had borrowed
anxiety and black misery worrying and suffering

TEACH & PRACTICE

D Analyze Visuals

About the Art Some French artists in the 1800s, including Andre Collin, who created this piece of art, painted and wrote about the living conditions of the poor in Europe.

Interpret and Respond What details in the painting suggest poverty?

E Critical Viewing: Effect

Analyze Effect Ask students to compare the painting to the one on p. 69.

Ask: How does the use of shadow affect the feeling of this painting?

Possible responses:

- *This painting is dark and gloomy. The people's faces are in the shadows, which makes them seem sad.*

Ask: How is the mood of this painting different from the one on p. 69? How is it like the mood of the Loisels' home?

Possible responses:

- *The mood of this painting is sad and gloomy. The mood of the other painting is happy and bright.*
- *The mood of the Loisels' home is gloomy like the painting.*

RL.9-10.7

F Reading Support

11 Clarify Vocabulary Ask students to explain what the husband does to pay for the necklace. Ask: What does *compromised* mean? What clues helped you understand the word?

Possible response:

- *The words* borrowed, ruin him, *and* pay back *show that* compromised *means "risked" or "put in danger."*

RL.9-10.4; L.9-10.4.a

Monitor Comprehension

Confirm Prediction Have students match their predictions with what the Loisels do to solve their problem. Ask: Can you confirm your prediction, or do you need to read on for more information?

RL.9-10.10

CCSS **Literacy.RL.9-10.4** Determine the meaning of words and phrases as they are used in the text, including figurative and connotative meanings; analyze the cumulative impact of specific word choices on meaning and tone (e.g., how the language evokes a sense of time and place; how it sets a formal or informal tone). **Literacy.RL.9-10.7** Analyze the representation of a subject or a key scene in two different artistic mediums, including what is emphasized or absent in each treatment (e.g., Auden's "Musée des Beaux Arts" and Breughel's Landscape with the Fall of Icarus). **Literacy.RL.9-10.10** By the end of grade 9, read and comprehend literature, including stories, dramas, and poems, in the grades 9-10 text complexity band proficiently, with scaffolding as needed at the high end of the range. By the end of grade 10, read and comprehend literature, including stories, dramas, and poems, at the high end of the grades 9-10 text complexity band independently and proficiently. **Literacy.L.9-10.4.a** Use context (e.g., the overall meaning of a sentence, paragraph, or text; a word's position or function in a sentence) as a clue to the meaning of a word or phrase.

OBJECTIVES

Vocabulary
- Key Vocabulary Ⓣ

Reading Strategy
- Plan and Monitor: Make Predictions

Comprehension & Critical Thinking
- Use Text Evidence Ⓣ

Literary Analysis
- Analyze Setting Ⓣ

Viewing
- Respond to and Interpret Visuals

Grammar
- Missing Verbs Ⓣ

TEACH & PRACTICE

A Chunking the Text

Predict Discuss how the Loisels might feel to be poor and in debt to help students predict how it will change Madame Loisel.

Read Have students read pp. 76–79. Support and monitor their comprehension using the reading support provided.
RL.9-10.10

B Critical Viewing: Design

Analyze Design Ask students to study the figure of the woman. Ask: What feeling does the artist create with his choice of colors?

Possible response:
- *The dark colors create a hopeless and lonely feeling.*

C Reading Support

12 **Setting** Ask: How have Madame Loisel's surroundings and lifestyle changed?

Possible response:
- *She went from living in a simple, comfortable home to living in a tiny attic and working hard.*

Ask: What is your opinion of her now? Why do you feel that way?

Possible response:
- *I feel sorry for her because her life is very difficult.*
RL.9-10.3

Madame Loisel learned what it was like to live in **poverty**. She did it, however, with a sudden **heroism**. The dreadful **debt** had to be paid. She would pay it. They dismissed their maid and moved into an attic under the roof.

She learned to do all the heavy housework chores, all the hateful duties of cooking. She washed dishes, wearing down her pink fingernails by scouring grease from pots and pans. She scrubbed dirty linen, shirts, and cleaning rags, which she hung on the line to dry. She took the garbage down to the street each morning and carried up the water, stopping at each floor to catch her breath. Dressed like a **peasant woman**, she went to the fruit store, the grocer, and the butcher with a basket on her arm. There she argued for each ***sou*** of her tiny funds.

Each month, some bills had to be paid, and others were renewed to give more time to pay. Her husband worked in the evenings for a shopkeeper. At night, he copied documents for five *sous* a page.

And this went on for ten years. 12

After ten years, they had finally paid back the whole debt.

Madame Loisel looked like an old woman now. She had become hard, rough, and coarse like a peasant. With her hair uncombed, her skirts

A Woman Ironing, 1873, Edgar Degas. Oil on canvas, The Metropolitan Museum of Art.

B ▲ Critical Viewing: Design What feeling is expressed by the dark colors the artist used for the woman?

12 **Setting** Describe how Madame Loisel's surroundings and lifestyle have changed. How do you feel about her now?

Key Vocabulary
poverty *n.*, being very poor

In Other Words
heroism bravery, fearlessness
debt money that was owed
peasant woman poor woman who lived in the countryside
sou penny (in French)

GRAMMAR

Fixing a Fragment: Add the Verb

Teach/Model Display the transparency. Ask students to identify each fragment. Model how to write one complete sentence for each fragment in the chart. For number 1, model adding more words to complete the predicate. Underline the verb in each complete sentence.

Practice A. Have students read the paragraph aloud. Ask the group to tell how to fix fragments and write their edits on the transparency. **B.** Have partners write their sentences and read a favorite sentence aloud. Choose one to write on the transparency. Ask the group to identify the verb. Underline it.
L.9-10.1

Grammar & Writing Practice Book, pp. 25–26

GRAMMAR SKILLS PATH

Grammar Transparency 13

What's Another Way to Fix a Fragment?

GRAMMAR FIXING A FRAGMENT: ADD THE VERB 13

Add a Predicate, and Be Sure It Has a Verb.

When you write a sentence, be sure to include the verb. If you leave out the verb, the words you wrote are a **fragment**.

Which of these are fragments?	Fix them.
1. Loisel's father.	Loisel's father gives him money.
2. Still, the Loisels more money.	Still, the Loisels need more money.
3. They move into an attic.	(correct)
4. Mathilde and her husband the debt.	Mathilde and her husband pay the debt.

Try It

A. Find five fragments. Add a verb or a predicate to form each fragment into a complete sentence. The first is done for you.

My friends and I earn money at work. Felipe and Luisa [work] in a music store. On Saturdays, I [sell] hot dogs in the park. Gretchen [makes] purses and sells them. We all save our money. Luisa and I [put] money in a bank account. Felipe's mother [keeps his money]. Gretchen hides her money in a secret place.

B. Now tell a partner more about saving money. Write your three best sentences. Include a verb in each sentence. Sentences will vary.

CCSS **Literacy.RL.9-10.3** Analyze how complex characters (e.g., those with multiple or conflicting motivations) develop over the course of a text, interact with other characters, and advance the plot or develop the theme. **Literacy.RL.9-10.10** By the end of grade 9, read and comprehend literature, including stories, dramas, and poems, in the grades 9-10 text complexity band proficiently, with scaffolding as needed at the high end of the range. By the end of grade 10, read and comprehend literature, including stories, dramas, and poems, at the high end of the grades 9-10 text complexity band independently and proficiently. **Literacy.L.9-10.1** Demonstrate command of the conventions of standard English grammar and usage when writing or speaking.

askew, her hands red, and her voice loud, she slopped water over the floors and scrubbed them. But sometimes, when her husband was at the office, she would sit by the window and think of that party long ago, when she had been so beautiful and so admired.

What would have happened if she had not lost that necklace? Who knows? Who can say? How strange and unpredictable life is! How little there is between happiness and sorrow!

> **How strange and unpredictable life is!**

Then one Sunday, she went for a walk on **the *Champs Elysées*** to relax from the week's work. Suddenly, she noticed a woman taking a child for a walk. It was Madame Forestier, still young, still beautiful, and still charming.

Madame Loisel felt a rush of emotion. Should she speak to her? Yes, of course she should. And now that she had paid everything back she would tell Madame Forestier the whole story. Why not?

She went toward her.

"Hello, Jeanne."

The other did not recognize her and seemed surprised that this common woman would speak to her **so familiarly**. She stammered, "But . . . madame! . . . I don't recognize . . . You must be mistaken."

"No. I am Mathilde Loisel."

Her friend cried out, "Oh, my poor Mathilde! How you have changed!" 13

"Yes, I've had a very hard time since I last saw you. I've had many troubles—and all because of you."

"Because of me? What do you mean?"

D

13 Setting
Why doesn't Madame Forestier recognize Mathilde? What does this tell you about the way people treated others at this time?

In Other Words
askew crooked, twisted around
the *Champs Elysées* a main street in Paris
so familiarly like a friend or family member

TEACH & PRACTICE

D Reading Support

13 **Setting** Have students find words in the text on pp. 76–77 that describe what Madame Loisel looks like now.

ELL Use Graphic Organizer
Record students' responses in a graphic organizer.

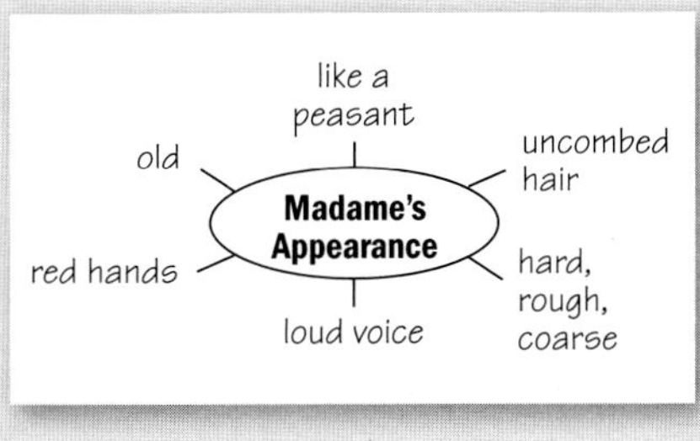

Ask: Why doesn't Madame Forestier recognize Madame Loisel?

Possible answer:
- *Madame Loisel looks like a peasant woman. She looks old and untidy.*

Madame Forestier is surprised that a poor woman would speak to her. Ask: What does this show about the way people treated others in that place and time?

Possible answer:
- *It shows that wealthy people of that time didn't know or want to be spoken to by poor people. There was a big difference between ways that poor and rich people were treated in the 1800s.*

RL.9-10.3; RL.9-10.6

CCSS **Literacy.RL.9-10.3** Analyze how complex characters (e.g., those with multiple or conflicting motivations) develop over the course of a text, interact with other characters, and advance the plot or develop the theme. **Literacy.RL.9-10.6** Analyze a particular point of view or cultural experience reflected in a work of literature from outside the United States, drawing on a wide reading of world literature.

READE

OBJECTIVES

Vocabulary
- Key Vocabulary Ⓣ
- Strategy: Use Contextual Analysis

Reading Strategy
- Plan and Monitor: Clarify Vocabulary; Review Strategies

Comprehension & Critical Thinking
- Use Text Evidence Ⓣ

Literary Analysis
- Analyze Setting Ⓣ

Viewing
- Respond to and Interpret Visuals

Writing
- Response to Literature

TEACH & PRACTICE

Ⓐ Reading Support

14 Clarify Vocabulary Ask: What does the phrase "stopped short" mean? Why does Madame Forestier stop short when talking to Mathilde?

Possible response:
- *It means that she suddenly stopped. She stops short because she hears something.*

RL.9-10.4; L.9-10.4.a

Review Strategies Have partners explain what other strategy they used as they read the text.

Possible response:
- *I know that sudden surprises can be upsetting. And so I think Madame Loisel probably changed from joy to horror after hearing the truth.*

RL.9-10.1

Ⓑ Analyze Visuals

About the Art Jan Zrzavy used shadows and long, curving lines to emphasize the subjects of his paintings.

Interpret and Respond Ask: Does this painting seem realistic? Explain.

Ⓒ Critical Viewing: Effect

Analyze Mood Point out how one woman seems to be comforting the other. Then ask students to explain the mood that the artist creates.

Possible response:
- *The room is dark and lit only by a single candle. This creates a sad mood.*

"Do you remember that diamond necklace you lent me to wear to the party at the Ministry?"

"Yes. What about it?"

"Well, I lost it."

"What do you mean? You returned it to me."

"I gave you another one that was just like it and it took us ten years to pay for it. You can imagine that wasn't easy for us, since we had nothing. Well, it's over now, and I am glad."

Ⓐ Madame Forestier stopped short. 14 "You say that you bought a diamond necklace to replace mine?"

14 Clarify Vocabulary What does the phrase "stopped short" mean? Why does Madame Forestier "stop short" when talking to Mathilde?

Friends, 1923, Jan Zrzavy. National Gallery, Prague, Czech Republic.

Ⓑ 

Ⓒ Critical Viewing: Effect What mood does the artist create with this painting? Explain.

VOCABULARY

Link Vocabulary and Concepts

Ask questions to link Key Vocabulary with the Essential Question.

EQ **ESSENTIAL QUESTION:**
What influences a person's choices?

Some possible questions:

- *What choice does Madame Loisel make to avoid a* **humiliating** *experience with her friend?*
- *How does Madame Loisel* **perceive** *the choices available to her?*
- *What item of* **luxury** *does Madame Loisel choose at her friend's home?*
- *Do you think the Loisels' choice might make them end up in* **poverty**?
- *How do Madame Loisel's choices show her* **values**?

As students answer, encourage the use of the highlighted Key Vocabulary.

L.9-10.6

CCSS **Literacy.RL.9-10.1** Cite strong and thorough textual evidence to support analysis of what the text says explicitly as well as inferences drawn from the text. **Literacy.RL.9-10.4** Determine the meaning of words and phrases as they are used in the text, including figurative and connotative meanings; analyze the cumulative impact of specific word choices on meaning and tone (e.g., how the language evokes a sense of time and place; how it sets a formal or informal tone). **Literacy.L.9-10.6** Acquire and use accurately general academic and domain-specific words and phrases, sufficient for reading, writing, speaking, and listening at the college and career readiness level; demonstrate independence in gathering vocabulary knowledge when considering a word or phrase important to comprehension or expression.

"Yes. You never noticed, then? They were exactly alike."

She smiled with proud, simple joy.

Madame Forestier, **quite moved**, took Mathilde's hands in her own.

"Oh, my poor Mathilde! Mine was an **imitation**. It was worth only five hundred francs at the most!" ❖

ANALYZE The Necklace

1. **Explain** How might the outcome of the story, or resolution, have changed if Madame Loisel had been more truthful? Support your response with details from the story.
2. **Vocabulary** How does the necklace change the way Madame Loisel **perceives** herself? Does it affect the way others at the party perceive her? Explain.
3. **Analyze Setting** With a partner, discuss how the settings and changing circumstances in the story affect Madame Loisel's choices. Record your ideas in a chart.

Setting/Circumstances	Choices
her shabby apartment	
the party	

4. **Focus Strategy Clarify Vocabulary** Tell a partner how you used a context clue to figure out a word's meaning.

Return to the Text

Reread and Write Madame Loisel's choices are influenced by what she **values** in life. Does her attitude toward these things change by the end of the story? Write your opinion using at least two pieces of evidence from the text.

Key Vocabulary

imitation *n.*, something that looks or acts like something else

• **perceive** *v.*, to see in a certain way

value *v.*, to think something is important or useful

In Other Words

quite moved feeling very emotional

APPLY

D ANALYZE

1. **Explain** Madame Loisel would have avoided a life of poverty if she had been truthful. Madame Forestier would have told her the necklace was an imitation.
RL.9-10.1; RL.9-10.5
2. **Vocabulary** The necklace makes her feel rich and admired. Other people at the party want to meet and dance with her.
L.9-10.6
3. **Analyze Setting** After partners complete their chart, have them use it to discuss how setting affects choices.

Setting/ Circumstances	Choices
her shabby apartment	refuses the invitation
the party	pretends to be rich
Madame Forestier's home	chooses the most valuable jewels
loses the necklace	chooses to lie
becomes poor	chooses to accept poverty
meets Madame Forestier	tells the truth

RL.9-10.3

4. **Focus Strategy: Clarify Vocabulary** Remind students that the words and phrases around an unknown word are clues to its meaning. Have partners model their use of context clues to determine word meanings.
RL.9-10.4; L.9-10.4.a

E Return to the Text

Students' opinions might reflect these influences and evidence:

- *When Madame Loisel loses the necklace, she decides to work very hard to pay for the necklace because that is the only choice she sees for herself. By the end of the story, she no longer values the things that make a person look rich. She values being truthful. She also decides to approach Madame Forestier and is honest with her about the past.*

W.9-10.9; W.9-10.10

Edge Interactive Practice Book, p. 38

CCSS **Literacy.RL.9-10.3** Analyze how complex characters (e.g., those with multiple or conflicting motivations) develop over the course of a text, interact with other characters, and advance the plot or develop the theme. **Literacy.RL.9-10.5** Analyze how an author's choices concerning how to structure a text, order events within it (e.g., parallel plots), and manipulate time (e.g., pacing, flashbacks) create such effects as mystery, tension, or surprise. **Literacy.W.9-10.9** Draw evidence from literary or informational texts to support analysis, reflection, and research. **Literacy.W.9-10.10** Write routinely over extended time frames (time for research, reflection, and revision) and shorter time frames (a single sitting or a day or two) for a range of tasks, purposes, and audiences. **Literacy.L.9-10.4.a** Use context (e.g., the overall meaning of a sentence, paragraph, or text; a word's position or function in a sentence) as a clue to the meaning of a word or phrase.

Lesson 20

BEFORE READING

OBJECTIVES

Reading Strategy
- Plan and Monitor: Clarify Vocabulary

Literary Analysis
- Determine Viewpoint T

TEACH STRATEGIES

A Determine Viewpoint

Introduce Read the introduction to define memoir and viewpoint. Explain that a memoir is nonfiction, but it has some features of a short story, such as a plot, or series of events. The narration is influenced by the writer's own viewpoint about his or her experiences.

Look Into the Text Use the callouts on p. 80 to teach about author's viewpoint. Point out the first-person pronouns and that most of the sentences begin with "I." Ask: How is the first-person narration in a memoir different from first-person narration in a short story?

Possible responses:
- *The narrator is the writer and not a fictional character.*
- *The events and feelings the narrator tells about are real and told from his or her viewpoint.*

RI.9-10.6

B Focus Strategy: Plan and Monitor

Clarify Vocabulary Review that students use a variety of strategies as they read. Then read the introduction with students. Define the strategy and work through the steps in the How To box.

Have partners reread Look Into the Text to figure out the meaning of *damaged*. Have them identify the context clues they used to figure out the meaning of the word.

Possible responses:
- *not well, broken, or injured; context clues: leg, and fall down*

RI.9-10.4; L.9-10.4.a

ONGOING ASSESSMENT
Have students explain how the writer's viewpoint might affect the kind of information a memoir contains.

BEFORE READING The Fashion Show

memoir by Farah Ahmedi with Tamim Ansary

Reading Strategies
- ▶ **Plan and Monitor**
- Determine Importance
- Make Inferences
- Ask Questions
- Make Connections
- Synthesize
- Visualize

Determine Viewpoint

A memoir is a writer's personal account of real events that happened in his or her life. It often has a plot like a short story. It also shares the writer's **viewpoint**, or thoughts and feelings about the events.

Look Into the Text

A **The author tells her own story. She is a first-person narrator. She uses *I* and *my* to tell the story. Many of the sentences have a similar structure.**

The first part of the show would be a dance performance by the kids from Mexico. The next part would be a fashion show. Kids from any country could be in the fashion show, and they would model clothes from their own culture, but no one had to do it.

I felt torn and confused. I could not take part in the dance, of course, but should I be in the fashion show? I really wanted to do it. I had two beautiful Afghan outfits I could model. But I was also thinking, *My leg is damaged. What if I fall down?*

The writing shows the author's feelings and opinions.

Focus Strategy ▶ Plan and Monitor

Sometimes a context clue in the sentence can help you understand an unknown word. Most other times, though, you will need to look at more than one sentence to figure out what a word means.

B

Focus Strategy

HOW TO CLARIFY VOCABULARY

1. **Read the sentences around the unknown word.** Read the sentence before the word, the sentence the word is in, and the sentence after the word.
2. **Look for a relationship between sentences.** Notice how the second sentence below is connected to the first: It gives an example of what the writer means by "torn and confused."

   I felt torn and confused. I could not take part in the dance, of course, but should I be in the fashion show?

   The author asks herself a question. Maybe confused means "questioning," or "unsure of the answer."
3. **Substitute your guess for the unknown word.** Check to see if it makes sense in the sentence.

   I felt torn and unsure of the answer. That meaning makes sense.

CCSS **Literacy.RI.9-10.4** Determine the meaning of words and phrases as they are used in a text, including figurative, connotative, and technical meanings; analyze the cumulative impact of specific word choices on meaning and tone (e.g., how the language of a court opinion differs from that of a newspaper). **Literacy.RI.9-10.6** Determine an author's point of view or purpose in a text and analyze how an author uses rhetoric to advance that point of view or purpose **Literacy.L.9-10.4.a** Use context (e.g., the overall meaning of a sentence, paragraph, or text; a word's position or function in a sentence) as a clue to the meaning of a word or phrase.

Connect Across Texts
In "The Necklace," Madame Loisel makes a choice because she worries about what others think. Now read this memoir. How do the opinions of others affect Farah's decision? D

THE FASHION SHOW

by Farah Ahmedi
with Tamim Ansary

C

At just 17, Farah Ahmedi entered an essay contest. Since then, her memoir, ***The Other Side of the Sky***, has inspired people everywhere with her life story as a proud Afghan American.

▲ Farah Ahmedi was a junior in high school when she published *The Other Side of the Sky: A Memoir.*

OBJECTIVES

Comprehension & Critical Thinking
- Use Text Evidence Ⓣ

Literary Analysis
- Determine Viewpoint Ⓣ

Cultural Perspectives
- Appreciate World Cultures

BUILD BACKGROUND

C Build Background

Explain Culture Read the title and text below it. Tell students that the photograph shows the author of the memoir, Farah Ahmedi. She is dressed in traditional Afghan clothing.

ELL Cultural Background Explain that an Afghan American is someone who is from Afghanistan and now lives in America.

Share information about Afghanistan.

- Afghanistan is a country in central Asia. Although it has a rich history of cultural traditions, today it is one of the poorest countries.
- After more than 40 years of being invaded and at war, much of Afghanistan's land is covered with unexploded landmines.
- Afghan American women might wear traditional clothing with detailed designs and bright colors like the author wears in the photograph for special occasions.

D Connect Across Texts

Ask students to predict what might have happened if Madame Loisel did not care about others' opinions.

Possible response:
- *She would not have borrowed the necklace and her whole life would have been different.*

Explain that in this memoir the author must choose whether to let others' opinions influence her decisions.

Read Have students read pp. 82–86. Support and monitor their comprehension using the reading support provided.

Comprehension Coach

Build Reading Power

Assign students to use the software, based on their instructional needs.

Read Silently
- Comprehension questions with immediate feedback
- Glossary support
- Review text evidence

RI.9-10.10

Listen
- Professional model of fluent reading

Record
- Oral reading fluency practice
- Ongoing fluency assessment with immediate feedback

CCSS Literacy.RI.9-10.10 By the end of grade 9, read and comprehend literary nonfiction in the grades 9–10 text complexity band proficiently, with scaffolding as needed at the high end of the range. By the end of grade 10, read and comprehend literary nonfiction at the high end of the grades 9–10 text complexity band independently and proficiently.

READ

OBJECTIVES

Vocabulary
- Strategy: Use Contextual Analysis
- Content Area Vocabulary: Media

Reading Strategy
- Plan and Monitor: Clarify Vocabulary
- Summarize
- Review Strategies

Comprehension & Critical Thinking
- Use Text Evidence Ⓣ

Literary Analysis
- Determine Viewpoint Ⓣ

Grammar
- Fixing a Fragment Ⓣ

Farah Ahmedi didn't have much of a childhood. She was still recovering from losing her leg in a land mine accident when a rocket attack destroyed her home in Kabul, Afghanistan. Four years and many challenges later, Farah and her mother found their way to a suburb of Chicago. Farah learned English, started high school, and began to make choices that would change her life. Despite her disability, she wanted to fit in. She wanted to "wear high-heeled shoes." Here, Farah remembers one of those choices.

During our second summer in America, I switched schools. The **ESL department** at my new high school had an international club. Kids from other countries met every Wednesday after school to play games, talk, and have fun. Ms. Ascadam, the teacher who sponsored this group, decided that the international kids should throw a party at the end of the year and present a show. [1] She told us each to bring food from our country to the party, and she encouraged us to think about participating in the show as well.

From Kabul to Chicago

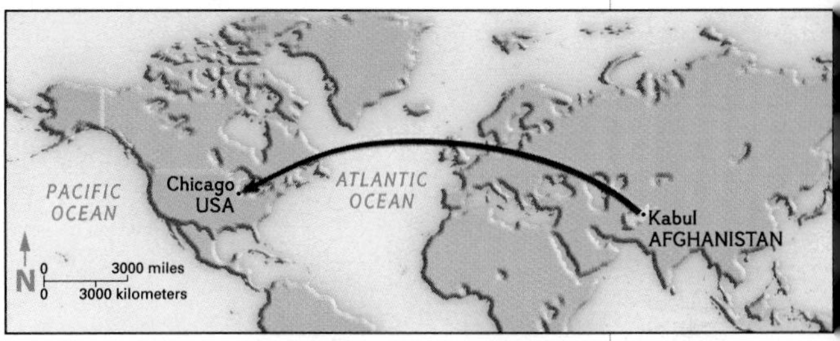

Ⓐ Interpret the Map Use the scale to calculate how far Farah and her mother traveled to their new home.

The first part of the show would be a dance performance by the kids from Mexico. The next part would be a **fashion show**. Kids from any country could be in the fashion show, and they would model clothes from their own culture, but no one had to do it.

[1] **Clarify Vocabulary** What does *sponsored* mean? What clues in the sentences before and after the word can help you figure it out?

In Other Words

a land mine accident an explosion caused by a bomb buried in the ground
suburb of town outside of
ESL department English classes for students who spoke other languages
fashion show display of special clothes

Historical Background

Afghanistan has been at war for more than forty years. In 2001, the U.S. and other countries invaded the country to force the Taliban, the ruling group, to leave.

TEACH & PRACTICE

Ⓐ Analyze Visuals

Interpret the Map Explain that a map scale lets you figure out distances between points on a map. Have students point to Chicago, U.S.A., and Kabul, Afghanistan, on the map. Ask: Using the scale, how far did Ahmedi and her mother travel from Kabul to Chicago?

Possible response:
- *about 13,500 miles*

Help students evaluate the information from this text feature. Ask: How do the map and the scale add to your understanding of the memoir?

Possible response:
- *The map and the scale show how far Farah has traveled from her childhood home.*

Ⓑ Reading Support

[1] **Clarify Vocabulary** Read the first paragraph. Then ask: What does *sponsored* mean? What clues in the paragraph help you figure it out?

Possible responses:
- *organized, supported; context clues: teacher, told us, encouraged us*

RI.9-10.4; L.9-10.4.a

GRAMMAR

Fixing a Fragment: Combine Sentences

Teach/Model Display the transparency. Suggest that reading a sentence aloud will help students hear when it makes sense to join a fragment to another sentence. Use the examples to illustrate how to combine fragments with preceding sentences.

Practice A. Read each item aloud. As students combine the fragments with the sentences, write the new sentence. **B.** Have partners write their sentences and read one aloud. Ask the group to identify the parts of each complete sentence.
L.9-10.1

Grammar & Writing Practice Book, pp. 27–28

GRAMMAR SKILLS PATH

11	Sentence Fragments
12	Fixing a Fragment: Add the Subject
13	Fixing a Fragment: Add the Verb
▶ 14	Fixing a Fragment: Combine Sentences — ELL Language & Grammar Lab
15	Review: Fix Sentence Fragments

Grammar Transparency 14

GRAMMAR FIXING A FRAGMENT: COMBINE SENTENCES 14

What's One More Way to Fix a Fragment?
Combine Neighboring Sentences.

Writers may create a fragment by starting a new sentence when they shouldn't. These fragments are easy to fix. Just combine the fragment with the sentence before it.

1. A rocket attack destroyed the house. (sentence) Where Farah lived. (fragment)
A rocket attack destroyed the house where Farah lived.
2. Farah had a hard childhood. (sentence) Because she lost her leg. (fragment)
Farah had a hard childhood because she lost her leg.

Try It

A. Find each fragment. Combine it with the other sentence.

1. Farah wants to be like everyone else. And be in the fashion show. Farah wants to be like everyone else and be in the fashion show.
2. She joins an international club at school. And meets students from different countries. She joins an international club at school and meets students from different countries.
3. The fashion show causes great excitement. Because many kids want to model clothes. The fashion show causes great excitement because many kids want to model clothes.
4. The teacher tells students to bring food. And to think about the show. The teacher tells students to bring food and to think about the show.

B. Now tell a partner about someone you know who is like Farah. Write your three best complete sentences. Sentences will vary.

CCSS Literacy.RI.9-10.4 Determine the meaning of words and phrases as they are used in a text, including figurative, connotative, and technical meanings; analyze the cumulative impact of specific word choices on meaning and tone (e.g., how the language of a court opinion differs from that of a newspaper). **Literacy.L.9-10.1** Demonstrate command of the conventions of standard English grammar and usage when writing or speaking. **Literacy.L.9-10.4.a** Use context (e.g., the overall meaning of a sentence, paragraph, or text; a word's position or function in a sentence) as a clue to the meaning of a word or phrase.

I felt **torn and confused**. I could not take part in the dance, of course, but should I be in the fashion show? I really wanted to do it. I had two beautiful **Afghan outfits** I could model. But I was also thinking, *My leg is damaged. What if I fall down?*

Finally, I said to myself, *Okay, next Wednesday I'll sit in on the practice session and see what it's like, and then I'll decide.*

WHAT IF I FALL DOWN?

That day the girl who always picked on me came to the practice session, because she was planning to be in the fashion show. The moment she saw me sitting there, she could tell I was thinking of entering the show, too. She didn't tell me to my face that I could not do it, but she immediately called out to the teacher. "Ms. Ascadam," she said, "when you model clothes at a fashion show, isn't this how you have to walk? **2** Isn't this how models walk on a **runway**?" **C**

Then she began to walk the way she thought a model should walk—with long strides, placing one foot in front of the other in a straight line that made her back end swing from side to side. "Is this the way you should walk?" she said. "If someone can't walk like this, should she be in the fashion show? She would just spoil the whole thing, wouldn't she?" And she kept walking back and forth, swinging from side to side.

It made me so angry, because I knew that she was really saying, *Farah can't do this. She has a problem with her legs. She shouldn't be in the fashion show.* She didn't say my name, but she was talking about me and only me, and everyone knew it.

That girl broke my heart. I felt as if somebody had punched me or slapped me. I felt as if someone had gotten into my throat and started pushing me and pressing me and choking me. I could not stay in that room. I turned and **fled**, my eyes stinging with tears. **3** At home I **D**

2 Clarify Vocabulary
What are some meanings for the word *model*? What context clues help you understand what the word means here?

3 Viewpoint
How is the author feeling? What images help you understand her feelings?

Monitor Comprehension
Summarize
How does Ahmedi feel about being a model in the fashion show?

In Other Words
torn and confused mixed up, upset
Afghan outfits sets of clothes from Afghanistan
runway stage
fled ran away

TEACH & PRACTICE

C Reading Support

2 Clarify Vocabulary Read the last two sentences in paragraph 3. Ask: What does the word *model* mean in this sentence?

Possible response:
- *to wear and show clothes to others*

Ask: What context clues help you understand what the word means?

Possible response:
- *fashion show, outfits*

RI.9-10.4; L.9-10.4.a

Review Strategies Have partners say which other strategy they used as they read the text.

Possible response:
- *I used details in the last paragraph of page 83 to visualize Farah's feelings after hearing the girl's comments. I read that she felt "punched" and "slapped" like someone was pushing and choking her. This helped me picture how upset and wounded Farah felt at the time.*

RI.9-10.10

D Reading Support

3 Viewpoint Read the beginning of the last paragraph. Ask: How is Ahmedi feeling? What images help you understand her feelings?

Possible responses:
- *She is very upset. Her heart is broken. She feels like someone punched or choked her.*

RI.9-10.6

Monitor Comprehension

Summarize Help students summarize the selection to this point. Ask: How does Ahmedi feel about being a model in the fashion show?

Possible response:
- *She wants to be a model very much.*

RI.9-10.2

VOCABULARY

MEDIA & TECHNOLOGY

Content Area Vocabulary: Fashion in the Media

Build vocabulary related to the content area of fashion in the media.

Teach/Model Use the Make Words Your Own routine (*see the Vocabulary tab*) and the sample sentences below to introduce these words from the selection.

outfit (**owt**-fit) ▸ p. 83

Models wear many different **outfits** *at a fashion show.*

runway (**run**-wā) ▸ p. 83

To walk on a **runway**, *you have to practice your balance and how to walk.*

pose (pōz) ▸ p. 85

Models **pose** *for the camera during the show.*

strutting (**strut**-ting) ▸ p. 85

The models are usually **strutting** *down the runway and looking very confident.*

cosmetics (coz-**met**-iks) ▸ p. 85

Sometimes, the lipsticks and other **cosmetics** *that models wear match the clothes.*

Practice Have students use the words to describe a celebrity in the film, fashion, or music industry.

Apply Have students find pictures in magazines that define these words and show their examples to the class.

L.9-10.6

CCSS **Literacy.RI.9-10.2** Determine a central idea of a text and analyze its development over the course of the text, including how it emerges and is shaped and refined by specific details; provide an objective summary of the text. **Literacy.RI.9-10.6** Determine an author's point of view or purpose in a text and analyze how an author uses rhetoric to advance that point of view or purpose. **Literacy.RI.9-10.10** By the end of grade 9, read and comprehend literary nonfiction in the grades 9–10 text complexity band proficiently, with scaffolding as needed at the high end of the range. By the end of grade 10, read and comprehend literary nonfiction at the high end of the grades 9–10 text complexity band independently and proficiently. **Literacy.L.9-10.6** Acquire and use accurately general academic and domain-specific words and phrases, sufficient for reading, writing, speaking, and listening at the college and career readiness level; demonstrate independence in gathering vocabulary knowledge when considering a word or phrase important to comprehension or expression.

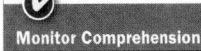

READ

OBJECTIVES

Vocabulary
- Key Vocabulary Ⓣ
- Strategy: Use Contextual Analysis

Reading Strategy
- Plan and Monitor: Clarify Vocabulary

Comprehension & Critical Thinking
- Use Text Evidence Ⓣ

Literary Analysis
- Determine Viewpoint Ⓣ

Research Skill
- Convert Data into Graphic Aids

TEACH & PRACTICE

Ⓐ Reading Support

4 Clarify Vocabulary Guide students in using the surrounding language in order to understand the phrase. Discuss Ahmedi's inner thoughts and worries about her self-image. Ask: What does she fear people will think about her?

ELL Use Graphic Organizer Ask: How did Farah feel when the girl picked on her in the practice sessions? List the details on a T Chart.

Girl's Words	Effect on Farah
models have to walk a certain way	weeping and feeling sorry for herself
if she can't, she will spoil it	lost her confidence

Possible response:
- *that she is not a complete woman*

Ask: What does Ahmedi mean by the phrase "getting through my defenses"?

Possible response:
- *getting through my tough outside to really hurt me inside*

Have students explain how the second part of the sentence helps explain the meaning of the phrase.

Possible response:
- *The words "poking me right where it hurt the most and where I would always hurt" tell that the girl found Ahmedi's most vulnerable feelings.*

RI.9-10.4; L.9-10.4.a

Farah Ahmedi shares her memoir with First Lady Laura Bush.

threw myself on my bed and just lay there, weeping and feeling sorry for myself—sorry about being only half a woman. I felt like everyone knew that I was not whole and that's what they thought about every time they looked at me. That girl had finally succeeded in getting through my defenses and poking me right where it hurt the most and where I would always hurt. 4 Ⓐ

And what happened just then?

My friend Alyce called.

"Hey," she said. "How are you, sweetie? Are you well?"

I started to **bawl**.

She said, "What is it? What are you crying about?"

I spilled the whole story.

Alyce said, "Now don't **get all hung up on** what other people say. You just go ahead and do it. You tell your teacher you want to be in the fashion show."

But I just went on crying. "You don't understand. It's not *just* what 'other people say.' The terrible thing is, that girl is right! I *can't* be in a fashion show! It's true. How can someone like me be in a fashion show? With my limp? I can't walk like a model." That girl's cruelty **wounded** me, to be sure, but what really hurt was the truth she was telling. "Why are you trying to **inspire** me to do something I should never even try?" I **ranted** at Alyce.

It was one of those moments, you see. And Alyce just let me rage.

4 Clarify Vocabulary What does the author mean by the phrase "getting through my defenses"? To figure it out, look at the second part of this sentence. Remember to always use the context to help you figure out a word or a phrase's meaning.

Key Vocabulary
inspire *v.*, to encourage someone to take action

In Other Words
bawl cry hard
I spilled the whole story. I told her everything.
get all hung up on worry about, feel upset about
wounded hurt
ranted yelled angrily

84 Unit 1 Choices

OUT-OF-SCHOOL LITERACY

SOCIOLOGY

Sharing World Cultures

Help students see how much prior knowledge they bring to the text by connecting the selection to students' experiences with their own cultures. Make a chart noting the different celebrations.

Country	Holidays	Traditions

- What holidays are celebrated in certain countries?
- How do people celebrate? What foods, clothes, and music are parts of these celebrations?
- What are traditions? How do we learn them?
- What special objects are part of a celebration or tradition?
- What **values** do these celebrations show? Why do people do these things?

Review the chart with students and ask them to note comparisons and differences among the different countries and celebrations.
SL.9-10.1.a

CCSS Literacy.RI.9-10.4 Determine the meaning of words and phrases as they are used in a text, including figurative, connotative, and technical meanings; analyze the cumulative impact of specific word choices on meaning and tone (e.g., how the language of a court opinion differs from that of a newspaper). Literacy.SL.9-10.1.a Come to discussions prepared, having read and researched material under study; explicitly draw on that preparation by referring to evidence from texts and other research on the topic or issue to stimulate a thoughtful, well-reasoned exchange of ideas. Literacy.L.9-10.4.a Use context (e.g., the overall meaning of a sentence, paragraph, or text; a word's position or function in a sentence) as a clue to the meaning of a word or phrase.

But then she said, "No, people aren't looking at you that way. Here, we **value** who you are as a person. You go right ahead and enter the fashion show fearlessly."

Well, I thought about it. I thought I should do it just to **spite** the girl who tried to keep me out of the show. I decided I had to do it, even if it meant falling down in the middle of the runway—because if I let that girl get away with talking about me as if I were half human, she would never stop. She would make me **her scapegoat**, and others would take up her view as well. I had to stand up for myself, because this was not just about a fashion show. It was about claiming my humanity. I had to do it. 5 **B**

I went to my teacher the next day and told her I wanted to enter the fashion show. She hugged me. "Farah," she said, "this makes me so, so happy!"

I HAD TO DO IT.

After that I started to practice walking. No, I started to practice *strutting* down a runway.

On the day of the fashion show, I hurried to the dressing room to get ready. I had two dresses to wear, an orange one and a purple one. Backstage the makeup people put cosmetics on my face and curled my hair, so that I looked really different than usual. The teacher saw me and said, "Oh my gosh, you look so pretty!"

The fashion show began. Each model was supposed to go out and walk around the stage in a diamond-shaped pattern. At each point of the diamond we were supposed to pause, face the audience, and **strike a pose**.

When my turn came, I went strutting out. 6 I threw my shoulders back and held my head up high so that my neck stretched long. I didn't fall, and I didn't shake. I didn't even feel nervous. **C**

5 Viewpoint
How does the author help you understand why she makes her decision?

6 Clarify Vocabulary
What does *strutting* mean? Look for clues in the paragraph.

Monitor Comprehension
Explain What makes Ahmedi change her mind about the show?

Key Vocabulary
value *v.*, to think something is important or useful

In Other Words
spite annoy, get back at
her scapegoat the one everyone blamed
strike a pose stand boldly for everyone to see

TEACH & PRACTICE

B Reading Support

5 Viewpoint Review what Alyce told Ahmedi. Then ask: How does Ahmedi help readers understand why she makes her decision?

Possible response:
- *Ahmedi describes her thoughts and feelings to readers. She lets readers know that she had to choose whether to let others influence her or to do what she believed was right.*

RI.9-10.6

C Reading Support

6 Clarify Vocabulary Help students identify clues in the last paragraph to define the word *strutting*. Ask: What does *strutting* mean?

Possible response:
- *throwing your shoulders back and holding your head up high as you walk proudly*

RI.9-10.4; L.9-10.4.a

Monitor Comprehension

Explain Remind students about the conflicting feelings and thoughts Ahmedi had about the show. Help students recall information from the text that explains why she decides to be in the show. Ask: What makes Ahmedi change her mind?

Possible response:
- *She decides to do what she wants and not to care about what others think about her or her decisions.*

RI.9-10.1

CONTENT AREA CONNECTIONS

HISTORY

Conduct Research Have students research Afghanistan's history and political situation over the last twenty years and use the information to answer the following questions:

- Where is Afghanistan located, who are its neighbors, and how did this affect its history?
- What ethnic groups make up Afghanistan's population and in what percentages?
- What happened in 1979, and how does this event affect Afghanistan today?
- What role did the Taliban play in Afghanistan's political situation before it was defeated?
- As a recently created democracy, what problems and challenges does Afghanistan face today?

Share and Compare Have students present their research to the class using charts, time lines, and graphs to present their information.

W.9-10.7

CCSS **Literacy.RI.9-10.1** Cite strong and thorough textual evidence to support analysis of what the text says explicitly as well as inferences drawn from the text. **Literacy.RI.9-10.4** Determine the meaning of words and phrases as they are used in a text, including figurative, connotative, and technical meanings; analyze the cumulative impact of specific word choices on meaning and tone (e.g., how the language of a court opinion differs from that of a newspaper). **Literacy.RI.9-10.6** Determine an author's point of view or purpose in a text and analyze how an author uses rhetoric to advance that point of view or purpose. **Literacy.W.9-10.7** Conduct short as well as more sustained research projects to answer a question (including a self-generated question) or solve a problem; narrow or broaden the inquiry when appropriate; synthesize multiple sources on the subject, demonstrating understanding of the subject under investigation. **Literacy.L.9-10.4.a** Use context (e.g., the overall meaning of a sentence, paragraph, or text; a word's position or function in a sentence) as a clue to the meaning of a word or phrase.

READ

OBJECTIVES

Vocabulary
- Key Vocabulary (T)
- Strategy: Use Contextual Analysis

Reading Strategy
- Plan and Monitor: Clarify Vocabulary

Comprehension & Critical Thinking
- Use Text Evidence (T)

Literary Analysis
- Determine Viewpoint (T)

Writing
- Response to Literature

APPLY

A ANALYZE

1. **Explain** Ahmedi is inspired by her friend's advice and her own desire to prove herself.
RI.9-10.1
2. **Vocabulary** Ahmedi perceives herself as damaged and half a woman at the start of the memoir. The girl who picks on her also thinks Ahmedi is different. Ahmedi's friend and teacher disagree. They encourage her to perceive herself as whole.
L.9-10.6
3. **Determine Viewpoint** A newspaper article would be written in third-person and include only facts about the fashion show. The memoir has a first-person narrator and includes her own opinions and feelings.
RI.9-10.6; RI-9-10.7
4. **Focus Strategy: Clarify Vocabulary** The words and phrases around the unknown word helped to figure out a word's meaning.
RI.9-10.4; L.9-10.4.a

B Return to the Text

Students' letters may vary but should include Ahmedi's thoughts and feelings about how the girl or Alyce affected her decision, as well as specific quotations embedded in the text as dialogue.
W.9-10.10

Alyce told me later that no one could tell about my legs. I moved in time to the music, showed the clothes off well, and smiled—I did just fine! My mother **beamed**. She didn't say much at the time, but later on, at home, she told me she felt proud of me. Imagine that! Proud that her daughter stood up before an audience of strangers and modeled our beautiful Afghan clothes: She, too, has come a long way since we arrived in America.

After the show the party began. We had all brought special foods from our various cultures. My mother had cooked a fancy Afghan rice dish. We ate and chatted and felt happy. That night, though it wasn't **literally** true, I felt that I was wearing high-heeled shoes at last. ❖

ANALYZE The Fashion Show

A

1. **Explain** Who or what **inspires** Ahmedi's final decision about the show? Provide specific evidence from the text that helps explain her decision.
2. **Vocabulary** How does Ahmedi **perceive** herself at the start of the memoir? Do others agree? Explain.
3. **Determine Viewpoint** With a partner, discuss how the viewpoint of a newspaper article about the fashion show would be different from the viewpoint in the memoir.
4. **Focus Strategy Clarify Vocabulary** Share one example of how you used context clues to figure out a word's meaning.

B

Return to the Text

Reread and Write Decide who inspires Ahmedi more—her friend Alyce or the girl who picks on her. Write a thank-you note from Ahmedi to that person. Quote remarks that the person made that affected Ahmedi's decision.

Key Vocabulary
- **perceive** *v.*, to see someone or something in a certain way

In Other Words
beamed smiled with joy
literally actually

Interactive Reading

Have students reread and mark "The Fashion Show" within the Edge Interactive Practice Book to apply their knowledge of author's viewpoint and to practice the Focus Strategy—Plan and Monitor: Clarify Vocabulary.

Edge Interactive Practice Book, pp. 39–44

Unit Project

Progress Check Allow time for students to work on their unit projects. Meet with individuals and/or groups to provide guidance and check on their progress.

myNGconnect.com
- **Unit Planning Tools**
- **Unit Project Evaluation Rubric**

CCSS **Literacy.RI.9-10.1** Cite strong and thorough textual evidence to support analysis of what the text says explicitly as well as inferences drawn from the text. **Literacy.RI.9-10.4** Determine the meaning of words and phrases as they are used in a text, including figurative, connotative, and technical meanings; analyze the cumulative impact of specific word choices on meaning and tone (e.g., how the language of a court opinion differs from that of a newspaper). **Literacy.RI.9-10.6** Determine an author's point of view or purpose in a text and analyze how an author uses rhetoric to advance that point of view or purpose. **Literacy.RI.9-10.7** Analyze various accounts of a subject told in different mediums (e.g., a person's life story in both print and multimedia), determining which details are emphasized in each account. **Literacy.W.9-10.10** Write routinely over extended time frames (time for research, reflection, and revision) and shorter time frames (a single sitting or a day or two) for a range of tasks, purposes, and audiences. **Literacy.L.9-10.4.a** Use context (e.g., the overall meaning of a sentence, paragraph, or text; a word's position or function in a sentence) as a clue to the meaning of a word or phrase. **Literacy.L.9-10.6** Acquire and use accurately general academic and domain-specific words and phrases, sufficient for reading, writing, speaking, and listening at the college and career readiness level; demonstrate independence in gathering vocabulary knowledge when considering a word or phrase important to comprehension or expression.

REFLECT AND ASSESS

- The Necklace
- The Fashion Show

EQ What Influences a Person's Choices?

Reading

Critical Thinking

1. **Interpret** What is Maupassant saying about the influence of society in "The Necklace"? Would Ahmedi agree with this message? Why or why not?
2. **Compare** The necklace in "The Necklace" and high-heeled shoes in "The Fashion Show" are both **symbols**. What is similar about the themes that the symbols represent? How are they different? Explain.
3. **Analyze** How do Ahmedi's and Madame Loisel's characters affect their decisions?
4. **Speculate** How would the theme of the memoir be different if it took place in France in the 1800s?
5. **Evaluate** Each of the selections in this unit deals with the things that influence us: our circumstances, our friends and families, and our communities. Which reason is the most positive? Use text examples to support your ideas.

Writing

Write About Literature

Response Log Write about a time when a choice you made had surprising consequences. Compare your experience to Madame Loisel's and Ahmedi's. Support your writing with examples from both texts.

Vocabulary

Key Vocabulary Review

Oral Review Work with a partner. Use these words to complete the paragraph.

humiliating	**luxuries**	**symbols**
imitations	**perceive**	**value**
inspire	**poverty**	

Some people think that money can buy happiness. They want __(1)__ that they don't really need, like big homes and cars. They think it's __(2)__ and embarrassing to wear inexpensive clothes. Some may even buy __(3)__ of other things because they are __(4)__ that represent happiness and wealth. But those things don't always make them happy. Sometimes, people who live in __(5)__ without enough money can be happier than rich people. It's because they __(6)__ things that are really important, like family and friends. They look at what they have and __(7)__ it as precious. These people __(8)__ me to be more like them.

Writing Application Write a paragraph about someone who **inspired** you. Use at least three Key Vocabulary words.

Fluency

Read with Ease: Intonation

Assess your reading fluency with the passage in the Reading Handbook, p. 753. Then complete the self-check below.

1. My intonation did/did not sound natural.
2. My words correct per minute: _____.

OBJECTIVES

Vocabulary
- Key Vocabulary T

Reading Fluency
- Intonation T

Comprehension & Critical Thinking
- Compare Across Texts
- Use Text Evidence T

Literary Analysis
- Evaluate Literature

Writing
- Form: Response Log
- Form: Paragraph

Reading

Critical Thinking

1. **Interpret** Maupassant is saying that society influences how people live their lives if they let it. Ahmedi might disagree because in the end, she did not let another girl's opinions about her change her mind about how she saw herself. RL.9-10.2; RI.9-10.2
2. **Compare** The shoes and the necklace both symbolize what others have and what society may see as important. They are different because the necklace represents wealth, and the shoes represent physical perfection. RL.9-10.2; RI.9-10.2
3. **Analyze** Both Ahmedi and Madame Loisel care too much about what other people think about them. Ahmedi was able to overcome her insecurities, but Madame Loisel was not. RL.9-10.3
4. **Speculate** French society was more class-conscious in the 1800s, so Ahmedi would have had a harder time finding support from others and proving herself. RL.9-10.2; RL.9-10.6
5. **Evaluate** Family and friends care about you and can help guide you to be the person you want to be. Family and friends are the most interested in your success and happiness. Ahmedi is influenced by her friend Alyce, who helps Ahmedi make the decision that is best for her. RL.9-10.1; RI.9-10.1

Writing

Write About Literature

Edge Interactive Practice Book, p. 45

Response Log Help students think of important choices they have made that resulted in surprising consequences: trusting a friend with a secret; helping a neighbor; choosing something despite other people's opinions. Invite volunteers to share their choices and compare them to Madame Loisel's and Ahmedi's choices.
W.9-10.3

Vocabulary

Key Vocabulary Review

1. *luxuries* **2.** *humiliating* **3.** *imitations* **4.** *symbols* **5.** *poverty* **6.** *value* **7.** *perceive* **8.** *inspire*
L.9-10.6

Fluency

Read with Ease: Intonation

Ensure that students complete the self-check.
RI.9.10-10

ASSESS & RETEACH

Assessments Handbook, pp. 1j–1m

Have students complete the **Reader Reflection**. Then give students the **Cluster Test** to measure their progress. Group students as needed for reteaching.

CCSS **Literacy.RL.9-10.1** Cite strong and thorough textual evidence to support analysis of what the text says explicitly as well as inferences drawn from the text. **Literacy.RL.9-10.2** Determine a theme or central idea of a text and analyze in detail its development over the course of the text, including how it emerges and is shaped and refined by specific details; provide an objective summary of the text. **Literacy.RL.9-10.3** Analyze how complex characters (e.g., those with multiple or conflicting motivations) develop over the course of a text, interact with other characters, and advance the plot or develop the theme. **Literacy.RL.9-10.6** Analyze a particular point of view or cultural experience reflected in a work of literature from outside the United States, drawing on a wide reading of world literature. **Literacy.RI.9-10.1** Cite strong and thorough textual evidence to support analysis of what the text says explicitly as well as inferences drawn from the text. **Literacy.RI.9-10.2** Determine a central idea of a text and analyze its development over the course of the text, including how it emerges and is shaped and refined by specific details; provide an objective summary of the text. **Literacy.RI.9-10.10** By the end of grade 9, read and comprehend literary nonfiction in the grades 9-10 text complexity band proficiently, with scaffolding as needed at the high end of the range. By the end of grade 10, read and comprehend literary nonfiction at the high end of the grades 9-10 text complexity band independently and proficiently. **Literacy.W.9-10.3** Write narratives to develop real or imagined experiences or events using effective technique, well-chosen details, and well-structured event sequences. **Literacy.L.9-10.6** Acquire and use accurately general academic and domain-specific words and phrases, sufficient for reading, writing, speaking, and listening at the college and career readiness level; demonstrate independence in gathering vocabulary knowledge when considering a word or phrase important to comprehension or expression.

2

GRATE THE NGUAGE ARTS

OBJECTIVES

Language Function
- Express Feelings and Intentions

Literary Analysis
- Analyze Setting and Theme

Grammar
- Fix Sentence Fragments

Grammar

Fix Sentence Fragments

Grammar Transparency 15

Review Use the transparency to review sentence fragments. Then conduct the activity on p. 88.

Oral Practice Students should remove the subject or verb from the complete sentence. Partners should replace the same element to fix the fragment.

Written Practice **6.** S **7.** F; She wants to be envied and admired. **8.** F; Mathilde feels sad and hopeless about her life. **9.** F; The invitation comes in a large envelope. **10.** S
L.9-10.1

Language Development

Express Feelings and Intentions

Evaluate students' acquisition of this language function with the Language Acquisition Rubric.
SL.9-10.4

Assessments Handbook, p. Io

Literary Analysis

Analyze Setting and Theme

1. Setting: Paris, France; 1800s; shabby apartment and fancy home. Choices: Madame Loisel borrows a necklace to look rich; she loses it and goes into extreme debt to replace it. Lesson: Choices based on others' opinions can have terrible consequences.

2. Possible response: Society can have a dramatic effect on a person's choices.
RL.9-10.2; RL.9-10.6

Edge Interactive Practice Book, p. 46

GRAMMAR SKILLS PATH
11 Sentence Fragments
12 Fixing a Fragment: Add the Subject
13 Fixing a Fragment: Add the Verb
14 Fixing a Fragment: Combine Sentences
15 Review: Fix Sentence Fragments ELL Language & Grammar Lab

INTEGRATE THE LANGUAGE ARTS

Grammar

Fix Sentence Fragments

This group of words begins with a capital letter and ends with a period, just like a sentence:

Dreams of a life of wealth.

The group of words looks like a sentence, but it is not complete. It is a **sentence fragment**. The fragment needs a **subject**:

The young wife dreams of a life of wealth.

A fragment may need a **verb**.

Fragment: The diamond necklace.
Sentence: The diamond necklace **sparkles**.

A fragment may need to become part of another sentence.

Fragment: Because she cannot afford fine clothes.
Sentence: Mathilde dresses plainly because she cannot afford fine clothes.

Oral Practice (1–5) Look at the selections you just read. Find five complete sentences. Break off a piece, and say it as a fragment. Ask your partner to change it back into a complete sentence.

Written Practice (6–10) Number your paper. Label each group of words with ***S*** for *Sentence* or ***F*** for *Fragment*. Then choose two fragments to write as complete sentences.

6. Mathilde wants to dress well.
7. To be envied and admired.
8. Feels sad and hopeless about her life.
9. A large envelope.
10. The couple is invited to a fancy party.

Language Development

Express Feelings and Intentions

Role-Play Take the role of Monsieur or Madame Loisel and tell about something you plan to do in the future. Tell how you feel about it, too.

Literary Analysis

Analyze Setting and Theme

Setting is the time and place in which a story unfolds. A story's setting affects the characters and the **theme**, or message, of the story. Think about the setting of "The Necklace."

- "The Necklace" is set in nineteenth century Paris. During this period, people could move from the lower class to the upper class if they had enough money or knew the right people.
- Madame Loisel wants to be wealthy. The setting feeds her desire and affects her decisions.
- Since the setting affects her actions, it also affects the story's theme. Here's how:

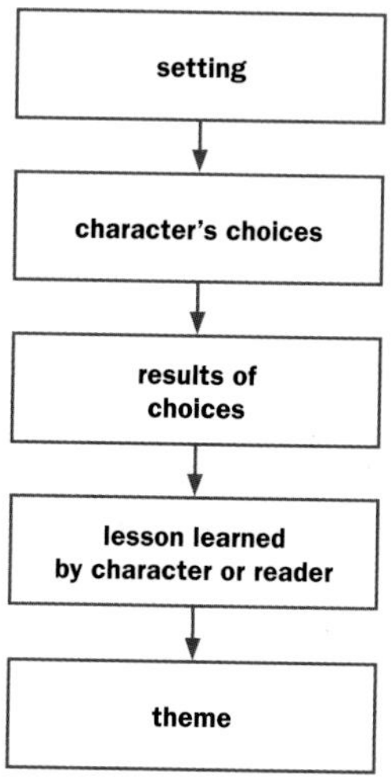

Discuss the following:

1. Use the diagram above to trace the development of the story's theme, starting with its setting.
2. State in your own words what you think the theme of this story is. How does the setting affect the theme?

GRAMMAR

Review: Fix Sentence Fragments

Review Display the transparency. Elicit the ways to identify and correct fragments. Have students read the examples aloud and tell how the fragment was fixed.

A. Oral Practice Have students suggest ways to fix each fragment. Write one of the suggestions on the transparency. Use the examples to provide corrective feedback as needed.

B. Written Practice Work through the example. Explain that some sentences have no errors. Have the group tell you how to edit the paragraph. Ask a volunteer to read the corrected paragraph aloud.
L.9-10.1

Grammar & Writing Practice Book, pp. 29–30

Grammar Transparency 15

Fix Sentence Fragments

GRAMMAR REVIEW: FIX SENTENCE FRAGMENTS 15

Remember: You can fix a fragment by adding a subject or a predicate that includes a verb. Or, you can combine the fragment with another sentence.

Fragment: Calls Farah on the telephone.
Sentence: Alyce calls Farah on the telephone.
Fragment: Farah's mother proud of her daughter.
Sentence: Farah's mother is proud of her daughter.
Fragment: A cruel girl hurts Farah's feelings. And makes her angry.
Sentence: A cruel girl hurts Farah's feelings and makes her angry.

Try It

A. Fix the fragments. Possible responses:

1. Influence our choices. Friends influence our choices.
2. A parent. A parent also influences us.
3. We ask for advice. When a choice is difficult. We ask for advice when a choice is difficult.
4. Have a responsibility to make the best choice. We have a responsibility to make the best choice.

B. Edit the paragraph. Fix five mistakes. The first is done for you.

Some students Plan a prank. The students ask you to join Because you have good ideas. They Think you will improve the prank. This prank is dangerous Even though it might make some people laugh. You want to say no And stop the prank. What will you do?

CCSS **Literacy.RL.9-10.2** Determine a theme or central idea of a text and analyze in detail its development over the course of the text, including how it emerges and is shaped and refined by specific details; provide an objective summary of the text. **RL.9-10.6** Analyze a particular point of view or cultural experience reflected in a work of literature from outside the United States, drawing on a wide reading of world literature. **Literacy.SL.9-10.4** Present information, findings, and supporting evidence clearly, concisely, and logically such that listeners can follow the line of reasoning and the organization, development, substance, and style are appropriate to purpose, audience, and task. **Literacy.L.9-10.1** Demonstrate command of the conventions of standard English grammar and usage when writing or speaking.

Vocabulary Study

Suffixes

A **suffix** is an affix, or word part, added at the end of a word. The suffix *-ify* comes from Latin. It means "to make." That's why the word *clarify* means "to make clear." Here are some other suffixes:

SUFFIX	ORIGIN	MEANING
-wise	Old English	in the direction of
-ion	Latin	act or process of
-logy	Greek	the study of

Copy each word below. Write what you think the word means based on the suffix. Then check the meaning in a dictionary. Use two of the words to tell a partner about "The Necklace."

1. biology **2.** attraction **3.** clockwise **4.** beautify

Writing Trait

Focus and Unity: Thesis or Central Idea

Every time you write, keep your central idea, or **thesis**, at the center of attention. To do this:

- state your central idea clearly
- choose examples that support the idea
- leave out unnecessary details or ideas

Just OK	Much Better
Madame Loisel was influenced too much by society. She admired wealthy people. Her friend loaned her a fancy necklace. She should have been content with her life instead of trying to be like rich people.	Madame Loisel was influenced too much by society. She admired wealthy people, so she sacrificed everything she had to be like them. ~~Her friend loaned her a fancy necklace.~~ She should have been content with her life.

Research / Writing

Research Report

Social Studies: Peers Under Pressure What is peer pressure—and are all of its influences bad? Work with a small group to brainstorm ideas, and then research the topic.

myNGconnect.com

- **Learn more about good and bad peer pressure.**
- **Find ways to deal with peer pressure.**

Pool your information to create a report about the positive and negative effects of peer pressure on teens today. Provide facts that support your thesis statement. Also tell stories with specific details that illustrate the influences of peer pressure.

Language and Learning Handbook, page 702

Writing Handbook, page 784

Read the paragraph below. Then brainstorm ways the writer could make the passage more focused. What would you add or take out?

> The most important lesson I've learned in high school is to always be myself. I used to try to be like the popular kids. They had expensive clothes and cars, and they all came from a school across town. Everybody thought they were cool. But whenever I tried to imitate them, I didn't feel right. They don't like to cook like me. I was really uncomfortable. I realized that to be really happy, I just had to be myself. I'm much happier now.

Identify the thesis. Then decide whether the details support or distract from the central idea.

Central Idea: It's important to be yourself.		
Detail	**Helps**	**Hurts**
She tried to be popular.	X	
They had expensive things.		

Writing Handbook, page 784

Lesson 23

INTEGRATE THE LANGUAGE ARTS

OBJECTIVES

Vocabulary
- Suffixes

Research Skill
- Organize Information from Multiple Sources

Writing
- Write Across the Curriculum
- Trait: Focus and Unity

Vocabulary Study

Suffixes

1. The study of life
2. The act of wearing away
3. In the direction that a clock moves
4. To make official

Have students make a list of additional words with affixes, specifically, the Latin suffix *-ion*, the Greek suffix *-logy*, and the Old English suffix *-wise*.
L.9-10.4.b

Edge Interactive Practice Book, p. 47

Research/Writing

Research Report

Social Studies: Peers Under Pressure
Make sure students understand the characteristics of a research report, and address both the positive and negative effects of peer pressure on teens today. Remind students that they should have a thesis statement and include facts that support it.
W.9-10.2; W.9-10.7; W.9-10.8

Writing Trait

Focus and Unity: Thesis or Central Idea

Help students identify characteristics that make the paragraph on the right much better than the paragraph on the left. Have partners brainstorm ways the passage could be improved and complete the Central Idea chart together.

Have students evaluate the samples using the Writing Rubric (*also online*).

See **Writing Handbook** p. 784 for further instruction.
W.9-10.5

Writing Rubric	Trait: Focus and Unity
Exceptional	• Writing addresses topic with a clear thesis. • Supporting details are relevant to the topic. • Sentences are complete.
Competent	• Writing addresses topic and includes a thesis. • Supporting details are adequate to the topic. • Sentences are complete with no more than one sentence error.
Developing	• Writing addresses topic adequately but thesis is weak. • Supporting details are loosely connected to the topic. • Sentences are sometimes incomplete.
Beginning	• Paragraph does not adequately address topic and thesis is poor. • Supporting details are not clearly connected to the topic. • Sentences are often incomplete.

CCSS Literacy.W.9-10.2 Write informative/explanatory texts to examine and convey complex ideas, concepts, and information clearly and accurately through the effective selection, organization, and analysis of content. **Literacy.W.9-10.5** Develop and strengthen writing as needed by planning, revising, editing, rewriting, or trying a new approach, focusing on addressing what is most significant for a specific purpose and audience. **Literacy.W.9-10.7** Conduct short as well as more sustained research projects to answer a question (including a self-generated question) or solve a problem; narrow or broaden the inquiry when appropriate; synthesize multiple sources on the subject, demonstrating understanding of the subject under investigation. **Literacy.W.9-10.8** Gather relevant information from multiple authoritative print and digital sources, using advanced searches effectively; assess the usefulness of each source in answering the research question; integrate information into the text selectively to maintain the flow of ideas, avoiding plagiarism and following a standard format for citation. **Literacy.L.9-10.4.b** Identify and correctly use patterns of word changes that indicate different meanings or parts of speech.

OBJECTIVES

Vocabulary
- Academic Vocabulary

Comprehension & Critical Thinking
- Determine Importance

Literary Analysis
- Analyze Characterization Ⓣ
- Use Text Evidence Ⓣ

TEACH & PRACTICE

Ⓐ Read for Understanding

Genre Display the **eEdition** and read aloud the selection and the Historical Background. Clarify that the characters in *The Grapes of Wrath* are not real people and that the *from* in the title means this is part of a longer work. Ask: What kind of text is this passage? How do you know?

Possible response:
- *part of a novel; while the setting is historical, the characters are invented*

Have students complete item 1 on **Interactive Practice Book** page 48.

Topic Display the prompt: This text mostly tells about ___ and [how/whether] ___. Have partners use the prompt to complete a topic sentence for item 2 on **Interactive Practice Book** page 48.

Ⓑ Reread and Summarize

Have partners read the selection. Encourage them to pause periodically to clarify ideas or vocabulary.

Word Choice Have partners choose words and note why each word is important to the big ideas in the section. Have students complete item 3 on **Interactive Practice Book** page 48.

Summary Have students use their notes with their topic sentence to create a summary of the selection. Have them complete item 4 on **Interactive Practice Book** page 48.
RL.9-10.2

Edge Interactive Practice Book, pp. 48–51

CLOSE READING

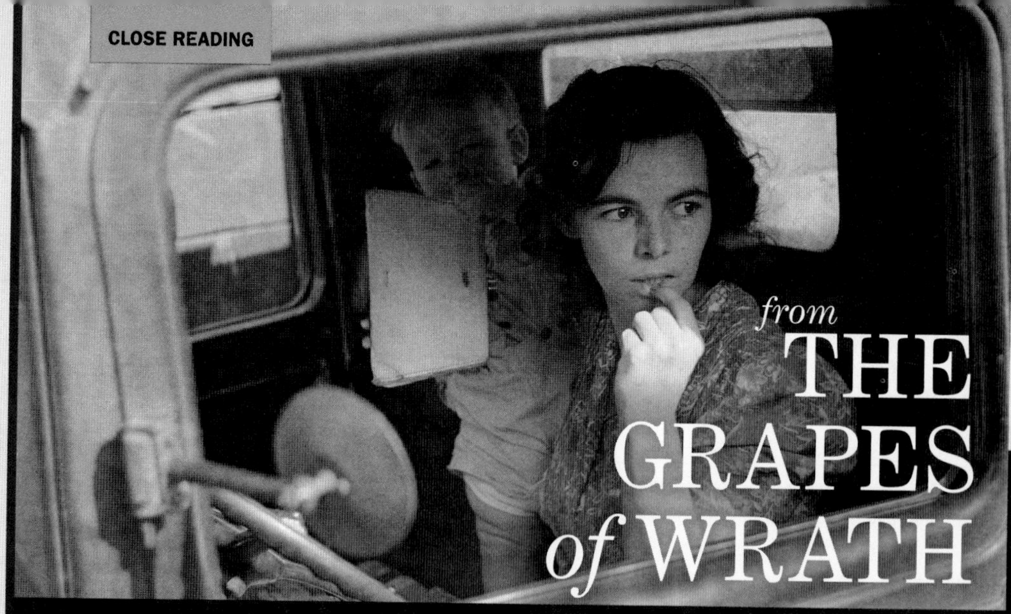

Farm wife waiting in the car while her husband attends the auction

from **THE GRAPES *of* WRATH**

By John Steinbeck

Critical Viewing: Mood What is the mood, or feeling, of this photograph? How did the photographer achieve the mood?

1 "...the road is full a them families goin' west. Never seen so many. Gets worse all a time. Wonder where the hell they all come from?"

2 "Wonder where they all go to," said Mae. "Come here for gas sometimes, but they don't hardly never buy nothin' else. People says they steal. We **ain't got nothin' layin'** around. They never stole nothin' from us."

3 Big Bill, munching his pie, looked up the road through the screened window. "Better tie your stuff down. I think you got some of 'em comin' now."

4 A 1926 Nash **sedan** pulled wearily off the highway. The back seat was piled nearly to the ceiling with sacks, with pots and pans, and on the very top, right up against the ceiling, two boys rode. On the top of the car, a mattress and a folded tent; tent poles tied along the running board. The car pulled up to the gas pumps. A dark-haired, hatchet-faced man got slowly out. And the two boys slid down from the load and hit the ground.

In Other Words

a them families goin' of those families going
ain't got nothin' layin' don't have anything lying
sedan medium-sized car

Historical Background

In the early 1930s, a drought hit the midwestern U.S. and farmers in the area lost all their crops. This area became known as the **Dust Bowl** because of the wind storms that swept dust over everything. Many families packed what little they had left and drove west to work in the fields of California.

ACADEMIC VOCABULARY — REVIEW

Use **Vocabulary Routine 3** (PD33) to help students create a word card for the academic vocabulary word *clarify*. Remind students that when you clarify something, you understand it much better.

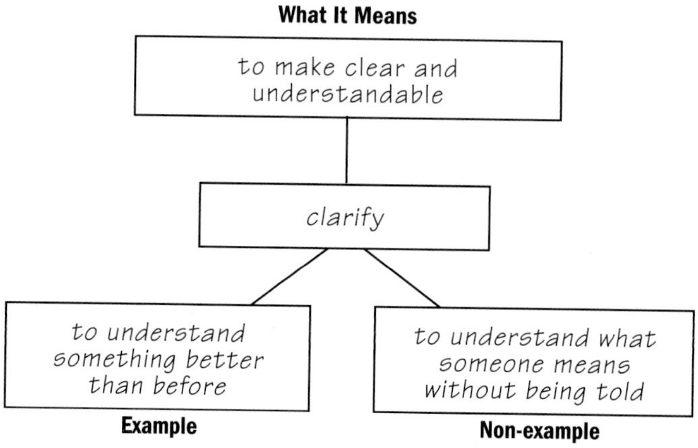

L.9-10.6

CCSS **Literacy.RL.9-10.2** Determine a theme or central idea of a text and analyze in detail its development over the course of the text, including how it emerges and is shaped and refined by specific details; provide an objective summary of the text. **Literacy.L.9-10.6** Acquire and use accurately general academic and domain-specific words and phrases, sufficient for reading, writing, speaking, and listening at the college and career readiness level; demonstrate independence in gathering vocabulary knowledge when considering a word or phrase important to comprehension or expression.

5 Mae walked around the counter and stood in the door. The man was dressed in gray wool trousers and a blue shirt, dark blue with sweat on the back and under the arms. The boys in overalls and nothing else, ragged patched overalls. Their hair was light, and it stood up evenly all over their heads, for it had been **roached**. Their faces were streaked with dust. They went directly to the mud puddle under the hose and dug their toes into the mud.

6 The man asked, "Can we **git** some water, ma'am?"

7 A look of annoyance crossed Mae's face. "Sure, go ahead." She said softly over her shoulder, "I'll keep my eye on the hose." She watched while the man slowly unscrewed the radiator cap and ran the hose in.

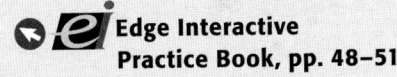

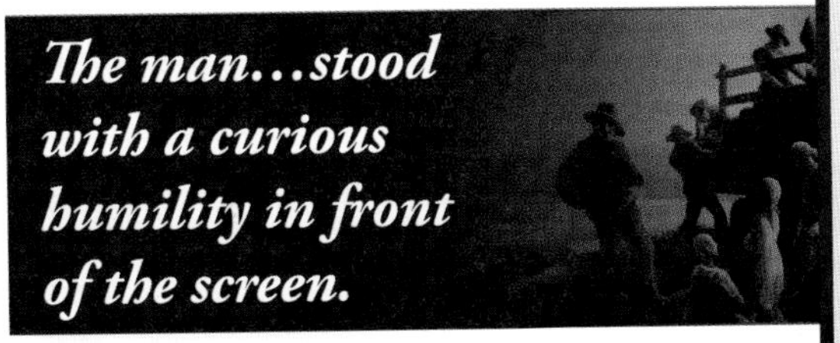

8 A woman in the car, a flaxen-haired woman, said, "See if you can't git it here."

9 The man turned off the hose and screwed on the cap again. The little boys took the hose from him and they upended it and drank thirstily. The man took off his dark, stained hat and stood with a curious **humility** in front of the screen. "**Could you see your way to** sell us a loaf of bread, ma'am?"

10 Mae said, "This ain't a grocery store. We got bread to make **san'widges**."

11 "I know, ma'am." His humility was **insistent**. "We need bread and there **ain't nothin' for quite a piece**, they say."

12 " 'F we sell bread we gonna run out." Mae's tone was **faltering**.

13 "We're hungry," the man said.

14 "**Whyn't** you buy a san'widge? We got nice san'widges, hamburgs."

15 "We'd sure **admire** to do that, ma'am. But we can't. We got to make a dime do all of us." And he said embarrassedly, "We **ain't got but** a little."

16 Mae said, "You can't get no loaf a bread for a dime. We only got fifteen-cent loafs."

17 From behind her Al growled, "God Almighty, Mae, give 'em bread."

18 "We'll run out 'fore the bread truck comes."

In Other Words

roached brushed to stand upright
git get
humility modesty, lack of pride
Could you see your way to Would you
san'widges sandwiches
insistent demanding, persistent
ain't nothin' for quite a piece isn't anything for quite a while
faltering uncertain, hesitating
Whyn't Why don't
admire like
ain't got but only have

PRACTICE & APPLY

C Reread and Analyze

Set a Purpose Explain that partners will reread the text in the **Interactive Practice Book** and determine how Steinbeck uses different techniques to reveal information about his characters.

Characterization Remind students: Authors often show what characters are like through descriptions of their appearance, their dialogue or speech, their actions, and how other characters react to them. Have students complete item 5 on **Interactive Practice Book** page 49.
RL.9-10.3

Details Explain: Authors often use physical descriptions to introduce characters. Have students complete item 6 on **Interactive Practice Book** page 49.

> If students have difficulty, ask: What does wearing ragged clothing with patched holes, instead of new clothing, show about the amount of money the family has?
> RL.9-10.3

Dialogue Review: In addition to physical descriptions, authors often use dialogue to show what characters are like. Direct students to complete items 7 and 8 on **Interactive Practice Book** page 49.

> If students have difficulty, ask: What does the man ask for? What does Mae say to his requests?
> RL.9-10.3

Edge Interactive Practice Book, pp. 48–51

CCSS Literacy.RL.9-10.3 Analyze how complex characters (e.g., those with multiple or conflicting motivations) develop over the course of a text, interact with other characters, and advance the plot or develop the theme.

OBJECTIVES

Comprehension & Critical Thinking
- Synthesize

Literary Analysis
- Analyze Characterization T
- Use Text Evidence T

Writing
- Write About Characterization

Research Skills
- Gather Information

PRACTICE & APPLY

C Reread and Analyze
(continued)

Characterization Remind students that authors also use characters' actions to show what they are like. Then have students complete items 9 and 10 on **Interactive Practice Book** page 50.

If students have difficulty, ask: How do the boys look at the candy? What does the father do when he sees his sons looking at the candy?
RL.9-10.3

Characterization Remind students that authors show what characters are like, not only through their actions, but also through the reactions of other characters. Then have students complete items 11 and 12 on **Interactive Practice Book** page 51.

If students have difficulty, ask: What do Big Bill and Mae know about the real price of the candy? What do Mae's actions show about her?
RL.9-10.3

Edge Interactive Practice Book, pp. 48–53

19 "Run out, then, goddamn it," said Al. And he looked sullenly down at the potato salad he was mixing.

20 Mae shrugged her plump shoulders and looked to the truck drivers to show them what she was up against.

21 She held the screen door open and the man came in, bringing a smell of sweat with him. The boys edged in behind him and they went immediately to the candy case and stared in—not with **craving** or with hope or even with desire, but just with a kind of wonder that such things could be. They were alike in size and their faces were alike. One scratched his dusty ankle with the toe nails of his other foot. The other whispered some soft message and then they straightened their arms so that their clenched fists in the overall pockets showed through the thin blue cloth.

The boys…went immediately to the candy case and stared in…

22 Mae opened a drawer and took out a long waxpaper-wrapped loaf. "This here is a fifteen-cent loaf."

23 The man put his hat back on his head. He answered with **inflexible** humility, "Won't you—can't you see your way to cut off ten cents' worth?"

24 Al said snarlingly, "Goddamn it, Mae. Give 'em the loaf."

25 The man turned toward Al. "No, we want ta buy ten cents' worth of it. We got it **figgered awful** close, mister, to get to California."

26 Mae said **resignedly**, "You can have this for ten cents."

27 "That'd be robbin' you, ma'am."

28 "Go ahead—Al says to take it." She pushed the waxpapered loaf across the counter. The man took a deep leather pouch from his rear pocket, untied the strings, and spread it open. It was heavy with silver and with greasy bills.

29 "May soun' funny to be so **tight**," he apologized. "We got a thousan' miles to go, an' we don' know if we'll make it." He dug in the pouch with a forefinger, located a dime, and pinched in for it. When he put it down on the counter he had a penny with it. He was about to drop the penny back into the pouch when **his eye fell on** the boys frozen before the candy counter. He moved slowly down to them. He pointed in the case at big long sticks of striped peppermint. "Is them penny candy, ma'am?"

In Other Words
craving want, hunger
inflexible unchanging
figgered awful counted very
resignedly giving up, yielding
tight worried about spending money
his eye fell on he saw

CONTENT AREA CONNECTIONS

Research the Dust Bowl

Conduct Research Have students research the Dust Bowl, finding answers to the following questions:
- What caused the Dust Bowl?
- How did it affect families in the United States?
- Why was the drought especially difficult for farm families?
- Why did so many Midwestern farm families decide to go to California?

Share and Discuss Have students share their findings with classmates and discuss why the Dust Bowl was an important event in U.S. history.

Explore the Okies of the 1930s

Share Facts Explain:
- During the Dust Bowl, thousands of families left a drought in the Midwest to find farm work in California.
- The workers were called "Okies" because many of them left farms in Oklahoma.

Predict and Discuss Have small groups discuss what they thought the Okies' experiences were like on the road to California.

Research and Confirm Have students research the Okies to find out what life was like on the road and what happened after they reached California. Then have them discuss whether their predictions were correct.
W.9-10.7

30 Mae moved down and looked in. "Which ones?"

31 "There, them stripy ones."

32 The little boys raised their eyes to her face and they stopped breathing; their mouths were partly opened, their half-naked bodies were **rigid**.

33 "Oh—them. Well, no—them's two for a penny."

34 "Well, gimme two then, ma'am." He placed the copper cent carefully on the counter. The boys **expelled** their held breath softly. Mae held the big sticks out.

35 "Take 'em," said the man.

36 They reached **timidly**, each took a stick, and they held them down at their sides and did not look at them. But they looked at each other, and their mouth corners smiled rigidly with embarrassment.

37 "Thank you, ma'am." The man picked up the bread and went out the door, and the little boys marched stiffly behind him, the red-striped sticks held tightly against their legs. They leaped like chipmunks over the front seat and onto the top of the load, and they burrowed back out of sight like chipmunks.

38 The man got in and started his car, and with a roaring motor and a cloud of blue oily smoke the ancient Nash climbed up on the highway and went on its way to the west.

39 From inside the restaurant the truck drivers and Mae and Al stared after them.

40 Big Bill **wheeled** back. "Them wasn't two-for-a-cent candy," he said.

41 "What's that to you?" Mae said fiercely.

42 "Them was nickel apiece candy," said Bill. ❖

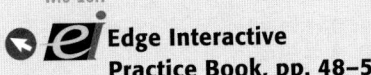

Part of an impoverished family of nine on a New Mexico highway, 1936, Dorthea Lange. Photographic negative, Library of Congress.

Critical Viewing: Setting
This photo was taken during the Dust Bowl. How do the setting details in the photo compare with the details in the story?

In Other Words
rigid stiff, not moving
expelled let out
timidly shyly, without confidence
wheeled turned the conversation

APPLY

D Discuss

Synthesize Ask: Based on your notes, what types of techniques does the author use to develop the character of Mae? Have students complete item 13 on **Interactive Practice Book** page 52.
SL.9-10.1.a; L.9-10.3

Write Prompt: Write a paragraph that explains the techniques authors use to portray characters. Have students complete item 14 on **Interactive Practice Book** page 52.
W.9-10.10

E Connect with the EQ

Viewpoint Help the class connect their understandings of the text to the Essential Question. Have students discuss what influences Mae's choices in the story. Be sure to have them use evidence and language from the selection to support their viewpoint. Then have students complete item 15 on **Interactive Practice Book** page 53.
SL.9-10.1.a

Theme Have students review the two quotations on the Unit Opener on pages 2–3. Ask: Which quotation applies more to Mae's choice in this selection? Explain. Then ask: What is the author's message about people's choices? Have students complete item 16 on **Interactive Practice Book** page 53.
RL.9-10.2; W.9-10.10

Research Have students generate research questions around the Close Reading content. Then have them do a short search for the answers and share their findings with the class.
W.9-10.7

Edge Interactive Practice Book, pp. 48–53

CCSS **Literacy.RL.9-10.3** Analyze how complex characters (e.g., those with multiple or conflicting motivations) develop over the course of a text, interact with other characters, and advance the plot or develop the theme. **Literacy.W.9-10.7** Conduct short as well as more sustained research projects to answer a question (including a self-generated question) or solve a problem; narrow or broaden the inquiry when appropriate; synthesize multiple sources on the subject, demonstrating understanding of the subject under investigation. **Literacy.RL.9-10.2** Determine a theme or central idea of a text and analyze in detail its development over the course of the text, including how it emerges and is shaped and refined by specific details; provide an objective summary of the text. **Literacy.W.9-10.10** Write routinely over extended time frames (time for research, reflection, and revision) and shorter time frames (a single sitting or a day or two) for a range of tasks, purposes, and audiences. **Literacy.SL.9-10.1.a** Come to discussions prepared, having read and researched material under study; explicitly draw on that preparation by referring to evidence from texts and other research on the topic or issue to stimulate a thoughtful, well-reasoned exchange of ideas. **Literacy.L.9-10.3** Apply knowledge of language to understand how language functions in different contexts, to make effective choices for meaning or style, and to comprehend more fully when reading or listening.

OBJECTIVES

Comprehension & Critical Thinking
- Compare Literature: Genre

Listening and Speaking
- Classroom Discussion

Media
- Deliver a Media Presentation T
- Evaluate Media Presentations

PRESENT & REFLECT

A Present Your Project

Suggest the following hints:

- Use notes on index cards. Include reminders to stay focused on the Essential Question.
- Be courteous during other shows.
- Be positive and constructive.

SL.9-10.1.c; SL.9-10.6

myNGconnect.com

Unit Project Evaluation Rubric

B Reflect on Your Reading

Genre Focus Point out that "The Fashion Show" and *Breaking Through* are memoirs.

Define *archetype* as a common character that occurs in literature. Review the characters in *The Trojan Horse* with students, and have students compare them with characters in the unit selections. SL.9-10.1.a

Focus Strategy Review the Plan and Monitor strategies:

- Preview/Predict; Set a Purpose
- Clarify Ideas
- Clarify Vocabulary

Have students use their bookmarks to "teach" the strategies to a partner. SL.9-10.1.a

C EQ Respond to the Essential Question

Discuss these questions:

- What were positive and negative influences on characters' choices?
- What choices would you have made, and why?

Encourage the use of examples from unit selections and **Edge Library**. SL.9-10.1.a

ONGOING ASSESSMENT

Have students write their responses to the Essential Question to assess understanding of the unit topic.

UNIT 1 WRAP-UP

CHOICES

EQ **ESSENTIAL QUESTION:**
What Influences a Person's Choices?

myNGconnect.com

Download the rubric.

EDGE LIBRARY

Present Your Project: TV Talk Show

It's time to host your TV talk show about the Essential Question for this unit: What Influences a Person's Choices?

A

1 Review and Complete Your Plan
- How will the host introduce the guests and the Essential Question?
- How will the host keep the focus on the Essential Question?
- How long will the guests discuss the topic?

Practice your talk show at least once. Be sure that everyone is prepared.

2 Give Your Talk Show

Seat the host and the guests so that the audience can see and hear them well. Follow the plan that you made to present the show.

3 Evaluate the Talk Shows

Use the online rubric to evaluate each of the talk shows, including yours.

Reflect on Your Reading

B

Many of the characters in the stories in this unit and in the Edge Library made important choices.

Think back on your reading of the unit selections, including your choice of Edge Library books. Then discuss the following with a partner or in a small group.

Genre Focus Compare and contrast the elements of a short story with the features of a memoir. Give examples, using the selections in this unit.

Think about classical archetypes you encountered in *The Trojan Horse,* such as the hero or the person who causes another's downfall. Did these archetypes appear in any of the unit selections? Explain how the archetypes in the selections are similar to the archetypes in *The Trojan Horse*.

Focus Strategy Pick a selection in this unit that you think might be difficult for some people to read. Choose three strategies that would help a person clarify his or her understanding and explain them on a bookmark that you can share with a partner. Use the bookmark as a reference as you continue to read more selections in this program.

EQ Respond to the Essential Question

C

Throughout this unit, you have been thinking about how people make choices. What have *you* decided? Support your response with evidence from your reading, discussions, research, and writing.

CUMULATIVE VOCABULARY REVIEW

Review Unit 1 Vocabulary:

affect	inspire
circumstances	juvenile
commit	luxury
conflict	maturity
consequences	motivation
contact	perceive
contribute	poverty
disrespect	privilege
empathy	responsible
generation	salvage
humiliating	symbol
imitation	value

Play one or more of the following games in pairs or small groups using Key Vocabulary:

20 Questions One student thinks of a word, and other students ask yes/no questions until they guess the word.

Categories One student thinks of a word to be a "category" and names words that relate to that category. Others try to guess the word. For example: For *contribute*, a student might say "charity, volunteer, participate."

Draw the Words One student has a word in mind and draws pictures to get another student to guess the word.

Edge Interactive Practice Book, pp. 54–55
L.9-10.6

CCSS **Literacy.SL.9-10.1.a** Come to discussions prepared, having read and researched material under study; explicitly draw on that preparation by referring to evidence from texts and other research on the topic or issue to stimulate a thoughtful, well-reasoned exchange of ideas. **Literacy.SL.9-10.1.c** Propel conversations by posing and responding to questions that relate the current discussion to broader themes or larger ideas; actively incorporate others into the discussion; and clarify, verify, or challenge ideas and conclusions. **Literacy.SL.9-10.6** Adapt speech to a variety of contexts and tasks, demonstrating command of formal English when indicated or appropriate. **Literacy.L.9-10.6** Acquire and use accurately general academic and domain-specific words and phrases, sufficient for reading, writing, speaking, and listening at the college and career readiness level; demonstrate independence in gathering vocabulary knowledge when considering a word or phrase important to comprehension or expression.

Assessment and Reteaching

Digital Assessment
- eAssessment
- ExamView
- online PDFs

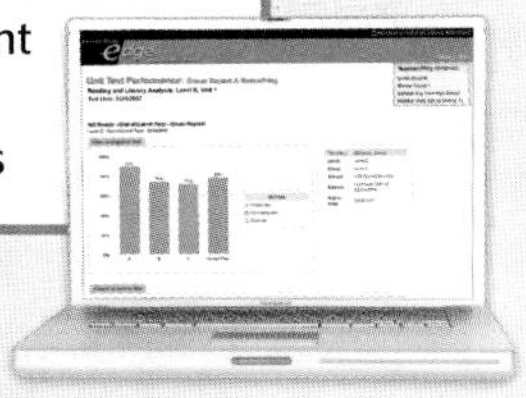

Administer the Assessments

Use the ***Assessments Handbook*** resources to measure the students' performance.

CLUSTER TESTS		
Cluster 1	**Cluster 2**	**Cluster 3**
READER REFLECTION p. 1b	**READER REFLECTION** p. 1f	**READER REFLECTION** p. 1j
READING AND LITERARY ANALYSIS pp. 1c–1e Key Vocabulary Analyze Plot Analyze Text Features: Article Use Text Evidence	**READING AND LITERARY ANALYSIS** pp. 1g–1i Key Vocabulary Analyze Characterization Analyze Text Features: Interview Use Text Evidence	**READING AND LITERARY ANALYSIS** pp. 1k–1m Key Vocabulary Analyze Setting Determine Viewpoint Use Text Evidence
READING FLUENCY *Student Edition p. 35*	**READING FLUENCY** *Student Edition p. 59*	**READING FLUENCY** *Student Edition p. 87*
ELL **LANGUAGE ACQUISITION RUBRIC** p. 1o Ask and Answer Questions	**LANGUAGE ACQUISITION RUBRIC** p. 1o Express Ideas and Opinions	**LANGUAGE ACQUISITION RUBRIC** p. 1o Express Feelings and Intentions

UNIT TESTS	
READING AND LITERARY ANALYSIS pp. 2–9 Use Word Parts: Prefixes, Roots, Suffixes Key Vocabulary Analyze Elements of Fiction Analyze Theme Use Text Evidence	**GRAMMAR AND WRITING** pp. 10–14 Sentences Subject-Verb Agreement Writing Trait: Focus and Unity Written Comprehension • Writing Traits • Written Conventions
UNIT SELF-ASSESSMENT p. 14	

PERFORMANCE ASSESSMENTS
WRITING PROJECT p. 124 Voice and Style • Self-Assessment: Written Composition p. 133 • Peer Assessment: Written Composition p. 134
LISTENING AND SPEAKING WORKSHOP *Student Edition pp. 86–87* Oral Response to Literature

Score and Reteach

- To hand-score: Use the Answer Keys and rubrics in the ***Assessments Handbook***, pp. 136–139. Download reteaching activities at myNGconnect.com.
- To take tests online: ***Edge* eAssessment** at myNGconnect.com. Online reports and reteaching offer immediate graphic displays of student performance to aid in making individualized instruction decision. Links to reteaching activities are included.

Affective and Metacognitive Measures

Help students commit to their own learning. Have students complete at least one reading and one writing form from the affective and metacognitive measures in the ***Assessments Handbook***:

- Personal Connections to Reading, pp. 106–107
- What Interests Me: Reading Topics, p. 108
- What I Do: Reading Strategies, pp. 109–110
- What I Do: Vocabulary Strategies, pp. 111–112
- Personal Connections to Writing, pp. 113–114
- What Interests Me: Writing Topics, pp. 115–117
- What I Do: Writing Strategy, p. 118

T = Tested on Cluster and/or Unit Reading and Literary Analysis Test
T = Tested on Language Acquisition Assessment
T = Tested on Unit Writing Test
T = Assessed with a Rubric
= Comprehension Coach

UNIT 1 Writing Project Overview

The Writing Form: Autobiographical Narrative

Your students will learn the features of an **autobiographical narrative**.

A good autobiographical narrative

- focuses on a specific experience or event and describes what happened as a result
- provides interesting background information for the experience or event
- establishes a clear controlling, or central, idea that reflects an insight gained
- tells what happened in a logical order
- uses precise language, sensory details, and dialogue

The Writing Trait: Focus and Unity

Students will learn to present a clear central idea or claim about the topic and support it with related ideas.

The Writing Portfolio

Have students collect their work in a portfolio. The portfolio provides a record of how students develop as writers.

Portfolio Evaluation Forms

Use the *Assessments* Handbook, pp. 129–134, myNGconnect.com.

Evaluation Guidelines

Use the complete **Good Writing Traits Rubric** to assess the work on all traits and summarize class results in the **Class Profile Chart**.

Rubrics & Reporting Forms

Use the *Assessments* Handbook, pp. 122–134, myNGconnect.com.

TARGETED TRAIT

SCALE	FOCUS AND UNITY	ORGANIZATION	DEVELOPMENT OF IDEAS	VOICE AND STYLE	WRITTEN CONVENTIONS
4	**Focus:** Clearly establishes and consistently maintains a central idea or claim. **Unity:** All facts, ideas, examples, and details are relevant and clearly connected to the central idea or claim.	**Structure:** The organizational pattern is appropriate to the audience, purpose, and task. **Coherence:** Includes a strong introduction and conclusion and leads the reader through a logical progression of ideas with varied and appropriate transitions.	**Content Quality:** Consistently presents meaningful ideas or claims in a logical way that is appropriate to the task, purpose, and audience. **Elaboration:** Includes relevant, clear reasoning, details, evidence, and/or description that are effective and comprehensive.	**Style and Voice:** Fully establishes and effectively maintains a voice that is appropriate to the audience, purpose, and task. **Words and Sentences:** Consistently chooses precise words and varied sentences that are appropriate to the audience and purpose and clearly convey the writer's meaning.	**Grammar and Usage:** Demonstrates strong command of English grammar and usage conventions. All sentences are formed correctly. **Mechanics and Spelling:** Demonstrates strong command of mechanics and spelling. Use of punctuation, capitalization, and spelling is effective and consistent.
3	**Focus:** Adequately establishes and mostly maintains a central idea or claim. **Unity:** Most facts, ideas, examples, and details are relevant and mostly connected to the central idea or claim.	**Structure:** The organizational pattern is mostly appropriate to the audience, purpose, and task. **Coherence:** Includes an introduction and conclusion and leads the reader through a progression of ideas with some transitions.	**Content Quality:** Mostly presents adequate ideas or claims that are appropriate to the task, purpose, and audience. **Elaboration:** Includes reasoning, details, evidence, and/or description that are adequate but incomplete.	**Style and Voice:** Mostly establishes and maintains a voice that is appropriate to the audience, purpose, and task. **Words and Sentences:** Mostly chooses precise words and a variety of sentences that are appropriate to the audience and purpose and adequately convey meaning.	**Grammar and Usage:** Demonstrates adequate command of English grammar and usage conventions. Errors are limited and do not impede understanding. Most sentences are formed correctly. **Mechanics and Spelling:** Demonstrates adequate command of mechanics and spelling. Use of punctuation, capitalization, and spelling is generally consistent.
2	**Focus:** Partially establishes a central idea or claim. **Unity:** Some facts, ideas, examples, and details are relevant and somewhat connected to the central idea or claim.	**Structure:** The pattern is inconsistent or less appropriate to the audience, purpose, or task. **Coherence:** Has an introduction and conclusion but leads the reader through loosely connected ideas that may be incomplete or not obvious to the reader.	**Content Quality:** Presents adequate ideas or claims that are less appropriate to the task, purpose, and audience. **Elaboration:** Includes weak reasoning, details, evidence, and/or description and may include extraneous or loosely related material.	**Style and Voice:** Inconsistently establishes and maintains a voice appropriate to the audience, purpose, and task. **Words and Sentences:** Demonstrates uneven word choice and limited sentence variety or chooses language mostly inappropriate to the audience and purpose. Meaning is vague or imprecise.	**Grammar and Usage:** Demonstrates partial command of English grammar and usage conventions. Frequent errors may impede understanding. Some sentences are formed incorrectly. **Mechanics and Spelling:** Demonstrates partial command of mechanics and spelling. Use of punctuation, capitalization, and spelling is inconsistent.
1	**Focus:** Lacks a central idea or claim. **Unity:** Few facts, ideas, examples, and details are relevant. Most do not support the central idea or claim or connections are unclear.	**Structure:** Lacks any organizational pattern. **Coherence:** Lacks an introduction or conclusion. Ideas are hard to understand.	**Content Quality:** Presents inappropriate or irrelevant ideas or claims. **Elaboration:** Lacks reasoning, details, evidence, and/or description.	**Style and Voice:** Does not establish and maintain a voice or uses a voice that is inappropriate to the audience, purpose, and task. **Words and Sentences:** Demonstrates little or no word choice and no sentence variety. Chooses language inappropriate to the audience, purpose, and task, hindering meaning.	**Grammar and Usage:** Demonstrates little or no command of English grammar and usage conventions. **Mechanics and Spelling:** Demonstrates little or no command of mechanics and spelling.

Write an Autobiographical Narrative

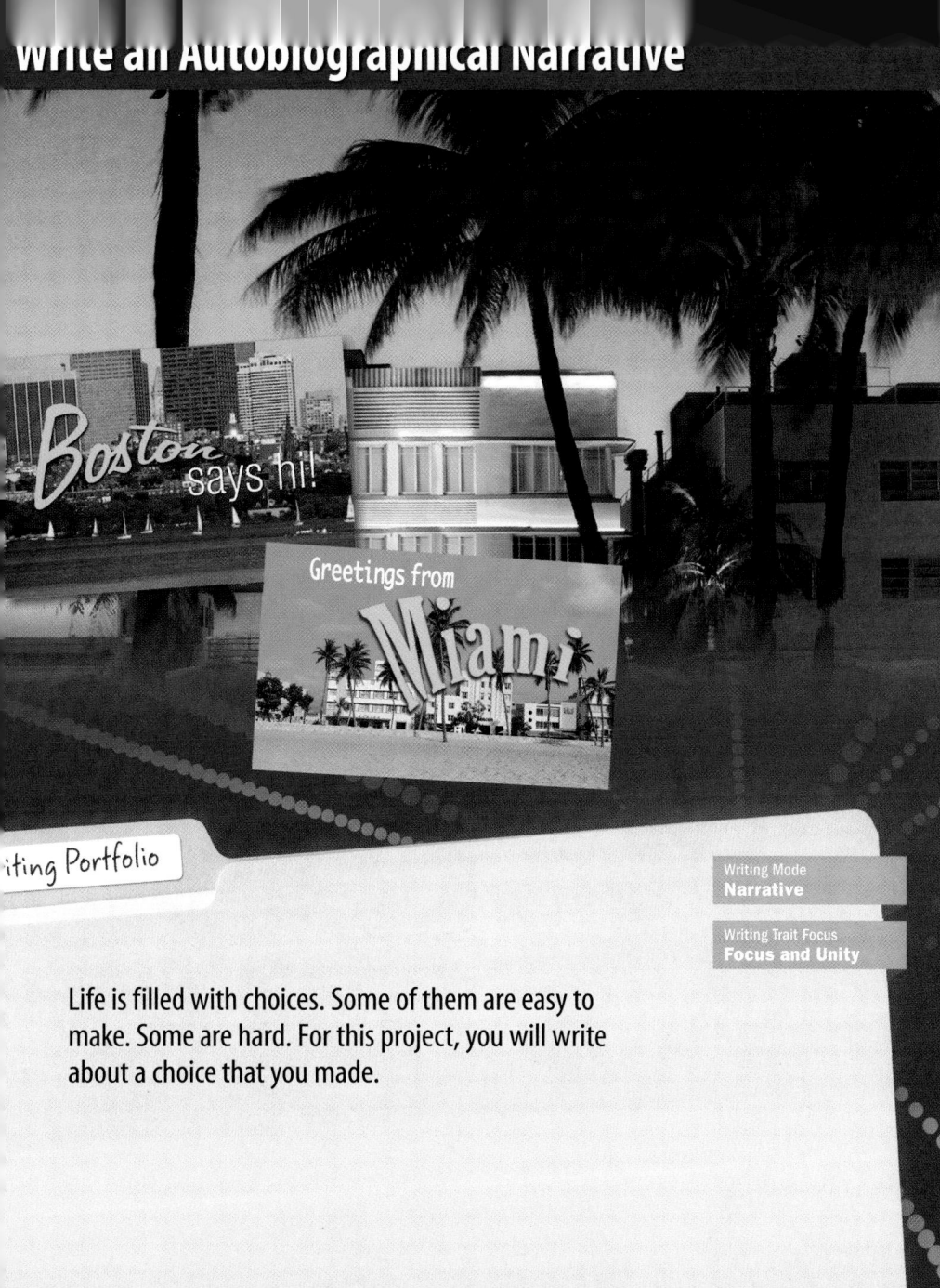

Writing Mode
Narrative

Writing Trait Focus
Focus and Unity

Life is filled with choices. Some of them are easy to make. Some are hard. For this project, you will write about a choice that you made.

Suggested Pacing

Each lesson in the Writing Project provides detailed instruction on the steps of the writing process. Here is a suggested daily sequence and pacing plan. Adjust as your schedule and student needs require.

Lesson 1	Study the Form and Prewrite
Lesson 2	Draft
Lesson 3	Revise
Lesson 4	Edit and Proofread
Lesson 5	Publish and Present

AUTOBIOGRAPHICAL NARRATIVE

OBJECTIVES

Writing
- Mode: Narrative
- Trait: Focus and Unity Ⓣ
- Process: Prewrite; Draft; Revise for Focus and Unity Ⓣ; Edit and Proofread Ⓣ; Publish and Present

Grammar, Usage, Mechanics, Spelling
- Capitalization: Proper Nouns and Adjectives
- Punctuation: Quotation Marks and Commas
- Spelling: Homonyms
- Complete Sentences Ⓣ

INTRODUCE

Writing Mode Identify the writing mode as narrative. Define narrative as writing that tells a story. Narratives can be fiction or nonfiction and are often used to entertain or to explain something that happened. Short stories, autobiographical narratives, memoirs, and biographical essays are some examples of narratives.

Explain to students that they will be writing an autobiographical narrative using the steps of the writing process.
W.9-10.3; W.9-10.10

Writing Trait Explain that writing traits are the characteristics of good writing. All good writing has effective organization; focus and unity; development of ideas; voice and style; and uses the written conventions of language correctly. For this project, students will learn to use the writing trait of **Focus and Unity** to plan, evaluate, and improve their writing.

Focus and unity help bring all ideas in a piece of writing together. Explain to students that a central or controlling idea creates focus for their writing. To create unity, they will learn to relate each main idea and detail to that controlling idea.

CCSS **Literacy.W.9-10.3** Write narratives to develop real or imagined experiences or events using effective technique, well-chosen details, and well-structured event sequences. **Literacy.W.9-10.10** Write routinely over extended time frames (time for research, reflection, and revision) and shorter time frames (a single sitting or a day or two) for a range of tasks, purposes, and audiences.

Lesson 1

STUDY THE FORM AND PREWRITE

OBJECTIVES

Writing
- Mode: Narrative
- Analyze Models

ENGAGE & CONNECT

Ⓐ Connect Writing to Your Life

Tell a Story Point out that there are times, such as filling out a school or job application, when students may need to tell about a significant experience in their lives. Have volunteers tell brief stories about recent choices they made. Explain that these stories are autobiographical narratives, which are told from the first-person point of view.

TEACH

Ⓑ Understand the Form

Explain that a narrative tells the events of a story in a logical sequence, usually chronological. Use a student's story to identify the beginning, the middle, and the end of the narrative. Use a chart like the one on p. 96 to show the organizational pattern.

Controlling Idea Explore the concept:

- A controlling idea is the central idea for a story. It tells the significance of the events of the story, or why the story is important.
- *My choice to join soccer changed my relationship with my dad* is a controlling idea. It tells that the choice led to an important change.

Have students identify controlling ideas in the examples they shared.

ELL **Sentence Frames** Provide frames for identifying controlling ideas:

- Topic: *The choice is about* _______.
- Controlling Idea: *The choice is significant because* _______.

Study Autobiographical Narratives

Autobiographical narratives are stories about events in your own life. Whenever you describe something that happened to you, such as a choice you made, you are telling an autobiographical narrative.

1 Connect Writing to Your Life

Ⓐ It is likely that you tell autobiographical narratives almost every day. You might tell classmates what you did over the weekend. You might tell friends about something funny that happened to you in school. You might trade stories with family about your day. This project builds on your personal storytelling skills.

2 Understand the Form

Remember that you are not writing just for yourself. Other people will read your narrative. Make it clear and interesting to them. Like all good stories, it needs a beginning, a middle, and an end.

Ⓑ

Beginning
Introduce the key choice that you made. Start with interesting background that leads to the decisions and choices that you made. Establish the **controlling idea** of your narrative.

Middle
Tell what happened in the **chronological order** that it happened. Use descriptive details and dialogue.

End
Tell what happened as a result of your choice.

Now look at these parts in action. Read an autobiographical narrative by a professional writer.

ACADEMIC VOCABULARY

Make a Definition Chart Use the sample sentences below to introduce these additional academic vocabulary words used in writing. Have students make a Definition Chart for the words.

- **establish** (is-**tab**-lish), *verb* ▶ page 96

I had to **establish** *the outline before I could write the paper.*

- **professional** (pruh-**fesh**-uhn-l), *adjective* ▶ page 96

He was so good at telling stories that he became a **professional** *writer.*

1. Write the word in the first column of the chart.
2. Read the sentences and then write what you think it means in the next column of the chart.
3. Then use a dictionary to determine the meaning of the word. Write the definition in the last column.

L.9-10.4.d; L.9-10.6

Word	What I Think It Means	What It Means
establish		
professional		

CCSS **Literacy.L.9-10.4.d** Verify the preliminary determination of the meaning of a word or phrase (e.g., by checking the inferred meaning in context or in a dictionary). **Literacy.L.9-10.6** Acquire and use accurately general academic and domain-specific words and phrases, sufficient for reading, writing, speaking, and listening at the college and career readiness level; demonstrate independence in gathering vocabulary knowledge when considering a word or phrase important to comprehension or expression.

B Analyze a Professional Model

As you read, look for the three main parts of the story.

The Bike

by Gary Soto

I was scared of riding on Sarah Street. Mom said hungry dogs lived on that street, and red anger lived in their eyes. Their throats were hard with extra bones from biting kids on bikes, she said.

Interesting background introduces the choice.

But I took the corner anyway. I didn't believe Mom. Once she had said that pointing at rainbows caused freckles, and after a rain had moved in and drenched the streets, a rainbow washed over the junkyard. I stood at the window, looking out, amazed and devious, with the devilish horns of my butch haircut standing up.

*The **choice** is stated here. The consequence of disbelieving and disobeying his mother is the **controlling idea**. Analyze the details that support and elaborate the controlling idea.*

I pedaled my squeaky bike around the curve onto Sarah Street, but returned immediately. I braked and looked back at where I had gone. My face was hot, my hair sweaty, but nothing scary seemed to happen. There ain't no dogs, I told myself. I began to think that maybe this was like one of those false rainbow warnings.

***Descriptive details** make the scene come alive, even if they aren't necessary to tell the story. Would you include them in a summary of the story? Why or why not?*

I stopped when I saw a kid my age come down a porch. His bike was a tricycle. Big baby, I thought, and said, "You can run over my leg with your trike if you want." I laid down on the sidewalk, and the kid, with fingers in his mouth, said, "OK."

He backed up and slowly, like a tank, advanced. When the tire climbed over my ankle, I sat up quickly, my eyes flinging tears like a sprinkler.

The writer tells what happened in the order that it happened.

The boy asked, "Did it hurt?"

"No," I said, almost crying.

The writer includes actual dialogue.

I got on my bicycle and pedaled mostly with the good leg.

Then the sudden bark of a dog scared me, and my pants leg fed into the chain, the bike coming to an immediate stop. I tugged at the cuff, gnashed and oil-black, until ripping sounds made me quit trying. I fell to the ground, bike and all, and let the tears lather my face. I then dragged the bike home with the pants leg in the chain. There was nothing to do except lie in the dirt because Mom saw me round the corner from Sarah Street. I just lay there when she came out, and I didn't blame the dog or that stupid rainbow.

What happened as a result of the narrator's choice?

C

FOCUS ON WRITER'S CRAFT

Understanding the Form

Teach Define autobiographical narrative as a written story of an important event in a person's life, told by that person. Add that it is told in a logical sequence and includes sensory details.

Explain that other forms of writing may use different organization or word styles. For example, a process description is written in a logical order, but the word choice may be more formal.

Model Use a student's oral example or one of your own to illustrate features of a narrative. Here are some examples.

- Organization: Apply transition words like *first*, *next*, and *then* to show the logical progression of events.
- Details: Answer these questions: *Does it show the scene with sensory details? Does it show actions and feelings?*

Practice In pairs, have students share brief narratives of a recent significant event. Have them follow your model to identify the organization and specific details.

Apply Have students identify the sequence of events and descriptive detail of an event from an autobiography they have read or an example you supply.

Extend Have students compare and contrast the narrative with another work. Answer these questions: *Does this form use transition words? What type of details are used?*

TEACH

C Analyze a Professional Model

Read and Evaluate Read aloud the whole narrative, and then have students read the narrative silently. Reread the first two paragraphs. Use the callouts to show the structure and key elements:

- the beginning of the narrative
- the background information
- the choice the writer made
- the controlling idea

Point out that these are some of the elements the writer used to make this a good narrative.

Identify Explain that writers often use precise language and sensory details. Have students identify and evaluate the effectiveness of any descriptive details in the third paragraph that describe the sights, sounds, smells, or physical feeling of the scene. Explain that you would not use the green highlighted phrases in a summary of the story.

Compare Explain that dialogue can help *show* the events in the story rather than just *tell* about them. Reread paragraphs four through seven using narrative text in place of dialogue. Have students discuss the difference between the scene with dialogue and without dialogue.

Discuss Explain that the controlling idea might not be stated directly by the writer but is shown by the narrative as a whole.

Ask: What makes the writer's choice important or significant? What is the controlling idea? Have students analyze the details that support and elaborate the controlling idea.

Possible response:

- *The writer faced consequences because of his choice to disbelieve and disobey his mother.*

Remind students that the controlling idea in an autobiographical narrative often reflects a personal insight gained from the experience described. Ask: What insight did the narrator gain?

ONGOING ASSESSMENT

Have students list three elements a good writer should include in an autobiographical narrative.

STUDY THE FORM AND PREWRITE

OBJECTIVES

Writing
- Writing Process: Prewrite
- Generate Ideas Before Writing
- Choose a Topic
- Identify Audience and Purpose
- Plan and Organize Ideas

TEACH

A Your Job as a Writer

Writing Prompt Read the prompt with students to help them better understand what is expected of them for this assignment.

B Choose Your Topic

Brainstorm Choices Have students make a list of incidents they've experienced in the last year. Have them list a significant event from each month. For example, *September: Tried out for the soccer team.* Then have students think about a choice they may have made about each event.

ELL **Sentence Frames** Provide frames for brainstorming choices:
- When I was ______, I chose to ______.
- Some choices were easy, such as ______. Some were very difficult, such as ______.

W.9-10.5

C Clarify Audience, Controlling Idea & Purpose

Controlling Idea Ask: What is the main idea you want to convey?

Provide this frame for expressing the controlling idea: *This choice is significant because (it showed)* ________.

D Gather Supporting Details

Describe Have students review their notes and add or cut details based on their partner's feedback. Remind students to use sensory details that describe scenes, feelings, and actions.
W.9-10.5

Your Job as a Writer

A **Prompt** Write an autobiographical narrative about a choice you made. Be sure to tell:
- what the choice was
- how or why you made the choice
- how you felt about the choice
- what happened as a result of the choice

✓ Prewrite

Now that you know the basics of autobiographical narratives, plan one of your own. Planning will make it easier for you to write later on. Making a Writing Plan helps you avoid the "blank page blues," when you can't think of anything to say.

1 Choose Your Topic

B Here are some good ways to choose a topic:
- Pick a decision that you have strong feelings about, one that you're proud of, or one that you regret.
- Pick a decision that you wonder about. Why did you make the choice? What would have happened if you had made a different choice?
- Brainstorm ideas with a friend or family member.

2 Clarify the Audience, Controlling Idea, and Purpose

C If you do any blogging, you probably choose the audience for the entries you make. Who will you be writing this paper for? Jot down your ideas.

Then think about the main point or central idea you want to get across about your choice. Write your notes about the controlling idea.

Finally, think about your purpose, or reason, for writing. Is your purpose to tell a story about yourself? To entertain your audience? Make them understand how you felt? Jot down your purpose.

Prewriting Tip

Ask yourself these questions to find your controlling idea:
- Was my choice good or bad?
- Did it change my life? If so, how?
- Did I learn something from the choice? If so, what?

3 Gather Supporting Details

D Next, gather details to support, or explain, your choice. Recall what happened and how you felt. Take notes.

Then tell your story to a partner. Have your partner take notes and ask questions to
- get more details that are specific, important, and on target
- help you clarify your ideas
- fill in background information.

98 Unit 1 Writing Project

DIFFERENTIATED INSTRUCTION

Addressing the Prompt As you teach the writing process in this unit, use these strategies to meet students' individual needs.

Struggling Readers

Freewrite Have students write the words *choice*, *important*, and *significant* on a blank sheet of paper. Using those words as prompts, have students write whatever comes to mind for five minutes without stopping.

English Language Learners ELL

Use Visuals Help students get started by creating a storyboard to tell their story. Use the sentence frames above to help students brainstorm topic ideas for their story.

Challenge

Develop Criteria Have students develop criteria for narrowing their topic. For example:
- *Were there circumstances that made the choice difficult or complicated?*
- *Did the choice have an effect on people?*
- *Did the choice result in new knowledge or understanding?*

CCSS Literacy W.9-10.5 Develop and strengthen writing as needed by planning, revising, editing, rewriting, or trying a new approach, focusing on addressing what is most significant for a specific purpose and audience.

4 Organize the Details

Organize the details in chronological order, the order in which they happened. Make a list, or use a time line like the one below. Put the turning point of your choice in the middle. Then add events on the left and right in time order.

Time Line

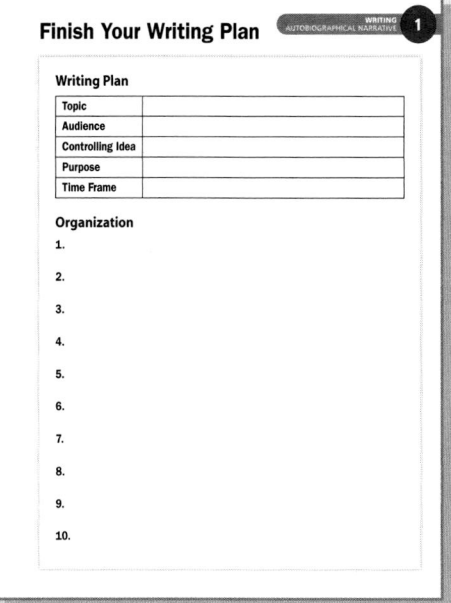

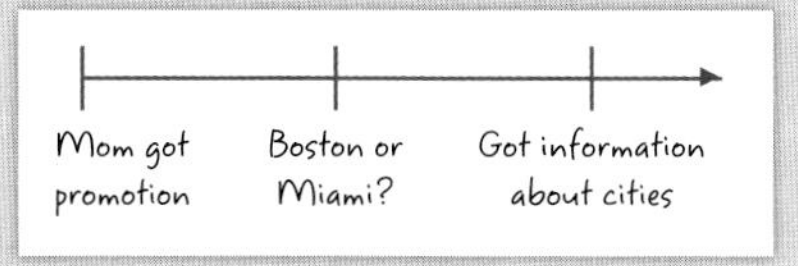

E

Technology Tip

List the details as phrases or sentences. Then use Cut and Paste from the Edit menu to move details around as you need to.

5 Finish Your Writing Plan

Make a Writing Plan like the one below to capture all the planning you have done. Show which details will go in the beginning, the middle, and the end.

Writing Plan

Topic	how I helped Mom choose where we would move
Audience	my teacher and my classmates
Controlling Idea	choosing Miami gave me a fresh start
Purpose	to tell the story of a choice; to entertain
Time Frame	a week from Monday

Beginning
1. Mom received a promotion.
2. We had to choose where to move, Boston or Miami.
3. My mom broke the news of the move to me at a restaurant. (Interesting! Use this in the beginning.)

Middle
4. I was in my freshman year and wanted a change.
5. We gathered information about both cities.
6. We chose Miami.
7. I found out about the New World School in Miami.

End
8. I have applied to the New World School.
9. I am glad that we chose Miami.
10. Living here is a fresh start for me and my mom.

F

Reflect on Your Writing Plan

- Do you have enough details for the beginning, the middle, and the end? Are you pleased with your topic and controlling idea? If not, now's the time to change them!

Writing Transparency 1

Finish Your Writing Plan

WRITING AUTOBIOGRAPHICAL NARRATIVE 1

Writing Plan

Topic	
Audience	
Controlling Idea	
Purpose	
Time Frame	

Organization
1.
2.
3.
4.
5.
6.
7.
8.
9.
10.

TEACH

E Organize the Details

Time Line Use the Student Model to show events in sequence on a time line. Show the writer's feelings at different points on the time line.

F Finish Your Writing Plan

Writing Transparency 1

Model the Plan Use the transparency to model creating a plan. Use a student example:

- **Topic:** What choice are you writing about?
- **Audience:** Who will read your narrative?
- **Controlling Idea:** Why is the choice meaningful or important? What was the result?
- **Purpose:** Why are you writing it?
- **Time Frame:** Set a deadline that allows time in and outside of class to fully complete the steps.

Manage the Steps Download this chart to help students manage their time.

myNGconnect.com

Date	Tasks
	1. Study the form. 2. Analyze a professional model. 3. Choose a topic. 4. Identify audience, controlling idea, and purpose. 5. Gather and organize details. 6. Create your Writing Plan.
	Write a draft using your Writing Plan.
	1. Revise for focus and unity. 2. Revise your draft, using the Revision Checklist. 3. Conduct a peer conference. 4. Make revisions based on peer conference.
	Review your draft for mistakes; check for capitalization, punctuation, spelling, and sentence completion.
	Print out your narrative, or write a clean copy by hand.

Model the Organization Have students list events in sequence, noting which events are in the beginning, the middle, and the end.
W.9-10.3.c; W.9-10.5

Have students turn in their Writing Plans. Use them to assess progress on prewriting.

CCSS Literacy.W.9-10.3.c Use a variety of techniques to sequence events so that they build on one another to create a coherent whole. Produce clear and coherent writing in which the development, organization, and style are appropriate to task, purpose, and audience. Literacy W.9-10.5 Develop and strengthen writing as needed by planning, revising, editing, rewriting, or trying a new approach, focusing on addressing what is most significant for a specific purpose and audience.

Lesson 2

WRITE A DRAFT

OBJECTIVES

Writing
- Writing Process: Draft
- Write a Draft
- Employ Literary Devices

TEACH

A Keep Your Ideas Flowing

Avoid "Writer's Block" Explain that the drafting step is not the time to worry about making everything perfect. A draft is for getting ideas down and will be polished later.

ELL **Demonstrate** Show the meaning of words related to the drafting process:

- **flowing:** Use the analogy of a water fountain that won't shut off: *During drafting, the writing keeps flowing.*
- **catchy:** Toss a ball of paper for a student to catch: *Your beginning should catch the reader right away.*
- **hook:** Use an index finger as a hook to grab your shirt collar: *Your writing should hook the reader's attention.*

Have students use a senses web to describe the setting of their narrative.
W.9-10.3; W.9-10.4; W.9-10.6

B Create a Catchy Beginning

Develop Details Have students choose something about their narrative to develop with detail, for example, setting. Ask: What details can you tell about the setting to get the reader engaged?

Suggest ways to use setting to catch the reader's attention. For example:

- Use words that appeal to the five senses to describe the setting.
- Describe something unusual about the setting.
- Use an analogy to compare the setting to something else.

W.9-10.3.d

✓Write a Draft

Now you are ready to write. Use your Writing Plan as a guide while you write your narrative. It's OK to make mistakes. You'll have chances to improve your draft. Just keep writing!

1 Keep Your Ideas Flowing

Sometimes writers get "stuck." They can't figure out what to say or how to say it. If you have trouble getting your ideas on paper, try these techniques:

- **Talk It Over** Tell someone what you want to say in your narrative. Together, find the words to say it.
- **Change Your Plan** If your plan is not helping, change it. Brainstorm, list, and organize new details.
- **Skip Over the Hard Part** If you have trouble writing one part of your paper, skip to a part that is easier to write. It will then be easier go back and finish it.
- **Do a Focused Freewrite** Write continuously about your topic for about five minutes. During that time, do not stop writing. If you can't think of anything to say, then say that. Then, reread what you wrote. Underline ideas that you might be able to use in your paper. Study the student example below.

A

> I was not sure what choice to make. I couldn't figure out what to do. What to do. What to do. I can't think of anything to say. Wait a minute. I remember. I remember. I felt as if I had information overload. Is there such a thing as too much information? There must be because I had it. I felt as if I were drowning in facts about Boston and Miami. The more I knew, the harder it was to choose.

Technology Tip

Make your text double- or triple-spaced, or as your teacher directs. (Use the Paragraph feature from the Format menu to change line spacing.) Print a copy of your draft to read later. The extra space between lines will give you room to mark changes.

2 Create a Catchy Beginning

How will you hook your readers' attention? What is an interesting detail that you can start out with? Sometimes coming up with a great beginning can help the rest of the writing flow. Here's an example:

B

OK	Better
My mom and I went to dinner. My mom told me that she got a promotion at work. We had to move.	My mom and I were eating Italian food at our favorite place, Tedesco's, when she told me the big news.

FOCUS ON WRITER'S CRAFT

Developing Ideas with Details

Teach/Model Explain that the main idea of a narrative needs to be developed and supported with details:

- Use **word choice** to precisely describe events, feelings, and moods: *I sprinted across the street; I strolled across the street; The gloomy fog hung over the silent street.*
- Use **sensory detail** to describe what is seen, heard, smelled, tasted, and touched: *icy ground; sour lemon; noisy crowd.*

Practice/Apply Have students use a variety of strategies to develop detail to include in their narratives. Here are some examples.

Word Choice: Make lists to help with word choice and precise language. Use a print or online thesaurus to help come up with alternate word choices. For example:

- Action verbs: List synonyms for important action verbs, and choose the most vivid and accurate.
- Feelings/Emotions: Replace general words like bad with specific words such as *devastated.*
- Tone/Mood: Brainstorm words for certain moods, such as *cheerful* or *somber.*

Sensory Detail: Use a cluster diagram.

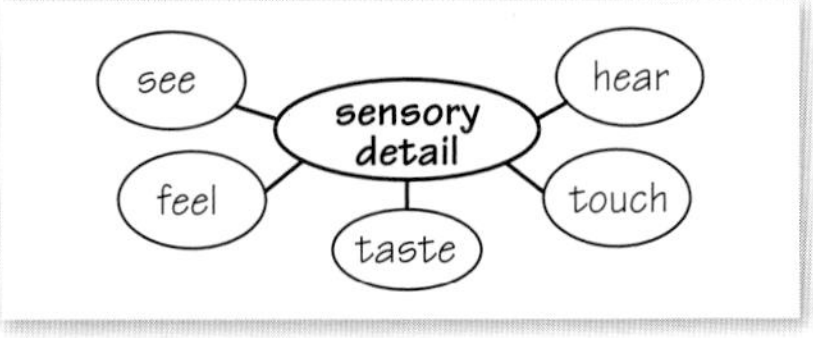

W.9-10.3.d; L.9-10.4.c

CCSS **Literacy.W.9-10.3** Write narratives to develop real or imagined experiences or events using effective technique, well-chosen details, and well-structured event sequences. **Literacy.W.9-10.3.d** Use precise words and phrases, telling details, and sensory language to convey a vivid picture of the experiences, events, setting, and/or characters. **Literacy.W.9-10.4** Produce clear and coherent writing in which the development, organization, and style are appropriate to task, purpose, and audience. **Literacy.W.9-10.6** Use technology, including the Internet, to produce, publish, and update individual or shared writing products, taking advantage of technology's capacity to link to other information and to display information flexibly and dynamically. **Literacy.L.9-10.4.c** Consult general and specialized reference materials (e.g., dictionaries, glossaries, thesauruses), both print and digital, to find the pronunciation of a word or determine or clarify its precise meaning, its part of speech, or its etymology.

3 Student Model

Read this draft to see how the student used the Writing Plan to get ideas down on paper. This first draft does not have to be perfect. As you will see, the student fixed the mistakes later.

A Fresh Start

My mom and I were eating italian food at our favorite place, Tedesco's restaurant, when she told me the big news. I love Tedesco's because the lasagna is so good. I always order it. She said that she had received a promotion at work. The company was opening two new branch offices, and her boss had asked her to open one of them. The only thing was, both branches were kind of far away from Baltimore, where we lived. One was in Boston, and the other was in Miami.

"We won't go if you don't want to go" she said.

Did I want to go? I wasn't sure. Did I want to stay? I wasn't sure about that either.

"It doesn't really matter to me whether its Boston or Miami," she added. Pick the one that will make you happy. It would be a fresh start for both of us."

"A fresh start is just what I need!" I said.

Wow. Picking a city to live in was quite a challenge—and quite an opportunity. I had only a month to make the choice. I went on the Internet right away. Soon, I was overloaded with information. I knew a lot about each city, but I didn't feel any closer to choosing between them. The more I knew, the harder it was to choose. I was just about ready to tell my mother that she was going to have to make the choice when I found out about Miami's New World School of the Arts (NWSA).

The NWSA has special high school programs in music, dance, theater, and visual arts. I explored it online, and I immediately began to fantasize about going there. I couldn't apply their if we lived out of state, but if we were living in Miami, I could apply for the next school year. My choice was made. "I'm ready," I said to my mother.

I gave her the full presentation. Telling her everything I'd found out about Boston and Miami. I finished with the NWSA.

"What if you don't get in?" she asked.

"At least I will have tried," I said.

"Done," she said. "We're moving to Miami."

Reflect on Your Draft

▶ Is your controlling idea clear? Do you have enough details, and are they in chronological order? Talk it over with a partner.

Autobiographical Narrative 201

Writing Transparency 2

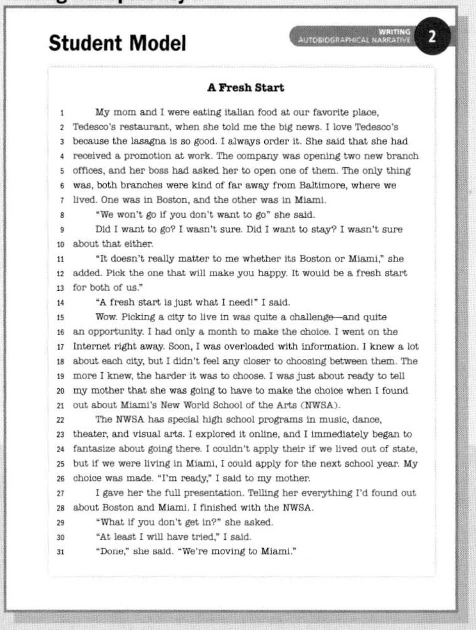

Student Model

WRITING AUTOBIOGRAPHICAL NARRATIVE 2

A Fresh Start

1 My mom and I were eating italian food at our favorite place,
2 Tedesco's restaurant, when she told me the big news. I love Tedesco's
3 because the lasagna is so good. I always order it. She said that she had
4 received a promotion at work. The company was opening two new branch
5 offices, and her boss had asked her to open one of them. The only thing
6 was, both branches were kind of far away from Baltimore, where we
7 lived. One was in Boston, and the other was in Miami.
8 "We won't go if you don't want to go" she said.
9 Did I want to go? I wasn't sure. Did I want to stay? I wasn't sure
10 about that either.
11 "It doesn't really matter to me whether its Boston or Miami," she
12 added. Pick the one that will make you happy. It would be a fresh start
13 for both of us."
14 "A fresh start is just what I need!" I said.
15 Wow. Picking a city to live in was quite a challenge—and quite
16 an opportunity. I had only a month to make the choice. I went on the
17 Internet right away. Soon, I was overloaded with information. I knew a lot
18 about each city, but I didn't feel any closer to choosing between them. The
19 more I knew, the harder it was to choose. I was just about ready to tell
20 my mother that she was going to have to make the choice when I found
21 out about Miami's New World School of the Arts (NWSA).
22 The NWSA has special high school programs in music, dance,
23 theater, and visual arts. I explored it online, and I immediately began to
24 fantasize about going there. I couldn't apply their if we lived out of state,
25 but if we were living in Miami, I could apply for the next school year. My
26 choice was made. "I'm ready," I said to my mother.
27 I gave her the full presentation. Telling her everything I'd found out
28 about Boston and Miami. I finished with the NWSA.
29 "What if you don't get in?" she asked.
30 "At least I will have tried," I said.
31 "Done," she said. "We're moving to Miami."

C Student Model

Read Have students read the Student Model.

ELL Read Aloud Read aloud the Student Model. Use illustrations, body language, gestures, or role-play to support meaning.

Writing Transparency 2

Analyze Display the transparency. Ask these questions to help students see the relationship between the Writing Plan on p. 99 and the draft. Mark answers on the transparency:

- Where does the writer tell what choice is being made? *[line 12]*
- What words or phrases show that the audience is the writer's classmates? *[lines 9-10 help a young person relate to the writer's indecision; line 15 uses informal language]*
- What does the writer say that shows you the controlling idea? *[line 14]*
- What words or phrases show that the story is meant to entertain? *[lines 1-2 help readers engage with the setting; lines 15-19 build excitement about the choice]*

Remind students that the Writing Plan is a place to start, and it may be revised as the draft is revised.

ONGOING ASSESSMENT

Have students explain how they would help a friend who was "stuck" in his or her writing.

Lesson 3

REVISE YOUR DRAFT

OBJECTIVES

Writing

- Writing Process: Revise
- Evaluate and Revise the Draft for Focus and Unity Ⓣ
- Participate in Peer Conferencing

TEACH

Ⓐ Revise for Focus and Unity

Define Elaborate on how the writing traits of focus and unity apply to an autobiographical narrative:

- **Focus:** The narrative concentrates on one event in the writer's life. The controlling idea is why the event is important to the writer.
- **Unity:** Everything in the narrative relates back to the controlling idea. Each paragraph, main idea, and detail helps explain the event's importance.

Try It Have partners use a cluster diagram to evaluate the draft for focus and unity.

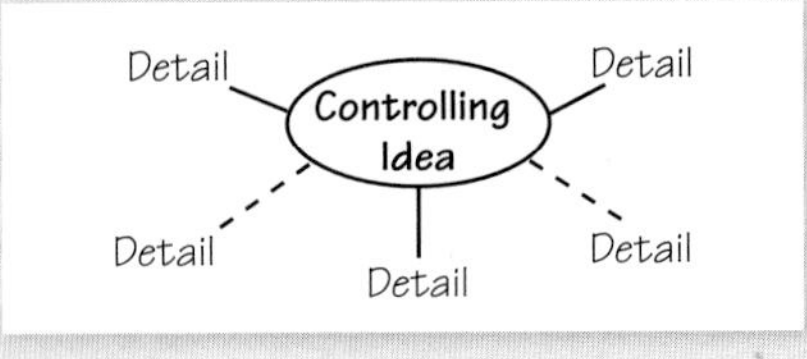

Tell them to write the controlling idea in the center and details on the branches. They should use a solid line to show which details support the controlling idea and a dotted line to show those that do not.

Ask the class:

- Does the controlling idea focus on one event and does it tell why it is important?
- Does everything relate back to the controlling idea? Is there any unrelated information?

Writing Handbook, p. 784

✔ Revise Your Draft

Your first draft is done. Now, polish it. Improve the focus and unity, and your choice of supporting details and words. Make what was just OK into something much better.

1 Revise for Focus and Unity

Any kind of good writing has a **focus**—it has a central, controlling idea. In an autobiographical narrative, the focus is telling the story of an important experience in the writer's life.

Good writing also has **unity**—that means that all of the parts tell about, or support, that controlling idea. In an autobiographical narrative, that means that the facts and events, descriptive details, and dialogue all go with the controlling idea.

Don't expect to achieve focus and unity with your first draft. Every writer expects and needs to rewrite. Time spent revising helps you sharpen your focus. Cut out any word, sentence, or even paragraph that doesn't relate to your controlling idea.

TRY IT ▸ With a partner, discuss which parts of the draft below do not support or relate to the writer's controlling idea.

Ⓐ

Student Draft

My mom and I were eating italian food at our favorite place, Tedesco's restaurant, when she told me the big news. I love Tedesco's because the lasagna is so good. I always order it. She said that she had received a promotion at work. The company was opening two new branch offices, and her boss had asked her to open one of them. The only thing was, both branches were kind of far away from Baltimore, where we lived. One was in Boston, and the other was in Miami. I had never been to either place.

"We won't go if you don't want to go" she said.

I stopped eating. I started playing with my food and wondering how they get that lasagna to be so good. Then I started to wonder about going. Did I want to go? I wasn't sure. Did I want to stay? I wasn't sure about that either...

Writing Plan

Controlling Idea	Choosing Miami gave me a fresh start.

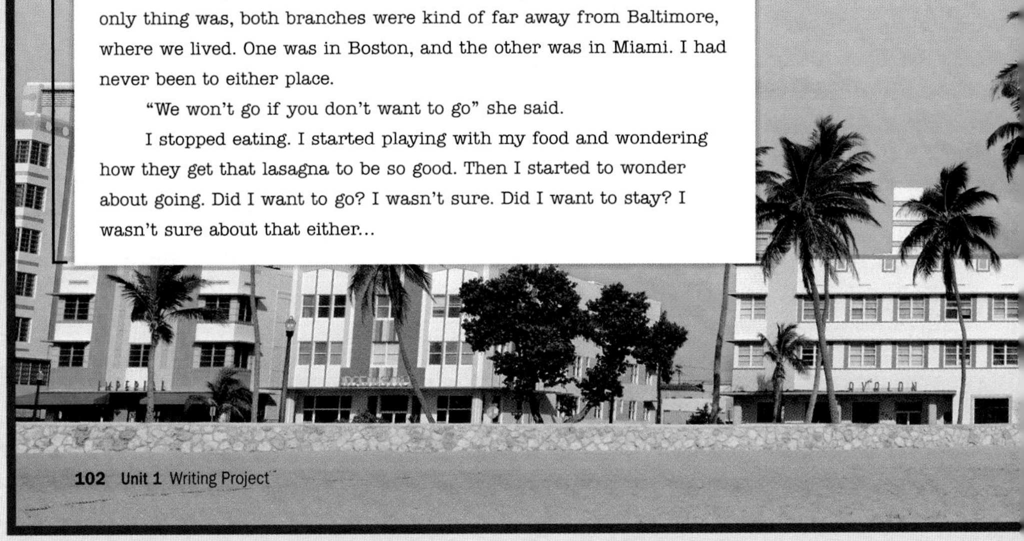

FOCUS ON WRITER'S CRAFT

Distinguishing Between Relevant and Irrelevant Support

Teach/Model Ask students if they sometimes go off-track in their conversations. Explain that it is just as easy for them to go off-track in their writing. One detail might flow into another detail that loosely goes with the topic but doesn't relate to the controlling idea. Show how to distinguish between relevant and irrelevant support using the student draft. Ask:

How does the first sentence about Tedesco's Restaurant relate to the controlling idea? *The first sentence relates to the controlling idea because it tells where the conversation about moving to a new city took place.*

The next two sentences are also about Tedesco's Restaurant. Why don't they relate to the controlling idea? *The next two sentences tell what the writer likes to eat at Tedesco's. They don't have anything to do with the idea of moving and having a fresh start.*

Practice Have students decide whether the following details would be relevant or irrelevant if added to the student draft:

1. My best friend moved to Denver last year. *[irrelevant]*
2. I had always dreamed about living in a new city. *[relevant]*
3. I love Boston cream pie. *[irrelevant]*

Apply Have students evaluate details for relevancy as they revise their narratives.
W.9-10.3.d; W.9-10.5

CCSS Literacy.W.9-10.3.d Use precise words and phrases, telling details, and sensory language to convey a vivid picture of the experiences, events, setting, and/or characters. Literacy.W.9-10.5 Develop and strengthen writing as needed by planning, revising, editing, rewriting, or trying a new approach, focusing on addressing what is most significant for a specific purpose and audience.

Now use the rubric to evaluate the focus and unity of your own draft. What score do you give your draft and why?

Focus and Unity

	How clearly does the writing present a central idea or claim?	How well does everything go together?
4 Wow!	**The writing expresses a clear central idea or claim about the topic.**	**Everything in the writing goes together.** • The main idea of each paragraph goes with the central idea or claim of the paper. • The main idea and details within each paragraph are related. • The conclusion is about the central idea or claim.
3 Ahh.	**The writing expresses generally clear central idea or claim about the topic.**	**Most parts of the writing go together.** • The main idea of most paragraphs goes with the central idea or claim of the paper. • In most paragraphs, the main idea and details are related. • Most of the conclusion is about the central idea or claim.
2 Hmm.	**The writing includes a topic, but the central idea or claim is not clear.**	**Some parts of the writing go together.** • The main idea of some paragraphs goes with the central idea or claim of the paper. • In some paragraphs, the main idea and details are related. • Some of the conclusion is about the central idea or claim.
1 Huh?	**The writing includes many topics and does not express one central idea or claim.**	**The parts of the writing do not go together.** • Few paragraphs have a main idea, or the main idea does not go with the central idea or claim of the paper. • Few paragraphs contain a main idea and related details • None of the conclusion is about the central idea or claim.

myNGconnect.com

- **Rubric: Focus and Unity**
- **Evaluate and practice scoring other student narratives.**

TEACH

B Use a Rubric

Model Model using a rubric to evaluate a draft. Read the Student Draft on p. 102 aloud. Ask: Where in the draft is the controlling idea? How clearly is it presented?

Possible response:
- *The writer tells why the choice is significant in lines 7–8.*

Work with students to evaluate the Student Draft and assign a score for focus. Instruct them to read the four descriptions in the left-hand column of the rubric and choose the score that best describes the draft.

Ask: How well does everything go together? Which lines show details that might not fit with the controlling idea?

Possible response:
- *It's hard to tell how the lasagna goes with the promotion in lines 2–3 and 10–11.*

Collaborative Evaluation Have students work in pairs to evaluate the Student Draft and assign a score for unity. Instruct them to read the four descriptions in the right-hand column of the rubric and choose the score that best describes the draft.

Then have students assign an overall score for focus and unity. The simplest way would be to have them find the average score and round down to the nearest whole number. For instance, if students assign a 4 for focus and a 3 for unity, the average would be 3.5, which rounds down to a score of 3.
SL.9-10.1

Self-Evaluation Have students follow the same steps to evaluate their own drafts. Try these suggestions:

- Evaluate the draft one paragraph at a time to check focus and then evaluate it as a whole.
- Answer yes or no to each criterion in the rubric to get a score.

W.9-10.5

myNGconnect.com

Evaluate more samples online.

DIFFERENTIATED INSTRUCTION

English Language Learners ELL

Create Analogies Help ELLs understand the traits of focus and unity:

- Make an analogy between focused writing and the spray of a garden hose. Say: *When writing is focused and unified, the ideas flow in one direction like a steady stream. Unfocused writing is like a hose with a broken nozzle. Ideas, like the water, are scattered in all different directions.* Show an illustration if possible.
- Have students look at objects in the classroom through an empty paper towel tube and say: *When writing is focused and unified, it centers on one thing. Ideas that are not about that one thing do not appear in the writing.*

CCSS **Literacy.W.9-10.5** Develop and strengthen writing as needed by planning, revising, editing, rewriting, or trying a new approach, focusing on addressing what is most significant for a specific purpose and audience. **Literacy.SL.9-10.1** Initiate and participate effectively in a range of collaborative discussions (one-on-one, in groups, and teacher-led) with diverse partners on grades 9–10 topics, texts, and issues, building on others' ideas and expressing their own clearly and persuasively.

REVISE YOUR DRAFT

TEACH

C Revise Your Draft

Interpret the Checklist Guide students through the process of using the Revision Checklist. Direct them to read the first box in the first row (*Is my narrative focused?*). Students should decide whether or not their own draft should be revised based on the criteria in the second box.

Have students read the options in the third box and choose what they think they should do to revise for focus.

Self-Evaluation Instruct students to follow the Revision Checklist to finish making revisions to their own drafts. Suggest that they use a different-color pen or the Comments feature in a word-processing program.

ELL Build Vocabulary Explain that sequence words and phrases can help improve unity by showing chronological order. Show examples in a list.

Past
Before that...
A long time ago...
Up to now...
Prior to this...

Present
Now...
At this point...
While...
Immediately...

Future
After that...
I'm looking forward to...
Later...
Someday...

Have students look at the beginning, middle, and end of their drafts to add transition words.
W.9-10.3.a; W.9-10.3.b; W.9-10.3.c

2 Revise Your Draft

You've now evaluated the focus and unity of your own draft. If you scored 3 or lower, how can you improve your work? Use the checklist below to revise your draft.

Revision Checklist

Ask Yourself	Check It Out	How to Make It Better
Is my narrative focused?	If your score is 3 or lower, revise.	☐ If you are telling about more than one choice, focus on just one. ☐ Decide on one idea or opinion about the choice and cut any others. ☐ If there is no central, or controlling, idea, add one.
Is my narrative unified?	If your score is 3 or lower, revise.	☐ Remove or replace any sentence or paragraph that is not about the central event. ☐ Consider adding a topic sentence to each paragraph to tell the main idea of the paragraph. ☐ Cut, move, or replace any details that do not really support a paragraph's main idea.
Does my narrative have a beginning, a middle, and an end?	Find and mark the boundaries between these parts.	☐ Add any part that is missing. ☐ Move any paragraph or sentence that is in the wrong part.
Are the supporting details vivid and interesting?	Underline descriptive details. **Highlight** dialogue. Are there enough details to make the writing come alive?	☐ Add sensory details or dialogue.
Will readers be able to follow my story?	Read it to someone or ask someone to read it. Ask about any parts that were hard to follow.	☐ Add any missing details. ☐ Add sequence words and phrases.

Writing Handbook, p. 784

FOCUS ON WRITER'S CRAFT

Using Transitional Devices

Teach/Model Review the organizational structure of a narrative and explain that sequence is shown by transitional devices, or sequence words between events. For example: *It all started when; but then; five seconds later; finally.* Have students brainstorm more transition words.

Ask: Have you ever felt like a brief moment lasted a long time? Explain that a writer can pace the presentation of actions to reflect this time and feeling. For example, a writer can take a page to tell about one important minute or use one sentence to describe five years.
W.9-10.3.a; W.9-10.3.b; W.9-10.3.c

Practice/Apply Have students follow these steps to revise their drafts for transitions and pacing:

1. **Transitions:** Look at one paragraph at a time. Do the sentences flow smoothly? Add transitional devices where necessary.
2. **Pacing:** Next to each paragraph, write how much time it describes. Be sure the important moments are not rushed.
   - **To slow down the pace:** Add sentences that describe the physical scene and the actions of the characters; tell what is going on inside the narrator's head.
   - **To speed up the pace or create suspense:** Use shorter sentences to build up to the most important moment.

CCSS Literacy.W.9-10.3.a Engage and orient the reader by setting out a problem, situation, or observation, establishing one or multiple point(s) of view, and introducing a narrator and/or characters; create a smooth progression of experiences or events. Literacy.W.9-10.3.b Use narrative techniques, such as dialogue, pacing, description, reflection, and multiple plot lines, to develop experiences, events, and/or characters. Literacy.W.9-10.3.c Use a variety of techniques to sequence events so that they build on one another to create a coherent whole.

3 Conduct a Peer Conference

It helps to get a second opinion when you are revising your draft. Ask a partner to read your draft and look for

- any part of the draft that is confusing
- any place where something seems to be missing
- anything that the reader doesn't understand.

Then talk with your partner about the draft. Focus on the items in the Revision Checklist. Use your partner's comments to make your narrative clearer, more complete, and easier to understand.

D

4 Make Revisions

Look at the revisions below and the peer-reviewer conversation on the right. Notice how the peer reviewer commented and asked questions. Notice how the writer used the comments and questions to revise.

Revised for Unity

My mom and I were eating italian food at our favorite place, Tedesco's restaurant, when she told me the big news. ~~I love Tedesco's because the lasagna is so good. I always order it.~~ While I was eating my lasagna, Mom told me she received a promotion. The company was opening two new branch offices.

Peer Conference

Reviewer's Comment: I think you went off track in the first paragraph. Your paper is about choices, not lasagna, isn't it?

Writer's Answer: Oops. I see what you mean. I'll delete that.

E

Revised Ending

I gave her the full presentation. Telling her everything I'd found out about Boston and Miami. I finished with the New World School of the Arts.

"What if you don't get in?" she asked.

"At least I will have tried," I said.

"Done," she said. "We're moving to Miami."

Now we're here, and I'm glad. I have applied to the NWSA, and I think I will be admitted. I'm looking forward to a new adventure. My mom and I made a fresh start—and we did it together.

Reviewer's Comment: This just sort of stops. Do you want to tell the result of the choice?

Writer's Answer: I was trying to be dramatic, but maybe it's not working. The assignment says to end with the result of the choice, so I'll add it.

Reflect on Your Revisions

▶ Think about the results of your peer conference. What are some of your strengths as a writer? What are some things that give you trouble?

TEACH

D Conduct a Peer Conference

Peer Response Instruct students to be sure their comments are about the writing and not about the choice the writer made.

ELL Sentence Frames Have students use these frames to respond to their partner's draft:

- I was confused about ______.
- It seems like you left out ______.
- I didn't understand ______.

SL.9-10.1.d

E Make Revisions

Model Have two students read aloud the Peer Conference in the margin. Then work with students to help them analyze and evaluate the writer's revisions. Ask:

- What did the writer do to improve the draft? What needed to be deleted, added, or changed?
- What are some other ways the writer could have revised the draft?

Use Feedback Have students follow the steps above for making revisions to their own drafts.
W.9-10.3.e; W.9-10.5

FOCUS ON WRITER'S CRAFT

Working Collaboratively

Teach Explain to students that even professional and established writers need the advice and opinions of others in order to improve their writing. Someone who has not seen the student's work will be able to point out confusing or missing information more easily than the writer who has read the draft many times.

Apply Advise students to practice active listening during their peer conferences. Have them take detailed notes on their reviewers' comments and summarize what they learned from the feedback.

Conference Notes	What I Learned

SL.9-10.1.d

ONGOING ASSESSMENT

Have students write a summary sentence about their revision: I improved my draft by ______.

CCSS Literacy.W.9-10.3.e Provide a conclusion that follows from and reflects on what is experienced, observed, or resolved over the course of the narrative. Literacy.W.9-10.5 Develop and strengthen writing as needed by planning, revising, editing, rewriting, or trying a new approach, focusing on addressing what is most significant for a specific purpose and audience. Literacy.SL.9-10.1.d Respond thoughtfully to diverse perspectives, summarize points of agreement and disagreement, and, when warranted, qualify or justify their own views and understanding and make new connections in light of the evidence and reasoning presented.

Lesson 4

EDIT AND PROOFREAD YOUR DRAFT

OBJECTIVES

Writing
- Writing Process: Edit and Proofread Ⓣ

Grammar
- Complete Sentences Ⓣ

Mechanics
- Capitalization: Proper Nouns and Adjectives
- Punctuation: Quotation Marks and Commas
- Spelling: Homonyms

TEACH

Writing Transparencies 3 and 4

Ⓐ Capitalize Proper Nouns and Adjectives

Try It Review the capitalization of proper nouns and adjectives. Use Proofreader's Marks to correct the errors on the transparency.

Possible response:
- *italian food; Tedesco's Restaurant*

Edit and Proofread Have students correct any capitalization errors in their own drafts.
L.9-10.2

Writing Handbook, p. 853

Ⓑ Punctuate Quotations Correctly

Try It Explain how to punctuate quotations.

Possible responses:

1. "We won't go if you don't want to go," Mom said.
2. I answered, "I'm not sure how I feel."
3. Correct

Edit and Proofread Remind students to look for areas in their drafts where they have used dialogue, irony, or sarcasm, and to check for correct punctuation.
L.9-10.2; L.9-10.3.a

✓ Edit and Proofread Your Draft

Your revision should now be complete. Before you share it with others, find and fix any mistakes that you made.

1 Capitalize Proper Nouns and Adjectives

Ⓐ Proper nouns are capitalized because they name specific people, places, and things. Common nouns, which are general, are not capitalized.

Common Noun	Proper Noun
teacher	Ms. Warner
city	Miami

Proper adjectives, which come from proper nouns, are also capitalized.

Proper Noun	Proper Adjective
Florida	Floridian
America	American

TRY IT ▸ Copy the sentences. Fix the two capitalization errors. Use proofreader's marks.

> My mom and I were eating italian food at our favorite place, Tedesco's restaurant, when she told me the big news.

2 Punctuate Quotations Correctly

Ⓑ Put quotation marks (" ") around the exact words that people speak. Do not use quotation marks when you describe what people said.

Quotation: "I'm ready," she said.
Description: She said that she was ready.

Use a comma to set off tags, or words that identify who is quoted.

I replied, "I believe that I am ready to make a choice."
"I believe that I am ready to make a choice**," I replied.**
"I believe that I am ready**," I replied, "**to make a choice."

TRY IT ▸ Copy the sentences. Add any necessary quotation marks and commas.

> 1. We won't go if you don't want to go Mom said.
> 2. I answered I'm not sure how I feel.
> 3. She said that I should help her choose.

Proofreader's Marks

Use proofreader's marks to correct capitalization and punctuation errors.

Capitalize:
My mother is asian.

Do not capitalize:
I enjoy Asian Music.

Add quotation marks:
My teacher said, Your narrative is good.

Add comma:
"Thank you" I replied.

Editing Tip

Quotation marks can also be used to show sarcasm or irony.

I found it hard to follow the "easy" directions.

Look in a style guide to find out more about how to use quotation marks.

Writing Transparency 3

WRITING AUTOBIOGRAPHICAL NARRATIVE 3

Edit and Proofread Your Draft

Proofreader's Marks		
≡	Capitalize	I love new york city.
/	Do not capitalize	I'm going shopping at my favorite Store.
∜ ∜	Add quotation marks	You are late, said the teacher.
∧	Add a comma	Amy how are you feeling today?
⊙	Add a period	Mr Lopez is our neighbor.
?	Add a question mark	Where is my black pen
↓	Add an exclamation mark	Look out
∧	Add a semicolon	This shirt is nice however, this one brings out the color of your eyes.
◇	Add a colon	He wakes up at 6 30 a.m.
⊼	Add a dash	Barney he's my pet dog has run away.
{ }	Add parentheses	I want to work for the Federal Bureau of Investigation FBI .
=	Add a hyphen	You were born in mid= September, right?
∨	Add an apostrophe	Im the oldest of five children.
#	Add a space	She likes him alot.
⁐	Close up a space	How much home work do you have?
∧	Add text	My keys are the table.
℘	Delete text	I am going too my friend's house.
∩∪	Transpose words, letters	Did you see thier new car?
(sp)	Spell out	Today he is turning 16.
¶	Begin a new paragraph	"I win!" I shouted. "No you don't," he said.
(ital) ___	Add italics	The Spanish word for table is mesa.
(u/s) ___	Add underlining	Little Women is one of my favorite books.

Writing Transparency 4

WRITING AUTOBIOGRAPHICAL NARRATIVE 4

Edit and Proofread Your Draft

1. Capitalize Proper Nouns and Adjectives

> My mom and I were eating italian food at our favorite place, Tedesco's restaurant, when she told me the big news.

2. Punctuate Quotations Correctly

> 1. We won't go if you don't want to go Mom said.
> 2. I answered I'm not sure how I feel.
> 3. She said that I should help her choose.

3. Check Your Spelling

> Their are two cities where we might move. They're both nice places to live. Its nice in Boston, but Miami is nice, too.

4. Check Sentences for Completeness

> Life is full of choices. Some of them easy. Some of them hard. I recently made a hard choice. Changed high schools. I needed a change. To learn more and get better grades.

CCSS Literacy.L.9-10.2 Demonstrate command of the conventions of standard English capitalization, punctuation, and spelling when writing. **Literacy.L.9-10.3.a** Write and edit work so that it conforms to the guidelines in a style manual (e.g., *MLA Handbook*, Turabian's *Manual for Writers*) appropriate for the discipline and writing type.

3 Check Your Spelling

Homonyms are words that sound alike but have different meanings and spellings. Spell these homonyms correctly when you proofread.

Homonyms and Their Meanings	Examples
it's (contraction) = it is; it has	**It's** hard to make a decision.
its (pronoun) = belonging to it	Every city has **its** good points.
there (adverb) = that place or position	I like Boston. I once lived **there**.
their (pronoun) = belonging to them	They sent me a map of **their** city.
they're (contraction) = they are	**They're** very friendly people.

TRY IT ▸ Copy the sentences. Find and fix the two homonym errors.

> Their are two cities where we might move. They're both nice places to live. Its nice in Boston, but Miami is nice, too.

Technology Tip

Most word-processing software includes a Spell-check feature and a Grammar feature. Always use these, but know their limits. Spell-checkers cannot find all homonym errors.

Proofreading Tip

Use a print or online dictionary to check your spelling and use of word endings.

C

4 Check Sentences for Completeness

You use complete sentences in your writing every day. You also routinely see them in written classroom materials. The structure of a complete sentence includes a subject and a predicate. A complete sentence expresses a complete thought.

Problem	Solution
Sentence is missing a subject. Had to choose a new home.	**Add the missing subject.** I had to choose a new home.
Sentence is missing a verb. Mom glad about her promotion.	**Add the missing verb.** Mom was glad about her promotion.
Sentence fragments do not express a complete thought. I gave her the full presentation. Telling her everything.	**Join the fragments to express a complete thought.** I gave her the full presentation, telling her everything.

TRY IT ▸ Copy the paragraph. Find and fix the structure of four incomplete sentences.

> Life is full of choices. Some of them easy. Some of them hard. I recently made a hard choice. Changed high schools. I needed a change. To learn more and get better grades.

Reflect on Your Corrections

▸ Look back over the changes you made. Do you see a pattern? If there are things you keep missing, make a checklist of what to watch in your writing.

D

Writing Handbook, p. 850

TEACH

C Check Your Spelling

Try It Explain the definition of homonyms. Discuss the differences between the following:

- **it's/its:** Point to the apostrophe in *it's* and explain that it means two words have been combined. *It's* is used in place of *it is*, and *its* shows possession.
- **there/their/they're:** Explain that *there* shows a location and is the opposite of *here; their* shows possession, like the way *its* does; *they're* shows that two words have been combined and is used in place of *they are*.

Ask: Where are the homonym errors in the sample? Mark corrections on the transparency.

Possible response:

- ~~Their~~ *There are two cities where we might move. They're both nice places to live.* ~~Its~~ *It's nice in Boston, but Miami is nice, too.*

Edit and Proofread Have students check their drafts for homonym errors and make corrections. Encourage students to use dictionaries and other sources to check their spelling and word endings.
W.9-10.6; L.9-10.1; L.9-10.2.c; L.9-10.3

D Check Sentences for Completeness

Try It Review the structure of a complete sentence. Work through the examples. Read the sample paragraph aloud. Have students work in pairs to correct the stucture of the incomplete sentences. Mark corrections on the transparency.

Possible response:

- *Life is full of choices. Some of them are easy, and some of them are hard. I recently made a hard choice. I changed high schools. I needed a change so I might learn more and get better grades.*

Edit and Proofread Have students read their drafts to identify sentence errors.
L.9-10.1

Grammar and Writing Practice Book, pp. 31–34

FOCUS ON WRITER'S CRAFT

Using Fragments for Effect

Teach Explain that grammar rules in English are complex and that most have exceptions. One exception to the rule of complete sentences is the use of fragments for effect. Tell students that in narrative writing, fragments are often used to illustrate a character's thoughts, to mimic conversational language, or to draw attention to a thought or action. Emphasize that intentional fragments should not be used in academic writing such as a research paper, a critical essay, or a professional report.

Practice Have students rewrite the following paragraph with intentional fragments:

We can move to Boston, or we can move to Miami. The names of the two cities lingered in my mind as I tried to picture what life would be like in either place. No matter what good images popped into my mind, I couldn't help but feel empty at the thought of leaving Baltimore, home of the "Star Spangled Banner" and my home.

[Boston or Miami. The names of the two cities lingered in my mind as I tried to picture what life would be like in either place. No matter what good images popped into my mind, I couldn't help but feel empty at the thought of leaving Baltimore, home of the "Star Spangled Banner." My home.]

Apply Have students review their drafts to look for instances when an intentional fragment might be used to create an effect.
L.9-10.1.b

CCSS **Literacy.W.9-10.6** Use technology, including the Internet, to produce, publish, and update individual or shared writing products, taking advantage of technology's capacity to link to other information and to display information flexibly and dynamically. **Literacy.L.9-10.1** Demonstrate command of the conventions of standard English grammar and usage when writing or speaking. **Literacy.L.9-10.1.b** Use various types of phrases (noun, verb, adjectival, adverbial, participial, prepositional, absolute) and clauses (independent, dependent; noun, relative, adverbial) to convey specific meanings and add variety and interest to writing or presentations. **Literacy.L.9-10.2.c** Spell correctly. **Literacy.L.9-10.3** Apply knowledge of language to understand how language functions in different contexts, to make effective choices for meaning or style, and to comprehend more fully when reading or listening.

EDIT AND PROOFREAD YOUR DRAFT

TEACH

E Edited Student Draft

Read and Discuss Read aloud the Edited Student Draft. Then go back and address the callouts. For example:

Ask: Where were the errors with quotation marks, and how did the writer correct them?

Possible response:
- *In the first quotation, the writer added a necessary comma between the last word of the quotation and the end quotation mark. In the second one, the writer added a beginning quotation mark to the second part of what the speaker was saying.*

Ask: How did the writer correct the fragment near the end?

Possible response:
- *The writer added the fragment to the previous sentence.*

Finally, ask: What other revision did the writer make?

Possible response:
- *The writer deleted the unrelated ideas about the lasagna.*

ONGOING ASSESSMENT
Have students write an example of each of the following on an "exit slip": a proper noun; correctly punctuated dialogue; correct use of the homonym *its* or *their*; one way to fix an incomplete sentence.

5 Edited Student Draft

Here's the student's draft, revised and edited. How did the writer improve it?

E

A Fresh Start

My mom and I were eating Italian food at our favorite place, Tedesco's Restaurant, when she told me the big news. She said that she had received a promotion at work. The company was opening two new branch offices, and her boss had asked her to open one of them. However, both branches were far away from Baltimore, where we lived. One was in Boston, and the other was in Miami.

"We won't go if you don't want to go," she said.

Did I want to go? I wasn't sure. Did I want to stay? I wasn't sure about that, either.

"It doesn't really matter to me whether it's Boston or Miami," she added. "Pick the one that will make you happy. It would be a fresh start for both of us."

"A fresh start is just what I need!" I said.

Wow. Picking a city to live in was quite a challenge—and quite an opportunity. I had only a month to make the choice. I went on the Internet right away. Soon, I was overloaded with information. I knew a lot about each city, but I didn't feel any closer to choosing between them. The more I knew, the harder it was to choose. That's when I found out about Miami's New World School of the Arts (NWSA).

The NWSA has special high school programs in music, dance, theater, and visual arts. I explored it online, and I immediately began to fantasize about going there. I couldn't apply there if we lived out of state, but if we were living in Miami, I could apply for the next school year. My choice was made. "I'm ready," I said to my mother.

I gave her the full presentation, telling her everything I'd found out about Boston and Miami. I finished with the NWSA.

"What if you don't get in?" she asked.

"At least I will have tried," I said.

"Done," she said. "We're moving to Miami."

Now we're here, and I'm glad. I have applied to the NWSA, and I think I will be admitted. I'm looking forward to a new adventure. My mom and I made a fresh start—and we did it together.

The writer capitalized the proper adjective and the complete name of the restaurant to fix the **capitalization** errors.

The writer deleted unrelated ideas.

The writer added the missing **comma** to the quotation.

The writer used the **right homonym** and added **quotation marks.**

The writer changed "their" to "there" to fix the **homonym error.**

The writer **fixed the fragment** to make a complete sentence.

Publish and Present

Print or write a clean copy of your narrative. You are now ready to publish and present it. Give your audience a chance to read or hear what you have to say. You may also want to present your work in a different way.

Alternative Presentations

Do a Reading Read aloud your narrative to the class. Make it come alive by reading with expression.

1. **Introduce Your Narrative** Tell your audience the subject. For example, you might say, "My narrative tells about a time when I had to choose between ______ and ______."
2. **Read with Expression** Use your tone of voice to show how you felt.
3. **Watch Your Pacing** Don't rush your presentation. Speak at a pace that is comfortable for your audience. Look up from time to time to see people's reactions. Does anyone look puzzled? If so, slow down.
4. **Make Eye Contact** Don't hide your face behind paper. Look over the paper at your audience to make eye contact from time to time.
5. **Ask for Feedback** When you are finished, thank your audience. Then ask for feedback:
   - Was the beginning interesting? If not, how could I improve it?
   - Was it easy to understand what choice I had to make? If not, how could I make it clearer?
   - Did the narrative feel complete? If not, what suggestions do you have for strengthening the ending?

Publish on the Internet Reach a wider audience. As your teacher directs, send your narrative to an appropriate Web site that publishes student writing.

1. **Find a Good Web Site** Post your paper on your own or the school's Web site, or another site.
   myNGconnect.com
   Directory of Online Publishers
2. **Send Your Writing** Follow any instructions to submit your writing.
3. **Ask for Feedback** If there is a comment box, ask readers to comment on your work. Use their suggestions to improve your writing.

Language and Learning Handbook, p. 702

A

Publishing Tip

Format your typed work according to your teacher's guidelines.

If you've handwritten your work, make sure your work is legible and clean.

Reflect on Your Work

- **Ask for and use feedback from your audience and your teacher to evaluate your strengths as a writer.**
  - What parts of your narrative did your audience like?
  - What parts of your narrative did your audience say need improvement?
  - What would you like to do better the next time you write? Set a goal for your next writing project.
- ☑ **Save a copy of your work in your portfolio.**

B

Lesson 5

PUBLISH AND PRESENT

OBJECTIVES

Writing

- Autobiographical Narrative
- Writing Process: Publish; Reflect and Evaluate

TEACH

Explain that the final stage in the writing process is to publish the work. Have students choose one of two ways of publishing and presenting their narrative: Do a Reading or Publish on the Internet.

A Alternative Presentations

Do a Reading Use the Edited Student Draft to model an oral reading. Demonstrate each of the four tips for reading aloud listed on page 109. After modeling the sample, ask students to respond to the feedback questions based on your reading.
SL.9-10.6

Publish on the Internet Review your school's Internet guidelines. Have students search the Directory of Online Publishers to find an appropriate Web site for publishing their narrative. After students have posted their work, have other students access the site to give feedback. Then have writers go back to read the feedback.
W.9-10.6

Language and Learning Handbook, p. 702

B Reflect on Your Work

Use Feedback Provide students with feedback before and after they publish. Next, have students write a short reflection in response to the questions, including a specific goal for their next writing project. For example: *In my next writing project I will try to use more descriptive details.*

Remind students to save a copy of their written narrative in their portfolio.
SL.9-10.1

ONGOING ASSESSMENT

Have students identify one thing they learned from publishing their work that they didn't learn from other steps in the writing process.

CCSS **Literacy.W.9-10.6** Use technology, including the Internet, to produce, publish, and update individual or shared writing products, taking advantage of technology's capacity to link to other information and to display information flexibly and dynamically. **Literacy.SL.9-10.1** Initiate and participate effectively in a range of collaborative discussions (one-on-one, in groups, and teacher-led) with diverse partners on grades 9–10 topics, texts, and issues, building on others' ideas and expressing their own clearly and persuasively. **Literacy.SL.9-10.6** Adapt speech to a variety of contexts and tasks, demonstrating command of formal English when indicated or appropriate.

UNIT 2 NONFICTION

THE ART OF EXPRESSION

EQ ESSENTIAL QUESTION:
Does Creativity Matter?

CLUSTER 1

Consider ways to express your creativity.

News Article
Creativity at Work
by Abe Louise Young

Interview
The Hidden Secrets of the Creative Mind
by Francine Russo

PROJECTS	WORKSHOPS
Writing Project Position Paper	**Workplace** Inside an Art Museum
Unit Project Demonstration	**Vocabulary** Use Context Clues
	Listening and Speaking Descriptive Presentation

CLUSTER 2

Explore the effect of music on our lives.

Essay

Hip-Hop as Culture
by Efrem Smith

Song

I Am Somebody
by Grandmaster Flash

CLUSTER 3

Discover one way to find your voice.

Essay

Slam: Performance Poetry Lives On
by Pooja Makhijani

Poetry

Euphoria
by Lauren Brown

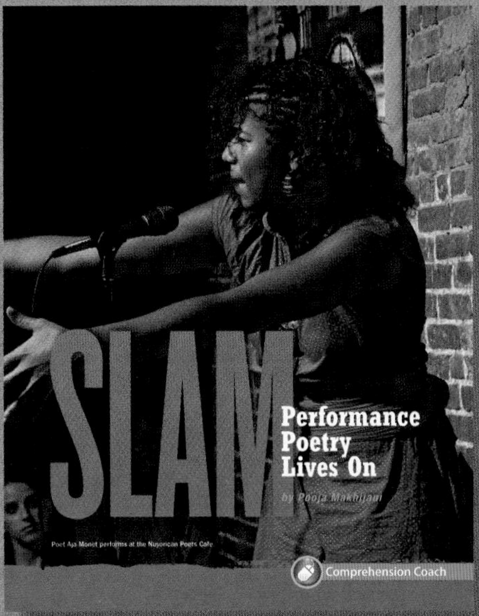

CLOSE READING

Investigate where creativity comes from.

Research Report

The Creativity Crisis
by Po Bronson & Ashley Merryman

EDGE LIBRARY

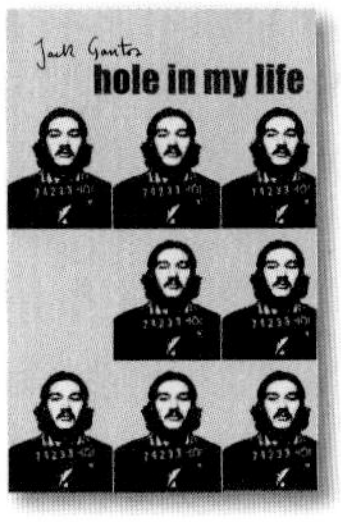

Hole in My Life ●
by Jack Gantos
Lexile® 840L
Genre/Length:
Autobiography; 224 pages

The Stone Goddess ●●
by Minfong Ho
Lexile® 1020L
Genre/Length:
Historical Fiction; 200 pages

Anthem ●●●
by Ayn Rand
Lexile® 880L
Genre/Length:
Science Fiction; 120 pages

UNIT 2 Edge Library

The **EDGE LIBRARY** provides an opportunity for student choice. Students self-select literature based on their interests and reading ability. Books support exploration of the **Essential Question**, forming an integral part of instruction.

1 Select

- Select a variety of appropriate materials to read

Self-Select Have students choose a book according to their interests and reading level.

Hole in My Life

by Jack Gantos

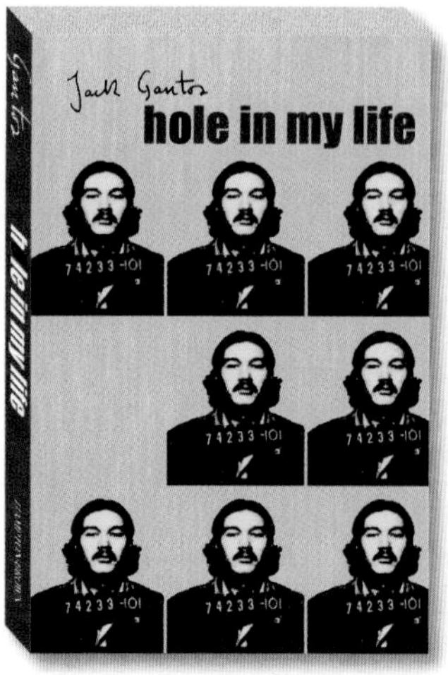

How can art destroy someone? How can it save someone?

Hole in My Life is Jack Gantos's autobiographical account of the crime he committed as a young adult and the time he spent in prison as a result. Students who read this book will learn about the negative consequences of committing a crime and the possibilities for turning one's life around.

- **Reading Level** Lexile® 840L

Genre: Autobiography

Length: 224 pages

Awards: Michael L. Prinz Award, Robert F. Gilbert Informational Book Award, Best Book for Young Adults, ALA

2 Read

- Read to develop and evaluate personal preferences

Download the **Teacher's Guide** and **Student Journals.** Have students read their chosen book independently or in small groups. Use the planner on **Student Journal, page 1**, to establish a reading schedule. RL.9-10.10; RI.9-10.10

myNGconnect.com

- **Unit 2 Resources**
- **Teacher's Guide**
- **Student Journal**

3 Use Strategies

- Identify, assess, and apply effective personal reading strategies

Have students identify the strategies they selected to use during reading. Use the prompts at the right to elicit student analysis and discussions.

Determine Importance
- How does Jack change during his time in prison? Which events play a key role in his transformation?

Visualize
- How does Jack's prison cell look similar to and different from the other places he has lived?

Make Inferences
- How does Jack's family life affect his decisions?

4 Discuss

- Exchange and extend ideas

EQ Does Creativity Matter?

Engage students in a discussion comparing how the texts address the **Essential Question**.

Consider ways to express your creativity. Jack wrote everything in his journal. He planned adventures and dreamed of becoming a famous writer.

Explore the effect of art on our lives. Jack's desire for adventure caused him to make a bad decision. Jack's love of writing helped him see a more positive future for himself.

Discover one way to find your voice. Jack became a writer. By expressing himself through writing, Jack realized he had the potential to turn his life around.

CCSS Literacy.RL.9-10.10 By the end of grade 9, read and comprehend literature, including stories, dramas, and poems, in the grades 9-10 text complexity band proficiently, with scaffolding as needed at the high end of the range. By the end of grade 10, read and comprehend literature, including stories, dramas, and poems, at the high end of the grades 9-10 text complexity band independently and proficiently.

READ ALOUD

Anthem Read aloud the introduction to engage students' interest in the book. Provide support for the highlighted key vocabulary. Use the feature about objectivism to explain the concept to students. Then model fluency by reading aloud pages 11–13.

The Stone Goddess

by Minfong Ho

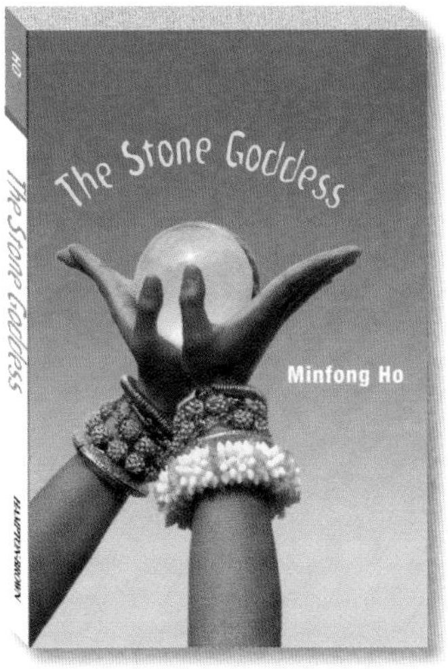

Do we need art in difficult times?

Set during Cambodia's Khmer Rouge, *The Stone Goddess* is told through the eyes of a young Cambodian girl, Nakri Sohka. After a rebel group seizes control of her country's government, Nakri's family is torn apart. Her courageous battle to survive reveals the importance of family, culture, and tradition.

● ● **Reading Level** Lexile® 1020L

Genre: Historical Fiction

Length: 200 pages

Determine Importance

- What does the art of classical dancing mean to Nakri and her family?

Synthesize

- What does the story suggest about the relationship between family and culture?

Make Connections

- How is the Cambodian conflict similar to a current conflict in the world?

Consider ways to express your creativity. Nakri dances and plays the flute.

Explore the effect of art on our lives. Traditional dancing brings Nakri closer to her family and culture. Playing the flute helps Nakri feel more comfortable in the United States.

Discover one way to find your voice. Dancing and playing music helps Nakri to better understand and appreciate her culture.

Anthem

by Ayn Rand

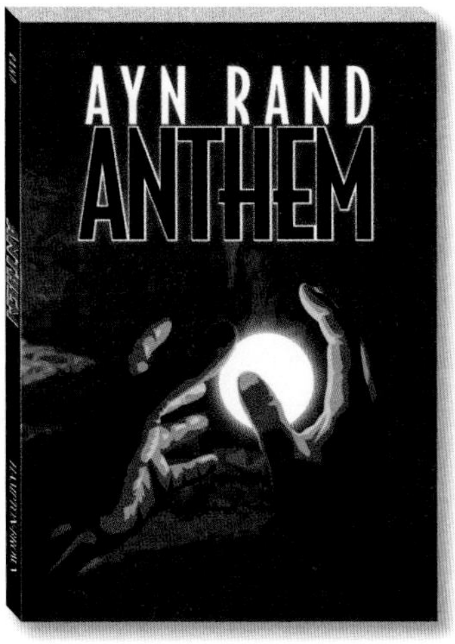

What is the greatest threat to creativity?

Anthem takes place in the future, long after war has destroyed modern society. The narrator, Equality 7-2521, describes a new society, in which individuality is illegal. Through the secret writing of Equality 7-2521, students will learn about the conflict between individuality and conformity and the lengths to which an individual will go for the freedom of expression.

● ● ● **Reading Level** Lexile® 880L

Genre: Science Fiction

Length: 120 pages

Determine Importance

- Why does Equality 7-2521 switch from using the pronoun "we" to the pronoun "I" when he talks about himself?

Plan and Monitor

- Predict how Equality 7-2521's curiosity will influence the events of the story.

Ask Questions

- How is the style of this story unique? Why do you think the author chose to write it this way?

Consider ways to express your creativity. Equality 7-2521 conducts scientific experiments in his secret tunnel.

Explore the effect of art on our lives. Innovation drives Equality 7-2521 to risk his life in the pursuit of knowledge.

Discover one way to find your voice. Equality 7-2521 cannot feel free without knowledge. His ability to create is his contribution to society.

CCSS Literacy.RI.9-10.10 By the end of grade 9, read and comprehend literary nonfiction in the grades 9-10 text complexity band proficiently, with scaffolding as needed at the high end of the range. By the end of grade 10, read and comprehend literary nonfiction at the high end of the grades 9-10 text complexity band independently and proficiently.

UNIT 2 Instructional Focus

EQ ESSENTIAL QUESTION:
Does Creativity Matter?

	UNIT LAUNCH How to Read Nonfiction	CLUSTER 1 Creativity at Work The Hidden Secrets of the Creative Mind
Reading		
Analyze Text Genre Focus **Kinds of Nonfiction**	Ⓣ **Analyze Author's Purpose** RI.9-10.6	Ⓣ **Analyze Author's Purpose** RI.9-10.6 Ⓣ **Analyze Development of Ideas** RI.9-10.3 Ⓣ **Analyze Description** RI.9-10.4 Ⓣ **Use Text Evidence** RI.9-10.1
Build Vocabulary	**Academic Vocabulary** L.9-10.6 • emphasize • summarize	Ⓣ **Key Vocabulary** L.9-10.6 career collaborate • commitment • evaluate expectation • insight talent • transform Ⓣ **Vocabulary Strategy** L.9-10.4.a • Context Clues Ⓣ **Reading Fluency** RL.9-10.10 Comprehension Coach
Writing		
Respond to Literature		Ⓣ **Writing on Demand** W.9-10.1 • Writing a Test Essay
Writing Project		Ⓣ **Writing Project** W.9-10.1.a-e; W.9-10.4-6; W.9-10.10 • Writing Trait: Focus and Unity
Language		
ELL **Develop Language**		Ⓣ **Describe People, Places, and Things** SL.9-10.4
Use Grammar Grammar Focus **Present Tense**		Ⓣ **Subject Pronouns: *I, You, He,* Etc.** L.9-10.1 Ⓣ **Subject Pronouns: *We, You, They*** L.9-10.1 Ⓣ **Pronouns in a Compound Sentence** L.9-10.1.b Ⓣ **Review: Subject Pronouns** L.9-10.1
Build Listening and Speaking Skills	**Unit Project** Ⓣ **Discuss the EQ** SL.9-10.4 • Plan Your Project: Demonstration	

• **Academic Vocabulary** Ⓣ = Tested on Cluster and/or Unit Reading and Literary Analysis Test Ⓣ = Tested on Unit Writing Test

Students explore the Essential Question "Does Creativity Matter?" through reading, writing, and discussion.
Each cluster focuses on a specific aspect of the larger question:
Cluster 1: Consider ways to express your creativity.
Cluster 2: Explore the effect of music on our lives.
Cluster 3: Discover one way to find your voice.
Close Reading: Investigate where creativity comes from.

CLUSTER 2

Hip-Hop as Culture
I Am Somebody

- **Analyze Author's Purpose** RI.9-10.6
- **Analyze Structure: Song Lyrics** RL.9-10.5
- **Analyze Style: Language and Word Choice** RL.9-10.4; RI.9-10.4
- **Use Text Evidence** RI.9-10.1

Key Vocabulary L.9-10.6
- • achieve
- assert
- • culture
- evolve
- heritage
- innovator
- • perspective
- self-esteem

Vocabulary Strategy L.9-10.4.a; L.9-10.5.a
- Context Clues for Idioms

Reading Fluency RI.9-10.10

Comprehension Coach

Writing Trait W.9-10.5
- Focus and Unity

Writing Project W.9-10.1.a-e; W.9-10.4-6; W.9-10.10
- Writing Trait: Focus and Unity

Describe Experiences SL.9-10.1

- **Action Verbs** L.9-10.1
- **Action Verbs in the Present Tense** L.9-10.1
- **Subject-Verb Agreement: -s** L.9-10.1; L9-10.2; L.9-10.2.c
- **Helping Verbs: *Can, Could, May, Might*** L.9-10.1.b
- **Review: Action Verbs in the Present Tense** L.9-10.1.b

Descriptive Presentation SL.9-10.4

CLUSTER 3

Slam: Performance Poetry Lives On
Euphoria

- **Analyze Author's Purpose** RI.9-10.6
- **Analyze Structure: Free Verse** RL.9-10.5
- **Use Text Evidence** RI.9-10.1

Key Vocabulary L.9-10.6
- compose
- euphoria
- expression
- improvisation
- • phenomenon
- recitation
- • structure
- transcend

Vocabulary Strategy L.9-10.4.a; L.9-10.5.a
- Context Clues for Idioms

Reading Fluency RI.9-10.10

Comprehension Coach

Written Composition W.9-10.2
- Write a How-To Paragraph

Writing Project W.9-10.1.a-e; W.9-10.4-6; W.9-10.10
- Writing Trait: Focus and Unity

Give and Follow Commands SL.9-10.6

- **Forms of *Be* in the Present Tense** L.9-10.1.b
- **Present Progressive Verb Forms** L.9-10.1.b
- **Present Tense of *Have*** L.9-10.1
- **Present Tense of *Do*** L.9-10.1.b
- **Review: Present Tense Verbs** L.9-10.1.b

CLOSE READING

The Creativity Crisis

- **Analyze Author's Purpose** RI.9-10.6
- **Use Text Evidence** RI.9-10.1

Academic Vocabulary L.9-10.6
- emphasize

UNIT WRAP-UP

Unit Project
Respond to the EQ SL.9-10.4
- Present Your Project: Demonstration

T = Tested on Language Acquisition Assessment   T = Assessed with a Rubric

UNIT 2 Resource Manager

Edge resources include practical, easy-to-use teaching tools
for comprehensive instruction, practice, assessment, and reteaching.

Reading & Writing

Reading Resources

UNIT LAUNCH

Edge Library

Hole in My Life

The Stone Goddess

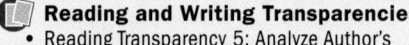

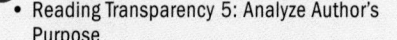

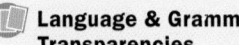

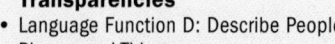

Anthem

Edge Library Resources
- Student Journals
- Teacher's Guides

CLUSTER 1

Creativity at Work
The Hidden Secrets of the Creative Mind

Cluster 1 Resources
- Learn more about Tony Carillo
- Selection summaries in eight languages
- Workplace Workshop resources

Comprehension Coach
- Creativity at Work
- The Hidden Secrets of the Creative Mind

Reading and Writing Transparencies
- Reading Transparency 5: Analyze Author's Purpose

Selection CD and MP3s
- Creativity at Work, CD 3 Track 1
- The Hidden Secrets of the Creative Mind, CD 3 Track 2
- The Hidden Secrets of the Creative Mind: Fluency Passage, CD 11 Track 4

Edge Interactive Practice Book
- Creativity at Work, pp. 56–60
- The Hidden Secrets of the Creative Mind, pp. 61–64
- Further Practice, pp. 65–67

Assessments Handbook
- Reader Reflection, p. 15b
- Cluster 1 Test, pp. 15c–15e

Reteaching Activities

Writing Project

Writing Project Tools
- Student Samples
- Scheduler
- Rubric

Reading and Writing Transparencies
- Writing Transparencies 5-8: Position Paper

Language & Grammar

UNIT LAUNCH

Unit Project Tools
- Planning Forms
- Scheduler
- Steps in the Demonstration Diagram
- Rubric

CLUSTER 1

Language & Grammar Lab Teacher's Edition, pp. 20–25

Language & Grammar Lab Transparencies
- Language Function D: Describe People, Places, and Things
- Grammar Transparencies 16–20 Subject Pronouns

Grammar & Writing Practice Book, pp. 35–44

Language CD and MP3
- Describe People, Places, and Things, Track 4

Assessments Handbook
- Language Acquisition Rubric p. 15o

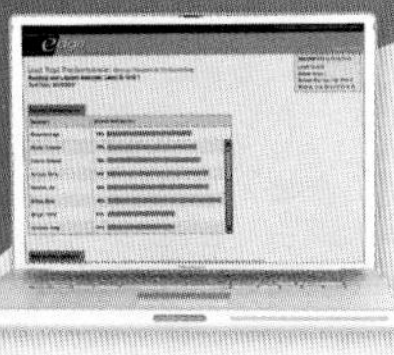

All Edge resources can be found online. Use the Online Lesson Tool, and all the relevant resources will automatically load into My Presentation Tool on myNGconnect.com.

CLUSTER 2

Hip-Hop as Culture
I Am Somebody

Cluster 2 Resources
- Learn more about Hip-Hop
- Selection summaries in eight languages

Comprehension Coach
- Hip-Hop as Culture
- I Am Somebody

Reading and Writing Transparencies
- Reading Transparency 6: Word Square
- Reading Transparency 7: Analyze Author's Purpose

Selection CD and MP3s
- Hip-Hop as Culture, CD 3 Track 3
- Hip-Hop as Culture: Fluency Passage, CD 11 Track 5
- I Am Somebody, CD 3 Track 4

Edge Interactive Practice Book
- Hip-Hop as Culture, pp. 68–72
- I Am Somebody, pp. 73–76
- Further Practice, pp. 77–79

Assessments Handbook
- Reader Reflection, p. 15f
- Cluster 2 Test, pp. 15g–15i

Reteaching Activities

Writing Project Tools
- Student Samples
- Scheduler
- Rubric

Reading and Writing Transparencies
- Writing Transparencies 5-8: Position Paper

Language & Grammar Lab Teacher's Edition, pp. 26-31

Language & Grammar Lab Transparencies
- Language Function E: Describe Experiences
- Grammar Transparencies 21-25: Action Verbs in the Present

Grammar & Writing Practice Book, pp. 45–54

Language CD and MP3
- Describe Experiences, Track 5

Assessments Handbook
- Language Acquisition Rubric p. 15o

Descriptive Presentation Rubric

CLUSTER 3

Slam: Performance Poetry Lives On
Euphoria

Cluster 3 Resources
- Learn more about slam poetry
- Selection summaries in eight languages

Comprehension Coach
- Slam: Performance Poetry Lives On
- Euphoria

Reading and Writing Transparencies
- Reading Transparency 8: Connotation Chart
- Reading Transparency 9: Analyze Author's Purpose

Selection CD and MP3s
- Slam: Performance Poetry Lives On, CD 3 Track 5
- Slam: Performance Poetry Lives On: Fluency Passage, CD 11 Track 6
- Euphoria, CD 3 Track 6

Edge Interactive Practice Book
- Slam: Performance Poetry Lives On, pp. 80–84
- Euphoria, pp. 85–86
- Further Practice, pp. 87–89

Assessments Handbook
- Reader Reflection, p. 15j
- Cluster 3 Test, pp.15k–15m

Reteaching Activities

Writing Project Tools
- Student Samples
- Scheduler
- Rubric

Reading and Writing Transparencies
- Writing Transparencies 5-8: Position Paper

Language & Grammar Lab Teacher's Edition, pp. 32-37

Language & Grammar Lab Transparencies
- Language Function F: Give and Follow Commands
- Grammar Transparencies 26-30: Present Tense Verbs

Grammar & Writing Practice Book, pp. 55-64

Language CD and MP3
- Give and Follow Commands, Track 6

Assessments Handbook
- Language Acquisition Rubric p. 15o

CLOSE READING

The Creativity Crisis

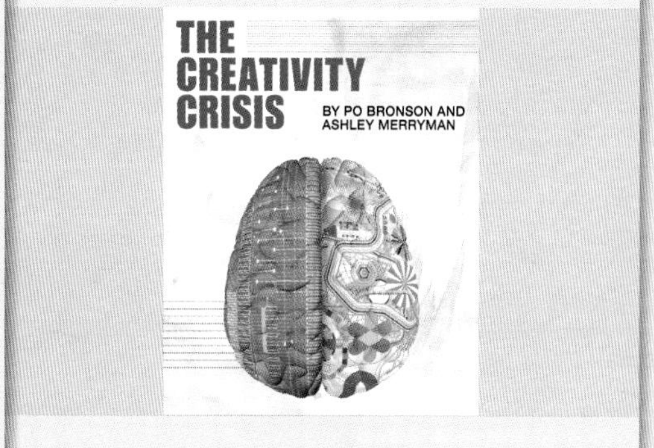

Selection CD and MP3s
- The Creativity Crisis, CD 12 Track 2

Edge Interactive Practice Book
- The Creativity Crisis, pp. 90–95

UNIT WRAP-UP

Unit Project
- Rubric

Assessments Handbook
- Reading and Literary Analysis, pp. 16–23
- Grammar and Writing, pp. 24–28
- Affective and Metacognitive Measures, pp. 105–119
- Self-Assessment: Written Composition, p. 133
- Peer Assessment: Written Composition, p. 134

Reteaching Activities

UNIT LAUNCH

OBJECTIVES

Listening and Speaking
- Classroom Discussion
- Evaluate a Speaker's Message

Viewing
- Respond to and Interpret Visuals

Cultural Perspectives
- Compare Cultures: Customs

ENGAGE & DISCUSS

A EQ Essential Question

Brainstorm and Map Define creativity as using imagination to develop new ideas. Chart how students express their creativity.
SL.9-10.1

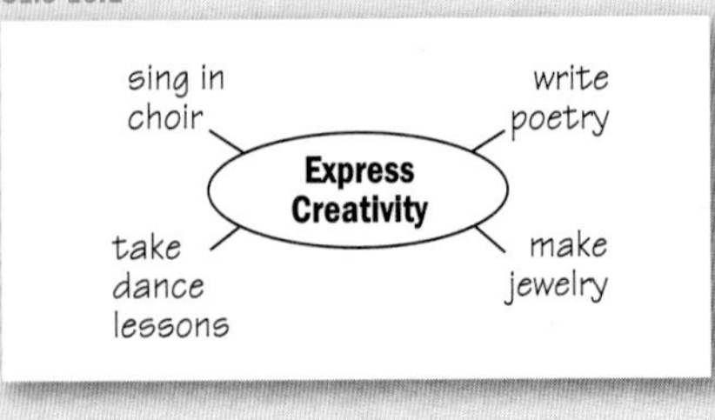

B Discuss the Quotations

Access Meaning Ask which words are most important in each quotation.

ELL Rephrase Language Explain that "keep an ear to the ground" means "pay attention to the world around you," and "keep an ear to your heart" means "listen to your feelings."

Evaluate a Speaker's Message What are Springsteen's and hooks's messages about art?

Possible response:
- *Springsteen says artists use their surroundings and feelings to create; hooks says artists also have to use their imaginations.*

Use the cooperative learning activity to explore different perspectives.
SL.9-10.1.b; SL.9-10.3

UNIT 2 **NONFICTION**

EQ **ESSENTIAL QUESTION:**

A **Does Creativity Matter?**

B

If you're an artist, you try to keep an ear to the ground and an ear to your heart.
—BRUCE SPRINGSTEEN

The function of art is to do more than tell it like it is—it's to imagine what's *possible*.
—BELL HOOKS

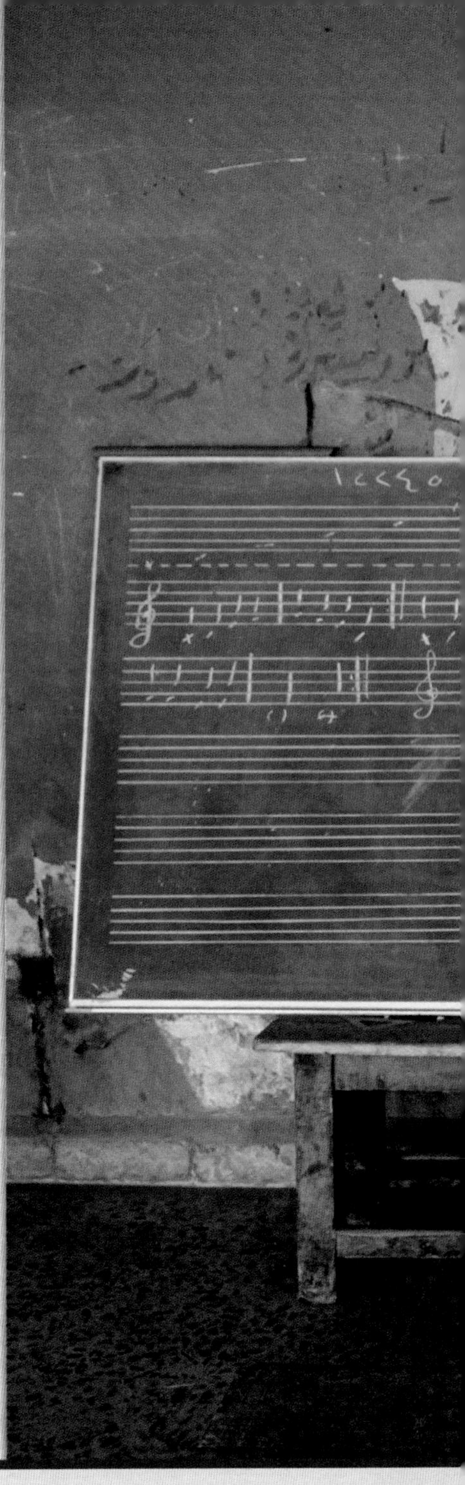

Critical Viewing
A boy practices violin at a music school in Sulaimaniya, Iraq. The school has been damaged by war, but he continues to make music there. Does his creativity matter?

110

COOPERATIVE LEARNING

Roundtable

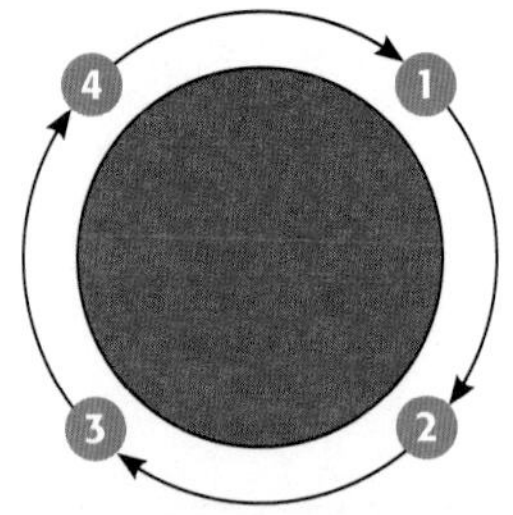

LISTENING AND SPEAKING

Evaluate a Speaker's Message

Use the Roundtable cooperative learning technique (*see the Best Practices tab*) to explore the quotations.

Discuss Form groups of four.

1. Have small groups work together to paraphrase the quotations by Bruce Springsteen and bell hooks. Work with groups to rephrase concepts, as needed.
2. Each group member pages through the book to identify a work of art, such as a painting, sculpture, or photograph, that expresses each idea.
3. Have students share and discuss their examples with the group and vote for the work that best illustrates each quotation.

Debrief Have groups share their findings with the class. Discuss:
- How does the art each group chose relate to the quotations?
- Which quotation is easier to show in a work of art?
- Does everyone respond to art in the same way? Explain.

Remind students to keep thinking about creativity and the art of expression as they read the selections and study the works of art in this unit.

CCSS **Literacy.SL.9-10.1** Initiate and participate effectively in a range of collaborative discussions (one-on-one, in groups, and teacher-led) with diverse partners on grades 9-10 topics, texts, and issues, building on others' ideas and expressing their own clearly and persuasively. **Literacy.SL.9-10.1.b** Work with peers to set rules for collegial discussions and decision-making (e.g., informal consensus, taking votes on key issues, presentation of alternate views), clear goals and deadlines, and individual roles as needed. **Literacy.SL.9-10.3** Evaluate a speaker's point of view, reasoning, and use of evidence and rhetoric, identifying any fallacious reasoning or exaggerated or distorted evidence.

ENGAGE & INTERPRET

C Critical Viewing

Observe Details Have students study the photograph. Draw their attention to details:

- What about this photograph is familiar or recognizable? What seems unfamiliar?
- What details do you notice about the boy? What do the details suggest about him?
- Can you imagine the sounds the boy is making? What are they like?

Interpret and Respond Have students consider whether the boy's creativity matters. Ask: Who do you think is listening to this boy's music? Why?

Possible responses:
- *I think the photographer is listening because she is inspired by his music.*
- *I think the boy's teacher or parents are listening because they want him to improve.*
- *I think the boy is playing for anyone who may pass by and will hear him. His music matters because it makes the environment more beautiful.*

D About the Photograph

Sulaimaniya is a city in the Kurdish region of Iraq, where wars have left a path of destroyed buildings. Still, the city remains an important cultural center and is considered by some to be the birthplace of modern Kurdish music. The boy in the photo and his classmates attend a crumbling music school where a single teacher instructs the hundred students for a minimal fee.

Interpret and Respond Have students think about how background information about Sulaimaniya has changed their answer to the Critical Viewing question.

Ask: Now that you know more about the history of Sulaimaniya, is your opinion about the boy's creativity different? If so, how?

Possible responses:
- *The boy's creativity seems more important knowing the history of violence in his city.*
- *The boy's creativity seems less unique knowing that it is part of a tradition in his community.*

CULTURAL PERSPECTIVES

Beliefs About Creativity

Explore how different cultures view creativity.

Collect Ideas Have students complete the following sentence frames:

In [name a culture to explore] …

- creativity is considered to be ______.
- ______ is considered to be the most important form of art.
- artists are treated as ______ people. For example, ______.
- all young women are expected to learn how to ______.
- all young men are expected to learn how to ______.

Compare Perspectives As a class, discuss the similarities and differences among the cultural perspectives. Be sure to discuss the roles of art and artists in society.

UNIT LAUNCH

OBJECTIVES

Listening and Speaking
- Debate

Viewing
- Analyze Design
- Analyze Meaning and Message

ENGAGE & DEBATE

EQ Essential Question

Students analyze the work of art and debate whether the creative arts are a luxury or a necessity in people's lives.

A Study the Painting

If students need help analyzing the work, preteach the Research Skills activity below. Then read the introductory paragraph with students. Ask:

- Why do you think an artist would paint cans of soup?
- Do you think paintings of soup cans should be called "art"?

Have students read the last sentence. Ask:

- Does it surprise you that one of Warhol's soup can paintings sold for so much money? Why or why not?

B Analyze and Debate

Have students respond in writing to the two questions.

ELL Sentence Frames Provide sentence frames to help ELLs respond:

1. Paintings like Warhol's are/are not creative because ______.
2. People need/do not need the arts in their lives because ______.

Then debate the questions in small groups. Have students share their ideas, supporting their ideas with evidence from the art and their own experiences.
SL.9-10.4

ONGOING ASSESSMENT
Have students complete this sentence: One reason that creativity is important to some people is that it ______.

UNIT 2

EQ ESSENTIAL QUESTION: Does Creativity Matter?

Study the Painting

A famous artist named Andy Warhol spent many years in the 1960s painting realistic images of canned soup, which he ate for lunch almost every day. Today, these paintings are displayed in important museums around the world and are considered very valuable. In May 2006, one of his soup can paintings was sold for $11,776,000. Study an example of Warhol's work.

A

Woman Admiring Andy Warhol's Campbell's Soup Cans, 2010, Museum of Modern Art, New York, New York, USA, Judie Long. Photograph ©Judie Long/Alamy.

Analyze and Debate

B

1. Art collectors believe that Warhol's paintings are important works of creativity. What do *you* think?
2. People express their creativity in many ways, including art, film, music, writing, dance, and more. Is creativity something that is necessary for society to survive? Or, is it something "extra" that we can live without?

With a small group, explain your opinions to others who may have a different point of view. Defend your ideas with reasons and examples from your own experience.

EQ ESSENTIAL QUESTION
In this unit, you will explore the **Essential Question** in class through reading, discussion, research, and writing. Keep thinking about the question outside of school, too.

RESEARCH SKILLS

Interpreting Paintings

Teach/Model Explain that when analyzing a painting or group of paintings, it can be useful to look at all of the elements individually: the colors, the composition (or arrangement), and the subject. Use subject as an example:

- The subject of the painting is soup cans.
- The can is repeated 32 times, but not all the cans have the same label.
- The cans are painted realistically.
- The subject is a common, everyday object.

Practice Discuss other elements of the group of paintings.

Apply Ask these questions about the group of paintings:

1. Which element—color, subject matter, or composition—makes the strongest statement to you? Explain.
2. What is the effect of the repetition of a single image?
3. How would the effect of the paintings be different if the cans were scattered around in no particular order?
4. What comment about modern culture do you think the artist is making?

Have students research more works by Warhol and answer these four questions about them.
W.9-10.7

CCSS **Literacy.W.9-10.7** Conduct short as well as more sustained research projects to answer a question (including a self-generated question) or solve a problem; narrow or broaden the inquiry when appropriate; synthesize multiple sources on the subject, demonstrating understanding of the subject under investigation. **Literacy.SL.9-10.4** Present information, findings, and supporting evidence clearly, concisely, and logically such that listeners can follow the line of reasoning and the organization, development, substance, and style are appropriate to purpose, audience, and task.

Plan a Project

Demonstration

In this unit, you will be giving a demonstration that relates to the Essential Question. Choose something creative to demonstrate, such as dancing, painting, or preparing a special food. To get started, choose an activity you enjoy and know about. Then think about

- steps needed to demonstrate the process
- materials or equipment you will need
- information and ideas you want to present.

Study Skills Start planning your demonstration. Use the forms on myNGconnect.com to plan your time and to prepare the content.

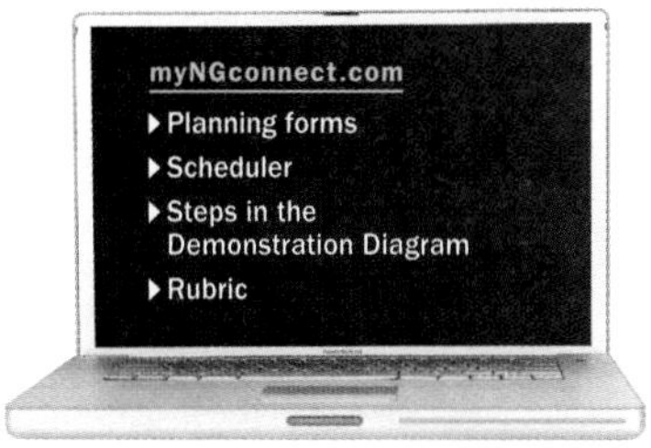

Choose More to Read

These readings provide different answers to the Essential Question. Choose a book and online selections to read during the unit.

Hole in My Life
by Jack Gantos

Jack wanted a writer's life of adventure and excitement. But instead of traveling around the world, he went to prison for smuggling drugs. By making the biggest mistake of his life, did Jack ruin his dream forever? Or did prison help him see what was really important?

▶ NONFICTION

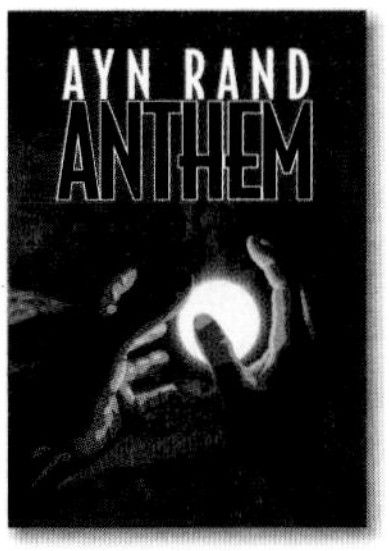

Anthem
by Ayn Rand

It is the future. Society as we know it was destroyed long ago. There is no "I" in this new society, only "we." But Equality 7-2521 seeks knowledge. Can he survive in a society that considers individual thought and creativity a crime?

▶ NOVEL

The Stone Goddess
by Minfong Ho

Cambodian sisters Nakri and Teeda love to dance. But life changes when a cruel rebel army takes control of Cambodia. The new government punishes Cambodians who dance. How will Nakri and Teeda survive when everything they love is at risk?

▶ NOVEL

myNGconnect.com

- **Read biographies of people who have found unique ways to express their creativity.**
- **Visit galleries of art, poetry, and music created by teens.**
- **Use programs that help you create your own artistic expressions.**

UNIT PROJECT & MORE TO READ

OBJECTIVES

Reading Behaviors
- Read Independently

Study Skill
- Use Writing as a Tool

Listening and Speaking
- Demonstration

1 Plan a Project

Demonstration Ask students about creative demonstrations they've seen:

- Did the demonstration follow steps? What were they?
- What information or ideas were presented during the demonstration?

Assign project groups and review the Unit Project Evaluation Rubric and other Project Tools (*available online*). Have groups follow these steps:

1. Choose an activity to demonstrate.
2. Decide what steps and/or materials are needed.
3. Brainstorm and write the information you want to present.

Project Support Teach the Study Skills lesson below.
SL.9-10.1.b

2 Choose More to Read

Guide students toward an independent reading choice from the **Edge Library**.

- ***Hole in My Life*** Lexile® 840L
- ***Anthem*** Lexile® 880L
- ***The Stone Goddess*** Lexile® 1020L

(Some titles may contain mature themes. Be sure to preview the books before assigning them to students.)

Distribute **Student Journals** and have students complete the time-management planning form on p. 1.
RL.9-10.10; RI.9-10.10

myNGconnect.com

- **Unit Project Planning Tools**
- **Unit Project Evaluation Rubric**
- **Edge Library Student Journals and Teacher's Guides**

STUDY SKILLS

Use Writing as a Tool

Help students use writing as a tool to build an effective presentation. Have them engage in the following writing activities to prepare for their demonstration:

1. List all the steps in the demonstration as if they were explaining it to a person who has never done it before. Include descriptions of materials and definitions of unfamiliar vocabulary.
2. Imagine giving the presentation, and write an interior monologue of the thoughts a person might have during each step.
3. Write out a step-by-step process for the demonstration, and highlight all the verbs.

Encourage students to use the writing they generate from these activities to help them plan their demonstration.

CCSS **Literacy RL.9-10.10** By the end of grade 9, read and comprehend literature, including stories, dramas, and poems, in the grades 9-10 text complexity band proficiently, with scaffolding as needed at the high end of the range. By the end of grade 10, read and comprehend literature, including stories, dramas, and poems, at the high end of the grades 9-10 text complexity band independently and proficiently. **Literacy RI.9-10.10** By the end of grade 9, read and comprehend literary nonfiction in the grades 9-10 text complexity band proficiently, with scaffolding as needed at the high end of the range. By the end of grade 10, read and comprehend literary nonfiction at the high end of the grades 9-10 text complexity band independently and proficiently. **Literacy.SL.9-10.1.b** Work with peers to set rules for collegial discussions and decision-making (e.g., informal consensus, taking votes on key issues, presentation of alternate views), clear goals and deadlines, and individual roles as needed.

OBJECTIVES

Vocabulary
- Academic Vocabulary

Reading Strategy
- Determine Importance: Identify Main Ideas and Details; Review Strategies

Literary Analysis
- Analyze Nonfiction: Author's Purpose (T)

Listening and Speaking
- Conversation and Classroom Discussion

ENGAGE & CONNECT

Nonfiction

In this lesson, students read three nonfiction texts about the same topic, examining details in each text to determine the author's purpose and main ideas. They then cite these details to show the type of information the author uses to support his or her purpose.

Introduce Genre

Engage students by asking about nonfiction topics that interest them.

- What types of nonfiction topics do you enjoy reading about? For example: historical events, people's life stories.
- Why are these topics useful or interesting to you?

Encourage students to share examples and name sources readers can use to learn about the topics.

(A) Focus on Demo Text

Preview Read each topic sentence to preview the Demo Text.

Read Students read Demo Text 1, Demo Text 2, and Demo Text 3.

ELL **Access Text** Read the Demo Texts aloud, rephrasing difficult words and demonstrating actions.

- Rephrase: *canvases* (cloth-like surfaces for painting), *stunned* (amazed), *studio* (artist's workplace)
- Demonstrate: *back and forth, dipping, flinging*

HOW TO READ NONFICTION

Genre Focus
Kinds of Nonfiction

One of the challenges of nonfiction is that there are so many kinds. Experienced readers approach each kind in a different way. Read these three nonfiction texts. Think about how the same topic works in each one.

DEMO TEXT #1

Lee Krasner first met Jackson Pollock in 1941. Like Pollock, she was a painter living and working in New York City. One day, she saw Pollock's canvases. "How could there be a painter like that who I didn't know about?" she wondered. Immediately recognizing his talent, she knew she had to meet him. As the two artists got to know one another, they soon fell in love. Four years later, they were married. The couple moved to the east end of Long Island and settled into a peaceful life on a farm. It was here that Jackson Pollock created the unusual paintings that made him famous. As for Lee, she became known as one of the best abstract painters of her generation.

(A)

DEMO TEXT #2

In the middle of the 20th century, a group of young artists in New York created a style that stunned the world. These painters brought new ideas to painting. They decided that a painting did not have to be a picture of something. A painting could just be colors and shapes. They also decided that a painting should show how the artist had put paint on the surface. If the artist used a brush, the viewer should see the brushstrokes.

The best-known artist in the group was Jackson Pollock. He won fame creating paintings by dripping paint onto canvas. The new style of art that he and these other young artists developed is often called *action painting.*

DEMO TEXT #3

Jackson Pollock is one of the greatest painters of all time. The way Pollock worked was truly amazing. He would run back and forth beside a huge canvas on the floor, dipping a brush in a can and flinging paint at the canvas. His method seems incredibly original. What other artist ever painted like that before? It is truly amazing to behold. He looks more like an athlete than an artist. Watching him surely would make anyone excited about the process of creating art.

OUT-OF-SCHOOL LITERACY

Media Literacies

Discuss various forms of nonfiction and differences in the type of information they provide; reminding students that authors chooses a form, based on their purpose for writing

- A **newspaper article** gives facts like *who, where, when, why,* and *how* about an event.
- An **autobiography** or **biography** tells the life story of a person through facts and real events.
- A film or television **documentary** gives history about a topic, usually focuses on a current dilemma that involves the topic, and shows ways the topic is relevant to viewers.
- **Web sites** provide factual information about a particular topic, sometimes in the form of visuals such as lists, charts, or graphs. There may be links to other sites, including sources of the factual information.

Have partners share information about a nonfiction topic they viewed or read about recently. Ask them to identify the main idea and tell if they think the purpose was to inform, entertain, persuade, or express personal feelings. Invite pairs to share key ideas from their discussion with the class. SL.9-10.1

CCSS Literacy.SL.9-10.1 Initiate and participate effectively in a range of collaborative discussions (one-on-one, in groups, and teacher-led) with diverse partners on grades 9-10 topics, texts, and issues, building on others' ideas and expressing their own clearly and persuasively.

Connect Reading to Your Life

Each of the following sentences belongs with one of the preceding Demo Texts. With a partner, figure out which sentences go with which texts.

Reading Strategies
- Plan and Monitor
- ▶ **Determine Importance**
- Make Inferences
- Ask Questions
- Make Connections
- Synthesize
- Visualize

	Demo Text #1	Demo Text #2	Demo Text #3
1. Action painting was an important art style throughout the 1950s.			
2. Some people say that Jackson Pollock's paintings are nothing special, but I disagree.			
3. Krasner worked hard to promote her husband's career.			

Focus Strategy ▶ Determine Importance

In the activity you just completed, your purpose was to match sentences with the Demo Texts. So you looked for important details in the sentences to help you.

You do this kind of thinking all the time in your life. Suppose that you're driving to Centerville. You see many road signs, but you only need to pay attention to the ones that point to Centerville. Experienced readers know that they can't pay attention to *everything* as they read. They only keep track of the important details.

Your Job as a Reader

What is important depends on why you are reading. You might, for example, be reading to prepare for a test. Then you need to determine what the author **emphasizes**, or says is important, and remember that. Or, you might be reading in order to solve a problem with a computer. In that case, you need to determine what is important to solving *your* problem. Your job as a reader of nonfiction is to know *why* you are reading and to determine what is important to help you meet your purpose.

Academic Vocabulary
- **emphasize** *v.*, to give special importance to, to stress; **emphasis** *n.*, special importance, force, stress

ACADEMIC VOCABULARY

Make Word Maps Present the Academic Vocabulary words. Have students make a Word Map for each.

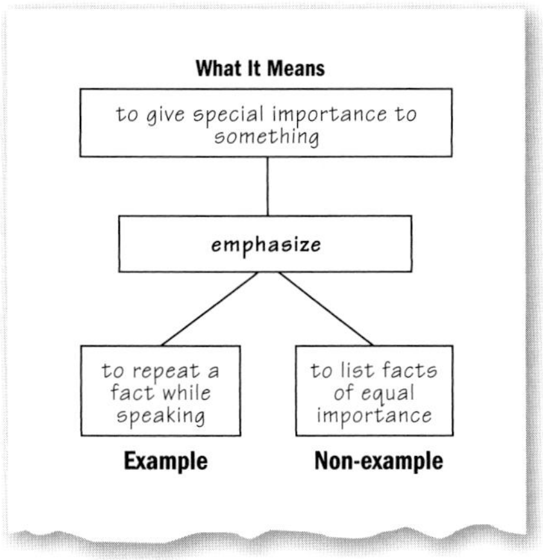

1. Write the word in the center. Write what it means in the top box. Give an example and a non-example in the boxes below.
2. Use a dictionary to check the information in your map.
3. Keep your Word Maps in a vocabulary notebook.

L.9-10.6

ENGAGE & CONNECT

B Connect Reading to Your Life

Have students connect the selections and the strategy to their own lives by identifying their response to the text. Ask: Which text did you find most interesting? What details in the text stood out to you?

Have students work in pairs to identify the Demo Text that each statement matches. Encourage them to use details from the text and their own reasoning to explain their responses.

Focus Strategy: Determine Importance
Read this section with students. Use the activity below to teach the Academic Vocabulary in this unit. Ask:

- How do you know which signs to pay attention to when you are driving?
- What are some ways you decide which parts of reading you need to pay attention to?

RI.9-10.2

Review Strategies Remind students that they use a variety of strategies as they read the text. Have students share a strategy they used when they read the Demo Texts.

Possible response:
- *While I read Demo Text I, I asked questions about how the text was organized. I realized that the sentences were organized in the order of events. This helped me realize that the text was narrative.*

RI.9-10.10

TEACH STRATEGIES

C Your Job as a Reader

Explain that good readers identify the purpose of reading a text and determine which details are important in meeting this purpose. Point out that students already are practicing this strategy when they identify statements that reflect main ideas of texts.

CCSS **Literacy.RI.9-10.2** Determine a central idea of a text and analyze its development over the course of the text, including how it emerges and is shaped and refined by specific details; provide an objective summary of the text. **Literacy.RI.9-10.10** By the end of grade 9, read and comprehend literary nonfiction in the grades 9–10 text complexity band proficiently, with scaffolding as needed at the high end of the range. By the end of grade 10, read and comprehend literary nonfiction at the high end of the grades 9–10 text complexity band independently and proficiently. **Literacy.L.9-10.6** Acquire and use accurately general academic and domain-specific words and phrases, sufficient for reading, writing, speaking, and listening at the college and career readiness level; demonstrate independence in gathering vocabulary knowledge when considering a word or phrase important to comprehension or expression.

TEACH STRATEGIES

Unpack the Thinking Process

Remind students of the nonfiction elements discussed on p. 115: different nonfiction texts and important details.

Read through and discuss kinds of nonfiction and author's purpose.

A Determine the Kind of Nonfiction Reread the first few sentences in each Demo Text on p. 114. Discuss the details in these sentences that provide clues about the type and purpose of the text.

Demo Text 1 Ask: Who is this text about? Have students identify names in the first sentence. Then ask: What do readers learn about these people's lives? In what order are the events presented?

Demo Text 2 Have students identify formal words and phrases from the text. Ask: What topic does this text explain?

Demo Text 3 Ask: What opinion words appear in this text? What main opinion does the text express?

B Determine Author's Purpose Read the examples of author's purposes and types of text in the first two columns. In the third column, have students identify the Demo Text that matches each purpose and type of text.

PURPOSE: The author chooses the type of nonfiction based on his or her purpose.

Purpose and Text: The author of Demo Text 1 wrote a biography, because the focus was on the life of Lee Krasner rather than her work or the type of art she created. An author wishing to focus on artistic technique, on the other hand, would probably choose to write expository nonfiction.

Unpack the Thinking Process

Determine the Kind of Nonfiction

When you read the Demo Texts, you were probably looking to see what was different about each text. Try looking at what the sentences are mostly about.

A

- **Demo Text #1:** The sentences tell a story about people. The events are told in time order. This usually means that the nonfiction text is a **narrative**. Its purpose is to tell a story—a biography—of a real person or group of people.
- **Demo Text #2:** These sentences sound pretty formal: "new style of art" and "best-known artist." Because they give facts and explain things, they are clues that the text is **expository**—or written to inform. Other clues include graphs, tables, and headings.
- **Demo Text #3:** Words like "one of the greatest" and "truly amazing" show strong opinions. The many opinions are clues that the nonfiction is an **argument**—written to argue a position.

Doing this is just like what you do when you go into a new store or restaurant. If you walk into a fast-food restaurant, you know that you have to go up to the counter and place your order. If you go into a fancier restaurant, you know that a waiter will come to take your order. It's the same principle with reading: if you know what kind of writing you're dealing with, you can figure out how to read it more effectively.

Determine Author's Purpose

There's another way to determine the kind of nonfiction you're about to read: figure out the **author's purpose**. Here are some of the most common purposes for writing nonfiction. Which Demo Text matches each purpose?

B

Author's Purpose	Type of Text	Demo Text #
To narrate	Narrative	
To explain	Expository	
To argue	Argument	

Elements of Literature
narrative *adj.*, that tells a story
expository *adj.*, that informs and explains
argument *n.*, a stated opinion or position defended with reasons
author's purpose *n.*, the reason an author has for writing a text

Determine What's Important

You've just learned some ways to approach nonfiction as you're reading. You pay attention to the kind of nonfiction it is, why the author wrote it, and your purpose for reading. But then what? The goal of determining importance as you read is to focus on important information. And how do you do that? You **summarize**. Here's one way to do that:

How to Summarize	
1. Tell what the passage is mostly about (the topic).	action painting
2. Tell what the passage is mostly saying about the topic.	how it brought new life to art
3. Combine your ideas into a complete sentence. Add details to make it complete.	Action painting, especially by Jackson Pollock, brought new life to art in the middle of the twentieth century.

C

Try an Experiment

Read this passage about the art world.

DEMO TEXT #4

Action painting is a unique style which began in New York around 1950. Unlike many other artistic styles, action painting does not require mastery of skills, such as showing perspective or rendering light. Instead, artists are concerned with the physical act of painting. They drip, splash, and splatter paint on a canvas. Jackson Pollock, the most famous of the action painters, even rode a bicycle across some of his canvases. Although these techniques were unusual, action painting played an important role in American art.

1. **Think:** What type of information is in this text? What is the author's purpose in writing it?
2. **Pair:** What is the main idea of the passage? Summarize it with a partner.
3. **Share:** Share your summary sentence with the class. Compare main ideas.

D

Monitor Comprehension

Expository Nonfiction
How can you tell when you're reading this kind of text?

Academic Vocabulary

- **summarize** *v.*, to briefly give the main points, to sum up; **summary** *n.*, a short statement that gives the main points

TEACH STRATEGIES

C Determine What's Important

Explain To recognize important ideas in texts, readers identify the type of nonfiction and why the author wrote it, and their own purposes for reading. After readers identify important ideas in a text, it is helpful to summarize them. Tell students they will learn and practice these strategies during this unit.

APPLY

D Try an Experiment

Have students read Demo Text 4.

Think, Pair, Share Students work in pairs to discuss and respond to the questions.

Discuss the questions as a class.

Possible responses:

1. *This is expository nonfiction. The author's purpose is to inform readers about action painting.*
2. *The main idea of the passage is that action painting involves unusual techniques and played an important role in American art.*

RI.9-10.6

Monitor Comprehension

Possible responses:

- *formal language that explains a topic; text may be labeled with headings*
- *might include graphs, tables, and other visuals*

DIFFERENTIATED INSTRUCTION

Teach Literary Elements As you teach the selections in this unit, use these strategies to meet students' individual needs.

Struggling Readers

Text Scanning Help students scan text for details that suggest nonfiction text type. Ask:

- What names and facts are in topic sentences?
- What visuals do texts contain?
- What opinion words do you see? (*awful, wonderful*)

Remind students of the types of nonfiction and reading purposes these clues signal.

English Language Learners ELL

Rephrase Language Rephrase heads to identify text organization and information.

- p. 123, "Pushing the Limits": passing limits or challenging them
- p. 145, "The Hip-Hop Influence": ways hip-hop music has changed people and culture
- p. 168, "Beating to the Sound of the Times": reciting poetry with a rhythm from the historical style called Beat poetry

Challenge

Compare and Contrast Provide language for students to use in comparing and contrasting the accomplishments and experiences of artists described in the articles:

- compare: both, similar, the same
- contrast: differ, dissimilar, vary, unlike

ONGOING ASSESSMENT

Have partners use the chart on p. 117 to summarize important information for each nonfiction selection in this unit.

CCSS **Literacy.RI.9-10.6** Determine an author's point of view or purpose in a text and analyze how an author uses rhetoric to advance that point of view or purpose.

UNIT 2 Cluster 1 Planner

EQ ESSENTIAL QUESTION:

Does Creativity Matter?

Consider ways to express your creativity.

Online Planner
myNGconnect.com

	LESSON 3 **Prepare to Read**	LESSON 4 **Creativity at Work** Main Selection
Reading		
Reading Strategies Focus Strategy **Determine Importance**	**Activate Prior Knowledge** SL.9-10.1 • Make a Connection: Anticipation Guide *T118*	**Determine Importance** RI.9-10.2 • Identify Main Ideas and Details *T119, T122–T127*
Literary Analysis Genre Focus **Kinds of Nonfiction**		**Analyze Author's Purpose** RI.9-10.6 *T119, T122–T127* **Recognize Author/Illustrator's Style** • Cartoonists' Inspiration *T120*
Vocabulary	**Key Vocabulary** RI.9-10.4; L.9-10.4.c; L.9-10.6 • Introduce *T118* career, collaborate, • commitment, • evaluate, expectation, • insight, talent, • transform	**Key Vocabulary** L.9-10.6 • Daily Routines *T123* • Link to Essential Question *T125* • Selection Reading *T122–T127* career, collaborate, • commitment, expectation, talent, • transform
Fluency		**Phrasing** RI.9-10.10 • Daily Routines *T123* **Accuracy and Rate** RI.9-10.10 Comprehension Coach *T121*
Writing		
Response to Literature		**Return to the Text** W.9-10.9.b; W.9-10.10 • **Reread and Write** Why do the students at AFH want and need to express themselves through art? *T127*
Writing Across the Curriculum		
Language		
ELL **Language Development**	**Describe People, Places, and Things** SL.9-10.4 • Language and Grammar Lab, Transparency D *LAB TE p. 20*	**Describe People, Places, and Things** SL.9-10.4 • Daily Routines *LAB TE p. 20*
Grammar Grammar Focus **Subject Pronouns**		**Subject Pronouns: *I, You, He*** *T124* L.9-10.1 **Subject Pronouns: *We, You, They*** *T126* L.9-10.1
Listening and Speaking	**Partner Talk** SL.9-10.1 • Ideas About Creativity *T118*	**Listen to a Selection** RI.9-10.10 Comprehension Coach *T121* *CD 3, Track 1*

T = Tested on Cluster and/or Unit Reading and Literary Analysis Test
T = Tested on Language Acquisition Assessment
T = Tested on Unit Writing Test
T = Assessed with a Rubric
• **Academic Vocabulary**

SELECTION SUMMARIES

Creativity at Work

Genre: News Article Lexile® 1020L

A nonprofit organization, Artists for Humanity, creates employment in the visual arts for public high school students who complete an apprenticeship. Teen artists at AFH learn skills to help them achieve their future career goals.

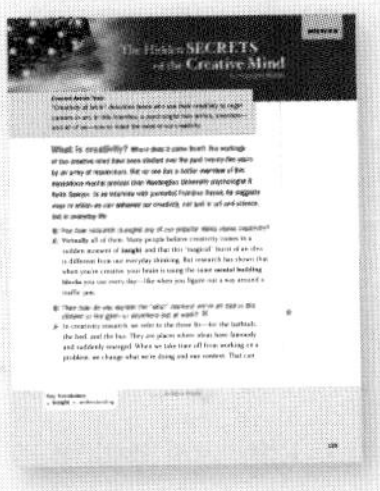

The Hidden Secrets of the Creative Mind

Genre: Interview Lexile® 980L

In this interview, psychologist and creativity researcher, R. Keith Sawyer explains ways to enhance the creative process. Drawing on new revelations about how the brain works, Sawyer explains that by using simple techniques, anyone can be creative.

LESSON 5 The Hidden Secrets of the Creative Mind	LESSON 6 Reflect and Assess	LESSONS 7 & 8 Integrate the Language Arts	LESSONS 9 & 10 Workshops
Determine Importance RI.9-10.2 • Identify Main Idea and Details *T128, T129–T132*	**Comprehension and Critical Thinking** RI.9-10.1; RI.9-10.10 *T133* • Compare Across Texts • Analyze, Interpret, Compare, Generalize, Draw Conclusions		
Analyze Development of Ideas RI.9-10.3 • Interview *T128, T129–T132*	**Interpret and Evaluate Literature** RI.9-10.10 **Use Text Evidence** RI.9-10.1 *T133*	**Analyze Description** RI.9-10.4 *T134*	
Key Vocabulary L.9-10.6 • Selection Reading *T129–T132* • evaluate • insight	**Key Vocabulary** L.9-10.6 • Review *T133* career, collaborate, • commitment, • evaluate, expectation, • insight, talent, • transform	**Vocabulary Strategy** L.9-10.4.a • Use Context Clues *T135*	**Vocabulary Workshop: Use Context Clues** L.9-10.4.a; L.9-10.4.d **Vocabulary Strategy** • Use Context Clues *T137*
Phrasing RI.9-10.10 • Daily Routines *T123* **Accuracy and Rate** RI.9-10.10 Comprehension Coach *T129*	**Phrasing** RI.9-10.10 • Peer Assessment *T133*		
Return to the Text RI.9-10.2; W.9-10.9; W.9-10.10 • **Reread and Write** Choose one question and answer from the interview. What was the main idea? *T132*	**Write About Literature** W.9-10.1 • **Opinion Paragraph** Have your thoughts and ideas about creativity changed? *T133*	**Writing on Demand for Tests** W.9-10.1 • **Test Essay** *T135*	
Research and Writing W.9-10.7 • **Art Connection** *T131*		**Research and Diagram** W.9-10.6; W.9-10.7; SL.9-10.5 • **Parts of the Brain** *T135*	**Workplace Workshop: Inside an Art Museum** W.9-10.7; W.9-10.10 **Research and Writing** • Research Jobs in Art Museums *T136*
Describe People, Places, and Things SL.9-10.4 • Daily Routines *LAB TE p. 20*		**Describe People, Places and Things** SL.9-10.4 • Pair Talk *T134*	
Pronouns in a Compound Subject *T128* L.9-10.1.b **Pronoun Agreement** *T130* L.9-10.1		**Subject Pronouns** *T134* L.9-10.1	
Listen to a Selection RI.9-10.10 Comprehension Coach *T129* *CD 3, Track 2*	**Participate in a Discussion** *T133* SL.9-10.1	**Interview** *T134* SL.9-10.4 **Oral Presentation** *T135* W.9-10.6; W.9-10.7; SL.9-10.5	

EDGE LIBRARY

Hole in My Life ●
by Jack Gantos

The Stone Goddess ● ●
by Minfong Ho

Anthem ● ● ●
by Ayn Rand

Lesson 3

PREPARE TO READ

OBJECTIVES

Vocabulary
- Key Vocabulary Ⓣ
- Strategy: Use Cognates; Use Reference Sources (thesaurus)
- Synonyms

Reading Strategy
- Activate Prior Knowledge

ELL Language & Grammar Lab

Language Function Transparency D
Describe People, Places, and Things Ⓣ

ENGAGE & CONNECT

Ⓐ EQ Essential Question

Focus on Creative Expression Ask: What are some ways that people can express their creativity?

Possible responses:
- *take photos, write plays, or play music*
- *build furniture or customize a car*

Ⓑ Make a Connection

Have students complete the Anticipation Guide and then compare their ideas about creativity with a partner.
SL.9-10.1

TEACH VOCABULARY

Ⓒ Learn Key Vocabulary

Study the Words Review the four steps of the Make Words Your Own routine (*see the Vocabulary tab*):

1. **Pronounce** Say a word and have students repeat it. Write the word in syllables and pronounce it, one syllable at a time: *ex-pec-ta-tion.* Ask what looks familiar in the word, and point out other forms, such as *expect.*

   ELL Use cognates to help Spanish speakers with the words (*see the Vocabulary tab*).

2. **Study Examples** Read the example in the chart. Provide more examples: Are *expectations* about the past or the future?

PREPARE TO READ

▸ Creativity at Work
▸ The Hidden Secrets of the Creative Mind

Ⓐ EQ Does Creativity Matter?

Consider ways to express your creativity.

Ⓑ Make a Connection

Anticipation Guide Think about all the ways that people express creativity, such as art, music, poetry, and drama. Then tell whether you agree or disagree with these statements. After reading the selections, see if you feel the same way.

ANTICIPATION GUIDE	Agree or Disagree
1. Creativity is important in everyday life.	_______
2. You are either born creative, or you're not.	_______
3. Some kinds of art are better than others.	_______
4. Students should be required to take a class like art or music.	_______

Ⓒ Learn Key Vocabulary

Study the Words Pronounce each word and learn its meaning. You may also want to look up the definitions in the Glossary.

• Academic Vocabulary

Key Words	Examples
career (ku-**rear**) *noun* ▸ page 122	A **career** is the kind of work a person does. The artist began her **career** by drawing comics in high school.
collaborate (ku-**lab**-u-rāt) *verb* ▸ pages 122, 133	To **collaborate** is to work together with one or more people on a specific task or project. My friends and I **collaborate** on group projects for class. 
• **commitment** (ku-**mit**-munt) *noun* ▸ page 123	You show your **commitment** by continuing to work on something, even when it is difficult. He shows his **commitment** to work by coming early every day.
• **evaluate** (i-**val**-ū-āt) *verb* ▸ page 131	When you **evaluate** something, you decide how good or valuable it is. The teacher will **evaluate** your presentation and then give you a final grade.
expectation (ek-spek-**tā**-shun) *noun* ▸ pages 122, 127	**Expectations** are beliefs about how things will turn out. If you have high **expectations,** you expect something to turn out well.
• **insight** (**in**-sīt) *noun* ▸ pages 129, 132, 133	When you have **insight,** you have a new or special understanding about something. The instruction sheet gave me **insight** into how to use the machine.
talent (**tal**-unt) *noun* ▸ page 124	Having **talent** means showing special ability or skill. She has a wonderful **talent** in music. 
• **transform** (trans-**form**) *verb* ▸ page 125	To **transform** something means to change it in an important way, or completely. I **transformed** my sketch into a painting.

Practice the Words Work with a partner to find synonyms for each of the Key Vocabulary words. Use a thesaurus for ideas.

Example: *Career = job, work, profession*

---

3. **Encourage Elaboration** Provide a sentence frame: *Teachers usually have expectations that their students will* ______.

4. **Practice the Words** Have students determine synonyms and alternate word choices for each Key Word by using a thesaurus. For example: *If you have high* ***hopes,*** *you expect something to turn out well.*
L.9-10.4.c

Edge Interactive Practice Book, pp. 56–57
RI.9-10.4; L.9-10.6

ONGOING ASSESSMENT
Have students complete an oral sentence for each word. For example: *Someone with* _______ *understands others' feelings.*

CCSS **Literacy.RI.9-10.4** Determine the meaning of words and phrases as they are used in a text, including figurative, connotative, and technical meanings; analyze the cumulative impact of specific word choices on meaning and tone (e.g., how the language of a court opinion differs from that of a newspaper). **Literacy.SL.9-10.1** Initiate and participate effectively in a range of collaborative discussions (one-on-one, in groups, and teacher-led) with diverse partners on grades 9-10 topics, texts, and issues, building on others' ideas and expressing their own clearly and persuasively. **Literacy.L.9-10.4.c** Consult general and specialized reference materials (e.g., dictionaries, glossaries, thesauruses), both print and digital, to find the pronunciation of a word or determine or clarify its precise meaning, its part of speech, or its etymology. **Literacy.L.9-10.6** Acquire and use accurately general academic and domain-specific words and phrases, sufficient for reading, writing, speaking, and listening at the college and career readiness level; demonstrate independence in gathering vocabulary knowledge when considering a word or phrase important to comprehension or expression.

BEFORE READING Creativity at Work

news article by Abe Louise Young

Reading Strategies

- Plan and Monitor
- ▶ **Determine Importance**
- Make Inferences
- Ask Questions
- Make Connections
- Synthesize
- Visualize

Analyze Author's Purpose

The purpose of a **news article** is to give information. The author describes people, places, and events using facts and supporting details from reliable sources.

Look Into the Text

Headlines and heads catch the reader's attention and give clues about the information in a section.

PUSHING THE LIMITS

The program began in 1991 as a collaboration between Susan Rodgerson—a white, middle-class artist—and five African American teen friends who started painting in her studio. The friends needed to sell their artwork in order to buy supplies and make more art. Sheer economics inspired an entrepreneurial zeal, and they approached Boston colleges, nonprofits, and corporations as potential customers. An audience was found and a program bloomed—with youth at the helm.

Details answer the 5Ws: *Who?, What?, Where? When?,* and *Why?* Which answers can you find?

D

Focus Strategy ▶ Determine Importance

A news article is filled with a lot of information and ideas, but not every fact has the same importance as others. As you read each paragraph, look for the important facts and details. They can help you identify the writer's most important idea.

Focus Strategy

HOW TO IDENTIFY MAIN IDEAS AND DETAILS

1. **Find the Important Details** Add them to a **5Ws Chart**.
2. **State the Main Idea** Ask yourself: If the author could say only one general thing in this paragraph, what would it be? Sometimes, this is very clear. Other times, it is implied, or hinted. In these cases, look at all the facts and say the idea in a few of your own words.

5Ws Chart

Who?	What?	Where?
Name the people.	Name the topic.	Name the location.

Why?	When?
Name the reason.	Name the time period.

Main Idea

State the topic and make a comment on what the author is saying about it.

E

Reading Transparency 5

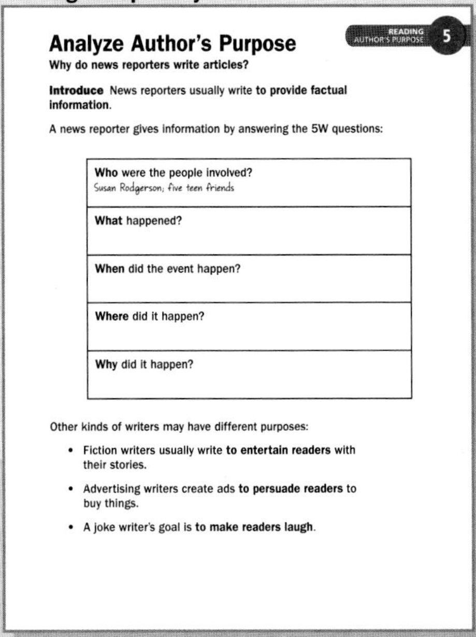
READING AUTHOR'S PURPOSE 5

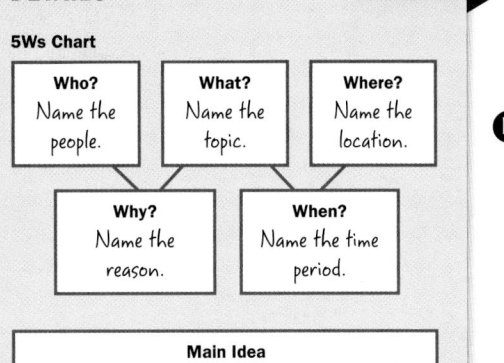

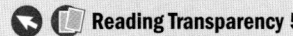

Analyze Author's Purpose

Why do news reporters write articles?

Introduce News reporters usually write **to provide factual information.**

A news reporter gives information by answering the 5W questions:

Who were the people involved? Susan Rodgerson; five teen friends
What happened?
When did the event happen?
Where did it happen?
Why did it happen?

Other kinds of writers may have different purposes:

- Fiction writers usually write **to entertain readers** with their stories.
- Advertising writers create ads **to persuade readers** to buy things.
- A joke writer's goal is **to make readers laugh**.

Lesson 4

BEFORE READING

OBJECTIVES

Reading Strategy
- Determine Importance: Identify Main Ideas and Details

Literary Analysis
- Analyze Author's Purpose T

TEACH STRATEGIES

D Author's Purpose

Look Into the Text Read the introduction to explain author's purpose in a news article. Read the text passage aloud. Use the callouts to discuss features of a news article. Ask: Which of the 5W questions are answered in the first sentence?

Possible response:
- *what; when; who; where; why*

Reading Transparency 5

Use the Transparency Reinforce author's purpose, and explain that news reporters write to inform. Ask: How did the reporter achieve this purpose in "Creativity at Work"?

Possible response:
- *by giving lots of facts*

Guide students in answering the 5W questions from the text passage. Explain the other three purposes.
RI.9-10.6

E Focus Strategy: Determine Importance

Identify Main Ideas and Details
Review that students use a variety of strategies as they read. Then read the introduction to review the strategy. Work through the steps in the How To box.

After completing the 5Ws Chart, lead students to determine the main idea by identifying relevant details. Ask: What is the most important idea in this paragraph?

Possible response:
- *Artists can earn a living while expressing their creativity.*
RI.9-10.2

Edge Interactive
Practice Book, pp. 58–59

ONGOING ASSESSMENT
Ask: What kinds of details do authors include to give information?

CCSS **Literacy.RI.9-10.2** Determine a central idea of a text and analyze its development over the course of the text, including how it emerges and is shaped and refined by specific details; provide an objective summary of the text. **Literacy.RI.9-10.6** Determine an author's point of view or purpose in a text and analyze how an author uses rhetoric to advance that point of view or purpose.

READ

OBJECTIVES

Literary Analysis
- Recognize Author/Illustrator's Style

Viewing
- Respond to and Interpret Visuals

BUILD BACKGROUND

A Creative Careers

Have students read the article on cartoonist Tony Carrillo.

> **ELL Use Visuals** Show students examples of cartoons from a newspaper. Explain that cartoons are usually funny drawings.

Cartoonists' Inspiration Share with students this information about how different cartoonists get their ideas.

One of the biggest challenges for cartoonists is getting good ideas. To do this, some rely on their own lives. For example, *Peanuts* creator Charles Shultz modeled his famous character Snoopy on his dog Spike. And *Zits* writer Jerry Scott says his character Jeremy is similar to himself as a teen, adding that "he's the kid I wished I had been." For cartoonists like Gary Larsen, creator of *The Far Side*, and Tony Carrillo, it's a certain perspective that gives them ideas. Larsen's cartoons are often written from the perspective of human-like animals, while Carrillo searches for the humor involved in everyday human activities.

Connect with Cartooning Have students share information about their favorite cartoonist and what they believe to be his or her main source of inspiration.

myNGconnect.com

Selection Summaries in eight languages

Creative Careers

An Accidental Cartoonist

Almost all my comics are about stupidity . . . I think most people can identify with being a loser. We've all been in that situation.

Cartoonist Tony Carrillo draws a character from his comic strip, "F Minus."

Like many artists who are just starting their careers, Tony Carrillo had an interesting series of day jobs. **A** They included pizza server, camel ride attendant, and orange cone-waver guy, directing planes at the airport.

Carillo didn't start out to be a professional cartoonist; he entered Arizona State University as an arts major. One day, he saw an ad in the student paper. That's when he discovered his creativity. The ad said, "'Can you draw—even just a little bit?'" recalls Carrillo. "It sounded like a fun job and I needed the money, so I drew three little cartoons and sent them in. They hired me over the phone, and I've been doing cartoons ever since."

And what's one of the secrets to Carrillo's success? "The rule is: If it's funny, I'll do it."

myNGconnect.com

See "F Minus" online.
Read Tony Carrillo's biography.

DIFFERENTIATED INSTRUCTION

English Language Learners ELL

Preview the selection:
- Show the photo on p. 121: *This is a young artist. The article is about a place where teens like him make art and sell it.*
- Show the photos on pp. 122–126. Say: *These young people are artists, too.*
- Write *Artists for Humanity (AFH)*. Explain: *The word* humanity *means "people." AFH helps young people. They get paid for making beautiful artwork.*
- Write *nonprofit*. Explain: *AFH is a nonprofit business. That means that it is there to help people, not to make money.*

Read Aloud to provide a supported listening experience:
- Play the **Selection Recording** as students track text in their books. **CD 3**
- Have students use the Listen feature in the **Comprehension Coach** where they see the text as it is read aloud.
- Read the selection aloud as you provide comprehensible input. For example, you can rephrase text in shorter, simpler sentences: (sentence 1 in the first paragraph on p. 122) *AFH wants to help kids by giving them jobs.*

CREATIVITY AT WORK

by Abe Louise Young

TEACH & PRACTICE

B Analyze Visuals

About the Photo Tell students that the teen in this photo is a member of a group called AFH, or Artists for Humanity. Explain that they will read more about him and teen artists like him.

> **ELL** **List Vocabulary** Write a list of words relating to creativity and the arts, including *studio*, *easel*, *paintbrush*, and *talent*. Encourage students to use the words during the discussion.

Interpret and Respond Ask: What do you think an artist looks like? How does this image compare with what you think about artists?

Comprehension Coach

Build Reading Power

Assign students to use the software, based on their instructional needs.

Read Silently
- Comprehension questions with immediate feedback
- Glossary support
- Review text evidence

Listen
- Professional model of fluent reading

Record
- Oral reading fluency practice
- Ongoing fluency assessment with immediate feedback

RI.9-10.10

CCSS Literacy.RI.9-10.10 By the end of grade 9, read and comprehend literary nonfiction in the grades 9-10 text complexity band proficiently, with scaffolding as needed at the high end of the range. By the end of grade 10, read and comprehend literary nonfiction at the high end of the grades 9 -10 text complexity band independently and proficiently.

READ

OBJECTIVES

Vocabulary
- Key Vocabulary T

Reading Fluency
- Phrasing T

Reading Strategy
- Determine Importance: Identify Main Ideas and Details

Comprehension & Critical Thinking
- Relate Main Ideas and Details
- Use Text Evidence T

Literary Analysis
- Analyze Author's Purpose T

TEACH & PRACTICE

A Reading Support

1 Main Ideas and Details Ask: What words and phrases in the first paragraph suggest that the subject of "art careers" is important in this article?

Possible responses:
- *for the hundreds of public high school students; becoming a thrilling reality*

Read Have students read pp. 122–126. Support and monitor their comprehension using the reading support provided. Use the Differentiated Instruction below to meet students' individual needs.
RI.9-10.2

B Reading Support

Author's Purpose Have students analyze and evaluate information from text features, including italicized text and subheads. Point out the different colors, styles, and sizes of type on p. 122.

Ask: What is the purpose of the red text "Creative Energy"?

Possible responses:
- *It is a subhead within the article.*
- *It tells what that section is about.*

Ask: Why does this news article include heads and subheads?

Possible response:
- *to catch the reader's attention and give clues about the next section of text*

RI.9-10.6

A **"Art"** is an **elusive** idea of a **career** for people young and old—a bit like basketball fame or becoming an astronaut. Yet for the hundreds of public high school students who **collaborate** on projects at Artists for Humanity (AFH), art careers are becoming a thrilling reality. 1

1 Main Ideas and Details What clues tell you that the subject of "art careers" is important in this article?

CREATIVE ENERGY

B The **nonprofit's mission** is to create meaningful employment for urban youth through creative arts. AFH is a study in **attainable dreams**: about what happens when high **expectations** for performance, discipline, and creativity meet the raw and eager energy of youth.

"Most of our participants come in off the sidewalk having never held a paintbrush," says Shane Hassey, who started at AFH when he was 15 years old and now works as the office manager. "After a few months, they are making full-scale paintings, selling their work, and developing their own visions."

At 3 p.m., teenagers from public schools all over Boston set up easels, mix their paints and photo developing chemicals, **rev up** woodcrafting tools, and settle down to sculpture tables and graphic-design computers. Hip-hop beats pulse through the studios, and small groups gather in the hallways to plan collaborative projects. Participants begin in the painting studio, and can branch out into sculpture, woodcrafting, photography, design, fashion, and **silkscreening**.

Portrait of an AFH Artist: Jose Guardarrama

"Here, I get to learn how to paint, draw, socialize. I wouldn't be able to do this anywhere else."

Key Vocabulary
career *n.*, job, occupation
collaborate *v.*, to work together with one or more people
expectations *n.*, beliefs about what will happen in the future

In Other Words
elusive difficult, challenging
nonprofit's mission goal of this people-centered group
attainable dreams dreams that can come true
rev up start
silkscreening printing art on cloth

122 Unit 2 The Art of Expression

DIFFERENTIATED INSTRUCTION

Interactive Reading As you conduct the interactive reading session with students, adjust your teaching strategies to their needs.

Struggling Readers

Reread Guide students to reread portions of the text that they do not understand. Suggest that they "plug in" phrases from the In Other Words feature to help them understand words and phrases in bold type. For example, "**start** woodcrafting tools" replaces "**rev up** woodcrafting tools."

For example:
- *"an elusive … career … like … becoming an astronaut" (a job that is very hard to get)*
- *"raw and eager energy" (pure, powerful energy)*
- *"branch out" (try something new)*

Discuss additional examples from the article and provide restatements.

English Language Learners ELL

Rephrase Language Rephrase comparisons, multiple-meaning words, and figurative language for students.

Challenge

Make Real-World Connections Ask students to display and/or describe for the class examples of computer art, wood sculpture, fashion design, and silk-screened T-shirts and posters.

CCSS Literacy.RI.9-10.2 Determine a central idea of a text and analyze its development over the course of the text, including how it emerges and is shaped and refined by specific details; provide an objective summary of the text. Literacy.RI.9-10.6 Determine an author's point of view or purpose in a text and analyze how an author uses rhetoric to advance that point of view or purpose.

Painters at work in the studio of AFH's EpiCenter building.

PUSHING THE LIMITS

The program began in 1991 as a collaboration between Susan Rodgerson—a white, middle-class artist—and five African American teen friends who started painting in her studio. The friends needed to sell their artwork in order to buy supplies and make more art. **Sheer economics inspired an entrepreneurial zeal**, and they approached Boston colleges, nonprofits, and corporations as potential customers. An audience was found, and a program bloomed—with youth at the helm.

Mars, 17, expresses his **commitment** this way: "You've just got to give all your might and create as much as you can. Do something that people have never seen before. That's what makes you an artist. Do something different."

Any public high school student in Boston can join AFH. After a period of **apprenticeship**, participants are paid seven dollars an hour to create. They clock in, clock out, and get a regular paycheck. When their art is sold, half of the **profit** goes to the program, and half to the artist's pocket. "We charge a fair dollar for the kids' work. We ask **market value**. We don't give it away or de-value the work," Rodgerson says. 2 (C)

Massiel Grullon began the program when she was 12 years old. "This is my home," she said. "To make art and get paid for it is the best job in the world. You can feel the love and creativity when you come in here." At 17, Grullon has sold thousands of dollars worth of her high-contrast, hyper-realistic paintings—and after

2 Main Ideas and Details These details describe AFH. Using only a few words, how would you say AFH works?

Monitor Comprehension

Explain What are some ways that AFH helps teens?

Key Vocabulary

- **commitment** *n.*, dedication, determination

In Other Words

Sheer economics inspired an entrepreneurial zeal The need for money encouraged them to start a business
apprenticeship practice and training
profit money made by selling the art
market value the price people are willing to pay

TEACH & PRACTICE

(C) Reading Support

2 Main Ideas and Details Help students identify the main idea and supporting details in the paragraph by using the 5Ws Chart on p. 119. Draw the chart and ask volunteers to create questions for each of the W squares.

> **ELL Questioning** Provide question starters, including *Who can ...*, *When do students ...*, and *What does AFH ...* .

Ask: How would you describe the way AFH works?

Possible responses:
- *Kids have to get trained when they join AFH.*
- *AFH pays kids for making art.*

Have students complete the main idea box in the 5Ws Chart. Ask: What is the main idea of the paragraph?

Possible response:
- *AFH is serious about helping teens become artists who earn money for their work.*

RI.9-10.2

Monitor Comprehension

Explain Have students think aloud to explain ways that AFH helps teens.

> **MODEL** Say:
> - *Teens are creative people. Any public high school student can join AFH to explore his or her creative energy. AFH pays artists seven dollars an hour plus half of the money from sales.*
> - *Working at AFH sounds like a fun way to learn about art and earn money. The program helps teens by giving them fun, creative, and educational jobs.*

Have students explain other ways AFH helps teens, such as what teens might learn from their experiences in the program.

RI.9-10.2

DAILY ROUTINES

Vocabulary

See the Vocabulary and Fluency Routines tab for more information.

Respond to Questions Compose questions using the words. For example: Would you like a *career* that allows you to work alone or *collaborate* with others?

Word Sorts Have students sort words by:

- parts of speech
- number of syllables

Connect with Students' Lives Have students describe experiences they have that feature the Key Vocabulary. For example: Describe a musician whose *talent* you admire.

L.9-10.6

Fluency: Phrasing

CD 11

This cluster's fluency practice uses a passage from "The Hidden Secrets of the Creative Mind" to help students practice appropriate phrasing. Use **Reading Handbook** T749 and the **Fluency Model CD** to teach or review the elements of fluent phrasing, and then use the daily fluency practice activities to develop students' oral reading proficiency.

RI.9-10.10

CCSS **Literacy.RI.9-10.2** Determine a central idea of a text and analyze its development over the course of the text, including how it emerges and is shaped and refined by specific details; provide an objective summary of the text. **Literacy.RI.9-10.10** By the end of grade 9, read and comprehend literary nonfiction in the grades 9-10 text complexity band proficiently, with scaffolding as needed at the high end of the range. By the end of grade 10, read and comprehend literary nonfiction at the high end of the grades 9-10 text complexity band independently and proficiently. **Literacy.L.9-10.6** Acquire and use accurately general academic and domain-specific words and phrases, sufficient for reading, writing, speaking, and listening at the college and career readiness level; demonstrate independence in gathering vocabulary knowledge when considering a word or phrase important to comprehension or expression.

OBJECTIVES

Vocabulary
- Key Vocabulary Ⓣ

Reading Strategy
- Determine Importance: Identify Main Ideas and Details; Review Strategies

Comprehension & Critical Thinking
- Relate Main Ideas and Details
- Use Text Evidence Ⓣ

Literary Analysis
- Analyze Author's Purpose Ⓣ

Viewing
- Respond to and Interpret Visuals

Grammar
- Subject Pronouns Ⓣ

TEACH & PRACTICE

Ⓐ Reading Support

3 Author's Purpose Ask: Why do you think the author includes this detail about how much money Grullon has made?

Possible responses:
- *to prove that the program is working*
- *to show that teens can make a living as artists*

RI.9-10.6

Ⓑ Reading Support

4 Author's Purpose Have volunteers read aloud the quotes.

ELL Rephrase Language Rephrase words and phrases in the students' descriptions of their art:
- *graffiti-influenced style*: a style of art that uses words and images
- *graphic, high-contrast realism*: drawings and paintings that look like photos and that use bright, bold colors.

Then ask: What do the quotes help you to understand about Michael and Massiel?

Possible responses:
- *They have very different styles, but they love working together.*
- *They have learned to work together because of AFH.*

RI.9-10.6

Ⓐ taking a fashion workshop at AFH, is outfitted in her own designs. 3

"You don't really know you're a visual artist until somebody pushes your limits," says Omar, a third-year participant. Christie, 17, reflects, "It's good to be able to get into a certain form of art. It makes you think, it makes you feel relaxed. It's a **talent** that you have for yourself that you earn and you don't have to give it to anyone. It feels like you own it. It gives you something to be proud of."

Rather than **formal instruction**, participants have a master artist as a **mentor** for each **medium** they choose to study. Mentor Ryan Conley says, "**Teaching here is very intuitive.** Every student has their own ideas and themes, and we work with everyone individually." Mentors also produce their own artwork side-by-side. Conley adds, "I work on my paintings right here; it shows that I'm focusing on my work. It's better to paint together than for me to just tell them things. And, the kids need a lot of room to make their own discoveries."

3 Author's Purpose Why do you think the author adds the detail that "Grullon has sold thousands of dollars worth" of her art?

Portrait of two AFH Artists: Michael Guardarrama and Massiel Grullon

Ⓑ *"I come here every single day. I got involved exactly one year ago—I fell in love with this place. I can't get enough of it. There's so much potential in it. One year ago today, I wouldn't have thought I'd do something like this painting—especially with her!"*

—Michael

"We decided to collaborate because our styles are very different. He does more of a graffiti-influenced style, and I do more of a graphic, high-contrast realism thing." 4

—Massiel

4 Author's Purpose The article includes quotes from AFH students. What do they help you understand?

Key Vocabulary
talent *n.*, ability or skill

In Other Words
formal instruction being taught in a classroom
mentor coach and teacher
medium different type of artwork
Teaching here is very intuitive. Teachers create lessons based on what they think will work best.

GRAMMAR

Subject Pronouns: *I, You, He,* Etc.

Teach/Model Display the transparency. Read each rule and its example sentence, pointing out the subject pronoun. For the last three rules, show how the pronoun refers to the noun in the prior sentence. Point out the match in gender.

Practice A. Have students say the sentence with the correct pronoun and explain their answer. **B.** Have partners write their sentences. Ask each student to read a pair of sentences aloud, and have the group identify the pronoun. L.9-10.1

Grammar & Writing Practice Book, pp. 35–36

GRAMMAR SKILLS PATH

▶ 16 Subject Pronouns: *I, You, He,* Etc. ELL Language & Grammar Lab
17 Subject Pronouns: *We, You, They*
18 Pronouns in a Compound Subject
19 Pronoun Agreement
20 Review: Subject Pronouns

Grammar Transparency 16

GRAMMAR SUBJECT PRONOUNS: I, YOU, HE, ETC. 16

Is the Subject of a Sentence Always a Noun?
No, It Can Be a Pronoun.

- Use **I** when you talk about yourself.
  I visit Artists for Humanity often.
- Use **you** when you talk to another person.
  You are an artist.
- Use **he** when you talk about one man or one boy.
  Michael paints every day. **He** paints with other students.
- Use **she** when you talk about one woman or one girl.
  Massiel sells her paintings. **She** makes her own clothing, too.
- Use **it** when you talk about one place, thing, or idea.
  The studio is a busy place. **It** is important to many students.

Subject Pronouns
Singular
I
you
he, she, it

Try It

A. Say each sentence. Use a subject pronoun from the chart.
1. I get to talk to a tour guide. Now __I__ know more about the program.
2. Susan Rodgerson is the founder. __She__ has original ideas.
3. The program is for teenagers. __It__ is popular.
4. José paints. __He__ spends time with other artists.
5. I told the tour guide, "__You__ are full of information!"

B. Now tell a partner about an art class you took. Tell about the teacher, yourself, and another student. Write three pairs of sentences. Use three pronouns from the chart. Sentences will vary.

CCSS Literacy.RI.9-10.6 Determine an author's point of view or purpose in a text and analyze how an author uses rhetoric to advance that point of view or purpose. Literacy.L.9-10.1 Demonstrate command of the conventions of standard English grammar and usage when writing or speaking.

AFH artists created a painting based on Paul Gauguin's work. Their finished painting now hangs in Boston's Logan Airport.

BEAUTIFYING BOSTON

The artwork that **emerges from** these discoveries beautifies buildings all over Boston. When a department store **commissioned** a store window for Black History Month this year, AFH students welded larger-than-life steel human figures in clothes **depicting** the history of black fashion.

Last year, a large Boston bank commissioned a large-scale painting of modern Boston. It was based on Paul Gauguin's signature masterpiece, *Where Do We Come From? What Are We? Where Are We Going?* After hanging alongside the colorful Gauguin original in the Museum of Fine Arts, this painting now greets travelers at Logan Airport, where it is on permanent display.

The very building that houses the program is perhaps the most **arresting** example of Boston urban landscape **transformed** in the hands of Artists for Humanity. The method of dreaming big—and collaborating with youth to make dreams into reality—resulted in the $6.8 million EpiCenter, the most environmentally-friendly building in Boston. 5 The EpiCenter **utilizes** solar panels, rainwater collection, and recycled

C

Yinetta Fuertes adds details to one of her paintings.

D

5 Main Ideas and Details The author says that AFH "beautifies buildings all over Boston." What details support the main idea of this section?

Key Vocabulary
- **transform** *v.*, to change from one thing to another

In Other Words
emerges from comes out of
commissioned hired them to create
depicting showing
arresting shocking, amazing
utilizes uses

Monitor Comprehension
Explain
How do AFH teens work together to help each other and their neighborhood?

TEACH & PRACTICE

C Reading Support

5 Main Ideas and Details Ask: What details in the text support the main idea that AFH artwork has made Boston more beautiful?

Possible response:
- *A Black History Month display in a store window, a large painting at Logan Airport, and AFH's own building all beautify Boston.*

RI.9-10.2

Review Strategies Have partners say what other strategies they used as they read the text.

Possible response:
- *I asked questions to understand main ideas: I read that the kids' artwork "beautifies buildings all over Boston." I asked: How can art beautify buildings? I read on and found out that their sculptures and paintings decorated a Boston department store and bank. This shows that Boston businesses support AFH.*

RI.9-10.1

D Analyze Visuals

About the Photo Point out that this and all the photos in the selection show students with their artwork.

Interpret and Respond Have students look at the photos in the selection and describe their impressions. Ask: What words would you use to describe the students and their work?

Possible responses:
- *The students look proud, focused, and comfortable as they work.*
- *Their work is bold and unique.*

Ask: Would you like to see artwork created by students displayed in your community? Where do you think are the best places to do this?

Monitor Comprehension

Explain Have students explain ways that AFH teens help each other and Boston.

Ask if students can think of any other ways that AFH teens might help their city.
RI.9-10.2

VOCABULARY

Link Vocabulary and Concepts

Ask questions to link Key Vocabulary with the Essential Question.

EQ **ESSENTIAL QUESTION:**
Does creativity matter?

Some possible questions:
- *How does AFH help teens to begin a* **career** *in art?*
- *What can young artists learn when they* **collaborate** *with each other on art projects?*
- *How does working with other artists help a young artist to make a strong* **commitment** *to his or her artwork?*
- *Is it possible to* **evaluate** *an artist's creativity?*
- *How do you think* **talent** *and creativity are related?*
- *Can creative expression* **transform** *a person's life?*

Have students use the Key Vocabulary words in their responses.
L.9-10.6

CCSS **Literacy.RI.9-10.1** Cite strong and thorough textual evidence to support analysis of what the text says explicitly as well as inferences drawn from the text. **Literacy.RI.9-10.2** Determine a central idea of a text and analyze its development over the course of the text, including how it emerges and is shaped and refined by specific details; provide an objective summary of the text. **Literacy.L.9-10.6** Acquire and use accurately general academic and domain-specific words and phrases, sufficient for reading, writing, speaking, and listening at the college and career readiness level; demonstrate independence in gathering vocabulary knowledge when considering a word or phrase important to comprehension or expression.

OBJECTIVES

Reading Strategy
- Determine Importance: Identify Main Ideas and Details

Comprehension & Critical Thinking
- Identify Main Idea
- Use Text Evidence T

Literary Analysis
- Analyze Author's Purpose T

Writing
- Response to Literature

Grammar
- Subject Pronouns T

TEACH & PRACTICE

A Reading Support

6 Main Ideas and Details Read the first full paragraph aloud.

Then ask: What main idea about the AFH program do the details support?

Possible response:
- *AFH is a successful program. It helps kids get a good education and good jobs.*

RI.9-10.2

B Reading Support

7 Author's Purpose Read aloud what Rassan Charles says about AFH.

ELL Use Graphic Organizer Have students use a cluster diagram to help them determine which of the 5W questions can be answered by the quote:

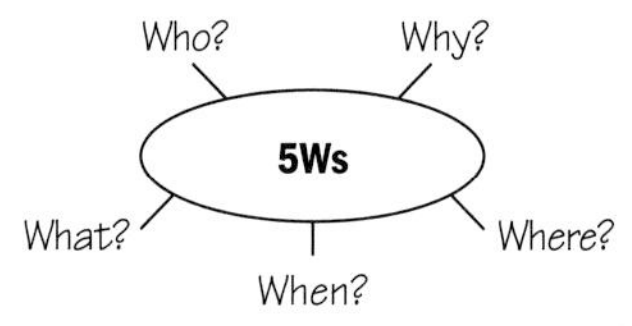

Ask: Is Rassan telling *who, what, where, when,* or *why?*

Possible responses:
- *He is telling why he is lucky to work at AFH and why it has helped him.*
- *He's telling about what career he has always wanted.*

RI.9-10.6

GRAMMAR SKILLS PATH
16 Subject Pronouns: *I, You, He,* Etc.
▶ 17 Subject Pronouns: *We, You, They* — ELL Language & Grammar Lab
18 Pronouns in a Compound Subject
19 Pronoun Agreement
20 Review: Subject Pronouns

A materials. Gallery balconies are lined with car windshields from **old Crown Victorias**. Industrial-sized toilet paper dispensers are cut from the bottoms of 5-gallon plastic water jugs. "The building represents who we are and what we do," says Susan Rodgerson.

Though most come from low-income families, 95 percent of AFH participants go on to college, and two-thirds of them **pursue careers in commercial or fine arts**. "I have the highest expectations for young people, and they have the highest expectations of me. Our entire **philosophy** is built on Respect, Responsibility, and Relationships," says Founding Director Susan Rodgerson. That, it appears, is a simple formula for brilliant success in **social entrepreneurship** with youth. 6 ❖

6 Main Ideas and Details Read for this paragraph's main idea. Then state it in your own words.

Portrait of an AFH Artist: Rassan Charles

B *"This painting reminds me of my homeland in Haiti. I left Haiti in June of 2003. In Haiti, after high school, I wouldn't be able to make any money at art. Art is the only thing I can do—I knew I wanted to be an artist since I was 11 [years old]! Working at AFH helps me a lot . . . By practicing painting every day, I'll be more skillful. I want to go to college, to the School of the Museum of Fine Arts."* 7

7 Author's Purpose Which of the 5W questions does this quote answer?

In Other Words
old Crown Victorias fancy old cars
pursue careers in commercial or fine arts look for jobs in the arts
philosophy belief about how to do things
social entrepreneurship creating positive businesses together

Geographic Background
Haiti a nation on an island in the Caribbean. It is one of the oldest countries in the Americas. Haiti has had many recent troubles. Jobs of any type can be difficult to find there.

GRAMMAR

Subject Pronouns: *We, You, They*

Teach/Model Display the transparency. Have students compare the two lists of pronouns. Elicit that *you* is included in both lists. Then read each rule and the examples, pointing out the subject pronoun. Remind students that pronouns match the gender and number of the nouns they refer to.

Practice A. As students say the correct subject pronoun, write it on the transparency. Use the chart to support students. **B.** After partners talk about an art project and write their sentences, have each student read his or her best sentence aloud and ask the group to say the subject pronoun. L.9-10.1

Grammar & Writing Practice Book, pp. 37–38

Grammar Transparency 17

GRAMMAR SUBJECT PRONOUNS: WE, YOU, THEY 17

Can a Pronoun Show "More Than One"?
Yes, It Can.

- Use **we** to talk about yourself and another person.
  My friend and I work at the EpiCenter.
  We work there after school.
- Use **you** to talk to one or more persons.
  You are a wonderful artist.
  You are all wonderful artists.
- Use **they** to talk about more than one person or thing.
  Artists for Humanity improve their city.
  They transform Boston.

Subject Pronouns	
Singular	Plural
I	we
you	you
he, she, it	they

Try It

A. Say each sentence with the correct subject pronoun.
1. The students create a painting. They work together.
2. My friends and I like art. We want to be artists.
3. An art career takes hard work. It requires training.
4. Your sister and you have talent. You are both talented artists.
5. Some young people have an interest in art. They deserve a chance to learn.

B. Now tell a partner about an art project you did with one or more people. Use subject pronouns. Write your four best sentences.
Sentences will vary.

CCSS Literacy.RI.9-10.2 Determine a central idea of a text and analyze its development over the course of the text, including how it emerges and is shaped and refined by specific details; provide an objective summary of the text. Literacy.RI.9-10.6 Determine an author's point of view or purpose in a text and analyze how an author uses rhetoric to advance that point of view or purpose. Literacy.L.9-10.1 Demonstrate command of the conventions of standard English grammar and usage when writing or speaking.

ANALYZE Creativity at Work

1. **Explain** What do most of the students from Artists for Humanity do after high school? Why do you think the program is so successful? Provide details from the article to support your answers.
2. **Vocabulary** What kind of **expectations** does Susan Rodgerson have for students in the program? What expectations should they have for *her*?
3. **Analyze Author's Purpose** In a news article, a reporter tries to provide the most important information about the article's subject. With a partner, compare the **5Ws Charts** you began on page 119. Then work together to create a **5Ws Chart** that identifies the most important details and main idea for the entire news article.
4. **Focus Strategy Determine Importance** Often, a main idea is implied, instead of stated directly in the text. With a partner, review a paragraph where you had difficulty deciding about the main idea. Find clues that point to the main idea that is implied.

C

Return to the Text

Reread and Write For kids in AFH, art is more than something to look at. Look back at the article and read all the things they say art does for them. List reasons why these students want and need to express themselves through art.

D

APPLY

C ANALYZE

1. **Explain** Most students go to college, and then they have art careers. AFH is successful because it helps students learn creative skills while having fun and making money.
RI.9-10.1
2. **Vocabulary** She has high expectations for students. She expects them to work hard and succeed. They should have high expectations for her because she is their link to a career in art.
L.9-10.6
3. **Analyze Author's Purpose** After partners complete their chart, have them use it to summarize the article.

Who? adult artist Susan Rodgerson other mentors and art teachers public high school students
What? Artists for Humanity, a program that supports student artwork
Where? the EpiCenter building Boston, Massachusetts
Why? to help kids make money from creative work to help low-income kids go to college and start art careers to help beautify Boston
When? from 1991 to the present
Main Idea AFH is very successful because it combines creativity, fun, friendship, and skill development.

RI.9-10.6

4. **Focus Strategy: Determine Importance** Have volunteers read aloud the paragraph they worked on. Ask them to explain how important details in the paragraph led them to discover the implied main idea.
RI.9-10.2

D Return to the Text

Students should list key statements the kids make. For example:

- *Art brings them closer to other artists.*
- *Making art makes them feel special or different in a good way.*
- *AFH feels like "home" to them.*
- *Making money from their work makes them feel more self-confident.*

W.9-10.2.b; W.9-10.10

Edge Interactive Practice Book, p. 60

CCSS **Literacy.RI.9-10.1** Cite strong and thorough textual evidence to support analysis of what the text says explicitly as well as inferences drawn from the text. **Literacy.RI.9-10.2** Determine a central idea of a text and analyze its development over the course of the text, including how it emerges and is shaped and refined by specific details; provide an objective summary of the text. **Literacy.RI.9-10.6** Determine an author's point of view or purpose in a text and analyze how an author uses rhetoric to advance that point of view or purpose. **Literacy.W.9-10.2.b** Develop the topic with well-chosen, relevant, and sufficient facts, extended definitions, concrete details, quotations, or other information and examples appropriate to the audience's knowledge of the topic. **Literacy.W.9-10.10** Write routinely over extended time frames (time for research, reflection, and revision) and shorter time frames (a single sitting or a day or two) for a range of tasks, purposes, and audiences. **Literacy.L.9-10.6** Acquire and use accurately general academic and domain-specific words and phrases, sufficient for reading, writing, speaking, and listening at the college and career readiness level; demonstrate independence in gathering vocabulary knowledge when considering a word or phrase important to comprehension or expression.

Lesson 5
BEFORE READING

OBJECTIVES

Reading Strategy
- Determine Importance: Identify Main Ideas and Details

Literary Analysis
- Analyze Development of Ideas Ⓣ

Grammar
- Pronouns in a Compound Subject Ⓣ

TEACH STRATEGIES

Ⓐ Analyze Development of Ideas

Introduce Read the definition of an interview and have students share their experiences with interviews.

Look Into the Text Use the callouts to present the features of an interview. Explain the Q-and-A text format and ask: How can a series of questions and answers help in the development of ideas?

Possible response:
- *The interviewer can ask several questions to develop an idea and add follow-up questions to learn more about a previous answer.* RI.9-10.3

Ⓑ Focus Strategy: Determine Importance

Identify Main Ideas and Details
Define the strategy and work through the steps in the How To box.

Have students fill in "Detail 2" with information from Look Into the Text.

Possible response:
- *Research shows that creativity is like regular problem solving.* RI.9-10.2

BEFORE READING The Hidden Secrets of the Creative Mind
interview by Francine Russo

Reading Strategies
- Plan and Monitor
- ▶ **Determine Importance**
- Make Inferences
- Ask Questions
- Make Connections
- Synthesize
- Visualize

Ⓐ Analyze Development of Ideas

An **interview** is a printed a conversation between an interviewer and someone who has something interesting to say. The interviewer develops ideas by asking questions designed to get information from the person interviewed.

Look Into the Text

The interviewer asks questions. The answers give the exact words of the person being interviewed.

Q: Has new research changed any of our popular ideas about creativity?

A: Virtually all of them. Many people believe creativity comes in a sudden moment of insight and that this "magical" burst of an idea is different from our everyday thinking. But research has shown that when you're creative, your brain is using the same mental building blocks you use every day—like when you figure out a way around a traffic jam.

Q: Then how do you explain the "aha!" moment we've all had in the shower or the gym—or anywhere but at work?

What information can you learn from this answer?

Answers can lead to new questions.

Ⓑ Focus Strategy ▶ Determine Importance

In an interview, you can often find main ideas in the questions and supporting details in the answers. As you read, find the main idea for each question-answer pair.

Focus Strategy

HOW TO IDENTIFY MAIN IDEA AND DETAILS

1. **Identify the Topic** Look for clues to find out what the passage is mostly about.
2. **Read for the Main Idea** Decide upon the writer's topic and look for details that give information about it. Use these to create a **Main Idea and Details Diagram** for each section.
3. **Sum Up the Information** Review all of your diagrams. Then decide upon one main idea for the entire interview.
4. **Think Beyond the Text** Ask yourself: What have I learned?

Main Idea and Details Diagram

Main Idea: Research has changed what we know about creativity.

Detail 1:	**Detail 2:**
People used to think that creativity was different from regular thinking.	

GRAMMAR
Pronouns in a Compound Subject

Teach/Model Display the transparency. Review subject-verb agreement in compound subjects with *and* or *or*. Have students identify the verb and explain why it is singular or plural. Elicit the placement of pronouns in compound subjects and read the rules below.

Practice A. As students give correct answers, underline them on the transparency. **B.** After partners write about creative moments, have them share their best sentences with the group. L.9-10.1.b

Grammar & Writing Practice Book, pp. 39–40

Grammar Transparency 18

GRAMMAR PRONOUNS IN A COMPOUND SUBJECT 18

Can a Compound Subject Include a Pronoun?
Yes, and the Pronoun Comes Last.

A **compound subject** can include nouns and pronouns joined by **and** or **or**.

1. Ms. Russo plans an interview. **Dr. Sawyer and she** talk for an hour.
2. The **class and I** read his responses.
3. The **researchers**, **Dr. Sawyer**, **and she** suggest ways to be creative.
4. **Dr. Sawyer or they** find creative places.
5. The **researchers or he** solves a problem on the bus.

How do you know where to place the pronoun?
- Nouns always come before pronouns.
- The pronoun **I** always comes last.

Try It

A. Say each sentence with the correct compound subject.
1. (Our teacher, I, and my friends / Our teacher, my friends, and I) meet with some scientists in a lab.
2. (The scientists and we / We and the scientists) study the brain.
3. (I and you / You and I) are creative thinkers.
4. (I and my lab partner / My lab partner and I) write questions.
5. (Claudia, I, or Bill / Claudia, Bill, or I) will research the questions.

B. Now tell a partner about a time when you and a friend had a sudden creative burst. Write your three best sentences with compound subjects. Sentences will vary.

ONGOING ASSESSMENT
Ask: Why would an interviewer ask a follow-up question on the same topic?

GRAMMAR SKILLS PATH
16 Subject Pronouns: *I, You, He,* Etc.
17 Subject Pronouns: *We, You, They*
▶ 18 Pronouns in a Compound Subject
ELL Language & Grammar Lab
19 Pronoun Agreement
20 Review: Subject Pronouns

CCSS **Literacy.RI.9-10.2** Determine a central idea of a text and analyze its development over the course of the text, including how it emerges and is shaped and refined by specific details; provide an objective summary of the text. **Literacy.RI.9-10.3** Analyze how the author unfolds an analysis or series of ideas or events, including the order in which the points are made, how they are introduced and developed, and the connections that are drawn between them. **Literacy.L.9-10.1.b** Use various types of phrases (noun, verb, adjectival, adverbial, participial, prepositional, absolute) and clauses (independent, dependent; noun, relative, adverbial) to convey specific meanings and add variety and interest to writing or presentations.

INTERVIEW

The Hidden SECRETS of the Creative Mind (C)

by Francine Russo

Connect Across Texts

"Creativity at Work" describes teens who use their creativity to begin careers in art. In this interview, a psychologist tells artists, inventors—and all of us—how to make the most of our creativity. (D)

What is creativity? Where does it come from? The workings of the creative mind have been studied over the past twenty-five years by an army of researchers. But no one has a better **overview** of this mysterious mental process than Washington University psychologist R. Keith Sawyer. In an interview with journalist Francine Russo, he suggests ways in which we can **enhance** our creativity, not just in art and science, but in everyday life.

Q: Has new research changed any of our popular ideas about creativity?

A: **Virtually** all of them. Many people believe creativity comes in a sudden moment of **insight** and that this "magical" burst of an idea is different from our everyday thinking. But research has shown that when you're creative, your brain is using the same **mental building blocks** you use every day—like when you figure out a way around a traffic jam. (E)

Q: Then how do you explain the "aha!" moment we've all had in the shower or the gym—or anywhere but at work? [1]

A: In creativity research, we refer to the three Bs—for the bathtub, the bed, and the bus. They are places where ideas have famously and suddenly emerged. When we take time off from working on a problem, we change what we're doing and **our context**. That can

[1] Development of Ideas
What idea from the first answer leads to the second question?

Key Vocabulary
- **insight** *n.*, understanding

In Other Words
overview understanding
enhance improve
Virtually Almost
mental building blocks ways of thinking
our context where and how we are doing it

Comprehension Coach

Build Reading Power

Assign students to use the software, based on their instructional needs.

Read Silently
- Comprehension questions with immediate feedback
- Glossary support
- Review text evidence

Listen
- Professional model of fluent reading

Record
- Oral reading fluency practice
- Ongoing fluency assessment with immediate feedback

RI.9-10.10

READ

OBJECTIVES

Vocabulary
- Key Vocabulary (T)

Comprehension & Critical Thinking
- Use Text Evidence (T)

Literary Analysis
- Analyze Development of Ideas (T)

BUILD BACKGROUND

(C) A Creativity Expert

Read the title and the introduction in the gray box.

ELL **Rephrase Language** Explain that a psychologist is a person who studies human behavior, emotions, and how the brain works. Tell students that they will read an interview with a psychologist who is studying creativity.

Ask: Why might it be useful to read a psychologist's view of creativity?

Possible response:
- *It might show new ways to explore our creativity.*

(D) Connect Across Texts

Ask students what R. Keith Sawyer might be able to teach the students at AFH.

Possible response:
- *He might be able to help them find even more ways to be creative.*

Read Have students read pp. 129–132. Support and monitor their comprehension using the reading support provided.

TEACH & PRACTICE

(E) Reading Support

[1] **Development of Ideas** Read the first answer and second question. Ask: What detail in the first answer does the second question ask more about?

Possible response:
- *It asks about the difference between the "mental building blocks" Sawyer just mentioned and the "sudden moment of insight" that he mentioned earlier.*

RI.9-10.3

CCSS **Literacy.RI.9-10.3** Analyze how the author unfolds an analysis or series of ideas or events, including the order in which the points are made, how they are introduced and developed, and the connections that are drawn between them. **Literacy.RI.9-10.10** By the end of grade 9, read and comprehend literary nonfiction in the grades 9–10 text complexity band proficiently, with scaffolding as needed at the high end of the range. By the end of grade 10, read and comprehend literary nonfiction at the high end of the grades 9–10 text complexity band independently and proficiently.

OBJECTIVES

Vocabulary
- Key Vocabulary Ⓣ
- Strategy: Use Contextual Analysis (jargon) Ⓣ

Reading Strategies
- Determine Importance: Identify Main Ideas and Details; Summarize; Review Strategies

Comprehension & Critical Thinking
- Identify Main Idea
- Use Text Evidence Ⓣ

Literary Analysis
- Analyze Development of Ideas Ⓣ
- Analyze Author's Style: Word Choice

Research Skills
- Formulate Research Questions; Gather Information

Grammar
- Pronoun Agreement

TEACH & PRACTICE

A Reading Support

2 Development of Ideas Paraphrase the concept of the "three Bs." Then ask: Why does Ms. Russo ask for an example?

Possible response:
- *An example can explain an idea that might be difficult to understand.*

RI.9-10.3

B Reading Support

3 Access Vocabulary Read the title and the text. Ask: How does the writer help readers figure out what *hemisphere* means?

Possible response:
- *Right after the word, it says "or sides." Also, the picture shows two sides of the brain.*

L.9-10.4.a

C Analyze Visuals

Interpret and Respond Tell students to study the diagram. Ask: What visual clues help you understand how the brain functions?

Possible response:
- *The diagram shows the two sides of the brain in different colors. It lists different functions on the right and left.*

GRAMMAR SKILLS PATH
16 Subject Pronouns: *I, You, He,* Etc.
17 Subject Pronouns: *We, You, They*
18 Pronouns in a Compound Subject
▶ 19 Pronoun Agreement ELL Language & Grammar Lab
20 Review: Subject Pronouns

activate different areas of our brain. If the answer wasn't in the part of the brain we were using, it might be in another. If we're lucky, in the next context we may hear or see something that relates to the problem that we had temporarily put aside.

A **Q: Can you give us an example of that?** 2

A: In 1990 a team of NASA scientists was trying to fix the lenses in the Hubble telescope, while it was already in orbit. An expert suggested that tiny mirrors could correct the images, but nobody could figure out how to fit them into the hard-to-reach space inside. Then

B

THE BRAIN: Use It or Lose It

There are two hemispheres, or sides, in the human brain. Both sides work together, although certain **mind functions** are only controlled by one hemisphere.

Take note: What we do during our teenage years may affect how our brains develop. If a skill is not used, the part of the brain needed for that skill dies. 3

Left Brain Functions	Right Brain Functions
Language and Reading	Insight
Math and Science	Art and Music
Reasoning	Imagination
Right-Hand Control	Left-Hand Control

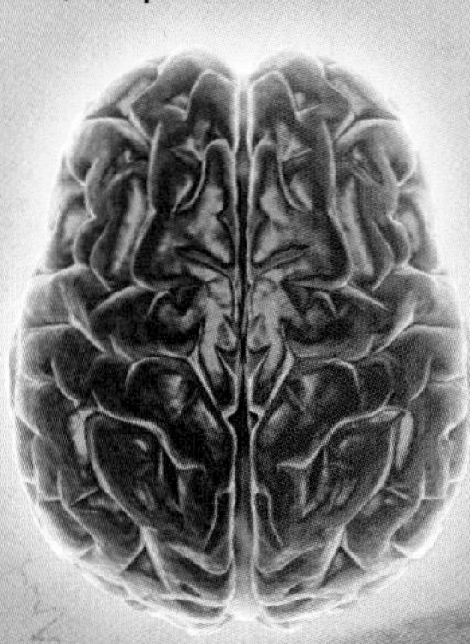

C Interpret the Diagram How does the diagram help you understand how the brain functions?

2 **Development of Ideas** Why do you think the interviewer asks Sawyer for an example of what he just said?

3 **Access Vocabulary** Many scientific experts use specialized words, or jargon, to describe ideas in their field. What clues do the text and diagram give about what the specialized term *hemisphere* means?

In Other Words
activate turn on
mind functions jobs done by the brain

GRAMMAR

Pronoun Agreement

Teach/Model Display the transparency. Use the questions to teach the rules for pronoun agreement. In the example for singular and plural pronouns, have students explain why one sentence is incorrect and the other correct.

Practice A. For each pair of sentences, have one student name the correct pronoun and another explain why the pronoun matches the underlined noun. **B.** After students complete their sentences, have them read a favorite aloud. Ask the group to name the pronoun. L.9-10.1

Grammar & Writing Practice Book, pp. 41–42

Grammar Transparency 19

GRAMMAR PRONOUN AGREEMENT 19

How Do You Avoid Confusion with Pronouns?
Match the Pronoun to the Noun.

If you're not sure which **pronoun** to use, first find the **noun** it goes with. Then ask yourself:
- Is the noun a man, a woman, or a thing? Use **he** for a man, **she** for a woman, and **it** for a thing.
- Is the noun singular or plural?

If a pronoun does not refer correctly to a noun, change the pronoun.

Incorrect: The **interview** is interesting. **They** is also useful.
Correct: The **interview** is interesting. **It** is also useful.

The pronouns in these sentences are correct. Tell why.
1. **Francine Russo** asks about creativity. **She** learns a lot.
2. Creative **people** work hard. **They** do not give up easily.

Try It

A. Say each pair of sentences. Add the pronoun that matches the underlined noun in the first sentence.
1. Dr. R. Keith Sawyer is a psychologist. ___He___ studies creative thinking.
2. A woman interviews him. ___She___ writes about creativity.
3. A creative idea often comes slowly. ___It___ takes time.
4. Creative people take risks. ___They___ make many mistakes.
5. The two sides of the brain differ. ___They___ work together.

B. Now write four pairs of sentences to tell about creative people you know. Use he, she, it, and they. Underline the noun each pronoun goes with. Sentences will vary.

CCSS Literacy.RI.9-10.3 Analyze how the author unfolds an analysis or series of ideas or events, including the order in which the points are made, how they are introduced and developed, and the connections that are drawn between them. **Literacy.L.9-10.1** Demonstrate command of the conventions of standard English grammar and usage when writing or speaking. **Literacy.L.9-10.4.a** Use context (e.g., the overall meaning of a sentence, paragraph, or text; a word's position or function in a sentence) as a clue to the meaning of a word or phrase.

engineer Jim Crocker, taking a shower in a German hotel, noticed the European-style showerhead on **adjustable rods**. He realized the Hubble's little mirrors could be **mounted onto** similar folding arms. And this **flash** was the key to fixing the problem.

Q: How have researchers studied this creative flash?

A: Some psychologists set up video cameras to watch creative people work, asking them to describe their thought processes out loud or interrupting them frequently to ask how close they were to a solution. In other experiments, subjects worked on problems that, when solved, tend to result in the sensation of sudden insight. In one experiment, they were asked to look at words that came up one at a time on a computer screen and to think of the one word that was associated with all of them. After each word they had to give their best guess. Although many swore they had no idea until a sudden burst of insight at about the twelfth word, their guesses got closer to the solution. Even when an idea seems sudden, our minds have actually been working on it all along.

Q: Are there other generalizations you can make about creative people?

A: Yes. They have tons of ideas, many of them bad. The trick is to **evaluate** them and **purge** the bad ones. But even bad ideas can be useful. Sometimes you don't know which sparks are important until later. But the more ideas you have, the better. 4 **D**

Q: So how can the average person get more ideas?

A: Ideas don't magically appear from nowhere. They always build on what came before. And collaboration is key. Look at what others are doing. Brainstorm with different people. Research and evidence suggest that this leads to new ideas.

4 **Main Idea and Details** What is the main idea of this question-and-answer set?

Monitor Comprehension

Summarize Summarize the important ideas and information in this passage.

Key Vocabulary

- **evaluate** *v.*, to decide how good or valuable something is

In Other Words

adjustable rods metal bars that can move back and forth
mounted onto placed on
flash idea, understanding
purge get rid of

TEACH & PRACTICE

D Reading Support

4 Main Ideas and Details Ask: What is the main point Sawyer makes about the "tons of ideas" that creative people have?

ELL Rephrase Language Help students focus in on the key concepts in Sawyer's answer. Then rephrase difficult language; for example:

- Key concept: The trick is to evaluate [many ideas] and purge the bad ones.
- Rephrase: It is important to decide if ideas are bad or good and then get rid of the bad ones.

Possible response:

- *It is good to have a lot of ideas as long as you can tell which ones are good and which ones are bad.*

RI.9-10.2

Review Strategies Have partners say what other reading strategy they used as they read the text.

Possible response:

- *I made a connection: I read that "collaboration is key" to creativity. I know that I do better on group projects because I can learn from my classmates' ideas. This helps me understand why it's helpful to "brainstorm with different people."*

RI.9-10.10

Monitor Comprehension

Summarize Have students paraphrase the important ideas from each question and answer. Then have them determine the main idea by summarizing the information in one or two sentences.

Possible responses:

- *Creativity works like regular thinking.*
- *Creative people sometimes think of good ideas when they aren't trying to.*
- *Creative people have lots of ideas. The hard part is figuring out which ones are good.*

RI.9-10.2

CONTENT AREA CONNECTIONS

Research Creativity and Language

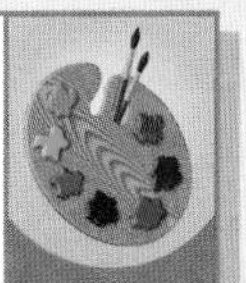
ART

Conduct Research Have students research the way that language learning takes place in the brain and use the information to answer the following questions:

- What areas of the brain are associated with language learning?
- How do the brain's hemispheres play a role in language learning?
- Is there a connection between creativity and language learning?
- Is language learning different for first and second languages?

Share and Discuss Students can share their findings with the class. Discuss the relationship between creativity and language learning. Ask: Does a person need to be creative to learn a second language?

W.9-10.7

CCSS **Literacy.RI.9-10.2** Determine a central idea of a text and analyze its development over the course of the text, including how it emerges and is shaped and refined by specific details; provide an objective summary of the text. **Literacy.RI.9-10.10** By the end of grade 9, read and comprehend literary nonfiction in the grades 9–10 text complexity band proficiently, with scaffolding as needed at the high end of the range. By the end of grade 10, read and comprehend literary nonfiction at the high end of the grades 9–10 text complexity band independently and proficiently. **Literacy.W.9-10.7** Conduct short as well as more sustained research projects to answer a question (including a self-generated question) or solve a problem; narrow or broaden the inquiry when appropriate; synthesize multiple sources on the subject, demonstrating understanding of the subject under investigation.

READ

OBJECTIVES

Vocabulary
- Key Vocabulary Ⓣ

Reading Strategy
- Determine Importance: Identify Main Ideas and Details

Comprehension & Critical Thinking
- Identify Main Idea
- Use Text Evidence Ⓣ

Literary Analysis
- Analyze Development of Ideas Ⓣ

Writing
- Response to Literature

TEACH & PRACTICE

Ⓐ Reading Support

5 Main Ideas and Details Have students use their own words to state the main idea.

Possible response:
- *Being creative depends on hard work, rest, being with other creative people, and not giving up.*

RI.9-10.2

APPLY

Ⓑ ANALYZE

1. **Explain** If you don't use a skill, the part of the brain needed for that skill stops working. RI.9-10.2
2. **Vocabulary** Crocker figured out how to fit mirrors into the Hubble telescope. This is an example of the "three Bs." L.9-10.6
3. **Analyze Development of Ideas** Yes, an interview presents an expert's exact words and allows follow-up questions to clarify information. RI.9-10.3
4. **Focus Strategy: Determine Importance** Make sure students include examples of main ideas and supporting details. RI.9-10.2

Ⓒ Return to the Text

Students can work in small groups to determine the main idea in a question-and-answer set.

RI.9-10.2; W.9-10.9; W.9-10.10

Ⓐ

Q: What advice can you give us nongeniuses to help us be more creative?

A: Take risks, and expect to make lots of mistakes. Work hard, and take frequent breaks, but stay with it over time. Do what you love, because creative breakthroughs take years of hard work. Develop a **network of colleagues**, and schedule time for free, unstructured discussions. Most of all, forget those romantic myths that creativity is all about being artsy and gifted and not about hard work. They **discourage** us because we're waiting for that one full-blown moment of inspiration. And while we're waiting, we may never start working on what we might someday create. 5 ❖

5 Main Idea and Details
In a few words, state the main idea of the advice offered here.

Ⓑ

ANALYZE The Hidden Secrets of the Creative Mind

1. **Explain** According to the diagram on page 130, why is it important to use all of your skills during your teen years?
2. **Vocabulary** What sudden **insight** came to engineer Jim Crocker in a hotel room? How does this example support the author's ideas?
3. **Analyze Development of Ideas** Are interviews a good way to present information? Share your opinions with a partner.
4. **Focus Strategy Determine Importance** In a few words, state the main idea of this interview and find two facts from the selection that support this idea. Compare your work with a partner's and discuss which facts best support the main ideas each of you found.

Ⓒ

Return to the Text

Reread and Write Choose a question and answer from the interview where you had difficulty finding the main idea. Reread the question and answer. Then try to write a sentence expressing the main idea.

In Other Words
network of colleagues group of people who are interested in working on the same things
discourage take hope away from

132 Unit 2 The Art of Expression

Interactive Reading

Have students reread and mark "The Hidden Secrets of the Creative Mind" within the Edge Interactive Practice Book to analyze the development of ideas and to practice the Focus Strategy—Determine Importance: Identify Main Ideas and Details.

Edge Interactive Practice Book, pp. 61–64

Unit Project

Progress Check Allow time for students to work on their unit projects. Meet with individuals and/or groups to provide guidance and check on their progress.

myNGconnect.com
- **Unit Planning Tools**
- **Unit Project Evaluation Rubric**

CCSS **Literacy.RI.9-10.2** Determine a central idea of a text and analyze its development over the course of the text, including how it emerges and is shaped and refined by specific details; provide an objective summary of the text. **Literacy.RI.9-10.3** Analyze how the author unfolds an analysis or series of ideas or events, including the order in which the points are made, how they are introduced and developed, and the connections that are drawn between them. **Literacy.W.9-10.9** Draw evidence from literary or informational texts to support analysis, reflection, and research. **Literacy.W.9-10.10** Write routinely over extended time frames (time for research, reflection, and revision) and shorter time frames (a single sitting or a day or two) for a range of tasks, purposes, and audiences. **Literacy.L.9-10.6** Acquire and use accurately general academic and domain-specific words and phrases, sufficient for reading, writing, speaking, and listening at the college and career readiness level; demonstrate independence in gathering vocabulary knowledge when considering a word or phrase important to comprehension or expression.

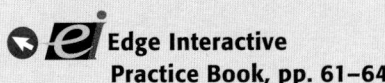

EQ Does Creativity Matter?

Reading

Critical Thinking

1. **Analyze** Review the **Anticipation Guide** on page 118. Explain how the selections supported or challenged your opinions.
2. **Interpret** According to the two selections, is it possible for people to improve their creativity? Give examples from both texts.
3. **Compare** What elements of the AFH program match R. Keith Sawyer's ideas about creativity?
4. **Generalize** Sawyer says that "collaboration is key." Consider what both selections say. Then explain how **collaborating** with others changes the creative experience.
5. **Draw Conclusions** Is creativity only useful in the arts? Base your conclusion on specific evidence from the text.

Writing

Write About Literature

Opinion Paragraph Choose one of the statements from the **Anticipation Guide** on page 118. Have your thoughts changed? Write a paragraph that explains your thoughts and feelings about the topic. Be sure to include support from both texts and your own experience.

Vocabulary

Key Vocabulary Review

Oral Review Work with a partner. Use these words to complete the paragraph.

career	**evaluate**	**talent**
collaborate	**expectations**	**transform**
commitment	**insight**	

It isn't easy to have a successful __(1)__ working as an artist. You need more than just natural skills and artistic __(2)__. You also need dedication and a __(3)__ to hard work. And forget about working alone. __(4)__ with other artists often so that you can study and __(5)__ the good and bad in each other's work. This can give you flashes of __(6)__ and understanding about how to improve. Above all, set high __(7)__ for a bright future. Over time, you will see yourself __(8)__ from a dreamer into a successful artist.

Writing Application Write about a time when you used your creativity or had a moment of sudden **insight**. Use at least 3–4 Key Vocabulary words.

Fluency

Read with Ease: Phrasing

Assess your reading fluency with the passage in the Reading Handbook, p. 754. Then complete the self-check below.

1. I did/did not pause appropriately for punctuation and phrases.
2. My words correct per minute: ____

Lesson 6

REFLECT AND ASSESS

OBJECTIVES

Vocabulary
- Key Vocabulary Ⓣ

Reading Fluency
- Phrasing Ⓣ

Comprehension & Critical Thinking
- Compare Across Texts
- Use Text Evidence Ⓣ

Literary Analysis
- Evaluate Literature

Writing
- Mode: Opinion
- Form: Paragraph

Reading

Critical Thinking

1. **Analyze** Have students review the Anticipation Guide and discuss how the selections supported or challenged their opinions.
2. **Interpret** Yes, the teens at AFH say that working together helps them to be more creative. Sawyer says that practice, rest, and hard work can improve creativity.
RI.9-10.1
3. **Compare** Sawyer says that being around other creative people and not giving up help creativity. The teens at AFH show that this is true.
4. **Generalize** Looking at others' ideas and working with different types of people help artists think of their own new ideas.
RI.9-10.10
5. **Draw Conclusions** No. Many people who aren't artists—such as businesspeople and scientists—can use creativity to find solutions to problems. The story about the NASA engineer who fixed the Hubble Telescope problem is a perfect example.
RI.9-10.1

Writing

Write About Literature

Edge Interactive Practice Book, p. 59

Opinion Paragraph Have students choose one of their Anticipation Guide statements and decide whether their opinion has changed. They can jot down details from both selections that support their opinion. Have them also take notes on related personal experiences. Have volunteers read aloud their completed paragraphs. Encourage debate.
W.9-10.1

Vocabulary

Key Vocabulary Review

1. *career* **2.** *talent* **3.** *commitment* **4.** *Collaborate* **5.** *evaluate* **6.** *insight* **7.** *expectations* **8.** *transform*
L.9-10.6

Fluency

Read with Ease: Phrasing

Ensure that students complete the self-check.
RI.9-10.10

ASSESS & RETEACH

Assessments Handbook, pp. 15b–15e

Have students complete the **Reader Reflection**. Then give students the **Cluster Test** to measure their progress. Group students as needed for reteaching.

CCSS **Literacy.RI.9-10.1** Cite strong and thorough textual evidence to support analysis of what the text says explicitly as well as inferences drawn from the text. **Literacy.RI.9-10.10** By the end of grade 9, read and comprehend literary nonfiction in the grades 9-10 text complexity band proficiently, with scaffolding as needed at the high end of the range. By the end of grade 10, read and comprehend literary nonfiction at the high end of the grades 9-10 text complexity band independently and proficiently. **Literacy.W.9-10.1** Write arguments to support claims in an analysis of substantive topics or texts, using valid reasoning and relevant and sufficient evidence. **Literacy.L.9-10.6** Acquire and use accurately general academic and domain-specific words and phrases, sufficient for reading, writing, speaking, and listening at the college and career readiness level; demonstrate independence in gathering vocabulary knowledge when considering a word or phrase important to comprehension or expression.

Lesson 7

INTEGRATE THE LANGUAGE ARTS

OBJECTIVES

Language Function
- Describe People, Places, and Things Ⓣ

Literary Analysis
- Analyze Description Ⓣ

Listening and Speaking
- Interview

Grammar
- Subject Pronouns Ⓣ

Grammar

Use Subject Pronouns

Grammar Transparency 20

Review Use the transparency to review subject pronouns. Then conduct the activity on p. 134.

Oral Practice 6. *We* **7.** *They* **8.** *She* **9.** *It* **10.** *He*

Written Practice Make sure subjects match subject pronouns.
L.9-10.1

Language Development

Describe People, Places, and Things

Evaluate students' acquisition of this language function with the Language Acquisition Rubric.

Assessments Handbook, p. 15o
SL.9-10.4

Literary Analysis

Analyze Description

Have students explain which description has the strongest impact. For example:

1. "They clock in, clock out" (hearing)
2. "welded larger-than-life steel human figures" (sight, touch)

RI.9-10.4

Edge Interactive Practice Book, p. 66

Listening / Speaking

Interview

Brainstorm with students about creative people and their effect on society.
SL.9-10.4

GRAMMAR SKILLS PATH

INTEGRATE THE LANGUAGE ARTS

Grammar

Use Subject Pronouns

A **subject pronoun** is used in the subject of a sentence.

- Use **I** to talk about yourself.
- Use **we** to talk about yourself and one or more than one other person.
- Use **you** to talk to one or more than one other person.
- Use **he**, **she**, **it**, and **they** to talk about other people or things. To choose which of these pronouns to use, think about number and gender.

One	More Than One	Male	Female
he she it	they	he	she

Oral Practice (1–5) Say each sentence with the correct subject pronoun.

1. Jill and I set out paints. ____ also set out paper.
2. Many artists work hard. ____ hope for success.
3. Maria is a sculptor. ____ loves to work with clay.
4. This painting is odd. ____ has only two colors.
5. Paul Gauguin was an artist. ____ was French.

Written Practice (6–10) Fix three more pronouns and rewrite the paragraph. Add two sentences.

Teens in Boston create art. ~~She~~ They earn money, too. An art piece is sold for a fair price. They is not sold for less. Susan Rodgerson started Artists for Humanity. He worked with five teens. Companies became interested. It gave AFH money.

Language Development

Describe People, Places, and Things

Pair Talk Describe an artist from the selection or an artist you know. Describe the places where the artist works and what he or she produces.

Literary Analysis

Analyze Description

When writers use **description**, they carefully choose words that will:

- help readers imagine people, places, and events.
- appeal to readers' senses of sight, smell, taste, touch, and hearing.
- give the selection a specific tone, or feeling.

In "Creativity at Work," the writer paints a picture of the sights and sounds at the AFH studio:

> teenagers . . . rev up wood-crafting tools and settle down to sculpture tables and graphic design computers. Hip-hop beats pulse through the studios . . .

Find three more descriptions in the selections where the writer's word choice helps you picture something or identify a certain tone.

Listening/Speaking

Interview

In "The Hidden Secrets of the Creative Mind," the writer interviews an expert on creativity. Now it's your turn. Interview a creative person you know.

1. **Prepare Interview Questions** Use what you learned in the articles to brainstorm questions you can ask about how the person uses creativity.
2. **Conduct the Interview** Take notes or ask for permission to record the conversation. Add follow-up questions if you need more information.
3. **Share Your Interview** Review your work. Then share the main ideas of what you learned with the class. If you recorded the interview, play short excerpts that support your ideas.

GRAMMAR

Review: Subject Pronouns

Review Display the transparency. Have students list the singular and plural pronouns in groups. Have a student tell something, naming a classmate. Another student tells more using the correct subject pronoun.

A. Oral Practice Have students choose the correct subject pronoun for each item and read the pair of sentences. Offer immediate corrective feedback as needed.

B. Written Practice Work through the example. Explain that some sentences have no errors. Have the group tell you how to edit the paragraph. Ask a volunteer to read the corrected paragraph aloud. L.9-10.1

Grammar & Writing Practice Book, pp. 43–44

Grammar Transparency 20

Use Subject Pronouns

GRAMMAR REVIEW: SUBJECT PRONOUNS 20

Remember: The subject of a sentence can be a pronoun. A **subject pronoun** can be singular or plural.

- Use **I** when you talk about yourself.
- Use **you** to talk to one or more persons.
- Use **we** to talk about another person and yourself.
- Use **he**, **she**, **it**, and **they** to talk about other people or things.

How do you know which pronoun to use? Look at the noun it goes with.

1. If the noun is a man or boy, use **he**. If it is a woman or girl, use **she**.
2. If the noun is a place or thing, use **it**. If the noun is plural, use **they**.

Try It

A. Say each sentence with the correct subject pronoun.

1. My best teachers are creative. (It / They) inspire us.
2. Ms. Stone teaches math. (She / They) explains ideas well.
3. Mr. Lee teaches painting. (He / She) uses bright colors.
4. Mr. Lee and I planned an exhibit. (We / They) hung art.

B. Edit the paragraph. Fix five pronoun mistakes. The first is done for you.

The theater is popular. ~~He~~ It is the creative center of school. Actors are always there. ~~It~~ They perform skits. Ted plays piano. ~~She~~ He plays jazz and classical music. Tanya and I sing together. ~~It~~ We always collaborate. The dancers rehearse for many hours. ~~She~~ They never stop!

CCSS **Literacy.RI.9-10.4** Determine the meaning of words and phrases as they are used in a text, including figurative, connotative, and technical meanings; analyze the cumulative impact of specific word choices on meaning and tone (e.g., how the language of a court opinion differs from that of a newspaper). **Literacy.SL.9-10.4** Present information, findings, and supporting evidence clearly, concisely, and logically such that listeners can follow the line of reasoning and the organization, development, substance, and style are appropriate to purpose, audience, and task. **Literacy.L.9-10.1** Demonstrate command of the conventions of standard English grammar and usage when writing or speaking.

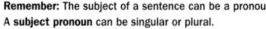

Vocabulary Study

Context Clues

Whenever you read an unfamiliar word, look for **context clues** in the words and phrases that are nearby. Many times, these will include:

- definitions of the word: "There are two **hemispheres**, or sides, in the human brain."
- examples of the word: "And **collaboration** is key. Look at what others are doing. Brainstorm with different people."

Work with a partner to review any unfamiliar words and phrases you have found in the two selections. Reread the context and find any definitions and examples that will make the meanings more clear.

Research / Speaking

Oral Presentation

Science: Parts of the Brain Learn more about the parts of the brain and the functions of each section.

myNGconnect.com

- **Study the PBS special, *The Secret Life of the Brain.***
- **Use magazine index databases to find articles about the brain in your local library.**

Use a computer program to create a web or a Venn diagram that organizes the results of your research. Then present your information to the class.

Language and Learning Handbook, page 702

Writing on Demand

Writing a Test Essay

A test may ask you to write about a topic using examples from your own experience.

1. **Unpack the Prompt** Study the writing prompt. As you read, underline words or phrases that show what you need to include in your essay.

> **Writing Prompt**
> What is creativity? Why is it important in our everyday lives? Write a short essay that gives your ideas about creativity. Include three examples of how people express themselves in creative ways.

2. **Plan** Organize your ideas in a cluster.

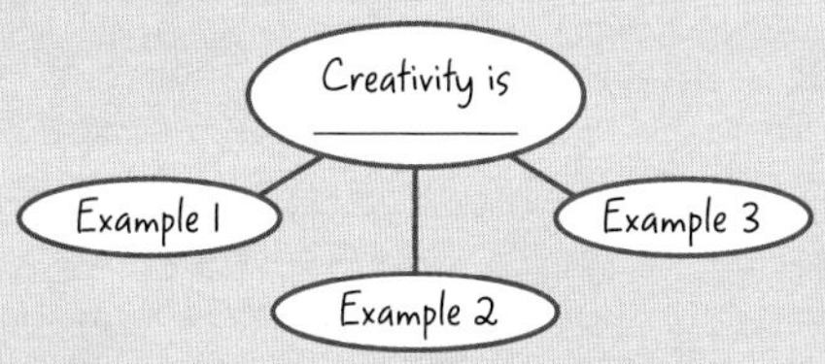

3. **Draft** Use these ideas to write your essay:

Essay Organizer

> I believe that creativity is [give your definition]. It is an important part of our lives because [give your reason].
>
> There are many ways to express your creativity. Some people [give example 1]. This helps them [support example 1].
>
> People also show creativity by [give example 2]. This helps them [support example 2].
>
> Other people express themselves through [give example 3]. This helps them show [support example 3].
>
> In conclusion, [summarize your ideas].

4. **Check Your Work** Reread your essay. Ask:
   - Does my essay address the writing prompt?
   - Do I give examples to support my ideas?
   - Do I use the correct subject pronouns?

Writing Handbook, page 784

Lesson 8

INTEGRATE THE LANGUAGE ARTS

OBJECTIVES

Vocabulary
- Context Clues

Research Skill
- Organize Information

Speaking
- Oral Presentation

Writing
- Writing Process
- Form: Test Essay

Vocabulary Study

Context Clues

Make sure students identify context clues that clarify meanings.
L.9-10.4.a

Edge Interactive Practice Book, p. 67

Research/Speaking

Oral Presentation

Science: Parts of the Brain
Students might create an idea web to list the parts of the brain and how they work.

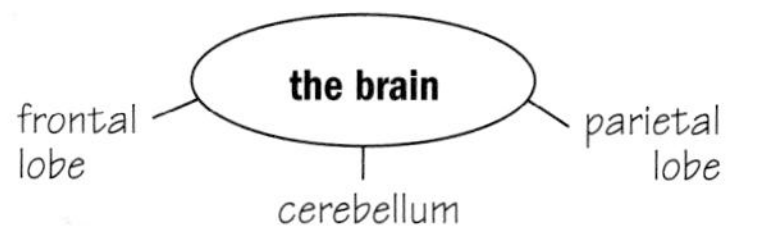

See **Language and Learning Handbook** p. 702 for further instruction.
W.9-10.6; W.9-10.7; SL.9-10.5

Writing on Demand

Writing a Test Essay

1. **Unpack the Prompt** Identify key words: creativity; important; three examples.
2. **Plan** Model completing a cluster.
3. **Draft** Have students use the Essay Organizer as a model.
4. **Check Your Work** Have students read their essays to a partner.
5. **Evaluate Your Work** Have students self-evaluate using the Writing Rubric (*also online*).

See **Writing Handbook** p. 784 for further instruction.
W.9-10.1

Writing Rubric Test Essay

Exceptional	• Essay addresses topic by showing a clear main idea. • Examples are detailed and relevant to main idea. • Sentences are complete.
Competent	• Essay pertains to topic and includes a main idea. • Examples are adequate. • Sentences are complete with no more than one sentence error.
Developing	• Essay may stray from topic. Main idea may be unclear. • Examples are loosely connected to topic. • Sentences are sometimes incomplete.
Beginning	• Essay does not address topic or include a main idea. • Examples are not clearly connected to topic. • Sentences are often incomplete.

CCSS **Literacy.W.9-10.1** Write arguments to support claims in an analysis of substantive topics or texts, using valid reasoning and relevant and sufficient evidence. **Literacy.W.9-10.6** Use technology, including the Internet, to produce, publish, and update individual or shared writing products, taking advantage of technology's capacity to link to other information and to display information flexibly and dynamically. **Literacy.W.9-10.7** Conduct short as well as more sustained research projects to answer a question (including a self-generated question) or solve a problem; narrow or broaden the inquiry when appropriate; synthesize multiple sources on the subject, demonstrating understanding of the subject under investigation. **Literacy.SL.9-10.5** Make strategic use of digital media (e.g., textual, graphical, audio, visual, and interactive elements) in presentations to enhance understanding of findings, reasoning, and evidence and to add interest. **Literacy.L.9-10.4.a** Use context (e.g., the overall meaning of a sentence, paragraph, or text; a word's position or function in a sentence) as a clue to the meaning of a word or phrase.

Lesson 9

WORKPLACE WORKSHOP

OBJECTIVES

Vocabulary
- Content Area Vocabulary: Jobs in Art Museums

Career Exploration
- Analyze the Job Outlook

ENGAGE & CONNECT

A Activate Prior Knowledge

Introduce Ask students what they know about art museums and the workers who are needed there. Then read the introduction.

TEACH & PRACTICE

B Jobs in Art Museums

Use the Chart Have students compare jobs in art museums. Discuss which career would be best if you:

- enjoy research about artwork
- like to build things
- like to restore artwork

C Research the Job Outlook

Brainstorm Ideas Ask: What do you want to know about the work done in an art museum or art gallery?

Possible responses:
- *What is a typical day like?*
- *How often do you talk to the public?*
- *How much art research does the job require?*

W.9-10.10

Computer Skills Show students how to use the Occupational Handbook Web site to research information about museum occupations. Point out how to use the A–Z Index and Search Box to research information on the positions. Then explain how to determine if the jobs have a positive or negative outlook.
W.9-10.7; SL.9-10.1

ONGOING ASSESSMENT
Have students use their charts to describe how they determined if their chosen job has a positive or negative outlook. Did they include all the necessary information and accurately analyze the job outlook?

Workplace Workshop

1

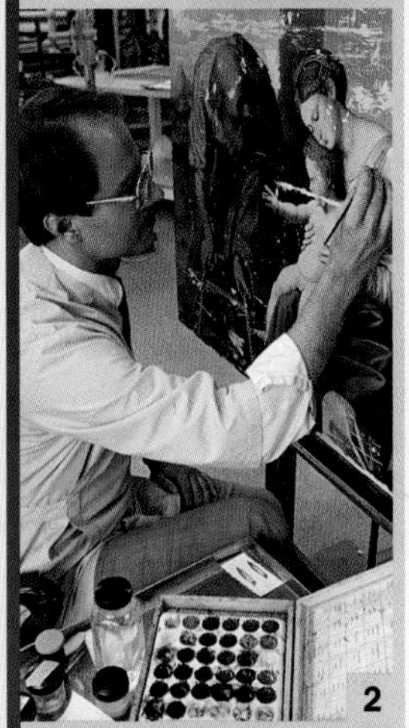
2

3

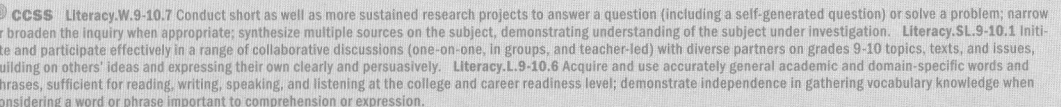

Inside an Art Museum

A People who work in art museums are responsible for preserving and displaying valuable works of art. Museum employees organize exhibitions and provide educational services to the public.

Jobs in Art Museums

B Art museums hire people for a variety of positions that require specific education and skills. Many employees are experts in a specific type of art or period of cultural history.

Job	Responsibilities	Education/Training Required
Museum Technician 1	• Builds, installs, and removes exhibits • Hangs and mounts works of art • Constructs cabinets and other displays for artwork • Moves, packs, and uncrates art shipments	• High school diploma • Shop or carpentry courses • Experience in designing and installing exhibits
Conservator 2	• Performs lab tests and uses special equipment to evaluate condition of art objects • Treats and repairs artwork	• College degree • Special knowledge about one kind of art • On-the-job training
Curator 3	• Researches and catalogs art collections • Directs purchases and exchanges of art objects and collection loans • Organizes exhibitions • Coordinates tours, lectures, and fundraisers	• Master's degree in art history or museum studies • Ph.D. desirable • Related work experience or internship in a museum

Research the Job Outlook

Analyze the job outlook for a job in an art gallery or museum.

C
1. Prepare a four-column chart with the following headings: *Job*, *Number of Employees in the Industry*, *Salary*, and *Job Outlook*.
2. Consult the Occupational Outlook Handbook. Read about your chosen job.
3. Fill in information about your chosen job in the chart. Work with a partner to determine if your job has a positive or negative job outlook. Save the information in a professional career portfolio.

myNGconnect.com
- Learn more about museum jobs.
- Download a form to evaluate whether you would like to work in this field.

Language and Learning Handbook, page 702

VOCABULARY

Content Area Vocabulary: Jobs in Art Museums

Build vocabulary related to the content area of art museums.

ART

Teach/Model Use the Make Words Your Own routine (*see the Vocabulary tab*) and the sample sentences below to introduce these words from the workshop.

• **display** (di-**splā**)

Cabinets are used to **display**, *or show, artwork.*

exhibit (ig-**zi**-bit)

An **exhibit** *is a collection of works of art that is displayed.*

install (in-**stawl**)

A technician sets up, or **installs**, *artwork in a museum.*

catalog (**ka**-tu-lawg)

A curator **catalogs**, *or organizes, detailed lists of art collections.*

Practice Have students use the words to describe a job they would like to do in an art gallery or museum.

Apply Have students work in teams of three or four to organize an art exhibit. Tell them to describe the type of artwork they would include in their exhibit. Then ask them to share how they would install and display the artwork.
L.9-10.6

• Academic Vocabulary

CCSS **Literacy.W.9-10.7** Conduct short as well as more sustained research projects to answer a question (including a self-generated question) or solve a problem; narrow or broaden the inquiry when appropriate; synthesize multiple sources on the subject, demonstrating understanding of the subject under investigation. **Literacy.SL.9-10.1** Initiate and participate effectively in a range of collaborative discussions (one-on-one, in groups, and teacher-led) with diverse partners on grades 9-10 topics, texts, and issues, building on others' ideas and expressing their own clearly and persuasively. **Literacy.L.9-10.6** Acquire and use accurately general academic and domain-specific words and phrases, sufficient for reading, writing, speaking, and listening at the college and career readiness level; demonstrate independence in gathering vocabulary knowledge when considering a word or phrase important to comprehension or expression.

Use Context Clues

Suppose you read the following in your school's newspaper: *The basketball star tore his anterior cruciate ligament. He will not return to the court until the tissue around his knee heals.* Can you figure out what the basketball player tore?

One way to figure out what unfamiliar words mean is to use **word clues** in the context of the sentence or paragraph where the unfamiliar words appear. Context clues are often **synonyms**. For example:

Exercise has a number of ***beneficial*** results. One ***positive*** result is sleeping better.

Positive is a synonym clue for *beneficial*. You can often, but not always, identify synonyms by signal words such as *like*, *another*, *also*, *as*, *for example*, and *likewise*.

A

Explore Words and Context Clues

Work with a partner to use context clues to determine word meanings.

1. Read the sentences on the right.
2. Look for context clues to determine the meaning of each highlighted word.
3. Check the meaning in a dictionary.

B

1. The river was full of **noxious**, dangerous materials such as chemicals from factories.
2. When going to a party, you should show your best **decorum**. For example, dress your best and thank the host.
3. As she got on the **off-roader**, she realized that the bicycle's tires were flat.

Put the Strategy to Work

When you see a word you don't know, use this strategy to look for context clues.

1. Look for punctuation clues or familiar words or ideas in the surrounding text that may mean something similar.
2. Look for signal words such as *or*, *like*, *also*, *as*, or *for example*.
3. Replace the unfamiliar word with the known one and see if it makes sense.

C

TRY IT ▸ Read the following sentence and use context clues to understand the meaning. Then rewrite the sentence using your own words.

▸ The middens of ancient people provide clues to their daily life, just as the trash heaps of today show how people live in modern times.

Reading Handbook, page 733

DIFFERENTIATED INSTRUCTION

Additional Vocabulary Practice
Use these strategies to help students practice using context clues.

Struggling Readers

Find Clues Have students tell what *salvaged* and *empathy* mean in the sentences below. Then ask which one uses a context clue and which uses a synonym clue.

- I **salvaged** my friendship by telling my friend I was sorry.
- I felt **empathy** and pity for the lonely boy.

English Language Learners ELL

Rephrase Have students try these words in place of the bolded words below: *strict, easy, did, pursued*. Then ask which one makes sense and why.

- The judge was too **lenient** on the thief, so he **committed** the crime again.

Challenge

Create Context Clues Have students work in pairs to write additional sentences about the exercise. Tell them to include the words *beneficial*, *positive*, and *precautions*. Ask pairs to swap papers and use context clues to understand the meaning.

Have students brainstorm other words and then look them up in the dictionary to learn the parts of speech and etymologies.

Lesson 10

VOCABULARY WORKSHOP

OBJECTIVES
Vocabulary
- Strategy: Use Contextual Analysis T

ENGAGE & CONNECT

A Build Background

Connect Explain: Imagine someone speaking to you in a language you don't understand. What could you do to figure out what the person is saying? You could use clues such as the person's gestures, expressions, and familiar-sounding words. Similarly, you can use clues when you read a word you don't understand. The clues are signal words and synonyms.

TEACH & PRACTICE

B Explore Words and Context Clues

Use Context Clues Have students identify word clues that can help in figuring out the meaning of each highlighted word. Verify the meaning of each word using a dictionary.

ELL **Sentence Frames** Use sentence frames to help students identify context clues:

- Dangerous chemical materials are ______.
- Dressing your best and thanking the host is good ______.
- An off-roader is a type of ______.

Point out that some words have several meanings depending on how they are used in a sentence. Tell students to substitute meanings in the context of the sentence until they find the one that makes the most sense.

C Put the Strategy to Work

Try It Remind students to review the steps of the strategy as they look for context clues. If students are having trouble understanding the meaning, encourage them to reference the dictionary.
L.9-10.4.a; L.9-10.4.c; L.9-10.4.d

ONGOING ASSESSMENT
Have students share and compare the sentences they wrote.

CCSS **Literacy.W.9-10.10** Write routinely over extended time frames (time for research, reflection, and revision) and shorter time frames (a single sitting or a day or two) for a range of tasks, purposes, and audiences. **Literacy.L.9-10.4.a** Use context (e.g., the overall meaning of a sentence, paragraph, or text; a word's position or function in a sentence) as a clue to the meaning of a word or phrase. **Literacy.L.9-10.4.c** Consult general and specialized reference materials (e.g., dictionaries, glossaries, thesauruses), both print and digital, to find the pronunciation of a word or determine or clarify its precise meaning, its part of speech, or its etymology. **Literacy.L.9-10.4.d** Verify the preliminary determination of the meaning of a word or phrase (e.g., by checking the inferred meaning in context or in a dictionary).

UNIT 2 Cluster 2 Planner

EQ ESSENTIAL QUESTION:

Does Creativity Matter?

Explore the effect of music on our lives.

Online Planner
myNGconnect.com

	LESSON 11 **Prepare to Read**	LESSON 12 **Hip-Hop as Culture** Main Selection
Reading		
Reading Strategies Focus Strategy **Determine Importance**	**Activate Prior Knowledge** SL.9-10.1 • Make a Connection: Discussion *T138*	**Determine Importance** RI.9-10.2 • Summarize Nonfiction *T139, T142–T149* • Identify Main Idea *T139, T142–T149*
Literary Analysis Genre Focus **Kinds of Nonfiction**		(T) **Analyze Author's Purpose** RI.9-10.6 *T139, T142–T149* **Analyze Historical and Social Context** • Hip-Hop and Popular Culture *T140*
Vocabulary	(T) **Key Vocabulary** RI.9-10.4; L.9-10.6 • Introduce *T138* • **achieve** **assert** • **culture** **evolve** **heritage** **innovator** • **perspective** **self-esteem**	(T) **Key Vocabulary** L.9-10.6 • Daily Routines *T143* • Link to Essential Question *T145* • Selection Reading *T142–T149* **assert** • **culture** **evolve** **innovator** • **perspective**
Fluency		(T) **Intonation** RI.9-10.10 • Daily Routines *T143* (T) **Accuracy and Rate** RI.9-10.10 Comprehension Coach *T141*
Writing		
Response to Literature		**Return to the Text** W.9-10.9.b; W.9-10.10 • **Reread and Write** Is it important to understand hip-hop as culture, not just as music, if you want to understand teen culture today? Why? *T149*
Writing Across the Curriculum		
Language		
ELL **Language Development**	(T) **Describe Experiences** SL.9-10.1 • Language and Grammar Lab, Transparency E *LAB TE p. 26*	(T) **Describe Experiences** SL.9-10.1 • Daily Routines *LAB TE p. 2*
Grammar Grammar Focus **Action Verbs in the Present**		(T) **Action Verbs** *T144* L.9-10.1 (T) **Action Verbs in the Present Tense** *T146* L.9-10.1 (T) **Subject-Verb Agreement: -s** *T148* L.9-10.1; L.9-10.2; L.9-10.2.c
Listening and Speaking	**Group Discussion** SL.9-10.1 • Types of Music *T138*	**Listen to a Selection** RI.9-10.10 Comprehension Coach *T141* • *CD 3, Track 3*

(T) = Tested on Cluster and/or Unit Reading and Literary Analysis Test
(T) = Tested on Language Acquisition Assessment
(T) = Tested on Unit Writing Test
(T) = Assessed with a Rubric
• **Academic Vocabulary**

Hip-Hop as Culture

Genre: Essay Lexile® 1060L

Efrem Smith describes the cultural relevance and influence of hip-hop in our society. Smith provides details about hip-hop's history, growth, and future to illustrate that hip-hop is more than just a musical genre.

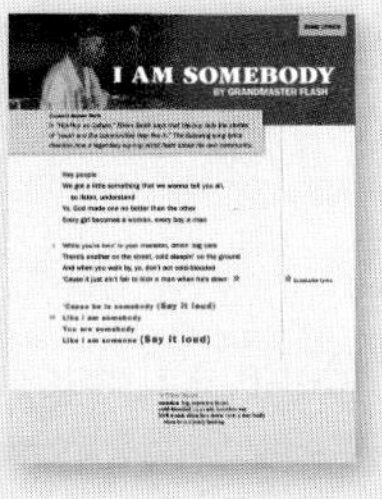

I Am Somebody

Genre: Song Lyrics

In these song lyrics, influential rap and hip-hop artist Grandmaster Flash expresses the value of self-esteem. Grandmaster Flash writes that even though each individual is different, every human being should be equally respected.

LESSON 13 **I Am Somebody** Second Selection	LESSON 14 **Reflect and Assess**	LESSONS 15 & 16 **Integrate the Language Arts**	LESSON 17 **Workshop**
Determine Importance RL.9-10.2 • Summarize Lyrics *T150, T151–T154* • Identify Main Idea *T150, T151–T154*	**Comprehension and Critical Thinking** *T155* RL.9-10.1; RI.9-10.1; SL.9-10.1 • Compare Across Texts • Analyze, Compare, Interpret, Predict, Evaluate		
Analyse Structure: Song Lyrics RL.9-10.2 • Song Lyrics *T150, T151–T154*	**Interpret and Evaluate Literature** RI.9-10.10 Ⓣ **Use Text Evidence** *T155* RI.9-10.1	Ⓣ **Analyze Style and Word Choice** *T156* RL.9-10.4; RI.9-10.4	
Ⓣ **Key Vocabulary** L.9-10.6 • Selection Reading *T151–T154* • **achieve** **heritage** **self-esteem**	Ⓣ **Key Vocabulary** L.9-10.6 • Review *T155* • **achieve** **assert** **heritage** **innovator** • **culture** **evolve** • **perspective** **self-esteem**	Ⓣ **Vocabulary Strategy** L.9-10.4.a; L.9-10.5.a • Use Context Clues: Idioms *T157*	
Ⓣ **Intonation** RL.9-10.10 • Daily Routines *T143* Ⓣ **Accuracy and Rate** RL.9-10.10 Comprehension Coach *T151*	Ⓣ **Intonation** RI.9-10.10 • Self Assessment *T155*		
Return to the Text W.9-10.9.a; W.9-10.10 • **Reread and Write** What message does the song have for the different people in our society? *T154*	**Write About Literature** RL.9-10.2; RI.9-10.2; W.9-10.10 • **Song Lyrics** What main idea fits both "Hip-Hop as Culture" and "I Am Somebody"? *T155*	Ⓣ **Writing Trait** W.9-10.5 • **Focus and Unity** *T157*	
Research and Writing W.9-10.7 • **Music Connection** *T153*		**Research and Record** W.9-10.7; SL.9-10.4 • **Teen Trend Survey** *T156*	
Ⓣ **Describe Experiences** SL.9-10.1 • Daily Routines *LAB TE p. 26*		Ⓣ **Describe Experiences** SL.9-10.1 • Group Talk *T156*	
Ⓣ **Helping Verbs: *Can, Could, May, Might*** *T152* L.9-10.1.b		Ⓣ **Action Verbs in the Present Tense** *T156* L.9-10.1.b	
Listen to a Selection RL.9-10.10 Comprehension Coach *T151* *CD 3, Track 4*	**Participate in a Discussion** *T155* SL.9-10.1	**Oral Presentation** *T156* SL.9-10.4	**Listening and Speaking Workshop** SL-9-10.3; SL-9-10.4; L.9-10.3 **Descriptive Presentation** • Plan, Practice, Give, and Evaluate a Presentation *T158–T159*

EDGE LIBRARY

Hole in My Life ●
by Jack Gantos

The Stone Goddess ● ●
by Minfong Ho

Anthem ● ● ●
by Ayn Rand

Lesson 11

PREPARE TO READ

OBJECTIVES

Vocabulary
- Key Vocabulary Ⓣ
- Strategy: Use Cognates; Relate Words

Reading Strategy
- Activate Prior Knowledge

ELL Language & Grammar Lab

Language Function Transparency E
Describe Experiences Ⓣ

ENGAGE & CONNECT

Ⓐ EQ Essential Question

Focus on Music Discuss how people are influenced by music. Ask: How has music affected your life?

Ⓑ Make a Connection

Discussion Brainstorm different types of music, such as country, classical, hip-hop, and pop. If possible, play samples of each type. Then have groups share how these genres influence their listeners.
SL.9-10.1

TEACH VOCABULARY

Ⓒ Learn Key Vocabulary

Study the Words Review the four steps of the Make Words Your Own routine (*see the Vocabulary tab*):

1. **Pronounce** Say a word and have students repeat it. Write the word in syllables and pronounce it, one syllable at a time: *in-no-va-tor*. Ask what looks familiar in the word, and point out other forms of the word (*innovate, innovative*).

   ELL Use cognates to help Spanish speakers with the words (*see the Vocabulary tab*).

2. **Study Examples** Read the examples. Provide more examples: Does an *innovator* follow the crowd or do something new?

3. **Encourage Elaboration** Teach synonyms for *innovator*, such as *leader* and *trendsetter*. Have students use the synonyms in sentences.

Reading Transparency 6

4. **Practice the Words** Use the transparency to model the completion of a Word Square for *innovator*. Have students complete a Word Square for each Key Vocabulary word.

Edge Interactive
Practice Book, pp. 68–69
RI.9-10.4; L.9-10.6

ONGOING ASSESSMENT
Have students complete an oral sentence for each word. For example: *If I work hard, I can _______ all of my future goals.*

Reading Transparency 6

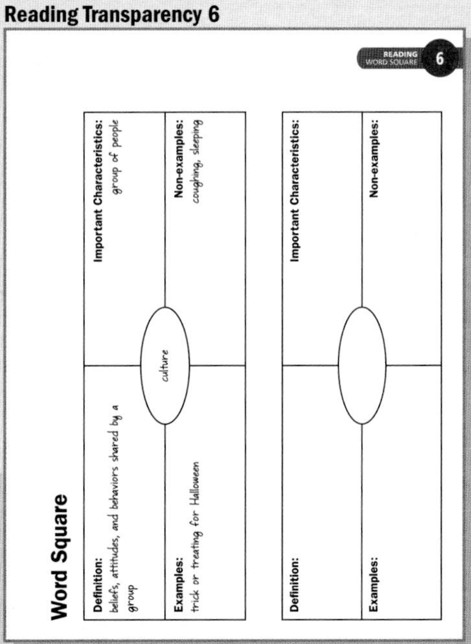

Ⓐ EQ Does Creativity Matter?

Explore the effect of music on our lives.

Ⓑ Make a Connection

Discussion Sometimes music can have a big influence on its listeners. With a group, talk about whether and how different kinds of music can affect the way people dress, talk, and even think.

Ⓒ Learn Key Vocabulary

Study the Words Pronounce each word and learn its meaning. You may also want to look up the definitions in the Glossary.

• Academic Vocabulary

Key Words	Examples
• **achieve** (u-**chēv**) *verb* ▸ pages 149, 153	To **achieve** means to succeed or do well. If you work hard, you can **achieve** your goals.
assert (u-**surt**) *verb* ▸ page 145	When you **assert** something, you insist on having your opinions and ideas heard. The song lyrics **assert** the band's ideas about the power of music.
• **culture** (**kul**-chur) *noun* ▸ pages 142, 149, 155	**Culture** includes the beliefs, attitudes, and behaviors that are shared by a group of people. Young people have a **culture** that appreciates creativity and independence.
evolve (ē-**valv**) *verb* ▸ page 144, 155	When something **evolves**, it changes over time. My taste in music has **evolved** over the years.
heritage (**her**-u-tij) *noun* ▸ page 152	Your **heritage** is your background. **Heritage** includes the traditions and beliefs given to you by your family, culture, and society.
innovator (in-nu-**vā**-tur) *noun* ▸ page 144	An **innovator** is someone who introduces something new. The new styles and sounds the musician uses make her an **innovator** of music.
• **perspective** (pur-**spek**-tiv) *noun* ▸ page 142	Your **perspective** is your point of view. Our teacher's background in classical music gives him a unique **perspective** when he hears our music.
self-esteem (**self** es-**tēm**) *noun* ▸ pages 153, 154	**Self-esteem** is the feeling that you are valuable. The confident girl has high **self-esteem**. *Synonyms*: confidence, self-respect

Practice the Words Complete a **Word Square** for each Key Vocabulary word.

Word Square

Definition: beliefs, attitudes, and behaviors shared by a group	**Important Characteristics:** large group of people
culture	
Examples: trick or treating for Halloween	**Non-Examples:** painting

CCSS **Literacy.RI.9-10.4** Determine the meaning of words and phrases as they are used in a text, including figurative, connotative, and technical meanings; analyze the cumulative impact of specific word choices on meaning and tone (e.g., how the language of a court opinion differs from that of a newspaper). **Literacy.SL.9-10.1** Initiate and participate effectively in a range of collaborative discussions (one-on-one, in groups, and teacher-led) with diverse partners on grades 9-10 topics, texts, and issues, building on others' ideas and expressing their own clearly and persuasively.

Before Reading Hip-Hop as Culture

essay by Efrem Smith

Reading Strategies
- Plan and Monitor
- ▶ **Determine Importance**
- Make Inferences
- Ask Questions
- Make Connections
- Synthesize
- Visualize

Analyze Author's Purpose

An **essay** is a short piece of writing about a subject. The author's **purpose** is usually to entertain, inform, persuade, or share opinions and ideas. The author presents details in a way that effectively achieves one or more of these purposes.

Look Into the Text

Smith gives facts to inform the reader about how hip-hop is often used.

Hip-hop has taken over the music industry in the same way the Williams sisters have taken over tennis. Look at the way the National Basketball Association uses hip-hop players like Shaquille O'Neal and Allen Iverson—and hip-hop culture in general—to sell soda, candy, and clothes to young people. To see hip-hop as simply rap is to not understand the impact and influence of a greater movement.

Rap music is just one element of hip-hop. In fact, true hip-hop heads understand that hip-hop isn't just about music. It's a culture, a way of life, a language, a fashion, a set of values, and a unique perspective.

What opinions does Smith include about hip-hop?

D

Focus Strategy ▶ Determine Importance

Once you have found the author's main ideas, it often helps to put them in your own words. As you read the rest of the essay, summarize the most important ideas.

Focus Strategy

How to Summarize Nonfiction

1. **Identify the Topic** Repeated words and ideas often point to the main topic.
2. **Read Carefully** Try to picture what the author is describing. Take notes.
3. **Summarize Each Section** Pause at the end of each section to decide upon the important details. Produce main idea statements.

Detail #1		Detail #2		Main Idea for Section 1
Hip-hop influences many industries.	+	It includes language, fashion, and values.	=	Hip-hop is an important culture today.

4. **Think Beyond the Text** After reading, ask yourself: What have I learned about the topic? How does this change my thinking?

E

Lesson 12
BEFORE READING

OBJECTIVES

Reading Strategy
- Determine Importance: Summarize Nonfiction

Literary Analysis
- Analyze Author's Purpose T

TEACH STRATEGIES

D Analyze Author's Purpose

Look Into the Text Read the introduction to define an essay and to explain author's purpose. Read the text passage aloud. Use the callouts to discuss the author's purpose. Ask: What facts and opinions does Smith include about hip-hop?

Possible responses:
- *fact: The NBA uses hip-hop players and culture to sell merchandise.*
- *opinion: Hip-hop is not just rap music. It's also a culture.*

Reading Transparency 7

Use the Transparency Explain how students can determine author's purpose. Ask: Which purpose does Smith have for writing his essay?

Possible responses:
- *to inform; to share opinions and ideas; to persuade*

Ask: What are some questions you can ask to help determine an author's purpose?

Possible responses:
- *Is the essay funny or entertaining?*
- *Does the writer want me to do or believe something?*

RI.9-10.6

E Focus Strategy: Determine Importance

Summarize Nonfiction Read the introduction to define the strategy. Work through the steps in the How To box.

Have students use the strategies to summarize the Look Into the Text passage in their own words.

RI.9-10.2

Edge Interactive Practice Book, pp. 70–71

ONGOING ASSESSMENT

Ask: What are three purposes authors may have for writing essays?

Reading Transparency 7

READING AUTHOR'S PURPOSE 7

Analyze Author's Purpose

What is the author's purpose in writing an essay?

Introduce Different authors have different purposes for writing essays:

- **to entertain** This type of essay should interest the reader. It might even be funny.
- **to inform** This type of essay teaches the reader something new or gives information about a topic. It usually contains lots of facts.
- **to share opinions and ideas** This type of essay gives the writer's ideas or viewpoint on a topic.
- **to persuade** This type of essay tries to convince a reader to do something or believe something.

Some essays have more than one purpose. For example, an essay written to share opinions and ideas may also try to entertain.

Here are some questions that can help you figure out the purpose or purposes of an essay:
- Does the writer want me to do something?
- Is the writer trying to teach me something?
- Is the essay mostly about the writer's ideas and views?
- Is the essay funny or entertaining?

CCSS **Literacy.RI.9-10.2** Determine a central idea of a text and analyze its development over the course of the text, including how it emerges and is shaped and refined by specific details; provide an objective summary of the text. **Literacy.RI.9-10.6** Determine an author's point of view or purpose in a text and analyze how an author uses rhetoric to advance that point of view or purpose. **Literacy.L.9-10.6** Acquire and use accurately general academic and domain-specific words and phrases, sufficient for reading, writing, speaking, and listening at the college and career readiness level; demonstrate independence in gathering vocabulary knowledge when considering a word or phrase important to comprehension or expression.

READ

OBJECTIVES

Literary Analysis
- Analyze Historical and Social Context

Viewing
- Respond to and Interpret Visuals

Cultural Perspectives
- U.S. Culture: Popular Culture

BUILD BACKGROUND

A A Moment in Time

Have students read the article "Hip-Hop High School."

Share this information about the origins of hip-hop to connect it to the selection "Hip-Hop as Culture":

You are about to read a selection that explores the ways that hip-hop culture has changed young people's lives—across the country and around the world.

Hip-hop music and culture haven't always been so widespread. Music historians generally agree that what people today call hip-hop began in the South Bronx area of New York City in the early 1970s. At that time, hip-hop didn't even have a name. It was just a style of music being created by local young people who came from many different backgrounds and cultures. Often, they would gather on the streets to show off original dance moves and share new songs that they spoke like poems. Over time, this developed into the musical style—and way of life—that we now call hip-hop.

Connect with Community
Guide students to make connections with their community.

Ask: How important is hip-hop culture in your community? Is it a big part of the culture of your school?

myNGconnect.com

Selection Summaries in eight languages

A Moment in Time

Hip-Hop High School

Chris "Kharma Kazi" Rolle created the Hip-Hop Project in 1999 when he was still a teenager. His goal was to create a "last chance" arts program for New York City teens. And the teens who come to the program have almost run out of second chances. Most of them are thinking about dropping out of high school. Some are homeless or have just been released from prison. Although these teens come from a variety of backgrounds, they do have something in common: hip-hop is a second language to them. Its rich poetry and power inspire their creativity and passion.

Recognizing the power of hip-hop to change lives, Rolle designed the Hip-Hop Project as a way to give students confidence in their abilities. (A) It also gives them knowledge and skills they can use in the future. The intensive program brings students together with professionals in the music industry who help them write, produce, market, and distribute their own collective hip-hop album. The money made from the album and all the related marketing materials they create—such as music videos, T-shirts, and posters—go into a special Scholarship/Enterprise Fund set up for the students.

In addition to recording their own music, the kids have performed at dozens of open-microphone and performance events. In 2000, they wrote, produced, and performed their own show to sold-out audiences in Manhattan. They also recorded their first demo album. Thanks to one teenager's vision, the kids of the Hip-Hop Project share the life-changing experience of transforming their own stories into powerful works of art.

myNGconnect.com

Listen to a song by members of the Hip-Hop Project.

Read more about teens and the arts.

DIFFERENTIATED INSTRUCTION

English Language Learners ELL

Preview the selection:
- Page through the illustrated time line throughout the selection: *This time line shows dates, people, and events that are important to hip-hop music.* Demonstrate reading the time line from left to right, then show how it continues on the next three pages.
- Point out the boxed text on p. 146: *This text is not part of Efrem Smith's essay. It is an interview with a hip-hop leader named Russell Simmons.*

Read Aloud to provide a supported listening experience:
- Play the **Selection Recording** as students track text in their books. **CD 3**
- Have students use the Listen feature in the **Comprehension Coach** where they see the text as it is read aloud.
- Read the selection aloud to students as you provide comprehensible input. Paraphrase quotations on pp. 145, 146, and 147.

Hip-Hop as Culture

by Efrem Smith

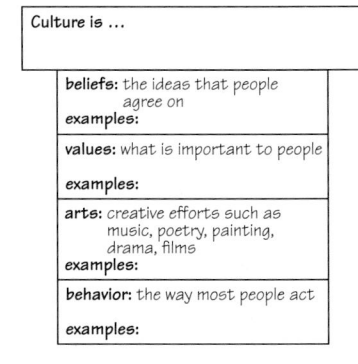

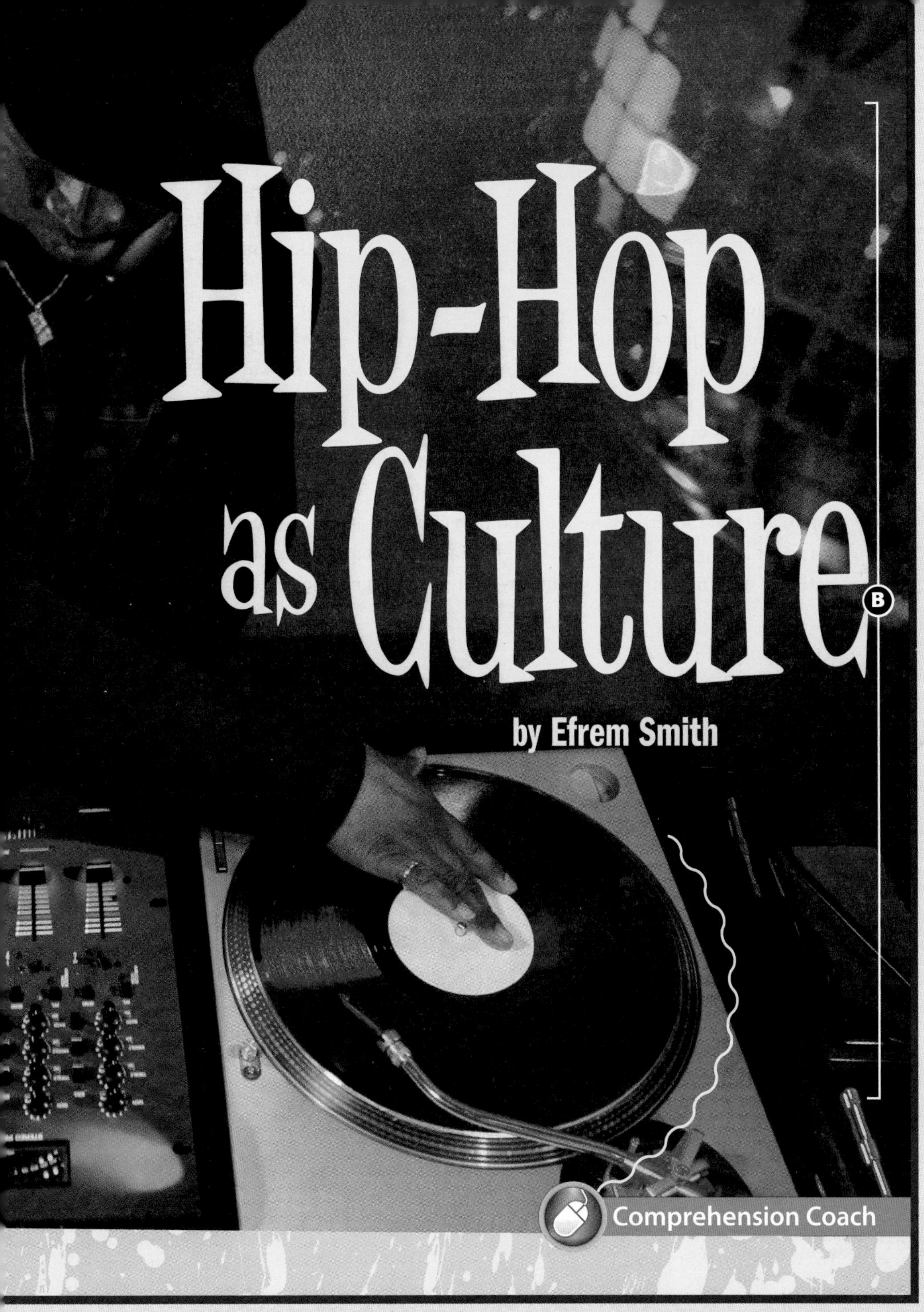

TEACH & PRACTICE

B Analyze Visuals

About the Image and Title This photograph shows a deejay playing music with turntables and an electronic board to mix, or blend, the sounds. The word *culture* refers to the beliefs, values, arts, and behavior that a group of people shares.

ELL Use Graphic Organizer Begin a main idea diagram and elicit ideas from students to create a more detailed description of each aspect of the hip-hop culture. Add to the chart as you read the selection.

Culture is ...
beliefs: the ideas that people agree on **examples:**
values: what is important to people **examples:**
arts: creative efforts such as music, poetry, painting, drama, films **examples:**
behavior: the way most people act **examples:**

Interpret and Respond Ask: What parts of this photo show hip-hop as culture?

Possible responses:

- *The record and music equipment show that hip-hop is a type of music. Hip-hop music can express people's values and beliefs.*

Comprehension Coach

Build Reading Power

Assign students to use the software, based on their instructional needs.

Read Silently
- Comprehension questions with immediate feedback
- Glossary support
- Review text evidence

Listen
- Professional model of fluent reading

Record
- Oral reading fluency practice
- Ongoing fluency assessment with immediate feedback

RI.9-10.10

CCSS Literacy.RI.9-10.10 By the end of grade 9, read and comprehend literary nonfiction in the grades 9-10 text complexity band proficiently, with scaffolding as needed at the high end of the range. By the end of grade 10, read and comprehend literary nonfiction at the high end of the grades 9-10 text complexity band independently and proficiently.

READ

OBJECTIVES

Vocabulary
- Key Vocabulary Ⓣ
- Strategy: Use Contextual Analysis Ⓣ

Reading Fluency
- Intonation Ⓣ

Reading Strategy
- Determine Importance: Summarize Nonfiction; Review Strategies

Comprehension & Critical Thinking
- Relate Main Ideas and Details
- Use Text Evidence Ⓣ

Literary Analysis
- Analyze Author's Purpose Ⓣ

TEACH & PRACTICE

Chunking the Text

Read Have students read pp. 142–148. Support and monitor their comprehension using the reading support provided. Use the Differentiated Instruction below to meet students' individual needs.
RI.9-10.10

Ⓐ Reading Support

1 Author's Purpose Remind students of the different purposes of essays. Ask: Does Efrem Smith seem to want to inform, entertain, persuade, or share opinions and ideas? Explain.

Possible response:
- *inform and share opinions and ideas; he gives a lot of information about rap and hip-hop—some are facts and some are opinions*

RI.9-10.6

Ⓑ Reading Support

2 Access Vocabulary Direct students to the photo of the young man with his legs in the air. Have them read its caption. Then ask: What do you think *breaking, popping,* and *locking* mean? What clues suggest their meanings?

Possible responses:
- *These are dance moves.*
- *The photo shows a young man break-dancing, and the caption says* breaking, popping, *and* locking *are done in dance clubs.*

L.9-10.4.a

Hip-Hop Today

Ⓐ

Hip-hop has taken over the music industry in the same way **the Williams sisters** have taken over tennis. Look at the way the National Basketball Association uses hip-hop players like Shaquille O'Neal and Allen Iverson—and hip-hop **culture** in general—to sell soda, candy, and clothes to young people. To see hip-hop as simply rap is to not understand the impact and influence of a greater movement.

Rap music is just one element of hip-hop. In fact, true hip-hop heads understand that hip-hop isn't just about music. It's a culture, a way of life, a language, a fashion, a set of values, and a unique **perspective**. Hip-hop is an **economy**. It's the ability to take the inner-city system and turn it into a multi-million—or possibly even billion—dollar business. Hip-hop **encompasses** groups like Public Enemy who use rap to address racism, oppression, and poverty. Their leader, "Chuck D," turned it into a new political movement that gets **urban young adults** active in ways **reminiscent of** the days of the civil rights movement. 1

1 Author's Purpose What does Smith do in the first two paragraphs to help establish the purpose of his essay? Explain.

2 Access Vocabulary How do the photo and caption give clues about what *breaking*, *popping*, and *locking* mean?

Breaking, popping, and locking become popular in dance clubs. 2

Ⓑ

A Brief History of Hip-Hop

▶ Early to Mid-1970s
DJs like Cool Herc perform at block parties and parks in the Bronx. Their mix of old funk, soul, and R&B becomes the foundation of hip-hop.

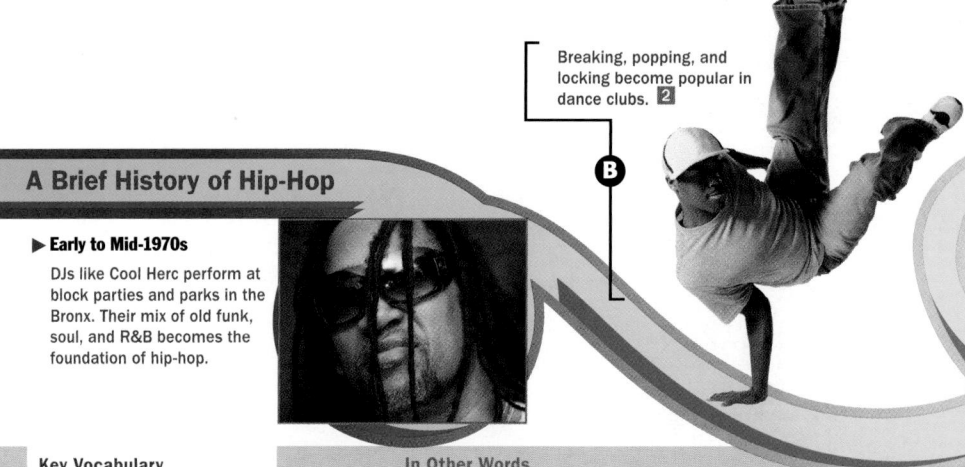

Key Vocabulary
- **culture** *n.*, the attitudes and behaviors of a group
- **perspective** *n.*, point of view

In Other Words
the Williams sisters tennis stars Venus and Serena Williams
economy organization of money and resources
encompasses includes
urban young adults young people in large cities
reminiscent of that are like

DIFFERENTIATED INSTRUCTION

Interactive Reading As you conduct the interactive reading session with students, adjust your teaching strategies to their needs.

Struggling Readers

Scan Text Explain that subheads tell readers what each section of the text is about. Read the subheads. Explain that they show that the selection talks about hip-hop at two different points in time: in the past ("Hip-Hop History") and in the present ("The Hip-Hop Influence").

English Language Learners ELL

Rephrase Language Model how to understand Smith's long sentences. Pause after examples and rephrase the main idea, omitting clauses in dashes and other extra details. For example, on p. 142:

The National Basketball Association uses popular hip-hop players in ads.

Challenge

Consider the Source On p. 144, Efrem Smith says he is "a part of the original hip-hop generation." Have students read the essay to determine whether Smith's ideas and opinions are reliable. Discuss ways that Smith presents himself in the article to show he is a credible source.

CCSS Literacy.RI.9-10.6 Determine an author's point of view or purpose in a text and analyze how an author uses rhetoric to advance that point of view or purpose. **Literacy.RI.9-10.10** By the end of grade 9, read and comprehend literary nonfiction in the grades 9-10 text complexity band proficiently, with scaffolding as needed at the high end of the range. By the end of grade 10, read and comprehend literary nonfiction at the high end of the grades 9-10 text complexity band independently and proficiently. **Literacy.L.9-10.4.a** Use context (e.g., the overall meaning of a sentence, paragraph, or text; a word's position or function in a sentence) as a clue to the meaning of a word or phrase.

Hip-hop culture is worldwide. Here, the group De La Soul performs in England.

Hip-Hop History

Hip-hop tells the stories of the **multiethnic** urban youth and the communities they live in. Hip-hop is about **inner-city and lower-class life**. It's about trying to live out the **American dream** from the bottom up. It's about trying to make something out of nothing. Hip-hop is about the youth culture of New York City taking over the world. Hip-hop is about dance, art, expression, pain, love, racism, sexism, broken families, hard times, **overcoming adversity**, and even the search for God. Anyone who looks at hip-hop and just sees rap music doesn't truly understand the history and the current influence hip-hop has on the whole youth culture. 3

3 Summarize Nonfiction
What is the author's main idea in this paragraph?

▶ **Late 1970s**
The focus of hip-hop moves from DJs to MCs, or rappers.

The Sugarhill Gang releases "Rapper's Delight," an early rap hit.

In Other Words
multiethnic varied backgrounds of
inner-city and lower-class life the lives of people in poor areas of large cities
American dream hope of being successful
overcoming adversity succeeding in spite of challenges

Monitor Comprehension
Explain
According to the author, what are some examples of today's hip-hop culture?

TEACH & PRACTICE

C Reading Support

3 Summarize Nonfiction Have students paraphrase the details in this paragraph to determine the main idea. Model paraphrasing an important detail. For example: *Hip-hop is about diverse youth and their urban communities.*

ELL Comprehensible Input
Point out the author's sentence structure, which repeats the phrase "Hip-hop/It's about …" Explain idiomatic language:

- *live out:* have
- *from the bottom up:* even if you're poor
- *make something out of nothing:* work hard to have a better life
- *taking over the world:* making themselves heard everywhere

Ask: What is the main idea of this paragraph?

Possible response:
- *Hip-hop is about the culture of young people.*

RI.9-10.2

Review Strategies Have partners say which other strategies they used as they read the text.

Possible response:
- *I synthesized what I read about hip-hop being an "economy," a "political movement," and the story of "multi-ethnic urban youth." This helped me to understand how hip-hop is more than just music.*

RI.9-10.1

Monitor Comprehension

Explain Review paragraph two on p. 142 and model thinking aloud to give examples of the hip-hop culture.

MODEL Say:
- *The author says that hip-hop is more than just rap music. That must mean that rap music is only one example of hip-hop in today's culture.*
- *I know that culture includes attitudes and beliefs. The author describes Chuck D's belief that hip-hop is a political movement.*

Have students complete the think aloud by explaining other examples Smith provides of the attitudes and beliefs of hip-hop culture.
RI.9-10.1

DAILY ROUTINES

Vocabulary

See the Vocabulary and Fluency Routines tab for more information.

Questions and Answers Have students prompt a partner with questions containing a Key Vocabulary word. Partners should answer with a sentence that uses a different Key Vocabulary word.

Antonym and Synonym Charts Have students think of one antonym or synonym for as many Key Vocabulary words as they can. They can use phrases or words.

Drama Have students act out or pantomime the action for each Key Vocabulary word that is a verb, such as *assert* and *evolve*.
L.9-10.6

Fluency: Intonation

CD 11

This cluster's fluency practice uses a passage from "Hip-Hop as Culture" to help students practice appropriate intonation. Use **Reading Handbook** T748 and the **Fluency Model CD** to teach or review the elements of fluent intonation, and then use the daily fluency practice activities to develop students' oral reading proficiency.
RI.9-10.10

CCSS Literacy.RI.9-10.1 Cite strong and thorough textual evidence to support analysis of what the text says explicitly as well as inferences drawn from the text. Literacy.RI.9-10.2 Determine a central idea of a text and analyze its development over the course of the text, including how it emerges and is shaped and refined by specific details; provide an objective summary of the text. Literacy.L.9-10.6 Acquire and use accurately general academic and domain-specific words and phrases, sufficient for reading, writing, speaking, and listening at the college and career readiness level; demonstrate independence in gathering vocabulary knowledge when considering a word or phrase important to comprehension or expression.

READ

OBJECTIVES

Vocabulary
- Key Vocabulary Ⓣ

Reading Strategy
- Determine Importance: Summarize Nonfiction

Comprehension & Critical Thinking
- Identify Main Idea
- Use Text Evidence Ⓣ

Literary Analysis
- Analyze Author's Purpose Ⓣ
- Analyze Style: Language and Word Choice Ⓣ

Grammar
- Action Verbs Ⓣ

TEACH & PRACTICE

A Reading Support

4 Author's Purpose Discuss reasons why a writer like Smith shares his own experiences with a topic.

Possible responses:
- *to show his knowledge*
- *to connect with his audience*

RI.9-10.6

B Reading Support

5 Language Ask: What words does Smith use to describe early hip-hop leaders?

Possible responses:
- *pioneers, innovators, architects*

ELL Use Visuals and Elaborate
If possible, show students pictures of early American pioneers, inventors, and architects, along with their work.

Ask: What do pioneers, innovators, and architects have in common?

Possible response:
- *They are all creating or exploring something new.*

Have students compare these leaders to musical "artists" and "producers."

Possible response:
- *Artists and producers work on individual projects, while pioneers, innovators, and architects create something new that influences a culture.*

RI.9-10.4

GRAMMAR SKILLS PATH

▶ 21	**Action Verbs** ELL Language & Grammar Lab
22	**Action Verbs in the Present Tense**
23	**Subject-Verb Agreement: *-s***
24	**Helping Verbs: *Can, Could, May, Might***
25	**Review: Action Verbs in the Present Tense**

A I was born in 1969, so I am a part of the original hip-hop generation. I watched hip-hop **evolve** from **underground** house parties in the basements of my friends' houses, to the first Run DMC video on cable television, to today's rap millionaires like Sean "Diddy" Combs, Master P, Suge Knight, and Russell Simmons. **4** These successful African Americans are more than just rappers. As a matter of fact, Russell Simmons doesn't even rap. **B** Simmons has been **behind the scenes of** hip-hop—developing it from rap artists and groups to films and clothing lines. Simmons, a true **pioneer** of the culture, opened the door so that others in the movement could start their own record labels and develop their own clothing lines.

These **innovators** are the **architects of** culture. **5** They started from the streets of the city and now influence suburban areas and even small rural towns. They took the hustle of the street and turned it into a Wall Street economy. It doesn't matter if you're in a city or suburb. It doesn't matter if you are Latino, Asian, or Irish. Hip-hop is influencing your situation.

I am part of the hip-hop generation

4 Author's Purpose Why does the author include his own experience with hip-hop? Explain.

5 Language Smith describes Russell Simmons as a "pioneer." What other words does he use to describe early hip-hop leaders? How is this different from calling them "artists" and "producers"?

▶ **Early to Mid-1980s**
Kurtis Blow's song, "The Breaks," becomes hip-hop's first gold single.

Rick Rubin and Russell Simmons form Def Jam Records, one of the top labels in hip-hop.

Key Vocabulary
evolve *v.*, to develop over time
innovator *n.*, person who introduces something new

In Other Words
underground secret
behind the scenes of working to support and help
pioneer early leader
architects of designers who plan and build

GRAMMAR

Action Verbs

Teach/Model Display the transparency. Provide an example of an action verb, and explain how it works in a sentence. Elicit more examples of action verbs from the students. As you work through the examples, review subject-verb agreement.

Practice A. Encourage students to suggest possible action verbs for each sentence, and together choose one to record. **B.** After partners write about music, have each student read a favorite sentence aloud. Ask the group to identify the action verb. L.9-10.1

Grammar & Writing Practice Book, pp. 45–46

Grammar Transparency 21

What Adds Action to a Sentence?
An Action Verb

GRAMMAR ACTION VERBS 21

- An **action verb** tells what the subject does.
  Some action verbs tell about an action that you cannot see.
  My friends **listen** to the lyrics.
  They **enjoy** the song.
- Make sure the action verb agrees with its subject. Add **-s** if the subject tells about one place, one thing, or one other person.
  Hip-hop **fashions change** over time.
  My **brother follows** hip-hop styles.
  He tells his friends about new fashions.
  I learn about hip-hop from him.

Try It

A. Say each sentence and add an action verb. Possible answers:

1. Hip-hop songs ___tell___ the stories of urban youth and their neighborhoods.
2. Some hip-hop groups ___write___ songs about social issues.
3. The music ___inspires___ people of all races and backgrounds.
4. The radio station in our city ___plays___ hip-hop all the time.
5. My friends ___enjoy___ the strong beat and lyrics.

B. Now tell a partner more about hip-hop music or another kind of music you like. Write your three best sentences with action verbs. Sentences will vary.

CCSS **Literacy.RI.9-10.4** Determine the meaning of words and phrases as they are used in a text, including figurative, connotative, and technical meanings; analyze the cumulative impact of specific word choices on meaning and tone (e.g., how the language of a court opinion differs from that of a newspaper). **Literacy.RI.9-10.6** Determine an author's point of view or purpose in a text and analyze how an author uses rhetoric to advance that point of view or purpose. **Literacy.L.9-10.1** Demonstrate command of the conventions of standard English grammar and usage when writing or speaking.

The Hip-Hop Influence

Kids may not love hip-hop, but they're being influenced by it. If teens are wearing oversized jeans with the tops of their boxers showing, oversized athletic jerseys, or long chains around their necks, this is hip-hop. Girls on a bus braiding their hair in the style of an Ethiopian queen, that's hip-hop. There are things around you that daily scream at you, "Long live hip-hop!" If you want to understand the culture teens live in today, it's important to understand hip-hop and understand it as culture, not just music.

In the book *Hip-Hop America,* Nelson George writes this:

"Now we know that rap music, and hip-hop style as a whole, has utterly broken through from **its ghetto roots** to **assert** a lasting influence on American clothing, magazine publishing, television, language, . . . and **social policy** as well as its obvious presence in records and movies. . . . [A]dvertisers, magazines, [television], fashion companies, . . . soft drink manufacturers, and **multimedia conglomerates** . . . have embraced hip-hop as a way to reach not just black young people, but *all* young people." 6 (C)

6 Summarize Nonfiction
What is the main idea of this paragraph from *Hip-Hop America*?

▶ **Mid to Late 1980s**
The Beastie Boys release the first rap album to reach #1 and the best-selling rap album of the decade.

DJ Jazzy Jeff & the Fresh Prince win the first Grammy Award for rap music.

Monitor Comprehension
Explain
According to Smith, how did leaders like Russell Simmons help later hip-hop artists?

Key Vocabulary
assert *v.*, to insist on having one's opinions and rights recognized

In Other Words
its ghetto roots where it began in poor areas
social policy the way the government and leaders treat different groups
multimedia conglomerates organizations that control TV, film, news, and advertising

TEACH & PRACTICE

C Reading Support

6 Summarize Nonfiction Remind students that this paragraph is a quote from another writer's work. Help them identify key phrases, such as "lasting influence," "way to reach," and "all."

ELL Rephrase Language Explain that the word *influence* means "effect" or "change." The "influence" of hip-hop is the way that hip-hop has changed how people act and think.

Ask: What is George's main idea?

Possible response:
- *Today, hip-hop affects and appeals to young people everywhere, not just those from poor cities.*

RI.9-10.2

Monitor Comprehension

Explain Have students compare the early years of hip-hop to today's hip-hop. Ask: What did Russell Simmons and other leaders do to help make these changes happen?

Possible responses:
- *They expanded hip-hop from rap artists to films and clothing lines.*
- *Russell Simmons provided more opportunities for future generations of hip-hop artists.*

RI.9-10.2

VOCABULARY

Link Vocabulary and Concepts

Ask questions to link Key Vocabulary with the Essential Question.

EQ ESSENTIAL QUESTION:
Does creativity matter?

Some possible questions:
- *In what way do artists and musicians affect* **culture** *with their creativity?*
- *How can a person's* **heritage** *influence his or her creativity?*
- *How does an* **innovator** *affect his or her society?*
- *What are some of the different* **perspectives** *people have about hip-hop?*
- *Do very creative people* **assert** *their right to their own ideas and beliefs?*
- *Can a person* **achieve** *creativity through hard work? Explain.*

Have students use the Key Vocabulary words in their responses.
L.9-10.6

CCSS Literacy.RI.9-10.2 Determine a central idea of a text and analyze its development over the course of the text, including how it emerges and is shaped and refined by specific details; provide an objective summary of the text. **Literacy.L.9-10.6** Acquire and use accurately general academic and domain-specific words and phrases, sufficient for reading, writing, speaking, and listening at the college and career readiness level; demonstrate independence in gathering vocabulary knowledge when considering a word or phrase important to comprehension or expression.

READ

OBJECTIVES

Vocabulary
- Strategy: Use Contextual Analysis Ⓣ
- Content Area Vocabulary: Music Business

Reading Strategy
- Synthesize

Comprehension & Critical Thinking
- Use Text Evidence Ⓣ

Literary Analysis
- Analyze Author's Purpose Ⓣ

Grammar
- Action Verbs in the Present Tense Ⓣ

TEACH & PRACTICE

Ⓐ Reading Support

Synthesize Explain that many critics complain that rap and hip-hop praise violence and insult women. Rephrase the interviewer's question: Are you worried that rap makes gangster life seem cool or fashionable?

Have students reread the second paragraph of Simmons's response and discuss the difference between a description and an endorsement.

Possible response:
- *A description tells what something is; an endorsement says that something is a good idea.*

Review that paraphrasing is explaining someone else's ideas in your own words. Have students paraphrase Russell Simmons's opinions to determine his main idea about rap.

Possible response:
- *Rap shows what life is like for a lot of people, but it doesn't tell you to go out and do the same thing.*

RI.9-10.2

Russell Simmons

Interview with a Hip-Hop Legend

Excerpt from Terry Gross's interview with Russell Simmons, from the program "Fresh Air," produced by WHYY, Philadelphia.

Terry Gross: Have you ever been concerned about the promotion of a gangster lifestyle through rap?

Russell Simmons: People are always surprised to know that I'm really proud of all of what rap stands for today. And I believe that what people say in their closed doors, they're shocked to hear it on the radio. They're shocked to hear a reflection of this reality, you know, broadcast. . . .

Ⓐ Almost all the records that people perceive as "gangster records" are about people frustrated—who don't perceive themselves as having any other opportunity—and it's a *description* of their lifestyle more than it is **an endorsement of** it. And so that's something that, you know, people who listen closely to the music can tell. And people from the outside, all they can hear is the language. Well, *real* language is OK by me, and descriptions of *real* situations and a *real* reflection of our society, a part of our society, is important by me.

◀ **Early to Mid-1990s**

Cypress Hill becomes one of the first Latino hip-hop groups to sell more than a million records.

In Other Words
an endorsement of a way to promote

GRAMMAR

Action Verbs in the Present Tense

Teach/Model Display the transparency. Elicit examples of action verbs. Use the time line to explain that verbs show tense, or the time an action happens. As you work through the examples, emphasize that the present tense expresses actions that happen now or as a habit.

Practice A. As volunteers substitute a new verb, have them read the sentence aloud. In number 3, point out the two verbs. **B.** After students write their own sentences, have them share one aloud and ask the group to identify the action verb. L.9-10.1

Grammar & Writing Practice Book, pp. 47–48

Grammar Transparency 22

GRAMMAR ACTION VERBS IN THE PRESENT TENSE 22

How Do You Know When the Action Happens?
Look at the Verb.

An **action verb** tells what the subject does. The tense of a verb tells when the action happens.

Past ← Earlier — Now — Later → Future

Present Tense
listen
listen**s**

Use the **present tense** to talk about actions that happen now or that happen on a regular basis.

Tanya **listens** to this radio station.
Marco **likes** the music, too.
They **listen** to hip-hop music every morning.

Try It

A. Find the present tense action verbs in the sentences. Then say the sentences again, using different verbs. Possible answers:

1. Russell Simmons makes albums. creates
2. He develops new hip-hop artists. coaches
3. He supports the hip-hop culture and forms new record labels. helps, starts
4. Simmons appreciates all hip-hop records. enjoys
5. He respects the real language of hip-hop. describes

B. Now write three sentences to tell more about how a hip-hop artist makes a hit album or performs songs. Use action verbs in the present tense. Sentences will vary.

GRAMMAR SKILLS PATH
21 Action Verbs
▶ 22 Action Verbs in the Present Tense — ELL Language & Grammar Lab
23 Subject-Verb Agreement: *-s*
24 Helping Verbs: *Can, Could, May, Might*
25 Review: Action Verbs in the Present Tense

CCSS Literacy.RI.9-10.2 Determine a central idea of a text and analyze its development over the course of the text, including how it emerges and is shaped and refined by specific details; provide an objective summary of the text. Literacy.L.9-10.1 Demonstrate command of the conventions of standard English grammar and usage when writing or speaking.

A rap artist who goes by the name KRS-One (Knowledge **Reigns Supreme** Over Nearly Everyone) presents the elements and history of hip-hop in his book, *Ruminations*. To him, hip-hop connects to philosophy, religion, government, and corporate America. It's a commentary from **the 'hood,** with urban artists serving as inner-city journalists who use their rap, dance, and urban art to report what's going on in the city and in the world at large. **7** KRS-One describes hip-hop as culture this way: **B**

> "True hip-hop is a term that describes the **independent collective consciousness of** a specific group of inner-city people. Ever growing, it is commonly expressed through such elements as: Breakin' (dance), Emceein' (rap), . . . Deejayin', Beatboxin', Street Fashion, Street Knowledge, and **Street Entrepreneurialism**. Discovered by Kool DJ Herc in the Bronx, New York around 1972, and established as a community of peace, love, unity, and having fun by Afrika Bambaataa through Zulu Nation in 1974, hip-hop is an independent and unique community, **an empowering behavior**, and an international culture." **8** **C**

7 Access Vocabulary
What is a "commentary"? First, decode the word by its syllables and word parts. Pronounce the word aloud. Look for words and phrases in the sentence that give you context clues about the word's meaning.

8 Author's Purpose
Why do you think the author includes this excerpt from KRS-One's book? Does it add or take away from the essay? Explain.

▶ Mid to Late 1990s
Queen Latifah wins the Grammy for best rap solo performance.

Lauryn Hill wins 5 Grammys. Her album is the first hip-hop album to win Album of the Year.

In Other Words
Reigns Supreme Has the Most Power
the 'hood neighborhood
independent collective consciousness of unique point of view that is shared by
Street Entrepreneurialism Business that began in the street
an empowering behavior a way to give people power and confidence

TEACH & PRACTICE

B Reading Support

7 Access Vocabulary Have students use sound-letter relationships and word parts to decode the word. Ask them to practice saying the word aloud. Circle the word *comment* inside *commentary*. Ask: What is a comment?

Possible response:
- *a statement of views about something*

Review the sentence and have students point out context clues that help them understand the word *commentary*.

Possible responses:
- *words and phrases: "journalists," "report what's going on in the city and the world at large"*
- *meaning: facts and opinions about news in the neighborhood*

L.9-10.4.a

C Reading Support

8 Author's Purpose Discuss KRS-One's ideas about hip-hop.

ELL Use Graphic Organizer Use a T Chart to rephrase ideas from the excerpt.

Excerpt Text	Restatement
independent collective consciousness ... inner-city people	ideas and values of people living in poor city neighborhoods
discovered by Kool DJ Herc	started by an artist named Kool DJ Herc
established ... by Afrika Bambaataa ...	this singer and band made hip-hop into a movement

Ask: What is the main purpose of this excerpt?

Possible response:
- *to share opinions and ideas*

Ask: Do you think the writer should have included this? Why or why not?

Possible responses:
- *Yes. It shows that other people view hip-hop the same way the author does.*

RI.9-10.6

VOCABULARY

MUSIC

Content Area Vocabulary: Music Business

Build vocabulary related to the content area of the music business.

Teach/Model Use the Make Words Your Own routine (see *the Vocabulary tab*) and the sample sentences below to introduce these words from the selection.

music industry ▸ p. 142

*The **music industry** includes bands, singers, radio stations, and record companies.*

rap music ▸ pp. 142, 148

*In **rap music**, the singer speaks the words but the words have rhythm.*

record labels ▸ p. 144

***Record labels** are companies that produce records and own the rights to them.*

records ▸ p. 145

*A **record** is a collection of music usually published today as a CD.*

Practice Have students use the words to describe their own feelings about music and business in America.

Apply Set up an office scene. Have pairs role-play a musician and a record label representative discussing whether to produce a record.

L.9-10.6

CCSS Literacy.RI.9-10.6 Determine an author's point of view or purpose in a text and analyze how an author uses rhetoric to advance that point of view or purpose. Literacy.L.9-10.4.a Use context (e.g., the overall meaning of a sentence, paragraph, or text; a word's position or function in a sentence) as a clue to the meaning of a word or phrase. Literacy.L.9-10.6 Acquire and use accurately general academic and domain-specific words and phrases, sufficient for reading, writing, speaking, and listening at the college and career readiness level; demonstrate independence in gathering vocabulary knowledge when considering a word or phrase important to comprehension or expression.

OBJECTIVES

Vocabulary
- Key Vocabulary Ⓣ

Reading Strategies
- Determine Importance: Summarize Nonfiction

Comprehension & Critical Thinking
- Identify Main Idea; Summarize
- Use Text Evidence Ⓣ

Literary Analysis
- Analyze Author's Purpose Ⓣ

Writing
- Form: Response to Literature

Grammar
- Subject-Verb Agreement: -s Ⓣ

TEACH & PRACTICE

Ⓐ Reading Support

9 **Summarize Nonfiction** Have students reread the paragraph to find the most important idea.

ELL **Sentence Frames** Have students complete this sentence frame in at least two ways to help describe aspects of hip-hop:

Hip-hop is more than music. It is also ______.

Ask: How would you express this idea in your own words?

Possible response:
- *Hip-hop helps young people in the cities feel like an important part of American culture as a whole.*

Then ask: How does the idea of this paragraph support the main idea of "Hip-Hop as Culture"?

Possible responses:
- *Hip-hop culture has influenced young people everywhere.*
- *The main idea in this paragraph gives an example of that influence from Smith's own life: hip-hop culture helps young people feel connected to mainstream culture.*

RI.9-10.2

Beyond Hip-Hop

The *American Heritage College Dictionary* gives hip-hop the following definition: "A popular urban youth culture, closely **associated with** rap music and with the style and fashions of African American inner-city residents."

Ⓐ Hip-hop moves beyond music into other forms: D.J., the M.C., dance, visual art, fashion, language, and big business. It's also culture because it encompasses the culture of African Americans, Latinos, and urban America. When I was in middle school and high school, hip-hop was more than just music for me—it was finally feeling like my voice, and the voice of urban youth culture, was **in the mainstream of** American culture. 9

Take into consideration that hip-hop evolved after a movement for civil rights, which had young people on the front lines. That isn't to say that hip-hop was the first movement to use the arts to speak to political, social, and spiritual issues. But it did so representing the underclass of urban America in a new way.

Things have changed since those early days. For today's teens, hip-hop is the mainstream culture—one that affects what they see, hear, and experience every day. The question is: What issues can hip-hop address today? How can its message reflect the realities of today's world? The answer is now, as it was then, for today's youth to decide. ❖

9 **Summarize Nonfiction** Summarize the main idea of this paragraph in your own words. How does it fit in with the rest of the essay?

▶ **Early to Mid-2000s**
Kanye West bursts onto the scene, delivering street-rap with a spirited message.

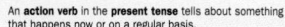

In Other Words
associated with related to
in the mainstream of accepted as an important part of

GRAMMAR

Subject-Verb Agreement: -s

Teach/Model Display the transparency. Elicit sentences with present tense verbs, using *I* as the subject. Then use the examples on the transparency to discuss when to add -s to a present tense verb. Teach the spelling rule for adding -es and ask for more examples.

Practice A. As students choose the correct verb, underline it and have them say the sentence aloud. **B.** After partners write about hip-hop, have each student read a favorite sentence. Ask the group to identify action verbs with -s. L.9-10.1; L.9-10.2; L.9-10.2.c

Grammar & Writing Practice Book, pp. 49–50

GRAMMAR SKILLS PATH
21 Action Verbs
22 Action Verbs in the Present Tense
▶ 23 Subject-Verb Agreement: -s ELL Language & Grammar Lab
24 Helping Verbs: *Can, Could, May, Might*
25 Review: Action Verbs in the Present Tense

Grammar Transparency 23

GRAMMAR SUBJECT-VERB AGREEMENT: -S 23

Which Action Verbs End in -s?
The Ones That Go with *He, She,* or *It*

- An **action verb** in the **present tense** tells about something that happens now or on a regular basis.
- Add -s to the action verb if the subject tells about one place, one thing, or one other person.
  Mina plays drums in our band. She keeps the beat for us.
  Our song gets attention. It brings energy to our concerts.
- If the verb ends in **sh**, **ch**, **ss**, **s**, **z** or **x**, add -es.
  A fan **rushes** on stage. She **reaches** for my guitar.
- Do not add -s to the action verb if the subject is **I**, **you**, **we**, **they**, or a plural noun.
  I **play** the guitar and you **sing**. We **perform** well together.
  The boys **perform** a breakdance. They **get** a lot of applause.

Try It

A. Say each sentence with the correct present tense verb.
1. We **(learn / learns)** that hip-hop is much more than just music.
2. The *American Heritage Dictionary* **(define / defines)** hip-hop as an urban culture.
3. Hip-hop **(influence / influences)** fashion, language, and advertising.
4. It **(include / includes)** the culture of African Americans, Latinos, and urban Americans.

B. Tell a partner about the influence of hip-hop in the world around you. Write your three best sentences with present tense verbs.
Sentences will vary.

CCSS **Literacy.RI.9-10.2** Determine a central idea of a text and analyze its development over the course of the text, including how it emerges and is shaped and refined by specific details; provide an objective summary of the text. **Literacy.L.9-10.1** Demonstrate command of the conventions of standard English grammar and usage when writing or speaking. **Literacy.L.9-10.2** Demonstrate command of the conventions of standard English capitalization, punctuation, and spelling when writing. **Literacy.L.9-10.2.c** Spell correctly.

ANALYZE Hip-Hop as Culture

1. **Explain** According to Efrem Smith, why is it important to understand hip-hop? Use examples from the text to support your answer.
2. **Vocabulary** What are the important parts of the hip-hop **culture**? How do these things influence our society?
3. **Analyze Author's Purpose** The goal of most essayists is to entertain, inform, persuade, and/or present opinions. Does Efrem Smith **achieve** each of these goals? Give examples from the text to support your analysis.
4. **Focus Strategy Determine Importance** Find a paragraph where the author's main idea was difficult to understand. Work with a partner to identify and summarize the main idea.

Return to the Text

Reread and Write Efrem Smith says, "If you want to understand the culture teens live in today, it's important to understand hip-hop and understand it as culture, not just music." Reread the text to find examples and details that support and elaborate this idea. Then summarize his idea in your own words and explain whether you agree.

▶ Mid-2000s

Grammy-winner Jill Scott establishes the Blues Babe Foundation, a program founded to help minority students between the ages of 16 and 21 pay for college.

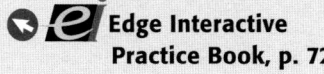

Key Vocabulary
- **achieve** *v.*, to succeed or do well

APPLY

B ANALYZE

1. **Explain** According to Efrem Smith, hip-hop is not just about music. It's also a culture that expresses the experiences of urban young people. This helps us understand young people everywhere. RI.9-10.1
2. **Vocabulary** Music and dance are important parts of hip-hop culture. Companies use hip-hop celebrities and culture to sell products, and hip-hop styles influence other music, dance, and fashion styles. L.9-10.6
3. **Analyze Literature: Author's Purpose** Efrem Smith informs readers with facts about hip-hop. He entertains readers with stories about hip-hop artists and his own life. He shares his opinions about the cultural importance of hip-hop in society. RI.9-10.6
4. **Focus Strategy: Determine Importance** Have volunteers explain how summarizing helped them to clarify the main idea of their paragraphs. RI.9-10.2

C Return to the Text

Students' paragraphs should summarize Smith's idea, analyzing details that support and elaborate his controlling idea, and then explain their own ideas about the topic. Their paragraphs may include ideas like these:

- *Smith believes hip-hop captures the culture of today's young people.*
- *Hip-hop is only one aspect of youth culture.*
- *The music reflects overcoming hard times, racism, and other adversities.*

W.9-10.9.b; W.9-10.10

Edge Interactive Practice Book, p. 72

CCSS Literacy.RI.9-10.1 Cite strong and thorough textual evidence to support analysis of what the text says explicitly as well as inferences drawn from the text. **Literacy.RI.9-10.2** Determine a central idea of a text and analyze its development over the course of the text, including how it emerges and is shaped and refined by specific details; provide an objective summary of the text. **Literacy.RI.9-10.6** Determine an author's point of view or purpose in a text and analyze how an author uses rhetoric to advance that point of view or purpose. **Literacy.W.9-10.9.b** Apply grades 9-10 Reading standards to literary nonfiction (e.g., "Delineate and evaluate the argument and specific claims in a text, assessing whether the reasoning is valid and the evidence is relevant and sufficient; identify false statements and fallacious reasoning"). **Literacy.W.9-10.10** Write routinely over extended time frames (time for research, reflection, and revision) and shorter time frames (a single sitting or a day or two) for a range of tasks, purposes, and audiences. **Literacy.L.9-10.6** Acquire and use accurately general academic and domain-specific words and phrases, sufficient for reading, writing, speaking, and listening at the college and career readiness level; demonstrate independence in gathering vocabulary knowledge when considering a word or phrase important to comprehension or expression.

Lesson 13
BEFORE READING

OBJECTIVES

Reading Strategy
- Determine Importance: Summarize Lyrics

Literary Analysis
- Analyze Structure: Song Lyrics Ⓣ

TEACH STRATEGIES

Ⓐ Analyze Structure: Song Lyrics

Introduce Read the introduction and explain that hip-hop is one form of music in which the lyrics, or words, are just as important as the music. In many cases the songs are like poems set to music.

Look Into the Text Use the callouts on p. 150 to identify and analyze structural elements of song lyrics.

Ask: Which images in verse 2 help you see the writer's ideas?

Possible response:
- *The image of a rich man kicking a homeless man shows how cruel it is to disrespect others.* RL.9-10.5

Ⓑ Focus Strategy: Determine Importance

Summarize Lyrics Define the strategy and work through the How To box to model how to summarize the main ideas in song lyrics.

Then have partners determine the main idea of the first verse in Look Into the Text.

Possible response:
- *All people are important no matter who they are.* RL.9-10.2

ONGOING ASSESSMENT
Ask: What question could you ask to help a partner analyze the structure of song lyrics?

BEFORE READING I Am Somebody

song lyrics by Grandmaster Flash

Reading Strategies
- Plan and Monitor
- ▶ **Determine Importance**
- Make Inferences
- Ask Questions
- Make Connections
- Synthesize
- Visualize

Analyze Structure: Song Lyrics

You're about to read the **lyrics**, or words, to a hip-hop song. Like most songs, "I Am Somebody" has a specific set of features that are very similar to poetry.

Look Into the Text

Ⓐ **A verse is a set of lines in a song or poem. Here each verse is four lines long.**

Hey people
We got a little something that we wanna tell you all, so listen, understand
Yo, God made one no better than the other
Every girl becomes a woman, every boy a man

Rhyme is a common structural element of song lyrics.

While you're livin' in your mansion, drivin' big cars
There's another on the street, cold sleepin' on the ground
And when you walk by, yo, don't act cold-blooded
'Cause it just ain't fair to kick a man when he's down

The chorus is a verse that is repeated at different times in the song.

'Cause he is somebody (Say it loud)
Like I am somebody
You are somebody
Like I am someone (Say it loud)

Imagery helps readers picture the writer's ideas. How do the images in the first line of verse 2 contrast with the image in the next line?

Focus Strategy ▶ Determine Importance

Song lyrics, like other texts, contain main ideas. Identify the main ideas in the song, and summarize them in your own words.

Ⓑ

Focus Strategy

HOW TO SUMMARIZE LYRICS

1. **Look for the clues about what's important.** Read for words or phrases that are repeated or very emotional words. Then determine the main idea that unites the important material. Record these in a **Main Idea Chart**.
2. **Check your understanding.** Compare your statement of the main idea against the other details of the song lyrics.

Main Idea Chart

Writer's Words	Main Idea
"don't act cold-blooded 'Cause it just ain't fair to kick a man when he's down" (lines 7-8)	Always treat others with respect.

CCSS **Literacy.RL.9-10.2** Determine a theme or central idea of a text and analyze in detail its development over the course of the text, including how it emerges and is shaped and refined by specific details; provide an objective summary of the text. **Literacy.RL.9-10.5** Analyze how an author's choices concerning how to structure a text, order events within it (e.g., parallel plots), and manipulate time (e.g., pacing, flashbacks) create such effects as mystery, tension, or surprise.

I AM SOMEBODY C

BY GRANDMASTER FLASH

Connect Across Texts D

In "Hip-Hop as Culture," Efrem Smith says that hip-hop tells the stories of "youth and the communities they live in." The following song lyrics describe how a legendary hip-hop artist feels about his own community.

Hey people
We got a little something that we wanna tell you all,
so listen, understand
Yo, God made one no better than the other
Every girl becomes a woman, every boy a man

While you're livin' in your mansion, drivin' big cars
There's another on the street, cold sleepin' on the ground
And when you walk by, yo, don't act cold-blooded
'Cause it just ain't fair to kick a man when he's down 1 E

'Cause he is somebody (Say it loud)
Like I am somebody
You are somebody
Like I am someone (Say it loud)

1 Summarize Lyrics
What is the main idea of verse 2? State it in your own words.

In Other Words
mansion big, expensive house
cold-blooded in a rude, heartless way
kick a man when he's down treat a man badly when he is already hurting

Comprehension Coach

Build Reading Power

Assign students to use the software, based on their instructional needs.

Read Silently
- Comprehension questions with immediate feedback
- Glossary support
- Review text evidence

Listen
- Professional model of fluent reading

Record
- Oral reading fluency practice
- Ongoing fluency assessment with immediate feedback

RL.9-10.10

CCSS **Literacy.RL.9-10.2** Determine a theme or central idea of a text and analyze in detail its development over the course of the text, including how it emerges and is shaped and refined by specific details; provide an objective summary of the text. **Literacy.RL.9-10.10** By the end of grade 9, read and comprehend literary nonfiction in the grades 9-10 text complexity band proficiently, with scaffolding as needed at the high end of the range. By the end of grade 10, read and comprehend literary nonfiction at the high end of the grades 9-10 text complexity band independently and proficiently.

READ

OBJECTIVES

Reading Strategies
- Determine Importance: Summarize Lyrics; Make Connections; Review Strategies

Comprehension & Critical Thinking
- Identify Main Idea
- Use Text Evidence T

Cultural Perspectives
- U.S. Culture: Popular Culture; Language

BUILD BACKGROUND

C Artistic Expression

Read the title and the author's name.

ELL **Build Background** Explain that *Somebody* in the title means "a person who is important." A *grandmaster* is a skilled expert.

Ask: What message does Grandmaster Flash give with this title and his artistic name?

Possible responses:
- *I am good at what I do and I am important. I will get people's attention.*

D Connect Across Texts

Remind students that part of the hip-hop culture includes its beliefs. Have students discuss how Grandmaster Flash can express part of the hip-hop culture.

TEACH & PRACTICE

E Reading Support

1 Summarize Lyrics Read verse 2 aloud and have students picture its images. Ask: What main idea do these images suggest?

Possible response:
- *Always treat others with respect.*

RL.9-10.2

Review Strategies Ask what other strategies students used as they read.

Possible response:
- *I read: "it ain't right to kick a man when he's down." When I visualize the scene, I understand the meaning: don't hurt someone who is already in trouble.*

RL.9-10.10

READE

OBJECTIVES

Vocabulary
- Key Vocabulary T

Comprehension & Critical Thinking
- Use Text Evidence T

Literary Analysis
- Analyze Structure: Song Lyrics T
- Analyze Style: Language and Word Choice T

Research Skill
- Analyze Information

Grammar
- Helping Verbs T

TEACH & PRACTICE

A Reading Support

2 Language Have students identify different examples of slang in lines 1–16.

ELL Rephrase Language Explain these idioms from lines 13–16:

- *you're here*: you are in a specific place; you agree with certain ideas
- *you're gone*: you are in a different place; you have different ideas
- *knock one another:* insult each other
- *be a brother:* treat people with respect

Ask: How do you think slang affects the message of this song?

Possible responses:
- *helps show that the writer really understands his listener or audience*
- *makes it hard for some people who don't know what the idioms mean*

RL.9-10.4

B Reading Support

3 Structure Have students reread lines 21–24 and identify images. Ask: What pictures do you see in your mind? How do these images relate to main ideas in the song?

Possible responses:
- *cold world, children crying, people looking down in shame, people standing proud, people rejoicing and celebrating*
- *The images help readers/listeners see real people who are going through what the writer describes.*

RL.9-10.5

GRAMMAR SKILLS PATH
21 Action Verbs
22 Action Verbs in the Present Tense
23 Subject-Verb Agreement: *-s*
▶ 24 Helping Verbs: *Can, Could, May, Might* ELL Language & Grammar Lab
25 Review: Action Verbs in the Present Tense

A

Whether you're here or you're gone, you're right or you're wrong
You were meant to be somebody from the second you were born
Don't criticize and knock one another
It ain't really that hard to just be a brother 2

So be good, speak up, don't wait for it to happen
Life is passing you by, and homeboy, you're cold nappin'
Don't be gettin' hung up on what you're not
Be proud of what you are and whatever you got

B

'Cause it's a cold, cruel world causing kids to cry
If you're hangin' your head, cold kiss it goodbye
Stand up for your heritage, rejoice in the fact
Whether you're red, white, tan, yellow, brown, or black 3

'Cause you are somebody (Say it loud)
Like I am somebody
He is somebody
Like I am someone (Say it loud)

There are firemen, bankers, messengers, preachers
Brokers, policemen, executives, teachers,
Journalists, janitors, architects, doctors,
Restaurant workers, nurses, chief rockers

2 Language
The author uses slang throughout the song. Is this effective? Find examples of how this helps or hurts his message.

3 Structure
What images does the author use in lines 21–24? How do they relate to other images in the song to help show his ideas?

Key Vocabulary
heritage *n.*, background, race, or ethnic group you belong to

In Other Words
criticize talk badly about
cold nappin' wasting your time
Don't be gettin' hung up on Don't worry about
rejoice in be happy about
Brokers People who trade stocks
Journalists News writers and reporters

GRAMMAR

Helping Verbs: *Can, Could, May, Might*

Teach/Model Display the transparency. Discuss how the helping verb in the second sentence changes the meaning of the action verb. Work through the other examples. As you discuss subject-verb agreement, contrast singular verbs without a helping verb (*sings*) and with (*can sing*).

Practice A. Before completing the sentences with students, point out that more than one answer is possible. **B.** After students write their lyrics, have them share the lyrics aloud. Repeat a line and ask the group to identify the helping verb. L.9-10.1.b

Grammar & Writing Practice Book, pp. 51–52

Grammar Transparency 24

What Kinds of Verbs Are *Can, Could, May,* and *Might*?

GRAMMAR HELPING VERBS: CAN, COULD, MAY, MIGHT 24

They Are Helping Verbs.

- An action verb can have two parts: a **helping verb** and a **main verb**. The main verb shows the action.
  I **lead** the band. I **can lead** the band.
- Some helping verbs change the meaning of the action verb.
  1. Use **can** or **could** to tell about an ability.
     Raphael **can play** the piano well. He **could play** for our show.
  2. Use **may**, **might**, or **could** to tell about a possibility.
     Raphael **may join** our band. He **might sing**, too.
     He **could become** the most popular performer in our band.
- **Can**, **could**, **may**, and **might** stay the same with all subjects. Do not add **-s**.
  Rafael **sings**. He **can play** the piano, too. He **may play** in the concert.

Try It

A. Say each sentence. Add the helping verb can, could, may, or might. More than one answer is possible. Possible responses:
1. Songs express feelings. They can, may, or might send a message.
2. Grandmaster Flash sings about pride. His songs may or might tell about your own actions.
3. He could or might help you have more pride.
4. If you ignore your heritage, you can, could, may, or might miss out on life.
5. You can, could, may, or might be proud of who you are.

B. Now write some song lyrics. Use can, could, may, and might.
Sentences will vary.

CCSS **Literacy.RL.9-10.4** Determine the meaning of words and phrases as they are used in the text, including figurative and connotative meanings; analyze the cumulative impact of specific word choices on meaning and tone (e.g., how the language evokes a sense of time and place; how it sets a formal or informal tone). **Literacy.RL.9-10.5** Analyze how an author's choices concerning how to structure a text, order events within it (e.g., parallel plots), and manipulate time (e.g., pacing, flashbacks) create such effects as mystery, tension, or surprise. **Literacy.L.9-10.1.b** Use various types of phrases (noun, verb, adjectival, adverbial, participial, prepositional, absolute) and clauses (independent, dependent; noun, relative, adverbial) to convey specific meanings and add variety and interest to writing or presentations.

If you feel you're somebody, be proud, and show it
'Cause everybody's somebody, (ugh) and ya know it
It doesn't matter if you're black, white, or Chinese
Livin' in the States or reside overseas

'Cause you and I are special, same as everyone else
If you don't believe me, you're only cheating yourself
We all got a purpose in life to achieve
That's a fact, and here's another that you better believe

That I am somebody (Say it loud)
Like you are somebody
He is somebody
Like I am someone (Say it loud) 4 C

You got wealth, good health, and you're stuck on yourself
Well let me tell you that you're better than nobody else
'Cause you got no self-esteem, so I'm richer
And when you leave this earth, you can't take money witcha

So play your dumb game, call me out my name,
But nothing you can do could make me feel shame
We're all created equal, we live and we die
So when you try to bring me down, I keep my head up high

4 Structure The words "I am somebody" are repeated in each chorus. Why do you think the author includes the direction to "Say it loud"?

Key Vocabulary
- **achieve** *v.*, to succeed or do well
- **self-esteem** *n.*, feeling that you are valuable, confidence in yourself

In Other Words
reside overseas living in another country
stuck on yourself too proud of yourself
call me out my name speak rudely about me

TEACH & PRACTICE

C Reading Support

4 Structure Ask: Why does the singer repeat "Say it loud"? What does he mean by it?

ELL Use Graphic Organizer Use a word web to help students list possible meanings for the word *loud* and choose the appropriate meaning for the context.

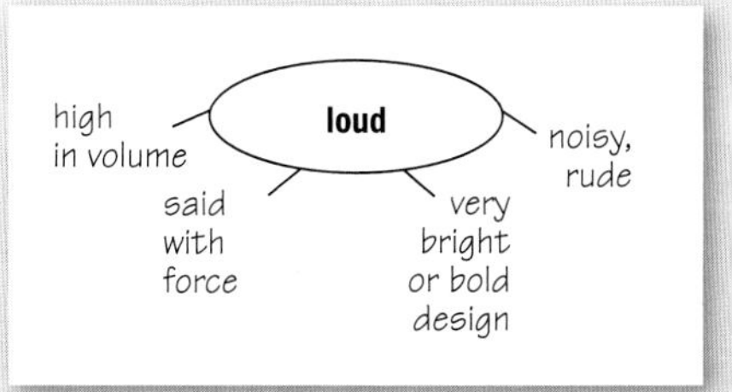

Possible responses:
- *This idea is important. Say it proudly so people will hear you.*

RL.9-10.5

D Reading Support

Language Ask students to identify the poet's use of English that is current or contemporary.

Possible responses:
- *brother, homeboy, cold-nappin', gettin' hung up on, call me out my name*

Have students discuss the way English has changed over time. For example, brainstorm words that might have been used to describe a close friend before *homeboy* or *brother* became popular.
RL.9-10.4

CONTENT AREA CONNECTIONS

MUSIC

Analyze Music

Share Information Recall with students the many reasons that people listen to music.

Conduct Research Have students research and take notes about their favorite musician to find out how they became involved in music, what formal training they have, and their particular talents and goals.

Discuss As a class, discuss the role of creativity in the lives of their favorite musicians:
- What are the different ways these artists got involved in music?
- What creative elements make each of these artists unique?
- Do most of them have formal training, or did they learn in other ways?
- What are some of the things these artists are trying to accomplish with their music?

W.9-10.7

CCSS Literacy.RL.9-10.4 Determine the meaning of words and phrases as they are used in the text, including figurative and connotative meanings; analyze the cumulative impact of specific word choices on meaning and tone (e.g., how the language evokes a sense of time and place; how it sets a formal or informal tone). Literacy.RL.9-10.5 Analyze how an author's choices concerning how to structure a text, order events within it (e.g., parallel plots), and manipulate time (e.g., pacing, flashbacks) create such effects as mystery, tension, or surprise. Literacy.W.9-10.7 Conduct short as well as more sustained research projects to answer a question (including a self-generated question) or solve a problem; narrow or broaden the inquiry when appropriate; synthesize multiple sources on the subject, demonstrating understanding of the subject under investigation.

READ

OBJECTIVES

Vocabulary
- Key Vocabulary Ⓣ

Reading Strategy
- Determine Importance: Summarize Lyrics

Comprehension & Critical Thinking
- Summarize
- Use Text Evidence Ⓣ

Literary Analysis
- Analyze Structure: Song Lyrics Ⓣ

Writing
- Form: Response to Literature; Letter

APPLY

Ⓐ ANALYZE

1. **Explain** Every person is important. We should be proud of who we are and respect others in the same way.
RL.9-10.2
2. **Vocabulary** Self-esteem gives a person pride and self-confidence. Low self-esteem makes you feel like you don't deserve respect.
L.9-10.6
3. **Analyze Structure: Song Lyrics** The images show how people from all walks of life show respect or disrespect for others.
RL.9-10.5
4. **Focus Strategy: Determine Importance** Have volunteers share their group's summary. Make sure students contrast the difficulty of summarizing ideas in "I Am Somebody" and "Hip-Hop as Culture."
RL.9-10.2; RI.9-10.2

Ⓑ Return to the Text

Students' letters should reflect:

- Grandmaster Flash's point of view
- views that say every person is valuable, no matter their circumstances

W.9-10.9.a; W.9-10.10

Don't judge a book by its cover
'Cause it's never what it seems
Now I know what I'm sayin',
And I feel I gotta scream

That I am somebody (Say it loud)
Like you are somebody
He is somebody
Like I am someone

So be yourself, HUH! ❖

ANALYZE I Am Somebody

Ⓐ

1. **Explain** What is the theme, or message, of the chorus?
2. **Vocabulary** According to Grandmaster Flash, what is important about **self-esteem**? What are the dangers of low self-esteem?
3. **Analyze Structure: Song Lyrics** Identify examples of imagery from the song. How do they help you understand the author's ideas?
4. **Focus Strategy Determine Importance** With a group, summarize the song's main idea. Discuss whether it is easier or harder to summarize ideas in song lyrics than in an essay.

Ⓑ

Return to the Text

Reread and Write What message does the song have for the different people in our society? Write a letter from Grandmaster Flash to one of the people he mentions. What ideas does he want them to know?

About the Songwriter

Grandmaster Flash (1958–), born Joseph Saddler, was one of the first musicians during rap and hip-hop music's early days. With his group, Grandmaster Flash and the Furious Five, he created some of the distinctive hip-hop sound effects that are still used today. In 2003, he received the Founder's Award for his achievements in hip-hop at the *Billboard* R&B/Hip-Hop Awards.

Interactive Reading

Have students reread and mark "I Am Somebody" within the Edge Interactive Practice Book to apply their knowledge of song lyric structure and to practice the Focus Strategy—Determine Importance: Summarize.

Edge Interactive Practice Book, pp. 73–76

Unit Project

Progress Check Allow time for students to work on their unit projects. Meet with individuals and/or groups to provide guidance and check on their progress.

myNGconnect.com

- **Unit Planning Tools**
- **Unit Project Evaluation Rubric**

CCSS **Literacy.RL.9-10.2** Determine a theme or central idea of a text and analyze in detail its development over the course of the text, including how it emerges and is shaped and refined by specific details; provide an objective summary of the text. **Literacy.RL.9-10.5** Analyze how an author's choices concerning how to structure a text, order events within it (e.g., parallel plots), and manipulate time (e.g., pacing, flashbacks) create such effects as mystery, tension, or surprise. **Literacy.RI.9-10.2** Determine a central idea of a text and analyze its development over the course of the text, including how it emerges and is shaped and refined by specific details; provide an objective summary of the text. **Literacy.W.9-10.9.a** Apply grades 9-10 Reading standards to literature (e.g., "Analyze how an author draws on and transforms source material in a specific work [e.g., how Shakespeare treats a theme or topic from Ovid or the Bible or how a later author draws on a play by Shakespeare]"). **Literacy.W.9-10.10** Write routinely over extended time frames (time for research, reflection, and revision) and shorter time frames (a single sitting or a day or two) for a range of tasks, purposes, and audiences. **Literacy.L.9-10.6** Acquire and use accurately general academic and domain-specific words and phrases, sufficient for reading, writing, speaking, and listening at the college and career readiness level; demonstrate independence in gathering vocabulary knowledge when considering a word or phrase important to comprehension or expression.

EQ Does Creativity Matter?

Reading

Critical Thinking

1. **Analyze** Think back to your discussion on page 138 about ways that music influences our lives. Explain whether the two selections support your ideas.
2. **Compare** Many people might think that hip-hop **culture** is all about clothes and money. Would Efrem Smith and Grandmaster Flash agree? Give examples from both selections.
3. **Interpret** Smith believes that no matter who you are, "Hip-hop is influencing your situation." What does he mean? Do you think Grandmaster Flash would agree?
4. **Predict** Over time, hip-hop **evolved** into an important culture. Do you think hip-hop will continue to be very popular? Why or why not?
5. **Evaluate** Music can have many effects on our lives. What effects might "I Am Somebody" have on a listener? Discuss your ideas with a group.

Writing

Writing: Write About Literature

Song Lyrics Think about the authors' important ideas in "Hip-Hop as Culture" and "I Am Somebody." Work with a partner to decide on one main idea that fits both texts. Then write a four-line verse that expresses the main idea. Read or perform your lyrics for the class.

Vocabulary

Key Vocabulary Review

Oral Review Work with a partner. Use these words to complete the paragraph.

achieve	**evolved**	**perspective**
asserts	**heritage**	**self-esteem**
culture	**innovator**	

Hip-hop style has __(1)__ and changed in many ways over the past few decades. It began in the 1970s with an __(2)__ who introduced a new way to combine many styles of music. Its __(3)__ includes influences from disco, funk, and reggae music. In the past, hip-hop lyrics included some negative messages. But much of today's hip-hop __(4)__ important ideas that come from the __(5)__, or point of view, of urban youth. It encourages young people to work hard in order to __(6)__ their goals, to have high __(7)__ and to believe that they are valuable. Hip-hop has become a __(8)__ that includes the beliefs, attitudes, and behaviors of many young people today.

Writing Application Write a short journal entry about a time when music had an effect on you. Use at least four Key Vocabulary words.

Fluency

Read with Ease: Intonation

Assess your reading fluency with the passage in the Reading Handbook, p. 755. Then complete the self-check below.

1. My intonation did/did not sound natural.
2. My words correct per minute: ____

Lesson 14

REFLECT AND ASSESS

OBJECTIVES

Vocabulary
- Key Vocabulary Ⓣ

Reading Fluency
- Intonation Ⓣ

Comprehension & Critical Thinking
- Compare Across Texts
- Identify Main Idea
- Use Text Evidence Ⓣ

Literary Analysis
- Evaluate Literature

Writing
- Form: Song Lyrics

Reading

Critical Thinking

1. **Analyze** Students should explain their original ideas and reflect on whether or not the selections supported or changed those ideas.
2. **Compare** Both writers would disagree. Efrem Smith says that hip-hop is a culture that began with "inner-city and lower-class life." Grandmaster Flash says that money doesn't merit status and "you can't take money witcha." RL.9-10.1; RI.9-10.1
3. **Interpret** Smith means that people buy clothes and listen to music that has been affected by hip-hop whether they listen to it or not. Grandmaster Flash might agree because he knows that his music and ideas can influence his fans.
4. **Predict** Students should make a clear prediction and give reasons for their ideas.
5. **Evaluate** Groups should discuss different effects that the song might have, such as changing people's attitudes about stereotypes and making people feel better about themselves. SL.9-10.1

Writing

Write About Literature

Edge Interactive Practice Book, p. 77

Song Lyrics Have partners brainstorm details and examples that reflect their shared main idea. Tell students to review some of the features common to song lyric structure, discussed on p.150. Invite volunteers to share their lyrics. RL.9-10.2; RI.9-10.2; W.9-10.10

Vocabulary

Key Vocabulary Review

1. *evolved* **2.** *innovator* **3.** *heritage* **4.** *asserts* **5.** *perspective* **6.** *achieve* **7.** *self-esteem* **8.** *culture*
L.9-10.6

Fluency

Read with Ease: Intonation

Ensure that students complete the self-check.
RI.9-10.10

ASSESS & RETEACH

Assessments Handbook, pp. 15f–15i

Have students complete the **Reader Reflection**. Then give students the **Cluster Test** to measure their progress. Group students as needed for reteaching.

CCSS **Literacy.RL.9-10.1** Cite strong and thorough textual evidence to support analysis of what the text says explicitly as well as inferences drawn from the text. **Literacy.RL.9-10.2** Determine a theme or central idea of a text and analyze in detail its development over the course of the text, including how it emerges and is shaped and refined by specific details; provide an objective summary of the text. **Literacy.RI.9-10.1** Cite strong and thorough textual evidence to support analysis of what the text says explicitly as well as inferences drawn from the text. **Literacy.RI.9-10.2** Determine a central idea of a text and analyze its development over the course of the text, including how it emerges and is shaped and refined by specific details; provide an objective summary of the text. **Literacy.W.9-10.10** Write routinely over extended time frames (time for research, reflection, and revision) and shorter time frames (a single sitting or a day or two) for a range of tasks, purposes, and audiences. **Literacy.SL.9-10.1** Initiate and participate effectively in a range of collaborative discussions (one-on-one, in groups, and teacher-led) with diverse partners on grades 9 -10 topics, texts, and issues, building on others' ideas and expressing their own clearly and persuasively. **Literacy.L.9-10.6** Acquire and use accurately general academic and domain-specific words and phrases, sufficient for reading, writing, speaking, and listening at the college and career readiness level; demonstrate independence in gathering vocabulary knowledge when considering a word or phrase important to comprehension or expression.

Lesson 15

INTEGRATE THE LANGUAGE ARTS

OBJECTIVES

Language Function
- Describe Experiences Ⓣ

Literary Analysis
- Analyze Style: Language and Word Choice Ⓣ

Research Skill
- Gather Information

Listening and Speaking
- Oral Presentation

Grammar
- Action Verbs in the Present Tense Ⓣ

Grammar

Use Action Verbs in the Present Tense

Grammar Transparency 25

Review Use the transparency to review action verbs. Conduct the activity on p. 156.

Oral Practice (1–5) Make sure students use present tense action verbs.

Written Practice **6.** listen **7.** unites **8.** can help

L.9-10.1.b

Language Development

Describe Experiences

Use the Language Acquisition Rubric to assess language function.

SL.9-10.1

Assessments Handbook, p. 15o

Literary Analysis

Analyze Style and Word Choice

Word choices should show writer's style.

RL.9-10.4; RI.9-10.4

Research/Speaking

Oral Presentation

Teens and Trends Give students the option of using visuals.

See **Language and Learning Handbook** p. 702 for further instruction.

W.9-10.7; SL.9-10.4

Edge Interactive Practice Book, p. 78

GRAMMAR SKILLS PATH
21 Action Verbs
22 Action Verbs in the Present Tense
23 Subject-Verb Agreement: *-s*
24 Helping Verbs: *Can, Could, May, Might*
▶ 25 Review: Action Verbs in the Present Tense ELL Language & Grammar Lab

INTEGRATE THE LANGUAGE ARTS

Grammar

Use Action Verbs in the Present Tense

An **action verb** tells what the subject does. An action verb in the **present tense** tells what the subject does now or does often.

My friends and I **listen** to music every day.
We **dance** to the beat.

Add **-s** to the action verb only when you talk about one other person, place, or thing.

That new song **amazes** me.
The singer **struts**.

An action verb can have a helping verb and a **main verb**. The helping verbs **can**, **could**, **may**, or **might** come before the main verb. Never add **-s** to them.

Music **can** **change** the world.
He **may** **write** a song.

Oral Practice (1–5) With a partner, take turns completing each sentence with a present tense verb.

1. Music ___ from the radio.
2. The DJ can ___ the songs.
3. Dancers ___ to the music.
4. Lyrics ___ a message.
5. I might ___ with my friends.

Written Practice (6–10) Rewrite the paragraph. Choose the correct present tense verb. Then add two sentences. Use action verbs in the present tense.

Today, many teens (listen/listens) to music on the Internet. Music (unite/unites) people from different cultures. A song (can help/cans help) people speak a common language.

Language Development

Describe Experiences

Group Talk What kind of music do you like? In a group with others who agree with you, describe a dance or music event you have experienced.

Literary Analysis

Analyze Style and Word Choice

Word choice is the kind of language a writer uses. It plays a big part in helping a writer develop his or her own **style**, or particular way of writing. Word choice often changes based on a writer's audience.

A hip-hop artist like Grandmaster Flash uses lots of informal language, or slang, choosing words and phrases that relate to his listeners:

- "yo, don't act cold-blooded"

An essayist like Efrem Smith mainly uses more formal writing to describe his experiences:

- "Hip-hop tells the stories of the multiethnic urban youth . . ."

Smith also adds slang that helps readers understand the time he is describing:

- "It's a commentary from the 'hood . . ."

Work with a partner to find more examples of the type of word choice that contributes to each writer's style. Discuss whether the author's message would be more effective with different style or word choice.

Research/Speaking

Oral Presentation

Teens and Trends Research how teens get their music today, such as: music stores and radio stations, over the Internet, or other ways.

1. **Survey** Ask students at your school where they get their music. Record your responses.
2. **Research** Find more information in newspaper, magazine, and online articles.
3. **Analyze** Compare your survey with research results. What trends or patterns do you see?
4. **Report** Share your findings with the class in a short oral report.

Language and Learning Handbook, page 702

156 Unit 2 The Art of Expression

GRAMMAR

Review: Action Verbs in the Present Tense

Review Display the transparency. Contrast the verbs in the items and reinforce when to add -s. Point out helping verbs and explain that it is not necessary to add -s to these verbs.

A. Oral Practice As students choose the correct verb, underline it and have them say the sentence aloud.

B. Written Practice Work through the example. Explain that some sentences have no errors. Have the group tell you how to edit the paragraph. Then ask a volunteer to read the corrected paragraph aloud. L.9-10.1.b

Grammar & Writing Practice Book, pp. 53–54

Grammar Transparency 25

GRAMMAR REVIEW: ACTION VERBS IN THE PRESENT TENSE 25

Use Action Verbs in the Present Tense

Remember: A verb must agree with its subject.

- Which subjects take -s on the **action verb**?

I **create** a song.	He **creates** a song.
You **sing** a song.	She **sings** a song.
We **get** applause.	It **gets** applause.
They **take** a bow.	A student **takes** a bow.

- Why don't these verbs change?
  He **may create** a song.
  She **could help** with the song.
  It **can become** popular.
  The student **might win** an award.

Try It

A. Say each sentence with the correct present tense verb.

1. Concerts often (**bring** / **brings**) people together.
2. One song (**may inspire** / **mays inspire**) people to kindness.
3. A group performance (**build** / **builds**) friendship among singers.
4. Others in the audience (**might sing** / **sings**) along.

B. Edit the paragraph. Fix four mistakes. The first is done for you.

Music ~~allow~~ allows everyone in my family to be creative. I write song lyrics. My dad ~~compose~~ composes the music. My brother ~~break-dance~~ break-dances to hip-hop. My sister ~~cans~~ can recite poetry to jazz.

CCSS **Literacy.RL.9-10.4** Determine the meaning of words and phrases as they are used in the text, including figurative and connotative meanings; analyze the cumulative impact of specific word choices on meaning and tone **Literacy.RI.9-10.4** Determine the meaning of words and phrases as they are used in a text, including figurative, connotative, and technical meanings; analyze the cumulative impact of specific word choices on meaning and tone (e.g., how the language of a court opinion differs from that of a newspaper). **Literacy.W.9-10.7** Conduct short as well as more sustained research projects to answer a question (including a self-generated question) or solve a problem; narrow or broaden the inquiry when appropriate; synthesize multiple sources on the subject, demonstrating understanding of the subject under investigation.

Vocabulary Study

Context Clues for Idioms

Expressions like "you're stuck on yourself" are called **idioms**. Idioms mean something different from the literal, or exact, meaning of their words.

To figure out the meaning of an unfamiliar idiom:

1. **Study the context of the phrase** The next line of the song says: "You're better than nobody else."
2. **Guess the meaning** The verse is about an overly proud or self-centered person.
3. **Test your guess** If it fits, you may have found your definition! If not, revise your guess.
4. **Use a resource** If all else fails, look up the phrase or ask a friend or teacher for help.

There may be times when these techniques do not work, and context clues may not always help you. Sometimes, it may help to skip over the phrase. The meaning may become clearer as you read on.

With a partner, find four unfamiliar idioms from both selections and add their meanings to a chart. You may even find more modern idioms that mean the same thing.

PAGE	IDIOM	CONTEXT	MEANING
153	you're stuck on yourself	"you're better than nobody else"	You're too proud of yourself.

Writing Trait

Focus and Unity

Whenever you write, you want to keep the reader focused on your main idea. To do this:

- avoid repeating yourself
- leave out unnecessary details
- remove ideas that take away from your point.

Just OK

Music is important to my family. Two of my four grandparents were singers. They have photos of tours to Europe. My parents fill our house with music all day. My sisters and I all take piano lessons, but I play sports, too.

Much Better

Music is important to my family. Two of my four grandparents were singers. ~~They have photos of tours to Europe.~~ My parents fill our house with music all day. My sisters and I all take piano lessons~~, but I play sports, too~~. Music is what brings our family together.

With a partner, analyze how to make the passage below more focused and unified.

Music is one way that people express their feelings and ideas. Other people may like to write letters or paint things to express their feelings and ideas. Loud music with a heavy beat shows strong emotions, such as anger and jealousy. Soft, slow music shows love or sadness. You don't have to be able to play an instrument to express yourself through music, either. There are times when I can tell how my friends are feeling by hearing what they're listening to. Just listening makes me know how they feel.

Sometimes a diagram helps you decide which details are focused and which are not.

Main Idea
Music expresses people's feelings.

Detail 1
Some music shows anger and jealousy.

Detail 2
Some music shows love or sadness.

Writing Handbook, page 784

Writing Rubric — Focus and Unity

Exceptional	• Rewritten passage clearly supports main idea. • Repetition and irrelevant statements are removed. • Action verbs are used correctly.
Competent	• Rewritten passage largely supports main idea. • Most repetition and irrelevant statements are removed. • Action verbs are used correctly with no more than one error.
Developing	• Rewritten passage may stray from supporting main idea. • Some repetition and irrelevant statements are retained. • Action verbs are sometimes used correctly.
Beginning	• Rewritten passage does not support main idea. • Many examples of repetition and irrelevant statements are retained. • Action verbs are not used correctly.

Lesson 16

INTEGRATE THE LANGUAGE ARTS

OBJECTIVES

Vocabulary
- Strategy: Use Contextual Analysis (idioms) T

Writing
- Trait: Focus and Unity T

Vocabulary Study

Context Clues for Idioms

Idiom	Context	Meaning
(p. 137) trying to live out the American dream from the bottom up	"trying to make something out of nothing"	trying to succeed even if you are poor
(p. 138) opened the door	"so that others ... could start"	made it easier for others to do something
(p. 147) bring me down	"could make me feel shame"	tell me I am worthless or no good

L.9-10.4.a; L.9-10.5.a

Edge Interactive Practice Book, p. 79

Writing Trait

Focus and Unity

Help students identify the ways that the Much Better paragraph is an improvement of the Just OK paragraph. For example: Unnecessary details were removed; additional sentence emphasizes main idea without repeating it.

Have partners use a main idea and details diagram to help identify which details are focused. Remind them to remove repeated ideas or details, unnecessary details, and ideas that take away from the main point.

See **Writing Handbook** p. 784 for further instruction.
W.9-10.5

CCSS **Literacy.SL.9-10.1** Initiate and participate effectively in a range of collaborative discussions with diverse partners on grades 9-10 topics, texts, and issues, building on others' ideas and expressing their own clearly and persuasively. **Literacy.SL.9-10.4** Present information, findings, and supporting evidence clearly, concisely, and logically such that listeners can follow the line of reasoning and the organization, development, substance, and style are appropriate to purpose, audience, and task. **Literacy.L.9-10.1.b** Use various types of phrases and clauses to convey specific meanings and add variety and interest to writing or presentations. **Literacy.W.9-10.5** Develop and strengthen writing as needed by planning, revising, editing, rewriting, or trying a new approach, focusing on addressing what is most significant for a specific purpose and audience. **Literacy.L.9-10.4.a** Use context as a clue to the meaning of a word or phrase. **Literacy.L.9-10.5.a** Interpret figures of speech in context and analyze their role in the text.

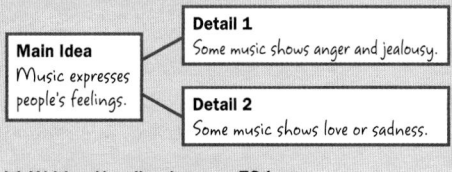

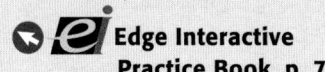

Lesson 17

LISTENING AND SPEAKING WORKSHOP

OBJECTIVES

Listening and Speaking

- Plan and Give a Descriptive Presentation Ⓣ
- Demonstrate Appropriate Body Language and Speaking Effectively for This Purpose
- Use a Rubric

BUILD BACKGROUND

A Descriptive Presentation

Introduce Point out that many commercials are examples of descriptive presentations. Explain how the speaker describes events in such a way that allows the listeners to feel like they are there.

Descriptive Presentation A descriptive presentation requires you to engage the listener in creative ways. Use detailed, descriptive words to connect with the audience.

TEACH & PRACTICE

B Plan Your Presentation

Brainstorm Tell students to think about a memorable event. Ask these questions:

- Where was the event and what did it look like?
- How would you describe the event to a friend who wasn't there?
- How did being there make you feel?

ELL **Use Visuals** Invite students to locate a photograph or draw illustrations that will help them describe the event.

Have students make a list of the most important details of the event they have selected. Remind them to choose an interesting and engaging way to start the presentation.

Descriptive Presentation

A Have you ever heard a speaker describe an event in a way that was so interesting, you could imagine the event as if you were there? You can be just as interesting of a speaker! All you need is the right subject, some great language, and a little practice. Here's how to give a great descriptive presentation:

B

1. Plan Your Presentation

Think about a memorable event, such as a dance or a sporting event that you have gone to or been a part of. Then do the following:

- List the most important details about the event.
- Write descriptive words or phrases about how the event looked, how being there made you feel, or what made it memorable.
- Choose details that support the impression you want to make.
- Write your presentation, including factual descriptions and sensory details.

C

2. Practice Your Presentation

Rehearse your presentation a few times to keep it smooth and interesting.

- Think of interesting ways to start—by role-playing a scenario, showing a photograph, or having the audience guess the event from your description.
- Practice using your voice and gestures in a way that keeps the audience focused on what you are saying.
- Practice speaking without your notes.
- Ask a classmate for helpful suggestions.

myNGconnect.com
Download the rubric.

D

3. Give Your Presentation

Keep your audience interested by doing the following:

- Make eye contact with your audience.
- Use your voice and gestures to keep your audience's attention.
- Stay focused on your topic and purpose.
- Speak clearly and loudly enough for the audience to understand.
- Look at your notes if you need to, but try to use them as little as possible.

FOCUS ON WRITER'S CRAFT

Using Active and Passive Voice

Teach Explain that knowing how to use active and passive voice can help you improve an oral presentation. Invite students to draft sample sentences for their descriptive presentations. Model how to express the same idea using passive and active voice. For example:

- The audience was spoken to by two actors. (passive) Two actors spoke to the audience. (active)
- The play was written by Gary Soto. (passive) Gary Soto wrote the play. (active)
- The theater was built last year. (passive) Some people built the theater last year. (active)

Practice/Apply Have students write active-passive sentence pairs in order to evaluate voice. Mention that active voice is usually easier to follow. Remind students to use passive voice when the subject does not perform the action (The theater was built last year) or when the subject is unknown (Some people).
L.9-10.1.b

CCSS Literacy.L.9-10.1.b Use various types of phrases (noun, verb, adjectival, adverbial, participial, prepositional, absolute) and clauses (independent, dependent; noun, relative, adverbial) to convey specific meanings and add variety and interest to writing or presentations.

4. Discuss and Rate the Presentation

Use the rubric to discuss and rate the descriptive presentations, including your own. Make sure your style and structure support your meaning and purpose.

Descriptive Presentation Rubric

Scale	Content of Descriptive Presentation	Student's Preparation	Student's Delivery
3 Great	• Made me really see the event • Was lively and held my attention throughout	• Included precise details about the event • Created a very clear impression of the event	• Spoke clearly and was easy to follow • Stayed focused on the purpose of describing the event
2 Good	• Gave me a fairly good picture of the event • Held my interest much of the time	• Included some details about the event • Created a general impression of the event	• Spoke clearly most of the time and was usually easy to follow • Was often focused on describing the event
1 Needs Work	• Did not help me imagine the event • Was not very interesting	• Included hardly any details about the event • Did not create an impression	• Was hard to hear and understand • Seemed to have no purpose

E

DO IT ▸ When you are finished preparing and practicing, give your descriptive presentation!

Language and Learning Handbook, page 702

How can you make a presentation even more descriptive?

DIFFERENTIATED INSTRUCTION

As you conduct the workshop with students, adjust your teaching strategies to their needs.

Struggling Readers

Graphic Organizer Help students complete a chart to help organize their ideas and details about the event they are describing.

What Did You See?	How Did You Feel?	What Did You Do?	What Made It Memorable?

Ask students to work with a partner to share their ideas and details. Encourage partners to extend their ideas together.

English Language Learners ELL

Demonstration Have students role-play and demonstrate the event they plan to use for their descriptive presentations. Encourage them to use their senses as they plan their descriptive presentations.

Challenge

Extend the Activity Have students prepare their descriptive presentations by using clues without naming the specific event. Invite this group to give their presentations first. Lead the other students to identify the event at the end of each presentation.

C Practice Your Presentation

Model Demonstrate a short descriptive presentation for students.

- Start the presentation in an interesting way, such as by role-playing a scenario or showing a photograph.
- Use descriptive word clues to describe a memorable event, such as a school dance. Have students guess the event.
- Include descriptive language that requires students to use their senses.
- Make eye contact and speak clearly, loudly, and with expression.
- Glance at your notes only occasionally.

SL.9-10.4; L.9-10.3

Prepare Have students rehearse their presentations. Remind them to use their voice in a way that keeps the audience interested.

Use a Rubric Discuss the rubric. Have teams of three students practice their presentations together and use the rubric to suggest feedback. Remind students to include any feedback from their team members into their presentations.

SL.9-10.4

myNGconnect.com

Descriptive Presentation Rubric

APPLY

D Give Your Presentation

Present Ask students to review the tips and give their descriptive presentations. Tell students to write notes while listening to summarize the speaker's ideas and help with feedback. Conclude by having students ask the presenter questions for clarification and elaboration.

SL.9-10.4; L.9-10.3

E Discuss and Rate the Presentation

Give Feedback Have students give written or oral feedback. Reviewers should rate the presenter with a 1, 2, or 3 and support their rating with comments about the content, preparation, and delivery. Students should also rate themselves. Remind students to evaluate if the style and structure support the meaning and purpose.

SL.9-10.3

ONGOING ASSESSMENT

Have students incorporate peer feedback into their descriptive presentations and describe how the feedback helped improve the presentation.

CCSS **Literacy.SL.9-10.3** Evaluate a speaker's point of view, reasoning, and use of evidence and rhetoric, identifying any fallacious reasoning or exaggerated or distorted evidence. **Literacy.SL.9-10.4** Present information, findings, and supporting evidence clearly, concisely, and logically such that listeners can follow the line of reasoning and the organization, development, substance, and style are appropriate to purpose, audience, and task. **Literacy.L.9-10.3** Apply knowledge of language to understand how language functions in different contexts, to make effective choices for meaning or style, and to comprehend more fully when reading or listening.

Cluster 3 Planner

EQ ESSENTIAL QUESTION:

Does Creativity Matter?

Discover one way to find your voice.

Online Planner
myNGconnect.com

	LESSON 18 **Prepare to Read**	LESSON 19 **Slam: Performance Poetry Lives On** Main Selection
Reading		
Reading Strategies Focus Strategy **Determine Importance**	**Activate Prior Knowledge** SL.9-10.1 • Make a Connection: Quickwrite *T160*	**Determine Importance** RI.9-10.2 • Determine What's Important *T161, T164–T173*
Literary Analysis Genre Focus **Kinds of Nonfiction**		T **Analyze Author's Purpose** RI.9-10.6 *T161, T164–T173* **Compare Themes and Time Periods** • Influential Modern Poets *T162*
Vocabulary	T **Key Vocabulary** RI.9-10.4; L.9-10.5.b; L.9-10.6 • Introduce *T160* **compose**, **euphoria**, **expression**, **improvisation**, • **phenomenon**, **recitation**, • **structure**, **transcend**	T **Key Vocabulary** L.9-10.6 • Daily Routines *T165* • Link to Essential Question *T167* • Selection Reading *T164–T173* **compose**, **expression**, **improvisation**, • **phenomenon**, **recitation**, • **structure**, **transcend**
Fluency		T **Expression** RI.9-10.10 • Daily Routines *T165* T **Accuracy and Rate** RI.9-10.10 Comprehension Coach *T163*
Writing		
Response to Literature		**Return to the Text** W.9-10.9.b; W.9-10.10 • **Reread and Write** Why are people attracted to creative expressions like slam poetry? *T173*
Writing Across the Curriculum		**Research and Writing** W.9-10.7 • **Music Connection** *T171*
Language		
ELL **Language Development**	T **Give and Follow Commands** SL.9-10.6 • Language and Grammar Lab, Transparency F *LAB TE p. 32*	T **Give and Follow Commands** SL.9-10.6 • Daily Routines *LAB TE p. 32*
Grammar Grammar Focus **Present Tense Verbs**		T **Present Tense of *Be*** *T166* L.9-10.1.b T **Present Progressive Verb Forms** *T168* L.9-10.1.b T **Present Tense of *Have*** *T170* L.9-10.1 T **Present Tense of *Do*** *T172* L.9-10.1.b
Listening and Speaking	**Partner Talk** SL.9-10.1 • Characteristics of Poetry *T160*	**Listen to a Selection** RI.9-10.10 Comprehension Coach *T163* *CD 3, Track 5*

T = Tested on Cluster and/or Unit Reading and Literary Analysis Test
T = Tested on Language Acquisition Assessment
T = Tested on Unit Writing Test
T = Assessed with a Rubric
• **Academic Vocabulary**

Slam: Performance Poetry Lives On

Genre: Essay Lexile® 970L

Slam poetry is a unique and modern style of spoken-word performance. This essay traces the roots of slam poetry from oral storytellers in ancient times to the major art form that it is today.

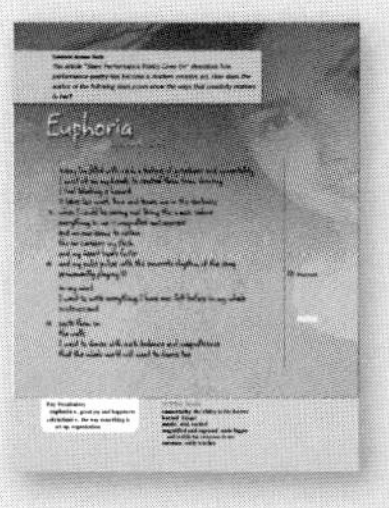

Euphoria

Genre: Poem

The author of this slam poem uses imagery and emotion to portray the excitement she feels about creativity. Her optimistic mood inspires her to share her happiness with other people.

LESSON 20 **Euphoria** Second Selection	LESSON 21 **Reflect and Assess**	LESSONS 22 & 23 **Integrate the Language Arts**	LESSON 24 **The Creativity Crisis** Close Reading
Determine Importance RL.9-10.2 • Determine What's Important *T174, T175–T176*	**Comprehension and Critical Thinking** *T177* RL.9-10.2; RI.9-10.2; RI.9-10.10 • Compare Across Texts • Explain, Analyze, Compare, Predict, Evaluate		
Analyze Structure: Free Verse *T174, T175–T176* RL.9-10.5	**Interpret and Evaluate Literature** RI.9-10.10 **Use Text Evidence** *T177* RI.9-10.1	**Analyze Literary Movements: Poetry Across Cultures** *T178* RI.9-10.1	**Analyze Author's Purpose** *T181* RI.9-10.6; L.9-10.3
Key Vocabulary L.9-10.6 • Selection Reading *T175–T176* **euphoria** • **structure** **expression**	**Key Vocabulary** L.9-10.6 • Review *T177* **compose** • **phenomenon** **euphoria** **recitation** **expression** • **structure** **improvisation** **transcend**	**Vocabulary Strategy** L.9-10.4.a; L.9-10.5.a • Use Context Clues: Idioms *T179*	**Academic Vocabulary** L.9-10.3; L.9-10.6 • Review *T180* • emphasize
Expression RI.9-10.10 • Daily Routines *T165* **Accuracy and Rate** RI.9-10.10 Comprehension Coach *T175*	**Expression** RI.9-10.10 • Peer Assessment *T177*		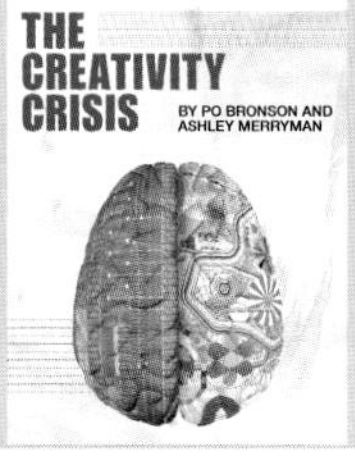
Return to the Text W.9-10.9.a • **Reread and Write** What forms of expression does the poet want to use to show her feelings and ideas? *T176*	**Write Poetry** RL.9-10.5; W.9-10.10 • **Write a Slam Poem** Create poems for a poetry slam, experimenting with different structures. *T177*	**Writing Form** W.9-10.2 • **How-To Paragraph** *T179*	**The Creativity Crisis** **Genre:** Research Report **Lexile® 1200L** *CD 11, Track 2*
Give and Follow Commands SL.9-10.6 • Daily Routines *LAB TE p. 32*		**Give and Follow Commands** SL.9-10.6 • Group Talk *T178*	LESSON 25 **UNIT WRAP-UP**
		Present Tense Verbs *T178* L.9-10.1.b	**Unit Project** SL.9-10.4 • Demonstration *T184*
Listen to a Selection RI.9-10.10 Comprehension Coach *T175* *CD 3, Track 6*	**Participate in a Discussion** *T177* SL.9-10.1	**Judging Panel** *T178* SL.9-10.1.d	

EDGE LIBRARY

Hole in My Life ●
by Jack Gantos

The Stone Goddess ● ●
by Minfong Ho

Anthem ● ● ●
by Ayn Rand

Lesson 18
PREPARE TO READ

OBJECTIVES

Vocabulary
- Key Vocabulary
- Strategy: Use Cognates; Relate Words

Reading Strategy
- Activate Prior Knowledge

ELL Language & Grammar Lab

Language Function Transparency F
Give and Follow Commands

ENGAGE & CONNECT

A EQ Essential Question

Focus on Personal Expression Ask: What are some ways that people can find and express their creative voice?

Possible responses:
- *They can paint or write.*
- *They perform; they act or sing.*

B Make a Connection

Have students complete the Quickwrite and compare their opinions with a partner about what does and does not qualify as poetry.
SL.9-10.1

TEACH VOCABULARY

C Learn Key Vocabulary

Study the Words Review the four steps of the Make Words Your Own routine (*see the Vocabulary tab*):

1. **Pronounce** Say one word and have students repeat it. Write *compose* and pronounce it, one syllable at a time: *com-pose*. Ask students what looks familiar in the word, and point out other forms of the word, such as *composition*.

   ELL Use cognates to help Spanish speakers with the words (*see the Vocabulary tab*).

2. **Study Examples** Read the example in the chart. Ask: Would you rather compose a poem or read a poem?

ONGOING ASSESSMENT
Have students complete an oral sentence for each word. For example: *She showed her ________ by leaping up in the air after scoring the game-winning goal.*

PREPARE TO READ

- Slam: Performance Poetry Lives On
- Euphoria

A **EQ** **Does Creativity Matter?**
Discover one way to find your voice.

Make a Connection

B **Quickwrite** As a student, you have encountered many kinds of poetry. Think about the different characteristics (if any) that they share. Then do a quickwrite about what you think poetry should and shouldn't be.

Learn Key Vocabulary

C **Study the Words** Pronounce each word and learn its meaning. You may also want to look up the definitions in the Glossary.

• Academic Vocabulary

Key Words	Examples
compose (kum-**pōz**) *verb* ▸ pages 167, 177	To **compose** means to create something by writing it. If you **compose** a poem, I'll compose music to go with it.
euphoria (ū-**for**-ē-u) *noun* ▸ pages 175, 176	**Euphoria** is great joy and happiness. Our team was filled with **euphoria** after we won the art contest. *Antonym*: depression
expression (eks-**pre**-shun) *noun* ▸ pages 166, 176, 179	The art of **expression** is the ability to communicate in a creative way. Poetry is one form of creative **expression**.
improvisation (im-prah-vu-**zā**-shun) *noun* ▸ page 171	**Improvisation** means something done without pre-planning. When I forgot to prepare a speech for class, **improvisation** was my only option.
• **phenomenon** (fi-**nahm**-u-nahn) *noun* ▸ pages 171, 173, 177	A **phenomenon** is something different that people get really excited about. The new music video is a real **phenomenon**; people everywhere are watching it.
recitation (re-su-**tā**-shun) *noun* ▸ page 164	A **recitation** involves speaking a poem or other text aloud in front of other people. For my class project, I will give a poetry **recitation**.
• **structure** (**struk**-chur) *noun* ▸ pages 166, 174, 175, 176	**Structure** is the way something is set up or organized. My poem has a **structure** that includes lots of rhyme.
transcend (tran-**send**) *verb* ▸ page 166	To **transcend** means to rise above or go beyond. Art is something that **transcends** the limits of language. *Synonyms*: outdo, exceed

Practice the Words Work with a partner to add a **Connotation Chart** entry for each Key Vocabulary word. If you think the word has a positive meaning, write +. If you think the word has a negative meaning, write –. If the word is neither, write =. Write your reason in the last column.

Connotation Chart

Word	Positive (+), Negative (–), or Neither (=)	Reason
compose	+	I always think it's good to create something new.

3. **Encourage Elaboration** Provide a frame: *When I have to compose an essay, I feel ______.*

Reading Transparency 8

4. **Practice the Words** Use the transparency to model how to complete a Connotation Chart. Have students work with a partner to make and complete a chart for each Key Vocabulary word.

Edge Interactive
Practice Book, pp. 80–81
RI.9-10.4; L.9-10.5.b; L.9-10.6

Reading Transparency 8

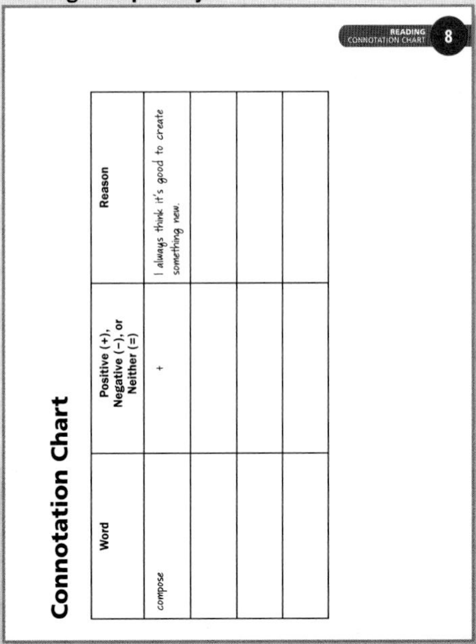

CCSS Literacy.RI.9-10.4 Determine the meaning of words and phrases as they are used in a text, including figurative, connotative, and technical meanings; analyze the cumulative impact of specific word choices on meaning and tone (e.g., how the language of a court opinion differs from that of a newspaper). Literacy.SL.9-10.1 Initiate and participate effectively in a range of collaborative discussions (one-on-one, in groups, and teacher-led) with diverse partners on grades 9-10 topics, texts, and issues, building on others' ideas and expressing their own clearly and persuasively. Literacy.L.9-10.5.b Analyze nuances in the meaning of words with similar denotations.

BEFORE READING Slam: Performance Poetry Lives On

essay by Pooja Makhijani

Reading Strategies
- Plan and Monitor
- ▶ **Determine Importance**
- Make Inferences
- Ask Questions
- Make Connections
- Synthesize
- Visualize

Analyze Author's Purpose

An **essay** is short piece of nonfiction writing that is about a single subject. The author writes from a limited point of view to inform, persuade, or entertain you about a certain topic. Be sure to think about the author's purpose for writing this essay and use it to decide whether he or she meets these goals effectively.

Look Into the Text

The author gives information about poetry.

Poetry doesn't have to be the twelve lines on a page in a book that is sitting in the dustiest corner of the library. Poetry doesn't have to be something you don't understand. Poetry is moving, breathing, ever changing.

How does the author want to persuade you to feel about poetry?

Want proof? Take a trip to the Urban Word Annual Teen Poetry Slam at the Nuyorican Poets Cafe in New York City.

Gathered in this tight space are hundreds of teens from every corner of the city. They've come together to compete for one of five top spots in Brave New Voices, the Eighth Annual National Youth Poetry Slam Festival.

The author informs you about an event.

Focus Strategy ▶ Determine Importance

Every text has a main idea. Details in the text help to support or explain that idea. As you read, ask yourself: Why is this detail important? How does it support the main idea of the text?

Focus Strategy

HOW TO DETERMINE IMPORTANCE

1. **Read Carefully** As you read, pause to ask yourself:
   - What is the main point of this section?
   - How do the details support this main idea?

Response Journal

Page	Details	Importance
164	"The slam is about words, rhythm, and performance, and it's a lot of fun."	The author includes this to show the important parts of slam.

2. **Record Your Ideas** Use a **Response Journal** to add details from the text and tell how they support the main idea. Note where you found the idea in the text.
3. **Summarize the Important Ideas** Retell the most important ideas in your own words.

Reading Transparency 9

Analyze Author's Purpose

READING AUTHOR'S PURPOSE 9

What does the writer include in an essay?

Introduce An essay shows an author's viewpoint on a single subject.

- **Authors provide information on the subject.**
  "Poetry doesn't have to be something you don't understand."
- **Authors show their viewpoint on the subject.**
  "Poetry is moving, breathing, ever changing."

Depending on their purpose and audience, writers may choose to write other types of text.

Purpose	Examples
to teach or inform	a nonfiction article about art history
to persuade	a letter to the editor about keeping music and art in public schools
to entertain	song lyrics

Lesson 19

BEFORE READING

OBJECTIVES

Reading Strategy
- Determine Importance

Literary Analysis
- Analyze Author's Purpose T

TEACH STRATEGIES

D Analyze Author's Purpose

Look Into the Text Read the introduction to explain essay and review author's purpose. Read the text passage aloud. Use the callouts to discuss the author's purpose for writing an essay about poetry. Ask: What does the author want you to feel or think about poetry?

Possible responses:
- *Poetry is exciting.*
- *Everyone can understand poetry.*

Reading Transparency 9

Use the Transparency Discuss different purposes an author might have for writing an essay. Review the information and point of view that an essay will show. Ask: Based on the information and the author's point of view so far, what do you think is the author's purpose for writing "Slam"?

Possible responses:
- *to provide information about slam poetry*
- *to persuade people to be excited about poetry*

RI.9-10.6

E Focus Strategy: Determine Importance

Determine What's Important Review that students use a variety of strategies as they read. Then read the introduction with students to define the strategy. Work through the steps in the How To box.

Have students use the strategies with Look Into the Text to determine what is important in the passage and why.

RI.9-10.2

Edge Interactive Practice Book, pp. 82–83

ONGOING ASSESSMENT

Have students tell what purposes an author may have for writing an essay and how an essay is different from other types of nonfiction, such as a news article or an interview.

CCSS Literacy.RI.9-10.2 Determine a central idea of a text and analyze its development over the course of the text, including how it emerges and is shaped and refined by specific details; provide an objective summary of the text. Literacy.RI.9-10.6 Determine an author's point of view or purpose in a text and analyze how an author uses rhetoric to advance that point of view or purpose. Literacy.L.9-10.6 Acquire and use accurately general academic and domain-specific words and phrases, sufficient for reading, writing, speaking, and listening at the college and career readiness level; demonstrate independence in gathering vocabulary knowledge when considering a word or phrase important to comprehension or expression.

READ

OBJECTIVES

Literary Analysis
- Compare Themes and Time Periods

Viewing
- Respond to and Interpret Visuals

BUILD BACKGROUND

A What You Should Know

Have students read "Never a Dull Friday Night."

Compare Themes Share information about these poets

- Dylan Thomas: Welsh poet; mid-1930s–early 1950s; themes of death, loss of innocence
- Bob Dylan: American musician/poet; mid-1960s; themes of social protest, restless youth
- Langston Hughes: American poet; mid-1930s–late 1950s; themes of racial identity and relations
- Marianne Moore: American poet; 1920s–1950s; themes of spirituality, love, animals, nature

Have students interpret the possible influences of the historical context on literary works. Ask: Do themes in poetry connect only to a certain culture or time period? Explain.

Possible response:
- *Most themes, like love or nature, would connect to any culture or time period. Other themes, like social protest, might be related to the time period.*

Connect to Themes Jesse Ibarra says poetry can be "a powerful weapon," especially for young people. Do you agree with him?

Help students connect to universal themes in poetry. Ask: If you wrote a poem, what would it be about?

myNGconnect.com

- Selection Summaries in eight languages

What You Should Know

Never a Dull Friday Night

by Katy Murphy, Oakland Tribune

It was a Friday night, and sounds of an electric guitar traveled down the hallways of San Leandro High School in San Leandro, CA.

But the music was just a warm-up. The teenagers who filled all the available chairs, desks, and tables of the drama room came for something else.

Poetry.

They came for Dylan Thomas and Bob Dylan. Langston Hughes and Marianne Moore. But most of all, they came to hear original works being read and sung by people they see every day and to share their art with a friendly audience.

"Love is like waking up on a beautiful Saturday morning because your house is on fire," Nicholas Morales, 16, delivered in perfect deadpan as the drumming stopped.

He strummed his guitar for a few beats.

Friday nights in San Leandro haven't been the same in the past few months, since Jesse Ibarra and his friends got tired of having nothing to do and nowhere to play their music.

Ibarra, a senior at San Leandro High School who says he writes "on a continuous basis," managed to secure a classroom with an adult chaperone. He called the monthly event "Friday Night of the Arts."

About 15 people showed up for the first run. The second drew about 20. By the fourth night more than 50 people—almost all high school students—came to whoop and laugh and cheer for anyone brave enough to take the stage, until it was their turn.

Ibarra advertises the event with signs asking people to help "break the mold of bad poetry," with strict instructions to leave all unicorn and rainbow poems at home. Poetry can be a powerful weapon, he said, and more young people need to realize that it's not all about rhyme and structure.

Increasingly, they do.

"I like that it's informal and completely unplanned for the most part," Morales said. "It's not like a show that you have to put on. It's like hanging out with friends."

myNGconnect.com

- Read about the founder of slam poetry.
- Listen to readings of poems by new and classic poets.

DIFFERENTIATED INSTRUCTION

English Language Learners ELL

Preview the selection:

- Show the photograph on p. 163: *The poets at a slam perform for an audience.*
- Read paragraph 4 on p. 164. Describe the slam as a combination of a sporting event, play, and concert all in one.
- Demonstrate the poses of the poets on pp. 163, 165, and 170: *The poets show their emotions throughout their performance.*

Read Aloud to provide a supported listening experience:

- Play the **Selection Recording** as students track text in their books. **CD 3**
- Have students use the Listen feature in the **Comprehension Coach** where they see the text as it is read aloud.
- Read the selection aloud to students as you provide comprehensible input. For example, you can provide visuals to depict the emotions expressed in the poems and excerpts.

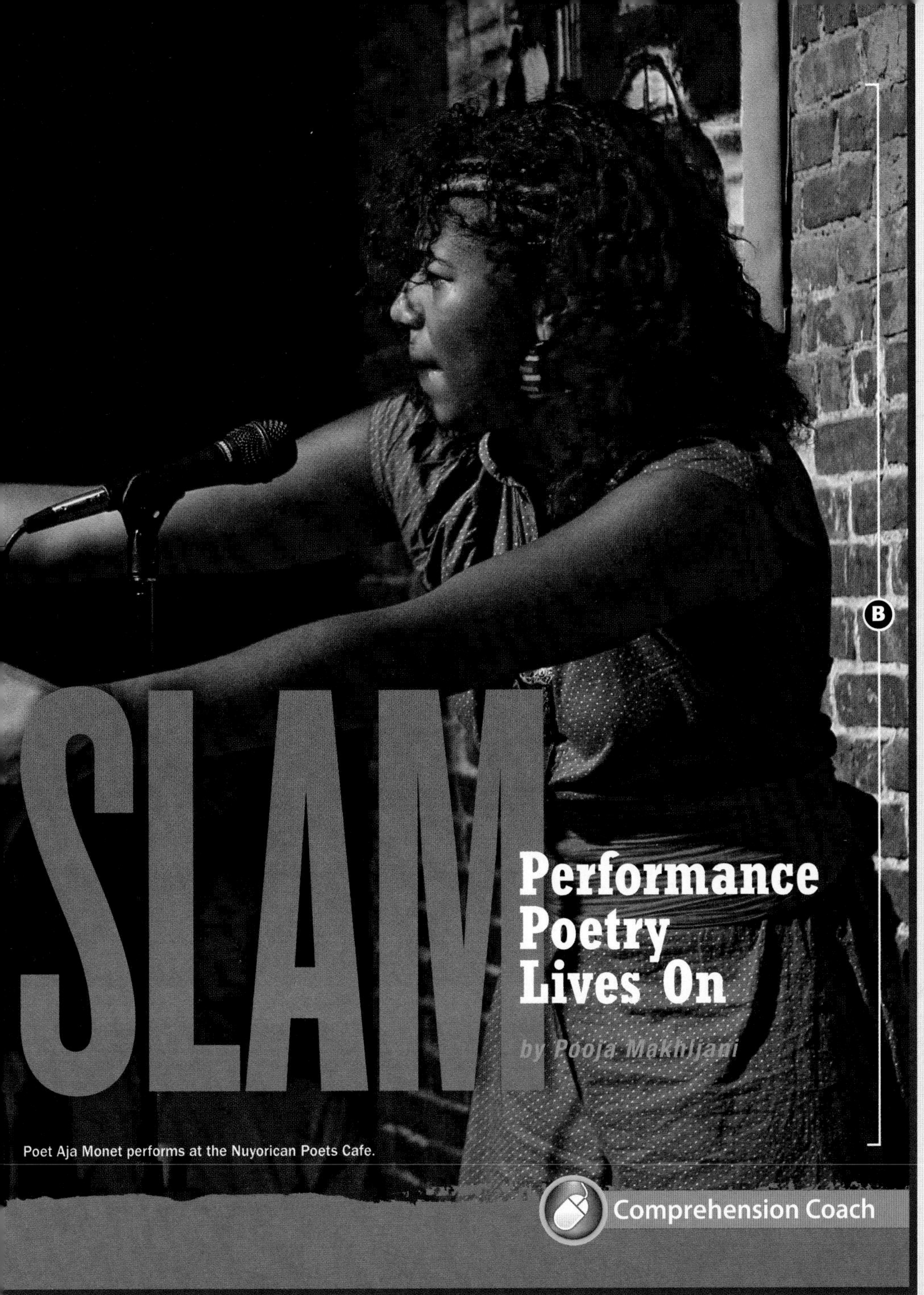

Poet Aja Monet performs at the Nuyorican Poets Cafe.

TEACH & PRACTICE

B Analyze Visuals

Analyze the Photograph Read the title of the selection and the caption as students study the photograph.

ELL Use Graphic Organizer Use a word web to show the different meanings of the word *slam*.

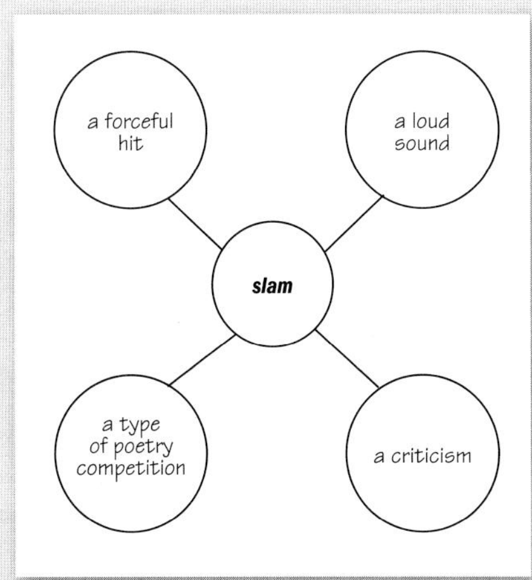

Ask: Based on the photograph, what can you tell about a poetry slam or performance poetry?

Possible responses:
- *Poets use gestures and facial expressions.*
- *The audience is watching carefully.*

Have students brainstorm other meanings they know for the word *slam*, such as those having to do with noise or criticism. Ask: Why do you think these poetry readings are called *slams?*

Possible responses:
- *The poets get evaluated or criticized.*
- *The poetry and the criticism are loud and forceful.*

L.9-10.5

Comprehension Coach

Build Reading Power

Assign students to use the software, based on their instructional needs.

Read Silently
- Comprehension questions with immediate feedback
- Glossary support
- Review text evidence

RI.9-10.10

Listen
- Professional model of fluent reading

Record
- Oral reading fluency practice
- Ongoing fluency assessment with immediate feedback

CCSS Literacy.RI.9-10.10 By the end of grade 9, read and comprehend literary nonfiction in the grades 9–10 text complexity band proficiently, with scaffolding as needed at the high end of the range. By the end of grade 10, read and comprehend literary nonfiction at the high end of the grades 9–10 text complexity band independently and proficiently. Literacy.L.9-10.5 Demonstrate understanding of figurative language, word relationships, and nuances in word meanings.

READ

OBJECTIVES

Vocabulary
- Key Vocabulary Ⓣ

Reading Fluency
- Expression Ⓣ

Comprehension & Critical Thinking
- Use Text Evidence Ⓣ

Literary Analysis
- Analyze Author's Purpose Ⓣ

Viewing
- Respond to and Interpret Visuals

TEACH & PRACTICE

Ⓐ Reading Support

1 Author's Purpose Ask: Why might the author start the essay by telling you what poetry is *not*?

Possible response:
- *The author may want to challenge readers' ideas about poetry.*

RI.9-10.6

Ⓑ Reading Support

2 Author's Purpose Point out the words and phrases "upbeat music," "people erupt into wild applause," and "hollers."

ELL Demonstrate Act out, or ask volunteers to act out, descriptive words and phrases in paragraph 4. For example, sit quietly and then clap and cheer suddenly to demonstrate "erupt into wild applause."

Ask: Why does the author include this description at the beginning of the essay?

Possible answer:
- *The author wants readers to feel the energy and excitement of a slam.*

RI.9-10.6

What Is Poetry?

Ⓐ Poetry doesn't have to be the twelve lines on a page in a book that is sitting in the dustiest corner of the library. Poetry doesn't have to be something you don't understand. Poetry is moving, breathing, ever changing. 1

Want proof? Take a trip to the **Urban** Word Annual Teen Poetry Slam at the Nuyorican Poets Cafe in New York City.

Gathered in this tight space are hundreds of teens from every corner of the city. They've come together to compete for one of five top spots in Brave New Voices, the Eighth Annual National Youth Poetry Slam Festival.

Ⓑ Sitting in the cafe feels like being at a sporting event. A DJ **revs up the crowd** with upbeat music. Young people erupt into wild applause as one of their own **hollers** his latest creation of slam before the microphone. 2

Take a listen to this **excerpt** from "Elementary Invasion," by 16-year-old slam poet Kai Zhang:

> "squeeze
> green putty oozing out of your hands
> and hugging your fingers cold and
> rubbery
> escaping
> your silly efforts to contain
> or hold"
>
> — *Kai Zhang*

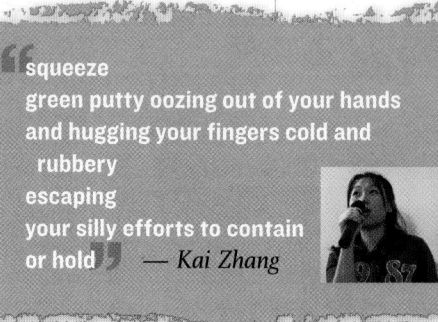

Zhang's **recitation** is a mix of **rant**, **rhetoric**, and stand-up comedy, with dashes of hip-hop and rap. Judges in the front row hold up cards with scores—10, 9.5, 10—as the crowd cheers her on, voting to keep her in the race.

The slam is about words, rhythm, and performance, and it's a lot of fun.

1 Author's Purpose The author begins by describing what poetry is not. What do you think is the author's purpose for starting this way?

2 Author's Purpose Why do you think Makhijani includes this lively scene near the beginning of the essay?

Key Vocabulary
recitation *n.*, speaking a poem or other text aloud in front of other people

In Other Words
Urban Big city
revs up the crowd gets the crowd excited
hollers shouts out
excerpt small part
rant, rhetoric opinion, argumentative style

DIFFERENTIATED INSTRUCTION

Interactive Reading As you conduct the interactive reading session with students, adjust your teaching strategies to their needs.

Struggling Readers

Make Connections Show how key ideas in the essay relate to students' experiences using the words *is like*; for example: *A poetry slam is like a sporting event.*

English Language Learners ELL

Figurative Language Explain that some language in the article is meant to create pictures in your mind. For example: *A poetry slam is like a lyrical boxing match.*

Encourage students to draw pictures to see the two things being compared.

Challenge

Compare and Contrast Have students compare and contrast aspects of poetry slams discussed in the article:
- a poetry slam and an athletic or other competition
- written poetry and spoken-word poetry

Have students share their ideas with the class and lead a discussion. For example: Do you think poetry should be competitive? Do you think poetry should be spoken or read?

CCSS Literacy.RI.9-10.6 Determine an author's point of view or purpose in a text and analyze how an author uses rhetoric to advance that point of view or purpose.

Slamming sequence at the Nuyorican Poets Cafe Friday Night Slam, performed by poet Ryler Dustin

Slam poet Ricardo Perez Gonzalez

C

TEACH & PRACTICE

C Analyze Visuals

Analyze the Photographs Discuss the photographs and read the caption. Ask: Why are there three photos of the same poet?

Possible response:

- *The photos show the poet's motion and different expressions.*

Ask: What do you notice about the poet's posture and gestures in the bottom picture?

Possible response:

- *The poet is using dramatic gestures, and moving as he performs.*

Then ask: How would you describe the audience's reaction?

Possible response:

- *The audience members are smiling and laughing, and seem very involved.*

Discuss students' impressions of poetry slams so far.

DAILY ROUTINES

Vocabulary

See the Vocabulary and Fluency Routines tab for more information.

Word Sorts Provide categories for sorting:

- Noun or verb? Suffix or no suffix?

Sentence Frames Write sentence frames; for example: *I will ______ a letter to my grandmother on the computer.*

Use Graphic Organizers Select a graphic organizer for practice; for example, a vocabulary log:

Word	Meaning	Sentence
expression	the ability to communicate in a creative way	Painting is a form of expression.

L.9-10.6

Fluency: Expression

CD 11

This cluster's fluency practice uses a passage from "Slam: Performance Poetry Lives On" to help students practice appropriate expression. Use **Reading Handbook** T750 and the **Fluency Model CD** to teach or review the elements of fluent expression, and then use the daily fluency practice activities to develop students' oral reading proficiency.

RI.9-10.10

CCSS **Literacy.RI.9-10.10** By the end of grade 9, read and comprehend literary nonfiction in the grades 9-10 text complexity band proficiently, with scaffolding as needed at the high end of the range. By the end of grade 10, read and comprehend literary nonfiction at the high end of the grades 9-10 text complexity band independently and proficiently. **Literacy.L.9-10.6** Acquire and use accurately general academic and domain-specific words and phrases, sufficient for reading, writing, speaking, and listening at the college and career readiness level; demonstrate independence in gathering vocabulary knowledge when considering a word or phrase important to comprehension or expression.

OBJECTIVES

Vocabulary
- Key Vocabulary Ⓣ

Reading Strategy
- Determine Importance

Comprehension & Critical Thinking
- Use Text Evidence Ⓣ

Literary Analysis
- Analyze Author's Purpose Ⓣ

Grammar
- Forms of *Be* in the Present Tense Ⓣ

TEACH & PRACTICE

Ⓐ Reading Support

3 Author's Purpose/Determine Importance Ask: What happened in 1984 that was important in slam history?

Possible responses:
- *Marc Smith started doing performance poetry.*
- *It was the beginning of competitive poetry slams.*

Ask: Why does the author include this information?

Possible response:
- *to let people know how slam got started*
- *to show that slam was started by ordinary people*

RI.9-10.2; RI.9-10.6

Ⓑ Reading Support

4 Determine Importance Ask: What older forms of poetry are connected to slam?

Possible response:
- *Slam is connected to the first storytellers, Shakespeare, the Beat poets of the 1960s, and hip-hop.*

Ask: Why does the author think it's important to tell where slam came from?

Possible responses:
- *to show that people have been doing something like slam for thousands of years*
- *to show that it's a serious way for people to express themselves*

RI.9-10.2

What Is Slam?

As the founders of the literary organization Youth Speaks put it, slam is a form of **expression**. It's "a generation of young people speaking for themselves; a generation . . . reciting struggles and successes on open microphones . . . **transcending traditional stereotypes** by speaking their truths and listening to the truths of others."

"A poetry slam is like a lyrical boxing match that pits poets against other poets in a **bout**," according to journalist Shilanda L. Woolridge. In simpler words, a slam is a competition in which poets perform original works alone or in teams. They recite their poems for an audience that boos and cheers as it votes on the best performers. Each poet's work is judged as much on the manner of its performance as on its content or style.

Ⓐ The **structure** of the traditional slam is a spoken-word performance of three minutes plus a ten-second **grace period**. This was started by construction worker and poet Marc Smith in 1984. 3 The **emphasis** on performance soon led to the energetic brand of poetry known as slam. Similar competitions quickly spread across the country and finally found a home at the Nuyorican Poets Cafe and in similar "slam cafes" around the country.

Ⓑ Really, though, the roots of slam can be traced from hip-hop back to the first storytellers, through Shakespeare, and to the Beat poets of the 1960s. 4

3 Author's Purpose/ Determine Importance What key moment in slam history is described here? Why does the writer include it?

4 Determine Importance What's an important way slam relates to older forms of poetry? How does the author show it's important?

Key Vocabulary

expression *n.*, way to get thoughts or feelings across to another person

transcend *v.*, to rise above or go beyond

• **structure** *n.*, way something is set up

In Other Words

traditional stereotypes old beliefs about other groups of people

bout contest

grace period time to think and get ready

emphasis focus

GRAMMAR

Forms of *Be* in the Present Tense

Teach/Model Display the transparency. Point out that the forms of *be* in the chart are in the present tense. As you work through the examples, ask students to come up with another example for each verb. Also elicit more examples for each contraction.

Practice A. As students choose the correct verb, underline it, and have them read the sentence aloud. **B.** After partners write about a competition, have each student read two sentences aloud. Ask the group to identify the forms of *be.* L.9-10.1.b

Grammar & Writing Practice Book, pp. 55–56

Grammar Transparency 26

GRAMMAR FORMS OF *BE* IN THE PRESENT TENSE 26

What Forms of *Be* Are Used in the Present?

Am, Is,* and *Are

- Use the form of the verb **be** that matches the subject.

  I **am** excited about the poetry slam.
  It **is** my favorite arts event.
  Pedro **is** a lively performer.
  Leora **is** amazing, too.
  They **are** talented.
  We **are** happy to be here. **Are** you?

Present Tense Forms of *Be*
I **am**
he, she, or it **is**
we, you, or they **are**

- Use **not** after the **verbs** **am**, **is**, and **are** to make a sentence negative. The short form of **is not** is **isn't**. The short form of **are not** is **aren't**.

  1. That poet **is** **not** ready.
     That poet **isn't** ready.
  2. They **are** **not** here yet.
     They **aren't** here yet.

Try It

A. Say each sentence with the correct verb form.

1. I like to go to poetry slams. They **(is / are)** like a boxing match.
2. Zhang **(is / are)** a fine poet and performer.
3. The audience at the slam **(am / is)** happy to hear her poetry.
4. I **(am / is)** a good poet, too, but my friends **(isn't / aren't)**.
5. They **(is / are)** good performers, though, and they read my poems at the slam.

B. Now imagine you are watching a poetry slam or other competition. Tell a partner your ideas. Write your four best sentences with forms of be. Sentences will vary.

GRAMMAR SKILLS PATH

- ▶ **26 Forms of *Be* in the Present Tense**
  ELL Language & Grammar Lab
- **27 Present Progressive Verb Forms**
- **28 Present Tense of *Have***
- **29 Present Tense of *Do***
- **30 Review: Present Tense Verbs**

CCSS Literacy.RI.9-10.2 Determine a central idea of a text and analyze its development over the course of the text, including how it emerges and is shaped and refined by specific details; provide an objective summary of the text. **Literacy.RI.9-10.6** Determine an author's point of view or purpose in a text and analyze how an author uses rhetoric to advance that point of view or purpose. **Literacy.L.9-10.1.b** Use various types of phrases (noun, verb, adjectival, adverbial, participial, prepositional, absolute) and clauses (independent, dependent, noun, relative, adverbial) to convey specific meanings and add variety and interest to writing or presentations.

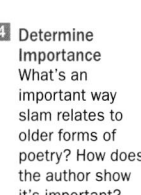

From Spoken Word to Written Word

Although slam draws on urban street rhythms like hip-hop, it is first a modern version of the oral **roots** of storytelling and poetry.

Oral storytelling is older than the written word. In ancient times, stories were passed from lips to ears and traveled from place to place. They changed as different storytellers forgot details, deliberately left things out, and added their own details. In ancient Greece, traveling **bards** performed to audiences across their land, reciting **epic poems**.

Over the course of history, there has been a change from the oral tradition to a written one. The earliest example of written poetry is Homer's *Odyssey*. **Composed** around the eighth century B.C.E., this epic poem was most likely the combination of several oral stories about the journey of **Odysseus**.

Perhaps the most famous poet of all is William Shakespeare. His written work was meant to be performed rather than read. He wrote 37 plays and 154 **sonnets** between 1588 and 1613. Like the ancient Greeks, Shakespeare wrote his plays in verse.

Students in the Shakespeare Theatre Company's Text Alive! program perform *A Midsummer Night's Dream*.

It is said that the beat of Shakespeare's poetry is modeled on the rhythm of the human heartbeat—bom-BOM bom-BOM bom-BOM bom-BOM bom-BOM. This separated it from the language of every day. 5 (C)

5 Author's Purpose
Why do you think the author "sounds out" the bom-BOM bom-BOM rhythm that Shakespeare used?

Monitor Comprehension

Explain
Does the author say slam is a totally new concept? Explain.

Key Vocabulary
compose *v.*, to write a poem or song

In Other Words
roots tradition
bards poets
epic poems long poems about heroes
Odysseus an Ancient Greek war hero
sonnets 14-line poems

Slam **167**

TEACH & PRACTICE

(C) Reading Support

5 Author's Purpose Read this paragraph aloud with the appropriate rhythm and volume.

ELL **Demonstrate** Some students may be unfamiliar with Shakespeare's language and rhythm. Read this line from Sonnet 13 by Shakespeare once, as marked for rhythm:

Shall **I** com**PARE** thee **TO** a **SUM**mer's **DAY**?

Then invite students to tap out the rhythm on their desks as you reread it.

Ask: Why do you think the author sounds out the rhythm that Shakespeare used?

Possible response:
- *to help readers hear the rhythm as they read*

RI.9-10.6

Monitor Comprehension

Explain Have students think aloud to explain whether the author says that slam is a totally new concept.

MODEL Say:
- *In the first section, the author describes a slam poetry event.*
- *The second section, "What is Slam?" explains more about slam and the competitions.*
- *This information so far doesn't tell whether slam is a new concept.*

Have students look at the rest of what they've read so far to complete the Think Aloud and answer the question.

Possible responses:
- *In the third section, right away the author relates slam poetry to oral storytelling and poetry of ancient times.*
- *This information shows that slam is not a new concept.*

RI.9-10.1

VOCABULARY

Link Vocabulary and Concepts

Ask questions to link Key Vocabulary with the Essential Question.

EQ **ESSENTIAL QUESTION:**
Does creativity matter?

Some possible questions:
- *Why is it important to be creative when you* **compose** *a poem?*
- *What did Marc Smith create as a* **structure** *for slam poetry?*
- *What are some examples of creative* **expression**?
- *How can a poet* **transcend** *the limits of language?*
- *What elements does a poet put in a* **recitation** *to make it unique?*
- *Do you think creativity can lead to* **euphoria**?

Have students use the Key Vocabulary words in their responses.
L.9-10.6

CCSS Literacy.RI.9-10.1 Cite strong and thorough textual evidence to support analysis of what the text says explicitly as well as inferences drawn from the text. Literacy.RI.9-10.6 Determine an author's point of view or purpose in a text and analyze how an author uses rhetoric to advance that point of view or purpose. Literacy.L.9-10.6 Acquire and use accurately general academic and domain-specific words and phrases, sufficient for reading, writing, speaking, and listening at the college and career readiness level; demonstrate independence in gathering vocabulary knowledge when considering a word or phrase important to comprehension or expression.

READ

OBJECTIVES

Vocabulary
- Content Area Vocabulary: Performance Art
- Synonyms

Reading Strategies
- Determine Importance; Summarize; Review Strategies

Comprehension & Critical Thinking
- Summarize
- Use Text Evidence T

Literary Analysis
- Analyze Author's Purpose T
- Analyze Style: Author's Word Choice

Grammar
- Present Progressive Verb Forms T

TEACH & PRACTICE

A Reading Support

6 Determine Importance Have volunteers summarize the main idea of the first paragraph.

Possible response:
- *Poetry is still influenced by the tradition of spoken poetry.*

Discuss how the details on this page support this main idea. RI.9-10.2

Review Strategies Have partners explain which other strategies they used, as they read the text.

Possible response:
- *I visualized the details of Allen Ginsberg performing "Howl." This helped me to understand what beat poetry looked like when it was performed.* RI.9-10.1

B Reading Support

7 Language Have students use a dictionary or a thesaurus to determine the precise meaning and use of the word *celebrated.*

Ask: What words in this paragraph are synonyms for *celebrated?*

Possible responses:
- *well-known, famous* RI.9-10.4; L.9-10.4.c; L.9-10.5.b

Beating to the Sound of the Times

A Although poetry has moved in many different directions since the time of Shakespeare, it has always kept a deep connection to the oral tradition. 6

In the 1950s and '60s, the Beat poets brought poetry directly to the people using the ancient ways of the traveling storyteller. Like today's slam artists, the Beats came to be known for their **unique** performance styles.

B Allen Ginsberg is one of the most **celebrated** poets of the Beat generation. He first read his most well-known poem, "Howl," in a series of famous readings in October 1955 in San Francisco. 7

It was Ginsberg's first **public performance**, and it made him instantly famous at the age of 29. After starting his recitation in a calm tone, the story goes, he soon gained confidence. He began to **sway rhythmically** with the music of his poetry, responding to the enthusiasm of the audience.

6 Determine Importance What is the main idea of paragraph 1? Explain how one detail on page 168 supports this main idea.

7 Language The author describes Ginsberg as a "celebrated" poet. What words in this paragraph are synonyms for *celebrated?*

Beat poet Allen Ginsberg once said, "Poetry is the one place where people can speak their original human mind. It is the outlet for people to say in public what is known in private."

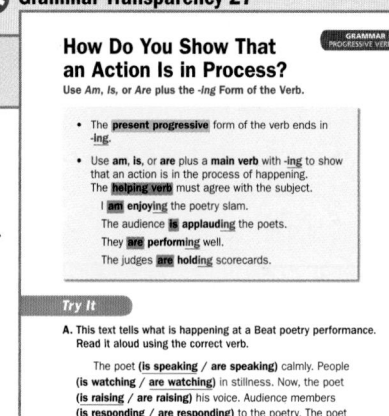

In Other Words
unique special, unusual
celebrated famous
public performance poetry reading in front of other people
sway rhythmically move back and forth to the beat

168 Unit 2 The Art of Expression

GRAMMAR

Present Progressive Verb Forms

Teach/Model Display the transparency. Perform and describe an action; for example: *I am opening a book.* Discuss how the verb *am opening* tells about an action that is in progress. Then work through the examples.

Practice A. As students choose the correct verb, underline it. Then have a volunteer read the paragraph aloud while the group acts out the scene. **B.** Have students complete and share the stories. Record some sentences with present progressive verbs, and ask the group to identify them. L.9-10.1.b

Grammar & Writing Practice Book, pp. 57–58

GRAMMAR SKILLS PATH

26 Forms of *Be* in the Present Tense
▶ 27 Present Progressive Verb Forms ELL Language & Grammar Lab
28 Present Tense of *Have*
29 Present Tense of *Do*
30 Review: Present Tense Verbs

Grammar Transparency 27

GRAMMAR PRESENT PROGRESSIVE VERB FORMS 27

How Do You Show That an Action Is in Process?

Use *Am, Is,* or *Are* plus the *-ing* Form of the Verb.

- The **present progressive** form of the verb ends in *-ing.*
- Use **am, is,** or **are** plus a **main verb** with *-ing* to show that an action is in the process of happening. The **helping verb** must agree with the subject.

I **am enjoying** the poetry slam.
The audience **is applauding** the poets.
They **are performing** well.
The judges **are holding** scorecards.

Try It

A. This text tells what is happening at a Beat poetry performance. Read it aloud using the correct verb.

The poet **(is speaking / are speaking)** calmly. People **(is watching / are watching)** in stillness. Now, the poet **(is raising / are raising)** his voice. Audience members **(is responding / are responding)** to the poetry. The poet **(is swaying / are swaying)**. Everyone in the audience is swaying.

B. Imagine that you are a slam poet about to present your poetry in a New York café. Write three more sentences with present progressive verbs. Sentences will vary.

I am waiting backstage.

CCSS **Literacy.RI.9-10.1** Cite strong and thorough textual evidence to support analysis of what the text says explicitly as well as inferences drawn from the text. **Literacy.RI.9-10.4** Determine the meaning of words and phrases as they are used in a text, including figurative, connotative, and technical meanings; analyze the cumulative impact of specific word choices on meaning and tone (e.g., how the language of a court opinion differs from that of a newspaper). **Literacy.L.9-10.4.c** Consult general and specialized reference materials (e.g., dictionaries, glossaries, thesauruses), both print and digital, to find the pronunciation of a word or determine or clarify its precise meaning, its part of speech, or its etymology. **Literacy.L.9-10.5.b** Analyze nuances in the meaning of words with similar denotations.

Ginsberg and other Beat poets, such as Jack Kerouac, were heavily influenced by jazz music. This is most obvious if you listen closely to the music of their words as you read them aloud. 8 **C**

8 Author's Purpose The author says a lot about the Beats. How are they connected with slam?

Poetry for the People

Slam has a **mission** for poetry that is similar to Ginsberg's. It seeks to bring poetry back to the people through rhythm, rhyme, and music. "What poetry is about is people," says Mike Henry. He **coordinates** the Austin National Slams, of Austin, Texas. "Slams have put the voice back into . . . the hands of the people."

Although the Beat poets were more influenced by jazz, slam poets have turned to hip-hop for inspiration. The godfather of popular slam, as we know it, is Russell Simmons. In 2001, the father figure to such rappers as Ludacris and Jay-Z created Def Poetry Jam (later called Def Poetry), a slam shown on television. The series **showcased** such artists as poet Ursula Rucker; the hip-hop spoken-word performer Saul Williams; and the British musical diva duo Floetry.

The first season of "def" (slang for *excellent*) poetry was hosted by hip-hop superstar Mos Def. He often opened the

Ursula Rucker is considered one of the pioneers of Slam poetry. She made her first spoken-word recording in 1994, and has performed all over the world.

In Other Words

mission goal, purpose
coordinates is in charge of, organizes
showcased gave the audience a chance to meet

Monitor Comprehension

Summarize How did music influence both the Beats and slam?

TEACH & PRACTICE

C Reading Support

8 Author's Purpose Point out that the author includes a whole section on the Beat poets.

ELL Use Graphic Organizer Use a Venn diagram to help students see the similarities between Beat poetry and slam poetry. Have students identify features of each and place them in the correct place in the diagram. For example:

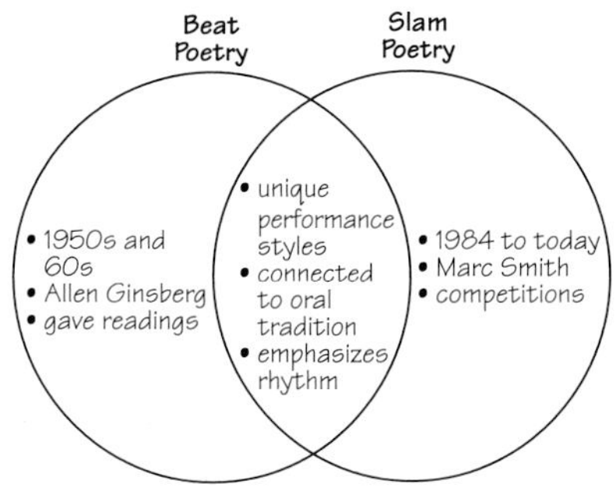

Ask: What qualities does slam poetry share with Beat poetry? What were they both trying to do?

Possible response:

- *emphasis on style and performance*
- *connected to oral tradition of poetry*

RI.9-10.6

Monitor Comprehension

Summarize Have students explain how music influenced the Beats and slam.

Possible response:

- *The Beats were influenced by the rhythms of jazz music; slam is influenced by the rhythms of hip-hop.*

RI.9-10.2

VOCABULARY

Content Area Vocabulary: Performance Arts

Build vocabulary related to the content area of the arts.

ART

Teach/Model Use the Make Words Your Own routine (*see the Vocabulary tab*) and the sample sentences below to introduce these words from the selection.

performance art (pur-**for**-muns art) ▸ p. 171

Musical concerts, plays, and ballet are examples of **performance art**.

venues (**ven**-yūz) ▸ p. 171

We went to the new concert hall, which is a new performance **venue** *in our city.*

rhyme (rīm) ▸ p. 169

When we were younger, we memorized nursery **rhymes**.

rhythm (**ri**-thum) ▸ p. 169

My favorite songs are those with a good beat and **rhythm**.

Practice Have students use the words to describe a music show, movie, or news story they've seen recently.

Apply Have students discuss their favorite form of performance art and describe a real venue they would like to visit some day.

L.9-10.6

CCSS **Literacy.RI.9-10.2** Determine a central idea of a text and analyze its development over the course of the text, including how it emerges and is shaped and refined by specific details; provide an objective summary of the text. **Literacy.RI.9-10.6** Determine an author's point of view or purpose in a text and analyze how an author uses rhetoric to advance that point of view or purpose. **Literacy.L.9-10.1.b** Use various types of phrases (noun, verb, adjectival, adverbial, participial, prepositional, absolute) and clauses (independent, dependent; noun, relative, adverbial) to convey specific meanings and add variety and interest to writing or presentations. **Literacy.L.9-10.6** Acquire and use accurately general academic and domain-specific words and phrases, sufficient for reading, writing, speaking, and listening at the college and career readiness level; demonstrate independence in gathering vocabulary knowledge when considering a word or phrase important to comprehension or expression.

OBJECTIVES

Vocabulary
- Key Vocabulary (T)

Reading Strategy
- Determine Importance

Comprehension & Critical Thinking
- Use Text Evidence (T)

Literary Analysis
- Analyze Author's Purpose (T)

Research Skill
- Evaluate and Draw Conclusions

Grammar
- Present Tense of *Have* (T)

TEACH & PRACTICE

(A) Reading Support

9 Determine Importance Ask: In your own words, what is the mission of slam?

Possible response:
- *Slam's mission is to make poetry something everyone can enjoy by turning it into a fun performance with singing, music, and poetry.*

Ask: How does the Def Poetry Slam help with this mission?

Possible response:
- *The Poetry Slam is a TV show with popular hip-hop artists singing and performing slam poetry. It makes slam poetry enjoyable for everyone.*

RI.9-10.2

(B) Reading Support

10 Author's Purpose Read Matthew Murray's quote aloud.

Ask: How does the author of this essay want people to feel about poetry? How does this quote support that message?

Possible response:
- *The author wants people to appreciate poetry. This quote shows that poetry doesn't have to be old and boring.*

RI.9-10.6

(A) night with a classic poem by **Byron, Shelley, Keats, or Wordsworth**. After that, the audience was treated to slam poetry such as Saul Williams's "Said the Shotgun to the Head": 9

CURRENTLY
MOON MARKED
AND
SUN SPARKED
UNMARKED BILLS
WILL I AM
CERTAIN
I SPEAK A NEW LANGUAGE
as is ALWAYS
THE FIRST SIGN
of a
NEW AGE — Saul Williams

Poet Saul Williams performs. He also records music and acts in films.

Def Poetry brought slam to **center stage**. In 2002, it **made its Broadway debut**. The show brought together a cast of poets as diverse as the United States itself: from Chinese American Beau Sia to Palestinian American Suheir Hammad.

(B) The success of DPJ has made people all around the country appreciate this form of expression. Theater critic Matthew Murray put it best when he wrote, "Def Poetry Jam on Broadway [is] dedicated to proving that poetry **needn't be ancient or stodgy**, but that it can still prove . . . inspiring to the current generation."

Whether it is being recited on Broadway, in a classroom, or in a local coffeehouse, the same is true of slam. 10

9 Determine Importance
What is "slam's mission for poetry"? How does the Def Poetry Jam help to support this concept?

10 Author's Purpose
Why does the author include Murry's quote? How does this quote support the author's main idea about poetry?

In Other Words

Byron, Shelley, Keats, or Wordsworth famous poets from hundreds of years ago
center stage everyone's attention
made its Broadway debut was first performed in one of New York City's famous theaters
needn't be ancient or stodgy doesn't have to be old and boring

GRAMMAR

Present Tense of *Have*

Teach/Model Display the transparency. Point out that the forms of the verb *have* are in the present tense. Use the chart to show how the forms change. Work through the example sentences. Then compare the subjects in the sentences that use *have* versus *has*. Ask a student to state a rule for using *has*.

Practice A. As students name the correct verb, underline it, and have them read the sentence aloud. **B.** Have partners complete the paragraph and read their versions aloud. Record some sentences on the transparency.
L.9-10.1

Grammar & Writing Practice Book, pp. 59–60

GRAMMAR SKILLS PATH

26 Forms of *Be* in the Present Tense
27 Present Progressive Verb Forms
▶ 28 Present Tense of *Have*
ELL Language & Grammar Lab
29 Present Tense of *Do*
30 Review: Present Tense Verbs

Grammar Transparency 28

GRAMMAR PRESENT TENSE OF *HAVE* 28

What Forms of *Have* Are Used in the Present?

Have* and *Has

Use the form of the verb **have** that matches the subject.
- I **have** a notebook for my poems.
- You **have** pages of original poetry.
- She **has** a beautiful poetry journal.
- He **has** a recording. It **has** poems from the Def Poetry Jam.
- We **have** plans to host a poetry jam.
- Several poets **have** an interest in performing.
- They **have** samples of their work on DVD.

Present Tense Forms of *Have*
I **have**
he, she, or it **has**
we, you, or they **have**

Try It

A. Say each sentence with the correct form of **have**.
1. Poetry slams **(have / has)** a mission.
2. Mike Henry plans a poetry slam. He **(have / has)** people in mind.
3. People **(have / has)** a voice with poetry.
4. They **(have / has)** the power to inspire audiences.

B. Talk with a partner about your favorite poet or songwriter. Use **have** or **has** in these sentences. Then add two more sentences.
Sentences will vary.
We __have__ many favorite poets and singers. They __have__ very different styles. Saul Williams uses strong images in his poetry. It __has__ interesting rhythms, too.

CCSS **Literacy.RI.9-10.2** Determine a central idea of a text and analyze its development over the course of the text, including how it emerges and is shaped and refined by specific details; provide an objective summary of the text. **Literacy.RI.9-10.6** Determine an author's point of view or purpose in a text and analyze how an author uses rhetoric to advance that point of view or purpose. **Literacy.L.9-10.1** Demonstrate command of the conventions of standard English grammar and usage when writing or speaking.

Slam Poetry FAQs by Cecily von Ziegesar

Cecily von Ziegesar

What's the difference between slam poetry and performance art?

Like performance art, slam poetry is entertaining. It makes you think, and, like all art, it tries to say something meaningful about **the human experience.** But a slam is a competition, so unlike presenting a set performance art piece, you have to do your best to win! In a slam there's always an element of **improvisation**. A good slam poet thinks on her feet and **delivers straight from the heart**.

Do slam poets really make a living doing this?

Writing poetry is **a labor of love**. Poets aren't paid to write or to slam, although there are sometimes cash prizes at slams. And there are always chances to get published, recorded, or filmed, especially at the bigger slam venues. Most slam poets have day jobs. But they make time to write poetry and to slam, because they love it. 11 C

Do you have to memorize your poems to compete in slams?

No. But the judges will be more impressed if you do. There's an actor inside of every successful slam poet. They love to *perform*.

Where can I find a slam near me?

Check out listings in your local paper or weekly area magazine. The poetry slam is a rapidly growing **phenomenon**, so there are most likely slams happening within a short traveling distance.

11 Determine Importance
Why do slam poets write and perform for little or no pay? What important idea does this detail tell you about slam poets?

Monitor Comprehension
Describe
What are slam poets like? Why do they choose to participate in slam?

Key Vocabulary
- **improvisation** *n.*, something done without pre-planning
- • **phenomenon** *n.*, something new that people get really excited about

In Other Words
FAQs Frequently Asked Questions
the human experience people and their lives
delivers straight from the heart says exactly what she really thinks and feels
a labor of love work that you do because you love it

TEACH & PRACTICE

C Reading Support

11 Determine Importance Ask: Why do slam poets write and perform?

Possible response:
- *They love to do it and they hope they'll get discovered and get published, recorded, or filmed. This shows that slam poets care about their art. It is a "labor of love" that they like to share.*

RI.9-10.2

Monitor Comprehension

Describe Have students review Slam Poetry FAQs on this page.

ELL Use Graphic Organizer
Visually display some characteristics and motivations of slam poets. Explain that "thinks on her feet" means that a person responds quickly to a changing situation.

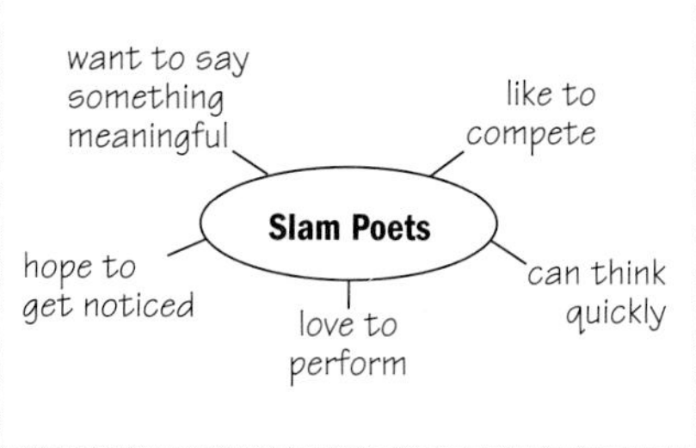

Ask: What are some characteristics of slam poets and some reasons that they participate in slam?

Possible responses:
- *They love to perform and compete.*
- *They are able to think quickly while performing.*

RI.9-10.1

CONTENT AREA CONNECTIONS

MUSIC

Research the Jazz Beats

Conduct Research Have students research the jazz musicians of the 1950s and 1960s and use the information to answer the following questions:
- What instruments did they use to compose their works?
- Which artists were the most famous?
- Was there a structure or form to the work of these jazz artists?
- What did the jazz musicians and the Beats have in common?
- Is improvisation a part of the work of these artists?
- Who is influenced by the jazz musicians today?

Share and Compare Students can share their findings with the class to compare jazz artists of the two decades.
W.9-10.7

CCSS Literacy.RI.9-10.1 Cite strong and thorough textual evidence to support analysis of what the text says explicitly as well as inferences drawn from the text. Literacy.RI.9-10.2 Determine a central idea of a text and analyze its development over the course of the text, including how it emerges and is shaped and refined by specific details; provide an objective summary of the text. Literacy.W.9-10.7 Conduct short as well as more sustained research projects to answer a question (including a self-generated question) or solve a problem; narrow or broaden the inquiry when appropriate; synthesize multiple sources on the subject, demonstrating understanding of the subject under investigation.

READ

OBJECTIVES

Vocabulary
- Key Vocabulary Ⓣ

Reading Strategy
- Determine Importance

Comprehension & Critical Thinking
- Use Text Evidence Ⓣ

Literary Analysis
- Analyze Author's Purpose Ⓣ

Writing
- Response to Literature

Grammar
- Present Tense of *Do* Ⓣ

TEACH & PRACTICE

Ⓐ Reading Strategy

12 **Determine Importance** Read the second item about judges.

ELL Comprehensible Input Clarify that a judge is usually an expert—that is, trained or educated—in the area he or she is judging. However, in a poetry slam, judges do not have to be experts.

Have students think about other situations at school, at sporting events, or on TV where judges give scores. Ask: What does having non-expert judges show about the competition? What qualities might these judges value?

Possible responses:
- *Slam is poetry everyone can understand and enjoy without being an "expert."*
- *The judges are also slam poets, so they might value creativity and energy.*

RI.9-10.2

Ⓑ Reading Support

13 **Author's Purpose** Point out the words after Beau Sia's name. Ask: Why do you think the author mentions Sia's awards?

Possible response:
- *The author wants readers to know that Sia's advice is good because he is a successful slam poet.*

RI.9-10.6

How Do You Have Your Own Slam?

by Felice Belle, *host of the Friday Night Slam at the Nuyorican Poets Cafe*

Felice Belle

A typical slam is five poets competing in three **rounds**. One poem per round. The highest **cumulative** score wins. So . . .

1. You need poets. You cannot have a poetry slam without poets.
2. You need judges. Judges should be **chosen at random** from the audience. Judges will score each poem on a scale of 0 to 10, 10 being the highest. Decimals are encouraged, because they prevent ties. A score of 30 is the highest score in slam. Larger slams usually have five judges and in calculating the score, the highest and lowest scores are dropped. If you select three judges all the scores should count. 12
3. You need a scorekeeper. Preferably a math major.
4. Poets choose numbers to decide the order. So as not to be unfair to the poet who has to perform first, we **sacrifice a poet on the altar of judgely ignorance**. This poet is not in the slam. She is called the sacrificial goat. Her purpose is to warm up the judges.

Now, you are ready to slam.

12 **Determine Importance** At a slam, anyone can be a judge and "expert." Why is this detail important? What does it show about slam?

How Do You Win a Slam?

by Beau Sia, *award-winning slam poet* 13

Beau Sia

That's easy. Be yourself. Once you get your **raw** self on stage, start to shape, mold, and **perfect it**. Most of the people who win slams are their poems **to the core**. And remember: it really isn't about the scores. It's about your voice and your poetry and having a stage to speak from.

13 **Author's Purpose** Why does the author mention Sia's awards?

In Other Words

rounds turns
cumulative total
chosen at random picked by chance
sacrifice a poet on the altar of judgely ignorance have a different poet read for the judges without getting a score that counts
raw true
perfect it make it the best it can be
to the core 100%, all the way

172 Unit 2 The Art of Expression

GRAMMAR

Present Tense of *Do*

Teach/Model Display the transparency. Use the chart to introduce the present tense forms of *do*. Review the concept of a helping verb and a main verb. Explain that the verb *do* can function as either. For each example, have students tell whether *do* is a helping verb or a main verb. Demonstrate how to form *doesn't* and *don't*.

Practice A. As students name the correct verb, underline it, and have them read the sentence aloud. **B.** After partners write their sentences, have each student read two aloud. Record some examples. Ask the group to identify the verbs. L.9-10.1.b

Grammar & Writing Practice Book, pp. 61–62

Grammar Transparency 29

GRAMMAR PRESENT TENSE OF *DO* 29

What Forms of *Do* Are Used in the Present?
Do and Does

- Use the form of **do** that matches the subject. You can use **do** as a **main verb** or as a **helping verb**.

You **do** excellent work.
Tina **does** the planning with Pedro and me.
We **do** try hard.
The poets **do** a great job.
They certainly **do perform** with energy.

Present Tense Forms of *Do*
I **do**
he, she, or it **does**
we, you, or they **do**

- The short form of **does not** is **doesn't**. The short form of **do not** is **don't**.

1. He **does not** speak loudly. He **doesn't** speak loudly.
2. We **do not** mind. We **don't** mind.

Try It

A. Say each sentence with the correct form of **do**.
1. Slam poets (**do** / **does**) their best on stage.
2. They really (**do** / **does**) want to win.
3. A judge from the audience (**do** / **does**) the scoring.
4. Some performers (**don't** / **doesn't**) memorize their poems.
5. A poem (**don't** / **doesn't**) always succeed.

B. Now tell a partner about a creative activity that you do for fun. Write your four best sentences with forms of **do**. Sentences will vary.

GRAMMAR SKILLS PATH
26 Forms of *Be* in the Present Tense
27 Present Progressive Verb Forms
28 Present Tense of *Have*
▶ 29 Present Tense of *Do* — ELL Language & Grammar Lab
30 Review: Present Tense Verbs

CCSS Literacy.RI.9-10.2 Determine a central idea of a text and analyze its development over the course of the text, including how it emerges and is shaped and refined by specific details; provide an objective summary of the text. Literacy.RI.9-10.6 Determine an author's point of view or purpose in a text and analyze how an author uses rhetoric to advance that point of view or purpose. Literacy.L.9-10.1.b Use various types of phrases (noun, verb, adjectival, adverbial, participial, prepositional, absolute) and clauses (independent, dependent; noun, relative, adverbial) to convey specific meanings and add variety and interest to writing or presentations.

How Do You Find Your Voice?

by Ishle Park, *2004 Poet Laureate, Queens, New York*

I write out of a fierce love for the people and places I care deeply about; I want them remembered, I want me remembered. No one else will speak for us if we don't do it ourselves.

Ishle Park

ANALYZE Slam: Performance Poetry Lives On

1. **Explain** What happens at a typical poetry slam? Include details from the text to describe the event and the people.
2. **Vocabulary** Slam may be a new **phenomenon**, but it is linked to older forms of poetry. Explain how traditional poetry contributed to slam.
3. **Analyze Author's Purpose** One purpose of this essay is to present information about the subject. Complete the sentences below with information from the article.
   - Slam poetry is __________.
   - Slam poetry has its roots in __________.
   - The mission of slam poetry is to __________.
4. **Focus Strategy Determine Importance** Look back at the **Response Journal** you began on page 161 about the essay's important ideas and details. With a partner, discuss the ideas and details you both listed and the reasons you found them important.

Return to the Text

Reread and Write Look back at the statements that describe how different people feel about slam poetry. Then write a short summary of reasons why people are attracted to creative expressions like slam.

In Other Words
Poet Laureate official poet

APPLY

C ANALYZE

1. **Explain** A DJ plays music and gets the crowd excited. A poet comes up first to get the audience warmed up. Then the competing poets perform and the audience claps and responds to each poet's performance. Judges score each poem and a winner is named.
   RI.9-10.1
2. **Vocabulary** Slam is a modern version of the ancient oral tradition of storytellers that made up epic poems, such as Homer's *Odyssey*. Slam also borrows from the rhythms of classical poetic forms, such as Shakespeare's sonnets.
   L.9-10.6
3. **Analyze Author's Purpose**
   - a form of creative expression
   - ancient storytelling, Shakespeare's writing, and Beat poetry
   - bring poetry back to the people
   RI.9-10.6
4. **Focus Strategy: Determine Importance** Have volunteers share the parts of the text that their partner found noteworthy. Then have a class discussion about how students felt about the essay.
   RI.9-10.2

D Return to the Text

Students' summaries might reflect these influences and evidence:

- *Slam poets believe they have an important voice that needs to be heard.*
- *Slam poets love to perform, compete, and write.*

W.9-10.9.b; W.9-10.10

Edge Interactive Practice Book, p. 84

CCSS **Literacy.RI.9-10.1** Cite strong and thorough textual evidence to support analysis of what the text says explicitly as well as inferences drawn from the text. **Literacy.RI.9-10.2** Determine a central idea of a text and analyze its development over the course of the text, including how it emerges and is shaped and refined by specific details; provide an objective summary of the text. **Literacy.RI.9-10.6** Determine an author's point of view or purpose in a text and analyze how an author uses rhetoric to advance that point of view or purpose. **Literacy.W.9-10.9.b** Apply grades 9-10 Reading standards to literary nonfiction (e.g., "Delineate and evaluate the argument and specific claims in a text, assessing whether the reasoning is valid and the evidence is relevant and sufficient; identify false statements and fallacious reasoning"). **Literacy.W.9-10.10** Write routinely over extended time frames (time for research, reflection, and revision) and shorter time frames (a single sitting or a day or two) for a range of tasks, purposes, and audiences. **Literacy.L.9-10.6** Acquire and use accurately general academic and domain-specific words and phrases, sufficient for reading, writing, speaking, and listening at the college and career readiness level; demonstrate independence in gathering vocabulary knowledge when considering a word or phrase important to comprehension or expression.

Lesson 20
BEFORE READING

OBJECTIVES
Reading Strategy
• Determine Importance
Literary Analysis
• Analyze Structure: Free Verse

TEACH STRATEGIES

A Analyze Structure: Free Verse

Introduce Read the introduction and ask students what they already know about poetry and poetic structure. Remind students that in most cases we read poetry in the same direction as any other English text.

Look Into the Text Read the excerpt aloud. Use the callouts to teach about the structure of free verse poetry. Ask: What do you notice about the structure of this poem?

Possible responses:
- *The lines are not the same length.*
- *None of the lines rhyme.*

Then ask: What words does the poet use to show her feelings?

Possible response:
- *filled with such a feeling of greatness and immortality*

Ask: What is unusual about the structure of the five lines?

Possible responses:
- *There is no punctuation. Except for the pronoun I, the first word of each line does not begin with a capital letter.*

RL.9-10.5

B Focus Strategy: Determine Importance

Determine What's Important
Define the strategy and work through the steps in the How To box.

Then have partners discuss the main idea of the excerpt from the poem.

Possible responses:
- *The images of hands dancing and manic colors make me feel excited.*
- *The speaker feels great, powerful., and excited.*

RL.9-10.2

ONGOING ASSESSMENT
Have students explain how the structure of a free verse poem is different from other types of poetry.

BEFORE READING Euphoria
poem by Lauren Brown

Reading Strategies
- Plan and Monitor
- ▶ **Determine Importance**
- Make Inferences
- Ask Questions
- Make Connections
- Synthesize
- Visualize

A Analyze Structure: Free Verse

Poetry comes in many forms. Some poems have a specific **structure** with rhythms (like bom-BOM) and regular rhymes. **Free verse poems** usually do not have set rhythms and regular rhymes. The poet is free to structure the free verse poem in any way. However, you will still read the poem in the usual way, from top to bottom and left to right.

Look Into the Text

Lines can be long or short.

Text doesn't always follow grammar rules.

today I'm filled with such a feeling of greatness and immortality
I must sit on my hands to control them from dancing
I find blinking a hazard
it takes too much time and leaves me in the darkness
when I could be seeing and living the manic colors

The poet chooses words that show her feelings.

Images paint pictures in the reader's mind.

B Focus Strategy ▶ Determine Importance

Like other literature, poems have main ideas. As you read a poem, think about how the details and images relate to the poet's main idea.

HOW TO DETERMINE IMPORTANCE

Focus Strategy

1. Read the poem once.
2. Read it again, pausing often to let the words linger, or stay, in your mind.
3. Think about the main idea of the poem.
4. Use a **Reading Journal** to record how details and images relate to the main idea of the poem.

Reading Journal

The speaker says:
"I must sit on my hands to control them from dancing"
(line 2)

This supports the main idea by:
showing how excited and happy the speaker feels

CCSS Literacy.RL.9-10.2 Determine a theme or central idea of a text and analyze in detail its development over the course of the text, including how it emerges and is shaped and refined by specific details; provide an objective summary of the text. Literacy.RL.9-10.5 Analyze how an author's choices concerning how to structure a text, order events within it (e.g., parallel plots), and manipulate time (e.g., pacing, flashbacks) create such effects as mystery, tension, or surprise.

Connect Across Texts

The article "Slam: Performance Poetry Lives On" describes how performance poetry has become a modern creative art. How does the author of the following slam poem show the ways that creativity matters to her?

C

D

Euphoria

by Lauren Brown

today I'm filled with such a feeling of greatness and immortality
I must sit on my hands to control them from dancing
I find blinking a hazard
it takes too much time and leaves me in the darkness
when I could be seeing and living the manic colors
everything in me is magnified and exposed
but no one seems to notice
the air caresses my flesh
and my heart beats faster
and my pulse pulses with the concrete rhythm of the song
permanently playing [1]
in my mind
I want to write everything I have ever felt before in my whole existence and
paste them on
the walls
I want to dance with such balance and magnificence
that the whole world will want to dance too

E

F

[1] **Structure** What features of free verse does the author use? How would the poem be different if it had a strict **structure** of rhythm and rhyme?

Key Vocabulary

euphoria *n.*, great joy and happiness

• **structure** *n.*, the way something is set up, organization

In Other Words

immortality the ability to live forever
hazard danger
manic wild, excited
magnified and exposed made bigger and visible for everyone to see
caresses softly touches

Comprehension Coach

Build Reading Power

Assign students to use the software, based on their instructional needs.

Read Silently
- Comprehension questions with immediate feedback
- Glossary support
- Review text evidence

RL.9-10.10

Listen
- Professional model of fluent reading

Record
- Oral reading fluency practice
- Ongoing fluency assessment with immediate feedback

OBJECTIVES

Vocabulary
- Key Vocabulary Ⓣ

Comprehension & Critical Thinking
- Use Text Evidence Ⓣ

Literary Analysis
- Analyze Structure: Free Verse Ⓣ

BUILD BACKGROUND

C The Poet

Tell students that Lauren Brown was 15 when she wrote "Euphoria." Ask: How does information about the poet change how you read a poem?

D Connect Across Texts

Have students suggest ways that this poem might be performed in a slam. Point out that reading poetry lets you focus on the emotions and images.

TEACH & PRACTICE

E Reading Support

Vocabulary Explain the meaning of *immortality, hazard, manic, magnified, caresses, concrete,* and *existence.*

ELL Use Graphic Organizer Visually display words and meanings.

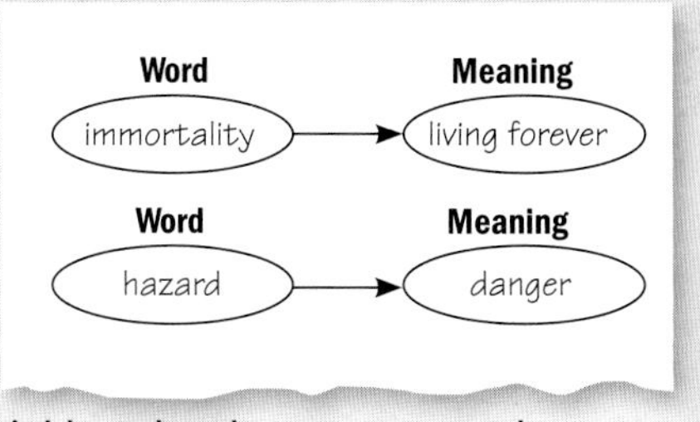

Add to the chart as you read.

RL.9-10.4

F Reading Support

[1] **Structure** Ask: How can you tell the poem is free verse?

Possible response:
- *There is no set rhythm or rhyme.*

Ask: How might the poem be different if it were structured in a more traditional way?

Possible response:
- *The emotions might not seem so free.*

RL.9-10.5

CCSS **Literacy.RL.9-10.4** Determine the meaning of words and phrases as they are used in the text, including figurative and connotative meanings; analyze the cumulative impact of specific word choices on meaning and tone (e.g., how the language evokes a sense of time and place; how it sets a formal or informal tone). **Literacy.RL.9-10.5** Analyze how an author's choices concerning how to structure a text, order events within it (e.g., parallel plots), and manipulate time (e.g., pacing, flashbacks) create such effects as mystery, tension, or surprise. **Literacy.RL.9-10.10** By the end of grade 9, read and comprehend literature, including stories, dramas, and poems, in the grades 9–10 text complexity band proficiently, with scaffolding as needed at the high end of the range. By the end of grade 10, read and comprehend literature, including stories, dramas, and poems, at the high end of the grades 9–10 text complexity band independently and proficiently.

READ

OBJECTIVES

Vocabulary
- Key Vocabulary Ⓣ

Reading Strategy
- Determine Importance

Comprehension & Critical Thinking
- Use Text Evidence Ⓣ

Literary Analysis
- Analyze Structure: Free Verse Ⓣ

Writing
- Response to Literature

TEACH & PRACTICE

Ⓐ Reading Support

2 Determine Importance Reread the poem and title. Ask: What is the poem's most important idea?

Possible response:
- *The speaker feels "euphoria" and wants to express it through her art.*

Have students identify specific details that support this main idea, such as the speaker wanting to write about everything she has ever felt.
RL.9-10.2

APPLY

Ⓑ ANALYZE

1. **Explain** She might plan to become a poet who explores other people's emotions.
RL.9-10.10
2. **Vocabulary** Creative expression has caused the euphoria. She plans to express herself through singing and dancing.
L.9-10.6
3. **Analyze Structure: Free Verse** The free verse structure lets her use the best words to express her feelings without worrying about rhyme or rhythm.
RL.9-10.5
4. **Focus Strategy: Determine Importance** Students should consider how their details relate to the speaker's feeling of euphoria.
RL.9-10.2

Ⓒ Return to the Text

Students' work might reflect that the poet wants to express herself through dancing and singing.
W.9-10.9.a

Ⓐ

I want to sing like the angels
to part my lips and have the loveliness of my song drip out of the corners of
my mouth
and to echo into everyone's ears and have a piece of my song glued into their minds
I want to be able to use my hands in ways I never have before
and to feel other people's emotions like sandpaper on my tongue . . .
. . . maybe I will 2

2 **Determine Importance** What is the speaker's most important idea? How do the details and images in the poem support this idea?

Ⓑ

ANALYZE Euphoria

1. **Explain** At the end of the poem, the speaker says, ". . . maybe I will." What do you think she plans to do? Why?
2. **Vocabulary** What do you think has caused the speaker's **euphoria**? How does she plan to express this?
3. **Analyze Structure: Free Verse** How does the free verse **structure** help the speaker express her ideas and feelings?
4. **Focus Strategy Determine Importance** With a partner, discuss two details from the poem that you recorded in your Response Journal. Consider how each detail supports the main idea of "euphoria."

Ⓒ **Return to the Text**

Reread and Write Reread the poem. Then write about how the speaker wants to show her feelings and ideas through different forms of **expression**.

Key Vocabulary
expression *n.*, creative communication

In Other Words
sandpaper rough paper used to make wood smooth

Interactive Reading

Have students reread and mark "Euphoria" within the Edge Interactive Practice Book to apply their knowledge of free verse structure and to practice the Focus Strategy—Determine Importance.

Edge Interactive Practice Book, pp. 85–86

Unit Project

Progress Check Allow time for students to work on their unit projects. Meet with individuals and/or groups to provide guidance and check on their progress.

myNGconnect.com
- **Unit Planning Tools**
- **Unit Project Evaluation Rubric**

CCSS Literacy.RL.9-10.2 Determine a theme or central idea of a text and analyze in detail its development over the course of the text, including how it emerges and is shaped and refined by specific details; provide an objective summary of the text. **Literacy.RL.9-10.5** Analyze how an author's choices concerning how to structure a text, order events within it (e.g., parallel plots), and manipulate time (e.g., pacing, flashbacks) create such effects as mystery, tension, or surprise. **Literacy.RL.9-10.10** By the end of grade 9, read and comprehend literature, including stories, dramas, and poems, in the grades 9-10 text complexity band proficiently, with scaffolding as needed at the high end of the range. By the end of grade 10, read and comprehend literature, including stories, dramas, and poems, at the high end of the grades 9-10 text complexity band independently and proficiently. **Literacy.W.9-10.9.a** Apply grades 9-10 Reading standards to literature (e.g., "Analyze how an author draws on and transforms source material in a specific work [e.g., how Shakespeare treats a theme or topic from Ovid or the Bible or how a later author draws on a play by Shakespeare]"). **Literacy.L.9-10.6** Acquire and use accurately general academic and domain-specific words and phrases, sufficient for reading, writing, speaking, and listening at the college and career readiness level; demonstrate independence in gathering vocabulary knowledge when considering a word or phrase important to comprehension or expression.

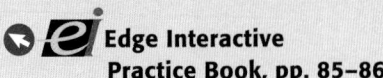

Reflect and Assess

EQ Does Creativity Matter?

Reading

Critical Thinking

1. **Explain** Return to the Quickwrite about poetry that you did before reading. Have your ideas changed? Discuss your responses with a partner.
2. **Analyze** Based on your reading of the essay and the poem, explain whether you think poetry matters in today's world.
3. **Compare** The author of "Slam: Performance Poetry Lives On" says "Poetry is moving, breathing, ever changing." Would the speaker of "Euphoria" agree? Why or why not?
4. **Predict** The recent **phenomenon** of slam poetry has its roots in many older forms of poetry. Do you think slam is here to stay? Why or why not?
5. **Evaluate** Why do you think popular kinds of poetry change over the years? How do they reflect the creativity of different times?

Writing

Write Poetry

Slam Poetry Imagine you are holding a poetry slam at your school. Write a slam poem using information from both texts for ideas. Try a variety of **structures** and styles, such as free verse or rhyme, for your slam poems. Highlight phrases you think will spark your listeners' interest. Then post the poems and judge them based on effectiveness and creativity. Which ones capture the joys of slam? Read or perform your poem for the class.

Vocabulary

Key Vocabulary Review

Oral Review Work with a partner. Use these words to complete the paragraph. You might see words like *structure*, *expression*, and *recitation* used in classroom materials in other subject areas.

compose	**improvisation**	**structure**
euphoria	**phenomenon**	**transcend**
expression	**recitation**	

Writing poetry is an exciting new __(1)__ that I just discovered. I love having a new form of __(2)__ that communicates my ideas and feelings. When I sit down at my computer to __(3)__ the words to a brand new poem, I usually use __(4)__ —which doesn't require a lot of pre-planning. Every time a poem comes out well, I feel great happiness, or __(5)__. Other times, I run into problems that I must rise above and __(6)__ through hard work. I think about my word choice and change the __(7)__ and organization of my poem until it looks just right. Next month, I'm reading two poems at a __(8)__ in front of my class.

Writing Application If you were to **compose** a song or poem, what would it be like? Use at least two Key Vocabulary words to write a song or poem.

Fluency

Read with Ease: Expression

Assess your reading fluency with the passage in the Reading Handbook, p. 756. Then complete the self-check below.

1. My expression did/did not sound natural.
2. My words correct per minute: ____

Lesson 21

REFLECT AND ASSESS

OBJECTIVES

Vocabulary
- Key Vocabulary Ⓣ

Reading Fluency
- Expression Ⓣ

Comprehension & Critical Thinking
- Compare Across Texts
- Use Text Evidence Ⓣ

Literary Analysis
- Evaluate Literature

Writing
- Form: Slam Poetry

Reading

Critical Thinking

1. **Explain** Discuss students' responses to the Quickwrite. Have students complete the activity and share their responses with a partner.
SL.9-10.1
2. **Analyze** Have students support their opinions with information from the article and the poem.
RL.9-10.2; RI.9-10.2
3. **Compare** The speaker of "Euphoria" would probably agree with the author of the essay. "Euphoria" is a poem that is free, moving, and breathing in its structure and rhythm.
RI.9-10.10
4. **Predict** Slam may be around for a while or it may evolve into some other form or structure of expression.
5. **Evaluate** Poets of every time period write about what they see in their world and they create a voice based on their experiences. Poetry changes with each generation, just like other popular forms of music, dance, and communication.

Writing

Write Poetry

Edge Interactive Practice Book, p. 87

Slam Poetry Show more examples of slam poems. Discuss the structures. Encourage students to refer to pages 174, 642, and 819 for additional tips on writing poetry. Invite volunteers to share their poems. Have the group vote to choose the most effective poems.
RL.9-10.5; W.9-10.10

Vocabulary

Key Vocabulary Review

1. *phenomenon* **2.** *expression*
3. *compose* **4.** *improvisation*
5. *euphoria* **6.** *transcend* **7.** *structure*
8. *recitation*
L.9-10.6

Fluency

Read with Ease: Expression

Ensure that students complete the self-check.
RI.9-10.10

ASSESS & RETEACH

Assessments Handbook, pp. 15j–15m

Have students complete the **Reader Reflection**. Then give students the **Cluster Test** to measure their progress. Group students as needed for reteaching.

CCSS **Literacy.RL.9-10.2** Determine a theme or central idea of a text and analyze in detail its development over the course of the text, including how it emerges and is shaped and refined by specific details; provide an objective summary of the text. **Literacy.RL.9-10.5** Analyze how an author's choices concerning how to structure a text, order events within it (e.g., parallel plots), and manipulate time (e.g., pacing, flashbacks) create such effects as mystery, tension, or surprise. **Literacy.RI.9-10.2** Determine a central idea of a text and analyze its development over the course of the text, including how it emerges and is shaped and refined by specific details; provide an objective summary of the text. **Literacy.RI.9-10.10** By the end of grade 9, read and comprehend literary nonfiction in the grades 9-10 text complexity band proficiently, with scaffolding as needed at the high end of the range. By the end of grade 10, read and comprehend literary nonfiction at the high end of the grades 9-10 text complexity band independently and proficiently. **Literacy.W.9-10.10** Write routinely over extended time frames (time for research, reflection, and revision) and shorter time frames (a single sitting or a day or two) for a range of tasks, purposes, and audiences. **Literacy.SL.9-10.1** Initiate and participate effectively in a range of collaborative discussions (one-on-one, in groups, and teacher-led) with diverse partners on grades 9-10 topics, texts, and issues, building on others' ideas and expressing their own clearly and persuasively. **Literacy.L.9-10.6** Acquire and use accurately general academic and domain-specific words and phrases, sufficient for reading, writing, speaking, and listening at the college and career readiness level; demonstrate independence in gathering vocabulary knowledge when considering a word or phrase important to comprehension or expression.

Lesson 22

INTEGRATE THE LANGUAGE ARTS

OBJECTIVES

Language Function
- Give and Follow Commands Ⓣ

Literary Analysis
- Analyze Literary Movements: Poetry Across Cultures

Media
- Evaluate and Critique the Effectiveness of Media Presentations

Grammar
- Present Tense Verbs Ⓣ

Grammar

Use Verbs to Talk About the Present

Grammar Transparency 30

Review Use the transparency lesson and the activity on p. 178 to review present tense verbs.

Oral Practice **1.** is **2.** are **3.** is **4.** is **5.** are

Written Practice **6.** has **7.** have **8.** are speaking

L.9-10.1.b

Language Development

Give and Follow Commands

Check that students' oral instructions are complete.

SL.9-10.6

Assessments Handbook, p. 15o

Literary Analysis

Literary Movements

Type sonnet; Beat

Period 1500s–1600s; 1950s and 1960s

Influence rhythm; poetry for people

RI.9-10.1

Media Study

Judging Panel

Performance Evaluation Have students justify the reasons for their scores.

See **Language and Learning Handbook** p. 702 for further instruction.

SL.9-10.1.d

Edge Interactive Practice Book, p. 88

GRAMMAR SKILLS PATH

26 Forms of *Be* in the Present Tense
27 Present Progressive Verb Forms
28 Present Tense of *Have*
29 Present Tense of *Do*
30 Review: Present Tense Verbs   ELL Language & Grammar Lab

INTEGRATE THE LANGUAGE ARTS

Grammar

Use Verbs to Talk About the Present

The verb **have** has two forms in the present.

I **have** poetry class today. You **have** class, too.
He **has** three favorite poets. She **has** four.

The verb **be** has three forms in the present.

I **am** a poet. She **is** a poet, too. We **are** creative.

Am, **is**, and **are** can also be **helping verbs**. A helping verb can come before a **main verb** that ends with **-ing**. The helping verb agrees with the subject.

I **am** **performing** my poetry.
The judge **is** **listening**.
They **are** **enjoying** the contest.

Oral Practice (1–5) With a partner, say each sentence with the correct helping verb.

1. The poetry contest ___ starting now.
2. We ___ waiting for the first poet.
3. The audience ___ applauding the poet.
4. She ___ reciting her poem with emotion.
5. The new poets ___ learning the art.

Written Practice (6–10) Rewrite the paragraph. Choose the correct present tense form of the verb. Add two more sentences. Use present tense verbs.

Poetry (have/has) rhythm. Poetry slams (have/has) action. Poets (is speaking/are speaking) their minds.

Language Development

Give and Follow Commands

Role-Play Using commands, write instructions telling a poet how to perform slam poetry. Start your commands with verbs such as *speak* and *express*. With a partner, take turns being the poet and the instructor. The instructor tells the poet what to do. The poet follows the directions. Each should ask and answer questions to clarify the directions.

Literary Analysis

Literary Movements: Poetry Across Cultures

In "Slam: Performance Poetry Lives On," author Pooja Makhijani says, "Poetry is living, moving, ever changing." That's because poetry, like many other forms of literature, changes across different times and cultures.

With a partner, reread the essay to find the many roots of slam poetry. Create a chart to track how these trends have led to the slam we know today.

Type of Poetry	Place and Time Period	Influence on Slam
epic poems	Ancient Greece c. 8th century B.C.E.	started the tradition of reciting poetry

Media Study

Judging Panel

Performance Evaluation With a group, conduct your own poetry slam or find video of a slam poetry performer. Search online poetry sites or check out the video collections of local libraries. Have each group member assign the performer a score from 1 to 10. Then take turns with group members in presenting and justifying the scores you gave. Discuss differences in opinion.

Language and Learning Handbook, page 702

GRAMMAR

Review: Present Tense Verbs

Teach/Model Display the transparency. Review the present tense forms of *be, have,* and *do*. Ask students for sentences, and use them to review subject-verb agreement.

A. Oral Practice Model how to choose the correct verb in the first sentence. Then have students work through the activity and explain each choice. Offer immediate corrective feedback.

B. Written Practice Work through the example. Explain that some sentences have no errors. Have the group tell you how to edit the paragraph. Then ask a volunteer to read the corrected paragraph to the class. L.9-10.1.b

Grammar & Writing Practice Book, pp. 63–64

Grammar Transparency 30

GRAMMAR REVIEW: PRESENT TENSE VERBS 30

Use Verbs to Talk About the Present

Remember: The verbs **be, have,** and **do** each have more than one form in the present. Use the form that goes with the subject.

Forms of *Be*	Forms of *Have*	Forms of *Do*
I **am**	I **have**	I **do**
he, she, or it **is**	he, she, or it **has**	he, she, or it **does**
we, you, or they **are**	we, you, or they **have**	we, you, or they **do**

Try It

A. Say each sentence with the correct verb form.

1. Authors often **(do / does)** express themselves well through poetry.
2. Some poets even **(do / does)** well on stage.
3. I **(am / is)** writing poems to show my imagination.
4. But I **(have / has)** all my poems in a private journal.
5. They **(is / are)** going to stay a secret!

B. Edit the paragraph. Fix five mistakes. The first is done for you.

Poets ~~is~~ are finding creative ways to share poetry. My friend Kim ~~have~~ has a Web site. One poet ~~do~~ does art around her poetry and then frames the work. A poet and a musician ~~is~~ are inspiring each other. Their first song is beautiful. I ~~does~~ do love it!

CCSS Literacy.RI.9-10.1 Cite strong and thorough textual evidence to support analysis of what the text says explicitly as well as inferences drawn from the text. Literacy.SL.9-10.1.d Respond thoughtfully to diverse perspectives, summarize points of agreement and disagreement, and, when warranted, qualify or justify their own views and understanding and make new connections in light of the evidence and reasoning presented. Literacy.SL.9-10.6 Adapt speech to a variety of contexts and tasks, demonstrating command of formal English when indicated or appropriate. Literacy.L.9-10.1.b Use various types of phrases (noun, verb, adjectival, adverbial, participial, prepositional, absolute) and clauses (independent, dependent; noun, relative, adverbial) to convey specific meanings and add variety and interest to writing or presentations.

Vocabulary Study

Context Clues for Idioms

An idiomatic expression is a word or phrase that has a meaning beyond its literal definition. Consider this example from "Euphoria":

I want to . . . have the loveliness of my song . . . echo into everyone's ears and have a piece of my song glued into their minds

1. **Study the context of the expression** The poet thinks her song is lovely.
2. **Make a guess about the meaning** If something is lovely or memorable, it sticks like glue. I think the poet wants people to remember her song.
3. **Test your guess** with the original passage. If it fits, you may have found your definition.
4. If all else fails, **look up the phrase or ask a friend or teacher for help**.

Use context to figure out the meaning of this idiom: The poet's voice filled the room as he screamed out his poem at the top of his lungs.

Writing

Write a How-To Paragraph

Imagine that you want to explain something to another person, like how to do well at a poetry slam. One way to do so is by writing an expository how-to paragraph. Read how to do it below. Then write a paragraph explaining how to do something you can do well.

1. **Identify the Topic** Be sure to include the main idea you want to express about the topic.

Topic: *Performing at a poetry slam*
Main Idea: *There are specific things you can do to perform at a poetry slam.*

2. **Brainstorm Details** Include ideas that support your main idea.

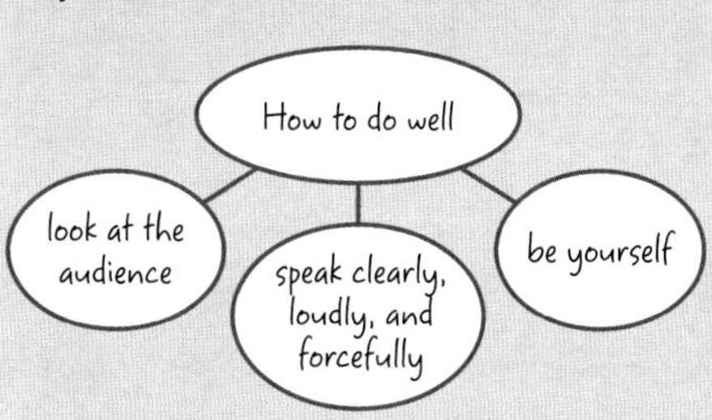

3. **Draft** First, introduce the topic and main idea. Then include supporting details. Use transition words to move from one detail to the next. Finally, sum up with a concluding sentence. Be aware that you have twenty minutes to complete your draft.

Model

If you want to do well at a poetry slam, there are things you can do to improve your chances. First, look at the audience while you perform. This will keep people focused on you. Second, be sure to speak loudly and clearly. You will not win if no one can hear your poems. Finally, relax and be yourself. If you like to move, move. Following these rules will help you do the best you can at a slam.

4. **Check Your Work** Reread your paragraph. Ask:
   - Do I identify my topic and main idea?
   - Do the details support the main idea?
5. **Publish** Share your work with others in written or oral form. Provide feedback.

Writing Handbook, page 784

Writing Rubric How-To Paragraph

Exceptional	• Paragraph addresses topic by showing clear main idea. • Details are relevant to topic. • Use of present tense verbs correct.
Competent	• Paragraph pertains to topic. • Details are adequate. • Use of present tense verbs correct.
Developing	• Essay may stray from topic. • Details are loosely connected to topic. • Use of present tense verbs often incorrect.
Beginning	• Paragraph does not address topic. • Details are not clearly connected to topic. • Use of present tense verbs incorrect.

Lesson 23

INTEGRATE THE LANGUAGE ARTS

OBJECTIVES

Vocabulary
- Context Clues Ⓣ

Writing
- Writing Process
- Form: Expository How-To Paragraph Ⓣ

Vocabulary Study

Context Clues for Idioms

Students' definitions may vary but should include that a slam is a competition where poets perform their work for an audience.

L.9-10.4.a; L.9-10.5.a

Edge Interactive Practice Book, p. 89

Writing

How-To Paragraph

1. **Identify the Topic** Help students express the main idea for the topic they select.
2. **Brainstorm Details** Model the completion of an idea web. Help students use a web to record details that support their main idea.
3. **Draft** Allow students twenty minutes to follow the model for introducing their topic and main idea and for writing sentences with supporting details and transition words. Make sure students sum up their paragraphs with a concluding sentence.
4. **Check Your Work** Have students read their paragraphs to a partner and answer the questions together.
5. **Publish** Have students write or orally present their work.
6. **Evaluate Your Work** Have students self-evaluate their how-to paragraph using the Writing Rubric (*also online*).

See **Writing Handbook** p. 784 for further instruction.

W.9-10.2

CCSS **Literacy.W.9-10.2** Write informative/explanatory texts to examine and convey complex ideas, concepts, and information clearly and accurately through the effective selection, organization, and analysis of content. **Literacy.L.9-10.4.a** Use context (e.g., the overall meaning of a sentence, paragraph, or text; a word's position or function in a sentence) as a clue to the meaning of a word or phrase. **Literacy.L.9-10.5.a** Interpret figures of speech (e.g., euphemism, oxymoron) in context and analyze their role in the text.

CLOSE READING

OBJECTIVES

Vocabulary
- Academic Vocabulary

Comprehension & Critical Thinking
- Determine Importance
- Use Text Evidence Ⓣ

Literary Analysis
- Determine Author's Purpose Ⓣ

TEACH & PRACTICE

Ⓐ Read for Understanding

Genre Display the **eEdition** and read aloud the selection. Ask: What kind of text is this passage? How do you know?

Possible response:
- *This is a nonfiction research report because the authors provide facts and conclusions from scientific studies.*

Have students complete item 1 on **Interactive Practice Book** page 90.

Topic Display the prompt: This text mostly tells about _____ and [how/what] _____. Have partners use the prompt to write a topic sentence for item 2 on **Interactive Practice Book** page 90.

Ⓑ Reread and Summarize

Have partners read the selection. Encourage them to pause periodically to clarify ideas or vocabulary.

Word Choice Have partners choose words and note why each word is important to the big ideas in the section. Have students complete item 3 on **Interactive Practice Book** page 90.

Summary Have students use their notes with their topic sentence to create a summary of the selection. Have them complete item 4 on **Interactive Practice Book** page 90.
RI.9-10.2

Edge Interactive Practice Book, pp. 90–95

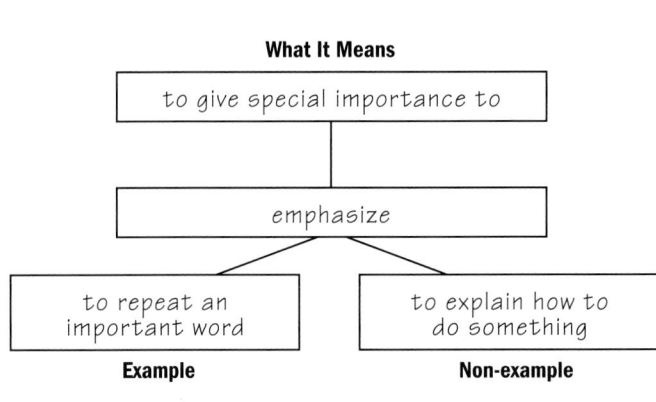

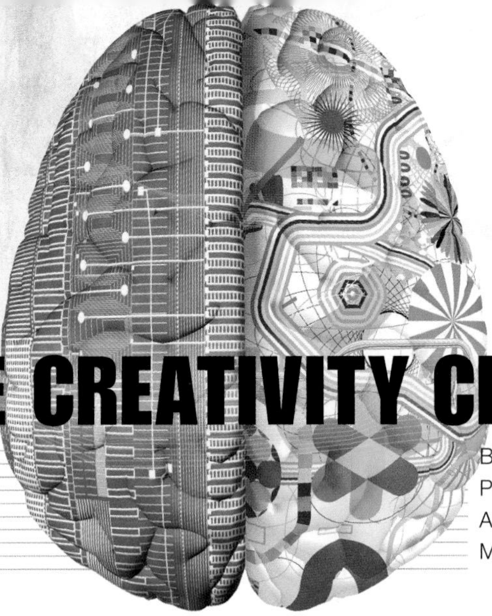

from
THE CREATIVITY CRISIS

BY PO BRONSON AND ASHLEY MERRYMAN

1 Back in 1958, Ted Schwarzrock was an 8-year-old third grader when he became one of the "Torrance kids," a group of nearly 400 Minneapolis children who completed a series of creativity tasks newly designed by professor E. Paul Torrance. Schwarzrock still vividly remembers the moment when a **psychologist** handed him a fire truck and asked, "How could you improve this toy to make it better and more fun to play with?" He recalls the psychologist being excited by his answers. In fact, the psychologist's session notes indicate Schwarzrock rattled off 25 improvements, such as adding a removable ladder and springs to the wheels. That wasn't the only time he impressed the scholars, who judged Schwarzrock to have "unusual visual perspective" and "an ability to synthesize diverse elements into meaningful products."

2 The accepted definition of creativity is production of something original and useful, and that's what's reflected in the tests. There is never one right answer. To be creative requires divergent thinking (generating many unique ideas) and then convergent thinking (combining those ideas into the best result).

In Other Words
psychologist doctor who studies the mind

ACADEMIC VOCABULARY — REVIEW

Use **Vocabulary Routine 3** (PD29) to help students create a word card for the academic vocabulary word **emphasize**. Remind students that when you emphasize something, you highlight or stress it.

What It Means
to give special importance to

emphasize

Example	Non-example
to repeat an important word	to explain how to do something

L.9-10.6

CCSS Literacy.RI.9-10.2 Determine a central idea of a text and analyze its development over the course of the text, including how it emerges and is shaped and refined by specific details; provide an objective summary of the text. Literacy.L.9-10.6 Acquire and use accurately general academic and domain-specific words and phrases, sufficient for reading, writing, speaking, and listening at the college and career readiness level; demonstrate independence in gathering vocabulary knowledge when considering a word or phrase important to comprehension or expression.

3 Nobody would argue that Torrance's tasks, which have become **the gold standard** in creativity assessment, measure creativity perfectly. What's shocking is how incredibly well Torrance's creativity index predicted those kids' creative accomplishments as adults. Those who came up with more good ideas on Torrance's tasks grew up to be **entrepreneurs**, inventors, college presidents, authors, doctors, diplomats, and software developers. The **correlation** to lifetime creative accomplishment was more than three times stronger for childhood creativity than childhood **IQ**.

4 Like intelligence tests, Torrance's test—a 90-minute series of discrete tasks, administered by a psychologist—has been taken by millions worldwide in 50 languages. Yet there is one crucial difference between IQ and CQ scores. With intelligence, there is a **phenomenon** called the Flynn effect—each generation, scores go up about 10 points. Enriched environments are making kids smarter. With creativity, a reverse trend has just been identified and is being reported for the first time here: American creativity scores are falling.

5 The potential consequences are sweeping. The necessity of human ingenuity is undisputed. A recent IBM poll of 1,500 CEOs identified creativity as the No. 1 "leadership competency" of the future. Yet it's not just about sustaining our nation's economic growth. All around us are matters of national and international importance that are crying out for creative solutions. Such solutions emerge from a healthy marketplace of ideas, sustained by a populace constantly contributing original ideas and receptive to the ideas of others.

American creativity scores are falling.

6 To understand exactly what should be done requires first understanding the new story emerging from **neuroscience**. The lore of pop psychology is that creativity occurs on the right side of the brain. But we now know that if you tried to be creative using only the right side of your brain, it'd be like living with ideas perpetually at the tip of your tongue, just beyond reach.

7 When you try to solve a problem, you begin by concentrating on obvious facts and familiar solutions, to see if the answer lies there. This is a mostly left-brain stage of attack. If the answer doesn't come, the right and left hemispheres of the brain activate together. **Neural networks** on the right side scan remote memories that could be vaguely relevant. A wide range of

Key Vocabulary

- **phenomenon** *n.*, something different that people get really excited about

In Other Words

the gold standard in known as the best
entrepreneurs creative business people
correlation connection
IQ intelligence
neuroscience the science of the brain
Neural networks Nerve connections

PRACTICE & APPLY

C Reread and Analyze

Set a Purpose Explain that partners will reread the text in the **Interactive Practice Book** and determine how Bronson and Merryman use different writing techniques to achieve their purpose.

Authors' Purpose Review: When analyzing a text, look for clues that show why the authors wrote the text. Ask: What was the authors' main purpose for writing this text? Have students complete item 5 on **Interactive Practice Book** page 91.

If students have difficulty, ask: Do the authors mainly give facts or opinions about the topic? Do they want to entertain or inform?
RI.9-10.6

Authors' Purpose Explain: Nonfiction authors include facts that support the information in their text. Direct students to complete items 6 and 7 on **Interactive Practice Book** page 91.

If students have difficulty, remind them that a fact is information that can be proved. Point out the data in paragraph 4 and ask how the data helps with the authors' purpose of informing the reader.
RI.9-10.6

Edge Interactive Practice Book, pp. 90–95

CCSS Literacy.RI.9-10.6 Determine an author's point of view or purpose in a text and analyze how an author uses rhetoric to advance that point of view or purpose.

CLOSE READING

OBJECTIVES

Vocabulary
- Content Area Vocabulary: Psychology

Comprehension & Critical Thinking
- Synthesize
- Use Text Evidence (T)

Literary Analysis
- Analyze Authors' Purpose (T)

Research Skill
- Gather Information

Writing
- Write About Author's Purpose

PRACTICE & APPLY

C Reread and Analyze

Details Explain: When authors explain a process in detail, it can help to identify the main steps of the process. Direct students to complete items 8 and 9 on **Interactive Practice Book** page 92.

If students have difficulty, say: To identify steps in a process, ask yourself: What happens at the beginning of the process? What happens after that?
RI.9-10.3

Authors' Purpose Review the steps of the process described in paragraphs 7 and 8. Then ask students to complete item 10 on **Interactive Practice Book** page 92.
RI.9-10.6

Word Choice Explain that nonfiction authors may include definitions to give information about important concepts. Then ask students to complete items 11 and 12 on **Interactive Practice Book** page 93.

If students have difficulty, remind them that definitions can be indicated with punctuation, such as commas, parentheses, and dashes.
RI.9-10.4; RI.9-10.6

Edge Interactive Practice Book, pp. 90–95

distant information that is normally **tuned out** becomes available to the left hemisphere, which searches for unseen patterns, alternative meanings, and **high-level abstractions**.

8 Having glimpsed such a connection, the left brain must quickly lock in on it before it escapes. The attention system must radically reverse gears, going from defocused attention to extremely focused attention. In a flash, the brain pulls together these **disparate shreds of thought** and binds them into a new single idea that enters consciousness. This is the "aha!" moment of **insight**, often followed by a spark of pleasure as the brain recognizes the **novelty** of what it's come up with.

9 Is this learnable? Well, think of it like basketball. Being tall does help to be a pro basketball player, but the rest of us can still get quite good at the sport through practice. In the same way, there are certain innate features of the brain that make some people naturally prone to divergent thinking. But convergent thinking and focused attention are necessary, too, and those require different neural gifts. Crucially, rapidly shifting between these modes is a top-down function under your mental control. University of New Mexico neuroscientist Rex Jung has concluded that those who diligently practice creative activities learn to recruit their brains' creative networks quicker and better. A lifetime of consistent habits gradually changes the neurological pattern.

This is the "aha!" moment of insight...

10 In early childhood, distinct types of free play are associated with high creativity. Preschoolers who spend more time in role-play (acting out characters) have higher measures of creativity: voicing someone else's point of view helps develop their ability to analyze situations from different **perspectives**. When playing alone, highly creative first graders may act out strong negative emotions: they'll be angry, hostile, anguished. **The hypothesis is** that play is a safe harbor to work through forbidden thoughts and emotions.

11 In middle childhood, kids sometimes create paracosms—fantasies of entire alternative worlds.

Iker Ayestaran.

Critical Viewing: Theme What comparison does the artist make here? What message does that send?

Key Vocabulary
- **insight** *n.*, understanding
- **perspective** *n.*, point of view

In Other Words
tuned out ignored
high-level abstractions complicated ideas
disparate shreds of thoughts separate ideas
novelty creative newness
The hypothesis is This may mean

VOCABULARY

Content Area Vocabulary: Psychology

Build vocabulary related to the content area of psychology.

PSYCHOLOGY

Teach/Model Use the Make Words Your Own routine (*see the Vocabulary tab*) and the sample sentences below to introduce these words.

assessment (u-**ses**-munt), p. 180
An **assessment** is a test that measures knowledge or ability.

innate (i-**nāt**), p. 182
Innate talents are skills that you are born with.

mental (**men**-tul), p. 182
Something **mental** is related to the mind.

neurological (nū-ru-**loj**-u-kul), p. 182 Something **neurological** is related to the body's nervous system.

Practice Have students use the content vocabulary words to describe how a psychologist conducts research or treats a patient.

Apply Have students use the words as they role-play a psychologist being interviewed about creativity on a radio or TV talk show.
L.9-10.6

CCSS **Literacy.RI.9-10.6** Determine an author's point of view or purpose in a text and analyze how an author uses rhetoric to advance that point of view or purpose. **Literacy.L.9-10.6** Acquire and use accurately general academic and domain-specific words and phrases, sufficient for reading, writing, speaking, and listening at the college and career readiness level; demonstrate independence in gathering vocabulary knowledge when considering a word or phrase important to comprehension or expression. **Literacy.RI.9-10.3** Analyze how the author unfolds an analysis or series of ideas or events, including the order in which the points are made, how they are introduced and developed, and the connections that are drawn between them. **Literacy.RI.9-10.4** Determine the meaning of words and phrases as they are used in a text, including figurative, connotative, and technical meanings; analyze the cumulative impact of specific word choices on meaning and tone (e.g., how the language of a court opinion differs from that of a newspaper).

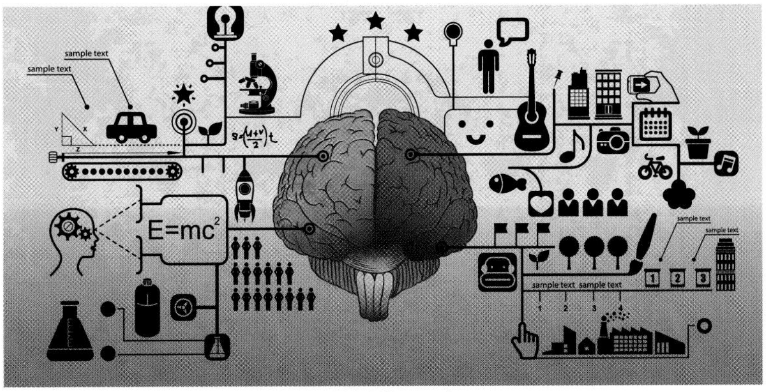

Left and right brain functions. Vector illustration, Doggygraph(alias)/Shutterstock.com.

Critical Viewing: Design What is the artist saying about the two parts of the brain?

Kids revisit their paracosms repeatedly, sometimes for months, and even create languages spoken there. This type of play peaks at age 9 or 10, and it's a very strong sign of future creativity. A Michigan State University study of MacArthur "genius award" winners found a remarkably high rate of paracosm creation in their childhoods.

12 From fourth grade on, creativity no longer occurs **in a vacuum**; researching and studying become an integral part of coming up with useful solutions. But this transition isn't easy. As school stuffs more complex information into their heads, kids get overloaded, and creativity suffers. When creative children have a supportive teacher—someone **tolerant of unconventional** answers, occasional disruptions, or detours of curiosity—they tend to **excel**. When they don't, they tend to underperform and drop out of high school or don't finish college at high rates.

13 Creativity has always been prized in American society, but it's never really been understood. While our creativity scores **decline unchecked**, the current national strategy for creativity consists of little more than praying for a Greek muse to drop by our houses. The problems we face now, and in the future, simply demand that we do more than just hope for inspiration to strike. Fortunately, the science can help: we know the steps to lead that **elusive muse** right to our doors. ❖

In Other Words

in a vacuum only when playing
tolerant of unconventional who likes unusual
excel succeed, do very well
decline unchecked keep going down
elusive muse difficult to find source of creativity

APPLY

D Discuss

Synthesize Ask: Based on your notes, how do authors present details and facts to inform their readers? Then have students complete item 13 on **Interactive Practice Book** page 94.
SL.9-10.1a; L.9-10.3

Write Prompt: Write a paragraph that explains how authors achieve their purpose of giving information. Have students complete item 14 on **Interactive Practice Book** page 94.
W.9-10.10; L.9-10.3

E Connect with the EQ

Viewpoint Help the class connect their understandings of the text to the Essential Question. Have students discuss what the research report says about the importance of creativity and supply evidence and language to support their responses. Then have students complete item 15 on **Interactive Practice Book** page 95.
SL.9-10.1.a

Theme Have students review the concepts about creativity in this selection and the comments in the final paragraph. Then ask: What is the authors' main message about creativity? Have students complete item 16 on **Interactive Practice Book** page 95.
W.9-10.10

Research Have students generate research questions around the Close Reading content. Then have them do a short search for the answers and share their findings with the class.
W.9-10.7

Edge Interactive Practice Book, pp. 90–95

CCSS **Literacy.W.9-10.7** Conduct short as well as more sustained research projects to answer a question (including a self-generated question) or solve a problem; narrow or broaden the inquiry when appropriate; synthesize multiple sources on the subject, demonstrating understanding of the subject under investigation. **Literacy.W.9-10.10** Write routinely over extended time frames (time for research, reflection, and revision) and shorter time frames (a single sitting or a day or two) for a range of tasks, purposes, and audiences. **Literacy.SL.9-10.1.a** Come to discussions prepared, having read and researched material under study; explicitly draw on that preparation by referring to evidence from texts and other research on the topic or issue to stimulate a thoughtful, well-reasoned exchange of ideas. **Literacy.L.9-10.3** Apply knowledge of language to understand how language functions in different contexts, to make effective choices for meaning or style, and to comprehend more fully when reading or listening.

Lesson 25

UNIT WRAP-UP

OBJECTIVES

Comprehension & Critical Thinking
- Compare Literature: Genre

Listening and Speaking
- Classroom Discussion

Media
- Deliver a Demonstration Ⓣ
- Evaluate Demonstrations

PRESENT & REFLECT

Ⓐ Present Your Project

Suggest the following hints:

- Review your list of steps before you begin your demonstration.
- Speak loudly and clearly.
- Keep track of time as you present your demonstration.

SL.9-10.4

myNGconnect.com

Unit Project Evaluation Rubric

Ⓑ Reflect on Your Reading

Genre Focus Remind students that an author's purpose for writing can be to entertain, inform, or persuade.

Possible response:

- *A news article gives factual information about a real person or event. An essay can include facts, but it can also try to persuade.*

SL.9-10.1.a

Focus Strategy Review the Determine Importance strategies:

- Identify Main Ideas and Details
- Summarize Nonfiction
- Summarize Lyrics

Have students share which strategies they used to summarize the selection.

SL.9-10.1.a

Ⓒ EQ Respond to the Essential Question

Discuss these questions:

- How did creativity matter to the authors of the selections you read?
- Does creativity matter to you? Why or why not?

Encourage the use of examples from unit selections and **Edge Library**.

SL.9-10.1.a

ONGOING ASSESSMENT

Have students write their responses to the Essential Question to assess understanding of the unit topic.

THE ART OF **EXPRESSION**

EQ **ESSENTIAL QUESTION:** Does Creativity Matter?

myNGconnect.com

Download the rubric.

Present Your Project: Demonstration

It's time to present your demonstration about the Essential Question for this unit: Does Creativity Matter?

1 Review and Complete Your Plan

Consider these points as you complete your project:

- What steps in the process will you emphasize in your demonstration?
- Will you need help? Can you get a volunteer from the class, or do you need someone to practice with you?
- How much time do you have for your demonstration?

Practice your demonstration at least once before you present it.

2 Give Your Demonstration

Position yourself so your audience can follow the demonstration clearly. Have any equipment or materials within easy reach.

3 Evaluate the Demonstrations

Use the online rubric to evaluate each of the demonstrations, including the one you presented.

EDGE LIBRARY

Reflect on Your Reading

Many of the people in the selections in this unit and in the Edge Library expressed themselves through creativity.

Think back on your reading of the unit selections, including your choice of Edge Library books. Then discuss the following with a partner or in a small group.

Genre Focus Compare and contrast the author's purpose in a news article and an essay. Give examples, using the selections in this unit.

Focus Strategy Choose a selection in this unit to describe to a family member or friend. Identify strategies that would help you determine the most important ideas and details. Then summarize the selection in your own words.

EQ Respond to the Essential Question

Throughout this unit, you have been thinking about whether creativity matters. What have *you* decided? Support your response with evidence from your reading, discussions, research, and writing.

CUMULATIVE VOCABULARY REVIEW

Review Unit 2 Vocabulary:

achieve	heritage
assert	improvisation
career	innovator
collaborate	insight
commitment	perspective
compose	phenomenon
culture	recitation
euphoria	self-esteem
evaluate	structure
evolve	talent
expectation	transcend
expression	transform

Play one or more of the following games in pairs or small groups using Key Vocabulary:

20 Questions One student thinks of a word, and other students ask yes/no questions until they guess the word.

Categories One student thinks of a word to be a "category" and names words that relate to that category. Others try to guess the word. For example: For *career*, a student might say "doctor, teacher, astronaut."

Draw the Words One student has a word in mind and draws pictures to get another student to guess the word.

Edge Interactive Practice Book, pp. 96–97

L.9-10.6

CCSS **Literacy.SL.9-10.1.a** Come to discussions prepared, having read and researched material under study; explicitly draw on that preparation by referring to evidence from texts and other research on the topic or issue to stimulate a thoughtful, well-reasoned exchange of ideas. **Literacy.SL.9-10.4** Present information, findings, and supporting evidence clearly, concisely, and logically such that listeners can follow the line of reasoning and the organization, development, substance, and style are appropriate to purpose, audience, and task. **Literacy.L.9-10.6** Acquire and use accurately general academic and domain-specific words and phrases, sufficient for reading, writing, speaking, and listening at the college and career readiness level; demonstrate independence in gathering vocabulary knowledge when considering a word or phrase important to comprehension or expression.

Assessment and Reteaching

Digital Assessment
- eAssessment
- ExamView
- online PDFs

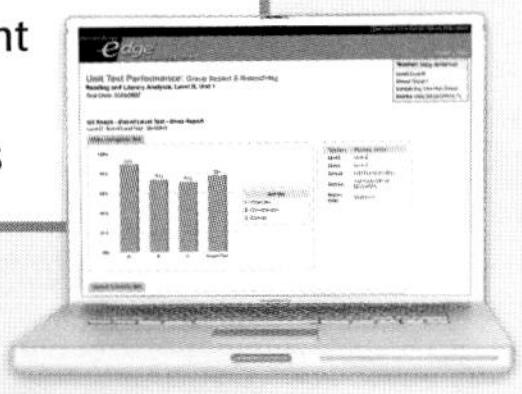

Administer the Assessments

Use the ***Assessments Handbook*** resources to measure the students' performance.

CLUSTER TESTS		
Cluster 1	**Cluster 2**	**Cluster 3**
READER REFLECTION p. 15b	**READER REFLECTION** p. 15f	**READER REFLECTION** p. 15j
READING AND LITERARY ANALYSIS pp. 15c–15e	**READING AND LITERARY ANALYSIS** pp. 15g–15i	**READING AND LITERARY ANALYSIS** pp. 15k–15m
Key Vocabulary Author's Purpose Anaylze Development of Ideas Use Text Evidence	Key Vocabulary Author's Purpose Analyze Structure: Song Lyrics Use Text Evidence	Key Vocabulary Analyze Purpose Analyze Structure: Free Verse Use Text Evidence
READING FLUENCY *Student Edition p. 754*	**READING FLUENCY** *Student Edition p. 755*	**READING FLUENCY** *Student Edition p. 756*
ELL **LANGUAGE ACQUISITION RUBRIC** p. 15o	**LANGUAGE ACQUISITION RUBRIC** p. 15o	**LANGUAGE ACQUISITION RUBRIC** p. 15o
Describe People, Places, and Things	Describe Experiences	Give and Follow Commands

UNIT TESTS	
READING AND LITERARY ANALYSIS pp. 16–23	**GRAMMAR AND WRITING** pp. 24–28
Key Vocabulary Context Clues Analyze Author's Purpose Analyze Word Choice: Style Analyze Development of Ideas Use Text Evidence	Present Tense Writing Trait: Focus and Unity Written Comprehension • Writing Traits • Written Conventions
UNIT SELF-ASSESSMENT p. 28c	

PERFORMANCE ASSESSMENTS
WRITING PROJECT p. 124
Focus and Unity • Self-Assessment: Written Composition p. 133 • Peer Assessment: Written Composition p.134
LISTENING AND SPEAKING WORKSHOP *Student Edition pp. 158–159*
Listening and Speaking Workshop: Descriptive Presentation

Score and Reteach

- To hand-score: Use the Answer Keys and rubrics in the **Assessments Handbook**, pp. 140–143. Download reteaching activities at myNGconnect.com.
- To take tests online: ***Edge* eAssessment** at myNGconnect.com. Online reports offer immediate graphic displays of student performance to aid in making individualized instruction decision. Links to reteaching activities are included.

Affective and Metacognitive Measures

Help students commit to their own learning. Have students complete at least one reading and one writing form from the affective and metacognitive measures in the ***Assessments Handbook***:

- Personal Connections to Reading, pp. 106–107
- What Interests Me: Reading Topics, p. 108
- What I Do: Reading Strategies, pp. 109–110
- What I Do: Vocabulary Strategies, pp. 111–112
- Personal Connections to Writing, pp. 113–114
- What Interests Me: Writing Topics, pp. 115–116
- What I Do: Writing Strategy, p. 118

T = Tested on Cluster and/or Unit Reading and Literary Analysis Test
T = Tested on Language Acquisition Assessment
T = Tested on Unit Writing Test
T = Assessed with a Rubric
= Comprehension Coach

Writing Project Overview

The Writing Form: Position Paper

Your students will learn the features of a **position paper**.

A good position paper
- identifies both sides of an issue
- clearly states the writer's position on the issue
- explains why the writer believes in the position
- provides reasons to support the position and evidence to support the reasons
- refutes the opposing position with reasons and evidence
- summarizes the writer's position in a memorable way

The Writing Trait: Focus and Unity

Students will learn to present a clear central idea or claim about the topic and support it with related ideas.

The Writing Portfolio

Have students collect their work in a portfolio. The portfolio provides a record of how students develop as writers.

Portfolio Evaluation Forms

Use the *Assessments* Handbook, pp. 129–134, myNGconnect.com.

Evaluation Guidelines

Use the complete **Good Writing Traits Rubric** to assess the work on all traits and summarize class results in the **Class Profile Chart**.

Rubrics & Reporting Forms

Use the *Assessments* Handbook, pp. 122–134, myNGconnect.com.

TARGETED TRAIT

SCALE	FOCUS AND UNITY	ORGANIZATION	DEVELOPMENT OF IDEAS	VOICE AND STYLE	WRITTEN CONVENTIONS
4	**Focus:** Clearly establishes and consistently maintains a central idea or claim. **Unity:** All facts, ideas, examples, and details are relevant and clearly connected to the central idea or claim.	**Structure:** The organizational pattern is appropriate to the audience, purpose, and task. **Coherence:** Includes a strong introduction and conclusion and leads the reader through a logical progression of ideas with varied and appropriate transitions.	**Content Quality:** Consistently presents meaningful ideas or claims in a logical way that is appropriate to the task, purpose, and audience. **Elaboration:** Includes relevant, clear reasoning, details, evidence, and/or description that are effective and comprehensive.	**Style and Voice:** Fully establishes and effectively maintains a voice that is appropriate to the audience, purpose, and task. **Words and Sentences:** Consistently chooses precise words and varied sentences that are appropriate to the audience and purpose and clearly convey the writer's meaning.	**Grammar and Usage:** Demonstrates strong command of English grammar and usage conventions. All sentences are formed correctly. **Mechanics and Spelling:** Demonstrates strong command of mechanics and spelling. Use of punctuation, capitalization, and spelling is effective and consistent.
3	**Focus:** Adequately establishes and mostly maintains a central idea or claim. **Unity:** Most facts, ideas, examples, and details are relevant and mostly connected to the central idea or claim.	**Structure:** The organizational pattern is mostly appropriate to the audience, purpose, and task. **Coherence:** Includes an introduction and conclusion and leads the reader through a progression of ideas with some transitions.	**Content Quality:** Mostly presents adequate ideas or claims that are appropriate to the task, purpose, and audience. **Elaboration:** Includes reasoning, details, evidence, and/or description that are adequate but incomplete.	**Style and Voice:** Mostly establishes and maintains a voice that is appropriate to the audience, purpose, and task. **Words and Sentences:** Mostly chooses precise words and a variety of sentences that are appropriate to the audience and purpose and adequately convey meaning.	**Grammar and Usage:** Demonstrates adequate command of English grammar and usage conventions. Errors are limited and do not impede understanding. Most sentences are formed correctly. **Mechanics and Spelling:** Demonstrates adequate command of mechanics and spelling. Use of punctuation, capitalization, and spelling is generally consistent.
2	**Focus:** Partially establishes a central idea or claim. **Unity:** Some facts, ideas, examples, and details are relevant and somewhat connected to the central idea or claim.	**Structure:** The pattern is inconsistent or less appropriate to the audience, purpose, or task. **Coherence:** Has an introduction and conclusion but leads the reader through loosely connected ideas that may be incomplete or not obvious to the reader.	**Content Quality:** Presents adequate ideas or claims that are less appropriate to the task, purpose, and audience. **Elaboration:** Includes weak reasoning, details, evidence, and/or description and may include extraneous or loosely related material.	**Style and Voice:** Inconsistently establishes and maintains a voice appropriate to the audience, purpose, and task. **Words and Sentences:** Demonstrates uneven word choice and limited sentence variety or chooses language mostly inappropriate to the audience and purpose. Meaning is vague or imprecise.	**Grammar and Usage:** Demonstrates partial command of English grammar and usage conventions. Frequent errors may impede understanding. Some sentences are formed incorrectly. **Mechanics and Spelling:** Demonstrates partial command of mechanics and spelling. Use of punctuation, capitalization, and spelling is inconsistent.
1	**Focus:** Lacks a central idea or claim. **Unity:** Few facts, ideas, examples, and details are relevant. Most do not support the central idea or claim or connections are unclear.	**Structure:** Lacks any organizational pattern. **Coherence:** Lacks an introduction or conclusion. Ideas are hard to understand.	**Content Quality:** Presents inappropriate or irrelevant ideas or claims. **Elaboration:** Lacks reasoning, details, evidence, and/or description.	**Style and Voice:** Does not establish and maintain a voice or uses a voice that is inappropriate to the audience, purpose, and task. **Words and Sentences:** Demonstrates little or no word choice and no sentence variety. Chooses language inappropriate to the audience, purpose, and task, hindering meaning.	**Grammar and Usage:** Demonstrates little or no command of English grammar and usage conventions. **Mechanics and Spelling:** Demonstrates little or no command of mechanics and spelling.

Write a Position Paper

iting Portfolio

Writing Mode
Argument

Writing Trait Focus
Focus and Unity

What issues make you want to speak out? Present an argument about an issue that matters to you by writing a position paper.

Position Paper **185**

Suggested Pacing

Each lesson in the Writing Project provides detailed instruction on the steps of the writing process. Here is a suggested daily sequence and pacing plan. Adjust as your schedule and student needs require.

Lesson 1	Study the Form and Prewrite
Lesson 2	Draft
Lesson 3	Revise
Lesson 4	Edit and Proofread
Lesson 5	Publish and Present

OBJECTIVES

Writing

- Mode: Argument
- Trait: Focus and Unity Ⓣ
- Process: Prewrite; Draft; Revise for Focus and Unity Ⓣ; Edit and Proofread Ⓣ; Publish and Present

Grammar, Usage, Mechanics, Spelling

- Capitalization: Names of Groups
- Punctuation: Colon
- Spelling: Homonyms
- Present Tense Verbs

INTRODUCE

Writing Mode Tell students that the writing mode for this unit is argument. Define argument as writing that presents, explains, and supports a viewpoint. The purpose of writing an argument is to prove something or to convince readers to understand or agree with the writer's claim. Examples of writing forms that may contain an argument include editorials and position papers.

Explain to students that they will be writing a position paper using the steps of the writing process.
W.9-10.1; W.9-10.10

Writing Trait Explain that writing traits are the characteristics of good writing. All good writing has effective organization; focus and unity; development of ideas; voice and style; and uses the written conventions of language correctly. For this project, students will learn to use the writing traits of **Focus and Unity** to plan, evaluate, and improve their writing.

Focus and unity in writing mean that ideas are connected and cohesive. Explain that students will focus their writing on conveying a clear viewpoint. To create unity, they will relate each main idea and detail to this viewpoint. Point out that this will make their message clearer and more persuasive.

CCSS Literacy.W.9-10.1 Write arguments to support claims in an analysis of substantive topics or texts, using valid reasoning and relevant and sufficient evidence. Literacy.W.9-10.10 Write routinely over extended time frames (time for research, reflection, and revision) and shorter time frames (a single sitting or a day or two) for a range of tasks, purposes, and audiences.

Lesson 1

STUDY THE FORM AND PREWRITE

OBJECTIVES

Writing
- Mode: Argument
- Analyze Models

ENGAGE & CONNECT

A Connect Writing to Your Life

Convince the Reader Ask students: When have you explained your viewpoint about an issue in your school, family, or community? Have volunteers share viewpoints they expressed and reasons behind them. Explain that writing a position paper involves stating a claim, or position, on an issue and giving valid and relevant reasons for it.

TEACH

B Understand the Form

Explain that a position paper clarifies and defends a writer's position on an issue. The writer presents the issue, identifies opposing views, and describes his or her position. Use a chart like the one on p. 186 to show how to organize the parts of a position paper.

Controlling Idea Explain that the controlling idea of a position paper is the author's position, or opinion, on an issue. All other parts of the writing explain this position and the reasons the writer believes it.

Write this example on the board: *People under age 16 should not be allowed to work*. Explain that this is the writer's position on the issue of the employment of minors.

Have students list other issues that affect the lives of young adults. As a class, discuss responses and form a controlling idea about each one.

Study Position Papers

Position papers contain claims, or positions, on important issues. Writers of position papers give reasons for their claims to make them sound credible, or believable, to the reader. They want the reader to fully understand and consider the issue.

A

1 Connect Writing to Your Life

You probably have argued for or against many things in your life. From debating a new school rule to convincing your parents to let you stay out late, you have stated your case many times. But how do you make a case believable? How do you get your point across? Learning to support an argument, or claim, with evidence will help you become a more convincing speaker and writer.

B

2 Understand the Form

A good position paper contains the following elements:

Introduction

Present the issue. Identify both sides. One side is your position, or claim. The other side is the opposing position. Your position is the **controlling idea** of your paper.

Body

Explain why you believe your position.

Support

Provide **reasons** to support your position and **evidence** to support your reasons. Address the **opposing position**, or other side of the argument, and provide reasons why that position is wrong.

Conclusion

Summarize your position in a memorable way.

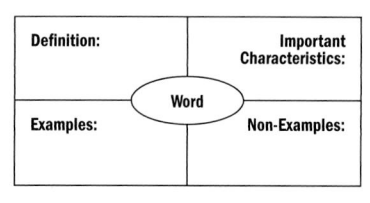

Now look at these parts in action. Read a position paper by a professional writer.

ACADEMIC VOCABULARY

Make a Word Square Use the sample sentences below to introduce these additional academic vocabulary words used in writing. Have students make a Word Square for each word.

- **position** (pu-**zi**-shun), noun ▶ page 176

He clearly established his **position** *that the legal voting age should be lowered to sixteen.*

- **summarize** (**su**-me-rīz), verb ▶ page 176

For our assignment, we had to watch a documentary and briefly **summarize** *it.*

1. Write the word in the center of the chart.
2. Look the word up in a dictionary or glossary and fill in the definition.
3. Provide a few characteristics, examples, and non-examples that help clarify the meaning.

Definition:	Important Characteristics:
Examples:	Non-Examples:

(Center: Word)

L.9-10.4.a

CCSS Literary.L.9-10.4.a Use context (e.g., the overall meaning of a sentence, paragraph, or text; a word's position or function in a sentence) as a clue to the meaning of a word or phrase.

B Analyze a Professional Model

As you read, look for the writer's position and supporting evidence.

Why Teens Need the Arts

by Oscar Delgado

Picture an environment in which young people do not dance or make music. Imagine a school where students do not put on plays, paint pictures, or take photographs. This situation may become a reality if the school board cannot balance its budget. To save money, the board has gone out on a limb and proposed cutting all arts funding for city high schools. While we must balance the budget and not spend more than we have, we should try to look elsewhere for the money. Visual and performing arts are a necessary part of our children's education.

> The writer states the issue and gives his **position**, as well as an **opposing position**,in the introduction.

For many students, art has helped them stay interested in school. Tara Sossa, for example, is a West High graduate who had planned to drop out as soon as she turned sixteen. A few months before her sixteenth birthday, an art teacher got her involved with oil painting. This opened up a bright new world to her—a world in which she could succeed. Little by little, she built self-confidence, and she stayed in school. In fact, she went on to get a degree in graphic design and a job at a magazine.

> These **reasons** support the writer's position. The writer elaborates on the reasons by providing examples as evidence.

The arts not only help keep teens in school but also teach them useful skills while they are there. Student artists learn problem-solving skills. Student actors, directors, and stage workers learn about teamwork. So do students in orchestra, chorus, and band. Student dancers learn the meaning of hard work, determination, and focus. Students involved in the arts learn the same skills as those who are members of a sports team.

> The writer uses **transition words** to connect ideas.

Perhaps most important of all, the arts encourage inventiveness and creative thinking. These are qualities our young people need if they are to become active members of government, business, and society. So, while many people think of the arts as a luxury we cannot afford, the truth is that the arts are as essential to students' learning as academics are.

> The writing style has a formal, academic **tone**.

> The writer addresses the **opposing position.**

The painter Robert Motherwell once said, "Art is much less important than life, but what a poor life without it!" For many of today's youth, art is the *only* chance they have for a successful life.

> What does the writer do to summarize his position in a memorable way?

TEACH

C Analyze a Professional Model

Read and Evaluate Read aloud the position paper. Then reread the highlighted sentences. Use the callouts to explain how the following elements work together in a position paper:

- opposing sides of an issue
- the writer's position on the issue
- reasons for the writer's position
- evidence to support the reasons
- a formal, or academic, tone
- summary of the writer's position

Point out that these are some of the elements the writer uses to explain and support a position on an issue.

ELL Use Visuals Draw a picture of a tennis court. Explain that an issue, like a game of tennis, has two players, or sides. A player tries to win by using skills to defeat the opponent. Similarly, people on each side of an issue try to win by proving their beliefs are more correct than those of their opponents.

Analyze Explain that after the writer states a position, he or she gives reasons and evidence that support it. Point to each highlighted main idea and identify it as a reason. The remaining sentences in each paragraph are evidence that support each reason. Discuss which evidence and reasons seem most valid and relevant to students and why.

Explore Ask questions to explore how the writer's controlling idea, reasons, and evidence work together. Point to the highlighted position. Ask: Why is it important that the writer states this position clearly to the reader?

Possible response:

- *The reader needs to know the central idea in order to understand the reasons and evidence that follows.*

Remind students that position papers are written to encourage readers to consider the writer's viewpoint. Ask: Do the writer's main ideas, reasons, and evidence help you understand his position? Why or why not?

ONGOING ASSESSMENT

Have students outline the main parts of a position paper and the function of each one.

FOCUS ON WRITER'S CRAFT

Writing the Hook

Teach Define the hook as the sentence or paragraph that grabs the reader's attention and shows why the issue is important. Explain that the hook offers a unique or surprising perspective on the issue.

List different types of hooks:

- **Question:** Ask a question readers had not considered before.
- **Consequence:** State a negative consequence of choosing the wrong position (or a positive consequence of choosing the right one).
- **Surprising Fact:** Present a fact to surprise readers and invite a new perspective.
- **Vivid Image:** Describe a vivid situation that might result from one view of the issue.

Practice Have students present an issue in the community, such as changing bus routes to accommodate a growing population. Have them write a position and two hooks related to the topic and read them aloud. Have the class classify them as a question, consequence, surprising fact, or vivid image.

Extend Have students identify the hook in the Professional Model and explain how it influences the reader. *What emotions does the hook cause readers to feel? How would the first paragraph be different without the hook? What type of details are used?*

STUDY THE FORM AND PREWRITE

OBJECTIVES

Writing
- Writing Process: Prewrite
- Generate Ideas Before Writing
- Choose and Justify Choice of Topic
- Identify Audience and Purpose
- Plan and Organize Ideas

TEACH

A Your Job as a Writer

Writing Prompt Read and explain the prompt to students.

B Choose Your Topic

Identify Issues Have pairs of students share the issues and questions they brainstormed. As they do, list each one and help students identify opposing sides. Have students choose a position on one of the issues listed.

ELL Use a Graphic Organizer Using simple language, record the issues and opposing sides:

Issue	*Side A*	*Side B*
School District Population	Change school boundaries	Build new school

W.9-10.5

C Clarify Audience, Controlling Idea & Purpose

Controlling Idea Ask: What position do you take on your issue? Say: This position is the controlling idea.

Audience and Purpose Remind students that their purpose is to help readers understand this position and the reasons behind it. Ask: Who is your audience? Why is it important to keep them in mind?

D Gather Your Support

Examine Ask students to record several reasons for their position. Have them choose the reasons that are most relevant and convincing. Have students consider the full range of the topic and issues and determine which information best supports their position.
W.9-10.1.a; W.9-10.1.b; W.9-10.5

Your Job as a Writer

A ▶ **Prompt** Write a position paper about an issue that affects your school or your community. Be sure to:
- state your position on the issue
- give reasons to support your position
- address the opposing position
- use a formal writing style
- end in a memorable way

✔ Prewrite

Now that you know the basics of position papers, plan one of your own. Planning will make it easier for you to write later on. When you are finished, you will have a detailed Writing Plan to guide you as you write.

B

1 Choose Your Topic

Think of an issue to write about. Here are some good ways to choose a topic:
- With a small group of students, brainstorm a list of issues that affect your school or community. Brainstorm questions related to this issue. Choose the issue that is most important to you.
- Skim the headlines of a school or community newspaper. What issues are in the news? Which could you write about?

C

2 Clarify the Audience, Controlling Idea, and Purpose

Your teacher and classmates will probably be your main audience. Who else might be interested in reading your paper? Jot down your ideas.

What is your position on the situation you are writing about? Do you want to encourage it or stop it? In a sentence or two, state your position. That is your **controlling idea**.

Finally, think about your reason for writing. What do you want your audience to understand? Your answer will be your purpose for writing.

Prewriting Tip

To make it easier to clarify your audience, ask yourself these questions:
- Who is affected by this issue?
- Who has the power to make things change the way I want them to?

These people could be part of your audience.

D

3 Gather Your Support

Next, gather reasons to support your position. List every reason your position is credible. Then choose the reasons that would be most understandable to your audience. Also think of the reasons someone might not support your position and then provide evidence to refute them, or prove them wrong. Remember, your purpose for writing is to make the audience understand and consider your position. Research the full range of information on the topic and determine which information best supports your position.

DIFFERENTIATED INSTRUCTION

Developing Prewriting Strategies As you teach the writing process, use these strategies to meet students' individual needs.

Struggling Readers

Guiding Questions Ask students to clearly state their position on the issue, using yes/no questions to help them fine tune it if necessary. Post additional questions to guide them in generating evidence for their position: *Why should readers believe your position? What reasons or evidence will help them understand and share your view?*

English Language Learners ELL

Elaborate Reinforce the link between the structure on p. 186 and the Professional Model on p. 187. Read and point to the introduction in the structure and draw your finger around the introduction paragraph in the Professional Model. Repeat the process with each part. Explain that students will use the same structure and form.

Challenge

Develop Criteria Have students develop a brief checklist to help them narrow down their lists of supporting reasons:
- *Does this statement help to explain and support my position?*
- *Does this statement seem true?*
- *Will this statement persuade the reader to consider my position?*

CCSS Literacy.W.9-10.1.a Introduce precise claim(s), distinguish the claim(s) from alternate or opposing claims, and create an organization that establishes clear relationships among claim(s), counterclaims, reasons, and evidence. **Literacy.W.9-10.1.b** Develop claim(s) and counterclaims fairly, supplying evidence for each while pointing out the strengths and limitations of both in a manner that anticipates the audience's knowledge level and concerns. **Literacy.W.9-10.5** Develop and strengthen writing as needed by planning, revising, editing, rewriting, or trying a new approach, focusing on addressing what is most significant for a specific purpose and audience.

4 Organize the Details

Build up to a strong conclusion. Present supporting information in order of importance. You can put your least important reason first and your most important reason last. Or you can put your most important reason first and your least important reason last. How can you tell which one is the most important? Decide which reason you have the most to say about. Presenting your data and factual support in this way will help to strengthen your position.

Reasons Why Uniforms Are Not for Us

2 Expensive
1 Not in other schools
3 Loss of freedom of expression

E

5 Finish Your Writing Plan

Choose a graphic organizer, such as an outline, to create a Writing Plan. Show which ideas will go in the introduction, the body, and the conclusion.

Writing Plan

Topic	uniform policy in district schools
Audience	my teacher, principal, and all students
Controlling Idea	school uniforms are not for us
Purpose	to explain why uniforms are not for us
Time Frame	one week from today

I. Introduction
- A. District wants to make students wear uniforms.
- B. School uniforms are not for us.

II. Body
- A. No other public school districts have uniforms.
- B. Uniforms are expensive.
- C. Uniforms equal loss of freedom of expression.
- D. Opposing position: Uniforms look neater, prevent kids from bad appearance. But we could have strict dress code instead.

III. Conclusion
- A. Summarize position.
- B. Ask a question.

F

Technology Tip

For help creating an outline, use the outline function of your word-processing program. Click on Outline from the View menu. To close the outline view, click on a different view, such as Page Layout.

Reflect on Your Writing Plan

Are your reasons likely to appeal to your audience? Are they organized by order of importance? If not, now is the time to change them.

Writing Transparency 5

Finish Your Writing Plan WRITING POSITION PAPER 5

Writing Plan

Topic	
Audience	
Controlling Idea	
Purpose	
Time Frame	

Organization

I. Introduction

II. Body

III. Conclusion

TEACH

E Organize the Details

Order of Importance List Use the Student Model to show how the writer rated the importance of each reason. Explain that this yields a logical progression of ideas that will better support a thesis statement.

F Finish Your Writing Plan

Writing Transparency 5

Model the Plan Use the transparency to model creating a plan. Use a student example:

- **Topic:** What issue and position are you writing about?
- **Audience:** Who will read your position paper?
- **Controlling Idea:** Why is the issue important? Why do you believe that your position is the right one?
- **Purpose:** Why are you writing it?
- **Time Frame:** Set a deadline that allows time both in and outside of class to fully complete the steps.

Manage the Steps Download this chart to help students manage their time.

W.9-10.5; W.9-10.6

myNGconnect.com

Date	Tasks
	1. Study the form. 2. Analyze a professional model. 3. Choose a topic. 4. Identify an audience, controlling idea, and purpose. 5. Gather and organize details. 6. Create your Writing Plan.
	Write a draft using your Writing Plan.
	1. Revise for focus and unity. 2. Revise your draft using the Revision Checklist. 3. Conduct a peer conference. 4. Make revisions based on peer conference.
	Review your draft for any mistakes; check for proper capitalization, punctuation, spelling, and verb forms.
	Print out the position paper, or write a clean copy by hand.

Model the Organization Have students list reasons, then number them in order of importance to the writer's position.

ONGOING ASSESSMENT

Have students evaluate a partner's Writing Plan. Students should place a check by the sections that are complete and a star by those that still need work.

CCSS Literacy.W.9-10.5 Develop and strengthen writing as needed by planning, revising, editing, rewriting, or trying a new approach, focusing on addressing what is most significant for a specific purpose and audience. Literacy.W.9-10.6 Use technology, including the Internet, to produce, publish, and update individual or shared writing products, taking advantage of technology's capacity to link to other information and to display information flexibly and dynamically.

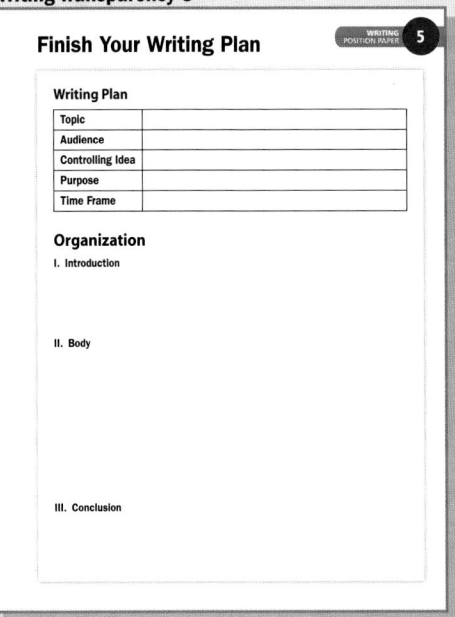

Lesson 2

WRITE A DRAFT

OBJECTIVES

Writing

- Writing Process: Draft
- Write a Draft
- Develop a Controlling Idea
- Provide Valid Evidence

TEACH

A Put Ideas Into Words

Express Ideas Have students express parts of their Writing Plan aloud to a partner, including the issue, their position, and key supporting reasons. Then ask them to write the ideas into a draft.

ELL Connect to Prior Learning Help students build on their existing knowledge and avoid getting "stuck" on language:

- Save time by using words you already know. Circle words you want to change, and use a thesaurus to do so later.
- If you cannot phrase a thought using language you know, draw a box to "reserve" the space and continue. If possible, jot down a few words in English or your first language to identify the idea you want to express. When you finish your draft, go back and use a dictionary to find the words you need.

W.9-10.1.a; W.9-10.4

B Use Evidence for Support

Develop Details Point out that details in a position paper should explain the main ideas convincingly. Read the definition of a fact, example, and analogy, and discuss an example of each in the paper on p. 187 or the sample on p. 190.

As students write their drafts, encourage them to support their main ideas with examples and facts that are concrete and relevant to their position. Also remind students to avoid emotional or informal language that may make them sound less credible.

W.9-10.1.a; W.9-10.1.b; W.9-10.1.d

✔Write a Draft

Now you are ready to write. Use your Writing Plan as a guide. You'll have chances to improve your draft later.

1 Put Ideas into Words

A

Sometimes writers look at a blank page and freeze. They do not know how to put their ideas into words. If you have this trouble, try these techniques:

- **Talk to Your Audience** Tell your ideas to one of your classmates. Ask the person to take notes. Use the notes to get your ideas down on paper.
- **Picture Your Audience** Choose one real person who will read your paper. Picture this person in your mind. Begin writing to this person alone. If it helps, you might write in the form of a letter. Underline the parts you can use in your draft.
- **Send Yourself an E-mail** If you are used to writing e-mails, begin your draft in an e-mail. It can be easier to write because it is less formal. Send yourself the e-mail. Underline the text you think you might use; then cut and paste the text into a document.

Technology Tip

Turn your outline into your draft. Copy your outline. Delete the numbers and letters and turn the list into a draft. Make each line a complete sentence. Combine related sentences into paragraphs.

2 Use Evidence for Support

B

One way to make your audience believe your position is to provide good supporting evidence. Supporting evidence should be clear and exact. Evidence that is presented objectively, or fairly, and is related to your position will help your audience better understand and believe it. Here are some kinds of evidence that you can use to support your position:

- **Facts** are statements that are proved to be true.
- **Examples** illustrate why your position is believable.
- **Analogies** are rhetorical devices that allow you to compare your position to something the audience might better understand.

OK

The worst consequence of a school uniform policy, however, would be the loss of freedom of expression. Clothing is an expression of students' personal identity, and it should stay that way.

Better

The worst consequence of a school uniform policy, however, would be the loss of freedom of expression. Clothes and jewelry allow us to be creative and confident about who we are as individuals. Putting us in uniforms would take away our personal identities. It would be like making everyone in the city paint their buildings the same color.

FOCUS ON WRITER'S CRAFT

Using Objective Language

Teach/Model Explain that writers can make reasons and evidence more believable by choosing the right words to describe them:

- **Modifiers to avoid:** *all, every, always, never, no one, nothing,* and *everything.* These words can be difficult to believe as there are nearly always exceptions to situations.
- **Modifiers to use instead:** *most of, many, the majority of, in many cases, often, more, few,* and *less.* Statements that include these words recognize exceptions, so they are easier to believe.

Practice Present the following reasons for a position, and guide a discussion on which reason is more believable and why:

- Teenagers should be allowed to work part-time because everyone has extra time after school that needs to be used wisely.
- Teenagers should be allowed to work part-time because many families need extra money.

Apply As they write reasons and details in their drafts, have students consider modifiers that acknowledge exceptions in order to invite readers to accept the writer's position.

W.9-10.1.d

CCSS **Literacy.W.9-10.1.a** Introduce precise claim(s), distinguish the claim(s) from alternate or opposing claims, and create an organization that establishes clear relationships among claim(s), counterclaims, reasons, and evidence. **Literacy.W.9-10.1.b** Develop claim(s) and counterclaims fairly, supplying evidence for each while pointing out the strengths and limitations of both in a manner that anticipates the audience's knowledge level and concerns. **Literacy.W.9-10.1.d** Establish and maintain a formal style and objective tone while attending to the norms and conventions of the discipline in which they are writing. **Literacy.W.9-10.4** Produce clear and coherent writing in which the development, organization, and style are appropriate to task, purpose, and audience.

B Student Model

Read this draft to see how the student used the Writing Plan to get ideas down on paper. This first draft does not have to be perfect. As you will see, the student fixed the mistakes later.

School Uniforms: Not Our Style

Because of a few students with bad judgment, all students in our school district may soon suffer the consequences. Administrators of South Regional school district 101 are considering adopting a school uniform policy to eliminate the problem of students dressing improperly. While something does need to be done, issuing school uniforms is a bad idea that would cause more harm than good.

First, having a school uniform will make us stand out from other School Districts. Most other districts have tackled the clothing problem by issuing dress codes like this one "You must dress in a manner that shows respect for other students and the school. You may not wear you're hats or caps indoors, and you may not wear clothing that could offend others." That is a sensible code. Choosing what students can wear, on the other hand, is *not* sensible, and that is why other districts does not do it.

Another problem with school uniforms is their cost. For many families in the area, school uniforms would be an additional strain on a budget that is already stretched to thin. What if a family have several children in high school at the same time? What if these children has a growth spurt? My friend Isaiah grew five inches in one year! The cost of new uniforms could grow out of control.

The worst consequence of a school uniform policy, however, would be the loss of our freedom of expression. Clothes and jewelry allow us to be creative and confident about who we are as individuals. Putting us in uniforms would take away our personal identities. It would be like making everyone in the city paint their buildings the same color.

It is true that uniforms are one way to prevent the distraction that could be caused by inappropriate clothing. However, a strictly enforced dress code could be just as effective, without costing students money and taking away their right to personal expression. Isn't rules supposed to help students instead of harm them? And on that note, how about getting rid of the "no-food-or-drink-in-class" policy, too?

Reflect on Your Draft

▶ What gave you trouble when you were writing? Was it hard to start? Was it hard to keep going? Think about what you might do differently next time.

TEACH

C Student Model

Read Have students read the Student Model.

Writing Transparency 6

Analyze Display the transparency. Ask these questions to help students see the relationship between the Writing Plan on p. 189 and the draft. Mark answers on the transparency:

- What is the controlling idea? [*The school should not require students to wear uniforms.*]
- Where does the writer state the issue and his or her position? [*Lines 2–4 and 5–6*]
- What three main ideas explain the writer's position? Where are they stated? [*Lines 7–8: Other districts do not have uniforms; Line 14: Uniforms are expensive; Lines 20–21: Uniforms take away freedom of expression.*]
- What is one detail the author uses to explain a main idea? [*Families with several children may have trouble buying uniforms.*]

Remind students that the Writing Plan is a place to start and may be revised as the draft is revised.

Writing Transparency 6

Student Model WRITING POSITION PAPER 6

School Uniforms: Not Our Style

Because of a few students with bad judgment, all students in our school district may soon suffer the consequences. Administrators of South Regional school district 101 are considering adopting a school uniform policy to eliminate the problem of students dressing improperly. While something does need to be done, issuing school uniforms is a bad idea that would cause more harm than good.

First, having a school uniform will make us stand out from other School Districts. Most other districts have tackled the clothing problem by issuing dress codes like this one "You must dress in a manner that shows respect for other students and the school. You may not wear you're hats or caps indoors, and you may not wear clothing that could offend others." That is a sensible code. Choosing what students can wear, on the other hand, is *not* sensible, and that is why other districts does not do it.

Another problem with school uniforms is their cost. For many families in the area, school uniforms would be an additional strain on a budget that is already stretched to thin. What if a family have several children in high school at the same time? What if these children has a growth spurt? My friend Isaiah grew five inches in one year! The cost of new uniforms could grow out of control.

The worst consequence of a school uniform policy, however, would be the loss of our freedom of expression. Clothes and jewelry allow us to be creative and confident about who we are as individuals. Putting us in uniforms would take away our personal identities. It would be like making everyone in the city paint their buildings the same color.

It is true that uniforms are one way to prevent the distraction that could be caused by inappropriate clothing. However, a strictly enforced dress code could be just as effective, without costing students money and taking away their right to personal expression. Isn't rules supposed to help students instead of harm them? And on that note, how about getting rid of the "no-food-or-drink-in-class" policy, too?

ONGOING ASSESSMENT

Have students explain to a partner the purpose of writing a draft and two strategies to produce main ideas and details for the draft.

Lesson 3

REVISE YOUR DRAFT

OBJECTIVES

Writing

- Writing Process: Revise
- Evaluate and Revise the Draft for Focus and Unity (T)
- Participate in Peer Conferencing

TEACH

(A) Revise for Focus and Unity

Define Elaborate on the writing traits of focus and unity:

- **Focus:** The position paper focuses on one issue. The controlling idea is the writer's position on the issue.
- **Unity:** Everything in the position paper relates back to the controlling idea. Each paragraph, main idea, and detail helps explain the writer's position. Relevant and precise evidence provides the best support for a position.

ELL Use a Graphic Organizer
Use Word Webs to help students understand the words *focus* and *unity*. Work together to expand each web with familiar words.

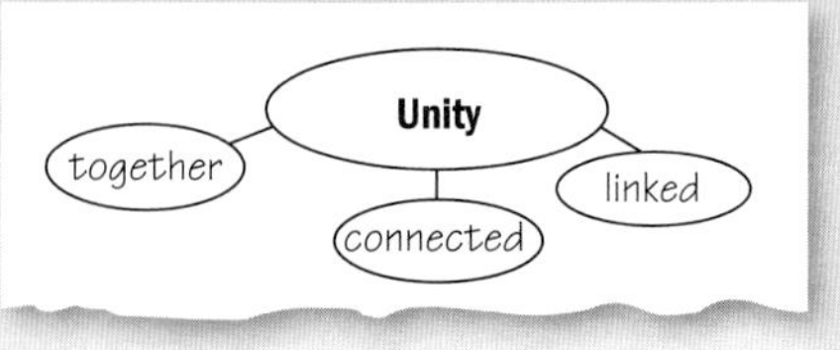

Remind students to use transition words and phrases between paragraphs to give their ideas unity.
W.9-10.1; W.9-10.1.c; W.9-10.5

Try It Have partners use a checklist.

1) The controlling idea focuses on one issue.	yes or no
2) The author clearly states his or her position.	yes or no
3) The main ideas and details explain and support the author's position.	yes or no
4) The conclusion addresses the idea in an interesting way.	yes or no

Tell students to read their partner's draft and circle yes for the statements that are true and no for those that are not. Have students suggest ways the writer can improve.

✔ Revise Your Draft

Your first draft is done. Now, you need to polish it. Improve the focus and unity. Make what was just OK into something much better.

1 Revise for Focus and Unity

Good writing has a **focus**—it has a central, controlling idea. In a position paper, the focus is the writer's position, or claim.

Good writing also has **unity**—that means that all of the parts support the controlling idea. In a position paper, that means that the reasons and evidence all relate to the writer's position. Good evidence is clear and exact. It is also related to your position.

Don't expect to have perfect focus and unity in your first draft. Time spent revising helps you sharpen your focus. Cut out any word, sentence, or even paragraph that doesn't relate to your controlling idea. It also helps to use transition words such as *first, also,* or *another* to unify your ideas. (A)

TRY IT ▸ With a partner, discuss which parts of the draft below do not support or relate to the writer's controlling idea.

Student Draft

Another problem with school uniforms is their cost. For many families in the area, school uniforms would be an additional strain on a budget that is already stretched to thin. What if a family have several children in high school at the same time? What if these children has a growth spurt? My friend Isaiah grew five inches in one year! The cost of new uniforms could grow out of control.

FOCUS ON WRITER'S CRAFT

Making Relationships Clear

Teach/Model Point out that it is the writer's responsibility to show the relationship between the controlling idea, main ideas, and details. Read these sentences:

- *Other local schools do not require uniforms. Students at our school already resent those at other local schools.*

Explain: These ideas are related, but the relationship is not clear. Have students write a sentence or two to explain the relationship. *[Possible response: They think other students have fewer rules to follow. If we wear uniforms, tensions will grow.]*

Practice/Apply Help students show relationships to give their papers a sense of completeness. Offer these steps:

1. **Examine each detail sentence:** If you were reading your paper for the first time, would you see the relationship between each detail sentence and the main idea?
2. **Add words, phrases, or sentences to explain relationships when necessary.** Encourage students to try to use words, phrases, and sentences to show relationships.

W.9-10.1.c

CCSS Literacy.W.9-10.1 Write arguments to support claims in an analysis of substantive topics or texts, using valid reasoning and relevant and sufficient evidence. **Literacy.W.9-10.1.c** Use words, phrases, and clauses to link the major sections of the text, create cohesion, and clarify the relationships between claim(s) and reasons, between reasons and evidence, and between claim(s) and counterclaims. **Literacy.W.9-10.5** Write arguments to support claims in an analysis of substantive topics or texts, using valid reasoning and relevant and sufficient evidence. Develop and strengthen writing as needed by planning, revising, editing, rewriting, or trying a new approach, focusing on addressing what is most significant for a specific purpose and audience.

Now use the rubric to evaluate the focus and unity of your own draft. What score do you give your draft and why?

Focus and Unity

	How clearly does the writing present a central idea or claim?	How well does everything go together?
4 Wow!	**The writing expresses a clear central idea or claim about the topic.**	**Everything in the writing goes together.** • The main idea of each paragraph goes with the central idea or claim of the paper. • The main idea and details within each paragraph are related. • The conclusion is about the central idea or claim.
3 Ahh.	**The writing expresses a generally clear central idea or claim about the topic.**	**Most parts of the writing go together.** • The main idea of most paragraphs goes with the central idea or claim of the paper. • In most paragraphs, the main idea and details are related. • Most of the conclusion is about the central idea or claim.
2 Hmm.	**The writing includes a topic, but the central idea or claim is not clear.**	**Some parts of the writing go together.** • The main idea of some paragraphs goes with the central idea or claim of the paper. • In some paragraphs, the main idea and details are related. • Some of the conclusion is about the central idea or claim.
1 Huh?	**The writing includes many topics and does not express one central idea or claim.**	**The parts of the writing do not go together.** • Few paragraphs have a main idea, or the main idea does not go with the central idea or claim of the paper. • Few paragraphs contain a main idea and related details • None of the conclusion is about the central idea or claim.

myNGconnect.com
- Rubric: Focus and Unity
- Evaluate and practice scoring other student papers.

TEACH

B Use a Rubric

Model Model using a rubric to evaluate a draft. Explain that students will first score the Student Model on focus. Read the statements in the left column of the rubric on p. 193 aloud. Then have a volunteer point to and read the controlling idea from the Student Model on p. 191. Ask: Would you give the Student Draft a score of 4, 3, 2, or 1 based on the criteria in the rubric?

Possible response:
- *I would give it a 4. The author clearly states the issue and a position.*

Next, explain that students will assign a score for unity. Read the first sentence in the right column. Tell students that the bulleted points below this and other statements provide specific points to guide them in assigning a score.

Collaborative Evaluation Have students work in small groups to compare their evaluations of the Student Model. Ask: How do your scores differ? Ask them to discuss the reasons for the differences and come up with a group consensus.

Then have students assign an overall score for focus and unity by averaging the two and rounding down to the nearest whole number. For instance, if students assign a 4 for focus and a 3 for unity, the average would be 3.5, which rounds down to a score of 3.
SL.9-10.1

Self-Evaluation Have students follow the same steps to evaluate their own drafts. Try these suggestions:

- First, evaluate the controlling idea. Did you state it? Is it clear? Score yourself using the left column of the rubric.
- Next, identify the main idea and details. Do they support the controlling idea? Does every detail belong? Rate yourself using the right column of the rubric.
W.9-10.5

myNGconnect.com
- **Evaluate more samples from peers or online.**

DIFFERENTIATED INSTRUCTION

English Language Learners ELL

Focus on Key Words Point out key words and text features to help students navigate points in the rubric:

- Point to the green tabs on top, and read the question in each. Explain: *These are the elements you are scoring.*
- Point to the underlined words in the left column. Reread and paraphrase each line: *The central idea is generally clear. This means "mostly clear."*
- Point to the boldfaced statements and underlined words in the right column. Reread them and define the underlined words: *Everything is more than most. Most is more than some.*

CCSS Literacy.W.9-10.5 Develop and strengthen writing as needed by planning, revising, editing, rewriting, or trying a new approach, focusing on addressing what is most significant for a specific purpose and audience. Literacy.SL.9-10.1 Initiate and participate effectively in a range of collaborative discussions (one-on-one, in groups, and teacher-led) with diverse partners on grades 9-10 topics, texts, and issues, building on others' ideas and expressing their own clearly and persuasively.

REVISE YOUR DRAFT

TEACH

C Revise Your Draft

Interpret the Checklist Guide students through the process of using the Revision Checklist. Read aloud the fourth question in the first column (*Do I address both sides of the issue?*). Students should then follow the instructions in the second column. If they are unable to find both sides to underline, they should revise based on the options in the third column.

Self-Evaluation Instruct students to follow the Revision Checklist to finish making revisions to their own drafts. Suggest that they first place a check by the questions that do not need extra attention and then focus on items that need revision.

ELL **Demonstrate** Demonstrate how to use the checklist by doing a think-aloud with the Student Model on p. 191.

- Point to the fourth question on the checklist: *Do I address both sides of the issue in my paper?*
- Read the introduction paragraph: *No, I see that I only gave my position on the issue. I need to add the other side.*
- Point to the suggestion in the central column: *I can't underline both sides, because my paper doesn't include both of them.*
- Point to the suggestion in the third column, and read it aloud: *I see. I need to add a sentence that tells why administrators think we need school uniforms. I will do that.*

Work with students to identify claims they make that are not supported by proof. Guide them in adding proof or deleting the unsubstantiated claim.
W.9-10.1.a; W.9-10.1.b; W.9-10.1.c; W.9-10.1.d

✓Revise Your Draft, continued

2 Revise Your Draft

You've now evaluated the focus and unity of your own draft. If you scored 3 or lower, how can you improve your work? Use the checklist below to revise your draft.

C

Revision Checklist

Ask Yourself	Check It Out	How to Make It Better
Is my paper focused?	Underline your controlling idea. Check that it states your position.	☐ Add a controlling idea if you don't have one. ☐ Rewrite your controlling idea if it is not clear.
Is my paper unified?	Check every paragraph to make sure you stay on topic.	☐ Cut or rewrite sections that do not support the controlling idea.
Does my position paper have an introduction, a body, and a conclusion?	Draw a box around each part.	☐ Add any part that is missing.
Do I address both sides of the issue?	Underline each side.	☐ State the opposing position in your introduction if you haven't done so. ☐ In the body, add reasons that explain why the opposing position is wrong.
Does the body contain two or more supporting reasons?	Underline each main reason. Count them.	☐ Add more reasons if you have just one.
Do I provide specific evidence to support those reasons?	Underline any examples, facts, or analogies that elaborate on your reasons.	☐ Add more specific evidence if needed.
Is my organizing structure appropriate to the purpose of the paper?	Check to see that you put your reasons in order of importance.	☐ Put your reasons in order from least to most important, or vice versa.
Have I used a formal style and presented my claims fairly?	Look for informal or overly emotional language.	☐ Replace informal language with academic-sounding language. ☐ Eliminate language that sounds emotional or exaggerated.
Can readers follow my train of thought?	Ask a classmate to read your paper.	☐ Reorganize your reasons. ☐ Add more supporting evidence. ☐ Add transition words and phrases.

Writing Handbook, p. 784

FOCUS ON WRITER'S CRAFT

Using Figurative Language in Evidence

Teach/Model Define figurative language as words that mean something different from the actual definition. Explain that figurative language helps readers envision the author's ideas and can freshen the expression of common themes. Discuss these forms of figurative language:

- **Metaphor:** a comparison in which an author names one thing or person as another to emphasize certain traits. Example: *She is a lamb. [She is gentle.]*
- **Idiom:** a word or phrase that says one thing literally but is used to mean another. Example: *I feel under the weather. [I feel sick.]*
- **Hyperbole:** an exaggeration to help communicate an idea. Example: *This is the longest tie in the world! [This is a very long tie.]*

Practice Have students identify the following words and phrases from p. 187 as a metaphor, idiom, or hyperbole:

1. To save money, the board has gone out on a limb and proposed cutting all arts funding for city high schools. (*idiom*)
2. This opened up a bright new world to her—a world in which she could succeed. (*metaphor*)
3. For many of today's youth, art is the only chance they have for a successful life. (*hyperbole*)

Apply Have students consider adding one or two examples of figurative language as they revise their position papers.
L.9-10.5

CCSS **Literacy.W.9-10.1.a** Introduce precise claim(s), distinguish the claim(s) from alternate or opposing claims, and create an organization that establishes clear relationships among claim(s), counterclaims, reasons, and evidence. **Literacy.W.9-10.1.b** Develop claim(s) and counterclaims fairly, supplying evidence for each while pointing out the strengths and limitations of both in a manner that anticipates the audience's knowledge level and concerns. **Literacy.W.9-10.1.c** Use words, phrases, and clauses to link the major sections of the text, create cohesion, and clarify the relationships between claim(s) and reasons, between reasons and evidence, and between claim(s) and counterclaims. **Literacy.L.9-10.5** Demonstrate understanding of figurative language, word relationships, and nuances in word meanings.

3 Conduct a Peer Conference

It helps to get a second opinion when you are revising your draft. Ask a partner to read your draft and look for the following:

- any part of the draft that is confusing
- any place where something seems to be missing
- anything that the person doesn't understand

Then talk with your partner about the draft. Focus on the items in the Revision Checklist. Use your partner's comments to make your position paper clearer, more complete, and easier to understand.

D

4 Make Revisions

Look at the revisions below and the peer-reviewer conversation on the right. Notice how the peer reviewer commented and asked questions. Notice how the writer used the comments and questions to revise.

Revised for Unity

Another problem with school uniforms is their cost. For many families in the area, school uniforms would be an additional strain on a budget that is already stretched to thin. ~~What if a family~~ This would be particularly hard on a family that have several children in high school at the same time? ~~What~~ It would also be a problem if these children has a growth spurt. ~~My friend Isaiah grew five inches in one year!~~ The cost of new uniforms could grow out of control.

Revised for Focus

It is true that uniforms are one way to prevent the distraction that could be caused by inappropriate clothing. However, a strictly enforced dress code could be just as effective, without costing students money and taking away their right to personal expression. Isn't rules supposed to help students instead of harm them? ~~And on that note, how about getting rid of the "no-food-or-drink-in-class" policy, too?~~

E

Peer Conference

Reviewer's Comment: You went off track in the third paragraph. The fact that Isaiah grew five inches doesn't really relate to your controlling idea.

Writer's Answer: You're right. I'll delete that sentence. I'll also change the "What if...?" questions. They sound more like informal speech than formal writing.

Reviewer's Comment: The last question introduces a whole new controlling idea. It doesn't belong.

Writer's Answer: I see your point. That's a whole other topic. I'll delete that sentence, too.

Reflect on Your Revisions

▶ Think about the results of your peer conference. What are your strengths as a writer? What do you need to improve?

TEACH

D Conduct a Peer Conference

Ask a Partner Provide questions for each student to ask the partner who reviewed his or her paper:

- Which parts seemed confusing?
- Which parts seemed incomplete?
- Which points were difficult for you to understand?
- Which ideas seem to be out of place?

Provide a simple but structured format for students to use to note their partner's responses. For example, distribute a table with sections labeled *Clarify*, *Add*, and *Explain*.
SL.9-10.1.d

E Make Revisions

Model Have two volunteers read aloud the first Peer Conference in the margin. Then work with students to help them analyze and evaluate the writer's revisions. Ask:

- What did the writer do to improve the draft?
- How did the revision make the draft better? Is there another way to revise the writing to achieve the same purpose?

Use Feedback Have students follow the steps above for making revisions to their own drafts.
W.9-10.1.d; W.9-10.5

FOCUS ON WRITER'S CRAFT

Gaining Perspective on Feedback

Teach Ask: Did you know that you provide some of the same types of feedback in ordinary conversations as you do in peer writing conferences? Point out that feedback in a conversation helps clarify the speaker's thoughts as feedback in writing helps clarify the writer's ideas. List common words and phrases people use in conversations to ask the speaker to clarify ideas:

- What do you mean?
- I don't understand.
- Can you give me an example?
- Why do you feel that way?

Suggest that when students receive feedback on their writing, they view clarifications they need to make in their writing similarly to those they make when speaking. For example, they might rephrase, add a detail, or offer an example. Their partner's feedback will reveal parts of their writing that might need these adjustments.

Apply After they receive feedback, have students apply it by rewording their ideas orally and then revising them in writing.

ONGOING ASSESSMENT

Have students list two revisions they made and why the revisions were necessary: *I revised* _______ *because* _______.

CCSS **Literacy.W.9-10.1.d** Establish and maintain a formal style and objective tone while attending to the norms and conventions of the discipline in which they are writing. **Literacy.W.9-10.5** Develop and strengthen writing as needed by planning, revising, editing, rewriting, or trying a new approach, focusing on addressing what is most significant for a specific purpose and audience. **Literacy.SL.9-10.1.d** Respond thoughtfully to diverse perspectives, summarize points of agreement and disagreement, and, when warranted, qualify or justify their own views and understanding and make new connections in light of the evidence and reasoning presented.

Lesson 4

EDIT AND PROOFREAD YOUR DRAFT

OBJECTIVES

Writing
- Writing Process: Edit and Proofread Ⓣ

Grammar
- Present Tense Verbs Ⓣ

Mechanics
- Capitalization: Names of Groups
- Punctuation: Colon
- Spelling: Homonyms

TEACH

Writing Transparencies 7 and 8

Ⓐ Capitalize the Names of Groups

Try It Review the capitalization of the names of groups.

ELL Build Background Explain that articles—words such as *a*, *an*, *of*, and *the*—are not capitalized unless they are the first word in a group name.

Have students work in pairs to correct the sentences. Then, use Proofreader's Marks to correct the errors on the transparency.

Possible response:
- *school district; School Districts*

Edit and Proofread Have students correct the capitalization errors in their own drafts.
L.9-10.2

Ⓑ Use Colons Correctly

Try It Explain the use of colons. Then on the transparency, underline the sentence that requires a colon. Ask: Where do we need to insert a colon? Why?

Possible responses:

Most other districts have tackled the clothing problem by issuing dress codes like this one:

Edit and Proofread Have students check the use of colons in their own drafts.
L.9-10.2.b; L.9-10.3.a

✔ Edit and Proofread Your Draft

Your revision should now be complete. Before you share it with others, find and fix any mistakes that you made.

1 Capitalize the Names of Groups

Ⓐ

The names of some groups are proper nouns. These include organizations and businesses. These also include institutions and government agencies.

Institution: First Bank of Newberg
Business: Cape Fuel Company
Organization: American Medical Association

The names of nonspecific groups should not be capitalized.

a bank   a company   an association

TRY IT ▸ Copy the sentences. Fix the capitalization errors. Use proofreader's marks.

1. Administrators of South Regional school district 101 are currently considering adopting a school uniform policy.
2. Having a school uniform will make us stand out from other School Districts.

Proofreader's Marks

Use proofreader's marks to correct errors.

Capitalize:
I joined the National Students' union.

Do not capitalize:
There are many different kinds of Unions in this country.

Add colon:
Your new uniform will consist of the following a white shirt, a red vest, and a blue skirt or blue pants.

2 Use Colons Correctly

Ⓑ

A colon (:) is used to set off a list, an explanation, or a quotation. It usually signals that important information is going to follow.

Students are forbidden to wear the following**:** baseball caps, sleeveless shirts, and ripped jeans.

There is only one solution to this problem**:** to require that students wear uniforms.

The principal read from a page in the student handbook**:** "Students must obey the dress code at all times, including during school-sponsored outings."

The first word after a colon is usually capitalized only if it is a proper noun or the first word of a complete sentence.

TRY IT ▸ Copy the sentence. Add a colon where necessary.

Most other districts have tackled the clothing problem by issuing dress codes like this one "You must dress in a manner that shows respect for other students and the school."

Proofreading Tip

If you are unsure of when to use a colon, look in a style manual for help and examples.

Writing Transparency 7

WRITING POSITION PAPER 7

Edit and Proofread Your Draft

Proofreader's Marks		
≡	Capitalize	I love new york city.
/	Do not capitalize	I'm going shopping at my favorite Store.
⌃⌄	Add a colon	He wakes up at 6:30 a.m.
⌄ ⌄	Add quotation marks	You are late, said the teacher.
∧	Add a comma	Amy how are you feeling today?
⊙	Add a period	Mr Lopez is our neighbor.
?	Add a question mark	Where is my black pen
↓	Add an exclamation mark	Look out
∧	Add a semicolon	This shirt is nice however, this one brings out the color of your eyes.
⊼	Add a dash	Barney he's my pet dog has run away.
{ }	Add parentheses	I want to work for the Federal Bureau of Investigation {FBI}.
=	Add a hyphen	You were born in mid=September, right?
⌄	Add an apostrophe	Im the oldest of five children.
#	Add a space	She likes him alot.
⌣	Close up a space	How much home work do you have?
∧	Add text	My keys are the table.
⌇	Delete text	I am going too my friend's house.
∩∪	Transpose words, letters	Did you see thier new car?
(sp)	Spell out	Today he is turning 16.
¶	Begin a new paragraph	"I win!" I shouted. "No you don't," he said.
(ital)	Add italics	The Spanish word for table is mesa.
(u/s)	Add underlining	Little Women is one of my favorite books.

Writing Transparency 8

WRITING POSITION PAPER 8

Edit and Proofread Your Draft

1. Capitalize the Names of Groups

1. Administrators of South Regional school district 101 are currently considering adopting a school uniform policy.
2. Having a school uniform will make us stand out from other School Districts.

2. Use Colons Correctly

Most other districts have tackled the clothing problem by issuing dress codes like this one "You must dress in a manner that shows respect for other students and the school."

3. Check Your Spelling

1. You may not wear you're hats or caps indoors.
2. School uniforms would be an additional strain on a budget that is already stretched to thin.

4. Use Correct Verb Forms in the Present Tense

1. That is why other districts does not do it.
2. It would be a problem if the children has a growth spurt.
3. Isn't rules supposed to help students instead of harm them?

CCSS Literacy.L.9-10.2 Demonstrate command of the conventions of standard English capitalization, punctuation, and spelling when writing. Literacy.L.9-10.2.b Use a colon to introduce a list or quotation. Literacy.L.9-10.3.a Write and edit work so that it conforms to the guidelines in a style manual (e.g., *MLA Handbook*, Turabian's *Manual for Writers*) appropriate for the discipline and writing type.

B Check Your Spelling

Homonyms are words that sound alike but have different meanings and spellings. Spell these homonyms correctly when you proofread.

Homonyms and Their Meanings	Examples
to (preposition) = toward **two** (adjective) = the number 2 **too** (adverb) = also, very	I walk **to** school. The rule has **two** parts. Your paper is **too** short.
your (adjective) = belonging to you **you're** (contraction) = you are	**Your** boots are like mine. **You're** in my art class.

TRY IT▶ Copy the sentences. Find and fix the homonym errors.

1. You may not wear you're hats or caps indoors.
2. School uniforms would be an additional strain on a budget that is already stretched to thin.

4 Use Correct Verb Forms in the Present Tense

The verbs *have, be,* and *do* are irregular verbs. They have different forms in the present tense than regular verbs do.

Have		Be		Do	
I have	we have	I am	we are	I do	we do
you have	you have	you are	you are	you do	you do
he, she, it has	they have	he, she, it is	they are	he, she, it does	they do

The key to using these verbs correctly in the present tense is to be sure the verb form agrees with the subject of the sentence.

I **have** a school uniform. She **has** one, too.

Are you angry about the decision? I definitely **am**.

I **do** not want to wear a uniform. Neither **does** he.

TRY IT▶ Copy the sentences. Find and fix any verb errors.

1. That is why other districts does not do it.
2. It would be a problem if the children has a growth spurt.
3. Isn't rules supposed to help students instead of harm them?

Reflect on Your Corrections

▶ How many errors did you find and fix? Notice what kinds of errors they were. If there are things you keep missing, make a checklist of what to watch in your writing.

Writing Handbook, pp. 840–841; 851

TEACH

C Check Your Spelling

Try It Explain the definition of homonyms. Read the definitions and examples and follow up with questions and tips such as the following:

- **to/two/too:** Hold up two fingers and ask: How many fingers do you see? *[two]* Give a pencil to a student, and ask: Whom did I give it to? *[to the student]* Then ask: What is another word for *also*? *[too]*
- **your/you're:** Tell students that if they have trouble remembering whether to use *your* or *you're*, replace the word with "you are." Say: If it makes sense, use the contraction *you're*, which is formed from *you are*. If it doesn't, then use *your*.

Ask: Where are the homonym errors in the sample? Mark corrections to the spelling/homonym errors on the transparency.

Possible responses:

- *~~you're~~ your hats*
- *~~to~~ too thin*

Edit and Proofread Have students check their drafts for homonym errors and make the necessary corrections.
L.9-10.2.c; L.9-10.3

D Use Correct Verb Forms in the Present Tense

Try It Read the examples in the chart. Then review the sentences with highlighted verb forms. Have students correct the sentences and compare answers with a partner. Then confirm the correct answers using the transparency.

Possible responses:

1) That is why other districts ~~does~~ do not do it.

2) It would be a problem if the children ~~has~~ have a growth spurt.

3) ~~Isn't~~ Aren't rules supposed to help students instead of harm them?

Edit and Proofread Have students scan their drafts and lightly circle forms of *have, be,* and *do*. Then ask them to review the sentences and correct any errors in the verb forms.
L.9-10.1

Grammar and Writing Practice Book, pp. 65–68
L.9-10.2.b

FOCUS ON WRITER'S CRAFT

Finding Words that Signal Colons

Teach Explain that signal words can help writers know when to use a colon, such as *the following, there is, there are, these,* and *this*:

- There is one person who can veto the policy: the superintendent of the school system.
- These are the reasons Alberto needs new clothes: he grew two inches and lost his jacket.

Also provide examples of situations in which students should avoid using colons, such as after the word *include* or *to be*:

- The people who agree with the new policy include our principal and vice principal. *[no colon after include]*

Practice Have students edit the following sentences by adding or omitting colons when necessary:

1) My favorite places include the neighborhood swimming pool, the mall, and a café near school. *[unchanged]*
2) The teacher asked students to do these tasks collect their things, line up, and walk to the gym. *[add colon after tasks]*
3) The only chore my parents asked me to do today was to clean my room. *[unchanged]*

Apply Have students review their drafts for signal words that show they need to add or omit colons in their sentences.
L.9-10.2.b

CCSS Literacy.L.9-10.1 Demonstrate command of the conventions of standard English grammar and usage when writing or speaking. **Literacy.L.9-10.2.b** Use a colon to introduce a list or quotation. **Literacy.L.9-10.2.c** Spell correctly. **Literacy.L.9-10.3** Apply knowledge of language to understand how language functions in different contexts, to make effective choices for meaning or style, and to comprehend more fully when reading or listening.

Lesson 4, continued

EDIT AND PROOFREAD YOUR DRAFT

TEACH

E Edited Student Draft

Read and Discuss Read aloud the Edited Student Draft. Then go back and address the callouts. For example:

Ask: What were the capitalization errors? How did the writer correct them?

Possible response:

- *In the first paragraph, the words* School *and* District *were capitalized, because they are part of the name of an organization. In the second paragraph,* school *and* district *were changed to lowercase since they refer to a nonspecific group.*

Ask: Which verb forms did the writer correct?

Possible response:

- *The writer changed* does *to* do *to match the subject* districts. *The verb* have *was changed to* has *to match the subject* family, *and the verb* has *was changed to* have *to match* children. *The contraction* isn't *was changed to* aren't *to match* rules.

Finally, ask: What other revisions did the writer make?

Possible responses:

- *The writer removed the unrelated sentence in the third paragraph. The writer also removed the question about an unrelated policy at the end of the paper.*
- *The writer fixed the writing style in the third paragraph.*
- *The writer added the transitional phrase* After all *at the beginning of the last sentence.*

ONGOING ASSESSMENT
Write sentences on the board that require corrections in capitalization, colons, present tense verb forms, and homonyms. Have students copy the sentences and use Proofreader's Marks to correct them.

5 Edited Student Draft

Here's the student's draft, revised and edited. How did the writer improve it?

School Uniforms: Not Our Style

Because of a few students with bad judgment, all students in our school district may soon suffer the consequences. Administrators of South Regional School District 101 are considering adopting a school uniform policy to eliminate the problem of students dressing improperly. While something does need to be done, issuing school uniforms is a bad idea that would cause more harm than good.

First, having a school uniform will make us stand out from other school districts. Most other districts have tackled the clothing problem by issuing dress codes like this one: "You must dress in a manner that shows respect for other students and the school. You may not wear your hats or caps indoors, and you may not wear clothing that could offend others." That is a sensible code. Choosing what students can wear, on the other hand, is *not* sensible, and that is why other districts do not do it.

Another problem with school uniforms is their cost. For many families in the area, school uniforms would be an additional strain on a budget that is already stretched too thin. This would be particularly hard on a family that has several children in high school at the same time. It would also be a problem if these children have a growth spurt. The cost of new uniforms could grow out of control.

The worst consequence of a school uniform policy, however, would be the loss of our freedom of expression. Clothes and jewelry allow us to be creative and confident about who we are as individuals. Putting us in uniforms would take away our personal identities. It would be like making everyone in the city paint their buildings the same color.

It is true that uniforms are one way to prevent the distraction that could be caused by inappropriate clothing. However, a strictly enforced dress code could be just as effective, without costing students money and taking away their right to personal expression. After all, aren't rules supposed to help students instead of harm them?

The writer fixed the **capitalization** error.

The writer fixed the **capitalization** error.

The writer added a **colon** to separate the quotation and used the correct **homonym**.

The writer used the correct **verb form**.

The writer used the correct **homonym** and **verb forms**. The writer also deleted the sentence that doesn't belong and revised the "What if...?" questions.

The writer added a **transitional phrase** and used the correct **verb form**. She also deleted the sentence that introduced a new controlling idea.

Publish and Present

You are now ready to publish and present your position paper. Print out your paper or write a clean copy by hand. You may also want to present your work in a different way.

Alternative Presentations

Submit a Guest Editorial Many publications have guest editorials. Most editorials are a type of position paper.

1. **Find a Publication** You are writing about a local issue, so check newspapers and magazines in your school and community.
2. **Check the Guidelines** Many publications have guidelines for writers. Ask for them if you can't find any.
3. **Send Your Work** Mail or e-mail your work. Include a way for the publisher to contact you. Ask for feedback on your work.

Create a Podcast A podcast is a radio-style program that is published on the Internet. Listeners subscribe to a podcast and can then download it to their computers or portable listening devices. You can easily reorganize and turn your position paper into a mini-podcast.

1. **Practice** Practice reading aloud before you record your podcast. Check with a dictionary if you are not sure how to pronounce a word.
2. **Record and Edit** Use a computer with a microphone and recording software to record your podcast. Speak clearly and slowly so your listeners can understand you. Use features of your software to add special effects, such as background noise and music.
3. **Listen** Carefully listen to your recording. Be sure it is clear and easy to follow. Ask a friend or classmate to listen and give feedback.
4. **Convert** Look at the file extension of your recording. If it is a WAV file, you need to convert it to a smaller file, such as an MP3. Certain recording software or media players will allow you to do this.
5. **Publish** Many schools provide free Web space to students who wish to publish school-related projects online. Check with your teacher or school Web administrator to see if your school has this policy.

Language and Learning Handbook, p. 714

A

Publishing Tip

Include a cover letter when you submit your position paper. Begin it with a highlight from the paper that will grab the publisher's attention. You want to stand out among all other submissions.

Reflect on Your Work

Ask for and use feedback from your audience and your teacher to evaluate your strengths as a writer.

- Did your audience clearly understand your position?
- Did your audience think you supported your position with strong reasons?
- What would you like to do better the next time you write? Set a goal for your next writing project.

☑ **Save a copy of your work in your portfolio.**

B

Lesson 5

PUBLISH AND PRESENT

OBJECTIVES

Writing
- Position Paper
- Writing Process: Publish; Reflect and Evaluate

TEACH

Have students choose one of two ways of publishing and presenting their position paper: Submit a Guest Editorial or Create a Podcast.

A Alternative Presentations

Submit a Guest Editorial Bring in local newspapers and magazines of interest to your students. Direct them to read the guidelines and to follow these closely as they write and submit their editorial. Remind students that they may need to reorganize their essays for publication.

Create a Podcast If it is compliant with the school's Internet policy, help students post their work online as podcasts. Then have classmates access and listen to the podcast. Have listeners provide feedback online if possible, and ask recipients to review each point.
W.9-10.6; SL.9-10.3; SL.9-10.4; SL.9-10.6

Language and Learning Handbook, p. 714

B Reflect on Your Work

Use Feedback Provide students with feedback before and after they publish. Next, have students write a short reflection in response to the questions, including a specific goal for their next writing project. For example: *In my next writing project I will try to include more specific evidence.*

Remind students to save a copy of their paper in their portfolio.

FOCUS ON WRITER'S CRAFT

Using Effective Speaking Strategies

Teach Explain that students should employ speaking strategies in both informal and formal situations to ensure that listeners understand their message and interpret it correctly:

- **Use Proper Volume:** Speaking too quietly may prevent listeners from hearing the message. Speaking too loudly may be distracting.
- **Stress Important Words:** Stress important words and ideas by saying them more slowly or emphatically than others.
- **Pace Yourself:** Speaking too quickly will make it difficult for listeners to process your words. Speaking too slowly will bore listeners.

Practice/Apply Have students work in pairs. Ask them to write a few sentences about an issue they might present in a podcast or presentation. Have them read the sentences and practice using the proper volume, stress, and pacing as if they were speaking in front of a group.
SL.9-10.6

ONGOING ASSESSMENT

Have students describe how publishing a persuasive work orally differs from a written presentation.

CCSS **Literacy.W.9-10.6** Use technology, including the Internet, to produce, publish, and update individual or shared writing products, taking advantage of technology's capacity to link to other information and to display information flexibly and dynamically. **Literacy.SL.9-10.3** Evaluate a speaker's point of view, reasoning, and use of evidence and rhetoric, identifying any fallacious reasoning or exaggerated or distorted evidence. **Literacy.SL.9-10.4** Present information, findings, and supporting evidence clearly, concisely, and logically such that listeners can follow the line of reasoning and the organization, development, substance, and style are appropriate to purpose, audience, and task. **Literacy.SL.9-10.6** Adapt speech to a variety of contexts and tasks, demonstrating command of formal English when indicated or appropriate.

UNIT 3 SHORT STORIES

THE HERO WITHIN

EQ **ESSENTIAL QUESTION:**
What Makes a Hero?

CLUSTER 1

Discover how legends begin.

Short Story
The Sword in the Stone
by Molly Perham

Historical Analysis
Was There a Real King Arthur?
by Robert Stewart

PROJECTS

Writing Project
Response to Literature

Unit Project
Documentary

WORKSHOPS

Workplace
Inside an Airport

Vocabulary
Find Familiar Words

Listening and Speaking
Panel Discussion

CLUSTER 2

Consider the everyday heroes in your community.

Short Story

A Job for Valentín
by Judith Ortiz Cofer

Song Lyrics

Hero
by Mariah Carey

Feature Article

In the Heart of a Hero
by Johnny Dwyer

CLUSTER 3

Explore how heroes change the world around them.

Short Story

The Woman in the Snow
by Patricia C. McKissack

Magazine Profile

Rosa Parks
by Rita Dove

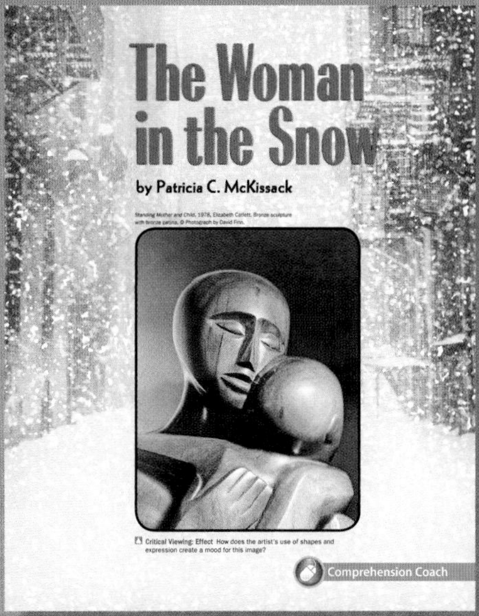

CLOSE READING

Consider the relationship between heroism and justice.

Speech

The American Promise
by Lyndon B. Johnson

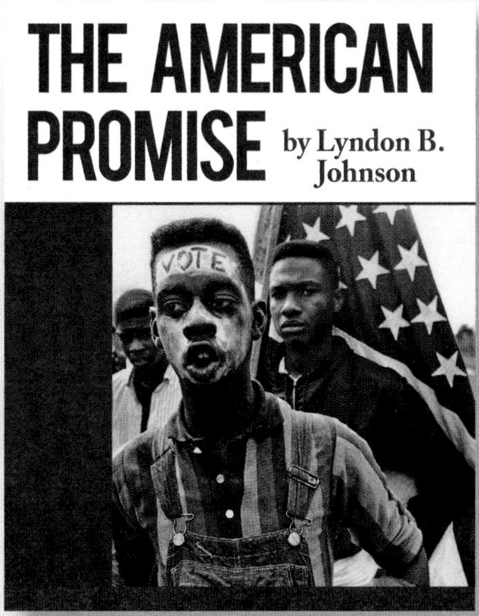

EDGE LIBRARY

Hercules ●
by Paul Storrie
Lexile® 540L
Genre/Length:
Graphic Novel; 52 pages

September 11, 2001 Attack on New York City ●●
by Wilborn Hampton
Lexile® 1060L
Genre/Length:
Nonfiction; 168 pages

Left Behind ●●●
by Velma Wallis
Lexile® 1030L
Genre/Length:
Legend; 112 pages

Edge Library

The **EDGE LIBRARY** provides an opportunity for student choice. Students self-select literature based on their interests and reading ability. Books support exploration of the **Essential Question**, forming an integral part of instruction.

1 Select

- Select a variety of appropriate materials to read

Self-Select Have students choose a book according to their interests and reading level.

Hercules
by Paul Storrie and Steve Kurth

Should a hero be loyal no matter what?

The graphic novel version of *Hercules* tells of the legendary hero Hercules and his twelve impossible labors. Students who read this story will also learn about Greek mythology and the traits of mythological characters.

- **Reading Level** Lexile® 540L

Genre: Graphic Novel

Length: 52 pages

2 Read

- Read to develop and evaluate personal preferences

Download the **Teacher's Guide** and **Student Journals.** Have students read their chosen book independently or in small groups. Use the planner on **Student Journal, page 1,** to establish a reading schedule. RL.9-10.10; RI.9-10.10

myNGconnect.com

- **Unit 3 Resources**
- **Teacher's Guide**
- **Student Journal**

3 Use Strategies

- Identify, assess, and apply effective personal reading strategies

Have students identify the strategies they selected to use during reading. Use the prompts at the right to elicit student analysis and discussions.

Make Inferences
- What qualities make Hercules successful in each challenge that he faces?

Synthesize
- What does the story say about loyalty and commitment?

Ask Questions
- How is Hercules similar to another character you have read about or seen on television or in a movie?

4 Discuss

- Exchange and extend ideas

EQ Does Creativity Matter?

Engage students in a discussion comparing how the texts address the **Essential Question**.

Discover how legends begin. The king challenges Hercules to perform twelve impossible tasks.

Consider the ways people show bravery in their community. Hercules is honest, brave, and strong, even when he faces great danger. He successfully conquers each task without jeopardizing his integrity.

Explore how heroes change the world around them. Hercules's bravery is legendary. Today, he is honored as one of the great heroes of ancient Greece.

CCSS Literacy.RL.9-10.10 By the end of grade 9, read and comprehend literature, including stories, dramas, and poems, in the grades 9-10 text complexity band proficiently, with scaffolding as needed at the high end of the range. By the end of grade 10, read and comprehend literature, including stories, dramas, and poems, at the high end of the grades 9-10 text complexity band independently and proficiently.

READ ALOUD

Left Behind Read aloud the introduction to engage students' interest in the book. Provide support for the highlighted key vocabulary. Study the map with students to show them where the story takes place. Then model fluency by reading aloud pages 15–18.

September 11, 2001

by Wilborn Hampton

What situations create heroes?

In *September 11, 2001,* powerful photographs are interwoven with personal accounts of the September 11 tragedy. Together, they show the shock people felt on September 11 and the deep impact of the attacks on American society.

• • **Reading Level** Lexile® 1060L

Genre: Journalistic Nonfiction

Length: 168 pages

Awards: Best Books for Young Adults, Bulletin Blue Ribbons, Capitol Choices

Make Inferences

- What influences people's choices during a tragedy?

Make Connections

- How are the people's experiences on September 11 similar to or different from your own?

Determine Importance

- What is the main reason people united and cooperated with one another on September 11?

Discover how legends begin. People reacted to the enormous tragedy of September 11 with acts of bravery.

Consider the ways people show bravery in their community. Passengers on hijacked planes try to save other people. Firefighters and everyday citizens risk their lives to help others.

Explore how heroes change the world around them. The New York City firefighters and rescue workers saved the lives of many people in the World Trade Center.

Left Behind

by Velma Wallis

How do challenges bring out the best and worst in people?

Left Behind is based on a Native American legend about two old women whose tribe leaves them to die in the Alaskan wilderness. Sa' and Ch'idzigyaak face starvation, loneliness, and the pain of abandonment, yet the old women gain wisdom and strength from their ordeal. They learn about the meaning of survival and the power and endurance of hope.

• • • **Reading Level** Lexile® 1030L

Genre: Legend

Length: 112 pages

Awards: Western States Book Award, Pacific Northwest Booksellers Association Book Award

Make Inferences

- Why do the women forgive their tribe after being abandoned?

Plan and Monitor

- How will the two old women survive without their tribe?

Visualize

- How would the women's experience have been different if the climate was warm, instead of cold?

Discover how legends begin. The tribe abandons the two old women. They decide to either survive on their own or to die trying.

Consider the ways people show bravery in their community. Sa' and Ch'idzigyaak support one another and survive the brutal wilderness when no one thought they would be able to.

Explore how heroes change the world around them. The two old women share food and knowledge with their tribe and inspire them to maintain hope.

CCSS Literacy.RI.9-10.10 By the end of grade 9, read and comprehend literary nonfiction in the grades 9-10 text complexity band proficiently, with scaffolding as needed at the high end of the range. By the end of grade 10, read and comprehend literary nonfiction at the high end of the grades 9-10 text complexity band independently and proficiently.

UNIT 3 Instructional Focus

EQ ESSENTIAL QUESTION:
What Makes a Hero?

	UNIT LAUNCH Short Stories: Viewpoint How to Read	CLUSTER 1 The Sword in the Stone Was There a Real King Arthur?
Reading		
Analyze Text Genre Focus **Short Stories: Viewpoint**	T **Viewpoint, Cultural Perspective** RL.9-10.6	T **Analyze Cultural Perspective** RL.9-10.6 T **Analyze Text Structures** RI.9-10.5 T **Use Text Evidence** RL.9-10.1; RI.9-10.1 T **Compare Character's Motives and Traits** RL.9-10.3
Build Vocabulary	T **Academic Vocabulary** L.9-10.6 • narrator • inference • reliable • third-person • omniscient • perception • perspective	T **Key Vocabulary** L.9-10.6 conscientiously endure • evidence genuine historian • investigation just skeptic T **Vocabulary Strategy** L.9-10.4.b; L.9-10.4.c; L.9-10.4.d • Word Families T **Reading Fluency** RL.9-10.10 Comprehension Coach
Writing		
Respond to Literature		T **Writing on Demand** W.9-10.1 • Write a Test Essay
Writing Project		T **Writing Project** W.9-10.2.a-f; W.9-10.4-6; W.9-10.9-10 • Writing Trait: Voice and Style
Language		
ELL **Develop Language**		T **Ask for an Give Information** SL.9-10.1.a
Use Grammar Grammar Focus **Verb Tenses; Subject and Object Pronouns**		T **Present and Past Tense** L.9-10.1.a T **Regular Past Tense Verbs** L.9-10.1; L.9-10.2.c T **Past Tense of *Be: Was Were*** L.9-10.1 T **Past Tense of *Have: Had*** L.9-10.1 T **Use Verb Tenses** L.9-10.1.a
Build Listening and Speaking Skills	**Unit Project** T **Discuss the EQ** SL.9-10.4; SL.9-10.5 • Plan Your Project: Documentary	

• **Academic Vocabulary** T = Tested on Cluster and/or Unit Reading and Literary Analysis Test T = Tested on Unit Writing Test

UNIT SUMMARY

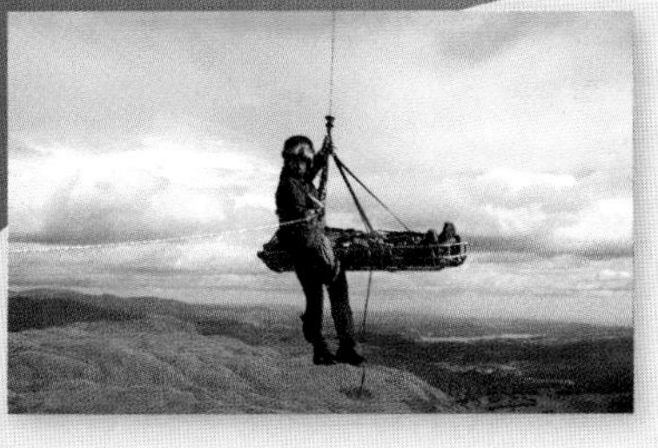

Students explore the Essential Question “What Makes a Hero?” through reading, writing, and discussion. Each cluster focuses on a specific aspect of the larger question:
Cluster 1: Discover how legends begin.
Cluster 2: Consider the everyday heroes in your community.
Cluster 3: Explain how heroes change the world around them.
Close Reading: Consider the relationship between heroism and justice.

CLUSTER 2

A Job for Valentín
In the Heart of a Hero

- **Analyze Viewpoint** RL.9-10.6
- **Analyze Structure: Feature Article** RI.9-10.5
- **Use Text Evidence** RL.9-10.1; RI.9-10.1

- **Key Vocabulary** L.9-10.6
  - anxiety
  - distracted
  - • inherent
  - • inhibit
  - prejudiced
  - protest
  - • survivor
  - tragedy
- **Vocabulary Strategy** L.9-10.4.c
  - Borrowed Words
- **Reading Fluency** RL.9-10.10
  - Comprehension Coach

- **Writing Trait** W.9-10.5
  - Voice and Style

- **Writing Project** W.9-10.2.a-f; W.9-10.4-6; W.9-10.9-10
  - Writing Trait: Voice and Style

- **Engage in Discussion** SL.9-10.1.b

- **Irregular Past Tense Verbs** L.9-10.1; L.9-10.2.c
- **Past Progressive Verb Forms** L.9-10.1.b
- **Future Tense Verbs** L.9-10.1.a; L.9-10.1.b
- **Use Verb Tenses** L.9-10.1.a; L.9-10.1.b

- **Panel Discussion** SL.9-10.1.b; SL.9-10.1.c; SL.9-10.1.d; SL.9-10.3; L.9-10.3

CLUSTER 3

The Woman in the Snow
Rosa Parks

- **Analyze Viewpoint** RL.9-10.6
- **Analyze Development of Ideas** RI.9-10.3
- **Use Text Evidence** RL.9-10.1; RI.9-10.1

- **Key Vocabulary** L.9-10.6
  - • authority
  - boycott
  - compassion
  - desperately
  - • discrimination
  - • persistent
  - provoke
  - segregation
- **Vocabulary Strategy** L.9-10.4.b; L.9-10.4.d
  - Word Families
- **Reading Fluency** RL.9-10.10
  - Comprehension Coach

- **Written Composition** W.9-10.1; W.9-10.5
  - Write an Opinion Paragraph

- **Writing Project** W.9-10.2.a-f; W.9-10.4-6; W.9-10.9-10
  - Writing Trait: Voice and Style

- **Elaborate During a Discussion** SL.9-10.1.a

- **Subject and Object Pronouns** L.9-10.1
- ***I* vs. *Me*** L.9-10.1
- **Subject and Object Pronouns** L.9-10.1
- **Use Subject and Object Pronouns** L.9-10.1

CLOSE READING

The American Promise

- **Analyze Viewpoint** RL.9-10.6

- **Academic Vocabulary** L.9-10.6
  - • perspective

UNIT WRAP-UP

Unit Project
- **Respond to the EQ** SL.9-10.5
  - Present Your Project: Documentary

(T) = Tested on Language Acquisition Assessment (T) = Assessed with a Rubric

UNIT 3 Resource Manager

Edge resources include practical, easy-to-use teaching tools for comprehensive instruction, practice, assessment, and reteaching.

Reading & Writing

Reading Resources

UNIT LAUNCH

Edge Library

Hercules

September 11, 2001

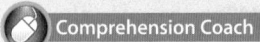

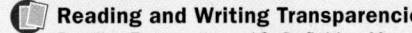

Left Behind

Edge Library Resources
- Student Journals
- Teacher's Guides

CLUSTER 1
The Sword in the Stone
Was There a Real King Arthur?

Cluster 1 Resources
- Learn more about the legend of King Arthur
- Selection summaries in eight languages
- Workplace Workshop resources

Comprehension Coach
- The Sword in the Stone
- Was There a Real King Arthur?

Reading and Writing Transparencies
- Reading Transparency 10: Definition Map
- Reading Transparency 11: Analyze Cultural Perspective

Selection CD and MP3s
- The Sword in the Stone, CD 4 Tracks 1–3
- The Sword in the Stone: Fluency Passage, CD 11 Track 7
- Was There a Real King Arthur?, CD 4 Track 4

Edge Interactive Practice Book
- The Sword in the Stone, pp. 98–102
- Was There a Real King Arthur?, pp.103–110
- Further Practice, pp. 111–113

Assessments Handbook
- Reader Reflection, p. 29b
- Cluster 1 Test, pp. 29c–29e

Reteaching Activities

Writing Project

CLUSTER 1

Writing Project Tools
- Student Samples
- Scheduler
- Rubric

Reading and Writing Transparencies
- Writing Transparencies 9–12: Response to Literature

Language & Grammar

UNIT LAUNCH

Unit Project Tools
- Planning Forms
- Scheduler
- Sequence-of-Events Chart
- Image Chart
- Rubric

CLUSTER 1

Language & Grammar Lab Teacher's Edition, pp. 38–43

Language & Grammar Lab Transparencies
- Language Function G: Ask for and Give Information
- Grammar Transparencies 31–35: Present and Past Tense Verbs

Grammar & Writing Practice Book, pp. 69–78

Language CD and MP3
- Ask for and Give Information, Track 7

Assessments Handbook
- Language Acquisition Rubric p. 29o

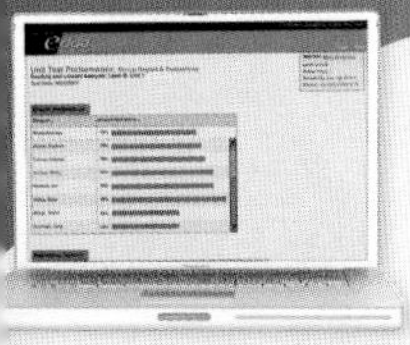

All Edge resources can be found online. Use the Online Lesson Tool, and all the relevant resources will automatically load into My Presentation Tool on myNGconnect.com.

CLUSTER 2

A Job for Valentín
In the Heart of a Hero

Cluster 2 Resources
- Learn more about Judith Ortiz Cofer
- Selection summaries in eight languages

Comprehension Coach
- A Job for Valentín
- In the Heart of a Hero

Reading and Writing Transparencies
- Reading Transparency 12: Analyze Viewpoint

Selection CD and MP3s
- A Job for Valentín, CD 4 Tracks 5-8
- A Job for Valentín: Fluency Passage, CD 11 Track 8
- In the Heart of a Hero, CD 4 Track 9

Edge Interactive Practice Book
- A Job for Valentín, pp. 114–118
- In the Heart of a Hero, pp. 119–122
- Further Practice, pp. 123–125

Assessments Handbook
- Reader Reflection, p. 29f
- Cluster 2 Test, pp. 29g-29i

Reteaching Activities

Writing Project Tools
- Student Samples
- Scheduler
- Rubric

Reading and Writing Transparencies
- Writing Transparencies 9–12: Response to Literature

Language & Grammar Lab Teacher's Edition, pp. 44–49

Language & Grammar Lab Transparencies
- Language Function H: Engage in Discussion
- Grammar Transparencies 36–40: Present, Past, and Future Tense Verbs

Grammar & Writing Practice Book, pp. 79–88

Language CD and MP3
- Engage in Discussion, Track 8

Assessments Handbook
- Language Acquisition Rubric p. 29o

Panel Discussion Rubric

CLUSTER 3

The Woman in the Snow
Rosa Parks

Cluster 3 Resources
- Learn more about African American oral tradition
- Selection summaries in eight languages

Comprehension Coach
- The Woman in the Snow
- Rosa Parks

Reading and Writing Transparencies
- Reading Transparency 13: Analyze Viewpoint

Selection CD and MP3s
- The Woman in the Snow, CD 5 Tracks 1–3
- The Woman in the Snow: Fluency Passage, CD 11 Track 9
- Rosa Parks, CD 5 Track 4

Edge Interactive Practice Book
- The Woman in the Snow, pp. 126–130
- Rosa Parks, pp. 131–136
- Further Practice, pp. 137–139

Assessments Handbook
- Reader Reflection, p. 29j
- Cluster 3 Test, pp. 29k-29m

Reteaching Activities

Writing Project Tools
- Student Samples
- Scheduler
- Rubric

Reading and Writing Transparencies
- Writing Transparencies 9–12: Response to Literature

Language & Grammar Lab Teacher's Edition, pp. 50–55

Language & Grammar Lab Transparencies
- Language Function I: Elaborate During a Discussion
- Grammar Transparencies 41–45: Subject and Object Pronouns

Grammar & Writing Practice Book, pp. 89–98

Language CD and MP3
- Elaborate During a Discussion, Track 9

Assessments Handbook
- Language Acquisition Rubric p. 29o

CLOSE READING

The American Promise

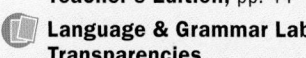

Selection CD and MP3s
- The American Promise: CD 12 Track 3

Edge Interactive Practice Book
- The American Promise, pp. 140–143

UNIT WRAP-UP

Unit Project
- Rubric

Assessments Handbook
- Reading and Literary Analysis, pp. 30–37
- Grammar and Writing, pp. 38–42
- Affective and Metacognitive Measures, pp. 105–119
- Self-Assessment: Written Composition, p. 133
- Peer Assessment: Written Composition, p. 134

Reteaching Activities

Lesson 1

UNIT LAUNCH

OBJECTIVES

Listening and Speaking
- Classroom Discussion
- Evaluate a Speaker's Message

Viewing
- Respond to and Interpret Visuals

Cultural Perspectives
- Compare Cultures: Points of View

ENGAGE & DISCUSS

A EQ Essential Question

Brainstorm and Map Ask students to think about one person they consider to be a hero and chart that person's traits.
SL.9-10.1

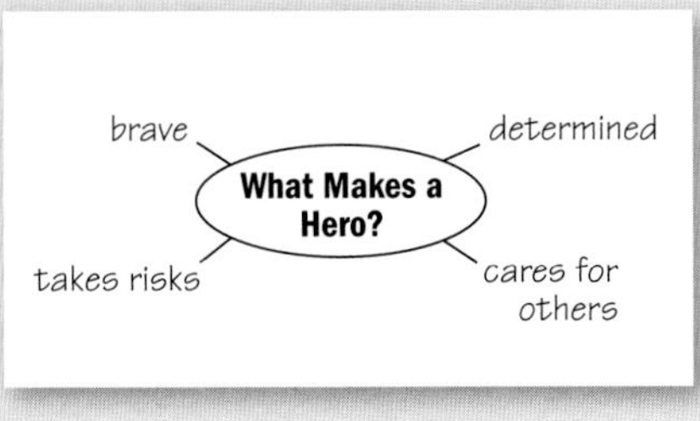

B Discuss the Quotations

Access Meaning Discuss and define unfamiliar words in the quotations.

ELL Rephrase Language Paraphrase each quotation as follows: Ashe: Real heroes are ordinary. They don't want to be better than others. They just want to help people. Fitzgerald: The story of a hero includes excitement and even sadness.

Evaluate a Speaker's Message
Ask: What is the difference between the two quotations?

Possible response:
- *Ashe says a hero is ordinary, not dramatic. Fitzgerald says a hero's story is full of drama.*

Use the cooperative learning activity to explore different perspectives.
SL.9-10.1.b; SL.9-10.3

COOPERATIVE LEARNING

Think Pair Share

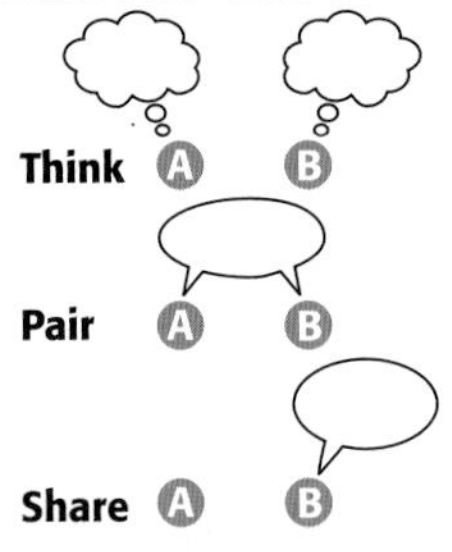

UNIT 3 SHORT STORIES

A

EQ ESSENTIAL QUESTION:

What Makes a Hero?

B

True heroism is remarkably sober, very undramatic. It is not the urge to surpass all others at whatever cost, but the urge to serve others at whatever cost.

—ARTHUR ASHE

Show me a hero and I will write you a tragedy.

—F. SCOTT FITZGERALD

Critical Viewing
Suspended in mid-air, a rescuer in Cumbria, England, guides an injured hiker to the safety of a helicopter overhead. What makes this airman a hero?

200

LISTENING AND SPEAKING

Evaluate a Speaker's Message

Use the Think Pair Share cooperative learning technique (*see the Best Practices tab*) to explore the quotations.

Think Provide time for students to think about how the qualities of an "ordinary" hero and a "dramatic" hero might differ.

Pair Have students discuss their ideas with a partner and work together to list at least two qualities for each type of hero.

Share Have students share their qualities with the class. List ideas in a T Chart.

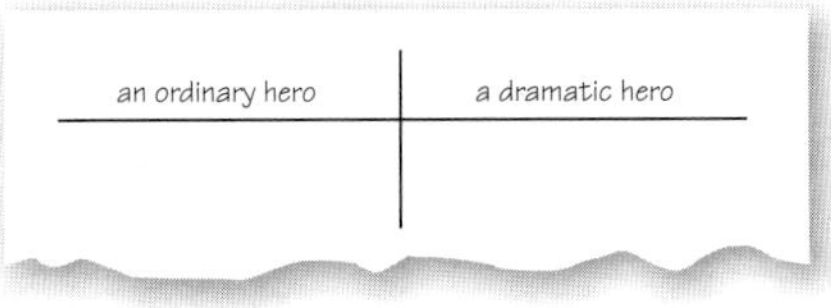

Debrief Discuss as a class:
- Are there any qualities that both kinds of heroes have?
- Which description of heroism do you believe is more accurate? Explain.
- Did the discussion change your ideas about heroes?

Remind students to keep thinking about what makes a hero as they read the selections in this unit.

CCSS **Literacy.SL.9-10.1** Initiate and participate effectively in a range of collaborative discussions (one-on-one, in groups, and teacher-led) with diverse partners on grades 9-10 topics, texts, and issues, building on others' ideas and expressing their own clearly and persuasively. **Literacy.SL.9-10.1.b** Work with peers to set rules for collegial discussions and decision-making (e.g., informal consensus, taking votes on key issues, presentation of alternate views), clear goals and deadlines, and individual roles as needed. **Literacy.SL.9-10.3** Evaluate a speaker's point of view, reasoning, and use of evidence and rhetoric, identifying any fallacious reasoning or exaggerated or distorted evidence.

ENGAGE & INTERPRET

C Critical Viewing

Observe Details Have students study the photograph. Draw their attention to details.

- What details do you notice about the setting? What did the photographer choose to include in the photo? Why?
- What does the man appear to be doing with the white rope? What might it be attached to?
- What is the man's expression? What does it show about him?

Interpret and Respond Explain that the white rope in the photo is attached to the side of a mountain. The rescuer is using it to stabilize himself as he and the person he is rescuing are drawn up into the helicopter. Ask: Do you think this man is heroic? Why or why not?

Possible responses:
- *He is not heroic because he appears to be a professional rescuer. He is just doing his job.*
- *He is heroic because he's risking his life to help others.*

D About the Photograph

The man in the yellow helmet is a member of the Royal Air Force (RAF) Mountain Rescue Service (MRS), a part of the British military. Unlike other military positions, these positions are voluntary; the rescuers choose to help save lives, often in addition to their other military duties. The job takes a year of intense training before volunteers are ready to become part of a rescue team. Still, MRS volunteers are sometimes killed during rescues. Despite the risks, the men and women of the MRS consider their job a privilege.

Interpret and Respond Have students think about how additional information may have changed their answer to the Critical Viewing question.

Ask: Now that you know more about the RAF Mountain Rescue Service, what makes the man in the photo a hero?

Possible response:
- *He is knowingly risking his life to save a stranger.*

CULTURAL PERSPECTIVES

Beliefs About Heroes

Explore how different cultures view what makes someone a hero.

Collect Ideas Have students complete the following sentence frames:

In [name a culture to explore] …

- people who work as _______ are often considered to be heroes.
- the important qualities of a hero are _______.
- a famous hero in literature or legend is _______.
- that character is considered to be a hero because he/she _______.
- young people admire _______ and treat them like heroes.

Compare Perspectives As a class, discuss the similarities and differences among the cultural perspectives. Be sure to discuss any qualities of heroes that are unique to each culture.

OBJECTIVES
Comprehension & Critical Thinking
- Read and Interpret a Bar Graph

Listening and Speaking
- Debate

ENGAGE & DEBATE

EQ Essential Question

Students analyze heroes and debate what makes someone a hero.

A Study the Facts

If students need help interpreting bar graphs, preteach the Research Skills activity below. Examine the top bar of the graph with students. Define public figures as people who are well known; for example: athletes, actors, or politicians. Ask:

- What percentage of people identified public figures as their heroes?
- Does this percentage surprise you, or is this what you would have guessed? Explain.

Have students review the rest of the bars in the graph. Ask:

- Did the information about family members surprise you? Why or why not?

B Debate and Vote

Have students respond in writing to the two questions.

ELL Sentence Frames Provide frames to help ELLs respond:

1. I think ______ and ______ are heroes because ______.
2. I think a hero must be ______ and ______.

Have small groups use the information to make and analyze a bar graph and to vote on a hero's most important quality.
SL.9-10.4

ONGOING ASSESSMENT
Have students draw a person whom they consider to be a hero and write three qualities that describe him or her.

UNIT 3

EQ ESSENTIAL QUESTION: What Makes a Hero?

Study the Facts

Most people have heroes, people whom they admire and respect. They may be world leaders, explorers, adventurers, sports stars, family members, or friends. When asked in a poll who their heroes were, people gave these responses:

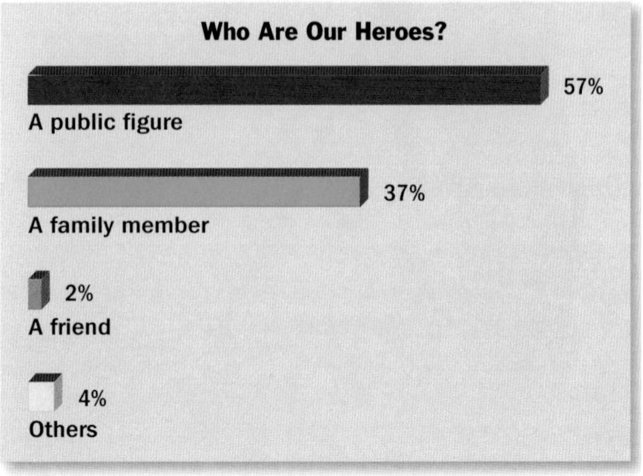

Source: Harris Interactive Inc. ©2001

Debate and Vote

1. Make a list of heroes that *you* admire. How does your list compare with the data in the bar graph above?
2. What are the most important qualities of a hero?

Share your list with a small group and use the information to make a bar graph that reflects the heroes you all admire. Analyze the results and discuss the qualities that make a hero. Then vote for the most important quality a hero must have. Defend your ideas with reasons and examples from your own knowledge, experience, and observations.

EQ ESSENTIAL QUESTION
In this unit, you will explore the **Essential Question** in class through reading, discussion, research, and writing. Keep thinking about the question outside of school, too.

RESEARCH SKILLS

Interpreting Bar Graphs

Teach/Model Explain that a bar graph is a useful tool to show data for comparing and contrasting. Point to each feature of the graph: the title, the labels, the bars, and the percentages as you explain it.

- The title tells what the graph is about. This graph will give information about who our heroes are.
- The labels underneath the bars name the categories, or types, of heroes. The first bar gives information about heroes who are public figures.
- The top bar is longer than the others. This shows that most people said their heroes were public figures.
- The number next to the bar shows that 57%, or 57 out of 100 people, said their heroes were public figures.

Practice Read through the rest of the choices in the bar graph. For each one, ask:

- What percentage of people said their hero was [a family member/a friend/someone else]?

Apply Ask these questions about the graph:

1. What percentage of the people asked said a family member was their hero? *(37%)*
2. Which category did the fewest number of people name as heroes? How do you know? *(friends; the bar is shorter than all the others; 2% is the smallest percentage)*

CCSS Literacy.SL.9-10.4 Present information, findings, and supporting evidence clearly, concisely, and logically such that listeners can follow the line of reasoning and the organization, development, substance, and style are appropriate to purpose, audience, and task.

1 Plan a Project

Documentary

In this unit, you will be creating a documentary about the Essential Question. Choose a hero of yours and create a documentary that presents a glimpse of the person's life and what makes the person a hero. To get started, watch a few documentaries on TV. Look for

- the types of information presented, such as interviews, photographs, and time lines
- the order in which information is given
- the narrator's role in the documentary.

Study Skills Start planning your documentary. Use the forms on myNGconnect.com to plan your time and to prepare the content.

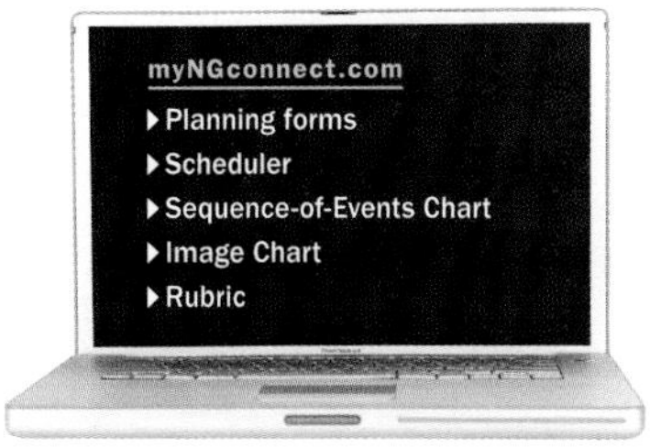

2 Choose More to Read

These readings provide different answers to the Essential Question. Choose a book and online selections to read during the unit.

September 11, 2001: Attack on New York City
by Wilborn Hampton

Wilborn Hampton describes the events of September 11, 2001, through the stories of those who lived through the attack on the World Trade Center. Their stories show that everyday people can turn into heroes and even the saddest stories can be full of hope.

▸ NONFICTION

Hercules
by Paul Storrie

Hercules is a hero of ancient Greece. His strength is legendary. But Hercules has a powerful enemy—the goddess Hera. She will do anything to defeat him. Hercules may be the strongest human alive, but is he stronger and more clever than an angry goddess?

▸ GRAPHIC CLASSIC

Left Behind
by Velma Wallis

Fighting to survive the harsh Alaskan winter, a Native American chief has to decide: Should he leave two old women behind or risk the lives of the entire group? The choice is a cruel one, but the decision is clear. Can the women survive alone?

▸ LEGEND

myNGconnect.com

- **Read about everyday heroes in your community and nominate some of your own.**
- **Take a personality quiz to find out how you match up to heroes of the past.**
- **Play an online game that takes you on a heroic adventure.**

UNIT PROJECT & MORE TO READ

OBJECTIVES

Reading Behaviors
- Read Independently

Study Skill
- Keep a Learning Log

Media
- Create and Deliver a Media Presentation (documentary)

1 Plan a Project

Documentary Ask students about documentaries they've seen:

- What is the purpose of a documentary?
- What is the usual tone, or mood, of a documentary?

Assign project groups and review the Unit Project Evaluation Rubric and other Project Tools (*available online*). Have groups follow these steps:

1. Decide on a subject and format.
2. Choose the kinds of information you would like to present.
3. Plan the order in which you want to present the information.

Project Support Teach the Study Skills lesson below.
SL.9-10.1.b

2 Choose More to Read

Guide students toward an independent reading choice from the **Edge Library**.

- ***Hercules*** Lexile® 540L
- ***September 11, 2001: Attack on New York City*** Lexile® 1030L
- ***Left Behind*** Lexile® 1060L

RL.9-10.10; RI.9-10.10

(Some titles may contain mature themes. Be sure to preview the books before assigning them to students.)

Distribute **Student Journals** and have students complete the time-management planning form on p. 1.

myNGconnect.com

- **Unit Project Planning Tools**
- **Unit Project Evaluation Rubric**
- **Edge Library Student Journals and Teacher's Guides**

STUDY SKILLS

Keep a Learning Log

Help students reflect on their learning during the project by using a learning log. Provide these guidelines:

1. Write regularly, at least each time you work on the project.
2. Date each entry.
3. Use a prompt to organize and focus your thinking:

   Topic/Content:
   - It is important or interesting for people to learn about …
   - New concepts and words I learned about are …

   Research:
   - I found the most useful information when I …
   - One idea we should find out more about is …

   Individual and Group Activity:
   - During this project, I hope to achieve …
   - Our group was most productive when we …

CCSS **Literacy.RL.9-10.10** By the end of grade 9, read and comprehend literature, including stories, dramas, and poems, in the grades 9-10 text complexity band proficiently, with scaffolding as needed at the high end of the range. By the end of grade 10, read and comprehend literature, including stories, dramas, and poems, at the high end of the grades 9-10 text complexity band independently and proficiently. **Literacy.RI.9-10.10** By the end of grade 9, read and comprehend literary nonfiction in the grades 9-10 text complexity band proficiently, with scaffolding as needed at the high end of the range. By the end of grade 10, read and comprehend literary nonfiction at the high end of the grades 9-10 text complexity band independently and proficiently. **Literacy.SL.9-10.1.b** Work with peers to set rules for collegial discussions and decision-making (e.g., informal consensus, taking votes on key issues, presentation of alternate views), clear goals and deadlines, and individual roles as needed.

Lesson 2

HOW TO READ

OBJECTIVES

Vocabulary
- Academic Vocabulary

Reading Strategy
- Make Inferences; Review Strategies

Literary Analysis
- Analyze Cultural Perspective (T)
- Analyze Viewpoint (T)

Listening and Speaking
- Retell a Story

Media
- Evaluate Various Media

ENGAGE & CONNECT

Short Stories

In this lesson, students explore how the viewpoints of narrators, characters, and authors influence stories. After reading a story told from three different points of view, students make inferences and evaluate the effects of the different viewpoints.

Introduce Genre

Engage students in talking about stories they like. Ask:

- Do you like to read stories that show the inner thoughts of characters? Why?
- Is it more interesting to read events told by a character in the story or by a narrator who watches the events? Why?

Encourage students to share examples of narrators from stories they have read.

(A) Focus on Demo Text

Read Students read Demo Texts 1, 2, and 3.

ELL Access Text Read the Demo Texts aloud, rephrasing difficult words and demonstrating actions.

- Rephrase: *raced* (moved quickly), *fragile* (easy to break), *defeated* (without success)
- Demonstrate: *put together, tipping, rushed out*

HOW TO READ SHORT STORIES

Genre Focus
Short Stories: Points of View

Authors can tell stories in many ways. One way to think about the way a story is told is to look at different versions of a familiar story.

DEMO TEXT #1

Humpty Dumpty sat on a wall.
Humpty Dumpty had a great fall.
All the King's horses
And all the King's men
Couldn't put Humpty together again.

DEMO TEXT #2

Humpty Dumpty sat on a wall. Thoughts raced through his mind: "You old fool. What is an egg like you doing on a wall? You always have to be the one to take risks. You always have to be the one who thinks that being fragile is no big deal."

Humpty looked out and saw the King's men sitting on their horses, waiting. Waiting for what? "For you to take a risk that will get you scrambled, that's what," Humpty thought. He sighed. He asked himself whether the view from the wall was worth it. Looking at the fields below him, he thought it was. Then the wind started to blow. He wondered what the King's men would think if he just climbed down. "I'll never give them the satisfaction."

Soon, Humpty felt himself tipping, then falling. As he fell, he thought that it hadn't been a bad life at all. At least not for an egg.

(A)

DEMO TEXT #3

Humpty Dumpty sat on a wall. Thoughts raced through his mind: "You old fool. What is an egg like you doing on a wall? You always have to be the one to take risks."

Humpty wasn't the only one whose mind was racing. For many of the King's men, the Humpty Dumpty job was no big deal. They had seen splattered eggs before. They made jokes about cracked eggs. For Joshua Jones, though, this was his first time. He was nervous. And queasy. He thought about all of the training he had received in fixing cracked eggs.

Joshua looked up. He saw Humpty teeter and then fall. His heart went out to the great egg. "He must be so frightened! He must be so disappointed to have it end this way," Joshua thought.

The crash echoed through the kingdom. People were concerned and rushed out of their houses. Joshua and the other King's men raced to fix Humpty. As he raced to the egg, he was certain he could help.

He rushed to the front to try some of the techniques he had learned. But nothing worked. The King's horses and King's men stood defeated. They couldn't put Humpty back together.

OUT-OF-SCHOOL LITERACY

Viewpoints in Media

Have students consider the different viewpoints offered by different media. Brainstorm the information and entertainment media students encounter regularly; for example: magazines and books, network news, Web sites, blogs, movies, sitcoms.

For each medium on the list, have students consider the following questions:

- Who is the audience? (for example: teens, adults, males, females)
- Where does the information come from, or who is telling the story? (for example: professional journalists, creative writers, an ordinary individual with a Web site)
- Is the information likely to be factual, or is it based on one person's opinion or point of view?

As a class, discuss the role of viewpoint in media by considering the following questions: Will a news show always be factual and accurate? Should you trust everything you read on a blog? Can you trust everything you read on a Web site?

Remind students to consider viewpoint when they use different media to obtain information.
SL.9-10.1.a

CCSS **Literacy.SL.9-10.1.a** Come to discussions prepared, having read and researched material under study; explicitly draw on that preparation by referring to evidence from texts and other research on the topic or issue to stimulate a thoughtful, well-reasoned exchange of ideas. **Literacy.RL.9-10.6** Analyze a particular point of view or cultural experience reflected in a work of literature from outside the United States, drawing on a wide reading of world literature.

Connect Reading to Your Life

Look at all three Demo Texts. Then rank the following statements. One (1) means you are *most sure* it is true. Five (5) means that you are *least sure* it is true.

Rank

- ____ Humpty Dumpty sat on a wall.
- ____ The view was worth the risks.
- ____ The King's men were very careful as they tried to put Humpty back together.
- ____ Humpty was frightened as he sat on the wall.
- ____ Joshua had learned many techniques for putting eggs back together.

Reading Strategies

- Plan and Monitor
- Determine Importance
- ▶ **Make Inferences**
- Ask Questions
- Make Connections
- Synthesize
- Visualize

Focus Strategy ▶ Make Inferences

To do that ranking, you had to make **inferences**. All the stories were told by a **narrator**. Some of the information came from the viewpoint of the characters. Some seemed to come from the author. Experienced readers make inferences about which information is **reliable**, or able to be trusted.

Think about two little kids playing with action figures. One kid says, "He's the greatest" and marches the action figure around. The other says, "He's the strongest" and marches the second action figure into battle with the first. After they fight for a while, one kid says, "There was an earthquake and the people were scared."

Like authors do, the little kids sometimes tell the story from the point of view of a character, even though they say *he* instead of *I*. They also make decisions about the plot—like the earthquake—that are beyond the scope of the characters to make.

Your Job as a Reader

One of your most important jobs as a reader is to figure out where you get your information from and which information to believe. You'll need to make a lot of inferences to do that.

Elements of Literature

narrator *n.*, the person who tells a story

Academic Vocabulary

- **inference** *n.*, good guess based on evidence and knowledge; **infer** *v.*, to make a good guess based on evidence and knowledge
- **reliable** *adj.*, trustworthy or believable; **rely** *v.*, to put trust in someone or something, to depend

ENGAGE & CONNECT

B Connect Reading to Your Life

Help students connect to the texts and strategy by comparing their perspective to that of the narrators. Ask: Which information sounds factual? Which sounds like a personal feeling or judgment?

Have students work in pairs to discuss each statement and then record their rankings individually. Encourage them to use information from the story and their own reasoning as they rank statements. RL.9-10.6

Focus Strategy: Make Inferences Read this section with students. Use the activity below to teach the Academic Vocabulary in this unit. Ask:

- If a child says that an action figure is strong, what might you infer about the way that action figure looks?
- Which Demo Text requires making the fewest inferences to understand? Which involves making the most? RL.9-10.1

Review Strategies Remind students that they use a variety of strategies as they read. Have students share a strategy they used when they read the Demo Texts.

Possible response:

- *While I read Demo Text 3, I tried to predict whether Joshua would use his training to help Humpty Dumpty. I read on and discovered that he tried the techniques he had learned, but he was not able to save Humpty Dumpty.* RL.9-10.10

TEACH STRATEGIES

C Your Job as a Reader

Explain that good readers make inferences, or guesses, based on details in the text. They also decide how different viewpoints affect how information is presented. Good readers know that characters can misunderstand, just as people do in real life. Tell students they will continue to make inferences about the text they read in this unit.

ACADEMIC VOCABULARY

Make Word Maps Present the Academic Vocabulary words. Have students make a Word Map for each.

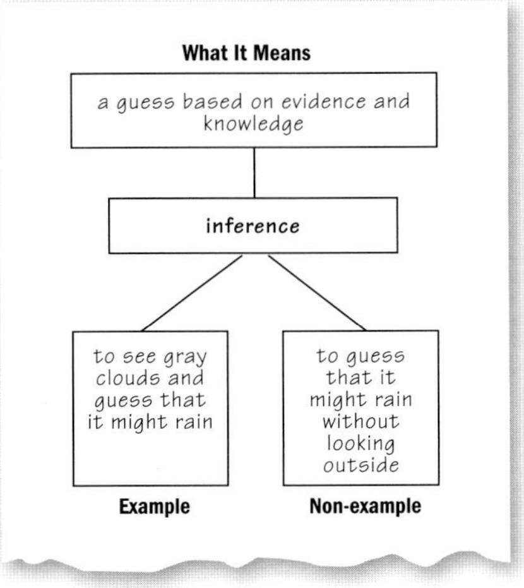

1. Write the word in the center. Write what it means in the top box. Give an example and a non-example in the boxes below.
2. Use a dictionary to check the information in your map.
3. Keep your Word Maps in a vocabulary notebook. L.9-10.6

CCSS **Literacy.RL.9-10.1** Cite strong and thorough textual evidence to support analysis of what the text says explicitly as well as inferences drawn from the text. **Literacy.RL.9-10.10** By the end of grade 9, read and comprehend literature, including stories, dramas, and poems, in the grades 9-10 text complexity band proficiently, with scaffolding as needed at the high end of the range. By the end of grade 10, read and comprehend literature, including stories, dramas, and poems, at the high end of the grades 9-10 text complexity band independently and proficiently. **Literacy.L.9-10.6** Acquire and use accurately general academic and domain-specific words and phrases, sufficient for reading, writing, speaking, and listening at the college and career readiness level; demonstrate independence in gathering vocabulary knowledge when considering a word or phrase important to comprehension or expression.

TEACH STRATEGIES

A Unpack the Thinking Process

Remind students of ways different narrators influence the versions of the story in the Demo Texts on p. 204. Then, explain and discuss these points of view:

Third-Person Limited Ask: Which Demo Texts are written in third-person limited point of view? How do you know?

Third-Person Omniscient Ask: Which Demo Text is written from the third-person omniscient point of view? What information does this version reveal that the others do not?

Making Inferences: Readers look for details in the text to help them determine how different viewpoints affect the information presented.

Interpret Viewpoint: The author chooses point of view carefully and uses it to inform readers about characters and events. Readers need to be aware that the way information is presented can be affected by an author's beliefs, experiences, or cultural background.

■ Unpack the Thinking Process

Viewpoint

Some stories are told by a narrator but focus on the **perceptions** of one character. These stories are told from the **third-person limited** point of view. When you read one of these stories, you have to make inferences about how that character's viewpoint affects the information, just as you have to do when one of the characters is telling the story (first-person point of view). A character's experiences and attitudes play a role in shaping his or her viewpoint. This is also true of an author's viewpoint. For example, authors from different cultures may have different ways of looking at the world, which can affect the way a story is told.

Stories told by narrators who can see into the minds of all of the characters are told from the **third-person omniscient** point of view. Even in these stories, the viewpoints of characters or the author may affect the information we learn and the way it is presented. So no matter what the point of view, you also have to figure out what you're *not* being told. It is your job as a reader to make inferences to fill in those blanks.

In the nursery rhyme version (Demo Text #1), the narrator only tells the facts. You trust that those facts are true, but there is a lot of information missing. If the nursery rhyme continued, experienced readers would look for details that would help them make inferences to fill in information such as:

- how Humpty got up on that wall in the first place
- why the King was so concerned about Humpty's safety.

You learn a lot more in Demo Text #2. The narrator chooses to let the reader in on Humpty's thoughts, so you know what Humpty thinks about himself. As a reader making inferences, you need to consider how Humpty's viewpoint affects the information. For example, Humpty considers it worth risking his life to see the view from the wall. You may wonder if the view is really so magnificent or if he is simply being stubborn because of his attitude toward the King's men.

Elements of Literature

third-person *adj.*, referring to a narrator who describes the action from outside the story

omniscient *adj.*, all-knowing

Academic Vocabulary

• **perception** *n.*, knowledge that comes from understanding or being aware; **perceive** *v.*, to be aware of, to observe, to notice

You get to see even more in Demo Text #3. You get to see *into* the thoughts of another character. Sometimes the narrator tells us the thoughts directly: Joshua was nervous.

But when things are told from Joshua's **perspective**, be careful. He thinks that he'll be able to put Humpty back together. That turns out not to be true.

Sometimes an omniscient narrator tells us things about the plot or setting that are beyond the knowledge of an individual character. When you read that the people in the kingdom rushed out in concern, you are learning information that neither Humpty Dumpty nor Joshua know.

B

Try an Experiment

Imagine that the story continues. Read on.

DEMO TEXT #3 *(continued)*

Someone would have to tell the Dumpty family about Humpty's accident. None of the King's men wanted that terrible job. Everyone knew that the Dumpty family was the most famous and well-loved family in the entire kingdom. The task fell to Joshua, since he was the newest of the King's men. Joshua was not happy, but he would do his duty.

Joshua rode swiftly to the family's house. As he neared their home, he slowed down so that he didn't scare the family. He took a deep breath and walked up to the enormous door. He knocked softly. Mrs. Dumpty and Humpty's young son looked at Joshua and then at each other. "They know," thought Joshua. "They already know."

Retell the Story Work with a small group to retell this new section of Demo Text #3. Use third-person *limited* point of view. Tell the story from the perspective of Joshua, Mrs. Dumpty, or the young son. Remember to use *he* or *she*, not *I*, to refer to the characters. Include illustrations to go along with your retelling.

Debrief After you retell the story, answer these questions:

1. What information did you leave out?
2. Which version requires you to make more inferences?

C

Monitor Comprehension

Viewpoint Why is knowing a narrator's viewpoint important?

Academic Vocabulary

- **perspective** *n.*, a specific angle from which something is viewed or observed

TEACH STRATEGIES

B Make Inferences

Explain Explain that good readers make inferences about details, including thoughts expressed by the narrator and characters in the story. Tell students they will learn and practice how to make inferences in this unit.

APPLY

C Try an Experiment

Have students read the continuation of the short story.

Retell the Story Have students work in small groups to retell the story from a third-person limited point of view.

Debrief Call on a volunteer from each group to share the group's story. Have the volunteer display the illustrations during the presentation.

Possible responses:

1. We told the story from the viewpoint of the young son, so we left out the detail about why Joshua was chosen to deliver the news.

2. Our version requires more inferences, since the young boy knows less background information than the adults would.

RL.9-10.6

Monitor Comprehension

Possible responses:

- *Readers need to know whether characters' thoughts are reliable.*
- *To evaluate the information in a story for believability, the reader must understand the viewpoint of the narrator.*

DIFFERENTIATED INSTRUCTION

Teach Literary Elements As you teach the selections in this unit, use these strategies to meet students' individual needs.

Struggling Readers

Reread and Question Reread and help students analyze important statements, such as (pp. 240–241): *I don't have anything against these handicapped people, but I don't want to spend my whole summer with one.* Ask:

- What is the narrator saying? (*I have no prejudice against people with handicaps.*)
- Is this statement reliable? (*no*)
- On what text is your inference based? (*She calls working with Valentín a "disaster."*)

English Language Learners ELL

Paraphrase Write important statements that narrators/characters make. Explain figurative language and offer elaboration to help interpret a character's meaning. Then, have students paraphrase each statement.

- *I don't have anything against: I don't dislike*
- *spend my whole summer: work all summer*
  I don't dislike handicapped people but I don't want to work with them all summer.

Challenge

Compare Stories Have students rewrite the first few sentences of a selection from a different viewpoint. Ask them to read a peer's writing and identify the point of view.

ONGOING ASSESSMENT

List statements a narrator could make. Have students label whether the statements are by a third-person limited or third-person omniscient narrator.

CCSS Literacy.RL.9-10.6 Analyze a particular point of view or cultural experience reflected in a work of literature from outside the United States, drawing on a wide reading of world literature.

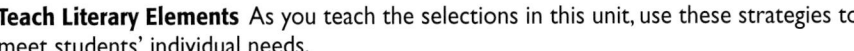

UNIT 3

Cluster 1 Planner

EQ **ESSENTIAL QUESTION:**

What Makes a Hero?

Discover how legends begin.

Online Planner

myNGconnect.com

	LESSON 3 **Prepare to Read**	LESSON 4 **The Sword in the Stone** Main Selection
Reading		
Reading Strategies Focus Strategy **Make Inferences**	**Activate Prior Knowledge** SL.9-10.1 • Make a Connection: Quickwrite *T208*	**Make Inferences** RL.9-10.1 • Make Inferences *T209, T212–T221*
Literary Analysis Genre Focus **Short Stories**		T **Analyze Cultural Perspective,** *T209, T212–T221* RL.9-10.6 **Recognize Genre: Folk Literature** • Analyze Symbols in Stories of King Arthur *T210*
Vocabulary	T **Key Vocabulary** RL.9-10.4; L.9-10.4.c; L.9-10.6 Introduce *T208* **conscientiously** **endure** • **evidence** **genuine** **historian** • **investigation** **just** **skeptic**	T **Key Vocabulary** L.9-10.6 • Daily Routines *T213* • Link to Essential Question *T215* • Selection Reading *T212–T221* **conscientiously** • **evidence** **just**
Fluency		T **Phrasing** RL.9-10.10 • Daily Routines *T213* T **Accuracy and Rate** RL.9-10.10 Comprehension Coach *T211*
Writing		
Response to Literature		**Return to the Text** W.9-10.9.a; W.9-10.10 • **Reread and Write** Is Arthur a hero? *T221*
Writing Across the Curriculum		
Language		
ELL **Language Development**	T **Ask for and Give Information** SL.9-10.1.a • Language and Grammar Lab, Transparency G *LAB TE p. 38*	T **Ask for and Give Information** SL.9-10.1.a • Daily Routines *LAB TE p. 38*
Grammar Grammar Focus **Present and Past Tense Verbs**		T **Present and Past Tense** *T214* L.9-10.1.a T **Regular Past Tense** *T218* L.9-10.1; L.9-10.2.c
Listening and Speaking	**Partner Talk** SL.9-10.1 • Opinions About Heroes *T208*	**Listen to a Selection** RL.9-10.10 Comprehension Coach *T211* *CD 4, Tracks 1–3* **Out-of-School Literacy** SL.9-10.1.a • Interpreting Movies *T220*

T = Tested on Cluster and/or Unit Reading and Literary Analysis Test
T = Tested on Language Acquisition Assessment
T = Tested on Unit Writing Test
T = Assessed with a Rubric
• **Academic Vocabulary**

The Sword in the Stone

Genre: Short Story Lexile® 960L

Only one individual can remove the sword from the stone and be crowned the King of England. Arthur shocks everyone when he pulls the sword out of the stone. He learns of his royal heritage and takes his rightful place as ruler of Camelot.

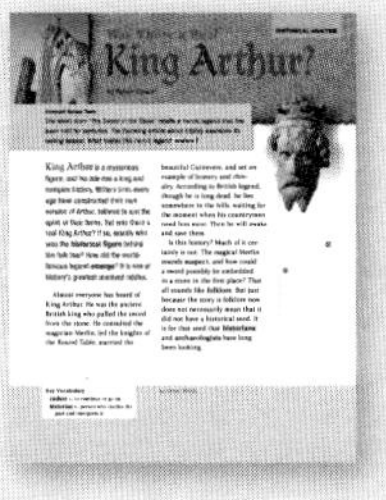

Was There a Real King Arthur?

Genre: Historical Analysis Lexile® 1040L

This article examines whether King Arthur really existed. Although stories make reference to him and researchers have discovered objects possibly linked to his existence, the truth remains a mystery. Still, people want to believe Arthur was real.

LESSON 5	LESSON 6	LESSONS 7 & 8	LESSON 9 & 10
Was There a Real King Arthur? Second Selection	**Reflect and Assess**	**Integrate the Language Arts**	**Workshops**
Make Inferences RI.9-10.1 • Make Inferences *T222, T223–T230*	**Comprehension and Critical Thinking** *T231* RL.9-10.1; RI.9-10.1 • Compare Across Texts • Analyze, Compare, Interpret, Speculate, Draw Conclusions		
Analyze Text Structures *T222, T223–T230* RI.9-10.5	**Interpret and Evaluate Literature** RL.9-10.10; RI.9-10.10 **Use Text Evidence** *T231* RL.9-10.1; RI.9-10.1	**Compare Character's Motives and Traits** *T232* RL.9-10.3	
Key Vocabulary L.9-10.6 • Selection Reading *T223–T230* endure, historian, • evidence, • investigation, genuine, skeptic	**Key Vocabulary** L.9-10.6 • Review *T231* conscientiously, historian, endure, • investigation, • evidence, just, genuine, skeptic	**Vocabulary Strategy** L.9-10.4.b; L.9-10.4.d • Word Families *T233*	**Vocabulary Workshop: Find Familiar Words** L.9-10.4.b; L.9-10.4.c; L.9-10.4.d **Vocabulary Strategy** • Relate Words: Use Word Families *T235*
Phrasing RL.9-10.10 • Daily Routines *T213* **Accuracy and Rate** RL.9-10.10 Comprehension Coach *T223*	**Phrasing** RL.9-10.10 • Peer Assessment *T231*		
Return to the Text W.9-10.9.b; W.9-10.10 • **Reread and Write** What is the most convincing evidence about a real King Arthur? *T230*	**Write About Literature** W.9-10.1 • **Interpretive Response:** What makes Arthur such an appealing hero? *T231*	**Writing on Demand for Tests** W.9-10.1 • **Test Essay** *T233*	
Research and Writing W.9-10.7 • **History Connection** *T226* • **Geography Connection** *T229*			**Workplace Workshop: Inside an Airport** W.9-10.7; W.9-10.10 **Research and Writing** • Explore the Job Market *T234* • Create a Career Chart *T234*
Ask for and Give Information SL.9-10.1.a • Daily Routines *LAB TE p. 38*		**Ask for and Give Information** SL.9-10.1.a • Pair Talk *T232*	
Past Tense: *Be* *T224* L.9-10.1 **Past Tense: *Have*** *T228* L.9-10.1		**Present and Past Tense** *T232* L.9-10.1.a	
Listen to a Selection RL.9-10.10 Comprehension Coach *T223* *CD 4, Track 4* **Out-of-School Literacy** SL.9-10.1.a • Research Online *T225*	**Participate in a Discussion** *T231* SL.9-10.1	**Art Gallery** *T233* W.9-10.7	

EDGE LIBRARY

Hercules ●
by Paul Storrie

September 11, 2001 Attack on New York City ● ●
by Wilbur Hampton

Left Behind ● ● ●
by Velma Wallis

Lesson 3
PREPARE TO READ

OBJECTIVES

Vocabulary
- Key Vocabulary T
- Strategy: Use Cognates; Use Reference Sources (dictionary)
- Word Families T

Reading Strategy
- Activate Prior Knowledge

ELL Language & Grammar Lab

Language Function Transparency G
Ask for and Give Information T

ENGAGE & CONNECT

A EQ Essential Question

Focus on Heroism Ask: Why are legends about heroes important?

Possible response:
- *They help us imagine being better than we are.*

B Make a Connection

Have students complete the Quickwrite and share answers with a partner to compare their opinions about Malamud's statement.
SL.9-10.1

TEACH VOCABULARY

C Learn Key Vocabulary

Study the Words Review the four steps of the Make Words Your Own routine (*see the Vocabulary tab*):

1. **Pronounce** Say one word and have students repeat it. Write the word in syllables and pronounce it, one syllable at a time: *his-to-ri-an*. Ask what looks familiar in the word, and point out the root word *history* and the suffix *-an*.

   ELL Use cognates to help Spanish speakers with the words (*see the Vocabulary tab*).

2. **Study Examples** Read the example in the chart. Provide more examples: The *historian* gave a talk about the history of Rome.

ONGOING ASSESSMENT
Have students complete an oral sentence for each word. For example: *Ernesto _______ checked his paper for spelling and grammar errors.*

PREPARE TO READ
- The Sword in the Stone
- Was There a Real King Arthur?

A EQ What Makes a Hero?
Discover how legends begin.

B Make a Connection

Quickwrite A writer named Bernard Malamud once said, "Without heroes, we are all plain people and don't know how far we can go." Write a response that explains what you think Malamud means and whether you agree or disagree. Then share your writing to see if others feel the same way.

C Learn Key Vocabulary

Study the Words Pronounce each word and learn its meaning. You may also want to look up the definitions in the Glossary.

• Academic Vocabulary

Key Words	Examples
conscientiously (kon-shē-**en**-shus-lē) *adverb* ▸ page 213	When you work **conscientiously**, you work carefully and thoroughly. Maribel **conscientiously** researched all the facts before writing her history essay.
endure (in-**dyur**) *verb* ▸ pages 223, 230, 233	Something **endures** if it continues to exist for a long time. Some old stories **endure** for centuries because people love to read and hear them.
• **evidence** (**e**-vu-duns) *noun* ▸ pages 221, 226, 230	**Evidence** is information that helps prove something. The detective looks for **evidence** that supports her ideas. 
genuine (**jen**-yū-win) *adjective* ▸ pages 228, 231	Something is **genuine** if it is real and not fake. He thought that the statue was **genuine** gold, but it was really made of brass.
historian (hi-**stor**-ē-un) *noun* ▸ pages 223, 230	A **historian** is someone who studies the events of the past and interprets them. The **historian** wrote an article about World War II.
• **investigation** (in-ves-ti-**gā**-shun) *noun* ▸ page 227	An **investigation** is a careful search or study that looks for facts. We only found out the truth about the event after we conducted our own **investigation**.
just (**just**) *adjective* ▸ pages 219, 221	A **just** person is guided by truth and fairness. I admire leaders who make decisions that are reasonable, fair, and **just**.
skeptic (**skep**-tik) *noun* ▸ page 229	A **skeptic** is someone who doubts beliefs that are generally accepted by others. My friends believe in the legend, but I'm a **skeptic** who needs more proof.

Practice the Words Work with a partner. Make a **Definition Map** for each Key Vocabulary word. Use a dictionary to find other forms of the word.

Definition Map

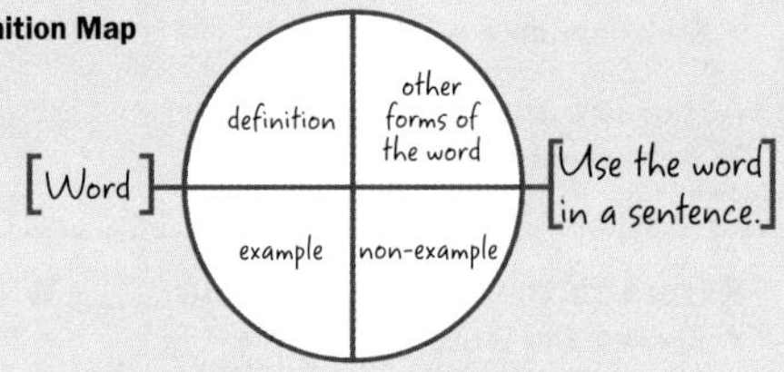

3. **Encourage Elaboration** Provide a sentence frame: *A historian is someone who studies the ______.*

Reading Transparency 10

4. **Practice the Words** Use the transparency to model a Definition Map. Then have students use a dictionary to increase learning as they work with a partner to make a Definition Map for each word.
L.9-10.4.c

Edge Interactive Practice Book, pp. 98–99
RL.9-10.4; L.9-10.6

Reading Transparency 10

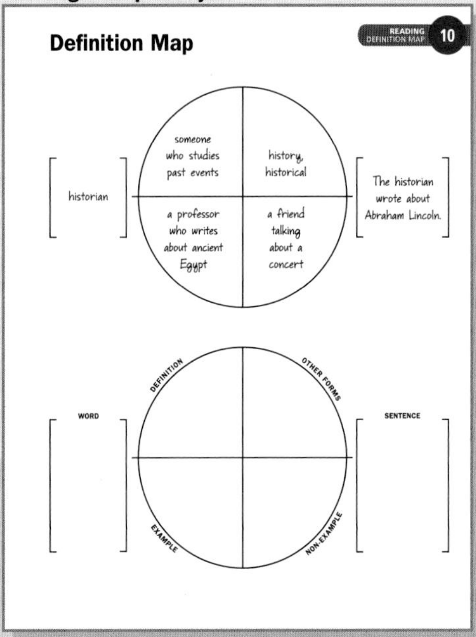

CCSS **Literacy.SL.9-10.1** Initiate and participate effectively in a range of collaborative discussions (one-on-one, in groups, and teacher-led) with diverse partners on grades 9-10 topics, texts, and issues, building on others' ideas and expressing their own clearly and persuasively. **Literacy.RL.9-10.4** Determine the meaning of words and phrases as they are used in the text, including figurative and connotative meanings; analyze the cumulative impact of specific word choices on meaning and tone (e.g., how the language evokes a sense of time and place; how it sets a formal or informal tone). **Literacy.L.9-10.4.c** Consult general and specialized reference materials (e.g., dictionaries, glossaries, thesauruses), both print and digital, to find the pronunciation of a word or determine or clarify its precise meaning, its part of speech, or its etymology.

BEFORE READING The Sword in the Stone

short story by Molly Perham

Reading Strategies

- Plan and Monitor
- Determine Importance
- ▶ **Make Inferences**
- Ask Questions
- Make Connections
- Synthesize
- Visualize

Analyze Cultural Perspective

Most stories are told from a **cultural perspective** that reflects the customs and attitudes of a particular society and era. "The Sword in the Stone" takes place in England during the Middle Ages. The cultural perspective of this time and place affects story elements, including plot, character, setting, and theme.

Look Into the Text

Farming is an important part of the culture in which the story takes place. It affects the plot, characters, and setting.

Everyone in the household had to get up early that morning because they were starting the hay-making.

This was Arthur's favorite time of year. Lessons were suspended so that he and Kay could join the men out in the fields. . . .

Tossing the hay onto the wagon was men's work. Arthur was not yet strong enough to lift a sheaf, but Kay had grown several inches in the last few months and was almost a man. In a few weeks' time he would leave the schoolroom for good to take up his duties as a squire.

Duties and roles are important in Arthur's society.

Focus Strategy ▶ Make Inferences

Sometimes understanding a text is like fitting together the pieces of a puzzle. Some pieces come from the author, who includes ideas and information about the subject. As a reader, you add your own experiences with the subject. You **make inferences** when you put these pieces together.

Focus Strategy

HOW TO MAKE INFERENCES

1. As you read about a subject, record the author's details in an **Inference Chart**.
2. Think about what you already know about the subject. Add your knowledge to the chart.
3. Consider all the information you now have about the subject. What new ideas can you infer, or put together, about the subject?
4. As you continue to read, see if the text proves or changes your inferences.

Inference Chart

Author's Details	My Knowledge	My Inferences
"Lessons were suspended so that he and Kay could join the men out in the fields."	School is suspended only for something important.	Hay-making is important to the characters and their society.

Reading Transparency 11

Analyze Cultural Perspective

READING CULTURAL PERSPECTIVE 11

How does cultural perspective affect the elements of a story?

Introduce Most stories have a **cultural perspective** that reflects the customs, beliefs, and attitudes of a particular society or era. The cultural perspective can affect many elements of the story.

Cultural Perspective: Farming is an important part of the community.

Plot
- Everyone in the household stops work to help with the hay-making.
- Kay and Arthur stop their lessons to work in the fields.

Setting
- The men work hard in the hot fields to finish the harvest before winter.
- The women cook all day in the kitchens to feed the workers.

Theme
- Everyone works together to help the community.

Character
- Kay is older and stronger, so he works like the farming men.
- Arthur is younger and weaker, so he helps less.

Stories may have multiple cultural perspectives. As you read, consider how they affect different elements of the story.

Lesson 4

BEFORE READING

OBJECTIVES

Reading Strategy
- Make Inferences

Literary Analysis
- Analyze Cultural Perspective

TEACH STRATEGIES

D Analyze Cultural Perspective

Look Into the Text Read the introduction to explain cultural perspective. Read aloud the passage. Use the callouts to identify details that reflect cultural perspective. Ask: What cultural perspective does this sample show?

Possible response:
- *England in the Middle Ages*

Point out that the cultural perspective of a story depends on the story's setting. The characters and events might change if the story was set in a place with different cultural perspectives.

Reading Transparency 11

Use the Transparency Read aloud the labeled example sentences to show how cultural perspective affects different story elements. Ask: How is the culture in the story different from our culture today?

Possible response:
- *Some boys leave school to become squires for knights.*

RL.9-10.6

E Focus Strategy: Make Inferences

Make Inferences Read the introduction to define the strategy. Work through the steps in the How To box to model making inferences. Have students try the strategy with another detail from Look Into the Text.

RL.9-10.1

Edge Interactive Practice Book, pp. 100–101

ONGOING ASSESSMENT

Have students discuss how cultural perspective might be reflected in a story set in America today.

CCSS **Literacy.RL.9-10.1** Cite strong and thorough textual evidence to support analysis of what the text says explicitly as well as inferences drawn from the text. **Literacy.RL.9-10.6** Analyze a particular point of view or cultural experience reflected in a work of literature from outside the United States, drawing on a wide reading of world literature. **Literacy.L.9-10.6** Acquire and use accurately general academic and domain-specific words and phrases, sufficient for reading, writing, speaking, and listening at the college and career readiness level; demonstrate independence in gathering vocabulary knowledge when considering a word or phrase important to comprehension or expression.

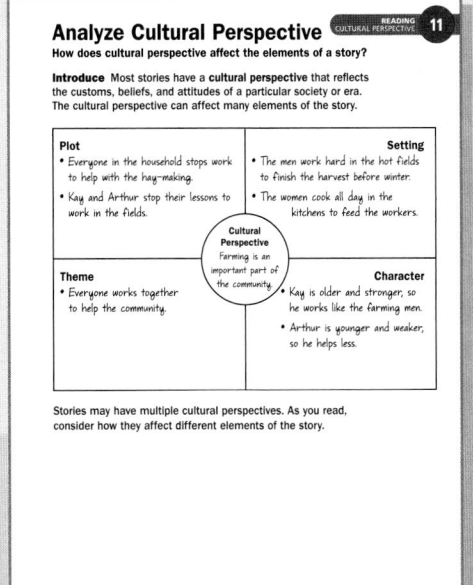

READ

OBJECTIVES

Literary Analysis
- Recognize Genre: Folk Literature
- Analyze Symbols

Viewing
- Respond to and Interpret Visuals

BUILD BACKGROUND

A Then and Now

Have students read the article on the legend of King Arthur.

Background History Share this information to place the legendary King Arthur in historical context:

From about 50 to 400 C.E. (Common Era), Britain was part of the Roman Empire. When Roman rule ended, the people of Britain were almost constantly attacked by neighboring armies. The stories of King Arthur are set in Britain around 500 C.E., during the beginning of what many call the "Dark Ages." Most historians agree that the legends are based on a real man who was a war leader during the Dark Ages.

Connect with History Have students identify and analyze the symbols associated with King Arthur across genres and historical periods by discussing the portrayal of knights in modern media, such as television commercials and video games. Ask: What symbols are associated with knights in all of these genres? What do they mean?

Possible responses:
- *sword: power; shield: protection; round table: equality*

Do you think these symbols meant the same during Arthur's time? What does this say about symbols?

Possible response:
- *Yes. Symbols can mean the same thing in any time period.*

myNGconnect.com

Selection Summaries in eight languages

Then and Now

A Legend Takes New Forms

A Your grandparents' generation may have first met the hero King Arthur in books with elegant illustrations by artists like Howard Pyle and Arthur Rackham.

Today's generation is discovering the King Arthur legend through computer games. In these games the players control the actions of characters with plenty of swordplay, archery, and fights on horseback. Some of the games let you play from Arthur's perspective, while others make you a character in his world.

Stories about King Arthur and his knights, or soldiers, have been part of popular culture for hundreds of years. Beginning in the 1900s, modern media have made it possible to enjoy his story in many forms besides books. For instance, Arthur's character has appeared in comic strips since the 1930s. One of the earliest and most successful strips was *Prince Valiant in the Days of King Arthur*, created by Harold Foster. A number of other comic books and strips are based on characters and events from the Arthur story.

The Arthur legend has been adapted in dozens of live-action and animated films. These movies deal not only with the central hero, Arthur, but also with his knights of the Round Table and the ladies of his court. There have been animated films for younger audiences, including *The Sword in the Stone*, released in 1963, and cartoon television series based on the legend.

Each generation finds ways to retell the story and interpret its events in new ways. What form will Arthur's story take for future generations?

myNGconnect.com

Read an encyclopedia entry about King Arthur.
View classic illustrations of the Arthur legend.

DIFFERENTIATED INSTRUCTION

English Language Learners ELL

Preview the selection:
- Show the art on p. 211: *The sword is an important part of the story.*
- Demonstrate Arthur cutting hay and tying it into sheaves, but struggling to stack them: *Arthur is a boy. He is not strong enough or tall enough to lift the heavy bundles of hay.*
- Show the image of the sword on p. 219: *This is the type of weapon knights would use to compete in contests and on the battlefield.*
- Show the image on p. 220: *Knights wore armor like this to fight in tournaments.*

Read Aloud to provide a supported listening experience:
- Play the **Selection Recording** as students track text in their books. **CD 4**
- Have students use the Listen feature in the **Comprehension Coach** where they see the text as it is read aloud.
- Read the selection aloud to students as you provide comprehensible input. For example, you can explain that the phrase "several more harvests came and went" on p. 213 means that the story skips a few years.

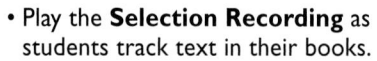

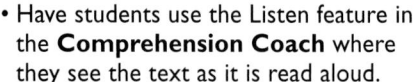

The Sword in the Stone

by Molly Perham

King Arthur's Sword in Stone, Richard T. Nowitz, ©1996.

▲ Critical Viewing: Effect How does the photographer use light and dark in this image? What effect does he create?

Comprehension Coach

TEACH & PRACTICE

B Analyze Visuals

About the Art The time that Arthur supposedly lived is often called the "Dark Ages." What can objects from a time period show about that time period?

Interpret and Respond Ask: What object would you choose to show something important about the present time? Why?

C Critical Viewing: Effect

Observe Details Ask: What details do you notice about the photograph?

ELL **Questioning** For less proficient students, ask yes/no questions or questions with embedded answer choices:

- Does the sword look important or not important? What makes it look this way?
- Does it look like it would be easy or hard to pull the sword from the stone? Why?

Ask: How does the photographer use light and dark in this image? What effect does he create?

Possible response:

- *The dark background looks scary, and the light on the sword makes it look important.*

Have students point out the parts of the image that support their observations.

Comprehension Coach

Build Reading Power

Assign students to use the software, based on their instructional needs.

Read Silently

- Comprehension questions with immediate feedback
- Glossary support
- Review text evidence

RL.9-10.10

Listen

- Professional model of fluent reading

Record

- Oral reading fluency practice
- Ongoing fluency assessment with immediate feedback

CCSS Literacy.RL.9-10.10 By the end of grade 9, read and comprehend literature, including stories, dramas, and poems, in the grades 9–10 text complexity band proficiently, with scaffolding as needed at the high end of the range. By the end of grade 10, read and comprehend literature, including stories, dramas, and poems, at the high end of the grades 9–10 text complexity band independently and proficiently.

READ

OBJECTIVES

Vocabulary
- Key Vocabulary Ⓣ

Reading Fluency
- Phrasing Ⓣ

Reading Strategies
- Make Inferences
- Plan and Monitor: Set a Purpose

Comprehension & Critical Thinking
- Make Inferences
- Use Text Evidence Ⓣ

Literary Analysis
- Analyze Cultural Perspective Ⓣ
- Analyze Style: Author's Word Choice

Viewing
- Respond to and Interpret Visuals

TEACH & PRACTICE

Ⓐ Chunking the Text

Set a Purpose Ask: What might you learn from a story about a young person who becomes a hero?

Possible response:
- *The story might have suspense and excitement.*

Read Have students read pp. 212–215. Support and monitor their comprehension using the reading support provided. Use the Differentiated Instruction below to meet students' individual needs.
RL.9-10.10

Ⓑ Reading Support

1 Language Have students look up the verb *loom* in a thesaurus and find synonyms to increase learning.

Ask: How does the phrase "loomed large" help you imagine the dragon?

Possible response:
- *It makes the dragon seem scary.*

RL.9-10.4; L.9-10.4.c

Ⓒ Reading Support

2 Cultural Perspective Ask: Based on details in the story, what does the culture consider to be valuable qualities for boys? Explain.

Possible responses:
- *The culture values strength and size, because boys are expected to help with farming and serve as squires.*

RL.9-10.6

Set a Purpose

Ⓐ ***Find out what change is on its way for Arthur and all of England.***

Ⓑ The dragon loomed large in front of Arthur's eyes, **1** then **wavered and disintegrated** and the smoke faded away.

Arthur sat up in his own bed and rubbed his eyes. He had been having the most wonderful dream. He started to tell his brother Kay about his strange adventures but just then someone knocked loudly at the door. Everyone in the household had to get up early that morning because they were starting the hay-making.

This was Arthur's favorite time of year. Lessons were suspended so that he and Kay could join the men out in the fields. **It was all hands to the wheel** to get the harvest in before the autumn rains.

Arthur loved to follow the men as they moved up and down with their scythes, cutting great swathes through the waist-high grass and sending scores of rabbits scurrying for cover into the nearby woods. He loved the smell of the new-mown hay, and the heat of the sun burning through the thin shirt on his back. He and Kay were responsible for tying the hay into **sheaves** and stacking them into stooks. Later these would be collected up and taken back to the barn just inside the castle gates.

Ⓒ Tossing the hay onto the wagon was men's work. Arthur was not yet strong enough to lift a sheaf, but Kay had grown several inches in the last few months and was almost a man. In a few weeks' time he would leave the schoolroom for good to take up his duties as a **squire**. Kay could toss the heavy sheaves as well as any of the farmhands. **2** At the end of the day he would climb up on top, pulling Arthur after him, and together they would ride back to the hay barn for supper—a splendid feast of rabbit stew and apple pies which the women had been preparing for most of the day, washed down with jugs of **frothing cider**.

1 Language
A dragon *loomed* large; it appeared in a frightening way. How does this help you picture Arthur's dream?

2 Cultural Perspective
What do the details show about the value this culture places on size and strength? Why is it so important to the boys of this era?

In Other Words

wavered and disintegrated went blurry and broke into small pieces
It was all hands to the wheel Everyone was hard at work
sheaves large piles
squire person who helped a knight or soldier get ready to fight
frothing cider bubbly apple juice

DIFFERENTIATED INSTRUCTION

Interactive Reading As you conduct the interactive reading session with students, adjust your teaching strategies to their needs.

Struggling Readers

Motivate Have students describe heroes in modern comic books, films, and other media.

Have students compare Arthur's actions in the story to the actions of present-day heroes.

English Language Learners ELL

Comprehensible Input Students may need help with words and phrases that are low frequency:
- *scythes* (p. 212): Draw a curved blade. Explain that a scythe is used to cut wheat or grass.
- *scores* (p. 212): a large group
- *Archbishop* (p. 213): Explain that an Archbishop is an important church official.
- *swore an oath* (p. 219): made a promise to do a job correctly

Challenge

Compare Characters Have students compare the characters of Arthur and Kay. Which boy has more of the qualities of a hero?

Have students share their ideas with the class and lead a discussion.

CCSS **Literacy.RL.9-10.4** Determine the meaning of words and phrases as they are used in the text, including figurative and connotative meanings; analyze the cumulative impact of specific word choices on meaning and tone (e.g., how the language evokes a sense of time and place; how it sets a formal or informal tone). **Literacy.RL.9-10.6** Analyze a particular point of view or cultural experience reflected in a work of literature from outside the United States, drawing on a wide reading of world literature. **Literacy.L.9-10.4.c** Consult general and specialized reference materials (e.g., dictionaries, glossaries, thesauruses), both print and digital, to find the pronunciation of a word or determine or clarify its precise meaning, its part of speech, or its etymology.

And so several more harvests came and went, and life went on much the same as usual, though it was a little dull for Arthur without his childhood companion. Kay was often away from the castle, acting as a squire to various knights at **tournaments** all over the country. A squire's task was to dress and **arm** his knight before an event, to carry all the **lances**, and generally to make sure that everything was kept in good order. Kay had been well trained in Sir Ector's household, and performed these tasks **conscientiously**. Rumor had it that Sir Ector was considering the possibility of making Kay a knight. 3

Meanwhile, Arthur grew tall and strong and waited impatiently for his school days to be over. This happened sooner than he expected. One day **an envoy** from the Archbishop arrived breathless at the castle gate with news from London.

On Christmas Day all the great **nobles** and knights had assembled in St. Paul's Cathedral to pray for a sign that would show who was the rightful King of England. When the service was over and they came out of the church they saw an amazing sight. There was a huge stone in the middle of the churchyard with

3 Make Inferences Using the text and what you know already, what is Kay learning? Make a note in your Inference Chart.

Mountain Dragon, 1992, Bob Eggleton. Acrylic on illustration board, private collection of Pat Wilshire, Pennsylvania.

Critical Viewing: Effect How do you think the artist wants the viewer to feel about this image? How does he create this mood?

Key Vocabulary
conscientiously *adv.*, very carefully and thoroughly

In Other Words
tournaments contests for knights, or soldiers
arm give weapons to
lances long-handled weapons with sharp metal points
an envoy a messenger
nobles people with high rank in royal society

TEACH & PRACTICE

D Reading Support

3 Make Inferences Ask students to tell what Kay is learning and to explain how they know.

Possible response:
- *Kay is learning to be a knight. The text says that Kay was doing his tasks well and that Sir Ector was thinking of making Kay a knight. When you learn well you usually end up reaching your goal.*

Have students add the information to their Inference Charts.
RL.9-10.1

E Analyze Visuals

About the Art Bob Eggleton creates illustrations for science fiction and fantasy books and magazines. His art has won many awards.

Interpret and Respond Ask students if they have seen pictures of dragons and, if so, where?

F Critical Viewing: Effect

Analyze Details Ask students to study the dragon's face and body.

ELL Build Background Tell students that in many stories set in the Middle or Dark Ages—when this story takes place—dragons have wings and are often evil.

Ask: How do you think the artist wants the viewer to feel about this image?

Possible response:
- *The artist wants viewers to feel afraid of the dragon.*

Ask: How does the artist create this mood?

Possible response:
- *The sharp teeth, sharp claws, and pointy wings make the dragon look scary.*

DAILY ROUTINES

Vocabulary

See the Vocabulary and Fluency Routines tab for more information.

Respond to Questions Compose yes/no questions using the words. You can use more than one word in a sentence, for example: Did the *evidence* turn the *historian* from a *skeptic* into a believer?

Word Sorts Provide categories for sorting words:
- Number of syllables
- Meaning: for example, which words describe people?

Drama Have students act out a skit that features the vocabulary words, such as *conscientiously*, *genuine*, and *skeptic*. L.9-10.6

Fluency: Phrasing

CD 11

This cluster's fluency practice uses a passage from "The Sword in the Stone" to help students practice appropriate phrasing. Use **Reading Handbook** T749 and the **Fluency Model CD** to teach or review the elements of fluent phrasing, and then use the daily fluency practice activities to develop students' oral reading proficiency.
RL.9-10.10

CCSS **Literacy.RL.9-10.1** Cite strong and thorough textual evidence to support analysis of what the text says explicitly as well as inferences drawn from the text. **Literacy.RL.9-10.10** By the end of grade 9, read and comprehend literature, including stories, dramas, and poems, in the grades 9–10 text complexity band proficiently, with scaffolding as needed at the high end of the range. By the end of grade 10, read and comprehend literature, including stories, dramas, and poems, at the high end of the grades 9–10 text complexity band independently and proficiently. **Literacy.L.9-10.6** Acquire and use accurately general academic and domain-specific words and phrases, sufficient for reading, writing, speaking, and listening at the college and career readiness level; demonstrate independence in gathering vocabulary knowledge when considering a word or phrase important to comprehension or expression.

READ

OBJECTIVES

Vocabulary
- Key Vocabulary Ⓣ
- Strategy: Use Contextual Analysis

Reading Strategy
- Make Inferences

Comprehension & Critical Thinking
- Make Inferences
- Use Text Evidence Ⓣ

Literary Analysis
- Analyze Cultural Perspective Ⓣ

Grammar
- Present and Past Tense Ⓣ

TEACH & PRACTICE

Ⓐ Reading Support

4 Make Inferences Ask students to share other stories they know in which a hero has to pass some kind of test.

ELL Read Aloud Call attention to important details by reading aloud the inscription on the anvil and the words of the Archbishop. Ask: What does the hero have to do to become king?

Ask: What does this test show about the man who will become king?

Possible response:
- *It will show that the man is strong or has special powers.*

Have students add this information to their Inference Charts.
RL.9-10.1

Ⓑ Reading Support

5 Access Vocabulary Ask: What is the root word in *expectant*?

Possible response:
- *expect*

Ask: What other word in the sentence helps you figure out the meaning? What do you think *expectant* means?

Possible responses:
- *excited; ready to go*

L.9-10.4.a; L.9-10.4.b

an anvil embedded in it. Pushed into the anvil was a magnificent sword, and written in golden letters were the words:

Whoever pulls this sword out of this stone
is born to be King of all England.

Ⓐ The nobles stood around the stone wondering about the words that were written on the sword. One of them went back to tell the Archbishop, who hurried out to see the **miracle**.

"God has given us a sign," he said. "We must pray once more and then those who think they are fit to be king may try to pull the sword out of the stone." 4

One by one the nobles tried to pull out the sword, but none of them succeeded.

"The man who will be King of England is not here," said the Archbishop. "But God will send him in his own good time."

Ten nobles were chosen to guard the sword until the right man was found. Then the Archbishop sent out messengers to all the knights in the land to invite them to a tournament.

Kay had just been made a knight, and Sir Ector agreed that this was a good opportunity for him to show off his skills. Arthur was to ride with them so he could act as Sir Kay's squire.

Ⓑ A very excited and expectant **party** set off for London that cold winter's morning. 5 The city was crowded with visitors and they had to **take lodgings** some distance from the center.

On New Year's Day Sir Ector, Sir Kay, and Arthur rode into town. But before they reached the field where the tournament was to be held, Kay discovered that he had forgotten his sword.

"Arthur," he gasped in horror, "I have left my sword at the house where we spent the night. I cannot fight without it. If I ride back, I will

4 Make Inferences Heroes in legends often pass tests. In this story, what do the characters believe this test will show about the man who will become king? Make a note in your Inference Chart.

5 Access Vocabulary What does the word *expectant* mean? Look for a root word and context clues that may give you an idea.

In Other Words
an anvil embedded in it a steel block stuck deep into the stone
miracle extraordinary event
party group of people
take lodgings find a place to stay

214 Unit 3 The Hero Within

GRAMMAR

Present and Past Tense

Teach/Model Display the transparency. Say the sentence pairs, emphasizing the pronunciations of the ending *-ed* and pointing out the parallel verbs in the second set of sentences.. Have students repeat.

Practice A. Have students say the past tense form of each verb before reading aloud the complete sentence. **B.** Suggest that students start their own sentences with a time phrase, such as *Five years ago*. Have students write about the childhood memory and read it aloud. Repeat a sentence from each memory, and ask the group to identify the past tense verb.
L.9-10.1.a

Grammar & Writing Practice Book, pp. 69–70

Grammar Transparency 31

GRAMMAR PRESENT AND PAST TENSE 31

How Do You Show That an Action Already Happened?
Add -*ed* to the Verb.

- Action in the **present tense** happens now or on a regular basis.
- Action in the **past tense** happened earlier.

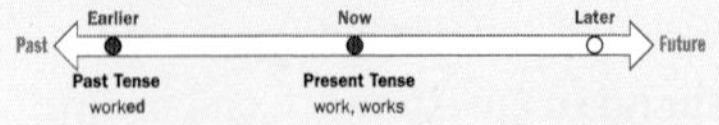

Add -ed to most verbs when you talk about a past action. If there is more than one verb in a sentence, they must all be in the same tense.

1. Today, Arthur and his brother **work** hard.
   Yesterday, they **worked** hard, too.
2. Today, the brothers **slash** hay, **collect** it in sheathes, and **stack** the bundles.
   Yesterday, they also **slashed** hay, **collected** it in sheathes, and **stacked** the bundles.

Try It

A. Say each sentence about Arthur's early memory. Use the past tense of the verb in parentheses.

1. Arthur remembered many good times with his brother. **(remember)**
2. At harvest time, Arthur and Kay __played__ together. **(play)**
3. Kay climbed onto the wagon, __pulled__ Arthur up, and waited for a ride to the barn. **(pull)**
4. Later, they all __feasted__ on stew and pies. **(feast)**

B. Now write three sentences about one of your childhood memories. Use verbs that end in -ed. Sentences will vary.

GRAMMAR SKILLS PATH

31	**Present and Past Tense** ELL Language & Grammar Lab
32	**Regular Past Tense Verbs**
33	**Past Tense of *Be*: *Was, Were***
34	**Past Tense of *Have*: *Had***
35	**Review: Present and Past Tense Verbs**

CCSS **Literacy.L.9-10.1** Demonstrate command of the conventions of standard English grammar and usage when writing or speaking. **Literacy.L.9-10.1.a** Use parallel structure. **Literacy.L.9-10.4.a** Use context (e.g., the overall meaning of a sentence, paragraph, or text; a word's position or function in a sentence) as a clue to the meaning of a word or phrase. **Literacy.L.9-10.4.b** Identify and correctly use patterns of word changes that indicate different meanings or parts of speech (e.g., analyze, analysis, analytical; advocate, advocacy).

be tired before the tournament starts. Please go and get it for me."

"Of course I will," said Arthur, who was always willing to help other people. In any case, it was his duty as a squire to serve his brother. 6 C

He rode back along the road as quickly as he could, but when he reached the lodging house he found that **it was locked and shuttered**. The landlady and all the other people who lived there had gone to watch the **jousting**.

Arthur was very upset. He rode slowly back to the jousting field wondering what he could do. Without a sword Kay would not be able to take part in the tournament.

Passing St. Paul's churchyard Arthur saw a magnificent sword gleaming in the sunlight. As he drew closer he saw that it was sticking out of an anvil on top of a huge stone. Arthur looked around but saw no one. The ten knights who were supposed to be keeping watch had also gone to the tournament.

. . . Arthur saw a magnificent sword gleaming in the sunlight.

"Well," thought Arthur, "whoever owns this sword can't want it very much if they leave it lying around like that."

He dismounted from his horse and climbed onto the stone. Grasping the sword by the **hilt** he pulled it out of the anvil. Then, delighted to have found a sword for his brother, Arthur spurred on his horse to catch up with Sir Ector's party.

6 Cultural Perspective
How does Arthur's cultural perspective affect his actions?

In Other Words

it was locked and shuttered the doors were shut and the windows were covered
jousting contests between knights riding on horses
hilt handle

Monitor Comprehension

Explain
How will the sword in the stone change the lives of everyone in England?

TEACH & PRACTICE

C Reading Support

6 Cultural Perspective Remind students that during Arthur's time, a squire was a knight's helper. Explain that knights were highly respected and that good knights followed a strict code of honor. Note that young squires like Arthur were usually knights in training and were also expected to display honorable behavior.

Ask: Based on Arthur's thoughts, what do you conclude were values important to knights and squires?

Possible response:
- *helping others, duty, and loyalty*

RL.9-10.6

Monitor Comprehension

Explain Remind students about the setting of the story. Have students think aloud to explain how the sword in the stone will change the lives of everyone in England.

MODEL Say:
- *This was a dark and dangerous time in England. There were many problems.*
- *So far I know that the knights and nobles prayed for a sign to help them find the real king of England.*

Have students answer the question.

Possible responses:
- *Once the real king is found, he'll be able to lead the country. He should be able to get the knights and nobles to work together for everyone.*

RL.9-10.1

VOCABULARY

Link Vocabulary and Concepts

Ask questions to link Key Vocabulary with the Essential Question.

EQ ESSENTIAL QUESTION:
What makes a hero?

Some possible questions:
- *How do you think a* **genuine** *hero behaves?*
- *Why is it important for a hero to act in a* **just** *manner?*
- *How would a hero* **conscientiously** *perform his or her duties? Give an example.*
- *Why do legends about heroes* **endure**?
- *Sometimes a person is not thought of as a hero during his or her lifetime. How might a* **historian** *prove that someone was a hero?*

Have students use the Key Vocabulary words in their responses.
L.9-10.6

CCSS **Literacy.RL.9-10.1** Cite strong and thorough textual evidence to support analysis of what the text says explicitly as well as inferences drawn from the text. **Literacy.RL.9-10.6** Analyze a particular point of view or cultural experience reflected in a work of literature from outside the United States, drawing on a wide reading of world literature. **Literacy.L.9-10.6** Acquire and use accurately general academic and domain-specific words and phrases, sufficient for reading, writing, speaking, and listening at the college and career readiness level; demonstrate independence in gathering vocabulary knowledge when considering a word or phrase important to comprehension or expression.

READ

OBJECTIVES

Vocabulary
- Content Area Vocabulary: Medieval Society

Reading Strategies
- Plan and Monitor: Predict
- Make Inferences

Comprehension & Critical Thinking
- Make Inferences
- Use Text Evidence (T)

Literary Analysis
- Analyze Cultural Perspective (T)

Viewing
- Respond to and Interpret Visuals

TEACH & PRACTICE

A Chunking the Text

Predict Review what students know about the significance of the sword.

Have students predict whether the legend of the sword will come true for a boy like Arthur.

Read Have students read pp. 216–218. Support and monitor their comprehension using the reading support provided.
RL.9-10.10

B Reading Support

7 Make Inferences Ask: What inference did you make about Kay when he took the sword?

Possible response:
- *Kay was planning to lie to become king, until he had to swear on the Bible.*

Then ask: Has your idea about Kay changed? Why or why not?
RL.9-10.1

C Reading Support

8 Make Inferences Ask: What word would you use to describe Sir Ector's character?

Possible responses:
- *honest, trustworthy, truthful*

Ask: What details in this scene help you make this inference?

Possible responses:
- *He is trying to prove who really pulled the sword from the stone.*

RL.9-10.1

Predict

(A) ***Do you think the legend of the sword will come true for a boy like Arthur?***

(B) "Kay! Kay!" he called. "The lodging house was all locked up, so I couldn't fetch your sword. But I found this one pushed into an anvil. It doesn't seem to belong to anyone. Will it be all right?"

When Kay saw the sword he realized immediately what it was and the **temptation** was too much for him. He took it to Sir Ector.

"Father," he said, "I have the sword from the stone. Therefore I must be King of England."

Sir Ector looked at the sword and looked at Kay. He knew that his son had no right to be king. He turned and took the two boys back to the churchyard.

Putting a Bible into Kay's hand he said, "Now, my son, tell me how you got the sword."

Kay sighed. "Arthur brought it to me," he said. **7**

(C) "And how did you get the sword, Arthur?"

"Kay forgot his sword, and I rode back to the lodging house to get it for him," Arthur explained, hoping that he was not going to get into trouble. "But the house was all locked up. On the way back I saw this sword in the churchyard. It didn't seem to belong to anyone, so I thought that Kay might as well have it. I'm sorry if I did wrong."

"Did anyone see you take the sword?"

"No, sir, there was no one there."

"Put the sword back and let us all try to pull it out."

"But it's easy," said Arthur, "anyone could do it."

"Just do as I say," said Sir Ector **sternly**. **8**

Arthur was **puzzled** by all this fuss over a sword, but he did as he was told and pushed it back into the anvil. Kay **seized** it by the hilt,

7 Make Inferences What inference did you make about Kay when he took the sword? Has your idea about him changed? Explain.

8 Make Inferences Choose one word to describe Sir Ector's character. What details in this scene help you make this inference?

In Other Words
temptation wish to do something wrong
sternly very seriously
puzzled confused
seized grabbed

VOCABULARY

HISTORY

Content Area Vocabulary: Medieval Society

Build vocabulary related to the content area of society in the Middle Ages.

Use the Make Words Your Own routine (*see the Vocabulary tab*) and the sample sentences below to introduce these words from the selection.

court (kort) ▸ p. 210

Sir Kay and Merlin were members of King Arthur's ***court****.*

knight (nīt) ▸ pp. 210, 213

The ***knight*** *fought in the king's army.*

Sir (sur) ▸ p. 213

When a man became a knight, he was addressed as ***Sir****.*

king (king) ▸ p. 213

A ***king*** *is the male ruler of a country.*

lords (lordz) ▸ p. 219

A ***lord*** *owned land and was loyal to the king.*

Have students use the words during a role-play of the scene on pp. 219–221.

Provide frames for students to contrast medieval and modern society. For example:

- *Medieval society had ______. Modern society has soldiers.*

L.9-10.6

CCSS **Literacy.RL.9-10.1** Cite strong and thorough textual evidence to support analysis of what the text says explicitly as well as inferences drawn from the text. **Literacy.RL.9-10.10** By the end of grade 9, read and comprehend literature, including stories, dramas, and poems, in the grades 9-10 text complexity band proficiently, with scaffolding as needed at the high end of the range. By the end of grade 10, read and comprehend literature, including stories, dramas, and poems, at the high end of the grades 9-10 text complexity band independently and proficiently.

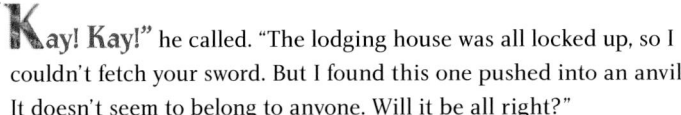

but though he pulled as hard as he could with both hands, he couldn't move it.

Then Sir Ector tried, but with no more success. "You try it, Arthur," he said.

So Arthur, wondering what this was all about, got hold of the sword and pulled it out easily.

Sir Ector stared in amazement at the boy he had brought up as his own. Then he dropped to his knees and motioned to Kay to do the same.

"Father!" Arthur cried in alarm. "Why are you kneeling before me?"

D "**It is God's will** that whoever pulls the sword from the stone must be King of England," said Sir Ector. "You know that I am not your real father, and Kay is not your brother, although we both love you dearly. **Merlin** brought you to me when you were a tiny baby, wrapped in a cloth of gold. I knew you were of noble blood, but I had no idea that you were born to be King." 9

"If I am really King," said Arthur **solemnly**, "then I swear to serve God and my people, to **put right any wrongs**, and to bring peace to the land. But please do not leave me, Father, for I will need your support and advice. And Kay, I want you to be a knight of my court and governor of my lands."

Merlin and Arthur, Sir William Goscombe John (1860–1952), Bronze, National Museum and Gallery of Wales, Cardiff, The Bridgeman Art Library.

E 9 Cultural Perspective
Why is Arthur surprised when Sir Ector kneels before him? What do Sir Ector's words and actions show about his culture?

F Critical Viewing: Effect
Look at the sculpture of Merlin holding Arthur as a baby. What does the artist show about their relationship?

In Other Words

It is God's will God's plan is
Merlin A wise wizard
solemnly seriously
put right any wrongs correct any problems or crimes

TEACH & PRACTICE

D Reading Support

9 **Cultural Perspective** Have students retell what Sir Ector reveals about Arthur's real family.

ELL **Build Background** Provide background information about certain features of medieval society:

- *God's will:* In medieval times, people believed that a person became king or queen because it was God's wish.
- *Merlin/wise wizard:* A wizard, or a man with magical powers, is a common character in literature set in this time period.
- *noble blood:* A person from an important family had an important position in society.

Ask: Based on what you know about the culture of the time, why is it unusual for Sir Ector to kneel before Arthur?

Possible response:

- *Fathers didn't kneel to their children, and a knight wouldn't kneel to a young squire.*

RL.9-10.6

E Analyze Visuals

About the Art Sir William Goscombe John lived from 1860 to 1952. He created sculptures of real people and characters from literature.

Interpret and Respond Ask: How has the artist made the figures realistic?

F Critical Viewing: Effect

Analyze Effect Ask students to study the expressions on the faces of Merlin and the baby Arthur.

Ask: What does the artist show about their relationship?

Possible responses:

- *Merlin looks like he loves the baby.*
- *Arthur looks like he trusts and pays attention to Merlin.*

CCSS Literacy.RL.9-10.6 Analyze a particular point of view or cultural experience reflected in a work of literature from outside the United States, drawing on a wide reading of world literature. **Literacy.L.9-10.6** Acquire and use accurately general academic and domain-specific words and phrases, sufficient for reading, writing, speaking, and listening at the college and career readiness level; demonstrate independence in gathering vocabulary knowledge when considering a word or phrase important to comprehension or expression.

OBJECTIVES

Vocabulary
- Key Vocabulary Ⓣ

Reading Strategies
- Make Inferences; Review Strategies
- Synthesize: Draw Conclusions

Comprehension & Critical Thinking
- Make Inferences
- Use Text Evidence Ⓣ

Literary Analysis
- Analyze Cultural Perspective Ⓣ

Grammar
- Regular Past Tense Verbs Ⓣ

TEACH & PRACTICE

Ⓐ Reading Support

10 Cultural Perspective Ask: What sort of person do the knights and nobles expect to be their king?

Possible response:
- *someone from a high-ranking family, not an "unknown youth"*

RL.9-10.6

Ⓑ Reading Support

11 Make Inferences Ask students why they think the nobles refuse to accept Arthur as their king.

Possible response:
- *Arthur is too young to even become a knight, so he has not proven that he will be able to be king.*

RL.9-10.1

Monitor Comprehension

Draw Conclusions Have students review the text and discuss who helped Arthur, such as Merlin and his knights. Then ask: Would Arthur have become a hero without help from other people?

Possible responses:
- *Yes, because Sir Ector said it was God's will.*
- *No, because Arthur first needed ordinary people, the nobles, and the knights to accept him as their king.*

RL.9-10.1

Sir Ector and Kay promised to stay with Arthur as long as he needed them.

Then they went to the Archbishop and told him what had happened. Arthur put the sword back into the stone again and invited anyone who wished to try and pull it out. No one succeeded. Only Arthur could pull it free.

Ⓐ The great nobles and knights refused to agree that this unknown youth should be king over them.

"We will come again **at Candlemas**," they said, as they mounted their horses and rode away. "Perhaps by then a man will have been found who is more worthy to be our King." 10

So at Candlemas there was another great gathering, but though all the nobles tried their hardest to draw the sword, none of them could move it. Once again Arthur put his hand on the hilt and at his touch it came out as easily as though it had never been stuck **fast** in the stone. Yet still the nobles would not accept such a boy for their king.

"We will pray to God again," they said. And at Easter, they made another trial, but none of them could move the sword except Arthur. By now the ordinary people, who had heard of the miracle and watched the trials eagerly, would be held back no longer.

> ... the nobles would not accept such a boy for their king.

Ⓑ "It is God's will that Arthur should be King—we will have Arthur for our King," they cried. And so the great nobles and knights **were obliged to** give in. 11

10 Cultural Perspective
What does the nobles' and knights' behavior toward Arthur show about attitudes in their society?

11 Make Inferences
Why do you think the nobles refuse to accept Arthur as King?

Monitor Comprehension
Draw Conclusions
Who helped Arthur become a hero? Would he have become a hero without help from other people?

In Other Words
at Candlemas on February 2, a Christian holiday
fast completely
were obliged to were forced to, had to

GRAMMAR

Regular Past Tense Verbs

Teach/Model Display the transparency. Explain that *-ed* appears at the end of most past tense verbs. After working through the spelling rules, add *-ed* to *hop*, and have students compare *hoped* and *hopped*.

Practice A. Tell students to refer to the rules as they form the past tense of each verb. Have students spell the verb as you write it. Then read aloud the complete sentence. **B.** Use the example about Sir Ector to model writing a reaction to a story. Have students write their reactions and read them aloud. Repeat a sentence from each, and ask the group to identify the past tense verb. L.9-10.1; L.9-10.2.c

Grammar & Writing Practice Book, pp. 71–72

GRAMMAR SKILLS PATH

31 Present and Past Tense
▶ 32 Regular Past Tense Verbs ELL Language & Grammar Lab
33 Past Tense of *Be: Was, Were*
34 Past Tense of *Have: Had*
35 Review: Present and Past Tense Verbs

Grammar Transparency 32

GRAMMAR REGULAR PAST TENSE VERBS 32

Can You Just Add *-ed* to Form a Verb in the Past?
Not Always

Most verbs end with -ed to show the past tense. Sometimes you have to change the spelling of the verb before you add -ed. Follow these rules:

1. If a verb ends in silent **e**, drop the **e**. Then add -ed.
   The knights hoped to be king. **(hope)**
   Sir Kay arrived without his sword. **(arrive)**
2. Some one-syllable verbs end in one vowel and one consonant. Double the consonant before you add -ed.
   Arthur stepped up to the stone. **(step)**
   He grabbed the sword. **(grab)**

Try It

A. Say each sentence about Arthur and the sword. Use the past tense form of the verb in parentheses. Spell the past tense verb.

1. Arthur ___tugged___ on the sword and pulled it out. **(tug)**
2. He ___raced___ back to Sir Kay with the sword. **(race)**
3. Sir Kay wanted to be king. He ___lied___ about the sword. **(lie)**
4. Sir Ector ___recognized___ the lie. He asked Arthur to put the sword back in the stone. **(recognize)**
5. Kay failed to pull out the sword, but Arthur ___removed___ it easily for the second time! **(remove)**

B. Now let's write a reaction to the story. Tell about a part of the story you liked or disliked. Add three more sentences. Use verbs with -ed.
Sentences will vary.
I liked the character of Sir Ector. He trusted Arthur's story.

CCSS **Literacy.RL.9-10.1** Cite strong and thorough textual evidence to support analysis of what the text says explicitly as well as inferences drawn from the text. **Literacy.RL.9-10.6** Analyze a particular point of view or cultural experience reflected in a work of literature from outside the United States, drawing on a wide reading of world literature. **Literacy.L.9-10.1** Demonstrate command of the conventions of standard English grammar and usage when writing or speaking. **Literacy.L.9-10.2.c** Spell correctly.

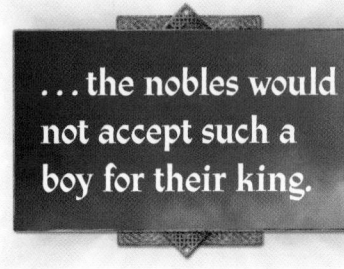

Predict

Arthur faces many new challenges. How will he work to win his people's support? **D**

Arthur went into the church and placed the sword on the **high altar**. The Archbishop took it up and touched Arthur on the shoulder with it to make him a knight. Then Arthur forgave the great nobles and knights for doubting him and swore an oath that he would be a **just** and true king for all his days.

He ordered the lords who held their land from the crown to fulfil the duties they owed him. Each one knelt before him in turn and promised to **abide by** the laws of the king. After this ceremony, Arthur said he would hear complaints about **injustices** and crimes committed in the land since the death of his father, **Uther Pendragon**. They told him of how lands and castles had been taken by force, and men murdered, and of how knights and ladies and common people were robbed and assaulted.

Arthur ordered that all lands and properties should be returned to their rightful owners and that everyone should respect the rights of others. **E** 12 When that was done, Arthur organized his government. Sir Kay was made High Steward of all Britain and the most trustworthy knights were **appointed to high office**. Merlin was **confirmed** as chief counsellor to the King.

Roman sword, Hod Hill fort, Dorset, Roman Britain, first century

12 Make Inferences Think about the decisions Arthur makes as king. How do they help you understand him?

Key Vocabulary

just *adj.*, guided by truth and fairness

In Other Words

high altar table in the church
abide by follow
injustices unfair actions
Uther Pendragon the old King
appointed to high office given important jobs
confirmed named

TEACH & PRACTICE

D Chunking the Text

Predict Review what students know about the challenges Arthur faces to help them predict how he might win his people's support.

Read Have students read pp. 219–221. Support and monitor their comprehension using the reading support provided.
RL.9-10.10

E Reading Support

12 **Make Inferences** Have students reread p. 219 to clarify Arthur's decisions and actions.

ELL **Use Graphic Organizer** Use a graphic organizer to display Arthur's actions and what they show about the kind of king he is. For example:

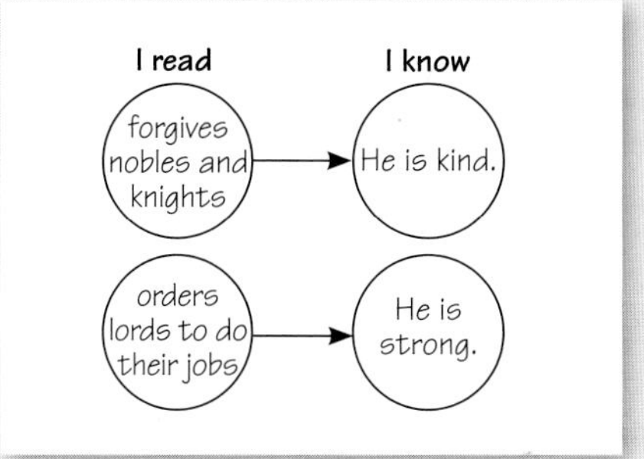

Ask: How do Arthur's decisions help you understand him?

Possible response:

- *Arthur's decisions make me understand that he wants to be as kind, fair, and strong as his father was.*

RL.9-10.1

Review Strategies Have partners say what other strategies they used as they read the text.

Possible response:

- *When I read about Arthur's behavior as a squire, I predicted that he would be a fine king. I read on and found out that my predictions were correct. Arthur showed that he would be a just, fair king.*

RL.9-10.1

CCSS **Literacy.RL.9-10.1** Cite strong and thorough textual evidence to support analysis of what the text says explicitly as well as inferences drawn from the text. **Literacy.RL.9-10.10** By the end of grade 9, read and comprehend literature, including stories, dramas, and poems, in the grades 9–10 text complexity band proficiently, with scaffolding as needed at the high end of the range. By the end of grade 10, read and comprehend literature, including stories, dramas, and poems, at the high end of the grades 9–10 text complexity band independently and proficiently.

READ

OBJECTIVES

Vocabulary
- Key Vocabulary Ⓣ

Reading Strategy
- Make Inferences

Comprehension & Critical Thinking
- Make Inferences
- Use Text Evidence Ⓣ

Literary Analysis
- Analyze Cultural Perspective Ⓣ

Viewing
- Respond to and Interpret Visuals

Writing
- Response to Literature

TEACH & PRACTICE

Ⓐ Analyze Visuals

Interpret and Respond Discuss whether students think the artist painted Arthur to look like a hero. Ask: Does this image of Arthur match what you imagined?

Ⓑ Critical Viewing: Design

Analyze Design Have students locate the gold on Arthur's crown, his sleeves, his cape, his belt, his leg armor, and around his neck.

ELL **Use Graphic Organizer** Show visually what gold symbolizes.

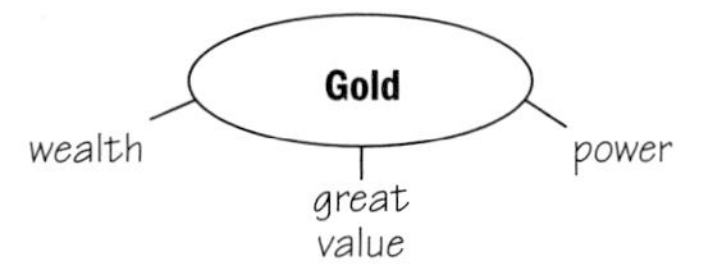

Ask: What does all the gold in the painting symbolize?

Possible response:
- *Arthur's power and heroic qualities*

Have students analyze the symbol of gold across historical periods. Ask: What are some modern-day examples of gold as a symbol of power, value, or wealth?

Possible responses:
- *jewelry, Olympic medals, "gold" credit cards*

King Arthur, 1903, Charles Ernest Butler. Oil on canvas, private collection, Christopher Wood Gallery, London, The Bridgeman Art Library.

Ⓐ

Ⓑ ▲ Critical Viewing: Design Why has the artist used so much gold in this painting? What is it a symbol for?

OUT-OF-SCHOOL LITERACY

MEDIA & TECHNOLOGY

Interpreting Movies

Help students see how much prior knowledge they bring to the text by connecting the selection to students' experience with watching movies about the time of King Arthur.

- Which movies about knights, kings, or the Dark Ages have you seen?
- What are some hardships that people of that time had to **endure**?
- Did the king act **conscientiously** toward the people in his kingdom?
- How might a **skeptic** be convinced that Arthur was a **just** ruler?
- Do you think the people had a **genuine** love and respect for the king? Did he feel that way about his people? Why or why not?

As students answer, encourage the use of the highlighted Key Vocabulary.
SL.9-10.1.a

CCSS Literacy.SL.9-10.1.a Come to discussions prepared, having read and researched material under study; explicitly draw on that preparation by referring to evidence from texts and other research on the topic or issue to stimulate a thoughtful, well-reasoned exchange of ideas.

Then Arthur proclaimed that the **Feast of Pentecost** would be his **coronation day**. When that day came, the Archbishop crowned him King of all **Britain**. He ruled his kingdom from **Camelot**, and everyone rejoiced that Britain once more had a King. ❖

ANALYZE The Sword in the Stone

1. **Explain** How do the nobles and the ordinary people treat Arthur at first? How do their attitudes compare by the end of the story? Cite evidence from the story to support your answer.
2. **Vocabulary** How does Arthur show that he will be a **just** and fair king?
3. **Analyze Cultural Perspective** With a partner, record how cultural perspectives affect the plot, characters, setting, and theme of the story.

Cultural Perspective	How It Affects the Story
Farming is important.	Everyone helps with the hay-making.

How would the story be different if it was told from a different cultural perspective?

4. **Focus Strategy Make Inferences** Do you think Arthur will make a good king? Consider what you know about kings or other leaders from stories you have read and heard. Then work with a partner to gather **evidence** from the story and make an inference about Arthur.

Return to the Text

Reread and Write Is Arthur a hero? Reread "The Sword in the Stone," and write your opinion. Include at least two details from the text to serve as evidence to support your ideas.

Key Vocabulary

- **evidence** *n.*, information that helps prove something

In Other Words

Feast of Pentecost Christian festival held on the seventh Sunday after Easter
coronation day day to become king
Britain England and all its lands
Camelot the capital city

APPLY

C ANALYZE

1. **Explain** The nobles do not want Arthur to be king, but the ordinary people do. By the end, they all accept that it is God's will.
RL.9-10.1
2. **Vocabulary** Arthur listens to people's complaints about injustices. He settles arguments and makes people respect each other's rights.
L.9-10.6
3. **Analyze Cultural Perspective** Have partners use their charts to describe what they learned about the cultural perspective of the story.

Possible responses:
- *People expect a sign to find out who will be king. Everyone waits for a king to pull the sword from the stone.*
- *The nobles expect a king who is "worthy." They do not accept Arthur because he is an "unknown youth."*
- *In other cultures, people vote for leaders. They might have different expectations for a king.*

RL.9-10.6

4. **Focus Strategy: Make Inferences** Have volunteers share their inferences and evidence with the class. Make sure students include details from the story that helped them make an inference.
RL.9-10.1

D Return to the Text

Students' opinions might reflect these influences and evidence:

- *Arthur is a hero because he treated the common people well.*
- *Arthur is a hero because he orders all lands to be returned to their rightful owners and for everyone to be respectful of the rights of others.*

W.9-10.9.a; W.9-10.10

Edge Interactive Practice Book, p. 102

CCSS **Literacy.RL.9-10.1 Cite** strong and thorough textual evidence to support analysis of what the text says explicitly as well as inferences drawn from the text. **Literacy.RL.9-10.6** Analyze a particular point of view or cultural experience reflected in a work of literature from outside the United States, drawing on a wide reading of world literature. **Literacy.L.9-10.6** Acquire and use accurately general academic and domain-specific words and phrases, sufficient for reading, writing, speaking, and listening at the college and career readiness level; demonstrate independence in gathering vocabulary knowledge when considering a word or phrase important to comprehension or expression. **Literacy.W.9-10.9.a** Apply grades 9-10 Reading standards to literature (e.g., "Analyze how an author draws on and transforms source material in a specific work [e.g., how Shakespeare treats a theme or topic from Ovid or the Bible or how a later author draws on a play by Shakespeare]"). **Literacy.W.9-10.10** Write routinely over extended time frames (time for research, reflection, and revision) and shorter time frames (a single sitting or a day or two) for a range of tasks, purposes, and audiences.

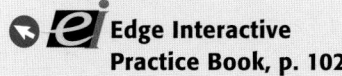

Lesson 5

BEFORE READING

OBJECTIVES

Reading Strategy
- Make Inferences

Literary Analysis
- Analyze Text Structures T

TEACH STRATEGIES

A Analyze Text Structures

Introduce Read the introduction to define text structures. Go over the chart of text structures and signal words. Explain that signal words can help readers identify an author's method of development.

Read the passage aloud. Ask: What phrase signals the time order of the events in these two paragraphs? What does it show?

Possible response:
- *At the same time; it shows the connection between stories of Arthur from different countries.*

Have students evaluate the effectiveness of this text structure. Ask: How do the signal words help you as you read?
RI.9-10.5

B Focus Strategy: Make Inferences

Make Inferences Define the strategy and work through the steps in the How To box. Tell students that readers have to think about the evidence and what they already know to make inferences.

Have partners discuss what they know that can help them make an inference about the subject of Look Into the Text.

Possible response:
- *We know that the stories of King Arthur are set in England during a time when life was really hard.*
RI.9-10.1

ONGOING ASSESSMENT
What are four common text structures and some words that signal them?

BEFORE READING Was There a Real King Arthur?

historical analysis by Robert Stewart

Reading Strategies
- Plan and Monitor
- Determine Importance
- ▶ **Make Inferences**
- Ask Questions
- Make Connections
- Synthesize
- Visualize

Analyze Text Structures

A

Nonfiction authors often organize their ideas into **text structures** that share information in a clear and interesting way. As you read, look for common signal words that show which text structure the author is using. These signal words will help you follow the author's thinking and find the information you need to know.

- Description: *for example, such as, one such, most important*
- Sequence or Time Order: *first, then, before, after, meanwhile, finally, on, in*
- Compare and Contrast: *like, while, but, on one hand, however, both, also*
- Cause and Effect: *therefore, so, because of, if . . . then, this led to, as a result*

Look Into the Text

A historian usually starts by looking for written evidence. The first mention of someone who might be Arthur is in a book called *The Overthrow of Britain* compiled by the British monk Saint Gildas (c. 516–570 C.E.)....

At the same time, bards in Wales and Brittany, in France, were entertaining their hosts with stories of a hero named Arthur. This one had a personality much like that of the Arthur we know, and he slew monsters and wicked giants.

Signal words can show how the author organizes events by time.

Which date does the author include to help you understand the order of events?

Focus Strategy ▶ Make Inferences

B

Most nonfiction authors provide evidence to support a big idea. But sometimes, reading the evidence is not enough. The reader must put together evidence to **make inferences** about the big idea.

Focus Strategy

HOW TO MAKE INFERENCES

1. As you read nonfiction, note important evidence from each section in an **Inference Diagram**.
2. Think about what the evidence proves. Sometimes, the author will state this directly.
3. If the big idea is not stated, summarize the evidence to make an inference about the author's big idea.
4. As you read on, make more inferences. See if the text supports or changes your inferences.

Inference Diagram

Evidence 1:	Historians look for clues about Arthur.
+	
Evidence 2:	Early written stories told about a hero like Arthur.
+	
Evidence 3:	Bards told stories about a hero named Arthur.
↓	
Inference:	Many old written and oral stories were about a hero like Arthur.

CCSS Literacy.RI.9-10.1 Cite strong and thorough textual evidence to support analysis of what the text says explicitly as well as inferences drawn from the text. Literacy.RI.9-10.5 Analyze in detail how an author's ideas or claims are developed and refined by particular sentences, paragraphs, or larger portions of a text (e.g., a section or chapter).

HISTORICAL ANALYSIS

Was There a Real King Arthur?

by Robert Stewart

Connect Across Texts

The short story "The Sword in the Stone" retells a heroic legend that has been told for centuries. The following article about history examines its lasting appeal. What makes this hero's legend ***endure****?*

Head of King Arthur, from the *Beautiful Fountain*, Nuremberg, Germany, fourteenth century 1

1 Make Inferences This photo and caption show a very old statue. How does this add to the text?

King Arthur is a mysterious figure, and his tale has a long and complex history. Writers from every age have constructed their own version of Arthur, tailored to suit the spirit of their times. But was there a real King Arthur? If so, exactly who was the historical figure behind the folk tale? How did the world-famous legend emerge? It is one of history's greatest unsolved riddles.

Almost everyone has heard of King Arthur. He was the ancient British king who pulled the sword from the stone. He consulted the magician Merlin, led the knights of the Round Table, married the beautiful Guinevere, and set an example of bravery and chivalry. According to British legend, though he is long dead, he lies somewhere in the hills, waiting for the moment when his countrymen need him most. Then he will awake and save them.

Is this history? Much of it certainly is not. The magical Merlin sounds **suspect**, and how could a sword possibly be embedded in a stone in the first place? That all sounds like **folklore**. But just because the story is folklore now does not necessarily mean that it did not have a historical seed. It is for that seed that **historians** and **archaeologists** have long been looking.

Key Vocabulary

endure *v.*, to continue or go on

historian *n.*, person who studies the past and interprets it

In Other Words

historical figure real person from the past
emerge come about
suspect hard to believe
folklore tales or beliefs shared by many people
archaeologists scientists who study past cultures

OBJECTIVES

Vocabulary
- Key Vocabulary T

Reading Strategy
- Make Inferences

Comprehension & Critical Thinking
- Make Inferences
- Use Text Evidence T

Literary Analysis
- Analyze Text Structures T
- Connect Across Texts

BUILD BACKGROUND

C King Arthur

Read the title, the introduction in the gray box, and the bolded introduction to the article.

ELL Rephrase Language
Explain:
- Many stories have been written about King Arthur.
- No one is sure if there was a real king named Arthur.
- Some people study old places, stories, and objects to find out if King Arthur was real.

D Connect Across Texts

Ask students to predict how people might feel if historians proved that King Arthur was real.

Possible response:
- *They might be more interested in reading the stories if they knew they were true.*

As students read, ask them to think about how the history supports what they read in the short story.

TEACH & PRACTICE

E Reading Support

1 Make Inferences Explain that the statue in the photo is more than 500 years old. Ask: How do the photo and caption add to the text?

Possible response:
- *It suggests King Arthur was real or that there must be some truth to the stories if there is a statue that is so old.*

RI.9-10.1; RI.9-10.5

Comprehension Coach

Build Reading Power

Assign students to use the software, based on their instructional needs.

Read Silently
- Comprehension questions with immediate feedback
- Glossary support
- Review text evidence

RL.9-10.10

Listen
- Professional model of fluent reading

Record
- Oral reading fluency practice
- Ongoing fluency assessment with immediate feedback

CCSS **Literacy.RL.9-10.10** By the end of grade 9, read and comprehend literature, including stories, dramas, and poems, in the grades 9–10 text complexity band proficiently, with scaffolding as needed at the high end of the range. By the end of grade 10, read and comprehend literature, including stories, dramas, and poems, at the high end of the grades 9–10 text complexity band independently and proficiently. **Literacy.RI.9-10.1** Cite strong and thorough textual evidence to support analysis of what the text says explicitly as well as inferences drawn from the text. **Literacy.RI.9-10.5** Analyze in detail how an author's ideas or claims are developed and refined by particular sentences, paragraphs, or larger portions of a text (e.g., a section or chapter).

OBJECTIVES

Comprehension & Critical Thinking
- Use Text Evidence Ⓣ
- Events in a Sequence

Viewing
- Respond to and Interpret Visuals

Grammar
- Past Tense of *Be: Was, Were* Ⓣ

Cultural Perspectives
- Compare Cultures

TEACH & PRACTICE

Ⓐ Analyze Visuals

About the Illustrations Read the title on p. 224, and show the illustrated time line on pp. 224–225.

Interpret and Respond Ask: Why might the time line be set up this way? What does it show?

Possible response:
- *It compares events in Britain and events in the rest of the world.*

Ⓑ Reading Support

Determine Sequence Read aloud the first four events and the caption at the top of the time line.

ELL Rephrase Language Point out the letter *c.* before the dates, and explain that it stands for the Latin word *circa,* which means "around" or "about." In the caption below the helmet, explain that "seventh century" refers to the years between 600 and 699.

Ask: About when was this helmet used?

Possible response:
- *sometime between 600 and 630*

Read the events and captions on the time line. Ask: What event on the time line happened first? When did it happen?

Possible response:
- *Tribes of Angles, Saxons, and Jutes invaded Britain around 390* C.E.

RI.9-10.5

British and World History Before 1100

Britain

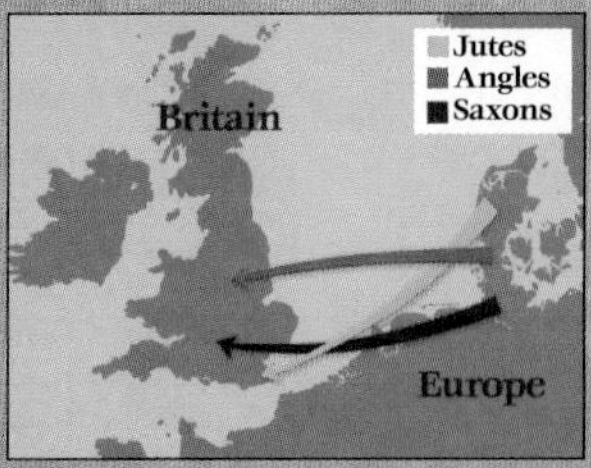

c. 390 C.E. (Common Era) Tribes of Angles, Saxons, and Jutes start to flood into Britain.

410 The Romans abandon Britain.

c. 500 Ambrosius, a Christian Roman-British leader, **makes a last stand** against an army of invading Saxons at the battle of Mount Badon.

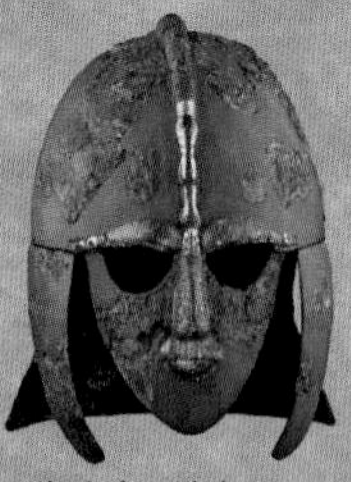

Anglo-Saxon helmet, Sutton Hoo, England, early seventh century

c. 547 The monk Gildas mentions Ambrosius in *The Overthrow of Britain.*

The World

c. 540 Buddhism reaches Japan.

Ethiopian monks **translate the Bible.**

Seated Buddha, Japan, Asuka Period, seventh century

Mosque, Baghdad, Iraq, Abbasid dynasty (749–1258)

570 Mohammed is born in Mecca.

c. 700 **Ancestors** of the Maori reach New Zealand.

Detail from an early twentieth-century Maori carving

711 Muslim **forces** cross the of Gibraltar and conquer

In Other Words

c. about (abbreviation used for estimated dates)
makes a last stand fights to defend his land
translate the Bible change the Bible from one language to another
Ancestors Family members from past generations
forces armies, soldiers

224 Unit 3 The Hero Within

GRAMMAR

Past Tense of *Be: Was, Were*

Teach/Model Display the transparency. Use the time line to review the present and past tense forms of *be.* Have students read the example sentences aloud. Then elicit more sentences using *was* and *were.*

Practice A. Have students read aloud the present tense sentence. Ask them to say the past tense form of the verb and then say each new sentence. **B.** After partners write their sentences about kings, have each student read aloud a sentence with the verb *was* or *were.*
L.9-10.1

Grammar & Writing Practice Book, pp. 73–74

Grammar Transparency 33

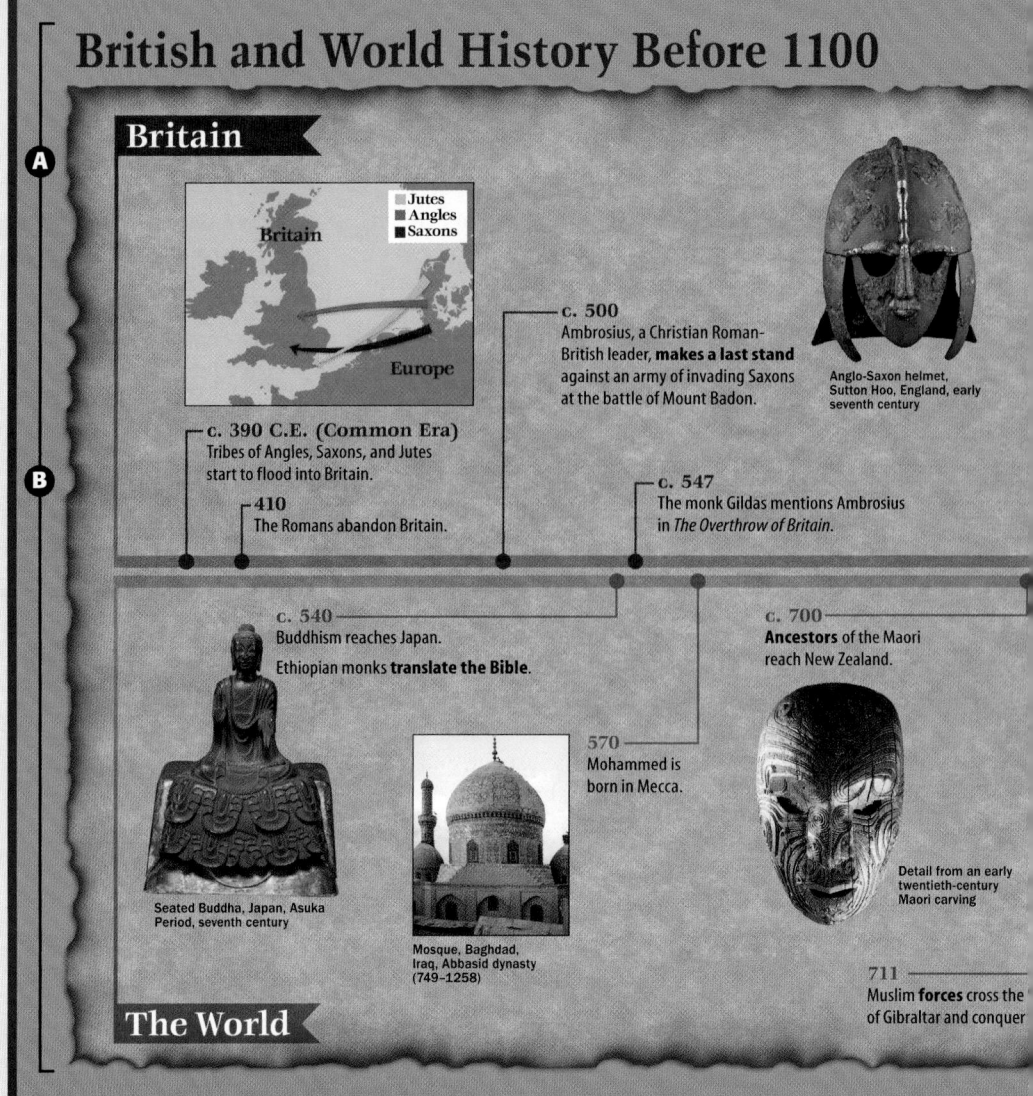

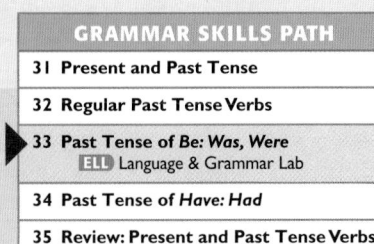

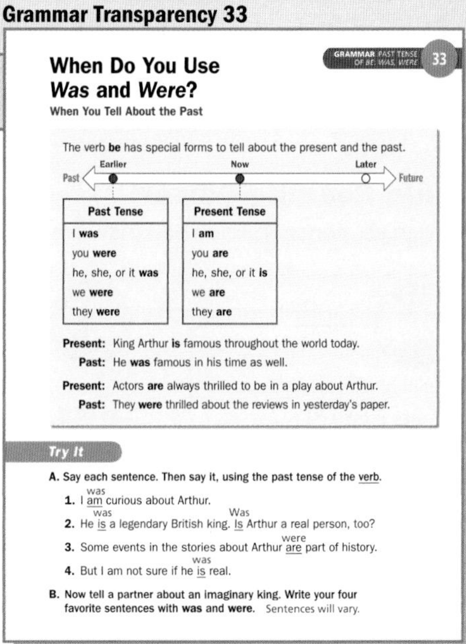

GRAMMAR PAST TENSE OF BE: WAS, WERE 33

When Do You Use *Was* and *Were?*
When You Tell About the Past

The verb **be** has special forms to tell about the present and the past.

Past — Earlier — Now — Later — Future

Past Tense	Present Tense
I **was**	I **am**
you **were**	you **are**
he, she, or it **was**	he, she, or it **is**
we **were**	we **are**
they **were**	they **are**

Present: King Arthur **is** famous throughout the world today.
Past: He **was** famous in his time as well.
Present: Actors **are** always thrilled to be in a play about Arthur.
Past: They **were** thrilled about the reviews in yesterday's paper.

Try It

A. Say each sentence. Then say it, using the past tense of the verb.
1. I am curious about Arthur. (was)
2. He is a legendary British king. Is Arthur a real person, too? (was, Was)
3. Some events in the stories about Arthur are part of history. (were)
4. But I am not sure if he is real. (was)

B. Now tell a partner about an imaginary king. Write your four favorite sentences with **was** and **were.** Sentences will vary.

GRAMMAR SKILLS PATH

- 31 Present and Past Tense
- 32 Regular Past Tense Verbs
- ▶ 33 Past Tense of *Be: Was, Were* — ELL Language & Grammar Lab
- 34 Past Tense of *Have: Had*
- 35 Review: Present and Past Tense Verbs

CCSS Literacy.RI.9-10.5 Analyze in detail how an author's ideas or claims are developed and refined by particular sentences, paragraphs, or larger portions of a text (e.g., a section or chapter). Literacy.L.9-10.1 Demonstrate command of the conventions of standard English grammar and usage when writing or speaking.

Portrait of Alfred the Great, 849–899

Norman coat of arms, c. 1066

c. 870 An army of Danes moving across England is defeated by Alfred the Great of Wessex.

Nennius names King Arthur as the hero of the Battle of Mt. Badon in his *History of the Britons.*

886 England is split between Danish **territory** to the east (the Danelaw), and Anglo-Saxon land to the west.

1013 King Swein of Denmark takes control of England. The Anglo-Saxon King Ethelred **flees** to Normandy.

1066 Normans from early France conquer Britain. The Norman Conquest leads to many changes in English language, culture, and government.

800 Charlemagne, king of the Franks, is crowned Holy Roman Emperor. His lands cover much of Europe.

873 Arab mathematicians invent the **concept** of zero.

1031 Christians begin to reconquer Spain.

1045 Printing with movable type is invented in China.

Charlemagne is crowned by Pope Leo III, December 25, 800.

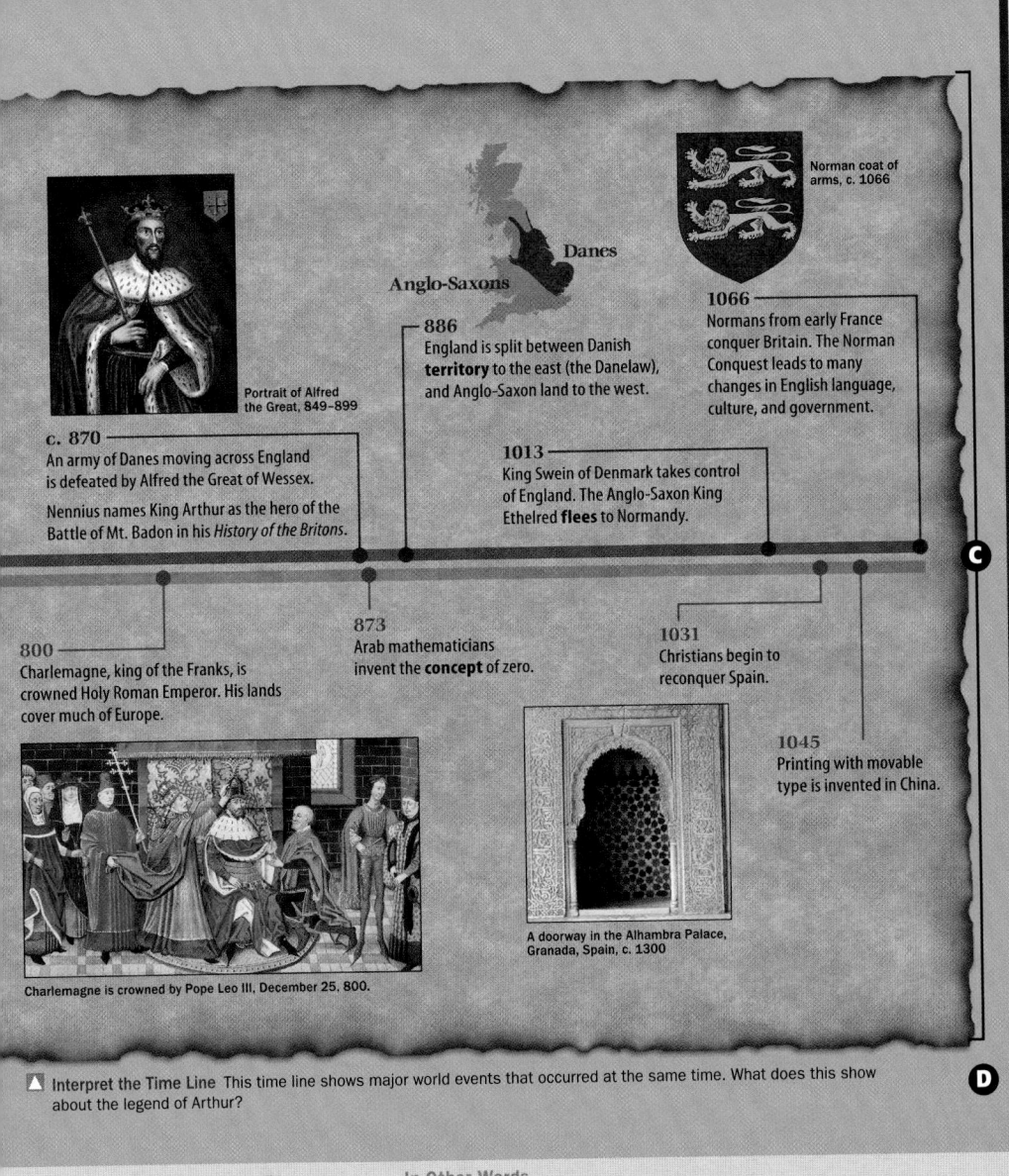

A doorway in the Alhambra Palace, Granada, Spain, c. 1300

C

D

▲ Interpret the Time Line This time line shows major world events that occurred at the same time. What does this show about the legend of Arthur?

In Other Words

concept idea or notion
territory land
flees escapes

TEACH & PRACTICE

C Reading Support

Determine Sequence Continue reading aloud the events and captions above and below the time line. Have students interpret the dates on the time line in conjunction with the related captions.

Ask: What is the last event that is shown on the time line? When did it happen?

Possible response:

- *Normans from France conquered Britain in 1066.*

RI.9-10.5

D Analyze Visuals

Interpret the Time Line Tell students to point to the date where Arthur is mentioned in the caption (870). Then have them look at the earlier caption that mentions Mount Badon. Ask: What does the time line show about the legend of Arthur?

Possible response:

- *Nennius says Arthur was the hero at the Battle of Mount Badon. Arthur may have been Ambrosius, or he may have been with Ambrosius.*

OUT-OF-SCHOOL LITERACY

MEDIA & TECHNOLOGY

Online Literacy

Connect the concept of legends to students' experiences with conducting Web searches and using online sources.

- What information do you get when you do a Web search on legends?
- How can you narrow your **investigation** to learn more about a specific legend?
- Were you a **skeptic** about the legend when you started your search? What about now?
- Did you find any **evidence** that the legend might be true? Explain.
- Describe the most useful source or site you found. Where did it come from? What made it useful?

As students answer, encourage the use of the highlighted Key Vocabulary.
SL.9-10.1.a

CCSS Literacy.RI.9-10.5 Analyze in detail how an author's ideas or claims are developed and refined by particular sentences, paragraphs, or larger portions of a text (e.g., a section or chapter). Literacy.SL.9-10.1.a Come to discussions prepared, having read and researched material under study; explicitly draw on that preparation by referring to evidence from texts and other research on the topic or issue to stimulate a thoughtful, well-reasoned exchange of ideas.

OBJECTIVES

Vocabulary
- Key Vocabulary T
- Content Area Vocabulary: History

Reading Strategy
- Make Inferences; Review Strategies

Comprehension & Critical Thinking
- Make Inferences
- Use Text Evidence T

Research Skill
- Gather and Use Information

Viewing
- Respond to and Interpret Visuals

TEACH & PRACTICE

A Reading Support

2 Make Inferences Have students reread the paragraph. Ask: How does the author feel about the evidence that Arthur Ambrosius and Arthur were the same person? What clues in the text show this?

Possible response:
- *The author is not sure. He ends the paragraph with a question instead of stating the information as fact.* RI.9-10.1

Review Strategies Have volunteers say what other strategies they used as they read the text.

Possible response:
- *I asked questions: After reading the first sentence, I asked: What written evidence can be found from so long ago? I read on and learned that there are historical books about that time.* RI.9-10.1

B Analyze Visuals

Interpret the Map Help students interpret the map in conjunction with the related text. Explain the legend at bottom right. Read each caption and tell students to point to the location it names on the map. Ask: What do the captions on the map show?

Possible response:
- *The captions show the places described in the article, where stories about Arthur and Ambrosius were mentioned.*

Where Is Arthur?

A A historian usually starts by looking for written **evidence**. The first mention of someone who might be Arthur is in a book called *The Overthrow of Britain* **compiled** by the British monk Saint Gildas (c. 516–570 C.E.). In this book, a British leader named Ambrosius slows the **advance** of the invading Angles and Saxons, who are later defeated at the Battle of Mount Badon in about 500 C.E. Gildas does not mention Arthur, nor say that Ambrosius fought at Badon. However, some historians have wondered if Ambrosius and Arthur are **one and the same**. This is historical evidence, but was it Arthur? 2

At the same time, **bards** in Wales and Brittany, in France, were entertaining their hosts with stories of a hero named Arthur. This one had a personality much like that of

2 Make Inferences How does the author feel about the evidence that Arthur and Ambrosius are the same person? How do you know?

B **Europe in the Early Middle Ages (c. 500–800 C.E.)**

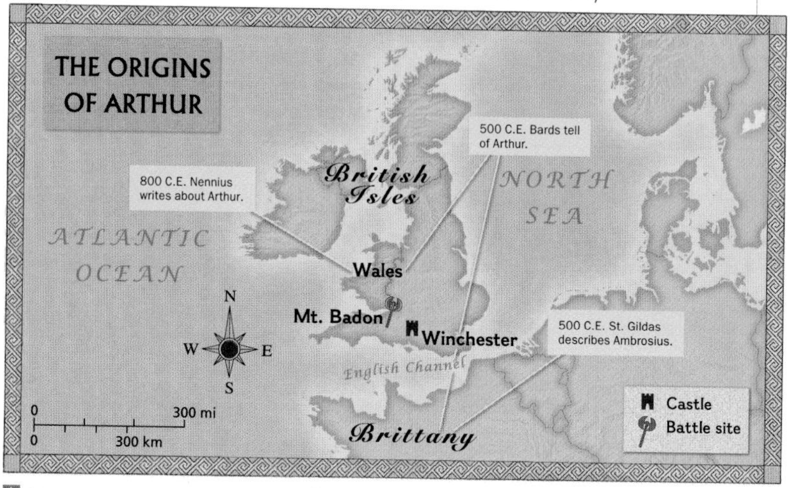

Interpret the Map What do the captions on the map show?

Key Vocabulary
- **evidence** *n.*, information that helps prove something

In Other Words
compiled put together from different sources
advance forward movement
one and the same the same person
bards storytellers from ancient times

CONTENT AREA CONNECTIONS

HISTORY

Research Early British History

Conduct Research Have students research the early history of Britain and use the information to answer the following questions:

- Who ruled Britain just before the time Arthur is supposed to have lived?
- What other groups were living in Britain at this time?
- Who were the Angles and Saxons, and where did they come from?
- Why were the Angles and Saxons able to defeat the rulers who were already in Britain?
- Describe the social class structure of early Britain.
- What was everyday life like?

Share and Compare Students can share their findings with the class to provide additional background information on the time that King Arthur supposedly lived and ruled.
W.9-10.7

CCSS **Literacy.RI.9-10.1** Cite strong and thorough textual evidence to support analysis of what the text says explicitly as well as inferences drawn from the text. **Literacy.W.9-10.7** Conduct short as well as more sustained research projects to answer a question (including a self-generated question) or solve a problem; narrow or broaden the inquiry when appropriate; synthesize multiple sources on the subject, demonstrating understanding of the subject under investigation.

the Arthur we know, and he **slew** monsters and wicked giants. Folk heroes are sometimes based on history. But was this Arthur real?

The next piece of written evidence comes from the early ninth century, when Arthur was named by the Welsh monk Nennius in his *History of the Britons*. According to Nennius, Arthur was a British war leader who fought a series of twelve battles against the Angles and Saxons, of which Badon was the last. The similarities with Ambrosius are unmistakable. 3 **C**

And that, together with poems and a few other writings of the same time, is all of the written evidence we have for King Arthur. All of the details—Lancelot, Guinevere, the sword in the stone, Camelot and the Round Table, Merlin the magician—appear only in literature. Much of it was written long after the Norman Conquest of 1066.

For hundreds of years after that, people were **content** to leave Arthur as a legend. Then, in the early twentieth century, some historians began to wonder. Could Arthur possibly be real after all? One popular view held by many scholars was that Arthur was actually a late-Roman **cavalry commander** who had led British forces against the invading Anglo-Saxons.

Archaeologists have also been looking around Britain for evidence of the real Arthur. One such **investigation** took place in 1976 in the city of Winchester in southern England. Hanging there, in the Great Hall of Winchester Castle, is an enormous round table-top. It is made of solid oak, is eighteen feet (5.4 meters) in diameter, weighs one-and-a-quarter tons (1,138 kilograms), and has places for twenty-five people marked on it. Many argued that it was the actual Round Table of legend. Historically, Winchester had become the capital of the Saxon kings of Wessex in the seventh century. Could the Saxons possibly have turned Arthur's capital into their own? 4 **D**

Unfortunately, the belief did not stand up to modern scientific investigation. **Tree-ring and radiocarbon dating**, plus a study

3 Make Inferences
What does this written evidence add to what you already know?

4 Make Inferences
How do the facts about the table support the inference that Arthur was real?

Monitor Comprehension

Explain
Why do some historians believe Arthur and Ambrosius are the same person?

Key Vocabulary
- **investigation** *n.*, careful search or study that looks for facts

In Other Words
slew killed
content happy, satisfied
cavalry commander leader of a group of soldiers riding on horses
Tree-ring and radiocarbon dating Scientific methods used to measure time

TEACH & PRACTICE

C Reading Support

3 Make Inferences Review the paragraph to find written evidence about Arthur's existence; also review the information from the first written evidence that was found.

ELL Word Parts Use word parts to define words that are essential to understanding:

- *similarities:* Point out the root word *similar* and provide synonyms: *the same, alike.* Explain that the suffix *-ities* makes it a plural noun. *Similarities* are things that are alike.
- *unmistakable:* Point out the root word *mistake* and provide synonyms: *error, something wrong.* Explain that the prefix *un-* means "not" and the suffix *-able* means "able." Something *unmistakable* cannot be wrong.

List the evidence. Ask: What does this add to what you know?

Possible response:
- *There are strong similarities between Ambrosius and Arthur.*

RI.9-10.1

D Reading Support

4 Make Inferences Have students clarify details.

Ask: Why did so many people believe this was the Round Table from the stories of Arthur's knights?

Possible responses:
- *I read that it was round with room for 25 people. It was located in what may have been Arthur's capital.*

RI.9-10.1

Monitor Comprehension

Explain Have students explain the evidence that Arthur and Ambrosius are the same person.

Possible responses:
- *At the time Ambrosius fought in the Battle of Mount Badon, bards were telling stories about Arthur.*
- *A description of Arthur in a ninth-century history book sounds like it's really describing Ambrosius.*

RI.9-10.2

VOCABULARY

HISTORY

Content Area Vocabulary: History

Build vocabulary related to the content area of history.

Teach/Model Use the Make Words Your Own routine (*see the Vocabulary tab*) and the sample sentences below to introduce these words from the selection.

overthrow (ō-vur-**thrō**) ▸ p. 226

When one group **overthrows** *another group, it takes control of something.*

invading (in-**vād**-ing) ▸ p. 226

An **invading** *army tries to take over the country it enters.*

defeated (di-**fēt**-ed) ▸ p. 226

If an army is **defeated**, *it loses a war or a battle.*

battles (**ba**-tilz) ▸ p. 227

When two armies have a **battle**, *they fight with each other.*

forces (**for**-siz) ▸ p. 227

Forces *is another word for a group of soldiers.*

Practice Have students use the words to describe a historic battle they have read about.

Apply Set up a TV news show scenario and have students role-play on-the-scene reporters who witness Arthur in battle against the Angles and Saxons.

L.9-10.6

CCSS **Literacy.RI.9-10.1** Cite strong and thorough textual evidence to support analysis of what the text says explicitly as well as inferences drawn from the text. **Literacy.RI.9-10.2** Determine a central idea of a text and analyze its development over the course of the text, including how it emerges and is shaped and refined by specific details; provide an objective summary of the text. **Literacy.L.9-10.6** Acquire and use accurately general academic and domain-specific words and phrases, sufficient for reading, writing, speaking, and listening at the college and career readiness level; demonstrate independence in gathering vocabulary knowledge when considering a word or phrase important to comprehension or expression.

OBJECTIVES

Vocabulary
- Key Vocabulary Ⓣ

Reading Strategy
- Make Inferences

Comprehension & Critical Thinking
- Make Inferences
- Use Text Evidence Ⓣ

Literary Analysis
- Analyze Text Structures Ⓣ

Research Skill
- Gather Information

Grammar
- Past Tense of *Have: Had* Ⓣ

TEACH & PRACTICE

A Reading Support

5 Text Structures Model how to analyze and evaluate information from text structures by helping students locate the signal words in the paragraph. Ask: What do those words tell you about how the author feels about Geoffrey of Monmouth's claim?

Possible response:
- *The words* although, but, unfortunately, *and* may have *signal that the author has doubts about Geoffrey's claim.*

RI.9-10.5

B Analyze Visuals

Interpret and Respond Have students look at the visual. Ask: What does this show?

Possible response:
- *the round table-top from Winchester Castle*

Then ask: How does the visual add to the information in the article?

Possible response:
- *It shows what archaeologists found and what the table in the legend might have looked like.*

of **medieval carpentry practices**, revealed that the table was actually constructed in the 1270s at the start of Edward I's **reign**. This was during a time when the king himself was taking a great interest in everything associated with Arthur. Experts now think that the table at Winchester was probably made to be used at the many knightly tournaments that Edward himself liked to hold.

Although no **genuine** Arthurian objects have ever been discovered, many possible Arthurian places have been investigated. Geoffrey of Monmouth, an author of the 1100s, said that Tintagel in Cornwall was Arthur's birthplace, and there is even a suitably ruined castle perched on a cliff there. But, unfortunately, the castle is no older than Geoffrey himself. Writers choose places as settings for their books for many different reasons. Geoffrey may have added the reference to Tintagel simply to please a rich local nobleman. 5 Ⓐ

In the 1960s, the search for Camelot heated up when archaeologists **excavated** an **Iron Age hill fort** at Cadbury Castle in southern England. Local legend held that Arthur and his knights lay sleeping under the hill. John Leland, a historian writing during King Henry VIII's reign, had stated that the local people often called the **fortified remains** "Camalat—King Arthur's palace."

Exhaustive excavations conducted by the archaeologist Leslie Alcock yielded evidence dating from about Arthur's time of a wall encircling an extensive hilltop

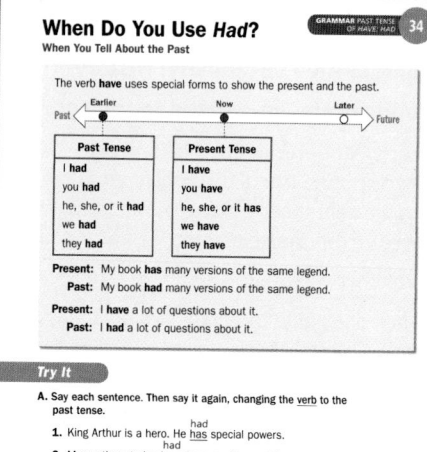

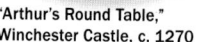

"Arthur's Round Table," Winchester Castle, c. 1270 Ⓑ

5 Text Structures Find the signal words in this paragraph. What do they tell you about how the author feels about Geoffrey of Monmouth's claim?

Key Vocabulary
genuine *adj.*, real, true

In Other Words
medieval carpentry practices ways carpenters worked in the Middle Ages
reign rule, time as king
excavated dug up
Iron Age hill fort fort built c. 1000 B.C.E.
fortified remains ruins

GRAMMAR

Past Tense of *Have: Had*

Teach/Model Display the transparency. Use the time line and chart to review the present tense forms of the verb *have* and introduce the past tense forms. Then read the example sentences aloud, and elicit more sentences using the verb *had*.

Practice A. Have students read each present tense sentence, change the verb to the past tense, and then say the new sentence. **B.** After students write their own sentences about modern heroes, have each student read aloud a sentence with the verb *had*. L.9-10.1

Grammar & Writing Practice Book, pp. 75–76

GRAMMAR SKILLS PATH

Grammar Transparency 34

When Do You Use *Had*?
When You Tell About the Past

GRAMMAR PAST TENSE OF *HAVE: HAD* 34

The verb **have** uses special forms to show the present and the past.

Past ← Earlier — Now — Later → Future

Past Tense	Present Tense
I **had**	I **have**
you **had**	you **have**
he, she, or it **had**	he, she, or it **has**
we **had**	we **have**
they **had**	they **have**

Present: My book **has** many versions of the same legend.
Past: My book **had** many versions of the same legend.
Present: I **have** a lot of questions about it.
Past: I **had** a lot of questions about it.

Try It

A. Say each sentence. Then say it again, changing the verb to the past tense.
1. King Arthur is a hero. He has (had) special powers.
2. Many other stories have (had) heroes with special powers, too.
3. Some legends have (had) descriptions of real events.
4. But often the events have (had) a twist.
5. That's when the hero has (had) a surprise for us.

B. Now write about a movie hero such as Superman, Spiderman, or Supergirl. Use **had** in four sentences. Sentences will vary.

CCSS **Literacy.RI.9-10.5** Analyze in detail how an author's ideas or claims are developed and refined by particular sentences, paragraphs, or larger portions of a text (e.g., a section or chapter). **Literacy.L.9-10.1** Demonstrate command of the conventions of standard English grammar and usage when writing or speaking.

Local legends held that Arthur and his knights lay sleeping under the hill at Cadbury Castle (left). Geoffrey of Monmouth claimed that Tintagel Castle (right) was Arthur's birthplace.

compound. At its center was a large aisled hall. Some see the remains of a stout defensive wall around a great feasting hall such as might befit a king named Arthur. But **skeptics** see only a moderately sized barn surrounded by walls barely able to contain horses and cattle, let alone keep determined enemies away.

So King Arthur remains a mystery. Though archaeologists can find no evidence for Arthur, this fact alone does not disprove his existence. Archaeologists are the first to explain that lack of proof is not a convincing argument against the existence of a person, place, or event. All it takes is one small piece of evidence—one small "voice"—to overcome the **accumulated** weight of silence. Such a discovery may well lie in the future. 6

6 Make Inferences
Do you think the author believes that we will find proof of Arthur? What parts of the text give you clues?

Monitor Comprehension

Explain What did the researchers at Cadbury Castle find? Explain their different ideas about the find.

Key Vocabulary

skeptic *n.*, person who doubts facts and beliefs that are generally accepted by others

In Other Words

compound group of buildings in an enclosed space
accumulated piled up

TEACH & PRACTICE

C Reading Support

6 Make Inferences Review the first full paragraph to look for clues to the author's opinion.

Ask: Do you think the author believes we will find proof of Arthur? What words in the text give you clues about that?

Possible responses:

- *The author believes it's possible that someone may make a discovery in the future. He says that even one small discovery about Arthur could convince people that he existed.*

RI.9-10.1

Monitor Comprehension

Explain Have students reread the section about the discovery at Cadbury Castle.

ELL Use Graphic Organizer Use a graphic organizer to display information about the find at Cadbury Castle. For example:

Evidence	Some Believe ...	Others Believe ...
a wall	It is strong enough to keep enemies out.	It is not strong enough to keep cows in.

Ask: What were the different ideas about the discovery of a wall at Cadbury Castle?

Possible response:

- *Researchers found a wall. Some people thought a hall at the center of the wall could have been a fort that was strong enough to keep enemies out, but others thought it wasn't even strong enough to keep cows in.*

RI.9-10.1; RI.9-10.2

CONTENT AREA CONNECTIONS

Research Geography of Britain

GEOGRAPHY

Conduct Research Have students research the geography of Britain in the early Middle Ages and use the information to answer the following questions:

- What was the country called at that time?
- How was the land divided?
- Were there any large cities? If so, where were they and what were their names?
- About how far apart were the largest towns/cities?
- What inferences can you make based on the geography of the country? Would it be easy to invade? Why?

Share and Compare Students can share their findings with the class and compare the information they found.
W.9-10.7

CCSS **Literacy.RI.9-10.1** Cite strong and thorough textual evidence to support analysis of what the text says explicitly as well as inferences drawn from the text. **Literacy.RI.9-10.2** Determine a central idea of a text and analyze its development over the course of the text, including how it emerges and is shaped and refined by specific details; provide an objective summary of the text. **Literacy.W.9-10.7** Conduct short as well as more sustained research projects to answer a question (including a self-generated question) or solve a problem; narrow or broaden the inquiry when appropriate; synthesize multiple sources on the subject, demonstrating understanding of the subject under investigation.

READ

OBJECTIVES

Reading Strategy
- Make Inferences

Comprehension & Critical Thinking
- Make Inferences
- Use Text Evidence Ⓣ

Literary Analysis
- Analyze Text Structures Ⓣ

Writing
- Response to Literature

TEACH & PRACTICE

Ⓐ Reading Support

7 Text Structures Review to find reasons the author feels we want to believe the legend of King Arthur is true.

Possible responses:
- *The story of Arthur has action, mystery, and romance.*
- *Other cultures have similar stories.*
- *Signal words are* one *and* and.

RI.9-10.5

APPLY

Ⓑ ANALYZE

1. **Recall and Interpret** Historians study old stories, structures, and books that may contain clues about whether Arthur was real.
   RI.9-10.1
2. **Vocabulary** Was he real? Did he pull the sword from the stone?
   L.9-10.6
3. **Analyze Text Structures** The author uses description, sequence, compare and contrast, and some cause-and-effect structures. Questions and signal words to indicate each type of structure.
   RI.9-10.5
4. **Focus Strategy: Make Inferences** Possible answer: Yes. He gives examples of texts that mention Arthur and describes places Arthur might have lived.
   RI.9-10.1

Ⓒ Return to the Text

After rereading the selection, students can note which statements in the selection match their own opinion about Arthur.

W.9-10.9.b; W.9-10.10

Why Do We Need Arthur?

Ⓐ But there is another Arthurian mystery. Why is it that we so much want King Arthur to be real? Why do historians and archaeologists continue this search? One of the great attractions of the Arthur story is that it contains something for everyone—action, mystery, romance, the struggle between good and evil. And the tales **have a ring of truth** because some have their roots in genuine ancient traditions.

And the idea of a once and future king, sleeping somewhere, awaiting his time to return, is not **unique to** the Arthur story. In Denmark, the knight Holger Danske sleeps. In Spain it is El Cid. In Germany it is Frederick Barbarossa. Arthur **embodies** real human needs and desires. We *want* him to be real. 7 ❖

7 Text Structures List three reasons the author feels we need Arthur. What signal word or phrase introduces each one?

ANALYZE Was There a Real King Arthur?

Ⓑ
1. **Recall and Interpret** According to the article, what kinds of **evidence** do **historians** study in the search for Arthur? What makes this evidence important?
2. **Vocabulary** What questions about King Arthur have **endured** over the centuries?
3. **Analyze Text Structures** With a partner, review the text and look for signal words that the author uses. What structure does the author use? How do you know?
4. **Focus Strategy Make Inferences** Does the author believe that King Arthur was real? Work with a partner to find details in the text to support your inference.

Ⓒ **Return to the Text**

Reread and Write Which information in the selection gives the most convincing evidence about a real King Arthur? Review that section and write a paragraph to explain why the evidence supports the belief that Arthur was real.

In Other Words

have a ring of truth sound like they might be true
unique to found only in
embodies represents, stands for

Interactive Reading

Have students reread and mark "Was There a Real King Arthur?" within the Edge Interactive Practice Book to apply their knowledge of text structures and to practice the Focus Strategy—Make Inferences.

Edge Interactive Practice Book, pp. 103–110

Unit Project

Progress Check Allow time for students to work on their unit projects. Meet with individuals and/or groups to provide guidance and check on their progress.

myNGconnect.com
- **Unit Planning Tools**
- **Unit Project Evaluation Rubric**

CCSS **Literacy.RI.9-10.1** Cite strong and thorough textual evidence to support analysis of what the text says explicitly as well as inferences drawn from the text. **Literacy.RI.9-10.5** Analyze in detail how an author's ideas or claims are developed and refined by particular sentences, paragraphs, or larger portions of a text (e.g., a section or chapter). **Literacy.W.9-10.9.b** Apply grades 9-10 Reading standards to literary nonfiction (e.g., "Delineate and evaluate the argument and specific claims in a text, assessing whether the reasoning is valid and the evidence is relevant and sufficient; identify false statements and fallacious reasoning"). **Literacy.W.9-10.10** Write routinely over extended time frames (time for research, reflection, and revision) and shorter time frames (a single sitting or a day or two) for a range of tasks, purposes, and audiences. **Literacy.L.9-10.6** Acquire and use accurately general academic and domain-specific words and phrases, sufficient for reading, writing, speaking, and listening at the college and career readiness level; demonstrate independence in gathering vocabulary knowledge when considering a word or phrase important to comprehension or expression.

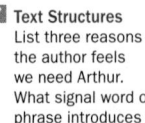

REFLECT AND ASSESS

▶ The Sword in the Stone
▶ Was There a Real King Arthur?

EQ What Makes a Hero?

Reading

Critical Thinking

1. **Analyze** Reread the **Quickwrite** you wrote about the quotation on page 208. How did the selection affect your thinking? Explain.
2. **Compare** How might a modern news story show a hero such as King Arthur differently than a legend from the Middle Ages?
3. **Interpret** According to Robert Stewart, "Arthur embodies real human needs and desires." Explain how Arthur's story influences the stories of other real heroes who have come after him.
4. **Speculate** Imagine that someone discovers **genuine** evidence proving that Arthur was a real person. Would this make people more or less interested in reading legends such as "The Sword in the Stone"? Explain.
5. **Draw Conclusions** Author Robert Stewart concludes his article by asking why we need heroes like Arthur to be real. What conclusions can you draw about whether *you* need heroes to be real?

Writing

Write About Literature

Interpretive Response Think about King Arthur's heroic qualities. Find specific examples from both texts that show these qualities. Then answer this question: What makes King Arthur such an appealing hero? Give evidence and embed quotations in your response.

Vocabulary

Key Vocabulary Review

Oral Review Work with a partner. Use these words to complete the paragraph.

conscientiously	**genuine**	**just**
endured	**historians**	**skeptics**
evidence	**investigations**	

The legend of King Arthur has __(1)__ over time because Arthur represents the qualities of a true hero. He is a __(2)__ and fair ruler who respects all of his people. Scientists and __(3)__ who study the past have begun many __(4)__ to see whether the legend is true. They look carefully and __(5)__ for any __(6)__ that would prove that Arthur was a real person. On the other hand, doubting __(7)__ do not believe that a __(8)__ object that proves Arthur's existence will ever be discovered.

Writing Application Think about a puzzle or problem you solved by making inferences. Write a paragraph about your experience. Use at least two Key Vocabulary words.

Fluency

Read with Ease: Phrasing

Assess your reading fluency with the passage in the Reading Handbook, p. 757. Then complete the self-check below.

1. I did/did not pause appropriately for punctuation and phrases.
2. My words correct per minute: _____

Lesson 6

REFLECT AND ASSESS

OBJECTIVES

Vocabulary
- Key Vocabulary Ⓣ

Reading Fluency
- Phrasing Ⓣ

Comprehension & Critical Thinking
- Compare Across Texts
- Use Text Evidence Ⓣ

Literary Analysis
- Evaluate Literature

Writing
- Form: Opinion Statement
- Form: Paragraph

Reading

Critical Thinking

1. **Analyze** Model looking through the selection to find examples of how it affected your thinking. Have students complete the activity and defend their answers. RL.9-10.1; RI.9-10.1
2. **Compare** A modern news story might show a hero as an everyday person instead of someone chosen by the will of God.
3. **Interpret** Arthur serves as a role model for heroes because he is strong and brave but seeks advice and help from others. He is also a just and caring leader. RL.9-10.1
4. **Speculate** People may become more interested in reading the tales about Arthur in order to compare them to what really happened. RL.9-10.10
5. **Draw Conclusions** Students may say that they need heroes to be real so they can have them as positive role models.

Writing

Write About Literature

Edge Interactive Practice Book, p. 111

Interpretive Response Have students use a graphic organizer to plan and write their response. Help them embed relevant quotations from the text as support within the response. Invite volunteers to share their responses. W.9-10.1

Vocabulary

Key Vocabulary Review

1. *endured* **2.** *just* **3.** *historians*
4. *investigations* **5.** *conscientiously*
6. *evidence* **7.** *skeptics* **8.** *genuine*
L.9-10.6

Fluency

Read with Ease: Phrasing

Ensure that students complete the self-check. RL.9-10.10

ASSESS & RETEACH

Assessments Handbook, pp. 29b–29e

Have students complete the **Reader Reflection**. Then give students the **Cluster Test** to measure their progress. Group students as needed for reteaching.

CCSS **Literacy.RL.9-10.1** Cite strong and thorough textual evidence to support analysis of what the text says explicitly as well as inferences drawn from the text. **Literacy.RL.9-10.10** By the end of grade 9, read and comprehend literature, including stories, dramas, and poems, in the grades 9-10 text complexity band proficiently, with scaffolding as needed at the high end of the range. By the end of grade 10, read and comprehend literature, including stories, dramas, and poems, at the high end of the grades 9-10 text complexity band independently and proficiently. **Literacy.RI.9-10.1** Cite strong and thorough textual evidence to support analysis of what the text says explicitly as well as inferences drawn from the text. **Literacy.W.9-10.1** Write arguments to support claims in an analysis of substantive topics or texts, using valid reasoning and relevant and sufficient evidence. **Literacy.L.9-10.6** Acquire and use accurately general academic and domain-specific words and phrases, sufficient for reading, writing, speaking, and listening at the college and career readiness level; demonstrate independence in gathering vocabulary knowledge when considering a word or phrase important to comprehension or expression.

Lesson 7

INTEGRATE THE LANGUAGE ARTS

OBJECTIVES

Language Function
- Ask for and Give Information T

Literary Analysis
- Compare Characters' Motives and Traits

Grammar
- Present and Past Tense Verbs T

Grammar

Use Verb Tenses

Grammar Transparency 35

Review Use the transparency to review. Then conduct the activity on p. 232.

Oral Practice Make sure students use past tense verbs and parallelism.

Written Practice *was, excavate, studied, argued, had*
L.9-10.1.a

Language Development

Ask for and Give Information

Evaluate students' acquisition of this language function with the Language Acquisition Rubric.

Assessments Handbook, p. 29o
SL.9-10.1.a

Literary Analysis

Compare Characters' Motives and Traits

Character	Arthur
Actions	He listened to his people.
Dialogue	"I swear to serve God and my people, to put right any wrongs, and to bring peace to the land."
Motives	He wanted everyone to respect the rights of others.
Traits	conscientious, just, fair

RL.9-10.3

Edge Interactive Practice Book, p. 112

INTEGRATE THE LANGUAGE ARTS

Grammar

Use Verb Tenses

Use the **present tense** to talk about an action that happens now or happens often. Use the **past tense** to talk about an action that already happened. If you use two or more verbs in the same sentence, they must all be in the same tense.

- **Present:** Archaeologists **search** for artifacts, **uncover** evidence, and **draw** conclusions.

  Past: In the 1960s, they **searched** for Camelot, **excavated** a hill, and **found** a hall.

The verbs **be** and **have** are irregular. They have special forms to show the past tense.

- **Present:** The story of Ambrosius **is** exciting.

  Past: Ambrosius **was** a real commander.

- **Present:** People **have** many ideas about Arthur.

  Past: In the legend, King Arthur **had** a palace.

In a list, all the verbs must be in the same tense.

Past: Arthur **ruled** fairly and **was** a just king.

Oral Practice (1–5) Tell a partner about a hero in history. Use at least five past tense verbs, with three in one sentence.

Written Practice (6–10) Rewrite the paragraph. Correct the underlined verbs to reflect parallel structure.

Arthur <u>is</u> an ancient British king. Today, scientists still search for sites, <u>excavated</u> hills, and uncover ruins. In 1976, a group <u>study</u> a round table, found places for 25 people, and <u>argue</u> that it was Arthur's. But even then, other scientists <u>have</u> their doubts.

Language Development

Ask for and Give Information

Pair Talk Ask a partner questions about King Arthur. For example, *Why do people want King Arthur to be real?* Give information to support your answer.

Literary Analysis

Compare Character's Motives and Traits

Just as there are many ways to get to know someone new, there are many ways to get to know a character in a story. These include:

- **actions:** what the character does
- **dialogue:** what the character says
- **motives:** why the character says and does certain things
- **traits:** how you describe the character and what makes him or her unique.

Study how Kay's motives and traits are shown in "The Sword in the Stone":

Character Chart

Character	Kay
Actions	He takes the sword from Arthur and pretends that he got it from the stone.
Dialogue	"I have the sword from the stone. Therefore I must be King of England."
Motives	He wants to be king, even if he must lie to do it.
Traits	ambitious, dishonest

Talk with a partner about Kay. How does his motivation affect what he does next? What are the consequences of his actions? As you read on, see if your understanding of the character changes.

Then create **Character Charts** for Arthur, Sir Ector, and the nobles in the story. Compare the characters from the text and discuss how their motivations affect what will happen in the story.

GRAMMAR

Review: Present and Past Tense Verbs

Teach/Model Display the transparency. Review regular past tense verbs and parallel structure. Use the examples to review spelling changes and forms of *be* and *have*.

A. Oral Practice In the first sentence, point out the clue that indicates the sentence requires the past tense form of the verb (*in the past*). Have students complete the remaining sentences.

B. Written Practice Work through the example. Explain that some sentences have no errors. Have the group tell you how to edit the paragraph. Ask a volunteer to read the corrected paragraph aloud.
L.9-10.1.a

Grammar & Writing Practice Book, pp. 77–78

Grammar Transparency 35

Use Verb Tenses

GRAMMAR REVIEW: PRESENT AND PAST TENSE VERBS 35

Remember: You have to change the verb to show the past tense. Be sure to use the same tense for all verbs in the same sentence.

Add **-ed** to most verbs. You may need to make a spelling change before you add **-ed**.

Present Tense	Past Tense
talk, talks	talked
act, acts	acted
plan, plans	planned
bake, bakes	baked

Use special forms for the past tense of **be** and **have**.

Forms of *Be*	
Present Tense	**Past Tense**
am, is, are	was, were

Forms of *Have*	
Present Tense	**Past Tense**
have, has	had

Try It

A. Say each sentence with the correct form of the verb.

1. In the past, heroes **(have / <u>had</u>)** and **(obey / <u>obeyed</u>)** a code of honor.
2. The heroes of long ago **(act / <u>acted</u>)** fairly toward others.
3. Heroes today **(<u>are</u> / were)** similar to the heroes of the past.

B. Edit the paragraph. Fix five mistakes. The first is done for you.

Yesterday, the newspaper had a story about a hero. The train ~~were~~ was almost in the station. A teenager ~~slips~~ slipped and ~~droped~~ dropped to the tracks. Just in time, a man ~~arriveed~~ arrived at the scene and ~~pulls~~ pulled the teenager up. The newspaper praised the man for his bravery.

GRAMMAR SKILLS PATH

CCSS **Literacy.RL.9-10.3** Analyze how complex characters (e.g., those with multiple or conflicting motivations) develop over the course of a text, interact with other characters, and advance the plot or develop the theme. **Literacy.SL.9-10.1.a** Come to discussions prepared, having read and researched material under study; explicitly draw on that preparation by referring to evidence from texts and other research on the topic or issue to stimulate a thoughtful, well-reasoned exchange of ideas. **Literacy.L.9-10.1.a** Use parallel structure.

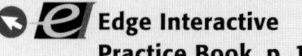

Vocabulary Study

Word Families

Word families are similar word forms related by meaning. While you read, a word may seem unfamiliar. But take a closer look. Sometimes, knowing the meaning of another member of a word family can help you understand the unfamiliar word.

endure	→	endurance
to endure or last for a long time		the ability to endure or last for a long time

The word *skeptical* is related to a Key Vocabulary word from this unit. What do you think the word means, based on what you already know? Check the meaning in a dictionary.

Media Study

Compare Visuals

Arthur Art Gallery Collect and display Arthurian images from books, magazines, and Web sites.

1. **Focus Your Search** Find two pieces of art that show an event or a character from the legend.
2. **Write Captions** Identify the images by title, artist, date created, and medium, such as painting or cartoon.
3. **Compare** Share the art that you found. Then compare how the different artists, times, or media affect how the art is presented.

Language and Learning Handbook, page 702

Writing Handbook, page 784

Writing on Demand

Write a Test Essay

An essay test may ask you to write a short response to a specific prompt.

1. **Unpack the Prompt** Underline key words that show what your response should include.

> **Writing Prompt**
> What makes a hero? In a short response, define the archetype of the hero. Then describe a character in traditional literature (such as the legend *Left Behind* from the Edge Library) whose heroic traits meet your definition.

2. **Plan Your Response** Choose a hero from traditional literature to write about. Then use a planning chart to organize your ideas in a clear way.

Hero	Ch'idzigyaak in *Left Behind*
Traits	courage and strength
Examples	She was brave in the face of certain death. Her determination helped her to survive.

3. **Draft** Organize your short response like this. Include specific ideas from your chart.

Short Response Organizer

To me, a hero is someone who is [name the traits here]. One person who is heroic is [hero's name]. He/She is [describe the hero].

[Your hero] is heroic because he/she is [give trait]. For example, [give an example of trait]. Another example of [your hero's] heroic traits is [give trait]. This was very important when [give examples of trait].

In conclusion, [restate the main idea of how the person fits your idea of a hero.]

4. **Check Your Work** Reread your response. Ask:
   - Do I address the writing prompt?
   - Do I give examples to support my ideas?
   - Do I use the correct past tense verbs?

Writing Handbook, page 784

Lesson 8

INTEGRATE THE LANGUAGE ARTS

OBJECTIVES

Vocabulary
- Word Families Ⓣ

Media
- Compare Across Media

Writing
- Writing Process
- Form: Test Essay Ⓣ

Vocabulary Study

Word Families

skeptical: doubtful about beliefs generally accepted by others

Edge Interactive Practice Book, p. 113

L.9-10.4.b; L.9-10.4.d

Media Study

Compare Visuals

Arthur Art Gallery Students should locate and write captions for two pieces of art that display Arthurian images. Then have partners use two sentences to compare their art.

See **Language and Learning Handbook** p. 702 and **Writing Handbook** p. 784 for further instruction.

W.9-10.7

Writing on Demand

Write a Test Essay

1. **Unpack the Prompt** Help students identify the Key Words: short response, define, archetype hero, character, traditional literature, heroic traits.
2. **Plan Your Response** Model the completion of a planning chart.
3. **Draft** Have students use the essay organizer as a model for writing test responses.
4. **Check Your Work** Have students read their essays to a partner and answer the questions together.
5. **Evaluate Your Work** Have students self-evaluate their essays using the Writing Rubric.

See **Writing Handbook** p. 784 for further instruction.

W.9-10.1

Writing Rubric — **Test Essay**

Exceptional	• Test response addresses topic by clearly naming a hero. • Examples are detailed and relevant to topic. • Past tense verbs are used correctly.
Competent	• Test response pertains to topic. • Examples are adequate. • Past tense verbs are correct with no more than one error.
Developing	• Test response may stray from topic. • Examples are loosely connected to topic. • Past tense verbs are sometimes incorrect.
Beginning	• Test response does not address topic. • Examples are not clearly connected to topic. • Past tense verbs are often incorrect.

CCSS **Literacy.W.9-10.1** Write arguments to support claims in an analysis of substantive topics or texts, using valid reasoning and relevant and sufficient evidence. **Literacy.W.9-10.7** Conduct short as well as more sustained research projects to answer a question (including a self-generated question) or solve a problem; narrow or broaden the inquiry when appropriate; synthesize multiple sources on the subject, demonstrating understanding of the subject under investigation. **Literacy.L.9-10.4.b** Identify and correctly use patterns of word changes that indicate different meanings or parts of speech (e.g., analyze, analysis, analytical; advocate, advocacy). **Literacy.L.9-10.4.d** Verify the preliminary determination of the meaning of a word or phrase (e.g., by checking the inferred meaning in context or in a dictionary).

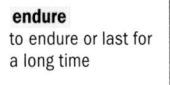

Lesson 9

WORKPLACE WORKSHOP

OBJECTIVES

Vocabulary

- Content Area Vocabulary: Airport Industry

Career Exploration

- Explore the Job Market

ENGAGE & CONNECT

A Activate Prior Knowledge

Introduce Invite students to share their knowledge about airports. Then read the introduction.

TEACH & PRACTICE

B Jobs in the Airport Industry

Use the Chart Lead a discussion comparing different jobs in the airport industry. Discuss which job would be best for a person with these interests:

- organizing traffic flow of airplanes
- ensuring safety of airline passengers
- helping airline customers with tickets, baggage, and questions

C Explore the Job Market

Generate Ideas Brainstorm with students additional jobs in the airport industry. Ask what job involves:

- serving people on an airplane
- flying an airplane
- transporting luggage for passengers

List student responses on a chart.

Research Skills Show students how to use a search engine to locate the individual Web sites for the airlines. Model how to navigate the career section of one of the sites. Then have students analyze the structure and format of the two Web sites. Ask them to compare and contrast any instructional text on the sites.
W.9-10.7

ONGOING ASSESSMENT
Ask students to share and compare the information they acquired about jobs in the airline industry.

Workplace Workshop

1

2

3

Inside an Airport

A Each year, millions of people pass through airports on business trips and vacations. Hundreds of people work inside an airport to help these travelers reach their destinations safely.

Jobs in the Airport Industry

B Most jobs in an airport require workers to have a high school diploma. Jobs that involve the safety of airline passengers also require on-the-job training and the completion of off-site classes and certification programs.

Job	Responsibilities	Education/Training Required
Ticket Agent 1	• Accepts tickets from passengers • Checks in passengers and baggage • Makes seat assignments • Answers customers' questions	• High school diploma • Company training programs and on-the-job training
Airport Security Screener 2	• Screens passengers, baggage, and cargo for dangerous or illegal objects using special equipment • Performs physical searches of passengers, baggage, and cargo	• High school diploma • Certification exam • On-the-job and off-site training
Air Traffic Controller 3	• Organizes flow of aircraft into and out of airport • Informs pilots of changes in weather conditions • Coordinates movement of air traffic to make sure planes stay a safe distance apart	• Pre-employment test • Three years of full-time work experience *or* • College degree • Twelve-week training program and two to four years of on-the-job training

Explore the Job Market

C Find out what other jobs are available in the airport industry.

1. Visit the Web site of a major U.S. airline. Click the "Careers" link. Check for information about careers available at that airline, other than those listed above.
2. Create a chart listing three or four available jobs. Include job description, responsibilities, and necessary qualifications. Share the chart with your classmates. Discuss which career you think is most interesting and why. Save the information in a professional career portfolio.

myNGconnect.com

- **Learn more about careers in the airport industry.**
- **Download a form to evaluate whether you would like to work in this field.**

Language and Learning Handbook, page 702

VOCABULARY

Content Area Vocabulary: Airport Industry

Build vocabulary related to the content area of the airport industry.

Teach/Model Use the Make Words Your Own routine (*see the Vocabulary tab*) and the sample sentences below to introduce these words from the workshop.

screen (skrēn)

Airport security employees **screen** *and check passengers and luggage.*

cargo (**kar**-gō)

The items carried in an airplane are called the **cargo**.

pilot (**pī**-lut)

A **pilot** *is a person qualified and licensed to fly an aircraft.*

controller (kun-**trō**-lur)

An air traffic **controller** *organizes and directs aircraft traffic in the air and on the ground.*

Practice Have students use the words to describe an experience they have had or might have when visiting an airport.

Apply Create an airport scenario and have students work in teams of four to role-play various jobs. Ask students to take turns as a pilot, screener, controller, and cargo customer service agent.
L.9-10.6

CCSS **Literacy.W.9-10.7** Conduct short as well as more sustained research projects to answer a question (including a self-generated question) or solve a problem; narrow or broaden the inquiry when appropriate; synthesize multiple sources on the subject, demonstrating understanding of the subject under investigation. **Literacy.L.9-10.6** Acquire and use accurately general academic and domain-specific words and phrases, sufficient for reading, writing, speaking, and listening at the college and career readiness level; demonstrate independence in gathering vocabulary knowledge when considering a word or phrase important to comprehension or expression.

Find Familiar Words

You probably know more words than you think. Even if you see a word you do not know, you have most likely seen part of the word before. **Word families** are words that share the same root word. For example, you may not know the word *dishonor.* However, you probably know the root word *honor.* You can then use your knowledge of prefixes and suffixes to get an idea of the word's meaning. The prefix *dis-* = *not or opposite*, so *dishonor* = *the loss of honor.*

Sometimes the root word has a slightly different spelling when a suffix is added. For example, *depth* = dee~~p~~ + pth. Usually, though, the spelling is close enough to recognize the root.

A

Use Word Families to Find Meaning

Work with another student to find familiar parts of words to figure out their meanings.

1. Copy the chart to the right onto a piece of paper.
2. Discuss what each word in the *honor* word family may mean.
3. Look up each word in the dictionary.
4. Think of other words in the *honor* word family and add them to the chart.

B

Words in the **Honor** Family	
honorable	honorary
dishonor	dishonorably

Put the Strategy to Use

When you come to a word you don't know, use this strategy to figure out its meaning:

1. Look for a root word.
2. Identify the other part or parts of the word.
3. Figure out how the part you know fits with the other part or parts.
4. Take a guess at the word's meaning.

TRY IT▸ Explore the words *untruthful* and *director.* Use a chart like the one below to define the word, determine the word family, and add additional words from the family. Look at the example for the word *dishonor.*

C

Word	Definition	Word Family	Additional Words
dishonor	the loss of honor	honor	honorable, honorary

▸ **Reading Handbook, page 733**

DIFFERENTIATED INSTRUCTION

Additional Vocabulary Practice
Use these strategies to help students practice structural analysis.

Struggling Readers

Use Word Families Make a list of the words in the *agree* family, such as *disagree*, *agreeable*, and *agreement*. Explain that the word *agree* can change meaning when you add *dis-*, *-able*, and *-ment* to it. For example, the prefix *dis-* means "not." The word *disagree* means "to fail to agree." Work with students to figure out the meaning of the other words in the *agree* family.

English Language Learners ELL

Understand Word Families List words in the *respect* family: *disrespect*, *respectful*, and *respectable*. Help students identify the root word and the prefix or suffix. Show them how to use a dictionary to figure out the word's meaning. Repeat the process with words in the *equal* word family.

Challenge

Create Word Families Have students work in pairs to create word families for the words *agree*, *attend*, and *direct*. Ask students to explain how they can use the word parts to understand the meanings.

Lesson 10

VOCABULARY WORKSHOP

OBJECTIVES
Vocabulary
- Strategy: Use Structural Analysis (word families, affixes) T

ENGAGE & CONNECT

A Build Background

Connect Explain: In families, all the members may have the same last name but different first names. In a word family, all the words have one part that is the same, such as *honor*. Then they have different parts, such as *dis-*, *-able*, or *-ary*. These are called prefixes and suffixes.

Give students examples where the pronunciation of vowel sounds differs among the words in the same family. Have students read these words and pronounce them aloud.

TEACH & PRACTICE

B Use Word Families

Create Word Families Have students list words in the *success* family. Have students verify meaning using a dictionary.

ELL Rephrase and Demonstrate Use the root word, prefixes, and suffixes to explain the meaning of *successful* and *unsuccessful*.

Say: Sometimes a root word has a different spelling when a suffix is added. For example: *happy* + *ness* = *happiness*. Have students discuss parts of speech and spelling as they use the dictionary.

C Put the Strategy to Use

Try It Tell students to follow the steps of the strategy as they define the words, determine the word family, and add words.
L.9-10.4.b; L.9-10.4.c; L.9-10.4.d

ONGOING ASSESSMENT
Have students write sentences using new words in the same family.

CCSS Literacy.L.9-10.4.b Identify and correctly use patterns of word changes that indicate different meanings or parts of speech (e.g., analyze, analysis, analytical; advocate, advocacy). **Literacy.L.9-10.4.c** Consult general and specialized reference materials (e.g., dictionaries, glossaries, thesauruses), both print and digital, to find the pronunciation of a word or determine or clarify its precise meaning, its part of speech, or its etymology. Literacy.L.9-10.4.d Verify the preliminary determination of the meaning of a word or phrase (e.g., by checking the inferred meaning in context or in a dictionary).

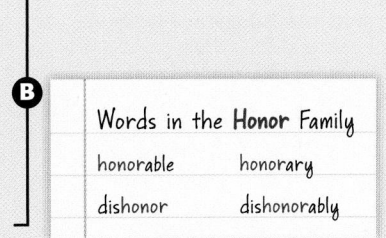

UNIT 3 Cluster 2 Planner

EQ **ESSENTIAL QUESTION:**

What Makes a Hero?

Consider the everyday heroes in your community.

Online Planner
myNGconnect.com

	LESSON 11 **Prepare to Read**	LESSON 12 **A Job for Valentín** Main Selection
Reading		
Reading Strategies Focus Strategy **Make Inferences**	**Activate Prior Knowledge** SL.9-10.1 • Make a Connection: Anticipation Guide *T236*	**Make Inferences** RL.9-10.1 • Make Inferences *T237, T240–T250*
Literary Analysis Genre Focus **Short Stories**		T **Analyze Viewpoint** RL.9-10.6 *T237, T240–T250* **Evaluate Author's Perspective** • Author's Background *T238*
Vocabulary	T **Key Vocabulary** RL.9-10.4; L.9-10.6 • Introduce *T236* **anxiety**, **prejudiced**, **distracted**, **protest**, • **inherent**, • **survivor**, • **inhibit**, **tragedy**	T **Key Vocabulary** L.9-10.6 • Daily Routines *T241* • Link to Essential Question *T243* • Selection Reading *T240–T250* **anxiety**, **prejudiced**, **distracted**, **protest**
Fluency		T **Expression** RL.9-10.10 • Daily Routines *T241* T **Accuracy and Rate** RL.9-10.10 Comprehension Coach *T239*
Writing		
Response to Literature		**Return to the Text** W.9-10.9.a; W.9-10.10 • **Reread and Write** Is Valentín a hero? How can challenged individuals become everyday heroes? *T250*
Writing Across the Curriculum		**Research and Writing** W.9-10.7 • **Sports Connection** *T245*
Language		
ELL **Language Development**	T **Engage in Discussion** SL.9-10.1.b • Language and Grammar Lab, Transparency H *LAB TE p. 44*	T **Engage in Discussion** SL.9-10.1.b • Daily Routines *LAB TE p. 44*
Grammar Grammar Focus **Present, Past, and Future Tense Verbs**		T **Irregular Past Tense Verbs** *T242, T244* L.9-10.1; L.9-10.2.c T **Past Progressive Verb Forms** *T248* L.9-10.1.b
Listening and Speaking	**Small Group Talk** SL.9-10.1 • Opinions About Heroes *T236*	**Listen to a Selection** SL.9-10.1 Comprehension Coach *T239* • *CD 4, Tracks 5–8* **Out-of-School Literacy** SL.9-10.1.a • Analyzing Friendships in Movies *T246*

T = Tested on Cluster and/or Unit Reading and Literary Analysis Test
T = Tested on Language Acquisition Assessment
T = Tested on Unit Writing Test
T = Assessed with a Rubric
• **Academic Vocabulary**

A Job for Valentín

Genre: Short Story Lexile® 750L

Teresa gets the perfect summer job until she has to work with Valentín, her mentally challenged assistant. She learns to appreciate his unique character and sees firsthand how unlikely individuals can become everyday heroes.

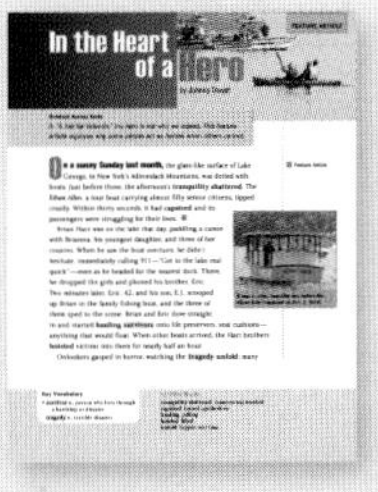

In the Heart of a Hero

Genre: Feature Article Lexile® 980L

This article features brothers Brian and Eric Hart, who demonstrated heroism when they saved a group of senior citizens from drowning. It examines the biological and situational factors that contribute to heroic actions.

LESSON 13 **In the Heart of a Hero** Second Selection	LESSON 14 **Reflect and Assess**	LESSONS 15 & 16 **Integrate the Language Arts**	LESSON 17 **Workshop**
Make Inferences RI.9-10.1 • Make Inferences *T252, T253–T256*	**Comprehension and Critical Thinking** *T257* RL.9-10.1; RI.9-10.1 • Compare Across Texts • Analyze, Interpret, Compare, Imagine, Synthesize		
Ⓣ **Analyze Structure: Feature Article** *T252, T253–T256* RI.9-10.3	**Interpret and Evaluate Literature** RL.9-10.10; RI.9-10.10 Ⓣ **Use Text Evidence** *T257* RL.9-10.10; RI.9-10.1	**Analyze Multiple Themes in a Text** *T248* RL.9-10.2	
Ⓣ **Key Vocabulary** L.9-10.6 • Selection Reading *T253–T256* • **inherent** • **survivor** • **inhibit** **tragedy**	Ⓣ **Key Vocabulary** L.9-10.6 • Review *T257* **anxiety** **prejudiced** **distracted** **protest** • **inherent** • **survivor** • **inhibit** **tragedy**	Ⓣ **Vocabulary Strategy** L.9-10.4.c • Use a Dictionary: Borrowed Words *T259*	
Ⓣ **Expression** RL.9-10.10 • Daily Routines *T241* Ⓣ **Accuracy and Rate** RI.9-10.10 Comprehension Coach *T253*	Ⓣ **Expression** RL.9-10.10 • Peer Assessment *T257*		
Return to the Text W.9-10.9.b; W.9-10.10 • **Reread and Write** What explanations does the author give for heroic behavior? *T256*	**Write About Literature** W.9-10.9.a • **Comparison** Write a paragraph explaining how the "heroes" in other stories are like Valentín. *T257*	Ⓣ **Writing Trait** W.9-10.5 • **Voice and Style** *T259*	
Research and Writing W.9-10.7 • **History Connection** *T255*		**Research and Writing** W.9-10.2.b; W.9-10.7 • **Historical Hero Profile** *T259*	
Ⓣ **Engage in Discussion** SL.9-10.1.b • Daily Routines *LAB TE p. 44*		Ⓣ **Engage in Discussion** SL.9-10.1.b • Group Talk *T258*	
Ⓣ **Future Tense Verbs** *T254* L.9-10.1.a; L.9-10.1.b		Ⓣ **Verb Tenses** *T258* L.9-10.1.a; L.9-10.1.b	
Listen to a Selection SL.9-10.1 Comprehension Coach *T253* *CD 4, Track 9*	**Participate in a Discussion** *T257* SL.9-10.1		**Listening and Speaking Workshop** SL.9-10.1; SL.9-10.1.b; SL.9-10.1.c; SL.9-10.1.d; SL.9-10.3; L.9-10.3 **Panel Discussion** • Plan, Practice, Hold, and Evaluate a Panel Discussion *T260–T261*

EDGE LIBRARY

Hercules ●
by Paul Storrie

September 11, 2001 Attack on New York City ● ●
by Wilbur Hampton

Left Behind ● ● ●
by Velma Wallis

Lesson 11

PREPARE TO READ

OBJECTIVES

Vocabulary
- Key Vocabulary Ⓣ
- Strategy: Use Cognates; Relate Words

Reading Strategy
- Activate Prior Knowledge

ELL **Language & Grammar Lab**

Language Function Transparency H
Engage in Discussion Ⓣ

ENGAGE & CONNECT

Ⓐ EQ Essential Question

Focus on Everyday Heroes Ask: Who are the everyday heroes in your community? What makes them heroes?

Possible responses:
- *firefighters and EMTs; they are brave*
- *community volunteers; they give their own time to help others*

Ⓑ Make a Connection

In small groups, have students support their opinions about heroes with examples from their own experiences.
SL.9-10.1

TEACH VOCABULARY

Ⓒ Learn Key Vocabulary

Study the Words Review the four steps of the Make Words Your Own routine (*see the Vocabulary tab*):

1. **Pronounce** Say one word and have students repeat it. Write the word in syllables and pronounce it, one syllable at a time: *sur-vi-vor*. Ask what looks familiar in the word. Point out the root word *survive* and the suffix *-or*.

   ELL Use cognates to help Spanish speakers with the words (*see the Vocabulary tab*).

2. **Study Examples** Read the example in the chart. Provide more examples: Is someone who escapes from a fire a *survivor* or a victim?

3. **Encourage Elaboration** Ask students to give an example of a person who can be called a survivor.

4. **Practice the Words** Have groups make a Vocabulary Study Card for each Key Vocabulary word.

Edge Interactive
Practice Book, pp. 114–115
RL.9-10.4; L.9-10.6

ONGOING ASSESSMENT
Have students complete an oral sentence for each word. For example: *If the TV is on, Sasha is _______ and can't do his homework.*

PREPARE TO READ

- A Job for Valentín
- Hero
- In the Heart of a Hero

Ⓐ EQ What Makes a Hero?

Consider the everyday heroes in your community.

Ⓑ Make a Connection

Anticipation Guide Write whether you agree or disagree with the statements. After reading the three selections, see if you still feel the same way.

ANTICIPATION GUIDE	Agree or Disagree
1. Anyone can become a hero in special circumstances.	_______
2. A hero is someone who is never afraid.	_______
3. Heroes are born, not made.	_______

Ⓒ Learn Key Vocabulary

Study the Words Pronounce each word and learn its meaning. You may also want to look up the definitions in the Glossary.

• Academic Vocabulary

Key Words	Examples
anxiety (ang-**zī**-ut-ē) *noun* ▸ pages 246, 250, 257	If people are nervous or worried they may show **anxiety**. I felt great **anxiety** before I started my new job. *Synonyms*: nervousness, worry; *Antonym*: calm 
distracted (di-**strakt**-id) *adjective* ▸ page 241	A person who is **distracted** isn't able to pay attention. If you are **distracted** by too many activities after school, you may not have time for homework.
• **inherent** (in-**hair**-unt) *adjective* ▸ pages 255, 256, 257	Something that is **inherent** is something that you are born with. She has always had an **inherent** sense of courage.
• **inhibit** (in-**hib**-it) *verb* ▸ pages 255, 257	When something **inhibits** you, it stops or holds you back from doing something. I want to swim but my fear of water **inhibits** me. *Antonym*: open
prejudiced (**prej**-u-dist) *adjective* ▸ page 241	**Prejudiced** people form opinions about others without thinking about the facts. I try not to be **prejudiced** about people who are different than me. *Antonym*: open-minded
protest (**prō**-test) *verb* ▸ page 242	When you **protest** something, you say or show that you are against it. We **protest** the unfair way the students are being treated. *Synonym*: object; *Antonym*: agree with 
• **survivor** (sur-**vī**-vur) *noun* ▸ page 253	A person who overcomes some hardship or manages to live through a disaster is a **survivor**. The police rescued the **survivors** of the car accident.
tragedy (**tra**-ju-dē) *noun* ▸ page 253	A **tragedy** is a terrible event or disaster. The earthquake **tragedy** left people homeless and many children became orphans. *Synonym*: misfortune; *Antonym*: good fortune

Practice the Words With a group, make a **Vocabulary Study Card** for each Key Vocabulary word. Write the word on the front of the card. On the back, write its definition, a synonym or antonym, and an example sentence. Take turns quizzing each other on the words.

CCSS **Literacy.RL.9-10.4** Determine the meaning of words and phrases as they are used in the text, including figurative and connotative meanings; analyze the cumulative impact of specific word choices on meaning and tone (e.g., how the language evokes a sense of time and place; how it sets a formal or informal tone). **Literacy.SL.9-10.1** Initiate and participate effectively in a range of collaborative discussions (one-on-one, in groups, and teacher-led) with diverse partners on grades 9-10 topics, texts, and issues, building on others' ideas and expressing their own clearly and persuasively. **Literacy.L.9-10.6** Acquire and use accurately general academic and domain-specific words and phrases, sufficient for reading, writing, speaking, and listening at the college and career readiness level; demonstrate independence in gathering vocabulary knowledge when considering a word or phrase important to comprehension or expression.

BEFORE READING A Job for Valentín

short story by Judith Ortiz Cofer

Reading Strategies

- Plan and Monitor
- Determine Importance
- ▶ **Make Inferences**
- Ask Questions
- Make Connections
- Synthesize
- Visualize

Analyze Viewpoint

A narrator's **viewpoint** is what he or she thinks and says about a situation. The viewpoint may be different depending on who is telling the story and can affect the way information is shared. If a story is told by one of the characters, it is called **first-person point of view**. First-person narrators tell the story using pronouns such as *I* and *me*. The reader sees everything through just that one person's eyes, so the information is limited by what the narrator knows and may be affected by the character's thoughts, experiences, and attitudes.

D

Look Into the Text

The narrator uses first-person pronouns.

The narrator reports only what she sees, hears, and feels.

Bob Dylan laughs and kisses my hand.

"My Chiquita banana," he says, "stay true to me. Don't give my whereabouts out to the enemy. I shall return."

"Bye," I say. I am such a great conversationalist, inside my own head.

But he's already looking away. We have both heard familiar giggles. It's Clarissa and Anne. I see him waving to them, letting them get a view of his entire, glorious self. He looks over his shoulder at me and winks, covering all the bases.

The narrator's viewpoint affects the information shared.

Focus Strategy ▶ Make Inferences

When you read fiction, you add information from your own knowledge and experiences. Use this information to **make inferences** that help you understand the text.

Focus Strategy

E

HOW TO MAKE INFERENCES

1. **Record Information and Ideas** Note things the narrator thinks, says, or does in an **"I Read," "I Know," "And So" Chart**. Then think about your own experience. Finally, make an inference by combining the information and ideas.
2. **Connect the Inferences** By adding up your inferences, you can form big ideas about the narrator.
3. **Read On** If your inferences turn out to be wrong, revise them.

"I Read," "I Know," "And So" Chart

I Read ...	I Know ...	And So ...
"I am such a great conversationalist, inside my own head." (page 244)	When I don't know what to say, I get all confused.	The narrator often feels confused when talking to people—especially boys.

Reading Transparency 12

READING VIEWPOINT 12

Analyze Viewpoint

How do you know who is telling a story?

Introduce Stories written from a **first-person** point of view are told by one of the characters.

- In the **first-person** point of view, the **narrator** experiences the events as one of the characters in the story.
- A **first-person narrator** uses pronouns like *I, me, we,* and *our* to tell about himself or herself. For example:

> One day last summer, *my* best friend, Shelby, and *I* went to the public pool. *We* both got terrible sunburns on *our* backs. Man, did it hurt!

- Remember: In the **third-person** point of view, the **narrator** is not one of the characters and does not experience the events in the story.
- **Third-person narrators** use pronouns like *she, her, they,* and *their* to tell about all the characters. For example:

> One day last summer, Carmina and *her* best friend, Shelby, went to the public pool. *They* both got terrible sunburns on *their* backs, which were very painful.

Lesson 12

BEFORE READING

OBJECTIVES

Reading Strategy
- Make Inferences

Literary Analysis
- Analyze Viewpoint **T**

TEACH STRATEGIES

D Analyze Viewpoint

Look Into the Text Read the introduction to explain viewpoint and first-person narrative. Read aloud the text passage. Use the callouts to discuss first-person narrators. Ask: What does this narrator tell about?

Possible responses:
- *what she thinks: that she is a great conversationalist only in her head*
- *what she sees, hears, and feels: her friends, laughing, her feelings about Bob Dylan*

Point out that information from first-person narrators is limited because they can only tell things through their own eyes.

Reading Transparency 12

Use the Transparency Distinguish the features of first-person and third-person narrators. Ask: How can you recognize a first-person narrator?

Possible responses:
- *The narrator uses* I, my, *and* we.
- *The narrator is a character in the story.*

RL.9-10.6

E Focus Strategy: Make Inferences

Make Inferences Read the introduction with students to define the strategy. Work through the steps in the How To box to model using information in the text ("I read") and what you already know ("I know") to make an inference ("And so").

Have students try the strategies to make an inference about what Bob Dylan is like.

RL.9-10.1

Edge Interactive Practice Book, pp. 116–117

ONGOING ASSESSMENT

Have students retell Look Into the Text using a third-person narrator.

CCSS **Literacy.RL.9-10.1** Cite strong and thorough textual evidence to support analysis of what the text says explicitly as well as inferences drawn from the text. **Literacy.RL.9-10.6** Analyze a particular point of view or cultural experience reflected in a work of literature from outside the United States, drawing on a wide reading of world literature.

OBJECTIVES
Literary Analysis
- Evaluate Author's Perspective

Viewing
- Respond to and Interpret Visuals

BUILD BACKGROUND

A The Writer and Her Influences

Have students read the biography of Judith Ortiz Cofer.

Author's Background Share these additional quotes from Ortiz Cofer:

"I have often felt like the oddball. . . . I was always the girl who had all *A*'s in school. . . . It was not that I was a genius, but books were all I had. I was a bookworm. So in many aspects of my life, in school, in Puerto Rico, being a navy brat, I felt like an outcast. Maybe my identification with eccentrics is because I saw myself as different."

ELL Rephrase Language Help students understand the meaning of the terms *infected, oddball, bookworm, navy brat, outcast,* and *identification with eccentrics*. For example: Infected *here means to become very interested in something.*

Ask: What do you think Cofer means when she says she was "infected" by the storytellers in her family?

Possible responses:
- *She was interested in the stories.*
- *The stories had a big effect on her.*

Connect with Author's Life Guide students to make connections with the author's life.

Then ask: How might feeling like an oddball have affected Cofer's writing?

Possible response:
- *She might write about characters who feel they are different.*

myNGconnect.com
- **Selection Summaries in eight languages**

The Writer and Her Influences

Judith Ortiz Cofer
(1952–)

The women in my family were wonderful storytellers who infected me at a very early age with the desire to tell stories.

For Judith Ortiz Cofer, storytelling is a family tradition.

Judith Ortiz Cofer uses growing up in two different worlds as the inspiration for much of her work.

A Born in Puerto Rico, Cofer and her family moved to the United States when she was two years old. Although most of her school years were spent in the United States, she often returned to Puerto Rico, where she lived with her grandmother, or *abuela*, who was a great storyteller. She remembers, "When my *abuela* sat us down to tell a story, we learned something from it, even though we always laughed."

Living in two countries led Cofer to see herself as "never quite belonging, because, after all, I speak English with a Spanish accent and Spanish with an American accent."

When Cofer began writing, her double heritage gave her many ideas for stories. In her fiction, Cofer deals with the challenges of moving between cultures and the possibility of using creativity to fit in. She says she often thinks about how being bilingual affects her understanding of the world. "Why do words have such an impact in one culture and not in another? Without being bilingual and bicultural I wouldn't know these things."

myNGconnect.com
- **Visit the author's Web site.**
- **Read a blog about being bilingual.**

238 Unit 3 The Hero Within

DIFFERENTIATED INSTRUCTION

English Language Learners ELL

Preview the selection:
- Show the art on p. 239: *The girl in the story works in a snack bar like this one.* Point out the watery background. *It is at a swimming pool.*
- Show the art on p. 243 and the rubber-band sculpture on p. 245: *An artistic man in the story makes animals with rubber bands.*
- Demonstrate by gestures and facial expressions what the following phrases from the selection mean:

flapping his arms and stuttering (p. 247)
moving in slow motion (p. 248)

Read Aloud to provide a supported listening experience:
- Play the **Selection Recording** as students track text in their books. **CD 4**
- Have students use the Listen feature in the **Comprehension Coach** where they see the text as it is read aloud.
- Read the selection aloud to students as you provide comprehensible input. For example, you might list and describe heroic traits shown by characters.

A Job for Valentín

by Judith Ortiz Cofer

Girl in Miami, 1999, Max Ferguson. Oil on panel, private collection, The Bridgeman Art Library.

▲ Critical Viewing: Effect What details in this scene remind you of summer? How do you think this artist feels about the place shown in the painting? C

Comprehension Coach

TEACH & PRACTICE

B Analyze Visuals

About the Art Max Ferguson, like Judith Ortiz Cofer, grew up near New York City during the 1960s. Some art critics call him a photorealist—a painter whose work is so realistic that it looks like a photograph. Ferguson is known for painting older New York City neighborhoods which he wants to preserve forever.

Respond Ask: What clues show that this is a painting and not a photograph?

Possible responses:
- *The colors are too pale and even.*
- *The details are too perfect.*

C Critical Viewing: Effect

Observe Details Ask: What in the painting shows it is summer? Have students point out details that support their observations and inferences.

Possible responses:
- *The girl wears shorts and a T-shirt.*
- *There are shadows made by a bright sun.*

Make Inferences Ask: What clues show how the artist feels about the place in the painting? How can you tell?

Possible responses:
- *The artist might think this place is pleasant and relaxing. Everything is clean, and the person looks relaxed.*

Comprehension Coach

Build Reading Power

Assign students to use the software, based on their instructional needs.

Read Silently
- Comprehension questions with immediate feedback
- Glossary support
- Review text evidence

RL.9-10.10

Listen
- Professional model of fluent reading

Record
- Oral reading fluency practice
- Ongoing fluency assessment with immediate feedback

CCSS Literacy.RL.9-10.10 By the end of grade 9, read and comprehend literature, including stories, dramas, and poems, in the grades 9-10 text complexity band proficiently, with scaffolding as needed at the high end of the range. By the end of grade 10, read and comprehend literature, including stories, dramas, and poems, at the high end of the grades 9-10 text complexity band independently and proficiently.

READ

OBJECTIVES

Vocabulary
- Key Vocabulary (T)

Reading Fluency
- Expression (T)

Reading Strategies
- Set a Purpose; Make Inferences

Comprehension & Critical Thinking
- Make Inferences
- Use Text Evidence (T)

Literary Analysis
- Analyze Viewpoint (T)
- Analyze Style: Author's Language

TEACH & PRACTICE

A Chunking the Text

Set a Purpose Remind students of their responses in the Anticipation Guide. Discuss challenges that teenagers might face when they work summer jobs.

Possible response:
- *working, instead of hanging out with friends*

Read Have students read pp. 240–241. Support and monitor their comprehension using the reading support provided. Use the Differentiated Instruction below to meet students' individual needs.
RL.9-10.10

B Reading Support

1 Viewpoint Work with students to brainstorm a list of information that the narrator gives about herself.

Possible responses:
- *She can't swim and has bad vision.*
- *She has a summer job at the city pool.*
- *She thinks the lifeguard is cute.*

RL.9-10.6

C Reading Support

2 Language Have students find and explain examples of slang on p. 240.

Possible response:
- *"Messing around" means not doing what you're supposed to.*

RL.9-10.4

A ***Set a Purpose***
A teenager gets a summer job, but it isn't perfect. Read to find out what challenges come up.

B **I can't swim very well,** mainly because my eyesight is so bad. The minute I take off my glasses to get in the pool, everything becomes a blob of color and I freeze. But I **managed** to talk my way into a summer job at the city pool anyway. All I'll be doing is selling drinks and snacks, and I get to talk to everyone since the little **concession stand** faces the pool and the cute lifeguard, Bob Dylan Kalinowski. His mother named him after the old singer from the sixties. 1

It's a good first day. Mrs. O'Brien says I don't need any training. I can run a cash register, I can **take inventory**, and I am very friendly with customers. The only thing I don't really like is that Mrs. O'Brien expects to be told if I ever see Bob Dylan messing around on the job.

"People's lives, *children's* lives, are in that young man's hands," she says. "Keep an eye on him, Teresa, and use that phone to call me, if you need to."

I say, "Yes, ma'am," even though I feel funny about being asked to spy on Bob Dylan. He's a senior at my school and, yeah, a crazy man sometimes. But if they gave him the job as a lifeguard, they ought to trust him to do it right.

C That was the first day. Except for O'Brien asking me to fink on Bob Dylan, I had a good time. 2 And one thing nobody knows: I'm interested in Bob Dylan, too. He flirts with every girl in school. Even me.

The second day is bad news. A disaster. I got assigned a **"mentally challenged" assistant** by the city. There's a new program to put retarded people to work at simple jobs so they can make some money, learn a skill, or something.

I don't have anything against these handicapped people, but I don't

1 Viewpoint
Who is the narrator of this story? What do you find out about him or her?

2 Language
The narrator uses slang, or informal language. What are some examples of slang used in the story so far? What do the words and phrases mean?

In Other Words
managed was able
concession stand stall for selling snacks and drinks
take inventory keep a record of things to be sold
"mentally challenged" assistant helper with mental disabilities

---

DIFFERENTIATED INSTRUCTION

Interactive Reading As you conduct the interactive reading with students, adjust your teaching strategies to their needs.

Struggling Readers

Picture the Text Show the characters' traits visually in a Character Chart:

Character	What the Character Does	What This Shows About the character
Teresa	acts friendly with customers	likes talking with people

English Language Learners ELL

Rephrase Language Explain that people use slang in relaxed conversations with friends. Every language, including English, has slang.

For example:

O'Brien asking me to fink on Bob Dylan (My boss asked me to tell her if I see Bob Dylan do something bad.)

Discuss additional examples from the story and provide restatements.

Challenge

Analyze Character Motivation Have students track Teresa's motivations throughout the story. For example: What is her motivation for taking a job at the pool? How do the reasons for her actions change as the story progresses? Discuss whether the changes make her more heroic.

CCSS Literacy.RL.9-10.4 Determine the meaning of words and phrases as they are used in the text, including figurative and connotative meanings; analyze the cumulative impact of specific word choices on meaning and tone (e.g., how the language evokes a sense of time and place; how it sets a formal or informal tone). **Literacy.RL.9-10.10** By the end of grade 9, read and comprehend literature, including stories, dramas, and poems, in the grades 9-10 text complexity band proficiently, with scaffolding as needed at the high end of the range. By the end of grade 10, read and comprehend literature, including stories, dramas, and poems, at the high end of the grades 9-10 text complexity band independently and proficiently.

want to spend my whole summer with one. Besides, how is it going to look to Bob Dylan and my other friends? They're not going to want to hang around the store with someone like that around. 3 **D**

But there he is. My new *partner* is being led in by Mrs. O'Brien. He is Puerto Rican like me, thirty years old, and mildly challenged. He has the **IQ** of a third grader, she tells me. A *bright* third grader. And he is an artist. I can't help but wonder what others are going to say about this guy. It's hard enough to get people to believe that you have normal intelligence when you're Puerto Rican, and my "assistant" will be a living proof for **prejudiced** people. **E**

"He's brought some of his creations," Mrs. O'Brien told me in a cheerful voice. "We're letting him sell them at the store. Valentín is gifted in art."

Old Valentín **has the posture of** a gorilla. And so much hair on his head and his arms that he is furry. And he's carrying a huge shopping bag that seems to drag him down. Great. Wonderful. **E**

I can't help but wonder what others are going to say about this guy.

Mrs. O'Brien takes Valentín's hand and guides him in. But then she is **distracted** by yelling and running at poolside. No running is allowed. Bob Dylan is nowhere in sight. Mrs. O'Brien takes off for the pool, and I'm left facing Valentín. He's standing there like a big hairy child waiting to be told what to do.

3 **Make Inferences** How would you describe Teresa's relationships with her friends? Look for evidence to support your inferences.

Monitor Comprehension

Describe What unexpected challenge does Teresa face at her new job?

Key Vocabulary

prejudiced *adj.*, ready to form opinions about others without thinking about the facts

distracted *adj.*, unable to pay attention

In Other Words

IQ level of intelligence

has the posture of stands like

TEACH & PRACTICE

D Reading Support

3 Make Inferences Tell students to find evidence in the text to help them describe Teresa's relationships with her friends.

Possible responses:

- *They are judgmental; "how is it going to look to ... my other friends?"*
- *They care about how they are seen by others; "They're not going to hang around the store with someone like that around."*

RL.9-10.1

E Reading Support

Viewpoint Have students identify the details Teresa uses to describe Valentín, including both physical and nonphysical details.

ELL Sentence Frame Use a sentence frame to help students understand Teresa's comments about Valentín. Explain difficult phrases, such as "mildly challenged" and "the posture of a gorilla." Point out that Teresa ends her description by saying, "Great. Wonderful." Then have students complete the sentences.

Teresa says ______. What she really means is ______.

Ask: Is the narrator's description of Valentín positive or negative?

Ask: What can you tell about Teresa from her description of Valentín?

Possible responses:

- *She is embarrassed by having to work with someone like Valentín.*
- *She probably doesn't have a lot of experience with people who have disabilities.*

RL.9-10.6

Monitor Comprehension

Describe Have students review what Teresa expected the job to be. Ask: What part of the job did Teresa not expect?

Possible response:

- *She didn't expect to be put in charge of a mentally challenged person who will be her assistant.*

RL.9-10.1

DAILY ROUTINES

Vocabulary

See the Vocabulary and Fluency Routines tab for more information.

Respond to Questions Compose yes/no questions using the words. You can use more than one word in a sentence. For example: Does *anxiety* cause people to feel *distracted* from their work?

Word Sorts Provide categories for sorting words:

- Endings
- Meaning

Make a Personal Connection Encourage students to imagine what their reactions would be in Teresa's situation. Ask: How would you react in this situation? L.9-10.6

Fluency: Expression

CD 11

This cluster's fluency practice uses a passage from "A Job for Valentín" to help students practice appropriate expression. Use **Reading Handbook** T750 and the **Fluency Model CD** to teach or review the elements of fluent expression, and then use the daily fluency practice activities to develop students' oral reading proficiency. RL.9-10.10

CCSS **Literacy.RL.9-10.1** Cite strong and thorough textual evidence to support analysis of what the text says explicitly as well as inferences drawn from the text. **Literacy.RL.9-10.6** Analyze a particular point of view or cultural experience reflected in a work of literature from outside the United States, drawing on a wide reading of world literature. **Literacy.L.9-10.6** Acquire and use accurately general academic and domain-specific words and phrases, sufficient for reading, writing, speaking, and listening at the college and career readiness level; demonstrate independence in gathering vocabulary knowledge when considering a word or phrase important to comprehension or expression.

READ

OBJECTIVES

Vocabulary
- Key Vocabulary Ⓣ

Reading Strategies
- Make Inferences
- Predict; Confirm Prediction

Comprehension & Critical Thinking
- Make Inferences
- Use Text Evidence Ⓣ

Literary Analysis
- Analyze Viewpoint Ⓣ

Viewing
- Respond to and Interpret Visuals

Grammar
- Irregular Past Tense Verbs Ⓣ

TEACH & PRACTICE

Ⓐ Chunking the Text

Predict Discuss what makes people get along. Review what students know about Teresa's first impressions of Valentín to help them predict how the two might get along at work.

Read Have students read pp. 242–243. Support and monitor their comprehension using the reading support provided.
RL.9-10.10

Ⓑ Reading Support

4 Make Inferences Ask: What does Valentín's way of talking to Teresa show about him?

Possible response:
- *He's shy and doesn't like to talk.*

RL.9-10.1

Ⓒ Reading Support

5 Make Inferences Tell students to use information in the text and what they already know to tell why Teresa doesn't answer Mrs. O'Brien.

Possible response:
- *Teresa likes Bob Dylan and probably wants him to like her back. Teresa is worried that if she tells Mrs. O'Brien about Bob Dylan, he won't like her.*

RL.9-10.1

Predict

Ⓐ *Teresa and Valentín start working together. How do you think they will get along?*

"I'm Terry," I say. Nothing. He doesn't even look up. This is going to be even worse than I thought.

"What's your name?" I say it real slow and loud.

Ⓑ "***Soy*** Valentín," he says in Spanish. His deep voice surprises me. Then he starts taking out these little animals. They are strange-looking things, all tan in color. They are made from rubber bands. Valentín takes them out one at a time: a giraffe, a teddy bear, an elephant, a dog, a fish, all kinds of animals. They are really kind of cute.

"Do you speak English?" I ask him. I can speak Spanish, but not that good.

"***Sí***," Valentín says. 4

This is going to be even worse than I thought.

He arranges his rubber-band **menagerie** on the counter, taking a long time to decide what goes next to what. Mrs. O'Brien walks in looking very upset.

"Teresa, does he do this often?"

I know she's talking about Bob Dylan taking off.

"This is only my second day here," I **protest**. And maybe my last, I think.

Ⓒ "Teresa, someone could drown while that boy is away from **his post**."

I don't say anything. 5 I was not hired to spy on Bob Dylan. Although I do plan to keep my eyes on him a lot for my own reasons. He's fun to watch.

Mrs. O'Brien turns to Valentín. "I see you two have met. Teresa, it is Valentín's goal to sell his art and make enough money to buy himself a bicycle. He lives in a **group home** on Green Street and he wants to have

4 Make Inferences What can you tell about Valentín from this first conversation? Read on to see if your inference is correct.

5 Make Inferences Why doesn't Teresa answer Mrs. O'Brien? Use what you already know to make sense of her silence.

Key Vocabulary
protest *v.*, to say or show that you are against something

In Other Words
Soy I am (in Spanish)
Sí Yes (in Spanish)
menagerie collection of animals
his post his station or place (the lifeguard's chair)
group home home for people with special needs

GRAMMAR

Irregular Past Tense Verbs

Teach/Model Display the transparency. Review the meaning of *past tense*, and elicit examples of regular past tense verbs. Use the chart to show how irregular verbs change forms. Have students say both forms aloud. Ask volunteers to read each sentence.

Practice A. Have students read each sentence aloud, identifying the present tense verb. If students do not remember the past tense form, refer them to the chart. **B.** After partners write sentences about a job, have them read a sentence aloud. Ask the group to identify the past tense verb.
L.9-10.1; L.9-10.2.c

Grammar & Writing Practice Book, pp. 79–80

Grammar Transparency 36

GRAMMAR IRREGULAR PAST TENSE VERBS 36

How Do You Show That an Action Already Happened?
Change the Verb.

Add **-ed** to most verbs to show that an action already happened. Use special past tense forms for **irregular verbs.**

Present	Past	Example in the Past
bring	brought	The pool closed, and I **brought** the chairs inside.
do, does	did	I **did** my chores to close up.
go, goes	went	Then I **went** home.
have, has	had	Everyone **had** a good time at the pool today.
make	made	We **made** a lot of money.
sell	sold	I **sold** 100 hot dogs and cold drinks!
spend	spent	I **spent** my own money on new sunglasses.
tell	told	Everyone **told** me how good I looked!

Try It

A. Say each sentence. Then say the sentence again, changing the verb to the past tense.
1. I sell food and soft drinks at the pool. (sold)
2. Teenagers often go to the pool. (went)
3. Mrs. O'Brien tells me about Valentín. (told)
4. Valentín makes animals out of rubber bands. (made)

B. Now tell a partner about a job you had. Write your four best sentences with irregular past tense verbs. Sentences will vary.

GRAMMAR SKILLS PATH

CCSS Literacy.RL.9-10.6 Analyze a particular point of view or cultural experience reflected in a work of literature from outside the United States, drawing on a wide reading of world literature. Literacy.RL.9-10.10 By the end of grade 9, read and comprehend literature, including stories, dramas, and poems, in the grades 9-10 text complexity band proficiently, with scaffolding as needed at the high end of the range. By the end of grade 10, read and comprehend literature, including stories, dramas, and poems, at the high end of the grades 9-10 text complexity band independently and proficiently. Literacy.L.9-10.1 Demonstrate command of the conventions of standard English grammar and usage when writing or speaking. Literacy.L.9-10.2.c Spell correctly.

transportation so that he can get a job in town. I think it's a wonderful idea, don't you?"

Mrs. O'Brien sighs, looking out at the pool again. Bob Dylan is back in his lifeguard chair. She says again, "Teresa, if anything goes wrong, use that phone there to call me. At five I'll come get Valentín. See if you can get your friends to buy his art. It's for a **worthy cause**!" 6

Valentín watches her leave the store with the look of a child left at school for the first time. His hands are **trembling** a little as he continues to line up his little rubber-band zoo.

Valentín moves around me cautiously. He acts like he's afraid I'm going to bite his head off. It's really annoying. He shows me a bunch of thick rubber bands. He smiles.

"*Trabajo*," he says. Work. It is his job.

"Yes. Make more ***animales***," I say. That will keep him busy and out of my way. I watch him wind a rubber band around his index finger into a tight little ball. He does it so slowly and carefully that it makes me want to scream.

6 Viewpoint
You see other characters from Teresa's point of view. What impression does she give you of Mrs. O'Brien?

Studies for a portrait, Federico Barocci (1526–1612)/Scala/Ministero per i Beni e le Attività culturali/Art Resource, NY

Critical Viewing: Effect
Why might the artist have chosen to use hands as the focus of this art? What feeling do these hands express?

Monitor Comprehension

Confirm Prediction
Was your prediction right? Why or why not?

In Other Words
worthy cause good goal
trembling shaking
animales animals (in Spanish)

TEACH & PRACTICE

D Reading Support

6 **Viewpoint** Have students find examples of how Teresa describes what Mrs. O'Brien says and does.

Possible responses:
- *She's bossy and nervous. She keeps asking Teresa to spy on Bob Dylan.*
- *She's nice to people with disabilities, like Valentín. She gives him a job and says good things about his artwork.*

RL.9-10.6

E Reading Support

Idioms Explain that an idiom is a group of words that means something different from the meaning of each individual word.

ELL **Rephrase Language** Explain the idioms. For example, "bite his head off" means "talk to him in an angry way."

Ask: What does Teresa think Valentín is afraid of?

Possible response:
- *that she'll yell at him or be angry with him*

RL.9-10.4; L.9-10.5.a

F Critical Viewing: Effect

Analyze Mood Have students brainstorm what hands might represent as they answer the question.

Possible responses:
- *Hands show strength and hard work.*
- *The artist might want to show hands to represent the sense of touch.*
- *These hands express the desire to connect with the world.*

Monitor Comprehension

Confirm Prediction Have students match their predictions with what they have read about Teresa and Valentín's interactions so far. Discuss reasons their predictions were right or wrong.

RL.9-10.1

VOCABULARY

Link Vocabulary and Concepts

Ask questions to link Key Vocabulary with the Essential Question.

EQ **ESSENTIAL QUESTION:**
What makes a hero?

Some possible questions:
- *Would a hero stay silent or* **protest** *unfair treatment of handicapped people?*
- *Who are some heroes who have overcome* **prejudiced** *people?*
- *What are some obstacles that might* **inhibit** *a person from acting heroically?*
- *What kind of* **tragedy** *could happen if a lifeguard is* **distracted** *at a swimming pool? What would a hero in this situation do?*

Have students use the Key Vocabulary words in their responses.
L.9-10.6

CCSS **Literacy.RL.9-10.1** Cite strong and thorough textual evidence to support analysis of what the text says explicitly as well as inferences drawn from the text. **Literacy.RL.9-10.4** Determine the meaning of words and phrases as they are used in the text, including figurative and connotative meanings; analyze the cumulative impact of specific word choices on meaning and tone. **Literacy.L.9-10.5.a** Interpret figures of speech (e.g., euphemism, oxymoron) in context and analyze their role in the text. **Literacy.L.9-10.6** Acquire and use accurately general academic and domain-specific words and phrases, sufficient for reading, writing, speaking, and listening at the college and career readiness level; demonstrate independence in gathering vocabulary knowledge when considering a word or phrase important to comprehension or expression.

READ

OBJECTIVES

Reading Strategies
- Make Inferences; Review Strategies
- Predict

Comprehension & Critical Thinking
- Make Inferences
- Use Text Evidence T

Literary Analysis
- Analyze Viewpoint T

Research Skill
- Gather Information

Viewing
- Respond to and Interpret Visuals

Grammar
- Irregular Past Tense Verbs

TEACH & PRACTICE

A Chunking the Text

Predict Have students draw from their own experiences to predict what would have to happen to make Teresa change her mind about Valentín.

ELL Comprehensible Input
Demonstrate "out of her way."

- Have a student stand in your path as you walk. Say, "I need you to get out of my way, please." Continue walking as the student steps aside.
- Explain that Teresa doesn't want the responsibility of watching over Valentín. He is "in her way" because she wants to do other things.

Read Have students read pp. 244–246. Support and monitor their comprehension using the reading support provided.
RL.9-10.10

B Reading Support

7 Make Inferences Ask: Do you know anyone who acts like Bob Dylan? What kind of person is he?

Possible responses:
- *He's conceited. He flirts with the girls because he's sure they all like him.*
- *He's mean. He talks to Valentín like he's not a whole person.*

RL.9-10.1

GRAMMAR SKILLS PATH

Predict
A Teresa is unhappy with Valentín and wants him out of her way. Do you think her attitude will change?

Bob Dylan's deep voice startles me.

"Hey, is that your new boyfriend there, Terry? I thought you were my girl." He pulls himself up onto the counter. The muscles on his arms are awesome.

"Hi." I cannot think of anything else to say.

"Give me **an o. j. on the rocks**, little mama. And introduce me to ***el hombre*** over there. And what are these . . . ?"

B "This is Valentín." I point to him, and Valentín quickly ducks his head like someone's going to punish him. "He makes them to sell."

Bob Dylan picks up the fish and makes his eyes cross. I have to laugh.

Valentín stops what he's doing to stare at us. He looks afraid. But he doesn't move. I take the fish back and put it in its place on the counter.

"VERY NICE, MY MAN!" Bob Dylan says, too loud. Valentín drops the little ball, and it bounces and rolls under the counter. I can tell that he's upset.

Bob Dylan laughs and kisses my hand.

"My Chiquita banana," he says, "stay true to me. Don't **give my whereabouts out to the enemy**. I shall return."

"Bye," I say. I am **such a great conversationalist**, inside my own head.

But he's already looking away. We have both heard familiar giggles. It's Clarissa and Anne. I see him waving to them, letting them get a view of his entire, glorious self. He looks over his shoulder at me and winks, covering all the bases. 7

Valentín has finally retrieved his rubber ball out from behind some cartons. He looks a little embarrassed, and I guess that he's really been hiding.

"Valentín, let me show you how to pour drinks. Those two girls will

7 Make Inferences Use evidence from the text and what you already know about people to describe the type of person Bob Dylan is.

In Other Words
an o.j. on the rocks orange juice with ice
el hombre the man (in Spanish)
give my whereabouts out to the enemy tell the boss where I am
such a great conversationalist so good at talking to people

GRAMMAR

Irregular Past Tense Verbs

Teach/Model Display the transparency. Elicit the difference between a regular and an irregular verb. Then have volunteers read aloud each present and past tense form on the chart, as well as the example sentences.

Practice A. If students cannot remember past tense forms, refer them to the chart. As they suggest each verb, write it in the blank.
B. Have partners continue the paragraph about the story and read their paragraph aloud. Repeat a sentence from each, and have the group identify the verb.
L.9-10.1; L.9-10.2.c

Grammar & Writing Practice Book, pp. 81–82

Grammar Transparency 37

GRAMMAR IRREGULAR PAST TENSE VERBS 37

How Do You Show That an Action Already Happened?
Change the Verb.

Add **-ed** to most verbs to show that an action already happened. Use special past tense forms **for irregular verbs.**

Present	Past	Example in the Past
buy	bought	"Who **bought** all the caps?" I asked.
feel	felt	I **felt** bad because I didn't get one.
get	got	Marco **got** all twelve of them from the store.
hide	hid	Then he **hid** the caps.
keep	kept	I knew that he **kept** them in his locker.
speak	spoke	I **spoke** to him and demanded to buy one.
give	gave	He **gave** me one instead!
teach	taught	That **taught** me a lesson.
write	wrote	I **wrote** Marco a thank-you note.

Try It

A. Say each sentence with the past tense form of the verb in parentheses.
1. Bob Dylan __spoke__ too loudly to Valentín. **(speak)**
2. Valentín __got__ very upset. **(get)**
3. He __kept__ away from Bob Dylan. **(keep)**
4. Terry __taught__ Valentín how to pour soft drinks. **(teach)**

B. Now tell a friend about the story. Add three more sentences. Use irregular past tense verbs. Sentences will vary.

Valentín hid. He felt unsafe.

CCSS **Literacy.RL.9-10.1** Cite strong and thorough textual evidence to support analysis of what the text says explicitly as well as inferences drawn from the text. **Literacy.RL.9-10.10** By the end of grade 9, read and comprehend literature, including stories, dramas, and poems, in the grades 9-10 text complexity band proficiently, with scaffolding as needed at the high end of the range. By the end of grade 10, read and comprehend literature, including stories, dramas, and poems, at the high end of the grades 9-10 text complexity band independently and proficiently. **Literacy.L.9-10.1** Demonstrate command of the conventions of standard English grammar and usage when writing or speaking. **Literacy.L.9-10.2.c** Spell correctly.

order a root beer and a diet cola. I'll do the cola and then you do the root beer. Watch."

He watches me very closely, following my hands with his eyes.

"Hey, Terry. How's the job going?" Clarissa booms out. I hear a crash behind me and see that Valentín has dropped ice all over everything. Both my friends start giggling. Valentín's turning red from his neck up. Embarrassed. 8

"This is Valentín," I say, not smiling. "He's helping me out, and he's selling these so that he can buy himself a bicycle."

"You make them yourself, right?" Anne is trying to be nice.

"***Dos dólares***," Valentín says to Anne.

Anne takes the giraffe and hands me a five-dollar bill. Valentín follows me to the cash register while I make change. I hand him two one-dollar bills. He smiles at me. Then he starts to pick up the ice cubes he dropped, one by one.

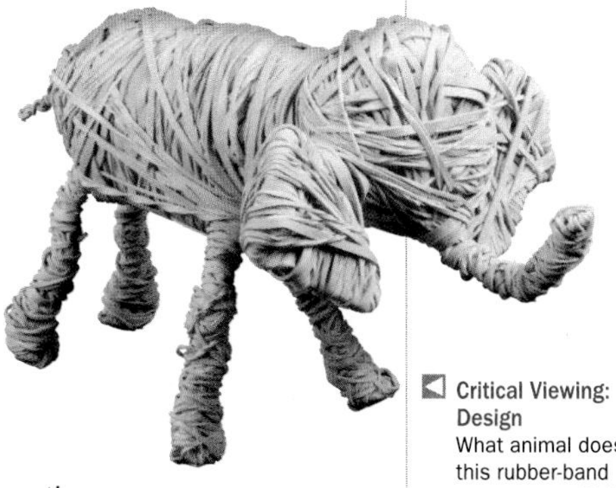

When I turn back to my friends, they are both grinning.

"Well, Teresa, you're going to have a *very interesting* summer," Clarissa says, looking pointedly in Valentín's direction.

Soon I get a crowd of kids all at once, so I have to get to work. Valentín really **gets the hang of** pouring drinks, but I'm hoping that he'll get tired of the work and quit. After we fill the orders, he sits down and closes his eyes. It must be tough to have to work so hard at every little thing you do. He takes the rubber-band ball he's been working on and starts a tail on it. But he just smiles at me and a peaceful look **settles over** his face. I guess that means he's happy. 9

C

8 Make Inferences
What do most people think about Valentín? From what you have read, do you think they are right? Explain.

D

Critical Viewing: Design
What animal does this rubber-band art represent? Tell what clues you used to identify it.

E

9 Viewpoint
How does Teresa feel about Valentín now? How do you know?

In Other Words
Dos dólares Two dollars (in Spanish)
gets the hang of becomes good at
settles over appears on

TEACH & PRACTICE

C Reading Support

8 Make Inferences Ask: What do Bob Dylan, Clarissa, and Anne probably think of Valentín? What kinds of words and actions show this?

Possible response:

- *They think he's clumsy and dumb. They laugh at his artwork and when he drops things.*

Ask: Do you agree with their opinions? Explain why or why not.

Possible response:

- *No, I drop things when I'm nervous, too, and I can't make rubber-band animals like Valentín makes.*

RL.9-10.1

Review Strategies Have partners say what other strategies they used as they read the text.

Possible response:

- *When the girls laugh at Valentín for dropping the ice, I made a connection to an article I read about bullies. This helped me to understand why the girls might have acted so rudely.*

RL.9-10.10

D Critical Viewing: Design

Analyze Design Ask students to study the animal's head and body.

Ask: What kind of animal do you think this is? What makes you think so?

Possible response:

- *It looks like a hippo—it has a big head and body.*
- *The big ears remind me of an elephant.*

E Reading Support

9 Viewpoint Ask: Has Teresa started to like Valentín better than she did at first? How do you know?

Possible response:

- *Yes, she feels sorry for him because he has to work so hard to do things right. She seems glad that he's happy.*

RL.9-10.6

CONTENT AREA CONNECTIONS

HEALTH & BIOLOGY

Explore Special Olympics

Share Facts Read students the following:

- The mission of the Special Olympics is "to provide year-round sports training and athletic competition in a variety of Olympic-type sports for children and adults with mental retardation, giving them continuing opportunities to develop physical fitness, demonstrate courage, experience joy, and participate in a sharing of gifts, skills, and friendship with their families, other Special Olympics athletes, and the community."

Discuss How could Special Olympics transform the life of someone like Valentín?

Research and Confirm Have students conduct research to confirm responses. Have them provide specific examples of Special Olympics athletes whose lives were changed for the better through their participation.

W.9-10.7

CCSS **Literacy.RL.9-10.6** Analyze a particular point of view or cultural experience reflected in a work of literature from outside the United States, drawing on a wide reading of world literature. **Literacy.W.9-10.7** Conduct short as well as more sustained research projects to answer a question (including a self-generated question) or solve a problem; narrow or broaden the inquiry when appropriate; synthesize multiple sources on the subject, demonstrating understanding of the subject under investigation.

OBJECTIVES

Vocabulary
- Key Vocabulary Ⓣ

Reading Strategies
- Make Inferences
- Predict; Confirm Prediction

Comprehension & Critical Thinking
- Make Inferences
- Use Text Evidence Ⓣ

Literary Analysis
- Analyze Viewpoint Ⓣ

TEACH & PRACTICE

A Reading Support

10 Viewpoint Remind students that first-person narrators are not always reliable. Have them explain why this might be true for Teresa and what she assumes about Maricela.

Possible response:
- *Teresa thinks Maricela is a bad parent, but Teresa may be jealous of Maricela.*

RL.9-10.6

B Reading Support

11 Make Inferences Ask: What does Teresa's reaction tell you about her?

Possible response:
- *She's a caring, responsible person who will defend people who are being mistreated.*

RL.9-10.1

Monitor Comprehension

Confirm Prediction Have students think aloud to confirm their predictions about Teresa's attitude.

MODEL Say:
- *I predicted Teresa's attitude wouldn't change. Her first reaction to Valentín was so negative that I thought she would never change her mind.*
- *Even after they started working together, she was mean to him and said he was annoying.*
- *My prediction was wrong, but I learned …*

Have students use your model to confirm their predictions and share what they learned about Teresa and Valentín.

RL.9-10.10

Everything settles into a routine for Valentín and me for the next few days. The only problem I have is Mrs. O'Brien, who calls me a lot to ask me about him and about Bob Dylan. I just say everything's okay, even though Bob Dylan has **zeroed in on** an older girl, and he's disappeared with her at least once that I know of. I found out after she left her two-year-old son alone, asleep on a lounge chair. When he woke up, he started crying so loud that I had to go out there and get him before someone called Mrs. O'Brien. I brought him into the store, and it was instant friendship between the kid and Valentín. The two of them played with the rubber-band animals until his mother, Maricela Nuñez, finally showed up looking like she'd been having a good time.

I was furious.

A "Is Pablito having fun with his new friend?" she says in a fake-friendly voice. She showed no **anxiety** over the fact that the kid could have drowned or just walked off into traffic while she was fooling around with Bob Dylan. 10

"Look at them," she says, laughing at the way Pablito and Valentín are lining up the animals back on the counter. "I think Pablito is teaching the dummy a few things."

. . . the kid could have drowned . . .

Valentín looks at me with such a hurt **expression** that I honestly had to count to five or I would have punched her. I lift Pablito over the counter to his mother. B "Maricela, you are the dummy. You listen up. If we hadn't been here to take care of your son, someone would have called **the family services** and they would have taken him away—which may be the best thing for him anyway." 11

She **storms off** and behind me I hear soft laughter. It's Valentín, apparently amusing himself with his new toy.

10 Viewpoint What does Teresa assume about Maricela? Do you think Teresa's comments about her are reliable? Explain.

11 Make Inferences Think about Teresa's reaction to Maricela's remarks. How does this help you understand Teresa?

Monitor Comprehension

Confirm Prediction Did your prediction turn out to be correct? What did you learn about Teresa and Valentín?

Key Vocabulary
anxiety *n.*, nervousness, worry

In Other Words
zeroed in on concentrated his attention on
expression look on his face
the family services an agency for helping and checking on families
storms off walks away angrily

OUT-OF-SCHOOL LITERACY

MEDIA & TECHNOLOGY

Analyzing Friendships in the Movies

Activate student's prior knowledge by connecting the selection to students' experience with movies about unlikely friendships. Explain that friendship is a universal theme that appears across genres.

- Name a movie you have seen about two very different people who form a friendship or partnership.
- How did the two characters feel about each other at first? Why?
- What brings the characters together?
- What happens to help them understand each other better?
- What problem do they solve as a team?

As a class, discuss the significance of friendship as a theme, and other genres in which it appears. Ask: Why might you see this theme explored across many different genres?

SL.9-10.1.a

CCSS **Literacy.RL.9-10.1** Cite strong and thorough textual evidence to support analysis of what the text says explicitly as well as inferences drawn from the text. **Literacy.RL.9-10.6** Analyze a particular point of view or cultural experience reflected in a work of literature from outside the United States, drawing on a wide reading of world literature. **Literacy.RL.9-10.10** By the end of grade 9, read and comprehend literature, including stories, dramas, and poems, in the grades 9–10 text complexity band proficiently, with scaffolding as needed at the high end of the range. By the end of grade 10, read and comprehend literature, including stories, dramas, and poems, at the high end of the grades 9–10 text complexity band independently and proficiently. **Literacy.SL.9-10.1.a** Come to discussions prepared, having read and researched material under study; explicitly draw on that preparation by referring to evidence from texts and other research on the topic or issue to stimulate a thoughtful, well-reasoned exchange of ideas.

Predict

Think about the different things you have learned so far about Teresa and Valentín. What will they do if there's a problem? **C**

By Friday afternoon, Maricela has been here every afternoon, and she, Pablito, and Bob Dylan leave together. Valentín is getting good at pouring drinks and cleaning up, so at least the job is easier. He works with his rubber bands and only talks when Maricela brings Pablito over for a snack.

Valentín is teaching Pablito the names of his animals in Spanish. "***Elefante, caballo, oso***"—Valentín points to each animal. Then Pablito tries to repeat the words. This makes Valentín smile big. I guess it makes him feel good to be able to teach someone else something for a change. 12 **D**

12 Viewpoint
As a narrator, Teresa can only describe what she sees and thinks. What does she guess about Valentín?

It's almost closing time on Friday when we hear a kind of little scream. It doesn't last very long, so I almost ignore it. I think it's some kid out in the street, since the pool is closed for the day. But Valentín has come out with a really scared look on his face. He is trying to see something in the water. I don't see anything, but Valentín is flapping his arms and stuttering "Pa . . . Pa . . . Pa . . ." His eyes look terrified. I start thinking he may be about to **have a fit** or something.

"What is it, Valentín? What do you see out there?"

"Pablito. Pablito." He is trembling so much I fear he's going to go out of control. But I don't have time to think. The water *is* moving, and it could be the kid. I don't see Bob Dylan anywhere.

"Get Mrs. O'Brien!" I yell to Valentín. But he **is frozen on the spot**. **E**

When I get to the pool, I see the kid is **thrashing wildly** near the edge. He's really scared and his kicking is only forcing him away toward the deep water. I jump into the shallow end and start walking in his direction. I cannot tell how deep it will be, and I feel scared that I may drown, but I have to reach Pablito. I keep going toward his voice.

In Other Words

Elefante, caballo, oso Elephant, horse, bear (in Spanish)
have a fit lose control
is frozen on the spot can't move
thrashing wildly moving his arms violently

TEACH & PRACTICE

C Chunking the Text

Predict Review what students know about Teresa's and Valentín's traits and about their relationship.

ELL Use Graphic Organizer Have students fill in a Character Description chart about Teresa and Valentín to help predict what they might do in a crisis.

Character	What the Character Does	What This Shows About the Character
Teresa	gets mad at Maricela	She is concerned about Pablito.
Valentín	spends time with Pablito	He likes Pablito.

Ask: What do you think Teresa and Valentín will do if there's a problem?

Possible responses:
- *Valentín will get very upset.*
- *Teresa will call Mrs. O'Brien.*

Read Have students read pp. 247–250. Support and monitor their comprehension using the reading support provided.
RL.9-10.3; RL.9-10.10

D Reading Support

12 Viewpoint Remind students that a first-person narrator knows only about his or her own thoughts and feelings. Ask: What does Teresa guess about Valentín?

Possible response:
- *that teaching Pablito makes Valentín feel good about himself*

RL.9-10.6

E Reading Support

Cause and Effect Discuss with students what might happen to Bob Dylan when Mrs. O'Brien finds out what happened. Ask: Does Teresa still care whether Bob Dylan gets in trouble? What has changed?

Possible response:
- *No. She is concerned with saving Pablito.*

RL.9-10.1

CCSS Literacy.RL.9-10.1 Cite strong and thorough textual evidence to support analysis of what the text says explicitly as well as inferences drawn from the text. **Literacy.RL.9-10.3** Analyze how complex characters (e.g., those with multiple or conflicting motivations) develop over the course of a text, interact with other characters, and advance the plot or develop the theme. **Literacy.RL.9-10.6** Analyze a particular point of view or cultural experience reflected in a work of literature from outside the United States, drawing on a wide reading of world literature. **Literacy.RL.9-10.10** By the end of grade 9, read and comprehend literature, including stories, dramas, and poems, in the grades 9-10 text complexity band proficiently, with scaffolding as needed at the high end of the range. By the end of grade 10, read and comprehend literature, including stories, dramas, and poems, at the high end of the grades 9-10 text complexity band independently and proficiently.

READ

OBJECTIVES

Reading Strategy
- Make Inferences

Comprehension & Critical Thinking
- Make Inferences
- Use Text Evidence (T)

Literary Analysis
- Analyze Viewpoint (T)

Viewing
- Respond to and Interpret Visuals

Grammar
- Past Progressive Verb Forms (T)

TEACH & PRACTICE

A Reading Support

13 **Viewpoint** Ask: What could someone watching tell about Teresa? What couldn't an outsider know?

Possible responses:
- *An outsider could hear her calling for help and see her struggling in the water.*
- *He or she couldn't know that Teresa can't see or swim well. That's what scares her so much.*

RL.9-10.6

B Reading Support

14 **Make Inferences** Reread paragraphs 2–3 aloud. Ask what Teresa's actions show about her.

Possible responses:
- *She is unselfish and brave.*
- *She knows what to do in an emergency.*

RL.9-10.1

C Critical Viewing: Effect

Analyze Artistic Effect Ask students to think about how Teresa feels while trying to save Pablito. Ask: How does the picture reflect Teresa's feelings when she's underwater?

Possible responses:
- *The hands below look like a drowning person's hands, and the one above looks like it belongs to a rescuer.*
- *All the hands look like they're trying desperately to reach each other.*

RL.9-10.7

A But I feel that I'm moving in slow motion, so I finally dive into the water. My glasses get wet and I can't see, so I throw them off, which makes it worse. I can't see a thing. I start screaming for help. I'm sinking and pushing up, stretching my hands in front of me to feel his body. 13

B Just when I feel that my lungs are going to burst, I feel Pablito and pull him up. I hear splashing behind me, and it's Valentín heading for us. He carries Pablito out of the pool in one arm and pulls me out with his free hand.

When I take him from Valentín's arms, his body **feels limp**, so I put him on the ground and push on his tiny chest until water comes out. Soon he is coughing and crying. 14

Then I see Bob Dylan and Maricela run up. Bob Dylan takes over while I run to call Mrs. O'Brien and the emergency rescue. Maricela **goes nuts** until Valentín guides her to a bench, where they sit holding hands until the ambulance drives up. She and Bob Dylan ride with Pablito to the hospital.

It's all over in minutes, but I feel like it's days while Valentín and I sit in Mrs. O'Brien's office, waiting for word from the hospital. I also expect to get fired for not **reporting** that Bob Dylan was not at his post. She comes in in a very solemn mood, and I look over at Valentín, who is

Reaching Hands, 2007, Jerry Lindemann. Digital illustration.

C **Critical Viewing: Effect** Explain how this image reflects how Teresa feels when she is underwater.

13 **Viewpoint** What does Teresa tell the reader about her feelings that an outsider couldn't know?

14 **Make Inferences** What do Teresa's actions with Pablito tell you about her?

In Other Words
feels limp is weak and lifeless
goes nuts is very upset (slang)
reporting telling someone

GRAMMAR

Past Progressive Verb Forms

Teach/Model Display the transparency. Review the past forms of the verb *be*. Model how to change a main verb to form the past progressive. Read the examples aloud. Have students suggest additional example sentences.

Practice A. Have students form the past progressive. Write each new verb on the transparency. **B.** Have partners write and share their reports. Other students identify a sentence with a past progressive form.

L.9-10.1.b

Grammar & Writing Practice Book, pp. 83–84

Grammar Transparency 38

GRAMMAR PAST PROGRESSIVE VERB FORMS 38

How Do You Show That an Action Was In Process?

Use *Was* or *Were* Plus the *-ing* Form of the Verb.

- Sometimes you want to show that an action was happening over a period of time in the past. Use the past progressive form of the verb.
- To form the past progressive, use the helping verb **was** or **were** plus a main verb that ends in -ing. The **helping verb** must agree with the subject.

I **was cleaning** the concession stand. I heard a sound and looked up.
Valentín **was flapping** his arms. He **was stuttering**.
He **was trying** to see something in the water.
I **was running** to Valentín. I **was standing** beside him.
We **were looking** down in horror.

Try It

A. Tell what happened when Pablito almost drowned and the teens were trying to save him. Say the sentences with the past progressive form of the verbs in parentheses.

1. Pablito was struggling in the water. **(struggle)**
2. Suddenly, I was jumping into the pool. **(jump)**
3. Soon I was swimming toward Pablito. **(swim)**
4. Then I was pulling the boy up, and Valentín was lifting him out of the pool. **(pull, lift)**
5. We were saving Pablito! **(save)**

B. Now tell a partner about an emergency you saw. What was happening? Use the past progressive form of the verbs.
Sentences will vary.

GRAMMAR SKILLS PATH

- 36 Irregular Past Tense Verbs
- 37 Irregular Past Tense Verbs
- ▶ 38 Past Progressive Verb Forms — ELL Language & Grammar Lab
- 39 Future Tense Verbs
- 40 Review: Verb Tenses

CCSS **Literacy.RL.9-10.1** Cite strong and thorough textual evidence to support analysis of what the text says explicitly as well as inferences drawn from the text. **Literacy.RL.9-10.6** Analyze a particular point of view or cultural experience reflected in a work of literature from outside the United States, drawing on a wide reading of world literature. **Literacy.RL.9-10.7** Analyze the representation of a subject or a key scene in two different artistic mediums, including what is emphasized or absent in each treatment (e.g., Auden's "Musée des Beaux Arts" and Breughel's Landscape with the Fall of Icarus). **Literacy.L.9-10.1.b** Use various types of phrases (noun, verb, adjectival, adverbial, participial, prepositional, absolute) and clauses (independent, dependent; noun, relative, adverbial) to convey specific meanings and add variety and interest to writing or presentations.

wringing his hands. I know he's only thinking of Pablito, and I feel a little guilty for worrying about myself so much.

"The boy is going to be fine," Mrs. O'Brien says, "thanks to both of you."

Then she does something that really surprises me. She kisses me on the forehead. She **fishes** my glasses out of her skirt pocket.

Then she goes over to Valentín.

"Valentín, you did a very good thing today. You and Teresa saved a little boy's life. You are a hero. Do you understand me?"

"*Sí,*" Valentín says. But I'm not sure about his English, so I start to translate: "Valentín, ***ella dice que eres un héroe***."

It's all over in minutes, but I feel like it's days . . .

"I know," Valentín says, and smiles real big.

"You speak English?" I cannot believe he's fooled me into thinking that he can barely speak a few words of Spanish, and here he understands two languages. **D**

"*Sí,*" Valentín answers, and laughs his funny quiet laugh. 15

Mrs. O'Brien looks at Valentín in a motherly way. "Valentín, how would you like to keep your job here year-round?"

Valentín slowly glances over at me, as if asking me what I think. He can communicate in total silence, and I'm learning his language.

"When the pool closes at the end of the summer, we are going to ask you, and yes, Teresa too, to come work in my office. We have many things that you both can do, such as helping out with after-school programs and **supervising** the playground. Are you interested?"

Valentín looks at me for an answer again. I can tell that we have

15 **Make Inferences** Why do you think Valentín hasn't spoken English before? How does this change what you think about Valentín?

In Other Words
wringing his hands twisting his hands together
fishes pulls
ella dice que eres un héroe she says that you are a hero (in Spanish)
supervising watching over

TEACH & PRACTICE

D Reading Support

15 Make Inferences Ask students why they think Valentín hasn't spoken English before.

ELL Use Graphic Organizer Have students use a graphic organizer to show how details lead to conclusions.

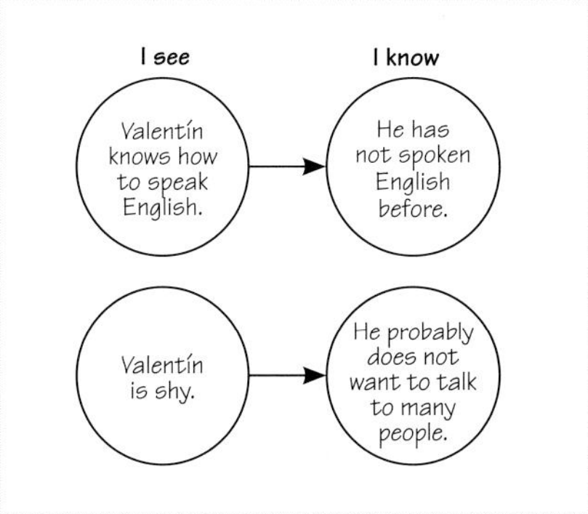

Ask: Why didn't Valentín speak English with Teresa before?

Possible responses:
- *because he was too shy*
- *because he didn't trust her*

Ask: How does this change your opinion of Valentín?

Possible response:
- *He's a more complicated person than I thought.*

RL.9-10.1

E Reading Support

Theme Ask: What lesson about heroes do you think the author wants to teach readers?

Possible responses:
- *that ordinary people can be heroes; that heroes care about other people; that anyone is capable of doing heroic things*

RL.9-10.2

CCSS Literacy.RL.9-10.1 Cite strong and thorough textual evidence to support analysis of what the text says explicitly as well as inferences drawn from the text. **Literacy.RL.9-10.2** Determine a theme or central idea of a text and analyze in detail its development over the course of the text, including how it emerges and is shaped and refined by specific details; provide an objective summary of the text.

READ

OBJECTIVES

Reading Strategy
- Make Inferences

Comprehension & Critical Thinking
- Make Inferences
- Use Text Evidence Ⓣ

Literary Analysis
- Analyze Viewpoint Ⓣ

Writing
- Form: Response to Literature

TEACH & PRACTICE

Ⓐ Reading Support

16 **Make Inferences** Ask what reason Teresa gives for taking the job. Is it her real reason?

Possible response:
- *so Valentín will take a job there, too; no, she really likes working with him and is proud to have a year-round job*

RL.9-10.1

APPLY

Ⓑ ANALYZE

1. **Explain** He is smart and good at teaching. He is caring and brave. RL.9-10.1; RL.9-10.3
2. **Vocabulary** She thinks her friends won't want to hang around with her. She's right; her friends do think that Valentín is strange. L.9-10.6
3. **Analyze Viewpoint** **Before/After:** "bad news … a disaster" (p. 240)/"He's helping me out." (p. 245); "I don't want to spend the whole summer with one." (p. 241)/"… it must be tough to have to work so hard." (p. 245); "a big hairy child" (p. 241)/"*ella dice que eres un héroe*" (p. 249). The reader has a bad impression of him at first because Teresa is unhappy that he is there. But as her opinion of him changes, she makes him seem more likeable. RL.9-10.6
4. **Focus Strategy: Make Inferences** Have volunteers share their partner's text evidence with the class. RL.9-10.1

Ⓐ to take the job as partners or he won't do it. I sneeze loudly and he practically falls out of his chair. Really, he's the most nervous human being I've ever met. I see that I'm going to have to put up with him in this new job, too. I don't think anyone else would have the patience. 16 ❖

16 **Make Inferences** Why does Teresa say she takes the job? Why do you think she takes it?

ANALYZE A Job for Valentín

Ⓑ

1. **Explain** What qualities does Valentín have? Think about his friendship with Pablito and his behavior during the accident. Include examples from the text to support your answer.
2. **Vocabulary** Why does Teresa experience **anxiety** when she learns that she is to work with Valentín? Do her fears come true? Explain.
3. **Analyze Viewpoint** Make a chart to compare the way Teresa describes Valentín at the beginning of the story with her ideas about him after the accident. How does Teresa's viewpoint affect the way we see him?

Before	After
"Valentín has the posture of a gorilla." (page 241)	"He can communicate in total silence, and I'm learning his language." (page 249)

4. **Focus Strategy** **Make Inferences** Find a passage where you as a reader understand something that the narrator doesn't realize. Tell a partner how you used evidence to make your inference.

Ⓒ **Return to the Text**

Reread and Write Is Valentín a hero? What does the story say about how challenged individuals can become everyday heroes? Write your opinion in a paragraph. Include two or three examples from the story to support your ideas.

Ⓒ Return to the Text

Possible examples:
- *Valentín takes good care of Pablito.*
- *He's the first to notice that Pablito is drowning. He pulls Teresa and Pablito out.*

W.9-10.9.a; W.9-10.10

Edge Interactive Practice Book, p. 118

CCSS **Literacy.RL.9-10.1** Cite strong and thorough textual evidence to support analysis of what the text says explicitly as well as inferences drawn from the text. **Literacy.RL.9-10.3** Analyze how complex characters (e.g., those with multiple or conflicting motivations) develop over the course of a text, interact with other characters, and advance the plot or develop the theme. **Literacy.RL.9-10.6** Analyze a particular point of view or cultural experience reflected in a work of literature from outside the United States, drawing on a wide reading of world literature. **Literacy.W.9-10.9.a** Apply grades 9-10 Reading standards to literature (e.g., "Analyze how an author draws on and transforms source material in a specific work [e.g., how Shakespeare treats a theme or topic from Ovid or the Bible or how a later author draws on a play by Shakespeare]"). Literacy.W.9-10.10 Write routinely over extended time frames (time for research, reflection, and revision) and shorter time frames (a single sitting or a day or two) for a range of tasks, purposes, and audiences. **Literacy.L.9-10.6** Acquire and use accurately general academic and domain-specific words and phrases, sufficient for reading, writing, speaking, and listening at the college and career readiness level; demonstrate independence in gathering vocabulary knowledge when considering a word or phrase important to comprehension or expression.

Hero

by Mariah Carey

There's a hero,
  if you look inside your heart.
You don't have to be afraid,
  of what you are.

There's an answer,
  if you reach into your soul.
And the sorrow that you know,
  will melt away.

Chorus
And then a hero comes along,
  with the strength to carry on.
And you cast your fears aside,
  and you know you can survive.
So when you feel like hope is gone,
  look inside you and be strong.
And you'll finally see the truth,
  that a hero lies in you.

It's a long road,
  when you face the world alone.
No one reaches out a hand
  for you to hold.

You can find love,
  if you search within yourself.
And the emptiness you felt,
  will disappear.

[Chorus]

Lord knows,
  dreams are hard to follow.
But don't let anyone
  tear them away.

Hold on,
  there will be tomorrow.
In time
  you'll find the way.

[Chorus]
...that a hero lies in you...
...that a hero lies in you...

READ

OBJECTIVES

Reading Strategies
- Make Connections
- Connect Across Texts

Listening and Speaking
- Listen Actively
- Respond to Literature

ENGAGE

Read the Lyrics Aloud If possible, play the song for students before reading the lyrics. Challenge students to listen for the song's theme, or lesson. Then read the lyrics two lines at a time. Have students echo you chorally.
RL.9-10.2

TEACH & PRACTICE

Listen Actively Check for understanding and elicit personal responses. Ask: Who is the speaker talking to?

Possible response:
- *to people who need to find strength inside themselves*

Ask: What message does the songwriter want to give listeners?

Possible response:
- *Don't wait for a hero to rescue you. Look inside yourself for strength.*
SL.9-10.1

Connect Across Texts Ask students to compare and contrast the song's theme to the theme in "A Job for Valentín."

Possible responses:
- *Both tell about ordinary heroes and being afraid.*
- *The story tells about people who act like heroes when they need to. The song tells about looking inside yourself to find a hero.*
RL.9-10.2

CCSS **Literacy.RL.9-10.2** Determine a theme or central idea of a text and analyze in detail its development over the course of the text, including how it emerges and is shaped and refined by specific details; provide an objective summary of the text. **Literacy.SL.9-10.1** Initiate and participate effectively in a range of collaborative discussions (one-on-one, in groups, and teacher-led) with diverse partners on grades 9-10 topics, texts, and issues, building on others' ideas and expressing their own clearly and persuasively.

Lesson 13

BEFORE READING

OBJECTIVES

Reading Strategy
- Make Inferences

Literary Analysis
- Analyze Structure: Feature Article Ⓣ

TEACH STRATEGIES

Ⓐ Analyze Structure: Feature Article

Introduce Read the introduction to define feature article. Ask students if they've ever read a feature article in a newspaper or magazine, and what it was about.

Ask: What is the main difference between a news story and a feature article?

Possible response:
- *A news story reports only facts about a current event. A feature article includes details about people's emotions, opinions, and problems.*

Look Into the Text Use the callouts on p. 252 to teach the elements of a feature article. Ask: Which words and phrases make the article sound emotional or dramatic?

Possible responses:
- *shattered, crazily, struggling for their lives, sped*

RI.9-10.5

Ⓑ Focus Strategy

Make Inferences Define the strategy and work through the steps in the How To box.

Then have partners reread Look Into the Text to infer Hart's reason for dropping off the girls. Have them complete an inference chart to show their process.

Possible response:
- *Probably the girls were too young to help, or they were not strong enough swimmers to save drowning people.*

RI.9-10.1

ONGOING ASSESSMENT

Have students explain in their own words how a feature article is different from a news article.

Before Reading In the Heart of a Hero

feature article by Johnny Dwyer

Reading Strategies
- Plan and Monitor
- Determine Importance
- ▶ **Make Inferences**
- Ask Questions
- Make Connections
- Synthesize
- Visualize

Analyze Structure: Feature Article

A **feature article**, or human interest story, is different from a **news story**, which reports just the facts about a current event. Feature articles go into more detail about real people and their emotions, opinions, and problems. There is often something dramatic or surprising about the stories feature articles tell.

Look Into the Text

On a sunny Sunday last month, the glass-like surface of Lake George, in New York's Adirondack Mountains, was dotted with boats. Just before three, the afternoon's tranquility shattered. The *Ethan Allen*, a tour boat carrying almost fifty senior citizens, tipped crazily. Within thirty seconds, it had capsized and its passengers were struggling for their lives.

Brian Hart was on the lake that day, paddling a canoe with Brianna, his youngest daughter, and three of her cousins. When he saw the boat overturn, he didn't hesitate, immediately calling 911—"Get to the lake real quick"—even as he headed for the nearest dock. There, he dropped the girls and phoned his brother, Eric. Two minutes later, Eric, 42, and his son, E.J., scooped up Brian in the family fishing boat, and the three of them sped to the scene.

These facts tell who, what, where, and when.

A quotation gives the exact words of a witness.

The emotional hook pulls in the reader.

How does the author use words and phrases that give a dramatic feeling to the story?

Focus Strategy ▶ Make Inferences

When you read nonfiction, like a feature article, you add information from your own knowledge and experiences. Use this information to **make inferences** that help you understand the text.

Focus Strategy

HOW TO MAKE INFERENCES

1. Think about what happens in the selection. Compare this to your own experiences, and record your thoughts in an **Inference Chart**.
2. Make an inference about a person or event in the selection.
3. Keep updating your ideas and inferences as you read.

Inference Chart

Think about what happened.	A boat turned over in the lake.
Think about what most people would do.	Most would call for help.
Think about what the hero did.	He called 911 and his family. Then they all jumped into a boat and sped to the scene.
My inference about the hero: Hart cares about other people and is a quick and clear thinker.	

CCSS **Literacy.RI.9-10.1** Cite strong and thorough textual evidence to support analysis of what the text says explicitly as well as inferences drawn from the text. **Literacy.RI.9-10.5** Analyze in detail how an author's ideas or claims are developed and refined by particular sentences, paragraphs, or larger portions of a text (e.g., a section or chapter).

In the Heart of a Hero

FEATURE ARTICLE

by Johnny Dwyer

Connect Across Texts
In "A Job for Valentín," the hero is not who we expect. This feature article explores why some people act as heroes when others cannot.

On a sunny Sunday last month, the glass-like surface of Lake George, in New York's Adirondack Mountains, was dotted with boats. Just before three, the afternoon's **tranquility shattered**. The *Ethan Allen*, a tour boat carrying almost fifty senior citizens, tipped crazily. Within thirty seconds, it had **capsized** and its passengers were struggling for their lives. 1

1 Feature Article What information in the opening paragraph tells who, what, when, and where?

It was a calm, beautiful day before the *Ethan Allen* capsized on Oct. 2, 2005.

Brian Hart was on the lake that day, paddling a canoe with Brianna, his youngest daughter, and three of her cousins. When he saw the boat overturn, he didn't hesitate, immediately calling 911—"Get to the lake real quick"—even as he headed for the nearest dock. There, he dropped the girls and phoned his brother, Eric. Two minutes later, Eric, 42, and his son, E.J., scooped up Brian in the family fishing boat, and the three of them sped to the scene. Brian and Eric dove straight in and started **hauling survivors** onto life preservers, seat cushions—anything that would float. When other boats arrived, the Hart brothers **hoisted** victims into them for nearly half an hour.

Onlookers gasped in horror, watching the **tragedy unfold**; many

Key Vocabulary
- **survivor** *n.*, person who lives through a hardship or disaster
- **tragedy** *n.*, terrible disaster

In Other Words
tranquility shattered calmness was wrecked
capsized turned upside down
hauling pulling
hoisted lifted
unfold happen over time

OBJECTIVES
Vocabulary
- Key Vocabulary T

Reading Strategies
- Connect Across Texts
- Make Connections

Comprehension & Critical Thinking
- Make Inferences
- Use Text Evidence T

Literary Analysis
- Analyze Structure: Feature Article

BUILD BACKGROUND

C Everyday Heroes
Read the title and the introduction.

ELL Comprehensible Input
Explain the multiple meanings of the word *fishing*:
- As a verb, *fishing* can mean "catching a fish" and "searching for," as in "fishing for my keys."
- In this article, *fishing* is also used as an adjective to describe a boat.

Ask: Would a man spending an afternoon in his boat expect to become a hero?

Possible response:
- *No—he's probably just having fun.*

D Connect Across Texts
Ask: Is a person more heroic if his or her actions are unexpected, like they were for Valentín and Teresa? What if they are a part of his or her personality, as for King Arthur?

Possible response:
- *Everyday heroes are braver and more heroic because they do more than they think they can.*

TEACH & PRACTICE

E Reading Support
1 Feature Article Ask: What event happened? Who did it happen to? When and where did it happen?

Possible response:
- *It is about an accident on a tour boat carrying senior citizens on Lake George one Sunday.*

RI.9-10.5

Comprehension Coach

Build Reading Power
Assign students to use the software, based on their instructional needs.

Read Silently
- Comprehension questions with immediate feedback
- Glossary support
- Review text evidence

RI.9-10.10

Listen
- Professional model of fluent reading

Record
- Oral reading fluency practice
- Ongoing fluency assessment with immediate feedback

CCSS Literacy.RI.9-10.10 By the end of grade 9, read and comprehend literary nonfiction in the grades 9–10 text complexity band proficiently, with scaffolding as needed at the high end of the range. By the end of grade 10, read and comprehend literary nonfiction at the high end of the grades 9–10 text complexity band independently and proficiently. **Literacy.RI.9-10.5** Analyze in detail how an author's ideas or claims are developed and refined by particular sentences, paragraphs, or larger portions of a text (e.g., a section or chapter).

OBJECTIVES

Vocabulary
- Key Vocabulary ⊤
- Strategy: Use Contextual Analysis

Reading Strategy
- Make Inferences; Review Strategies

Comprehension & Critical Thinking
- Make Inferences
- Use Text Evidence ⊤

Literary Analysis
- Analyze Structure: Feature Article ⊤

Research Skill
- Analyze Information

Viewing
- Respond to and Interpret Visuals

Grammar
- Future Tense Verbs ⊤

TEACH & PRACTICE

Ⓐ Analyze Visuals

Interpret the Visuals Ask: What does the map help you understand about the event shown in the photo?

Possible response:
- *It helps me understand where in the United States New York State is located and where the boat sank.*

Ask: What information do you learn from reading the caption?

Possible response:
- *I learned that divers were called to search for the boat after it sank.*
RI.9-10.7

Ⓑ Reading Support

2 Feature Article Ask: What kind of behavior does Farley think DNA may determine?

Possible response:
- *thrill-seeking; risk-taking*

ELL List Vocabulary Explain that *thrill-seeking* and *risk-taking* are compound adjectives. List and explain the meaning of other adjectives to describe this type of personality: *daring, bold, adventurous, risky, courageous.* Encourage students to use the words during their discussions.
RI.9-10.5

GRAMMAR SKILLS PATH
36 Irregular Past Tense Verbs
37 Irregular Past Tense Verbs
38 Past Progressive Verb Forms
▶ **39** Future Tense Verbs — ELL Language & Grammar Lab
40 Review: Verb Tenses

called for help. Those who saw the brothers' actions surely wondered at their uncommon courage: *Do they know what they're doing? Will they be able to save anyone? Will they die trying?* Later—over dinner, perhaps, or just before they drifted off to sleep—these **bystanders** likely pondered another set of questions both simple and complex: *What makes a hero? Why do some of us dive in when others simply cannot?*

In Brian's case, the answer may lie in his **biological makeup**. "I guess my boys were always fearless," says Donald Hart, 71, Brian and Eric's father. "Not only that day, but in childhood, with the motorbikes, snowmobiles. I wasn't surprised they would do something like that."

Recovery divers prepare to search for the *Ethan Allen* after it sank in Lake George, New York, in October 2005.

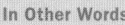

Dr. Frank Farley, a psychologist who has studied heroic behavior, says that something literally in a hero's **DNA** may contribute to brave actions. Heroes, he says, often have what he calls "Big T"—or thrill-seeking, risk-taking personalities. "They're not satisfied with normal levels of **stimulation**, so they seek out more of it," says Farley. **2**

Ⓐ **Interpret the Visuals** What additional information do the map and caption give you about the photo?

2 Feature Article What ideas does the quotation support?

In Other Words
bystanders people who stood by and watched
biological makeup nature
DNA genetic code
stimulation excitement

254 Unit 3 The Hero Within

GRAMMAR

Future Tense Verbs

Teach/Model Display the transparency. Explain the future tense, using the time line and example sentences. Discuss the two options for forming the future tense. Generate more examples of future tense parallel structure: *Eric will answer the phone, get his son, and speed to the lake.*

Practice A. Point out that students may use either option to complete the sentences.
B. Have students write and share their predictions about Brian. Choose one to write, and ask the group to identify the future tense verb.
L.9-10.1.a; L.9-10.1.b

 Grammar & Writing Practice Book, pp. 85–86

Grammar Transparency 39

How Do You Tell About the Future?
Use *Will* **Before the Verb.**

- The **future tense** of a verb shows that an action will happen later.

Past ◄—— Earlier ○ —— Now ○ —— Later ● ——► Future
Future Tense

To form the future tense, use **will** before the main verb.
Survivors **will grab** the life preservers.

Or use **am, is,** or **are** plus **going to** before the main verb.
Survivors **are going to grab** the life preservers.

- If **will** or **am, is,** or **are** plus **going to** comes before the first verb in a series, all three verbs are in the future tense.
Brian **will head** to a dock, **drop off** the children, and **call** his brother.

Try It

A. Say each sentence. Use the future tense of the verb in parentheses. More than one answer is possible. *Possible responses:*
1. Brian _____ will dive _____ in, swim out, and save people. **(dive)**
2. He _____ is going to save _____ as many people as possible. **(save)**
3. People _____ are going to recover _____ on shore. **(recover)**
4. Brian's daughter _____ will wait _____ for him on shore. **(wait)**

B. Now let's write a prediction about Brian. Write three sentences to tell what you think Brian will say about the event. Use future tense verbs. *Sentences will vary.*

CCSS Literacy.RI.9-10.5 Analyze in detail how an author's ideas or claims are developed and refined by particular sentences, paragraphs, or larger portions of a text (e.g., a section or chapter). Literacy.RI.9-10.7 Analyze various accounts of a subject told in different mediums (e.g., a person's life story in both print and multimedia), determining which details are emphasized in each account. Literacy.L.9-10.1.a Use parallel structure. Literacy.L.9-10.1.b Use various types of phrases (noun, verb, adjectival, adverbial, participial, prepositional, absolute) and clauses (independent, dependent; noun, relative, adverbial) to convey specific meanings and add variety and interest to writing or presentations.

When Brian plunged into the lake and swam into the crowd of struggling passengers, he remained calm and focused. "Situational heroes," as Farley refers to regular people who **rise to the occasion** in emergencies, simply aren't **inhibited** by "**uncertainty**, which is one of the biggest sources of human fear." 3 **C**

Brian had something else, too, that **complemented** his **inherent** fearlessness: his comfort in the water, particularly this water. As a boy, he'd learned to paddle and fish on Lake George, and later scuba dived and piloted his first motorboat there. "We always used to horse around, brothers grabbing you in the water. I'm sure a lot of people who came [to the scene] in boats didn't jump in because they didn't have the comfort level I had." **D**

And beyond that? Perhaps empathy. 4

Is it **a coincidence** that this man who dove into the water had once been rescued on Lake George? In 1978, Brian was thrown from a motorboat. He floated dazed—but uninjured—for fifteen minutes until a boater fished him out.

Donald wonders about the circumstances of rescues—a man with the heart of a hero finding himself in the right place at the right time—and **speculates on** what his boys might have taken from hearing about his own experience: "Something like this, it's a series of events that happens, and if there's

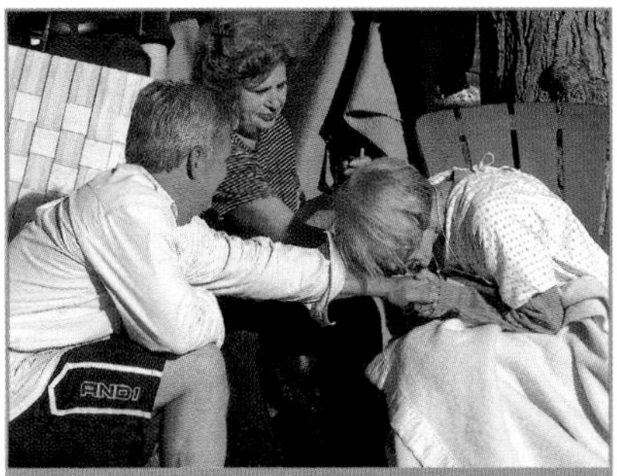

Ethan Allen survivor Carol Charlton holds Brian Hart's hand.

3 Access Vocabulary Why are people like Brian called "situational heroes"? Look for root words and context clues for ideas.

4 Make Inferences Use what you already know about rescuers. Do they "dive in" with the same kind of attitude presented here?

Key Vocabulary
- **inhibit** *v.*, to stop or hold a person back from doing something
- **inherent** *adj.*, natural, basic

In Other Words
rise to the occasion do more than they thought they could
uncertainty doubt
complemented added to
a coincidence just chance
speculates on guesses about

TEACH & PRACTICE

C Reading Support

3 Access Vocabulary Have students identify word parts they may know in the word *situational.* Use a think-aloud to model the process: A *situation* is something that happens at a certain time. Situations can be good or bad.

Possible response:
- *A situational hero must be someone who only acts like a hero at a certain place or time.*

L.9-10.4.a; L.9-10.4.b

D Reading Support

4 Make Inferences Have students reread the first three paragraphs.

ELL Rephrase Language Explain that *dive in* means to "jump head-first into water." The idiom "dive in" can also mean to get involved in something.

Ask: From what you know about rescuers, do they "dive in" for the same reasons presented in the text?

Possible response:
- *Yes, Brian feels calm under pressure. He also feels comfortable in the water. These seem like good reasons why he and other rescuers would "dive in" to dangerous situations.*

RI.9-10.1

Review Strategies Have partners discuss other strategies they used as they read the text.

Possible response:
- *As I read about Brian's actions, I asked myself: Other than DNA, why would Brian risk his life to rescue the passengers? I read on and learned that he had once been rescued on Lake George. Now I want to know more about his experiences.*

RI.9-10.1

CONTENT AREA CONNECTIONS

HISTORY

Research the *Ethan Allen* Tragedy

Conduct Research Have students do research to answer the following questions:
- Who owned the *Ethan Allen* at the time of the tragedy?
- Why did the boat capsize?
- Why were most of the passengers senior citizens?
- How many survivors were there? How many people died?
- Besides the Harts, who helped with the rescue? Were the other rescuers similar to the Harts in some ways?

Share and Compare After sharing their findings, students might debate the following question: *Should the people who owned the boat pay damages to the victims' families?*

W.9-10.7

CCSS **Literacy.RI.9-10.1** Cite strong and thorough textual evidence to support analysis of what the text says explicitly as well as inferences drawn from the text. **Literacy.W.9-10.7** Conduct short as well as more sustained research projects to answer a question (including a self-generated question) or solve a problem; narrow or broaden the inquiry when appropriate; synthesize multiple sources on the subject, demonstrating understanding of the subject under investigation. **Literacy.L.9-10.4.a** Use context (e.g., the overall meaning of a sentence, paragraph, or text; a word's position or function in a sentence) as a clue to the meaning of a word or phrase. **Literacy.L.9-10.4.b** Identify and correctly use patterns of word changes that indicate different meanings or parts of speech (e.g., analyze, analysis, analytical; advocate, advocacy).

OBJECTIVES

Vocabulary
- Key Vocabulary Ⓣ

Reading Strategy
- Make Inferences

Comprehension & Critical Thinking
- Make Inferences
- Use Text Evidence Ⓣ

Literary Analysis
- Analyze Structure: Feature Article

Writing
- Form: Response to Literature

TEACH & PRACTICE

A Reading Support

5 Make Inferences Ask: Does Hart answer Brianna's questions truthfully? What does this tell you about him?

Possible responses:
- *He doesn't tell her everything. He wants to protect his daughter from knowing about tragedy.*
- *He believes he should help others.*

RI.9-10.1

APPLY

B Analyze

1. **Recall and Interpret** Probably not—to Brian, what he did was just the right thing to do. RI.9-10.1
2. **Vocabulary** A psychologist who has studied heroic behavior said acting like a hero might be in our DNA. L.9-10.6
3. **Analyze Structure: Feature Article** The photos, captions, and map give more information about the event that took place. RI.9-10.5
4. **Focus Strategy: Make Inferences** The rescuers showed heart, or empathy, when they risked their lives to save people. RI.9-10.1

C Return to the Text

Before they begin writing, encourage students to tell which explanation for heroism they chose, and why.
W.9-10.1.b; W.9-10.10

---

a lesson, maybe it's that there's an outside source, a God above."

Whether **Providence** or circumstance, when Hart, exhausted, finally returned to shore, Brianna asked, "Did you save everybody?"

"Yes," he lied. She's 8 years old; there's time yet for truth.

"Daddy, why did you go back?" she asked.

"The people needed my help."

For some—for heroes—it's as simple as that. 5 ❖

5 Make Inferences Think about Hart's answers to his daughter's questions. What does it tell you about him?

Analyze In the Heart of a Hero

1. **Recall and Interpret** Would Brian Hart consider himself to be a hero? Include examples of his words and actions to explain your answer.
2. **Vocabulary** What information in the article supports the idea that heroic behavior is **inherent**? Do you agree? Explain.
3. **Analyze Structure: Feature Article** Review the article and identify several ways that the author gives information. Explain the information and tell how it helps you understand the selection.
4. **Focus Strategy Make Inferences** Why would the author include the word *heart* in the title of this article? Explain your reasons to a partner.

Return to the Text

Reread and Write What explanations does the author give for heroic behavior? Write a paragraph to describe the explanation that you agree with most. Support your opinion with examples from the text.

In Other Words
Providence God's plan

Interactive Reading

Have students reread and mark "In the Heart of a Hero" within the Edge Interactive Practice Book to apply their knowledge of feature articles and to practice the Focus Strategy—Make Inferences.

Edge Interactive Practice Book, pp. 119–122

Unit Project

Progress Check Allow time for students to work on their unit projects. Meet with individuals and/or groups to provide guidance and check on their progress.

myNGconnect.com
- **Unit Planning Tools**
- **Unit Project Evaluation Rubric**

CCSS **Literacy.RI.9-10.1** Cite strong and thorough textual evidence to support analysis of what the text says explicitly as well as inferences drawn from the text. **Literacy.RI.9-10.5** Analyze in detail how an author's ideas or claims are developed and refined by particular sentences, paragraphs, or larger portions of a text (e.g., a section or chapter). **Literacy.W.9-10.1.b** Apply grades 9-10 Reading standards to literary nonfiction (e.g., "Delineate and evaluate the argument and specific claims in a text, assessing whether the reasoning is valid and the evidence is relevant and sufficient; identify false statements and fallacious reasoning"). **Literacy.W.9-10.10** Write routinely over extended time frames (time for research, reflection, and revision) and shorter time frames (a single sitting or a day or two) for a range of tasks, purposes, and audiences. **Literacy.L.9-10.6** Acquire and use accurately general academic and domain-specific words and phrases, sufficient for reading, writing, speaking, and listening at the college and career readiness level; demonstrate independence in gathering vocabulary knowledge when considering a word or phrase important to comprehension or expression.

REFLECT AND ASSESS

- A Job for Valentín
- Hero
- In the Heart of a Hero

What Makes a Hero?

Reading

Critical Thinking

1. **Analyze** Review the **Anticipation Guide** on page 236 and explain whether you still agree or disagree with the statements after reading the selections. Use examples from the selections to support your answer.
2. **Interpret** Do you think Valentín fits the description of a "situational hero" who acts bravely in emergencies? Review the definition on page 255, then give reasons to support your answers to a group.
3. **Compare** The author of "In the Heart of a Hero" compares people with **inherent** courage to others who are **inhibited** by fear and **anxiety**. How would Brian Hart, Teresa, and Valentín respond to this idea? Support your ideas with details from the texts.
4. **Imagine** Think of the scene that takes place between Mrs. O'Brien and Bob Dylan after the pool accident. Choose a partner and role-play the scene, using what you have learned about both characters in the story.
5. **Synthesize** Imagine Brian Hart wasn't successful in saving anyone. Would he still be a hero? Include details from the article to help you explain your answer.

Writing

Write About Literature

Comparison In "A Job for Valentín," the hero is not who we expect. The unlikely hero is a common archetype that appears often in traditional literature. Think about the two old women in the legend *Left Behind* or the characters in a familiar fable, such as "The Tortoise and the Hare." Write a paragraph explaining how the "heroes" in these stories are like Valentín.

Vocabulary

Key Vocabulary Review

Oral Review Work with a partner. Use these words to complete the paragraph.

anxiety	**inhibited**	**survivor**
distracted	**prejudiced**	**tragedy**
inherent	**protest**	

My friend believes that heroes are different from everyone else. He says that ordinary people get too __(1)__ by the excitement around them to think clearly and help. He thinks that their __(2)__, or nervousness, will cause more harm than good. Some people may want to help, but they are too __(3)__ by their own doubts to step forward and help. However, I disagree and __(4)__ this idea because it gives a negative opinion that is __(5)__ against everyday people. Just ask a __(6)__, like Pablito, who lived through an accident. I bet he'd say that although some people are born with the __(7)__ qualities of a hero, almost anyone can be trained to help in a disaster or __(8)__.

Writing Application Recall a time when you felt anxiety. Write a paragraph about the situation that uses at least three Key Vocabulary words.

Fluency

Read with Ease: Expression

Assess your reading fluency with the passage in the Reading Handbook, p. 758. Then complete the self-check below.

1. My expression did/did not sound natural.
2. My words correct per minute: _____

Lesson 14 REFLECT AND ASSESS

OBJECTIVES

Vocabulary
- Key Vocabulary Ⓣ

Reading Fluency
- Expression Ⓣ

Comprehension & Critical Thinking
- Compare Across Texts
- Use Text Evidence Ⓣ

Literary Analysis
- Evaluate Literature

Writing
- Form: Paragraph
- Form: Comparison

Reading

Critical Thinking

1. **Analyze** Have students examine how the selections relate to the ideas in the Anticipation Guide. Have them explain how the selections influenced their ideas.
RL.9-10.1; RI.9-10.1
2. **Interpret** Valentín acts bravely in an emergency, which makes him a situational hero. But he also feels uncertain. He may not respond in the same way in other emergencies.
RL.9-10.1; RI.9-10.1
3. **Compare** Brian Hart might agree, but Teresa and Valentín would probably disagree. Both of them are "inhibited by uncertainty," but they still act like heroes when the need arises.
RL.9-10.1; RI.9-10.1
4. **Imagine** Before they role-play the scene, have students reread the scene. Tell them to pay close attention to words, actions, and emotions of the character whom they will portray.
5. **Synthesize** Students might cite the following point in their explanations:
   - *Even if he hadn't saved anyone, Brian risked his life to try to save people in danger. He would still be a hero.*

   RI.9-10.1

Writing

Write About Literature

Edge Interactive Practice Book, p. 123

Comparison Review the term *archetype* with students. Then review the plot and characters in *Left Behind* with students, or help them brainstorm other types of traditional literature. Have students read their paragraphs aloud.
W.9-10.9.a

Vocabulary

Key Vocabulary Review

1. *distracted* 2. *anxiety* 3. *inhibited* 4. *protest* 5. *prejudiced* 6. *survivor* 7. *inherent* 8. *tragedy*
L.9-10.6

Fluency

Read with Ease: Expression

Ensure that students complete the self-check.
RL.9-10.10

ASSESS & RETEACH

Assessments Handbook, pp. 29f–29i

Have students complete the **Reader Reflection**. Then give students the **Cluster Test** to measure their progress. Group students as needed for reteaching.

CCSS **Literacy.RL.9-10.1** Cite strong and thorough textual evidence to support analysis of what the text says explicitly as well as inferences drawn from the text. **Literacy.RL.9-10.10** By the end of grade 9, read and comprehend literature, including stories, dramas, and poems, in the grades 9-10 text complexity band proficiently, with scaffolding as needed at the high end of the range. By the end of grade 10, read and comprehend literature, including stories, dramas, and poems, at the high end of the grades 9-10 text complexity band independently and proficiently. **Literacy.RI.9-10.1** Cite strong and thorough textual evidence to support analysis of what the text says explicitly as well as inferences drawn from the text. **Literacy.W.9-10.9.a** Apply grades 9–10 Reading standards to literature (e.g., "Analyze how an author draws on and transforms source material in a specific work [e.g., how Shakespeare treats a theme or topic from Ovid or the Bible or how a later author draws on a play by Shakespeare]"). **Literacy.L.9-10.6** Acquire and use accurately general academic and domain-specific words and phrases, sufficient for reading, writing, speaking, and listening at the college and career readiness level; demonstrate independence in gathering vocabulary knowledge when considering a word or phrase important to comprehension or expression.

Lesson 15

INTEGRATE THE LANGUAGE ARTS

OBJECTIVES

Language Function
- Engage in Discussion Ⓣ

Literary Analysis
- Analyze Theme

Grammar
- Verb Tenses Ⓣ

Grammar

Use Verb Tenses

Grammar Transparency 40

Review Use the transparency to review verb tenses and parallel structure. Then conduct the activity on p. 258.

Oral Practice Check students' examples of parallel structure and that they correctly identify the tenses.

Written Practice 6. Valentín *will live* in a group home. **7.** He *shows* his animal art to Teresa. **8.** He *will make* animals and *work* with Teresa. **9.** Teresa and Valentín *will do* a good job. **10.** Valentín and Teresa *will help* in the office.
L.9-10.1.a; L.9-10.1.b

Language Development

Engage in Discussion

Encourage each group to write down their plan for consensus-building and decision-making and refer to it frequently during their discussion.

Evaluate students' acquisition of this language function with the Language Acquisition Rubric.
SL.9-10.1.b

Assessments Handbook, p. 29o

Literary Analysis

Multiple Themes in a Text

Brainstorm with students some possible themes, such as standing up for oneself. Have students provide text evidence and examples to support the themes they identify.
RL.9-10.2

Edge Interactive Practice Book, p. 124

GRAMMAR SKILLS PATH
36 Irregular Past Tense Verbs
37 Irregular Past Tense Verbs
38 Past Progressive Verb Forms
39 Future Tense Verbs
▶ 40 Review: Verb Tenses ELL Language & Grammar Lab

INTEGRATE THE LANGUAGE ARTS

Grammar

Use Verb Tenses

Regular past tense verbs end in **-ed**. Irregular verbs have special forms to show the past tense.

Present: Lifeguards **do** an important job.

Past: In the story, Valentín **did** something heroic.

Here are some common irregular verbs.

Present	Past	Present	Past
am, is, are	was, were	make	made
do, does	did	say	said
eat	ate	see	saw
have, has	had	write	wrote

Use the **future tense** to tell about an action that has not yet happened. Use **will** before the main verb to tell about the future. If there is more than one main verb in a sentence, use **will** only before the first verb.

Present: Valentín **works** at the pool, **makes** toys, and **saves** a child.

Future: Later, Valentín **will buy** a bike, **ride** to the pool, and **work** in the office.

Oral Practice (1–5) With a partner, find one or two examples of parallel structure on pages 243–245. Tell the tense of each verb.

Written Practice (6–8) Rewrite each sentence. Change the verb to the tense shown in parentheses.

6. Valentín showed his animal art. (present)
7. He makes animals and works. (future)
8. Teresa and Valentín did a good job. (future)

Language Development

Engage in Discussion

Group Talk Discuss and list Teresa and Vaentín's strengths and faults. Make ground rules for the discussion and decide what to add to your list.

Literary Analysis

Multiple Themes in a Text

A **theme** is a main idea or lesson in a story. The author uses characters, dialogue, and plot events to make a general statement that is true about people or life.

Many stories include more than one theme. Study these examples from "A Job for Valentín":

Theme	Examples
Don't judge others by their appearance.	• Teresa assumes that Valentín can't speak English, even though he says he can. • People treat Valentín as if he doesn't understand anything, although he does.
Even ordinary people can be heroes.	• Teresa overcomes her fears to try to save Pablito. • Valentín jumps into the water to save Pablito and Teresa.

With a partner, add at least two more themes that you can find from the story. Include evidence and examples that support your ideas.

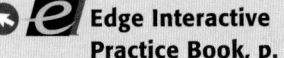

NO LIFEGUARD
ON DUTY
SWIM AT YOUR
OWN RISK

GRAMMAR

Review: Verb Tenses

Review Display the transparency. Remind students about the formation of present, past, and future tense verbs. Have students read the example sentences aloud. Elicit more examples.

A. Oral Practice Model how to change the verb to the past progressive in the first sentence. Then have students change the form for the remaining verbs.

B. Written Practice Work through the example. Explain that some sentences have no errors. Have the group tell you how to edit the paragraph. Ask a volunteer to read the corrected paragraph aloud.
L.9-10.1.a; L.9-10.1.b

Grammar & Writing Practice Book, pp. 87–88

Grammar Transparency 40

Use Verb Tenses

GRAMMAR REVIEW: VERB TENSES 40

Remember: You have to change the verb to show when an action happens. The action can happen in the **present**, **past**, or **future**.

The **tense** of a verb tells when an action happens.

Past ← Earlier (Past Tense) — Now (Present Tense) — Later (Future Tense) → Future

Present: Every day, news articles **describe** heroic actions.
Past: Yesterday, one article **described** an act of bravery.
Future: Tonight, the evening news **will describe** the incident. The report **is going to describe** the woman's actions.

Try It

A. Say each sentence. Change each verb to the tense in parentheses.

1. A car slides [was sliding] on a patch of ice. **(past progressive)**
2. The car goes [went] into a post and knocks [knocked] it over. **(past)**
3. A teen calls [called] 9-1-1, describes [described] the scene, and waits [waited]. **(past)**
4. The teenager waits [will wait] for the police. **(future)**

B. Edit the paragraph. Fix five mistakes. The first is done for you.

Sometimes ordinary people act with great courage. Last fall, we ~~are~~ were at a football game. Everyone ~~standed~~ stood up and several bleachers collapsed. Two children were trapped underneath. My brother immediately ~~goed~~ went to their rescue. He ~~bringed~~ brought them to safety. I predict the children will remember my brother always.

CCSS Literacy.RL.9-10.2 Determine a theme or central idea of a text and analyze in detail its development over the course of the text, including how it emerges and is shaped and refined by specific details; provide an objective summary of the text. Literacy.SL.9-10.1.b Work with peers to set rules for collegial discussions and decision-making (e.g., informal consensus, taking votes on key issues, presentation of alternate views), clear goals and deadlines, and individual roles as needed. Literacy.L.9-10.1.a Use parallel structure. Literacy.L.9-10.1.b Use various types of phrases (noun, verb, adjectival, adverbial, participial, prepositional, absolute) and clauses (independent, dependent; noun, relative, adverbial) to convey specific meanings and add variety and interest to writing or presentations.

Vocabulary Study

Borrowed Words

Borrowed words come into one language from another language. Dictionaries tell you the language or languages a word has been borrowed from. For example, the entry below describes the word *banana*. It originated in Africa. Portuguese borrowed it; then Spanish borrowed it from Portuguese. English borrowed it from one of those languages.

banana [< Sp or Pg; Sp from Pg of African origin]

Use a print or online dictionary, glossary, or thesaurus to trace the source of these borrowed words: *chic*, *patio*, *chocolate*.

Research / Writing

Profile

Historical Hero Who are the historical heroes in your community? Research local sources, such as newspaper archives, regional histories, and Internet articles to identify local, historical heroes.

myNGconnect.com

Find biographies of courageous people in history.

Write a profile of your local hero that you can share with your class. Be sure to use specific details to describe the person and explain why he or she is a hero.

Language and Learning Handbook, page 702

Writing Handbook, page 784

Writing Trait

Voice and Style

Think about the **voice and style** of your work. Ask:

- **Voice:** Is my voice clear and interesting? Does it express who I am and what I think?
- **Style:** Is the style right for my audience and purpose? How can I improve my word choice and sentence structure?

Just OK

> **News Report for Older Readers**
> Brian Hart is a total hero in New York. Brian saw a boat tip over. He jumped right in. He helped a lot of people.

Much Better

> **News Report for Older Readers**
> Brian Hart is one of New York's many heroes. When Hart saw the *Ethan Allen* tour boat capsize in Lake George, he immediately dove in and pulled many of the elderly passengers to safety. Thanks to Hart, there were many more survivors of this dreadful tragedy.

Read the paragraph below. Talk with a partner about what the writer can do to improve the voice and style.

> **Personal Narrative for Your Classmates**
> I think that a hero is someone who tries to help others. Even when it's dangerous. I was three years old when I fell in the pool. No one noticed except for my neighbor, Nia. She dove in and pulled me out. She made sure I was breathing. She said that she couldn't just stand by and do nothing. Nia is my biggest hero. I wouldn't even be here without her.

After you make your revisions, use a chart to evaluate the voice and style.

The voice and style...	Yes	Not Yet
are clear and interesting		
don't change too much		
are right for the audience and purpose		
show great word choices		
show sentence variety		

Writing Handbook, page 784

Lesson 16

INTEGRATE THE LANGUAGE ARTS

OBJECTIVES

Vocabulary
- Borrowed Words T

Research Skill
- Use the Research Process

Writing
- Trait: Voice and Style T
- Form: Profile

Vocabulary Study

Borrowed Words

chic	[French origin]
patio	[Spanish origin]
chocolate	[Sp < Nahuatl origin]

Edge Interactive Practice Book, p. 125
L.9-10.4.c

Research/Writing

Profile

Historical Hero Suggest that students search the Web site of a local newspaper to identify additional subjects. Remind students to use specific details such as personality, height, and hair color to describe the person. Tell them to give examples of things the person has done to explain why he or she is a hero. If students do not understand the search words and phrases, have them look up their meanings in a dictionary, glossary, or thesaurus.
W.9-10.2.b; W.9-10.7

Writing Trait

Voice and Style

Help students identify how the "Much Better" example was improved.

- "total hero" changed to "one of New York's many heroes": more mature language
- specific details added about where and when the event happened
- more vivid and dramatic wording in final sentence

Have students suggest ways to improve the personal narrative sample. Then have them complete the chart to evaluate the voice and style.
W.9-10.5

See **Writing Handbook** p. 784 for further instruction.

Writing Rubric Voice and Style

Exceptional	• Voice and word choice well suited to the audience. • Style is appropriate to the audience. • Ideas are relevant to topic.
Competent	• Voice and word choice mostly suited to the audience. • Style is generally appropriate to the audience. • Ideas are adequate to topic.
Developing	• Voice and word choice often not suited to the audience. • Style is often inappropriate to the audience. • Ideas are loosely connected to topic.
Beginning	• Voice and word choice not suited to the audience. • Style is generally inappropriate to the audience. • Ideas not clearly connected to the topic.

CCSS **Literacy.W.9-10.2.b** Develop the topic with well-chosen, relevant, and sufficient facts, extended definitions, concrete details, quotations, or other information and examples appropriate to the audience's knowledge of the topic. **Literacy.W.9-10.5** Develop and strengthen writing as needed by planning, revising, editing, rewriting, or trying a new approach, focusing on addressing what is most significant for a specific purpose and audience. **Literacy.W.9-10.7** Conduct short as well as more sustained research projects to answer a question (including a self-generated question) or solve a problem; narrow or broaden the inquiry when appropriate; synthesize multiple sources on the subject, demonstrating understanding of the subject under investigation. **Literacy.L.9-10.4.c** Consult general and specialized reference materials (e.g., dictionaries, glossaries, thesauruses), both print and digital, to find the pronunciation of a word or determine or clarify its precise meaning, its part of speech, or its etymology.

Lesson 17

LISTENING AND SPEAKING WORKSHOP

OBJECTIVES

Listening and Speaking

- Express Ideas, Opinions, and Supporting Information
- Hold a Panel Discussion Ⓣ
- Use a Rubric

BUILD BACKGROUND

Ⓐ Panel Discussion

Introduce Explain that in a panel discussion, a group of people discuss a topic before an audience.

Panel Discussion Explain that the moderator's job is to help the panel discussion proceed smoothly but not to take sides or offer opinions. Audience members may ask panelists questions after the discussion.

TEACH & PRACTICE

Ⓑ Plan Your Panel Discussion

Generate Ideas Organize students into groups of four or five. Ask all students to think about the qualities of a hero. Discuss the different ways groups might structure their discussion, and list student responses on a chart:

- How would you describe a hero?
- What heroes have you read about or seen in movies or on TV? Why were they heroes?
- Are there qualities that all heroes have in common?

Invite groups to share ideas for decision-making and consensus-building with the class.

ELL Use Visuals Encourage students to look through the selection for images that will help them think about and expand on the main idea of heroism.

Encourage students to write notes and to incorporate feedback from their group members in their notes.

Listening and Speaking Workshop

Panel Discussion

Ⓐ **A panel discussion offers the perfect forum to explore different sides of a topic, such as "What makes a hero?" In a panel discussion, each group member focuses on a different part of a given topic. After the panelists present their views, the moderator opens the discussion to the audience. Here is how to plan and conduct a panel discussion:**

1. Plan Your Panel Discussion

Discuss the question "What makes a hero?" with a group of four or five classmates. Then do the following:

Ⓑ
- Set the ground rules your group will follow to reach agreements and make decisions. Then, decide on an approach. For example, each panelist might give his or her own definition of a hero.
- Choose a moderator, who will introduce the speakers and take questions from the audience afterward.
- Have each panelist write notes on his or her main idea about heroism with supporting examples and other information.

myNGconnect.com

Download the rubric.

How can practicing and providing feedback to your group improve your panel discussion?

CCSS **Literacy.SL.9-10.1** Initiate and participate effectively in a range of collaborative discussions (one-on-one, in groups, and teacher-led) with diverse partners on grades 9-10 topics, texts, and issues, building on others' ideas and expressing their own clearly and persuasively. **Literacy.SL.9-10.1.b** Work with peers to set rules for collegial discussions and decision-making (e.g., informal consensus, taking votes on key issues, presentation of alternate views), clear goals and deadlines, and individual roles as needed. **Literacy.SL.9-10.1.c** Propel conversations by posing and responding to questions that relate the current discussion to broader themes or larger ideas; actively incorporate others into the discussion; and clarify, verify, or challenge ideas and conclusions.

2. Practice Your Panel Discussion

Work together to make the presentations go as smoothly as possible.

- Make sure each panelist speaks within the amount of time given.
- Practice speaking without your notes.
- Provide positive feedback about how the panelists explain their ideas.
- Ask questions and make comments to clarify and elaborate on others' ideas.

3. Hold Your Panel Discussion

Have the panelists sit at a long table, with the moderator in the center, in front of the audience. Keep your presentation interesting and lively by doing the following:

- Make eye contact with your audience.
- Speak clearly and loudly enough for the audience to understand.
- Look at your notes if you need to, but try to use them as little as possible.
- Listen attentively and respectfully to the rest of your group, so that you can help answer the audience's questions.

4. Discuss and Rate the Panel Discussion

Use the rubric to discuss and rate the discussions, including your own.

Panel Discussion Rubric

Scale	Content of Panel Discussion	Participants' Preparation	Participants' Delivery
3 Great	• Thoroughly covered the topic with many good examples • Taught me something and made me think	• Seemed to know a lot about the topic • Presentation was well coordinated	• All spoke clearly and were easy to follow • Responded to questions and comments very well
2 Good	• Gave good coverage of the topic with some good examples • Had some effect on my ideas	• Seemed somewhat well-informed about the topic • Presentation was fairly well coordinated	• Most spoke clearly and were usually easy to follow • Responded to questions and comments fairly well
1 Needs Work	• Gave little coverage of the topic • Didn't make me think and didn't influence my opinions	• Did not seem familiar with subject • Presentation was disorganized	• Most were hard to understand • Did not respond to questions and comments well

DO IT ▸ When your group is finished preparing and practicing, hold your panel discussion, and keep it lively!

Language and Learning Handbook, page 702

DIFFERENTIATED INSTRUCTION

As you conduct the workshop with students, adjust your teaching strategies to their needs.

Struggling Readers

Make Connections Ask students to identify a person they consider a hero. Guide students to name specific reasons they consider this person a hero. Then lead them to generate descriptive examples and supporting information they can include on the outlines they will use for their panel discussion.

English Language Learners ELL

Role-Play Ask students to role-play a hero. Help students verbalize why they consider this person a hero to help with their input for the panel discussion.

Challenge

Research a Hero Have students research a hero from the past or present to focus on during their panel discussion. Tell them to cite specific examples that show why the person is considered a hero.

C Practice Your Panel Discussion

Model Model a short panel discussion for students.

- Model both the role of a panelist and a moderator.
- Use specific ideas about heroes.
- Speak clearly and make eye contact with your audience.

Prepare Have students practice their panel discussions. Remind them to glance only occasionally at their notes.

Use a Rubric Discuss the rubric. Have groups rehearse their panel discussions together and use the rubric to suggest feedback.
SL.9-10.1; SL.9-10.1.b; SL.9-10.1.c; SL.9-10.1.d; L.9-10.3

myNGconnect.com

Panel Discussion Rubric

Guided Support Circulate around the room as groups practice. Ensure that students incorporate the elements of a panel discussion into their presentations.

APPLY

D Hold Your Panel Discussion

Present Have all groups hold their panel discussions. Remind students in the audience to take notes during the presentations to help generate questions they will ask the panelists.
SL.9-10.1; SL.9-10.1.b; SL.9-10.1.c; SL.9-10.1.d; L.9-10.3

E Discuss and Rate the Panel Discussion

Give Feedback Have students give written or oral feedback to each group. Reviewers should rate the groups with a 1, 2, or 3 and support their rating with comments about the content, preparation, and delivery. Encourage students to also rate themselves.
SL.9-10.3

ONGOING ASSESSMENT
Ask students to compare notes about each panel discussion. Have them explain how the discussions had an influence on their personal opinions.

CCSS **Literacy.SL.9-10.1.d** Respond thoughtfully to diverse perspectives, summarize points of agreement and disagreement, and, when warranted, qualify or justify their own views and understanding and make new connections in light of the evidence and reasoning presented. **Literacy.SL.9-10.3** Evaluate a speaker's point of view, reasoning, and use of evidence and rhetoric, identifying any fallacious reasoning or exaggerated or distorted evidence. **Literacy.L.9-10.3** Apply knowledge of language to understand how language functions in different contexts, to make effective choices for meaning or style, and to comprehend more fully when reading or listening.

UNIT 3 Cluster 3 Planner

EQ ESSENTIAL QUESTION:

What Makes a Hero?

Explore how heroes change the world around them.

Online Planner
myNGconnect.com

	LESSON 18 **Prepare to Read**	LESSON 19 **The Woman in the Snow** Main Selection
Reading		
Reading Strategies Focus Strategy **Make Inferences**	**Activate Prior Knowledge** SL.9-10.1 • Make a Connection: Brainstorming *T262*	**Make Inferences** RL.9-10.1 • Make Inferences *T263, T266–T277*
Literary Analysis Genre Focus **Short Stories**		T **Analyze Viewpoint** RL.9-10.6 *T263, T266–T277* **Identify Historical Themes** • Racial Struggles *T264*
Vocabulary	T **Key Vocabulary** RI.9-10.4; L.9-10.4.b; L.9-10.6 Introduce *T262* • authority, boycott, compassion, desperately, • discrimination, • persistent, provoke, segregation	T **Key Vocabulary** L.9-10.6 • Daily Routines *T267* • Link to Essential Question *T270* • Selection Reading *T266–T277* boycott, compassion, desperately, • discrimination
Fluency		T **Intonation** RL.9-10.10 • Daily Routines *T267* T **Accuracy and Rate** RL.9-10.10 Comprehension Coach *T265*
Writing		
Response to Literature		**Return to the Text** W.9-10.9.a; W.9-10.10 • **Reread and Write** What qualities make Ray Hammond a hero? *T277*
Writing Across the Curriculum		**Research and Writing** W.9-10.7 • **History Connection** *T273*
Language		
ELL **Language Development**	T **Elaborate During a Discussion** SL.9-10.1.a • Language and Grammar Lab, Transparency I *LAB TE p. 50*	T **Elaborate During a Discussion** SL.9-10.1.a • Daily Routines *LAB TE p. 50*
Grammar Grammar Focus **Subject and Object Pronouns**		**Direct Objects** *T268* L.9-10.1 T **Subject and Object Pronouns** *T272* L.9-10.1 T ***I* vs. *Me*** *T274* L.9-10.1
Listening and Speaking	**Group Talk** SL.9-10.1 • Ideas About Real-Life Heroes *T262*	**Listen to a Selection** RL.9-10.10 Comprehension Coach *T265* *CD 5, Tracks 1–3* **Out-of-School Literacy** SL.9-10.1.a • Use and Discuss Online Reading *T276*

T = Tested on Cluster and/or Unit Reading and Literary Analysis Test
T = Tested on Language Acquisition Assessment
T = Tested on Unit Writing Test
T = Assessed with a Rubric
• **Academic Vocabulary**

The Woman in the Snow

Genre: Short Story Lexile® 730L

Ray hears rumors that a ghost named Eula Mae is haunting his new bus route. In the past, another bus driver refused to give Eula Mae and her sick child a ride, and they died in the snow. Ray breaks the curse with an act of kindness.

Rosa Parks

Genre: Magazine Profile Lexile® 980L

This article focuses on Rosa Parks's historic fight for a seat on an Alabama bus in 1955. Her action was a bold move at a pivotal time. The writer speaks of the impact and lasting effects that this simple act had on our nation.

LESSON 20	LESSON 21	LESSONS 22 & 23	LESSON 24
Rosa Parks Second Selection	**Reflect and Assess**	**Integrate the Language Arts**	**The American Promise** Close Reading
Make Inferences RI.9-10.1 • Make Inferences *T278, T280–T284*	**Comprehension and Critical Thinking** *T285* RL.9-10.1; RL.9-10.2; RI.9-10.1; RI.9-10.2; • Compare Across Texts RL.9-10.6 • Interpret, Analyze, Compare, Speculate, Synthesize		
❶ **Analyze Development of Ideas** *T278, T280–T284* RI.9-10.3	**Interpret and Evaluate Literature** RL.9-10.10 ❶ **Use Text Evidence** *T285* RL.9-10.1	**Compare Themes** *T286* RL.9-10.2	❶ **Analyze Viewpoint** *T289* RI.9-10.6; RI.9-10.9; L.9-10.3
❶ **Key Vocabulary** L.9-10.6 • Selection Reading *T280–T284* • authority provoke • persistent segregation	❶ **Key Vocabulary** L.9-10.6 • Review *T285* • authority • discrimination boycott • persistent compassion provoke desperately segregation	❶ **Vocabulary Strategy** L.9-10.4.b; L.9-10.4.d • Relate Words: Word Families *T287*	**Academic Vocabulary** L.9-10.6 • Review *T288* • perspective
❶ **Intonation** RL.9-10.10 • Daily Routines *T267* ❶ **Accuracy and Rate** RI.9-10.10 ⊙ Comprehension Coach *T279*	❶ **Intonation** RL.9-10.10 • Peer Assessment *T285*		or... **THE AMERICAN PROMISE** by Lyndon B. Johnson
Return to the Text W.9-10.10 • **Reread and Write** Why was Rosa Parks's protest on the bus important? *T284*	**Write About Literature** W.9-10.2 • **Theme Statement** What do both selections say about the struggle to overcome prejudice? *T285*	❶ **Writing Form** W.9-10.1; W.9-10.5 • Opinion Paragraph *T287*	**The American Promise** **Genre:** Speech **Lexile® 1000L** CD 12, Track 3
Research and Writing W.9-10.7; SL.9-10.2 • **History Connection** *T283*			LESSON 25
❶ **Elaborate During a Discussion** SL.9-10.1.a • Daily Routines *LAB TE p. 50*		❶ **Elaborate During a Discussion** SL.9-10.1.a • Pair Talk *T286*	**UNIT WRAP-UP**
❶ **Subject and Object Pronouns** *T280* L.9-10.1		❶ **Subject and Object Pronouns** *T286* L.9-10.1	
Listen to a Selection RI.9-10.10 ⊙ Comprehension Coach *T279* CD 5, Track 4 **Out-of-School Literacy** SL.9-10.1.a; L.9-10.b • Transportation *T282*	**Participate in a Discussion** *T285* SL.9-10.1	**Oral Interpretation** *T287* SL.9-10.6	❶ **Unit Project** SL.9-10.5 • Documentary *T290*

EDGE LIBRARY

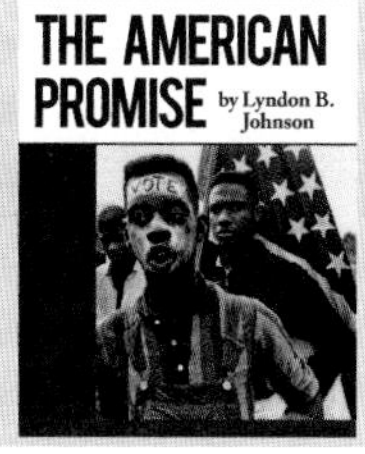

 Hercules ●
by Paul Storrie

 September 11, 2001 Attack on New York City ● ●
by Wilbur Hampton

 Left Behind ● ● ●
by Velma Wallis

Lesson 18

PREPARE TO READ

OBJECTIVES

Vocabulary
- Key Vocabulary (T)
- Strategy: Use Cognates; Relate Words

Reading Strategy
- Activate Prior Knowledge

ELL Language & Grammar Lab

Language Function Transparency I
Elaborate During a Discussion (T)

ENGAGE & CONNECT

(A) EQ Essential Question

Focus on Positive Change Ask: How can a hero influence others?

Possible responses:
- *by changing things that are unfair*
- *by being a positive role model*

(B) Make a Connection

Have students work in groups to make their lists. Invite groups to share and discuss.
SL.9-10.1

TEACH VOCABULARY

(C) Learn Key Vocabulary

Study the Words Review the four steps of the Make Words Your Own routine (*see the Vocabulary tab*):

1. **Pronounce** Say a word and have students repeat it. Write the word in syllables and pronounce it, one syllable at a time: *au-thor-i-ty*. Point out the familiar word *author* within *authority*.

   ELL Use cognates to help Spanish speakers with the words (*see the Vocabulary tab*).

2. **Study Examples** Read the example in the chart. Provide more examples: The principal of our school is a person with *authority*.

PREPARE TO READ

- The Woman in the Snow
- Rosa Parks

(A) EQ What Makes a Hero?

Explore how heroes change the world around them.

Make a Connection

(B) **Brainstorming** List the names of people who have helped break down barriers in such fields as sports, education, and employment. Work in small groups to explore how these heroes have changed the world around them.

Learn Key Vocabulary

Study the Words Pronounce each word and learn its meaning. You may also want to look up the definitions in the Glossary.

(C)

• Academic Vocabulary

Key Words	Examples
• **authority** (u-**thor**-u-tē) *noun* ▸ pages 282, 285, 287	People in **authority** can have power over others. Government leaders have the **authority** to make laws. *Synonym*: power
boycott (**boi**-kot) *noun* ▸ page 266	A **boycott** is a way to punish an organization by refusing to use its product or service. We will hold a **boycott** of the company's products because we don't like the way it treats its workers.
compassion (kum-**pash**-un) *noun* ▸ pages 274, 277	When you show **compassion** for others, you care deeply about their suffering and troubles. I felt **compassion** for the sad, lonely girl. *Synonym*: pity; *Antonym*: unkindness
desperately (**des**-pur-it-lē) *adverb* ▸ page 270	When you act **desperately**, you make a big effort because you feel a great need. The doctors worked **desperately** to save the child's life. *Synonym*: frantically; *Antonym*: calmly
• **discrimination** (di-skrim-u-**nā**-shun) *noun* ▸ pages 266, 284, 285	**Discrimination** is treating people in a particular group unfairly. Racism is a form of **discrimination** that focuses on a person's skin color.
• **persistent** (pur-**sis**-tunt) *adjective* ▸ page 282	If you are **persistent**, you keep trying in spite of challenges. The **persistent** woman kept asking for help even though everyone ignored her.
provoke (pru-**vōk**) *verb* ▸ page 283	To **provoke** means to force a person or thing to act. We hope our protests against the unfair law will **provoke** the government to make a change. *Synonym*: stir up
segregation (seg-ri-**ga**-shun) *noun* ▸ page 280	**Segregation** keeps some people apart from others because of race. In the past, **segregation** didn't allow black and white children to go to the same schools. *Synonyms*: divided, separated; *Antonym*: united

Practice the Words Create a **Vocabulary Study Card** for each Key Vocabulary word. Write the word on one side. On the other side, write an example sentence for the word, but leave the word out. Then take turns quizzing a partner.

Vocabulary Study Card

authority

Police officers, judges, and mayors are some people who have _______ in a community.

---

3. **Encourage Elaboration** Provide a frame: *My teacher has the* authority *to* _____.

4. **Practice the Words** Have students create Vocabulary Study Cards for each word, then prompt a partner with example sentences.

Edge Interactive
Practice Book, pp. 126–127
RI.9-10.4; L.9-10.4.b; L.9-10.6

ONGOING ASSESSMENT
Have students complete an oral sentence for each word. For example: *Jana wanted to see this movie so _______ that she waited hours in line to get a ticket.*

CCSS **Literacy.RI.9-10.4** Determine the meaning of words and phrases as they are used in the text, including figurative and connotative meanings; analyze the cumulative impact of specific word choices on meaning and tone (e.g., how the language evokes a sense of time and place; how it sets a formal or informal tone). **Literacy.SL.9-10.1** Initiate and participate effectively in a range of collaborative discussions (one-on-one, in groups, and teacher-led) with diverse partners on grades 9-10 topics, texts, and issues, building on others' ideas and expressing their own clearly and persuasively. **Literacy.L.9-10.4.b** Identify and correctly use patterns of word changes that indicate different meanings or parts of speech (e.g., analyze, analysis, analytical; advocate, advocacy). **Literacy.L.9-10.6** Acquire and use accurately general academic and domain-specific words and phrases, sufficient for reading, writing, speaking, and listening at the college and career readiness level; demonstrate independence in gathering vocabulary knowledge when considering a word or phrase important to comprehension or expression.

BEFORE READING The Woman in the Snow

short story by Patricia C. McKissack

Reading Strategies

- Plan and Monitor
- Determine Importance
- ▶ **Make Inferences**
- Ask Questions
- Make Connections
- Synthesize
- Visualize

Analyze Viewpoint

The **third-person omniscient** narrator tells the story as an outsider. Because the narrator is omniscient, or all-knowing, he or she can reveal what the characters think and feel, include information that the characters do not know, and describe past and future events.

Although a third-person narrator does not reflect the thoughts and feelings of one character, he or she may reflect a cultural **viewpoint**. For example, this story is set in the South, before African Americans had equal rights. The culture affects how the narrator shares information with the reader.

D

Look Into the Text

The narrator knows how characters feel and what they think.

Grady Bishop had just been hired as a driver for Metro Bus Service. When he put on the gray uniform and boarded his bus, nothing mattered, not his obesity, not his poor education, not growing up the eleventh child of the town drunk. Driving gave him power. And power mattered.

What does the narrator tell about Grady that other characters might not know?

Why does the narrator explain who Billy is?

One cold November afternoon Grady clocked in for the three-to-eleven shift. "You've got Hall tonight," Billy, the route manager, said matter-of-factly.

Focus Strategy ▶ Make Inferences

As you read, look for new ideas and information that the author provides. Use this to build on the inferences you have already made.

E

Focus Strategy

HOW TO MAKE INFERENCES

1. As you read, make an inference about a character or an event in the story. Record this in an **Inference Chart**.
2. Add information from the story that supports your inferences.
3. Add ideas and information from the text to form a new, revised inference.

Inference Chart

Initial Inference	Grady Bishop doesn't feel good about himself.
New Information	"Driving gave him power."
New Inference	Having power makes him feel good.

Reading Transparency 13

READING VIEWPOINT 13

Analyze Viewpoint

Introduce Authors use narrators to tell stories. Narrators can be one of the following:

Narrator	Pronouns Used	Story Told from View of
first person	*I, we*	character in the story
third person	*he, she, they*	someone outside the story

A third-person narrator may be limited or omniscient. The word *omniscient* means "all-knowing." An omniscient narrator knows everything about the characters, including what they think and feel. For example:

Most Metro drivers didn't like the Hall Street assignment in the best weather, because the road twisted and turned back on itself like a retreating snake. When slick with ice and snow, it was even more hazardous. But Grady had his own reason for hating the route. The Hall Street Express serviced black domestics who rode out to the fashionable west end in the mornings and back down to the lower east side in the evening.

Lesson 19

BEFORE READING

OBJECTIVES

Reading Strategy
- Make Inferences

Literary Analysis
- Analyze Viewpoint T

TEACH STRATEGIES

D Analyze Viewpoint

Look Into the Text Read the introduction to review viewpoint and third-person narrators. Read aloud the text passage. Use the callouts to discuss what an omniscient narrator tells about a character like Grady. Ask: What does this narrator know about Grady that other characters might not?

Possible responses:
- *He had a poor education.*
- *He cares about power.*

Reading Transparency 13

Use the Transparency Reinforce the features of third-person omniscient narrators. Ask: How are first- and third-person different?

Possible responses:
- *A third-person narrator is not a character and can tell you what all characters think and feel, including things characters don't know.*
- *A third-person narrator uses the pronouns* he, she, it, *and* they.

Explain the difference between a third-person omniscient narrator and a third-person limited narrator.
RL.9-10.6

E Focus Strategy: Make Inferences

Make Inferences Read the introduction with students to define the strategy. Work through the How To box to model making inferences. Have students try the strategies to make another new inference from Look Into the Text.
RL.9-10.1

Edge Interactive Practice Book, pp. 128–129

ONGOING ASSESSMENT
Have partners discuss how the passage might change if it was told by Billy.

CCSS Literacy.RL.9-10.1 Cite strong and thorough textual evidence to support analysis of what the text says explicitly as well as inferences drawn from the text. Literacy.RL.9-10.6 Analyze a particular point of view or cultural experience reflected in a work of literature from outside the United States, drawing on a wide reading of world literature.

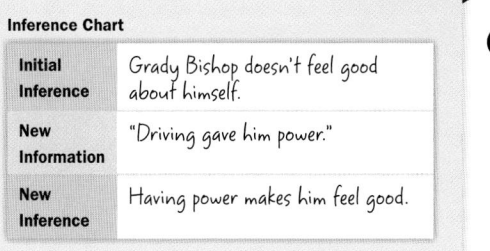

READ

OBJECTIVES

Literary Analysis
- Identify Historical Themes

Viewing
- Respond to and Interpret Visuals

BUILD BACKGROUND

A The Writer and Her Experience

Have students read the biography of Patricia C. McKissack.

Historical Themes Share this information to identify themes and subjects in Patricia C. McKissack's work:

Patricia C. McKissack bases her stories on the African American oral traditions she grew up with, which include her African American heritage. She and her husband, Frederick L. McKissack, have written several books that describe the challenges and successes that African Americans have faced and address the theme of racial struggles. *Days of Jubilee* is a story about the end of slavery. *Black Hands, White Sails: The Story of African-American Whalers* tells about free black sailors and the Underground Railroad during the movement to end slavery.

Connect with Themes Guide students to make connections with universal themes across time periods.

Ask: Do you think the theme of racial struggles is significant today? Discuss how stories about racial struggles today might compare to those from the time of slavery.

myNGconnect.com

- Selection Summaries in eight languages

The Writer and Her Experience

Patricia C. McKissack

(1944–)

Patricia McKissack says, "It's quite interesting how your youth shapes how you think in the future."

Patricia C. McKissack was born in Nashville, Tennessee, in the 1940s, and lived through both segregation and the civil rights movement. Although the outside world might have been challenging, her family life was full of wonderful stories and poems. "Long before I became a writer," she says, "I was a listener and an observer."

A Her family gathered on the porch during the hot summer evenings of her childhood. They took turns telling ghost stories, reciting poetry, or remembering their own younger days. The ghost stories took place during the "dark-thirty," the thirty minutes just before darkness falls, and they made a big impression on McKissack.

As an adult, McKissack felt drawn to create stories that have their roots in the experiences of her youth, both good and bad. "I write because there's a need to have books for, by, and about the African American experience and how we helped to develop this country," she has said.

McKissack has written over 100 books, many of which deal with the lives and contributions of African Americans. "The Woman in the Snow" first appeared in her award-winning book *The Dark-Thirty: Southern Tales of the Supernatural*, which draws on the African American oral traditions she grew up with.

myNGconnect.com

- Listen to a traditional African American story.
- Explore the world of oral traditions.

DIFFERENTIATED INSTRUCTION

English Language Learners ELL

Preview the selection:
- Show the art on p. 265: *The story includes a mother and her baby.*
- Show the art on p. 266: *The story is set during a time when African Americans, or "coloreds," sat in a different part of the bus from whites.*
- Demonstrate looking a person over and judging him or her on appearance only. Then explain: *The story gets started when a character makes a decision based on another character's race.*

Read Aloud to provide a supported listening experience:
- Play the **Selection Recording** as students track text in their books. **CD 5**
- Have students use the Listen feature in the **Comprehension Coach** where they see the text as it is read aloud.
- Read the selection aloud to students as you provide comprehensible input. For example, you can pantomime body language, such as bowing one's head on p. 274.

The Woman in the Snow

by Patricia C. McKissack

Standing Mother and Child, 1978, Elizabeth Catlett. Bronze sculpture with bronze patina, © Photograph by David Finn.

B

C

△ **Critical Viewing: Effect** How does the artist's use of shapes and expression create a mood for this image?

Comprehension Coach

TEACH & PRACTICE

B Analyze Visuals

About the Art Elizabeth Catlett, like Patricia C. McKissack, focuses on African American subjects and uses her art for social change.

Interpret and Respond Ask: If you made paintings or sculptures of people who are important to you, who would you show?

C Critical Viewing: Effect

Observe Characteristics of Mood Have students describe the shapes and expression in the sculpture.

ELL Questioning For less proficient students, ask questions with embedded answer choices:

- Is this woman happy or sad?
- Is she being careful or careless with her child?

For more proficient students, ask open-ended questions:

- What shapes do you see in this sculpture?
- How does this woman feel? How does she feel about her child?

Have students point out the parts of the image that support their observations.

Possible response:

- *The woman looks sad or worried.*

Ask: What does the artist do to create a mood in this art?

Possible responses:

- *The shapes are very simple and powerful. They don't get in the way of the emotions. The woman's expression gives the sculpture a sad or dark mood.*

Comprehension Coach

Build Reading Power

Assign students to use the software, based on their instructional needs.

Read Silently

- Comprehension questions with immediate feedback
- Glossary support
- Review text evidence RL.9-10.10

Listen

- Professional model of fluent reading

Record

- Oral reading fluency practice
- Ongoing fluency assessment with immediate feedback

CCSS Literacy.RL.9-10.10 By the end of grade 9, read and comprehend literature, including stories, dramas, and poems, in the grades 9–10 text complexity band proficiently, with scaffolding as needed at the high end of the range. By the end of grade 10, read and comprehend literature, including stories, dramas, and poems, at the high end of the grades 9–10 text complexity band independently and proficiently.

READ

OBJECTIVES

Vocabulary
- Key Vocabulary Ⓣ

Reading Fluency
- Intonation Ⓣ

Reading Strategies
- Make Inferences
- Plan and Monitor: Set a Purpose

Comprehension & Critical Thinking
- Make Inferences
- Use Text Evidence Ⓣ

Literary Analysis
- Analyze Viewpoint Ⓣ

Viewing
- Respond to and Interpret Visuals

TEACH & PRACTICE

Ⓐ Reading Support

1 Make Inferences Explain that this introduction was written by the author for context. It will help students build background knowledge in order to comprehend the story. Point out the bolded terms. Ask: What clues can you find about the "bus story"? What do they suggest the story will be about?

Possible responses:
- *what was happening in real life at the time the story takes place*
- *It will be about African Americans demanding their rights.*

Read aloud the last sentence. Ask: Why does the author include this phrase?

Possible response:
- *to show that this story is fiction*

RL.9-10.1

Ⓑ Critical Viewing: Effect

Analyze Effect Ask: What is the effect of seeing the figures from the back? What do you think the artist wanted the viewer to feel?

Possible response:
- *The artist might have wanted the viewer to feel like part of the line of people and part of the event.*

Ⓐ The year-long Montgomery, Alabama, bus **boycott** in 1955–56 was a **pivotal** event in the **American civil rights movement**. Blacks refused to ride the buses until their demand of fair and equal treatment for all **fare-paying passengers** was met. Today the right to sit anywhere on a public bus may seem a small victory over racism and **discrimination**. But that single issue changed the lives of African Americans everywhere. After the successful boycott in Montgomery, blacks in other cities challenged bus companies, demanding not only the right to sit wherever they chose but also employment opportunities for black bus drivers. Many cities had their own "bus" stories. **1** Some are in history books, but this story is best enjoyed by the fireplace on the night of the first snowfall.

Pools of Defiance, Colin Bootman, 2001. Oil on canvas, private collection. The Bridgeman Art Library.

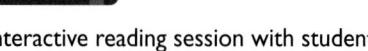

Ⓑ **Critical Viewing: Effect** Why do you think the artist chose to show these men and women from the back? What emotions does the artist want the viewer to feel?

1 Make Inferences The author has provided you with necessary background information. What might this "bus story" be about? Form an initial inference.

Key Vocabulary

boycott *n.*, punishment of an organization by refusing to use its services

• **discrimination** *n.*, unfair treatment of people in a particular group

In Other Words

pivotal very important, key
American civil rights movement effort to gain equal rights for all Americans
fare-paying passengers riders who paid to ride the bus

DIFFERENTIATED INSTRUCTION

Interactive Reading As you conduct the interactive reading session with students, adjust your teaching strategies to their needs.

Struggling Readers

Retelling Ask questions to help students retell events in the story and make inferences: Who is in this scene? What is happening? What does he/she mean when he/she says that? What does the author tell you about what he/she is like?

English Language Learners ELL

Rephrase Idioms Explain that the text includes expressions that do not mean what the individual words in the expression mean.

For example:
- *Grady clocked in (checked in; started work)*
- *cutting their conversation short (keeping the conversation brief)*

Discuss additional examples from the story and provide restatements.

Challenge

Compare and Contrast Have students compare and contrast the two bus drivers, Grady Bishop and Ray Hammond. Discuss: How do these characters illustrate the changes that took place in society over the 25 years that pass during the story?

CCSS Literacy.L.9-10.6 Acquire and use accurately general academic and domain-specific words and phrases, sufficient for reading, writing, speaking, and listening at the college and career readiness level; demonstrate independence in gathering vocabulary knowledge when considering a word or phrase important to comprehension or expression. **Literacy.RL.9-10.1** Cite strong and thorough textual evidence to support analysis of what the text says explicitly as well as inferences drawn from the text.

Set a Purpose

Find out what happens when a bus driver goes down a lonely road one snowy night. **C**

Grady Bishop had just been hired as a driver for Metro Bus Service. When he put on the gray uniform and **boarded** his bus, nothing mattered, not his **obesity**, not his poor education, not growing up the eleventh child of the town drunk. Driving gave him power. And power mattered. **2** **D**

One cold November afternoon Grady **clocked in** for the three-to-eleven shift. "You've got Hall tonight," Billy, the route manager, said **matter-of-factly**.

"The Blackbird Express." Grady didn't care who knew about his nickname for the route. "Not again." He turned around, slapping his hat against his leg.

"Try the *Hall Street Express*," Billy corrected Grady, then hurried on, cutting their conversation short. "Snow's predicted. Try to keep on schedule, but if it gets too bad out there, forget it. Come on in."

Grady popped a fresh stick of gum into his mouth. "You're the boss. But tell me. How am I s'posed to stay on schedule? What do those people care about time?"

Most Metro drivers didn't like the Hall Street assignment in the best weather, because the road twisted and turned back on itself like a retreating snake. When slick with ice and snow, it was even more **hazardous**. But Grady had his own reason for hating the route. The Hall Street Express serviced black **domestics** who rode out to the fashionable west end in the mornings and back down to the lower east side in the evenings.

"You know I can't stand being a chauffeur for a bunch of colored maids and cooks," he **groused**. **3** **E**

2 Viewpoint What does the omniscient narrator tell about the driver's character in the first paragraph?

3 Make Inferences What does this sentence add to your initial inference of what the story is about?

In Other Words

boarded got on
obesity heavy weight
clocked in got to work
matter-of-factly without emotion
hazardous dangerous
domestics maids or cooks
groused complained

TEACH & PRACTICE

C Chunking the Text

Set a Purpose Discuss how heroes come from ordinary situations, as well as from difficult ones, such as the Civil Rights Movement. Then ask: What might you learn by reading a story about a bus driver during this time?

Possible response:
- *You might see how people coped with discrimination.*

Read Have students read pp. 267–270. Support and monitor their comprehension using the reading support provided. Use the Differentiated Instruction below to meet students' individual needs.
RL.9-10.10

D Reading Support

2 Viewpoint Have students reread the first paragraph on p. 267. Ask: How does the narrator describe Grady?

Possible response:
- *Grady is fat, not well educated, from a large and troubled family, and he wants to feel powerful.*

RL.9-10.6

E Reading Support

3 Make Inferences Read aloud the last sentence of dialogue on the page.

ELL Rephrase Language Point out and rephrase informal language in the text:

- I can't stand *(I really don't like)*
- being a chauffeur for *(driving)*
- bunch of *(group of)*

Have students rephrase the sentence in their own words before making an inference.

Ask: What do Grady's words tell you about this story?

Possible response:
- *This story is probably about racism or discrimination.*

RL.9-10.1

DAILY ROUTINES

Vocabulary

See the Vocabulary and Fluency Routines tab for more information.

Connect to Meaning Have students connect the Key Vocabulary words to their own lives. For example: *I have seen acts of* compassion *when* _______.

Use Graphic Organizers Select a graphic organizer for practice:

Semantic Map: Relate words about how people react to one another.

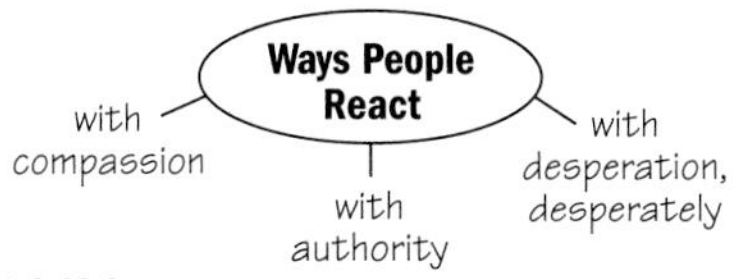

L.9-10.6

Fluency: Intonation

CD 11

This cluster's fluency practice uses a passage from "The Woman in the Snow" to help students practice appropriate intonation. Use **Reading Handbook** T748 and the **Fluency Model CD** to teach or review the elements of fluent intonation, and then use the daily fluency practice activities to develop students' oral reading proficiency.
RL.9-10.10

CCSS Literacy.RL.9-10.1 Cite strong and thorough textual evidence to support analysis of what the text says explicitly as well as inferences drawn from the text. Literacy.RL.9-10.6 Analyze a particular point of view or cultural experience reflected in a work of literature from outside the United States, drawing on a wide reading of world literature. Literacy.RL.9-10.10 By the end of grade 9, read and comprehend literature, including stories, dramas, and poems, in the grades 9-10 text complexity band proficiently, with scaffolding as needed at the high end of the range. By the end of grade 10, read and comprehend literature, including stories, dramas, and poems, at the high end of the grades 9-10 text complexity band independently and proficiently.

READE

OBJECTIVES

Reading Strategy
- Make Inferences

Comprehension & Critical Thinking
- Make Inferences
- Use Text Evidence Ⓣ

Literary Analysis
- Analyze Viewpoint Ⓣ

Viewing
- Respond to and Interpret Visuals

Grammar
- Direct Objects

TEACH & PRACTICE

Ⓐ Reading Support

4 Make Inferences Read paragraph 3 and highlight details that describe the setting: *frosted wonderland; winding, twisting, and bending street; nightmare.* Then ask: How could the setting of the bus route affect the plot?

Possible response:
- *Snow on a dangerous road might cause an accident.*

RL.9-10.1; RL.9-10.6

Ⓑ Critical Viewing: Design

Analyze Design Have students describe the people and setting in the painting. Ask: How can their positions show their feelings?

Possible responses:
- *The image shows three women on a city train.*
- *Two women are seated together talking. They are probably friends.*
- *The third woman is sitting alone and sits very straight. She seems tense, as if she is uncomfortable. Her shoes are off, as if her feet are tired.*

"Take it or leave it," Billy said, walking away in disgust.

Grady started to say something but thought better of it. He was still **on probation**, lucky even to have a job, especially during such hard times.

Ⓐ Snow had already begun to fall when Grady pulled out of the garage at 3:01. It fell steadily all afternoon, creating a frosted wonderland on the **manicured** lawns that lined West Hall. But by nightfall the winding, twisting, and bending street was a driver's nightmare. 4

> 4 **Make Inferences** The narrator describes the bus route in detail. How might the setting affect the plot of the story?

The temperature **plummeted**, too, adding a new challenge to the mounting snow. "Hurry up! Hurry up! I can't wait all day," Grady snapped at the boarding passengers. "Get to the back of the bus," he **hustled** them on impatiently. "You people know the rules."

Ⓑ **Critical Viewing: Design** How would you describe this image? Are there features in the image that tell you how the passengers feel? Explain.

The regulars recognized Grady, but except for a few muffled groans they paid **their fares** and rode **in sullen silence** out to the east side loop.

"Auntie! Now, just why are you taking your own good time getting off this bus?" Grady grumbled at the last passenger.

The woman struggled down the wet, slippery steps. At the bottom she looked over her shoulder. Her dark face held no clue of any emotion. "Auntie? Did you really call me *Auntie*?" she said, laughing **sarcastically**. "Well, well, well! I never knew

In Other Words

on probation in danger of being fired if he did anything wrong
manicured carefully and evenly trimmed
plummeted dropped quickly
hustled hurried
their fares the price for the bus ride
in sullen silence angrily but quietly
sarcastically in a rude way

GRAMMAR

Direct Objects

Teach/Model Display the transparency. Show how nouns can function as subjects or objects in a sentence. Model how to ask a question to find the object of the verb. Discuss the common sentence patterns in English. Have students suggest other statements and mark the pattern.

Practice A. Have students identify the underlined noun as a subject or an object. Ask questions such as: Who is the sentence about? Grady drove what? **B.** Have partners finish the paragraph about Grady and share their work. Have the group identify objects in several sentences. L.9-10.1

Grammar & Writing Practice Book, pp. 89–90

Grammar Transparency 41

GRAMMAR DIRECT OBJECTS 41

How Do Nouns Work in a Sentence?
They Can Be the Subject or the Object.

- Nouns can be the **subject** of a sentence.
  In the 1950s, **laws** (subject) required black people to sit at the back of the bus.
- Nouns can also be the **object** of an action verb. To find the object, turn the verb into a question like: "Upheld what?" Your answer is the object.
  Bus drivers upheld (verb) the **laws** (object).
- Many English sentences follow this pattern: **subject → verb → object.**
  People (subject) boycotted (verb) buses (object) from 1955 to 1956.
  The boycotts (subject) changed (verb) history (object).

Try It

A. Say each sentence and tell the job of the underlined noun. Is it a subject or an object?
1. Patricia McKissick (subject) wrote a story about a racist bus driver.
2. Grady drove a bus (object).
3. The passengers (subject) recognized Grady.
4. Grady treated the people (object) with disrespect.
5. One night, snow created a challenge (object).

B. Now let's tell what happened on Grady's route. Add an object to complete each sentence. Then add two more sentences. Sentences will vary.

Grady uses a _nickname_ for the route. The manager corrects _him_. Grady dislikes the _route_.

GRAMMAR SKILLS PATH
41 Direct Objects — ELL Language & Grammar Lab
42 Subject and Object Pronouns
43 *I* vs. *Me*
44 Subject and Object Pronouns
45 Review: Subject and Object Pronouns

CCSS Literacy.RL.9-10.1 Cite strong and thorough textual evidence to support analysis of what the text says explicitly as well as inferences drawn from the text. Literacy.RL.9-10.6 Analyze a particular point of view or cultural experience reflected in a work of literature from outside the United States, drawing on a wide reading of world literature. Literacy.L.9-10.1 Demonstrate command of the conventions of standard English grammar and usage when writing or speaking.

my brother had a white son." And she hurried away, chuckling.

Grady's face flushed with surprise and anger. He shouted out the door, "Don't get **uppity** with me! Y'all know *Auntie* is what we call all you old colored women." Furious, he slammed the door against the bitter cold. He shook his head in disgust. "It's a waste of time trying to be nice," he told himself. 5 **C**

But one look out the window made Grady refocus his attention to a more immediate problem. The weather had worsened. He checked his watch. It was a little past nine. Remarkably, he was still on schedule, but that didn't matter. He had decided to close down the route and take the bus in.

> **"It's a waste of time trying to be nice," he told himself.**

That's when his headlights picked up the **figure** of a woman running in the snow, without a hat, gloves, or boots. Although she'd pulled a shawl over the lightweight jacket and **flimsy** dress she was wearing, her clothing offered very little protection against the **elements**. As she pressed forward against the driving snow and wind, Grady saw that the woman was very young, no more than twenty. And she was clutching something close to her body. What was it? Then Grady saw the baby, a small bundle wrapped in a faded pink blanket. 6 **D**

"These people," Grady sighed, opening the door. The woman stumbled up the steps, escaping the wind that **mercilessly** ripped at her **petite frame**.

"Look here. I've closed down the route. I'm taking the bus in."

In big gulping sobs the woman laid her story before him. "I need help, please. My husband's gone to Memphis looking for work. Our baby's

5 **Viewpoint** Explain how Grady's remarks reflect a cultural viewpoint about African Americans. Use specific examples.

6 **Make Inferences** Think about the inferences you have made about Grady so far. What do you think he will do?

In Other Words

uppity too bold
figure shape
flimsy thin and poorly made
elements weather
mercilessly cruelly, harshly
petite frame slim body

TEACH & PRACTICE

C Reading Support

5 **Viewpoint** How might Grady's response to the woman reflect a cultural perspective?

Possible response:

- *He is a white man living in the segregated South, where many white people were racist toward black people. His response shows that he thinks he is better than African Americans.* RL.9-10.6

D Reading Support

6 **Make Inferences** Have students summarize what they know about Grady so far.

ELL Use Graphic Organizer List the details students have noticed about Grady and use a graphic to help students understand how these details lead to inferences.

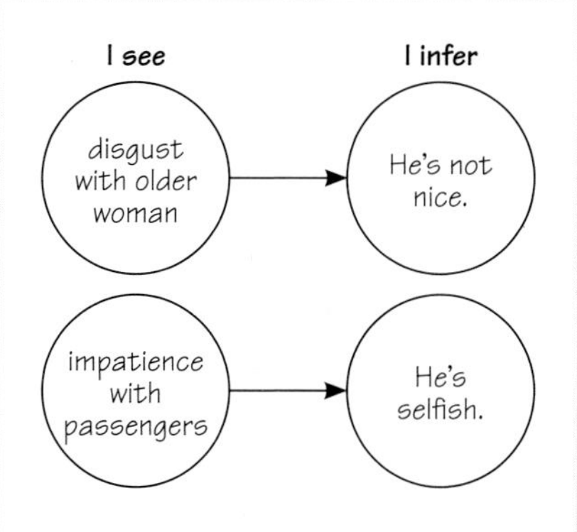

Ask: What do you think Grady will do? What clues from his actions so far helped you make an inference?

Possible responses:

- *He is selfish, not very nice, and doesn't like African Americans.*
- *He will hurt someone else.* RL.9-10.1

CCSS **Literacy.RL.9-10.1** Cite strong and thorough textual evidence to support analysis of what the text says explicitly as well as inferences drawn from the text. **Literacy.RL.9-10.6** Analyze a particular point of view or cultural experience reflected in a work of literature from outside the United States, drawing on a wide reading of world literature.

READ

OBJECTIVES

Vocabulary
- Key Vocabulary T

Reading Strategies
- Make Inferences
- Plan and Monitor: Predict

Comprehension & Critical Thinking
- Make Inferences
- Use Text Evidence T

Literary Analysis
- Analyze Style: Language and Word Choice

Viewing
- Respond to and Interpret Visuals

TEACH & PRACTICE

A Reading Support

7 **Make Inferences** Ask: How does Grady act toward the woman with the baby? How do these actions compare with the way he has treated the other African American passengers?

Possible response:
- *Grady has treated all the African American passengers rudely and without compassion or understanding.* RL.9-10.1

Monitor Comprehension

Explain Have students think aloud to explain what Grady discovers.

MODEL Say:
- *Grady forgets all about what happened until he notices a small article in the paper the next morning.*
- *He discovers …*
- *We know that Grady knows …*

Have students complete the think aloud to answer the question.

Possible responses:
- *He discovers that the woman he turned away froze to death with her child.*
- *We know that Grady knows what really happened: She froze because he wouldn't let her on the bus.* RL.9-10.10

sick, real sick. She needs to get to the hospital. I know she'll die if I don't get help."

"Well, I got to go by the hospital on the way back to the garage. You can ride that far." Grady nodded for her to pay. The woman looked at the floor. "Well? Pay up and get on to the back of the bus so I can get out of here."

A "I—I don't have the fare," she said, quickly adding, "but if you let me ride, I promise to bring it to you in the morning."

"**Give an inch, y'all want a mile.** You know the rules. No money, no ride!" 7

"Oh, please!" the young woman cried. "Feel her little head. It's so hot." She held out the baby to him. Grady **recoiled**.

Desperately the woman looked for something to bargain with. "Here," she said, taking off her wedding ring. "Take this. It's gold. But please don't make me get off this bus."

He opened the door. The winds howled savagely. "Please," the woman begged.

"Go on home, now. You young gals get **hysterical** over a little fever. Nothing. It'll be fine in the morning." As he shut the door the last sounds he heard were the mother's sobs, the baby's wail, and the moaning wind.

Grady **dismissed** the incident until the next morning, when he read that it had been a record snowfall. His eyes were drawn to a small article about a colored woman and child found frozen to death on Hall Street. No one seemed to know where the woman was going or why. No one but Grady.

"That gal should have done like I told her and gone on home," he said, turning to the comics.

7 Make Inferences Is Grady's answer consistent with the inferences you have made about him so far? Why or why not? Add the new information to your Inference Chart.

Key Vocabulary
desperately *adv.*, frantically, with great need

In Other Words
Give an inch, y'all want a mile. If I do you a small favor, you will want even more.
recoiled pulled back in disgust
hysterical very upset
dismissed forgot about

Monitor Comprehens
Explain What does Grady discover happened on Hall Street that snowy night?

VOCABULARY

Link Vocabulary and Concepts

Ask questions to link Key Vocabulary with the Essential Question.

EQ **ESSENTIAL QUESTION:**
What makes a hero?

Some possible questions:
- *Can everyday people who show* **compassion** *for others be considered heroic?*
- *Does someone need* **authority** *to be considered a hero? Why or why not?*
- *Is it important for someone to be* **persistent** *in trying to change things for the better? Why?*
- *In what ways can heroes inspire and* **provoke** *others to do good things?*

Have students use the Key Vocabulary words in their responses. L.9-10.6

CCSS Literacy.RL.9-10.1 Cite strong and thorough textual evidence to support analysis of what the text says explicitly as well as inferences drawn from the text. Literacy.L.9-10.6 Acquire and use accurately general academic and domain-specific words and phrases, sufficient for reading, writing, speaking, and listening at the college and career readiness level; demonstrate independence in gathering vocabulary knowledge when considering a word or phrase important to comprehension or expression.

Predict
A year later Grady is assigned to the same bus route. What do you think will happen? **B**

It was exactly one year later, on the anniversary of the record snowstorm, that Grady was assigned the Hall Street Express again. Just as before, a storm heaped several inches of snow onto the city in a matter of hours, making driving extremely hazardous. **8** **C**

By nightfall Grady decided to close the route. But just as he was making the turnaround at the east side loop, his headlight picked up a woman running in the snow—the same woman he'd seen the previous year. Death hadn't **altered** her desperation.

8 Language
What words and phrases give clues about what might happen next?

Balzac, Towards the Light, Midnight, 1908, Edward Steichen (1879–1973). Direct carbon print
©The Metropolitan Museum of Art/Art Resource, NY.

D

▲ **Critical Viewing: Effect** How does this image express the feeling and mood of the story? **E**

In Other Words
altered changed

TEACH & PRACTICE

B Chunking the Text

Predict Review what students know about Grady to help them predict what might happen next.

Read Have students read pp. 271–272. Support and monitor their comprehension using the reading support provided.
RL.9-10.10

C Reading Support

8 Language Highlight *exactly* and *anniversary*, which make the date sound important, and *just as before*. Point out descriptions of the weather and compare them to the ones on pp. 268–269.

ELL Sketch the Scene Point out words and phrases that create a picture of the scene: *snowstorm, Hall Street Express, several inches of snow, driving extremely hazardous.*

Have students sketch the scene to create visual clues about what might happen next.

Ask: How do these words and phrases help you tell what might happen next?

Possible responses:
- *The words* exactly, anniversary, *and* just as before *suggest a repeat of last year's events.*
- *Descriptions of the snow and the roads suggest danger.*

RL.9-10.4

D Analyze Visuals

About the Image Photographer George H. Seeley used a printing method that allowed him to change the light in an image and create unusual effects.

Interpret and Respond Ask: Do you think the title fits the image? What other titles might work, especially in relation to the story?

E Critical Viewing: Effect

Analyze Mood Ask: How are the moods in the story and the image the same?

Possible response:
- *The image has an unreal feeling. This reflects the ghostly mood when Grady sees the woman again, a year after her death.*

RL.9-10.7

CCSS **Literacy.RL.9-10.4** Determine the meaning of words and phrases as they are used in the text, including figurative and connotative meanings; analyze the cumulative impact of specific word choices on meaning and tone (e.g., how the language evokes a sense of time and place; how it sets a formal or informal tone). **Literacy.RL.9-10.7** Analyze the representation of a subject or a key scene in two different artistic mediums, including what is emphasized or absent in each treatment (e.g., Auden's "Musée des Beaux Arts" and Breughel's Landscape with the Fall of Icarus). **Literacy.RL.9-10.10** By the end of grade 9, read and comprehend literature, including stories, dramas, and poems, in the grades 9-10 text complexity band proficiently, with scaffolding as needed at the high end of the range. By the end of grade 10, read and comprehend literature, including stories, dramas, and poems, at the high end of the grades 9-10 text complexity band independently and proficiently.

OBJECTIVES

Reading Strategies
- Make Inferences; Review Strategies
- Plan and Monitor: Confirm Prediction

Comprehension & Critical Thinking
- Make Inferences
- Use Text Evidence Ⓣ

Literary Analysis
- Analyze Viewpoint Ⓣ
- Literary Device: Personification

Research Skills
- Convert Data into Graphic Aids; Evaluate and Draw Conclusions

Grammar
- Subject and Object Pronouns Ⓣ

TEACH & PRACTICE

Ⓐ Reading Support

9 Make Inferences Have students reread from p. 271. Ask: What suggests these events are unusual?

Possible responses:
- *Grady closes his eyes but can't keep them shut.*
- *The narration includes a question.*

RL.9-10.1

Ⓑ Reading Support

Literary Device Point out the author's use of personification: "The gray coldness of Fear slipped into the driver's seat." Ask: What effect does personification have in this paragraph?

Possible response:
- *It makes the fear seem very real.*

RL.9-10.4

Ⓒ Reading Support

10 Viewpoint Ask: What can an omniscient narrator tell us about the accident that the driver cannot?

Possible response:
- *Grady crashed because he thought he saw a ghost.*

RL.9-10.6

Monitor Comprehension

Confirm Prediction Have students match their predictions with what happens to Grady. Discuss the accuracy of their predictions.

RL.9-10.10

Ⓐ Still holding on to the blanketed baby, the small-framed woman **pathetically** struggled to reach the bus.

Grady closed his eyes but couldn't keep them shut. She was still coming, but from where? The answer was too horrible to consider, so he chose to let his mind find a more reasonable explanation. 9 From some dark corner of his childhood he heard his father's voice, **slurred** by alcohol, **mocking** him. *It ain't the same woman, dummy. You know how they all look alike!*

Grady remembered his father with bitterness and swore at the thought of him. This *was* the same woman, Grady argued with his father's memory, taking no comfort in being right. Grady watched the woman's movements breathlessly as she stepped out of the headlight beam and approached the door. She stood outside the door waiting . . . waiting.

Ⓑ The gray coldness of Fear slipped into the driver's seat. Grady sucked air into his lungs in big gulps, feeling out of control. Fear moved his foot to the gas pedal, **careening** the bus out into oncoming traffic. Ⓒ Headlights. A truck. Fear made Grady hit the brakes. The back of the bus went into a sliding spin, slamming into a tree. Grady's stomach crushed against the steering wheel, **rupturing** his liver and spleen. *You've really done it now, lunkhead.* As he drifted into the final darkness, he heard a woman's sobs, a baby **wailing**—or was it just the wind? 10

She stood outside the door waiting . . . waiting.

9 Make Inferences What clues tell you that these events are unusual?

10 Viewpoint How would this part of the story be different if the narrator had been the truck driver, rather than a third-person omniscient narrator? Explain.

Monitor Comprehension

Confirm Prediction Was your prediction accurate? Explain whether it met or didn't meet your expectations.

In Other Words

pathetically pitifully
slurred made unclear
mocking making fun of
careening wildly swaying, tilting
rupturing cutting a hole in
wailing crying loudly

GRAMMAR

Subject and Object Pronouns

Teach/Model Display the transparency. Compare the subject and object pronouns in the chart. Use the examples to show how subject pronouns and object pronouns work in a sentence. Point out that *it* and *you* are both subject and object pronouns.

Practice A. As students suggest the correct pronoun, write it and ask them to identify the noun it refers to. Underline the noun.

B. Have students write and share their sentences. Repeat a sentence from each, and ask the group to identify the pronoun, telling if it is a subject or object pronoun. L.9-10.1

Grammar & Writing Practice Book, pp. 91–92

Grammar Transparency 42

GRAMMAR SUBJECT AND OBJECT PRONOUNS 42

Why Are There So Many Pronouns?

Some Work as Subjects, and Some Work as Objects.

- Use a **subject pronoun** as the subject of a sentence.

  Jon enjoys nonfiction. **He** (subject) reads history.

  Jon bought a **book** about the boycott. **It** (subject) told about the protest.

- Use an **object pronoun** as the object of the verb.

  I like **historical fiction**. I prefer **it** (object) to nonfiction.

  Sonia likes books about civil rights. This one interests **her** (object).

- Which pronouns stay the same no matter how they are used?

Pronouns	
Subject	Object
I	me
you	you
he	him
she	her
it	it

Try It

A. Say each pair of sentences about the story. Add a pronoun, and tell the noun that it refers to.

1. Grady saw a woman. He did not know ___her___.
2. Grady told the woman to get off the bus. ___He___ was rude.
3. The woman pleaded with Grady. She begged ___him___.
4. Grady closed the door. He shut ___it___ in the woman's face.
5. The bus began to spin. ___It___ spun out of control.

B. Write two pairs of sentences about kind or cruel characters in stories that you know. Use a pronoun in each pair. Sentences will vary.

GRAMMAR SKILLS PATH
41 Direct Objects
▶ 42 Subject and Object Pronouns — ELL Language & Grammar Lab
43 *I* vs. *Me*
44 Subject and Object Pronouns
45 Review: Subject and Object Pronouns

CCSS **Literacy.RL.9-10.4** Determine the meaning of words and phrases as they are used in the text, including figurative and connotative meanings; analyze the cumulative impact of specific word choices on meaning and tone (e.g., how the language evokes a sense of time and place; how it sets a formal or informal tone). **Literacy.RL.9-10.10** By the end of grade 9, read and comprehend literature, including stories, dramas, and poems, in the grades 9-10 text complexity band proficiently, with scaffolding as needed at the high end of the range. By the end of grade 10, read and comprehend literature, including stories, dramas, and poems, at the high end of the grades 9-10 text complexity band independently and proficiently. **Literacy.L.9-10.1** Demonstrate command of the conventions of standard English grammar and usage when writing or speaking.

Predict
What will happen now that a new driver has been assigned to the Hall Street Express? **D**

Twenty-five years later, Ray Hammond, a war hero with two years of college, became the first black driver Metro hired. A lot of things had happened during those two and a half decades to pave the way for Ray's new job. The military had **integrated its forces** during the Korean War. In 1954 the Supreme Court had ruled that **segregated** schools were unequal. And one by one, unfair laws were being challenged by civil rights groups all over the South. Ray had watched the Montgomery bus boycott with interest, especially the boycott's leader, Dr. Martin Luther King, Jr. **E**

Ray soon found out that progress on the day-to-day level can be painfully slow. Ray was given the Hall Street Express.

"The white drivers call my route the Blackbird Express," Ray told his wife. "I'm the first driver to be given that route as a permanent assignment. The others wouldn't take it." 11

"What more did you expect?" his wife answered, tying his bow tie. "Just do your best so it'll be easier for the ones who come behind you."

In November, Ray worked the three-to-eleven shift. "Snow's predicted," the route manager barked one afternoon. "Close it down if it gets bad out there, Ray."

The last shift on the Hall Street Express.

Since he was a boy, Ray had heard the story of the haunting of that bus route. Every first snowfall passengers and drivers testified that they'd seen the ghost of Eula Mae Daniels clutching her baby as she ran through the snow.

"Good luck with Eula Mae tonight," one of the drivers said, **snickering**.

"I didn't know white folk believed in **haints**," Ray shot back.

But parked at the east side loop, staring into the swirling snow mixed

11 **Make Inferences** Think about the information on this page. What initial inferences can you make about Ray Hammond?

In Other Words
integrated its forces allowed soldiers of different races to serve together
segregated racially separate
snickering laughing meanly
haints spirits or ghosts

TEACH & PRACTICE

D Chunking the Text

Predict Ask: Are the same events likely to happen again? Why or why not? Predict what might happen with a new driver on the same route.

Read Have students read pp. 273–277. Support and monitor their comprehension using the reading support provided.
RL.9-10.10

E Reading Support

11 **Make Inferences** Have students reread the first three paragraphs on p. 273, and then describe Ray Hammond.

ELL **Use Graphic Organizer** List the details students identify about Ray Hammond and use a graphic to show how these details lead to an inference.

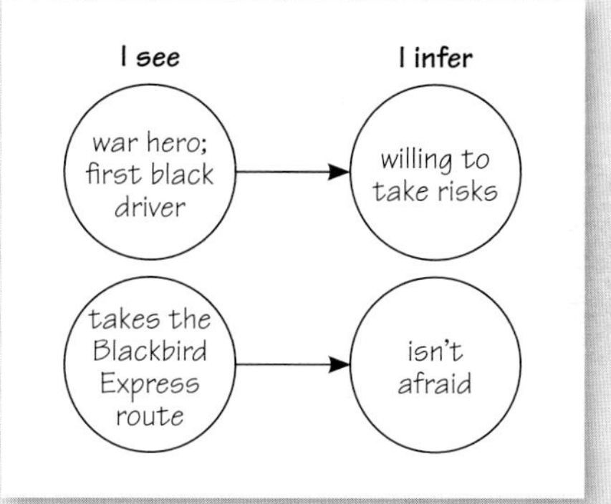

Have students combine the information to make inferences about Ray.

Ask: What inferences can you make about Ray?

Possible responses:
- *He is a brave war hero. He is not afraid to take risks.*

RL.9-10.1

Review Strategies Have partners say what other strategy they used as they read the text.

Possible responses:
- *I made a connection between what the story said about civil rights at the time and Ray being the first black bus driver. This helped me understand how unfair it was for African Americans in the South.*

RL.9-10.10

CONTENT AREA CONNECTIONS

HISTORY

Research the Civil Rights Movement

Conduct Research Have student groups research key events of the civil rights movement and make a time line of these events. Have students label each event to describe its importance and have them use these questions to guide their research:

- Who were the main civil rights leaders?
- What were some major boycotts or other organized protests?
- What key civil rights laws were passed and when?
- What other major events occurred, and what were the effects?

Share and Compare Have groups share time lines to compare key events and make inferences about the effects of civil rights activism in America.
W.9-10.7

CCSS Literacy.RL.9-10.1 Cite strong and thorough textual evidence to support analysis of what the text says explicitly as well as inferences drawn from the text. Literacy.W.9-10.7 Conduct short as well as more sustained research projects to answer a question (including a self-generated question) or solve a problem; narrow or broaden the inquiry when appropriate; synthesize multiple sources on the subject, demonstrating understanding of the subject under investigation.

READ

OBJECTIVES

Vocabulary
- Key Vocabulary Ⓣ

Reading Strategy
- Make Inferences

Comprehension & Critical Thinking
- Make Inferences
- Use Text Evidence Ⓣ

Literary Analysis
- Analyze Viewpoint Ⓣ

Grammar
- *I* vs. *Me* Ⓣ

TEACH & PRACTICE

Ⓐ Reading Support

12 Viewpoint Help students recall Grady's response to the woman from pp. 270 and 272. Then look at Ray's response on p. 274. Point out phrases such as "overruling his fear," "she deserves better," and "pushed fear aside." Ask: How does the narrator use this to contrast the ways Grady and Ray respond?

Possible responses:
- *Grady responds first with anger and then with fear. Ray is able to push fear aside and respond with compassion and concern.*

Ask: How might the drivers' cultural viewpoints affect their decisions?

Possible responses:
- *Grady is prejudiced toward African Americans and only sees the woman's color. Ray is African American and sees her as a human being.*

RL.9-10.6

Ⓑ Reading Support

13 Viewpoint Discuss why Ray's history as a soldier is important to know. Ask: Why does the narrator tell readers that Ray spent Christmas in a Korean foxhole?

Possible response:
- *The narrator shares information about Ray's past to show that he is familiar with death, fear, and cold.*

RL.9-10.6

with ice, Ray felt tingly, as if he were dangerously close to an electrical charge. He'd just made up his mind to close down the route and head back to the garage when he saw her. Every hair on his head stood on end.

He wished her away, but she kept coming. He tried to think, but his thoughts were jumbled and confused. He wanted to look away, but curiosity fixed his gaze on the advancing horror.

Just as the old porch stories had described her, Eula Mae Daniels was a small-framed woman frozen forever in youth. "So young," Ray whispered. "Could be my Carolyn in a few more years." He watched as the ghost came around to the doors. She was out there, waiting in the cold. Ray heard the baby crying. "**There but for the grace of God goes one of mine**," he said, **compassion** overruling his fear. "Nobody deserves to be left out in this weather. Ghost or not, she deserves better." And he swung open the doors.

Ⓐ The woman had form but **no substance**. Ray could see the snow falling *through* her. He pushed fear aside. "Come on, honey, get out of the cold," Ray said, waving her on board. 12

Eula Mae stood stony still, looking up at Ray with dark, questioning eyes. The driver understood. He'd seen that look before, not from a dead woman but from plenty of his passengers. "It's okay. I'm for real. Ray Hammond, the first Negro to drive for Metro. Come on, now, get on," he coaxed her gently.

Ⓑ Eula Mae moved soundlessly up the steps. She held the infant to her body. Ray couldn't remember ever feeling so cold, not even the Christmas he'd spent in a Korean **foxhole**. He'd seen so much death, but never anything like this. 13

The ghost mother consoled her crying baby. Then with her head bowed she told her story in quick bursts of sorrow, just as she had twenty-five years earlier. "My husband is in Memphis looking for

12 Viewpoint How does the narrator explain the difference between Ray's and Grady's responses to the woman?

13 Viewpoint What does the narrator tell you about Ray's past? Why do you think the narrator chooses to share this information?

Key Vocabulary
compassion *n.*, care for the suffering and troubles of others

In Other Words
There but for the grace of God goes one of mine That could be someone in my family
no substance no body or flesh
foxhole hole that protects a soldier in battle

GRAMMAR

I vs. *Me*

Teach/Model Display the transparency. Move through the examples and rules for the subject pronoun *I*. Then show how the object pronoun *me* functions. Fix the errors in the incorrect sentences for each pronoun.

Practice A. As students choose the correct pronoun, underline it on the transparency. **B.** After partners write sentences about stories they both liked, have each student read a favorite sentence aloud. Ask the group to identify each pronoun and tell whether it is a subject or object pronoun. L.9-10.1

Grammar & Writing Practice Book, pp. 93–94

Grammar Transparency 43

Do You Ever Talk About Yourself?
Then Learn to Use the Words *I* and *Me*.

GRAMMAR *I* VS. *ME* 43

Subject Pronoun: I
- Use the pronoun **I** in the **subject** of a sentence.
  I started to read the story.
- In a compound subject, name yourself last.
  Joey and I finished the story.
  He and I liked it.
- What's wrong with this sentence?
  Me and Joey will read another book together.

Object Pronoun: me
- Use the pronoun **me** as the **object**.
  The story interested **me**.
- In a compound object, name yourself last.
  The story scared **Joey and me.**
  The story scared **him and me.**
- What's wrong with these sentences?
  The characters surprised Joey and I.
  The ending also surprised me and him.

Try It

A. Say each sentence about "The Woman in the Snow." Use I or me.
1. The librarian invited another girl and **(I / me)** to read the story aloud to a group.
2. The ghost surprised her and **(I / me)**.
3. Ray Hammond's kindness pleased my friend and **(I / me)**.
4. The group and **(I / me)** liked Ray Hammond's kind ways.

B. Now talk with a partner about a story you both liked. Write your four best sentences. Include I and me in your sentences.
Sentences will vary.

GRAMMAR SKILLS PATH

41	Direct Objects
42	Subject and Object Pronouns
▶ 43	*I* vs. *Me* — ELL Language & Grammar Lab
44	Subject and Object Pronouns
45	Review: Subject and Object Pronouns

CCSS Literacy.RL.9-10.6 Analyze a particular point of view or cultural experience reflected in a work of literature from outside the United States, drawing on a wide reading of world literature. Literacy.L.9-10.1 Demonstrate command of the conventions of standard English grammar and usage when writing or speaking.

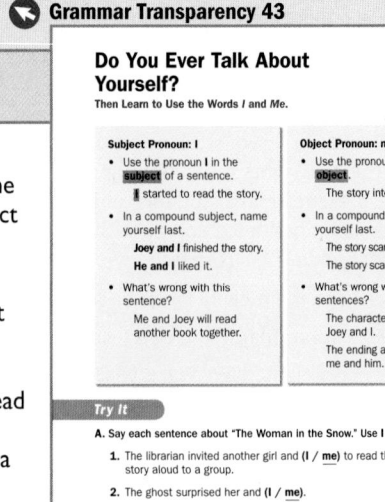

work. Our baby is sick. She'll die if I don't get help."

"First off," said Ray. "Hold your head up. **You got no cause for shame.**"

"I don't have any money," she said. "But if you let me ride, I promise to bring it to you tomorrow. I promise."

Ray sighed deeply. "The rule book says no money, no ride. But the book doesn't say a word about a personal loan." He took a handful of change out of his pocket, fished around for a dime, and dropped it into the pay box. "**You're all paid up.** Now, go sit yourself down while I try to get this bus back to town."

The rule book says no money, no ride.

Eula Mae started to the back of the bus.

"No you don't," Ray stopped her. "You don't have to sit in the back anymore. You can sit right up front."

The ghost woman moved to a seat closer, but still not too close up front. The baby **fretted**. The young mother comforted her as best she could.

They rode in silence for a while. Ray checked in the rearview mirror every now and then. She gave no reflection, but when he looked over his shoulder, she was there, all right. "Nobody will ever believe this," he mumbled. "*I* don't believe it. 14 (C)

"Things have gotten much better since you've been . . . away," he said, wishing immediately that he hadn't opened his mouth. Still he couldn't—or wouldn't—stop talking.

"I owe this job to a little woman just about your size named Mrs. Rosa Parks. Down in Montgomery, Alabama, one day, Mrs. Parks refused to give up a seat she'd paid for just because she was a colored woman."

14 Make Inferences Think about the new information on these pages. What more can you infer about Ray Hammond?

In Other Words

You got no cause for shame. You have no reason to be embarrassed.
You're all paid up. Your ticket is paid for.
fretted cried and moved around

TEACH & PRACTICE

C Reading Support

14 Make Inferences Review the surprising events recounted on this page and Ray's reaction to them.

ELL Use Graphic Organizer Use a two-column chart to help students list and understand informal words and phrases that describe what Ray says and does.

Character's Words and Actions	What They Mean
"First off … hold your head up."	*The first thing I want to tell you is that you have no reason to be ashamed.*
"fished around for a dime"	*looked for a dime*
"right up front"	*all the way at the front*
"she was there, all right"	*she was really there*

Ask: What does Ray do to help the woman? What does he tell her about how she should act?

Possible responses:
- *Ray gives the woman a ride and pays for her fare.*
- *He tells her not to be ashamed and not to sit in the back of the bus.*

Ask: What do his words and actions tell you about the kind of person Ray Hammond is?

Possible response:
- *He cares about individual people, is proud of being African American, and believes in equal rights for African Americans.*

RL.9-10.1

CCSS Literacy.RL.9-10.1 Cite strong and thorough textual evidence to support analysis of what the text says explicitly as well as inferences drawn from the text.

OBJECTIVES

Vocabulary
- Key Vocabulary Ⓣ

Reading Strategy
- Make Inferences

Comprehension & Critical Thinking
- Make Inferences
- Use Text Evidence Ⓣ

Literary Analysis
- Analyze Viewpoint Ⓣ

Writing
- Form: Response to Literature

TEACH & PRACTICE

A Reading Support

15 Make Inferences Have students recall what they know about Ray.

ELL Sentence Frames Provide frames to help students review their inferences about Ray and to understand his actions:

- From Ray's background, I can tell he is ______.
- When Ray pays the woman's bus fare, it shows ______.
- The last thing he does for Eula Mae is ______.

Have students explain whether or not Ray's actions are consistent with the inferences they have made.

Possible response:

- *Taking the ghost woman to the hospital is consistent with all of Ray's previous kind and compassionate actions.*

RL.9-10.1

A Eula Mae sat **motionless**. There was no way of telling if she had heard or not. Ray kept talking. "Well, they arrested her. So the colored people decided to boycott the buses. Nobody rode for over a year. Walked everywhere, formed **carpools**, or just didn't go, rather than ride a bus. The man who led the boycott was named Reverend King. Smart man. We're sure to hear more about him in the future. . . . You still with me?" Ray looked around. Yes, she was there. The baby had quieted. It was much warmer on the bus now.

Slowly Ray **inched along** the icy road, holding the bus steady, trying to keep the back wheels from racing out of control. "Where was I?" he continued. "Oh yeah, things changed after that Montgomery bus boycott. This job opened up. More changes are on the way. Get this: They got an Irish Catholic running for President. Now, what do you think of that?"

About that time Ray pulled the bus over at Seventeenth Street. The lights at Gale Hospital sent a welcome message to those in need on such a frosty night. "This is it." 15

Eula Mae raised her head. "You're a kind man," she said. "Thank you."

Ray opened the door. The night air **gusted** up the steps and **nipped** at his ankles. Soundlessly, Eula Mae stepped off the bus with her baby.

"Excuse me," Ray called politely. "About the bus fare. No need for you to make a special trip . . . back. Consider it a gift."

He thought he saw Eula Mae Daniels smile as she vanished into the swirling snow, never to be seen again. ❖

15 Make Inferences Review the inferences you have made about Ray. Are his actions consistent? Explain.

In Other Words
motionless without moving
carpools groups to share rides
inched along moved a little at a time on
gusted blew strongly
nipped felt like little bites

Historical Background
The Reverend Martin Luther King Jr., organized the Montgomery bus boycott and eventually became the leader of the civil rights movement. He was shot and killed in 1968.

OUT-OF-SCHOOL LITERACY

MEDIA & TECHNOLOGY

Using Online Reading

Have small groups investigate online resources that can help bring the civil rights movement to life in new ways. Students may choose to:

- visit virtual civil rights museums
- read biographies and first-person accounts of key figures in the civil rights movement
- investigate blogs and podcasts to find different perspectives about key people and events
- play online history games about the time period
- view and hear historical clips of speeches, interviews, and newscasts.

Have groups share the new knowledge they gain and evaluate how effectively different online resources convey information.

SL.9-10.1.a

CCSS Literacy.RL.9-10.1 Cite strong and thorough textual evidence to support analysis of what the text says explicitly as well as inferences drawn from the text. Literacy.SL.9-10.1.a Come to discussions prepared, having read and researched material under study; explicitly draw on that preparation by referring to evidence from texts and other research on the topic or issue to stimulate a thoughtful, well-reasoned exchange of ideas

ANALYZE The Woman in the Snow

1. **Recall and Interpret** What happens to Eula Mae after her bus ride with Ray? What is responsible for the change? Use details from the text to support your answer.
2. **Vocabulary** How does Grady's background explain his lack of **compassion**? Does he show any signs of feeling guilty or sorry? Explain.
3. **Analyze Viewpoint** Talk with a partner about how having a third-person omniscient narrator affects the story. How would the story be different if the author had written it using a first-person narrator?
4. **Focus Strategy Make Inferences** Choose a passage that you think suggests the story's message, or theme. Explain to a partner the theme you infer and the details that support your inference.

Return to the Text

Reread and Write What qualities make Ray Hammond a hero? Reread the story and find at least two details from the text. Write your opinion.

APPLY

B ANALYZE

1. **Recall and Interpret** She no longer visits the bus route because her spirit is "healed" by Ray's fair and compassionate treatment. RL.9-10.1
2. **Vocabulary** Grady's childhood made him feel insecure, so he may have a hard time feeling compassion for others. When he reads about her death, he pretends he didn't have anything to do with it. L.9-10.6
3. **Analyze Viewpoint** A first-person narrator would not include as much insight into all the characters. A first-person narrator would also offer his or her own attitudes and opinions. The narrator might not know about the history. RL.9-10.6
4. **Focus Strategy: Make Inferences** Have volunteers share their partner's passage and inference with the class. Make sure students include details that support their thinking. RL.9-10.1

C Return to the Text

Students' opinions might reflect these influences and evidence:

- *Ray is brave to be the first African American driver on that route. He shows compassion by helping someone who may appear to be frightening to others. He is a leader for other African Americans.* W.9-10.9.a; W.9-10.10

Edge Interactive Practice Book, p. 130

CCSS **Literacy.RL.9-10.1** Cite strong and thorough textual evidence to support analysis of what the text says explicitly as well as inferences drawn from the text. **Literacy.RL.9-10.6** Analyze a particular point of view or cultural experience reflected in a work of literature from outside the United States, drawing on a wide reading of world literature. **Literacy.W.9-10.9.a** Apply grades 9-10 Reading standards to literature (e.g., "Analyze how an author draws on and transforms source material in a specific work [e.g., how Shakespeare treats a theme or topic from Ovid or the Bible or how a later author draws on a play by Shakespeare]".) **Literacy.W.9-10.10** Write routinely over extended time frames (time for research, reflection, and revision) and shorter time frames (a single sitting or a day or two) for a range of tasks, purposes, and audiences. **Literacy.L.9-10.6** Acquire and use accurately general academic and domain-specific words and phrases, sufficient for reading, writing, speaking, and listening at the college and career readiness level; demonstrate independence in gathering vocabulary knowledge when considering a word or phrase important to comprehension or expression.

Lesson 20

BEFORE READING

OBJECTIVES

Reading Strategy
• Make Inferences

Literary Analysis
• Analyze Development of Ideas Ⓣ

TEACH STRATEGIES

Ⓐ Analyze Development of Ideas

Introduce Read the paragraph to define magazine profiles, how they are usually structured, and how the author develops his or her ideas. Ask students what they already know about articles in magazines.

Look Into the Text Use the callouts on p. 278 to teach the development of ideas in a magazine profile. Ask: What time words can you find in the text?

Possible response:
• *Eight months earlier; then in October; Six weeks later; December 1, 1955*

Then ask: What names are given in the text?

Possible response:
• *Claudette Colvin, Mary Louise Smith, Mrs. Rosa Parks*

Have students identify more factual details that help develop ideas about the events.
RI.9-10.3

Ⓑ Focus Strategy: Make Inferences

Make Inferences Define the strategy and work through the How To box.

Have students read the Cultural Background note on p. 281 to learn about the N.A.A.C.P.

Then have partners make an inference to answer the question at the end of Look Into the Text.

Possible response:
• *Yes. Her work for the N.A.A.C.P. had taught her the best way to fight for her rights.*
RI.9-10.1

ONGOING ASSESSMENT
Have students explain what kind of details might be found in a magazine profile of a famous person.

BEFORE READING Rosa Parks

magazine profile and poem by Rita Dove

Reading Strategies
· Plan and Monitor
· Determine Importance
▶ **Make Inferences**
· Ask Questions
· Make Connections
· Synthesize
· Visualize

Analyze Development of Ideas

A **magazine profile** is a short article that tells about one aspect, or part, of a person's life. Authors usually tell events in time order and use facts, quotations, and other details to develop important ideas about the person's life. In this profile of Rosa Parks, the writer focuses on Parks's role in the civil rights movement.

Look Into the Text

Ⓐ The profile shows the sequence of events with time order words.

Parks was not the first to be detained for this offense. Eight months earlier, Claudette Colvin, 15, refused to give up her seat and was arrested. And then in October, a young woman named Mary Louise Smith was arrested. Smith paid the fine and was released.

Six weeks later, the time was ripe. The facts, rubbed shiny for retelling, are these: On December 1, 1955, Mrs. Rosa Parks, seamstress for a department store, boarded the Cleveland Avenue bus. She took a seat in the fifth row—the first row of the "Colored Section." ... [H]ad her work in the N.A.A.C.P. sharpened her sensibilities so that she knew what to do—or more precisely, what not to do: Don't frown, don't struggle, don't shout, don't pay the fine?

What facts develop the idea in the first sentence?

What names, events, and details do these two paragraphs include?

Focus Strategy ▶ Make Inferences

As you read, ask yourself why the author includes certain details. Use your own knowledge and experience to **make inferences** about Parks and the civil rights movement.

Ⓑ

Focus Strategy

HOW TO MAKE INFERENCES

Use an **Inference Map** to collect information from the key points of the text and your own experience. Then use that information to make an inference.

1. Jot down an important idea from the text.
2. Identify details that support that idea.
3. Add what you know about the idea from your own experience.
4. Combine the information to make an inference.

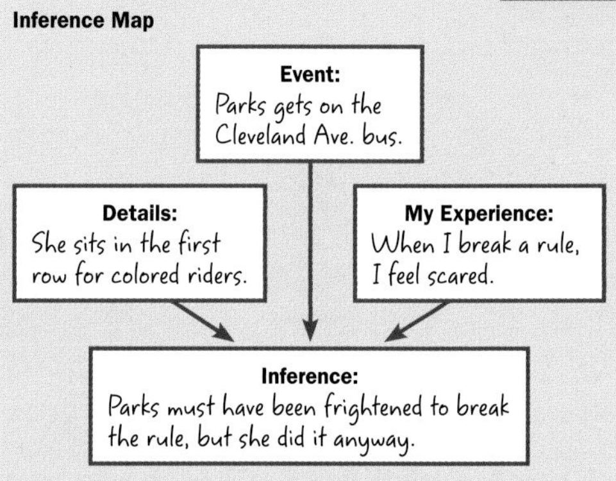

Inference Map
Event:
Parks gets on the Cleveland Ave. bus.
Details:
She sits in the first row for colored riders.
My Experience:
When I break a rule, I feel scared.
Inference:
Parks must have been frightened to break the rule, but she did it anyway.

CCSS Literacy.RI.9-10.1 Cite strong and thorough textual evidence to support analysis of what the text says explicitly as well as inferences drawn from the text. Literacy.RI.9-10.3 Analyze how the author unfolds an analysis or series of ideas or events, including the order in which the points are made, how they are introduced and developed, and the connections that are drawn between them.

Connect Across Texts
In "The Woman in the Snow," an ordinary person makes an extraordinary choice. Read this profile about another person's extraordinary choice.

D

Rosa Parks

by Rita Dove

"Our mistreatment was just not right, and I was tired of it."
—Rosa Parks

C

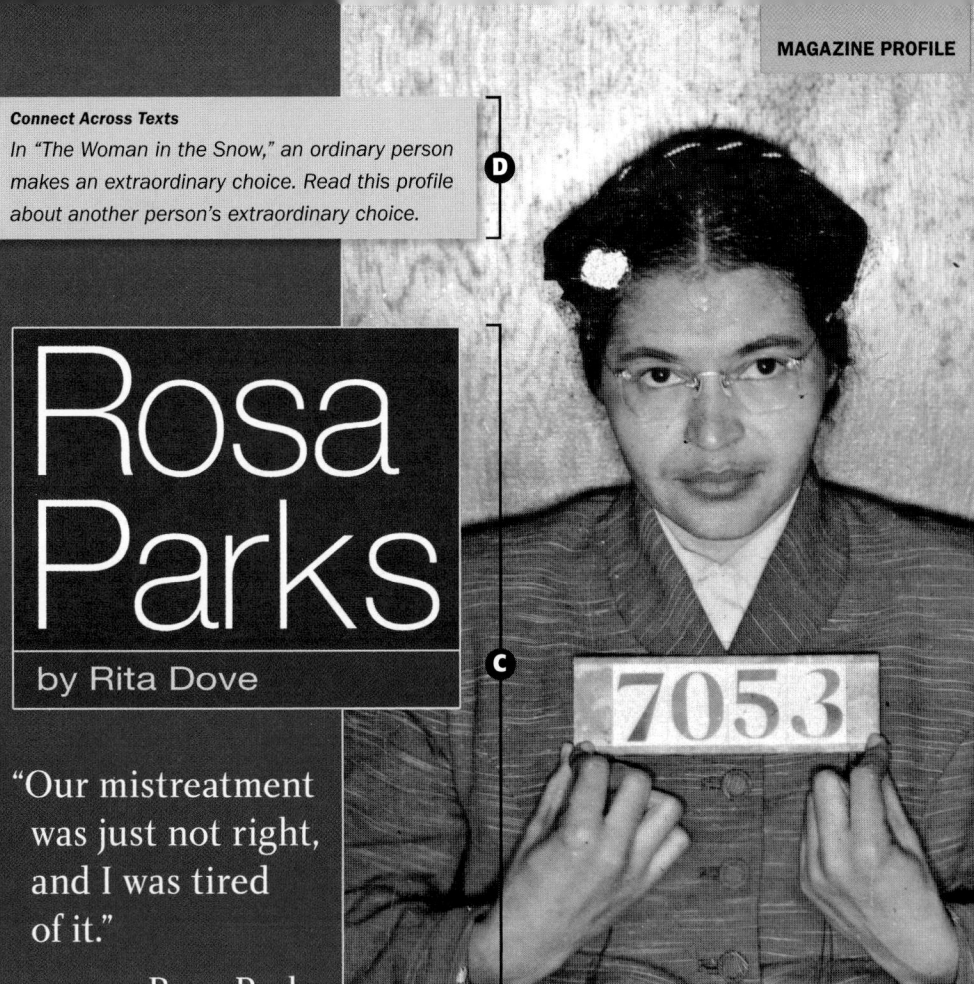

OBJECTIVES
Reading Strategy
- Make Connections

Cultural Perspectives
- U.S. Culture: Customs
- Compare Cultures: History

BUILD BACKGROUND

C Civil Disobedience
Read the title and quotation.

ELL **Build Background** Tell students that when people are arrested in the United States they are given an identification number, photographed, and fingerprinted. In this photo, Rosa Parks is in the process of being arrested and taken to jail.

Explain that many people in history have used civil disobedience to work for social change. Civil disobedience is a way to protest unjust laws with peaceful acts such as marching or writing letters. In many cases, this includes breaking or refusing to obey an unfair law. In the United States in the 1800s, writer Henry David Thoreau refused to pay a tax and was jailed. In India in the 1920s, Mahatma Gandhi was also jailed for acts of civil disobedience.

D Connect Across Texts
Have students review p. 268 and discuss how many African American bus passengers were treated unfairly. Study Parks's quote again and have students predict what act of civil disobedience she may have used.

Read Have students read pp. 279–284. Support and monitor their comprehension using the reading support provided.

Comprehension Coach

Build Reading Power
Assign students to use the software, based on their instructional needs.

Read Silently
- Comprehension questions with immediate feedback
- Glossary support
- Review text evidence

RI.9-10.10

Listen
- Professional model of fluent reading

Record
- Oral reading fluency practice
- Ongoing fluency assessment with immediate feedback

CCSS Literacy.RI.9-10.10 By the end of grade 9, read and comprehend literary nonfiction in the grades 9–10 text complexity band proficiently, with scaffolding as needed at the high end of the range. By the end of grade 10, read and comprehend literary nonfiction at the high end of the grades 9–10 text complexity band independently and proficiently.

READ

OBJECTIVES

Vocabulary
- Key Vocabulary Ⓣ
- Content Area Vocabulary: Criminal Justice

Reading Strategy
- Make Inferences; Review Strategies

Comprehension & Critical Thinking
- Make Inferences
- Use Textual Evidence Ⓣ

Literary Analysis
- Analyze Development of Ideas Ⓣ

Viewing
- Respond to and Interpret Visuals

Grammar
- Subject and Object Pronouns Ⓣ

TEACH & PRACTICE

Ⓐ Reading Support

1 Development of Ideas Have students name the events step by step. Ask: What is important about these events?

Possible response:
- *They led to Rosa Parks's decision to stay seated. This decision led to a new era in the Civil Rights Movement.*

RI.9-10.3

Ⓑ Reading Support

2 Make Inferences Have students name the events step by step. Ask: What is important about these events?

Possible response:
- *Rosa Parks unexpectedly challenges a very powerful force.*

RI.9-10.1

Ⓒ Analyze Visuals

Interpret and Respond Read the caption. Have students describe how people are seated. Ask: How does this seating plan create different treatment for blacks and whites?

Possible responses:
- *The white people get the better seats.*
- *Black people aren't treated with respect.*

Ⓐ **We know the story.** One December evening, a woman left work and boarded a bus for home. She was tired; her feet ached. But this was Montgomery, Alabama, in 1955. As the bus became crowded, the woman, a black woman, was ordered to give up her seat to a white passenger. When she remained seated, that simple decision eventually led to the end of **segregation** in the South, **ushering in** a new era of the civil rights movement. 1

This, anyway, was the story I had heard from the time I was curious enough to **eavesdrop on** adult conversations. I was 3 years old when a white bus driver warned Rosa Parks, "Well, I'm going to have you arrested," and she replied, "You may go on and do so." As a child, I Ⓑ didn't understand how doing nothing had caused so much activity, but I recognized the **template**: David slaying the giant Goliath, or the boy who saved his village by sticking his finger in the **dike**. 2 And perhaps it is the **lure of fairy-tale retribution** that colors the lens we look back through. Parks was 42 years old when she refused to give up her seat. She has insisted that her feet were not aching; she was, by her own testimony, no more tired than usual. And she did not plan her fateful act: "I did not get on the bus to get arrested," she has said. "I got on the bus to go home."

Montgomery's segregation laws were complex. Blacks were required to pay their fare to the driver, then get off and reboard through the back door. Sometimes the bus would drive off before the paid-up customers made it to the back entrance. If the white section was full and another white customer entered, blacks were

Ⓒ 

In Alabama in the 1950s, by law, if the white section of the bus was full, blacks had to give up their seats to allow whites to sit down.

1 Development of Ideas What idea is the author trying to tell about here? How does she use time-ordered events to develop her idea?

2 Make Inferences Writers often reference well-known stories in their works. In the Bible, a young boy named David defeats the giant Goliath with a small stone. How is Rosa Parks's action similar?

Key Vocabulary
segregation *n.*, the act of separating or keeping apart

In Other Words
ushering in introducing, beginning
eavesdrop on listen secretly to
template pattern, model
dike barrier to prevent flooding
lure of fairy-tale retribution appeal of evil people being punished

280 Unit 3 The Hero Within

GRAMMAR

Subject and Object Pronouns

Teach/Model Display the transparency. Show how to use plural pronouns as subjects or objects. Provide an example of a compound object with a noun and a pronoun (*Her story inspires my sister and me*). Point out that *you* can be used four ways: singular, plural, subject, and object. Provide example sentences..

Practice A. As students suggest the correct pronoun, write it and ask them to identify the noun it refers to. **B.** Have partners write and share their sentences about the civil rights movement. Repeat a sentence from each, and ask the group to identify a pronoun, telling whether it is a subject or object pronoun.

L.9-10.1

Grammar & Writing Practice Book, pp. 95–96

GRAMMAR SKILLS PATH

Grammar Transparency 44

GRAMMAR SUBJECT AND OBJECT PRONOUNS 44

Which Pronouns Refer to More Than One Person?
We, You, They,* and *Us, You, Them

With so many pronouns, how do you know which one to use in a sentence?

- Use a **subject pronoun** as the subject.
  The **officers** arrived. **They** (subject) arrested Rosa.
  Riders and bystanders watched. **They** (subject) were upset.
- Use an **object pronoun** as the object of the verb.
  Rosa hated unfair **laws**. She challenged **them** (object).
  We (subject) admire Rosa. Her story inspires **us** (object).

Pronouns	
Subject	Object
we	us
you	you
they	them

Try It

A. Say each pair of sentences. Add a pronoun, and tell what the pronoun refers to.

1. The civil rights movement affects you and me. It teaches __us__ about equality.
2. Some people protest unjust laws. The laws anger __them__.
3. My class and I read about Rosa Parks. __We__ admire her.
4. Other leaders of the civil rights movement also inspire us. __They__ worked tirelessly.
5. They got new laws passed and worked to enforce __them__.

B. Now talk with a partner about the civil rights movement. Write your three best sentences. Use pronouns. Sentences will vary.

CCSS Literacy.RI.9-10.1 Cite strong and thorough textual evidence to support analysis of what the text says explicitly as well as inferences drawn from the text. Literacy.RI.9-10.3 Analyze how the author unfolds an analysis or series of ideas or events, including the order in which the points are made, how they are introduced and developed, and the connections that are drawn between them. Literacy.L.9-10.1 Demonstrate command of the conventions of standard English grammar and usage when writing or speaking.

required to give up their seats and move farther to the back. A black person was not even allowed to sit across the aisle from whites. At the time, two-thirds of the bus riders in Montgomery were black. 3 **D**

Parks was not the first to be **detained for this offense**. Eight months earlier, Claudette Colvin, 15, refused to give up her seat and was arrested. And then in October, a young woman named Mary Louise Smith was arrested. Smith paid the fine and was released.

Six weeks later, the time was ripe. The facts, rubbed shiny for retelling, are these: On December 1, 1955, Mrs. Rosa Parks, **seamstress** for a department store, boarded the Cleveland Avenue bus. She took a seat in the fifth row—the first row of the "Colored Section." The driver was the same one who had put her off a bus twelve years earlier for refusing to get off and reboard through the back door. ("He was still mean-looking," she has said.) Did that make her stubborn? Or had her work in the N.A.A.C.P. sharpened her **sensibilities** so that she knew what to do—or more precisely, what not to do: Don't frown, don't struggle, don't shout, don't pay the fine?

She was arrested on a Thursday; **bail was posted** by Clifford Durr, the white lawyer whose wife had employed Parks as a seamstress.

After her first arrest in December, 1955, Rosa Parks was arrested again in February, 1956. This time the charge was helping organize a bus boycott. **E**

3 Make Inferences
The author says the laws "were complex." How else could the laws be described?

Monitor Comprehension

Explain
Why was Rosa Parks arrested?

In Other Words

detained for this offense held in jail for breaking this law
seamstress a woman who sewed clothes
sensibilities awareness and understanding
bail was posted money to release Rosa from jail was paid

Cultural Background

The **National Association for the Advancement of Colored People** (N.A.A.C.P.) was founded in 1909. Over the years, it has fought for the civil rights of schoolchildren, leaders, and ordinary men and women.

TEACH & PRACTICE

D Reading Support

3 Make Inferences Review the paragraph, photo, and caption on p. 280. Have students discuss how they would feel in this situation.

Possible responses:
- *The laws were unfair. The black passengers paid the same fare but didn't have the same rights.*

RI.9-10.1

Review Strategies Have students tell what other strategies they used as they read the text.

Possible response:
- *I made a connection to books I have read about girls being treated unfairly. This helped me to understand how African Americans riding the bus felt.*

RI.9-10.10

E Analyze Visuals

Interpret and Respond Have students analyze the photo, including Rosa Parks's posture and expression.

Monitor Comprehension

Explain Review the events leading up to Rosa Parks's arrest.

ELL Use Graphic Organizer Have students reread pp. 280–281 to find the actual events leading to Parks's arrest. Help them list what happens in a sequence chain.

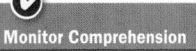

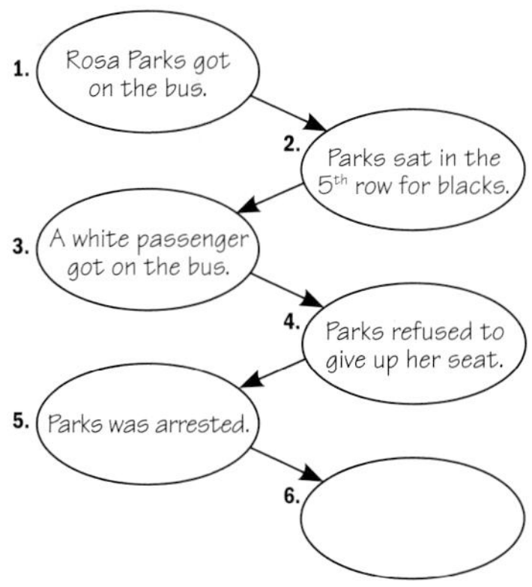

Have students summarize reasons for Parks's arrest.

Possible response:
- *She refused to give up her seat to a white person.*

RI.9-10.2

VOCABULARY

Content Area Vocabulary: Civics/Government

Build vocabulary related to the content area of criminal justice.

POLITICAL SCIENCE

Teach/Model Use the Make Words Your Own routine (see *the Vocabulary tab*) and the sample sentences below to introduce these words from the selection.

detained (dē-**tānd**) ▸ p. 281

She was **detained** *and couldn't leave.*

offense (u-**fens**) ▸ p. 281

Her **offense** *was not following a law about seating on buses.*

arrested (u-**rest**-id) ▸ pp. 280, 281

If you are **arrested**, *the police may take you to jail.*

charge (charj) ▸ p. 281

Her **charge** *in 1956 was helping to organize a bus boycott.*

conviction (con-**vik**-shun) ▸ p. 282

No one was surprised by Rosa Parks's **conviction**. *They knew she would be found guilty.*

Practice Have students scan a newspaper for the words, then explain what each word means in the context of the article.

Apply Ask students to describe a recent news event using the vocabulary.

L.9-10.6

CCSS Literacy.RI.9-10.2 Determine a central idea of a text and analyze its development over the course of the text, including how it emerges and is shaped and refined by specific details; provide an objective summary of the text. **Literacy.RI.9-10.10** By the end of grade 9, read and comprehend literary nonfiction in the grades 9–10 text complexity band proficiently, with scaffolding as needed at the high end of the range. By the end of grade 10, read and comprehend literary nonfiction at the high end of the grades 9–10 text complexity band independently and proficiently. **Literacy.L.9-10.6** Acquire and use accurately general academic and domain-specific words and phrases, sufficient for reading, writing, speaking, and listening at the college and career readiness level; demonstrate independence in gathering vocabulary knowledge when considering a word or phrase important to comprehension or expression.

READ

OBJECTIVES

Vocabulary
- Key Vocabulary (T)

Reading Strategy
- Make Inferences

Comprehension & Critical Thinking
- Make Inferences
- Use Text Evidence (T)

Literary Analysis
- Analyze Development of Ideas (T)

Research Skill
- Gather Information

TEACH & PRACTICE

(A) Reading Support

4 Development of Ideas Have students use a T-chart to record facts and comments about Parks's life.

Facts	Comments
She was arrested on December 1, 1955.	"Oh, she's so sweet. They've messed with the wrong one now."

Discuss how the profile would be different if it only included facts. Then have students synthesize the facts and comments to understand Parks's life.

Possible response:
- *Dove describes how Parks acted and how others viewed her.*

RI.9-10.3

(A) That evening, after talking it over with her mother and husband, Rosa Parks agreed to challenge Montgomery's segregation laws. Thirty-five thousand handbills were distributed to all black schools the next morning. The message was simple:

"We are . . . asking every Negro to stay off the buses Monday in protest of the arrest and trial . . . You can afford to stay out of school for one day. If you work, take a cab, or walk. But please, children and grown-ups, don't ride the bus at all on Monday. Please stay off the buses Monday."

Monday came. Rain threatened, yet the black population of Montgomery stayed off the buses, either walking or catching one of the black cabs stopping at every **municipal** bus stop for ten cents per customer—standard bus fare. Meanwhile, Parks was scheduled to appear in court. As she made her way through the throngs at the courthouse, a girl in the crowd caught sight of her and cried out, "Oh, she's so sweet. They've messed with the wrong one now!"

Yes, indeed. The trial lasted thirty minutes, with the expected **conviction and penalty**. That afternoon, the Montgomery Improvement Association was formed. The members elected as their president a **relative newcomer to** Montgomery, the young minister of Dexter Avenue Baptist Church: the Reverend Martin Luther King Jr. That evening, addressing a crowd, King declared in that ringing voice millions the world over would soon thrill to: "There comes a time that people get tired." When he was finished, Parks stood up so the audience could see her. She did not speak; there was no need to. Here I am, her silence said, among you. 4

And she has been with us ever since—a **persistent** symbol of human dignity in the face of brutal **authority**. The famous **U.P.I.** photo (actually taken more than a year later, on December 21, 1956, the day

4 Development of Ideas Dove gives facts and comments about Rosa Parks's life. What does she add to help you understand Parks's actions?

Key Vocabulary
- **persistent** *adj.*, continuing in spite of challenges, unchanging
- **authority** *n.*, people with power over others

In Other Words
municipal city
conviction and penalty decision and punishment
relative newcomer to person who hadn't lived long in
U.P.I. United Press International (a news agency)

OUT-OF-SCHOOL LITERACY

SOCIOLOGY

Estimating the Value of Transportation

Help students see how much prior knowledge they bring to the text by connecting the selection to their own experience with transportation systems.

- What forms of public transportation do your school and larger community use?
- How do these forms of transportation benefit the community?
- What might happen if these forms of transportation were no longer functioning?
- Who has **authority** over this form of transportation?

As students answer, encourage the use of the highlighted Key Vocabulary.

SL.9-10.1.a

CCSS Literacy.RI.9-10.3 Analyze how the author unfolds an analysis or series of ideas or events, including the order in which the points are made, how they are introduced and developed, and the connections that are drawn between them. **Literacy.SL.9-10.1.a** Come to discussions prepared, having read and researched material under study; explicitly draw on that preparation by referring to evidence from texts and other research on the topic or issue to stimulate a thoughtful, well-reasoned exchange of ideas.

Montgomery's public transportation system was legally integrated) is a study of calm strength. She is looking out the bus window, her hands resting in the folds of her checked dress. **B** [5] A white man sits calmly in the row behind her. That clear profile, the neat eyeglasses and sensible coat—she could have been my mother, anybody's favorite aunt. History is often portrayed **as a grand opera, all baritone intrigues and tenor heroics**. Some of the most **tumultuous** events, however, have been **provoked** by **serendipity**—the assassination of an archduke spawned World War I, a kicked-over lantern may have sparked the Great Chicago

[5] Make Inferences
What do Rosa Parks's actions tell you about her?

Rosa

How she sat there,
the time right inside a place
so wrong it was ready.

That trim name with
its dream of a bench
to rest on. Her sensible coat. **C**

Doing nothing was the doing:
the clean flame of her gaze
carved by a camera flash.

How she stood up
when they bent down to retrieve
her purse. That courtesy. [6]

—Rita Dove

[6] Make Inferences
Study the poem. What words or phrases can you use from it to describe this picture?

Key Vocabulary
provoke *v.*, to force a person or thing to act

In Other Words
as a grand opera, all baritone intrigues and tenor heroics as if it were an exciting drama played out on a stage
tumultuous wild and noisy
serendipity a lucky accident

Monitor Comprehension
Explain
How did blacks in Montgomery show that they supported the fight against segregation?

TEACH & PRACTICE

B Reading Support

[5] **Make Inferences** Have students list facts they know about Parks. Use each fact to make an inference about her character. Ask: What do Parks's actions tell you about her?

Possible responses:
- *She was polite and cooperated with police; she was a dignified, well-mannered, and strong person.*

RI.9-10.1

C Reading Support

[6] **Make Inferences** Have students highlight words in the poem that describe Rosa Parks.

ELL **Read Aloud** Have students listen as you read the poem aloud. Emphasize words that describe Parks, as shown in the picture, and point to the picture for any words that are visually represented.

Read the poem again, one line at a time, and have students repeat in a choral reading.

Ask: Which words or phrases describe Rosa Parks?

Possible responses:
- *trim name, sat there, sensible coat, doing nothing, clean flame of her gaze*

RI.9-10.1

Monitor Comprehension

Explain Review p. 282 to find examples of the fight against segregation. Ask: What did black citizens in Montgomery do to fight segregation?

Possible responses:
- *The citizens formed an association and organized a bus boycott.*
- *They made sacrifices to boycott the buses.*

RI.9-10.1

CONTENT AREA CONNECTIONS

Research History

HISTORY

Conduct Research Have students research the role of Reverend Martin Luther King, Jr., in the Montgomery bus boycott. Use the information to answer these questions:

- What were some reasons that Reverend King was a good choice to lead the boycott?
- What happened to Dr. King and his family during the boycott?
- What did the boycott involve?
- How did the white population in Montgomery react to the boycott?
- What other movements for freedom did the Montgomery boycott inspire?
- How did the boycott end bus segregation in Montgomery?

Share and Profile Students can share their findings with the class to create a mini-profile of Dr. Martin Luther King, Jr.

W.9-10.7

CCSS Literacy.RI.9-10.1 Cite strong and thorough textual evidence to support analysis of what the text says explicitly as well as inferences drawn from the text. Literacy.W.9-10.7 Conduct short as well as more sustained research projects to answer a question (including a self-generated question) or solve a problem; narrow or broaden the inquiry when appropriate; synthesize multiple sources on the subject, demonstrating understanding of the subject under investigation.

READ

OBJECTIVES

Vocabulary
- Key Vocabulary Ⓣ

Reading Strategy
- Make Inferences

Comprehension & Critical Thinking
- Make Inferences
- Use Text Evidence Ⓣ

Literary Analysis
- Analyze Development of Ideas Ⓣ

Writing
- Form: Response to Literature

APPLY

Ⓐ ANALYZE

1. **Recall and Interpret** Rosa Parks's actions are important for helping to move the bus boycott forward, fueling the civil rights movement, and for the quiet and courteous way that they occurred. RI.9-10.1; RI.9-10.2
2. **Vocabulary** Segregated buses discriminated against African Americans because they were denied equal services. L.9-10.6
3. **Analyze Development of Ideas** Dove uses facts about the Montgomery bus boycott and world and U.S. history to help explain the significance of this event. RI.9-10.3
4. **Focus Strategy: Make Inferences** Answers may vary but should reflect that students' inferences about Parks changed during their reading. RI.9-10.1

Ⓑ Return to the Text

Have volunteers share their letters with the class. Make sure students explain why Rosa Parks is a traditional hero and include at least two examples from the selection. W.9-10.10

Fire. One cannot help wondering what role Martin Luther King Jr. would have played in the civil rights movement if the opportunity had not presented itself that first evening of the boycott—if Rosa Parks had chosen a row farther back from the outset, or if she had missed the bus altogether. Today, it is the modesty of Rosa Parks's example that **sustains us**. It is no less than the belief in the power of the individual, that **cornerstone** of the American Dream, that she inspires, along with the hope that all of us—even the least of us—could be that brave, that **serenely** human, when crunch time comes. ❖

ANALYZE Rosa Parks

Ⓐ

1. **Recall and Interpret** According to author Rita Dove, what is it about Rosa Parks's actions that makes them important? Include evidence from the profile to support your ideas.
2. **Vocabulary** How were segregated buses an example of **discrimination** against African Americans?
3. **Analyze Development of Ideas** What facts does Dove use to develop ideas about Rosa Parks and her achievement?
4. **Focus Strategy Make Inferences** List a few of the inferences you made while reading the profile. Which ones changed as you gained new information about Parks?

Ⓑ

Return to the Text

Reread and Write When Rita Dove was a child, she heard about Rosa Parks as a traditional hero. Write a letter to young Rita Dove to explain why Rosa Parks's protest on the bus was so important to so many people. Use at least two examples from the selection.

In Other Words

sustains us gives us hope and support
cornerstone foundation
serenely calmly

About the Writer

Rita Dove (1952–) is one of the best-known modern American poets. She has published seven books of poetry as well as a novel and a short story collection. In 1993 she became the youngest person ever to be named the Poet Laureate of the United States.

Interactive Reading

Have students reread and mark "Rosa Parks" within the Edge Interactive Practice Book to apply their knowledge of development of ideas and to practice the Focus Strategy—Make Inferences.

Edge Interactive Practice Book, pp. 131–136

Unit Project

Progress Check Allow time for students to work on their unit projects. Meet with individuals and/or groups to provide guidance and check on their progress.

myNGconnect.com

- **Unit Planning Tools**
- **Unit Project Evaluation Rubric**

CCSS **Literacy.RI.9-10.1** Cite strong and thorough textual evidence to support analysis of what the text says explicitly as well as inferences drawn from the text. **Literacy.RI.9-10.2** Determine a central idea of a text and analyze its development over the course of the text, including how it emerges and is shaped and refined by specific details; provide an objective summary of the text. **Literacy.RI.9-10.3** Analyze how the author unfolds an analysis or series of ideas or events, including the order in which the points are made, how they are introduced and developed, and the connections that are drawn between them. **Literacy.W.9-10.10** Write routinely over extended time frames (time for research, reflection, and revision) and shorter time frames (a single sitting or a day or two) for a range of tasks, purposes, and audiences. **Literacy.L.9-10.6** Acquire and use accurately general academic and domain-specific words and phrases, sufficient for reading, writing, speaking, and listening at the college and career readiness level; demonstrate independence in gathering vocabulary knowledge when considering a word or phrase important to comprehension or expression.

Reflect and Assess

▶ The Woman in the Snow
▶ Rosa Parks

EQ What Makes a Hero?

Reading

Critical Thinking

1. **Interpret** In the poem "Rosa," Rita Dove writes, "Doing nothing was the doing." Tell what you think she means. Reread the profile to find details that support your interpretation.
2. **Analyze** What conditions in people's lives can lead them to show **discrimination** against a particular group of people? Find details in both texts that suggest explanations.
3. **Compare** Identify the different types of narrators in "The Sword in the Stone," "A Job for Valentín," and "The Woman in the Snow." How does the choice of a narrator affect each story's character, plot, and tone? How does it influence the story's credibility? Explain.
4. **Speculate** How is Eula Mae's experience similar to Rosa Parks's? How would Parks respond to a driver like Grady Bishop?
5. **Synthesize** How does the traditional heroism of Rosa Parks affect Ray Hammond? Discuss how one individual's courage or heroism can influence the world.

Writing

Write About Literature

Theme Statement What do both selections say about the struggle to overcome prejudice? Write a brief statement of their shared theme and support it with examples from both texts. Use a **T Chart** to keep track of your examples.

T Chart

Overcoming Prejudice

"The Woman in the Snow"	"Rosa Parks"

Vocabulary

Key Vocabulary Review

Oral Review Work with a partner. Use these words to complete the paragraph.

authority	**desperately**	**provoke**
boycott	**discrimination**	**segregation**
compassion	**persistent**	

During the Montgomery bus __(1)__, African American passengers refused to use city buses. This fought the __(2)__ laws that kept black passengers separated from white passengers. After this protest, the civil rights movement went on to fight racial __(3)__ that treated people differently in schools and jobs. They were determined and __(4)__, working for long, hard years to improve the lives of __(5)__ poor people who felt sad and helpless. These leaders felt great __(6)__ for others in need. They did not hesitate to __(7)__ the anger of the leaders in __(8)__ who wished to keep things the way they were.

Writing Application Write a paragraph about when you think it is right to challenge people in **authority**. Use at least two Key Vocabulary words in your paragraph.

Fluency

Read with Ease: Intonation

Assess your reading fluency with the passage in the Reading Handbook, p. 759. Then complete the self-check below.

1. My intonation did/did not sound natural.
2. My words correct per minute: ____

Lesson 21

REFLECT AND ASSESS

OBJECTIVES

Vocabulary
- Key Vocabulary Ⓣ

Reading Fluency
- Intonation Ⓣ

Comprehension & Critical Thinking
- Compare Across Texts
- Make Inferences Ⓣ

Literary Analysis
- Compare Literature
- Evaluate Literature

Writing
- Form: Theme Statement
- Form: Paragraph

Reading

Critical Thinking

1. **Interpret** "Doing nothing was the doing" means that Parks's small act of not getting up was the act that started a lot more action, or "doing," in the civil rights movement. She acted by refusing to obey an unfair law. RL.9-10.1
2. **Analyze** Answers should include that lack of education and compassion can lead people to discriminate. RL.9-10.1; RI.9-10.1
3. **Compare** "The Sword in the Stone" and "The Woman in the Snow" have a third-person narrator; "A Job for Valentín" has a first-person narrator. The third-person narrator can tell the reader about all the characters and plot events; the tone is more objective. The first-person narrator tells only what he or she knows, so the story might be one-sided or have incomplete information. RL.9-10.6; RL.9-10.10
4. **Speculate** Both Eula Mae and Rosa Parks are treated unfairly by white bus drivers. Parks might have refused to cooperate with a bus driver like Grady.
5. **Synthesize** The traditional heroism of Rosa Parks inspires Ray to be a leader for civil rights. If one person takes a courageous step forward, others will notice and may follow. RL.9-10.2; RI.9-10.2

Writing

Write About Literature

Edge Interactive Practice Book, p. 137

Theme Statement Have students use the T-chart to plan and write the theme statement. Advise students to state the theme as the topic sentence and use their examples as evidence and support. W.9-10.2

Vocabulary

Key Vocabulary Review

1. *boycott* 2. *segregation* 3. *discrimination* 4. *persistent* 5. *desperately* 6. *compassion* 7. *provoke* 8. *authority* L.9-10.6

Fluency

Read with Ease: Intonation

Ensure that students complete the self-check. RL.9-10.10

ASSESS & RETEACH

Assessments Handbook, pp. 29j–29m

Have students complete the **Reader Reflection**. Then give students the **Cluster Test** to measure their progress. Group students as needed for reteaching.

CCSS **Literacy.RL.9-10.1** Cite strong and thorough textual evidence to support analysis of what the text says explicitly as well as inferences drawn from the text. **Literacy.RL.9-10.2** Determine a theme or central idea of a text and analyze in detail its development over the course of the text, including how it emerges and is shaped and refined by specific details; provide an objective summary of the text. **Literacy.RL.9-10.6** Analyze a particular point of view or cultural experience reflected in a work of literature from outside the United States, drawing on a wide reading of world literature. **Literacy.RL.9-10.10** By the end of grade 9, read and comprehend literature, including stories, dramas, and poems, in the grades 9-10 text complexity band proficiently, with scaffolding as needed at the high end of the range. By the end of grade 10, read and comprehend literature, including stories, dramas, and poems, at the high end of the grades 9-10 text complexity band independently and proficiently. **Literacy.RI.9-10.1** Cite strong and thorough textual evidence to support analysis of what the text says explicitly as well as inferences drawn from the text. **Literacy.RI.9-10.2** Determine a central idea of a text and analyze its development over the course of the text, including how it emerges and is shaped and refined by specific details; provide an objective summary of the text. **Literacy.W.9-10.2** Write arguments to support claims in an analysis of substantive topics or texts, using valid reasoning and relevant and sufficient evidence. **Literacy.L.9-10.6** Acquire and use accurately general academic and domain-specific words and phrases, sufficient for reading, writing, speaking, and listening at the college and career readiness level; demonstrate independence in gathering vocabulary knowledge when considering a word or phrase important to comprehension or expression.

Lesson 22

INTEGRATE THE LANGUAGE ARTS

OBJECTIVES

Language Function
- Elaborate During a Discussion (T)

Literary Analysis
- Compare Themes

Grammar
- Subject and Object Pronouns (T)

Grammar

Use Subject and Object Pronouns

Grammar Transparency 45

Review Use the transparency to review subject and object pronouns. Then conduct the activity on p. 286.

Oral Practice **1.** *She* **2.** *it* **3.** *him* **4.** *We* **5.** *us*

Written Practice **6.** *She* **7.** *She* **8.** *them* **9.** *They* **10.** *It*
L.9-10.1

Language Development

Elaborate During a Discussion

Evaluate students' acquisition of this language function with the Language Acquisition Rubric.

Assessments Handbook, p. 29o
SL.9-10.1.a

Literary Analysis

Compare Themes

Students' discussions should reflect an understanding that heroes inspire people in all cultures.
RL.9-10.2

Edge Interactive Practice Book, p. 138

INTEGRATE THE LANGUAGE ARTS

Grammar

Use Subject and Object Pronouns

Pronouns can take the place of nouns. Use a **subject pronoun** to replace a subject. Use an **object pronoun** to replace an object.

Rosa Parks started **the boycott**.
subject — object

She started **it** in 1955.

Subject Pronouns	I, you, he, she, it, we, they
Object Pronouns	me, you, him, her, it, us, them

Oral Practice (1–5) With a partner, change the underlined subject or object to the correct pronoun.

1. Rosa Parks boarded the bus. (She/Her)
2. She rode the bus every day. (it/them)
3. The passengers paid the driver. (he/him)
4. My friends and I admire Rosa Parks. (We/Us)
5. She inspires my friends and me. (them/us)

Written Practice (6–10) Fix four more pronouns and rewrite the paragraph below. Then add a sentence about the boycott.

They
The laws were unjust. ~~Them~~ treated people differently. One day, Rosa Parks took a seat on a bus. He refused to give up her seat. They was arrested. Citizens boycotted buses. Them won. The boycott changed the law. They changed America.

Language Development

Elaborate During a Discussion

Pair Talk Tell what Rosa Parks did on the bus. Then tell more about what the event meant.

Literary Analysis

Compare Themes

Theme is the most important idea in a work of literature. Many themes are universal, which means that they deal with issues that all people can relate to, such as looking for love or experiencing loss.

Both "The Sword in the Stone" and "The Woman in the Snow" deal with the universal theme of heroism, but each selection focuses on a different aspect of heroism.

Read these lines from "The Sword and the Stone." How do they help express the theme that true heroes are honest and trustworthy?

> Arthur … got hold of the sword and pulled it out easily.
>
> Arthur … swore an oath that he would be a just and true king for all his days.

Now read these lines from "The Woman in the Snow." How do they support the theme that an everyday act of kindness can turn an ordinary person into a hero?

> Eula Mae raised her head. "You're a kind man," she said. "Thank you."

In a small group, discuss these questions:

- Why is heroism a universal theme?
- What do *you* think the author says about heroism in each story?

286 Unit 3 The Hero Within

GRAMMAR

Review: Subject and Object Pronouns

Review Display the transparency. Use the chart to review subject and object pronouns. Have volunteers read the paragraph, and tell why each pronoun is correct.

A. Oral Practice Model how to replace the underlined words in the first sentence. As students provide the correct pronoun, write it on the transparency by its referent. Ask students to explain their answers.

B. Written Practice Work through the example. Explain that some sentences have no errors. Have the group tell you how to edit the paragraph. Then ask a volunteer to read the corrected paragraph aloud. L.9-10.1

Grammar & Writing Practice Book, pp. 97–98

GRAMMAR SKILLS PATH
41 Direct Objects
42 Subject and Object Pronouns
43 *I* vs. *Me*
44 Subject and Object Pronouns
▶ 45 Review: Subject and Object Pronouns ELL Language & Grammar Lab

Grammar Transparency 45

Use Subject and Object Pronouns

GRAMMAR REVIEW: SUBJECT AND OBJECT PRONOUNS 45

Remember: Use a subject pronoun as the subject of a sentence. Use an object pronoun as the object of the verb.

Subject Pronouns	I	you	he	she	it	we	you	they
Object Pronouns	me	you	him	her	it	us	you	them

I like heroes. Heroes inspire **me.** Rosa Parks is a hero. **She** took a stand. Do you admire **her**? Martin Luther King, Jr., is also a hero. **He** fought for his people and helped **them.**

Try It

A. Say each sentence. Then say it again replacing the underlined words with the correct pronoun.

1. Rosa Parks broke the law and went to jail. (She)
2. Martin Luther King, Jr., spoke out on unjust laws. (He)
3. His speeches inspired many people. (them)
4. He also made enemies. One angry person killed King. (him)

B. Edit the paragraph. Fix five mistakes. The first is done for you.

My friends and ~~me~~ I wrote a play. ~~Us~~ We created a story about soldiers in the Civil War. ~~Them~~ They experienced great suffering. In the play, President Lincoln spoke to the soldiers. He inspired ~~they~~ them. President Lincoln has inspired ~~we~~ us as well.

CCSS Literacy.RL.9-10.2 Determine a theme or central idea of a text and analyze in detail its development over the course of the text, including how it emerges and is shaped and refined by specific details; provide an objective summary of the text. Literacy.SL.9-10.1.a Come to discussions prepared, having read and researched material under study; explicitly draw on that preparation by referring to evidence from texts and other research on the topic or issue to stimulate a thoughtful, well-reasoned exchange of ideas. Literacy.L.9-10.1 Demonstrate command of the conventions of standard English grammar and usage when writing or speaking.

Vocabulary Study

Word Families

Knowing the meaning of one word can help you understand other related words. For example, you know that **authority** means "power" or "control." When you see the new word *authoritarian*, you can guess that it means "showing a lot of power or control."

Here are some words related to words in the selections. Guess what each word means before confirming the definition in a dictionary.

WORD	WHAT I THINK IT MEANS	WHAT IT MEANS
desperation		
compassionate		
persist		

Listening/Speaking

Oral Interpretation

Literature: Poetry Presentation Prepare Rita Dove's poem "Rosa" for an oral presentation to classmates or a group of friends. You might practice with a partner or tape your reading as you rehearse before your recitation.

1. Practice reading the poem aloud, paying attention to the meaning of the words as well as their sound. The punctuation of the poem will give you clues about where to pause.
2. Think about your intonation. Decide where you should raise or lower your voice. How will you emphasize key words or change the tone in your voice?
3. Ask your audience to review your performance.

Language and Learning Handbook, page 702

Writing

Write an Opinion Paragraph

In an **opinion paragraph**, you tell what you think about a subject. Write an opinion paragraph about this quote by James A. Autry: "I believe it is the nature of people to be heroes, given the chance."

1. **Prewrite** Organize your ideas by completing these sentences:
   - The quote means that ________________.
   - I agree/disagree because ________________.
   - An example of this is ________________.
2. **Draft** Arrange your sentences into a paragraph that states your opinion clearly.
3. **Revise** Add, move, or replace examples to make your opinion clearer.
4. **Edit and Proofread** With a partner, fix spelling and grammar mistakes. Match sounds to letters or use rules to make corrections.
5. **Publish** Share your work with the class. Then compare opinions in a group discussion.

Model Opinion Paragraph

James A. Autry once said: "I believe it is the nature of people to be heroes, given the chance." The quote means that everyone is brave enough to be a hero, we just don't have many chances to be heroic in our everyday lives. I agree with Autry that we all can be heroes, but I disagree that we don't have chances to be heroes. I think that we can be heroes all the time—in big and small ways. My mom and grandma are always making sacrifices for our family. My best friend spends a lot of his free time helping out at a homeless shelter. Sure, one of them might save someone from a speeding bus someday, but even if they don't, they'll still be heroes to me.

The writer gives his opinion.

These examples support the main opinion.

The conclusion restates the writer's opinion.

Writing Handbook, page 784

Lesson 23

INTEGRATE THE LANGUAGE ARTS

OBJECTIVES

Vocabulary
- Word Families T

Listening and Speaking
- Oral Interpretation

Writing
- Writing Process
- Form: Opinion Paragraph T

Vocabulary Study

Word Families

desperation: state of being very needful compassionate: caring deeply; persist: to keep trying

L.9-10.4.b; L.9-10.4.d

Edge Interactive Practice Book, p. 139

Listening / Speaking

Oral Interpretation

Literature: Poetry Presentation

Provide recordings of Rita Dove's work. Guide students to practice their reading for tone, pacing, and volume.

See **Language and Learning Handbook** p. 702 for further instruction.

SL.9-10.6

Writing

Opinion Paragraph

1. **Prewrite** Point out the important ideas in the quote: the nature of people, what heroes do, and how chance represents opportunities for change.
2. **Draft** Check that students have a topic sentence with a main idea, supporting details, and a conclusion. Have students use the model as a reference.
3. **Revise** Remind students to choose the most relevant examples.
4. **Edit and Proofread** Have partners use a dictionary to check spelling. Have them discuss the mistakes they see, especially those involving orthographic patterns and common spelling rules.
5. **Publish** Have students share and discuss their opinions.

See **Writing Handbook** p. 784 for further instruction.

W.9-10.1; W.9-10.5

Writing Rubric Opinion Paragraph

Exceptional	• Paragraph addresses topic by showing a clear opinion. • Examples are detailed and relevant to topic. • Pronouns are correct.
Competent	• Paragraph pertains to topic. • Examples are adequate. • Pronouns are correct with no more than one error.
Developing	• Paragraph may stray from topic. • Examples are loosely connected to topic. • Pronouns are sometimes incorrect.
Beginning	• Paragraph does not address topic. • Examples are not clearly connected to topic. • Pronouns are often incorrect.

CCSS **Literacy.W.9-10.1** Write arguments to support claims in an analysis of substantive topics or texts, using valid reasoning and relevant and sufficient evidence. **Literacy.W.9-10.5** Develop and strengthen writing as needed by planning, revising, editing, rewriting, or trying a new approach, focusing on addressing what is most significant for a specific purpose and audience. **Literacy.SL.9-10.6** Adapt speech to a variety of contexts and tasks, demonstrating command of formal English when indicated or appropriate. **Literacy.L.9-10.4.b** Identify and correctly use patterns of word changes that indicate different meanings or parts of speech (e.g., analyze, analysis, analytical; advocate, advocacy). **Literacy.L.9-10.4.d** Verify the preliminary determination of the meaning of a word or phrase (e.g., by checking the inferred meaning in context or in a dictionary).

OBJECTIVES

Vocabulary
- Academic Vocabulary

Comprehension & Critical Thinking
- Determine Importance
- Synthesize
- Use Text Evidence (T)

Literary Analysis
- Analyze Viewpoint (T)

Research Skills
- Gather Information

Writing
- Write About Viewpoint (T)

Cultural Perspectives
- U.S. Culture: Analyze Seminal Documents

TEACH & PRACTICE

A Read for Understanding

Genre Display the **eEdition** and read aloud the selection. Ask: What kind of text is this passage? How do you know?

Possible response:
- *It is a speech; it is the text of what the president said to mark a historic event.*

Explain that the speech is a seminal, or important, document in U.S. history. Have students complete item 1 on **Interactive Practice Book** page 140.

Topic Display: This text mostly tells about ___ and why ___. Have partners write a topic sentence to complete item 2 on **Interactive Practice Book** page 140.

B Reread and Summarize

Have partners read the selection, pausing to clarify ideas.

Word Choice Have partners choose words or phrases and note why they are important to the big ideas in the section. Have students complete item 3 on **Interactive Practice Book** page 140.

Finally, have students complete item 4 on **Interactive Practice Book** page 140.
RI.9-10.2

Edge Interactive Practice Book, pp. 140–143

from
THE AMERICAN PROMISE
by Lyndon B. Johnson
March 15, 1965

Selma March, Selma, Alabama, USA, 1965, Bruce Davidson. Photograph © Bruce Davidson/Magnum Photos.

1 . . . At times history and fate meet at a single time in a single place to shape a turning point in man's unending search for freedom. So it was at **Lexington and Concord**. So it was a century ago at **Appomattox**. So it was last week in Selma, Alabama.

2 There, long-suffering men and women peacefully **protested** the denial of their rights as Americans. Many were brutally assaulted. One good man, a man of God, was killed. . . .

3 In our time we have come to live with moments of great crisis. Our lives have been marked with debate about great issues; issues of war and peace, issues of prosperity and depression. But rarely in any time does an issue lay bare the secret heart of America itself. Rarely are we met with a challenge, not to our growth or abundance, our welfare or our security, but rather to the values and the purposes and the meaning of our beloved nation.

4 The issue of equal rights for American Negroes is such an issue. And should we defeat every enemy, should we double our wealth and conquer the stars, and still be unequal to this issue, then we will have failed as a people and as a nation. . . .

5 This was the first nation in the history of the world to be founded with a purpose. The great phrases of that purpose still sound in every American

Key Vocabulary
protest *v.*, to say or show you are against something

In Other Words
Lexington and Concord the first battles of the American Revolution
Appomattox the last battle of the Civil War

Historical Background
In March 1965, African Americans in Selma, Alabama marched to protest laws preventing them from voting. Authorities attacked the marchers, killing one of them.

ACADEMIC VOCABULARY — REVIEW

Use the **Graphic Organizer** vocabulary routine (PD43). Remind students that the specific angle from which something is viewed is called *perspective*.

What It Means: a specific angle from which something is viewed or observed

• **perspective**, noun p. 197

Example: a speaker's opinion about a topic

Non-example: a mental image of the speaker's description

L.9-10.6

CCSS RI.9-10.2 Determine a central idea of a text and analyze its development over the course of the text, including how it emerges and is shaped and refined by specific details; provide an objective summary of the text. **Literacy.L.9-10.6** Acquire and use accurately general academic and domain-specific words and phrases, sufficient for reading, writing, speaking, and listening at the college and career readiness level; demonstrate independence in gathering vocabulary knowledge when considering a word or phrase important to comprehension or expression.

heart, North and South: "All men are created equal"—"government by consent of the governed"—"give me liberty or give me death." Well, those are not just clever words, or those are not just empty theories. In their name Americans have fought and died for two centuries, and tonight around the world they stand there as guardians of our liberty, risking their lives.

6 Those words are a promise to every citizen that he shall share in the **dignity** of man. This dignity cannot be found in a man's possessions; it cannot be found in his power, or in his position. It really rests on his right to be treated as a man equal in opportunity to all others. It says that he shall share in freedom, he shall choose his leaders, educate his children, and provide for his family according to his ability and his merits as a human being.

7 To apply any other test—to deny a man his hopes because of his color or race, his religion or the place of his birth—is not only to do injustice, it is to **deny** America and to dishonor the dead who gave their lives for American freedom. . . .

8 Every American citizen must have an equal right to vote. . . .

9 Wednesday I will send to Congress a law designed to eliminate illegal barriers to the right to vote. . . .

10 But even if we pass this bill, the battle will not be over. What happened in Selma is part of a far larger movement which reaches into every section and state of America. It is the effort of American Negroes to secure for themselves the full blessings of American life.

11 Their cause must be our cause too. Because it is not just Negroes, but really it is all of us, who must overcome the crippling legacy of **bigotry** and injustice.

12 And we shall overcome.

13 The real hero of this struggle is the American Negro. His actions and protests, his courage to risk safety and even to risk his life, have awakened the **conscience** of this nation. His demonstrations have been designed to call attention to injustice, designed to provoke change, designed to stir reform.

14 He has called upon us to make good the promise of America. And who among us can say that we would have made the same progress were it not for his **persistent** bravery, and his faith in American democracy. . . . ❖

Key Vocabulary

- **persistent** *adj.*, continuing in spite of challenges, unchanging

In Other Words

dignity value and worthiness
deny reject
bigotry hating another person because of ethnic background, racism
conscience sense of right and wrong

Research Have students generate research questions around the Close Reading content. Then have them do a short search for the answers and share their findings with the class. W.9-10.7

PRACTICE & APPLY

C Reread and Analyze

Set a Purpose Explain that partners will reread the text in the **Interactive Practice Book** and identify how Johnson states and supports his viewpoint.

Author's Viewpoint Review: An author's viewpoint is his or her way of thinking about the topic. Authors support their viewpoints with facts, specific pieces of information, and examples. Have students complete items 5–7 on **Interactive Practice Book** page 141.

Ask: Based on this seminal U.S. document, how does Johnson feel about the topic of civil rights for African Americans?
RI.9-10.1; RI.9-10.6; RI.9-10.9

D Discuss

Synthesize Have students discuss the ways Johnson supports his viewpoint. Have them complete item 8 on **Interactive Practice Book** page 142.
SL.9-10.1.a; L.9-10.3

Write Write a paragraph to explain how authors use details to support their viewpoints. Have students complete item 9 on **Interactive Practice Book** page 142.
RI.9-10.1; W.9-10.10

E Connect with the EQ

Viewpoint Have students analyze the historical document and discuss whether Johnson would agree with the EQ. Have them complete item 10 on **Interactive Practice Book** page 143.
RI.9-10.9; SL.9-10.1.a

Theme Ask: Based on Johnson's comments, how do you think he would define heroism? Then have students complete item 11 on **Interactive Practice Book** page 143.
RI.9-10.9; W.9-10.10

Edge Interactive Practice Book, pp. 140–143

CCSS **Literacy.RI.9-10.1** Cite strong and thorough textual evidence to support analysis of what the text says explicitly as well as inferences drawn from the text. **Literacy.RI.9-10.6** Determine an author's point of view or purpose in a text and analyze how an author uses rhetoric to advance that point of view or purpose. **Literacy.RI.9-10.9** Analyze seminal U.S. documents of historical and literary significance (e.g., Washington's Farewell Address, the Gettysburg Address, Roosevelt's Four Freedoms speech, King's "Letter from Birmingham Jail"), including how they address related themes and concepts. **Literacy.W.9-10.7** Conduct short as well as more sustained research projects to answer a question (including a self-generated question) or solve a problem; narrow or broaden the inquiry when appropriate; synthesize multiple sources on the subject, demonstrating understanding of the subject under investigation. **Literacy.W.9-10.10** Write routinely over extended time frames (time for research, reflection, and revision) and shorter time frames (a single sitting or a day or two) for a range of tasks, purposes, and audiences. **Literacy.SL.9-10.1.a** Come to discussions prepared, having read and researched material under study; explicitly draw on that preparation by referring to evidence from texts and other research on the topic or issue to stimulate a thoughtful, well-reasoned exchange of ideas. **Literacy.L.9-10.3** Apply knowledge of language to understand how language functions in different contexts, to make effective choices for meaning or style, and to comprehend more fully when reading or listening.

Lesson 25

UNIT WRAP-UP

OBJECTIVES

Comprehension & Critical Thinking
- Compare Literature: Viewpoint

Listening and Speaking
- Classroom Discussion

Media
- Deliver a Documentary T
- Evaluate Documentaries

PRESENT AND REFLECT

A Present Your Project

Suggest the following hints:

- Make a list of equipment you need.
- Take time to consider classmates' questions before you answer.
- Offer an introduction to engage the audience in the topic.

SL.9-10.5

myNGconnect.com

Unit Project Evaluation Rubric

B Reflect on Your Reading

Genre Focus Review that "The Sword in the Stone" and "The Woman in the Snow" are told in third-person omniscient, and "A Job for Valentín" is told in first-person point of view.

SL.9-10.1.a

Focus Strategy Review the Make Inferences strategies:

- Use what the author says.
- Use what you already know.
- Figure out what is not stated.

SL.9-10.1.a

C EQ Respond to the Essential Question

Discuss these questions:

- What qualities do the heroes in the unit selections share?
- What are different versions of the heroic archetype?

Encourage the use of examples from unit selections and the traditional and mythic literature in the **Edge Library**.

SL.9-10.1.a

ONGOING ASSESSMENT

Have students write their responses to the Essential Question to assess understanding of the unit topic.

UNIT 3 WRAP-UP

THE HERO WITHIN

EQ ESSENTIAL QUESTION: What Makes a Hero?

myNGconnect.com

Download the rubric.

Present Your Project: Documentary

It's time to present your documentary about the Essential Question for this unit: What Makes a Hero?

1 Review and Complete Your Plan

Consider these points as you complete your project:

- How will you present your documentary? Will you show it as a movie or perform it live?
- Is your script organized in a logical order, and does it answer the Essential Question?
- What materials, such as photographs and interviews, do you need?

2 Give Your Documentary

Present your documentary to your classmates. Be prepared to answer questions afterward.

3 Evaluate the Documentaries

Use the online rubric to evaluate each of the documentaries, including the one you presented.

EDGE LIBRARY

Reflect on Your Reading

Many of the characters in the selections in this unit and in the Edge Library showed heroic qualities.

Think back on your reading of the unit selections, including your choice of Edge Library books. Then discuss the following with a partner or in a small group.

Genre Focus Compare and contrast the different perspectives used in first-person and third-person omniscient narrators. Give examples, using the selections in this unit.

Focus Strategy Choose a selection in this unit that doesn't reveal everything about a character or event. Identify three strategies that would help you make inferences and write them on an index card that you can share with a partner.

EQ Respond to the Essential Question

Throughout this unit, you have been thinking about the archetype of the hero. What different types of heroes have you come across in contemporary and traditional literature? Support your response with evidence from the unit selections and Edge Library books.

CUMULATIVE VOCABULARY REVIEW

Review Unit 3 Vocabulary:

anxiety	inherent
authority	inhibit
boycott	investigation
compassion	just
conscientiously	persistent
desperately	prejudiced
discrimination	protest
distracted	provoke
endure	segregation
evidence	skeptic
genuine	survivor
historian	tragedy

Play one or more of the following games in pairs or small groups using Key Vocabulary:

20 Questions One student thinks of a word, and other students ask yes/no questions until they guess the word.

Categories One student thinks of a word to be a "category" and names words that relate to that category. Others try to guess the word. For *authority*, a student might say "policeman, judge, principal."

Draw the Words One student has a word in mind and draws pictures to get another student to guess the word.

Edge Interactive Practice Book, pp. 140–141

L.9-10.6

CCSS **Literacy.SL.9-10.1.a** Come to discussions prepared, having read and researched material under study; explicitly draw on that preparation by referring to evidence from texts and other research on the topic or issue to stimulate a thoughtful, well-reasoned exchange of ideas. **Literacy.SL.9-10.5** Make strategic use of digital media in presentations to enhance understanding of findings, reasoning, and evidence and to add interest. **Literacy.L.9-10.6** Acquire and use accurately general academic and domain-specific words and phrases, sufficient for reading, writing, speaking, and listening at the college and career readiness level; demonstrate independence in gathering vocabulary knowledge when considering a word or phrase important to comprehension or expression.

UNIT 3 Assessment and Reteaching

Digital Assessment
- eAssessment
- ExamView
- online PDFs

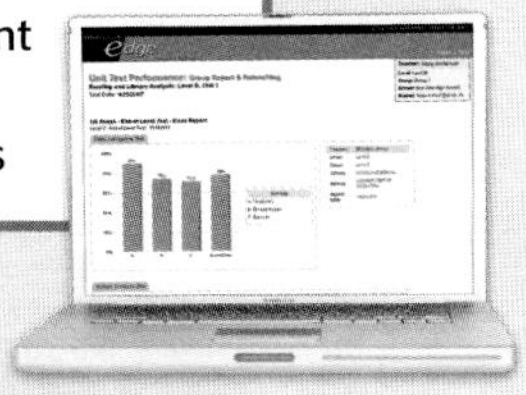

Administer the Assessments

Use the ***Assessments Handbook*** resources to measure the students' performance.

CLUSTER TESTS		
Cluster 1	**Cluster 2**	**Cluster 3**
READER REFLECTION p. 29b	**READER REFLECTION** p. 29f	**READER REFLECTION** p. 29j
READING AND LITERARY ANALYSIS pp. 29c–29e	**READING AND LITERARY ANALYSIS** pp. 29g–29i	**READING AND LITERARY ANALYSIS** pp. 29k–29m
Key Vocabulary Analyze Cultural Perspective Analyze Text Structure Use Text Evidence	Key Vocabulary Analyze Viewpoint Analyze Structure: Feature Article Use Text Evidence	Key Vocabulary Analyze Viewpoint Analyze Development of Ideas Use Text Evidence
READING FLUENCY *Student Edition p. 757*	**READING FLUENCY** *Student Edition p. 758*	**READING FLUENCY** *Student Edition p. 759*
ELL **LANGUAGE ACQUISITION RUBRIC** p. 29o	**LANGUAGE ACQUISITION RUBRIC** p. 29o	**LANGUAGE ACQUISITION RUBRIC** p. 29o
Ask for and Give Information	Engage in Discussion	Elaborate During a Discussion

UNIT TESTS	
READING AND LITERARY ANALYSIS pp. 30–37	**GRAMMAR AND WRITING** pp. 38–42
Use Context Clues Analyze Viewpoint Analyze Elements of Fiction: Characters Use Text Evidence	Verb Tenses Subject and Object Pronouns Writing Trait: Voice and Style Written Comprehension • Writing Traits • Written Conventions
UNIT SELF-ASSESSMENT p. 42c	

PERFORMANCE ASSESSMENTS
WRITING PROJECT p. 127
Voice and Style • Self-Assessment: Written Composition p. 133 • Peer Assessment: Written Composition p. 134
LISTENING AND SPEAKING WORKSHOP *Student Edition pp. 260-261*
Panel Discussion

Score and Reteach

- To hand-score: Use the Answer Keys and rubrics in the **Assessments Handbook**, pp. 144–147. Download reteaching activities at myNGconnect.com.
- To take tests online: ***Edge* eAssessment** at myNGconnect.com. Online reports offer immediate graphic displays of student performance to aid in making individualized instruction decision. Links to reteaching activities are included.

Affective and Metacognitive Measures

Help students commit to their own learning. Have students complete at least one reading and one writing form from the affective and metacognitive measures in the ***Assessments Handbook***:

- Personal Connections to Reading, pp. 106–107
- What Interests Me: Reading Topics, p. 108
- What I Do: Reading Strategies, pp. 109–110
- What I Do: Vocabulary Strategies, pp. 111–112
- Personal Connections to Writing, pp. 113–114
- What Interests Me: Writing Topics, pp. 115–117
- What I Do: Writing Strategy, p. 118

T = Tested on Cluster and/or Unit Reading and Literary Analysis Test
T = Tested on Language Acquisition Assessment
T = Tested on Unit Writing Test
T = Assessed with a Rubric
= Comprehension Coach

UNIT 3 Writing Project Overview

The Writing Form: Response to Literature

Your students will learn the features of a **response to literature**.

A good essay in response to literature
- is written in the first-person
- shares personal thoughts and interpretations about a specific work of literature
- states the significant idea in the literature and explains its impact
- relates the literature to personal experience
- establishes a clear controlling, or central, idea that reflects an insight gained
- supports interpretations with accurate and detailed references from the text
- makes a personal observation about life based on the literature and the author's style

The Writing Trait: Voice and Style

Students will learn to engage the reader with a voice and style that are interesting, unique to the writer, and appropriate to the audience and purpose.

The Writing Portfolio

Have students collect their work in a portfolio. The portfolio provides a record of how students develop as writers.

Portfolio Evaluation Forms

Use the *Assessments* Handbook, pp. 129–134, myNGconnect.com.

Evaluation Guidelines

Use the complete **Good Writing Traits Rubric** to assess the work on all traits and summarize class results in the **Class Profile Chart**.

Rubrics & Reporting Forms

Use the *Assessments* Handbook, pp. 122–134, myNGconnect.com.

TARGETED TRAIT: VOICE AND STYLE

SCALE	FOCUS AND UNITY	ORGANIZATION	DEVELOPMENT OF IDEAS	VOICE AND STYLE	WRITTEN CONVENTIONS
4	**Focus:** Clearly establishes and consistently maintains a central idea or claim. **Unity:** All facts, ideas, examples, and details are relevant and clearly connected to the central idea or claim.	**Structure:** The organizational pattern is appropriate to the audience, purpose, and task. **Coherence:** Includes a strong introduction and conclusion and leads the reader through a logical progression of ideas with varied and appropriate transitions.	**Content Quality:** Consistently presents meaningful ideas or claims in a logical way that is appropriate to the task, purpose, and audience. **Elaboration:** Includes relevant, clear reasoning, details, evidence, and/or description that are effective and comprehensive.	**Style and Voice:** Fully establishes and effectively maintains a voice that is appropriate to the audience, purpose, and task. **Words and Sentences:** Consistently chooses precise words and varied sentences that are appropriate to the audience and purpose and clearly convey the writer's meaning.	**Grammar and Usage:** Demonstrates strong command of English grammar and usage conventions. All sentences are formed correctly. **Mechanics and Spelling:** Demonstrates strong command of mechanics and spelling. Use of punctuation, capitalization, and spelling is effective and consistent.
3	**Focus:** Adequately establishes and mostly maintains a central idea or claim. **Unity:** Most facts, ideas, examples, and details are relevant and mostly connected to the central idea or claim.	**Structure:** The organizational pattern is mostly appropriate to the audience, purpose, and task. **Coherence:** Includes an introduction and conclusion and leads the reader through a progression of ideas with some transitions.	**Content Quality:** Mostly presents adequate ideas or claims that are appropriate to the task, purpose, and audience. **Elaboration:** Includes reasoning, details, evidence, and/or description that are adequate but incomplete.	**Style and Voice:** Mostly establishes and maintains a voice that is appropriate to the audience, purpose, and task. **Words and Sentences:** Mostly chooses precise words and a variety of sentences that are appropriate to the audience and purpose and adequately convey meaning.	**Grammar and Usage:** Demonstrates adequate command of English grammar and usage conventions. Errors are limited and do not impede understanding. Most sentences are formed correctly. **Mechanics and Spelling:** Demonstrates adequate command of mechanics and spelling. Use of punctuation, capitalization, and spelling is generally consistent.
2	**Focus:** Partially establishes a central idea or claim. **Unity:** Some facts, ideas, examples, and details are relevant and somewhat connected to the central idea or claim.	**Structure:** The pattern is inconsistent or less appropriate to the audience, purpose, or task. **Coherence:** Has an introduction and conclusion but leads the reader through loosely connected ideas that may be incomplete or not obvious to the reader.	**Content Quality:** Presents adequate ideas or claims that are less appropriate to the task, purpose, and audience. **Elaboration:** Includes weak reasoning, details, evidence, and/or description and may include extraneous or loosely related material.	**Style and Voice:** Inconsistently establishes and maintains a voice appropriate to the audience, purpose, and task. **Words and Sentences:** Demonstrates uneven word choice and limited sentence variety or chooses language mostly inappropriate to the audience and purpose. Meaning is vague or imprecise.	**Grammar and Usage:** Demonstrates partial command of English grammar and usage conventions. Frequent errors may impede understanding. Some sentences are formed incorrectly. **Mechanics and Spelling:** Demonstrates partial command of mechanics and spelling. Use of punctuation, capitalization, and spelling is inconsistent.
1	**Focus:** Lacks a central idea or claim. **Unity:** Few facts, ideas, examples, and details are relevant. Most do not support the central idea or claim or connections are unclear.	**Structure:** Lacks any organizational pattern. **Coherence:** Lacks an introduction or conclusion. Ideas are hard to understand.	**Content Quality:** Presents inappropriate or irrelevant ideas or claims. **Elaboration:** Lacks reasoning, details, evidence, and/or description.	**Style and Voice:** Does not establish and maintain a voice or uses a voice that is inappropriate to the audience, purpose, and task. **Words and Sentences:** Demonstrates little or no word choice and no sentence variety. Chooses language inappropriate to the audience, purpose, and task, hindering meaning.	**Grammar and Usage:** Demonstrates little or no command of English grammar and usage conventions. **Mechanics and Spelling:** Demonstrates little or no command of mechanics and spelling.

LITERATURE

...ting Portfolio

Writing Mode
Informative/Explanatory

Writing Trait Focus
Voice and Style

Thinking about great literature can give you new insight into life, other people—and yourself. For this project, you will write an essay in response to a work of literature.

Suggested Pacing
Each lesson in the Writing Project provides detailed instruction on the steps of the writing process. Here is a suggested daily sequence and pacing plan. Adjust as your schedule and student needs require.

Lesson 1	Study the Form and Prewrite
Lesson 2	Draft
Lesson 3	Revise
Lesson 4	Edit and Proofread
Lesson 5	Publish and Present

OBJECTIVES

Writing
- Mode: Informative/Explanatory
- Trait: Voice and Style Ⓣ
- Process: Prewrite; Draft; Revise for Voice and Style Ⓣ; Edit and Proofread Ⓣ; Publish and Present

Grammar, Usage, Mechanics, Spelling
- Capitalization: Days of the Week and Months
- Punctuation: Comma (appositives and nouns of direct address)
- Active Voice
- Consistent Verb Tense Ⓣ

INTRODUCE

Writing Mode Identify the writing mode as informative/explanatory. Define *informative/explanatory* as writing that explains a topic or an idea. Writers of informative/explanatory texts present accurate details and information to help the reader fully understand the topic or idea. Examples of informative/explanatory writing include essays, research reports, textbooks, and news articles.

Explain to students that they will be writing an essay in response to a work of literature using the steps of the writing process.
W.9-10.2; W.9-10.9; W.9-10.10

Writing Trait Explain that writing traits are the characteristics of good writing. All good writing has effective organization; focus and unity; development of ideas; voice and style; and uses the written conventions of language correctly. For this project, students will learn to use the writing traits of **Voice and Style** to plan, evaluate, and improve their writing.

Voice and style help writers express themselves more powerfully in a piece of writing. Explain to students that letting their personality come through will give their writing an individual and engaging voice. To create style, they will learn to use vivid words and vary their sentences.

CCSS **Literacy.W.9-10.2** Write informative/explanatory texts to examine and convey complex ideas, concepts, and information clearly and accurately through the effective selection, organization, and analysis of content. **Literacy.W.9-10.9** Draw evidence from literary or informational texts to support analysis, reflection, and research. **Literacy.W.9-10.10** Write routinely over extended time frames (time for research, reflection, and revision) and shorter time frames (a single sitting or a day or two) for a range of tasks, purposes, and audiences.

Lesson 1

STUDY THE FORM AND PREWRITE

OBJECTIVES
Writing
- Mode: Informative/Expository
- Analyze Models

ENGAGE & CONNECT

A Connect Writing to Your Life

Respond to a Story Have students freewrite for five minutes to express their thoughts about a movie or book. Ask: Which part was the most significant to you? How did this part relate to your experience? Explain that these responses are similar to a response to literature, since they offer a personal written response to a work.

TEACH

B Understand the Form

Explain that an essay shares and supports a main point. Use a volunteer's freewrite to model the three main parts of an essay. Show students how to shape the writing so that it has a clear introduction, body, and conclusion. Use a chart like the one on p. 292 to clarify the organization.

Conclusion Explore the concept:

- While the introduction introduces the significant idea of the literature, the conclusion describes the writer's personal insight gained from that idea.
- The conclusion shares a personal observation that leaves readers thinking about their own lives: *This story taught me that keeping an open mind leads to new experiences and fair treatment of others.*

Have students share conclusions from their written responses.

ELL **Sentence Frames** Provide frames for identifying impact:

- *The main idea of the story is* ______.
- *This story taught me that* ______.

Study a Response to Literature

When you write an essay about something you have read, you are writing a response to literature. You summarize the main ideas in the text and you share your personal thoughts about the writer's work.

A

1 Connect Writing to Your Life

Sometimes an interesting article opens your eyes to a whole new way of looking at the world, or a work of fiction prompts you to think about a similar experience in your own life. When you write an essay in response to literature, you carefully consider ideas and details in the text and then share your personal interpretation of their significance.

B

2 Understand the Form

When you write a response to literature, be sure to:

Introduction
- Write in the first person.
- Identify the work of literature.
- Briefly state the significant idea in the literature and its impact on you.

Body of Essay
- Tell how that idea or event relates to your experience.
- Support your interpretation with accurate and detailed examples from the literature.
- Identify any uncertainty the literature created in your mind and show how you dealt with that.

Conclusion
- Make a personal observation about life based on the author's work and the effect the author's ideas and style created.

Now look at an essay by a professional writer, writing in response to a short story, "The Woman in the Snow."

ACADEMIC VOCABULARY

Make a Vocabulary Example Chart Use the sample sentence below to introduce an additional academic vocabulary word used in writing. Have students make a Vocabulary Example Chart for the word.

- **accurate** (**ak**-yur-it), adjective ▸ p. 292

It is important to give the reader ***accurate*** *information about your topic.*

1. Write the word in the first column of the chart.
2. Then use a dictionary to determine the meaning of the word. Write the definition in the next column of the chart.
3. Think about how the word relates to something in your own life. Write the example in the last column of the chart.

Word	Definition	Example from My Life

L.9-10.4.c; L.9-10.6

CCSS **Literacy.L.9-10.4.c** Consult general and specialized reference materials (e.g., dictionaries, glossaries, thesauruses), both print and digital, to find the pronunciation of a word or determine or clarify its precise meaning, its part of speech, or its etymology. **Literacy.L.9-10.6** Acquire and use accurately general academic and domain-specific words and phrases, sufficient for reading, writing, speaking, and listening at the college and career readiness level; demonstrate independence in gathering vocabulary knowledge when considering a word or phrase important to comprehension or expression.

B Analyze a Professional Model

In this essay, the writer reflects on the significance of a short story in her own life.

Response to "The Woman in the Snow"

by Ana Jacobs

Sometimes in life we must rely on the kindness of others. In the short story "The Woman in the Snow" by Patricia McKissack, a young mother cannot get the help she needs to save her baby. Even though she desperately pleads for a ride to the hospital, a prejudiced bus driver turns her away. This story reminded me of a time when my family was also turned away unfairly.

The writer states a ***significant idea*** *and identifies the* ***literary work*** *that prompted it.*

The writer relates the literature to a ***personal experience.***

Several years ago, a landlord had refused to rent to us. He claimed that the vacant apartment we had an appointment to see had just been rented by someone else. Yet, it stood empty for months.

Likewise, the racist bus driver of McKissack's short story wields power instead of practicing fairness. When Grady Bishop "put on the gray uniform and boarded his bus, nothing mattered, not his obesity, not his poor education, not growing up the eleventh child of the town drunk. Driving gave him power. And power mattered."

The writer supports her interpretation with detailed examples from the literature.

Grady treats "his bus" as if it were his own exclusive world. Perhaps this demonstrates how excluded Grady feels from the larger world, but I think what's most important is that in the narrow world of Grady's bus, there is no room for kindness. "It's a waste of time," he says.

The writer deals with an ***uncertainty*** *the literature created in her mind.*

By contrast, Ray Hammond, "the first black driver Metro hired," welcomes the title character onboard. By this point in the story, 25 years have passed and the woman in the snow is a ghost. But with "compassion overruling his fear," Hammond grasps what Grady cannot or will not—that "nobody deserves to be left out in this weather."

Reading this story again, I realize that life offers us all the chance to be kind, and that refusing to be kind hurts us as well as others. After all, the man who shut the door on my family will never know the friendship that we would gladly have shown him. Fortunately, just two blocks away, we were able to rent an apartment from a kind woman who became a lifelong family friend.

The writer concludes with an insight she gained through ***further reflection*** *on the literature.*

After all, what matters most, McKissack suggests, is that nobody deserves to be left out, period.

C

FOCUS ON WRITER'S CRAFT

Understanding the Form

Teach Explain that a response to literature, unlike many other types of informative/expository writing, includes the writer's personal thoughts and interpretations. Add that an essay uses details from the text and personal experiences to support these insights.

Explain that one way writers can establish their insights is by using a cause and effect chart. Writers can list experiences and then write the impact those experiences had on them.

Model Use a student's freewrite or an essay of your own to illustrate the cause and effect of the details from the text and personal experiences. For example, cause: I missed the bus this morning; effect: I was late to school.

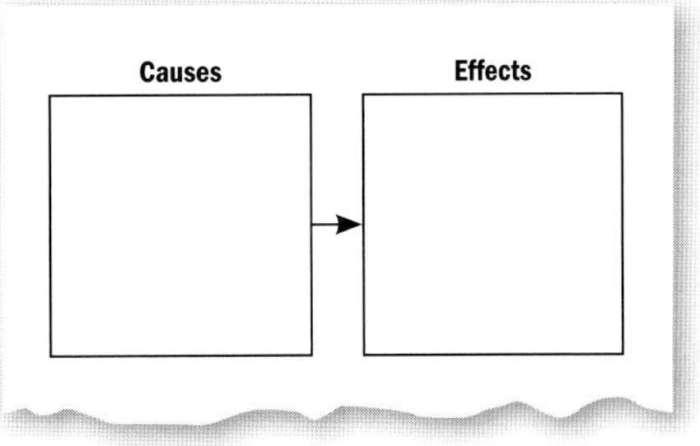

Practice/Apply Have students work in pairs to identify personal experiences and details from the Professional Model and the effects, or impact, of those experiences.

TEACH

C Analyze a Professional Model

Read and Evaluate Read aloud the whole essay. Then reread the first paragraph. Use the callouts to show the structure and key elements:

- first-person point of view
- the significant idea in the literature and its impact
- the controlling, or central, idea
- the link between the literature and the writer's life

Point out that, unlike other informative/explanatory texts such as research reports and news articles, an essay is written in first person because it includes a writer's thoughts, conclusions, and experiences. Other types of nonfiction, on the other hand, are written in third person because their purpose is to present information objectively, in a neutral voice.

Identify Tell students that the writer also refers to details from the literature such as "driving gave him power" to support significant ideas in the text and connect them to her own thoughts. Have students identify the text details that support the writer's interpretation of the literature in paragraphs two and three. Explain that writers also express uncertainties, or doubts, they have as they read literature. Have students review paragraphs four and five to identify a question that the literature raised for the writer.

Discuss Explain that the writer concluded with insights about the significant ideas that she had about the literature.

Ask: What personal observation about life does the writer make?

Possible responses:

- *We all have an opportunity to be kind; nobody deserves to be left out.*

Remind students that the insights shared in a reflective essay might be different for each writer. Ask: How would a writer with a different personal experience have a different response to the literature?

ONGOING ASSESSMENT

Have students list three parts a good writer should include in a reflective essay.

Lesson 1, continued

STUDY THE FORM AND PREWRITE

OBJECTIVES

Writing
- Writing Process: Prewrite
- Use Strategies to Generate Ideas
- Choose a Topic
- Identify Audience and Purpose
- Plan and Organize Ideas

TEACH

A Your Job as a Writer

Writing Prompt Read the prompt with students to help them better understand what is expected of them.

B Choose Your Topic

Brainstorm Ideas Have students list significant ideas from favorite works of literature. For example, *"William's Run": Main character overcomes hardships to win a race.* Then have students circle the title of the work they feel most relates to their own lives.

ELL Sentence Frames Provide frames for brainstorming choices:
- I responded strongly to the selection about ______ because ______.
- A significant idea in the literature was ______. It made a big impression on me because ______.

W.9-10.5

C Clarify Audience, Controlling Idea & Purpose

Controlling Idea Ask: Does your controlling idea build on your first impression about the literature?

Provide this frame for expressing the controlling idea: *The significant idea that impressed me about this work was ______. That idea is important to me because (I also) ______.*

D Gather Supporting Details

Identify Explain to students that as they gather details from the literature to support the main idea, they can look for direct quotations from the story.

W.9-10.2.b

Your Job as a Writer

A ▶**Prompt** Write an essay in response to literature. Make sure to:
- show that you grasp the significant ideas in the text
- support your interpretation with detailed examples
- identify any uncertainty the literature created in your mind and show how you dealt with that

✔ Prewrite

Now that you have analyzed the elements of an effective essay in response to literature, make a Writing Plan. This will help you demonstrate your grasp of significant ideas about the literature as you write.

1 Choose Your Topic

B Try these strategies to find a topic for your essay:
- List works of literature that made a strong impression on you.
- Note which literature has the strongest connection to your life, and why.
- Review any written responses you have already made to the literature.

2 Clarify the Audience, Controlling Idea, and Purpose

C Are your readers familiar with the literary work? If not, consider what information they will need and what details should be kept a surprise.

Turn your first impression and later reflections into a clear **controlling idea**. This main point should be true to the literature as well as to your own experience.

Remember that your purpose is to demonstrate your grasp of a significant idea in a literary work and to show what effect the work has on you, and why.

3 Gather Supporting Details

D To trap details from the story that support your controlling, or main idea, you can use a **Cluster Map** like the one shown. It's based on a student's response to "A Job for Valentín" (pp. 238–250). The controlling idea is in the center. Supporting details surround the main idea.

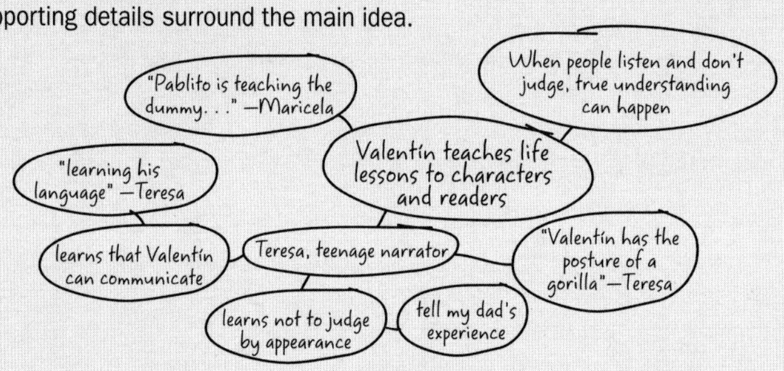

Prewriting Tip

To clarify significant ideas in the literature:
- List details about the characters, the conflict, and the plot.
- Accurately note quotations that make an impression on you.
- State what is important about each item on your list.
- Write the message, or idea, about the literature that best sums up your details.

DIFFERENTIATED INSTRUCTION

Addressing the Prompt As you teach the writing process in this unit, use these strategies to meet students' individual needs.

Struggling Readers

Freewrite Have students write the words *my life* on a sheet of paper. Using those words as prompts, have students write for five minutes without stopping about any personal thoughts or experiences the story brings to mind.

English Language Learners ELL

Use Quotations Help students locate and correctly list quotations from the literature that could support their controlling idea. Review the use of quotation marks and remind students that quotations should be written exactly as they appear in the story.

Challenge

Create Questions Have students write question starters for addressing uncertainties in the literature. For example:
- *What uncertainty, or question, do you have about the story?*
- *Which detail or details from the story addresses the question you have?*

CCSS Literacy.W.9-10.2.b Develop the topic with well-chosen, relevant, and sufficient facts, extended definitions, concrete details, quotations, or other information and examples appropriate to the audience's knowledge of the topic. Literacy.W.9-10.5 Develop and strengthen writing as needed by planning, revising, editing, rewriting, or trying a new approach, focusing on addressing what is most significant for a specific purpose and audience.

4 Organize the Details

Organize the details in a way that best supports your controlling idea. The student writer organized details in order of importance.

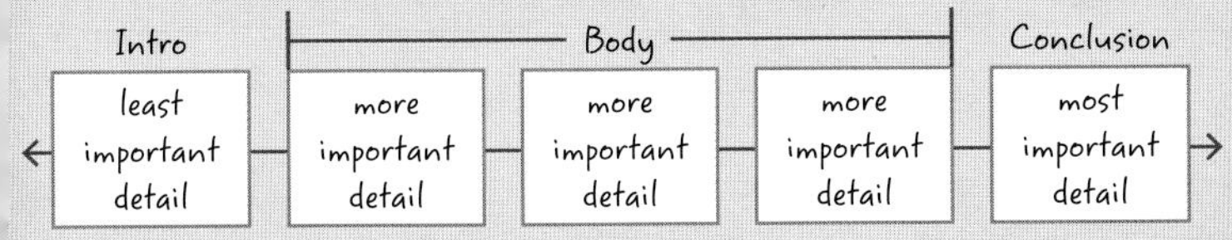

E

5 Finish Your Writing Plan

Before you actually begin drafting your essay, make a final plan. Decide how you will begin your essay, how you will organize it, and how you will conclude. Your **Cluster Map** will provide information for the body of your essay.

Writing Plan

Topic	response to "A Job for Valentín"
Audience	my teacher and my classmates
Controlling Idea	Valentín teaches other characters and readers valuable life lessons.
Purpose	to reflect on the story's significant ideas
Time Frame	due in ten days
Organization	order of importance
Introduction Include least important detail	Briefly summarize the story; connect to my life; engage readers' attention with dramatic example from story. State controlling idea.
Body Include more important details	Valentín teaches the other characters; present my ideas in order of importance; support them with detailed examples and accurate quotations.
Conclusion Include most important detail	When people listen and stop judging, true understanding can take place.

F

Technology Tip

If you use a computer, save your Writing Plan, draft, and other notes for the essay in one folder. That way, you can quickly locate everything you need.

Reflect on Your Plan

▶ Does your plan include accurate and detailed examples from the literature? Do you make a clear observation? Share your plan with a partner. Ask for suggestions. Make any changes you think would improve the plan for your essay.

Writing Transparency 9

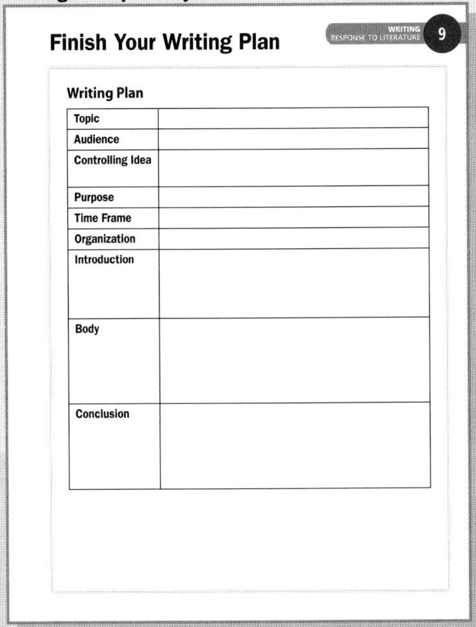
Finish Your Writing Plan

WRITING RESPONSE TO LITERATURE 9

Writing Plan

Topic	
Audience	
Controlling Idea	
Purpose	
Time Frame	
Organization	
Introduction	
Body	
Conclusion	

TEACH

E Organize the Details

Detail Chart Use the Student Model to list supporting details on a detail chart. Point out that the details are listed from least to most important on the chart. The least important detail is used in the introduction, and the most important detail is used in the essay's conclusion.

F Finish Your Writing Plan

Writing Transparency 9

Model the Plan Use the transparency to model creating a plan. Use a student example:

- **Topic:** What literary work are you writing about?
- **Audience:** Who will read your essay?
- **Controlling Idea:** What is the most important idea?
- **Purpose:** Why are you writing it?
- **Time Frame:** Set a deadline that allows time both in and outside of class to fully complete the steps.

Manage the Steps Download this chart to help students manage their time.

myNGconnect.com

Date	Tasks
1	1. Study the form. 2. Analyze a professional model. 3. Choose a work of literature. 4. Identify an audience, controlling idea, and purpose. 5. Gather and organize details. 6. Create your Writing Plan.
2	Write a draft using your Writing Plan.
3	1. Revise for voice and style. 2. Revise your draft, using the Revision Checklist. 3. Conduct a peer conference. 4. Make revisions based on peer conference.
4	Review draft for mistakes; check for capitalization, punctuation, spelling, active voice, verb tense, and sentence completion.
5	Print essay, or write a clean copy.

Model the Organization Have students list details in order, noting which details are in the introduction, the body, and the conclusion. W.9-10.2.a; W.9-10.5; W.9-10.6

ONGOING ASSESSMENT

Have students submit their Writing Plans. Make sure they have gathered enough details to support a main idea.

CCSS **Literacy.W.9-10.2.a** Introduce a topic; organize complex ideas, concepts, and information to make important connections and distinctions; include formatting (e.g., headings), graphics (e.g., figures, tables), and multimedia when useful to aiding comprehension. **Literacy.W.9-10.5** Develop and strengthen writing as needed by planning, revising, editing, rewriting, or trying a new approach, focusing on addressing what is most significant for a specific purpose and audience. **Literacy.W.9-10.6** Use technology, including the Internet, to produce, publish, and update individual or shared writing products, taking advantage of technology's capacity to link to other information and to display information flexibly and dynamically.

Lesson 2

WRITE A DRAFT

OBJECTIVES

Writing
- Writing Process: Draft
- Write a Draft
- Employ Literary Devices

TEACH

A Keep Your Ideas Flowing

Organize Impressions Explain that organizing their impressions will help students later as they write their draft. Have students number their sticky notes or lists by the literary paragraph that inspired the thought.

ELL Use Graphic Organizer Use a chart to post target words and restate their meaning related to the drafting process.

Target Words	Meaning
evokes	*Sometimes a literary work causes or creates strong feelings in you.*
impressions	*Jot down whatever first thoughts or feelings come to mind.*
established	*Has the writer created or described a viewpoint you share?*

W.9-10.2; W.9-10.4; W.9-10.6; W.9-10.9

B Create a Compelling Opening

Choose a Strong Opening Discuss the examples provided for each rhetorical device. Ask: What makes the detail so compelling? Would many readers be interested in the question? Does the quotation catch your attention?

Suggest ways to use these same techniques. For example:
- Use vivid details from the text.
- Choose an open-ended, thought-provoking question.
- Use a quotation that will make readers curious about the text.

W.9-10.2.a

✓Write a Draft

Let your Writing Plan guide you as you write your essay. Don't worry if you're still thinking over some of the details. You'll have a chance to clarify your writing later.

1 Keep Your Ideas Flowing

A

Sometimes a literary work evokes strong feelings in you, yet you aren't sure how to turn those feelings into more considered thought. If so, try these techniques:

- **Save Those First Impressions** Reread the literary work, pausing to jot down whatever impressions come to mind. Use sticky notes to attach your responses to important examples in the text. Then go back and see what your responses have in common. Write notes about it.
- **Link Impressions to Your Life** What personal experience or connection comes to mind as you read the literature, and why? Has the writer established a viewpoint you share? Jot down your ideas.
- **Go Deeper** Reflect further on your first impressions. Make notes. Then discuss your ideas with another student who has read the literary work. Upon further reflection, what seems most significant to you about the literature? How does this idea apply to life in general?
- **Do a Focused Freewrite** If you're on the verge of an idea and aren't sure how to say it, just freewrite to talk to yourself about it.

2 Create a Compelling Opening

B

How will you engage the attention of readers who may not have read the literature? A compelling, or strong, opening is one that makes readers want to find out more. Consider using different rhetorical devices in the introduction of your essay, as shown below. Choose the one that will lead most easily to the main point that you want to make and that will help your readers grasp the effect the literature had on you.

Rhetorical Device	Example
Start with a simile.	Pablito was like a fish without fins
Start with a question.	Why are people so quick to see differences between themselves and others?
Start with a thought-provoking quotation.	"I think Pablito is teaching the dummy a few things." —Maricela

Drafting Tip

Use transition words to help readers better understand your ideas and experiences. For example:
- Use time order words such as *several years ago, at first, afterward,* and *later* to show when an experience took place.
- Use transitions such as *likewise, in the same way,* and *after all* to show how two ideas go together or are similar.
- Use transitions like *however, instead,* and *yet* to emphasize a contrast or difference.

Technology Tip

If you try two different ways to begin your essay, save them both. You might want to name one file *Intro1* and another *Intro2*. You can later determine which version works better for you and then delete the one you don't want.

FOCUS ON WRITER'S CRAFT

Creating a Compelling Opening

Teach/Model Explain that one of the main ways to make the beginning of an essay compelling is to create questions in the readers' mind. Use the examples in the chart on p. 296 to illustrate how each technique engages readers.

- The **specific detail** about Pablito invites readers to ask: *Why is Pablito struggling? Will he be rescued?*
- The **question** might make readers apply it to their own experiences: *Am I quick to see differences between myself and others?*
- The **quotation** might make readers wonder: *Why does Maricela call Valentín a dummy?*

Practice/Apply Have students share the details, questions, and quotations they have chosen for their essays. Students should write a question about their partner's examples.

Use the following sentence frame to help students list their responses to each example:

- This **detail/question/quotation** makes me want to know more about ______.

Partners can share responses and discuss the examples they found to be the most compelling. Students can use their partner's responses to help them choose elements for their introductions.

W.9-10.2.a

CCSS Literacy.W.9-10.2 Write informative/explanatory texts to examine and convey complex ideas, concepts, and information clearly and accurately through the effective selection, organization, and analysis of content. Literacy.W.9-10.2.a Introduce a topic; organize complex ideas, concepts, and information to make important connections and distinctions; include formatting (e.g., headings), graphics (e.g., figures, tables), and multimedia when useful to aiding comprehension. Literacy.W.9-10.4 Produce clear and coherent writing in which the development, organization, and style are appropriate to task, purpose, and audience. Literacy.W.9-10.6 Use technology, including the Internet, to produce, publish, and update individual or shared writing products, taking advantage of technology's capacity to link to other information and to display information flexibly and dynamically. Literacy.W.9-10.9 Draw evidence from literary or informational texts to support analysis, reflection, and research.

B Student Model

Here is the first draft of the essay written in response to "A Job for Valentín." There are some mistakes. Those can be fixed later.

Lessons to Learn

This story is called "A Job for Valentín." This story is about a man named Valentín. This man is disabled. A Summer job at a pool is gotten by him. This man looks after a little boy. The boy's mother says something mean. She says how Valentín is a dummy. But it is Valentín who teaches the other characters.

For example, Teresa the teenage narrator of the story learns not to judge others by their appearance. At the beginning of the story, Teresa says, "Valentín has the posture of a gorilla." She assumes that he is helpless. My dad who uses a wheelchair sometimes deals with similar assumptions. Last tuesday a new neighbor expressed surprise that Dad manages the city animal shelter. He was spoken to loudly and slowly by her as if he could not hear or comprehend.

As this experience and Cofer's story show, assumptions can get in the way of real communication. For example, Teresa thinks that Valentín has trouble understanding things and that he can't speak English even after he tells her he can. At first I was uncertain about him, too. When he sees Pablito in the water and tries to tell her, Teresa says, "I guess he's having a fit or something."

Teresa changed. She will change at end of the story. Teresa realized that Valentín can do something she thinks he can't. Communicate in total silence. Teresa will learn something from this. In both of the two things I'm thinking about the significance of this is clear. Only when people listened actively and stopped judging others by their appearance can true understanding take place.

Reflect on Your Draft

▶ Does your paper have a clear introduction, body, and conclusion? Did you provide details from the story that demonstrate the significant ideas and style of the writer and the effects on you? Talk them over with a partner.

C

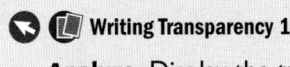

Writing Transparency 10

Student Model

WRITING RESPONSE TO LITERATURE 10

Lessons to Learn

This story is called "A Job for Valentín." This story is about a man named Valentín. This man is disabled. A Summer job at a pool is gotten by him. This man looks after a little boy. The boy's mother says something mean. She says how Valentín is a dummy. But it is Valentín who teaches the other characters.

For example, Teresa the teenage narrator of the story learns not to judge others by their appearance. At the beginning of the story, Teresa says, "Valentín has the posture of a gorilla." She assumes that he is helpless. My dad who uses a wheelchair sometimes deals with similar assumptions. Last tuesday a new neighbor expressed surprise that Dad manages the city animal shelter. He was spoken to loudly and slowly by her as if he could not hear or comprehend.

As this experience and Cofer's story show, assumptions can get in the way of real communication. For example, Teresa thinks that Valentín has trouble understanding things and that he can't speak English even after he tells her he can. At first I was uncertain about him, too. When he sees Pablito in the water and tries to tell her, Teresa says, "I guess he's having a fit or something."

Teresa changed. She will change at end of the story. Teresa realized that Valentín can do something she thinks he can't. Communicate in total silence. Teresa will learn something from this. In both of the two things I'm thinking about the significance of this is clear. Only when people listened actively and stopped judging others by their appearance can true understanding take place.

TEACH

C Student Model

Read Have students read the Student Model.

ELL Read aloud the Student Model. Use illustrations, body language, gestures, or role-play to support meaning.

Writing Transparency 10

Analyze Display the transparency. Ask these questions to help students see the relationship between the Writing Plan on p. 295 and the draft. Mark answers on the transparency:

- Where does the writer tell what literary work he or she is responding to? *[line 1]*
- What does the writer say that shows you the controlling idea? *[lines 4–5 show that Valentín teaches other characters; lines 19–21 show that Valentín's silence helped him teach others]*
- Which lines summarize the story? *[lines 1–5 tell readers what the story is about]*
- Which lines present the body of the essay with story details and quotations? *[lines 6–16 present the body of the story]*
- What words or phrases show that the essay is meant to reflect on a literary work's significant ideas? *[lines 20–22 point out important ideas that the story illustrates]*
- How does the essay writer organize details from the story? *[from least important to most important; lines 6–9 describe an example that supports a less important idea than the most important idea at the end]*
- Which words or phrases contain the most important story detail for the conclusion? *[lines 17–21 present the details about Valentín communicating with silence]*

Remind students that the Writing Plan is a place to start, and may be revised as the draft is revised.

ONGOING ASSESSMENT

Have students explain how they would help a friend who was having trouble organizing details for his or her writing.

Lesson 3

REVISE YOUR DRAFT

OBJECTIVES

Writing

- Writing Process: Revise
- Evaluate and Revise the Draft for Voice and Style Ⓣ
- Participate in Peer Conferencing

TEACH

Ⓐ Revise for Voice and Style

Define Elaborate on how the writing traits of voice and style apply to a response to literature:

- **Voice:** An essay written in a strong, expressive voice helps convey a writer's unique viewpoint and his or her personal response to a literary work.
- **Style:** The choice of words and sentence types used in an essay help make the writing compelling to readers.

Try It Have partners use a checklist to help them evaluate the draft for voice and style. Have them check each draft to assess:

- the variety of descriptive details and quotations
- how unique, real, and expressive the writer's voice sounds
- how the sentences begin
- the length of the sentences

Ask:

- Which draft has more interesting descriptive details? Which includes a quotation from the story?
- Which draft best expresses the writer's unique personality?
- Do most of the sentences begin in similar ways, or do the beginnings vary?
- Which draft has more sentences of different lengths?

✔ Revise Your Draft

The word *revise* is made from word parts that mean "see again." Look at your draft with fresh eyes. You can then improve your essay's voice and style.

1 Revise for Voice and Style

Because a response to literature is a type of informative writing that also presents your personal thoughts, ideas, and experiences, it is important to let your writing sound like you. This doesn't just happen. A good writer uses **voice** to make the writing sound real and unique. Writing with an effective voice shows a mature command of language and has freshness of expression. Just as an engaging speaking voice makes someone want to keep listening, effective voice in writing fully engages the reader and lets the writer's personality shine through.

Good writing also has **style**. That means that the words and sentences are appropriate to the purpose and the audience. The word choices are vivid and precise. As for the sentences, they don't all begin in the same way, have the same end punctuation, or run the same length. The writer can vary the sentence length and structure by using a longer sentence to discuss a complex aspect of the text or a shorter sentence to emphasize a point.

Revising Tip

Make sure that your ending fits your purpose and reflects your voice and style. For example, if you want to share an insight, state it clearly and in your own words.

TRY IT ▸ With a partner, evaluate the voice and style of the two drafts below. Which draft uses words that are more powerful and engaging? Explain. Ⓐ

Draft 1

> This story is called "A Job for Valentín." This story is about a man named Valentín. This man is disabled. A Summer job at a pool is gotten by him. This man looks after a little boy. The boy's mother says something mean. She says how Valentín is a dummy.

Draft 2

> In "A Job for Valentín," a story by Judith Ortiz Cofer, the main character is a developmentally disabled man who gets a summer job at a pool. The man makes friends with a 2-year-old boy, Pablito. But others are not so kind. How does the boy's mother, Maricela, respond? She laughs. "I think Pablito is teaching the dummy a few things," she says meanly.

FOCUS ON WRITER'S CRAFT

Incorporating Variety in Sentence Structure

Teach/Model Explain that just as some people have engaging ways of speaking, writers have their own style of writing. Discuss the qualities that make a speaker engaging and how those qualities apply to writing. Point out that sentence variety adds interest because readers won't expect similar types or lengths of sentences. Use the student draft to show how to distinguish between dull and varied sentences.

- Which draft has more variety in sentence length? How does this add interest for the reader? *[The sentences in Draft 2 are much more varied, with a very long first sentence and a very short third sentence. This makes each sentence unique and engaging.]*
- What are other ways in which the sentences in Draft 1 are alike? How are sentences in Draft 2 different? *[Two sentences begin with "This story" and two begin with "This man." There are no questions or quotations in that draft. In the second draft, sentences begin in different ways and there is a question and a quotation.]*

Practice Have students relate each of these sentences to Draft 1 or Draft 2:

1. The boy was upset. *[Draft 1]*
2. By the end of the story, Teresa understood that she had misjudged Valentín. *[Draft 2]*
3. The woman changed her mind. *[Draft 1]*

Apply Have students evaluate sentence length and variety as they revise their essays. L.9-10.1.b

CCSS Literacy.L.9-10.1.b Use various types of phrases (noun, verb, adjectival, adverbial, participial, prepositional, absolute) and clauses (independent, dependent; noun, relative, adverbial) to convey specific meanings and add variety and interest to writing or presentations.

Now use the rubric to evaluate the voice and style of your own draft. What score do you give your draft and why?

Voice and Style

	Does the writing have a clear voice and is it the best style for the type of writing?	Is the language interesting and are the words and sentences appropriate for the purpose, audience, and type of writing?
4 Wow!	**The writing fully engages the reader with its individual voice. The writing style is best for the type of writing.**	**The words and sentences are interesting and appropriate to the purpose and audience.** • The words are precise and engaging. • The sentences are varied and flow together smoothly.
3 Ahh.	**Most of the writing engages the reader with an individual voice. The writing style is mostly best for the type of writing.**	**Most of the words and sentences are interesting and appropriate to the purpose and audience.** • Most words are precise and engaging. • Most sentences are varied and flow together.
2 Hmm.	**Some of the writing engages the reader, but it has no individual voice and the style is not best for the writing type.**	**Some of the words and sentences are interesting and appropriate to the purpose and audience.** • Some words are precise and engaging. • Some sentences are varied, but the flow could be smoother.
1 Huh?	**The writing does not engage the reader.**	**Few or none of the words and sentences are appropriate to the purpose and audience.** • The words are often vague and dull. • The sentences lack variety and do not flow together.

Writing Handbook, p. 784

myNGconnect.com
- Rubric: Voice and Style
- Evaluate and practice scoring other student responses to literature.

TEACH

B Use a Rubric

Model Model using a rubric to evaluate a draft.

ELL Rephrase Language Clarify terms from the rubric:

- **unique:** special; not like other people
- **tone:** the writer's attitude or feelings about the topic and story
- **consistent:** the same throughout

Read the Student Model on p. 297 aloud. Ask: Does the writing sound consistent throughout? Is the voice engaging?

Possible response:
- *The writing is not consistent. Some is engaging and unique, but some is repetitive and not very interesting.*

Work with students to evaluate the Student Model and assign a score for voice. Instruct them to read the four descriptions in the left-hand column of the rubric and choose the score that best describes the draft.

Ask: Are the words and sentences varied or do they all sound the same?

Possible response:
- *The writer uses varied words and sentences.*

Collaborative Evaluation Have partners evaluate the Student Model by reading the four descriptions in the right-hand column of the rubric and choosing the score that describes the draft.

Then have students assign an overall score for voice and style. Model how to find the average score and round down to a whole number, for example, a 4 for voice and a 3 for style yields an average of 3.5, which rounds down to 3.
SL.9-10.1

Self-Evaluation Have students follow the same steps to evaluate their own drafts. Try these suggestions:

- Evaluate sentences one element at a time (sentence length, type, and word variety), then as a whole.
- Answer yes or no to each criterion in the rubric to get a score.
- Evaluate more samples online.

myNGconnect.com
W.9-10.4; L.9-10.1.b

DIFFERENTIATED INSTRUCTION

English Language Learners ELL

Be Specific Help ELLs understand the traits of voice and style:

- Explain that specific words help make writing more expressive and vivid. Write: *The man looks after the boy. A disabled man named Valentín looks after 2-year-old Pablito.* Ask students which sentence paints a more vivid picture in their minds. Point out how words like *disabled, 2-year-old,* and *Pablito* give the writer's voice more power by providing readers with details about the characters' age and physical description.
- Have partners take turns talking for three minutes about a favorite after-school activity. Explain that they are limited to only using sentences beginning with the word *I*, for example: *I like to play ball. I play with my friends.* After each partner has had a turn, discuss as a class whether the limited variety of sentence starters was dull or interesting to use and to listen to. Ask: How could you make the sentences more interesting?

CCSS Literacy.SL.9-10.1 Initiate and participate effectively in a range of collaborative discussions (one-on-one, in groups, and teacher-led) with diverse partners on grades 9–10 topics, texts, and issues, building on others' ideas and expressing their own clearly and persuasively. Literacy.W.9-10.4 Produce clear and coherent writing in which the development, organization, and style are appropriate to task, purpose, and audience. Literacy.L.W.9-20.1.b Use various types of phrases (noun, verb, adjectival, adverbial, participial, prepositional, absolute) and clauses (independent, dependent; noun, relative, adverbial) to convey specific meanings and add variety and interest to writing or presentations.

REVISE YOUR DRAFT

TEACH

C Revise Your Draft

Interpret the Checklist Guide students through the process of using the Revision Checklist. Direct them to read the first box in the first row (which begins *Does my introduction ...*) and answer each bulleted question. Students should decide whether or not their draft should be revised based on the criteria in the second box.

Have students read the options in the third box and identify any ways in which they could revise to improve the introduction.

Self-Evaluation Instruct students to follow the Revision Checklist to make revisions to their own drafts. Suggest that they save a paper or electronic copy of their first draft in case they want to refer to their original essay as they revise.

ELL **Rephrase Language** Clarify terms from the checklist, rephrasing as necessary. For example: *State the link between the literature and your own life* might be rephrased as: *Explain how something in the literature is like something in your own life.*
W.9-10.2.a; W.9-10.2.b; W.9-10.2.d; W.9-10.2.f; W.9-10.5; L.9-10.1.b

✓Revise Your Draft, continued

2 Revise Your Draft

You've now evaluated the voice and style of your own draft. If you scored 3 or lower, use the checklist below to revise your draft.

Revision Checklist

Ask Yourself	Check It Out	How to Make It Better
Does my introduction: • introduce the work and the author? • state my main idea? • engage readers' attention?	Put a checkmark by the author's name, the name of the work, and your main idea.	☐ Add missing details. ☐ Rewrite the opening to be more compelling.
Does the body of my essay refer to significant ideas in the literature? Do I refer to my own experience?	Read each paragraph. Look for a reference to an idea in the literary work. Reread the body to find a reference to your experience.	☐ If specific ideas from the literature are missing, add them. ☐ State the link between the literature and your life.
C Do I support significant ideas with accurate and detailed examples from the literature, including quotations?	Read each body paragraph. Underline examples. Compare quotations in your essay with quotations in the text.	☐ If examples are missing, or lack detail, add them. ☐ Match the wording and punctuation of your quotations to the literature.
Does my essay reflect effective voice? Did I adjust the style to fit the purpose and the audience?	Examine the sentence length and structure for sameness. Mark word choices that are dull or vague. Read the essay aloud to a partner. Ask for feedback.	☐ Rewrite some sentences to vary the structure and length. ☐ Replace weak language with precise and vivid words. ☐ Rewrite some parts to be clearer and more interesting.
Does my conclusion show the progress of my thinking?	Read the conclusion aloud. Find a sentence that leaves readers with your most important idea.	☐ Write the conclusion to include the idea you want readers to remember. ☐ Briefly sum up the content of your essay.

Writing Handbook, p. 784

FOCUS ON WRITER'S CRAFT

Supporting Main Ideas

Teach/Model Remind students that in a response to literature, the significant ideas from a work of literature are supported with accurate and detailed examples from the story. Ask: What are some types of examples or details that a writer uses to support main ideas? *[quotations, a character's actions]*

Explain that each paragraph of the essay should include a supportive detail from the text. For example, the main idea of the Professional Model is that kindness matters. Direct quotations from the story, such as "compassion overruling his fear," support this idea.

Practice/Apply Have students revise their drafts to add details and examples from the text to support the main idea. Ask: Did they include dialogue and quotations? Which descriptions of characters or settings might help support the main idea? How can the actions or feelings of the characters support the main idea?
W.9-10.2.b; W.9-10.5

CCSS **Literacy.W.9-10.2.a** Introduce a topic; organize complex ideas, concepts, and information to make important connections and distinctions; include formatting (e.g., headings), graphics (e.g., figures, tables), and multimedia when useful to aiding comprehension. **Literacy.W.9-10.2.b** Develop the topic with well-chosen, relevant, and sufficient facts, extended definitions, concrete details, quotations, or other information and examples appropriate to the audience's knowledge of the topic. **Literacy.W.9-10.2.d** Use precise words and phrases, telling details, and sensory language to convey a vivid picture of the experiences, events, setting, and/or characters. **Literacy.W.9-10.2.f** Provide a concluding statement or section that follows from and supports the information or explanation presented (e.g., articulating implications or the significance of the topic).

3 Conduct a Peer Conference

Exchanging essays with a partner will help each of you revise your draft. Look for any part that:

- seems to be missing important details
- is difficult to understand
- seems very different from the rest of the writing

Discuss the draft with your partner. Focus on the items in the Revision Checklist. Use your partner's comments to make your essay more engaging, more complete, and easier to understand.

4 Make Revisions

Look at the revisions below and the peer-reviewer conversation on the right. Notice how the peer reviewer commented and asked questions. Notice how the writer used the comments and questions to revise the essay.

Revised for Voice and Style

Teresa [has] changed. She ~~will change at the end of the story.~~ ~~Teresa~~ realize[s] that Valentín can ~~do something she thinks he can't.~~ [c]ommunicate in total silence, [and I'm learning his language."] ~~Teresa will learn something from this.~~ In both [life and literature,] ~~of the two things I'm thinking about~~ the significance of this is clear. Only when people listened actively and stopped judging others by their appearance can true understanding take place.

Revised for Accuracy and Detail

As this experience and Cofer's story show, assumptions can get in the way of real communication. For example, Teresa thinks that Valentín has trouble understanding things and that he can't speak English even after he tells her he can. At first I was uncertain about him, too. When he sees Pablito in the water and tries to tell her, Teresa says, "I ~~guess he's having~~ [start thinking he may be about to have] a fit or something." [Upon further reflection, I realize that it's Teresa who misunderstands Valentín.]

Peer Conference

Reviewer's Comment: I don't hear your voice, because the sentences are repetitive and the word choice is vague.

Writer's Answer: I'll vary the structure and length of sentences. I'll also add specific details.

Reviewer's Comment: You say you were uncertain about Valentín as you first read this. Can you show how you dealt with that?

Writer's Answer: Yes. I'll also fix the quotation so that it accurately reflects the text.

Reflect on Your Revisions

▶ Think about the results of your peer conference. Then, in a journal or notebook, write down what you think are your strengths and where you can improve. What did you learn by revising this essay that you can use again?

TEACH

D Conduct a Peer Conference

Discuss with a Peer Instruct students to share comments about the details and not about the specific responses and insights.

Have students ask these questions to help them evaluate their partner's draft:

- Where is more information needed?
- Which part of the essay was most difficult to understand?
- Did one part of the essay sound very different from the rest?

Instruct students to make sure their partner knows which word, sentence, or paragraph each comment refers to.
SL.9-10.1.d

E Make Revisions

Model Have volunteers role-play the Peer Conference in the margin. Then use questions to help students analyze and evaluate the writer's revisions. Ask:

- What did the writer do to improve the draft? How did he or she change the sentences?
- What information did the writer add to the draft? Why did the writer need to change a quotation?

Use Feedback Have students follow the steps above for making revisions to their own drafts.
W.9-10.2.b.; W.9-10.5; L.9-10.1.b

FOCUS ON WRITER'S CRAFT

Working Collaboratively

Teach Explain to students that sometimes writers have questions about their own writing. They may wonder if a particular sentence or idea is clear enough or if it will hold a reader's interest. Encourage students to write down any questions they have about their own work before their conference. They can ask their questions after the conference, if needed.

Apply Challenge students to identify one or more questions they have about their draft. Have them write down their questions and then present them during their peer conferences. They can fill in what they learned from their partner's feedback.

Questions About My Draft	What I Learned

SL.9-10.1.a

ONGOING ASSESSMENT
Have students write a list of three or more improvements in their revision.

CCSS Literacy.W.9-10.5 Develop and strengthen writing as needed by planning, revising, editing, rewriting, or trying a new approach, focusing on addressing what is most significant for a specific purpose and audience. Literacy.SL.9-10.1.a Come to discussions prepared, having read and researched material under study; explicitly draw on that preparation by referring to evidence from texts and other research on the topic or issue to stimulate a thoughtful, well-reasoned exchange of ideas. Literacy.L.9-10.1.b Use various types of phrases (noun, verb, adjective, adverbial, participial, prepositional, absolute) and clauses (independent, dependent; noun, relative, adverbial) to convey specific meanings and add variety and interest to writing or presentations.

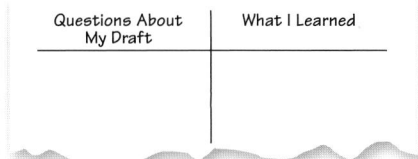

Lesson 4

EDIT AND PROOFREAD YOUR DRAFT

OBJECTIVES

Writing
- Writing Process: Edit and Proofread Ⓣ

Grammar
- Active Voice
- Consistent Verb Tense

Mechanics
- Capitalization: Days of Week and Months
- Punctuation: Comma (appositives and nouns of direct address)

TEACH

Writing Transparencies 11 and 12

Ⓐ Capitalize Days of the Week and Months

Try It Review the capitalization of days of the week and months. Use Proofreader's Marks to correct the errors on the transparency.

Possible response:
- *Last tuesday; a Summer job*

Edit and Proofread Have students correct the capitalization errors in their own drafts.
L.9-10.2

Ⓑ Punctuate Appositives and Nouns of Direct Address Correctly

Try It Explain punctuating appositives and nouns of direct address. Use Proofreader's Marks to correct the errors on the transparency.

Possible responses:
1. The narrator, a teenage girl named Teresa, learns a lesson.
2. Valentín, could you please help me?

Edit and Proofread Have students check the punctuation of appositives and nouns of direct address in their own drafts.
L.9-10.2; L.9-10.3.a

✔ Edit and Proofread Your Draft

When you have revised your draft, find and fix any mistakes that you made.

Ⓐ

1 Capitalize Days of the Week and Months

Capitalize specific days of the week and the names of months because they are proper nouns.

Common Nouns	Proper Nouns
day, night, today, summer, spring, autumn, winter	**Days of the Week**: Monday, Tuesday, Wednesday, Thursday, Friday, Saturday, Sunday
	Months: January, February, March, April, May, June, July, August, September, October, November, December

TRY IT ▸ Copy the sentences. Fix the two capitalization errors. Use proofreader's marks.

1. Last tuesday, a new neighbor visited.
2. In the story, Valentín gets a Summer job.

Proofreader's Marks

Use proofreader's marks to correct capitalization and punctuation errors.

Capitalize:
School lets out in june.

Do not capitalize:
The Winter of 2006 was unusually cold.

Add comma:
Valentín's animals all made from rubber bands were on display.

Ⓑ

2 Punctuate Appositives and Nouns of Direct Address Correctly

An appositive is a noun or pronoun placed next to another noun to identify it or to give more information about it. An appositive phrase is an appositive plus any words that modify it. You should usually use commas to set off an appositive or an appositive phrase.

"A Job for Valentín," **a story by Judith Ortiz Cofer,** is about a mentally challenged man.

Use commas to set off a noun of direct address, or the person to whom one is speaking.

Pablito, stay away from the water!

I'm coming to help you, Pablito!

TRY IT ▸ Copy the sentences. Add commas where they are needed.

1. The narrator a teenage girl named Teresa learns a lesson.
2. Valentín could you please help me?

Proofreading Tip

If you are unsure of whether you need to set off a word or phrase with commas, look in a style manual for help.

302 Unit 3 Writing Project

Writing Transparency 11

WRITING RESPONSE TO LITERATURE 11

Edit and Proofread Your Draft

Proofreader's Marks

≡	Capitalize	I love new york city.
/	Do not capitalize	I'm going shopping at my favorite Store.
^	Add a comma	Amy how are you feeling today?
∨ ∨	Add quotation marks	You are late, said the teacher.
⊙	Add a period	Mr Lopez is our neighbor.
?	Add a question mark	Where is my black pen
!	Add an exclamation mark	Look out
^	Add a semicolon	This shirt is nice however, this one brings out the color of your eyes.
:	Add a colon	He wakes up at 6 30 a.m.
—	Add a dash	Barney he's my pet dog has run away.
( )	Add parentheses	I want to work for the Federal Bureau of Investigation FBI .
=	Add a hyphen	You were born in mid September, right?
∨	Add an apostrophe	Im the oldest of five children.
#	Add a space	She likes him alot.
⌒	Close up a space	How much home work do you have?
^	Add text	My keys are the table.
↗	Delete text	I am going too my friend's house.
∩∪	Transpose words, letters	Did you see thier new car?
sp	Spell out	Today he is turning 16
¶	Begin a new paragraph	"I win!" I shouted. "No you don't," he said.
ital	Add italics	The Spanish word for table is mesa
un	Add underlining	Little Women is one of my favorite books.

Writing Transparency 12

WRITING RESPONSE TO LITERATURE 12

Edit and Proofread Your Draft

1. Capitalize Days of the Week and Months

1. Last tuesday, a new neighbor visited.
2. In the story, Valentín gets a Summer job.

2. Punctuate Appositives and Nouns of Direct Address Correctly

1. The narrator a teenage girl named Teresa learns a lesson.
2. Valentín could you please help me?

3. Check Sentences for Active Voice

1. A wheelchair is used by Dad.
2. Short stories are read by us every week.

4. Check for Consistency of Verb Tense

1. I remembered now that last year we travel to California.
2. Yesterday I check the computer and it work.

CCSS Literacy.L.9-10.2 Demonstrate command of the conventions of standard English capitalization, punctuation, and spelling when writing. Literacy.9-10.3.a Write and edit work so that it conforms to the guidelines in a style manual (e.g., *MLA Handbook*, Turabian's *Manual for Writers*) appropriate for the discipline and writing type.

3 Check Sentences for Active Voice

Use the **active voice** when the subject of the sentence performs the action described by the verb. Use the **passive voice** when you want to focus on the result (or the receiver) of the action. Read the following sentences aloud.

Passive Voice	Active Voice
He was **spoken** to by her.	She **spoke** to him.
It **has been decided** by the group to see a movie.	The group **has decided** to see a movie.
The test **had been given** before by the teacher.	The teacher **has given** the test before.

The passive voice can be awkward and hard to follow. It also drains energy from the writing. Use it only when it is necessary.

TRY IT ▸ Copy the sentences. Identify whether the sentence is active or passive voice. Rewrite each sentence, using the active voice if passive, and passive voice if active.

1. A wheelchair is used by Dad.
2. The way we gather information has been changed by the Internet.
3. The teacher had already helped him.
4. The family agreed to get a dog.

C

Editing Tip

Ask someone to read your essay aloud, or read it aloud yourself. You can often notice choppy sentences more clearly when they are read aloud.

4 Check for Consistency of Verb Tense

Check that you have used the correct verb tense and that you haven't switched from tense to tense. Change tense only if you talk about something that happened before or after the time you are writing about. The present tense of a verb tells about an action that is happening now. The past tense of a verb tells about an action that happened earlier or in the past.

I remember (present) what I learned (past), last June, when I volunteered (past) at the animal shelter.

TRY IT ▸ Copy these sentences. Rewrite them, using the correct verb tense.

1. I remembered now that last year we travel to California.
2. Yesterday I check the computer and it work.

D

Reflect on Your Corrections

▸ Proofread your essay more than once. You can often find mistakes you missed the first time. If there are things you keep missing, make a checklist of what to watch in your writing.

Writing Handbook, p. 835

TEACH

C Check Sentences for Active Voice

Try It Explain the definitions of *active voice* and *passive voice*:

Ask: Who is doing the action, *using*, in the first sentence, the *wheelchair* or *Dad*? How can you rewrite the sentence to actively show Dad using the wheelchair?

Possible response:
- *Dad uses the wheelchair.*

Use items 2 and 3 to point out the more complex verb tenses. Item 2 uses present perfect tense and item 3 uses past perfect tense.

Edit and Proofread Have students check their drafts for passive voice and make the necessary corrections.
L.9-10.1; L.9-10.3

D Check for Consistency of Verb Tense

Try It Work through the examples of verbs used correctly, and discuss why the present or past tense is used for each verb. Read the sample sentences aloud. Have students work in pairs to correct the incorrect verb tenses in each sentence. Mark corrections on the transparency.

Possible responses:
1. I remembered ~~now~~ that last year we traveled to California.
2. Yesterday, I checked the computer and it worked.

Edit and Proofread Have students read their drafts aloud and listen for verb tense errors. Review the use of each tense and how to correct verb tenses.
L.9-10.1

Grammar and Writing Practice Book, pp. 99–102

FOCUS ON WRITER'S CRAFT

Checking Subject-Verb Agreement

Teach Explain that not only must verb tense be correct but each verb must also agree with its subject. For example, in the sentence *Maria want to hear about the trip I took last summer*, the verb *want* is in the present tense, which is correct; but the verb does not agree with the noun *Maria* because *want* goes with a first-person singular *(I)* or third-person plural *(they)* form and Maria is a third-person singular noun. Model how to correct the sentence by replacing *want* with *wants*.

Practice Have students rewrite the following sentences for tense and subject-verb agreement:

I likes to draw. Yesterday I draw a picture of Joan. She like the picture. Now Ben want me to draw a picture of him.

[I like to draw. Yesterday I drew a picture of Joan. She liked the picture. Now Ben wants me to draw a picture of him.]

Apply Have students review their drafts to make sure they have used the correct verb tenses and to check that each verb agrees with its subject.
L.9-10.1

CCSS Literacy.L.9-10.1 Demonstrate command of the conventions of standard English grammar and usage when writing or speaking.
Literacy.L.9-10.3 Apply knowledge of language to understand how language functions in different contexts, to make effective choices for meaning or style, and to comprehend more fully when reading or listening.

EDIT AND PROOFREAD YOUR DRAFT

TEACH

E Edited Student Draft

Read and Discuss Read aloud the Edited Student Draft. Then go back and address the callouts.

Ask: How did the writer use the first four sentences from the original draft in the revised draft? What precise word did the writer add that tells more about Valentín's disability?

Possible response:
- *The writer combined the first four sentences to make one longer sentence for the revised draft. The writer added the word* developmentally.

Ask: How did the writer fix errors with punctuating appositives?

Possible response:
- *The writer added commas to set off appositive phrases about Teresa being the teenage narrator and about the father's wheelchair.*

Ask: How did the writer correct errors in capitalization?

Possible response:
- *The writer capitalized the first letter in* Tuesday. *Days of the week should always be capitalized.*

Ask: How did the writer correct the passive voice in the second paragraph?

Possible response:
- *The writer reorganized the sentence to show who is doing the action and who is receiving the action.*

Finally, ask: How did the writer change verb tenses?

Possible response:
- *The writer corrected verb tenses so that the form of each verb matches the time it refers to.*

Guide students in copying the sentences with active verb tenses and underlining the complete verb.

ONGOING ASSESSMENT
Have students identify the item they found most difficult to correct: appositive punctuation; capitalization; active voice; verb tenses. Have them write four examples of the correct use of that skill.

5 Edited Student Draft

Here's the student's draft, revised and edited. Read the draft aloud. How did the writer improve it? Copy the sentences highlighted in blue and underline the complete verb.

E

Lessons to Learn

In "A Job for Valentín," a short story by Judith Ortiz Cofer, a developmentally disabled man gets a summer job at a pool. The man makes friends with a 2-year-old boy, Pablito. But others are not so kind. How does the boy's mother, Maricela, respond? She laughs. "I think Pablito is teaching the dummy a few things," she says meanly. In my opinion, it is Valentín who teaches the other characters—and readers, too.

For example, Teresa, the teenage narrator of the story, learns not to judge others by their appearance. At the beginning of the story, Teresa says, "Valentín has the posture of a gorilla." She assumes that he is helpless. My dad, who uses a wheelchair, sometimes deals with similar assumptions. Last Tuesday, a new neighbor expressed surprise that Dad manages the city animal shelter. She spoke to him loudly and slowly as if he could not hear or comprehend her.

As this experience and Cofer's story show, assumptions can get in the way of real communication. For example, Teresa thinks that Valentín has trouble understanding things and that he can't speak English even after he tells her he can. At first, I was uncertain about him, too. Upon further reflection, I realize that it's Teresa who has been misunderstanding Valentín. When he sees Pablito in the water and tries to tell her, using verbal and body language, Teresa says, "I start thinking he may be about to have a fit or something."

By the end of the story, Teresa has changed. She realizes that Valentín "can communicate in total silence, and I'm learning his language." In both life and the literature, the significance of this is clear. Only when people listen actively and stop judging others by their appearance can true understanding take place.

The writer created a compelling opening and improved the voice and style by using precise word choices and varying sentence structure.

The writer used **commas** to set off appositives.

The writer **capitalized** a day of the week.

The writer replaced passive voice with **active voice** and more complex tenses to make sentences stronger.

To convey the significant ideas in the literature, the writer added detailed examples from the text. The writer also fixed a **quotation** for accuracy.

The writer fixed the **verb tenses** for consistency.

Publish and Present

You are now ready to publish and present your work. Print out your essay or write a clean copy by hand. You may also want to present your work in a different way.

Alternative Presentations

Make an Illustrated Booklet Create a booklet that presents your essay along with quotations from the work of literature. Add illustrations that complement the work.

1. **Create a Cover** Put the title of your essay on a cover page. Find or make an illustration from the work of literature for the cover as well.
2. **Body** Print a clean copy of your essay. If you like, leave room to add illustrations.
3. **About the Writer** On the inside back cover, write a paragraph or two to share what you know about the writer. Include biographical details and titles of some of his or her other writing.
4. **Share Your Booklet** Exchange booklets with another student, or share your booklet with a friend or family member. Ask for feedback.

Create a Web Site With your teacher's supervision, make a class Web site to showcase each student's essay. Follow school rules. Work in groups to complete the following steps.

1. **Design a Home Page** Find out if your school computer lab has Web authoring software, or work with an online template from a source approved by your teacher. Make sure the content of your home page is organized and easy to follow. Don't use a lot of different font styles or divide the page into too many sections. Include links to each student's essay on the home page.
2. **Prepare a Template** Create a model page for the essays. Have each essay follow that design. Decide what font to use, how many lines to run on each page, and whether to add graphics.
3. **Publicize Your Web Site** Send out an e-mail to friends and family with the link to the Web site. Check with your teacher about school guidelines.
4. **Ask for Feedback** If appropriate, invite readers to e-mail comments about the Web site to your teacher that he or she can share with the class. Be sure to ask your teacher's permission.

Language and Learning Handbook, p. 702

Publishing Tip

You can design, lay out, and print a cover using desktop publishing software.

Technology Tip

Choose the booklet, pamphlet, guide, or photo-essay format on the computer to access graphic features. These features let you set up the size, spacing, and layout of elements on a page. Create three different layouts and then discuss them with a group to evaluate which layout is best.

Reflect on Your Work

- Use the feedback from your teacher and peers to improve your ongoing writing. Write a brief summary of the positive comments you got.
- **In your portfolio, save a copy of your essay in response to literature.**

Lesson 5

PUBLISH AND PRESENT

OBJECTIVES

Writing
- Response to Literature
- Writing Process: Publish, Reflect, and Evaluate

TEACH

Have students choose one of two ways of publishing and presenting their essay.

A Alternative Presentations

Make an Illustrated Booklet Model how to make a booklet cover by folding an 11 × 17 piece of paper in half. After students share their completed booklets, invite them to share feedback about their booklets.

ELL **Demonstrate** Use models and gesture to clarify terms such as *booklet* and *inside back cover.*
W.9-10.2.a

Create a Web Site Review your school's guidelines for creating Web sites. After students have prepared the homepage, have each student assemble a list with e-mail addresses of people to review the site. Have students check the site for feedback.
W.9-10.6; SL.9-10.1

Language and Learning Handbook, p. 702

B Reflect on Your Work

Use Feedback Provide students with feedback before and after they publish. Next, have students write a short reflection on the questions, including a writing goal. For example: *In my next writing project I will write in a more engaging voice.*

Remind students to save a copy of their written essay in their portfolios.

ONGOING ASSESSMENT

Have students discuss one aspect of publishing they found difficult and how they resolved that.

FOCUS ON WRITER'S CRAFT

Illustrating Written Work

Teach Explain that there are many approaches to illustrating a piece of writing. Share examples, such as magazine articles or literary Web sites. Point out that some illustrations are decorative, capturing the mood of an essay, while others are informative, showing characters from a story or clarifying a connection to the essay writer.

Have students use the following questions to help them choose illustrations or other graphics they locate in books or online.

- For the cover illustration: What important action or idea of the story or essay do I want to show?
- For main points: What aspects of the story and its impact on me do I want to show? How can I show this with a picture?

Practice/Apply Have students reread the Edited Student Draft on p. 304. Ask students to use the bulleted questions to choose an idea from the story or essay for a cover illustration. They can then write a sentence to describe the proposed illustration. Have students share their ideas in small groups, explaining why they chose the idea for their cover.
W.9-10.2.a

CCSS **Literacy.W.9-10.2.a** Introduce a topic; organize complex ideas, concepts, and information to make important connections and distinctions; include formatting (e.g., headings), graphics (e.g., figures, tables), and multimedia when useful to aiding comprehension. **Literacy.W.9-10.6** Use technology, including the Internet, to produce, publish, and update individual or shared writing products, taking advantage of technology's capacity to link to other information and to display information flexibly and dynamically. **Literacy.SL.9-10.1** Initiate and participate effectively in a range of collaborative discussions (one-on-one, in groups, and teacher-led) with diverse partners on grades 9–10 topics, texts, and issues, building on others' ideas and expressing their own clearly and persuasively.

UNIT 4 NONFICTION

OPENING DOORS

EQ ESSENTIAL QUESTION:

How Can Knowledge Open Doors?

CLUSTER 1

Consider how learning can give you power.

Biography

Curtis Aikens and the American Dream
by Dan Rather

Brochure

Think You Don't Need an Education?

Opinion Essay

Go For It!
by Earvin "Magic" Johnson

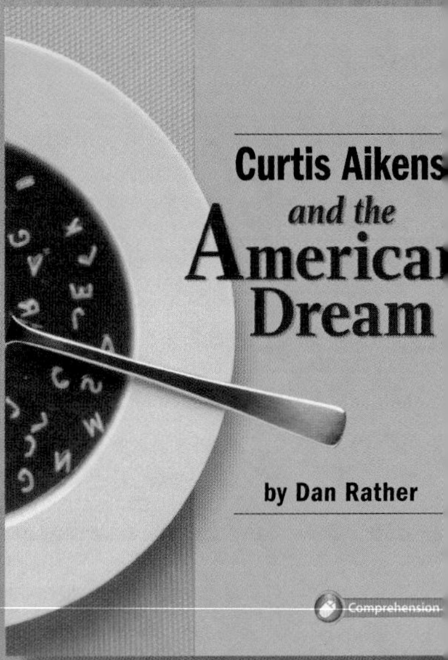

PROJECTS

Writing Project
Research Report

Unit Project
Class Newspaper or Magazine

WORKSHOPS

Workplace
Inside a Restaurant

Vocabulary
Access Words During Reading

Listening and Speaking
Oral Report

CLUSTER 2

Consider how books can take you places.

Essay

Superman and Me
by Sherman Alexie

Short Fiction

A Smart Cookie
by Sandra Cisneros

Memoir

It's Our Story, Too
by Yvette Cabrera

CLUSTER 3

Explore how knowledge changes the world.

News Feature

The Fast and the Fuel-Efficient
by Akweli Parker

Cartoon

The Hybrid
by Mick Stevens

Article

Teens Open Doors
by Richard Thompson

CLOSE READING

Investigate the role of knowledge in reaching your goals.

The Sky Is Not the Limit

Congressional Resolution

U.S. House of Representatives, 110th Congress, 1st Session, Resolution 661

Online News Article

Miami Pilot Makes History, Inspires Others
by Daniela Guzman, *The Miami Herald*

EDGE LIBRARY

The Outsiders ●
by S. E. Hinton
Lexile® 750L
Genre/Length: Classic Fiction; 208 pages

Parrot in the Oven: Mi Vida ●●
by Victor Martínez
Lexile® 990L
Genre/Length: Contemporary Fiction; 184 pages

Narrative of the Life of Frederick Douglass: An American Slave ●●●
by Frederick Douglass
Lexile® 1030L
Genre/Length: Autobiography; 152 pages

UNIT 4 Edge Library

The **EDGE LIBRARY** provides an opportunity for student choice. Students self-select literature based on their interests and reading ability. Books support exploration of the **Essential Question**, forming an integral part of instruction.

1 Select

- Select a variety of appropriate materials to read

Self-Select Have students choose a book according to their interests and reading level.

2 Read

- Read to develop and evaluate personal preferences

Download the **Teacher's Guide** and **Student Journals.** Have students read their chosen book independently or in small groups. Use the planner on **Student Journal, page 1**, to establish a reading schedule. RL.9-10.10; RI.9-10.10

myNGconnect.com

- **Unit 4 Resources**
- **Teacher's Guide**
- **Student Journal**

The Outsiders

by S. E. Hinton

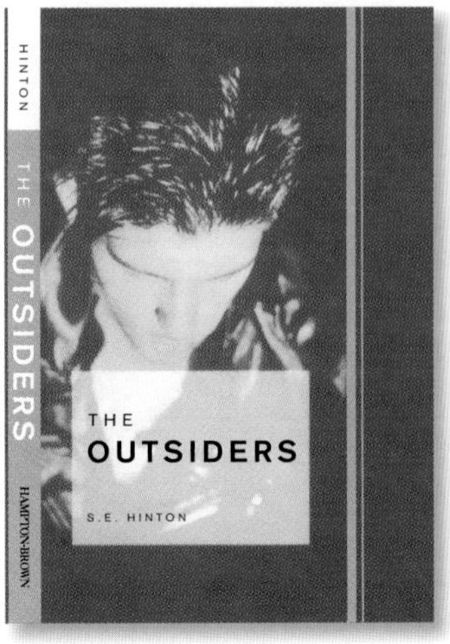

What can life teach us that school cannot?

The Outsiders explores gang and class rivalry in the 1960s between a gang of social misfits, called the Greasers, and their affluent rivals, the Socials. Its narrator, a young greaser named Ponyboy, struggles to make sense of life and learns he is not alone.

- **Reading Level** Lexile® 750L

Genre: Classic Fiction

Length: 208 pages

Awards: ALA Best Books for Young Adults, Massachusetts Children's Book Award, Books I Love Best Yearly Awards

3 Use Strategies

- Identify, assess, and apply effective personal reading strategies

Have students identify the strategies they selected to use during reading. Use the prompts at the right to elicit student analysis and discussions.

Ask Questions
- How does knowing that the book's author was a teenage girl affect how you read the story?

Make Connections
- How are the problems that the characters in the book face similar to the problems teenagers face today?

Visualize
- What do the Greasers and the Socials look like? How does their appearance affect how people treat them?

4 Discuss

- Exchange and extend ideas

EQ How Can Knowledge Open Doors?

Engage students in a discussion comparing how the texts address the **Essential Question.**

Consider how learning can give you power. Johnny writes a letter to Ponyboy reminding him of what is important in life. Randy learns violence doesn't solve problems.

Consider how books can take you places. Johnny reads *Gone with the Wind* and learns about bravery and honor. Ponyboy learns about the loss of innocence from the poem, "Nothing Gold Can Stay."

Explore how knowledge changes the world. Ponyboy decides to write about the Greasers to help people understand what everyone shares in common.

CCSS Literacy.RL.9-10.10 By the end of grade 9, read and comprehend literature, including stories, dramas, and poems, in the grades 9-10 text complexity band proficiently, with scaffolding as needed at the high end of the range. By the end of grade 10, read and comprehend literature, including stories, dramas, and poems, at the high end of the grades 9-10 text complexity band independently and proficiently.

READ ALOUD

Parrot in the Oven Read aloud the introduction to engage students' interest in the book. Provide support for the highlighted key vocabulary. Use the feature on the history of gang violence in Los Angeles to give students background information about the topic. Then model fluency by reading aloud pages 13–15.

Parrot in the Oven

by Victor Martinez

What is the best way to get respect?

Parrot in the Oven tells the story of Manny, a Mexican American youth struggling to form his identity and learn about respect. Victor Martinez draws from his own experiences of growing up with poverty, racial discrimination, and violence.

● ● **Reading Level** Lexile® 990L

Genre: Contemporary Fiction

Length: 184 pages

Awards: Pura Belpré Award, National Book Award, Americas Award

Ask Questions
- What questions does Manny have about his life?

Make Inferences
- How does Manny's home life influence his ideas about respect?

Determine Importance
- What does Manny learn about respect? Who or what played a key role in teaching him?

Consider how learning can give you power. Manny learns he does not need to act tough to earn respect. Manny's mother wants him to attend a better school, so he can have a brighter future.

Consider how books can take you places. *Parrot in the Oven* explores coming of age issues from different cultural and economic perspectives.

Explore how knowledge changes the world. Manny learns to earn respect by treating others respectfully.

Narrative of the Life of Frederick Douglass

by Frederick Douglass

What is an education worth?

Narrative of the Life of Frederick Douglass chronicles the life of Frederick Douglass from his childhood as a slave to his life as a free man. Douglass speaks out against the institution of slavery, while emphasizing the theme of knowledge as a path to freedom.

● ● ● **Reading Level** Lexile® 1030L

Genre: Autobiography

Length: 152 pages

Ask Questions
- Do I understand who the narrator is and when and where the events of his life took place?

Plan and Monitor
- What is difficult about the language the author uses? What can I do to help clarify my understanding?

Synthesize
- According to the narrator's account, what was daily life like for a slave?

Consider how learning can give you power. Education freed Frederick Douglass from slavery. Education helped Douglass and other slaves understand and articulate their plight.

Consider how books can take you places. Books gave Douglass a thirst for knowledge. Reading *The Liberator* helped Douglass to better understand slavery and how to argue against it.

Explore how knowledge changes the world. Douglass helped to educate other slaves. He became a leader in the abolitionist movement and would witness the end of slavery before he died.

Literacy.RI.9-10.10 By the end of grade 9, read and comprehend literary nonfiction in the grades 9-10 text complexity band proficiently, with scaffolding as needed at the high end of the range. By the end of grade 10, read and comprehend literary nonfiction at the high end of the grades 9-10 text complexity band independently and proficiently.

UNIT 4 Instructional Focus

EQ ESSENTIAL QUESTION:
How Can Knowledge Open Doors?

	UNIT LAUNCH How to Read Nonfiction: Text Structure	CLUSTER 1 Curt Aikens and the American Dream Go For It!
Reading		
Analyze Text Genre Focus **Nonfiction: Text Structure**	T Analyze Text Structure RI.9-10.5	T Analyze Text Structure: Chronology RI.9-10.5 T Analyze Text Features RI.9-10.7 T Use Text Evidence RI.9-10.1
Build Vocabulary	Academic Vocabulary L.9-10.6 • clarify • orient • sequence	T Key Vocabulary L.9-10.6 ambitious cause confession discourage fate literacy • profession reputation T Vocabulary Strategy L.9-10.4.c; L.9-10.4.d • Dictionary and Jargon T Reading Fluency RI.9-10.10 Comprehension Coach
Writing		
Respond to Literature		T Writing Trait W.9-10.2; W.9-10.5 • Development of Ideas
Writing Project		T Writing Project W.9-10.2.a-f; W.9-10.4-8; W.9-10.10 • Writing Trait: Development of Ideas
Language		
ELL **Develop Language**		T Define and Explain SL.9-10.1.a
Use Grammar Grammar Focus **Possessive Words; Pronouns**		T Possessive Nouns L.9-10.1.b; L.9-10.2.c T Possessive Adjectives: *My, Our,* Etc. L.9-10.1.b T Possessive Pronouns: *Mine, Ours,* Etc. L.9-10.1 T Possessive Words L.9-10.1.b
Build Listening and Speaking Skills	**Unit Project** T Discuss the EQ W.9-10.2; W.9-10.4; W.9-10.6 • Plan Your Project: Class Newspaper or Magazine	

• **Academic Vocabulary** T = Tested on Cluster and/or Unit Reading and Literary Analysis Test T = Tested on Unit Writing Test

UNIT SUMMARY

Students explore the Essential Question "How Can Knowledge Open Doors?" through reading, writing, and discussion. Each cluster focuses on a specific aspect of the larger question:

Cluster 1: Consider how learning can give you power.
Cluster 2: Consider how books can take you places.
Cluster 3: Explore how knowledge changes the world.
Close Reading: Investigate the role of knowledge in reaching your goals.

CLUSTER 2

Superman and Me
A Smart Cookie/It's Our Story, Too

- **Analyze Text Structure: Cause and Effect** RI.9-10.5
- **Analyze Text Structure: Chronology** RI.9-10.5
- **Use Text Evidence** RI.9-10.1

- **Key Vocabulary** L.9-10.6
  - arrogant
  - • assume
  - • constant
  - disgusted
  - prodigy
  - recall
  - shame
  - standard
- **Vocabulary Strategy** L.9-10.4; L.9-10.4.c
  - Multiple-Meaning Words
- **Reading Fluency** RI.9-10.10

- **Written Composition** W.9-10.2; W.9-10.5
  - Social Science: Write a Case Study

- **Writing Project** W.9-10.2.a-f; W.9-10.4-8; W.9-10.10
  - Writing Trait: Development of Ideas

- **Clarify** SL.9-10.1.cw

- **Object Pronouns After a Preposition** L.9-10.1.b
- **Compound Object Pronouns** L.9-10.1.b
- **Pronouns in Prepositional Phrases** L.9-10.1.b

- **Oral Report** SL.9-10.2; SL.9-10.3; SL.9-10.4; L.9-10.3

CLUSTER 3

The Fast and the Fuel-Efficient
Teens Open Doors

- **Analyze Text Structure: Problem and Solution** RI.9-10.5
- **Analyze Development of Ideas** RI.9-10.3
- **Use Text Evidence** RI.9-10.1

- **Key Vocabulary** L.9-10.6
  - aggressive
  - • assemble
  - • device
  - efficient
  - • environment
  - obstacle
  - solution
  - • technology
- **Vocabulary Strategy** L.9-10.4.c
  - Multiple-Meaning Words
- **Reading Fluency** RI.9-10.10
  - Comprehension Coach

- **Writing on Demand** W.9-10.1; W.9-10.4
  - Write a Problem-Solution Essay

- **Writing Project** W.9-10.2.a-f; W.9-10.4-8; W.9-10.10
  - Writing Trait: Development of Ideas

- **Verify or Confirm Information** SL.9-10.1.a

- **Indefinite Pronouns & Singular Verbs** L.9-10.1
- **Indefinite Pronouns & Plural Verbs** L.9-10.1
- **Indefinite Pronouns and Verbs** L.9-10.1.b
- **Pronoun Agreement** L.9-10.1

CLOSE READING

The Sky Is Not the Limit

- **Analyze Text Structure: Cause and Effect** RI.9-10.5
- **Analyze Text Structure: Chronology** RI.9-10.5
- **Analyze Text Features** RI.9-10.3
- **Use Text Evidence** RI.9-10.1

Academic Vocabulary L.9-10.6
- • sequence

UNIT WRAP-UP

Unit Project
- **Respond to the EQ** W.9-10.2; W.9-10.4; W.9-10.6
  - Present Your Project: Class Newspaper or Magazine

T = Tested on Language Acquisition Assessment   T = Assessed with a Rubric

UNIT 4 Resource Manager

Edge resources include practical, easy-to-use teaching tools for comprehensive instruction, practice, assessment, and reteaching.

Reading & Writing

Reading Resources

UNIT LAUNCH

Edge Library

The Outsiders

Parrot in the Oven

Narrative of the Life of Frederick Douglass

Edge Library Resources
- Student Journals
- Teacher's Guides

CLUSTER 1
Curtis Aikens and the American Dream
Go For It!

Cluster 1 Resources
- Learn more about literacy in the United States
- Selection summaries in eight languages
- Workplace Workshop resources

Comprehension Coach
- Curtis Aikens and the American Dream
- Go For It!

Reading and Writing Transparencies
- Reading Transparency 14: Vocabulary T-Chart
- Reading Transparency 15: Analyze Test Structure: Chronology

Selection CD and MP3s
- Curtis Aikens and the American Dream, CD 6 Tracks 1–2
- Curtis Aikens and the American Dream: Fluency Passage, CD 11 Track 10
- Go For It!, CD 6 Track 3

Edge Interactive Practice Book
- Curtis Aikens and the American Dream, pp. 146–150
- Go For It!, pp. 151–154
- Further Practice, pp. 155–157

Assessments Handbook
- Reader Reflection, p 43b
- Cluster 1 Test, pp. 43c–43e

Reteaching Activities

Writing Project

CLUSTER 1

Writing Project Tools
- Student Samples
- Scheduler
- Rubric

Reading and Writing Transparencies
- Writing Transparencies 13-16: Research Report

Language & Grammar

UNIT LAUNCH

Unit Project Tools
- Planning Forms
- Scheduler
- School newspaper and magazine sites
- Interview forms
- Rubric

CLUSTER 1

Language & Grammar Lab Teacher's Edition, pp. 56–61

Language & Grammar Lab Transparencies
- Language Function J: Define and Explain
- Grammar Transparencies 46–50: Possession

Grammar & Writing Practice Book, pp. 103–112

Language CD and MP3
- Define and Explain, Track 10

Assessments Handbook
- Language Acquisition Rubric p. 43o

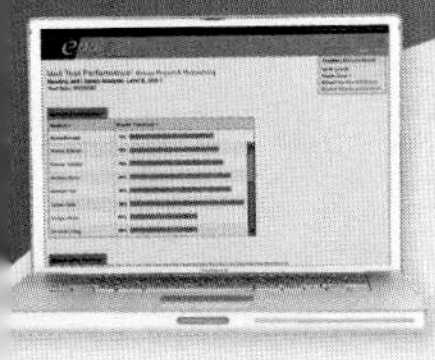

All Edge resources can be found online. Use the Online Lesson Tool, and all the relevant resources will automatically load into My Presentation Tool on myNGconnect.com.

CLUSTER 2

Superman and Me
A Smart Cookie; It's Our Story, Too

Cluster 2 Resources
- Learn more about Sherman Alexie
- Selection summaries in eight languages
- Superman and Me
- A Smart Cookie; It's Our Story, Too

Reading and Writing Transparencies
- Reading Transparency 16: Synonym-Antonym Chart
- Reading Transparency 17: Analyze Text Structure: Cause and Effect

Selection CD and MP3s
- A Smart Cookie; It's Our Story, Too, CD 6 Track 6
- A Smart Cookie: Fluency Passage, CD 11 Track 11

Edge Interactive Practice Book
- Superman and Me, pp. 158–162
- A Smart Cookie/It's Our Story, Too, pp. 163–168
- Further Practice, pp. 169–171

Assessments Handbook
- Reader Reflection, p. 43f
- Cluster 2 Test, pp. 43g–43i

Reteaching Activities

Writing Project Tools
- Student Samples
- Scheduler
- Rubric

Reading and Writing Transparencies
- Writing Transparencies 13–16: Research Report

Language & Grammar Lab Teacher's Edition, pp. 62–67

Language & Grammar Lab Transparencies
- Language Function K: Clarify
- Grammar Transparencies 51–55: Pronouns and Prepositional Phrases

Grammar & Writing Practice Book, pp. 113–122

Language CD and MP3
- Clarify, Track 11

Assessments Handbook
- Language Acquisition Rubric p. 43o

CLUSTER 3

The Fast and the Fuel-Efficient
Teens Open Doors

Cluster 3 Resources
- Learn more about alternative fuels
- Selection summaries in eight languages

Comprehension Coach
- The Fast and the Fuel-Efficient
- Teens Open Doors

Reading and Writing Transparencies
- Reading Transparency 18: Analyze Test Structure: Problem-Solution

Selection CD and MP3s
- The Fast and the Fuel-Efficient, CD 6 Tracks 7–8
- The Fast and the Fuel-Efficient: Fluency Passage, 11 Track 12
- Teens Open Doors, CD 6 Track 9

Edge Interactive Practice Book
- The Fast and Fuel-Efficient, pp. 172–176
- Teens Open Doors, pp. 177–180
- Further Practice, pp. 181–183

Assessments Handbook
- Reader Reflection, p. 43j
- Cluster 3 Test, pp. 43k–43m

Reteaching Activities

Writing Project Tools
- Student Samples
- Scheduler
- Rubric

Reading and Writing Transparencies
- Writing Transparencies 13–16: Research Report

Language & Grammar Lab Teacher's Edition, pp. 68–73

Language & Grammar Lab Transparencies
- Language Function L: Verify or Confirm Information
- Grammar Transparencies 56–60: Pronouns

Grammar & Writing Practice Book, pp. 123–132

Language CD and MP3
- Verify or Confirm Information, Track 12

Assessments Handbook
- Language Acquisition Rubric p. 43o

CLOSE READING

The Sky Is Not the Limit

Selection CD and MP3s
- The Sky Is Not the Limit: CD 12 Track 4

Edge Interactive Practice Book
- The Sky Is Not the Limit pp. 184–189

UNIT WRAP-UP

Unit Project
- Rubric

Assessments Handbook
- Reading and Literary Analysis, pp. 44–53
- Grammar and Writing, pp. 54–61
- Affective and Metacognitive Measures, pp. 105–119
- Self-Assessment: Written Composition, p. 133
- Peer Assessment: Written Composition, p. 134

Reteaching Activities

Lesson 1

UNIT LAUNCH

OBJECTIVES

Listening and Speaking
- Classroom Discussion
- Evaluate a Speaker's Message

Viewing
- Respond to and Interpret Visuals

Cultural Perspectives
- Compare Cultures: Education

ENGAGE & DISCUSS

A EQ Essential Question

Brainstorm and Map Chart ways to acquire knowledge and the doors that are opened.
SL.9-10.1

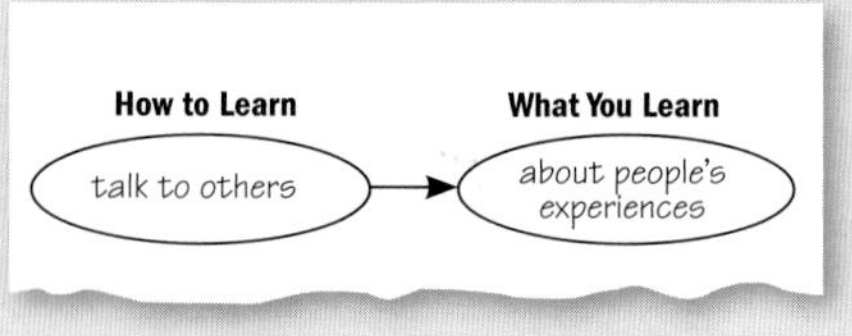

B Discuss the Quotations

Access Meaning Help students to identify a cause-and-effect and a comparison-contrast relationship.

ELL Elaborate Explain the sentence structure:
- Repetition of *I change* connects the two things that are changed: *myself* and *the world.*
- *what one cannot do ... what one can:* This structure places opposite ideas together.

Evaluate a Speaker's Message What are the speakers' attitudes about change?

Possible responses:
- *Anzaldua believes change is possible.*
- *Yutang thinks people are limited by what they cannot do.*

Use the cooperative learning activity to explore different perspectives.
SL.9-10.1.b; SL.9-10.3

UNIT 4 NONFICTION

A EQ ESSENTIAL QUESTION:

How Can Knowledge Open Doors?

B

I change myself, I change the world.

—GLORIA ANZALDUA

Sometimes it is more important to discover what one cannot do, than what one can.

—LIN YUTANG

Critical Viewing ▶
A Buddhist monk enters part of an ancient temple in Angkor, Cambodia. This site is part of a large city that was mysteriously abandoned in the mid-1500s. How does knowledge about the past open doors today?

306

COOPERATIVE LEARNING

Numbered Heads

LISTENING AND SPEAKING

Evaluate a Speaker's Message

Use the Numbered Heads cooperative learning technique (*see the Best Practices tab*) to explore the quotations.

Understand the Quotations Assign a number to each student in the group. Have students review the quotations as a group and paraphrase each one. Then have students discuss which quotation they agree with and why, and list reasons for each opinion.

Discuss Quotations Call a number and have the student with that number provide the group's paraphrase of the first quotation. Call another number for a student to provide the group's paraphrase of the second quotation. As a class, discuss the differences between the paraphrases, in both language and meaning. Call another number, and have that student summarize the group's discussion of the quotations and their reasons for agreeing and disagreeing with each quotation.

Debrief the Content As a class, discuss how paraphrasing the quotations helped their understanding. Then ask students whether the discussion influenced their initial opinions about knowledge and change.

Remind students to keep thinking about the ways in which knowledge can open doors as they read the selections in this unit.

CCSS **Literacy.SL.9-10.1** Initiate and participate effectively in a range of collaborative discussions (one-on-one, in groups, and teacher-led) with diverse partners on grades 9 -10 topics, texts, and issues, building on others' ideas and expressing their own clearly and persuasively. **Literacy.SL.9-10.1.b** Work with peers to set rules for collegial discussions and decision-making (e.g., informal consensus, taking votes on key key issues, presentation of alternate views), clear goals and deadlines, and individual roles as needed. **Literacy.SL.9-10.3** Evaluate a speaker's point of view, reasoning, and use of evidence and rhetoric, identifying any fallacious reasoning or exaggerated or distorted evidence.

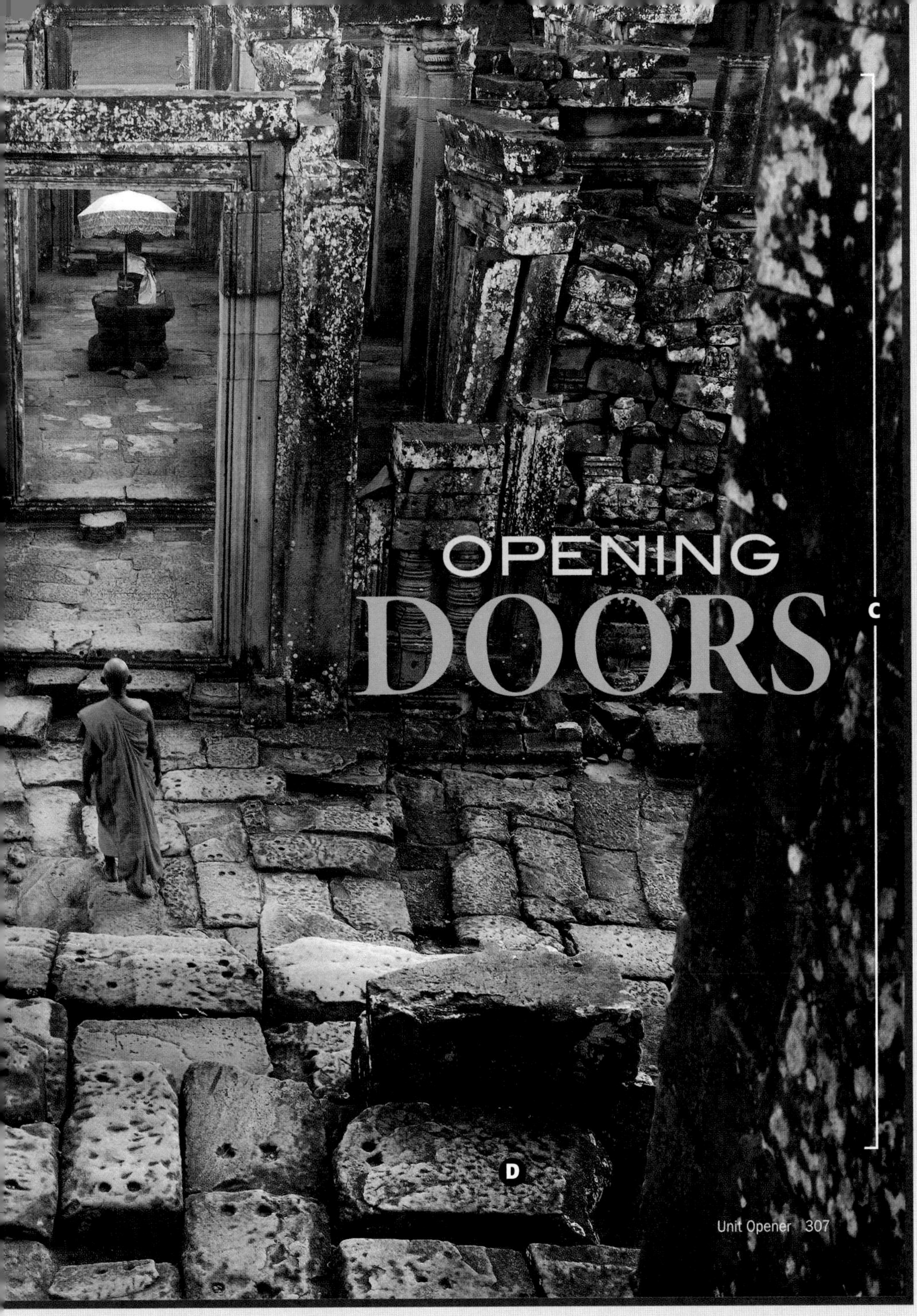

ENGAGE & INTERPRET

C Critical Viewing

Observe Details Have students study the photograph. Draw their attention to details:

- What do you notice about the building? What does it suggest about the people who built it?
- Where does the monk appear to be going? What might be his purpose?
- What role does color play in the photo? How does it help you differentiate between the past and present?

Interpret and Respond Ask: What would help you better understand this site and why it was abandoned?

Possible responses:
- *Knowledge of the history, geography, and religion of Cambodia might help me.*
- *Knowledge of the kinds of scientific studies taking place at the site might help me.*

D About the Photograph

The city of Angkor was the capital of the Khmer Empire, one of the largest kingdoms in the history of Southeast Asia. Many theories exist about why it was left to crumble. Some scholars point to ancient texts describing wars. Others say religious changes in the 1200s caused the downfall of Khmer kings, along with their greatest city. In the 1990s, special scans revealed that deforestation caused flooding, which may have caused the city's end.

Interpret and Respond Have students think about how additional information about Angkor has changed their answer to the Critical Viewing question.

Ask: How does knowledge about Angkor's past help people today?

Possible responses:
- *Knowledge about its political history helps explain how the city might have been destroyed. It shows that wars can destroy even mighty cities.*
- *Knowledge about its geography has helped us understand how it might have overused its resources. It can teach us to be careful of our resources today.*

CULTURAL PERSPECTIVES

Beliefs About Knowledge

Explore how different cultures view the importance of knowledge and learning.

Collect Ideas Have students complete these sentence frames:

In [name a culture to explore] …

- knowledge is ______.
- most people get their knowledge through ______.
- women and men have ______ access to knowledge.
- it is ______ for people to get a college degree.
- having a college education means ______.

Compare Perspectives As a class, discuss the similarities and differences among the cultural perspectives. Be sure to discuss how social position, gender, and personal determination affect the acquisition of knowledge.

UNIT LAUNCH

OBJECTIVES

Comprehension & Critical Thinking
- Read and Interpret a Bar Graph
- Use Text Evidence Ⓣ

Listening and Speaking
- Debate

ENGAGE & DEBATE

EQ Essential Question

Students analyze college enrollment figures and debate the long-term effects of higher enrollments.

Ⓐ Study the Facts

If students need help interpreting bar graphs, preteach the Research Skills activity below. Then examine the first set of bars with students. Ask:

- About how many Native American students were enrolled in college in 1993?
- Was enrollment higher or lower for Native Americans in 2003? How do you know?

Ⓑ Analyze and Debate

Have students respond in writing to the three questions.

ELL Questioning Ask questions with embedded choices. For example:

1. Did college enrollment go up or down for each group?
2. How will society change if more minority students go to college?
3. Is getting a good job harder or easier for people with a college education?

Then debate the questions in small groups and share some examples. Tell students to include data analysis of the graph to support their arguments. After the debate, have students identify similar and different opinions about the issue of getting a college education.
SL.9-10.4

ONGOING ASSESSMENT

Have students ask an open-ended question about knowledge or education. For example: *How does a college education open doors?*

UNIT 4

EQ ESSENTIAL QUESTION:
How Can Knowledge Open Doors?

Ⓐ

Study the Facts

More and more teens are choosing college as an option after high school. Study the numbers of U.S. students who enrolled in college in one decade.

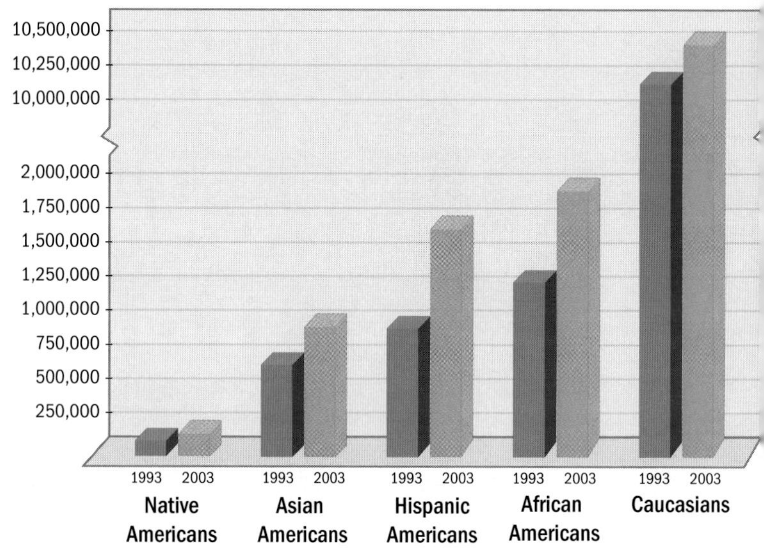

Source: American Council on Education, 2006

Ⓑ

Analyze and Debate

1. How did college enrollment change between 1993 and 2003? Why do you think so many more students were able to attend college in 2003?
2. Overall, minority enrollment increased 50.7% during these years. How might the increase in the number of minority students who attended college affect our society?
3. How can a college education affect a person's life after high school? Is getting an education the same thing as getting knowledge?

Talk about the facts and the questions with a group. Give reasons to support your opinions. Identify how your opinions differ from the viewpoints of others in your group.

ESSENTIAL QUESTION

EQ In this unit, you will explore the **Essential Question** in class through reading, discussion, research, and writing.

RESEARCH SKILLS

Interpreting Bar Graphs

Teach/Model Explain that a bar graph is a useful tool to show data for comparing and contrasting. Point to each feature of the graph: the labels, the numbers, and the bars. Use the first two bars as an example:

- The numbers on the left side of the graph represent a number of students. The smallest number—250,000—is at the bottom. The greatest number—10,500,000—is at the top.
- The first set of bars is for Native American students.
- The bar on the left shows how many Native American students enrolled in college in 1993. The bar on the right shows how many Native Americans enrolled in college in 2003.

Practice Read through the rest of the choices in the graph. For each one, ask:

- Was the number of [Asian American] students who enrolled in college higher or lower in 2003 than in 1993?

Apply Ask these questions about the graph:

1. In which group did the fewest number of students enroll in college in 2003? *(Native Americans)*
2. About how many Hispanic American students were enrolled in college in 2003? *(over 1.5 million)*

CCSS Literacy.SL.9-10.4 Present information, findings, and supporting evidence clearly, concisely, and logically such that listeners can follow the line of reasoning and the organization, development, substance, and style are appropriate to purpose, audience, and task.

1 Plan a Project

Class Newspaper or Magazine

In this unit, you'll be creating a class newspaper or magazine about the Essential Question. Choose the subjects you'll develop in your articles. To get started, review some magazines and newspapers. Look for

- the kinds of subjects that are covered
- how the headlines capture readers' interest
- how the articles are organized
- how images and diagrams help tell the story.

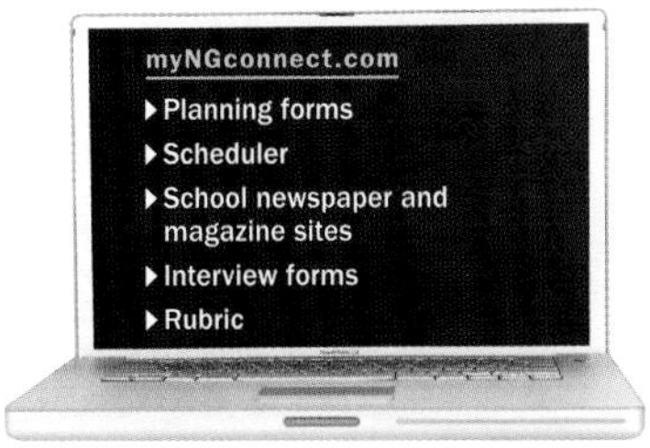

Study Skills Start planning your newspaper or magazine. Use the forms on myNGconnect.com to plan your time and to prepare the content.

2 Choose More to Read

These readings provide different answers to the Essential Question. Choose a book and online selections to read during the unit.

Narrative of the Life of Frederick Douglass: An American Slave
by Frederick Douglass

Frederick Douglass was born a slave in 1817, but he never stopped dreaming of freedom. Douglass discovered that education was the key to overcoming the obstacles that stood in his way. Education also gave Douglass the voice to help others.

▸ NONFICTION

The Outsiders
by S. E. Hinton

Life has been hard for Ponyboy and his brothers ever since their parents died. But they are not alone as long as "the Greasers" are there to protect them from their enemies, the Socs. Will Ponyboy be trapped in a life of violence, or will he learn to open doors to a new future?

▸ NOVEL

Parrot in the Oven: Mi Vida
by Victor Martínez

Manny's friends think school is not the place to get the kind of education they need. To them, gangs are the best teachers. That's where they learn the really valuable lesson—how to get respect. But is that really the education Manny wants?

▸ NOVEL

myNGconnect.com

- Read about men and women whose lives have opened doors for others.
- Learn how educational options can change your life.
- Play a game to explore how your choices can open doors to success.

UNIT PROJECT & MORE TO READ

OBJECTIVES

Reading Behaviors
- Read Independently

Study Skill
- Complete Tasks in an Efficient Order

Writing
- Write in a Variety of Forms (newspaper or magazine)

1 Plan a Project

Class Newspaper or Magazine Ask:

- What subjects are covered in the newspapers/magazines you read?
- How are newspapers and magazines different?

Assign project groups and review the Unit Project Evaluation Rubric and other Project Tools (*available online*). Have groups follow these steps:

1. Choose a format (newspaper or magazine) and subjects to cover.
2. Write articles with interesting headlines and decide on an order for the articles.

Project Support Teach the Study Skills lesson below.
SL.9-10.1.b

2 Choose More to Read

Guide students toward an independent reading choice from the **Edge Library**.

- ***The Outsiders*** Lexile® 750L
- ***Parrot in the Oven: Mi Vida*** Lexile® 1000L
- ***Narrative of the Life of Frederick Douglass: An American Slave*** Lexile® 1030L

(Some titles may contain mature themes. Be sure to preview the books before assigning them to students.)
RL.9-10.10; RI.9-10.10

Distribute **Student Journals** and have students complete the time-management planning form on p. 1.

myNGconnect.com

- **Unit Project Planning Tools**
- **Unit Project Evaluation Rubric**
- **Edge Library Student Journals and Teacher's Guides**

STUDY SKILLS

Complete Tasks in an Efficient Order

Have students use a chart to help them complete the Unit Project. Encourage them to write tasks in the first column and then write a check in the second column when a step is completed:

Tasks	Completed
gather information	✓
write headline and article	✓
put articles in order	

Tell students to refer to their chart as they begin each group meeting for the project. The group can decide together which of the remaining tasks should be worked on next.

Inform students of the date the Unit Project will be due. Have students check off each task as it is completed to be sure they stay on schedule.

CCSS **Literacy.RL.9-10.10** By the end of grade 9, read and comprehend literature, including stories, dramas, and poems, in the grades 9-10 text complexity band proficiently, with scaffolding as needed at the high end of the range. By the end of grade 10, read and comprehend literature, including stories, dramas, and poems, at the high end of the grades 9-10 text complexity band independently and proficiently. **Literacy.RI.9-10.10** By the end of grade 9, read and comprehend literary nonfiction in the grades 9-10 text complexity band proficiently, with scaffolding as needed at the high end of the range. By the end of grade 10, read and comprehend literary nonfiction at the high end of the grades 9-10 text complexity band independently and proficiently. **Literacy.SL.9-10.1.b** Work with peers to set rules for collegial discussions and decision-making (e.g., informal consensus, taking votes on key issues, presentation of alternate views), clear goals and deadlines, and individual roles as needed.

Lesson 2

HOW TO READ

OBJECTIVES

Vocabulary
- Academic Vocabulary

Reading Strategy
- Ask Questions; Review Strategies

Literary Analysis
- Analyze Text Structure Ⓣ

Media
- Analyze Factors That Impact Media Content

ENGAGE & CONNECT

Nonfiction

In this lesson, students learn to use text structures and features to navigate nonfiction texts. They read a text that outlines steps for completing a college application and use the strategy of asking questions to understand sequence.

Introduce Genre

Discuss processes that are important and familiar to students. Ask:

- What have you learned to do by following step-by-step instructions?
- Why is it important to be able to read and understand steps in a process?

Show texts that outline steps to a process, such as assembly instructions, order forms, or product manuals. Have students compare and contrast the features of these consumer materials.

Ⓐ Focus on Demo Text

Read Have students read "How to Complete a College Application."

Then have student pairs orally retell the instructions for the college application process to each other. Check that their instructions are complete.

HOW TO READ NONFICTION

Genre Focus
Nonfiction: Text Structure

Nonfiction texts organize information in certain ways. One way to make sense of a nonfiction text is to read one like this.

DEMO TEXT #1

How to Complete a College Application

Filling out a college application can be a time-consuming and difficult task, but you can make the process easier by following a few suggestions.

Before you begin, skim the application to find out whether an essay is required. If so, leave plenty of time to write your essay. Organize your ideas and be concise. Be honest about yourself, too. Don't exaggerate your accomplishments.

The next step is to gather all the information and materials you will need to complete the application:

- personal and family information (names, addresses, Social Security numbers)
- educational information (schools you've attended and when, courses you've taken)
- test scores
- honors and awards
- information about extracurricular activities
- examples of outstanding work that you have done
- personal essay
- recommendations from teachers and counselors
- high school transcript
- check or credit card information for the processing fee

Ⓐ

Now that you have everything you need, choose a time and a place to complete the application. Allow plenty of time. Read all the directions carefully. Answer every question. Don't leave anything blank unless you are given the option to do so.

After you finish, proofread your application. Then sign your name. Finally, attach all supporting materials (letters of recommendation, your transcript, examples of your work, etc.). Make sure you also include payment for the processing fee.

OUT-OF-SCHOOL LITERACY

Functional Literacy

Discuss sources students can use to learn about steps in a process, such as:

- instructions for joining a club or team
- a recipe for a dish or beverage
- a booklet on getting a driver's license
- directions for setting up a computer or installing software

Have students find examples of written instructions and read them aloud to a partner, who should follow the instructions if possible. Then, have students discuss the following details:

- the process the source describes and the main steps involved
- the action verbs used in the description of each step in the process
- how the steps are outlined; for example: by numbers, bullets, or in paragraphs
- special features of the instructions, such as materials lists, diagrams, graphics, and cross-referencing
- questions students had as they reviewed or followed the steps and how they found the answers

Review results as a class and note similarities among the texts. Link the similarities to Demo Text 1.
SL.9-10.1.a

CCSS Literacy.9-10.1.a Come to discussions prepared, having read and researched material under study; explicitly draw on that preparation by referring to evidence from texts and other research on the topic or issue to stimulate a thoughtful, well-reasoned exchange of ideas.

■ Connect Reading to Your Life

Here are some extra steps for completing an application. Work with a partner to decide where each one could go in Demo Text #1.

Where do you think item A belongs?
I think it should go at the very end.

A. Make a copy for your records.
B. Ask a parent or friend to proofread your application as well.
C. Be sure to edit and proofread your essay so that the final version is ready to attach to your application.
D. Select a workspace that is quiet and uncluttered.

B

Focus Strategy ▶ Ask Questions

When you placed the steps, you and your partner probably asked each other questions like these: Where does this go? Where does it make sense? What should this come after? You also probably figured out that the text is organized in a logical **sequence**. This helped you figure out where to insert the extra steps.

When you read, you also ask questions—of the author, yourself, and the text. Asking questions is an important reading strategy. It helps you understand what you're reading, as well as how the information in a text is organized.

Reading Strategies

- Plan and Monitor
- Determine Importance
- Make Inferences
- ▶ **Ask Questions**
- Make Connections
- Synthesize
- Visualize

■ Your Job as a Reader

C

Experienced readers know that one of the best ways to read is to question the author, themselves, and the text. Your job as a reader is to get involved with the text and think along with the author. *Who? What? When? Where? How?* and *Why?* are some of a good reader's favorite questions.

Academic Vocabulary

- **sequence** *n.*, an arrangement, or order, in which one thing comes after another; **sequential** *adj.*, forming a sequence

ENGAGE & CONNECT

B Connect Reading to Your Life

Help students connect the strategy to their own lives by recalling how they have completed other applications, such as for a job. Ask: Which parts could you complete by yourself, and which parts did you need help with? Would instructions like those on p. 310 have been useful? Explain.

After students carefully review the text, have them work in pairs to determine where to insert the extra steps.

Focus Strategy: Ask Questions Read this section with students. Use the activity below to teach the Academic Vocabulary in this unit. Ask:

- What types of questions did you ask your partner, and vice versa?
- How did questioning help you understand some steps more clearly?
- How can you tell the sequence of steps in the application instructions?

RI.9-10.1

Review Strategies Remind students that they use a variety of strategies as they read a text. Have them share a strategy they used when they read Demo Text 1.

Possible response:

- *When I read the list of things you need to gather to apply for college in "How to Complete a College Application," I made an inference that applying for schools takes a lot of hard work. This helped me to understand why it is important to begin your applications as soon as possible and do your best in school.*

RI.9-10.1

TEACH STRATEGIES

C Your Job as a Reader

Explain that good readers interact with text by asking questions as they read. Tell students they have already begun practicing this strategy by inserting extra steps into a sequence. They will continue to practice the strategy during this unit.

ACADEMIC VOCABULARY

Make Word Maps Present the Academic Vocabulary words. Have students make a Word Map for each.

1. Write the word in the center. Write what it means in the top box. Give an example and a non-example in the boxes below.
2. Use a dictionary to check the information in your map.
3. Keep your Word Maps in a vocabulary notebook.

L.9-10.6

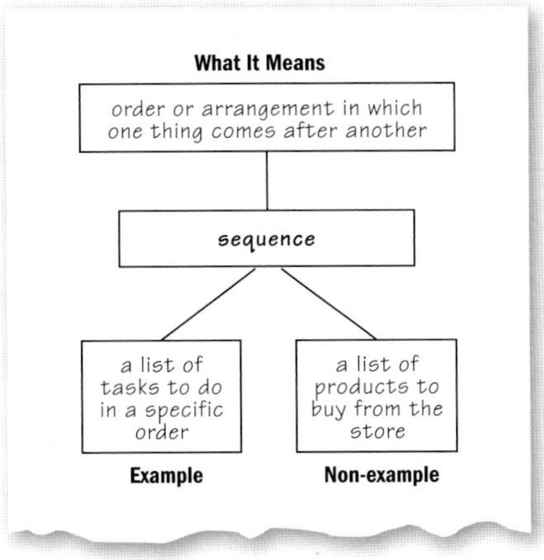

a list of tasks to do in a specific order
a list of products to buy from the store

CCSS Literacy.RI.9-10.1 Cite strong and thorough textual evidence to support analysis of what the text says explicitly as well as inferences drawn from the text. Literacy.L.9-10.6 Acquire and use accurately general academic and domain-specific words and phrases, sufficient for reading, writing, speaking, and listening at the college and career readiness level; demonstrate independence in gathering vocabulary knowledge when considering a word or phrase important to comprehension or expression.

TEACH STRATEGIES

A Unpack the Thinking Process

Review Demo Text 1 on p. 310, and go over features students noted while discussing it.

Text Structure: Sequence Explain that sequential order and chronological order may overlap, but that chronological order typically refers to events across a period of real time, such as hours or days. Ask: Are the steps in the application sequential or chronological? Confirm that the text is sequential because it lists steps in a process.

Read the numbered steps. Then ask: Why is it helpful to see these steps numbered rather than written in paragraph form?

Review the signal words in the chart. Then ask students to scan the text on p. 310 for examples.

Sequence: A sequence is a text structure that includes ordered steps and words that show order.

Numbered Steps and Signal Words: These are features of a sequential text structure. They are tools readers can use to guide them through a process.

■ Unpack the Thinking Process

Authors can organize nonfiction texts in many ways. Experienced readers know that authors put their ideas together in certain patterns, or text structures, and that analyzing those text structures can help them understand the ideas.

Text Structure: Sequence

Sequence is one kind of text structure. Writers use a **chronological** (by time) or sequential (by steps in a process) text structure when they want to explain how to do something or show how or why something happened.

To identify a sequential text structure, look for:

☑ **Numbered Steps**

1. Write, edit, and proofread your essay.
2. Gather the information and materials you will need.
3. Choose a time and a place to complete the application.

A

☑ **Signal Words**

after	first	next	soon
afterward	following	not long after	then
as soon as	immediately	now	third
before	initially	on [date]	today
during	later	preceding	until
finally	meanwhile	second	when

Signal words are useful during all stages of the reading process.

- Before Reading: Skim for signal words to help you identify the text structure.
- During Reading: Use the signal words as anchors to keep track of all the steps or events.
- After Reading: Use the signal words to review.

Elements of Literature
chronological *adj.*, in the order in which events occur

Asking Questions

Experienced readers also ask questions to help identify the text structure and to **clarify** a sequence of steps or events in their minds. Here are some questions a reader might ask about Demo Text #1:

Question the Author	*Why did you organize the text like this?* *Why are you telling about this now?*
Question Yourself	*Do I understand that step?* *What will I read about next?*
Question the Text	*Where is the signal word in this sentence?* *Why is this a new paragraph?*

B

With a partner, take turns reading aloud Demo Text #1. As you listen, imagine you are following the instructions in the text. Then, ask questions to clarify the sequence of steps.

■ Try an Experiment

Here are two texts that explain how to do something.

DEMO TEXT #2

Dear Elena:

Your **orientation** date for Rutherford College is September 12. Please follow the instructions in this letter carefully. First, complete the attached form and mail it back with the $50 fee by July 31. Then wait for a confirmation letter. It will be sent along with information about check-in and the day's activities. After receiving confirmation, you can finalize your travel plans. We look forward to meeting you.

DEMO TEXT #3

When you read a textbook, do you have trouble remembering all the information? These steps can help you study effectively:

1. When you come to each chapter, glance at headings, pictures, and captions to get an idea of what the text is about.
2. Read the first and last paragraphs of the chapter and the chapter questions.
3. Describe each passage in your own words.
4. Review the entire chapter. Refer to the book if you need help.

Think, Pair, Share With a partner, reread Demo Text #2 and #3. Identify the structure of each text. Tell what signal words helped you identify the structure. C

Monitor Comprehension

Text Structure Describe two ways to identify sequential text structure.

Academic Vocabulary

- **clarify** *v.*, to make something clear or understandable
- **orient** *v.*, to adjust yourself to a new situation; **orientation** *n.*, the act or process of orienting

TEACH STRATEGIES

B Asking Questions

Explain Asking questions about a text can help readers to clarify and understand steps in a sequence. Questions can be about an author's purpose, a reader's own understanding, or the text itself. Tell students they will learn and practice this strategy during this unit.

APPLY

C Try an Experiment

Have students read the letter in Demo Text 2 and the instructions in Demo Text 3 and compare and contrast the features of each.

Think, Pair, Share Have students work in pairs to determine whether each text is chronological or sequential and explain how they know, identifying any signal words that help them determine the structure.

Possible responses:

- *Demo Text 2: The text is chronological. It uses time order signal words, such as* first, then, *and* after.
- *Demo Text 3: This text shows steps in a process. It shows a bulleted list and uses phrases, such as* "before you begin," *and* "the next step."

Practice Have students work in pairs to give and follow the instructions in Demo Text 3. Ask one student to read the steps aloud while the other follows, using a chapter from any textbook. Then have students exchange roles and repeat the activity, using a different chapter. RI.9-10.5; SL.9-10.1

Monitor Comprehension

Possible responses:

- *Look for numbered steps.*
- *Search for signal words that show order.*

DIFFERENTIATED INSTRUCTION

Teach Text Features and Structures As you teach the selections in this unit, use these strategies to meet students' individual needs.

Struggling Readers

Identify Signal Words Before reading each main selection, preview how identifying signal words can help a reader identify the type of nonfiction text structure used. For example, read aloud the first two paragraphs on p. 320 and have students note time and signal words that indicate that the selection is organized in chronological order.

English Language Learners ELL

Preview Main Ideas Before reading each section, point out text structures and explain signal words. For example, before reading the section "CRAZY PILES" on p. 344, tell students that the section outlines a cause and effect. Explain that *since,* in the last sentence of the section, means "because."

Challenge

Use Visuals and Text Pair students, and assign them a text structure in the selection. Have students use a graphic organizer to show information visually and then describe the information in paragraph form using signal words.

ONGOING ASSESSMENT

Have partners create a numbered list to show sequential steps of a process they know. Next, have them take turns telling the same steps, using signal words.

CCSS Literacy.RI.9-10.5 Analyze in detail how an author's ideas or claims are developed and refined by particular sentences, paragraphs, or larger portions of a text (e.g., a section or chapter). Literacy.SL.9-10.1 Initiate and participate effectively in a range of collaborative discussions (one-on-one, in groups, and teacher-led) with diverse partners on grades 9-10 topics, texts, and issues, building on others' ideas and expressing their own clearly and persuasively.

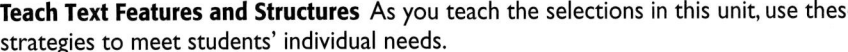

UNIT 4 Cluster 1 Planner

EQ ESSENTIAL QUESTION:

How Can Knowledge Open Doors?

Consider how learning can give you power.

Online Planner
myNGconnect.com

	LESSON 3 **Prepare to Read**	LESSON 4 **Curtis Aikens and the American Dream** Main Selection
Reading		
Reading Strategies Focus Strategy **Ask Questions**	**Activate Prior Knowledge** SL.9-10.1 • Make a Connection: Think-Pair-Share *T314*	**Ask Questions** RI.9-10.1 • Self-Question *T315, T318–T328*
Literary Analysis Genre Focus **Nonfiction**		T **Analyze Text Structure: Chronology** *T315, T318–T328* RI.9-10.5
Vocabulary	T **Key Vocabulary** RI.9-10.4; L.9-10.6 • Introduce *T314* ambitious, cause, confession, discourage, fate, literacy, • profession, reputation	T **Key Vocabulary** L.9-10.6 • Daily Routines *T319* • Link to Essential Question *T321* • Selection Reading *T318–T328* cause, confession, fate, literacy, reputation
Fluency		T **Phrasing** RI.9-10.10 • Daily Routines *T319* T **Accuracy and Rate** RI.9-10.10 Comprehension Coach *T317*
Writing		
Response to Literature		**Return to the Text** W.9-10.9.b; W.9-10.10 • **Reread and Write** What everyday things was Curtis unable to do because of his illiteracy? *T328*
Writing Across the Curriculum		**Research and Writing** W.9-10.7 • **Sociology Connection** *T327*
Language		
ELL **Language Development**	T **Define and Explain** SL.9-10.1.a • Language and Grammar Lab, Transparency J *LAB TE p. 56*	T **Define and Explain** SL.9-10.1.a • Daily Routines *LAB TE p. 56*
Grammar Grammar Focus **Possessive Words**		T **Possessive Nouns** *T320* L.9-10.1.b; L.9-10.2.c T **Possessive Adjectives** *T322* L.9-10.1.b T **Possessive Pronouns** *T326* L.9-10.1
Listening and Speaking	**Partner and Class Talk** SL.9-10.1 • Opinions on Knowledge as Power *T314*	**Listen to a Selection** RI.9-10.10 Comprehension Coach *T317* *CD 6, Tracks 1–2* **Out-of-School Literacy** SL.9-10.1.a • Household Literacy *T324*

T = Tested on Cluster and/or Unit Reading and Literary Analysis Test
T = Tested on Language Acquisition Assessment
T = Tested on Unit Writing Test
T = Assessed with a Rubric
• **Academic Vocabulary**

Curtis Aikens and the American Dream

Genre: Biography Lexile® 900L

Curtis Aikens never learned how to read, but he was always too ashamed to tell anyone. Curtis realized that he needed help. He learned how to read, and now Curtis shares his experience with others to promote the importance of literacy.

Go For It!

Genre: Opinion Essay Lexile® 680L

Basketball star Magic Johnson encourages readers of this essay to complete school and go to college. He advises young people to pursue a variety of professions that are beneficial to society and not just to focus on a career in the NBA.

LESSON 5 **Go For It!** Second Selection	LESSON 6 **Reflect and Assess**	LESSONS 7 & 8 **Integrate the Language Arts**	LESSONS 9 & 10 **Workshops**
Ask Questions RI.9-10.1 *T330, T331–T334*	**Comprehension and Critical Thinking** *T335* RI.9-10.1; RI.9-10.2; RI.9-10.8; RI.9-10.10 • Compare Across Texts • Analyze, Compare, Interpret, Speculate, Evaluate		
(T) **Analyze Text Features** RI.9-10.7 *T330, T331–T334*	**Interpret and Evaluate Literature** RI.9-10.10 (T) **Use Text Evidence** RI.9-10.1 *T335*		
(T) **Key Vocabulary** L.9-10.6 • Selection Reading *T331–T334* **ambitious** • **profession** **discourage**	(T) **Key Vocabulary** L.9-10.6 • Review *T335* **ambitious**, **cause**, **confession**, **discourage**, **fate**, **literacy**, • **profession**, **reputation**	(T) **Vocabulary Strategy** L.9-10.4.c • Use Reference Sources: Dictionary (Jargon) *T337*	**Vocabulary Workshop: Access Words During Reading** L.9-10.4; L.9-10.4.d **Vocabulary Strategy** • Clarify Word Meanings *T339*
(T) **Phrasing** RI.9-10.10 • Daily Routines *T319* (T) **Accuracy and Rate** RI.9-10.10 Comprehension Coach *T331*	(T) **Phrasing** RI.9-10.10 • Peer Assessment *T335*		
Return to the Text W.9-10.9.b; W.9-10.10 • **Reread and Write** What things help you with or distract you from achieving your educational goals? *T334*	**Write About Literature** W.9-10.10 • **PS Announcement** How can you promote education after high school? *T335*	(T) **Writing Trait** W.9-10.2; W.9-10.5 • **Development of Ideas** *T337*	
Research and Writing W.9-10.7; SL.9-10.1.a • **Sociology Connection** *T333*		**Research and Writing** W.9-10.7 • **Literacy in the United States** *T336*	**Workplace Workshop: Inside a Restaurant** W.9-10.2; W.9-10.4; W.9-10.10 **Writing** • Write a Business Memo *T338*
(T) **Define and Explain** SL.9-10.1.a • Daily Routines *LAB TE p. 56*		(T) **Define and Explain** SL.9-10.1.a • Pair Talk *T336*	
Reflexive Pronouns L.9-10.1 *T332*		(T) **Possessive Words** L.9-10.1.b *T336*	
Listen to a Selection RI.9-10.10 Comprehension Coach *T331* *CD 6, Track 3*	**Participate in a Discussion** *T335* SL.9-10.1	**Deliver a Media Presentation** *T336* W.9-10.7; SL.9-10.3	

EDGE LIBRARY

The Outsiders ●
by S. E. Hinton

Parrot in the Oven ● ●
by Victor Martinez

Narrative of the Life of Frederick Douglass ● ● ●
by Frederick Douglass

Lesson 3

PREPARE TO READ

OBJECTIVES

Vocabulary
- Key Vocabulary
- Strategy: Use Cognates; Relate Words

Reading Strategy
- Activate Prior Knowledge

ELL Language & Grammar Lab

Language Function Transparency J
Define and Explain

ENGAGE & CONNECT

A EQ Essential Question

Focus on Learning Ask: How is knowledge powerful?

Possible responses:
- *If you have knowledge, you can get a better job.*
- *When you know more, people respect you and turn to you for help.*

B Make a Connection

Have students discuss the quotation with a partner and then share their examples with the class.
SL.9-10.1

TEACH VOCABULARY

C Learn Key Vocabulary

Study the Words Review the four steps of the Make Words Your Own routine (*see the Vocabulary tab*):

1. **Pronounce** Say one word and have students repeat it. Write the word in syllables and pronounce it, one syllable at a time: *am-bi-tious*. Ask what looks familiar in the word, and point out other forms of the word, such as *ambition*.

   ELL Use cognates to help Spanish speakers with the words (*see the Vocabulary tab*).

2. **Study Examples** Read the example in the chart. Provide more examples: Are you *ambitious* when you do extra credit work to improve your grade or when you don't do your homework?

3. **Encourage Elaboration** Provide students with a sentence frame to complete, such as *I showed I was* ambitious *when I* ______.

Reading Transparency 14

4. **Practice the Words** Use the transparency to model completing a Vocabulary T Chart. Have students complete a Chart and share their lists with a group.

Edge Interactive Practice Book, pp. 146–147
RI.9-10.4; L.9-10.6

ONGOING ASSESSMENT

Have students complete an oral sentence for each word. For example: *When you believe in a* ______, *you might fight for it.*

PREPARE TO READ

- Curtis Aikens and the American Dream
- Think You Don't Need an Education?
- Go For It!

A EQ How Can Knowledge Open Doors?

Consider how learning can give you power.

B Make a Connection

Think-Pair-Share An English writer named Francis Bacon once said, "Knowledge is power." What does this statement mean to you? With a partner, talk about people who have used knowledge as power. Then share your example with the class.

C Learn Key Vocabulary

Study the Words Pronounce each word and learn its meaning. You may also want to look up the definitions in the Glossary.

• Academic Vocabulary

Key Words	Examples
ambitious (am-**bi**-shus) *adjective* ▸ page 332	If you are **ambitious**, you have big goals that you want to achieve. The **ambitious** student studied day and night to win the science prize.
cause (**kawz**) *noun* ▸ page 327	A **cause** is an idea you believe in and are willing to fight for. I volunteer my time and money to the **cause** of helping the homeless. *Synonym*: goal
confession (kun-**fe**-shun) *noun* ▸ pages 326, 328	You make a **confession** when you tell someone something private or secret. *Synonyms*: telling the truth, owning up; *Antonyms*: keeping a secret, denial
discourage (dis-**kur**-ej) *verb* ▸ pages 332, 334	When someone or something **discourages** you, it makes you not want to do something. His laughter **discouraged** me from painting any more pictures.
fate (**fāt**) *noun* ▸ page 322	**Fate** is the future that is expected to happen. Many people believe that you cannot change your **fate**, while others think that you can change it with hard work.
literacy (**li**-tu-ru-sē) *noun* ▸ pages 318, 328, 335, 336	**Literacy** is the ability to read and write. Without **literacy**, it is difficult to complete a job application, use the Internet, or read a map.
• **profession** (pru-**fe**-shun) *noun* ▸ pages 332, 334	A **profession** is a job that you need special training to do. Because he chose the medical **profession**, he spent years studying to be a doctor. *Synonyms*: career, work
reputation (re-pyu-**tā**-shun) *noun* ▸ pages 321, 335	Your **reputation** is the way people think about you. He had a **reputation** as a shy person because he was always so quiet in class.

Practice the Words Complete a **Vocabulary T Chart** to compare whether the Key Vocabulary words mean something positive or negative to you. Then share your chart with a group, and discuss how you grouped the words in similar or different ways.

Vocabulary T Chart

Positive (+)	Negative (-)
ambitious	discourage

Reading Transparency 14

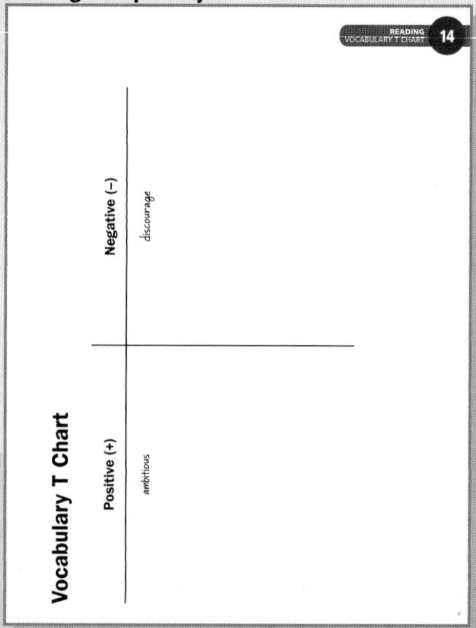

CCSS Literacy.SL.9-10.1 Initiate and participate effectively in a range of collaborative discussions (one-on-one, in groups, and teacher-led) with diverse partners on grades 9-10 topics, texts, and issues, building on others' ideas and expressing their own clearly and persuasively. Literacy.L.9-10.6 Acquire and use accurately general academic and domain-specific words and phrases, sufficient for reading, writing, speaking, and listening at the college and career readiness level; demonstrate independence in gathering vocabulary knowledge when considering a word or phrase important to comprehension or expression.

BEFORE READING Curtis Aikens and the American Dream

biography by Dan Rather

Reading Strategies

- Plan and Monitor
- Determine Importance
- Make Inferences
- ▶ **Ask Questions**
- Make Connections
- Synthesize
- Visualize

Analyze Text Structure: Chronology

A biography is the true story of someone's life. It includes information about the most important events and people in the person's life. Authors often organize biographies in **chronological order**. This describes the events in the order that they happened.

D

Look Into the Text

Dates and times tell when events happened.

Sequence words, such as *first*, *then*, *later*, signal the order of events.

In the third grade, Curtis made a decision that would determine the course of his life. As he sat through a parent-teacher conference, he heard his teacher praise him: "'I just love having your boy in my class,'" Curtis remembers her saying. "'He's a great kid, he's sweet,' and then I heard a 'but.' And I thought, 'Oh no. What's this? But he's dumb? He's stupid?'" Well, no. She didn't say anything close to that, but she did say that he had some reading trouble, and she thought it would be best for him to repeat the third grade.

What happens here? Who are the people involved?

Focus Strategy ▶ Ask Questions

It's natural to have questions about what you're reading. In fact, learning to ask useful questions is a good way to find new information, solve problems, and learn more. As you read, ask yourself about the people, places, and events in each section.

E

Focus Strategy

HOW TO SELF-QUESTION

1. As you read, ask yourself questions to add to your understanding of the passage.
2. Ask questions about the passage based on the 5Ws and H: *Who?*, *What?*, *Where?*, *When?*, *Why?*, and *How?* Record these on a **Question-Answer Chart**.
3. Reread the text to see if you can find the answers. If you don't find them, ask a classmate or teacher.

Question-Answer Chart

My Questions	My Answers
Curtis seems really worried about what his teacher tells his parents. Why is he so worried?	The author includes Curtis's thoughts. Curtis is scared that people will think that he is "dumb" and "stupid."

Reading Transparency 15

Analyze Text Structure: Chronology

READING TEXT STRUCTURE: CHRONOLOGY 15

What is one way that authors organize biographies?

Introduce Authors usually organize biographies in **chronological order**. This describes the events in the order that they happened, from first to last. Some words and numbers can give clues about chronological order:

- **Dates** and **times** tell when events happened.

  Paul was born on **August 17, 1983**, at **6:20 A.M.**

- **Sequence words**, such as *first*, *then*, *later*, and *finally*, signal the order of events.

  After Paul's birth, Mrs. Choy had two more boys. **Then** she **finally** had a girl.

In "Curtis Aikens and the American Dream," the words *In the third grade* indicate a time. They tell when Curtis made an important decision.

In the third grade, Curtis made a decision that would determine the course of his life.

The word *then* is a sequence word. It tells when Curtis heard something his teacher said.

"'He's a great kid, he's sweet,' and **then** I heard a 'but.'"

CCSS **Literacy.RI.9-10.1** Cite strong and thorough textual evidence to support analysis of what the text says explicitly as well as inferences drawn from the text. **Literacy.RI.9-10.5** Analyze in detail how an author's ideas or claims are developed and refined by particular sentences, paragraphs, or larger portions of a text (e.g., a section or chapter). **Literacy.RI.9-10.4** Determine the meaning of words and phrases as they are used in a text, including figurative, connotative, and technical meanings; analyze the cumulative impact of specific word choices on meaning and tone (e.g., how the language of a court opinion differs from that of a newspaper).

Lesson 4

BEFORE READING

OBJECTIVES

Reading Strategy
- Ask Questions: Self-Question

Literary Analysis
- Analyze Text Structure: Chronology **T**

TEACH STRATEGIES

D Analyze Text Structure: Chronology

Look Into the Text Read the introduction to define biography and explain chronological order. Read aloud the text passage. Use the callouts to discuss the text structure. Ask: When did Curtis make a big decision?

Possible response:
- *in the third grade*

Ask: Why is chronological order used in a biography?

Possible response:
- *It helps the reader keep track of the events in a person's life.*

Reading Transparency 15

Use the Transparency Reinforce the features of chronological order in a biography. Ask: Did Curtis's teacher describe his problems to his mother before or after she said he was a great kid? How can you tell?

Possible response:
- *after; the sequence word* then

RI.9-10.5

E Focus Strategy: Ask Questions

Self-Question Review that students use a variety of strategies as they read. Then read the introduction with students to define the strategy. Work through the steps in the How To box to model self-questioning.

Have students add to their Question-Answer Charts as they read.

RI.9-10.1

Edge Interactive Practice Book, pp. 148–149

ONGOING ASSESSMENT

Have partners share time-order signal words and other clues they can use to identify chronological text structure.

OBJECTIVES

Reading Strategy
- Make Connections

Viewing
- Respond to and Interpret Visuals

Cultural Perspectives
- U.S. Culture: Education
- Connect Personal Experiences

BUILD BACKGROUND

A Broader Horizons

Have students read the letter about a teen literacy program.

Discuss Changes in Literacy Rates Worldwide Share this additional information about literacy around the world:

Studies show that if a country has high rates of literacy, its people are healthier and its economy is stronger. Because many countries still have low rates of literacy, in 2003, the United Nations declared 2003–2012 the "United Nations Literacy Decade" and announced that literacy is a basic human right.

In 2003, there were over 861 million adults who were not literate. By 2015, estimates project this number going down to 800 million, bringing the total literacy rate to 85% worldwide.

Make Connections Guide students to make connections with the text.

Ask: How would your life be different if you couldn't read or write at all? What other problems does illiteracy cause?

Possible responses:
- *It would be hard to find my way around if I couldn't read signs.*
- *I wouldn't be able to graduate or get a good job; illiteracy limits your future.*

myNGconnect.com

Selection Summaries in eight languages

Broader Horizons

Literacy Volunteers

A

TEENS *for* LITERACY!

Dear **Teens for Literacy! Volunteer,**

Thank you for your interest in Teens for Literacy! You are making a difference in the world by helping an adult or child learn to read.

By volunteering each week, you are helping to change these statistics:

- 38% of American 4th graders read below the "basic" level.
- Forty million adults in the U.S. aren't able to read a simple story to a child.
- From 1983 to 1999, over ten million Americans reached the 12th grade without learning to read at a basic level. In the same time period, six million Americans dropped out of high school.

Though these numbers are scary, we can do something about them! The time you spend teaching others to read will change their lives and make sure that they don't become another statistic.

Again, thank you for your interest in Teens for Literacy! We're looking forward to seeing you at our orientation. If you have any questions, please contact me, Jenny Ramirez, at (650) 555-6545.

Sincerely,

Jenny

myNGconnect.com

Learn about the problem of illiteracy in the U.S.

Read stories about adults who learned to read.

DIFFERENTIATED INSTRUCTION

English Language Learners ELL

Preview the selection:

- Show the book cover on p. 327: *This biography tells about a man named Curtis Aikens. He is a famous chef.*
- Show the art on p. 317: *The bowl of alphabet soup shows letters that can make words.*
- Show the photograph on p. 321: *This is a bridge in San Francisco. Part of the story takes place in San Francisco, California.*

Read Aloud to provide a supported listening experience:

- Play the **Selection Recording** as students track text in their books. **CD 6**
- Have students use the Listen feature in the **Comprehension Coach** where they see the text as it is read aloud.
- Read the selection aloud to students as you provide comprehensible input. For example, you can pantomime identifying things based on only a few letters, or cooking without reading a recipe.

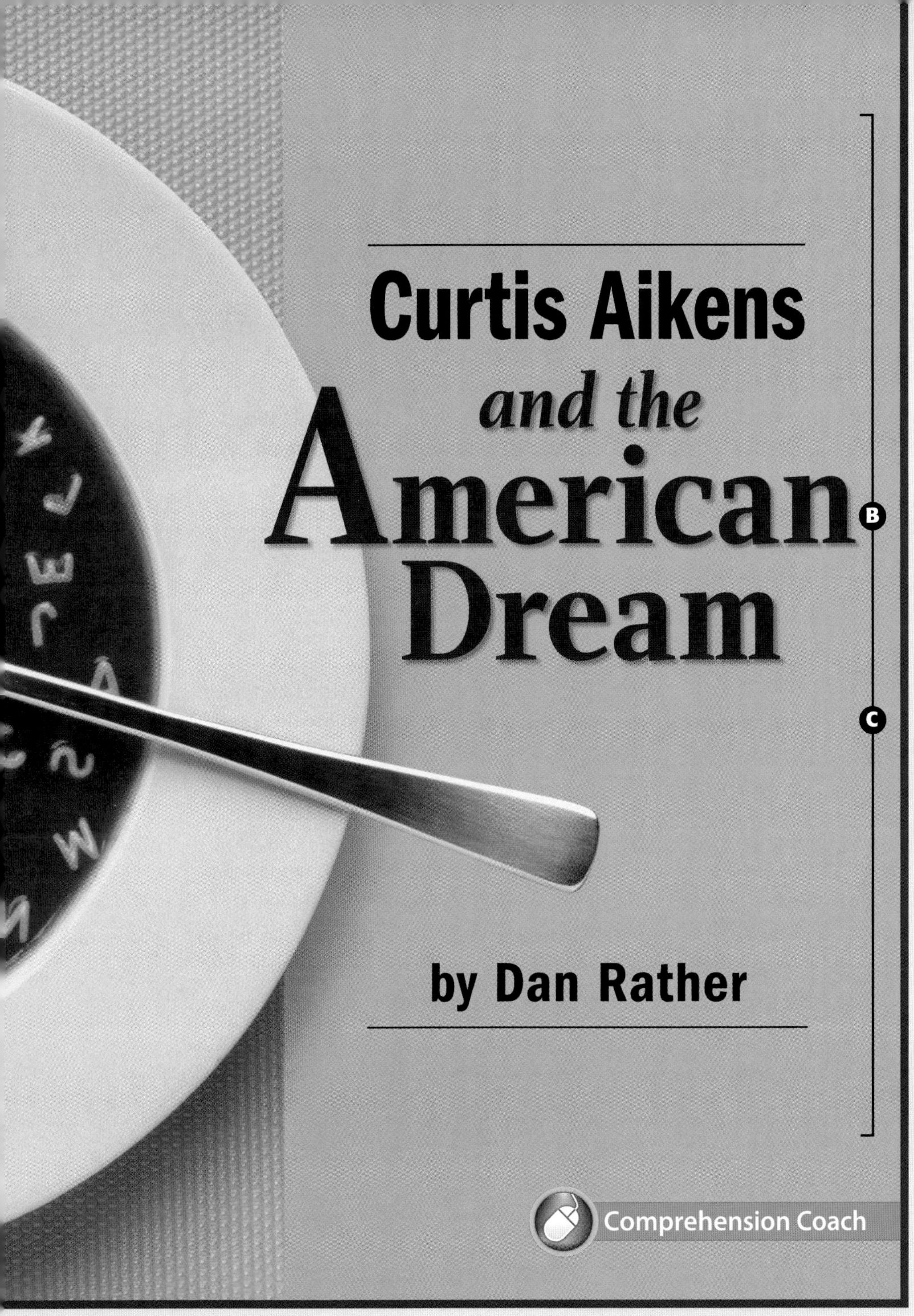

Curtis Aikens *and the* American Dream

by Dan Rather

Comprehension Coach

TEACH & PRACTICE

B Reading Support

The American Dream Discuss the meaning of the term "American dream." Explain that it refers to the idea that with hard work, people who live in America can have anything they dream of having. Ask students what they think Americans dream of having. Display students' ideas in a graphic organizer.

C Analyze Visuals

About the Photo Point out the alphabet soup, and have students make a connection between the literacy letter on p. 316 and the image.

ELL Cultural Background Some students may not be familiar with alphabet soup:

- Explain that the alphabet letters are made from pasta and can be eaten.
- Explain that alphabet soup is a popular food in the United States, especially with children.

Interpret and Respond Ask: How does this photo symbolize illiteracy?

Possible response:

- *When you can't read, written words look unconnected, like they do in the soup.*

Comprehension Coach

Build Reading Power

Assign students to use the software, based on their instructional needs.

Read Silently
- Comprehension questions with immediate feedback
- Glossary support
- Review text evidence

RI.9-10.10

Listen
- Professional model of fluent reading

Record
- Oral reading fluency practice
- Ongoing fluency assessment with immediate feedback

CCSS Literacy.RI.9-10.10 By the end of grade 9, read and comprehend literary nonfiction in the grades 9–10 text complexity band proficiently, with scaffolding as needed at the high end of the range. By the end of grade 10, read and comprehend literary nonfiction at the high end of the grades 9–10 text complexity band independently and proficiently.

READ

OBJECTIVES

Vocabulary
- Key Vocabulary (T)
- Strategy: Use Contextual Analysis (idioms)

Reading Strategy
- Ask Questions: Self-Question

Comprehension & Critical Thinking
- Use Text Evidence (T)

Literary Analysis
- Analyze Text Structure: Chronology (T)

TEACH & PRACTICE

(A) Reading Support

Vocabulary Read the introduction aloud. Work with students to paraphrase "would have disappeared completely."

Possible response:
- *He would have failed.*

Read Have students read pp. 318–328. Support and monitor their comprehension using the reading support provided.
RI.9-10.10

(B) Reading Support

1 Text Structure: Chronology
Review the main events of Curtis's biography. Point out where the main action begins.

ELL Use Graphic Organizer
Record the main events in a time line to help students keep track of the selection's chronology:

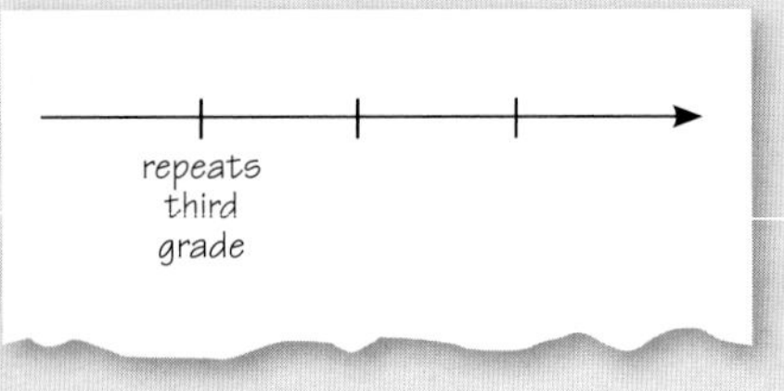

Ask: When do the main events of the biography start?

Possible response:
- *when Curtis is in the third grade*
RI.9-10.5

Hiding the Truth

(A) Curtis Aikens puts a face to **statistics about literacy** that we hear but sometimes cannot believe: he went through high school and five semesters of college without learning how to read or write, one of millions of Americans who **fall through the cracks and keep falling**. Curtis believes today that he would have disappeared completely if he hadn't, at age twenty-six, finally asked for help. Now, at age forty-one, he's **molded himself into a celebrity chef**, with three cookbooks to his name and his own show on the Food Network. Of his literacy tutors, he says, "They didn't change my life, they *saved* my life."

Elementary School Days

Conyers, Georgia, was a small rural town when Curtis was growing up, but he says his parents always encouraged their children to think beyond the way their lives were then.

(B) In the third grade, Curtis made a decision that would determine the course of his life. As he sat through a parent-teacher conference, he heard his teacher praise him: "'I just love having your boy in my class,'" Curtis remembers her saying. "'He's a great kid, he's sweet,' and then I heard a 'but.' And I thought, 'Oh no. What's this? But he's dumb? He's stupid?'" Well, no. She didn't say anything close to that, but she did say that he had some reading trouble, and she thought it would be best for him to repeat the third grade. 1

1 Text Structure: Chronology
When do the main events of Curtis's story start? How do you know?

Key Vocabulary
literacy *n.*, ability to read and write

In Other Words
statistics about literacy studies showing numbers of people who cannot read
fall through the cracks and keep falling have problems but never get the help they need
molded himself into a celebrity chef turned himself into a famous cook on television

DIFFERENTIATED INSTRUCTION

Interactive Reading As you conduct the interactive reading session with students, adjust your teaching strategies to their needs.

Struggling Readers

Picture the Text Show visually how key ideas relate. Pause after each major choice that Curtis makes and complete a choice-and-consequence diagram. For example:

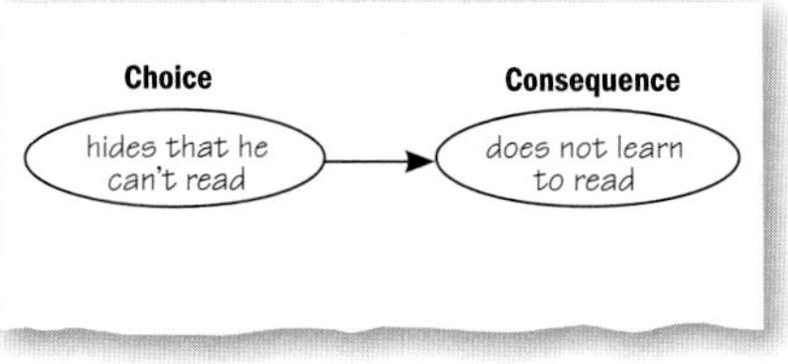

English Language Learners ELL

Rephrase Idioms Remind students that idioms are phrases that have a meaning that is different from the meaning of each individual word.

For example:
puts a face to is an example of

Challenge

Make Real-World Connections As students read Curtis's biography, have them make connections to their own choices and consequences.

CCSS Literacy.RI.9-10.5 Analyze in detail how an author's ideas or claims are developed and refined by particular sentences, paragraphs, or larger portions of a text (e.g., a section or chapter). Literacy.RI.9-10.10 By the end of grade 9, read and comprehend literary nonfiction in the grades 9-10 text complexity band proficiently, with scaffolding as needed at the high end of the range. By the end of grade 10, read and comprehend literary nonfiction at the high end of the grades 9-10 text complexity band independently and proficiently.

"I was shocked. I was floored. **2** I'm thinking to myself, 'Well, I'm not gonna let anyone ever call me dumb or stupid again.' So instead of learning to read, I learned to hide the fact that I couldn't read." **C**

Bad choice, as Curtis would find out. Faking it took a good deal more effort than if he had simply asked for help. As he grew older, he felt that if anyone found out his secret, the label "stupid, dumb" would be much bigger and harder to shake. So he dug himself deeper and deeper into a hole.

I learned to hide the fact that I COULDN'T READ.

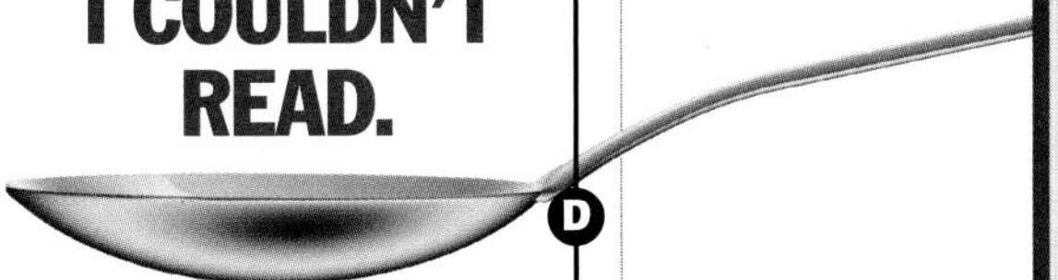

We've all heard of children graduating from high school, and even going on to college, with little or no reading and writing skills, and most often it is the schools that get blamed. Curtis, however, **declines to point a finger, except at himself**. Most of his teachers, he feels, were ready to give him a hand if he asked. But they were also completely fooled by what Curtis calls "the tricks of the trade." The trade, in this case, was about **conning** everyone. "I had two things going for me," the younger Curtis realized. "I remembered stuff—I had pretty much total recall—and I had a likeable personality." **3** **D**

"One of the things I remember thinking about was, if you sound smart, people think you're smart. So I had this great **facade** of being this smart, confident boy." He says he built his vocabulary and **charisma** by watching TV and listening to recordings of great black entertainers—Flip Wilson, Richard Pryor, Bill Cosby, Redd Foxx, Sidney Poitier. They used big words, they were likeable, and they projected the confidence that Curtis needed to **pull off his scam**. And, Curtis adds,

2 Language
The phrase "I was floored" is an idiom. Find clues that tell you what it means. Where do you think this expression comes from?

3 Ask Questions
Pause here. Think of a *what* question that will help you understand this paragraph. Record it in your Question-Answer Chart.

Monitor Comprehension

Explain
What secret does Curtis hide? Why doesn't he ask someone for help?

In Other Words

declines to point a finger, except at himself only blames himself
conning fooling
facade fake appearance
charisma charm
pull off his scam make people believe he could read

TEACH & PRACTICE

C Reading Support

2 Language Explain that in many cases, we can figure out the meaning of an idiom by studying the words and phrases around it. Work with students to identify clues.

ELL Demonstrate Demonstrate how people look when they are "shocked."

Ask: What clues tell you what the phrase "I was floored" means? Where do you think the expression comes from?

Possible responses:
- *"I was shocked" is a clue. It means, "I was surprised."*
- *It comes from being so surprised that you fall to the floor.*

L.9-10.4

D Reading Support

3 Ask Questions List students' questions. Ask students to answer their questions and tell how their questions helped them to understand the paragraph.

Possible response:
- *What is Curtis's opinion about his teachers? He thinks his teachers would have helped him if he had asked for help.*

Have students add their questions and answers to their Question-Answer Charts.

RI.9-10.1

Monitor Comprehension

Explain Discuss reasons why someone would want to hide a problem.

Possible response:
- *Curtis can't read. He might be embarrassed about asking for help or afraid of letting people down.*

RI.9-10.10

DAILY ROUTINES

Vocabulary

See the Vocabulary and Fluency Routines tab for more information.

Word Wall Display the Key Vocabulary words on a Word Wall. Give students clues for a word, challenging them to guess it in as few clues as possible.

Word Sort Provide categories for sorting:
- Parts of speech
- Similar meanings

Use Graphic Organizer Relate words about people's work lives:

L.9-10.6

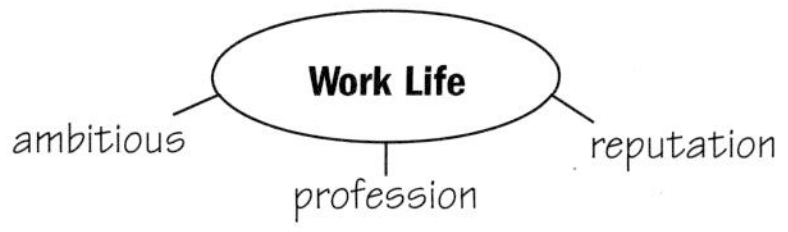

Fluency: Phrasing

CD 11

This cluster's fluency practice uses a passage from "Curtis Aikens and the American Dream" to help students practice appropriate phrasing. Use **Reading Handbook** T749 and the **Fluency Model CD** to teach or review the elements of fluent phrasing, and then use the daily fluency practice activities to develop students' oral reading proficiency.

RI.9-10.10

CCSS **Literacy.RI.9-10.1** Cite strong and thorough textual evidence to support analysis of what the text says explicitly as well as inferences drawn from the text. **Literacy.L.9-10.4** Determine or clarify the meaning of unknown and multiple-meaning words and phrases based on grades 9-10 reading and content, choosing flexibly from a range of strategies. **Literacy.L.9-10.6** Acquire and use accurately general academic and domain-specific words and phrases, sufficient for reading, writing, speaking, and listening at the college and career readiness level; demonstrate independence in gathering vocabulary knowledge when considering a word or phrase important to comprehension or expression.

OBJECTIVES

Vocabulary
- Key Vocabulary Ⓣ
- Strategy: Use Contextual Analysis (unfamiliar words)

Reading Strategy
- Ask Questions: Self-Question

Comprehension & Critical Thinking
- Analyze Information
- Use Text Evidence Ⓣ

Literary Analysis
- Analyze Text Structure: Chronology Ⓣ

Viewing
- Interpret Visuals (information graphics)

Grammar
- Possessive Nouns Ⓣ

TEACH & PRACTICE

Ⓐ Reading Support

4 Text Structure: Chronology Have students look at text, headings, and graphics for clues about Curtis's age.

Possible responses:
- *"went on to high school," "The High School Years," "The game changed in high school," and the student schedule*
- *He's a teenager.*

RI.9-10.5

Ⓑ Analyze Visuals

About the Schedule Have students analyze the format of the schedule, including the headers, and explain how these features make the schedule more clear.

Interpret the Schedule Ask: Which courses are academic and which are electives?

Possible response:
- *Basic math and reading are academics. Home economics, physical education, band, lunch, nutrition, and study hall are electives.*

Have students make an inference about Curtis's school experience. Ask: How would you describe a typical school day for Curtis?

Possible response:
- *Curtis's school day seems pretty undemanding, especially after lunch.*

"When they really wanted to **do the Anglo talk,** they did it."

Most of his grade school teachers **were completely taken**. In the fifth grade, however, Curtis met up with a teacher who wouldn't be fooled. So he adjusted his game plan—he started acting up. He realized that being a pain in the neck was also a sure way to be passed over. Once again, he advanced, and went on to high school with **no one the wiser**. Sadly, Curtis was no wiser himself.

The High School Years

Ⓐ The game changed in high school, with Curtis discovering that a course load **heavy on electives and light on academics**, coupled with athletics and student government, could bring him a diploma. He could do basic math, he could guess at multiple choice. 4

It would have been hard indeed to fail Curtis Aikens: star football player, student council member, winner of a statewide cooking competition (he was the only boy in his **Home Economics class**). And now, though he doesn't blame his teachers, he does have some lessons for them. "Now when I talk to teachers," he explains, "I say, listen, it's not just the bad kids that you gotta worry about. Sometimes it's those sugar sweet kids who are having problems, too, but they're afraid to talk to you about

Ⓑ **Conyers High School 1975–1976 Student Schedule**

Name: **AIKENS, CURTIS**
Student ID: **472344**

Course	Days	Time	Room	Instructor
HOME ECONOMICS	MTWRF	8:15 – 9:05 AM	F35	MORRIS
BASIC MATH	MTWRF	9:10 – 10:00 AM	M122	MCCRACKEN
PHYSICAL EDUCATION	MWF	10:05 – 10:55 AM	GYM	SCHMIDT
BAND	TR	10:05 – 10:55 AM	MUS	BENSON
READING 2	MTWRF	11:00 – 11:50 AM	B17	GOLDBERG
LUNCH	ALL	12:00 – 12:50 PM	CAF	LILLY
NUTRITION	MTWRF	12:55 – 1:45 PM	F38	TAYLOR
STUDY HALL	MTWRF	2:00 – 2:50 PM	LIB	SANTINI

Interpret the Schedule Curtis's course load is "heavy on electives and light on academics." What examples of these can you find on the course schedule?

4 Text Structure: Chronology The biography begins when Curtis is a child. How old is Curtis now? What clues on the page let you know this?

In Other Words

do the Anglo talk talk like many successful white people do
were completely taken never knew he couldn't read
no one the wiser no one knowing the truth
heavy on electives and light on academics filled with easy classes
Home Economics class class that taught students how to cook and sew

GRAMMAR

Possessive Nouns

Teach/Model Display the transparency. Review singular and plural nouns. Then use the example sentences to focus on their possessive forms, stressing the placement of the apostrophe and, when needed, the letter *s*. Also have volunteers name the owner/owners and the thing/things owned.

Practice A. Model the first sentence. Then have students name the owner, tell how to use the apostrophe and *s*, and say the remaining revised sentences aloud. **B.** After partners talk and write their sentences, have each student read one sentence aloud and ask the group to identify the possessive noun. L.9-10.1.b; L.9-10.2.c

Grammar & Writing Practice Book, pp. 103–104

GRAMMAR SKILLS PATH

Grammar Transparency 46

How Do I Show Possession?

GRAMMAR POSSESSIVE NOUNS 46

One Way Is to Use a Possessive Noun.

- Use a **possessive noun** to show that someone owns, or possesses, something. Add **'s** if the possessive noun names one owner.
  - Ms. Gibbs taught the class. **Ms. Gibbs's** class was fun.
  - One **student's** goal was to finish this book.
  - **Dan's** voice trembled as he read aloud.
- A possessive noun can name more than one owner. Follow these rules:
  1. Add only an apostrophe if the plural noun ends in **-s**.
     The **listeners'** applause pleased Dan.
  2. Add **'s** if the plural noun does not end in **-s**.
     Dan saw the **children's** smiles, too.

Try It

A. Turn the underlined words into a possessive noun. Then say each sentence.

1. The story about Curtis makes a point. Curtis's story
2. The struggles of the student were hidden. The student's struggles
3. Curtis cared about the opinions of people. people's opinions
4. He risked the disappointment of his parents by using tricks. his parents' disappointment
5. Records by entertainers gave him confidence. Entertainers' records

B. Now tell a partner more about Curtis's secret. Write two more sentences. Use a possessive noun in each sentence. Sentences will vary.

Curtis's behavior fooled most teachers.

CCSS Literacy.RI.9-10.5 Analyze in detail how an author's ideas or claims are developed and refined by particular sentences, paragraphs, or larger portions of a text (e.g., a section or chapter). **Literacy.L.9-10.1.b** Use various types of phrases (noun, verb, adjectival, adverbial, participial, prepositional, absolute) and clauses (independent, dependent; noun, relative, adverbial) to convey specific meanings and add variety and interest to writing or presentations. **Literacy.L.9-10.2.c** Spell correctly.

it because they have the **reputation** of being a nice kid. That was me. I was that nice kid, who really wanted a teacher to grab him and say, 'What's up?'"

On top of being nice, Curtis was headed for a football scholarship. He remembers a photograph of himself signing his **letter of intent** to Southern University, **ringed by** his beaming family. He was supposed to be the first in the family to graduate from college, and he represented their hopes and dreams. Curtis should have been beaming along with them. "But my face just looked like this sheer face of horror: 'Oh, no. Here I go again. Four more years of having to fake this.'" 5

C

5 Ask Questions
Ask and answer a *why* question to check your understanding of this paragraph. Record the question and answer in your chart.

Facing the Facts

College and Work

The ploys of high school were **evidently not going to play** in college. He barely made it through his first year at Southern, and halfway through his sophomore year, he dropped out. 6

D

6 Access Vocabulary
What is a *ploy*? Look for clues in the text. Then check your guess in a dictionary.

"My dad, he was so heartbroken that I had left college. . . Everybody thought I was supposed to be a success, but no one knew I couldn't read. Not my mom, not my dad, not my brothers and sisters, not my school. And I remember, I wanted to say, 'Dad, you know what, your kid can't read, man. I can't read! I'm just faking.'"

The American dream seemingly out of reach, Curtis thought he could settle for a California dream instead. The Golden State's promise

Key Vocabulary
reputation *n.*, what people think about another person

In Other Words
letter of intent acceptance letter
ringed by surrounded by
evidently not going to play not going to work
The American dream The idea that anyone can succeed through hard work and determination

Monitor Comprehension
Explain
What does Curtis want to tell teachers? Why doesn't he tell them this?

TEACH & PRACTICE

C Reading Support

5 Ask Questions List students' *why* questions. Ask students to read aloud the portion of the text that answers their question.

Possible response:
- *Why did Curtis look horrified? He had to fake being able to read for four more years.*

Have students add their questions and answers to their Question-Answer Charts.
RI.9-10.1

D Reading Support

6 Access Vocabulary Have students identify context clues and guess the meaning of *ploys*.

ELL Use Graphic Organizer Use a graphic organizer to help students identify the ploys Curtis uses to get through high school.

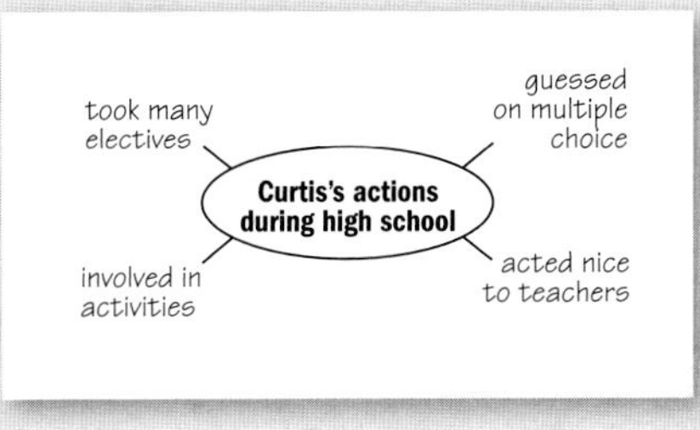

Explain that these actions were meant to hide something, or to trick people.

Possible response:
- *A ploy is a dishonest act, or a trick; clues: "light on academics"; "guess at multiple choice"; "He barely made it through his first year."*

L.9-10.4

Monitor Comprehension

Explain Model a think aloud to explain what Curtis wants to tell teachers and why he does not do this.

MODEL Say:
- *Curtis wants to tell his teachers that he can't read.*
- *If I were in his situation, I would be afraid that my teachers wouldn't think as well of me if they found out.*

Have students continue the think aloud to identify more reasons why Curtis doesn't tell his teachers about his problem.
RI.9-10.1

VOCABULARY

Link Vocabulary and Concepts

Ask questions to link Key Vocabulary with the Essential Question.

EQ ESSENTIAL QUESTION:
How can knowledge open doors?

Some possible questions:
- *How can being* **ambitious** *help a person succeed?*
- *What events or circumstances might* **discourage** *a person from trying to succeed?*
- *Do you think that* **fate** *plays a part in a person's success?*
- *Why is* **literacy** *such an important skill to have?*
- *What things does having a good* **reputation** *depend on?*
- *What knowledge do you need in the* **profession** *you are interested in?*

Have students use the Key Vocabulary words in their responses.
L.9-10.6

CCSS **Literacy.RI.9-10.1** Cite strong and thorough textual evidence to support analysis of what the text says explicitly as well as inferences drawn from the text. **Literacy.L.9-10.4** Determine or clarify the meaning of unknown and multiple-meaning words and phrases based on grades 9–10 reading and content, choosing flexibly from a range of strategies. **Literacy.L.9-10.6** Acquire and use accurately general academic and domain-specific words and phrases, sufficient for reading, writing, speaking, and listening at the college and career readiness level; demonstrate independence in gathering vocabulary knowledge when considering a word or phrase important to comprehension or expression.

READ

OBJECTIVES

Vocabulary
- Key Vocabulary Ⓣ
- Content Area Vocabulary: Economics

Reading Strategy
- Ask Questions; Review Strategies

Comprehension & Critical Thinking
- Use Text Evidence Ⓣ

Literary Analysis
- Analyze Text Structure: Chronology Ⓣ

Viewing
- Respond to and Interpret Visuals

Grammar
- Possessive Adjectives: *My, Our,* Etc. Ⓣ

TEACH & PRACTICE

A Reading Support

7 Text Structure: Chronology Have students list the events Curtis describes. Discuss how they lead to his next decision. Ask: What happens after Curtis leaves college?

Possible responses:
- *His family is disappointed in him.*
- *His dreams are fading.*
- *He goes to California and gets a job in a grocery store.*

RI.9-10.5

B Reading Support

8 Ask Questions List students' *wh-* questions. Ask volunteers for answers.

ELL Sentence Frames Provide sentence frames to help students formulate *wh-* questions:
- ______ does Curtis not get along with?
- ______ does Curtis decide to start a produce company?
- ______ doesn't Curtis write his idea?

Possible responses:
- *Why does Curtis decide to start a produce company? It was the first idea he thought of.*
- *Why doesn't he write his idea? He didn't know how to write the words.*

Have students add their questions and answers to their Question-Answer Charts.

RI.9-10.1

GRAMMAR SKILLS PATH

46	Possessive Nouns
▶ 47	Possessive Adjectives: *My, Our,* Etc. ELL Language & Grammar Lab
48	Possessive Pronouns: *Mine, Ours,* Etc.
49	Reflexive Pronouns
50	Review: Possessive Words

A of **rebirth had strong appeal**, and with both San Diego and the San Francisco Bay area tugging on him, he flipped a coin to decide. His **fate** settled, he headed north and got a job in a grocery store. 7

B Life should have been much easier than it was in school. Curtis says he had little trouble telling the difference between smooth and chunky peanut butter, between two-percent and nonfat milk. It was all in the packaging. But his manager turned out to be one of the few people he wasn't able to win over, and the two fought constantly. After one particularly bad argument, he went home to plot a new course. When he got there, he did something strange.

"I got a pad and paper like I could write something. I don't know why I took it out, but that's what smart people do. They write down their ideas. This is one of the things I'd learned—that smart people write down their ideas. And the first idea that came to my head was to start a **produce company**. I wrote the number one down. But I never wrote the idea out. I didn't know how in the world to write that." 8

I DIDN'T KNOW HOW in the world to write that.

His idea was to go into a business that he could run on, as he says, "a handshake and a smile," with a minimum of letters. He'd noticed buyers from restaurants coming in for produce. He could do that. He could selectively pick produce from **wholesalers** and deliver it to restaurants. He knew little about produce, but he knew plenty about talking to people. The grocers at the produce market were happy to share:

7 Text Structure: Chronology What is life like for Curtis after leaving college? What decision does he make next?

8 Ask Questions Use *wh-* questions to check your understanding of Curtis's actions after he leaves school. Make notes in your Question-Answer Chart.

Key Vocabulary
fate *n.*, the future that will happen

In Other Words
rebirth had strong appeal a new beginning seemed like a good idea
produce company company that sells fruits and vegetables
wholesalers other companies that sell things in large amounts

---

GRAMMAR

Possessive Adjectives: *My, Our,* Etc.

Teach/Model Display the transparency. Read the examples and point out that the possessive adjectives *my, his,* and *their* refer to *I, Carlos,* and *students*. Refer to the chart for support. Elicit that *my* describes *friend, his* describes *stories,* and *their* describes *opinion*. Discuss the next examples and draw an arrow from *his* back to *Carlos*, and from *her* back to *she*.

Practice A. Underline the correct word as students read aloud. Have students name the word that each possessive adjective refers to. **B.** After the class starts the reaction paragraph, have students write three more sentences and read one aloud. L.9-10.1.b

Grammar & Writing Practice Book, pp. 105–106

Grammar Transparency 47

GRAMMAR POSSESSIVE ADJECTIVES: MY, OUR, ETC. 47

What's a Possessive Adjective?

It's an Ownership Word.

- Use a **possessive adjective** to tell who has or owns something. Put the possessive adjective before the **noun**.
  - I like Carlos. He is **my friend**.
  - **His stories** tell about real life.
  - Several students at the library listened to one of Carlos's stories.
  - What was **their opinion** of it?
- Match the possessive adjective to the **noun** or **pronoun** that it goes with.
  - **Carlos** (noun) told a story about **his** mother.
  - **She** (pronoun) worked hard. **Her** life was not easy.

Subject Pronoun	Possessive Adjective
I	my
you	your
he	his
she	her
it	its
we	our
they	their

Try It

A. Tell about Curtis. Use the correct form.

Curtis still could not read. **(He / His)** problem remained a secret. Mr. and Mrs. Aikens were proud parents, and **(they / their)** hopes for Curtis were high. Curtis hoped to be the first person in **(her / his)** family to graduate from college. College proved impossible for him, though. **(It / Its)** demands were just too great.

B. Now let's write a reaction to "Hiding the Truth." Add three more sentences. Use three possessive adjectives. Sentences will vary.

I think that many people might act like Curtis did. Their ability to talk hides the truth.

CCSS **Literacy.RI.9-10.1** Cite strong and thorough textual evidence to support analysis of what the text says explicitly as well as inferences drawn from the text. **Literacy.RI.9-10.5** Analyze in detail how an author's ideas or claims are developed and refined by particular sentences, paragraphs, or larger portions of a text (e.g., a section or chapter). **Literacy.L.9-10.1.b** Use various types of phrases (noun, verb, adjectival, adverbial, participial, prepositional, absolute) and clauses (independent, dependent; noun, relative, adverbial) to convey specific meanings and add variety and interest to writing or presentations.

"These guys taught me everything about buying mushrooms and onions and tomatoes. It was like being in the college of fruits and vegetables."

Curtis even developed a **microlanguage of produce** to help him deal with crates. He learned to recognize that two Ps meant the box contained apples, two Ts meant lettuce. An apex followed by a vertex, AV, stood for avocados. Curtis couldn't sound out the letters, but he didn't make many mistakes.

A Interpret the Graphic
Use the visual details to help you comprehend the language. What does Curtis use to identify what is inside crates?

C

At the wholesale end, he couldn't have run his business without trust. He could pretend to read **an invoice** but ultimately had to believe that it was right. To pay the wholesalers, he usually had to leave a blank check: "There's no way I could have pulled off my scam if I had to write a check to [for example] Crescent Produce. I couldn't spell 'crescent,'" Curtis recalls, adding, "but every single **purveyor** had become a friend. They wanted to help me, they wanted me to succeed. They trusted me and I had to trust them." 9

D

9 Ask Questions
What questions will deepen your understanding of this part of the selection? Record them in your Question-Answer chart.

As Curtis says, he could have **strung this tiny enterprise along indefinitely** as long as it remained tiny. But he soon found himself with seven employees, serving seventy-five **accounts**. The larger companies in the business started to **take notice**. They could afford to lower their prices. Curtis couldn't, and more quickly than it had grown, his business crumbled.

Monitor Comprehension

Describe
How does Curtis's business succeed even when he cannot read?

In Other Words

microlanguage of produce special way to read the boxes of fruits and vegetables
an invoice a bill
purveyor seller
strung this tiny enterprise along indefinitely kept his small business going forever
accounts customers, companies he worked with
take notice pay attention, know about

TEACH & PRACTICE

C Analyze Visuals

About the Graphic Explain that the photo shows a wooden crate in which fruits and vegetables are shipped. Guide students in using the surrounding language in order to understand the word.

Interpret the Graphic Review the text to remind students of the clues Curtis uses to decipher words.

Possible response:
- *He uses two Ps for apples, 2 Ts for lettuce, and the points on the AV for avocados.*

D Reading Support

9 Ask Questions Work with students to form several questions about the selection. List them and have students choose the most effective ones.

Possible responses:
- *What happens when Curtis starts to succeed?*
- *How does his inability to read affect his business?*

Have students add their questions and answers to their Question-Answer Charts.
RI.9-10.1

Review Strategies Have partners say what other strategies they used as they read the text.

Possible response:
- *I read the description of the words on the crate and visualized what they looked like to Curtis. This helped me to understand how difficult it must have been for Curtis to run his business without revealing his secret.*
RI.9-10.10

Monitor Comprehension

Describe Have students describe the success that Curtis has. They can read aloud the lines from the text that support their answer.

Possible responses:
- *Curtis is good at talking to people.*
- *Curtis avoids any situations that require reading or writing.*
- *Curtis has clients he can trust.*
RI.9-10.1

VOCABULARY

Content Area Vocabulary: Economics

ECONOMICS

Build vocabulary related to the content area of business/economics.

Teach/Model Use the Make Words Your Own routine (see *the Vocabulary tab*) and the sample sentences below to introduce these words from the selection.

buyers (bī-urz) ▸ p. 322

Buyers *were unhappy with the quality of the produce.*

manager (**ma**-ni-jur) ▸ p. 322

The ***manager*** *who ran the store didn't get along well with Curtis.*

company (**kum**-pu-nē) ▸ p. 322

A ***company*** *is a group of people who work together.*

business (**biz**-nus) ▸ pp. 322, 323

If you have a ***business****, you buy or sell goods or services.*

check (chek) ▸ p. 323

A ***check*** *is a piece of paper that tells the bank to take money from your bank account.*

employees (im-**ploi-ēz**) ▸ p. 323

The people who work for a business are the ***employees****.*

Practice Have students use the words to describe a business they know.

Apply Set up a business scenario and have students role-play the employees and owner.
L.9-10.6

CCSS **Literacy.RI.9-10.10** By the end of grade 9, read and comprehend literary nonfiction in the grades 9–10 text complexity band proficiently, with scaffolding as needed at the high end of the range. By the end of grade 10, read and comprehend literary nonfiction at the high end of the grades 9–10 text complexity band independently and proficiently. **Literacy.L.9-10.6** Acquire and use accurately general academic and domain-specific words and phrases, sufficient for reading, writing, speaking, and listening at the college and career readiness level; demonstrate independence in gathering vocabulary knowledge when considering a word or phrase important to comprehension or expression.

READ

OBJECTIVES

Reading Strategy
- Ask Questions: Self Question

Comprehension & Critical Thinking
- Use Text Evidence Ⓣ

Literary Analysis
- Analyze Text Structure: Chronology Ⓣ

TEACH & PRACTICE

Ⓐ Reading Support

10 **Text Structure: Chronology** Point out the phrase "at the same time" as a way of determining chronology. Ask: What events made Curtis realize that his literacy problem was serious?

Possible responses:
- *His business crumbled.*
- *He was driving and could not read the road signs.*
- *He was in the airport and could not read the monitors with flight times.*

Have students evaluate the method of development. Ask: What is the effect of telling the reader that these things happened at the same time?

Possible response:
- *It shows the dramatic effect that Curtis's illiteracy was having on his life.* RI.9-10.5

Curtis Aikens works with businesses and organizations around the U.S. to promote literacy.

Reaching Out for Help

Ⓐ At the same time, Curtis was feeling the **undertow of his illiteracy**. Driving across the country, he found himself stuck on the side of the road, unsure if he was headed in the right direction, simply because he couldn't read the word "Arkansas." In the airport, he found himself staring at the **arrival and departure monitors** until he got the courage to ask someone where his connecting flight was. The world started to look like a very limited place. 10

Deep in debt, with all his employees let go, Curtis seldom left his apartment except to **service** his few remaining accounts or work his part-time job: "You don't date anyone when you don't feel good about yourself. You don't really have friends to **socialize** with. . . . So a bag of chips and a Coke and my television were my friends." One night, a **public service announcement from Literacy Volunteers of America**

10 Text Structure: Chronology When does Curtis finally realize that not being able to read is a problem? What makes him realize it?

In Other Words

undertow of his illiteracy effects of not being able to read and write
arrival and departure monitors TV screens that show when planes land and take off
service work on
socialize spend time
public service announcement from Literacy Volunteers of America TV commercial about an organization that teaches people how to read

OUT-OF-SCHOOL LITERACY

Household Literacy

Help students understand the meaning of the selection by connecting it with prior authentic literacy experiences in English, such as reading a recipe from a cookbook.

"Easy Chocolate Chip Cookies"

2 cups	flour
1 1/2 cups	sugar
1/2 bag	chocolate chips
2 sticks	butter, melted
2 eggs	

Combine ingredients, mix well.
Grease cookie sheet.
Preheat oven to 350 degrees.
Spoon-drop cookies onto cookie sheet, and bake at 350 degrees for 8 to 10 minutes.

Ask these questions to demonstrate how literacy is important in daily life:

- What do you need 1 1/2 cups of? (*sugar*) What might happen if you put in 1 1/2 cups of salt?
- What do you need to do with the butter? (*melt it*) What might happen if you froze it instead?
- How do you need to prepare the cookie sheet? (*grease it*) What might happen if you skip this step because you can't read it?

Brainstorm with students other household activities that require reading instructions, such as using cleaning products. What might be the consequences of trying to do these activities without being able to read? SL.9-10.1.a

CCSS **Literacy.RI.9-10.5** Analyze in detail how an author's ideas or claims are developed and refined by particular sentences, paragraphs, or larger portions of a text (e.g., a section or chapter). **Literacy.SL.9-10.1.a** Come to discussions prepared, having read and researched material under study; explicitly draw on that preparation by referring to evidence from texts and other research on the topic or issue to stimulate a thoughtful, well-reasoned exchange of ideas.

came on that spoke directly to Curtis: "It said, 'Don't be ashamed, don't be embarrassed. We can teach you how to read.'" And, Curtis adds, they knew the secret to getting him to make that call when they said: "'And we won't tell anybody.'" 11

He was hooked up with a husband-and-wife team he only remembers as "Steve and Ginny." Steve was a student, Ginny a nurse. They were the first people Curtis felt he could tell his secret to: "It was like the world was lifted off my shoulders when I said 'You know what? I can't read, and I want to be able to read.' To be able to say that to somebody and not have them laugh or pick at me or think I was dumb or stupid . . . was my biggest fear, and they didn't do it." 12

11 Ask Questions The ad for the literacy organization says, "And we won't tell anybody." What questions will help you understand this more fully? Record them in your chart.

12 Ask Questions Ask questions to understand more about Curtis's tutors. Record the questions in your chart.

Sharing the Lessons

Building a New Life

Curtis flew through the literacy training program, in part, he was told, because he already had a large vocabulary. But he could also feel the way his life was about to change, and that, more than anything, **impelled him forward**. He says he now reads about a book a week and has read maybe close to a thousand books since he learned how it's done. He carries a **laptop** with him on his frequent trips. He enjoys a laugh every time a conversation turns to books because he can participate without faking it.

On the surface, Curtis's life changed little. He didn't tell anyone that he had just learned how to read—it was still **a stigma**. After a few years in New York, working for a market that **catered to upscale** restaurants,

Monitor Comprehension

Describe
How does literacy change Curtis's life?

In Other Words
impelled him forward made him continue, motivated him
laptop light, moveable computer
a stigma something he was ashamed of
catered to upscale sold things to expensive

TEACH & PRACTICE

B Reading Support

11 Ask Questions Discuss with students the feelings Curtis had about not being able to read. Then ask students what kinds of questions might help them understand the importance of the ad saying "And we won't tell anybody."

Possible responses:
- *Why is it important to people who can't read that others not find out?*
- *If I couldn't read, how would I feel about others knowing?*

Discuss possible answers to these questions.
RI.9-10.1

C Reading Support

12 Ask Questions Reread paragraph 2. Then ask students what else they would like to understand about the tutors.

Possible responses:
- *How did the tutors help him to learn so quickly?*
- *What made the tutors interested in literacy?*

Have students add to the Question-Answer Charts they began on p. 315.
RI.9-10.1

Monitor Comprehension

Describe Review what problems Curtis faced with illiteracy. Ask: How does being able to read and write change Curtis's life?

ELL Use Graphic Organizer Display responses in a graphic organizer. For example:

Before Literacy	After Literacy
can't read or write	reads a book every week
feels ashamed	feels proud
uses tricks to fool people	doesn't have to fake

Possible responses:
- *Curtis reads constantly and uses a laptop.*
- *He can enjoy talking about books.*
RI.9-10.10

CCSS **Literacy.RI.9-10.1** Cite strong and thorough textual evidence to support analysis of what the text says explicitly as well as inferences drawn from the text. **Literacy.RI.9-10.10** By the end of grade 9, read and comprehend literary nonfiction in the grades 9-10 text complexity band proficiently, with scaffolding as needed at the high end of the range. By the end of grade 10, read and comprehend literary nonfiction at the high end of the grades 9-10 text complexity band independently and proficiently.

READ

OBJECTIVES

Vocabulary
- Key Vocabulary Ⓣ

Reading Strategy
- Ask Questions: Self-Question

Comprehension & Critical Thinking
- Use Text Evidence Ⓣ

Literary Analysis
- Analyze Text Structure: Chronology Ⓣ

Research Skills
- Gather and Use Information; Evaluate and Draw Conclusions

Grammar
- Possessive Pronouns: *Mine, Ours,* Etc. Ⓣ

TEACH & PRACTICE

Ⓐ Reading Support

13 Text Structure: Chronology Ask students to find the sentence that tells when Curtis went back to Georgia. Have them find two things he did after he went back. Ask them to point out the sequence words they used as clues.

Possible responses:
- *once, before, now, eventually*

ELL Rephrase Language Explain that the idiom "sold himself" means that he made himself look good to the editor.

Ask: What are two things that Curtis does after returning to Georgia?

Possible response:
- *He starts a produce company and studies French.*

RI.9-10.5

Ⓑ Reading Support

14 Ask Questions Ask: What questions will help you understand what Curtis is doing?

Possible responses:
- *Why does Curtis want to help others?*
- *How does his honesty about his problem help him reach his goal?*

Have students add their questions and answers to their Question-Answer Charts.

RI.9-10.1

GRAMMAR SKILLS PATH
46 Possessive Nouns
47 Possessive Adjectives: *My, Our,* Etc.
▶ 48 Possessive Pronouns: *Mine, Ours,* Etc. ELL Language & Grammar Lab
49 Reflexive Pronouns
50 Review: Possessive Words

Ⓐ he returned to Georgia. Once back in Conyers, he started a produce company with his family and took French lessons. Before he could read, he says, his confidence was just for show. Now it was brimming over, looking for **an outlet**.

Eventually, he sold himself as a **food columnist** to the editor of the local paper. He wrote his first column on how to pick the perfect fig. 13

13 **Text Structure: Chronology** What are two things Curtis does *after* he goes back to Georgia?

Helping Others

Ⓑ As his writing developed, Curtis started to see how he could use it as a **platform for** more than just his ideas about produce. He decided to become a celebrity, to help those who couldn't read. Curtis knew enough about the game to use his connections. He called an old high school friend who was then in theater in Atlanta, and told her everything: how he fooled her and everyone else, how he finally learned to read and write, and why he wanted to get on television. His tearful **confession** moved her to call and write every station in Atlanta, and one called back. 14

14 **Ask Questions** What *wh*–questions will help you fully understand what Curtis is doin[g] here? Record the questions in your chart.

. . . he FOOLED her and everyone else . . .

The personality he had developed to hide his illiteracy made him perfect for television. He was outgoing, funny, **somewhat self-effacing**. His appearances kept getting longer and went out to larger audiences, especially after he published his first cookbook. His audiences were growing, as was his confidence. But it took years before he could muster the courage to confess his own illiteracy on camera. He finally talked

Key Vocabulary
confession *n.*, something you say about a thing you have kept private or secret

In Other Words
an outlet a new way to use and express itself
food columnist person who writes about food
platform for way to tell others about
somewhat self-effacing and sometimes made fun of himself

326 Unit 4 Opening Doors

GRAMMAR

Possessive Pronouns: *Mine, Ours,* Etc.

Teach/Model Display the transparency. Use the chart to review the possessive adjectives and teach possessive pronouns. Read the sentences aloud, one row at a time. Point out the difference between the use of possessive adjectives and possessive pronouns. Invite students to provide more examples.

Practice A. Have students name the possessive pronoun that can replace the underlined words. Read each new sentence aloud. **B.** After partners talk and write their own sentences, have each student read one pair of sentences aloud, and ask the group to identify the possessive pronoun. L.9-10.1

Grammar & Writing Practice Book, pp. 107–108

Grammar Transparency 48

GRAMMAR POSSESSIVE PRONOUNS: MINE, OURS, ETC. 48

What Are the Possessive Pronouns?

Mine, Yours, His, Hers, Ours,* and *Theirs

Possessive Adjectives	my	your	his	her	our	their
Possessive Pronouns	mine	yours	his	hers	ours	theirs

Possessive adjectives are used before a **noun**. **Possessive pronouns** stand alone.

All **my books** are here.	All the books here are **mine**.
My brother likes mysteries. These are **his books**.	This book is **his**.
My sister reads magazines. These are **her magazines**.	These magazines are **hers**.
Our reviews are published in the newspaper.	The review in today's paper was **ours**.
Other people share **their opinions**.	Do our opinions match **theirs**?

Try It

A. **Say each sentence. Change the underlined words to the correct possessive pronoun.**

1. After Curtis could read, new dreams became his dreams. his
2. Curtis thought, "I don't know other people's futures, but my future is shining brightly." mine
3. Reading is a gift, and it is a gift for you. Can it be our gift, too? yours, ours

B. **Now write about a favorite book or character. Write three pairs of sentences. Use three possessive pronouns.** Sentences will vary.

CCSS **Literacy.RI.9-10.1** Cite strong and thorough textual evidence to support analysis of what the text says explicitly as well as inferences drawn from the text. **Literacy.RI.9-10.5** Analyze in detail how an author's ideas or claims are developed and refined by particular sentences, paragraphs, or larger portions of a text (e.g., a section or chapter). **Literacy.L.9-10.1.** Demonstrate command of the conventions of standard English grammar and usage when writing or speaking.

a producer into doing **a segment** on illiteracy, and he felt he was ready to let the world know that he had learned to read in his twenty-sixth year. He did it on *The Home Show* on ABC, as a guest host with Sarah Purcell. 15

"We were doing a story on how television can help people learn to read. It was about using **closed captioning**. And I actually misread the **teleprompter**. On live television. I actually asked Sarah Purcell a word on TV. . . . I wasn't even thinking about the fact that I asked until two or three seconds after I did it. I broke down and started crying on national TV." There was nothing left to hide, and no way to hide it: "The whole thing just blew up."

Aikens donates part of the profits from his cookbook sales to literacy programs across the country.

15 Text Structure: Chronology
When does Curtis finally feel he's ready to talk about his problem on TV?

Curtis thought he had really screwed up, that no one would listen to him, that his television career was over, and that if the show had reached any illiterate adults, they would only be more convinced to hide their problem. But the opposite was true. Curtis's "screwup" had been one of those moments where television was at its best, where everything was real. The phone lines lit up, at the station and at literacy centers across the country. "It was a great day for literacy," Curtis concludes, without a hint of embarrassment or regret.

His story finished, the TV chef **climbs up on his soapbox**. The only reason he wanted to share all of this is because he has a **cause**: "Illiteracy is a problem that all of America can unite around. It doesn't

Monitor Comprehension
Explain
How is Curtis able to help others in an unexpected way?

Key Vocabulary
cause *n.*, an idea you believe in and are willing to fight for

In Other Words
a segment part of a TV show
closed captioning a feature that shows the words the people on TV are saying
teleprompter script
climbs up on his soapbox tells people about the importance of learning to read

TEACH & PRACTICE

C Reading Support

15 Text Structure: Chronology
Have students locate the sentence on p. 327 that tells when Curtis talked about his problem on TV. Tell them to look back at the previous paragraphs to find out what changed in Curtis's life.

Possible responses:
- *He told a surprised but supportive friend about his problem.*
- *His TV shows were popular.*
- *He was becoming more confident.*

Then ask: How does the chronological text structure help the reader better understand Curtis's progress?

Possible response:
- *It shows how Curtis's confidence developed over time.*

RI.9-10.5

Monitor Comprehension

Explain Ask students how they think someone who could not read might feel if they saw Curtis talking about his struggles on TV. Discuss how his revelation helped others.

Have students explain what Curtis expected to happen after his "screwup," and what happened instead.

Possible response:
- *Curtis thought he had made things worse for illiterate adults. Instead, they were inspired to read and write.*

RI.9-10.10

CONTENT AREA CONNECTIONS

SOCIOLOGY

Research Illiteracy

Conduct Research Have students research statistics about illiteracy in America to answer the following questions:

- How many people graduate from high school without knowing how to read?
- What kinds of jobs are available for people who can't read?
- What programs are there to help adults learn to read?

Have students also find human-interest feature articles about people facing their illiteracy and overcoming it by learning to read and write. How were they able to do it?

Share and Discuss Students can share their findings with the class. Have them convert literacy statistics into a graphic aid. Graphics can be accompanied by a summary of a real-life story of triumph over illiteracy.

W.9-10.7

CCSS **Literacy.RI.9-10.10** By the end of grade 9, read and comprehend literary nonfiction in the grades 9-10 text complexity band proficiently, with scaffolding as needed at the high end of the range. By the end of grade 10, read and comprehend literary nonfiction at the high end of the grades 9-10 text complexity band independently and proficiently. **Literacy.W.9-10.7** Conduct short as well as more sustained research projects to answer a question (including a self-generated question) or solve a problem; narrow or broaden the inquiry when appropriate; synthesize multiple sources on the subject, demonstrating understanding of the subject under investigation.

READ

OBJECTIVES

Reading Strategy
- Ask Questions: Self-Question

Comprehension & Critical Thinking
- Use Text Evidence Ⓣ

Literary Analysis
- Analyze Text Structure: Chronology Ⓣ

Writing
- Form: Response to Literature

TEACH & PRACTICE

Ⓐ Reading Support

16 **Ask Questions** Discuss that *why* and *how* questions usually require deeper responses than *where* and *when* questions. List students' questions and have the class answer them.

Have students complete their Question-Answer Charts.
RI.9-10.1

APPLY

Ⓑ ANALYZE

1. **Explain** After Curtis learns to read, he becomes more confident.
RI.9-10.1
2. **Vocabulary** His confession encouraged others who had similar problems.
L.9-10.6
3. **Analyze Text Structure: Chronology** Have students use their charts to summarize the selection.
RI.9-10.5
4. **Focus Strategy: Ask Questions** Have volunteers share their Question-Answer Charts with the class.
RI.9-10.1

Ⓒ Return to the Text

Students should find facts like these:
- *Curtis could not finish college.*
- *He could not write a note to himself.*

W.9-10.9.b; W.9-10.10

Edge Interactive Practice Book, p. 150

Ⓐ know race, it doesn't know money, it doesn't know **boundaries**. This is one thing we can all get together on." That cause fully and completely contains Curtis's version of the American dream: "I don't get bored anymore, because I can read. I don't get lonely anymore, because I can read. I'm never out of friends anymore, because I can read. But I'm still trying to **obtain the American dream**, because I want to give everybody the ability to read. I know that sounds **hokey**, but there it is." 16 ❖

16 **Ask Questions** What questions help you think deeply about Curtis and the American dream? Record the questions in your chart.

Ⓑ ANALYZE Curtis Aikens and the American Dream

1. **Explain** How does **literacy** change Curtis's life? What kind of power does he gain by learning how to read? Cite evidence from the text to support your answers.
2. **Vocabulary** How does Curtis's **confession** help other people?
3. **Analyze Text Structure: Chronology** This **Sequence Chain** shows some events in Curtis's life in the order that they happened. Add more events, including signal words or phrases to show the order of events.

Sequence Chain

First	Then	Later
Curtis's business fails.	He sees a commercial about adult illiteracy.	

4. **Focus Strategy Ask Questions** Review the **Question-Answer Chart** you began on page 315 and add any answers you may have found. Then put a star by questions that helped you understand the biography. Put an "X" by any questions that weren't so helpful.

Ⓒ **Return to the Text**

Reread and Write Many doors were closed to Curtis because he couldn't read. Reread the section "Facing the Facts" to find and describe several everyday things that Curtis could not do because of his illiteracy.

In Other Words

boundaries the imaginary lines that divide people or things into groups
obtain the American dream make my dreams of success come true
hokey silly and cheerful

CCSS **Literacy.RI.9-10.1** Cite strong and thorough textual evidence to support analysis of what the text says explicitly as well as inferences drawn from the text. **Literacy.RI.9-10.5** Analyze in detail how an author's ideas or claims are developed and refined by particular sentences, paragraphs, or larger portions of a text (e.g., a section or chapter). **Literacy.W.9-10.9.b** Apply grades 9-10 Reading standards to literary nonfiction (e.g., "Delineate and evaluate the argument and specific claims in a text, assessing whether the reasoning is valid and the evidence is relevant and sufficient; identify false statements and fallacious reasoning"). **Literacy.W.9-10.10** Write routinely over extended time frames (time for research, reflection, and revision) and shorter time frames (a single sitting or a day or two) for a range of tasks, purposes, and audiences. **Literacy.L.9-10.6** Acquire and use accurately general academic and domain-specific words and phrases, sufficient for reading, writing, speaking, and listening at the college and career readiness level; demonstrate independence in gathering vocabulary knowledge when considering a word or phrase important to comprehension or expression.

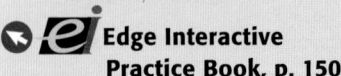

Think You Don't Need an Education?

There are many options for your life after high school. Your education is one choice that makes a big difference—a difference that can add up to millions of dollars over your lifetime.

Here are some of your choices:

Technical/Vocational School
1–2 years for an applied degree or certificate in computers, mechanics, firefighting, etc.

Community/Junior College
(high school diploma required) 2 years for an associate's degree in electronics, healthcare, social work, etc.

College or University
(high school diploma required) 4 years for a bachelor's degree in most fields

Graduate School
(bachelor's degree required) 1–4 years for a master's degree, 4–8 years for a doctorate in most fields

Other
time varies for a professional degree in architecture, law, medicine, etc.

For most people in the United States, education may decide whether or not they will have a job—and how much that job will pay. What is that difference worth to you? Think about it.

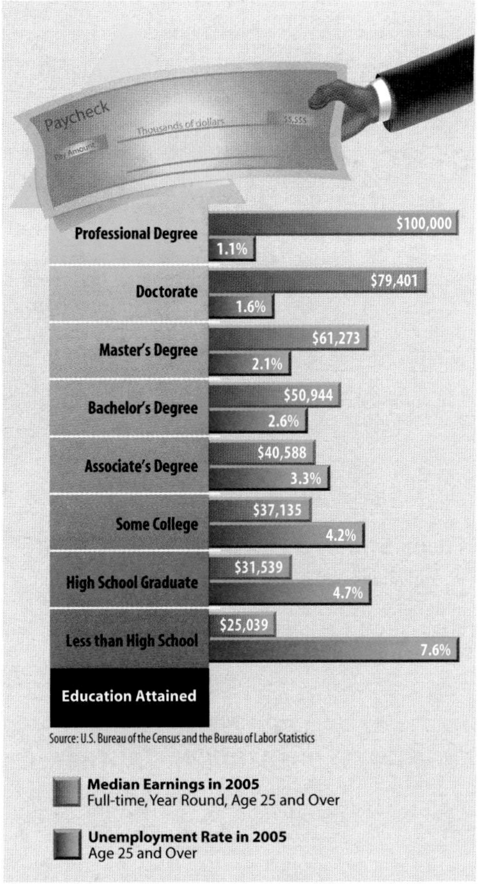

In Other Words
Median Average

Lesson 4, continued

POSTSCRIPT

OBJECTIVES

Reading Strategy
- Make Connections

Literary Analysis
- Analyze Text Features (T)

Viewing
- Interpret Visuals (information graphics)

TEACH & PRACTICE

A Reading Support

Read the Text Aloud Read aloud the descriptions of educational opportunities that students have after high school, pausing to clarify unfamiliar terms.

B Analyze Visuals

Introduce the Graph Explain how to use the graph key and define "Median Earnings" and "Unemployment Rate." Make connections between the labels on the graph and the heads in the text, for example: *If you go to community or junior college, you would have some college. This is where you would look on the graph.*

Ask: What information does the graph show?

Possible response:
- *It shows how education affects how much you earn and how likely it is you will find a good job.*

Interpret the Graph Ask: What inference can you make about the connection between education, salary, and unemployment?

Possible response:
- *The more education you have, the more you will earn and the safer your job will be.*

Connect Across Texts Have students interpret the graph in conjunction with the article about Curtis Aikens. Ask: What do you think Curtis Aikens might say about these numbers?

Possible response:
- *He would agree that educated people are more successful and secure.*

RI.9-10.1; RI.9-10.3

CCSS **Literacy.RI.9-10.1** Cite strong and thorough textual evidence to support analysis of what the text says explicitly as well as inferences drawn from the text. **Literacy.RI.9-10.3** Analyze how the author unfolds an analysis or series of ideas or events, including the order in which the points are made, how they are introduced and developed, and the connections that are drawn between them.

Lesson 5

BEFORE READING

OBJECTIVES

Reading Strategy
• Ask Questions: Question the Author

Literary Analysis
• Analyze Text Features Ⓣ

TEACH STRATEGIES

Ⓐ Analyze Text Features

Introduce Read the introduction to present text features such as visuals, captions, and text boxes. Discuss how authors use each feature to present and clarify information. Have students page through earlier units to identify text features they have seen and used.

Look Into the Text Use the callouts on p. 330 to teach some of the text features of an opinion essay. Ask: How are photos captions, and text boxes helpful in a text?

Possible responses:
- *Photos show readers what the real people and places look like.*
- *Captions describe who is in the photo, where they are, and what they are doing.*
- *Text boxes give more information or clarify important information already in the text.*

RI.9-10.7

Ⓑ Focus Strategy: Ask Questions

Question the Author Define the strategy and work through the steps in the How To box.

Then have partners identify a question they want to ask the author of the essay, based on the photograph in Look Into the Text.

As they read, have students write questions they want to ask the author on the Question the Author Chart.

RI.9-10.1

ONGOING ASSESSMENT
Have students identify and describe text features they use when reading their school textbooks.

BEFORE READING Go For It!

opinion essay by Earvin "Magic" Johnson

Reading Strategies
- Plan and Monitor
- Determine Importance
- Make Inferences
- ▶ **Ask Questions**
- Make Connections
- Synthesize
- Visualize

Analyze Text Features

Nonfiction writers can use many devices to develop and present their ideas. Many writers use a variety of **text features**. These are simple ways to give information clearly and quickly. Some text features include:

- **visuals** such as photographs, drawings, diagrams, charts, and graphs
- **captions** that give more information about the visuals
- **text boxes** that add or highlight information.

Ⓐ

Look Into the Text

This photo shows Magic working with teens at a computer center.

What kinds of information can a photo show easily?

Magic Johnson spends time with students at his computer center in Philadelphia, PA.

A caption explains what is shown in the photo. What information does this caption give?

Focus Strategy ▶ Ask Questions

In nonfiction texts such as opinion essays, the author provides more than just information or facts about a topic. The author also includes his or her beliefs and ideas. As you read this type of writing, **ask questions** to see if you understand the author's opinion.

Ⓑ

Focus Strategy

HOW TO QUESTION THE AUTHOR

1. Read the selection carefully.
2. Use a **Question the Author Chart** to list questions you have about the author and the selection.
3. Find evidence in the text to support your answers. This evidence may be clearly stated, or it may be hinted at in words and phrases.
4. Review your chart to decide if the author effectively gives information, ideas, and opinions.

Question the Author Chart

What is the author's most important message?	Go to college.
How does the author state his beliefs and ideas?	
Why does the author include this detail?	
Does the author change opinions in the selection?	

CCSS Literacy.RI.9-10.1 Cite strong and thorough textual evidence to support analysis of what the text says explicitly as well as inferences drawn from the text. Literacy.RI.9-10.7 Analyze various accounts of a subject told in different mediums (e.g., a person's life story in both print and multimedia), determining which details are emphasized in each account.

OPINION ESSAY

Connect Across Texts

"Curtis Aikens and the American Dream" describes how one person reaches for success by learning. In this essay, what does basketball star Magic Johnson say to people about success in life? (D)

Go For It!

by Earvin "Magic" Johnson
with William Novak

Basketball was my ticket to success. But if I hadn't been good enough at basketball, I would have been successful in something else.

Magic Johnson at the 1992 Olympics in Barcelona, Spain

OBJECTIVES

Reading Strategy
- Make Connections

Listening and Speaking
- Conversation and Classroom Discussion

Cultural Perspectives
- U.S. Culture: Sports Celebrities

BUILD BACKGROUND

C Athletes as Role Models

Discuss with students whether they think professional athletes are good role models for children and teens. Ask: What behaviors of pro athletes make them positive role models? What behaviors make them negative role models?

Read the title of the article and the quotation from Magic Johnson.

> **ELL** **Rephrase Language** Explain that "Basketball was my ticket to success" means "Basketball was my way to find success."

Ask: What do you think Magic Johnson means by this?

Possible response:
- *He was determined to be successful, whether it was because of basketball or something else.*

D Connect Across Texts

Ask students to suppose what Curtis Aikens and Magic Johnson might talk about if they met.

Possible response:
- *They might talk about ways to help convince students to stay in school and get a good education.*

Comprehension Coach

Build Reading Power

Assign students to use the software, based on their instructional needs.

Read Silently
- Comprehension questions with immediate feedback
- Glossary support
- Review text evidence

RI.9-10.10

Listen
- Professional model of fluent reading

Record
- Oral reading fluency practice
- Ongoing fluency assessment with immediate feedback

CCSS **Literacy.RI.9-10.10** By the end of grade 9, read and comprehend literary nonfiction in the grades 9–10 text complexity band proficiently, with scaffolding as needed at the high end of the range. By the end of grade 10, read and comprehend literary nonfiction at the high end of the grades 9–10 text complexity band independently and proficiently.

READ

OBJECTIVES

Vocabulary
- Key Vocabulary Ⓣ

Reading Strategy
- Ask Questions; Review Strategies

Comprehension & Critical Thinking
- Use Text Evidence Ⓣ

Literary Analysis
- Analyze Text Features Ⓣ

Research Skill
- Gather Information

Grammar
- Reflexive Pronouns

TEACH & PRACTICE

Reading Support

Read Have students read pp. 332–334. Support and monitor their comprehension using the reading support provided.
RI.9-10.10

Ⓐ Reading Support

1 Ask Questions Have students identify a sentence that summarizes Johnson's main message. ("Basketball is not the best way to get ahead," "Your chances of playing basketball for a living are minuscule.") Point out that Johnson uses several numbers and statistics to make his point. Suggest asking questions starting with *How many* to better understand Johnson's message.

Possible responses:
- *How many college seniors play ball at any one time?*
- *How many of them make it to the NBA?*

RI.9-10.1

Ⓑ Reading Support

2 Syntax Point out the use of repetition. Point out the sentences that use italics. Explain that italic type and repetition are used to show that the author considers these to be important points in the essay.

Ask volunteers to role-play Johnson as they read the sentences aloud.
RI.9-10.4

Ⓐ I would have gone to college, and worked hard, and made something of myself. You can do that, too. Basketball is not the best way to get ahead. It's probably the most difficult path you could take. There are thirty teams in the **NBA**, and each team has twelve players. That makes 360 players who are in the league at any one time. In a country as big as ours, that's not a big number. There are about 1,800 college seniors who play ball, and only a few of them are good enough to be **drafted**. So even if you're good enough and fortunate enough to play in college, what makes you think you're going to play in the NBA? You have to understand that your chances of playing basketball for a living are **miniscule**. 1

Ⓑ *The black community already has enough basketball players.* And enough baseball players, and football players. But there are a lot of other people we could really use. We need more teachers. We need more lawyers. We need more doctors. We need more accountants. We need more nurses. We need more pilots. And more scientists. And more carpenters. And more professors. And more police officers. And more bankers. And more computer programmers. And more mechanics. And more **social workers**. And more car dealers. And more politicians. 2

We need more teachers . . . And more scientists.

And every single one of these **professions** *—including doctor and lawyer—is easier to get into than the NBA.*

If you can possibly go to college, go! I know it's hard. I know that some kids you know will **discourage** you. If you're **ambitious**, if you

1 Ask Questions
What questions help you fully understand Johnson's message? Record them in your Question the Author Chart.

2 Syntax
How does Johnson's use of repetitive phrases, such as "We need..." affect the tone of the essay?

Key Vocabulary
- **profession** *n.*, job that requires education or training
- **discourage** *v.*, to make someone not want to do something
- **ambitious** *adj.*, having big goals

In Other Words
- **NBA** National Basketball Association
- **drafted** chosen to play on a professional team
- **miniscule** tiny
- **social workers** people who work for a city or state to help other people

GRAMMAR

Reflexive Pronouns

Teach/Model Display the transparency. Use the first set of example sentences to show that reflexive pronouns reflect, or point back, to the subject. Explain the spelling rule for the plural reflexive pronouns (self/selves). Discuss the mistakes. Elicit that *theirselves* and *hisself* do not appear in the chart.

Practice A. Have students explain their pronoun choices and underline the correct answers on the transparency. **B.** After partners talk about career plans and write their own sentences, have each student read his or her best sentence aloud. Ask the group to identify the reflexive pronoun. L.9-10.1

Grammar & Writing Practice Book, pp. 109–110

GRAMMAR SKILLS PATH

46	Possessive Nouns
47	Possessive Adjectives: *My, Our,* Etc.
48	Possessive Pronouns: *Mine, Ours,* Etc.
▶ 49	Reflexive Pronouns ELL Language & Grammar Lab
50	Review: Possessive Words

Grammar Transparency 49

What's a Reflexive Pronoun?

GRAMMAR REFLEXIVE PRONOUNS 49

It's a Word for the Same Person.

- Use a **reflexive pronoun** to talk about the same person or thing twice in a sentence. Reflexive pronouns end in -**self** or -**selves**.

  Luisa treated **herself** to a pro-basketball game with some friends.

  The players prepare **themselves** to compete for their fans.

Reflexive Pronouns	
Singular	**Plural**
myself	ourselves
yourself	yourselves
himself, herself, itself	themselves

- Avoid these common mistakes with reflexive pronouns.
  1. The friends saw ~~theirselves~~ themselves on the big screen.
  2. Bob bought ~~hisself~~ himself a program.

Try It

A. Say the sentence using the correct pronoun.
1. Magic Johnson expresses **(himself / hisself)** clearly.
2. You need to apply **(you / yourself)** to career and educational goals.
3. After all, even professional athletes may hurt **(themselves / theirselves)** and lose a job.
4. Because sports is not a reality for most people, we need to prepare **(ourselves / us)** for a career.
5. I play hockey now, but I will prepare **(myself / herself)** to be a chef.

B. Now tell a partner about career plans you have for yourself. Write three sentences. Use reflexive pronouns. Sentences will vary.

CCSS Literacy.RI.9-10.4 Determine the meaning of words and phrases as they are used in a text, including figurative, connotative, and technical meanings; analyze the cumulative impact of specific word choices on meaning and tone (e.g., how the language of a court opinion differs from that of a newspaper). **Literacy.RI.9-10.10** By the end of grade 9, read and comprehend literary nonfiction in the grades 9-10 text complexity band proficiently, with scaffolding as needed at the high end of the range. By the end of grade 10, read and comprehend literary nonfiction at the high end of the grades 9-10 text complexity band independently and proficiently. **Literacy.L.9-10.1** Demonstrate command of the conventions of standard English grammar and usage when writing or speaking.

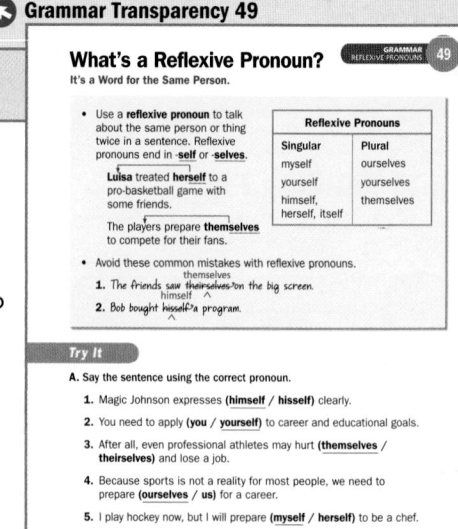

Magic lives up to his name.

Earvin "Magic" Johnson got his nickname in high school after a local sportswriter saw him in action on the basketball court. Johnson went on to play basketball for two years at Michigan State University in East Lansing. Then in 1979, he was drafted by the NBA to play for the Los Angeles Lakers. From there, he went on to make NBA history. He was named to the NBA All-Star team twelve times and was voted both league and NBA Finals Most Valuable Player three times. He retired from the NBA in 1991. Johnson was a member of the USA's famous "Dream Team," which won a gold medal at the 1992 Olympics. He was voted into the Naismith Memorial Basketball Hall of Fame in 2002. **D**

Magic Johnson spends time with students at his computer center in Philadelphia, PA. **3** **C**

His basketball career over, Johnson continues to amaze. He is the head of Magic Johnson Enterprises, a company that tries to bring business to urban areas. It is estimated that he is worth $800 million from his post-basketball activities. But Johnson gives back to the community through his charity, The Magic Johnson Foundation. He provides scholarships and develops community centers and technology training centers. Johnson lives up to his own advice: Go for it! **4** **5** **E**

study hard, if your goals are high, some people may tell you you're "acting white." Stay away from these people! They are not your friends. If the people around you aren't going anywhere, if their dreams are no bigger than hanging out on the corner, or if they're **dragging you down**, get rid of them. Negative people can **sap your energy** so fast, and they can take your dreams from you, too.

3 Text Features
What information do the photo and caption give about Johnson?

4 Text Features
What kind of information does this text box provide? How can you tell that it was not written by Johnson?

5 Ask Questions
What *wh-* questions do you still have for the author of the text box? Record them in your chart.

In Other Words
dragging you down making it harder for you to succeed
sap your energy take away your desire to reach your goals

TEACH & PRACTICE

C Reading Support

3 Text Features Ask students: What can you learn about Johnson from the photo and caption?

Possible response:
- *The photo shows how the people and computer center look. The caption tells where it is.*

RI.9-10.7

D Reading Support

4 Text Features Point out the text box and read aloud the first sentence. Explain that the text is no longer in the first person because it was written by another person. Ask: Why is it included in this selection?

Possible response:
- *It gives more information about Johnson.*

RI.9-10.7

E Reading Support

5 Ask Questions List students' *wh-* questions on the board. Work with students to form *wh-* questions based on information about Johnson's life from the text box.

ELL Sequence Chain Work with students to complete a sequence chain about Magic Johnson's life.

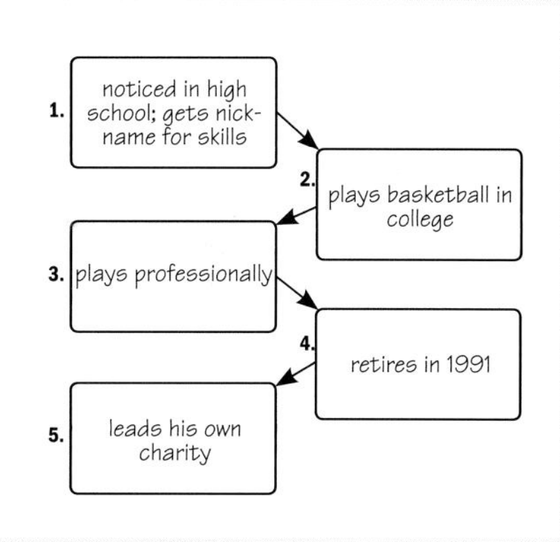

Possible responses:
- *Why is Earvin called "Magic"?*
- *What does Johnson do now?*

RI.9-10.1

Review Strategies Have partners discuss other strategies they used as they read the text.

Possible response:
- *I synthesized the text that mentions Johnson's charity work with the photo and caption. Now, I understand how important charity work is to Johnson since basketball.*

RI.9-10.1

CONTENT AREA CONNECTIONS

Research Professions

Conduct Research Have students research one profession mentioned on p. 332 to answer the following questions:

- How many members are there in this profession?
- How many of these members are black?
- What does this profession do to encourage new black members and to support the black members already there?

Share and Discuss Students can share their findings with the class. Discuss these questions as a class: Do any of these findings surprise you? Why might Magic Johnson want to encourage young African Americans to pursue these professions?

W.9-10.7

CCSS **Literacy.RI.9-10.1** Cite strong and thorough textual evidence to support analysis of what the text says explicitly as well as inferences drawn from the text. **Literacy.RI.9-10.7** Analyze various accounts of a subject told in different mediums (e.g., a person's life story in both print and multimedia), determining which details are emphasized in each account. **Literacy.W.9-10.7** Conduct short as well as more sustained research projects to answer a question (including a self-generated question) or solve a problem; narrow or broaden the inquiry when appropriate; synthesize multiple sources on the subject, demonstrating understanding of the subject under investigation.

READ

OBJECTIVES

Reading Strategy
- Ask Questions: Question the Author

Comprehension & Critical Thinking
- Use Text Evidence Ⓣ

Literary Analysis
- Analyze Text Features Ⓣ

Writing
- Form: Response to Literature

APPLY

Ⓐ ANALYZE

1. **Explain** "The government will not save you. The black leadership will not save you." You are the only one who can make a difference and save yourself.
RI.9-10.1
2. **Vocabulary** Very few people can have a career in basketball. Other professions are easier to get into, and the black community needs more people in those professions.
L.9-10.6
3. **Analyze Text Features** The pictures support the text. Photos of other black professionals might help the reader understand Johnson's opinions.
RI.9-10.7
4. **Focus Strategy: Ask Questions** Sample answer: Yes, the questions helped and I was able to find many of the answers.
RI.9-10.1

Ⓑ Return to the Text

Before they begin writing, encourage students to make a list of things that have helped and distracted them from achieving their goals. Then have them compare the information in the text with their own experience.
W.9-10.9.b; W.9-10.10

I don't mean to tell you it's easy. It's *not* easy. Growing up today is hard. I know that. It's much harder than when I was your age. We've got to quit making excuses. Quit feeling sorry for ourselves. We have to go to college. Think about business. Work hard. Support one another, like other groups do.

The government will not save you.
The black leadership will not save you.
You're the only one who can make the difference.
Whatever your dream is, go for it. ❖

ANALYZE Go For It!

Ⓐ

1. **Explain** What reasons does Magic Johnson give for continuing one's education?
2. **Vocabulary** Why does Johnson **discourage** readers from seeking a career in basketball? What does he say about other **professions**?
3. **Analyze Text Features** Talk with a partner about the photos used in this essay. Explain whether the pictures support the text or add new information. What other photo ideas would you have included to help readers understand Johnson's opinions?
4. **Focus Strategy Ask Questions** Share your **Question the Author Chart** with a small group. Did these questions help you? Were you able to find answers?

Ⓑ

Return to the Text

Reread and Write According to Magic Johnson, there are many things that either help us or distract us from achieving our goals. Find one of these examples in the text and write a paragraph about how this relates to your own experiences with education.

Interactive Reading

Have students reread and mark "Go For It!" within the Edge Interactive Practice Book to apply their knowledge of text features and to practice the Focus Strategy—Ask Questions.

Edge Interactive Practice Book, pp. 151-154

Unit Project

Progress Check Allow time for students to work on their unit projects. Meet with individuals and/or groups to provide guidance and check on their progress.

myNGconnect.com
- **Unit Planning Tools**
- **Unit Project Evaluation Rubric**

CCSS **Literacy.RI.9-10.1** Cite strong and thorough textual evidence to support analysis of what the text says explicitly as well as inferences drawn from the text. **Literacy.RI.9-10.7** Analyze various accounts of a subject told in different mediums (e.g., a person's life story in both print and multimedia), determining which details are emphasized in each account. **Literacy.W.9-10.9.b** Apply grades 9-10 Reading standards to literary nonfiction (e.g., "Delineate and evaluate the argument and specific claims in a text, assessing whether the reasoning is valid and the evidence is relevant and sufficient; identify false statements and fallacious reasoning"). **Literacy.L.9-10.6** Acquire and use accurately general academic and domain-specific words and phrases, sufficient for reading, writing, speaking, and listening at the college and career readiness level; demonstrate independence in gathering vocabulary knowledge when considering a word or phrase important to comprehension or expression. **Literacy.W.9-10.10** Write routinely over extended time frames (time for research, reflection, and revision) and shorter time frames (a single sitting or a day or two) for a range of tasks, purposes, and audiences.

EQ How Can Knowledge Open Doors?

Reading

Critical Thinking

1. **Analyze** Think back to the quotation: "Knowledge is power." Give examples of how Curtis Aikens's experiences and Magic Johnson's opinions support this idea.
2. **Compare** Find evidence in both selections that shows how Aikens and Johnson have used their fame and success to help others.
3. **Interpret** Curtis Aikens says that his literacy coaches "didn't change my life, they *saved* my life." What do you think he means by this? In what way does Magic Johnson try to do the same thing for others?
4. **Speculate** Do you think Curtis Aikens would agree with Magic Johnson that college is the best way to open doors? Explain.
5. **Evaluate** Explain whether the selections give convincing reasons for learning to read and going to college. Describe the ideas that connected most to your own experiences and opinions.

Writing

Write About Literature

Public Service Announcement Watching a public service announcement about **literacy** changed Curtis Aikens's life. Work with a partner to write a public service announcement that encourages high school students to go to a technical school or college. Include information and quotations from both texts to describe how knowledge can open doors to success in the future.

Vocabulary

Key Vocabulary Review

Oral Review Work with a partner. Use these words to complete the paragraph.

ambitious	**discouraged**	**profession**
cause	**fate**	**reputation**
confession	**literacy**	

Last year, my cousin Amy made a __(1)__ about a secret she had hidden for years. "I can't read," she said. "In school, I got a __(2)__ as a lazy student because that's how everyone saw me. This __(3)__ me so much that I didn't want to tell anyone the truth. Now I'll never have a good job or a __(4)__ that I like." After that, Amy and I found a program for adult __(5)__ that taught her to read and write. Soon she saw that her __(6)__ was not set—she is very __(7)__ and filled with big goals for the future. I've also changed because now I have a __(8)__ that I am dedicated to help: I'm working with schools to teach teens how to read!

Writing Application What are some things you can do to earn a good **reputation** with classmates or teachers? Write a paragraph about it. Use at least five Key Vocabulary words.

Fluency

Read with Ease: Phrasing

Assess your reading fluency with the passage in the Reading Handbook, p. 760. Then complete the self-check below.

1. I did/did not pause appropriately for punctuation and phrases.
2. My words correct per minute: _____.

Lesson 6

REFLECT AND ASSESS

OBJECTIVES

Vocabulary
- Key Vocabulary Ⓣ

Reading Fluency
- Phrasing Ⓣ

Comprehension & Critical Thinking
- Compare Across Texts
- Use Text Evidence Ⓣ

Literary Analysis
- Evaluate Literature

Writing
- Mode: Persuasive
- Form: Paragraph

Reading

Critical Thinking

1. **Analyze** Have students make a two-column chart and list examples from both texts. Have students support their examples.
RI.9-10.1
2. **Compare** Aikens donates money to literacy programs and talks about his own struggles. Johnson uses his own money to support business and educational programs.
RI.9-10.1
3. **Interpret** The literacy coaches saved Aikens from a life of limited opportunities. Johnson does the same thing for others by providing scholarships and technology training.
RI.9-10.2
4. **Speculate** Yes, they both agree that a college education is important. A good education is the best way to achieve the American dream.
5. **Evaluate** The selections give convincing reasons for learning to read. Aikens's life got much better after he learned to read. Johnson would not have his two successful careers if he could not read. There are some convincing reasons for going to college, such as increased opportunities.
   - Aikens is never bored or lonely because he can read.
   - A good education helps a person feel confident and successful.

   RI.9-10.8; RI.9-10.10

Writing

Write About Literature

Edge Interactive Practice Book, p. 155

Public Service Announcement
Discuss examples of public service announcements students have seen on television. Have students make a list of facts and quotations from the texts to support the idea that knowledge opens doors to success. Remind them to include these in their public service announcement.
W.9-10.10

Vocabulary

Key Vocabulary Review

1. *confession* 2. *reputation*
3. *discouraged* 4. *profession* 5. *literacy*
6. *fate* 7. *ambitious* 8. *cause*
L.9-10.6

Fluency

Read with Ease: Phrasing

Ensure that students complete the self-check.
RI.9-10.10

ASSESS & RETEACH

Assessments Handbook, pp. 43b–43e

Have students complete the **Reader Reflection**. Then give students the **Cluster Test** to measure their progress. Group students as needed for reteaching.

CCSS **Literacy.RI.9-10.1** Cite strong and thorough textual evidence to support analysis of what the text says explicitly as well as inferences drawn from the text. **Literacy.RI.9-10.2** Determine a central idea of a text and analyze its development over the course of the text, including how it emerges and is shaped and refined by specific details; provide an objective summary of the text. **Literacy.RI.9-10.8** Delineate and evaluate the argument and specific claims in a text, assessing whether the reasoning is valid and the evidence is relevant and sufficient; identify false statements and fallacious reasoning. **Literacy.RI.9-10.10** By the end of grade 9, read and comprehend literary nonfiction in the grades 9-10 text complexity band proficiently, with scaffolding as needed at the high end of the range. By the end of grade 10, read and comprehend literary nonfiction at the high end of the grades 9-10 text complexity band independently and proficiently. **Literacy.W.9-10.10** Write routinely over extended time frames (time for research, reflection, and revision) and shorter time frames (a single sitting or a day or two) for a range of tasks, purposes, and audiences. **Literacy.L.9-10.6** Acquire and use accurately general academic and domain-specific words and phrases, sufficient for reading, writing, speaking, and listening at the college and career readiness level; demonstrate independence in gathering vocabulary knowledge when considering a word or phrase important to comprehension or expression.

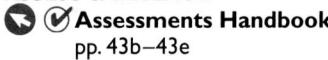

Lesson 7

INTEGRATE THE LANGUAGE ARTS

OBJECTIVES

Language Function
- Define and Explain Ⓣ

Research/Writing
- Visual Presentation

Media
- Deliver a Media Presentation; Analyze the Effect of the Media

Grammar
- Possessive Words Ⓣ

Grammar

Show Possession

Grammar Transparency 50

Review Review the transparency. Then conduct the activity on p. 336.

Oral Practice 1. his **2.** their **3.** their **4.** hers **5.** its

Written Practice 6. his **7.** His **8.** Their
L.9-10.1.b

Language Development

Define and Explain

Use the Language Acquisition Rubric to assess this language function.
SL.9-10.1.a

Assessments Handbook, p. 43o

Research/Writing

Visual Presentation

Be sure students include photos, illustrations, and text on their posters that connect to their school, home, or town. Model how to describe images in a formal presentation.

See **Language and Learning Handbook** p. 702 for further instruction.
W.9-10.7

Media Study

Evaluate PSAs

Media Presentation Have students evaluate their presentations.

See **Language and Learning Handbook** p. 702 for further instruction.
W.9-10.7; SL.9-10.3

Edge Interactive Practice Book, p. 156

GRAMMAR SKILLS PATH
46 Possessive Nouns
47 Possessive Adjectives: *My, Our,* Etc.
48 Possessive Pronouns: *Mine, Ours,* Etc.
49 Reflexive Pronouns
▶ 50 Review: Possessive Words ELL Language & Grammar Lab

INTEGRATE THE LANGUAGE ARTS

Grammar

Show Possession

Use **possessives** to show who owns something.

	Possessive Nouns	Possessive Adjectives	Possessive Pronouns
One Owner	Curtis's Ginny's teacher's school's	my your his, her, its	mine yours his, hers, its
More Than One Owner	teachers' schools'	our your their	ours yours theirs

Curtis's problem was hidden. **His** family didn't know.

Illiteracy is **our** problem. The problem is **ours**.

Ask your **teachers'** help. Ask for **their** help.

This is **your** choice. The choice is **yours**.

Oral Practice (1–5) With a partner, say each sentence with the correct possessive word.

1. Curtis tried to fool (his/their) teachers.
2. He watched actors and copied (his/their) speech.
3. Many adults cannot read. The problem is often (their/theirs) secret.
4. My aunt learned how to read as an adult. This story reminds me of (his/hers).
5. Curtis's story and (its/our) message are powerful.

Written Practice (6–10) Choose the correct possessive word. Rewrite the paragraph. Add two more sentences. Use possessive words.

Curtis's problem of illiteracy held him back. He lost (his/her) business. (His/Their) secret was too big. He found literacy coaches. (Our/Their) help changed his life.

Language Development

Define and Explain

Pair Talk What is **literacy**? Give a simple definition of literacy, and explain why it is so important.

Research / Writing

Visual Presentation

Social Studies: Literacy in the United States

Curtis Aikens helps fight the problem of illiteracy. How widespread is this problem? And what are people doing to solve it?

Work with a small group to research the problems and solutions for illiteracy. Then create a poster that uses illustrations, photos, and text. Try to include images that connect to your school, home, or town.

myNGconnect.com

- **Look for statistics and data about illiteracy in the U.S.**
- **Search for literacy programs in your community or state.**

Display your poster in your neighborhood to provide information for people who may need help.

Language and Learning Handbook, page 702

Media Study

Evaluate Public Service Announcements

Media Presentation Celebrities often participate in public service announcements (PSAs), which inform the public about different causes, like literacy, education, and health issues.

With a partner, create a media presentation that evaluates different public service announcements:

1. Research PSAs on the Internet. Choose three causes that are meaningful to you.
2. Evaluate the effectiveness of the PSAs. What kind of language, tone, and voice do they use? How do you think they affect the viewers?
3. Present your findings to the class. If possible, role-play or show each PSA, and see if your classmates agree with your critiques.

Language and Learning Handbook, page 702

GRAMMAR

Review: Possessive Words

Review Display the transparency. Have students explain the use of possessive adjectives and possessive pronouns.

A. Oral Practice Model how to choose the correct possessive word. Then have students choose the remaining possessive words. Use the charts to provide immediate corrective feedback.

B. Written Practice Work through the example. Explain that some sentences have no errors. Have the group tell you how to edit the paragraph. Then ask a volunteer to read the corrected paragraph to the class. L.9-10.1.b

Grammar & Writing Practice Book, pp. 111–112

Grammar Transparency 50

Show Possession

GRAMMAR REVIEW: POSSESSIVE WORDS 50

Remember: Use possessive words to show that someone owns something. A possessive adjective comes before a noun. A possessive pronoun stands alone.

Possessive Adjectives	my	your	his	her	its	our	your	their
Possessive Pronouns	mine	yours	his	hers		ours	yours	theirs

Try It

A. Say each sentence with the correct possessive word.

1. I was talking to **(my / mine)** friends, Leah and Emily.
2. They want to have **(its / their)** own clothing store one day.
3. I told them **(my / mine)** goal is to become a chef.
4. Leah and Emily invited me to join **(their / theirs)** business class.
5. If you have a goal and work hard, success will be **(your / yours)** someday.

B. Edit the paragraph. Fix five mistakes. The first is done for you.

Friendliness can help open doors. Friendliness is one of ~~mine~~ my best traits. It helps me greet people and become ~~theirs~~ their friend. A new student joined ~~ours~~ our class last week. It was easy to see he was nervous. ~~My~~ Mine was the first greeting he heard. ~~He~~ His grin made my efforts worthwhile!

CCSS **Literacy.W.9-10.7** Conduct short as well as more sustained research projects to answer a question (including a self-generated question) or solve a problem; narrow or broaden the inquiry when appropriate; synthesize multiple sources on the subject, demonstrating understanding of the subject under investigation. **Literacy.SL.9-10.1.a** Come to discussions prepared, having read and researched material under study; explicitly draw on that preparation by referring to evidence from texts and other research on the topic or issue to stimulate a thoughtful, well-reasoned exchange of ideas. **Literacy.SL.9-10.3** Evaluate a speaker's point of view, reasoning, and use of evidence and rhetoric, identifying any fallacious reasoning or exaggerated or distorted evidence.

Vocabulary Study

Dictionary and Jargon

An English **dictionary** gives the meanings of words in the English language. Many English words have an everyday meaning and a specialized meaning in a career field. The meanings of words also vary according to part of speech.

produce (pruh-**düs**) *v.* to make

produce (**prö**-düs) *n.* fruit and vegetables

Jargon is the specialized language of a career field. The following words have special meanings related to cooking: *beat, batter, dress, fold, skim, toss.*

With a partner, look up each of the six words in a print or online dictionary. Then answer the following questions:

- How many meanings does the word have?
- Which meaning relates to the field of cooking?
- What part of speech is it?

With your partner, research and list jargon in other fields, such as sports, education, or government. For each word, give an everyday meaning and the specialized meaning.

Writing Trait

Development of Ideas

Good writers develop their ideas in organized and creative ways. They begin by stating a clear main idea. Then they add thoughtful, relevant details that help support the main idea.

Just OK

> Education is one of the most important things that will influence your future. Some other things are your family and your interests. Education gives you the skills you need for a successful career, and it prepares you to face the world with confidence.

Much Better

> Education is one of the most important things that will influence your future. ~~Some other things are your family and your interests.~~ Doing well in school shows that you are willing to sacrifice your time and energy to achieve goals that you set for yourself. Education gives you the skills you need for a successful career, and it prepares you to face the world with confidence. Education can open doors to a brighter future.

With a partner, revise the student model below. Look for ways to state the main idea clearly, include more details to support the main idea, and remove details that are unnecessary or distracting.

Model Paragraph

> Something that people should think about is literacy. People graduate from high school and can't read—there are even statistics that show this. But even if you get through school without learning how to read, that doesn't mean that you will do well. A few people probably do it, but most people need to read in order to survive in daily life. There are many times you can't do things if you can't read. It's important to have good math skills, too, because you may get cheated when you shop. Reading is also very fun. We should all do what we can to help people become literate because reading is something we should all be able to do well.

Write your own paragraph that describes another way that people can open doors to the future. State a clear main idea, and then add details that develop your main idea in a clear, thoughtful way.

Writing Handbook, page 784

Lesson 8

INTEGRATE THE LANGUAGE ARTS

OBJECTIVES

Vocabulary
- Strategy: Use Reference Sources (dictionary); Jargon T

Writing
- Writing Process
- Trait: Development of Ideas T

Vocabulary Study

Dictionary and Jargon

Have students use a dictionary to determine the meaning and part of speech of specialized language.

- *beat*: 8+; to mix by stirring; verb
- *batter*: 2; a mixture of flour and liquid; noun
- *dress*: 6+; to kill and prepare for market; verb
- *fold*: 6+; to incorporate into a mixture; verb
- *skim*: 5+; to remove cream; verb
- *toss*: 7+; to stir or mix lightly; verb

L.9-10.4.c

Edge Interactive Practice Book, p. 157

Writing Trait

Development of Ideas

Help students understand why the second paragraph is much better than the first because it has a clear main idea and relevant details.

Have students use the second paragraph as a model for revising the student model.

Have students read their revised paragraph to a partner and together identify the main idea and details. Then have them write their own paragraph.

Have students self-evaluate their paragraph using the Writing Rubric (*also online*).

See **Writing Handbook** p. 784 for further instruction.

W.9-10.2; W.9-10.5

Writing Rubric — **Development of Ideas**

Exceptional	• Paragraph addresses topic by showing clear main idea and supporting details. • Examples are detailed and relevant to topic. • Possessive words are correct.
Competent	• Paragraph pertains to topic. • Examples are adequate. • Possessive words are correct with no more than one error.
Developing	• Paragraph may stray from topic. • Examples are loosely connected to topic. • Possessive words are sometimes incorrect.
Beginning	• Paragraph does not address topic. • Examples are not clearly connected to topic. • Possessive words are often incorrect.

CCSS **Literacy.W.9-10.2** Write informative/explanatory texts to examine and convey complex ideas, concepts, and information clearly and accurately through the effective selection, organization, and analysis of content. **Literacy.W.9-10.5** Develop and strengthen writing as needed by planning, revising, editing, rewriting, or trying a new approach, focusing on addressing what is most significant for a specific purpose and audience. **Literacy.L.9-10.4.c** Consult general and specialized reference materials (e.g., dictionaries, glossaries, thesauruses), both print and digital, to find the pronunciation of a word or determine or clarify its precise meaning, its part of speech, or its etymology. **Literacy.L.9-10.1.b** Use various types of phrases (noun, verb, adjectival, adverbial, participial, prepositional, absolute) and clauses (independent, dependent; noun, relative, adverbial) to convey specific meanings and add variety and interest to writing or presentations.

Lesson 9

WORKPLACE WORKSHOP

OBJECTIVES

Vocabulary
- Content Area Vocabulary: Restaurant Industry

Writing
- Write a Business Memo

Comprehension & Critical Thinking
- Analyze and Compare Information

ENGAGE & CONNECT

A Activate Prior Knowledge

Introduce Ask students what they know about restaurants. Then read the introduction.

TEACH & PRACTICE

B Jobs in the Restaurant Industry

Use the Chart Compare jobs in the restaurant industry. Ask: Which career would be best for a person with these qualities:

- friendly, outgoing personality
- supervisory ability

C Write a Business Memo

Brainstorm Questions A memo informs the reader about new information. Ask: Why might an assistant manager write a memo to staff at a restaurant?

Possible responses:
- *to inform employees of new schedules*
- *to inform cooks of new menu items*

Writing Skills Model how to write an effective business memo:

1. Explain that memos are divided into sections.
2. Begin the body of a memo by stating the purpose clearly.
3. Describe the purpose with details.
4. Close a memo with an ending that explains what action the reader should take.

Then have students critique the logic and format of some actual memos.
W.9-10.2; W.9-10.4; W.9-10.10

ONGOING ASSESSMENT
Tell students to share the memos they wrote. Did they follow the steps to write an effective business memo?

Workplace Workshop

1

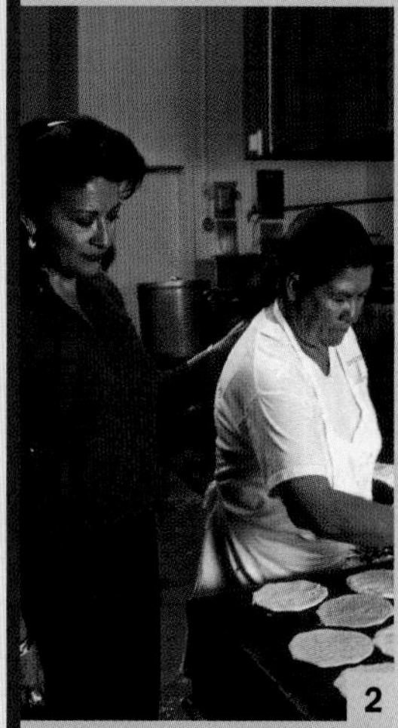
2

3

Inside a Restaurant

A In a full-service restaurant, a greeter seats customers at a table where menus, drinks, and food are provided. Some full-service restaurants are part of a national chain. Others are run independently.

Jobs in the Restaurant Industry

B A restaurant employs a team of workers for different responsibilities. The amount of training and experience each employee needs depends on the type of restaurant. Here are some jobs found in a typical full-service restaurant.

Job	Responsibilities	Education/Training Required
Greeter 1	• Greets customers and shows them to tables • Takes phone reservations • Acts as cashier when necessary	• On-the-job training
Assistant Manager 2	• Supervises servers and kitchen staff • Ensures quality of food preparation and service	• Previous experience working in food service • On-the-job training
Manager 3	• Hires, trains, and supervises all staff • Performs clerical and financial tasks • Handles customer complaints	• Experience in food service (often as an assistant manager) • Completion of a restaurant management program

Write a Business Memo

Practice writing a general business memo to the staff at a restaurant.

C
1. Imagine you are an assistant manager at a restaurant. You need to write a memo to your staff telling them about a new policy. Choose a topic for your memo: new uniforms, how to greet customers, or telling customers about daily specials.
2. Write your memo. Include the date the memo was written and when the new policy will start. Make sure you use a professional tone.
3. Read your memo to a classmate. Ask for feedback about how to improve it. Save the information in a professional career portfolio.

myNGconnect.com
- **Learn more about the restaurant industry.**
- **Download a form to evaluate whether you would like to work in this field.**
- **Download a memo form.**

Writing Handbook, page 784

READING

Workplace Documents: Understanding a Memo

Write a business memo.

Teach/Model Download a practice memo and model completing it.

- Discuss each section of the memo and the information that should be included.
- Tell students that sometimes the abbreviation *RE:* is substituted for "SUBJECT." *RE:* stands for "regarding" or "referencing."
- Complete each section of the memo as students follow along. Remind students that the body of the memo should be organized by main ideas and details.
- Emphasize the importance of using professional language.

Practice Display a blank memo form. Ask volunteers to describe the information they will include in each section of the memo.

Apply Have students work with a partner to write a memo. Then have them exchange memos with another set of partners. Have students compare and contrast the structure of the memos. Tell them to revise their memos based on the feedback they receive and add them to their portfolios.

myNGconnect.com

CCSS Literacy.W.9-10.2 Write informative/explanatory texts to examine and convey complex ideas, concepts, and information clearly and accurately through the effective selection, organization, and analysis of content. Literacy.W.9-10.4 Produce clear and coherent writing in which the development, organization, and style are appropriate to task, purpose, and audience. Literacy.W.9-10.10 Write routinely over extended time frames (time for research, reflection, and revision) and shorter time frames (a single sitting or a day or two) for a range of tasks, purposes, and audiences.

Access Words During Reading

When you read, you may not understand some parts of the text. Use this set of strategies to help you access the meaning.

A

Use Strategies During Reading

1. What unfamiliar word should I figure out in order to understand the selection? Can I decode the word by sounding out the letters or breaking up the word by its parts?
2. Have I seen this word before? What do I know about it already? *Now do I understand the word well enough to continue?*
3. Does this part of the selection help me understand the word? Do other parts of the selection help me understand the word? *Now do I understand the word well enough to continue?*
4. Do any parts of the word help me understand it? *Now do I understand the word well enough to continue?*
5. Who or what can help me understand the word right away? *If I still don't understand the word, I'll mark it and come back to it later.*

B

TRY IT ▸ Read the passage below and apply the five strategies above. Then answer these questions: What does it take to become a paramedic? Why do you think turnover, or the number of people who leave this job, is high?

C

▸ Paramedics go through a lot of training to become certified. Some are called upon to perform difficult prehospital procedures. Paramedics put in long hours and do not get much pay. Job turnover is fairly high, so there are often job openings.

Reading Handbook, page 733

Lesson 10

VOCABULARY WORKSHOP

OBJECTIVES

Vocabulary

- Clarify Word Meanings T

ENGAGE & CONNECT

A Build Background

Connect Explain: As you read, there will be words you cannot figure out. Look for parts of the word you know or for clues near the word. If you still don't understand, make a good guess and keep reading.

TEACH & PRACTICE

B Use Strategies During Reading

Use Strategies Have students first decode the words using knowledge of sound-letter relationships, affixes, and root words. Ask students to underline familiar word parts and context clues that can help them understand unfamiliar words.

ELL Rephrase Language

Rephrase idiomatic expressions: "go through a lot" as *do*; "called upon" as *asked*; and "put in" as *work*. Ask students what clues help them understand the idioms (*training* for "go through a lot"; *perform* for "called upon"; and *long hours* for "put in"). Ask what context clues they can use for "job turnover" (*job openings*).

Explain to students that they should use the underlined clues and what they already know about the topic to make good guesses about the meanings of the words.

C Put the Strategy to Work

Try It Tell students to review the steps of the strategy when they come to words they do not know. Remind them to use the dictionary to confirm their understanding.
L.9-10.4; L.9-10.4.d

ONGOING ASSESSMENT

Have partners describe the strategies they used to understand words they did not know.

DIFFERENTIATED INSTRUCTION

Additional Vocabulary Practice

Use these strategies to help students clarify word meanings.

Struggling Readers

Use Graphic Organizer Work with students to complete a two-column chart to understand how using strategies helped them clarify word meanings.

Strategy I Used	How It Helped

Finally, have students use the word meanings to summarize the passage.

English Language Learners ELL

Guided Rereading Work with students to reread the passage aloud. After each sentence, help them identify and highlight familiar word parts and context clues they can use to help understand the meaning. Then make a summary chart.

Challenge

Extend the Passage Have students work with a partner to write sentences to explain why job turnover for paramedics is fairly high. Ask pairs to share their sentences with the whole class.

CCSS Literacy.L.9-10.4 Determine or clarify the meaning of unknown and multiple-meaning words and phrases based on grades 9-10 reading and content, choosing flexibly from a range of strategies. Literacy.L.9-10.4.d Verify the preliminary determination of the meaning of a word or phrase (e.g., by checking the inferred meaning in context or in a dictionary).

UNIT 4 Cluster 2 Planner

EQ ESSENTIAL QUESTION:
How Can Knowledge Open Doors?
Consider how books can take you places.

Online Planner
myNGconnect.com

	LESSON 11 **Prepare to Read**	LESSON 12 **Superman and Me** Main Selection
Reading		
Reading Strategies Focus Strategy **Ask Questions**	**Activate Prior Knowledge** SL.9-10.1 • Make a Connection: Anticipation Guide *T340*	**Ask Questions** RI.9-10.1 • Find Question-Answer Relationships *T341, T344–T349*
Literary Analysis Genre Focus **Nonfiction**		**Analyze Text Structure: Cause and Effect** *T341, T344–T349* RI.9-10.5 **Identify Author's Influences and Perspective** • Influential British and American Writers *T342*
Vocabulary	**Key Vocabulary** RI.9-10.4; L.9-10.4.c; L.9-10.6 Introduce *T340* arrogant, • assume, • constant, disgusted, prodigy, recall, shame, standard	**Key Vocabulary** L.9-10.6 • Daily Routines *T345* • Link to Essential Question *T347* • Selection Reading *T344–T349* arrogant, • assume, prodigy, recall, standard
Fluency		**Intonation** RI.9-10.10 • Daily Routines *T345*
Writing		
Response to Literature		**Return to the Text** W.9-10.1; W.9-10.9.b; W.9-10.10 • **Reread and Write** Does reading really have the power to save people's lives? *T349*
Writing Across the Curriculum		
Language		
ELL **Language Development**	**Clarify** SL.9-10.1.c • Language and Grammar Lab, Transparency K *LAB TE p. 62*	**Clarify** SL.9-10.1.c • Daily Routines *LAB TE p. 62*
Grammar Grammar Focus **Pronouns in Prepositional Phrases**		**Prepositions** *T346* L.9-10.1.b **Prepositional Phrases** *T348* L.9-10.1.b
Listening and Speaking	**Partner Talk** SL.9-10.1 • Opinions About Reading *T340*	

T = Tested on Cluster and/or Unit Reading and Literary Analysis Test
T = Tested on Language Acquisition Assessment
T = Tested on Unit Writing Test
T = Assessed with a Rubric
• **Academic Vocabulary**

SELECTION SUMMARIES

Superman and Me

Genre: Essay   Lexile® 910L

Growing up on the Spokane Indian Reservation, writer Sherman Alexie taught himself to read using comic books. He was determined not to fail in life. As an adult, Alexie inspires young people to strive for their goals and to keep reading.

A Smart Cookie/It's Our Story, Too

Genre: Short Fiction/Memoir   Lexile® 920L

In an excerpt from *The House on Mango Street*, a mother reflects on the mistakes she made in her life and gives advice to her daughter. In "It's Our Story, Too," a writer describes how *The House on Mango Street* changed her life.

LESSON 13 **A Smart Cookie/It's Our Story, Too** Second Selection	LESSON 14 **Reflect and Assess**	LESSONS 15 & 16 **Integrate the Language Arts**	LESSON 17 **Workshop**
Ask Questions RL.9-10.1; RI.9-10.1 • Find Question-Answer Relationships *T350, T352–T356*	**Comprehension and Critical Thinking** *T357* RI.9-10.1; RI.9-10.10 • Compare Across Texts • Analyze, Compare, Interpret, Speculate, Assess		
Analyze Text Structure: Chronology *T350, T352–T356* RL.9-10.5; RI.9-10.5	**Interpret and Evaluate Literature** RI.9-10.10 **Use Text Evidence** *T357* RI.9-10.1	**Analyze Imagery** *T358* RL.9-10.4; RI.9-10.4	
Key Vocabulary L.9-10.6 • Selection Reading *T352–T356* • **constant** **shame** **disgusted**	**Key Vocabulary** L.9-10.6 • Review *T357* **arrogant** **prodigy** • **assume** **recall** • **constant** **shame** **disgusted** **standard**	**Vocabulary Strategy** L.9-10.4; L.9-10.4.c • Use Context Clues: Multiple-Meaning Words *T359*	
Intonation RI.9-10.10 • Daily Routines *T345* **Accuracy and Rate** RI.9-10.10 Comprehension Coach *T351*	**Intonation** RI.9-10.10 • Peer Assessment *T357*		
Return to the Text W.9-10.9.a; W.9-10.10 • **Reread and Write** What advice did the daughter get from her mother, and how has the advice opened doors? *T356*	**Write About Literature** W.9-10.9.a; W.9-10.9.b • **E-mail Message** What can students do to change their attitudes toward school and reading? *T357*	**Writing Form** W.9-10.2; W.9-10.5 • **Case Study** *T359*	
Research and Writing W.9-10.7 • **Sociology Connection** *T355*			
Clarify SL.9-10.1.c • Daily Routines *LAB TE p. 62*		**Clarify** SL.9-10.1.c • Pair Talk *T358*	
Object Pronouns After a Preposition *T352* L.9-10.1.b **Compound Object Pronouns** *T354* L.9-10.1.b		**Pronouns in Prepositional Phrases** *T358* L.9-10.1.b	**Listening and Speaking Workshop** **Oral Report** W.9-10.7; SL.9-10.2; SL.9-10.3; SL.9-10.4; L.9-10.3 • Plan, Practice, Give, and Evaluate an Oral Report *T360–T361*
Listen to a Selection RI.9-10.10 Comprehension Coach *T351* *CD 6, Track 6*	**Participate in a Discussion** *T357* SL.9-10.1	**Oral Presentation** *T359* SL.9-10.1.a; SL.9-10.4	

EDGE LIBRARY

The Outsiders •
by S. E. Hinton

Parrot in the Oven • •
by Victor Martinez

Narrative of the Life of Frederick Douglass • • •
by Frederick Douglass

Lesson 11
PREPARE TO READ

Vocabulary
- Key Vocabulary Ⓣ
- Strategy: Use Cognates
- Synonyms and Antonyms

Reading Strategy
- Activate Prior Knowledge

ELL Language & Grammar Lab

Language Function Transparency K
Clarify Ⓣ

ENGAGE & CONNECT

Ⓐ EQ Essential Question

Focus on Books Ask: How can reading change people's lives?

Possible responses:
- *Reading can help people learn about the world.*
- *Reading can show people a world outside their own.*

Ⓑ Make a Connection

Have students share their Anticipation Guides with a partner to compare their opinions about reading.
SL.9-10.1

TEACH VOCABULARY

Ⓒ Learn Key Vocabulary

Study the Words Review the four steps of the Make Words Your Own routine (see *the Vocabulary tab*):

1. **Pronounce** Say one word and have students repeat it. Write the word in syllables and pronounce it, one syllable at a time: *dis-gust-ed*. Point out other forms of the word such as *disgust* and *disgusting*.

   ELL Use cognates to help Spanish speakers with the words (*see the Vocabulary tab*).

2. **Study Examples** Read the example in the chart. Provide more examples: If you get a compliment, do you feel pleased or *disgusted?*

3. **Encourage Elaboration** Provide students with a sentence frame: *I feel* disgusted *when* ______.

Reading Transparency 16

4. **Practice the Words** Use the transparency to model the completion of a Synonym-Antonym Chart. Have students work in groups to complete a Synonym-Antonym Chart for each word.
L.9-10.4.c

Edge Interactive Practice Book, pp. 158–159
RI.9-10.4; L.9-10.6

ONGOING ASSESSMENT
Have students complete an oral sentence for each word. For example:
We stay in _______ *contact with our grandma by phone.*

PREPARE TO READ

- Superman and Me
- A Smart Cookie
- It's Our Story, Too

Ⓐ EQ How Can Knowledge Open Doors?

Consider how books can take you places.

Ⓑ Make a Connection

Anticipation Guide People read for many reasons. Some read for school or work, while others only read for entertainment. What do you think about reading? Tell whether you agree or disagree with the statements in the **Anticipation Guide**.

ANTICIPATION GUIDE	Agree or Disagree
1. Reading books is more important than reading papers or magazines.	________
2. Magazines are more interesting than books.	________
3. It's more important to read a lot about one topic than a little about many topics.	________

Ⓒ Learn Key Vocabulary

Study the Words Pronounce each word and learn its meaning. You may also want to look up the definitions in the Glossary.

• Academic Vocabulary

Key Words	Examples
arrogant (**ar**-u-gunt) *adjective* ▸ pages 347, 357	If you are **arrogant**, you are overly proud. That **arrogant** girl acts like she is better than everyone else.
• **assume** (u-**sūm**) *verb* ▸ page 346	When you **assume** something, you think it is true even though you do not know that it is. He **assumes** that I am poor because my clothes are old.
• **constant** (**kon**-stunt) *adjective* ▸ pages 355, 356	Something that is **constant** stays the same. No matter what else changes, my love for my family will always stay **constant**.
disgusted (di-**skus**-tid) *adjective* ▸ pages 352, 356	If you are **disgusted**, you feel turned off or very upset. I felt **disgusted** when I saw the rude way he treated others.
prodigy (**prah**-du-jē) *noun* ▸ page 346	A **prodigy** is a young person who has unusual skills for his or her age. The **prodigy** could play the violin when she was four years old.
recall (rē-**kawl**) *verb* ▸ pages 344, 357, 359	To **recall** means to remember something from the past. I **recall** many happy memories from my childhood.
shame (**shām**) *noun* ▸ page 352	**Shame** is a painful feeling that is caused by embarrassment or guilt. He felt **shame** about a mistake that he had made.
standard (**stan**-durd) *noun* ▸ pages 344, 349	A **standard** is a way of judging or measuring things. According to the teacher's high **standards**, she was a great student.

Practice the Words Work with a small group to complete a **Synonym-Antonym Chart** for the Key Vocabulary words. Use a thesaurus to find ideas and check your work.

Synonym-Antonym Chart

Word	Synonyms	Antonyms
arrogant	proud, stuck up	humble, modest

Reading Transparency 16

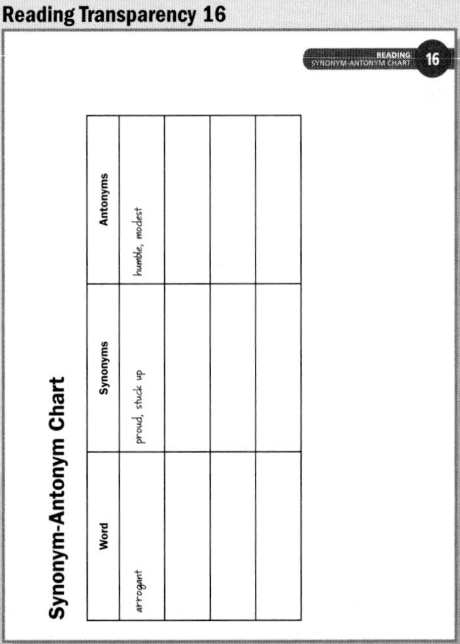

CCSS Literacy.RI.9-10.4 Determine the meaning of words and phrases as they are used in a text, including figurative, connotative, and technical meanings; analyze the cumulative impact of specific word choices on meaning and tone (e.g., how the language of a court opinion differs from that of a newspaper). Literacy.SL.9-10.1 Initiate and participate effectively in a range of collaborative discussions (one-on-one, in groups, and teacher-led) with diverse partners on grades 9-10 topics, texts, and issues, building on others' ideas and expressing their own clearly and persuasively. Literacy.L.9-10.4.c Consult general and specialized reference materials (e.g., dictionaries, glossaries, thesauruses), both print and digital, to find the pronunciation of a word or determine or clarify its precise meaning, its part of speech, or its etymology.

BEFORE READING Superman and Me

essay by Sherman Alexie

Reading Strategies

- Plan and Monitor
- Determine Importance
- Make Inferences
- ▶ **Ask Questions**
- Make Connections
- Synthesize
- Visualize

Analyze Text Structure: Cause and Effect

Some nonfiction writers use **cause and effect** to structure, or organize, their ideas. A **cause** is an event that leads to another event, which is called the **effect**. Authors use cause and effect to explain why something happens and how one thing leads to another.

Look Into the Text

In a fit of unemployment-inspired creative energy, my father built a set of bookshelves and soon filled them with a random assortment of books about the Kennedy assassination, Watergate, the Vietnam War, and the entire twenty-three-book series of the Apache westerns. My father loved books, and since I loved my father with an aching devotion, I decided to love books as well.

This effect has more than one cause.

Signal words like *since*, *so*, and *because* show how events relate.

You can begin a **Cause-and-Effect Chart** to show how events relate.

Cause-and-Effect Chart

Cause	Effect
Father loves books.	Author loves books.
Author loves his father.	

Focus Strategy ▶ Ask Questions

It's not only important to ask questions about a text. When you read, you also need to find the answers. Sometimes the answer to a question is "right there" in the text.

Focus Strategy

HOW TO FIND QUESTION-ANSWER RELATIONSHIPS

1. As you read, ask yourself how important events relate. Your questions may begin with *Who, What, Where, When, Why,* and *How*.

   QUESTION: Why does Alexie explain that his father loved books?

2. Reread the section to find any answers that are "right there."

   IN THE TEXT: "My father loved books, and since I loved my father … I decided to love books as well."

   ANSWER: He explains that his father's love of books causes him to love books, too.

   Record these relationships on your **Cause-and-Effect Chart**.

3. If the answer cannot be found in this section, keep reading. You may find the answer you need in later sections.

Reading Transparency 17

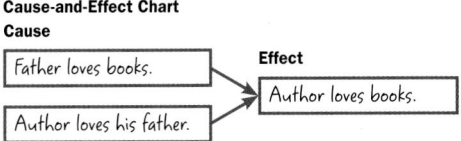

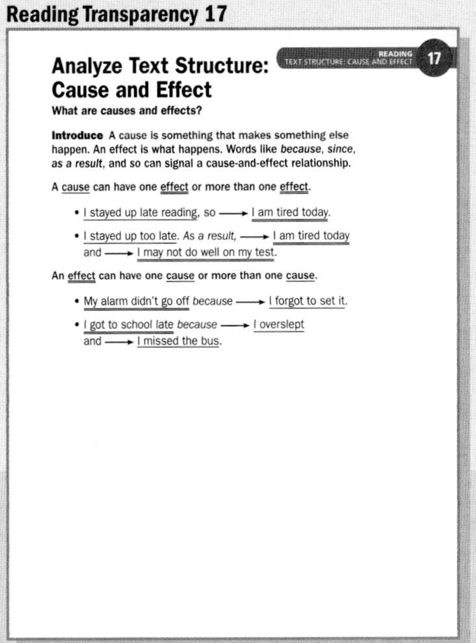

Analyze Text Structure: Cause and Effect

READING 17 TEXT STRUCTURE: CAUSE AND EFFECT

What are causes and effects?

Introduce A cause is something that makes something else happen. An effect is what happens. Words like *because, since, as a result,* and *so* can signal a cause-and-effect relationship.

A cause can have one effect or more than one effect.

- I stayed up late reading, so → I am tired today.
- I stayed up too late. *As a result,* → I am tired today and → I may not do well on my test.

An effect can have one cause or more than one cause.

- My alarm didn't go off *because* → I forgot to set it.
- I got to school late *because* → I overslept and → I missed the bus.

Lesson 12
BEFORE READING

OBJECTIVES

Reading Strategy
- Ask Questions: Find Question-Answer Relationships

Literary Analysis
- Analyze Text Structure: Cause and Effect T

TEACH STRATEGIES

D Analyze Text Structure: Cause and Effect

Look Into the Text Use the callouts to locate an example of multiple causes for the author's love of books. Ask: How many causes for his love of books does the author mention?

Possible response:
- *two—father loves books and the author loves his father*

Reading Transparency 17

Use the Transparency Display the transparency. Help students use signal words to spot cause-and-effect relationships. Have them complete sentence frames such as these to reinforce the features of cause-and-effect relationships:

- *I can't ______ **because** I'm sick.*
- ***Since** she works late tonight, Mom can't ______.*

Possible responses:
- *go to the party; come over*
- *pick me up; make dinner*

RI.9-10.5

E Focus Strategy: Ask Questions

Find Question-Answer Relationships Review that students use a variety of strategies as they read. Then read the introduction with students to define the strategy. Work through the How To box to model finding question-answer relationships.

Have students try the strategy to find another question-answer relationship in Look Into the Text.

RI.9-10.1

Edge Interactive Practice Book, pp. 160–161

ONGOING ASSESSMENT

Have students discuss words and phrases that signal a cause-and-effect structure.

CCSS Literacy.RI.9-10.1 Cite strong and thorough textual evidence to support analysis of what the text says explicitly as well as inferences drawn from the text. Literacy.RI.9-10.5 Analyze in detail how an author's ideas or claims are developed and refined by particular sentences, paragraphs, or larger portions of a text (e.g., a section or chapter). Literacy.L.9-10.6 Acquire and use accurately general academic and domain-specific words and phrases, sufficient for reading, writing, speaking, and listening at the college and career readiness level; demonstrate independence in gathering vocabulary knowledge when considering a word or phrase important to comprehension or expression.

READ

OBJECTIVES

Literary Analysis
- Identify Author's Influences and Perspective

Viewing
- Respond to and Interpret Visuals

BUILD BACKGROUND

A The Writer and His World

Have students read the article about Sherman Alexie.

Author's Influences Share this information about the writers Alexie mentions in the article:

- Walt Whitman and Emily Dickinson are considered to be two of the greatest poets in all of American literature.
- William Shakespeare, who was British, is often referred to as the greatest playwright who ever lived.
- Denis Johnson and James Wright are influential modern American writers.

Point out to students that selections from Whitman and Shakespeare appear later in this book.

Ask: Why does Alexie mention these writers when he talks about the need for Native American authors?

Possible responses:
- *These writers inspired him to become a great writer.*
- *There is room for a great Native American writer.*

Connect with Author's Life Guide students to make connections with the author's life. Ask: Why do you think it is important for young people to know about artists from their own culture?

Discuss the ways that reading books by authors both within and outside of one's own culture can "open doors."

myNGconnect.com

Selection Summaries in eight languages

Sherman Alexie
(1966–)

Sherman Alexie has said, "I have no answers. I just hope I'm asking the right questions."

Sherman Alexie says, "The percentage of Indian kids doing some sort of artistic work is much higher than in the general population—painting, drawing, dancing, singing . . . It's not a big leap from a kid who dances to a kid who writes poems. It's the same impulse. It just needs a little push."

A Alexie should know. He was born into a poor Native American community on the Spokane Indian Reservation in Washington. As described in the essay, "Superman and Me," Alexie took it upon himself to improve his situation. He developed an early love of books and later decided to attend high school off the reservation, where he says, "I was the only Indian, besides the mascot."

In a literary world with few Native American authors, Alexie has created his own place. "It's selfish in a sense that we haven't had our Emily Dickinson or Walt Whitman; we haven't had our Shakespeare or Denis Johnson or James Wright."

However, that doesn't stop him from looking to the future to motivate the next generation. "There's a kid out there, some boy or girl who will be that great writer, and hopefully they'll see what I do and get inspired by that."

myNGconnect.com

Listen to interviews with the writer.

Read reviews of films the writer has written, such as *Smoke Signals*.

DIFFERENTIATED INSTRUCTION

English Language Learners ELL

Preview the selection:

- Show the map on p. 344: *In the 1800s, the U.S. government forced Native Americans to live in places called reservations. The writer is Native American and grew up poor on an Indian reservation.*
- Point to Superman on p. 343: *Superman is a famous hero in comic books, TV, and films. Many children look up to him for his strength, courage, and honesty.* If possible, show an example of a comic book.
- Point out the quotations on pp. 345, 347, and 348. The quotations on these pages show important ideas in the selection.

Read Aloud to provide a supported listening experience:

- Read the selection aloud to students as you provide comprehensible input. Example for p. 346: Show a comic book and read aloud as you point to *panels, dialogue balloons,* and *narrative* (storytelling).

SUPERMAN and Me

by Sherman Alexie

Superman from the *Myths* series, Andy Warhol © 1981.

Critical Viewing: Cause and Effect Think of what you know about Superman. What feelings does this image and title create?

TEACH & PRACTICE

B Analyze Visuals

About the Art This painting was one of 10 that Andy Warhol included in his 1981 *Myths* series. The *Myths* paintings show imaginary characters loved and recognized by people all over the world.

Interpret and Respond Ask: Other than Superman, what imaginary characters do you think people all over the world would recognize?

C Critical Viewing: Cause and Effect

Analyze Details Help students to brainstorm words and phrases that describe Superman.

ELL Use Graphic Organizer Use a graphic organizer to display students' ideas. Explain them, and allow students to use the words during the discussion.

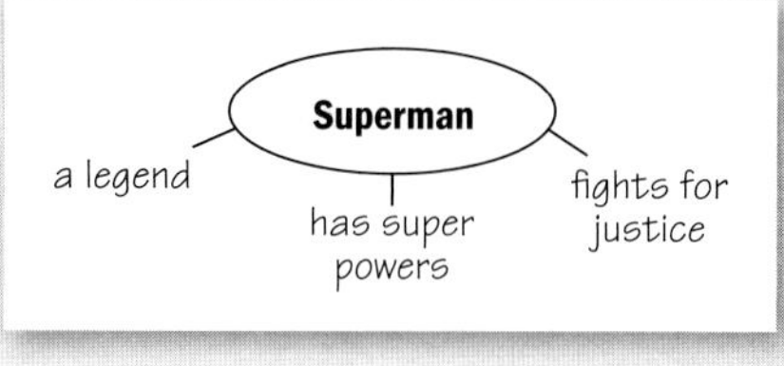

Ask: What feelings does this image and title create?

Possible responses:

- *a feeling of power because Superman is strong*
- *a sense of what is good or right because Superman always does the right thing*

OBJECTIVES

Vocabulary
- Key Vocabulary (T)

Reading Fluency
- Intonation (T)

Reading Strategy
- Ask Questions: Find Question-Answer Relationships

Comprehension & Critical Thinking
- Use Text Evidence (T)

Literary Analysis
- Analyze Text Structure: Cause and Effect (T)

TEACH & PRACTICE

Reading Support

Read Have students read pp. 344–349. Support and monitor their comprehension using the reading support provided. Use the Differentiated Instruction below to meet students' individual needs.
RI.9-10.10

(A) Analyze Visuals

About the Map Explain that the smaller map shows where Washington state is located. The larger map gives a closer view of Washington, including large cities and landforms.

Interpret the Map Have students describe the land around the reservation.

Possible response:
- *The only large city near the reservation is Spokane.*

Have students use information from the text and the map to make an inference about what might have affected Alexie as he was growing up.

Possible responses:
- *He might have felt isolated.*
- *The surroundings might have made him more creative.*

(B) Reading Support

1 Ask Questions Have students review details about Alexie before asking their questions.

Possible response:
- *Does he have any brothers or sisters? (He has one brother and three sisters.)*

RI.9-10.1

POOR BY MOST STANDARDS

I learned to read with a *Superman* comic book. Simple enough, I suppose. I cannot **recall** which particular *Superman* comic book I read, nor can I remember which villain he fought in that issue. I cannot remember the plot, nor **the means by which I obtained** the comic book. What I can remember is this: I was three years old, a Spokane Indian boy living with his family on the **Spokane Indian Reservation** in eastern Washington state. We were poor by most **standards**, but one of my parents usually managed to find some **minimum-wage job** or another, which made us middle-class by reservation standards. I had a brother and three sisters. We lived on a combination of irregular paychecks, hope, fear, and **government-surplus food**. 1

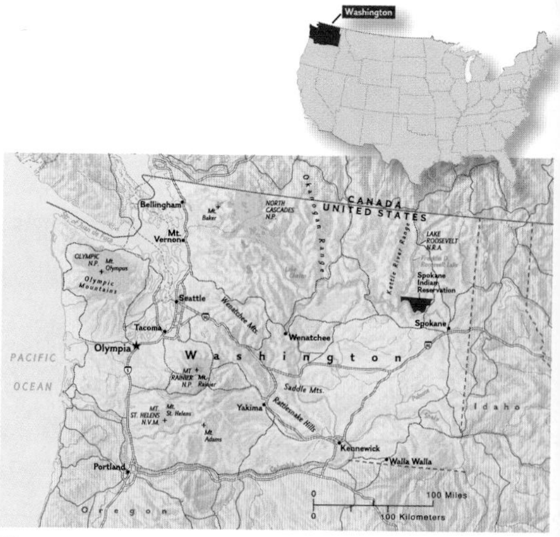

(A) Interpret the Map What does this map show you about the cities and land near the Spokane Indian Reservation?

1 **Ask Questions** Check your understanding by asking a question about this section with an answer that is "Right There" on the page.

CRAZY PILES

My father, who is one of the few Indians who went to Catholic school on purpose, was an **avid** reader of westerns, spy thrillers, murder mysteries, gangster epics, basketball-player biographies, and anything else he could find. He bought his books by the pound at Dutch's Pawn

Key Vocabulary
recall *v.*, to remember something from the past
standard *n.*, way of judging or measuring things

In Other Words
the means by which I obtained the way I got
Spokane Indian Reservation land where the Spokane Tribe lives
minimum-wage job low-paying job
government-surplus food free food
avid eager, regular

DIFFERENTIATED INSTRUCTION

Interactive Reading As you conduct the interactive reading session with students, adjust your teaching strategies to their needs.

Struggling Readers

Build Background Further explain terms that describe the economic situation:
- *Minimum wage* is the lowest wage that the law requires must be paid to workers.
- The *middle class* is neither the highest nor the lowest in society. Alexie is saying that on the reservation, being middle-class places them above most other families.
- *Government-surplus food* is extra food produced by farmers.

English Language Learners ELL

Define Multiple-Meaning Words Help students understand the meanings of words with more than one definition.

Example on p. 344:
- As a noun, *a state* is one of 50 states in the U.S. We live in the state of ______. As a verb, *to state* means "to say."

Discuss additional examples from the story such as *means* and *class*. Work together to provide restatements.

Challenge

Lead the Discussion Have students lead the discussion during reading, posing additional questions for the group. Help leaders model use of the Ask Questions reading strategy.

CCSS **Literacy.RI.9-10.1** Cite strong and thorough textual evidence to support analysis of what the text says explicitly as well as inferences drawn from the text. **Literacy.RI.9-10.10** By the end of grade 9, read and comprehend literary nonfiction in the grades 9-10 text complexity band proficiently, with scaffolding as needed at the high end of the range. By the end of grade 10, read and comprehend literary nonfiction at the high end of the grades 9-10 text complexity band independently and proficiently.

Shop, Goodwill, Salvation Army, and Value Village. When he had extra money, he bought new novels at supermarkets, convenience stores, and hospital gift shops. Our house was filled with books. They were stacked in crazy piles in the bathroom, bedrooms, and living room. **In a fit of unemployment-inspired creative energy,** my father built a set of bookshelves and soon filled them with a random assortment of books about the Kennedy assassination, Watergate, the Vietnam War, and the entire twenty-three-book series of the Apache westerns. My father loved books, and since I loved my father with an aching devotion, I decided to love books as well. 2

Our house was filled with books.

2 Cause and Effect What changes in Alexie's life because of his father's love of books? Give two examples. Add them to your Cause-and-Effect Chart.

BREAKING DOWN THE DOOR

I can remember picking up my father's books before I could read. The words themselves were mostly **foreign**, but I still remember the exact moment when I first understood, **with a sudden clarity,** the purpose of a paragraph. I didn't have the vocabulary to say "paragraph," but I realized that a paragraph was a fence that held words. The words inside a paragraph worked together for a common purpose. They had some specific reason for being inside the same fence. This knowledge delighted me. I began to think of everything in terms of paragraphs. Our reservation was a small paragraph within the United States. My family's house was a paragraph, distinct from the other paragraphs of the LeBrets to the north, the Fords to our south, and the Tribal School

Monitor Comprehension

Describe What is the author's childhood like on the reservation?

In Other Words

In a fit of unemployment-inspired creative energy, Once, when he was unemployed,
foreign impossible to understand
with a sudden clarity, and it was suddenly clear,

Historical Background

The **Kennedy assassination, Watergate,** and the **Vietnam War** were important events in U.S. history. In 1963, President Kennedy was killed. In the 1970s, President Nixon was forced to quit because of the Watergate scandal. The U.S. was also fighting a very unpopular war in Vietnam.

TEACH & PRACTICE

C Reading Support

2 Cause and Effect Help students to speculate about an effect.

ELL Use Graphic Organizer Help students recognize cause-and-effect relationships.

Cause		Effect
Alexie's father loved books.	→	Alexie decided to love books.

Ask students to name two things in Alexie's life that change because of his father's love of books.

Possible responses:
- *There are books all over the house.*
- *Alexie decides to love books, too.*

RI.9-10.5

Monitor Comprehension

Describe Have students consider the family's economic situation, Alexie's father's influence, and Alexie's own thoughts to help describe his childhood.

Possible responses:
- *Alexie's family sometimes had financial difficulties.*
- *His house was filled with books, and he developed a love of reading.*

RI.9-10.1

DAILY ROUTINES

Vocabulary

See the Vocabulary and Fluency Routines tab for more information.

Word Wall Display the words on a Word Wall. Ask a question or give a clue for each word, such as *This word means the opposite of* forget.

Use Vocabulary Cards Make a card for each word. Have students take turns saying cloze sentences for the words. Other students choose and take the words that complete the sentences.

Word Sorts Provide categories for sorting words:
- Parts of speech
- Related meanings

L.9-10.6

Fluency: Intonation

CD 11

This cluster's fluency practice uses a passage from "It's Our Story, Too" to help students practice appropriate intonation. Use **Reading Handbook** T748 and the **Fluency Model CD** to teach or review the elements of fluent intonation, and then use the daily fluency practice activities to develop students' oral reading proficiency.
RI.9-10.10

CCSS **Literacy.RI.9-10.1** Cite strong and thorough textual evidence to support analysis of what the text says explicitly as well as inferences drawn from the text. **Literacy.RI.9-10.5** Analyze in detail how an author's ideas or claims are developed and refined by particular sentences, paragraphs, or larger portions of a text (e.g., a section or chapter). **Literacy.L.9-10.6** Acquire and use accurately general academic and domain-specific words and phrases, sufficient for reading, writing, speaking, and listening at the college and career readiness level; demonstrate independence in gathering vocabulary knowledge when considering a word or phrase important to comprehension or expression.

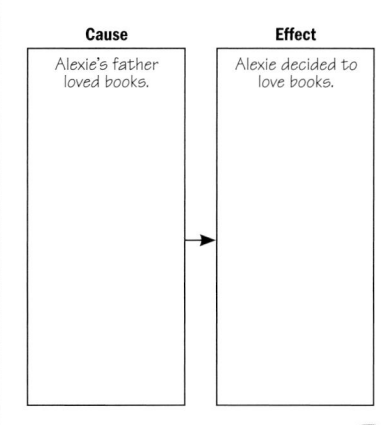

OBJECTIVES

Vocabulary
- Key Vocabulary Ⓣ

Reading Strategy
- Ask Questions; Review Strategies

Comprehension & Critical Thinking
- Use Text Evidence Ⓣ

Literary Analysis
- Analyze Text Structure: Cause and Effect Ⓣ

Grammar
- Prepositions

TEACH & PRACTICE

Ⓐ Reading Support

3 Cause and Effect Ask: How does Alexie see the world in paragraphs?

Possible response:
- *He thinks of how people and things belong together, like the words and ideas in a paragraph.* RI.9-10.5

Ⓑ Reading Support

4 Ask Questions Have students ask and answer their *wh-* questions with information in the text.

Possible response:
- *What helps Alexie learn to read? (looking at a* Superman *comic book)* RI.9-10.1

Review Strategies Ask what other strategies students used as they read.

Possible response:
- *I read that smart children were treated like oddities on the reservation. I made an inference that Alexie's pain came from being teased.* RI.9-10.1

Ⓒ Reading Support

Build Background Explain that *The Grapes of Wrath* is a novel that students usually read in high school, and that "Dick and Jane" are simple books that young children use when they begin to read.

Point of View Explain that Alexie sometimes speaks about himself in the third person, as if he is talking about someone else. RI.9-10.1

Ⓐ to the west. Inside our house, each family member existed as a separate paragraph, but still had **genetics** and common experiences to link us. Now, using this logic, I can see my changed family as an essay of seven paragraphs: mother, father, older brother, the deceased sister, my younger twin sisters, and our adopted little brother. 3

Ⓑ At the same time I was seeing the world in paragraphs, I also picked up that *Superman* comic book. Each **panel, complete with picture, dialogue, and narrative, was a three-dimensional paragraph**. In one panel, Superman breaks through a door. His suit is red, blue, and yellow. The brown door shatters into many pieces. I look at the narrative above the picture. I cannot read the words, but I **assume** it tells me that Superman is breaking down the door. Aloud, I pretend to read the words and say "Superman is breaking down the door." Words, dialogue, also float out of Superman's mouth. Because he is breaking down the door, I assume he says, "I am breaking down the door." Once again, I pretend to read the words and say aloud, "I am breaking down the door." In this way, I learned to read. 4

3 Cause and Effect The author learns what paragraphs are. What effect does this have on the way he looks at the world? Add it to your Cause-and-Effect Chart.

4 Ask Questions Ask *wh-* questions about Alexie learning how to read. How do asking and answering these questions add to your understanding? Find clues in this paragraph.

PRODIGY OR ODDITY?

This might be an interesting story all by itself. Ⓒ A little Indian boy teaches himself to read at an early age and advances quickly. He reads *Grapes of Wrath* in kindergarten when other children are struggling through Dick and Jane. If he'd been anything but an Indian boy living on the reservation, he might have been called a **prodigy**. But he is an Indian boy living on the reservation, and is simply **an oddity**. He grows into a man who often speaks of his childhood in the third-person, as if it will somehow dull the pain and make him sound more modest about his talents.

Key Vocabulary
- **assume** *v.*, to think that something is true even if you're not sure
- **prodigy** *n.*, young person with advanced (or specialized) skills

In Other Words
- **genetics** the same family
- **panel, complete with picture, dialogue, and narrative, was a three-dimensional paragraph** square of the comic had a picture, words, and a story that went together like a paragraph
- **an oddity** someone who is very strange

346 Unit 4 Opening Doors

GRAMMAR

Prepositions

Teach/Model Display the transparency. Work through each group of prepositions. Read the example sentences aloud, emphasizing the prepositions. Then elicit or say a sentence for a few more prepositions in the group.

Practice A. Elicit one or more prepositions to complete each sentence, and record students' responses on the transparency. **B.** After partners talk about Sherman Alexie and write their own sentences, have each student read a favorite sentence aloud and ask the group to identify the preposition. L.9-10.1.b

Grammar & Writing Practice Book, pp. 113–114

Grammar Transparency 51

GRAMMAR PREPOSITIONS 51

What Kinds of Things Do Prepositions Show?

Location, Direction, and Time

Prepositions That Show Location: in, on top of, on, at, over, under, above, below, next to, beside, in front of, in back of, behind
- Use a preposition of **location** to tell where something is.
  Stacked books sat **in** the bathroom.
  Some books are **on top of** the closet.

Prepositions That Show Direction: into, throughout, up, down, through, across, to
- Use a preposition of **direction** to tell where something is going.
  More books spread **throughout** the house.
  They spilled **into** the yard!

Prepositions That Show Time: after, until, before, during
- Use a preposition of **time** to tell when something happens.
  After dinner, I will read this book. I may read **until** bedtime.

Try It

A. Say each sentence about Sherman Alexie. Add a preposition.
Possible answers:
1. Sherman Alexie got books __at__ the library.
2. He read them __during__ recess.
3. He read __in__ the car.
4. He often read while his family drove __up__ the street.
5. In fact, Sherman Alexie read any paper with words __on__ it.

B. Now tell a partner something about Sherman Alexie. Write your three best sentences with prepositions. Sentences will vary.

GRAMMAR SKILLS PATH

51	**Prepositions** ELL Language & Grammar Lab
52	**Prepositional Phrases**
53	**Object Pronouns After a Preposition**
54	**Compound Object Pronouns**
55	**Review: Pronouns in Prepositional Phrases**

CCSS **Literacy.RI.9-10.1** Cite strong and thorough textual evidence to support analysis of what the text says explicitly as well as inferences drawn from the text. **Literacy.RI.9-10.5** Analyze in detail how an author's ideas or claims are developed and refined by particular sentences, paragraphs, or larger portions of a text (e.g., a section or chapter). **Literacy.L.9-10.1.b** Use various types of phrases (noun, verb, adjectival, adverbial, participial, prepositional, absolute) and clauses (independent, dependent, noun, relative, adverbial) to convey specific meanings and add variety and interest to writing or presentations.

A smart Indian is a dangerous person, widely feared and **ridiculed by** Indians and non-Indians alike. I fought with my classmates on a daily basis. They wanted me to stay quiet when the non-Indian teacher asked for answers, for volunteers, for help. We were Indian children who were expected to be stupid. Most lived up to those expectations inside the classroom, but **subverted them** on the outside. They struggled with basic reading in school, but could remember how to sing a few dozen **powwow songs**. They **were monosyllabic** in front of their non-Indian teachers, but could tell complicated stories and jokes at the dinner table. They **submissively** ducked their heads when confronted by a non-Indian adult, but would slug it out with the Indian bully who was ten years older. As Indian children, we were expected to fail in the non-Indian world. Those who failed were ceremonially accepted by other Indians and appropriately pitied by non-Indians. 5

D

5 Cause and Effect How do the other Indian boys at school react to Alexie's talent for reading? What causes their reaction towards him? Add this to your Cause-and-Effect Chart.

WITH JOY AND DESPERATION

I refused to fail. I was smart. I was **arrogant**. I was lucky. I read books late into the night, until I could barely keep my eyes open. I read books at recess, then during lunch, and in the few minutes left after I had finished my classroom assignments. I read books in the car when my family traveled to powwows or basketball games. In shopping malls, I ran to the bookstores and read bits and pieces of as many books as I could. I read the books my father brought home from the pawnshops and

I refused to fail.

Monitor Comprehension

Explain Why was Alexie considered an "oddity" at his school?

Key Vocabulary

arrogant *adj.*, overly proud

In Other Words

ridiculed by teased by
subverted them went against them
powwow songs traditional Native American songs
were monosyllabic hardly spoke at all
submissively meekly, timidly

VOCABULARY

Link Vocabulary and Concepts

Ask questions to link Key Vocabulary with the Essential Question.

EQ **ESSENTIAL QUESTION:**
How can knowledge open doors?

Some possible questions:

- *How can setting a high* **standard** *for yourself open doors for you?*
- *How can being a* **prodigy** *change your life in good and bad ways?*
- *How might being* **arrogant** *affect your opportunities in life?*
- *What does Alexie say non-Indian teachers* **assume** *about their Indian students?*
- *Why doesn't Alexie feel* **shame** *when the other kids tease him for doing well in school?*

Have students use the Key Vocabulary words in their responses.
L.9-10.6

TEACH & PRACTICE

D Reading Support

5 Cause and Effect Discuss what Alexie means when he says, "A smart Indian is a dangerous person."

ELL Use Graphic Organizer Use a Venn diagram to compare behaviors accepted in the "Indian" and "non-Indian" worlds the author describes:

Ask: How do the other Indian kids react to him?

Possible response:
- *They fight with him to stop him from showing the teacher that he is smart.*

Then ask: Why don't they like it when Alexie shows that he is smart?

Possible responses:
- *They don't like anyone who's different.*
- *They might be jealous of him or think he's conceited.*

RI.9-10.5

Monitor Comprehension

Explain Have students think aloud to explain why Alexie was considered an "oddity" at his school.

MODEL Say:
- *I know that someone with interests or ideas that aren't like everyone else's will stand out, but not always in a good way.*
- *Alexie acted in ways that were not typical for an Indian boy at school.*

Have students continue your model with details about how Alexie was different from his classmates:

Possible responses:
- *He could read at an early age. He read different books than his classmates did.*
- *He didn't stay quiet in class like other Indian students did.*
- *Indian children are expected to fail, but he refused to fail.*

RI.9-10.1

CCSS Literacy.RI.9-10.1 Cite strong and thorough textual evidence to support analysis of what the text says explicitly as well as inferences drawn from the text. Literacy.RI.9-10.5 Analyze in detail how an author's ideas or claims are developed and refined by particular sentences, paragraphs, or larger portions of a text (e.g., a section or chapter). Literacy.L.9-10.6 Acquire and use accurately general academic and domain-specific words and phrases, sufficient for reading, writing, speaking, and listening at the college and career readiness level; demonstrate independence in gathering vocabulary knowledge when considering a word or phrase important to comprehension or expression.

OBJECTIVES

Vocabulary
- Key Vocabulary Ⓣ

Reading Strategy
- Ask Questions : Find Question-Answer Relationships

Comprehension & Critical Thinking
- Use Text Evidence Ⓣ

Literary Analysis
- Analyze Text Structure: Cause and Effect Ⓣ
- Analyze Author's Language and Word Choice

Writing
- Form: Response to Literature

Grammar
- Prepositional Phrases

TEACH & PRACTICE

Ⓐ Reading Support

6 Language Read aloud the passage. Point out the common structures Alexie uses. Ask: What does he show by repeating *I read*?

Possible response:
- *that reading was a huge part of his life*

RI.9-10.4

Ⓑ Reading Support

7 Ask Questions Say that Alexie is surprised he became a writer.

ELL Comprehensible Input
Restate abstract ideas:
- *I was trying to save my life:* I was trying to make my life better.

Have students ask and answer questions about Alexie's statement.

Possible response:
- *Why was he surprised? He was never taught how to write poetry, short stories, or novels in school. He had no role models.*

Students learn that some people outside of the reservation mistakenly think that Native Americans cannot be writers. Discuss how this opinion shaped Alexie as a writer.

RI.9-10.1

GRAMMAR SKILLS PATH

51 Prepositions
▶ 52 Prepositional Phrases ELL Language & Grammar Lab
53 Object Pronouns After a Preposition
54 Compound Object Pronouns
55 Review: Pronouns in Prepositional Phrases

Ⓐ secondhand stores. I read the books I borrowed from the library. I read the backs of cereal boxes. I read the newspaper. I read the **bulletins** posted on the walls of the school, the clinic, the **tribal offices**, the post office. I read junk mail. I read auto-repair manuals. I read magazines. I read anything that had words and paragraphs. I read **with equal parts joy and desperation**. I loved those books, but I also knew that love had only one purpose. I was trying to save my life. 6

Ⓑ Despite all the books I read, I am still surprised I became a writer. I was going to be a **pediatrician**. These days, I write novels, short stories, and poems. I visit schools and teach creative writing to Indian kids. In all my years in the reservation school system, I was never taught how to write poetry, short stories, or novels. I was certainly never taught that Indians wrote poetry, short stories, and novels. Writing was something beyond Indians. 7 I cannot recall a single time that a guest teacher visited the reservation. There must have been visiting teachers. Who were they? Where are they now? Do they exist? I visit the schools as often as possible. The Indian kids crowd the classroom. Many are writing their own poems, short stories, and novels. They have read my books. They have read many other books. They look at me with bright eyes and arrogant wonder. They are trying to save their lives. Then there are the **sullen** and already defeated Indian kids who sit in the back rows and ignore me **with theatrical precision**.

I was trying to save my life.

6 Language
Notice the common structures the author uses in this paragraph. What effect does the author create by repeating the phrase *I read* so many times in this paragraph?

7 Ask Questions
Ask yourself questions about Alexie's surprise at becoming a writer. As you read this, what do you learn about how some people viewed Native Americans?

In Other Words

bulletins announcements, fliers
tribal offices buildings where the leaders of the Spokane Indians worked
with equal parts joy and desperation out of love and out of need
pediatrician doctor for children
sullen quiet and angry
with theatrical precision as if they are playing bad students in a play

GRAMMAR

Prepositional Phrases

Teach/Model Display the transparency. Define *phrase*. Then use the example sentences to show the structure of prepositional phrases. Point out that sometimes a sentence can contain more than one prepositional phrase. Have students locate the noun at the end of the prepositional phrases.

Practice A. As students say each sentence with a prepositional phrase, record them and discuss how the prepositional phrase adds information. **B.** After students write about a classroom scene, have each student read one sentence aloud and ask the group to identify the prepositional phrase. L.9-10.1.b

Grammar & Writing Practice Book, pp. 115–116

Grammar Transparency 52

GRAMMAR PREPOSITIONAL PHRASES 52

How Do You Recognize a Prepositional Phrase?
Look for the Preposition.

- A **phrase** is a group of related words. A **prepositional phrase** begins with a preposition and ends with a noun or pronoun. Use prepositional phrases to add information to your sentences.

  Alexie walked **into the school** (noun).

  He looked **around the room** (noun) **at his classmates** (noun).

- The **noun** at the end of a prepositional phrase is called the **object of the preposition**.

Try It

A. Say each pair of sentences. Add a prepositional phrase to tell more. Possible responses:

1. Sherman Alexie read bulletins.
   He read the bulletins ___on school walls___.
2. Alexie never read poetry.
   He never read poetry ___in school___.
3. Now Alexie teaches.
   He teaches creative writing ___to Indian students___.
4. Some students sit. They sit ___in the back rows___.
5. Many students write poems.
   They write poems ___in notebooks___.

B. Write three sentences that describe a classroom scene. Use prepositional phrases to add details. Sentences will vary.

CCSS **Literacy.RI.9-10.1** Cite strong and thorough textual evidence to support analysis of what the text says explicitly as well as inferences drawn from the text. **Literacy.RI.9-10.4** Determine the meaning of words and phrases as they are used in a text, including figurative, connotative, and technical meanings; analyze the cumulative impact of specific word choices on meaning and tone (e.g., how the language of a court opinion differs from that of a newspaper). **Literacy.L.9-10.1.b** Use various types of phrases (noun, verb, adjectival, adverbial, participial, prepositional, absolute) and clauses (independent, dependent; noun, relative, adverbial) to convey specific meanings and add variety and interest to writing or presentations.

The pages of their notebooks are empty. They carry neither pencil nor pen. They stare out the window. They refuse and **resist**. "Books," I say to them. "Books," I say. I throw my weight against their locked doors. The door **holds**. I am smart. I am arrogant. I am lucky. I am trying to save our lives. 8 ❖

C

8 Language
What might the metaphor of the locked door suggest about Native American culture in the present day?

ANALYZE Superman and Me

1. **Explain** Why does Sherman Alexie return to reservation schools as an adult? What is his hope for the young students there? Cite evidence from the text to support your responses.
2. **Vocabulary** According to Alexie, why did many of his childhood classmates resist books and have low **standards** for their schoolwork?
3. **Analyze Text Structure: Cause and Effect** Review the **Cause-and-Effect Chart** you began on page 341. Name two causes and two effects that Alexie gives for his love of reading.
4. **Focus Strategy Ask Questions** As you read, there may be times when you ask yourself: "Why does the author include this?" or "Why is this event or detail important?" Talk with a partner about which questions most helped you understand Alexie's essay. Make a rule about what makes good and bad questions.

D

Return to the Text

Reread and Write Sherman Alexie believes that reading can save people's lives. Do you agree? Reread the text to see how Alexie supports his ideas and consider your own experiences. Then write a short opinion statement about whether reading really has the power to save lives.

E

In Other Words
resist fight against me
holds stays shut against me

APPLY

C Reading Support

8 Language Explain that the metaphor of the locked door represents the minds of the "already defeated" students. Say: *The writer feels that these students are resistant to change. They don't want to be like him.* Then ask students what this metaphor implies about Native American culture in the present day. (It paints a picture of a place that is resistant to change. Many of the young people have already given up and refuse to try and improve their lives.)
RI.9-10.4

D ANALYZE

1. **Explain** Alexie wants to be a role model for Native American students. He wants to change their lives by encouraging them to read and write well.
RI.9-10.1
2. **Vocabulary** His classmates had low expectations for themselves and each other.
L.9-10.6
3. **Analyze Text Structure: Cause and Effect** After students complete their chart, have them compare the causes and effects they cited.

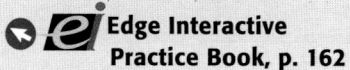

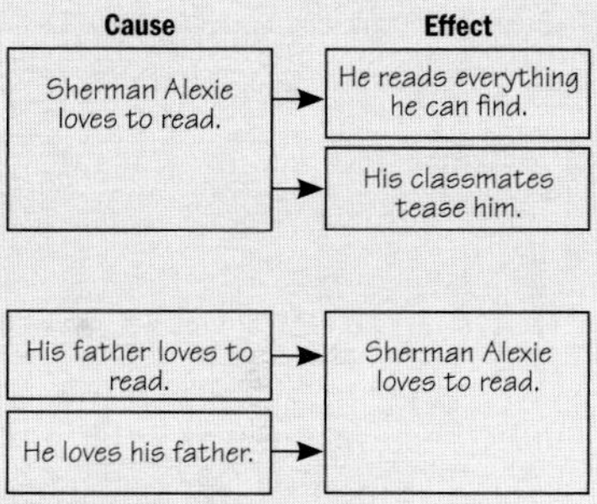

Cause
Effect
Sherman Alexie loves to read.
He reads everything he can find.
His classmates tease him.
His father loves to read.
He loves his father.
Sherman Alexie loves to read.

RI.9-10.5
4. **Focus Strategy: Ask Questions** Have volunteers share their partner's ideas about effective and ineffective questions.
RI.9-10.1

E Return to the Text

Students' statements should reflect both the author's viewpoint and their own experiences.
W.9-10.1; W.9-10.9.b; W.9-10.10

Edge Interactive Practice Book, p. 162

CCSS **Literacy.RI.9-10.1** Cite strong and thorough textual evidence to support analysis of what the text says explicitly as well as inferences drawn from the text. **Literacy.RI.9-10.4** Determine the meaning of words and phrases as they are used in a text, including figurative, connotative, and technical meanings; analyze the cumulative impact of specific word choices on meaning and tone (e.g., how the language of a court opinion differs from that of a newspaper). **Literacy.RI.9-10.5** Analyze in detail how an author's ideas or claims are developed and refined by particular sentences, paragraphs, or larger portions of a text (e.g., a section or chapter). **Literacy.W.9-10.1** Write arguments to support claims in an analysis of substantive topics or texts, using valid reasoning and relevant and sufficient evidence. **Literacy.W.9-10.9.b** Apply grades 9-10 Reading standards to literary nonfiction (e.g., "Delineate and evaluate the argument and specific claims in a text, assessing whether the reasoning is valid and the evidence is relevant and sufficient; identify false statements and fallacious reasoning"). **Literacy.W.9-10.10** Write routinely over extended time frames (time for research, reflection, and revision) and shorter time frames (a single sitting or a day or two) for a range of tasks, purposes, and audiences. **Literacy.L.9-10.6** Acquire and use accurately general academic and domain-specific words and phrases, sufficient for reading, writing, speaking, and listening at the college and career readiness level; demonstrate independence in gathering vocabulary knowledge when considering a word or phrase important to comprehension or expression.

Lesson 13
BEFORE READING

OBJECTIVES

Reading Strategies
- Ask Questions: Find Question-Answer Relationships

Comprehension & Critical Thinking
- Use Text Evidence T

Literary Analysis
- Analyze Text Structure: Chronology T

TEACH STRATEGIES

A Analyze Text Structure: Chronology

Introduce Read the introduction about text structures together. Ask students to give an example of a type of text in which the author tells the events chronologically.

Ask: Why is chronological order effective for a biography?

Possible response:
- *It clearly shows the order of events.*

Look Into the Text Use the callouts on p. 350 to teach flashback. Ask: Which phrases tell you that the author is "flashing back" in time?

Possible response:
- *memories of childhood weekends; back then*

RI.9-10.5

B Focus Strategy: Ask Questions

Find Question-Answer Relationships Remind students how to use the strategy by guiding them through the steps in the How To box. Show the difference between "right there" and "think and search" answers by pointing to parts in the text that answer the sample questions.

Then ask: What other questions do you have about this text? Can you find answers here, or will you have to read more?

Possible response:
- *Why does the word mango remind the author of trips to Olvera Street's plaza? (read more to find out)*

RI.9-10.1

ONGOING ASSESSMENT
Have students tell about a flashback in a book or film and explain why it was included.

BEFORE READING A Smart Cookie/ It's Our Story, Too

short fiction by Sandra Cisneros
memoir by Yvette Cabrera

Reading Strategies
- Plan and Monitor
- Determine Importance
- Make Inferences
- ▶ **Ask Questions**
- Make Connections
- Synthesize
- Visualize

Analyze Text Structure: Chronology

A

As you have seen, writers choose from a variety of text structures, such as cause and effect, chronological order, or problem-solution, to organize their writing. In **chronological order**, writers describe the events in the order that they happened. Other writers may use **flashback**, which is a kind of chronological order that tells about events further in the past, often by relating memories, dreams, or conversations. Or writers may shift to the present time to tell about what is happening now. Signal words and phrases are good clues that the events are heading in a different direction.

Look Into the Text

The author describes time passing.

She uses flashback to tell about a time before high school.

It was that way all through high school. Then one day in college I was assigned to read *The House on Mango Street.*

Mango. The word alone evoked memories of childhood weekends. Back then my family and I would pile into our sky-blue Chevrolet Malibu and head to Olvera Street's plaza in downtown Los Angeles.

Signal words and phrases show how time changes.

Focus Strategy ▶ Ask Questions

As you **ask questions** about a selection, you may find that some answers are "right there" in the text. Other answers may not be so easy to answer. In many cases, you will need to consider how different ideas in a text are connected before you think and search for the answer you are looking for.

B

Focus Strategy

HOW TO FIND QUESTION-ANSWER RELATIONSHIPS

1. As you read, record questions you have about the text in a **Question-Answer Journal**.
2. Record any answers that can be found "right there" in the text.
3. For other questions, find the part of the selection that the question is asking about. Consider how the information or ideas fit together and see if you can find an answer.
4. If you cannot find an answer, keep reading. You may find an answer later.

Question-Answer Journal

Question	Answer
When did the author read The House on Mango Street?	Right There: in college
Why did the book remind the author of her childhood?	Think and Search: The people, places, and things (like mangos) were like her memories of the past.

CCSS Literacy.RI.9-10.1 Cite strong and thorough textual evidence to support analysis of what the text says explicitly as well as inferences drawn from the text. Literacy.RI.9-10.5 Analyze in detail how an author's ideas or claims are developed and refined by particular sentences, paragraphs, or larger portions of a text (e.g., a section or chapter).

Connect Across Texts
In "Superman and Me," Sherman Alexie describes how a comic book changed his life. Read "A Smart Cookie" and "It's Our Story, Too" to learn how Cisneros's book changed the life of one of her readers. **D**

A Smart Cookie

by Sandra Cisneros

C

Do words have the power to change lives? Author Sandra Cisneros's characters (and her readers) certainly think so.

Comprehension Coach

Build Reading Power

Assign students to use the software, based on their instructional needs.

Read Silently
- Comprehension questions with immediate feedback
- Glossary support
- Review text evidence

RI.9-10.10

Listen
- Professional model of fluent reading

Record
- Oral reading fluency practice
- Ongoing fluency assessment with immediate feedback

OBJECTIVES

Reading Strategies
- Ask Questions
- Make Connections

Literary Analysis
- Evaluate Literature (author's perspective)

BUILD BACKGROUND

About the Authors

Share this information about the authors with students: Sandra Cisneros is a Mexican American writer of novels, short stories, and poetry. When she was a child, her family moved often. Cisneros learned that writing helped overcome those painful experiences. "A Smart Cookie" is an excerpt from *The House on Mango Street,* a novel in which the main character also hates moving.

Also Mexican American, Yvette Cabrera is a news reporter who writes about the Hispanic community in California. In this selection, Cabrera tells how Cisneros's writing affected her life.

C Reading Support

Ask Questions Read the title and text below it.

> **ELL Rephrase Language** Explain that a "smart cookie" is someone who is clever and good at dealing with difficult situations.

Ask students what questions they hope to have answered as they read the selections.

Possible responses:
- *Who is the smart cookie?*
- *How does Cisneros affect her readers' lives?*

RI.9-10.1

D Connect Across Texts

Say: Predict how Cisneros's book changed Cabrera's life.

Possible response:
- *by showing Cabrera that a Hispanic woman can be a successful writer*

CCSS **Literacy.RI.9-10.1** Cite strong and thorough textual evidence to support analysis of what the text says explicitly as well as inferences drawn from the text. **Literacy.RI.9-10.10** By the end of grade 9, read and comprehend literary nonfiction in the grades 9–10 text complexity band proficiently, with scaffolding as needed at the high end of the range. By the end of grade 10, read and comprehend literary nonfiction at the high end of the grades 9–10 text complexity band independently and proficiently.

READ

OBJECTIVES

Vocabulary
- Key Vocabulary Ⓣ
- Content Area Vocabulary: Performing Arts

Reading Strategy
- Ask Questions: Find Question-Answer Relationships

Comprehension & Critical Thinking
- Use Text Evidence Ⓣ

Literary Analysis
- Analyze Text Features: Art
- Analyze Text Structure: Chronology Ⓣ

Viewing
- Respond to and Interpret Visuals

Grammar
- Object Pronouns After a Preposition Ⓣ

TEACH & PRACTICE

Ⓐ Reading Support

1 Ask Questions Ask: What *wh*-questions about the first sentence can help you understand it better?

Possible responses:
- *What does the mother mean by "somebody"?*

Ⓑ Critical Viewing: Design

Analyze Design Ask: How do the colors and light relate to the painting's title and meaning?

Possible response:
- *Light shines from the girl's head, showing that she is dreaming.*

Ⓒ Reading Support

2 Chronology Ask: Which signal words tell you that the mother is talking about the past? The present?

Possible responses:
- *Past: then; Present: Today*

RL.9-10.5

Monitor Comprehension

Explain Ask: How does the mother see herself in the past and now?

Possible response:
- *In the past, she thought she was "a smart cookie." She thinks she is "nobody" because she didn't stay in school.*

RL.9-10.1

GRAMMAR SKILLS PATH
51 Prepositions
52 Prepositional Phrases
▶ 53 Object Pronouns After a Preposition ELL Language & Grammar Lab
54 Compound Object Pronouns
55 Review: Pronouns in Prepositional Phrases

Ⓐ **I could've been somebody, you know?** my mother says and sighs. 1 She has lived in this city her whole life. She can speak two languages. She can sing an opera. She knows how to fix a T.V. But she doesn't know which subway train to take to get downtown. I hold her hand very tight while we wait for the right train to arrive.

She used to draw when she had time. Now she draws with a needle and thread, little knotted rosebuds, tulips made of silk thread. Someday she would like to go to the ballet. Someday she would like to see a play. She borrows opera records from the public library and sings with **velvety lungs powerful as morning glories**.

Ⓒ Today while cooking oatmeal she is **Madame Butterfly** until she sighs and points the wooden spoon at me. I could've been somebody, you know? Esperanza, you go to school. Study hard. That Madame Butterfly was a fool. She stirs the oatmeal. Look at my ***comadres***. She means Izaura whose husband left and Yolanda whose husband is dead. Got to take care all your own, she says shaking her head.

Then out of nowhere:

Shame is a bad thing, you know. **It keeps you down**. You want to know why I quit school? Because I didn't have nice clothes. No clothes, but I had brains.

Yup, she says **disgusted**, stirring again. I was a smart cookie then. 2

Ⓑ 

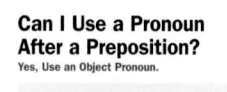

The Dreamer, 2002, Patssi Valdez. Acrylic on canvas.

Critical Viewing: Design What is the title of this work? How do the colors and light contribute to its meaning?

1 Ask Questions What *wh*–questions help you understand this sentence better? Record them in your Question-Answer Journal.

2 Chronology Which signal words tell you when the mother talks about the past and the present?

Monitor Comprehension

Explain The mother in "A Smart Cookie" remembers her youth. How did she see herself then? How does she see herself now?

Key Vocabulary

shame *n.*, a painful feeling that is caused by embarrassment or guilt

disgusted *adj.*, feeling very upset

In Other Words

velvety lungs powerful as morning glories a strong and beautiful voice
Madame Butterfly a famous opera character
comadres very good friends (in Spanish)
It keeps you down. It keeps you from being happy and doing what you want to do.

352 Unit 4 Opening Doors

GRAMMAR

Object Pronouns After a Preposition

Teach/Model Display the transparency. Ask volunteers to read aloud the example sentences, replacing *me* with each of the other object pronouns from the chart. Encourage pairs of students to create and share additional example sentences.

Practice A. Point out that object pronouns are not the only pronouns in the paragraph. As students add the object pronouns, write them on the transparency. **B.** Have students write and read their sentences aloud. Choose some to write on the transparency and ask the group to identify the prepositions and object pronouns. L.9-10.1.b

Grammar & Writing Practice Book, pp. 117–118

Grammar Transparency 53

GRAMMAR OBJECT PRONOUNS AFTER A PREPOSITION 53

Can I Use a Pronoun After a Preposition?
Yes, Use an Object Pronoun.

- Use an **object pronoun** after a preposition.
  Mom wants the best **for me**.
  That's why she discusses the future **with me**.

Object Pronouns	
Singular	Plural
me	us
you	you
him, her, it	them

Try It

A. Read this paragraph about one mother's advice. Add object pronouns.

My mom has many plans for __me__. I wonder if her parents talked to __her__ about staying in school. Last week, she saw Miguel and had advice for __him__. She speaks to __us__ out of love, so we don't mind. But look out, friends! If you visit, she may have words of wisdom for __you__, too!

B. Now tell a partner about giving or getting advice. Write three sentences. Use prepositional phrases with object pronouns.
Sentences will vary.

CCSS Literacy.RL.9-10.1 Cite strong and thorough textual evidence to support analysis of what the text says explicitly as well as inferences drawn from the text. Literacy.RL.9-10.5 Analyze how an author's choices concerning how to structure a text, order events within it (e.g., parallel plots), and manipulate time (e.g., pacing, flashbacks) create such effects as mystery, tension, or surprise. Literacy.L.9-10.1.b Use various types of phrases (noun, verb, adjectival, adverbial, participial, prepositional, absolute) and clauses (independent, dependent; noun, relative, adverbial) to convey specific meanings and add variety and interest to writing or presentations.

It's Our Story, Too

by Yvette Cabrera

The Orange County Register (Santa Ana, California)
April 15, 2002

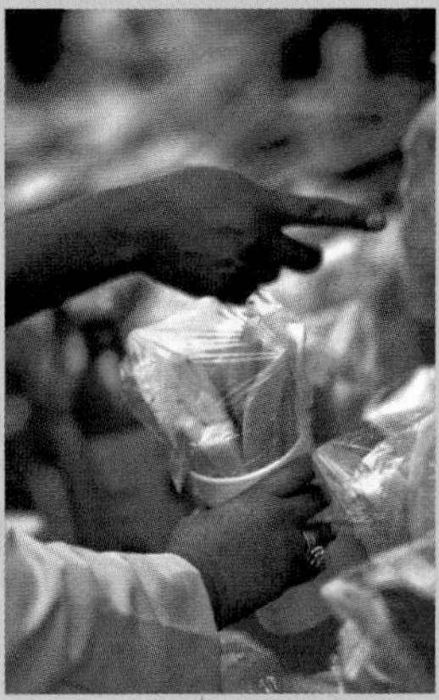

Fresh fruit from a fruit stand at the Olvera Street plaza in Los Angeles, California

Growing up, I studied books my high school English teachers said were must reads for a well-rounded education. Books like J. D. Salinger's *Catcher in the Rye*, Fyodor Dostoyevsky's *Crime and Punishment*, and Thomas Hardy's *Tess of the d'Urbervilles*.

It was literature with great meaning that taught important lessons. But still, I **felt a disconnection**. *Beowulf* was an epic poem. But as my high school teacher went into great detail explaining what **a mail shirt** was, I wondered what that had to do with my life.

It was that way all through high school. Then one day in college I was assigned to read *The House on Mango Street*.

Mango. The word alone **evoked memories** of childhood weekends. Back then my family and I would pile into our sky-blue Chevrolet Malibu and head to **Olvera Street's plaza** in downtown Los Angeles. 3

For my sisters and me, the treat for behaving ourselves was a juicy mango on a stick sold at a fruit stand in the plaza. We would squeeze lemon and sprinkle chile and salt over the bright yellow slices.

As an adult, whenever I had a reporting assignment near Olvera Street, I'd always take a minute to stop. Standing amid the smell of sizzling ***carne asada***, the sounds of **vendors negotiating** prices in Spanish, and children licking a rainbow of *raspados* (shaved ice treats), I would bite into my mango and feel at home. 4

That's what *The House on Mango Street* did for me.

D

E

3 Chronology
Look for the phrases that signal what time periods the author is describing.

4 Author's Purpose
Why does the author switch to Spanish words?

In Other Words

felt a disconnection couldn't relate to the stories
a mail shirt armor in old battles
evoked memories reminded me
Olvera Street's plaza an outdoor shopping area that is famous for its Hispanic products
carne asada grilled steak (in Spanish)
vendors negotiating sellers arguing about

TEACH & PRACTICE

D Reading Support

3 Chronology Remind students that signal words and phrases are clues to help readers understand chronology as they read.

ELL Use Graphic Organizer Use a Sequence Chain to help students visualize the order of story events. For example:

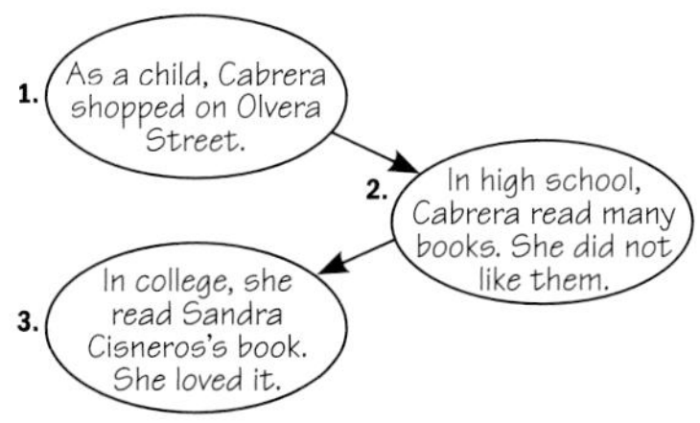

1. As a child, Cabrera shopped on Olvera Street.
2. In high school, Cabrera read many books. She did not like them.
3. In college, she read Sandra Cisneros's book. She loved it.

Add to the sequence chart as you read the selection.

Ask: Which phrases tell about time?

Possible responses:
- *Growing up, all through high school, one day in college, Back then, As an adult, whenever*

Have students evaluate the effectiveness of signal words in a chronological text structure. Ask: What do the signal words help the reader to understand about the author of this memoir?

Possible response:
- *The signal words show how books affected her over time and the childhood memories brought up by* The House on Mango Street.

RI.9-10.5

E Reading Support

4 Author's Purpose Review the meaning of the two Spanish phrases. Ask: Why did the author use Spanish words here instead of English?

Possible response:
- *The story evokes childhood memories of Olvera Street, including hearing Spanish. She can relate to* The House on Mango Street.

RI.9-10.6

VOCABULARY

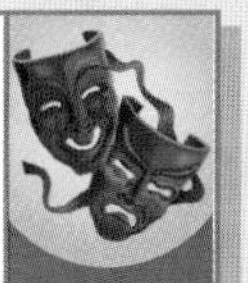

DRAMA

Content Area Vocabulary: Performing Arts

Build vocabulary related to the content area of performing arts.

Teach/Model Use the Make Words Your Own routine (*see the Vocabulary tab*) and the sample sentences below to introduce these words from the selection.

ballet (**ba**-lā) ▸ p. 352

The graceful dancers in the **ballet** *wore beautiful costumes.*

play (plā) ▸ p. 352

Actors study hard to memorize their lines in a **play**.

opera (**ah**-prah) ▸ p. 352

The music in an **opera** *is usually very dramatic and full of emotion.*

review (re-**vyū**) ▸ p. 355

Critics **review** *plays to help people decide if they should see the play or not.*

Practice Have students use the words to describe types of performances they enjoy or would like to see.

Apply Have students review a movie, television show, or theatrical performance and share it with the class.

L.9-10.6

CCSS **Literacy.RI.9-10.5** Analyze in detail how an author's ideas or claims are developed and refined by particular sentences, paragraphs, or larger portions of a text (e.g., a section or chapter). **Literacy.RI.9-10.6** Determine an author's point of view or purpose in a text and analyze how an author uses rhetoric to advance that point of view or purpose. **Literacy.L.9-10.6** Acquire and use accurately general academic and domain-specific words and phrases, sufficient for reading, writing, speaking, and listening at the college and career readiness level; demonstrate independence in gathering vocabulary knowledge when considering a word or phrase important to comprehension or expression.

OBJECTIVES

Vocabulary
- Key Vocabulary Ⓣ

Reading Strategy
- Ask Questions; Review Strategies

Comprehension & Critical Thinking
- Use Text Evidence Ⓣ

Literary Analysis
- Analyze Text Features: Art
- Analyze Text Structure: Chronology Ⓣ

Research Skills
- Choose and Narrow a Topic

Viewing
- Respond to and Interpret Visuals

Grammar
- Compound Object Pronouns Ⓣ

TEACH & PRACTICE

A Analyze Visuals

About the Art Frank Romero has made many lively paintings in which he celebrates L.A.'s busy freeways—the part of Los Angeles that most people complain about!

Interpret and Respond Ask: What does Romero like about the freeway?

Possible responses:
- *the colors; the movement*

B Critical Viewing: Effect

Analyze Effect Ask: What mood do the painting's colors and lines create? How might this painting reflect the feeling of a large city like Los Angeles?

Possible responses:
- *a busy, fast-moving, happy mood*
- *The city is busy, and the different ethnic communities make it colorful.*

C Reading Support

5 Ask Questions Ask: What questions do you have about the first two paragraphs? Can you answer them or will you have to read on?

Possible response:
- *Why does everyone except Cabrera's parents pronounce her last name "haltingly"? (need to read on)*

RI.9-10.1

GRAMMAR SKILLS PATH

51	Prepositions
52	Prepositional Phrases
53	Object Pronouns After a Preposition
▶ 54	Compound Object Pronouns ELL Language & Grammar Lab
55	Review: Pronouns in Prepositional Phrases

A

East on the 10, 2001, Frank Romero. Oil on wood, private collection.

B △ Critical Viewing: Effect What mood do the colors and lines create? How might this reflect the feeling of a large city like Los Angeles?

C

On the first page, Esperanza explains how at school they say her name funny, "as if the syllables were made out of tin and hurt the roof of your mouth." I was **hooked**.

I knew nothing of the East Coast **prep schools** or the English **shires** of the books I had read before. But like Esperanza, I could remember how different my last name sounded when it was **pronounced melodically** by my parents but **so haltingly** by everyone else. 5

Cisneros's hometown of Chicago may have been hundreds of miles away from the palm-tree lined streets of Santa Barbara, California, where I grew up. But in her world I was no longer **the minority**.

5 Ask Questions Check your understanding by asking questions about this text. Reread the text to find the answer. Record them in your Question-Answer Journal.

In Other Words

hooked so interested I couldn't stop reading it
prep schools expensive private schools
shires villages
pronounced melodically said in a musical way
so haltingly said in a jerky, ugly way
the minority part of the small group that no one seemed to notice or care about

GRAMMAR

Compound Object Pronouns

Teach/Model Display the transparency. Review subject and object pronouns. Read the examples, and have students identify the compound objects. Read the last example sentence and elicit why the prepositional phrase is at the start (*to emphasize it*). Work through the sentences with mistakes.

Practice A. As students say each sentence, underline the correct pronoun and have them explain their choice. **B.** After partners talk about a memory and write their own sentences, have each student read a sentence aloud and ask the group to identify prepositional phrases. L.9-10.1.b

Grammar & Writing Practice Book, pp. 119–120

Grammar Transparency 54

In a Prepositional Phrase, Where Does the Pronoun Go?

GRAMMAR COMPOUND OBJECT PRONOUNS 54

It Goes Last.

- A **prepositional phrase** starts with a preposition and ends with a noun or a pronoun. Sometimes, it ends with both. Put the pronoun last.
  I remember the day Mom went out **with my sisters and me**.
  We met Dad **on Olvera Street**. He bought mangos **for Mom and us**.
- You can put a prepositional phrase at the start of the sentence to emphasize your idea.
  To my sisters and me, Olvera Street still feels like home.
- Avoid these common mistakes in a prepositional phrase:
  1. Use **me,** not **I**:
     Olvera Street was a magical place for my sisters and ~~I~~ me.
  2. Put **me** last:
     Memories of that place are special to ~~me and my sisters~~ my sisters and me.

Try It

A. Say the sentences. Use the correct pronouns.

1. Vendors sold fruit to local shoppers and **(we / us)**.
2. For Ana and **(I / me)**, mangos with salt and chile were a treat.
3. Dad said, "Olvera Street means a lot to **(me and you / you and me)**.
4. That day together was great for my family and **(I / me)**.
5. To other families and **(we / us)**, these childhood memories are more than just good times.

B. Now tell a partner about a childhood memory. Write three sentences. Use prepositional phrases. Sentences will vary.

CCSS Literacy.RI.9-10.1 Cite strong and thorough textual evidence to support analysis of what the text says explicitly as well as inferences drawn from the text. Literacy.L.9-10.1.b Use various types of phrases (noun, verb, adjectival, adverbial, participial, prepositional, absolute) and clauses (independent, dependent; noun, relative, adverbial) to convey specific meanings and add variety and interest to writing or presentations.

That was a dozen years ago. Today, Latinos are the **majority** in cities like Santa Ana, California, where Cisneros spoke at Valley High School.

Today, these students can pick from bookstore shelves filled with authors such as Julia Álvarez, Victor Villaseñor, and Judith Ortiz Cofer. These are authors who go beyond **census numbers** to explain what U.S. Latino life is about. 6

Cisneros provided an hour of humorous storytelling that had the students busting with laughter. They crowded in line afterward, **giddily** waiting to get her autograph.

"Everything she explains, what she says is true," Jessica Cordova, a 10th-grader at Valley High School, says of *The House on Mango Street*. "She puts a lot of emotion, feeling, and thought into the book." 7

Later, as I talk to Cisneros, she explains how much **the literary world** has changed since she finished writing *The House on Mango Street* twenty years ago. Back then, forget trying to get *The New York Times* to review your book if you were Latino—or getting a major bookseller to carry it, she says.

One thing has remained **constant**, something that Cisneros can see by the question that's most asked by students.

Sandra Cisneros
The House on Mango Street
"Sandra Cisneros is one of the most brilliant of today's young writers. Her work is sensitive, alert, nuanceful... rich with music and picture."—Gwendolyn Brooks

The House on Mango Street is a book by Sandra Cisneros. The narrator is a Latina girl named Esperanza, who describes people and events in her neighborhood.

D

E

6 **Chronology** How have schools, students, and books changed since the author first read the book?

7 **Ask Questions** What questions might the students have asked Cisneros? Record them in your Question-Answer Journal.

Key Vocabulary

- **constant** *adj.*, the same, without any change

In Other Words

majority group which has the most people
census numbers the official number of people who live in the country
giddily excitedly
the literary world the book-selling and publishing businesses

D Reading Support

6 Chronology Point out that there have been many changes since the author first read the book.

ELL Use Graphic Organizer
Have students use a time line to understand changes that have taken place:

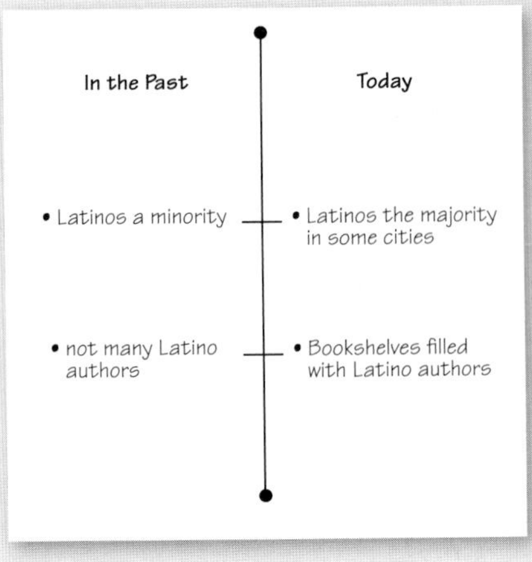

In the Past
Today
• Latinos a minority
• Latinos the majority in some cities
• not many Latino authors
• Bookshelves filled with Latino authors

Ask: What has changed since Cabrera was in high school?

Possible responses:

- *In some places, Latinos are the majority.*
- *Students can easily find books by Latino authors.*

Have students evaluate the author's use of past events as part of the method of development. Ask: How does reading about past events help your understanding?

Possible response:

- *It shows how much society has changed over the years.*

RI.9-10.5

E Reading Support

7 Ask Questions Ask: If Cisneros came to your school, what would you ask her?

Possible responses:

- *Is Esperanza really you?*
- *Why was moving hard for you?*

RI.9-10.1

Review Strategies Ask what other strategies students used as they read.

Possible response:

- *I read the author's description of eating a mango and visualized the experience. This helped me understand the memories she pictures when she thinks of home.*

RI.9-10.1

CONTENT AREA CONNECTIONS

Research Hispanic Authors

Conduct Research Have students research one of the authors that Cabrera lists or other Hispanic writers. Ask them to answer the following:

- When and where was the author born? Where did he or she grow up? Were there many other Hispanics in the neighborhood?
- What are some of the author's most famous books? Does he or she write poetry, fiction, or another literary genre?
- What interesting quotes from the author can you find?
- How does the author feel about his or her Hispanic heritage? Has he or she faced discrimination in the U.S.?
- Does he or she visit schools to talk with students?

Share and Compare Students can share their findings with the class to compare the authors they researched.

W.9-10.7

CCSS **Literacy.RI.9-10.1** Cite strong and thorough textual evidence to support analysis of what the text says explicitly as well as inferences drawn from the text. **Literacy.RI.9-10.5** Analyze in detail how an author's ideas or claims are developed and refined by particular sentences, paragraphs, or larger portions of a text (e.g., a section or chapter). **Literacy.W.9-10.7** Conduct short as well as more sustained research projects to answer a question (including a self-generated question) or solve a problem; narrow or broaden the inquiry when appropriate; synthesize multiple sources on the subject, demonstrating understanding of the subject under investigation.

READ

OBJECTIVES

Vocabulary
- Key Vocabulary Ⓣ

Reading Strategy
- Ask Questions

Comprehension & Critical Thinking
- Use Text Evidence Ⓣ

Literary Analysis
- Analyze Text Structure: Chronology Ⓣ

Writing
- Form: Response to Literature

APPLY

Ⓐ ANALYZE

1. **Explain** Cabrera realizes that there are books that reflect her own experience and that describe her world. RI.9-10.1
2. **Vocabulary** She's disgusted with herself for quitting school and not becoming everything she could have. L.9-10.6
3. **Analyze Text Structure: Chronology** Changes: Today some schools are mostly Hispanic and the students have no trouble finding books by Hispanic writers. Constant: Kids still want authors to write about their own lives. RI.9-10.5
4. **Focus Strategy: Ask Questions** Ask a group spokesperson to share a sampling of each group's questions, answers, and reasoning processes. RI.9-10.1

Ⓑ Return to the Text

Remind students that a journal entry tells the inner thoughts and feelings of the writer. Writing from the daughter's point of view, students may express things the daughter wouldn't want her mother or anyone else to know. W.9-10.9.a; W.9-10.10

"They want to know, 'Is this real? Did this happen to you?'" Cisneros says. "They're so concerned and want to make sure this is my story, because it's their story, too." ❖

ANALYZE A Smart Cookie/It's Our Story, Too

Ⓐ

1. **Explain** How does the idea of reading change for Yvette Cabrera after she reads *The House on Mango Street*? Support your answer with details from the text.
2. **Vocabulary** Why does the mother in "A Smart Cookie" feel **disgusted**? Who or what is she upset about?
3. **Analyze Text Structure: Chronology** According to Cabrera, how have schools changed since her childhood? What has remained **constant**?
4. **Focus Strategy Ask Questions** Work with a group to share your questions from the **Question-Answer Journal** you began on page 350. Discuss how you found details and connected ideas to answer your questions.

Ⓑ

Return to the Text

Reread and Write Reread "A Smart Cookie" by Sandra Cisneros. Then write a journal entry from the daughter's point of view. Describe the advice she has gotten from her mother and how it has opened doors.

About the Writer

Sandra Cisneros (1954–) is one of the leading Latina voices in contemporary American literature. She has published two novels, a collection of short stories, and three books of poetry. "A Smart Cookie" is from her famous book, *The House on Mango Street*, which is often taught in high schools and colleges today.

Interactive Reading

Have students reread and mark "A Smart Cookie" and "It's Our Story, Too" within the Edge Interactive Practice Book to apply their knowledge of Text Structure: Chronology and to practice the Focus Strategy—Ask Questions: Find Question-Answer Relationships.

Edge Interactive Practice Book, pp. 163–168

Unit Project

Progress Check Allow time for students to work on their unit projects. Meet with individuals and/or groups to provide guidance and check on their progress.

myNGconnect.com
- **Unit Planning Tools**
- **Unit Project Evaluation Rubric**

CCSS **Literacy.RL.9-10.1** Cite strong and thorough textual evidence to support analysis of what the text says explicitly as well as inferences drawn from the text. **Literacy.RI.9-10.1** Cite strong and thorough textual evidence to support analysis of what the text says explicitly as well as inferences drawn from the text. **Literacy.RI.9-10.5** Analyze in detail how an author's ideas or claims are developed and refined by particular sentences, paragraphs, or larger portions of a text (e.g., a section or chapter). **Literacy.W.9-10.9.a** Apply grades 9-10 Reading standards to literature (e.g., "Analyze how an author draws on and transforms source material in a specific work [e.g., how Shakespeare treats a theme or topic from Ovid or the Bible or how a later author draws on a play by Shakespeare]"). **Literacy.W.9-10.10** Write routinely over extended time frames (time for research, reflection, and revision) and shorter time frames (a single sitting or a day or two) for a range of tasks, purposes, and audiences. **Literacy.L.9-10.6** Acquire and use accurately general academic and domain-specific words and phrases, sufficient for reading, writing, speaking, and listening at the college and career readiness level; demonstrate independence in gathering vocabulary knowledge when considering a word or phrase important to comprehension or expression.

Reflect and Assess

- Superman and Me
- A Smart Cookie
- It's Our Story, Too

EQ How Can Knowledge Open Doors?

Reading

Critical Thinking

1. **Analyze** How does reading have the power to open doors in people's lives? Support your ideas with examples from each selection.
2. **Compare** Both Sandra Cisneros and Sherman Alexie talk with high school students about writing. How are the students' responses similar or different? Explain.
3. **Interpret** According to the selections, why do some students resist reading or working hard in school? What do you think can be done to change the way these students view school?
4. **Speculate** What might Esperanza's mother tell the "sullen" and "defeated" students at Alexie's school? What advice do you think Alexie and Yvette Cabrera would give these students?
5. **Assess** Each of these authors addresses the importance of education and reading. Which selection do you relate to the most? Why?

Writing

Write About Literature

E-mail Message Write an e-mail to one of the struggling students you have read about, such as one of Alexie's students, Esperanza's mother, and young Yvette Cabrera. Offer advice from one of the three authors about what the student can do to change his or her attitude toward school and reading.

Vocabulary

Key Vocabulary Review

Oral Review Work with a partner. Use these words to complete the paragraph.

arrogant	**disgusted**	**shame**
assumed	**prodigy**	**standards**
constant	**recall**	

My little brother Eddie is a true __(1)__ who could read and write when he was only three years old. As I __(2)__ from memories of his childhood, he was a __(3)__ reader who always had a book open. People who didn't know the truth __(4)__ that everything came easily for him. But he just set such high __(5)__ for himself that he worked harder than everyone else. He became __(6)__ and upset if he made one mistake on a test. If he made two mistakes, he'd feel great __(7)__, guilt, and embarrassment. But even though Eddie is a really smart kid, he's always humble and never __(8)__. It's just another reason why I'm so proud of my little brother.

Writing Application **Recall** a time when you met someone who was **arrogant**. Write a paragraph about it. Use at least four Key Vocabulary words.

Fluency

Read with Ease: Intonation

Assess your reading fluency with the passage in the Reading Handbook, p. 761. Then complete the self-check below.

1. My intonation did/did not sound natural.
2. My words correct per minute: ____.

Lesson 14

REFLECT AND ASSESS

OBJECTIVES

Vocabulary
- Key Vocabulary T

Reading Fluency
- Intonation T

Comprehension & Critical Thinking
- Compare Across Texts
- Use Text Evidence T

Literary Analysis
- Evaluate Literature

Writing
- Form: E-mail Message
- Form: Paragraph

Reading

Critical Thinking

1. **Analyze** Reading helped Alexie and Cisneros escape difficult childhoods and become successful writers. It helped Cabrera to feel like a valued member of a group.
RI.9-10.1
2. **Compare** Similar: Many students are excited to talk with famous writers. Different: When Alexie visits reservations, some Native American students do not seem happy or excited to see him.
3. **Interpret** Some students might resist it because they don't want to seem smarter than other students or because they can't find books that they can relate to.
4. **Speculate** Esperanza's mother would probably tell them that she is very sorry now that she dropped out of school and that she could have been successful if she had stayed. Alexie might explain how reading and writing helped him to have a happier life—and to make money. Cabrera might encourage them to find good books by Native American authors.
RI.9-10.10
5. **Assess** Ask students to support the reasons that they identify most strongly with Alexie, Cisneros, or Cabrera.

Writing

Write About Literature

Edge Interactive Practice Book, p. 169

E-mail Message Have students choose a "sullen" student of Alexie's, Esperanza's mother (when she was a student), or young Cabrera. Before they begin to write, have them note advice that each author might give a struggling student. Invite students to share their e-mail messages.
W.9-10.9.a; W.9-10.9.b

Vocabulary

Key Vocabulary Review

1. *prodigy* 2. *recall* 3. *constant* 4. *assumed* 5. *standards* 6. *disgusted* 7. *shame* 8. *arrogant*
L.9-10.6

Fluency

Read with Ease: Intonation

Ensure that students complete the self-check.
RI.9-10.10

ASSESS & RETEACH

Assessments Handbook, pp. 43f–43i

Have students complete the **Reader Reflection**. Then give students the **Cluster Test** to measure their progress. Group students as needed for reteaching.

CCSS **Literacy.RI.9-10.1** Cite strong and thorough textual evidence to support analysis of what the text says explicitly as well as inferences drawn from the text. **Literacy.RI.9-10.10** By the end of grade 9, read and comprehend literary nonfiction in the grades 9-10 text complexity band proficiently, with scaffolding as needed at the high end of the range. By the end of grade 10, read and comprehend literary nonfiction at the high end of the grades 9-10 text complexity band independently and proficiently. **Literacy.W.9-10.9.a** Apply grades 9-10 Reading standards to literature (e.g., "Analyze how an author draws on and transforms source material in a specific work [e.g., how Shakespeare treats a theme or topic from Ovid or the Bible or how a later author draws on a play by Shakespeare]"). **Literacy.W.9-10.9.b** Apply grades 9-10 Reading standards to literary nonfiction (e.g., "Delineate and evaluate the argument and specific claims in a text, assessing whether the reasoning is valid and the evidence is relevant and sufficient; identify false statements and fallacious reasoning"). **Literacy.L.9-10.6** Acquire and use accurately general academic and domain-specific words and phrases, sufficient for reading, writing, speaking, and listening at the college and career readiness level; demonstrate independence in gathering vocabulary knowledge when considering a word or phrase important to comprehension or expression.

Lesson 15

INTEGRATE THE LANGUAGE ARTS

OBJECTIVES

Language Function
- Clarify T

Literary Analysis
- Analyze Imagery

Grammar
- Pronouns in Prepositional Phrases T

Grammar

Use Pronouns in Prepositional Phrases

Grammar Transparency 55

Review Use the transparency to review pronouns in prepositional phrases. Then conduct the activity on p. 358.

Oral Practice **1.** it **2.** them **3.** her **4.** him **5.** us

Written Practice ~~them~~ him/~~her~~ them/ ~~us~~ them
L.9-10.1.b

Language Development

Clarify

Evaluate using the Language Acquisition Rubric.
SL.9-10.1.c

Assessments Handbook, p. 43o

Literary Analysis

Analyze Imagery

Imagery	Sense(s)	Effect
(Alexie, p. 333) "Our house was filled with books. They were stacked in crazy piles in the bathroom, bedrooms, and living room."	sight	I can picture tall, wobbly, uneven stacks of books all over the house.

Read aloud partners' written examples and analyses. Discuss as a class which images are strongest.
RL.9-10.4; RI.9-10.4

Edge Interactive Practice Book, p. 170

GRAMMAR SKILLS PATH

INTEGRATE THE LANGUAGE ARTS

Grammar

Use Pronouns in Prepositional Phrases

Prepositions show how words relate. Some common prepositions are **about**, **for**, **from**, **in**, **on**, **to**, and **with**.

A **prepositional phrase** is a group of words that begins with a preposition and ends with a noun or an object pronoun. **Object pronouns** are **me**, **you**, **him**, **her**, **it**, **us**, and **them**.

The books were **for Sherman Alexie**.

The books were **for him**.

When a prepositional phrase ends with both a noun and an object pronoun, put the object pronoun last.

Books were important **to our father and us**.

I wrote **about Superman and me**.

Oral Practice (1–5) With a partner, replace the underlined word or words with an object pronoun.

1. Sherman Alexie tells about <u>his home</u>.
2. The house was filled with <u>books</u>.
3. The boy learned from both his father and <u>mother</u>.
4. Many of the books came from <u>his father</u>.
5. What does Alexie's message mean to <u>my friends and me</u>?

Written Practice (6–10) Fix three more pronouns and rewrite the paragraph. Then add two more sentences. Use prepositional phrases.

Sherman Alexie's culture is important to ~~he~~ **him**. Alexie wants young Indians to learn from them. He talks to students. He hopes to be a help to her. Alexie visits schools and wants other speakers to go to us, too.

Language Development

Clarify

Pair Talk Read a paragraph from "Superman and Me." Use everyday, informal English to ask questions to clarify its meaning.

Literary Analysis

Analyze Imagery

Imagery is language that appeals to the senses. Authors use imagery to help readers

- "picture" what is being described
- imagine how things taste, smell, look, feel, and sound
- understand how characters feel or what they experience
- experience ideas or emotions.

In "It's Our Story, Too," Cabrera uses imagery to show readers what her childhood was like and to help readers imagine the trips her family took to Olvera Street's plaza. She uses phrases that appeal to the five senses to help readers

- smell the "sizzling *carne asada*"
- see the "bright yellow slices" of mango
- taste the slices of mango sprinkled with "chile and salt."

With a partner, create an **Imagery Chart** to record examples of how Alexie, Cisneros, and Cabrera use imagery in their selections. Discuss and write about how the images help you understand and relate to the text.

Imagery Chart

Author	Imagery	Sense	Effect
Cabrera	"children licking a rainbow of <u>raspados</u>" (p. 353)	sight, taste, touch	I can picture what it's like to be at Olvera Street.

GRAMMAR

Review: Pronouns in Prepositional Phrases

Review Display the transparency. Review prepositions, prepositional phrases, and object pronouns in single and compound objects.

A. Oral Practice Model how to complete the first sentence with a noun. Have students complete the remaining sentences.

B. Written Practice Work through the example. Explain that some sentences have no errors. Have the group tell you how to edit the paragraph. Then ask a volunteer to read the corrected paragraph to the class. L.9-10.1.b

Grammar & Writing Practice Book, pp. 121–122

Grammar Transparency 55

GRAMMAR REVIEW: PRONOUNS IN PREPOSITIONAL PHRASES 55

Use Pronouns in Prepositional Phrases

Remember: You can use prepositions to add details to your sentences. If you need a pronoun in a prepositional phrase, use an object pronoun.

Sentences with Prepositional Phrases
- Books open doors **into other worlds.**
- A good book is a treasure **to me.**
- The librarian found some books **for Jamal and me.**
- I think this book includes a story **for us.**

Object Pronouns	
Singular	Plural
me	us
you	you
him, her, it	them

Try It

A. Add a noun or an object pronoun to complete each prepositional phrase.
Possible responses:
1. I am looking for books about dogs.
2. The librarian counts the books and gives them to me.
3. A book about my city is for my mom and me.
4. She reads a book to us every night.

B. Edit the paragraph. Fix five mistakes. The first is done for you.

My brother Todd says that books are important to ~~he~~ him. I agree! I think the library is fun for ~~me and Todd~~ Todd and me. Today, one librarian shelved new books. I walked over to ~~they~~ them and read their titles. "Todd," I said, "here's a book for you and ~~I~~ me. It's about Egypt. Kim would like it, too. Let's check it out for ~~she~~ her and us!"

CCSS **Literacy.RL.9-10.4** Determine the meaning of words and phrases as they are used in the text, including figurative and connotative meanings; analyze the cumulative impact of specific word choices on meaning and tone. **Literacy.RI.9-10.4** Determine the meaning of words and phrases as they are used in a text, including figurative, connotative, and technical meanings; analyze the cumulative impact of specific word choices on meaning and tone. **Literacy.SL.9-10.1.c** Propel conversations by posing and responding to questions that relate the current discussion to broader themes or larger ideas; actively incorporate others into the discussion; and clarify, verify, or challenge ideas and conclusions. **Literacy.L.9-10.1.b** Use various types of phrases and clauses to convey specific meanings and add variety and interest to writing or presentations.

Vocabulary Study

Multiple-Meaning Words

Many English words have more than one meaning. In the dictionary, these meanings are numbered.

recall (verb):
1. to remember something
2. to take something back

Since *recall* is always spelled the same way, the best way to figure out the correct meaning is to study the context clues near the word. Which meaning of *recall* is used on page 344?

Look up the words below in a dictionary and list the meanings for each word. Then find the words on page 344 and tell which meaning applies.

1. plot	**3.** reservation
2. state	**4.** pound

Listening/Speaking

Oral Presentation

Book Recommendation Share about a book that you would recommend, or suggest, for others.

1. **Choose a Book** Think of a book that has affected your life.
2. **Share** Display the book and describe it to the class. Include your opinions, ideas, and how it has affected you in some way.
3. **Discuss** Listen respectfully to other presentations. Pay attention to the way your classmates describe their books. Then talk about the books you have each read and heard about. Make a reading list of books you would like to read.

Language and Learning Handbook, page 702

Writing

Social Science: Write a Case Study

A **case study** presents research information about how a specific person, event, or situation relates to a larger issue. Write a short case study about the role of education in the life of someone you know.

1. **Prewrite** Interview your subject about how education has affected his or her life.
2. **Draft** Write a topic sentence that explains why the person is a good subject for a case study. Describe events and ideas in a logical way, such as chronological order. Use specific details in your description.
3. **Revise** Ask yourself:
   - Is my topic sentence clear?
   - Do I use specific details to describe events and ideas?
4. **Edit and Proofread** Check your work carefully for spelling, grammar, and punctuation.
5. **Publish** Add your paragraph to a class case study book about education.

Model Case Study

My cousin Lenny's life was changed by a great teacher. He never was a good student. Then he took Ms. Gonzalez's Spanish class. She didn't just teach Spanish grammar and vocabulary. She brought the culture alive for Lenny and the other students. Lenny loved the field trips to museums and historical sites. He started going to Spanish music concerts, where he enjoyed the fast-paced rhythms. After graduation, Lenny got a job with a health care organization in Mexico City. Now every year he visits Ms. Gonzalez's class and tells how what he learned has helped both himself and others.

The topic sentence gives the main idea.

Events are presented in chronolgical order.

Specific details add to the description.

Writing Handbook, page 784

Lesson 16

INTEGRATE THE LANGUAGE ARTS

OBJECTIVES

Vocabulary
- Multiple-Meaning Words Ⓣ

Listening and Speaking
- Oral Presentation

Writing
- Writing Process
- Form: Case Study Ⓣ

Vocabulary Study

Multiple-Meaning Words

1. plot: 1. a small area of land; 2. *the main story;* 3. a secret plan
2. state: 1. a condition of being; 2. a social position; 3. *one of the units of a nation having a federal government*
3. reservation: 1. the act of reserving; 2. *something reserved for a special use;* 3. misgiving
4. pound: 1. *unit of mass and weight;* 2. an enclosure for animals; 3. to reduce to powder by beating

L.9-10.4; L.9-10.4.c

Edge Interactive Practice Book, p. 171

Listening / Speaking

Oral Presentation

Book Recommendation Ask volunteers to describe the book and give reasons for recommending it. Provide frames, such as *I recommend this book because* ________. Ask the audience to listen for these words to help them understand.

SL.9-10.1.a; SL.9-10.4

See **Language and Learning Handbook** p. 702.

Writing

Write a Case Study

1. **Prewrite** Help students write open-ended questions for the interview.
2. **Draft** Model using a time line.
3. **Revise** Use the Model to show a strong topic sentence and evidence.
4. **Edit and Proofread** Partners check spelling, grammar, and punctuation.
5. **Publish** Have students self-evaluate using the Writing Rubric.

W.9-10.2; W.9-10.5

Also see **Writing Handbook** p. 784.

Writing Rubric Case Study

Exceptional	• Case study begins with a strong topic sentence. • Events are presented in clear chronological order. • Pronouns in prepositional phrases correct.
Competent	• Case study topic sentence adequate. • Events are presented in chronological order. • Pronouns in prepositional phrases correct with no more than one pronoun error.
Developing	• Case study topic sentence vague. • Chronological order is loosely presented. • Pronouns in prepositional phrases are sometimes used incorrectly.
Beginning	• Case study does not include a topic sentence. • Events are not presented in chronological order. • Pronouns in prepositional phrases are often used incorrectly.

CCSS **Literacy.W.9-10.2** Write informative/explanatory texts to examine and convey complex ideas, concepts, and information clearly and accurately through the effective selection, organization, and analysis of content. **Literacy.W.9-10.5** Develop and strengthen writing as needed by planning, revising, editing, rewriting, or trying a new approach, focusing on addressing what is most significant for a specific purpose and audience. **Literacy.SL.9-10.1.a** Come to discussions prepared, having read and researched material under study; explicitly draw on that preparation by referring to evidence from texts and other research on the topic or issue to stimulate a thoughtful, well-reasoned exchange of ideas. **Literacy.SL.9-10.4** Present information, findings, and supporting evidence clearly, concisely, and logically such that listeners can follow the line of reasoning and the organization, development, substance, and style are appropriate to purpose, audience, and task. **Literacy.L.9-10.4** Determine or clarify the meaning of unknown and multiple-meaning words and phrases based on grades 9-10 reading and content, choosing flexibly from a range of strategies. **Literacy.L.9-10.4.c** Consult general and specialized reference materials, both print and digital, to find the pronunciation of a word or determine or clarify its precise meaning, its part of speech, or its etymology.

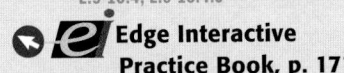

Lesson 17

LISTENING AND SPEAKING WORKSHOP

OBJECTIVES

Listening and Speaking
- Research an Invention
- Incorporate Technology
- Present an Oral Report (T)
- Use a Rubric

BUILD BACKGROUND

(A) Oral Report

Introduce Explain that in an oral report, the speaker presents information about a specific topic to an audience.

Oral Report Describe how planning an oral report and planning a written report are very similar. They both have the same three basic parts: introduction, body, and conclusion. The speaker can use gestures and his or her voice to enhance the report.

TEACH & PRACTICE

(B) Plan Your Oral Report

Brainstorm Tell students to choose an invention that he or she considers important. Have them take notes while answering these questions:

- Why is this invention important?
- Who was the inventor?
- How does the invention work? How does it make our lives easier?

ELL Use Graphic Organizer Work with students to complete a two-column chart to list questions about the invention. Help them answer the questions to organize the ideas, facts, and examples for their oral report.

Show students reference sources they can use to gather research. Ask them to study headings, an index, and the table of contents in a reference source. Have students write an outline of their report.
W.9-10.7

ORAL REPORT

(A) It would be very difficult to imagine our lives without most of the technology tools we take for granted—the automobile, the telephone, the television, the computer. Choose one invention that is really important to you, and learn as much as you can about it. You can impress your classmates with your special knowledge by giving an oral report about it. Here is how to plan and give an oral report:

1. PLAN YOUR ORAL REPORT

(B) **Brainstorm about various inventions that you use and that interest you. Then do the following:**

- Choose an invention you want to tell your audience about.
- Summarize how the invention contributes to your life.
- Write questions you have about the invention: who created it, how it works, and what need it fulfills. Do research to answer your questions.
- Use your notes to write your report. Focus on three or four important points, and write facts and examples to develop each point.
- Use multimedia in your report, if appropriate.

2. PRACTICE YOUR ORAL REPORT

(C) **Rehearse your report several times before your presentation.**

- Experiment with different ways to introduce your subject. If the invention is portable, you might demonstrate it.
- Look at your notes if you need to, but try to use them as little as possible.
- If you include multimedia, practice with that, too.
- Ask a friend to listen to your report and ask you questions.
- Use formal English, but avoid lengthy technical explanations.
- Make sure you speak within the given time limit.

CCSS Literacy.W.9-10.7 Conduct short as well as more sustained research projects to answer a question (including a self-generated question) or solve a problem; narrow or broaden the inquiry when appropriate; synthesize multiple sources on the subject, demonstrating understanding of the subject under investigation.

3. GIVE YOUR ORAL REPORT

Keep your presentation lively by doing the following:

- Make eye contact with your audience.
- Speak clearly and loudly enough for the audience to understand. Use your notes as little as possible.
- Answer questions and comments from the audience.

4. DISCUSS AND RATE THE ORAL REPORT

Use the rubric to discuss and rate the oral reports, including your own.

ORAL REPORT RUBRIC

Scale	Content of Oral Report	Student's Preparation	Student's Delivery
3 Great	• Thoroughly covered the invention • Taught me a lot about the invention	• Gathered good information about the invention • Presented a clear, well-focused explanation of the invention	• Spoke clearly and was easy to follow • Responded to questions and comments very well
2 Good	• Gave somewhat good coverage about the invention • Taught me a few new things about the invention	• Gathered an adequate amount of information about the invention • Presented a reasonably focused explanation of the invention	• Spoke clearly most of the time and was usually easy to follow • Responded to questions and comments fairly well
1 Needs Work	• Gave poor coverage about the invention • Taught me nothing new	• Did not seem very familiar with the invention • Presented confusing or disorganized explanations of the invention	• Was hard to hear and understand • Was not able to handle questions and comments well

DO IT ▸ When you are finished preparing and practicing, give your oral report, and be informative!

Language and Learning Handbook, page 702

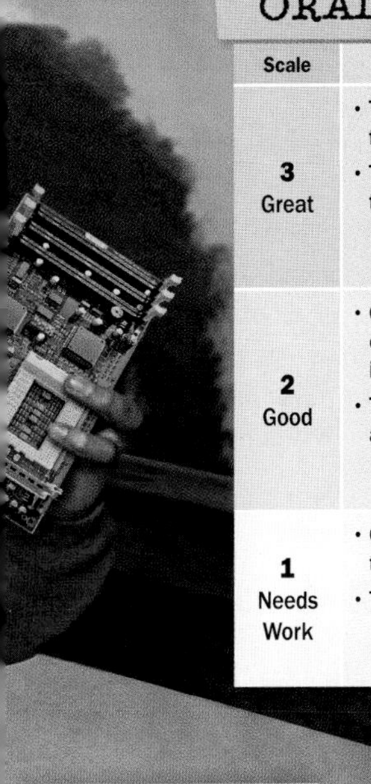

How can showing the invention help your presentation?

myNGconnect.com
Download the rubric.

C Practice Your Oral Report

Model Model an oral report for students.

- Select a modern invention to report about.
- Begin the report in an innovative, creative way.
- Focus on three important points. Provide supporting examples.
- Stand up straight, and speak clearly and loudly.
- Use gestures and your voice effectively to enhance the report.
- Glance at your notes only occasionally. Make eye contact.

Prepare Have students rehearse their oral reports. Remind them to use a creative, exciting introduction that will grab the audience's attention. Encourage students to review their word choices to ensure they are using formal English in their reports.

Use a Rubric Review the rubric. Ask partners to practice their reports together. They should then use the rubric to suggest feedback. Remind students to incorporate any feedback from their partner in their reports.
SL.9-10.2; SL.9-10.4; L.9-10.3

myNGconnect.com
Oral Report Rubric

APPLY

D Give Your Oral Report

Present Review the presentation tips with students and have them present their oral reports. Encourage students to provide feedback by taking notes while listening to the reports.
SL.9-10.2; SL.9-10.4; L.9-10.3

E Discuss and Rate the Oral Report

Give Feedback Ask students to give written or oral feedback to the presenter. Reviewers should rate the presenter with a 1, 2, or 3 and support their rating with comments about the content, preparation, and delivery. Students should also rate themselves.
SL.9-10.3

DIFFERENTIATED INSTRUCTION

As you conduct the workshop with students, adjust your teaching strategies to their needs.

Struggling Readers

Graphic Organizer Guide students to complete an idea web.

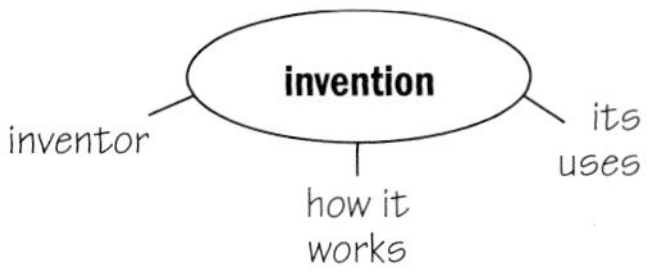

Students can share webs with a partner. Have partners develop examples for each key point.

English Language Learners ELL

Use Visuals Help students locate or draw pictures that support the facts about the inventions. Tell them to use the pictures as they plan and present their oral reports.

Challenge

Create an Invention Ask students to brainstorm about and draw a diagram of an invention they would like to create. Then have them research the steps it would take to produce their invention. Tell them to use the facts they find to plan and outline their oral reports.

ONGOING ASSESSMENT
Ask students to share what they learned about their inventions. Then have them explain what they could teach a family member about this invention.

CCSS Literacy.SL.9-10.2 Integrate multiple sources of information presented in diverse media or formats (e.g., visually, quantitatively, orally) evaluating the credibility and accuracy of each source. Literacy.SL.9-10.3 Evaluate a speaker's point of view, reasoning, and use of evidence and rhetoric, identifying any fallacious reasoning or exaggerated or distorted evidence. Literacy.SL.9-10.4 Present information, findings, and supporting evidence clearly, concisely, and logically such that listeners can follow the line of reasoning and the organization, development, substance, and style are appropriate to purpose, audience, and task. Literacy.L.9-10.3 Apply knowledge of language to understand how language functions in different contexts, to make effective choices for meaning or style, and to comprehend more fully when reading or listening.

UNIT 4 Cluster 3 Planner

EQ ESSENTIAL QUESTION:

How Can Knowledge Open Doors?

Explore how knowledge changes the world.

Online Planner
myNGconnect.com

	LESSON 18 **Prepare to Read**	LESSON 19 **The Fast and the Fuel-Efficient** Main Selection
Reading		
Reading Strategies Focus Strategy **Ask Questions**	**Activate Prior Knowledge** SL.9-10.1 • Make a Connection: Brainstorm *T362*	**Ask Questions** RI.9-10.1 • Find Question-Answer Relationships *T363, T366–T374*
Literary Analysis Genre Focus **Nonfiction**		(T) **Analyze Text Structure: Problem and Solution** *T363, T366–T374* RI.9-10.5 **Apply Literature to Personal Life** • Alternate Energy Sources *T364*
Vocabulary	(T) **Key Vocabulary** RI.9-10.4; L.9-10.6 Introduce *T362* aggressive • assemble • device efficient • environment obstacle solution • technology	(T) **Key Vocabulary** L.9-10.6 • Daily Routines *T367* • Link to Essential Question *T369* • Selection Reading *T366–T374* aggressive • assemble efficient • environment obstacle solution
Fluency		(T) **Expression** RI.9-10.10 • Daily Routines *T367* (T) **Accuracy and Rate** RI.9-10.10 Comprehension Coach *T365*
Writing		
Response to Literature		**Return to the Text** W.9-10.9.b; W.9-10.10 • **Reread and Write** What dreams does the West Philly team have? *T374*
Writing Across the Curriculum		
Language		
ELL **Language Development**	(T) **Verify or Confirm Information** SL.9-10.1.a • Language and Grammar Lab, Transparency L *LAB TE p. 68*	(T) **Verify or Confirm Information** SL.9-10.1.a • Daily Routines *LAB TE p. 68*
Grammar Grammar Focus **Pronoun Agreement**		(T) **Indefinite Pronouns and Verbs** *T368 ,T370, T372* L.9-10.1; L.9-10.1.b
Listening and Speaking	**Small Group/Class Discussion** SL.9-10.1 • Benefits of Technology *T362*	**Listen to a Selection** RI.9-10.10 Comprehension Coach *T365* *CD 6, Tracks 7-8* **Out-of-School Literacy** SL.9-10.1.a • Interpreting Competitions *T373*

(T) = Tested on Cluster and/or Unit Reading and Literary Analysis Test
(T) = Tested on Language Acquisition Assessment
(T) = Tested on Unit Writing Test
(T) = Assessed with a Rubric
• **Academic Vocabulary**

SELECTION SUMMARIES

The Fast and the Fuel-Efficient

Genre: News Feature Lexile® 1040L

A group of West Philadelphia high school students work hard to build a fuel-efficient, eco-friendly car for the 2006 Tour de Sol competition. Their hard work eventually pays off when they win the competition.

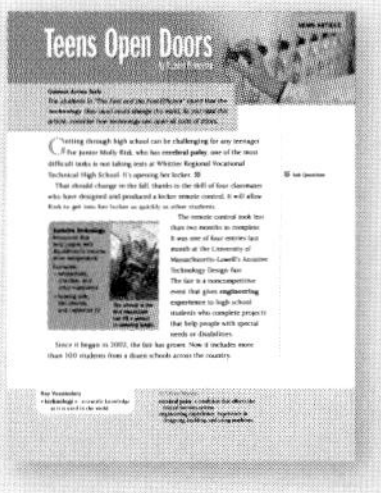

Teens Open Doors

Genre: Magazine Profile Lexile® 980L

A group of high school students use their technological skills and compassion for a disabled classmate to build a remote control to open lockers. The successful device may be used to develop similar devices for broader use.

LESSON 20	LESSON 21	LESSONS 22 & 23	LESSON 24
Teens Open Doors Second Selection	**Reflect and Assess**	**Integrate the Language Arts**	**The Sky Is Not the Limit** Close Reading
Ask Questions RI.9-10.1 • Find Question-Answer Relationships *T376, T377–T380*	**Comprehension and Critical Thinking** *T381* RI.9-10.1; RI.9-10.2; • Compare Across Texts RI.9-10.10 • Analyze, Interpret, Compare, Speculate, Synthesize		
Ⓣ **Analyze Development of Ideas** RI.9-10.3 *T376, T377–T380*	**Interpret and Evaluate Literature** RI.9-10.10 Ⓣ **Use Text Evidence** RI.9-10.1 *T381*		Ⓣ **Analyze Text Structure** RI.9-10.5; L.9-10.3 Ⓣ **Analyze Text Features** RI.9-10.3 Ⓣ **Use Text Evidence** RI.9-10.1
Ⓣ **Key Vocabulary** L.9-10.6 • Selection Reading *T377–T380* • **device** • **technology**	Ⓣ **Key Vocabulary** L.9-10.6 • Review *T381* **aggressive** • **assemble** • **device** **efficient** • **environment** **obstacle** **solution** • **technology**	Ⓣ **Vocabulary Strategy** L.9-10.4.c • Use a Dictionary: Multiple-Meaning Words *T383*	Ⓣ **Academic Vocabulary** L.9-10.6 • Review *T384* • sequence 
Ⓣ **Expression** RI.9-10.10 • Daily Routines *T367* Ⓣ **Accuracy and Rate** RI.9-10.10 Comprehension Coach *T377*	Ⓣ **Expression** RI.9-10.10 • Peer Assessment *T381*		
Return to the Text W.9-10.4; W.9-10.10 • **Reread and Write** What challenge might high school pose for Molly Rizk, and how might she meet the challenge? *T380*	**Write About Literature** W.9-10.1; W.9-10.9.b • **Opinion Statement** Which student group's work is more important? Why? *T381*	Ⓣ **Writing on Demand for Tests** W.9-10.1; W.9-10.4 • **Problem-Solution Essay** *T383*	**The Sky Is Not The Limit** **U.S. House of Representatives, 110th Congress, 1st Session, Resolution 661** **Genre:** Congressional Resolution
		Research Viewing W.9-10.2; W.9-10.7 • **Assistive Technology** *T382*	**Miami Pilot Makes History, Inspires Others** **Genre:** Online News Article Lexile® 1390L
Ⓣ **Verify or Confirm Information** SL.9-10.1.a • Daily Routines *LAB TE p. 68*		Ⓣ **Verify or Confirm Information** SL.9-10.1.a • Pair Talk *T382*	*CD 12, Track 4*
Pronouns and Antecedents L.9-10.1 *T378*		Ⓣ **Pronoun Agreement** L.9-10.1 *T382*	**LESSON 25** **UNIT WRAP-UP**
Listen to a Selection RI.9-10.10 Comprehension Coach *T377* *CD 6, Track 9*	**Participate in a Discussion** SL.9-10.1 *T381*	**Speech** *T382* SL.9-10.4; SL.9-10.6	Ⓣ **Unit Project** W.9-10.2; W.9-10.4; W.9-10.6 • Class Newspaper or Magazine *T388*

EDGE LIBRARY

The Outsiders •
by S. E. Hinton

Parrot in the Oven • •
by Victor Martinez

Narrative of the Life of Frederick Douglass • • •
by Frederick Douglass

PREPARE TO READ

OBJECTIVES

Vocabulary
- Key Vocabulary (T)
- Strategy: Use Cognates; Relate Words

Reading Strategy
- Activate Prior Knowledge

ELL Language & Grammar Lab

Language Function Transparency L
Verify or Confirm Information (T)

ENGAGE & CONNECT

A **EQ Essential Question**

Focus on Knowledge Ask: How can knowledge and new discoveries change the world? Explain.

Possible responses:
- *They can make the world better, like when scientists find a cure for a disease.*
- *They can make the world worse, like when someone invents a new weapon.*

B **Make a Connection**

Have small groups list ways that technology makes the world a better place. Then have groups compare their lists with the class.
SL.9-10.1

TEACH VOCABULARY

C **Learn Key Vocabulary**

Study the Words Review the four steps of the Make Words Your Own routine (*see the Vocabulary tab*):

1. **Pronounce** Say a word and have students repeat it. Write the word in syllables and pronounce it, one syllable at a time: *ag-gres-sive*. Ask what looks familiar in the word, such as *aggression*.

   ELL Use cognates to help Spanish speakers with the words (*see the Vocabulary tab*).

2. **Study Examples** Read the example in the chart. Provide more examples: Is an angry dog *aggressive* or peaceful?

PREPARE TO READ

▸ The Fast and the Fuel-Efficient
▸ Teens Open Doors

A **EQ How Can Knowledge Open Doors?**
Explore how knowledge changes the world.

B

Make a Connection

Brainstorm Advances in areas like science and medicine help to make life easier, keep people healthier, and make the world a better place. Work with a group to brainstorm a list of specific ways that technology opens doors to the future.

C

Learn Key Vocabulary

Study the Words Pronounce each word and learn its meaning. You may also want to look up the definitions in the Glossary.

• Academic Vocabulary

Key Words	Examples
aggressive (u-**gre**-siv) *adjective* ▸ page 374	**Aggressive** means forceful, bold, and willing to take strong action. She is an **aggressive** soccer player who scores lots of goals. *Synonym*: assertive; *Antonym*: shy
• **assemble** (u-**sem**-bul) *verb* ▸ pages 371, 380	When you **assemble** something, you put it together. **Assemble** the model car out of the pieces in the box. *Synonym*: build
• **device** (di-**vīs**) *noun* ▸ pages 378, 380, 382	A **device** is a machine or tool that is used to do a particular job. A cell phone is a **device** that makes it easy to communicate.
efficient (i-**fi**-shunt) *adjective* ▸ pages 366, 374, 381	Someone or something that is **efficient** works well without wasting energy. My **efficient** car gets 35 miles per gallon of gas. *Antonym*: wasteful
• **environment** (in-**vī**-ru-munt) *noun* ▸ page 368	Your **environment** includes all the things that surround you. The race car driver's work **environment** is noisy and stressful.
obstacle (**ahb**-sti-kul) *noun* ▸ pages 368, 374, 380, 381	An **obstacle** is something that gets in your way or causes trouble for you. The fallen tree was an **obstacle** on the road.
solution (su-**lü**-shun) *noun* ▸ pages 363, 366, 380, 381, 383	A **solution** is an answer that solves, or fixes, a problem. My team found a **solution** to our problem with the project. *Antonym*: problem
• **technology** (tek-**nah**-lu-jē) *noun* ▸ pages 374, 377, 380, 381	**Technology** is scientific knowledge as it is used in the world. **Technology** can include machines, equipment, and systems that are created by science. The car doesn't run on gas; it uses a battery-powered **technology**.

Practice the Words Write each Key Vocabulary word on an index card. Then take turns with a partner to group two or more words at a time. Explain how the words go together.

assemble | device

Some devices must be assembled before they can work.

---

3. **Encourage Elaboration** Write the headings *Adjectives*, *Verbs*, and *Nouns*. Write *aggressive* under *Adjectives*. Have students sort and list the remaining words under the headings. Then use each word in a sentence.

4. **Practice the Words** Have partners use index cards to group words and explain how they are related.

Edge Interactive Practice Book, pp. 172–173
RI.9-10.4; L.9-10.6

ONGOING ASSESSMENT
Have students complete an oral sentence for each word. For example: *A can opener is a _______ used to open things in the kitchen.*

CCSS **Literacy.RI.9-10.4** Determine the meaning of words and phrases as they are used in a text, including figurative, connotative, and technical meanings; analyze the cumulative impact of specific word choices on meaning and tone (e.g., how the language of a court opinion differs from that of a newspaper). **Literacy.SL.9-10.1** Initiate and participate effectively in a range of collaborative discussions (one-on-one, in groups, and teacher-led) with diverse partners on grades 9-10 topics, texts, and issues, building on others' ideas and expressing their own clearly and persuasively. **Literacy.L.9-10.6** Acquire and use accurately general academic and domain-specific words and phrases, sufficient for reading, writing, speaking, and listening at the college and career readiness level; demonstrate independence in gathering vocabulary knowledge when considering a word or phrase important to comprehension or expression.

BEFORE READING The Fast and the Fuel-Efficient

news feature by Akweli Parker

Reading Strategies
- Plan and Monitor
- Determine Importance
- Make Inferences
- ▶ **Ask Questions**
- Make Connections
- Synthesize
- Visualize

Analyze Text Structure: Problem and Solution

Some nonfiction authors use a **problem and** solution text structure. The author introduces a problem and then describes how the problem is solved. Some selections also include smaller problems that must be solved along the way.

Look Into the Text

This paragraph describes the team's problem.

A student got under the car to pop the axle in. Kinsler yanked on the suspension to create clearance. But, after many tries, it hadn't connected.

Quietly, Calvin Cheeseboro … took over.…

First, the wheel-facing side popped into place. Then, with Kinsler again pulling on the suspension, the inboard side connected with the transmission with a satisfying clunk.…

The team had hopefully resolved their most difficult problem.

They'd find out soon if their solution had worked.

Signal words help to show how the passage is organized. D

Begin a **Problem-and-Solution Chart** to record information as you read.

Problem-and-Solution Chart

Problem	Solution	Question
The team needs to connect an axle.	Calvin sets it in place.	Why was he able to do it?

Focus Strategy ▶ Ask Questions

There are many times when the answer isn't something you can find in the text. In these cases, look for ways to figure out the answers for yourself.

Focus Strategy

HOW TO FIND QUESTION-ANSWER RELATIONSHIPS

As you read the selection, add notes to your **Problem-and-Solution Chart**. Include questions you have about each problem-and-solution pair. To answer:

1. **"Right There" or "Think and Search" questions:** Look in the text.
2. **"Author and You" questions:** Use what you have already read. Your answers should make sense with the rest of the author's ideas.

You read: There could be scholarships and well-paying jobs—and badly needed grants.

How does the author feel about the team's goal?

He says money is "badly needed." He wants them to win.

E

Reading Transparency 18

READING TEXT STRUCTURE: PROBLEM AND SOLUTION 18

Analyze Text Structure: Problem and Solution

How do writers organize texts to present a problem and a solution?

Introduce Authors include several kinds of information in problem and solution writing. These include the:

- **problem**, or what is wrong or needs to be changed
- **causes**, or the reasons for the problem
- **effects**, or events that happen because of the problem
- **solution**, or how the problem is fixed, including all the steps taken to fix the problem.

Authors use **signal words** to show the relationship of ideas. Signal words can tell about sequence, time, and contrast.

sequence	*first, then, after many tries*
time	*soon*
contrast	*but*

Lesson 19
BEFORE READING

OBJECTIVES

Reading Strategy
- Ask Questions: Find Question-Answer Relationships

Literary Analysis
- Analyze Text Structure: Problem and Solution T

TEACH STRATEGIES

D Text Structure: Problem and Solution

Look Into the Text Read the introduction to explain the problem-and-solution text structure. Read the text passage aloud. Use the callouts to signal words that show the organization. Ask: What is the team's problem?

Possible response:
- *They have trouble connecting an axle.*

Reading Transparency 18

Use the Transparency Review the problem-and-solution text structure. Ask: Which signal words show how words and ideas relate?

Possible response:
- *The word* first *shows the order of events; the word* but *shows a contrast of ideas.*

RI.9-10.5

E Focus Strategy: Ask Questions

Find Question-Answer Relationships Read the introduction with students to define the strategy. Work through the How To box to model "Right There," "Think and Search," and "Author and You" questions.

Mention that some questions might be answered "On Your Own," using students' own knowledge and experience.

Have students try to ask and answer a question about Look Into the Text.

RI.9-10.1

Edge Interactive Practice Book, pp. 174–175

ONGOING ASSESSMENT

Have students name topics and explain why they seem suited to a problem and solution text structure.

CCSS Literacy.RI.9-10.1 Cite strong and thorough textual evidence to support analysis of what the text says explicitly as well as inferences drawn from the text. Literacy.RI.9-10.5 Analyze in detail how an author's ideas or claims are developed and refined by particular sentences, paragraphs, or larger portions of a text (e.g., a section or chapter).

READ

OBJECTIVES

Vocabulary
- Jargon and Specialized Vocabulary

Literary Analysis
- Apply Literature to Personal Life

Viewing
- Respond to and Interpret Visuals

BUILD BACKGROUND

A What You Should Know

Have students read the text about alternative fuels and hybrid vehicles.

ELL **Read Aloud** Read the text aloud, pausing frequently to clarify.
- Show pictures of the vehicles.
- Refer to classroom technology as examples of electricity as fuel.

Alternate Energy Sources Share this information related to alternative fuels:

Renewable resources include the sun, wind, waves, and products that are grown on farms. Nonrenewable resources like coal, gas, and oil cannot be replaced when they have been used up. Most "traditional fuel options" are nonrenewable and can also harm the environment by causing pollution, global warming, and other problems.

Have students discuss which of the alternative fuels on the list are renewable. *(hydrogen, electricity, biodiesel)*

Connect to Students' Lives Have students brainstorm a list of their everyday activities that require the use of energy, such as driving to school. Ask: How can you decrease your use of nonrenewable energy?

myNGconnect.com
- **Selection Summaries in eight languages**

What You Should Know

Alternatives and Hybrids

A

What Is Alternative Fuel? An *alternative* fuel is any fuel other than the traditional options, such as gasoline and diesel. Many alternative fuels are also renewable, so they'll never run out.

- **Alcohols** are mainly methanol and ethanol. They are made mostly from coal and grain.
- **Blends** are mixtures of traditional and alternative fuels, such as E85 (85% ethanol and 15% gasoline).
- **Hydrogen** is mostly made from petroleum. It can also be made by passing electricity through water.
- **Electricity** is created by traditional or alternative fuel sources. It is stored in a rechargeable battery.
- **Biodiesel** is a diesel fuel replacement or additive. It is made from vegetable oil or animal fat.

Why Go Alternative? Alternative fuels reduce exhaust emissions like carbon monoxide and carbon dioxide, which cause air pollution and contribute to global warming. Some alternative fuels also cost less.

What Is a Hybrid? A hybrid car uses at least two different fuel sources. For example, it can combine gasoline with electricity.

Why Go Hybrid? Because of their special technology, hybrid cars get much higher gas mileage than the average U.S. vehicle and they are better for the environment.

myNGconnect.com
- **Discover how hybrid cars work.**
- **Learn more about alternative fuels.**

DIFFERENTIATED INSTRUCTION

English Language Learners ELL

Preview the selection:
- Show the photo on p. 366: *The news feature focuses on cars that save fuel, or energy.*
- Show the diagram and charts on pp. 367, 370, and 372: *The diagram on p. 367 shows different parts of a car. Charts on pp. 370 and 372 give more information.*
- Demonstrate a look of disappointment. Then explain: *The selection begins when a team of people find a big problem with a racecar they have built.*

Read Aloud to provide a supported listening experience:
- Play the **Selection Recording** as students track text in their books. **CD 6**
- Have students use the Listen feature in the **Comprehension Coach** where they see the text as it is read aloud.
- Read the selection aloud to students as you provide comprehensible input. For example, use photos on pp. 366, 368, 369, 371, and 373 to point out the sequence of events: building the car, checking the car, and racing the car.

THE FAST AND THE Fuel-Efficient

by Akweli Parker

TEACH & PRACTICE

B The Fast and the Fuel-Efficient

About the Title Point out that the title of the article is a variation on the phrase "the fast and the furious," which students may recognize from popular movies about racing cars. Explain that the phrase originated in a poem written in 1793 by Robert Burns, a famous Scottish poet. A synonym for the phrase might be "quickly and intensely."

Interpret and Respond Ask: Why do you think the author chose this title for the feature article? *(to attract readers interested in cars; to show a little of what the article is about)*

C Analyze Visuals

About the Photograph This photo shows some members of a team that built a fuel-efficient car.

Interpret and Respond Have students describe the perspective from which this photo was taken. Ask: Where was the photographer when taking this photo? What does it help you understand?

Possible response:

- *The photographer must have been under the engine. It shows what it is like to work on the car.*

Have students focus on the faces of the subjects in this image. Ask: What can you tell about how they work together?

Possible response:

- *The team is focused on the same issue and working together.*

Comprehension Coach

Build Reading Power

Assign students to use the software, based on their instructional needs.

Read Silently

- Comprehension questions with immediate feedback
- Glossary support
- Review text evidence

RI.9-10.10

Listen

- Professional model of fluent reading

Record

- Oral reading fluency practice
- Ongoing fluency assessment with immediate feedback

CCSS Literacy.RI.9-10.10 By the end of grade 9, read and comprehend literary nonfiction in the grades 9–10 text complexity band proficiently, with scaffolding as needed at the high end of the range. By the end of grade 10, read and comprehend literary nonfiction at the high end of the grades 9–10 text complexity band independently and proficiently.

READ

OBJECTIVES

Vocabulary
- Key Vocabulary Ⓣ

Reading Fluency
- Expression Ⓣ

Reading Strategy
- Ask Questions; Review Strategies

Comprehension & Critical Thinking
- Use Text Evidence Ⓣ

Literary Analysis
- Analyze Text Structure: Problem and Solution Ⓣ
- Analyze Text Features Ⓣ

TEACH & PRACTICE

Reading Support

Read Have students read pp. 366–374. Support and monitor their comprehension using the reading support provided. Use the Differentiated Instruction below to meet students' individual needs.
RI.9-10.10

Ⓐ Reading Support

1 Problem and Solution Read the introduction with students. Then ask: What is the team's main problem?

Possible response:
- *They want to win the 2006 Tour de Sol competition.*

RI.9-10.5

Ⓑ Reading Support

2 Ask Questions Ask: What questions do you have? How can you answer them from the text?

Possible responses:
- *Question: How could the students or school benefit from a win? Answer: Students could get high-paying jobs or scholarships; school could get grants and sponsorships.*

RI.9-10.1

Review Strategies Have partners say what other strategies they used as they read the text.

Possible response:
- *When I read that the Tour de Sol was "the Olympics of environmental auto competitions," I used what I know about the Olympics to infer that this was an important event.*

RI.9-10.1

Ⓐ **The Tour de Sol is an annual competition that honors the "greenest vehicles." The goal is to produce a vehicle that reduces gasoline use and greenhouse gas emissions by 100%. West Philadelphia High School's Electric Vehicle Team won the Tour's category for student-built vehicles in 2002 and 2005—could they win again in 2006?** 1

A Test Run

Clayton Kinsler, auto mechanics teacher at West Philadelphia High School, scanned Locust Street to make sure there were no **pedestrians**. Then he hammered the throttle, rocketing the mean little coupe down the block. The car was the Attack—the country's fastest, most **efficient**, **eco-friendly** sports car. And it was created by a West Philadelphia High School team.

The asphalt-hugging, gunmetal-gray roadster was preparing for the Olympics of environmental auto competitions—the Tour de Sol in upstate New York. And much was riding on this car.

Ⓑ The car had won the race in 2002 and 2005, earning national attention for the team of about a dozen mostly African American **vocational education students**. If it won more Tour de Sol victories, there could be **scholarships** and well-paying jobs in the auto industry for the students—and badly needed **grants**, sponsorships, or even partnerships with major automakers for the city school's automotive academy.

Maybe Hollywood would come knocking. 2

The Attack in the shop. It is arguably the country's fastest, most efficient sports car.

For the moment, though, on Locust Street, it was time to cut loose and show off. At each high-speed pass by Kinsler, 47, the car's student builders whooped and cheered. Then, zooming down Locust, Kinsler suddenly felt a loss of power. When he pushed the pedal, the engine revved, but nothing happened at the wheels. He coasted to a stop at 48th Street. And sat there.

1 Problem and Solution The author begins by introducing the team's main problem. What is it? Add this to your Problem-and-Solution Chart.

2 Ask Questions What questions and answers help you understand this section more fully?

Key Vocabulary
- **efficient** *adj.*, working well without wasting energy
- **solution** *n.*, the answer that solves or fixes a problem

In Other Words
- **pedestrians** people walking on the street
- **eco-friendly** environmentally safe
- **vocational education students** students learning technical skills
- **scholarships** awards that help pay for college
- **grants** money to pay for the project

366 Unit 4 Opening Doors

DIFFERENTIATED INSTRUCTION

Interactive Reading As you conduct the interactive reading session with students, adjust your teaching strategies to their needs.

Struggling Readers

Scan Text Features Model scanning text to preview content and identify text features. For example, point to these features on pp. 366–367:
- Introductory text gives background information.
- Subheads tell what sections will be about.
- Photos and captions give information.
- Diagrams show how something works.

Have students scan the rest of the article to prepare for reading.

English Language Learners ELL

Comprehensible Input Explain subheads:
- *A Test Run* (p. 366): a practice
- *Under the Hood* (p. 367): how the car works
- *A Lesson for Detroit Automakers* (p. 370): Detroit is a city in Michigan where many American cars are made
- *One Solution at a Time* (p. 371): don't try to solve every problem at once

Challenge

Verify Information Have students make true-or-false statements based on the article. Partners must verify or disprove statements using information in the text.

CCSS **Literacy.RI.9-10.1** Cite strong and thorough textual evidence to support analysis of what the text says explicitly as well as inferences drawn from the text. **Literacy.RI.9-10.5** Analyze in detail how an author's ideas or claims are developed and refined by particular sentences, paragraphs, or larger portions of a text (e.g., a section or chapter). **Literacy.RI.9-10.10** By the end of grade 9, read and comprehend literary nonfiction in the grades 9-10 text complexity band proficiently, with scaffolding as needed at the high end of the range. By the end of grade 10, read and comprehend literary nonfiction at the high end of the grades 9-10 text complexity band independently and proficiently.

The students looked at one another and began walking, then running toward the car, as they realized that something had gone horribly wrong. They moved around the car **with pit crew precision** and removed the engine cover. 3

Simon Hauger, 36-year-old head of the school's Electric Vehicle Team and mastermind of the project, looked into the tangle of wires, pipes, and hoses. "The axle's done," he announced. As he had feared might happen, the car's axle had broken in two.

3 **Problem and Solution** How do the students realize there is a problem with the car before they even get there?

Under the Hood

West Philadelphia High School's **hybrid electric and biodiesel car** goes from 0 to 60 m.p.h. in under 4 seconds and gets over 50 miles to the gallon. It is built mainly from a car kit, **donor parts**, and also has a number of **custom innovations**.

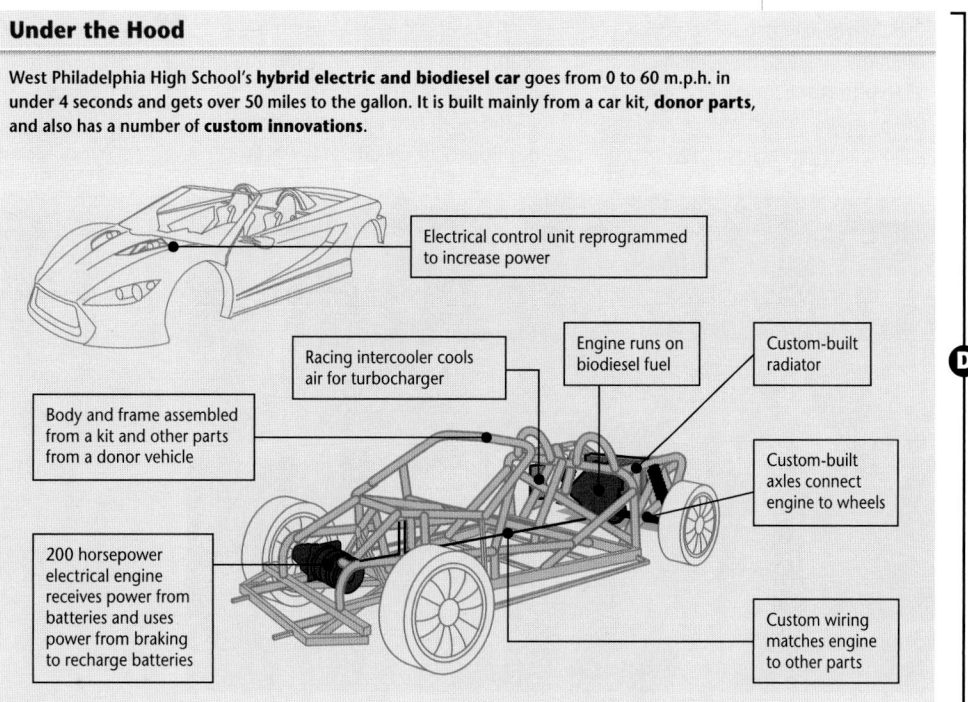

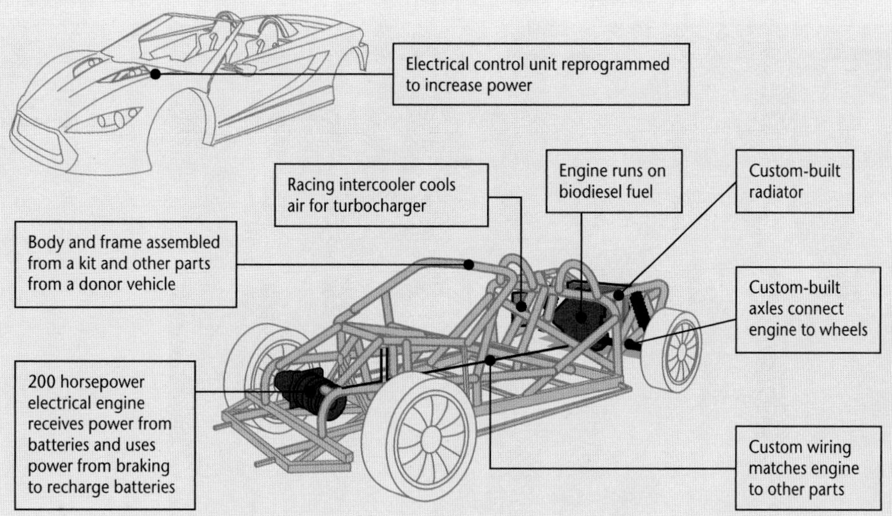

D

Interpret the Diagram What does the diagram show about the amount of work the students put into the car?

Monitor Comprehension

Explain What is the Attack? What happens during its test run on Locust Street?

In Other Words

with pit crew precision like expert teams that work on racecars during races
hybrid electric and biodiesel car car that runs on battery power and fuel made from vegetable oils and/or animal fats
donor parts parts from other cars
custom innovations special features designed for this particular car

TEACH & PRACTICE

C Reading Support

3 Problem and Solution Read the last paragraph on p. 366 and the text on p. 367. Ask: What happens to the car? How do students see the problem? Have students review the text to search for clues.

Possible response:
- *They know how the car should work and notice when it suddenly stops.*

RI.9-10.5

D Analyze Visuals

About the Diagram This diagram labels and describes main parts of the Attack. Explain that the smaller image shows the body, which would fit on top of the frame.

Interpret the Diagram Read the caption and each of the diagram labels. Discuss what the diagram means and what it shows about the students who built it.

ELL Build Background Explain technical vocabulary related to automotive parts, and use gestures to show how the parts are connected: *horsepower:* how much power a car has; *intercooler:* a device that keeps fluid cool; *turbocharger:* a device that gives an engine extra power; *radiator:* a part that uses fluid to cool the engine.

Have students use information from the diagram to make an inference about the Attack. Ask: How much work would it take to build something with so many custom parts?

Possible response:
- *Something with so many custom parts would take a great deal of work.*

Monitor Comprehension

Explain Have students summarize what has happened so far. Ask: What is the Attack and what happens during its test run on Locust Street?

Possible responses:
- *The Attack is the hybrid car built by a high school team.*
- *It loses power on its test run.*

RI.9-10.2

DAILY ROUTINES

Vocabulary

See the Vocabulary and Fluency Routines tab for more information.

Word Wall Display the words to provide a visual scaffold. Use questions to connect the words to the selection. For example: *Which words can describe the Attack?*

Drama Have students use skits or pantomime to show the meanings of words such as *assemble, obstacle,* and *aggressive.*

Word Hunt Provide visual or tactile representations of Key Vocabulary. Invite students to match the representations to the Key Words, then to suggest other words that relate to the selection vocabulary.

L.9-10.6

Fluency: Expression

CD 11

This cluster's fluency practice uses a passage from "The Fast and the Fuel-Efficient" to help students practice appropriate expression. Use **Reading Handbook** T750 and the **Fluency Model CD** to teach or review the elements of fluent expression, and then use the daily fluency practice activities to develop students' oral reading proficiency.

RI.9-10.10

CCSS **Literacy.RI.9-10.2** Determine a central idea of a text and analyze its development over the course of the text, including how it emerges and is shaped and refined by specific details; provide an objective summary of the text. **Literacy.L.9-10.6** Acquire and use accurately general academic and domain-specific words and phrases, sufficient for reading, writing, speaking, and listening at the college and career readiness level; demonstrate independence in gathering vocabulary knowledge when considering a word or phrase important to comprehension or expression.

READ

OBJECTIVES

Vocabulary
- Key Vocabulary Ⓣ
- Strategy: Use Contextual Analysis (technical and specialized vocabulary)

Comprehension & Critical Thinking
- Use Text Evidence Ⓣ

Literary Analysis
- Analyze Text Structure: Problem and Solution Ⓣ

Grammar
- Indefinite Pronouns & Singular Verbs Ⓣ

TEACH & PRACTICE

Ⓐ Reading Support

4 Problem and Solution Point out the colon at the end of the first paragraph and the repeated phrases beginning "How to …" Mention that each paragraph relates to problems that could keep the team from succeeding. Ask: What problems must team leaders solve?

Possible responses:
- *poor motivation; lack of money; the need for unconventional thinking*

RI.9-10.5

Ⓑ Reading Support

5 Language Explain that each profession, like engineering or medicine, uses specialized vocabulary. To help students define *axle*, point out dashes that cue word explanations and the label that points to the axle on the diagram. Ask: What clues in the text and the diagram on p. 367 help you understand what *axle* means?

Possible responses:
- *The phrase inside the dashes describes an axle as a rod connected to the wheels.*
- *The diagram shows how an axle connects the car's wheels to its engine.*

Provide students with examples of school jargon, such as *graphic organizer* and *worksheet*. List common expressions used in the classroom and the school environment.

L.9-10.4.a; L.9-10.6

Overcoming Obstacles

Over the last year, the team and their instructors—Kinsler, Hauger, and shop teacher Ron Preiss—had overcome all kinds of **obstacles**:

Ⓐ How to **instill in these urban students** the value of hard work, responsibility, and a passion for learning when their **environment** outside of school often encouraged the opposite.

How to get the money to support the **endeavor**, which was beyond the school district's ability to pay for.

And how to use **unconventional** thinking not just to succeed, but to blow away the world's expectations of them. 4

Ⓑ The axle—a thick metal rod that transfers engine power to the wheels—had required a lot of unconventional thinking. This was the fourth time in less than a year that it had broken. 5

The team had **custom built the car** from a kit called the K-1 Attack,

4 Problem and Solution
What are some of the **obstacles** that the team leaders face if they want the team to succeed?

5 Language
This article uses jargon, or special words, often used by engineers. What clues tell you what an *axle* is? How does the diagram on page 367 help? How do you use jargon at school?

The team, in a rare moment together (clockwise from left): Terrie Gabe, Bruce Harmon, Oceansey Tete, Victor Webster, Tyson Drummond (in passenger seat), teacher Clayton Kinsler (rear), Calvin Cheeseboro (in driver's seat), Tyshona Lovett, Joseph Pak, and Kevin McKnight.

Key Vocabulary
obstacle *n.*, something that gets in the way or causes trouble
• **environment** *n.*, the surroundings or conditions a person lives in

In Other Words
instill in these urban students make these city kids believe in
endeavor project
unconventional unusual, creative
custom built the car worked together to build their unique car

GRAMMAR

Indefinite Pronouns & Singular Verbs

Teach/Model Display the transparency. In the first set of example sentences, elicit that the subjects are *Everybody* and *Something* (not *car*). Emphasize that these words are not modifiers (as in, for example, *each car*). Have students use the pronoun chart to replace the subjects in the example sentences with a different one. Point out the verbs in the second set of examples.

Practice A. As students say each correct verb, underline it on the transparency. **B.** After partners talk and write their own sentences, have each student read a sentence and ask the group to identify the indefinite pronoun. L.9-10.1

Grammar & Writing Practice Book, pp. 123–124

GRAMMAR SKILLS PATH
- ▶ **56 Indefinite Pronouns & Singular Verbs** ELL Language & Grammar Lab
- **57 Indefinite Pronouns & Plural Verbs**
- **58 Indefinite Pronouns & Verbs**
- **59 Pronouns and Antecedents**
- **60 Review: Pronoun Agreement**

Grammar Transparency 56

GRAMMAR INDEFINITE PRONOUNS & SINGULAR VERBS 56

When Do You Use an Indefinite Pronoun?
When You Can't Be Specific

- When you are not talking about a specific person or thing, you can use an **indefinite pronoun**.
  Everybody loves an auto race.
  Something in that car is broken.
- Some indefinite pronouns are always singular, so they need a **singular verb** that ends in **-s**.
  Now **everything looks** fine for the big race.
  Nobody expects a problem.

Singular Indefinite Pronouns			
another	each	everything	nothing
anybody	either	neither	somebody
anyone	everybody	nobody	someone
anything	everyone	no one	something

Try It

A. Say each sentence. Use the correct form of the verb.
1. The teams are competing, and each **(build / builds)** a car.
2. Everyone **(want / wants)** to watch the race.
3. Someone suddenly **(give / gives)** the signal to start.
4. Now somebody **(is / are)** fixing the blue car.
5. Nothing **(seem / seems)** wrong with the engine.

B. Now tell a partner about a race. Write three sentences. Use indefinite pronouns from the chart above. Sentences will vary.

CCSS **Literacy.RI.9-10.5** Analyze in detail how an author's ideas or claims are developed and refined by particular sentences, paragraphs, or larger portions of a text (e.g., a section or chapter). **Literacy.L.9-10.1** Demonstrate command of the conventions of standard English grammar and usage when writing or speaking. **Literacy.L.9-10.4.a** Use context (e.g., the overall meaning of a sentence, paragraph, or text; a word's position or function in a sentence) as a clue to the meaning of a word or phrase. **Literacy.L.9-10.6** Acquire and use accurately general academic and domain-specific words and phrases, sufficient for reading, writing, speaking, and listening at the college and career readiness level; demonstrate independence in gathering vocabulary knowledge when considering a word or phrase important to comprehension or expression.

with parts coming from different car manufacturers. The axle presented a peculiar engineering challenge—the car's Volkswagen engine needed a way to spin its Honda rear wheels.

And so, the two rear axles are a combination of Volkswagen, Honda, and other parts welded together. The left one, shorter and less flexible, is constantly breaking. A section of cheap steel pipe held its VW and Honda ends together, but the pipe tore during acceleration. (The car goes from zero to sixty in four seconds.) A thicker, higher-quality sleeve might do the trick, Hauger thought.

A half-dozen team members pushed the car backwards, uphill to the school's garage, and gently rolled it onto a **power car lift**. The only thing to do now was saw off new axle halves from whole VW and Honda units, send them out to be welded . . . and wait. 6

"We didn't expect it to break again," said a disappointed Joseph Pak, a **lanky**, earringed tenth-grader with gel-spiked hair. Still, he said, he was relieved that it had happened well before the May competition.

For Pak and other team members who'd struggled with school, the car was **an "in-your-face" affirmation of**

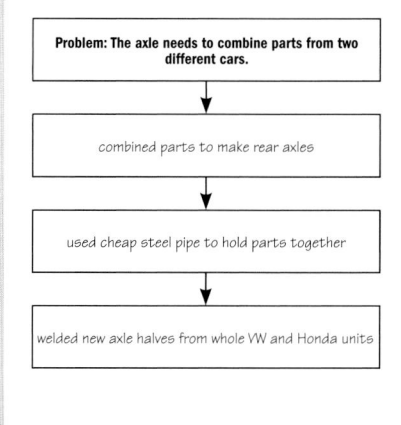

Student Tyson Drummond cuts pipe for a roof frame he and classmates will affix to the hybrid car they're assembling. Winning the national Tour de Sol race for eco-friendly cars could fulfill their dreams.

their talents and dreams. Pak, the team's only Asian member, admits he used to skip more school than he attended. "I was just hanging out." Now he gets straight As and wants to be an engineer.

"I've seen the **extreme** of not doing things when you should," Pak said. With the Attack, he said he's seen the extreme of what happens when you **stay the course**.

Hauger, though, was optimistic. "This is actually pretty good news," Hauger said. Their more complex engineering of the axle had held. This was a simple weld.

6 **Problem and Solution**
Why has the axle been a challenging problem? How has the team worked to solve it?

Monitor Comprehension

Explain
How does the Electric Vehicle program help students?

In Other Words

power car lift machine that lifts the car
lanky tall and thin
an "in-your-face" affirmation of their talents and dreams real proof that they were talented and could reach their goals
extreme worst side
stay the course keep doing what you plan to do

TEACH & PRACTICE

C Reading Support

6 Problem and Solution Have students review the text to describe the problem the team faces.

ELL Use Graphic Organizer
Use a sequence chain to show the problem and the steps students took to address it:

Problem: The axle needs to combine parts from two different cars.
↓
combined parts to make rear axles
↓
used cheap steel pipe to hold parts together
↓
welded new axle halves from whole VW and Honda units

Ask: Why is the axle a problem? How has the team tried to solve the problem?

Possible responses:
- *The axle is made of parts from many manufacturers.*
- *They tried many options before they sawed off new axle halves and sent them out to be welded.*

RI.9-10.5

Monitor Comprehension

Explain Use the text on pp. 368–369 to help students draw conclusions about ways that the Electric Vehicle program helps its students.

Possible responses:
- *instills key values, chance to use talents and build dreams, motivation to stay in school*

RI.9-10.1

VOCABULARY

Link Vocabulary and Concepts

Ask questions to link Key Vocabulary with the Essential Question.

EQ **ESSENTIAL QUESTION:**
How can knowledge open doors?

Some possible questions:

- *How does the team overcome* **obstacles** *to gain new knowledge?*
- *How does the Electric Vehicle program provide a supportive* **environment** *for students?*
- *What* **solutions** *does the team find to its problem?*
- *How can the use of* **technology** *lead to a more* **efficient** *and faster car?*
- *What knowledge can you gain if you* **assemble** *a machine yourself?*

Have students use the Key Vocabulary words in their responses.
L.9-10.6

CCSS **Literacy.RI.9-10.1** Cite strong and thorough textual evidence to support analysis of what the text says explicitly as well as inferences drawn from the text. **Literacy.RI.9-10.5** Analyze in detail how an author's ideas or claims are developed and refined by particular sentences, paragraphs, or larger portions of a text (e.g., a section or chapter). **Literacy.L.9-10.6** Acquire and use accurately general academic and domain-specific words and phrases, sufficient for reading, writing, speaking, and listening at the college and career readiness level; demonstrate independence in gathering vocabulary knowledge when considering a word or phrase important to comprehension or expression.

READ

OBJECTIVES

Vocabulary
- Key Vocabulary Ⓣ
- Content Area Vocabulary: Engineering
- Strategies: Use Contextual Analysis; Use Structural Analysis

Reading Strategy
- Ask Questions: Find Question-Answer Relationships

Comprehension & Critical Thinking
- Use Text Evidence Ⓣ

Literary Analysis
- Analyze Text Features: Chart

Grammar
- Indefinite Pronouns & Plural Verbs Ⓣ

TEACH & PRACTICE

Ⓐ Reading Support

7 Ask Questions Help students question: What are the students' lofty ambitions? Have them Think and Search in the second paragraph to answer.

ELL Use Visuals Draw a bar graph to show $1 billion, $100,000, and $50,000. Note that $1 billion = 100 × $100,000; $100,000 = 2 × $50,000. Point out the contrast between $100,000 and $1 billion as a development cost.

Ask: What do you learn from the answers to your questions?
RI.9-10.1

Ⓑ Analyze Visuals

Interpret the Chart Read the chart head and caption. Demonstrate how to find information for different vehicles. Have students use text features such as row and column heads to interpret the chart. Ask: In what main ways are standard models and hybrids different?

Possible response:
- *Hybrids get much better gas mileage and create fewer emissions.*

A Lesson for Detroit Automakers

The ideas that come out of West Philly's auto shop aren't **rocket science**, Hauger says, but they do require imagination and some risk-taking—traits he thinks Detroit could use. He dreams of the high school program sharing the team's know-how of building hybrid cars cheaply. No major automaker sells a performance car that **gets such outrageously high mileage**. With oil prices high and demand for hybrids soaring, the timing could not be better.

Developing a car model costs automakers about $1 billion. Even adding back the discounts and **freebies** the school team received—such as carbon-fiber body panels and custom wheels—the Attack would still have **clocked in well under** $100,000. Ⓐ Hauger estimated their two-seater, if **mass-produced**, could sell for about $50,000.

But before **such lofty ambitions** could become reality, the Attack's axle had to be repaired. 7

7 Ask Questions Ask yourself, "What does the author mean by 'lofty ambitions'? Which ambitions are they?" How do your answers add to your understanding?

Do Hybrid Cars Make A Difference? Ⓑ

A hybrid car combines a gas engine with one or more electric motors. This limits the amount of gas used and the emissions that are released into the environment. This chart shows the difference in fuel consumption between a regular engine and a hybrid engine.

Type	Model	Miles Per Gallon City	Miles Per Gallon Hwy	Emissions Category
SUV	2006 Brand A Standard	13	17	LEV II (Low)
	2006 Brand A Hybrid	31	27	SULEV (Super-Ultra-Low)
sedan	2006 Brand B Standard	22	31	U-LEV II (Ultra-Low)
	2006 Brand B Hybrid	60	51	AT-PZEV (Advanced Technology Partial Zero)
coupe	2006 Brand C Standard	23	33	U-LEV II
	2006 Brand C Hybrid	60	66	SULEV

Sources: The California Air Resources Board
The U.S. Environmental Protection Agency

Interpret the Chart According to this chart, what are the main differences between standard models and hybrids?

In Other Words

rocket science too difficult for everyday people to think of or understand
gets such outrageously high mileage can drive so many miles on such little gas
freebies free things
clocked in well under cost much less than
mass-produced built in large numbers by car companies
such lofty ambitions his great dreams

370 Unit 4 Opening Doors

GRAMMAR

Indefinite Pronouns & Plural Verbs

Teach/Model Display the transparency. Have students tell the pronoun subjects in the first set of example sentences; then review plural verb forms. Ask students to replace the subjects in the example sentences with another pronoun from the chart. Verify that each new subject requires a plural verb.

Practice A. Ask students to explain their verb choices by identifying the pronoun subject of each sentence. **B.** After the class starts the paragraph, have students write two more sentences and share one with the class. Record some sentences on the transparency. Verify that the verb is plural in their sentences.
L.9-10.1

Grammar & Writing Practice Book, pp. 125–126

Grammar Transparency 57

GRAMMAR INDEFINITE PRONOUNS & PLURAL VERBS 57

Which Indefinite Pronouns Are Plural?
Both, Few, Many,* and *Several

- Use an **indefinite pronoun** when you are not talking about a specific person or thing.
  Many of the students are quite talented.
  Several work on cars as a hobby.
- Some **indefinite pronouns** are always plural, so they need a **plural verb**.
  Both of the instructors **help** their team.
  A **few** of the team members **know** how to fix the axle.

Plural Indefinite Pronouns	
both	many
few	several

Try It

A. Say each sentence about the Electric Vehicle Team. Use the correct form of the verb.

1. Many of the students **(understand / understands)** the value of hard work.
2. A few **(study / studies)** car engines during their free time.
3. Both of those students **(have / has)** high hopes for the future.
4. A few of their ideas **(is / are)** highly imaginative.
5. Several of the team members **(dream / dreams)** of building a record-breaking car.

B. Now tell more about the group of students from West Philly. Write two more sentences. Use pronouns from the chart above.
Sentences will vary.
Many of the students have a chance to work for a big car company.

GRAMMAR SKILLS PATH

CCSS Literacy.RI.9-10.1 Cite strong and thorough textual evidence to support analysis of what the text says explicitly as well as inferences drawn from the text. Literacy.L.9-10.1 Demonstrate command of the conventions of standard English grammar and usage when writing or speaking. Literacy.L.9-10.6 Acquire and use accurately general academic and domain-specific words and phrases, sufficient for reading, writing, speaking, and listening at the college and career readiness level; demonstrate independence in gathering vocabulary knowledge when considering a word or phrase important to comprehension or expression.

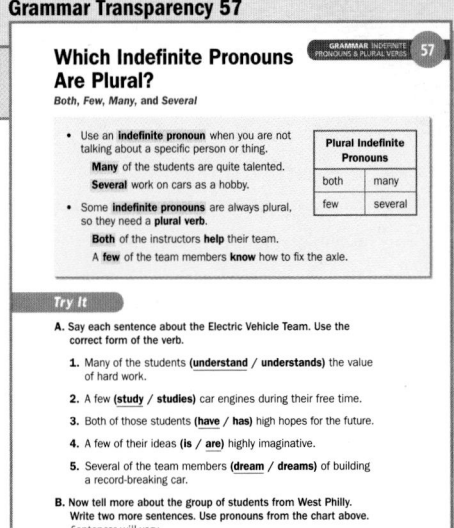

Students Terrie Gabe (left) and Tyson Drummond (right) peering under the hood for some last minute inspections and troubleshooting during the beginning of the Tour de Sol.

One Solution at a Time

Sixteen days later, during fourth-period auto mechanics class, a handful of team members gathered in the school shop. On a metal worktable sat the newly welded axle assembly.

A student got under the car to pop the axle in. Kinsler **yanked on the suspension to create clearance**. But, after many tries, it hadn't connected.

Quietly, Calvin Cheeseboro, a tall, athletic-looking eleventh-grader with neatly twisted braids, took over. Cheeseboro, who'd twice **installed** axles in the Attack and can practically **assemble** some of its complicated parts in his sleep, now wrestled with the greasy metal rod.

First, the wheel-facing side popped into place. Then, with Kinsler again pulling on the suspension, the inboard side connected with the transmission with a satisfying clunk. 8 **C**

Cheeseboro, who has struggled to maintain passing grades so he can work with the team, said it felt good to be the guy to put in the **critical part**. Still, he said, he'd sooner not face such drama, especially with the May race coming up soon. "I don't want to break another axle."

D The team had hopefully resolved their most difficult problem.

They'd find out soon if their solution had worked. 9

8 **Ask Questions** Ask yourself questions to add to your understanding of what the article says about Calvin. Read on to look for the answers.

9 **Access Vocabulary** What do you think the word *resolved* means? What root word and context clues help you figure it out?

Key Vocabulary
- **assemble** *v.*, to put something together

In Other Words
yanked on the suspension to create clearance made room to work
installed put in
critical part important piece

Monitor Comprehension
Explain How does the team solve the axle problem?

TEACH & PRACTICE

C Reading Support

8 Ask Questions Write the words *appearance* and *skills*. Help students develop questions about Calvin for each category. Lead them to the third paragraph to find answers.

Possible responses:
- *Questions: What does Calvin look like? What is Calvin good at?* RI.9-10.1

D Reading Support

9 Access Vocabulary Guide students in using the surrounding language to figure out the word. Tell students to reread the final two sentences on p. 371 for clues about what *resolved* means. Ask: What root word and context clues help you define *resolved*?

Possible response:
- *The word* solve *is the root word.* Resolve *must mean "to answer a problem." Context clues are:* most difficult problem *and* solution had worked. L.9-10.4.a; L.9-10.4.b

Monitor Comprehension

Explain Have students think aloud to show their understanding of the problem and the solution.

MODEL Say:
- *When the car lost power in the test run, I thought it would be an engine problem.*
- *But then when I read about the rear axle, it made sense to me that parts from different cars might cause a problem.*
- *To fix the axle problem, students ...*

Have students complete the think aloud to answer the question.

Possible response:
- *Had axle halves from a VW and a Honda welded together.*

Evaluate Text Structure Have students use their Problem-and-Solution Chart to evaluate text structure. Ask: How does the problem-solution method of development help you better understand the article?

Possible response:
- *It shows each problem the team faces and how they work to solve it.* RI.9-10.5

VOCABULARY

Content Area Vocabulary: Auto Engineering

Build vocabulary related to the content area of auto engineering.

Teach/Model Use the Make Words Your Own routine (*see the Vocabulary tab*) and the sample sentences below to introduce these words from the selection.

suspension (su-**spen**-shun) ▸ p. 371

The system that supports the upper part of the car is called the **suspension***.*

transmission (tranz-**mi**-shun) ▸ p. 371

The **transmission** *controls the gears.*

radiator (**rā**-dē-ā-tur) ▸ p. 367

The **radiator** *is a series of pipes or tubes.*

horsepower (**hors**-pau-ur) ▸ p. 367

The powerful car has a 200 **horsepower** *engine.*

carbon-fiber (**kar**-bun-**fī**-bur) ▸ p. 370

To make cars weigh less, mechanics use **carbon-fiber** *panels for the body of the car.*

prototype (**prō**-tu-tīp) ▸ p. 372

The engineer showed his designs for the **prototype** *of a new kind of car.*

Practice Have students use the words to describe the Attack vehicle.

Apply Have students draw a simple design of a vehicle that shows how the parts contribute to the vehicle. L.9-10.6

CCSS Literacy.RI.9-10.5 Analyze in detail how an author's ideas or claims are developed and refined by particular sentences, paragraphs, or larger portions of a text (e.g., a section or chapter). Literacy.L.9-10.4.a Use context (e.g., the overall meaning of a sentence, paragraph, or text; a word's position or function in a sentence) as a clue to the meaning of a word or phrase. Literacy.L.9-10.4.b Identify and correctly use patterns of word changes that indicate different meanings or parts of speech (e.g., analyze, analysis, analytical; advocate, advocacy).

READ

OBJECTIVES

Reading Strategy
- Ask Questions: Find Question-Answer Relationships

Comprehension & Critical Thinking
- Use Text Evidence T

Literary Analysis
- Analyze Text Features: Chart
- Analyze Text Structure: Problem and Solution T

Grammar
- Indefinite Pronouns & Verbs T

TEACH & PRACTICE

A Reading Support

10 Ask Questions Suggest the five Ws (*Who, What, Why, When, Where*) plus *How* to help students generate questions.

Possible responses:
- *What events are in the competition? How long is the Tour? How does a team win? How does a team earn points?*

RI.9-10.1

B Analyze Visuals

About the Chart This chart shows the categories of competition in the Tour de Sol. It tells the number of possible points in each category and the number of points earned by the Attack.

Interpret and Respond Ask: Do you think this information is more clear in a chart format or written out as text? Explain.

C Interpret the Chart

Compare Read the column heads and category names. Have students compare numbers in the second and third columns. Then ask: In which categories do the Attack's points match or come close to matching the maximum possible points?

Possible responses:
- *Range, Acceleration, Hill climb, 41-mile trip, GHG/mile, Autocross*
56 Indefinite Pronouns & Singular Verbs
57 Indefinite Pronouns & Plural Verbs
▶ **58** Indefinite Pronouns & Verbs **ELL** Language & Grammar Lab
59 Pronouns and Antecedents
60 Review: Pronoun Agreement

The Final Test of Mind, Spirit—and Car

The three-day Tour de Sol competition had begun.

Of the sixty or so Tour de Sol **entrants**, West Philadelphia was directly competing with only four others, all in the powerful **"prototype alternative fuel and hybrids" division**. But the team aimed to earn the most points overall as well—as it had done last year.

Between Wednesday and Friday, the team's **ranking** had never dropped beyond third, and it had **dominated** the driving event. The point spread was narrow. With each challenge, though, the team had found ways to stay in the running.

On Thursday night, Hauger explained the next day's 200-mile run to his team. They'd have to do a good job

The Tour de Sol Competition: How It Works

Vehicles entered in the Tour de Sol Championship participate in four days of events that **assess the "green-ness" of the vehicle** and give points for accomplishment. Events also assess **conventional** vehicle performance such as acceleration, braking, and handling. 10

Category / WPHS 2006 Results	Maximum Possible Points	Points Scored by "Attack"
Technology / Internal Combustion Engine: Biodiesel	100	64
Range (total distance covered) / 198 miles	100	100
Acceleration / 5 seconds	75	73
Hill climb / 10 seconds	75	72
41-mile trip to STEP* & back / 41 miles	100	100
Efficiency event / 55 mpg	250	105
Greenhouse gas per mile / 58 GHG per mile	250	242
Autocross (handling) / 31 seconds	100	100
TOTAL POINTS	1050	865.8

*STEP = Saratoga Technology + Energy Park

Interpret the Chart Which categories does the Attack score well in?

10 **Ask Questions** Ask and answer questions to develop your understanding of the Tour de Sol's events.

In Other Words
entrants competing teams, competitors
"prototype alternative fuel and hybrids" division category of cars that don't run on regular gasoline
ranking place in the competition
dominated easily beat the others in
assess the "green-ness" of the vehicle test how the car protects the environment
conventional regular, typical

GRAMMAR

Indefinite Pronouns & Verbs

Teach/Model Display the transparency. Review prepositional phrases. As you discuss each example sentence, invite a volunteer to explain its singular or plural meaning. Elicit that if a prepositional phrase follows one of these pronoun subjects, the object of the preposition determines the choice of a singular or plural verb.

Practice A. As students choose each correct verb, underline it on the transparency.
B. After partners talk and write their own sentences, have each student read one sentence aloud and ask the group to identify the indefinite pronoun as singular or plural.
L.9-10.1.b

Grammar & Writing Practice Book, pp. 127–128

GRAMMAR SKILLS PATH

Grammar Transparency 58

GRAMMAR INDEFINITE PRONOUNS & VERBS 58

Which Indefinite Pronouns Are Tricky?

The Ones That Can Be Singular or Plural

- The **indefinite pronouns** in the chart can be either singular or plural.
- The prepositional phrase after the pronoun shows whether the sentence talks about one thing or more than one thing. Use the correct **verb**.

Singular or Plural Indefinite Pronouns	
all	none
any	some
most	

Singular: **Most** of the car **is** blue.
Plural: **Most** of the parts **are** metal.
Singular: **Some** of the oil **is** on the ground.
Plural: **Some** of the students **are** in the shop.
Singular: **All** of the group **waits** patiently.
Plural: **All** of the students **are** waiting.

Try It

A. Say each sentence. Use the correct form of the verb.
1. All of the teams **(build / builds)** cars.
2. Most of their time **(go / goes)** into designing the car.
3. Some of the students **(works / work)** at putting the parts together.
4. All of the cars are efficient. None of the cars **(uses / use)** petroleum.
5. Some of the power **(come / comes)** from batteries.

B. Now tell a partner your opinion about cars and the environment. Write three sentences. Use pronouns from the chart. Sentences will vary.

CCSS Literacy.RI.9-10.1 Cite strong and thorough textual evidence to support analysis of what the text says explicitly as well as inferences drawn from the text. Literacy.L.9-10.1.b Use various types of phrases (noun, verb, adjectival, adverbial, participial, prepositional, absolute) and clauses (independent, dependent; noun, relative, adverbial) to convey specific meanings and add variety and interest to writing or presentations.

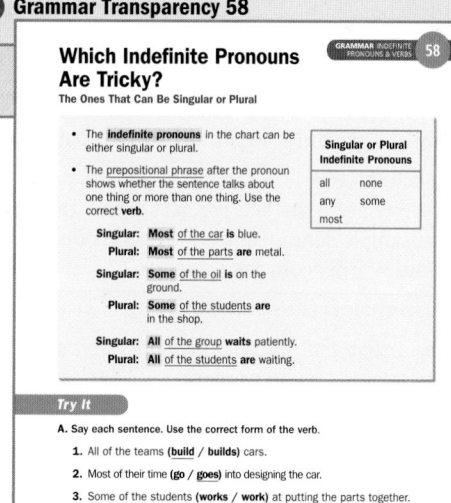

of attaching the Plexiglas top to their open-air car. **Navigation** had to be perfect. And **conserving** fuel would challenge the **lead-footed** Hauger.

"The idea is to drive as slowly as possible," Hauger would say. "Without losing your sanity."

The next day, **fatigue**, cold, wet weather, and **inconsiderate** drivers all threatened Hauger and student Joseph Pak on their trip. A scary **hydroplaning incident** brought Hauger to attention around the 150-mile mark.

"I was praying, praying, 'God, please let us finish,'" he said later. 11

After Hauger and Pak pulled into the parking lot, a Tour official measured the biodiesel fuel left in their tank to calculate miles per gallon.

With the race tight, West Philly had one event still to complete. It was the afternoon's autocross, which involved zipping through a cone-marked path.

It was the Attack's **strong suit**, provided the car could hold together. The event could decide the overall winner.

Amazingly, West Philadelphia's **miniature muscle car** had logged the highest mileage out of its closest competitors in the total points standings—55 miles per gallon.

In total points, West Philly stood at 665.8 points, compared with the next team's 652.6.

Shortly before the race, Hauger pointed to the number "1" under the "Position" heading next to his team's listing on the score sheet.

"Heh, heh," he said. "It's ours to lose." 12 **E**

After the West Philly student crew helped him into the cramped Attack, Hauger pulled up to the start line. An official dropped his arm and the Attack sprang to life, with its characteristic whistling roar.

On the first run, Hauger seemed **tentative**, but managed to complete the course in a respectable 32.3 seconds.

11 **Ask Questions** What questions help you better understand this test of mind, spirit, and car?

12 **Problem and Solution** What is the main challenge that the team has to meet? How is the team doing so far? What does Hauger mean when he says "It's ours to lose"?

West Philadelphia High School teacher Simon Hauger drives the Attack during the technical test of the 2006 Tour de Sol in Saratoga Springs, NY.

Monitor Comprehension

Describe What are some of the challenges that the team faces at the competition?

In Other Words

Navigation The car's direction
conserving not using too much
lead-footed fast-driving
fatigue exhaustion
inconsiderate rude, impatient
hydroplaning incident moment when the car skidded on a wet road
strong suit best category
miniature muscle car tiny sports car
tentative cautious, hesitant

TEACH & PRACTICE

D Reading Support

11 Ask Questions Point out that the test is about more than the car's performance. Have students consider what else is being tested. Then have them reread from the end of p. 372 for answers.

ELL Questioning Briefly review the meanings of *mind, spirit,* and *car.* Then post question starters: *How was the 200-mile run hard for the _____? How did the drive test the driver's _____? How did the drive affect the _____?*

Possible responses:

- *Why is it hard to drive very slowly? How does being tired and cold make it hard to drive? Why is driving for 200 miles hard on a car?*

RI.9-10.1

E Reading Support

12 Problem and Solution Point out that these questions help clarify the main idea. Have students review the text to answer "Right There" and "Think and Search" questions. Ask: What challenge does the team face? In what position is the team on the score sheet? Have students use their answers to tell what "It's ours to lose" means.

Possible responses:

- *winning the final event*
- *in first place with the most points*
- *The team will lose only if they make mistakes.*

RI.9-10.5

Monitor Comprehension

Describe Review what pp. 372–373 say about the events at the race. Then ask: What are some of the challenges that the team faces at the competition?

Possible responses:

- *must carefully attach Plexiglas top, use good navigation, drive patiently; car must hold together*

RI.9-10.1

OUT-OF-SCHOOL LITERACY

MEDIA & TECHNOLOGY

Interpreting Competitions

Help students see how much prior knowledge they bring to the text by connecting the selection to students' experiences with other types of competitions they have seen or participated in (sports, reality TV shows, political races).

- What kinds of competitions have you seen or been part of recently?
- How do people show their **aggressive** spirit in the competition?
- What **environment** do the teams or individuals play in?
- Is there any **technology** involved in the competition?
- What are some of the **obstacles** to winning?

As students answer, encourage the use of the highlighted Key Vocabulary words.

SL.9-10.1.a

CCSS Literacy.RI.9-10.1 Cite strong and thorough textual evidence to support analysis of what the text says explicitly as well as inferences drawn from the text. Literacy.RI.9-10.5 Analyze in detail how an author's ideas or claims are developed and refined by particular sentences, paragraphs, or larger portions of a text (e.g., a section or chapter). Literacy.SL.9-10.1.a Come to discussions prepared, having read and researched material under study; explicitly draw on that preparation by referring to evidence from texts and other research on the topic or issue to stimulate a thoughtful, well-reasoned exchange of ideas.

READ

OBJECTIVES

Vocabulary
- Key Vocabulary T

Reading Strategy
- Ask Questions: Find Question-Answer Relationships

Comprehension & Critical Thinking
- Use Text Evidence T

Literary Analysis
- Analyze Text Structure: Problem and Solution T

Writing
- Form: Response to Literature

TEACH & PRACTICE

A Reading Support

13 **Problem and Solution** Review the team's original goal of winning the Tour de Sol. Discuss what they did to meet it. Ask: How does the team solve their problems and meet their original goal?

Possible response:
- *They focus on solutions and don't feel discouraged.*
RI.9-10.5

APPLY

B ANALYZE

1. **Explain** The Tour de Sol is very competitive. The West Philly team performs the best overall.
RI.9-10.1
2. **Vocabulary** The Attack gets good gas mileage with low emissions. It uses alternative fuel and an electric engine.
L.9-10.6
3. **Analyze Text Structure: Problem and Solution** the axle; by identifying signal words that show sequence or key ideas
RI.9-10.5
4. **Focus Strategy: Ask Questions** Have volunteers share their questions and strategies with the class.
RI.9-10.1

Moritz, the Jetta from St. Mark's High School in Southborough, Massachusetts, took to the course. Its driver navigated expertly, hitting 32.2 seconds on his second try.

Viking 32 of Western Washington University, a top car-design school, **snared** the low 30s.

Again, West Philly's Attack sprinted out onto the course. As Hauger swung it around each corner and accelerated, the gray missile seemed to grow more **aggressive** and confident.

With a final grunt, it shot through the finish line, and the announcer said, "30.895."

West Philly's team **erupted**. The numbers didn't lie. West Philly had won itself another Tour de Sol championship. 13 ❖ A

13 **Problem and Solution** Consider the team's original goal. Do the team members meet it? How? Add these notes to your Problem-and-Solution Chart.

ANALYZE The Fast and the Fuel-Efficient

B

1. **Explain** What is the Tour de Sol competition like? How does the West Philly team perform in the different challenges? Use evidence from the text to find details.
2. **Vocabulary** What makes West Philly's Attack an **efficient** car? What kind of **technology** does the car use?
3. **Analyze Text Structure: Problem and Solution** What was the continuing mechanical problem that became an **obstacle** for the team? Explain how you used the structure of the text to identify the problem.
4. **Focus Strategy Ask Questions** Talk with a partner about how your knowledge of the topic and your own experiences helped you to answer a question you had about the news feature.

C

Return to the Text

Reread and Write Simon Hauger and the West Philly team have dreams that go beyond winning the Tour de Sol. Identify more examples of things the team wants to achieve and write a paragraph that describes their dreams.

Key Vocabulary
aggressive *adj.*, forceful and bold

In Other Words
snared completed the course in
erupted cheered

C Return to the Text

Students' paragraphs may include:
- *scholarships, sponsorships, jobs, grants, movies, and car sales*
W.9-10.9.b; W.9-10.10

Edge Interactive Practice Book, p. 176

CCSS **Literacy.RI.9-10.1** Cite strong and thorough textual evidence to support analysis of what the text says explicitly as well as inferences drawn from the text. **Literacy.RI.9-10.5** Analyze in detail how an author's ideas or claims are developed and refined by particular sentences, paragraphs, or larger portions of a text (e.g., a section or chapter). **Literacy.W.9-10.9.b** Apply grades 9-10 Reading standards to literary nonfiction (e.g., "Delineate and evaluate the argument and specific claims in a text, assessing whether the reasoning is valid and the evidence is relevant and sufficient; identify false statements and fallacious reasoning"). **Literacy.W.9-10.10** Write routinely over extended time frames (time for research, reflection, and revision) and shorter time frames (a single sitting or a day or two) for a range of tasks, purposes, and audiences. **Literacy.L.9-10.6** Acquire and use accurately general academic and domain-specific words and phrases, sufficient for reading, writing, speaking, and listening at the college and career readiness level; demonstrate independence in gathering vocabulary knowledge when considering a word or phrase important to comprehension or expression.

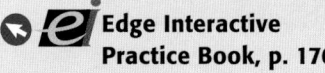

by Mick Stevens

"It runs on its conventional gasoline-powered engine until it senses guilt, at which point it switches over to battery power."

Critical Viewing What is happening in the comic? Describe it to a partner.

READ

OBJECTIVES

Comprehension & Critical Thinking
- Use Text Evidence T

Literary Analysis
- Recognize Genre: Humor
- Compare Literature (points of view across texts)

Viewing
- Respond to and Interpret Visuals

TEACH & PRACTICE

D Critical Viewing: Comic Strip

Interpret the Art and Text Have students study the comic strip and describe the situation. Tell students to describe it as if they are telling a story. Ask them to not only retell what is happening, but also to describe the characters and setting. The text is dialogue spoken by the car salesman.

ELL **Use Graphic Organizer** Read the text to students and help them use a Cause-and-Effect Chart to clarify the salesman's points.

Reason	Result
car is fuel efficient	buy the car
car cares about the environment	buy the car

Ask: What makes this cartoon funny?

Possible response:
- *Cars don't feel guilt or responsibility about the environment—people do.*

Compare Across Texts Compare the salesman to the students of the Attack team. Ask: How are their views about protecting the environment the same or different?

Possible response:
- *The team cares very much about protecting the environment; the salesman just wants to sell a car.*

Discuss which point of view best represents most people's attitudes toward the environment.
RL.9-10.10

CCSS **Literacy.RL.9-10.10** By the end of grade 9, read and comprehend literature, including stories, dramas, and poems, in the grades 9–10 text complexity band proficiently, with scaffolding as needed at the high end of the range. By the end of grade 10, read and comprehend literature, including stories, dramas, and poems, at the high end of the grades 9–10 text complexity band independently and proficiently.

Lesson 20

BEFORE READING

OBJECTIVES

Reading Strategy
- Ask Questions: Find Question-Answer Relationships

Comprehension & Critical Thinking
- Use Text Evidence T

Literary Analysis
- Analyze Development of Ideas T

TEACH STRATEGIES

A Analyze Development of Ideas

Introduce Read the introduction to describe how quotations are used as nonfiction text features.

Look Into the Text Read the callouts on p. 376. Ask: How are Moskevitz's words shown in the first paragraph compared to the second?

Possible responses:
- *The first paragraph tells his exact words, so quotation marks are used.*
- *The second paragraph describes what he said and is not exact.*

Then ask: How do you know you can believe what the speaker says?

Possible response:
- *The text explains that he is a machine technology instructor. He is a reliable source of information for this topic.*

RI.9-10.3

B Focus Strategy: Ask Questions

Find Question-Answer Relationships Define the strategy and work through the How To box.

Then have students ask a question about Look Into the Text and identify the strategy they can use to answer it.

Possible responses:
- *What kind of teacher is Moskevitz?*
- *Think and Search: He is a mentor; he encourages real-world experiences.*

Have students use a Question Chart to record their questions and strategies as they read.

RI.9-10.1

myNGconnect.com

Selection Summaries in eight languages

ONGOING ASSESSMENT

Have students explain two ways that quotations add to a text.

BEFORE READING Teens Open Doors

article by Richard Thompson

Reading Strategies
- Plan and Monitor
- Determine Importance
- Make Inferences
- ▶ **Ask Questions**
- Make Connections
- Synthesize
- Visualize

Analyze Development of Ideas

A

Nonfiction writers often include **quotations** in order to develop their ideas. Quotations show the exact words a person says about a subject. Writers use quotations in nonfiction articles to:

- provide facts and opinions from a reliable expert
- add details and elaborate on ideas
- help the reader relate to the subject and person
- give the viewpoint of someone who was there.

Compare how the speaker's words are presented in the first two paragraphs below.

Look Into the Text

Quotation marks signal where the quotation begins and ends.

"We tried to run this like it was a real-world project that an engineering company would go through," said Paul Moskevitz, a machine technology instructor who was a mentor to the group.

More than a dozen students at Whittier contributed to the final product, Moskevitz said. He added that he liked how a variety of the school's programs, including carpentry, electronics, robotics, and metal fabrication were involved.

"We have lots of capabilities at this school, and it was good for folks to see the other disciplines," Moskevitz said.

The text explains who the speaker is and why you can believe him.

Focus Strategy ▶ Ask Questions

B

You've learned many ways to **ask questions** as you read. Now choose the strategy that works best for each question.

Focus Strategy

HOW TO FIND QUESTION-ANSWER RELATIONSHIPS

As you read, record your questions in a **Question Chart**. Then identify the strategy or strategies you can use to find each answer. Use the following strategies:

- **Right There:** when the answer is found in the text
- **Think and Search:** when you need to relate separate information you find in the text
- **Author and You:** when the answer is not in the text, use what you know about the text to form new ideas
- **On My Own:** when you can answer the question based on what you already know

Question Chart

Question	Strategy
How could the different school programs contribute to the project?	I can use "Author and You" to combine clues in the text with what I know to find an answer.

CCSS Literacy.RI.9-10.1 Cite strong and thorough textual evidence to support analysis of what the text says explicitly as well as inferences drawn from the text. Literacy.RI.9-10.3 Analyze how the author unfolds an analysis or series of ideas or events, including the order in which the points are made, how they are introduced and developed, and the connections that are drawn between them.

NEWS ARTICLE

Teens Open Doors

by Richard Thompson

Connect Across Texts

The students in "The Fast and the Fuel-Efficient" found that the ***technology*** *they used could change the world. As you read this article, consider how technology can open all sorts of doors.*

Getting through high school can be challenging for any teenager. For junior Molly Rizk, who has **cerebral palsy**, one of the most difficult tasks is not taking tests at Whittier Regional Vocational Technical High School. It's opening her locker. 1

That should change in the fall, thanks to the skill of four classmates who have designed and produced a locker remote control. It will allow Rizk to get into her locker as quickly as other students.

Assistive Technology: Resources that help people with disabilities to become more independent.

Examples:
- wheelchairs, crutches, and other equipment
- hearing aids, text phones, and captioned TV

The wheels of the iBot wheelchair can lift a person to standing height.

The remote control took less than two months to complete. It was one of four entries last month at the University of Massachusetts-Lowell's Assistive Technology Design Fair. The fair is a noncompetitive event that gives **engineering experience** to high school students who complete projects that help people with special needs or disabilities.

Since it began in 2002, the fair has grown. Now it includes more than 100 students from a dozen schools across the country.

1 **Ask Questions** Ask yourself a question about Molly Rizk. What strategy will help you answer it as you read? Record the question and strategy in your Question Chart.

Key Vocabulary
- **technology** *n.*, scientific knowledge as it is used in the world

In Other Words
- **cerebral palsy** a condition that affects the central nervous system
- **engineering experience** experience in designing, building, and using machines

OBJECTIVES

Vocabulary
- Key Vocabulary T

Reading Strategies
- Ask Questions
- Make Connections

Comprehension & Critical Thinking
- Use Text Evidence T

Cultural Perspectives
- U.S. Culture: Government

BUILD BACKGROUND

C Assistive Technology

Read the title and introduction. Then review the photo, sidebar, and caption.

ELL **Use Visuals** Use photos to explain common assistive technology, such as wheelchairs, hearing aids, and text phones.

Explain that people with disabilities make up one-fifth of the U.S. population. Federal laws require businesses, schools, and other facilities to provide access and services to those with disabilities. For example, all government buildings must provide ramps and elevators.

D Connect Across Texts

Ask students to predict how a group of teenagers like the Attack team might use technology to "open doors" (or change the world) in a high school.

Read Have students read pp. 377–380. Support and monitor their comprehension using the reading support provided.

TEACH & PRACTICE

E Reading Support

1 **Ask Questions** Read the first paragraph and have students ask a question about Molly Rizk. Then ask: Which strategy helped you find the answer to your question?

Possible response:
- *Question: Why is high school especially challenging for Molly?*
- *Right There: She has cerebral palsy.*

RI.9-10.1

Comprehension Coach

Build Reading Power

Assign students to use the software, based on their instructional needs.

Read Silently
- Comprehension questions with immediate feedback
- Glossary support
- Review text evidence

RI.9-10.10

Listen
- Professional model of fluent reading

Record
- Oral reading fluency practice
- Ongoing fluency assessment with immediate feedback

CCSS Literacy.RI.9-10.1 Cite strong and thorough textual evidence to support analysis of what the text says explicitly as well as inferences drawn from the text. Literacy.RI.9-10.10 By the end of grade 9, read and comprehend literary nonfiction in the grades 9-10 text complexity band proficiently, with scaffolding as needed at the high end of the range. By the end of grade 10, read and comprehend literary nonfiction at the high end of the grades 9-10 text complexity band independently and proficiently.

READ

OBJECTIVES

Vocabulary
- Key Vocabulary Ⓣ

Reading Strategy
- Ask Questions; Review Strategies

Comprehension & Critical Thinking
- Use Text Evidence Ⓣ

Literary Analysis
- Analyze Development of Ideas Ⓣ

Research Skills
- Formulate Research Questions; Convert Data into Graphic Aids

Viewing
- Respond to and Interpret Visuals

Grammar
- Pronouns and Antecedents

TEACH & PRACTICE

Ⓐ Reading Support

2 Development of Ideas Ask: Which of Moskevitz's exact words help you fully understand the project?

Possible response:
- *"Real-world project" and "engineering company" show that the project is like a real engineer's job.* RI.9-10.3

Ⓑ Reading Support

3 Ask Questions Ask: What "Think and Search" questions help you understand this section?

Possible response:
- *How does the remote control open the correct locker? Its signal matches the one on the lock.* RI.9-10.1

Review Strategies Have partners say what other strategies they used as they read the text.

Possible response:
- *As I read details about the device, I visualized what it looks like. This helped me understand how it works and how it helps Molly to open her locker.* RI.9-10.10

For juniors Zachary Drapeau and Tom Smallwood, and seniors Casey Hansen and Nathan Lindberg, their work could make getting through college easier to afford. If they choose to **enroll** at University of Massachusetts-Lowell, each student will be able to apply for a $2,000 grant for each of the four years.

Ⓐ "We tried to run this like it was a real-world project that an engineering company would go through," said Paul Moskevitz, 2 a machine technology instructor who was a **mentor** to the group.

More than a dozen students at Whittier contributed to the final product, Moskevitz said. He added that he liked how a variety of the school's programs, including carpentry, electronics, robotics, and metal fabrication, were involved.

"We have lots of capabilities at this school, and it was good for folks to see the other **disciplines**," Moskevitz said.

Students must use keys to unlock their lockers at Whittier. The **device** developed by the four students lets Rizk use a remote control. It automatically slides the bolt out of the lock. They have also given her a specially designed key. It is molded to fit her grasp, in case the batteries in the remote stop working.

The remote control uses **an infrared signal**. It ensures that if more than one is used in a hallway, the signal will only be able to open the locker **programmed to** Ⓑ **the same encryption**. 3

Assistive Technology: Resources that help people with disabilities to become more independent.

More examples:
- voice recognition, Braille, and other touch technology
- symbols-based computer software, switch technology, speech-generators
- prosthetic limbs

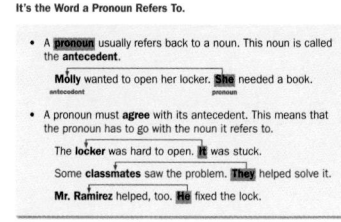

High school senior Ryan Patterson invented a glove that deaf people can wear to send messages to a screen for others to read.

2 Development of Ideas How does this quotation help you understand what it is like to be a part of the project?

3 Ask Questions Ask and answer "Think and Search" questions to deepen your understanding of this part of the selection. Record the question and how you use the strategy in your chart.

Key Vocabulary
- **device** *n.*, machine or tool that is used to do a particular job

In Other Words
enroll go to school
mentor teacher and guide
disciplines types of classes and studies
an infrared signal a powerful beam of light
programmed to the same encryption that has the same code

GRAMMAR

Pronouns and Antecedents

Teach/Model Display the transparency. Use the example to illustrate pronoun-antecedent agreement. Carefully work through the next three sentences. Invite students to identify additional pronouns and their antecedents in "Teens Open Doors."

Practice A. Have students explain their choices and record the correct answers on the transparency. Record one new sentence on the transparency. **B.** After partners talk and write their own sentences, have each student read one sentence aloud and ask the group to identify each pronoun and antecedent. L.9-10.1

Grammar & Writing Practice Book, pp. 129–130

GRAMMAR SKILLS PATH
56 Indefinite Pronouns & Singular Verbs
57 Indefinite Pronouns & Plural Verbs
58 Indefinite Pronouns & Verbs
▶ 59 Pronouns and Antecedents ELL Language & Grammar Lab
60 Review: Pronoun Agreement

Grammar Transparency 59

GRAMMAR PRONOUNS AND ANTECEDENTS 59

What's an "Antecedent"?

It's the Word a Pronoun Refers To.

- A **pronoun** usually refers back to a noun. This noun is called the **antecedent**.

  Molly wanted to open her locker. **She** needed a book.
  antecedent — pronoun

- A pronoun must **agree** with its antecedent. This means that the pronoun has to go with the noun it refers to.

  The **locker** was hard to open. **It** was stuck.
  Some **classmates** saw the problem. **They** helped solve it.
  Mr. Ramirez helped, too. **He** fixed the lock.

Try It

A. Name the antecedent for the underlined pronoun. Then add a new sentence or two. Use a pronoun and tell its antecedent. New sentences will vary.

1. My brother invents gadgets. They are very useful. antecedent: gadgets
2. He made a kitchen tool for Mom. She uses it to turn oranges into sculptures. antecedent: Mom
3. He also invented a door opener. It pulls the door open by itself. antecedent: door opener
4. Some of his ideas are very creative. They show a good imagination. antecedent: ideas

B. Tell a partner about another invention. Write three sentences. Underline each pronoun and circle its antecedent. Sentences will vary.

CCSS **Literacy.RI.9-10.1** Cite strong and thorough textual evidence to support analysis of what the text says explicitly as well as inferences drawn from the text. **Literacy.RI.9-10.3** Analyze how the author unfolds an analysis or series of ideas or events, including the order in which the points are made, how they are introduced and developed, and the connections that are drawn between them. **Literacy.RI.9-10.10** By the end of grade 9, read and comprehend literary nonfiction in the grades 9–10 text complexity band proficiently, with scaffolding as needed at the high end of the range. By the end of grade 10, read and comprehend literary nonfiction at the high end of the grades 9–10 text complexity band independently and proficiently. **Literacy.L.9-10.1** Demonstrate command of the conventions of standard English grammar and usage when writing or speaking.

Molly Rizk tests the new device.

C

"There was a lot of **trial and error** along the way," Smallwood said. "Especially trying to fit the parts together and trying to get things to work and to have everything centered so the **deadbolt** would come across and strike the plate at the right time." 4 D

In the last few weeks, the students have been in the process of **patenting** their device. David Cunningham, the school's technology chairman, said he hopes that the device could have **broader application**. It's a realistic possibility, he said, given that the setup can be easily **duplicated and maintained**.

Next year, school officials plan to "check with local **nursing homes** . . . to see if this device could be used" to help **their residents**, Cunningham said.

Mike Hart, president of the Haverhill Rotary Club, saw the remote control in action last month when the students sat in on one of his

4 **Development of Ideas**
What does this quotation tell you about Smallwood? Why do you think he worked so hard?

In Other Words

trial and error testing new ideas and then fixing them if they didn't work
deadbolt metal bar in the lock
patenting getting ownership of
broader application many more uses
duplicated and maintained made again and taken care of
nursing homes homes for people with very serious health problems
their residents the people who live there

TEACH & PRACTICE

C Analyze Visuals

Connect to Experience Read the caption for the photo. Ask students what Molly Rizk is doing. Then have them describe places they have seen assistive technologies used.

ELL **Build Background** Tell students that:

- Braille is a system of writing for the blind that uses an alphabet and other characters made up of raised dots.
- Speech-generators allow people to type words that are then spoken by a machine.
- Prosthetic limbs are artificial devices to replace a missing part of the body.

Possible responses:
- *Molly is using a new remote control to open her locker.*
- *Braille is used in elevators and on ATMs.*

D Reading Support

4 Development of Ideas Rephrase the questions: What can you learn about Smallwood from what he says? What does it tell you about someone when he or she is willing to work very hard at a task?

Possible responses:
- *Smallwood is very careful and interested in details. He doesn't give up easily.*
- *He worked hard because he cared a lot and wanted his invention to work.*

RI.9-10.3

CONTENT AREA CONNECTIONS

Design Technology to Support Disabilities

MEDIA & TECHNOLOGY

Discuss Brainstorm examples of ways that homes, cars, and businesses are already outfitted with technology to make life easier, faster, safer, and more independent for people with disabilities.

Brainstorm and Draw Have small groups brainstorm devices that can help people with disabilities. Students may list real devices they have seen or used, or suggest new devices that address different needs. Have the group draw a floor plan for one room that uses assistive technology to make the room accessible for people with disabilities. Use icons to show the different devices that could be used in that room. A legend should explain each icon and the device's use.

CCSS Literacy.RI.9-10.3 Analyze how the author unfolds an analysis or series of ideas or events, including the order in which the points are made, how they are introduced and developed, and the connections that are drawn between them.

group's weekly meetings. Hart said he was "very impressed." The presentation "really added a lot to the meeting . . . I was amazed at **the sophistication and the complexity of** the device," he said. "It was just beyond what you would've expected their achievements to be."

Rizk said she was moved by the commitment of her classmates.

A "When I first saw the actual locker, I was touched that the kids had built this for me," said Rizk. "I really appreciated that they took the time out of their busy schedules to do this for me, and I've learned that people can be very caring once you get to know them." 5

5 Development of Ideas Why does the author end with a quotation by Molly Rizk? What effect does this have on the article?

B

ANALYZE Teens Open Doors

1. **Explain** What inspired the students to invent their **device**? How does the device also help the students who invented it? Support your answer with details from the text.
2. **Vocabulary** How long did it take the students to **assemble** the locker device? What kinds of **technology** did they use?
3. **Analyze Development of Ideas** Many nonfiction authors include quotations from witnesses, experts, and other people involved in the events. Find two quotations in the article and think about why the author includes them. Look at the list on page 376 for the possible reasons.
4. **Focus Strategy Ask Questions** Share your **Question Chart** with a partner. Discuss the strategies you used to answer each question. Ask your partner whether he or she would have used the same strategies.

C

Return to the Text

Reread and Write Return to the section that describes Molly Rizk and her disability. Then brainstorm a list of other challenges that going to high school might pose for Rizk. Write a paragraph that describes one **obstacle** in detail and suggest **solutions** that would help her overcome it.

In Other Words

the sophistication and the complexity of the professional quality and hard work that was shown in

OBJECTIVES

Vocabulary
- Key Vocabulary T

Reading Strategy
- Ask Questions: Find Question-Answer Relationships

Comprehension & Critical Thinking
- Use Text Evidence T

Literary Analysis
- Analyze Development of Ideas T

Writing
- Form: Response to Literature

TEACH & PRACTICE

A Reading Support

5 Development of Ideas Ask: Why does the author include Molly Rizk's point of view?

Possible responses:
- *He wants to bring readers back to the real person so they can connect with her experience.*
- *It makes a scientific article more human.*

RI.9-10.3

APPLY

B ANALYZE

1. **Explain** A classmate was in need of help. The students are eligible for college grant money and maybe rights to a patent.
RI.9-10.1
2. **Vocabulary** It took less than two months. They used remote control and infrared technology.
L.9-10.6
3. **Analyze Development of Ideas** Students should include quotations from the article.
RI.9-10.3
4. **Focus Strategy: Ask Questions** Lists should include at least two of the three strategies listed on p. 376.
RI.9-10.1

C Return to the Text

Have students visualize their own progress through a typical school day, then match tasks against Molly's situation.
W.9-10.4; W.9-10.10

Interactive Reading

Have students reread and mark "Teens Open Doors" within the Edge Interactive Practice Book to apply their knowledge of text features and to practice the Focus Strategy—Ask Questions: Find Question-Answer Relationships.

Edge Interactive Practice Book, pp. 177–180

Unit Project

Progress Check Allow time for students to work on their unit projects. Meet with individuals and/or groups to provide guidance and check on their progress.

myNGconnect.com
- **Unit Planning Tools**
- **Unit Project Evaluation Rubric**

CCSS **Literacy.RI.9-10.1** Cite strong and thorough textual evidence to support analysis of what the text says explicitly as well as inferences drawn from the text. **Literacy.RI.9-10.3** Analyze how the author unfolds an analysis or series of ideas or events, including the order in which the points are made, how they are introduced and developed, and the connections that are drawn between them. **Literacy.W.9-10.4** Produce clear and coherent writing in which the development, organization, and style are appropriate to task, purpose, and audience. **Literacy.W.9-10.10** Write routinely over extended time frames (time for research, reflection, and revision) and shorter time frames (a single sitting or a day or two) for a range of tasks, purposes, and audiences. **Literacy.L.9-10.6** Acquire and use accurately general academic and domain-specific words and phrases, sufficient for reading, writing, speaking, and listening at the college and career readiness level; demonstrate independence in gathering vocabulary knowledge when considering a word or phrase important to comprehension or expression.

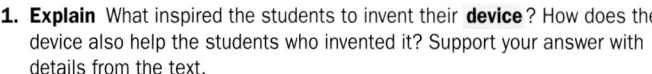

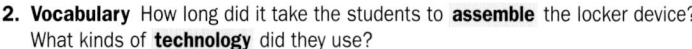

Lesson 21
REFLECT AND ASSESS

OBJECTIVES

Vocabulary
- Key Vocabulary Ⓣ

Reading Fluency
- Expression Ⓣ

Comprehension & Critical Thinking
- Compare Information
- Use Text Evidence Ⓣ

Literary Analysis
- Evaluate Literature

Writing
- Mode: Opinion
- Form: Paragraph

EQ How Can Knowledge Open Doors?

Reading

Critical Thinking

1. **Analyze** Review the brainstorm you began on page 362 and consider the students you read about in both selections. Why are people motivated to use **technology** to make improvements?
2. **Interpret** In "The Fast and the Fuel-**Efficient**," student Joseph Pak says: "I've seen the extreme of not doing things when you should" (page 369). What does he mean? How does this idea also apply to "Teens Open Doors"?
3. **Compare** How does each team overcome **obstacles** to find **solutions** to their problems? How are their experiences different?
4. **Speculate** How do you think these students' experiences will affect them in the future? What have they learned from the process of finding solutions for their problems?
5. **Synthesize** Considering the examples in these two selections, describe ways that technology can help open doors for people in the future.

Writing

Write About Literature

Opinion Statement Consider the work both groups of students are doing. Which do you think is more important? Write an opinion statement that explains your choice and support it with examples from both texts. Use the cluster below to organize your ideas.

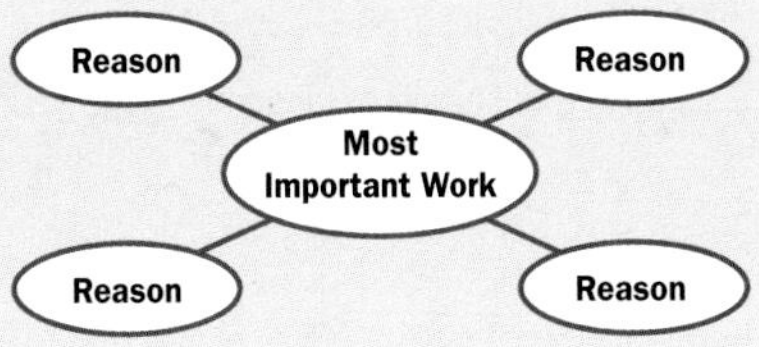

Vocabulary

Key Vocabulary Review

Oral Review Work with a partner. Use these words to complete the paragraph.

aggressive	efficient	solutions
assembling	environment	technology
devices	obstacles	

Advances in science and __(1)__ improve our lives in many ways. Many __(2)__ car companies are taking strong action to help protect the __(3)__ that surrounds us. They are __(4)__, or putting together, new hybrid cars that are more __(5)__ because they use less gas and release fewer emissions. New machines and __(6)__ also help people with disabilities overcome __(7)__ and difficulties that get in their way. Our world still isn't perfect, but if we continue to identify problems and find __(8)__, tomorrow will be even better than today.

Writing Application What example of technology would you have trouble living without? Write a paragraph about it that uses at least four Key Vocabulary words.

Fluency

Read with Ease: Expression

Assess your reading fluency with the passage in the Reading Handbook, p. 762. Then complete the self-check below.

1. I did/did not sound natural.
2. My words correct per minute: ____.

Reading

Critical Thinking

1. **Analyze** People use technology to help people, to improve the world, and to reach personal goals.
2. **Interpret** He means that not doing a job thoroughly can lead to extreme failures. In "Teens Open Doors," the students learn that doing things right makes a big difference. RI.9-10.2
3. **Compare** The Attack team didn't give up on fixing the axle—and they won the race. The other team used trial and error—and perfected their device. The Attack team is in a competitive environment; the other team is not. RI.9-10.1; RI.9-10.10
4. **Speculate** Students' experiences will help them face challenges in the future. They have learned to be good problem solvers and to be persistent. Their experiences and successes could open doors to more opportunities in the future.
5. **Synthesize** Technology can make the world safer, easier, and healthier. RI.9-10.1

Writing

Write About Literature

Edge Interactive Practice Book, p. 181

Opinion Statement Have students use the organizer to write the opinion statement. Remind students to state their opinion with evidence.

Invite volunteers to share their statements. Chart the supporting reasons and have the group vote to choose the strongest statement. W.9-10.1; W.9-10.9.b

Vocabulary

Key Vocabulary Review

1. *technology* 2. *aggressive*
3. *environment* 4. *assembling*
5. *efficient* 6. *devices* 7. *obstacles*
8. *solutions*
L.9-10.6

Fluency

Read with Ease: Expression

Ensure that students complete the self-check. RI.9-10.10

ASSESS & RETEACH

Assessments Handbook, pp. 43j–43m

Have students complete the **Reader Reflection**. Then give students the **Cluster Test** to measure their progress. Group students as needed for reteaching.

CCSS **Literacy.RI.9-10.1** Cite strong and thorough textual evidence to support analysis of what the text says explicitly as well as inferences drawn from the text. **Literacy.RI.9-10.2** Determine a central idea of a text and analyze its development over the course of the text, including how it emerges and is shaped and refined by specific details; provide an objective summary of the text. **Literacy.RI.9-10.10** By the end of grade 9, read and comprehend literary nonfiction in the grades 9-10 text complexity band proficiently, with scaffolding as needed at the high end of the range. By the end of grade 10, read and comprehend literary nonfiction at the high end of the grades 9-10 text complexity band independently and proficiently. **Literacy.W.9-10.1** Write arguments to support claims in an analysis of substantive topics or texts, using valid reasoning and relevant and sufficient evidence. **Literacy.W.9-10.9.b** Apply grades 9-10 Reading standards to literary nonfiction (e.g., "Delineate and evaluate the argument and specific claims in a text, assessing whether the reasoning is valid and the evidence is relevant and sufficient; identify false statements and fallacious reasoning"). **Literacy.L.9-10.6** Acquire and use accurately general academic and domain-specific words and phrases, sufficient for reading, writing, speaking, and listening at the college and career readiness level; demonstrate independence in gathering vocabulary knowledge when considering a word or phrase important to comprehension or expression.

Lesson 22

INTEGRATE THE LANGUAGE ARTS

OBJECTIVES

Language Function
- Verify or Confirm Information Ⓣ

Research Skill
- Convert Data into Graphic Aid

Listening and Speaking
- Speech

Grammar
- Pronoun Agreement Ⓣ

Grammar

Use the Correct Pronoun

Grammar Transparency 60

Review Use the transparency lesson and the activity on p. 382 to review pronouns. Explain that reciprocal pronouns are used to show that two people are carrying out the same action at the same time. See also p. 830.

Oral Practice Pronouns should correctly replace antecedent nouns.

Written Practice **6.** *He* **7.** *it* **8.** *They* **9.** *each other*
L.9-10.1

Language Development

Verify or Confirm Information

Have students clarify ideas, details, and language by listening carefully and asking questions.
SL.9-10.1.a

Assessments Handbook, p. 43o

Research/Viewing

Descriptive Diagram

Science: Assistive Technology
Remind students to include specific details in their explanation.
W.9-10.2; W.9-10.7

Listening/Speaking

Speech

Tech Talk Brainstorm the goals and criteria for building the hybrid car.
SL.9-10.4; SL.9-10.6

Edge Interactive Practice Book, p. 182

GRAMMAR SKILLS PATH
56 Indefinite Pronouns & Singular Verbs
57 Indefinite Pronouns & Plural Verbs
58 Indefinite Pronouns & Verbs
59 Pronouns and Antecedents
▶ 60 Review: Pronoun Agreement ELL Language & Grammar Lab

INTEGRATE THE LANGUAGE ARTS

Grammar

Use the Correct Pronoun

The pronoun you use depends on the **noun** it refers to. To choose the correct pronoun, ask yourself:

- Does the noun name a male, a female, or a thing?
- Does the noun name one or more than one?
- Do you need a **subject pronoun** or an **object pronoun**?
- Do you need a **reciprocal pronoun**: **each other** or **one another**?

Study these examples:

The **girl** is smart. **She** plans to be an engineer.

The factory built many **cars**. I like **them**.

The actors help **each other** remember lines.

The students looked at **one another**.

Oral Practice (1–5) With a partner, take turns using each pair of words below in sentences about "The Fast and the Fuel-Efficient." **Example:** *Mr. Preiss is the shop teacher. Students talk to him about cars.*

teacher, him	girl, her
race, it	future, they

Written Practice (6–10) Rewrite the paragraph using the correct pronouns. Add one sentence.

Clayton Kinsler test drove the car. (He/Him) sped down the street. Students who built (them/it) cheered. (They/He) were shocked when the car stopped. The axle was broken. Students whispered to (it/each other).

Language Development

Verify or Confirm Information

Pair Talk What do you think are the most fuel-efficient cars on the road today? Check a reliable source and report your findings: *I thought* __________, *and found out that it was (true/not true).*

Research / Writing

Descriptive Diagram

Science: Assistive Technology Assistive technology helps improve the lives of many people with disabilities. Work with a group to research one important assistive **device**, such as text-to-speech software, Braille printers, or text telephones.

myNGconnect.com

- **Find information about how the device looks and works.**
- **Read firsthand accounts by people who have used it.**

Create a diagram that explains the different parts of the device and how the device works. Then write a paragraph describing the device. Be sure to use specific details and technical language in your paragraph.

Listening / Speaking

Speech

Tech Talk Imagine that you are Simon Hauger and you have been asked to give a presentation about the Attack to auto company executives. What would you say about your project?

1. **Brainstorm Ideas** Jot down the ideas that are most important to discuss, such as the dream of building inexpensive hybrids.
2. **Outline Ideas** Organize your ideas into a point-by-point outline.
3. **Rehearse** Practice your speech. Remember your audience. Use formal language and jargon from the selection. Speak clearly and be polite.
4. **Speech** Deliver your speech to your classmates. Then, listen to their speeches and take notes to summarize their ideas.

Language and Learning Handbook, page 702

GRAMMAR

Review: Pronoun Agreement

Review Display the transparency. Remind students that pronouns must agree with their antecedents. Use the examples to review pronoun agreement. Show how the arrows point out the pronoun's antecedent.

A. Oral Practice Model how to choose the correct pronoun in the first sentence. Underline students' correct choices on the transparency, and have them explain their choice.

B. Written Practice Work through the example. Explain that some sentences have no errors. Have the group tell you how to edit the paragraph. Then ask a volunteer to read the corrected paragraph to the class. L.9-10.1

Grammar & Writing Practice Book, pp. 131–132

Grammar Transparency 60

Use the Correct Pronoun

GRAMMAR REVIEW: PRONOUN AGREEMENT 60

Remember: When you use a pronoun, be sure it fits correctly into the sentence. Also be sure it goes with the noun it refers to.

- Use a **subject pronoun** in the subject of a sentence.
  Use an **object pronoun** after the verb or after a preposition.

  Mr. Ross tutors **Diana**. **He** helps **her** with algebra.

  The **students** are learning a new **formula**. **They** understand **it**.

- Every **pronoun** must agree with the **noun** it refers to. This noun is called the antecedent.
  1. If the noun names a male, use **he** or **him**.
  2. If the noun names a female, use **she** or **her**.
  3. If a noun names one thing, use **it** or **it**.
  4. If a noun names "more than one," use **they** or **them**.

Try It

A. Read the paragraph aloud. Say the correct pronouns.

Mr. Ross helps his students explore careers in the computer industry. **(He / They)** takes **(him / them)** to visit a software company. **(It / They)** is near the school.

B. Edit the paragraph. Fix four mistakes. The first is done for you.

Diana has two brothers. ~~Them~~ They are in college. Oscar is studying computers. ~~Him~~ He works part-time at a software company. Silvino works there, too. Diana admires her brothers. Maybe ~~her~~ she will join ~~they~~ them at work someday.

CCSS **Literacy.W.9-10.2** Write informative/explanatory texts to examine and convey complex ideas, concepts, and information clearly and accurately through the effective selection, organization, and analysis of content. **Literacy.W.9-10.7** Conduct short as well as more sustained research projects to answer a question (including a self-generated question) or solve a problem; narrow or broaden the inquiry when appropriate; synthesize multiple sources on the subject, demonstrating understanding of the subject under investigation. **Literacy.SL.9-10.1.a** Come to discussions prepared, having read and researched material under study; explicitly draw on that preparation by referring to evidence from texts and other research on the topic or issue to stimulate a thoughtful, well-reasoned exchange of ideas. **Literacy.L.9-10.1** Demonstrate command of the conventions of standard English grammar and usage when writing or speaking.

Vocabulary Study

Multiple-Meaning Words

Many **multiple-meaning words** have specialized meanings in different subject areas. Review the chart. What does the word *power* mean in each subject area?

Word	Social Studies	Science	Math
power	authority, influence, control	a source of energy, such as electricity	the result of a number multiplied by itself one or more times

Copy the chart. For each word below, look in a dictionary to find specialized definitions in two or more subject areas. Add the definitions to the chart.

1. ruler **2. landslide** **3. revolution** **4. solution**

Writing on Demand

Write a Problem-Solution Essay

An essay test in a social science class may ask you to find a solution for a problem that is described in a prompt.

❶ **Unpack the Prompt** Read the prompt and underline key words.

> Your school library cannot afford to provide a large selection of audio books for blind and disabled students. Describe the best solution to the problem. Explain why your solution is the best.

❷ **Plan Your Response** Put your ideas in a chart. First, describe the problem. Then list possible solutions. Provide specific details to describe why each solution will or won't work. Finally, choose the best solution. Add additional specific details to make the solution strong.

Problem	
Possible Solutions	**Why They Work or Don't Work**
1.	1.
2.	2.
3.	3.
Best Solution and Reasons	

❸ **Draft** Use this organizer to plan your essay. Keep in mind that your paragraphs should flow from one idea to another. Limit your writing time to fifteen minutes, as if it was a test.

Essay Organizer

> A current problem in our school is [describe the problem]. This is important to solve because [explain].
>
> I believe the best way to solve this problem is to [describe your solution]. This solution would work because [explain how the solution solves the problem].
>
> My solution is better than other options because [give specific reasons and examples].
>
> In conclusion, I believe the best solution is to [restate the best option].

❹ **Check Your Work** Reread your work. Ask:

- Does my response address the prompt?
- Does my essay suggest good solutions?
- Do I use the correct pronouns?
- Do I use rhetorical devices?

Writing Handbook, page 784

INTEGRATE THE LANGUAGE ARTS

OBJECTIVES

Vocabulary
- Multiple-Meaning Words Ⓣ
- Strategy: Use Reference Sources (dictionary)

Writing
- Writing Process
- Form: Problem-Solution Essay Ⓣ

Vocabulary Study

Multiple-Meaning Words

Social Studies	Science	Math
(ruler) one that rules	machine that lines paper	strip used for measurement
(landslide) election win by a large number of votes	avalanche of rock	a large number
(revolution) major political change	circular movement	movement around an axis
(solution) process of solving a problem	mixture of solids, liquids, or gases	answer to or the process of solving a problem

L.9-10.4.c

Edge Interactive Practice Book, p. 183

Writing on Demand

Problem-Solution Essay

1. **Unpack the Prompt** Help students identify Key Words.
2. **Plan Your Response** Model the completion of the chart.
3. **Draft** Limit students to 15 minutes writing time. Tell students to pay attention to the order of their paragraphs, transitions, and rhetorical devices to convey meaning. Also remind them to include specific details in the description of the solution.
4. **Check Your Work** Have students read their essays to a partner and answer the questions together.
5. **Evaluate Your Work** Have students self-evaluate their essays using the Writing Rubric.

See **Writing Handbook** p. 784 for further instruction.

W.9-10.1; W.9-10.4

Writing Rubric Problem-Solution Essay

Exceptional	• Essay addresses topic by describing a clear problem and solution. • Solutions are clear and relevant to topic. • Pronouns are used correctly.
Competent	• Essay pertains to topic. • Solutions are adequate but not very descriptive. • Sentence pronouns are used correctly with no more than one error.
Developing	• Essay may stray from topic. • Solutions are occasionally unclear and are not descriptive. • Pronouns are sometimes not used correctly.
Beginning	• Essay does not address topic. • Solutions are unclear and non-descriptive. • Pronouns are often not used correctly.

CCSS **Literacy.W.9-10.1** Write arguments to support claims in an analysis of substantive topics or texts, using valid reasoning and relevant and sufficient evidence. **Literacy.W.9-10.4** Produce clear and coherent writing in which the development, organization, and style are appropriate to task, purpose, and audience. **Literacy.L.9-10.4.c** Consult general and specialized reference materials (e.g., dictionaries, glossaries, thesauruses), both print and digital, to find the pronunciation of a word or determine or clarify its precise meaning, its part of speech, or its etymology. **Literacy.SL.9-10.4** Present information, findings, and supporting evidence clearly, concisely, and logically such that listeners can follow the line of reasoning and the organization, development, substance, and style are appropriate to purpose, audience, and task. **Literacy.SL.9-10.6** Adapt speech to a variety of contexts and tasks, demonstrating command of formal English when indicated or appropriate.

Lesson 24

CLOSE READING

OBJECTIVES

Vocabulary
- Academic Vocabulary

Comprehension & Critical Thinking
- Determine Importance
- Use Text Evidence (T)

Literary Analysis
- Analyze Text Structure: Chronology (T)
- Analyze Text Features (T)

TEACH & PRACTICE

A Read for Understanding

Genre Display the **eEdition** and read aloud the two-part selection. Ask: What kind of text is each part? How do you know?

Possible response:
- *congressional resolution, as indicated by the title and heading*
- *online news article, as indicated by the Internet features, newspaper name, and posting date*

Have students complete item 1 on **Interactive Practice Book** p. 184.

Topic Display the prompt: The two parts of the selection mostly tell about ___ and [how/what] ___. Have partners use the prompt to write a topic sentence. Then have students complete item 2 on **Interactive Practice Book** p. 184.

B Reread and Summarize

Have partners read the selection, pausing to clarify ideas.

Key Ideas Have partners choose important words or phrases from each part of the selection and note why each word is important. Have students complete item 3 on **Interactive Practice Book** p. 184.

Finally, have students use their notes with their topic sentences to complete item 4 on **Interactive Practice Book** page 184.
RI.9-10.2

Edge Interactive Practice Book, pp. 184–187

CLOSE READING

The Sky Is Not the Limit

110th CONGRESS
1st Session
H. RES. 661

House Calendar No. 158

RESOLUTION

1 *Honoring the accomplishments of Barrington Antonio Irving, the youngest pilot and first person of African descent ever to fly solo around the world.*

2 **Whereas** Barrington Irving was born in 1983 in Kingston, Jamaica, and raised in inner-city Miami, Florida;

3 Whereas Irving discovered his passion for aviation at the age of 15 when Captain Gary Robinson, a Jamaican airline pilot who has since served as his mentor, took him to tour the **cockpit of a Boeing 777**;

4 Whereas Irving overcame financial hardship to pursue his dream to become a pilot by working miscellaneous jobs and working for private aircraft owners in exchange for flying lessons;

5 Whereas Irving was the recipient of a joint Air Force/Florida Memorial University Flight Awareness Scholarship to cover college tuition and flying lessons for his tireless volunteer efforts and commitment to community service;

6 Whereas in 2003, Irving contacted companies including aircraft manufacturer Columbia, which agreed to provide him with a plane to fly around the world if he could secure **donations and components**;

7 Whereas over several years, Irving visited **aviation trade shows** throughout the country and secured more than $300,000 of cash and donated components including the engine, tires, cockpit systems, and seats for a Columbia 400, one of the world's fastest single-engine piston airplanes;

In Other Words

Whereas Since
cockpit of a Boeing 777 steering area of a large airplane
donations and components money and parts
aviation trade shows meetings of companies that sell airplane parts

Social Studies Background

Resolutions are documents created by members of the United States Congress. Unlike bills, simple resolutions are not laws. Instead, they may give advice, honors, or opinions.

ACADEMIC VOCABULARY **REVIEW**

Use the **Graphic Organizer** (**Word Web**) vocabulary routine (PD44). Remind students that *sequence* means an arrangement, or order, in which one thing comes after another. Point out that ideas in congressional resolutions and events in news articles are usually presented in sequential, or chronological, order.

- **sequence (n.)**
  - an arrangement, or order, in which one thing comes after another
  - dates on a calendar
  - cognate: secuencia (Spanish)
  - sequence (v.), sequential (adj.), sequentially (adv.), unsequenced (adj.)
  - consequence, something that follows something else

L.9-10.6

CCSS Literacy.RI.9-10.2 Determine a central idea of a text and analyze its development over the course of the text, including how it emerges and is shaped and refined by specific details; provide an objective summary of the text. Literacy.L.9-10.6 Acquire and use accurately general academic and domain-specific words and phrases, sufficient for reading, writing, speaking, and listening at the college and career readiness level; demonstrate independence in gathering vocabulary knowledge when considering a word or phrase important to comprehension or expression.

8 Whereas in the process of pursuing his dream of an around the world flight, Irving founded a nonprofit organization in 2005 to address the significant shortage of youth pursuing careers in aviation and aerospace;

9 Whereas Irving's efforts have **garnered** widespread community support and sponsorship as an effective model to expose young people and underrepresented groups to opportunities in aviation;

10 Whereas on March 23, 2007, Irving embarked from Miami, Florida, on a 24,600-mile flight around the world in an airplane named "Inspiration" at 23-years of age while still a senior majoring in aerospace at Florida Memorial University;

11 Whereas on June 27, 2007, Irving concluded his flight in Miami, Florida, after stopping in 27 cities throughout the world; and

12 Whereas Irving continues to inspire youth and adults alike with his achievements and work to increase the accessibility of opportunities in aviation and aerospace: Now, therefore, be it

13 Resolved, that the House of Representatives—

14 (1) honors the accomplishments of Barrington Irving, the youngest pilot and first person of African **descent** ever to fly solo around the world and founder of a nonprofit organization that inspires youth to pursue careers in aviation and aerospace;

15 (2) encourages young people and minorities to pursue educational opportunities in preparation for careers in aviation and related industries; and

16 (3) encourages museums throughout the Nation related to aviation to commemorate the historic achievements of Captain Barrington Irving.

In Other Words
garnered gotten
descent ancestry

PRACTICE & APPLY

C Reread and Analyze

Set a Purpose Explain that partners will reread each text in the **Interactive Practice Book** and determine how the authors use text structures and features to organize and present information.

Text Structure: Chronology Review: Nonfiction authors often organize information using a chronological text structure. They present events in the order that they happened in real life. Then have students complete items 5 and 6 on **Interactive Practice Book** p. 185.

If students have difficulty, remind them to look for clues in dates and people's ages. Ask: What year was Irving born? What happened 15 years later?
RI.9-10.5

Text Features Remind students that texts often use features such as headings or bulleted lists to help organize information or highlight key ideas. Then have students complete item 7 on **Interactive Practice Book** p. 185.

If students have difficulty, say: Point out the numbers in paragraphs 14–16. What do these numbers show?
RI.9-10.3

Edge Interactive Practice Book, pp. 184–187

CCSS Literacy.RI.9-10.3 Analyze how the author unfolds an analysis or series of ideas or events, including the order in which the points are made, how they are introduced and developed, and the connections that are drawn between them. Literacy.RI.9-10.5 Analyze in detail how an author's ideas or claims are developed and refined by particular sentences, paragraphs, or larger portions of a text (e.g., a section or chapter).

CLOSE READING

OBJECTIVES

Comprehension & Critical Thinking
- Synthesize

Literary Analysis
- Analyze Text Structure: Chronology Ⓣ
- Analyze Text Features Ⓣ
- Use Text Evidence Ⓣ

Research Skills
- Gather Information

Writing
- Write About Text Structures and Features

PRACTICE & APPLY

C Reread and Analyze

Text Structure: Chronology Remind students that news articles often present events in a chronological, or sequential, order. Have students complete items 8–9 and 13–14 on **Interactive Practice Book** pp. 186 and 187.

If students have difficulty, remind them to look for time-order words that signal sequence, such as: *when, upon, while.*
RI.9-10.5

Text Features Review: News articles often include text features like photos, captions, and quotations in order to add more information about the subject. Then have students complete items 10–12 on **Interactive Practice Book** pp. 186 and 187.

If students have difficulty, ask: What kind of additional information can you learn from a photo, caption, or quotation?
RI.9-10.3

Edge Interactive Practice Book, pp. 184–187

http://myNGconnect.com/Pilot

HOME NEWS SPORTS ENTERTAINMENT BUSINESS LIVING OPINION JOBS

Posted on Tuesday, 06.05.12 A A | Share 21 email print comment reprints

Miami Pilot Makes History, Inspires Others

Barrington Irving

2007, John Ross.

BY DANIELA GUZMAN
The Miami Herald

1 As a young man at Miami Northwestern Senior High School, Barrington Irving knew he had **potential**. He imagined a football scholarship to a state school would fulfill that potential. When the Opa-locka **native** was offered a full **ride** to the University of Florida, he was set.

2 But another dream took off. Before turning 29 years old, Irving became the youngest person and the first black pilot to fly around the world, the founder of a non-profit organization and most recently, one of 15 National Geographic Emerging Explorers in 2012.

3 His journey began in Miami, long before he took off on his first flight.

4 Irving was sixteen and working at his parents' bookstore in Miami Gardens when he met Gary Robinson, a customer and a commercial pilot. Robinson told Irving about the life of a pilot. Although the **salary was intriguing**, Irving didn't feel he was smart enough.

5 "I never had that confidence," Irving said.

6 But his confidence soared when Robinson invited Irving to take a test flight with him in a training plane from the Opa-locka airport. Flying above his own neighborhood, from the airport he lived so close to, Irving **became enamored** with aviation. Robinson gave Irving a handheld radio that could tune into airport traffic control, helping Irving tune into his own calling. Upon graduating, Irving rejected the UF football scholarship and started working odd jobs. He cleaned pools. He bagged groceries. But he dreamed of the skies. While he saved up, Irving started studying aeronautical science at Florida Memorial University in Miami Gardens.

In Other Words
potential the ability to become successful
native resident
ride scholarship
salary was intriguing pay was interesting
became enamored fell in love

CONTENT AREA CONNECTIONS

Explore the History of Aviation

Share Facts Tell students the following:

- In 1903, two Ohio brothers named Wilbur and Orville Wright developed the first successful airplane.
- Since then, many people have tried to achieve different "firsts" in flight. For example, in 1927, Charles Lindbergh became the first person to fly solo across the Atlantic Ocean without stopping. His feat made him such a cultural hero that he even had a popular dance named for him—the Lindy Hop.

Discuss What are some other "firsts" that different pilots might have wanted to achieve in the history of aviation, or flight?

Research and Share Have partners use the research process to learn more about famous heroes of American aviation, such as Amelia Earhart, Charles "Chuck" Yeager, and Neil Armstrong. Invite students to report their findings to the class.
W.9-10.7

CCSS **Literacy.RI.9-10.3** Analyze how the author unfolds an analysis or series of ideas or events, including the order in which the points are made, how they are introduced and developed, and the connections that are drawn between them. **Literacy.RI.9-10.5** Analyze in detail how an author's ideas or claims are developed and refined by particular sentences, paragraphs, or larger portions of a text (e.g., a section or chapter). **Literacy.W.9-10.7** Conduct short as well as more sustained research projects to answer a question (including a self-generated question) or solve a problem; narrow or broaden the inquiry when appropriate; synthesize multiple sources on the subject, demonstrating understanding of the subject under investigation.

7 With the help of his mentor, Irving started learning how to fly planes, first with simulator software, which he now uses with students grades 3 through 12 in his after-school and summer camp program, Experience Aviation. The non-profit educational program is based at Opa-locka Airport and the newly restored Glen Curtiss Mansion in Miami Springs. Through the program, which he started in 2008, he has mentored hundreds of students in the South Florida area. Because of Irving's success in aviation, he decided to give back by encouraging young people to pursue careers in science, **technology**, engineering and mathematics.

8 "My ultimate goal is to show young people that they can do amazing things," said Irving.

9 It's something that Irving showed the world when he flew around the world in a plane put together from over $300,000 worth of donated parts. Irving reached out to aviation companies, telling them about his passion for flying and aerospace engineering. The companies saw the young man's effort as remarkable. The airplane, a Cessna 400, is named the "Inspiration," and was manufactured and **assembled** by the Columbia Aircraft Mfg. Co. in 2005. Without a de-icing system or weather radar, the 23-year-old pilot took off from Miami making the unprecedented journey around the globe.

10 Upon landing, Irving felt the accomplishment would not be complete without teaching minority youth that they could do the same. Under his guidance, 60 high school students built a plane in 10 weeks—from scratch. Then, Barrington tested it out with a flight over Miami. The program evolved into Experience Aviation. There are some students in the program that are coming straight from jail, and some that are straight-A students. But according to Irving, you wouldn't be able to tell the difference when they're learning how to fly on a simulator, or building an engine.

11 Daniel Diaz, 14, an incoming ninth-grader at Coral Park Senior High, has participated in Experience Aviation for three years. While he had never seen aviation as a **field** before, he has his mind set on being an aeronautical engineer.

12 "I have a chance to do things that a lot of people my age don't have," said Diaz, who flew with Irving in a small plane last year, sealing his love for flying. "I never thought I could feel what it's like to be in the sky. Now that's all I want to do." ❖

Key Vocabulary

- **technology** *n.*, scientific knowledge as it is used in the world
- **assemble** *v.*, to put something together

In Other Words

field career option

APPLY

D Discuss

Synthesize Based on your notes, explain how authors use text structures and features to organize and present information. Then have students complete item 15 on **Interactive Practice Book** p. 188.
SL.9-10.1.a; L.9-10.3

Write Prompt: Write a paragraph to explain how the structures and features of texts can help convey important information. Have students complete item 16 on **Interactive Practice Book** p. 188.
RI.9-10.1; W.9-10.10

E Connect with the EQ

Opinion Help students connect their understandings of the text to the Essential Question. Encourage students to focus on specific details from the text about Barrington Irving's life and whether or not those details apply in general to the ideas about opening doors. Then have students complete item 17 on **Interactive Practice Book** p. 189.
SL.9-10.1.a

Theme Have students review the two quotations in the Unit Opener (p. 306). Ask: Do Barrington Irving's experiences support either of these quotations? Then have students complete item 18 on **Interactive Practice Book** p. 189.
RI.9-10.1; W.9-10.10

Research Have students generate research questions around the Close Reading content. Then have them do a short search for the answers and share their findings with the class.
W.9-10.7

Edge Interactive Practice Book, pp. 184–187

CCSS **Literacy.RI.9-10.1** Cite strong and thorough textual evidence to support analysis of what the text says explicitly as well as inferences drawn from the text. **Literacy.W.9-10.7** Conduct short as well as more sustained research projects to answer a question (including a self-generated question) or solve a problem; narrow or broaden the inquiry when appropriate; synthesize multiple sources on the subject, demonstrating understanding of the subject under investigation. **Literacy.W.9-10.10** Write routinely over extended time frames (time for research, reflection, and revision) and shorter time frames (a single sitting or a day or two) for a range of tasks, purposes, and audiences. **Literacy.SL.9-10.1.a** Come to discussions prepared, having read and researched material under study; explicitly draw on that preparation by referring to evidence from texts and other research on the topic or issue to stimulate a thoughtful, well-reasoned exchange of ideas. **Literacy.L.9-10.3** Apply knowledge of language to understand how language functions in different contexts, to make effective choices for meaning or style, and to comprehend more fully when reading or listening.

Lesson 25

UNIT WRAP-UP

OBJECTIVES

Comprehension & Critical Thinking
- Compare Literature: Text Features
- Use Text Evidence T

Listening and Speaking
- Classroom Discussion

Writing
- Present a Class Newspaper or Magazine T
- Evaluate Class Newspapers or Magazines

PRESENT AND REFLECT

A Present Your Project

Suggest the following hints:

- Write an attention-grabbing headline.
- Make sure each item in your newspaper or magazine is focused on the Essential Question.

W.9-10.4; W.9-10.6

myNGconnect.com

Unit Project Evaluation Rubric

B Reflect on Your Reading

Genre Focus Remind students that "Curtis Aikens and the American Dream" is a biography and "Superman and Me" is an essay.

Possible responses:

- *A biography is the true story of a person's life. An essay includes both facts and opinions about a subject.*
- *"Curtis Aikens and the American Dream" gives facts about Aikens's life. In "Go For It!" Johnson cites facts to support his opinion: "There are about 1,800 college seniors who play ball, and only a few of them are good enough to be drafted."*

SL.9-10.1.a

Reading Strategy Review the Ask Questions strategies. Have students use self-stick notes.

SL.9-10.1.a

C EQ Respond to the Essential Question

Discuss these questions:

- How did knowledge open doors for the people or characters you have read about in this unit?
- What doors has knowledge opened for you?

SL.9-10.1.a

ONGOING ASSESSMENT

Have students write their responses to the Essential Question to assess understanding of the unit topic.

UNIT 4 WRAP-UP

OPENING

DOORS

EQ ESSENTIAL QUESTION: How Can Knowledge Open Doors?

myNGconnect.com

Download the rubric.

EDGE LIBRARY

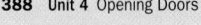

Present Your Project: Class Newspaper or Magazine

It's time to present your class newspaper or magazine about the Essential Question for this unit: How Can Knowledge Open Doors?

A

1 Review and Complete Your Plan

Consider these points as you complete your project:

- What kinds of stories interest your readers?
- What materials, such as photographs and interviews, do you need?
- What are the best ways to present the information?

2 Publish Your Newspaper or Magazine

Consider ways to get your newspaper or magazine out. You might publish it electronically on your school computer network. You could also photocopy and distribute it to classmates.

3 Evaluate the Newspaper or Magazine

Use the online rubric to evaluate the class newspaper or magazine.

Reflect on Your Reading

Many of the people in the selections in this unit and in the Edge Library found ways that knowledge could open doors to success.

Think back on your reading of the unit selections, including your choice of Edge Library books. Then discuss the following with a partner or in a small group.

B

Genre Focus Compare and contrast the elements of a biography with an essay. Write your interpretive response using quotations and relevant evidence from the selections. Give examples, using the selections in this unit.

Focus Strategy Choose a selection in this unit that might be difficult for someone to read. Think of three places where asking questions about self, the text, or the author could help readers understand the text. Mark these places with self-stick notes to remind readers to ask questions as they read.

EQ Respond to the Essential Question

C

Throughout this unit, you have been thinking about how knowledge can open doors. What have *you* decided? Support your response with evidence from your reading, discussions, research, and writing.

CUMULATIVE VOCABULARY REVIEW

Review Unit 4 Vocabulary:

aggressive	environment
ambitious	fate
arrogant	literacy
assemble	obstacle
assume	prodigy
cause	profession
confession	recall
constant	reputation
device	shame
discourage	solution
disgusted	standard
efficient	technology

Play games in pairs or small groups:

20 Questions One student thinks of a word, and other students ask yes/no questions until they guess the word.

Categories One student names words that relate to a category. Others try to guess the word. For *technology*, a student might say "computer, internet, DVD."

Draw the Words One student draws pictures to get a partner to guess a word.

Edge Interactive Practice Book, pp. 190-191

L.9-10.6

CCSS **Literacy.W.9-10.4** Produce clear and coherent writing in which the development, organization, and style are appropriate to task, purpose, and audience. **Literacy.W.9-10.6** Use technology, including the Internet, to produce, publish, and update individual or shared writing products, taking advantage of technology's capacity to link to other information and to display information flexibly and dynamically. **Literacy.SL.9-10.1.a** Come to discussions prepared, having read and researched material under study; explicitly draw on that preparation by referring to evidence from texts and other research on the topic or issue to stimulate a thoughtful, well-reasoned exchange of ideas. **Literacy.L.9-10.6** Acquire and use accurately general academic and domain-specific words and phrases, sufficient for reading, writing, speaking, and listening at the college and career readiness level; demonstrate independence in gathering vocabulary knowledge when considering a word or phrase important to comprehension or expression.

Assessment and Reteaching

Digital Assessment
- eAssessment
- ExamView
- online PDFs

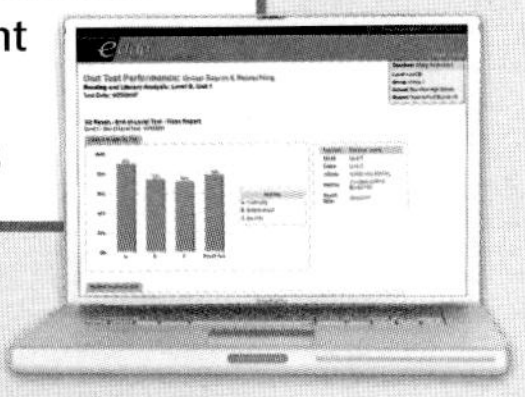

Administer the Assessments

Use the ***Assessments Handbook*** resources to measure the students' performance.

CLUSTER TESTS		
Cluster 1	**Cluster 2**	**Cluster 3**
READER REFLECTION p. 43b	**READER REFLECTION** p. 43f	**READER REFLECTION** p. 43j
READING AND LITERARY ANALYSIS pp. 43c–43e	**READING AND LITERARY ANALYSIS** pp. 43g–43i	**READING AND LITERARY ANALYSIS** pp. 43k–43m
Key Vocabulary Analyze Text Structure: Chronology Analyze Text Features Use Text Evidence	Key Vocabulary Analyze Text Structure: Cause and Effect Analyze Text Structure: Chronology Use Text Evidence	Key Vocabulary Analyze Text Structure: Problem and Solution Analyze Development of Ideas Use Text Evidence
READING FLUENCY *Student Edition* p. 760	**READING FLUENCY** *Student Edition* p. 761	**READING FLUENCY** *Student Edition* p. 762
ELL **LANGUAGE ACQUISITION RUBRIC** p. 43o	**LANGUAGE ACQUISITION RUBRIC** p. 43o	**LANGUAGE ACQUISITION RUBRIC** p. 43o
Define and Explain	Clarify	Verify or Confirm Information

UNIT TESTS	
READING AND LITERARY ANALYSIS pp. 44–53	**GRAMMAR AND WRITING** pp. 54–61
Use Context Clues Key Vocabulary Analyze Text Structures Analyze Text Features Use Text Evidence	Subject Pronouns Progressive Words Object Pronouns Writing Trait: Development of Ideas Written Comprehension • Writing Traits • Written Conventions
UNIT SELF-ASSESSMENT p. 61c	

PERFORMANCE ASSESSMENTS
WRITING PROJECT p. 61b
Development of Ideas • Self-Assessment: Written Composition p. 133 • Peer Assessment: Written Composition p. 134
LISTENING AND SPEAKING WORKSHOP *Student Edition pp. 360–361*
Oral Report

Score and Reteach

- To hand-score: Use the Answer Keys and rubrics in the **Assessments Handbook**, pp. 148–151. Download reteaching activities at myNGconnect.com.
- To take tests online: ***Edge* eAssessment** at myNGconnect.com. Online reports offer immediate graphic displays of student performance to aid in making individualized instruction decision. Links to reteaching activities are included.

Affective and Metacognitive Measures

Help students commit to their own learning. Have students complete at least one reading and one writing form from the affective and metacognitive measures in the ***Assessments Handbook***:

- Personal Connections to Reading, pp. 106–107
- What Interests Me: Reading Topics, p. 108
- What I Do: Reading Strategies, pp. 109–110
- What I Do: Vocabulary Strategies, pp. 111–112
- Personal Connections to Writing, pp. 113–114
- What Interests Me: Writing Topics, pp. 115–116
- What I Do: Writing Strategy, p. 118

T = Tested on Cluster and/or Unit Reading and Literary Analysis Test
T = Tested on Language Acquisition Assessment
T = Tested on Unit Writing Test
T = Assessed with a Rubric
= Comprehension Coach

Writing Project Overview

The Writing Form: Research Report

Your students will learn the features of a **research report**.

A good research report
- presents a thoughtful and interesting thesis statement
- supports the thesis with accurate evidence and information from primary and secondary sources
- makes distinctions between the value and importance of supporting evidence
- anticipates and addresses readers' potential misunderstandings, biases, and expectations
- correctly cites sources according to a proper style
- includes a list of works cited that is formatted according to a style manual

The Writing Trait: Development of Ideas

Students will learn to present meaningful ideas in an interesting and thoughtful way and support those ideas with relevant and specific information.

The Writing Portfolio

Have students collect their work in a portfolio. The portfolio provides a record of how students develop as writers.

Portfolio Evaluation Forms

Use the *Assessments* Handbook, pp. 129–134, myNGconnect.com.

Evaluation Guidelines

Use the complete **Good Writing Traits Rubric** to assess the work on all traits and summarize class results in the **Class Profile Chart**.

Rubrics & Reporting Forms

Use the *Assessments* Handbook, pp. 122–134, myNGconnect.com.

TARGETED TRAIT: DEVELOPMENT OF IDEAS

SCALE	FOCUS AND UNITY	ORGANIZATION	DEVELOPMENT OF IDEAS	VOICE AND STYLE	WRITTEN CONVENTIONS
4	**Focus:** Clearly establishes and consistently maintains a central idea or claim. **Unity:** All facts, ideas, examples, and details are relevant and clearly connected to the central idea or claim.	**Structure:** The organizational pattern is appropriate to the audience, purpose, and task. **Coherence:** Includes a strong introduction and conclusion and leads the reader through a logical progression of ideas with varied and appropriate transitions.	**Content Quality:** Consistently presents meaningful ideas or claims in a logical way that is appropriate to the task, purpose, and audience. **Elaboration:** Includes relevant, clear reasoning, details, evidence, and/or description that are effective and comprehensive.	**Style and Voice:** Fully establishes and effectively maintains a voice that is appropriate to the audience, purpose, and task. **Words and Sentences:** Consistently chooses precise words and varied sentences that are appropriate to the audience and purpose and clearly convey the writer's meaning.	**Grammar and Usage:** Demonstrates strong command of English grammar and usage conventions. All sentences are formed correctly. **Mechanics and Spelling:** Demonstrates strong command of mechanics and spelling. Use of punctuation, capitalization, and spelling is effective and consistent.
3	**Focus:** Adequately establishes and mostly maintains a central idea or claim. **Unity:** Most facts, ideas, examples, and details are relevant and mostly connected to the central idea or claim.	**Structure:** The organizational pattern is mostly appropriate to the audience, purpose, and task. **Coherence:** Includes an introduction and conclusion and leads the reader through a progression of ideas with some transitions.	**Content Quality:** Mostly presents adequate ideas or claims that are appropriate to the task, purpose, and audience. **Elaboration:** Includes reasoning, details, evidence, and/or description that are adequate but incomplete.	**Style and Voice:** Mostly establishes and maintains a voice that is appropriate to the audience, purpose, and task. **Words and Sentences:** Mostly chooses precise words and a variety of sentences that are appropriate to the audience and purpose and adequately convey meaning.	**Grammar and Usage:** Demonstrates adequate command of English grammar and usage conventions. Errors are limited and do not impede understanding. Most sentences are formed correctly. **Mechanics and Spelling:** Demonstrates adequate command of mechanics and spelling. Use of punctuation, capitalization, and spelling is generally consistent.
2	**Focus:** Partially establishes a central idea or claim. **Unity:** Some facts, ideas, examples, and details are relevant and somewhat connected to the central idea or claim.	**Structure:** The pattern is inconsistent or less appropriate to the audience, purpose, or task. **Coherence:** Has an introduction and conclusion but leads the reader through loosely connected ideas that may be incomplete or not obvious to the reader.	**Content Quality:** Presents adequate ideas or claims that are less appropriate to the task, purpose, and audience. **Elaboration:** Includes weak reasoning, details, evidence, and/or description and may include extraneous or loosely related material.	**Style and Voice:** Inconsistently establishes and maintains a voice appropriate to the audience, purpose, and task. **Words and Sentences:** Demonstrates uneven word choice and limited sentence variety or chooses language mostly inappropriate to the audience and purpose. Meaning is vague or imprecise.	**Grammar and Usage:** Demonstrates partial command of English grammar and usage conventions. Frequent errors may impede understanding. Some sentences are formed incorrectly. **Mechanics and Spelling:** Demonstrates partial command of mechanics and spelling. Use of punctuation, capitalization, and spelling is inconsistent.
1	**Focus:** Lacks a central idea or claim. **Unity:** Few facts, ideas, examples, and details are relevant. Most do not support the central idea or claim or connections are unclear.	**Structure:** Lacks any organizational pattern. **Coherence:** Lacks an introduction or conclusion. Ideas are hard to understand.	**Content Quality:** Presents inappropriate or irrelevant ideas or claims. **Elaboration:** Lacks reasoning, details, evidence, and/or description.	**Style and Voice:** Does not establish and maintain a voice or uses a voice that is inappropriate to the audience, purpose, and task. **Words and Sentences:** Demonstrates little or no word choice and no sentence variety. Chooses language inappropriate to the audience, purpose, and task, hindering meaning.	**Grammar and Usage:** Demonstrates little or no command of English grammar and usage conventions. **Mechanics and Spelling:** Demonstrates little or no command of mechanics and spelling.

Write a Research Report

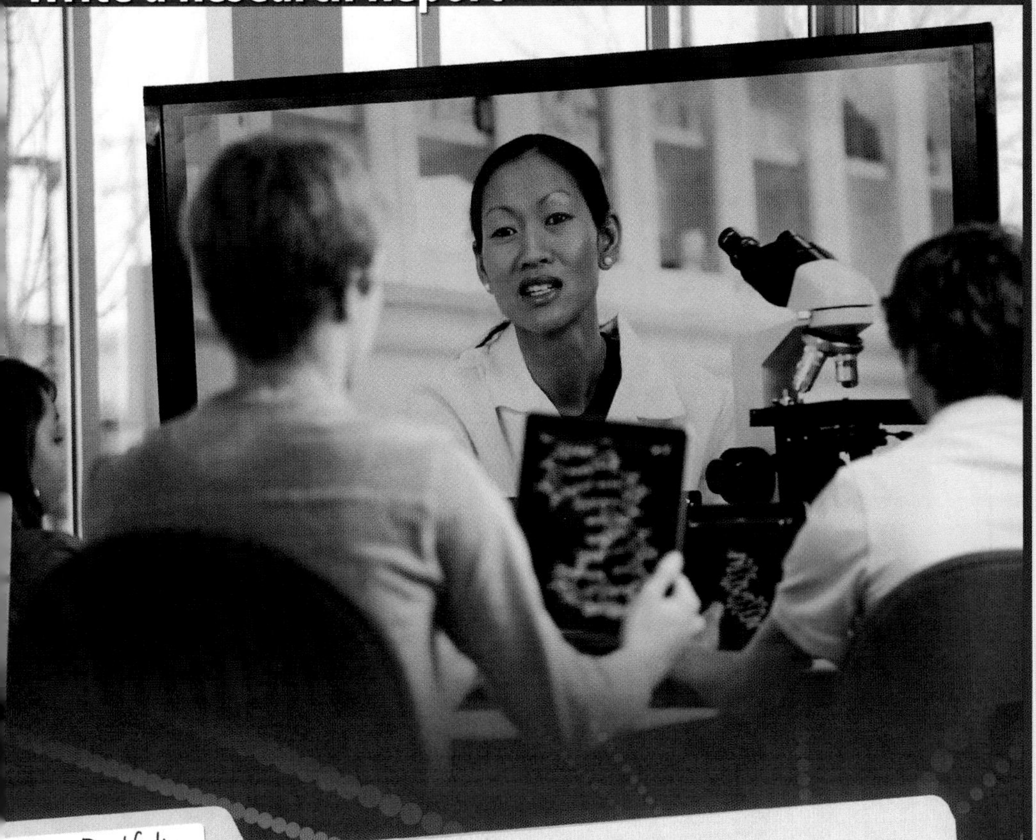

riting Portfolio

Writing Mode
Informative/Explanatory

Writing Trait Focus
Development of Ideas

How do you find out more about something that interests you? You do research, or gather information about it. You also ask research questions that can be changed as you go along. Here's your chance to learn more about technology as you write a research report.

Suggested Pacing

Each lesson in the Writing Project provides detailed instruction on the steps of the writing process. Here is a suggested daily sequence and pacing plan. Adjust as your schedule and student needs require.

Lesson 1	Study the Form and Prewrite
Lesson 2	Draft
Lesson 3	Revise
Lesson 4	Edit and Proofread
Lesson 5	Publish and Present

Unit 4 Writing Project

RESEARCH REPORT

OBJECTIVES

Writing
- Mode: Informative/Explanatory
- Trait: Development of Ideas Ⓣ
- Process: Prewrite; Draft; Revise for Development of Ideas Ⓣ; Edit and Proofread Ⓣ; Publish and Present

Grammar, Usage, Mechanics, Spelling
- Capitalization: Titles of Publications
- Punctuation: Parentheses
- Pronoun Agreement Ⓣ
- Consistent Verb Tense

INTRODUCE

Writing Mode Identify the writing mode as informative/explanatory. Define *informative/explanatory* as writing that informs readers about a topic. Writers of informative/explanatory pieces provide accurate, factual details to explain the topic, as well as sources that can be checked. Examples of informative/explanatory writing include research reports, nonfiction books, and newspaper and magazine articles.

Explain to students that they will be writing a research report using the steps of the writing process. W.9-10.2; W.9-10.10

Writing Trait Explain that writing traits are the characteristics of good writing. All good writing has effective organization; focus and unity; development of ideas; voice and style; and uses the written conventions of language correctly. For this project, students will focus on using the **Development of Ideas** to plan, evaluate, and improve their writing.

Development of ideas makes writing thorough and clear. Tell students that they will develop the main idea of their topic by supporting it with information and evidence. Students will change and adjust research questions as part of their research plan. By developing ideas fully, writers teach readers about a topic and avoid leaving them with unanswered questions.

CCSS **Literacy.W.9-10.2** Write informative/explanatory texts to examine and convey complex ideas, concepts, and information clearly and accurately through the effective selection, organization, and analysis of content. **Literacy.W.9-10.10** Write routinely over extended time frames (time for research, reflection, and revision) and shorter time frames (a single sitting or a day or two) for a range of tasks, purposes, and audiences.

Lesson 1

STUDY THE FORM AND PREWRITE

OBJECTIVES

Writing
- Mode: Informative/Explanatory

Research Skills
- Formulate Research Questions
- Choose Appropriate Resources
- Take Notes

ENGAGE & CONNECT

A Connect Writing to Your Life

Research a Topic Have volunteers share experiences with everyday research, such as reading a book or magazine to learn more about a hobby, or finding directions using the Internet.

TEACH

B Understand the Form

Tell students that the controlling idea of a research report is expressed in the thesis statement. Explain that this idea is developed in the body paragraphs using topic sentences, appropriate transitions, and supporting facts and data.

Thesis Statement Explore the concept:

- A thesis statement tells readers what aspect of the main topic the writer will develop in the body of the research report.
- *Several inexpensive cars on the market are extremely reliable, safe, and fuel-efficient* is an example of a thesis statement. The paragraphs that follow it should address different aspects of this statement.

Have partners form thesis statements about hobbies, musical genres, or other topics they've identified through everyday research.

Study Research Reports

Research reports present a synthesis, or compilation, of information about a topic. In a research report, you combine and organize facts from different sources. You put the information in your own words and let your readers know where you found it.

A

1 Connect Writing to Your Life

How do you find the location of a new restaurant? You look it up on the Internet or in the phone book. How do you find a part-time job? You read the want ads in the paper or look for "now hiring" signs in store windows. All of these methods, no matter how simple, are a form of research. What other kinds of research do you perform in everyday life?

B

2 Understand the Form

Like other kinds of informative/explanatory writing, a research report has an introduction, a body, and a conclusion. It is written with a formal voice that presents the information clearly and objectively. An additional feature of a research report is a list of Works Cited at the end. This list includes the sources of information you cite, or use, in your report. A good research report must contain the following elements.

1. Thesis Statement	A **thesis statement** consists of one or two sentences that state the **controlling**, or main, **idea** that you will develop in your report or essay. It usually appears in the introduction and is restated in the conclusion.
2. Supporting Information and Evidence	Supporting information and evidence come from your research on your topic and make up the body of the paper. They should both relate to the thesis statement and provide background or proof.
3. Citations	Citations are references to the sources from which you gathered your information and evidence. They appear with the supporting information and evidence you are citing, or using, in your paper.
4. Conclusion	In the conclusion, you restate your thesis statement and briefly summarize your supporting ideas.
5. Works Cited	This list appears after the conclusion and shows all the sources you used to write your report. Use a style guide to learn how to format and arrange your sources.

Before you get started, you need to become familiar with the research process.

Thesis Tip

A good thesis statement should be thoughtful and interesting. It should make your audience want to learn more about your topic.

The following are examples of what to avoid when writing your thesis:

- a long list of everything you are going to cover in the paper
- a statement that most people already know to be true

390 Unit 4 Writing Project

ACADEMIC VOCABULARY

Complete an Extended Meaning Map Use the sentences below to introduce these additional academic vocabulary words used in research. Have students complete an Extended Meaning Map for each word.

- **citation** (sī-**tā**-shun), *noun* ▸ p. 390

I used information in the **citation** *to find the book and double check the fact.*

- **topic** (**tah**-pik), *noun* ▸ p. 390

He decided to research the **topic** *of sea life because he lives near the ocean.*

1. Write the word in the center of the word map.
2. Use a dictionary to check the meaning of the word and write the definition above the word.
3. Write an example of the word and what the word is like on either side of the word.

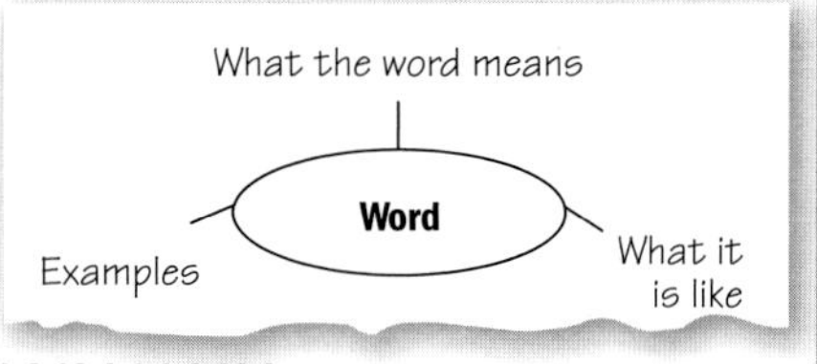

L.9-10.4.d; L.9-10.6

CCSS Literacy.L.9-10.4.d Verify the preliminary determination of the meaning of a word or phrase (e.g., by checking the inferred meaning in context or in a dictionary). Literacy.L.9-10.6 Acquire and use accurately general academic and domain-specific words and phrases, sufficient for reading, writing, speaking, and listening at the college and career readiness level; demonstrate independence in gathering vocabulary knowledge when considering a word or phrase important to comprehension or expression.

B Understand the Research Process

When you research a topic, you look for useful, accurate, and trustworthy information about it.

- **Decide What You Need to Know** What do you want to know about your topic? Make a list of questions that you would like to answer. Look at the most important words in your questions. Those are **key words** that you can use to find information.
- **Locate Resources** Find sources of information about your topic. Typical resources are print materials, such as books, magazines, and newspapers, and electronic media, such as documentaries or Web sites.
- **Include Primary and Secondary Resources** There are two kinds of resources: primary and secondary sources. **Primary sources** give firsthand information about a topic. Some examples are historical documents, diaries, and letters. **Secondary sources** give explanations and interpretations of a topic. Some examples are encyclopedias, books, and journal articles.
- **Evaluate the Resources** Not everything in print or online is useful, accurate, and trustworthy. To check the validity of your resources, answer the questions below. The more you can answer with a "yes," the more likely that you can use the resource.
  1. Will this resource answer at least some of my questions?
  2. Does this resource explain my topic in ways that I can understand?
  3. Can I tell who the author is?
  4. Is the author an expert on my topic?
  5. Is the information up to date?
- **Gather Information and Take Notes** Use tables of contents, indexes, and Internet search engines to locate your key words. This will help you save time as you look for information. While you read, jot down important ideas on note cards along with their sources.

Language and Learning Handbook, pp. 725–727

C

Research Tip

Paraphrase, or take notes in your own words, to avoid **plagiarizing**. This occurs when you use someone else's words or ideas without giving the person credit.

TEACH

C Understand the Research Process

Read and Discuss Read aloud each bulleted point. Explain that these are steps writers use to research a topic:

- deciding what information to research
- locating a variety of resources
- evaluating resources
- taking notes

Resources Show examples of primary resources, such as letters, taped television interviews, and diaries. Read aloud the examples of secondary resources, and ask volunteers to point to examples they see in the classroom.

Discuss questions students should ask while evaluating resources. Show parts of print and electronic resources that researchers use to locate information, including the table of contents, index, inside cover, title page, and pages about the author or Web site. Have students identify parts they can use to answer the evaluation questions. For example, ask: What part of a book or Web site can I use to learn if the information is up to date?

Possible response:

- *copyright/publication date or last update*

Remind students of the importance of paraphrasing information when taking notes. This would also be a good time to review with students your school's policy on plagiarism.

ELL **Culture Share** In many Asian, Middle Eastern, and African cultures, the concept of plagiarism does not exist. Instead, knowledge is believed to belong to society as a whole and can therefore be used accordingly.

Have students with different cultural backgrounds share their culture's views of intellectual property. Discuss as a class how these views are similar to or different from U.S. views.

FOCUS ON WRITER'S CRAFT

Writing a Thesis Statement

Teach Explain that after reading the thesis statement, readers should have a solid idea of what the upcoming paragraphs will cover. Reread the Thesis Tip on p. 390, and share these examples to clarify an effective thesis:

- **Do not simply list everything you will cover:** *Several players in the history of baseball improved batting methods and pitching techniques, promoted the game on a national and personal level, and still managed to have fun.*

  Instead, make it concise: *Several players in the history of baseball changed the way the game is played and viewed.*
- **Do not tell readers what they already know:** *Baseball is a sport in which players hit a ball with a bat and run around bases.*

  Instead, focus on something unique: *Modern baseball contrasts sharply with the game that was once known as "America's pastime."*

Practice List three examples of poor thesis statements. Have students revise them in one or two ways to make them stronger. Record students' answers, and work together to make further improvements.

ONGOING ASSESSMENT

Have students identify two types of resources and explain why it is important to evaluate them.

Lesson 1, continued

STUDY THE FORM AND PREWRITE

OBJECTIVES

Writing
- Writing Process: Prewrite
- Use Strategies to Generate Ideas
- Choose a Topic
- Identify Audience and Purpose
- Conduct Research
- Plan and Organize Ideas

TEACH

A Your Job as a Writer

Writing Prompt Read the prompt carefully with students to help them better understand what is expected of them for this assignment.

ELL **List Vocabulary** Provide synonyms and brief definitions of key words to help students understand the prompt:

- *origin*: start, beginning
- *invention*: new tool or technology
- *everyday*: normal, ordinary

B Choose Your Topic

Brainstorm Ideas Pair students to list technologies they use daily. List students' responses. Have them choose an invention to research.
W.9-10.5

C Clarify Audience, Thesis Statement & Purpose

Thesis Statement Help students narrow their focus. Ask: Do you want to know how the invention has changed? How it has made life easier? Explain that this focus will guide the thesis statements and research. If students have trouble finding information based on their initial research questions, encourage them to revise their questions.
W.9-10.7

D Do Your Research

Describe Remind students to record publication information as well as facts. Show them where to find this information in books, magazines, and other resources.
W.9-10.8

A

Your Job as a Writer

Prompt Write a research report about the origin or history of an everyday invention. Be sure to tell:
- what the invention is and how it originated
- how it developed into what we use today
- how it has changed the way people live and why it matters

Tip

Throughout this project, refer to the Writing Handbook, pp. 812–815.

✓ Prewrite

Once you know the basics of research reports, you can plan one of your own. Planning will make it easier for you to write later on.

B

1 Choose Your Topic

Think of an everyday tool or gadget that you want to learn more about.
- Pick something that you enjoy using.
- Pick something that puzzles or interests you.
- Brainstorm with friends or family members about which inventions interest them.

Prewriting Tip

Be sure that your topic isn't too broad, or general, to cover in a short report.

Also be sure that your topic will be of interest to your audience. Ask the question "Why should we care?" about your topic. If you can't come up with a reason, you might want to choose a different topic.

C

2 Clarify the Audience, Thesis Statement, and Purpose

Your teacher and your classmates will probably be part of your audience. Who else would like to know about your topic? Jot down your ideas.

What aspect of your topic will you focus on? Write one or two sentences that summarize what your research will be about. These sentences will form your **thesis statement**.

Think about your purpose for writing. Is it to inform? Why else might you write about your topic? Write down your ideas.

D

3 Do Your Research

Use questions to drive your research. How did the invention originate? How has it changed everyday life? If you are unable to find sources based on your research questions, revise your questions and refocus your research. Be sure to take detailed notes on cards. Use a separate card for each piece of information. Remember to paraphrase. Use quotation marks if you write an exact quotation. Include the source information, too.

author	*Robert V. Bellamy, Jr., and James R. Walker*
title	*Television and the Remote Control*
where and when published	*New York: Guilford Press, 1996*
	Zenith Space Command first sold in 1956 (p. 50)

Prewriting Tip

Read your note cards carefully and pull out the ones that are related to your thesis statement. Sort these note cards into groups based on common ideas. The idea for each group will become a main point in your research paper.

392 Unit 4 Writing Project

DIFFERENTIATED INSTRUCTION

Taking Notes As you teach the prewriting step of the writing process, use these strategies to meet students' individual needs.

Struggling Readers

Key Words Explain that notes should be brief. Encourage students to focus on recording key details rather than copying lots of text. Point out that they must be sure to copy enough to understand what the note says. Provide a few examples of poor notes, and show students how to correct them.

English Language Learners ELL

Demonstrate Model steps in the research process. Show an example of an invention such as a stapler. Together, develop questions to investigate, such as: When was this invented? Who invented it? Use preselected sources such as an encyclopedia or Web page. Finally, model taking a few brief notes from the sources, along with publication information, on note cards.

Challenge

Develop Criteria Have students brainstorm primary and secondary sources besides books and magazines. Offer suggestions, such as museum brochures, notes from a lecture, or a factual television miniseries. Encourage them to work in pairs and work together to brainstorm sources for each partner's topic.

CCSS **Literacy.W.9-10.5** Develop and strengthen writing as needed by planning, revising, editing, rewriting, or trying a new approach, focusing on addressing what is most significant for a specific purpose and audience. **Literacy.W.9-10.7** Conduct short as well as more sustained research projects to answer a question (including a self-generated question) or solve a problem; narrow or broaden the inquiry when appropriate; synthesize multiple sources on the subject, demonstrating understanding of the subject under investigation. **Literacy.W.9-10.8** Gather relevant information from multiple authoritative print and digital sources, using advanced searches effectively; assess the usefulness of each source in answering the research question; integrate information into the text selectively to maintain the flow of ideas, avoiding plagiarism and following a standard format for citation.

4 Evaluate Your Sources

As you conduct your research and choose your sources, evaluate the credibility, or believability, of the source and what is said. To check the validity of your sources, consider the following:

- Who wrote the information? Is the source written by an authority on the topic?
- How recent is the information? Check the publication date to see if the source reflects the most current research on your topic.
- Is it a reliable resource? Some popular-interest magazines or Web sites may not be considered credible sources. More reliable sources include an approved encyclopedia, a scholarly Web site, or a respected newspaper or magazine.

Refer to the **Language and Learning Handbook** on page 727 for information about evaluating and citing sources.

E

5 Finish Your Writing Plan

Choose a graphic organizer, such as an outline, to create a Writing Plan. Use your groupings to help organize your main points.

Writing Plan

Topic	the history of the remote control
Audience	my teacher and classmates
Thesis Statement	Many people deserve credit for inventing the remote control.
Purpose	to inform
Time Frame	two weeks from today

I. Introduction
  A. remotes used for many things today
  B. who's responsible
II. Body
  A. Eugene McDonald's invention
  B. Eugene Polley's improvement
  C. Robert Adler's invention
III. Conclusion
  A. restate thesis
  B. summarize key points

F

Technology Tip

Use the Outline feature in a word-processing program to help create your plan.

Reflect on Your Writing Plan

Are your main points organized in a way that will make your report easy to understand? Do you have enough research to support your thesis statement?

Writing Transparency 13

Finish Your Writing Plan

WRITING RESEARCH REPORT 13

Writing Plan

Topic	
Audience	
Thesis Statement	
Purpose	
Time Frame	

Organization

I. Introduction

II. Body

III. Conclusion

TEACH

E Evaluate Your Sources

Examine Use the bulleted questions and both credible and unreliable samples to guide students in evaluating sources.
W.9-10.8

F Finish Your Writing Plan

Writing Transparency 13

Model the Plan Use the transparency to model creating a plan. Use a student example:

- **Topic:** What invention are you writing about?
- **Audience:** Who will read your report?
- **Thesis Statement:** What is the main focus of your research?
- **Purpose:** Why are you writing?
- **Time Frame:** Set a deadline that allows time both in and outside of class to fully complete the steps.

Manage the Steps Download this chart to help students manage their time.

myNGconnect.com

Date	Tasks
	1. Study the form. 2. Analyze the research process. 3. Choose a topic. 4. Identify an audience, thesis, and purpose. 5. Conduct research and evaluate sources. 6. Create your Writing Plan.
	Write a draft using your Writing Plan.
	1. Revise for development of ideas. 2. Revise your draft using the Revision Checklist. 3. Conduct a peer conference. 4. Make revisions based on peer conference.
	Review your draft for any mistakes; check for capitalization, punctuation, spelling, verb tenses, and pronouns.
	Print out your research report or write a clean copy by hand.

Model the Organization Have students arrange their note cards and begin thinking about which notes best fit in the introduction, body, and conclusion of the paper.
W.9-10.2.a; W.9-10.5; W.9-10.6

ONGOING ASSESSMENT

Have students turn in their Writing Plans and note cards. Review them to ensure students understand the process and have taken sufficient and accurate notes.

CCSS **Literacy.W.9-10.2.a** Introduce a topic; organize complex ideas, concepts, and information to make important connections and distinctions; include formatting (e.g., headings), graphics (e.g., figures, tables), and multimedia when useful to aiding comprehension. **Literacy.W.9-10.5** Develop and strengthen writing as needed by planning, revising, editing, rewriting, or trying a new approach, focusing on addressing what is most significant for a specific purpose and audience. **Literacy.W.9-10.6** Use technology, including the Internet, to produce, publish, and update individual or shared writing products, taking advantage of technology's capacity to link to other information and to display information flexibly and dynamically.

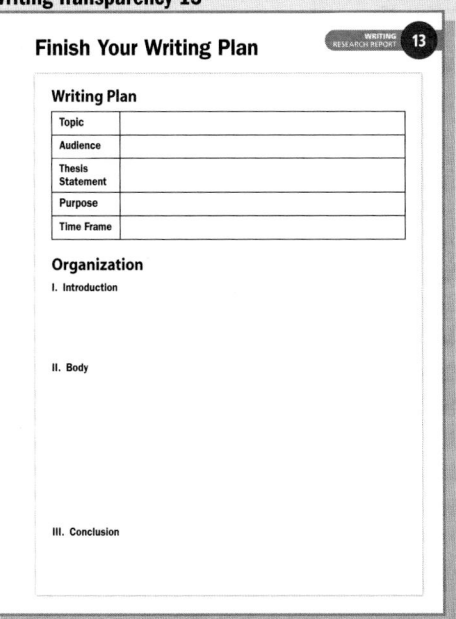

Lesson 2

WRITE A DRAFT

OBJECTIVES

Writing
- Writing Process: Draft
- Write a Draft
- Develop a Thesis

Research Skill
- Cite Sources

TEACH

A Keep Your Ideas Flowing

Stay Focused Remind students to refer to the outline in their Writing Plan as they draft each paragraph. If they get stuck, encourage them to ask questions to help them continue: What do I want to say? What do I want to teach readers in this part of my report? Mention that after they have drafted the report, they will still have the opportunity to rearrange the order of the paragraphs to create a strong and cohesive piece.
W.9-10.2; W.9-10.2.a; W.9-10.4

B Cite Your Sources

Create Citations Present and clarify the citation style students should use. Point out exactly what information is included in each example. Specify where students should place punctuation.

Post examples of different types of citations students may need to format:

- no author
- two or more authors
- single author with different titles and publication dates

Refer students also to Web sites that catalog both MLA and other citation formats. Such sites offer guidance on how to format citations for nearly every variation, including electronic sources. Tell students to refer to appropriate models as they write their drafts. If they are unsure how to format a particular citation, encourage them to write the name of the author and title and return to it later. Explain that this will help them maintain a steady writing momentum.
W.9-10.2.a; W.9-10.8; L.9-10.3.a

✓Write a Draft

Use your Writing Plan as a guide while you write your report. It's OK to make mistakes. You'll have chances to improve your draft later on.

1 Keep Your Ideas Flowing

A

If you took good notes during your research, you have a head start on the writing. Use your notes to write your draft. As you write each section, your draft will grow. Also, keep in mind the way your paragraphs work together. You want your draft to flow smoothly from one idea to another and one paragraph to another.

2 Cite Your Sources

B

As you write, cite your sources. That is, tell where you got information, ideas, or words that are not your own. For example, put the author's name in parentheses after the information, along with the page number on which the information was found. This is called the parenthetical method. Check with your teacher to find out what citation style you should use.

> Robert Adler is known as "the father of the remote" (Gregory 3).

After you finish writing, create your Works Cited list. Include all the sources that you cited in your paper. Sources are listed in alphabetical order by authors' last names.

Language and Learning Handbook, p. 729.

Drafting Tip

Some of your sources may not have a listed author. In this case, you should use part of the title in your parenthetical element. You can also use it when alphabetizing your Works Cited list.

Format the titles of books, journals, Web sites, and newspapers with underlining or italics. The MLA format (shown in the student model) gives preference to underlining, but if you type your research paper, you may use italics instead, if your teacher allows it.

3 Student Model

C

Read this draft to see how the student used the Writing Plan to get ideas down on paper. The student will fix any mistakes later.

> **A History of the Remote Control**
>
> Today, a person can turn on the TV, adjust the volume, play a video game, or fast-forward through a movie without ever getting out of their chair. One revolutionary device has made this possible. What is it? Duh, they're remote controls! Several people deserve credit for this life-changing invention.
>
> The story of the remote's development begins with Eugene McDonald, founder of Zenith Radio Corporation now known as Zenith

FOCUS ON WRITER'S CRAFT

Creating Topic Sentences

Teach/Model Remind students that the thesis statement tells readers what to expect in the body paragraphs of a research report. Specify that each paragraph's topic sentence should address a different aspect of the thesis statement. Give these tips to help students write strong topic sentences:

- Use a *key word* from the thesis statement.
- Use a *synonym* of a key word from the thesis statement.
- Use a word that names a specific *example* or *subgroup* of a key word from the thesis statement.

Give examples:

Thesis statement: Consumers buying Magic Gadget are younger every year.

Topic Sentence #1: The first year Magic Gadget hit the market, the majority of consumers were over age 30. *(key word)*

Topic Sentence #2: As the product became more popular and affordable, buyers in their early 20s began to purchase them. *(synonym)*

Topic Sentence #3: Now studies show that teenagers and young adults make up a large group of buyers. *(subgroup)*

Practice/Apply Have students use these strategies as they draft the topic sentences of their body paragraphs.
W.9-10.2.c

CCSS **Literacy.W.9-10.2** Write informative/explanatory texts to examine and convey complex ideas, concepts, and information clearly and accurately through the effective selection, organization, and analysis of content. **Literacy.W.9-10.2.a** Introduce a topic; organize complex ideas, concepts, and information to make important connections and distinctions; include formatting (e.g., headings), graphics (e.g., figures, tables), and multimedia when useful to aiding comprehension. **Literacy.W.9-10.2.c** Use appropriate and varied transitions to link the major sections of the text, create cohesion, and clarify the relationships among complex ideas and concepts. **Literacy.W.9-10.4** Produce clear and coherent writing in which the development, organization, and style are appropriate to task, purpose, and audience. **Literacy.W.9-10.8** Gather relevant information from multiple

Electronics Corporation. Late in the 1940s, McDonald decided that Zenith ought to give people a way to control their TVs from their couches. By 1950, Zenith's engineers had created a device that McDonald called the Lazy Bones.

McDonald wanted something better. He specifically told his engineers that it should enable viewers to avoid commercials. ("Five Decades" 1) One engineer, Eugene Polley, created a remote that used a light beam. It became known as the Flashmatic. The viewer pointed their Flashmatic at the TV controls and pressed a button, and flashes of light turned the picture on or off and the sound up or down. The Flashmatic's drawback was that they would not work in bright light. If sunlight hit the targets, the TV might turn on and off by itself.

McDonald again called on Zenith's engineers to come up with something better. This time, Robert Adler invented a remote that uses sound instead of light. It is a small box with a number of keys on top. In some ways it is like a miniature piano. By pressing the keys, the user played musical tones. A receiver in the TV detected the sounds and responds to them. People do not notice the sounds because they were too high-pitched for the human ear. Adler's device went on sale in 1956 as the Zenith Space Command (Bellamy and Walker 50).

In the end, Polley's invention was the one that led to the modern remote. Today's remotes use light, not sound, to communicate with the TV. The light it uses is infrared, so bright light is not a problem anymore. In popular histories of television, Adler is known as "the father of the remote (Gregory 3)". Polley has said that his invention was first and he should have gotten more recognition. Adler seems to have agreed. When he was interviewed in 2006 at the age of 92, Adler said, "I don't believe that it has a single father" (3).

Works Cited

Bellamy, Robert V., Jr., and James R. Walker. Television and the Remote Control: grazing on a vast wasteland. New York: Guilford, 1996.

Gregory, Ted. "Meet your Maker, Couch Potatoes." Chicago Tribune 5 Feb. 2006: 1.

"Five Decades Of Channel Surfing: History Of The TV Remote Control." Zenith.com. 2006. Zenith Electronics Corp. 14 Dec. 2006 <http://www.zenith.com/sub_about/about_remote.html>.

C

Reflect on Your Draft

- Is your thesis statement clear? Have you used your note cards and followed your Writing Plan?

TEACH

C Student Model

Read Have students read the Student Model.

Writing Transparency 14a and b

Analyze Display the transparencies. Ask these questions to help students see the relationship between the Writing Plan on p. 393 and the draft. Mark answers on the transparencies:

- Where is the thesis statement? *[lines 4–5]*
- Where are examples of citations? *[lines 13–14, 27, and 32]*
- What key words link the body paragraphs to the thesis statement? *[The names Eugene McDonald, Eugene Polley, and Robert Adler link to the key words "several people" in the thesis statement.]*
- How many sources did the author use? How do you know? *[three sources; I counted the entries on the Works Cited page]*

ELL Comprehensible Input As volunteers answer each question, underline the parts they reference on the transparency, and then briefly restate their points. For example:

- After a volunteer points out the thesis statement, underline it in the model, and say: Here is the thesis statement.
- After the third question, underline the phrase "several people" in the thesis statement and the names of people in the topic sentences. Say: The phrase "several people" refers to these men.

If possible, use different colors to help students visually distinguish different elements of the report.

Remind students that the Writing Plan is a place to start, and it may be revised as the draft is revised.

ONGOING ASSESSMENT

Have students explain how each of their topic sentences relates to their thesis statement.

Writing Transparency 14a

Student Model

WRITING RESEARCH REPORT 14a

A History of the Remote Control

Today, a person can turn on the TV, adjust the volume, play a video game, or fast-forward through a movie without ever getting out of their chair. One revolutionary device has made this possible. What is it? Duh, they're remote controls! Several people deserve credit for this life-changing invention.

The story of the remote's development begins with Eugene McDonald, founder of Zenith Radio Corporation now known as Zenith Electronics Corporation. Late in the 1940s, McDonald decided that Zenith ought to give people a way to control their TVs from their couches. By 1950, Zenith's engineers had created a device that McDonald called the Lazy Bones.

McDonald wanted something better. He specifically told his engineers that it should enable viewers to avoid commercials. ("Five Decades" 1) One engineer, Eugene Polley, created a remote that used a light beam. It became known as the Flashmatic. The viewer pointed their Flashmatic at the TV controls and pressed a button, and flashes of light turned the picture on or off and the sound up or down. The Flashmatic's drawback was that they would not work in bright light. If sunlight hit the targets, the TV might turn on and off by itself.

McDonald again called on Zenith's engineers to come up with something better. This time, Robert Adler invented a remote that uses sound instead of light. It is a small box with a number of keys on top. In some ways it is like a miniature piano. By pressing the keys, the user played musical tones. A receiver in the TV detected the sounds and responds to them. People do not notice the sounds because they were too high-pitched for the human ear. Adler's device went on sale in 1956 as the Zenith Space Command (Bellamy and Walker 50).

In the end, Polley's invention was the one that led to the modern remote. Today's remotes use light, not sound, to communicate with the

continue on 14b

Writing Transparency 14b

Student Model, continued

WRITING RESEARCH REPORT 14b

TV. The light it uses is infrared, so bright light is not a problem anymore. In popular histories of television, Adler is known as "the father of the remote (Gregory 3)". Polley has said that his invention was first and he should have gotten more recognition. Adler seems to have agreed. When he was interviewed in 2006 at the age of 92, Adler said, "I don't believe that it has a single father" (3).

Works Cited

Bellamy, Robert V., Jr., and James R. Walker. Television and the Remote Control: grazing on a vast wasteland. New York: Guilford, 1996.

Gregory, Ted. "Meet your Maker, Couch Potatoes." Chicago Tribune 5 Feb. 2006: 1.

"Five Decades Of Channel Surfing: History Of The TV Remote Control." Zenith.com. 2006. Zenith Electronics Corp. 14 Dec. 2006 <http://www.zenith.com/sub_about/about_remote.html>.

authoritative print and digital sources, using advanced searches effectively; assess the usefulness of each source in answering the research question; integrate information into the text selectively to maintain the flow of ideas, avoiding plagiarism and following a standard format for citation. **Literacy. L.9-10.3.a** Write and edit work so that it conforms to the guidelines in a style manual (e.g., *MLA Handbook*, Turabian's *Manual for Writers*) appropriate for the discipline and writing type.

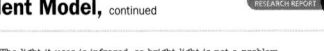

Lesson 3

REVISE YOUR DRAFT

OBJECTIVES

Writing
- Writing Process: Revise
- Evaluate and Revise the Draft for Development of Ideas Ⓣ
- Participate in Peer Conferencing

TEACH

Ⓐ Revise for Development of Ideas

Develop Explain that in a research report, writers develop, or build on, ideas using facts and details.

ELL **Use a Graphic Organizer** List and compare writing that exemplifies and falls short of the trait.

Complete Development of Ideas	Incomplete Development of Ideas
All ideas are explained.	Some ideas are not fully explained.
Examples and details help readers understand ideas.	Readers may feel confused about ideas.
The writing answers important questions that clarify the main ideas.	Readers have important questions that were not answered in the writing.

Try It Have partners ask and answer questions to find out if the ideas in the two drafts are clearly and fully developed:

- Can I identify the thesis statement?
- Does each main idea help to develop the thesis statement?
- Are any ideas not fully explained?
- Which ideas seem confusing?
- What questions do I still have after reading the draft?

Ask each pair of students to briefly answer the questions, and then explain their answers to the class.

✓ Revise Your Draft

Your first draft is done. Now, you need to polish it. Improve the development of ideas and your choice of supporting details.

1 Revise for Development of Ideas

Good writing contains **well-developed ideas**. A good writer **elaborates**, or builds, on his or her ideas by providing specific details for support.

In a good research report, the writer elaborates on the thesis statement by supporting it with specific facts and data gathered from his or her research. The writer also makes sure that each piece of information supports the thesis statement and removes any information that does not.

Don't expect to fully develop all of your ideas in your first draft. As you read your draft, you may notice that some of your body paragraphs need more details. Adding specific facts such as names, dates, and places will help you better narrate the story of the scientific invention you chose to write about.

Ⓐ **TRY IT ▸ Evaluate the drafts below. Does either one contain facts or data that do not support the thesis statement? Which one needs more development? Discuss them with a partner, using the rubric to decide.**

Draft 1

The story of the remote's development begins with Eugene McDonald, founder of Zenith Radio Corporation now known as Zenith Electronics Corporation. Late in the 1940s, McDonald decided that Zenith ought to give people a way to control their TVs from their couches. By 1950, Zenith's engineers had created a device that McDonald called the Lazy Bones.

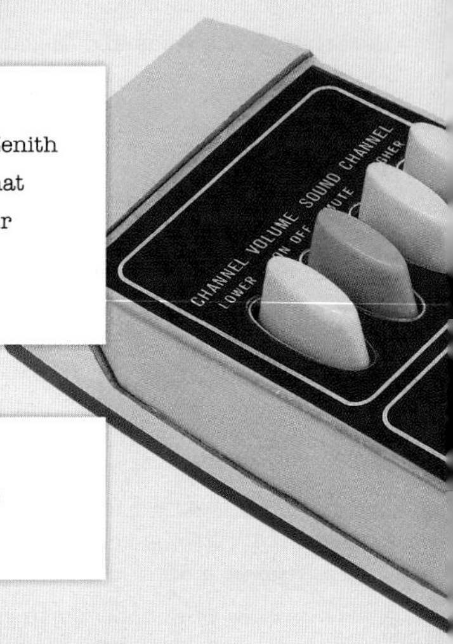

Draft 2

The story of the remote's development begins with Eugene McDonald, founder of Zenith Radio Corporation. He had Zenith's engineers create a device that he called the Lazy Bones.

FOCUS ON WRITER'S CRAFT

Choosing Relevant Details

Teach/Model Explain that facts and data in a research report must not only relate to the topic sentence and main idea of each paragraph, but that they must also work together to explain the main idea.

Practice Have students read the following details and explain which support the following main idea: Telephones have changed in numerous ways since they were first invented.

1. The first telephones didn't have buttons but had a crank instead. *[supports]*
2. Many companies sell modern telephones that look like antique phones in appearance. *[does not support]*
3. Early telephones were much larger than the ones we use today. *[supports]*
4. Early telephones were used for the same purpose contemporary phones are used—to call friends, family, and associates. *[does not support]*

As you review answers, point out that all of the details relate to the main idea, but only a few develop and explain it.

Apply Have students evaluate facts and data for relevancy as they revise their research reports.
W.9-10.2.b

CCSS Literacy.W.9-10.2.b Develop the topic with well-chosen, relevant, and sufficient facts, extended definitions, concrete details, quotations, or other information and examples appropriate to the audience's knowledge of the topic.

Now use the rubric to evaluate the development of ideas in your own draft. What score do you give your draft and why?

Development of Ideas

	How thoughtful and interesting is the writing?	How well are the ideas or claims explained and supported?
4 Wow!	**The writing engages the reader with meaningful ideas or claims and presents them in a way that is interesting and appropriate to the audience, purpose, and type of writing.**	**The ideas or claims are fully explained and supported.** • The ideas or claims are well developed with important details, evidence, and/or description. • The writing feels complete, and the reader is satisfied.
3 Ahh.	**Most of the writing engages the reader with meaningful ideas or claims and presents them in a way that is interesting and appropriate to the audience, purpose, and type of writing.**	**Most of the ideas or claims are explained and supported.** • Most of the ideas or claims are developed with important details, evidence, and/or description. • The writing feels mostly complete, but the reader still has some questions.
2 Hmm.	**Some of the writing engages the reader with meaningful ideas or claims and presents them in a way that is interesting and appropriate to the audience, purpose, and type of writing.**	**Some of the ideas or claims are explained and supported.** • Only some of the ideas or claims are developed. Details, evidence, and/or description are limited or not relevant. • The writing leaves the reader with many questions.
1 Huh?	**The writing does not engage the reader. It is not appropriate to the audience, purpose, and type of writing.**	**The ideas or claims are not explained or supported.** The ideas or claims lack details, evidence, and/or description, and the writing leaves the reader unsatisfied.

myNGconnect.com
- **Rubric: Development of Ideas**
- **Evaluate and practice scoring other student reports.**

TEACH

B Use a Rubric

Model Model using a rubric to evaluate a draft. Read the Student Model on pp. 394–395 aloud. Guide students in assessing the Student Model. Ask: Is the writing thoughtful and interesting? Read aloud the boldfaced statements in the rubric's left column. Ask: Which statement best describes the model and why?

Possible response:
- *I assigned the model a score of 3, because I found only one idea that didn't seem interesting.*

Collaborative Evaluation Have students work in pairs to assign a score for explaining and supporting ideas. Instruct students to read the boldfaced sentences and then review the bulleted criteria below each one for further guidance. Suggest that they first rule out any statements that clearly do not apply. Ask: Which statement best describes the model and why?

Possible response:
- *We scored it as 3, because the device called Lazy Bones was mentioned but not described further.*

Next, have students assign an overall score for development of ideas. If both columns had different scores, tell students to find the average score and round down to the nearest whole number. For instance, if students assign a 4 for the first column and a 3 for the second column, the average would be 3.5, which rounds down to a score of 3. SL.9-10.1

Self-Evaluation Have students follow the same steps to evaluate their own drafts. Try these suggestions:
- To check that ideas are explained and supported, read each paragraph as if you are seeing it for the first time.
- After adjusting to support ideas more completely, edit to make sure the report is presented in a way that will engage readers. W.9-10.5

myNGconnect.com
- **Evaluate more samples online.**

FOCUS ON WRITER'S CRAFT

Writing a Strong Conclusion

Teach Explain that the conclusion gives writers a final chance to communicate the main point to readers and encourage students to extend their evaluation to include how well their conclusion develops their ideas.

The conclusion should:
- Restate the thesis statement in an interesting way.
- Summarize key points of the research report.
- Put a new perspective on the same topic.

The conclusion should not:
- Introduce new ideas.
- Repeat the thesis sentence without a new perspective, suggestion, or phrasing.
- Be longer than three or four sentences.

Practice Review the Student Model and show examples of each point above. Then, ask a few volunteers to share their thesis statements. As a class, review ways to rephrase them in an interesting way.

Apply Ask students to review their conclusion paragraphs and make any necessary revisions. W.9-10.2.f

CCSS **Literacy.W.9-10.2.f** Provide a concluding statement or section that follows from and supports the information or explanation presented (e.g., articulating implications or the significance of the topic). **Literacy.W.9-10.5** Develop and strengthen writing as needed by planning, revising, editing, rewriting, or trying a new approach, focusing on addressing what is most significant for a specific purpose and audience. **Literacy.SL.9-10.1** Initiate and participate effectively in a range of collaborative discussions (one-on-one, in groups, and teacher-led) with diverse partners on grades 9–10 topics, texts, and issues, building on others' ideas and expressing their own clearly and persuasively.

REVISE YOUR DRAFT

TEACH

C Revise Your Draft

Interpret the Checklist Guide students through the process of using the Revision Checklist. Read aloud the first and second questions in the checklist (*Are the ideas in my report clear? Have I answered my major research question?*). Students should decide whether or not their own draft should be revised based on the criteria in the second column.

Direct them to the instructions in the third column to decide how to revise.

Self-Evaluation Instruct students to follow the Revision Checklist to finish making revisions to their own drafts. Suggest that they complete the entire checklist before they make changes. Point out that some revisions, such as adding details, need to be completed before others, such as using a style manual to format citations.

ELL Use a Graphic Organizer Explain the steps for using the Revision Checklist by rewriting one row as a flow chart.

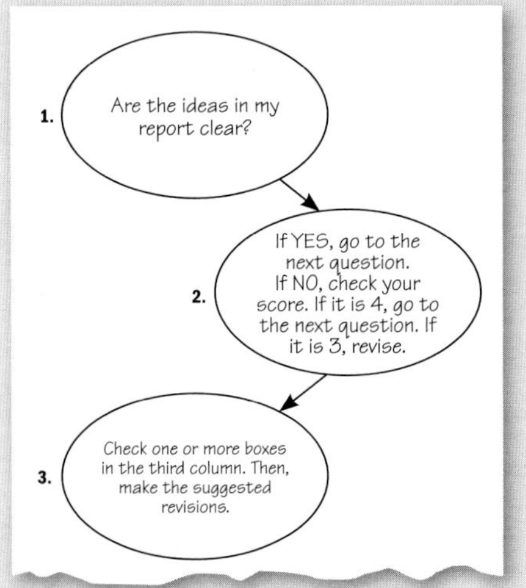
1.
Are the ideas in my report clear?
2.
If YES, go to the next question. If NO, check your score. If it is 4, go to the next question. If it is 3, revise.
3.
Check one or more boxes in the third column. Then, make the suggested revisions.

W.9-10.2.a; W.9-10.2.b; W.9-10.2.d; W.9-10.2.e; W.9-10.7; L.9-10.3.a

✓Revise Your Draft, continued

2 Revise Your Draft

You've now evaluated the development of ideas in your own draft. If you scored 3 or lower, how can you improve your work? Use the checklist below to revise your draft.

C

Revision Checklist

Ask Yourself	Check It Out	How to Make It Better
Are the ideas in my report clear?	If your score is 3 or lower, revise.	☐ If your report does not have a thesis statement, add one. ☐ Be sure that each body paragraph relates to the thesis. ☐ Make the main idea of each paragraph easy to identify. If necessary, add topic sentences.
Have I answered my major research question?	If your score is 3 or lower, revise.	☐ Look back at your note cards and see if there is information you may have overlooked while writing your draft. ☐ Add more specific details appropriate to the content area, such as scientific or technical facts, names, dates, and places. ☐ If necessary, change your question and do more research.
Does my report have an introduction, a body, and a conclusion?	Find and mark the boundaries between the parts.	☐ Add any part that is missing.
Have I used a formal tone?	Look for informal language, including contractions.	☐ Spell out contractions. ☐ Replace slang with more formal language and academic terms.
Do I cite everything that I need to cite in my report?	Reread your report to be sure that any ideas or words that are not your own are properly cited.	☐ Add citations where necessary. These should be included for quotations and information that you summarized or paraphrased. ☐ Use a style manual to make sure you have correctly formatted your citations.
Is every source cited included on a Works Cited list?	Compare your Works Cited list with your citations.	☐ Add any missing information.

Writing Handbook, pp. 785–802; 812–815

FOCUS ON WRITER'S CRAFT

Choosing Specific Details

Teach/Model Explain that using specific details helps writers develop ideas concisely and clearly. It also helps them narrate a clearer, more interesting story. Give these examples and point out how the specific details answer questions:

General	*Specific*
thing	invention (what kind of thing?)
change	revolutionize (changed in what way?)
world	people's lives (what part of the world?)

- **General:** This thing changed the world.
- **Specific:** This invention revolutionized people's lives.

Ask: Which sentence is more fully developed? Which gives you a better picture of what the writer meant? Which is a better narration? Stress that specific details develop the idea in the second sentence.

Practice/Apply As students revise their drafts, tell them to consider using more specific details as one way to develop their ideas.
W.9-10.2.b

CCSS Literacy.W.9-10.2.a Introduce a topic; organize complex ideas, concepts, and information to make important connections and distinctions; include formatting (e.g., headings), graphics (e.g., figures, tables), and multimedia when useful to aiding comprehension. **Literacy.W.9-10.2.b** Develop the topic with well-chosen, relevant, and sufficient facts, extended definitions, concrete details, quotations, or other information and examples appropriate to the audience's knowledge of the topic. **Literacy.W.9-10.2.d** Use precise language and domain-specific vocabulary to manage the complexity of the topic. **Literacy.W.9-10.2.e** Establish and maintain a formal style and objective tone while attending to the norms and conventions of the discipline in which they are writing. **Literacy.L.9-10.3.a** Write and edit work so that it conforms to the guidelines in a style manual (e.g., *MLA Handbook*, Turabian's *Manual for Writers*) appropriate for the discipline and writing type.

3 Conduct a Peer Conference

It helps to get a second opinion when you are revising your draft. Ask a partner to read your draft and look for the following:

- any part of the draft that is confusing
- any element that seems to be missing or out of place
- any place where the tone seems inappropriate for a research report
- anything that the person doesn't understand

Then talk with your partner about the draft. Focus on the items in the Revision Checklist. Use your partner's comments to make your report clearer, more complete, and easier to understand.

D

4 Make Revisions

Look at the revisions below and the peer-reviewer conversation on the right. Notice how the peer reviewer commented and asked questions. Notice how the writer used the comments and questions to revise.

Revised for Development of Ideas and Tone

The story of the remote's development begins with Eugene McDonald, founder of Zenith Radio Corporation now known as Zenith Electronics Corporation. Late in the 1940s, McDonald decided that Zenith ought to give people a way to control their TVs from their couches. By 1950, Zenith's engineers had created a device that McDonald called the Lazy Bones. The Lazy Bones worked, but it had one big drawback: It was connected to the TV by a cable.

McDonald wanted something better. He specifically told ~~his engineers~~ them that it should enable viewers to avoid commercials. ("Five Decades" 1) One engineer, Eugene Polley, created a remote that used a light beam. It became known as the Flashmatic. The viewer pointed their Flashmatic at the TV controls and pressed a button, and flashes of light turned the picture on or off and the sound up or down. The Flashmatic's drawback was that they ~~wouldn't~~ would not work in bright light. If sunlight hit the targets, the TV might turn on and off by itself, ~~which was pretty weird~~. He challenged his engineers to come up with a remote that worked without wires.

E

Peer Conference

Reviewer's Comment: I'm a little confused. Why did McDonald want something better? What was wrong with the Lazy Bones?

Writer's Answer: That's a good question I hadn't really thought about. I'll need to do some more research to answer it.

Reviewer's Comment: Do you really need to say that it "was pretty weird" in the last sentence? It doesn't sound very academic, and I don't think it adds much.

Writer's Answer: You're right. I'll also spell out the contraction "wouldn't," since "would not" will sound more formal.

Reflect on Your Revisions

▸ Which revisions improved your paper the most? Take note of them. The next time you write, refer to your notes to remember which areas you most want to improve.

TEACH

D Conduct a Peer Conference

Peer Response Have partners exchange drafts. Tell students to ask each other questions prompted by the Revise Your Draft checklist on p. 398 and the bulleted items on p. 399. Then tell them to make notes in their draft as partners provide answers and suggestions. Describe this example: If your partner asks what a certain part means, lightly circle the section and note "confusing."

E Make Revisions

Model Have two students read aloud the Peer Conference in the margin. Then work with students to help them analyze and evaluate the writer's revisions. Ask:

- Why did the writer add the last sentence to the introductory paragraph?
- How did the additional sentence improve the second paragraph?
- Why did the writer take out the phrase *which was pretty weird?*

Use Feedback Have students follow the steps above for making revisions to their own drafts.
W.9-10.2.c; W.9-10.2.e; W.9-10.5; W.9-10.7

FOCUS ON WRITER'S CRAFT

Using Visuals

Teach/Model Explain that visuals can help writers develop and convey their ideas clearly. Present this list of different visuals and discuss their appropriate uses. Students may want to add visuals as they revise.

- **Graphics** such as maps, time lines, and diagrams can help readers locate places, find dates, and identify parts of a whole.
- **Tables** organize numerical or statistical information in easy-to-read formats.
- **Charts and Graphs** such as circle charts, bar graphs, and webs can show relationships of ideas and changes over time.
- **Illustrations** can show steps in a process or what an item looks like.

Practice Have students work in pairs to brainstorm visuals that could help them clarify confusing parts of their draft.

Apply Have students look for an appropriate way to add at least one visual to their report.
W.9-10.2.a

ONGOING ASSESSMENT
Have students name revisions they made to different parts of their research reports and why.

CCSS **Literacy.W.9-10.2.c** Use appropriate and varied transitions to link the major sections of the text, create cohesion, and clarify the relationships among complex ideas and concepts. **Literacy.W.9-10.2.e** Establish and maintain a formal style and objective tone while attending to the norms and conventions of the discipline in which they are writing. **Literacy.W.9-10.5** Develop and strengthen writing as needed by planning, revising, editing, rewriting, or trying a new approach, focusing on addressing what is most significant for a specific purpose and audience. **Literacy.W.9-10.7** Conduct short as well as more sustained research projects to answer a question (including a self-generated question) or solve a problem; narrow or broaden the inquiry when appropriate; synthesize multiple sources on the subject, demonstrating understanding of the subject under investigation.

Lesson 4

EDIT AND PROOFREAD YOUR DRAFT

OBJECTIVES

Writing
- Writing Process: Edit and Proofread T

Grammar
- Pronoun Agreement T
- Consistent Verb Tense

Mechanics
- Capitalization: Titles of Publications
- Punctuation: Parentheses

TEACH

Writing Transparencies 15 and 16a and b

A Capitalize the Titles of Publications

Try It Review capitalization. Have students correct the capitalization errors in the exercise.

Possible responses:

- *grazing on a vast wasteland; Of The TV Remote*

Edit and Proofread Have students check capitalization in their drafts.
L.9-10.2; L.9-10.3.a

B Use Parentheses Correctly

Try It Explain the use of parentheses. Clarify that parentheses should *not* interrupt a thought.

ELL **Read Aloud** Use intonation and pausing to distinguish the train of thought from the interruption:

- It was raining outside. I really needed an umbrella. (What genius invented umbrellas anyway?) I looked everywhere and finally found one.

Have students correct the errors.

Possible responses:

- *(now known as Zenith Electronics Corporation); ("Five Decades" 1). "the father of the remote" (Gregory 3).*

Edit and Proofread Have students check parentheses in their drafts.
L.9-10.2

✔ Edit and Proofread Your Draft

Your revision should now be complete. Before you share it with others, find and fix any mistakes that you made.

1 Capitalize the Titles of Publications

Capitalize all main words in the titles of resources. Do not capitalize small words such as *a*, *on*, *the*, and *of*. The first word in a title should always be capitalized, even if it's a small word.

Book: *Television: Critical Methods*
Magazine: *TV Guide*
Newspaper: *The Washington Post*
Article: "You Watched It!"

A

TRY IT ▸ Copy the titles. Fix the capitalization errors. Use proofreader's marks.

1. *Television and the Remote Control: grazing on a vast wasteland*
2. "Five Decades Of Channel Surfing: History Of The TV Remote"

2 Use Parentheses Correctly

Parentheses ( ) can be used to set off a sentence, phrase, or citation.

- If the words in parentheses interrupt the train of thought or are a citation, the end punctuation goes after the end parenthesis.

  Half a billion remote controls are in use (Bellamy and Walker 1–2**).**

  Many different devices can now be operated with one remote control (called a universal remote**).**

- When you are citing a direct quotation, the citation comes after the end quotation and before the end punctuation.

  He is "the greatest inventor on the planet**" (Smith 53).**

B

TRY IT ▸ Copy the sentences. Correct any errors with parentheses.

1. The story of the remote's development begins with Eugene McDonald, founder of Zenith Radio Corporation now known as Zenith Electronics Corporation.
2. He specifically told his engineers that it should enable viewers to avoid commercials. ("Five Decades" 1)
3. In popular histories of television, Adler is known as "the father of the remote (Gregory 3)".

Proofreading Tip

If you are unsure about whether a word in a title should be capitalized or not, look in a style manual to see if there is a similar example.

Proofreader's Marks

Use proofreader's marks to correct errors.

Capitalize:
An article in newsweek discussed the remote control.

Do not capitalize:
The book *How The Remote Changed TV* mentioned Adler.

Add parentheses:
Polley is the real father of the remote (Gregory 3).

Writing Transparency 15

Edit and Proofread Your Draft

WRITING RESEARCH REPORT 15

Proofreader's Marks		
≡	Capitalize	I love new york city.
/	Do not capitalize	I'm going shopping at my favorite Store.
{ }	Add parentheses	I want to work for the Federal Bureau of Investigation (FBI).
∜ ∜	Add quotation marks	You are late, said the teacher.
^	Add a comma	Amy how are you feeling today?
⊙	Add a period	Mr Lopez is our neighbor.
?	Add a question mark	Where is my black pen
↓	Add an exclamation mark	Look out
^	Add a semicolon	This shirt is nice however, this one brings out the color of your eyes.
⇕	Add a colon	He wakes up at 6 30 a.m.
⊼	Add a dash	Barney he's my pet dog has run away.
=	Add a hyphen	You were born in mid September, right?
∨	Add an apostrophe	Im the oldest of five children.
#	Add a space	She likes him alot.
⌢	Close up a space	How much home work do you have?
^	Add text	My keys are on the table.
℘	Delete text	I am going too my friend's house.
∩∪	Transpose words, letters	Did you see thier new car?
(sp)	Spell out	Today he is turning 16.
¶	Begin a new paragraph	"I win!" I shouted. "No you don't," he said.
(ital)	Add italics	The Spanish word for table is mesa.
(u/s)	Add underlining	Little Women is one of my favorite books.

CCSS Literacy.L.9-10.2 Demonstrate command of the conventions of standard English capitalization, punctuation, and spelling when writing.
Literacy.9-10.3.a Write and edit work so that it conforms to the guidelines in a style manual (e.g., *MLA Handbook*, Turabian's *Manual for Writers*) appropriate for the discipline and writing type.

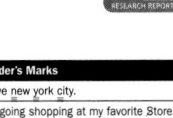

3 Use Consistent Verb Tense

A paragraph or essay that has shifting verb tenses can be difficult to follow. When you write, you need to choose a tense and stick to it. Change tense only to talk about something that happened before or after the time that you are writing about. Here are some general tips:

- Use the past tense to tell a story and to talk about historical events.
- Use the present tense to talk about facts, literary works, actions that continually happen, and your own ideas.

TRY IT ▸ Rewrite the paragraph, correcting any inconsistencies in verb tense.

McDonald again called on Zenith's engineers to come up with something better. This time, Robert Adler invented a remote that uses sound instead of light. It is a small box with a number of keys on top. In some ways it is like a miniature piano. By pressing the keys, the user played musical tones. A receiver in the TV detected the sounds and responds to them. People do not notice the sounds because they were too high-pitched for the human ear. Adler's device went on sale in 1956 as the Zenith Space Command (Bellamy and Walker 50).

C

4 Make Pronouns Agree with Their Antecedents

A pronoun takes the place of a noun. The pronoun you use depends on its antecedent, or the noun it replaces. To choose the correct pronoun, you need to decide if the antecedent is male or female and if it is singular or plural.

The **man** said **he** broke the TV's remote.

The **remote** is broken. **It** needs to be repaired.

In paragraphs and essays, the antecedent may not always appear in the same sentence as the pronoun. Check your work to be sure you are not switching from singular to plural pronouns, or vice versa, to describe the same antecedent.

D

TRY IT ▸ Copy the sentences. Correct any pronoun agreement errors.

1. What is it? They're remote controls.
2. The viewer pointed their Flashmatic at the TV controls and pressed a button.
3. The Flashmatic's drawback was that they would not work in bright light.

Writing Handbook, p. 784

Reflect on Your Corrections

▸ Look back at any edits you made. Do you see a pattern? If there are things you keep missing, make a list of what to watch in your writing. Then review the grammar concepts to make sure you understand them and can use them correctly in your writing.

TEACH

C Use Consistent Verb Tense

Try It Explain that using consistent verb tense helps insure that readers will not become confused. Ask what tense a person should use when:

- telling part of a favorite book *(present: talking about literary works)*
- telling a story versus talking about one *(past: telling a story)*
- describing how a historical figure gained power or fame *(past: talking about a historical event)*

Ask: Where is verb tense in this paragraph inconsistent? Have students rewrite and correct the paragraph. Mark corrections on the transparency.

Possible responses:

- *that ~~uses~~ used sound; It ~~is~~ was a small box; it ~~is~~ was like a miniature piano; and ~~responds~~ responded to them; People ~~don't~~ didn't notice*

Edit and Proofread Have students check their drafts for consistent use of verb tense and make corrections.
L.9-10.1

D Make Pronouns Agree with Their Antecedents

Try It Read the examples and point out the pronouns and their antecedents. Write a few sentences that contain singular and plural nouns and ask volunteers to name the correct pronoun to replace each noun. Then have them correct the pronoun agreement errors on the transparency. Discuss different ways to fix item 2, such as making the subject plural to avoid the need for *his or her.*

Possible responses:

1. *What is it? It's a remote control.*
2. *The viewer pointed his or her Flashmatic at the TV controls and pressed a button.*
3. *The Flashmatic's drawback was that it wouldn't work in bright light.*

L.9-10.1

Edit and Proofread Have students skim their drafts for pronouns and check that each matches its antecedent. Remind them to use grammatical structures correctly, such as verb tenses, pronoun and antecedent agreement, and others they have learned in their grade level.

Grammar and Writing Practice Book, pp. 133–136

Writing Transparency 16a

WRITING RESEARCH REPORT 16a

Edit and Proofread Your Draft

1. Capitalize the Titles of Publications

1. *Television and the Remote Control: grazing on a vast wasteland*
2. "Five Decades Of Channel Surfing: History Of The TV Remote"

2. Use Parentheses Correctly

1. The story of the remote's development begins with Eugene McDonald, founder of Zenith Radio Corporation now known as Zenith Electronics Corporation.
2. He specifically told his engineers that it should enable viewers to avoid commercials. ("Five Decades" 1)
3. In popular histories of television, Adler is known as "the father of the remote (Gregory 3)".

continue on 16b

Writing Transparency 16b

WRITING RESEARCH REPORT 16b

Edit and Proofread Your Draft, continued

3. Use Consistent Verb Tense

McDonald again called on Zenith's engineers to come up with something better. This time, Robert Adler invented a remote that uses sound instead of light. It is a small box with a number of keys on top. In some ways it is like a miniature piano. By pressing the keys, the user played musical tones. A receiver in the TV detected the sounds and responds to them. People do not notice the sounds because they were too high-pitched for the human ear. Adler's device went on sale in 1956 as the Zenith Space Command (Bellamy and Walker 50).

4. Make Pronouns Agree with Their Antecedents

1. What is it? They're remote controls.
2. The viewer pointed their Flashmatic at the TV controls and pressed a button.
3. The Flashmatic's drawback was that they would not work in bright light.

CCSS Literacy.L.9-10.1 Demonstrate command of the conventions of standard English grammar and usage when writing or speaking.

EDIT AND PROOFREAD YOUR DRAFT

TEACH

E Edited Student Draft

Read and Discuss Read aloud the Edited Student Draft. Then go back and address the callouts. For example:

Ask: What errors did the writer make in pronoun agreement? How did the writer correct them?

Possible responses:
- *changed* their *to* his or her *to match the pronoun antecedent* person; *changed* they're *to* It is; *changed* their *to* his or her *to match* viewer; *changed* it *to* they *to match* remotes *and the verb* uses *to* use

ELL Questioning Use questions with embedded answers or open-ended questions depending on the student's proficiency level. For example, point to the word *viewer*, and ask:

- Is this noun singular or plural?
- Why was the pronoun *their* changed to *his or her*?

Repeat the strategy for each type of revision noted in the callouts.

Ask: How did the writer revise to improve the development of ideas?

Possible response:
- *added two sentences to develop the idea of the Lazy Bones gadget*

ONGOING ASSESSMENT
Provide sentences that contain errors in pronoun agreement, use of parentheses, consistent verb tense, capitalization of titles, and development of ideas. Ask students to correct each error.

5 Edited Student Draft

Here's the student's draft, revised and edited. How did the writer improve it?

A History of the Remote Control

Today, a person can turn on the TV, adjust the volume, play a video game, or fast-forward through a movie without ever getting out of his or her chair. One revolutionary device has made this possible. What is it? It is the remote control, and several people deserve credit for this life-changing invention.

The writer corrected the **pronoun agreement** error and changed the **tone** to make it more formal.

The story of the remote's development begins with Eugene McDonald, founder of the Zenith Radio Corporation (now known as Zenith Electronics Corporation). Late in the 1940s, McDonald decided that Zenith ought to give people a way to control their TVs from their couches. By 1950, Zenith's engineers had created a device that McDonald called the Lazy Bones. The Lazy Bones worked, but it had one big drawback. It was connected to the TV by a cable.

The writer used **parentheses** to set apart a phrase that interrupts the train of thought.

The writer added more details to develop an idea.

McDonald wanted something better. He challenged his engineers to come up with a remote that worked without wires. He specifically told them that it should enable viewers to avoid commercials ("Five Decades" 1). One engineer, Eugene Polley, created a remote that used a light beam. It became known as the Flashmatic. The viewer pointed his or her Flashmatic at the TV controls and pressed a button, and flashes of light turned the picture on or off and the sound up or down. The Flashmatic's drawback was that it would not work in bright light. If sunlight hit the targets, the TV might turn on and off by itself.

The writer correctly used end punctuation with **parentheses**.

The writer corrected the **pronoun agreement** error.

McDonald again called on Zenith's engineers to come up with something better. This time, Robert Adler invented a remote that used sound instead of light. It was a small box with a number of keys on top. In some ways it was like a miniature piano. By pressing the keys, the user played musical tones. A receiver in the TV detected the sounds and responded to them. People did not notice the sounds because they were too high-pitched for the human ear. Adler's device went on sale in 1956 as the Zenith Space Command (Bellamy and Walker 50).

The writer used **consistent verb tense.**

In the end, Polley's invention was the one that led to the modern remote. Today's remotes use light, not sound, to communicate with the TV. The light they use is infrared, so bright light is not a problem anymore. In popular histories of television, Adler is known as "the father of the remote" (Gregory 3). Polley has said that his invention was first and he should have

The writer corrected the **pronoun agreement** error (and changed the verb form).

The writer correctly used quotation marks and end punctuation with **parentheses**.

gotten more recognition. Adler seems to have agreed. When he was interviewed in 2006 at the age of 92, Adler said, "I don't believe that it has a single father" (3).

Works Cited

Bellamy, Robert V., Jr., and James R. Walker. Television and the Remote Control: Grazing on a Vast Wasteland. New York: Guilford, 1996.

Gregory, Ted. "Meet Your Maker, Couch Potatoes." Chicago Tribune 5 Feb. 2006: 1.

"Five Decades of Channel Surfing: History of the TV Remote Control." Zenith.com. 2006 Zenith Electronics Corp. 14 Dec. 2006 <http://www.zenith.com/sub_about/about_remote.html>.

E The writer corrected **capitalization** errors in the titles.

Publish and Present

You are now ready to publish and present your report. Print out your research report or write a clean copy by hand. You may also want to present your work in a different way.

Alternative Presentations

Read Your Written Report Read your research report aloud to your class.

1. Print a hard copy of your report.
2. Bind it using a folder, binder, or adhesive.
3. Read the report to your class.
4. Lead a question-and-answer session about your report.

Deliver a Presentation Use information from your report to give a presentation on your topic.

1. Use presentation software to create a slide show.
2. Gather images to illustrate your presentation.
3. Use your report as a script as you present the slide show.
4. Lead a question-and-answer session about your presentation.

Language and Learning Handbook, pp. 719; 724

A

Publishing Tip

Format your typed work according to your teacher's guidelines.

If you've handwritten your work, be sure your work is legible and clean.

Reflect on Your Work

Ask for and use feedback from your audience and your teacher to evaluate your strengths as a writer.

- Did your audience find your report to be interesting? What did they learn?
- What did your audience think was the strongest point of your report? What did they think was the weakest point?
- What would you like to do better the next time you write? Set a goal for your next writing project.

Save a copy of your work in your portfolio.

B

Lesson 5

PUBLISH AND PRESENT

OBJECTIVES

Writing

- Research Report
- Writing Process: Publish; Reflect and Evaluate

TEACH

Have students choose one of two ways of publishing and presenting their report: Prepare a Written Report or Deliver a Presentation.

A Alternative Presentations

Read Your Written Report Use the Edited Student Draft to model an oral reading and a question-and-answer session. Provide class time for students to practice.
SL.9-10.4; SL.9-10.6

Deliver a Presentation Review techniques of slide show presentations. For example: *Do use brief bulleted points. Do not use a small font.* Encourage students to use graphics, tables, charts, or illustrations in their presentations. Have students practice in small groups before speaking in front of the class. Have presenters collect and review feedback.
W.9-10.2.a; W.9-10.6; SL.9-10.5; SL.9-10.6

Language and Learning Handbook, p. 719; 724

B Reflect on Your Work

Reflect Provide students with feedback before and after they publish. Next, have students use the questions to gather feedback from their classmates.

- Did your audience understand the purpose of your report? What did they learn?
- Did each paragraph cover a specific topic from your outline?
- What was the conclusion of your report? Did the audience find the conclusion interesting?

Remind students to save a copy of their written report in their portfolio.
SL.9-10.1

ONGOING ASSESSMENT

Have students identify one thing they learned about using visual aids while speaking in front of a large group.

CCSS **Literacy.W.9-10.2.a** Introduce a topic; organize complex ideas, concepts, and information to make important connections and distinctions; include formatting (e.g., headings), graphics (e.g., figures, tables), and multimedia when useful to aiding comprehension. **Literacy.W.9-10.6** Use technology, including the Internet, to produce, publish, and update individual or shared writing products, taking advantage of technology's capacity to link to other information and to display information flexibly and dynamically. **Literacy.SL.9-10.1** Initiate and participate effectively in a range of collaborative discussions (one-on-one, in groups, and teacher-led) with diverse partners on grades 9–10 topics, texts, and issues, building on others' ideas and expressing their own clearly and persuasively. **Literacy.SL.9-10.4** Present information, findings, and supporting evidence clearly, concisely, and logically such that listeners can follow the line of reasoning and the organization, development, substance, and style are appropriate to purpose, audience, and task. **Literacy.SL.9-10.5** Make strategic use of digital media (e.g., textual, graphical, audio, visual, and interactive elements) in presentations to enhance understanding of findings, reasoning, and evidence and to add interest. **Literacy.SL.9-10.6** Adapt speech to a variety of contexts and tasks, demonstrating command of formal English when indicated or appropriate.

Language and Learning Handbook

Language, Learning, Communication

Reading Handbook

Reading, Fluency, Vocabulary

Writing Handbook

Writing Process, Traits, Conventions

RESOURCES

The **Resources** include:

- handbooks
- glossaries
- indices

Each handbook has its own table of contents. For more information about what is covered in each handbook, see the following:

- **Language and Learning Handbook**, p. 702
- **Reading Handbook**, p. 733
- **Writing Handbook**, p. 784

Resources can be used alone by the student or along with the teacher, a partner, or the whole class. Each handbook includes three teaching options with specific purposes:

- **Reinforce** This option includes additional instructions pertaining to a skill. Often, the reinforcing lessons include modeling.
- **Expand** This option takes a specific skill or example from the student book and expands the teaching.
- **Practice** This option gives the students an opportunity to practice the skill with additional texts or visuals that are not included in the student book.

In addition to these options, special English language learner support is provided.

LANGUAGE AND LEARNING HANDBOOK

The **Language and Learning Handbook** guides students to effectively use language in all aspects of communication:

- **Strategies for Learning and Developing Language** Students learn strategies to build their English language skills and how to most efficiently use language to communicate in any situation.
- **Listening and Speaking** Students learn effective listening strategies and how to choose and use language to present ideas and information.
- **Viewing and Representing** Students learn to interpret visuals and how to use them to share ideas and information.
- **Technology and Media** Students learn how to use technology to communicate. They also learn how to distinguish the purposes, accuracy, and reliability of information from multiple media forms.
- **Research** Students learn how to use the research process to research, organize, and present information about a topic.
- **Test-Taking Strategies** Students learn test-taking strategies to help them prepare for and complete tests.

Language and Learning Handbook

How Do I *Learn* Language?

1 Listen actively and try out language.

What to Do	Examples
Listen to others and use their language.	**You hear:** "When did our teacher say that the assignment is due?" **You say:** "Our teacher said that the assignment is due May 1."
Listen to yourself to perfect pronunciation of new words.	**You say:** "I see the word *privacy. Privacy* has a long *i* sound. Let me practice the long i sound to make sure I'm saying the word correctly."
Incorporate language chunks into your speech.	**You hear:** "Send me an e-mail or a text message on my cell." **You think:** I know what an e-mail is. So a text message must be an e-mail that you send on a phone. **You say:** "I'll e-mail you. I don't think I can send text messages on my cell."
Make connections across content areas. Use the language you learn in one subject area in other subject areas and outside of school.	**You read this in science class:** Studies show that each person in the U.S. produces more than 4 pounds of garbage each day. We don't have enough landfill space. Recycling is essential. **You write this in your reading journal:** Maybe I'll do my persuasive paper for English class on recycling. I have strong feelings about why it is good to recycle. **At home, you might say:** Mom, did you recycle the empty cans and bottles?
Take risks. Use words or phrases you know and use them in another way.	**All of these statements mean the same thing:** My teacher helps me push my thinking. My teacher helps me stretch my mind to see different viewpoints. Before I make a decision, my teacher suggests I role-play different choices in my imagination.
Memorize new words. They will help you build the background knowledge you need to understand more difficult language.	**Make flash cards:** Flash cards are a great way to memorize new words, phrases, or expressions. Write the English meaning on one side of a note card and the meaning in your language on the other side. Look at the words or phrases in your language and try to say the English meaning. Flip the card over to check your answer.

(Rows 1–3: A; Row 4: B; Row 5: C)

A Use Others' Language

Expand Remind students to listen carefully in order to distinguish the various sounds of English as well as the intonation patterns. This will help them reflect what they hear. Explain to students that by incorporating the language of the speaker into their response, listeners show that they understood what the speaker said. Point out the repetition of the key words "Our teacher said that the assignment is due," noting the change in the tense of the verb *say*. Have students respond to the question: What do you plan to do after school?
L.9-10.1

B Make Connections

Expand Tell students that using language in a variety of contexts can help them better understand the concepts and ideas they are expected to understand at their grade level. Ask students to define the word *culture* as they learn it in a social studies class. Then ask: How might you use this word in a science class? How might you use it outside of school?
L.9-10.6

C Say It in a New Way

Reinforce Point out that figures of speech and other types of figurative language can often be used to express a familiar idea in a different way. Explain to students that because you cannot actually "push a mind" or "stretch an imagination," the speaker is using this language to create a mental picture for the listener. Generate additional examples, such as "think outside the box," and help students analyze figurative meanings.

ELL Elaborate Model making flash cards for the phrases noted above and their meanings. Ask students for additional English words or phrases that they may not fully understand, and help them generate more flash cards. Encourage students to write the meanings of the words or phrases in their own languages underneath the English meanings.
L.9-10.5.a

CCSS Literacy.L.9-10.1 Demonstrate command of the conventions of standard English capitalization, punctuation, and spelling when writing or speaking. Literacy.L.9-10.5.a Interpret figures of speech (e.g., euphemism, oxymoron) in context and analyze their role in the text. Literacy.L.9-10.6 Acquire and use accurately general academic and domain-specific words and phrases, sufficient for reading, writing, speaking, and listening at the college and career readiness level; demonstrate independence in gathering vocabulary knowledge when considering a word or phrase important to comprehension or expression.

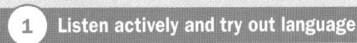

A Ask Questions

Expand Remind students that when they don't understand a word or phrase, asking a teacher or a classmate is a good way to clarify the meaning. Brainstorm with students a generic list of questions they might ask, such as *What does this word mean?* and *Could you please repeat that?* Post the questions in a visible place for students to refer to.

B Use Gestures

Expand Explain that gestures often can be used instead of words. Ask students to use gestures to show the following: *yes, hello, I don't know, look over there,* and *wait.*

- cues showing agreement (nodding, smiling, thumbs up)
- cues showing disagreement (frown, head shake, crossed arms)
- cues that show confusion (furrowed brow, head tilt)
- cues to encourage others to join the discussion (welcome gestures, eye contact)

Point out that gestures vary across cultures, so students should be sure the gestures they are using are appropriate for their audience.

C Identify and Respond to Nonverbal Clues

Practice Tell students that speakers frequently use facial expressions and gestures that match their words. Show students images of a variety of facial expressions and gestures. Have partners practice interpreting and miming the images. Ask them to provide a line of dialogue to accompany each nonverbal clue.
SL.9-10.1.c

2 Ask for help, feedback, and clarification.

What to Do	Examples	
A Ask questions about how to use language.	Did I say that right? / Did I use that word the right way?	Which is right: "brang" or "brought"?
Use your native language or English to ask for clarification. Use what you learned to correct your mistakes.	**You say:** "Wait! Could you go over that point again, a little more slowly, please?"	**Other examples:** "Does 'have a heart' mean 'to be kind'?" "Is 'paper' another word for 'essay'?"
Use context clues to confirm your understanding of difficult words.	**You hear:** "The team united, or came together, after they lost the game."	**You think:** "I hear the word *or* after the word *united*, so *united* must mean 'came together.'"

3 Use nonverbal clues.

What to Do	Examples
B Use gestures and mime to show an idea.	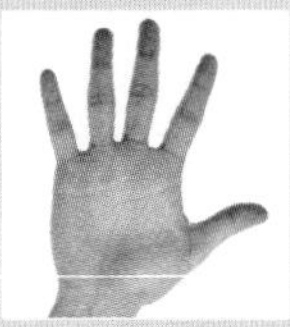 I will hold up five fingers to show that I need five minutes.
C Look for nonverbal clues.	 María invited me to a concert where her favorite band will be playing. They are electrifying! / Electrifying must mean "good." She looks good.
Identify and respond appropriately to nonverbal and verbal clues.	Let's give him a hand. / Everyone is clapping. "Give him a hand" must mean to clap for him. I should clap for him, too.

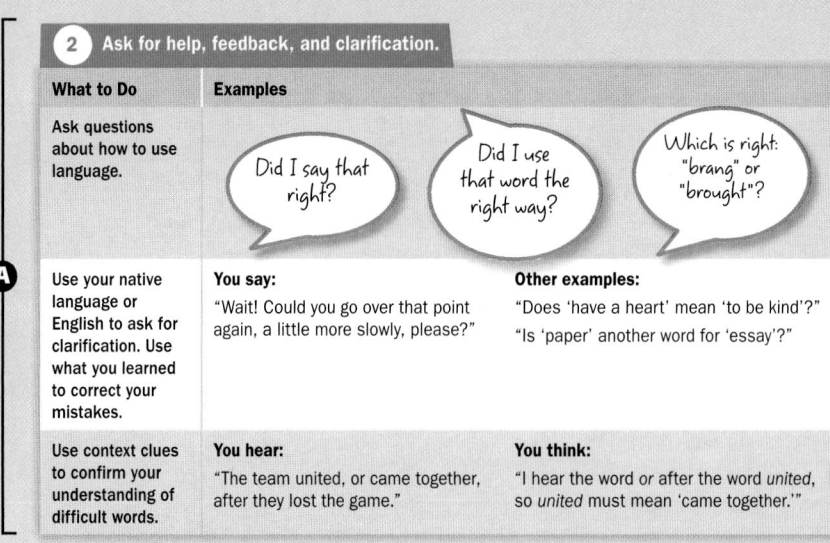

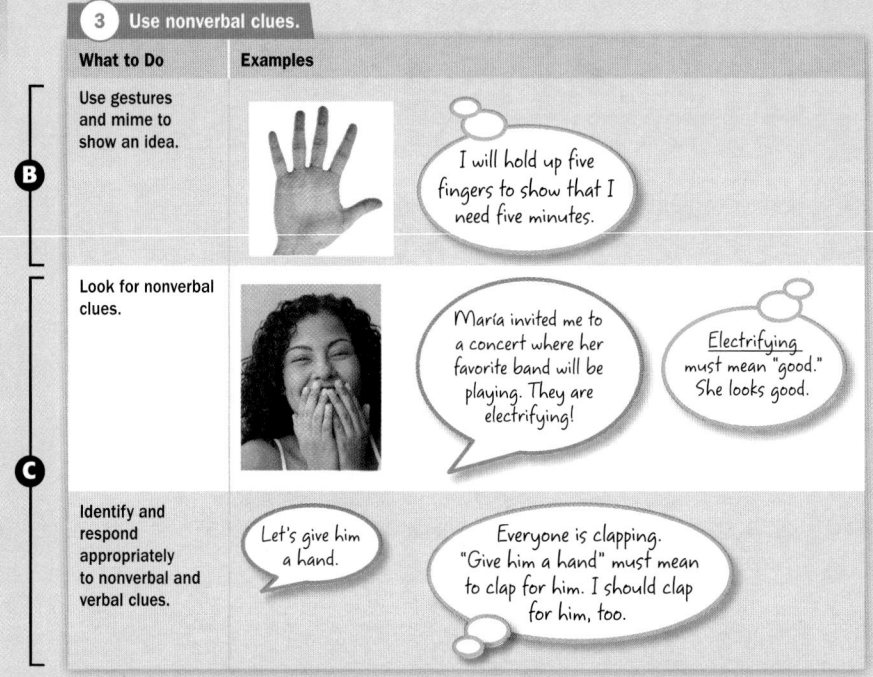

CCSS Literacy.SL.9-10.1.c Propel conversations by posing and responding to questions that relate the current discussion to broader themes or larger ideas; actively incorporate others into the discussion; and clarify, verify, or challenge ideas and conclusions.

4 Verify how language works.

What to Do	Examples
Test hypotheses about how language works.	**You can try out what you learned:** *I can add -ation to the verb observe to get the noun observation. So maybe I can make a noun by adding -ation to some verbs that end in -e. Let's see.* *Prepare and preparation. Yes, that is right!* *Compare and comparation. That doesn't sound correct. I will see what the dictionary says . . . Now I understand–it's comparison.*
Use spell-checkers, dictionaries, and other available reference aids, such as the Internet.	**You just finished your draft of an essay, so you think:** *Now I'll use spell-check to see what words I need to fix.*
Use prior knowledge.	You can figure out unfamiliar words by looking for or remembering words you do know or experiences you've learned about previously. Use this prior knowledge to figure out new words. **Example:** We felt embarrassed for Tom when he behaved like a clown. *I know the word "clown." Maybe "embarrassed" means the way I feel when one of my friends starts acting like a clown.*
Use contrastive analysis to compare how your language works to how English works.	**You hear:** "She is a doctor." **You think:** *In English, an article, such as a or an, is used before the title of a job. In my native language, no article is used: "She is doctor."*
Use semantic mapping to determine the relationship between the meanings of words.	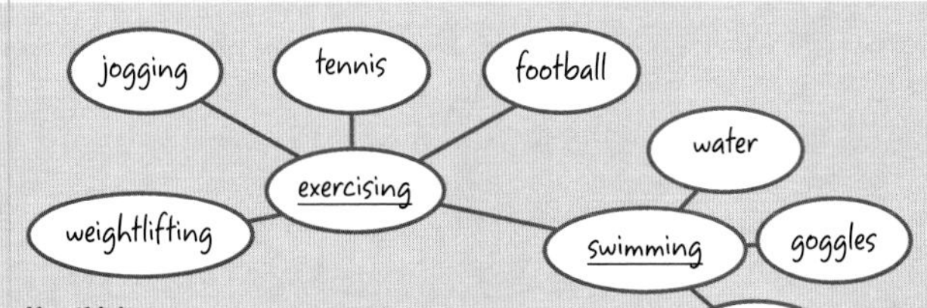 **You think:** *Where should I place the word ball? It can attach to football or tennis because both activities use a kind of ball.*
Use imagery.	Use descriptive language to form a picture in your imagination in order to figure out a word you don't know. You can draw pictures of what you imagined to remind you of the meaning of the word. Say the words while looking at the pictures to make connections.

Use References

Reinforce Point out the various reference sources students can access including classroom dictionaries, references. Display and demonstrate how to use online tools such as dictionary web sites or word meaning tools that are integrated into word processing software.
L.9-10.4.c

Contrastive Analysis

Reinforce Tell students that they can use their understanding of how words, phrases, and sentences are formed in their own languages to better understand how to construct English words, phrases, and sentences. Model using contrastive analysis. First read the example aloud.

MODEL Say:

- *To contrast two things, I look at how they are different. I notice that in English, the article* a *is used before the word* doctor. *In my native language, an article is not used before the job title. When I write or talk in English about a person's job title, I should use* a *before jobs that begin with a consonant and* an *before jobs that begin with a vowel.*
- *I can also look at ways my native language is similar to English. In English, the subject of the sentence comes first, followed by the predicate. This is also how sentences are organized in my native language. When I write or say sentences in English, I will begin with the subject of the sentence.*
- *Some words in English are similar to words in other languages. The English word* doctor *looks similar to the German word* doktor *and the Spanish word* doctor. *If I know what a word means in my native language, I can often use it to help me figure out the meanings of similar English words.*

Practice Write the following question: Did Ana study for the exam?

Then draw a Venn diagram with the heads *My Language*, *Both*, and *English*. Invite volunteers to write the question in their native languages. Guide students to use contrastive analysis to analyze similarities and differences in punctuation, word order, and sentence structure.
L.9-10.4

CCSS Literacy.L.9-10.4 Determine or clarify the meaning of unknown and multiple-meaning words and phrases based on grades 9–10 reading and content, choosing flexibly from a range of strategies. Literacy.L.9-10.4.c Consult general and specialized reference materials (e.g., dictionaries, glossaries, thesauruses), both print and digital, to find the pronunciation of a word or determine or clarify its precise meaning, its part of speech, or its etymology.

A Self-Assess and Take Notes

Expand Remind students that good speakers and writers ask themselves questions to make sure that they expressed themselves correctly, clearly, and appropriately. Model making note cards with information about language use. Then write a sentence and model asking self-assessment questions aloud.

B Use Visuals

Reinforce Write these sentences: Some movies are dramas. Some movies are comedies or documentaries. There are many kinds of movies. Model using an idea web to arrange the details. Remind students to use the Index of Graphic Organizers on page 860 if they need assistance constructing a visual.

> **ELL** **Elaborate** Use the sentences above to model for students the process of self-assessing and then using visuals. Say: I think I need to put my main idea sentence first. Putting the main idea sentence first helps the reader understand that the paragraph is about movie types. Use a main-idea diagram to show students how to organize the information.

5 Monitor and evaluate your learning.

What to Do	Examples
A Self-monitor and self-assess language use.	Did I use the correct verb form to tell what my plans are for the future? Was it all right to use informal language only? Did I use transitions to show how my ideas were connected?
A Take notes about language.	Active Voice Compared to Passive Voice • I should write most sentences in active voice. This is the most common way to construct sentences. The "doer," or actor, of the verb in the sentence should be the subject. **Incorrect**: The race was won by Jon. **Correct**: Jon won the race.
B Use visuals to construct or clarify meaning.	This paragraph is confusing. Maybe I can use a graphic organizer to organize the main ideas.
Review.	Do I understand everything that was taught? I should review my notes and graphic organizers.

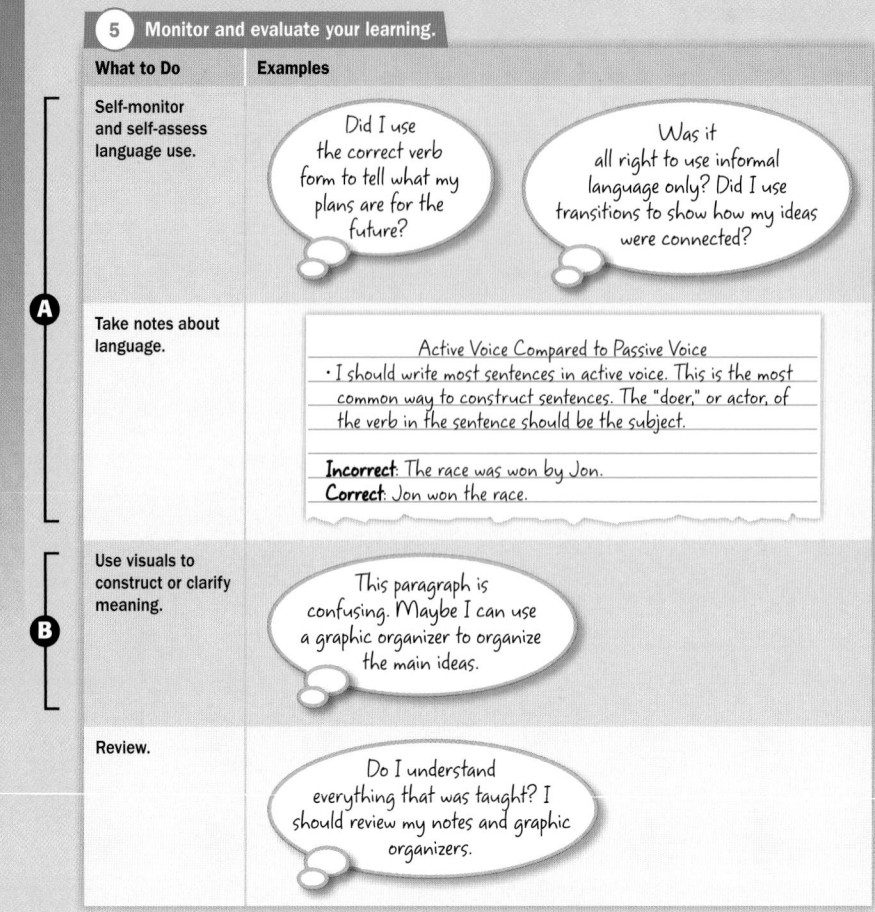

How Do I *Use* Language?

Sometimes you use language to clarify ideas or to find out about something. Other times you will want to share information.

How to Ask Questions

Ask about a person: *Who* is the girl in the photograph?

Ask about a place: *Where* are the people standing?

Ask about a thing: *What* is she holding?

Ask about a time: *When* do you think Anna plays tennis?

Ask about reasons: *Why* is the woman interviewing Anna?

How to Express Feelings

Name an event: I won the game.

Name a feeling: I was so happy when I won the game.

Tell more: I held the trophy over my head with pride!

Use the subjunctive mood: If you weren't here, I would be concerned.

How to Express Likes and Dislikes

Tell what you think: I like this painting. I think this painting is creative. In my opinion, this is a great painting.

How to Express Ideas, Needs, Intentions, and Opinions

Use words that express your needs: I need (require, must have) something to eat.

Be specific about what you need: I need a fire extinguisher now!

Elaborate on why you need something: I need some tape because I need to attach these two pieces of paper.

Use words that signal your intentions: I plan (intend, expect) to arrive at 6:00 p.m.

Use words that tell your opinions: I believe (think) the movie is great.

How to Give Oral Directions

Tell the first thing to do: Go to the board.

Tell the next step. Use a time order word: Now pick up the chalk.

Tell another step. Use another time order word: Next, write your name.

Tell the last thing to do: Go back to your seat.

Receive feedback on directions: Ask listeners if they were able to follow the directions. Repeat directions as needed.

How to Give Directions

Give information: The meeting begins at 3:15 p.m. at the library on Main Street.

Give one step directions: Go south on Ridge Road, then turn left on Main Street.

Provide directions to peers: The meeting is at the library on Main Street. It is on the same block as the school where last week's football game was held.

Oral and Written Directions

Reinforce Point out that both oral and written directions should be specific, given in order, and use numbers or sequence words to make them easier to understand.

MODEL Say:

- *To give written directions, I make a list of numbered steps. For example: 1. From our school, turn left on Maple Street. 2. When you get to the stop sign, turn right onto Elm Ave.*
- *In written directions, I can include more details and even visuals because people can reread my directions.*
- *When I give oral directions, I still tell the steps in order. However, instead of saying the numbers, I replace them with words such as* first *and* second. *For example, I say, "First, turn left on Maple Street."*
- *I give simple or less detailed oral directions because I know listeners will have to remember them.*

Practice Have students write a set of complex, multi-step instructions for a task that can be accomplished in the classroom. Remind students to replace cardinal numbers, such as 2, with ordinal numbers, such as *second*. Then organize students into pairs and have them practice giving and following their instructions orally. Invite students to give feedback about the organization and clarity of the instructions.

ELL **Elaborate** Make sure students understand the difference between ordinal numbers and cardinal numbers by drawing a two-column chart with cardinal numbers on the left and the corresponding ordinal numbers on the right.
L.9-10.1

CCSS Literacy.L.9-10.1 Demonstrate command of the conventions of standard English grammar and usage when writing or speaking.

A Respond and Converse

Expand Tell students that requests and conversations usually require both verbal and nonverbal communication. Point out that words such as *please* and *thank you* communicate a polite and pleasant tone, while gestures such as nodding, smiling, and making eye contact show that you are engaged in the discussion. Invite a pair of students to demonstrate a conversation they might have about a favorite book, story, or movie. Point out polite words and nonverbal cues the students use to show engagement.

ELL Provide examples of words and phrases that propel conversation and incorporate others:

- Why do you think that?
- Tell me more.
- Do you agree?
- What do you think about that?
- Can anyone add a different option or idea?

SL.9-10.1.c

B Tell and Describe

Expand Tell students to use precise words and details to help listeners form mental pictures of story events or places they are describing, such as home or school. Use the adjectives from this section to point out examples of specific words, such as *tall* and *modern*. Then invite students to take turns using adjectives and interesting details to describe their favorite activities.

Practice Provide students with illustrations from a familiar fairy tale. Ask students to retell the story, based on the pictures, to a partner.

ELL **Define** Explain to students that "small talk" is casual conversation about simple subjects. Tell students that people generally use informal English when making small talk. Provide examples of common small talk topics: sports, weather, music, etc. Invite students to use informal English to make small talk with a partner.

L.9-10.1

How to Give and Respond to Requests and Commands

Make polite requests: Could you please give me a pen? May I read aloud?

Respond to a request: Of course. You're welcome.

Make a polite command: Please listen carefully.

Make a strong command: Do not follow me!

Respond to a command: Of course. Certainly.

A

How to Engage in Conversation and Small Talk

Engage in small talk: How are you today? Nice weather we're having, isn't it?

Use social courtesies: May I borrow your pen, please? Thank you.

Ask and answer questions: Do you play baseball? Yes, I do.

Use verbal cues to show that you are listening: Uh-huh. Yes, I see. OK.

Use nonverbal language skills: For example, nod your head, smile at something funny, or make eye contact.

How to Tell an Original Story

Give the main idea of the story first: I want to tell you about my trip to Chicago.

Tell the important events of the story: I visited my cousin at her office. She showed me what her job is like.

Use transition words: First, I got off the bus. Then, I walked down into a tall, modern building.

Give details to make the story interesting: It was very cold that day. I remember I was wearing a big, warm jacket.

Retell a story: Maria said she was on her way to the library when she noticed something strange. Someone was following her.

How to Describe

B

Be specific by using descriptive words or phrases: I like the actor with the bright red hair.

Use descriptive imagery when possible: The room was as dark as a mountain cave. The butterfly floated gracefully through the air.

Describe a favorite activity: Playing volleyball is exciting and competitive.

Describe people: Marta has long, brown hair. She is wearing a blue t-shirt.

Describe places: The building on the corner had its windows covered with wood, and its yard was filled with trash.

Describe things: My house is large and brown. It looks like a barn.

Describe events: The jazz band is playing in the auditorium tonight.

Describe ideas: We plan to have a car wash next Saturday.

Describe feelings: I was bored, but happy.

Describe experiences: Playing guitar is relaxing for me.

Describe immediate surroundings: There are 28 desks in my English classroom.

Describe wishes using the subjunctive mood: I wish that my brother were nicer to me.

CCSS **Literacy.SL.9-10.1.c** Propel conversations by posing and responding to questions that relate the current discussion to broader themes or larger ideas; actively incorporate others into the discussion; and clarify, verify, or challenge ideas and conclusions. **Literacy.L.9-10.1** Demonstrate command of the conventions of standard English grammar and usage when writing or speaking.

How to Elaborate an Idea

Give examples to support your ideas: All students should participate in an activity to fully experience their high school years. For example, people could join the chess club, a sports team, or the school band.

Give details about your ideas: I want to organize a group trip to the museum. We can take the city bus there. We will bring our own lunches to save money. There are many new, exciting exhibits to see at the museum.

Be as specific as possible: It takes several years of school to become a lawyer. First, you have to get a college degree. Then, you need to go to law school. Getting a law degree usually takes about three years.

A

How to Ask for and Give Information

Use polite requests to ask for information: Can you please tell me your name again?

Give the exact information someone is asking for: To get to the bus stop, walk down this street, then turn left at Carter Avenue.

How to Recognize, Express, and Respond Appropriately to Humor

Listen and watch for clues: For example, a change in a person's voice or facial expression might mean that the person is joking or using humor. Also, watch for more obvious clues such as smiling and laughing.

Use verbal or nonverbal responses to recognize humor: A smile or a nod of the head is a good nonverbal response to humor. You might also respond by saying, "I get it!" or "That's funny!"

Watch others to see how they react: If other people are responding to a humorous situation, then it is usually appropriate to respond to the humor, too.

B

LANGUAGE AND LEARNING HANDBOOK

A Elaborate an Idea

Reinforce Explain that elaborating means giving more information about a topic or idea. Read aloud the first example.

MODEL Say:

- *In order to elaborate, I need to support my ideas and give specific details.*
- *The first sample tells me that all students should participate in an activity to fully experience high school.*
- *I have an idea that students should try to meet a lot of new people in high school to make their experiences even better.*
- *To elaborate on my idea, I will say that meeting people that are older or younger than me, or meeting students that are from many different cultures, will provide opportunities to make new, exciting friendships and learn more about the world.*
- *The sample also tells me that I need to be specific. I will say that students can meet new people by saying hello in the hallways or sitting down with a different group in the lunchroom.*

Practice Have students use examples and details to elaborate this statement: Sometimes, it can be difficult to study for a test.
SL.9-10.1.c

B Recognize Humor

ELL **Elaborate** Humor can be challenging for English language learners because many jokes are based on clever use of language. Explain that students should focus on gestures and facial expressions to determine if someone is joking. Encourage students to ask for clarification about jokes they don't understand. Then help them build language skills by suggesting that they offer to tell and explain a joke they know.
SL.9-10.6

CCSS **Literacy.SL.9-10.1.c** Propel conversations by posing and responding to questions that relate the current discussion to broader themes or larger ideas; actively incorporate others into the discussion; and clarify, verify, or challenge ideas and conclusions. **Literacy.SL.9-10.6** Adapt speech to a variety of contexts and tasks, demonstrating command of formal English when indicated or appropriate.

Ⓐ Make Comparisons

Expand Read aloud each example. Then draw a two-column chart. In the first column, list words that signal a comparison (*similarly, like*). In the second column, list words that signal contrasts (*on the contrary, but*). Then work with students to add words to each column, such as *also*, *and*, and *both* for comparisons and *however*, *unlike*, and *in contrast* for contrasts.

Practice Ask volunteers to add another sentence comparing or contrasting: cats/dogs, cities/towns, football/basketball. Encourage them to use words from the chart.
L.9-10.1

Ⓑ Clarify Information

Expand Tell students that unfamiliar words will often be clarified by the words that follow it. Read the examples. Point out that the words and phrases *In other words*, *meaning*, and *or* are often signals that a word or idea will be further explained. Remind them that if they still aren't sure they understand an explanation or definition, they should ask for it to be repeated or restated. Then they should confirm their understanding by restating what they heard.

For additional information about using context clues to understand new words, have students study the Vocabulary section of the **Reading Handbook**, page 690.

Ⓒ Confirm Information

Reinforce Explain to students that retelling or summarizing spoken messages will help ensure that they understand all aspects of the information received even when the topic or context is unfamiliar.

How to Make Comparisons

Ⓐ

Use compare and contrast words: The eagle is a majestic animal. Similarly, many people love dolphins. On the contrary, rats are pests and have few admirers.

Explain with details: The first math problem was difficult. But the second math problem was much more difficult. It required students to read a graph with data.

How to Define and Explain

Give a clear definition: A peacock is a large bird that is known for its colorful feathers.

Give details or examples to clarify: The large tail feathers of the male peacock are often bright green, gold, and blue.

Use a logical order for explanations: The house needs to be cleaned. First, pick up all of the toys and clothes and put them away. Then, vacuum and mop the floors.

Use graphic organizers to help explain: See the Index of Graphic Organizers on p. 772 for graphic organizers you can use to explain and define words and ideas.

How to Clarify Information

Ⓑ

Restate your words with new words: The job is a volunteer position. In other words, you do not receive payment for doing the work.

Define some confusing words: Math class is intriguing, meaning it is very interesting.

Use synonyms and antonyms: The information in the memo is confidential, or secret. It is not public information, or common knowledge.

How to Verify and Confirm Information

Ⓒ

Ask for repetition: Could you repeat that, please? Would you rephrase that for me?

Restate what you just heard: So, you're saying that it is OK to wear jeans to school?

How to Express Doubts, Wishes, and Possibilities

Understand the subjective mood: Verbs in the subjunctive mood describe doubts, wishes, and possibilities.

Use the subjunctive mood correctly:

- In the present tense, third-person singular verbs in the subjunctive mood do not have the usual -s or -es ending: She demands that he *play* outside.
- In present tense, the subjunctive mood of *be* is *be* (instead of *is* or *are*): She insists that the boys be quiet.
- In past tense, the subjunctive mood of *be* is *were*, regardless of the subject: If she *were* kinder, the boys might listen to her.

How to Understand Basic Expressions

Consider the social context:

This video game is so cool!

It's rather cool out today. It's 55 degrees.

Consider the language context: Turn right on Maple Street. The gas station will be just ahead on the left.

CCSS Literacy.L.9-10.1 Demonstrate command of the conventions of standard English grammar and usage when writing or speaking.

How to Justify with Reasons

State your claim clearly: I should be the class president.

Support your claim with evidence: This year I created a scholarship drive, organized career night, and spoke up for students at a school board meeting.

Give clear reasons that connect the evidence and your claim: My actions show that I can be a strong class president.

Combine your sentences to make the logic clear: I should be voted president of our class because I have worked hard to give students new opportunities this year.

A

How to Persuade or Convince

Use persuasive words: You can be a positive force in your community.

Give suggestions to others: You should listen to what the people in your community believe. You ought to consider all options available.

Give strong support for your persuasive idea: Everyone should ride his or her bicycle to work or school. It will lessen pollution and give people daily exercise.

B

How to Negotiate

Show that you know both sides of an issue: I see your point about the need for a new parking lot, but a park and soccer field would be more useful.

Use persuasive language: I believe you will agree with me if you consider these facts.

Clearly state your goals: We want to raise $2,000 by April and donate the money to the park fund.

How to Adjust Communication for Your Audience, Purpose, Occasion, and Task

Make sure your language is appropriate for your audience and the situation: You should choose a formal or informal manner of speaking depending on whom you are speaking to and the situation.

If you are addressing your teacher, an employer, or another adult, you might speak in this manner:

Excuse me, Mr. Johnson. May we please talk about my research paper?

If you are speaking to a friend, you can be less formal:

Hey Bob, can we talk about my research paper?

If you do not know whether a situation will call for formal or informal language, ask your teacher to help you.

Focus on your purpose: I want to make it very clear to you why that behavior could be hazardous to your health.

A Justify with Reasons and Logic

Reinforce Explain to students that when they state an opinion without supporting it, their opinion loses meaning to their readers or listeners. Give an example of an unsupported opinion, such as *yellow is the best color.* Have students discuss ways to justify this opinion. Point out that opinions should be supported with reasons and logical details. Say: To support an opinion, tell *why* you think as you do and *what* you want your audience to do. Use the examples to model.

MODEL Say:

- *The writer says that everyone should make an effort to protect the environment. I am not sure if I agree with this opinion.*
- *The writer says that if everyone takes action, we can save our environment. Then the writer gives examples. Now I understand why the writer thinks everyone should make an effort and how I can help.*
- *Combining sentences clarifies the ideas. The word* because *tells me exactly why the speaker thinks he or she should be voted president.*

Practice Have students state their opinions about a current event using the word *because.*
SL.9-10.4

B Persuade or Convince

Expand Tell students that the words *should, ought,* and *everyone* are often used to convince people to do something. Positive words, such as *improve* and *help,* encourage people to take action.

Practice Display and read aloud the following claim: We need to take care of the schoolyard. Everyone should pick up their trash. Have pairs identify supporting details and craft sentences to support the claim. Ask listeners to pay attention to supporting evidence and logic. Have partners take turns presenting the claim and their persuasive sentences. Invite the listeners to vote for the pair with the strongest argument.
SL 9-10.3, SL.9-10.4

CCSS Literacy.SL.9-10.3 Evaluate a speaker's point of view, reasoning, and use of evidence and rhetoric, identifying any fallacious reasoning or exaggerated or distorted evidence. Literacy.SL.9-10.4 Present information, findings, and supporting evidence clearly, concisely, and logically such that listeners can follow the line of reasoning and the organization, development, substance, and style are appropriate to purpose, audience, and task.

Ⓐ Academic Conversation

Reinforce Remind students that they speak more formally in the classroom than they do in casual situations among friends. Use the examples to model the difference between casual and academic conversation.

MODEL Say:

- *Academic conversation is more formal than a conversation with friends. When I am speaking with friends, I might say, "Take a look at this when you have a second." But when I speak to other teachers, I would say, "Please review the information at your convenience."*
- *When I use academic conversation, I will use facts and accurate information. I will talk about topics I know well and politely ask for information about topics I am unfamiliar with.*
- *I will express respect for others by listening to others and thanking them for information.*

Practice Ask students to brainstorm a list of situations that call for the use of formal English and a list of those that call for the use of informal English. Then, have students provide examples of comments they might make in each situation.
SL.9-10.6

Ⓑ Social Courtesies, Business Transactions, and Nonverbal Communication

Expand Explain that expressing social courtesies and conducting business transactions both require speakers to clearly state their ideas and use polite expressions, such as *please*, *thank you*, and *you're welcome.* Model saying these words using a formal tone and appropriate facial expressions and gestures.

Practice Have students role-play purchasing an item from a local store. Listen for them to clearly state their purpose and suggest polite terms they might use while conversing. Also have them notice nonverbal cues that other students use.
SL.9-10.6

How to Engage in an Academic Discussion

Ⓐ

Use formal speech: Please review the information at your convenience.

Refer to evidence: In the article we read, the author says that only 40 percent of newspapers have minorities as editors.

Ask questions: Why do you think that? What other options are there? What might have caused that?

Involve others: What do you think?

Express respect for what others say: I understand your opinion. Thank you for sharing that information.

Clarify and verify what others say: Can you explain that in a another way? What evidence supports that opinion?

How to Express Social Courtesies

Ⓑ

Listen politely and show interest: Yes, I see. Oh, what a good idea!

Wait your turn to speak: May I ask a question? I would just like to say that I disagree.

Use polite terms: Please. Thank you. That was nice of you. You are so welcome.

Use informal language when interacting with friends and family: Hi! How's it going? Thanks! No problem. Bye!

How to Conduct a Transaction or Business Deal

Clearly state numbers, dollar amounts, and other important details: Yes, I would like three textbooks. I cannot spend more than $50.

Be polite and professional: Thank you for your time. I appreciate your help.

Consider the context of the situation: Consider where you are and what is going on. For example, you can infer that when you are asked for your identification at a bank, the teller means your driver's license rather than a school ID.

How to Demonstrate and Interpret Nonverbal Communication

Watch for and use gestures, eye contact, or other visual or nonverbal communication.
Some examples include the following:

- waving to say "hello" or "good-bye"
- direct eye contact to show attention
- nodding to show understanding or approval
- using hands to show a number or a sign, like "stop"
- winking or smiling to show you are joking

Look for clues by combining verbal and nonverbal communication. You can often guess what someone means by watching how they communicate nonverbally while they speak. For example, you will have an easier time understanding someone's directions by watching where he or she points.

CCSS Literacy.SL.9-10.6 Adapt speech to a variety of contexts and tasks, demonstrating command of formal English when indicated or appropriate.

Listening and Speaking

Listening

Good listeners are able to learn new information and avoid confusion.

How to Listen Actively and Respectfully

- Set a purpose and prepare for listening.
- Pay close attention to the speaker. Demonstrate appropriate body language by sitting up straight and looking at the speaker as you listen.
- Connect texts or ideas that you are hearing to personal knowledge and experience—this will help you understand.
- Don't interrupt, unless you need to ask the speaker to speak more loudly.
- When the speaker is finished, ask him or her to explain things you did not understand. If the speaker did not talk enough about a topic, ask him or her to tell you more about it.

A

How to Overcome Barriers to Listening

- Pay close attention to the speaker.
- Try to ignore other noises or distractions around you.
- Politely ask any other people who are talking to be quiet.
- Close the classroom door or any windows if outdoor noises are distracting.
- Raise your hand, and ask the speaker to speak louder if necessary.
- Take notes on the topic being discussed. This will help you stay focused and self-monitor what you hear and track your understanding.
- In your notes, summarize the speaker's main idea and details. Were they effective enough to keep you interested? Was the speech's main idea easy to understand? Did the supporting ideas confirm the speech's main idea?

B

How to Use Choral Reading and Readers Theater

Choral Reading is a group activity that involves people reading a selection aloud, together. Readers Theater takes a story and treats it like a play. Students are assigned to read different parts, such as the narrator or a character.

During Choral Reading

- Listen carefully to how other readers pronounce words and phrases.
- Listen to how the intonation of the words changes.
- Listen to hear if your pitch and pronunciation sound like everyone else's.

C

During Readers Theater

- Listen to how different characters have different voices and expressions.
- Watch the speakers for gestures or acting.
- If you are the one who narrates or reads the stage directions, focus on describing where the action takes place.

D

A Listening Respectfully

Reinforce Explain that students can listen responsively by asking questions for clarification, or understanding the speaker's ideas, and elaboration, or building on the speaker's ideas.

Practice Have students identify good examples and bad examples of effective listening behaviors. For example, ask if whispering during a presentation is a good or bad example of an effective listening behavior. Remind students that they will need to continue to improve their listening skills in order to meet expectations at their grade level.
SL.9-10.1

B Barriers to Listening

Expand Tell students that note-taking is useful both during and after listening. Point out that students can refer back to their notes to guide their critical reflection on the speaker's ideas.

C Choral Reading

Reinforce Tell students that when they read chorally, they should track the print and read aloud with the group, using the same expression and intonation as the group. Explain that *expression* means varying one's tone to show the meaning and emotion of the words, and *intonation* is the rise and fall of one's voice.

Write these sentences: Susan groaned when she heard the news. How could her mother make her baby-sit on the night of Rosa's party? Model reading the sentences with proper intonation and expression, emphasizing the word *groaned* and using your intonation to indicate the question. Then have students read the sentences chorally.

D Readers Theater

Reinforce Tell students that Readers Theater is performed from a script. Say: Readers use their voices to bring the characters to life. Think about how the character might feel, act, and sound, and use your voice to reflect those characteristics.

CCSS Literacy.SL.9-10.1 Initiate and participate effectively in a range of collaborative discussions (one-on-one, in groups, and teacher-led) with diverse partners on grades 9–10 topics, texts, and issues, building on others' ideas and expressing their own clearly and persuasively.

Manage Discussions and Presentations

Reinforce Tell students that in a discussion, they must be both a listener and a speaker. Explain that an effective discussion requires speakers to adapt to their listeners' needs and concerns. Tell students that they should:

- avoid topics that may be unpleasant or sensitive to others
- state differing opinions in a respectful way
- avoid being argumentative or too personal
- include everyone by speaking clearly and making eye contact
- acknowledge the ideas and opinions of others

Point out that when people disagree, they are critiquing ideas, not people. Model some ways to address the needs and concerns of others.

MODEL Say:

- *I don't want Kai to feel bad, so I will explain why I disagree: Kai's idea for a bake sale is a good one, but I think a car wash might also be a good fund-raiser. Some people might not have the resources to bake, but we can all help wash the cars.*
- *When I have an idea, I will encourage others to share theirs, too. I will say: I think we should play soccer after school, but I'd like to hear what everyone else wants to do.*

Practice Organize students into small groups. Ask them to share their opinions about a book the class has read recently. After conducting discussions, invite students to share how they used discussion techniques to propel conversation and respond thoughtfully.

ELL **Explain** Tell students that part of speaking responsibly and ethically is being *politically correct*, or *P. C.* Explain that it is important to be politically correct in group discussions, and that failing to do so could cause hurt feelings or fights. Remind students that a phrase or word that might be acceptable in one language might not be in another.

SL.9-10.1.c, SL.9-10.1.d

Speaking

Speaking is saying aloud what you are thinking. Good speakers choose their words and use language effectively. They also choose an appropriate organizational strategy for their ideas. You may be required to speak in class during a discussion or when giving a presentation. Always speak responsibly and ethically. When you speak ethically, you are careful not to offend or upset anyone who is listening to you.

How to Manage Discussions and Presentations

To be a good speaker, you need to effectively share your ideas in class, in a group, or with a partner. There will be times when it is necessary to have a conference with your teacher or another student. In any discussion, whether it is formal or informal, there are things you can do to make it a productive meeting. Discussions are good ways to find information, check your understanding, and share ideas.

- In discussions, make positive comments about the ideas of others. Connect your ideas to what others say.

Interesting point! That is a good idea. Thank you for sharing your opinion.
I agree that people should recycle and I also think we should focus on saving water.

- Think about the topic that is being discussed. Give ideas about that topic, and exclude nonessential information.

He is talking about how climate and weather are different in other parts of the world.
There are many tropical climates near the equator.

- Ask questions if you need more information.
- Ask questions to verify or challenge ideas.

Can you please repeat that? I do not understand. Can you explain that again?
Can you give me evidence to support that idea? I respect your opinion but I think the character was shy, not scared.

- Anticipate, recognize, and adjust to listeners' needs and concerns.

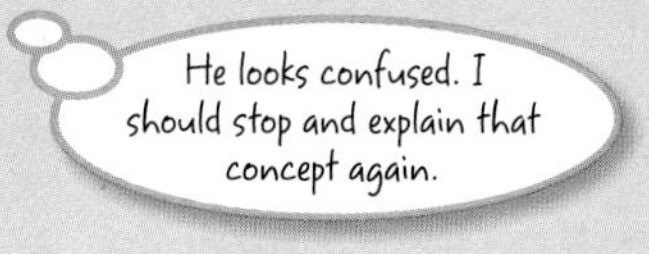
He looks confused. I should stop and explain that concept again.

CCSS Literacy.SL.9-10.1.c Propel conversations by posing and responding to questions that relate the current discussion to broader themes or larger ideas; actively incorporate others into the discussion; and clarify, verify, or challenge ideas and conclusions. Literacy.SL.9-10.1.d Respond thoughtfully to diverse perspectives, summarize points of agreement and disagreement, and, when warranted, qualify or justify their own views and understanding and make new connections in light of the evidence and reasoning presented.

How to Give Presentations

Choose an interesting topic that will engage listeners' attention. You may make a speech, share a poem, or give a performance or report to share your ideas. Be sure to justify your choice of performance technique. That is, does it fit your purpose and audience?

Use an engaging and effective introduction and conclusion. Keep your audience interested by changing your tone and volume and by using varied sentence structure to emphasize meaning. Speak using standard English grammar and syntax. It is fine to make your audience laugh, but be careful to use effective and appropriate humor that does not upset or offend your listeners. Use audience feedback to improve future presentations.

- Change your rate and volume for your audience or purpose. Be sure to speak with appropriate pitch, stress, intonation, and enunciation.

  I will be speaking about how dangerous chemicals are in the chemistry lab. I should use a serious tone during the presentation.

- Use body language such as gestures, facial expressions, and posture while you are speaking to show what you mean.

  I want to show how tall and wide a hockey goal is. I'll use my hands.

- Occasionally make eye contact with specific audience members.

  I do not want to appear nervous or unprepared. If I make eye contact with my audience, my presentation will be natural and relaxed.

A

How to Overcome Anxiety

Some people get a bit nervous or anxious about speaking in front of others. There are simple ways you can avoid this.

- **Be prepared.** If you plan your presentation well, you can be confident that you will speak well. Practice presenting in front of a mirror or a family member.
- **Use notes.** Use notes, graphic aids, and props as memory aids and to support the message. Notes can guide your speech or presentation. You can refer to the notes if you get confused or forget a topic you want to discuss. See the example on the right for the type of information you can keep track of in notes.

> Civil Wars Around the World
> — Mexico, 1857–1861
> — U.S., 1861–1865
> — Greece, 1946–1949
> — Yugoslavia, 1991–2001

B

A Give a Presentation

Reinforce Tell students that effective speakers match their tone and their body language to their words. Read each bulleted point with students. Then model using appropriate tone and body language.

MODEL Say:

- *When I give a presentation on traffic safety, I will start by introducing my topic in clear language. This is a serious topic, so I will use a serious tone:* Many accidents can be avoided if people use caution.
- *I will use gestures to show what I mean:* Before you cross the street, stop and look both ways to make sure no cars are coming. *I raised my hand to illustrate* "stop" *and turned my head both ways as I said* "look both ways."
- *Before I move on to the next point, I will pause to look up at my audience and check for understanding. I will also make eye contact with my audience.*

B Use Note Cards

Expand Explain that organized notes can make speakers feel more prepared. Point out the note card on the student page. Say:

- Note cards should not include every detail. They should just list the important ideas you want to cover.
- Notice how the events are arranged in time order. Organizing information in a logical way helps both the presenter and the listener keep track of important information.

Practice Have students make a set of note cards for a presentation on the organization and decoration of the classroom. Then have them practice delivering the information to a partner. Tell them to focus on looking up from their note cards and using appropriate facial expressions and gestures.
SL.9-10.4

CCSS Literacy.SL.9-10.4 Present information, findings, and supporting evidence clearly, concisely, and logically such that listeners can follow the line of reasoning and the organization, development, substance, and style are appropriate to purpose, audience, and task.

Use Rhetorical Devices

Reinforce Read aloud the definitions and examples of rhetorical devices. Then say:

- Allusions are most effective when they reference a work that is familiar to the audience. Remember that not everyone has read the same stories you have read. Try to make allusions with very common works, such as fairy tales, folk tales, or classic works of literature.
- Facial expressions can help you determine whether someone is being ironic or serious. Watch and listen for the difference in my tone and facial expression as I say, "Today must be your lucky day!" as a sincere statement and an ironic one.
- A pun is also called a "play on words." The example is amusing because writing with a pencil without a point, or tip, has no point, or purpose. Speakers will often emphasize the multiple-meaning word to help listeners recognize the pun. Notice how I emphasize the word *point* when I read the example.
- Parallelism creates a sense of balance and shows that a series of things are equally important. Notice the repetition of "We can" in the example. Use parallelism only for emphasis, or the presentation can become too repetitive.

Practice Have students name rhetorical devices used in these examples:

- I wished my fairy godmother would bring me a new dress. (allusion)
- I woke up with a sore throat. I felt like a million bucks. (irony)

ELL Explain To help English language learners better understand irony, explain that irony can also be referred to as sarcasm, satire, mockery, or wit. Model additional examples of ironic statements that students can understand at their grade level.

Elaborate Point out that parallelism usually involves the repetition of the subject and the verb. Write the following sentence: Everyone should help others. Guide students to write two more parallel sentences to match the example.

L.9-10.1.a, L.9-10.5

How to Self-Monitor

Monitoring is watching or noticing what is happening as you speak. It is important to monitor your audience's reactions, so you can adjust your presentation if necessary. If possible, tape your speech so you can listen to it before you give it. Analyze the tape to discover anything that might be confusing or inappropriate for the listeners. Use a rubric to prepare, critique, and improve your speech. Create a scoring guide that you can use to self-monitor. For sample rubrics and scoring guides, see page 720–722 and 792–800.

How to Use Rhetorical Devices

Rhetorical devices are ways to use language to make your presentation more interesting, engaging, or effective. Look at the examples below. Then produce one or two examples of your own.

Rhetorical Device	Example
Alliteration: The repetition of the same consonant sounds at the beginning of words.	Pablo prefers pecan pie.
Allusion: A form of literary language in which one text makes the reader think about another text that was written before it.	When Hannah wrote in her essay that vanity was the main character's weak point, or "Achilles' heel," her teacher understood that Hannah was referring to a character in a Greek myth.
Analogy: A way of illustrating or explaining a thing or an idea by comparing it with a more familiar thing or idea.	*Blogs* are to the *Internet* as *journals* are to *paper*.
Irony: When you say one thing, but want the listeners to understand something different. You may say the opposite of what is really true.	Your friend says to you after you trip and fall, "Today must be your lucky day!"
Mood: The attitude or feeling of your presentation. You create this for your listeners with the words you choose.	Slowly the car approached. It rolled to a stop, and a strange looking character stepped out of the back seat.
Quotation: Repeating the exact words of someone using quotation marks.	As Franklin D. Roosevelt said, "The only thing we have to fear is fear itself."
Pun: A humorous use of words that have more than one meaning.	To write with a broken pencil is *point*-less.
Parallelism: Similarity of structure in a pair or series of related words, phrases, or sentences.	We can change our school. We can make a difference. We can do this together.
Repetition: Repeating words, phrases, or ideas. Using this device shows your listeners that you believe the idea is very important.	All people are entitled to freedom. Freedom is something everyone deserves. Freedom will make the world a better place.
Tone: A speaker's attitude toward the topic, audience, or self.	I am definitely not in favor of a shorter lunch period.

CCSS Literacy.L.9-10.1.a Use parallel structure. Literacy.L.9-10.5 Demonstrate understanding of figurative language, word relationships, and nuances in word meanings.

Viewing and Representing

Monitoring Your Understanding of Visuals

You encounter visual elements constantly–in print, on TV, on the Internet, and in movies. How can you make sure you accurately understand and interpret what you see? Does the visual enhance your understanding of the oral presentation? Use the following strategies to self-monitor, or check that you understand, what you are viewing.

How to View and Look for Details

Study the image below. Ask these kinds of questions:

- Who or what does the image show? Are there other details that answer *when*, *where*, *why*, or *how* questions about the image?
- How does the image make me feel? Do I enjoy looking at it? Does it worry me, make me laugh, or give me a good or bad feeling?
- What do the details and elements (such as shape, color, and size of the image) add to the meaning?

How to Respond to and Interpret Visuals and Informational Graphics

When you view visuals and informational graphics, think about why they are included and what information they provide. Informational graphics often present facts or statistics. For example, you will sometimes see illustrations or informational graphics used in an oral presentation. Ask yourself:

- What message or information is the visual showing?
- Why did the artist, designer, or illustrator create and include the visual?
- Does the visual represent information accurately and fairly? What information did the creator choose to include or leave out? Why?

How to Self-Correct Your Thoughts as You View

Examine your understanding of visuals to correct any faulty thinking. Always question the validity and accuracy of visuals.

- Be aware of racial, cultural, and gender stereotyping. A **stereotype** is a general opinion that is not always true. A stereotype does not look at the differences between individual people or things. For example, "All cats are lazy." This is a stereotype because although some cats are lazy, some are very active.
- Look again at the image or graphic for more information and details that may change your understanding and for things you did not notice at first.
- Watch for **bias**. Is the writer or creator presenting information that is slanted or manipulated to show a particular point of view?

A Interpret Informational Graphics

Expand Display a chart or graph that accompanies an ad for a product. Define propaganda. Point out that informational graphics can be biased. Say: Speakers and presenters may choose to only show information that supports *their* point of view. Pay attention to what the author or presenter does *not* show in addition to what he or she *does* show to help determine if the author is being truthful.
SL.9-10.2

B Self-Correct Stereotypes and Bias

Reinforce Display a stereotypical picture of a grandmother. Ask students to point out stereotypical characteristics. Then explain that all grandmothers do not look like this grandmother.

Say: Stereotypes often occur because the creator of the image wants viewers to quickly and easily understand the image. However, these stereotypes can lead to misunderstandings. Remember while viewing that some images may be unfair or incorrect. Ask yourself if the visual could be changed to be more accurate.

Bias can also occur in the way information is presented. A graphic may contain a diagram that exclaims; "35% of Americans prefer Fizzy Pop!" This may seem positive, but it also means that 65% prefer something else.

Practice Have students work in groups to find examples of stereotypes in magazines and books. Ask them to describe the stereotype and then discuss an image that would correct it.

Then show students some advertisements containing statistics. Have them create ads that counter the original message.
SL.9-10.2

CCSS Literacy.SL.9-10.2 Integrate multiple sources of information presented in diverse media or formats (e.g., visually, quantitatively, orally) evaluating the credibility and accuracy of each source.

A Maps

Expand Have students study the map. Ask them what location it shows and how they know. Explain that many maps have labels and keys that help viewers understand the symbols and locations on the map. Use a map to show features, such as the compass rose, key, and legend.

Practice Have students find maps online, on mobile devices, or in content-area textbooks. Ask students to show and explain the map symbols and features.
RI.9-10.7

B Charts and Graphs

Expand Point out that charts and graphs are often used when the author or speaker wants to show a comparison of information. Ask: Which classification has the greatest number of endangered species? Which sport do most students prefer?

Practice Create a chart and graph collection. Set up a display area or folder. Have each student find charts and graphs from newspapers, magazines, content-area textbooks, or online. Have students write a summary of what they learned from the chart or graph. Pull out an example once a week to display for the class. Invite the student who located the chart or graph to read aloud their summary and elaborate about why they selected the chart or graph.
RI.9-10.7

C Artwork

Practice Have students describe the artwork and the illustration by telling how each makes them feel and what its purpose might be.

Review Have students work in small groups to find examples of a map, a chart, and artwork. Ask them to share their examples with the class and describe what information the graphics convey.

Practice Access the National Geographic Web site. Preview and display the National Geographic Photograph of the Day. Invite students to describe the information the graphic conveys. Then have partners work together to write captions that augment, restate, or clarify the message.
RI.9-10.7

How to Understand Different Kinds of Visuals

It is important to be familiar with the different kinds of visuals that illustrate ideas for a text or spoken presentation. You will be expected to respond to and interpret these different visuals. Some examples are maps, charts, graphs, photographs, illustrations, and other artwork. As you look at a visual, decide what it is telling you. Visuals should help you better understand the information, especially if the language is elaborate or complex.

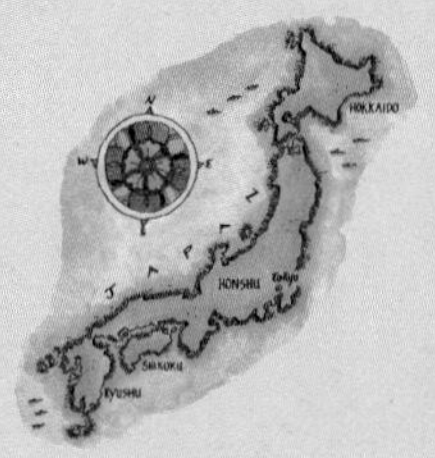

Map

A

A map is a visual layout of a specific location. Maps are an excellent way to gain more information about an idea presented in text.

Graphic Displays

A chart or a graph can show comparisons or provide information more clearly than if the same statistics were only presented in a text. Be sure to evaluate the credibility of the source of the data.

B

Chart

Number of Endangered Species in the United States	
Classification	Number of Species
Mammals	70
Birds	76
Reptiles	13
Fish	74
Insects	47

Graph

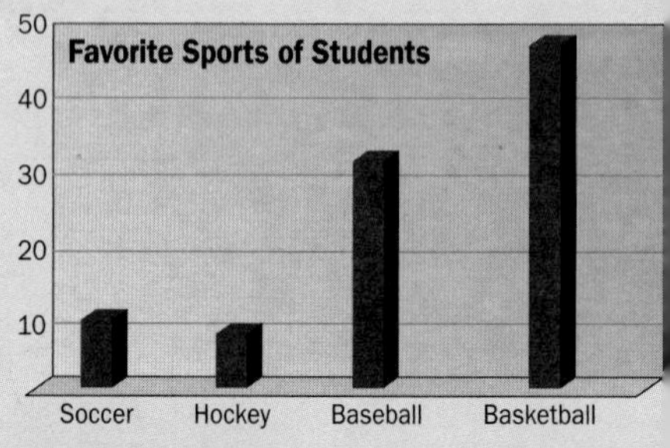

Photographs, Illustrations, Video, Sound, and Artwork

C

Photographs, illustrations, and other artwork can have a variety of purposes:

- to share an opinion
- to elicit, or draw out, emotions
- to make people think
- to entertain

Multimedia resources include sound, motion, special effects, audio, and visuals. Use what you see and hear. Think about how the creator of a video or media presentation uses music or effects to make a point. Animations and other interactive media change based on what you click or touch.

CCSS Literacy.RI.9-10.7 Analyze various accounts of a subject told in different mediums (e.g., a person's life story in both print and multimedia), determining which details are emphasized in each account.

Using Visuals and Multimedia in Writing and Presenting

Here are some key points to keep in mind when you choose to represent your ideas by using a visual or other media.

Representing Your Ideas Through Visuals

Using visuals in your writing and oral presentations can help you make your point more clearly. Choose visuals that match your purpose and your topic. Strong visuals will make a strong impression. Music and sound effects in multimedia presentations also impact tone and can be used to emphasize ideas or information. For example, if you choose to illustrate a poem about nature, include a picture that will help readers picture the place or feel the mood of the poem. **A**

How Key Elements of Design Create Meaning and Influence the Message

Different visuals share information in different ways.

- If your goal is to entertain, choose a humorous picture.

Source: ©Terry Warner/Cartoon Stock, Ltd.

"Is this seat taken?"

- If your goal is to inform, use a visual that gives additional information about your topic or clarifies the information in some way. See the Index of Graphic Organizers on page 772 for ideas of ways to share information in graphic form.

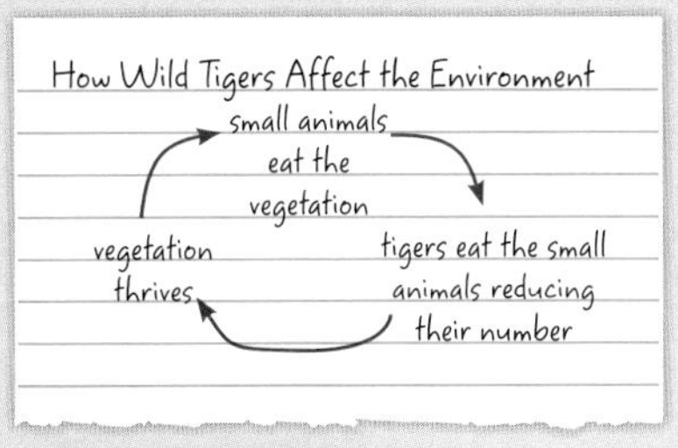

B

- If your goal is to persuade, or to make people feel or think a certain way, you may want to choose a visual that will appeal to emotions.
- If you use a visual from another source, be sure to identify the source.

Source: ©Jeff Rotman/Getty Images.

C

A Use Visuals

Expand Have students study the sunset picture. Ask: What adjectives would you use to describe this photo? What kind of text would you use with a photo like this?

Advise students that if they choose the wrong visual to go with their presentations, listeners may not fully understand the message. Visuals should be chosen that reflect or emphasize the topic.

B Create Graphics

Expand Have students study the note card. Then explain how the note card is only showing a sketch of the writer's graphic organizer. Encourage students to create stimulating graphics for presentations by:

- using large, colorful paper
- experimenting with different fonts or clip art on the computer
- drawing or painting images to go with the graphic organizer
- cutting images or statements from magazines, newspapers, or advertising materials
- making an interactive visual, such as one that includes a spinner, pockets, or pull-tabs

C Cite Sources

Reinforce Explain to students that sources for photos and cartoons are often placed on the side of the image, as shown on this page. Say: Image sources must be cited. Sources should be cited according to *Modern Language Association* or *Chicago Manual of Style* guidelines. Share the sample below and say: Fine art, such as paintings, often use captions. This caption is for an oil painting:

> *City Heights,* 2001, Kadir Nelson. Oil on canvas, collection of the artist.

Practice Have each student select a piece of writing from their journal or portfolio. Ask them to select a visual to accompany their writing. Have partners share and respond to the text and visuals. Have each student add a citation.
W.9-10.8, SL.9-10.5

CCSS Literacy.W.9-10.8 Gather relevant information from multiple authoritative print and digital sources, using advanced searches effectively; assess the usefulness of each source in answering the research question; integrate information into the text selectively to maintain the flow of ideas, avoiding plagiarism and following a standard format for citation. **Literacy.SL.9-10.5** Make strategic use of digital media (e.g., textual, graphical, audio, visual, and interactive elements) in presentations to enhance understanding of findings, reasoning, and evidence and to add interest.

Ⓐ The Effects of Visuals

Expand Explain that the diagram of the U.S. government is an effective visual because it shows the information in a clear, concise way. Discuss with students what other kinds of visuals they might use to show the same information in humorous, serious, edgy, or artistic ways to create different moods.

Ⓑ Interpret and Analyze Media

Expand Remind students that you can't believe everything you see. Explain that because media is often used to sell a product or promote a point of view, images are often selected and even altered for a particular purpose. Point out the following:

- Many periodicals show attention-grabbing photos with misleading headlines to grab viewers' attention.
- Images in magazines may be airbrushed or altered to make people look different.

Suggest that students use a checklist to analyze the credibility of media:

- ☑ Who is the creator of the image? What hidden motive might the creator have?
- ☑ Does the image "tell the whole story," or is it used to support one point of view?
- ☑ Does the image contradict information or images you've seen elsewhere?

Tell students that by analyzing the validity of media images, they can arrive at the true purpose, or message, of the media and make an informed decision about the information presented.

Practice Display the checklist. Have students identify examples of questionable media images including printed images, information on the radio or television, online media, and information encountered via social networks. Invite individuals to share examples of how they determined whether or not the message was valid. Expand the checklist as appropriate to integrate student input.
SL.9-10.2

The Effects of Visual Arts on Mood

Ⓐ When you choose a visual to represent information in an essay or an oral presentation, make sure it is a visual that your particular audience will understand. A complex graph may not work well if your viewers do not know a lot about your topic. Creating a simple visual is especially important if you have an elaborate presentation. Your audience should be able to use the visual to make sense of the presentation. Make sure it is a visual you would want to view yourself.

In addition, consider the mood that you want the visual to create. The mood should be appropriate to your purpose and audience, such as a classroom of students listening to your oral presentation. If the mood of a presentation or essay is serious, do not use humorous or distracting visuals. For example, if you are giving a presentation on the United States government, you might display a graphic showing the legislative, executive, and judicial branches of government.

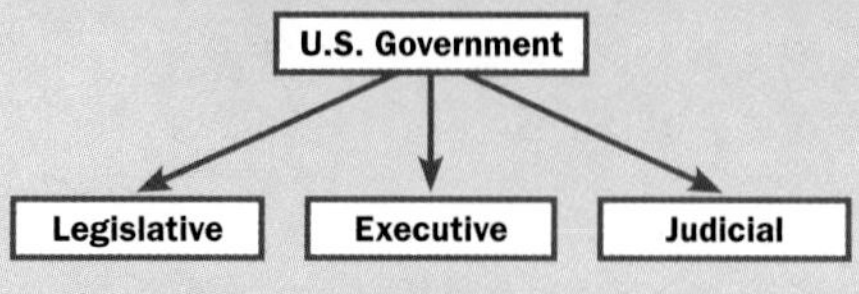

Interpreting and Analyzing Media

Media is the term used to describe the many forms of technology used today to provide communication to a large number of people. As you view media around you, such as the Internet, television, movies, magazines, and newspapers, make sure you remember the key points that are presented. What information is being presented in the visuals that are used? How is it presented? Make decisions about the information you are presented with by the media.

Ⓑ The information and visuals presented may be trustworthy, or they may be suspicious. In today's world, we are surrounded by images and information that we need to analyze and make decisions about. Keep in mind that visual media can easily influence our cultural and social expectations because it is much more visual than traditional texts. Be aware that you can make judgments and decisions while viewing the images and form your own opinions about the information they present.

Sometimes, the same event can be interpreted differently, based on the way the event is covered and the medium in which it is shown. Find a news event discussed in a newspaper and the same event on the Internet or TV. Then compare what is similar and what is different.

- What is the message?
- How do I know it is believable or valid?
- What information is included and what is left out?
- Is the information objective, or is it biased?

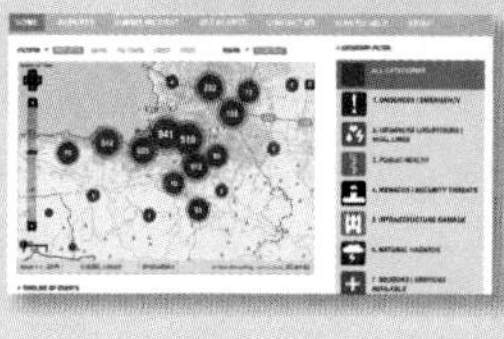

CCSS Literacy.SL.9-10.2 Integrate multiple sources of information presented in diverse media or formats (e.g., visually, quantitatively, orally) evaluating the credibility and accuracy of each source.

How to Use Technology to Communicate

This section provides examples of the technology used today to communicate in school, in the workplace, and with friends and family.

Cell Phone

A **cell phone** does not need a wire connection to a phone network. It can be used anywhere there is a wireless phone network signal. It is completely portable. Cell phones can allow you to send text messages, connect to the Internet, play music, take photos, and make phone calls.

Personal Computer

A **personal computer** is an electronic tool that helps you create, save, and use information. You can also use a computer to communicate with e-mail, browse the Internet, work with digital photos or movies, or listen to music.

A **desktop computer** is not portable. It has several parts, including a monitor, a mouse, a keyboard, and a CD drive.

A **laptop computer** is smaller than a desktop computer. It is designed to be portable. A laptop computer usually fits in a travel case.

A **tablet computer** is typically even smaller than a laptop computer. You can use your fingers or a stylus pen to make most tablet computers work.

Use Technology to Communicate

Expand Invite students to share some types of technology they use in their everyday lives. Then briefly discuss each type of technology:

- Point out that cell phones are a useful way of keeping in touch with people at all times. However, cell phones should be turned off in quiet public places, such as libraries and movie theaters.
- Tell students that offices often use fax machines to quickly send important documents. Many offices use computers or photocopiers that have fax machines built into them.
- Use the photograph or a classroom computer to point out the features of a desktop computer. Explain that unlike a laptop, a desktop computer also has a tower that houses the disk drives, as well as the microprocessing unit, or "brains," of the computer. Then point out the features of the laptop computer. Discuss with students the advantages and disadvantages of laptops and desktops.

Practice Draw a three-column chart with the headings *School*, *Workplace*, and *Friends and Family*. Have students give examples of technology, including the ones named in the student book, that they use in each situation. Have them explain how they use each type.
W.9.10-6

CCSS Literacy.W.9-10.6 Use technology, including the Internet, to produce, publish, and update individual or shared writing products, taking advantage of technology's capacity to link to other information and to display information flexibly and dynamically.

Other Sources of Information

Expand Point out that there are a variety of print and nonprint sources that can be used in research. Explain that the following sources are usually reliable, accurate, and objective:

- Magazines, newspapers, news sources, and almanacs are good sources of information about current events and topics. Almanacs are annual publications that contain statistical data for a variety of topics. Past issues of magazines and newspapers are often stored on microfiche, or film, at your local library.
- Professional and scholarly journals contain articles, research, and field studies about specific professions or academic areas. Often reading the abstract, or brief summary, at the beginning of articles can provide you with useful information.
- Political speeches and press conferences are additional sources of information about current events. Often transcripts of these events are available through a press organization or online.
- Technical documents include manuals and blueprints. These types of materials often include visuals that may be useful in your research.

How to Select and Use Media to Research Information

Modern technology allows us to access a wide range of information. The Internet is a popular source for research and finding information for academic, professional, and personal reasons. Another source for research is your local library. It contains databases where you can gain access to many forms of print and nonprint resources, including audio and video recordings and many other sources of information.

The Internet

The **Internet** is an international network, or connection, of computers that share information with each other. The **World Wide Web** is a part of the Internet that allows you to find, read, and organize information. Using the Web is a fast way to get the most current information about many topics.

Any series of words or phrases can be typed into the "search" section of a search engine, and multiple Web sites with those words will be listed for you to investigate. Once you are at a Web site, you can perform a word or phrase search of the page you are on. This will help direct you to the information you are researching.

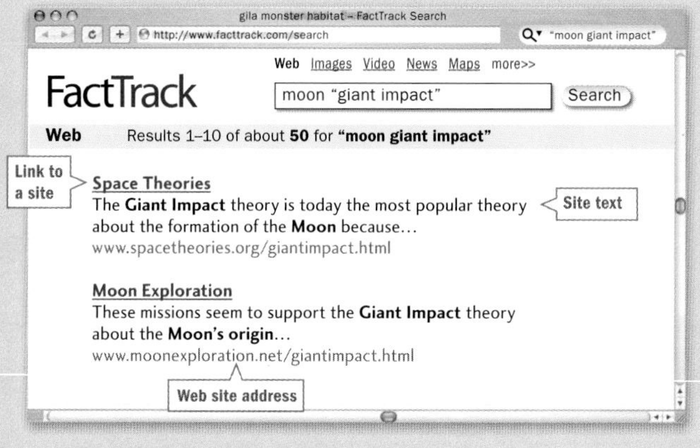

Other Sources of Information

There are many other reliable print and nonprint sources of information to use in your research. For example:

- magazines
- newspapers
- professional or scholarly journal articles
- experts
- political speeches
- press conferences

Most of the information from these sources is also available on the Internet. You should be careful to evaluate and choose the best sources for this information. It is important to double-check the source. Does the source show a bias? Is the source from a professor or from an anonymous blog post?

How to Evaluate the Quality of Information

There is so much information available on the Internet it can be hard to comprehend. It is important to be sure that the information you use as support or evidence is reliable and can be trusted. Use the following checklist as a guideline to decide if a Web page you are reading is reliable and a credible source.

Checklist to Determine Reliable Web Sites

- ☑ The information is from a well-known and trusted source. For example, Web sites that end in ".edu" are part of an educational institution and usually can be trusted. Other cues for reliable Web sites are sites that end in ".org" for "organization" or ".gov" for "government."
- ☑ The people who write or are quoted on the Web site are experts, not just everyday people expressing ideas or opinions.
- ☑ The Web site gives evidence, not just opinions.
- ☑ The Web site is free of grammatical and spelling errors. This is often a hint that the site was carefully constructed and will not have factual errors.
- ☑ The Web site is not trying to sell a product or persuade people. It is trying to provide accurate information.

If you are uncertain about the quality of a Web site, contact your teacher for advice.

A

How to Organize and Discuss Information From Various Media

Devise a system to organize the information you find from various forms of media, such as newspapers, books, and the Internet. You can make photocopies of important newspaper and magazine articles or pages from books and keep them in labeled folders. Web pages can be printed out or bookmarked on your computer for reference. You can discuss the information you find from various media with your classmates or teachers to evaluate its reliability. In fact, explaining aloud what you've gathered from a variety of media is one way to better understand the information. It will also help you to learn how to use specific language and vocabulary related to certain types of media.

How to Analyze and Interpret Information from Various Media

You should always try to analyze and interpret the information you find from various media sources. Many times the same event can be interpreted differently depending on the medium in which it is presented. Ask yourself if the source is reliable or if the information you find shows any bias or opinion. Some writers may only mention facts that support their ideas or opinions and not mention details that are not supportive of their arguments. Find an event that is covered both in your local newspaper and on television. Compare the differences between the coverage in the two media. Do you notice a difference in bias or opinion? Comparing two sources of information about the same topic may help you see that one is more biased than the other. It can help you see ways that different people present similar information.

B

A Evaluate Information

Expand Review with students the checklist for determining reliable sources. Then point out the following "red flags" to the reliability of a source:

- makes "important" claims or covers "important" recent events that have not been covered by reliable news sources
- attributes statements to a person that seem out of character or against the way that person typically speaks
- makes claims such as "find out what others don't want you to know"
- is covered with advertisements for the product it is discussing
- claims to be developed by a large, well-known company but doesn't have links to or trademarks from that company

B Analyze and Interpret Media

Expand Tell students that they should always analyze media for bias. Reliable facts should be free from the author's or speaker's opinions. Students should look for these signs of bias:

- Glittering generalities are vague, unsupported statements that appeal to emotions. Politicians and public representatives often use glittering generalities, such as "I will fight for our freedom," in formal speeches to sway their audience.
- Logical fallacies are structured like a supported argument but end in an incorrect conclusion. For example, an activist might say, "If you don't support our movement, you don't value freedom." You might support freedom but simply not agree with the activist's approach.
- Many advertisements will use symbols to suggest something about their product. A car company might include an eagle to give consumers the impression they are supporting the U. S. when they buy the product. However, the cars may actually be made in other countries.

Ⓐ Electronic Media

Reinforce Tell students that word-processing programs are a good way to design newsletters, reports, brochures, or other printed texts. If possible, read aloud each step and model completing it on a classroom computer. Point out that word-processing proofreading tools can be helpful, but they will not catch every error. This is because word-processing programs cannot account for every grammar situation, nor do their spelling lists contain every word in the English language. Students should be sure to proofread their work before printing a final copy.

ELL **Elaborate** Clarify terminology that may be unfamiliar, such as *file*, *document*, *template*, *font*, *desktop*, *shortcut*, *import*, *clip art*, etc. Also name the programs available on your school's computers that may be referred to in a shortened form.

Ⓑ Multimedia Presentation

Expand Explain that visuals add interest to a presentation. Share these tips for using visuals:

- Practice speaking with your visuals so that you can show a photograph or point to a diagram without interrupting the flow of your speech.
- Use words and phrases that signal the audience that you are about to use media. For example, you might say, "Let's listen to what a noted scientist has to say."
- Make sure your materials are organized and your videos or recordings are set to the correct place and ready to be played.

Practice Have individuals select one of the Unit Projects that used multimedia elements. Ask them to share with the class which media format they chose and how the media impacted their presentation. If students have not integrated multimedia, adjust the activity to invite them to augment their prior project by adding a media element.
SL.9-10.5

How to Use Technology to Create Final Products

Technology allows people to create interesting final products to share information. Once you become comfortable with the appropriate equipment and software, there are many ways to create, change, and individualize your work using technology. Here are two examples of products that can be made with technology today.

Electronic Media

Ⓐ

Electronic media, or a **word-processing document**, allows you to create and save written work. You can use it to:

- store ideas, plans, and essays
- write drafts of your work
- revise, edit, and proofread your writing
- format, publish, and share your work

There are many different kinds of word-processing programs. If you are not familiar with word-processing programs, talk to your teacher about learning one that will work well for you in class. Review or learn the following basic steps:

1. **Start a File or Document** Open a new document, and choose a place to save it.

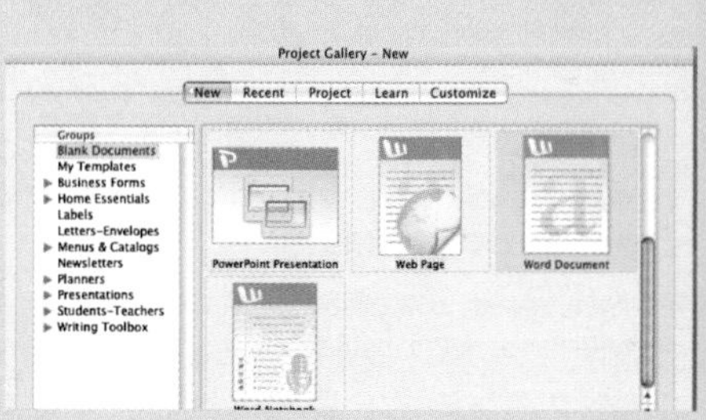

2. **Type and Format Your Work** Review how to do basic tasks, such as change a font, highlight words in color, and make type bold or underlined.
3. **Save and Share Your Work** Continually click the Save icon on the toolbar to ensure your work is not lost by computer error. Once you have a finished document, talk to your teacher about printing or using e-mail options.

Multimedia Presentation

Ⓑ

A **multimedia presentation** allows your audience to read, see, and hear your work. You may choose to include visuals, videos, photographs, or audio recordings in your presentation to make the information more interesting for your audience. Be sure to carefully plan and practice your presentation. This will help you avoid errors during your presentation.

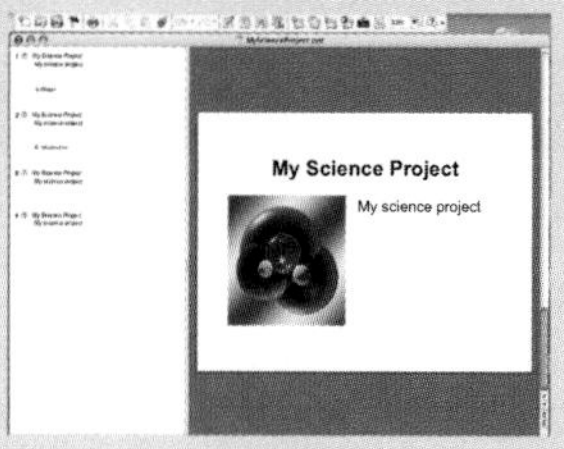

CCSS Literacy.SL.9-10.5 Make strategic use of digital media (e.g., textual, graphical, audio, visual, and interactive elements) in presentations to enhance understanding of findings, reasoning, and evidence and to add interest.

What Is Research?

Research is collecting information about a specific subject. When you research, you are trying to find the answer to a question.

How to Use the Research Process

When you research, you search for information about a specific topic. You can use the information you find to write a story, an article, or a research report.

Choose and Narrow Your Topic

The best way to choose your research topic is to think of something you want to learn more about and that interests you. Make sure your teacher approves your topic. Pick a topic that is not too general. A specific topic is easier to research and write about. It also is more interesting to read about in a report.

Discover What Is Known and What Needs to Be Learned

Get to know your topic. Are there recent articles or reports in the news that relate to your topic? What are researchers and scientists currently working on that relates to the topic?

Formulate Research Questions

What do you know about your topic? What do you want to learn? Write down some questions about your topic that you want to find the answers to. Look at the most important words in your questions, or the key words. These are the words that will be the focus of your research.

Is there life on Mars?
Is water or oxygen found on Mars?
Can life forms live on the surface of Mars?
What have space missions to Mars discovered about possible life there?

Narrowing the Topic

A Outer Space: This is a very large topic. There are too many things to research in outer space, such as planets, stars, and meteors. There is too much information to cover in one report.

↓

B Planets: This topic is better, but it is still too large. There are many planets in our solar system. It is best to pick a specific planet, and decide on one thing you want to learn about that planet.

↓

C Life on Mars: This topic is more specific than researching the entire planet of Mars. The research can focus just on whether or not plants and animals exist on Mars, or if they ever existed there in the past.

A Narrow Your Topic

Practice Read aloud the information about narrowing a topic. Brainstorm with students narrowing this topic: Painting. Have students use a diagram like the one in the student book.
W.9-10.7

B Get to Know the Topic

Reinforce Explain to students that getting an overview of their topic can help them decide what they want to know about their topic. Use the topic you brainstormed as you model.

MODEL Say:

- *A good overview has two parts. First, I will start by locating general background information about the topic. Textbooks, nonfiction books, and encyclopedias are good sources.*
- *Next, I will look for current articles and information about the topic. A periodical database or an Internet search engine will help me find sources of up-to-date information.*
- *Then, I will use a two-column chart to organize the information about what I know and what I need to learn. I will underline information that I might want to research further.*

Suggest that students record the bibliographic information of sources they might want to look at more closely when they begin their formal research.

C Formulate Research Questions

Expand Tell students that they may find it helpful to organize their research questions in a KWL chart. Elicit from students information about the topic you brainstormed and add it to the chart.

CCSS Literacy.W.9-10.7 Conduct short as well as more sustained research projects to answer a question (including a self-generated question) or solve a problem; narrow or broaden the inquiry when appropriate; synthesize multiple sources on the subject, demonstrating understanding of the subject under investigation.

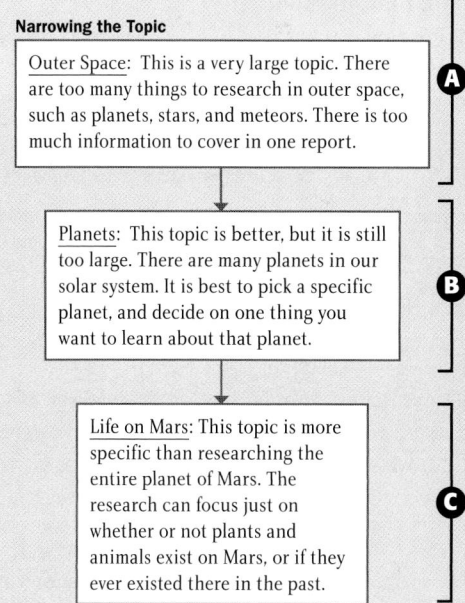

Ⓐ Choose Appropriate Resources

Expand Ask students to give examples that would fit in each category. Explain that in each of these categories, they will find a variety of resources with a variety of purposes. Review the distinction between objective and subjective sources—particularly Internet sources.

Ⓑ Take Notes and Avoid Plagiarism

Reinforce Refer to the sample notecard as you point out the research question, the title and page number of the source, and the details and facts related to the topic. Explain to students that when they take notes, they should record only information that is directly related to their topic. Explain to students that it is ethically wrong to copy another person's work and, in most cases, is illegal. Define the following regarding mass media and digital resources: libel, slander, copyright, plagiarism. Encourage students to research the consequences of not following state and federal laws.

Demonstrate paraphrasing by displaying this sentence: *In 1998, NASA launched two missions to Mars.*

MODEL Say:

- *To paraphrase this text, I will replace key words with synonyms and rearrange the order of the words in the sentence.*
- *I'll replace the word* launched *with* sent. *Then I'll move the prepositional phrase* In 1998 *to the end of the sentence. Now the sentence reads "NASA sent two missions to Mars in 1998."*
- *Even though I have put the text in my own words, I still need to make sure I credit the source of this fact in order to avoid plagiarism and copyright infringement.*

Practice Display new sentences: In 2012, NASA landed a new rover on Mars. It was named *Curiosity*. Have each student practice paraphrasing the sentence. Invite individuals to read their paraphrased sentence to a partner.
W.9-10.8

Choose Appropriate Resources to Support Your Topic

Ⓐ Resources can be people you interview, such as experts or teachers. Textbooks, magazines, newspapers, videos, photographs, and the Internet are also resources. The four main types of resources are:

- print
- electronic
- audio visual
- graphic aids

Create a rubric to rate the reliability of your sources. Rate each source on a scale of 1 to 4; 4 is the most reliable, 1 is the least reliable. If you are unsure of the reliability of your sources, ask your teacher, your parents, or a partner.

Gather Information

You may need to survey, skim, or scan a variety of sources to pick the best ones. Use the research questions you formulated to guide your reading.

To Skim Read the title to see if the article is useful for your topic. Read the beginning sentences of the main paragraphs, or any subheads. See if the article may give details about your topic. Read the last paragraph. At the end, there is usually a conclusion that will summarize the main points of the article.

To Scan Look for key words or details. They may be underlined or in bold type. This will tell you if the article will discuss your topic.

Take Notes

Ⓑ As you read, take notes. You will gather the specific information you need from each source. For each resource:

1. Include the key words or important phrases about your topic.
2. Write down the source to record where you found the facts.
   - For a book, list the title, author, page number, publisher, and year of publication.
   - For a magazine or newspaper article, list the name, date, volume, and issue number of the source. Also list the title of the article and the author.
   - For an Internet site, list the Web address, the name of the site, the author (if there is one listed), and the date of the latest site update.
3. List the details and facts that are important to your topic. Be certain to summarize or paraphrase the information in your own words. If you use exact words from a source, you must put the words in quotation marks and note the page you copied it from. If you exactly copy someone else's words, you will be plagiarizing. **Plagiarism** is illegal and can be punished by law.

Notecard for a book

Is there life on Mars?
Mars by Seymour Simon, page 27
–Viking spacecraft supposed to find out if there's life
–Some think experiments showed there isn't

CCSS Literacy.W.9-10.8 Gather relevant information from multiple authoritative print and digital sources, using advanced searches effectively; assess the usefulness of each source in answering the research question; integrate information into the text selectively to maintain the flow of ideas, avoiding plagiarism and following a standard format for citation.

LANGUAGE AND LEARNING HANDBOOK

Organize Information from Multiple Sources

After you have taken notes from several sources, **organize** them to see what information is the most important. See how the information from different sources is related.

One of the best ways to organize your information is to use a graphic organizer called an outline. You can also organize your information by using technology. For example, you could type up your notes and save them in a word processing document. It also allows you to choose which data (like dates or times), facts, or ideas are the most relevant.

Analyze, Evaluate, and Use Information

Review your rubric that showed which sources were the most reliable. After you check the reliability, usefulness, relevance, and accuracy of the information, **analyze** and **evaluate** the information. All resources are either primary or secondary sources. A **primary source** is an account of an event by someone who was actually there. A primary source might be a journal, letter, or photograph. A **secondary source** is an account of an event by someone who was not present at the event but that describes the event for other people. A secondary source could be a textbook or an article.

Primary Sources	Secondary Sources
• a soldier's journal	• a book about World War I
• a photograph of a volcano erupting	• a documentary that tells the story of the day a volcano erupted

Synthesize Information from Multiple Sources

Convert your data into graphic aids. Make an outline to **synthesize**, or organize and summarize, your research findings and draw conclusions. Doing this will allow you to identify complexities and discrepancies. You can also use your outline and notes to organize your Works Cited page at the end of your paper. Include the author, title, and page number or Web address.

How to Make an Outline:

1. Put all your notes that have the same keywords or phrases together.
2. Make the first question from your notes into a main idea statement. This will be Roman numeral I.
3. Each of your key research questions will be a Roman numeral heading.
4. Find details that explain each main idea statement. Each important detail about that idea should go below it, and be listed with capital letters.
5. More specific details can be listed with numbers under each capital letter detail.
6. Give your outline a title. This title should state the overall or main idea. It may be a good title to use for your report.

Sample Outline

The Mystery of Life on Mars
I. Life on Mars
  A. How Mars is like Earth
    1. Volcanoes
    2. Giant canyons
  B. Fact-finding missions
    1. Viking
    2. Pathfinder
II. Signs of life on Mars
  A. Studied by David McKay's team
  B. Meteorite
    1. Might contain bacteria fossils
    2. Found in Antarctica
    3. Probably from Mars
III. Continued search for life on Mars
  A. Look underground
  B. More study
    1. Mission planned for future
    2. Gases in atmosphere
    3. What rocks are made of.

Ⓐ Analyze and Evaluate Information

Expand Tell students that primary sources are most useful for original research. For example, letters and interviews are primary sources that might be useful in a research project about the history of a community. To report on a topic such as how volcanoes erupt, secondary sources, such as encyclopedias and textbooks, are good sources of information. Remind students to cite all sources.

Support Your Thesis Statement Remind students that all of the evidence they assemble from their sources should be in support of a clear thesis statement. Reiterate the difference between objective and subjective information.

Ⓑ Outline

Reinforce Model the outline in the student book.

MODEL Say:

- *Before I begin my outline, I group related ideas together. Then I arrange the groups in the order in which I want to write about them.*
- *Then I need to turn my research questions into main idea statements. "How is Mars like Earth?" can be restated as "How Mars is like Earth." I use a Roman numeral followed by a period for each main topic.*
- *Under each main idea, I use a capital letter and a period for each subtopic. Subtopics are the most important details I plan to discuss about each main idea.*
- *Under each detail, I list more specific ideas I plan to discuss. I keep these short. I will expand them when I write the report.*
- *Finally, I look at what all my subtopics have in common and write a title that best summarizes the topic, or focus, of my report.*

ELL Explain to students that in many English-speaking countries, Roman numerals are commonly used in outlines, the beginnings of books, clock faces, movie or video game sequels, and to identify successive political leaders. Ask students to share any special ways that Roman numerals are used in their home countries.

A Write the Introduction

Expand Have students read the introduction. Explain that a good introduction serves two purposes: it captures the reader's attention and tells the reader what the report will be about. Point to each feature as you say:

- Begin with a title that tells what your report will be about.
- Next, write a sentence or two that grabs the reader's attention. Ask a thought-provoking question or state an interesting fact. In this sample, the writer is asking the readers to think about how they feel about life on other planets.
- Finally, write a topic sentence that tells what your report will be about.

B Write the Body

Expand Share the following suggestions for writing from an outline:

- Follow the outline, but feel free to make changes if you find the order of ideas isn't working. Make sure that you include all of the details under a main idea in the paragraph.
- Begin a new paragraph for each section of your outline.
- Remember to add transition words and details to show the connections among ideas.

> **ELL** **Elaborate** Provide students with support in writing sentences by providing simple sentence frames such as: *Mars is like Earth because* ______. Then explain that they can write this sentence in another way by replacing the word *like* with the words *similar to*.

C Write a Conclusion

Expand Tell students that they can use their introduction and their outline as a guide for writing their conclusion. Provide additional samples of ways to end reports that will keep readers thinking.

Design and Write a Research Report

Before you write, ask your teacher to show you which style guide to use. Follow the style guide to learn the proper formatting of the paper. It will also show you how to format your sources into a works cited page. Use the following techniques to complete your research paper.

Write the Title and Introduction

Copy the **title** from your outline. You can make it more interesting if you want. Make sure it gives the main idea of your topic. Next you should write an interesting **introduction** that will explain what the rest of your report will be about. Write an introduction that will get your readers' attention.

A

Outline

The Mystery of Life on Mars

Title and Introduction

The Mystery of Life on Mars

Perhaps you have heard stories about life on other planets. Or perhaps, you may have only thought about life here on Earth. I am going to explore the research on the planet Mars and discuss with you the studies that have been done to see if there is life on "the red planet."

Write the Body

The body is the main portion of your report. Use your main ideas to write topic sentences for each paragraph. Then use your research details to write sentences about each topic.

B

Outline

I. Life on Mars
  A. How Mars is like Earth
    1. Volcanoes
    2. Giant canyons

Topic Sentence and Detail

People have always wondered if there is life on other planets, especially Mars. Because Mars is similar to Earth with features like volcanoes and giant canyons, it seems possible that there is life on Mars.

Write the Conclusion

C

Write about the main ideas of your report in the **conclusion**. This will summarize your report. You can also include an interesting fact or opinion to end your report. This will keep your audience thinking after they have finished reading. For example, "I believe that with all the research still being done on Mars, perhaps in the near future, we will learn more about life on that mysterious planet."

Design Your Report: Graphic and Multimedia Aids

After you write your report, you should consider its **design**, or how it will look on a printed page. This includes choosing the font of the text and deciding whether you will use **graphic aids** to make the information in your report easier to understand or more interesting. Do you want to include illustrations or photographs? Does your audience need a time line or diagram to understand the text better? Is there a video or audio file that might support your ideas? Choose visuals or media that will make your presentation more effective.

Integrate Quotations and Citations

Adding **quotations** and including **citations** are important ways of sharing the information you find during your research. Any words that are not your own must be in quotation marks and the source must be given in the running text in order to avoid plagiarism. If you use an idea that is not your own, even if you paraphrase it in your own words, you must **cite** the source for that information.

To cite a source means to list the information of your source. This helps you to properly note where you found your information. Citing allows other readers to look at the source, too. Use the citation style your teacher tells you to use. Two commonly used citation styles were developed by the Modern Language Association (MLA) and the American Psychological Association (APA). Both of these associations publish style manuals that can help you write research papers. They are available at www.mla.org and www.apastyle.org. **A**

A common way to cite is to use the MLA style for author and page citation. List the author and the page number of your source right after you use the words or idea of that author. The author's name should be either in the sentence itself or in parentheses following the quotation or paraphrase. The page number(s) should always appear in parentheses, not in the text of your sentence. For example:

> The writer T. S. Eliot has said that poetry expresses an "overflow of powerful feelings" (263).

> Poetry expresses an "overflow of powerful feelings" (Eliot 263).

At the end of your report create a separate **"Works Cited"** page. **B**

> Works Cited
>
> Ackroyd, Peter. *T. S. Eliot: A Life.* London: Simon and Schuster, 1985.
>
> Vendler, Helen. "T. S. Eliot." *Time* 8 June 1998. 70–72.
>
> "T. S. Eliot." *Microsoft Encarta Online Encyclopedia.* 2006.
> <http://encarta.msn.com>

A Integrate Quotations and Citations

Expand Tell students that they must take care to accurately credit the sources they use. Explain to students which type of citation style you want them to use for papers in your classroom. Remind students to ask their other teachers which style they prefer since it might be different for different classrooms. Have students create at least one illustration or visual that will help readers better understand the information in their report.

B MLA and Works Cited

Reinforce Point out the two examples of citations. Say:

- In the first citation, Eliot's name is mentioned in the sentence, so it does not appear in the end citation. Eliot's exact words are enclosed in quotations.
- In the second citation, Eliot's name is not mentioned in the sentence, so it is included in the end citation.
- Be sure to accurately quote a text or a person, and make sure that someone double-checking the reference will find the quote on the page you cited.

Then share the Works Cited example. Say:

- Works cited are listed in alphabetical order by the author's last name. If no author is given, alphabetize by title.
- To cite a book, list the author, last name first. Then give the title. The city where the book was published comes next, followed by a colon and the name of the publisher. The year the book was published comes last.

Follow a similar procedure to point out the features of the magazine and electronic source citations. Point out that if a Web site has no author or organization associated with it, it is probably not a reliable source and should not be used as a reference.

Practice Have students create a set of citation note cards, one for a book, one for a periodical, and one for an electronic source. Encourage them to refer to these cards to create Works Cited pages.
L.9-10.3.a

CCSS Literacy.L.9-10.3.a Write and edit work so that it conforms to the guidelines in a style manual (e.g., *MLA Handbook*, Turabian's *Manual for Writers*) appropriate for the discipline and writing type.

Ⓐ Evaluate and Draw Conclusions

Expand Read aloud the bulleted checklist with students. Revisit each section of the report in the student book and decide together if it meets the listed criteria. Emphasize to students that they should revise any weak sections of their report before publishing it or presenting it. Ask: How might you revise an introduction that does not clearly state the main idea of the report? (*Add a topic sentence.*)

Encourage students to use rubrics to evaluate their writing. For rubric examples, have them see the **Writing Handbook**, page 707.

> **ELL** **Elaborate** Tell students that they might find it helpful to read aloud their writing to a partner or teacher. As they come to a section of their report that needs revision, students and their partners can work together to make the necessary corrections. Encourage students to build fluency by reading the revised text aloud.

Ⓑ Questions for Further Study

Expand Suggest that students keep a notebook with their ideas for future research.

Evaluate Your Research Report and Draw Conclusions

After you complete your research report, you should **evaluate** it, or check its quality. Ask questions about how well you did each step of the report. Look at the paper overall. Does it accomplish what you want it to do? Do you have to do more research or adjust your main idea to achieve the goal of your paper? This will help you to decide if the end product is presented correctly.

Checklist to Evaluate Ⓐ

- ☑ The title tells what the report is about.
- ☑ The introduction is interesting, gets the attention of the reader, and gives the main idea of the report.
- ☑ The body gives the facts you found.
- ☑ Each paragraph covers a specific topic from your outline.
- ☑ Each topic in the body paragraphs is connected to the main idea.
- ☑ Other sentences give specific details about the topic.
- ☑ The conclusion is a summary of the most important information on your topic.
- ☑ The conclusion is interesting for the reader.
- ☑ The paper is formatted according to the style guide used.
- ☑ All sources are properly formatted per the style guide used.

Share Your Report Ⓑ

Publish your report. You can choose different media for publishing. You can print the final report in paper, put it online, create a poster or display of your final paper, or attach it to an email and send it to trusted friends or adults. Be sure to check your school's Acceptable Use Policy before posting your work.

Questions for Further Study

Now that you have finished the report, you may have questions based on the conclusions you drew. You can consider these questions as other research ideas for the future.

During Your Research

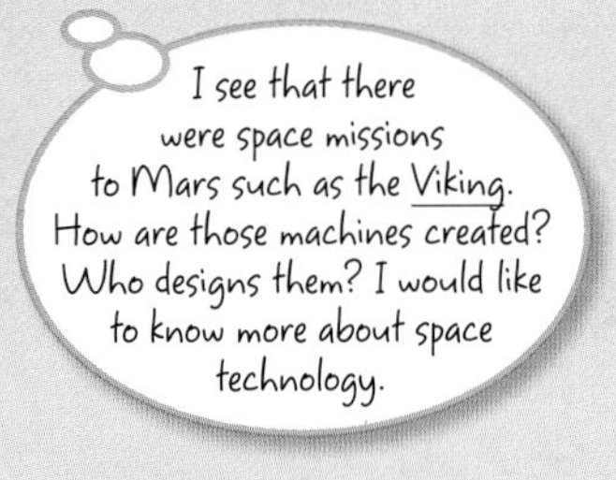
I see that there were space missions to Mars such as the Viking. How are those machines created? Who designs them? I would like to know more about space technology.

Now

Maybe my next research report will be about space technology. I could study who designs the machines that go into space and how they work.

What Are Test-Taking Strategies?

Test-taking strategies are skills to help you effectively complete a test. These strategies will help you to show what you know on a test without making mistakes.

What to Do Before a Test

Use the following strategies to help you prepare for a test.

- Find out if the test will be multiple-choice, short answers, or essay. Noting the format will allow you to select an appropriate strategy.
- Ask your teacher for practice tests or examples to try before the test day.
- Carefully study the material that will be on the test.
- Make sure you get a good night of rest before a test. This will help you focus.
- Eat a nutritious meal before the test. This will give you energy to get through the test.

(A)

What to Do During a Test

Use the following strategies as you complete the test.

Relax: Relax and think carefully during the test. If you feel stressed, take a few deep breaths. Remind yourself that you are prepared.

Plan Your Time: Survey the test to estimate difficulty and plan time. See what questions you can answer easily. Do not work on one question for too long because you might not have enough time to finish the test if you only focus on one question.

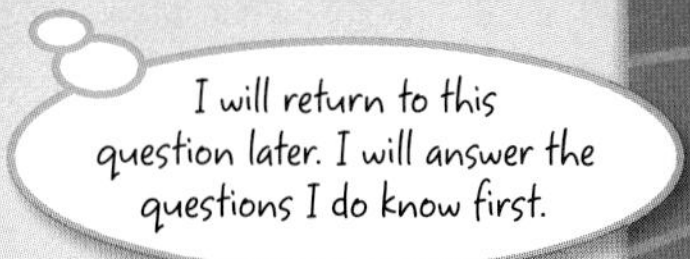

Read: Read the directions for each section of the test. Then, read each question carefully. Underline key words in the directions and questions to focus on the most important information. Be certain that you are doing what the question asks. For example, if a question says to "describe," give more than a definition. You may need to give specific details.

(B)

Clarify: Tests ask logical questions. If something seems strange, reread the directions, question, or passage to clarify information. Think about words carefully to be certain you understand their meaning. Use typographic and visual clues to find meaning.

Mark Answers: Carefully mark your answers on the test and check for legibility. This can affect your test grade! Be sure to use the correct writing utensil. For example, some multiple choice tests require the use of a #2 pencil.

Check Completeness: Check to make sure all questions are answered (if there is no penalty for guessing). Always reread your answers or answer choices, if you have time. Finish any questions you may not have finished before.

You think:

> This question is difficult. I cannot answer this right now.

Then you decide:

> I will return to this question later. I will answer the questions I do know first.

Language and Learning Handbook **731**

LANGUAGE AND LEARNING HANDBOOK

(A) What to Do Before a Test

Expand Read aloud the bulleted suggestions with students. Then ask them which of these strategies they already use and which they would like to try. Invite volunteers to add strategies to the list.

(B) What to Do During a Test

Reinforce Tell students they should read directions carefully and underline key words and phrases. Write these directions: Choose the word that means the same thing as the underlined word. Then mark the space for the answer you have chosen.

> **MODEL** Say:
> - *The first words I underline are choose the word because they tell me what I need to do. Then I underline means the same thing because this tells me what kind of word I'm looking for. Next I underline underlined word because this is the word I need to focus on. Finally, I underline mark the space because this is what I need to do once I've made my choice.*
> - *For other types of questions, I will pay attention to underlined words, italic words, words on their own line, and words in boxes. Focusing on these important words can help me answer questions quickly and correctly.*

Practice Write these directions: Read the sentence. There may be a mistake in punctuation, capitalization, or word usage. If you find a mistake, choose the answer that is the best way to rewrite it. If there is no mistake, choose "Correct as is." Guide students to underline important words and then restate what the directions are asking them to do.

A Narrow Choices and Rephrase Questions

Expand Tell students that to narrow the answer choices, they should first eliminate obviously incorrect answers. Explain the following:

- Obviously incorrect answers are often not mentioned in the passage, may include generalizations such as *everyone*, *always*, and *never*, or are grammatically different from the other choices.
- To choose the correct answer, make sure the answer you are considering completely addresses the question.
- It is sometimes helpful to restate a question and try to answer it before looking at the answer choices. Write this example: Something that is significant is ______. A. minor B. useless C. important D. confusing.

MODEL Say:

- *This question is asking for the meaning of* significant. *I know* significant *means "special."*
- *Now I'll look for* special *or a similar word in the answer choices. Answer choice C gives a word similar to* special, *so that is the answer I will choose.*

Practice Have students restate and answer this question: The root word of energized is ______. A. energy B. general C. gize D. nerve

B Tips for Essay Tests

Expand Tell students that they should first read the question, underline key words, and then determine their purpose and audience for writing. Next, they should budget the amount of time they plan to spend on each part of the writing process. Typically, most time should be spent drafting and revising. Remind them to be sure to address each part of the question in their answer. Finally, remind them to stay on topic. Explain that they must answer the question they were asked.

Tips for Objective Tests

Use the following strategies to help you complete objective tests.

Easy First: Answer the easy questions first. Leave the most difficult ones for last.

A

Narrow the Choices: If you are uncertain of an answer, determine which choices are definitely not correct. Choose the two that are closest to correct. This will narrow your number of answers to choose from to only two.

Rephrase Questions and Answer Them Mentally: Try to put the question in your own words and think about how you will answer. Then, look at the answer choices to see which one matches your own answer the best.

Make Changes If Needed: Ask yourself if you answered each question correctly. Check your work by reading through the test a second time. Change your answer only if the question was initially misunderstood.

Shuttle Among the Passage, the Question, the Choices: Read the passage, the questions, and the choices until you fully understand what is being asked.

Tips for Essay Tests

B

Use the following strategies to help you complete essay tests.

Outline: Make an outline of your answer before you write. This way, you can make sure you discuss all the important points of your essay.

Plan: Plan the time for your essay. Know how long you have to write your essay. Mark on your outline how long you plan to spend writing each section of your essay.

Write: Only include information in your essay that you know is accurate and is about your topic. If you are uncertain if it is factual or important, do not include it. Use a topic sentence and supporting details for each paragraph.

Proofread: Carefully proofread your writing. Check for grammar, punctuation, and capitalization. Most importantly, make sure all parts of your essay can be read clearly.

Tips for Online Tests

Use the following strategies to help you complete tests on a computer.

- Find out how the test is designed—Can you go back to questions you have already answered? Can you change your answers? Is there a time limit? Is there a glossary? Audio? Some tests will show you this information on the introduction screen. You can also ask your teacher.
- Find out if this is an adaptive test. When you take adaptive tests, the questions get harder or easier based on whether you are getting answers correct or incorrect. So when you take an adaptive test, take your time and be careful as you answer the first several questions.
- Have a pencil and paper in addition to your computer test. Use your paper to jot down an idea or organize your thoughts with a graphic organizer.

Reading Strategies

Reading Fluency

Study Skills and Strategies

Vocabulary

READING HANDBOOK

The **Reading Handbook** guides students in all aspects of reading and vocabulary comprehension:

- **Reading Strategies** Students learn reading strategies and their purposes, along with detailed explanations of how to apply the seven reading strategies presented in this program.
- **Reading Fluency** Students learn how to improve reading fluency through accuracy and rate, intonation, phrasing, and expression. Excerpts for student practice are included in this section.
- **Study Skills and Strategies** Students learn skills and strategies to help them develop efficient and productive study habits.
- **Vocabulary** Students learn routines and skills that can help them improve and expand their vocabulary.

A Basic Reading Strategy

Expand Explain to students that they must recognize the directionality of English reading before tackling any of the more advanced prereading and reading strategies. Review the left-to-right directionality of English and point out that when readers get to the end of a line of text, they move down to the next line to continue.

B Preview

Reinforce Use a magazine article that includes photographs and captions to model how to use visual information when previewing a selection.

MODEL Say:

- *When I preview, I ask myself, "What is this article about?" I look for photographs and captions to help me answer that question.*
- *The photographs in this article show details about the subject of the text. I can use them to help me decide what the article is about.*
- *Many of the photographs have captions. The captions describe the photographs, and they also give me clues about what is in the article.*
- *I also look for nonfiction text features, like headings, subheadings, or transitional devices.*
- *When I'm reading fiction, I look for chapter titles or section titles to tell me more about the text.*

Make a prediction about the content of the article based on your preview.

ELL **Elaborate** Using a photograph from a magazine article, ask questions to help students make a prediction. For example: Is this article about the desert or the forest? Do you get clues from viewing the cactus or the sky? Remind students to look for specific parts of photographs or artwork, such as people's expressions, unusual focal points, or minute details, for more clues.

Reading Strategies

What Are Reading Strategies?

A

Reading strategies are hints or techniques you can use to help you become a better reader. They help you interact with the text and take control of your own reading comprehension. Reading strategies can be used before, during, and after you read.

Plan and Monitor

Before you read, plan how to approach the selection by using prereading strategies. **Preview** the selection to see what it is about and try to make a prediction about its content. Keep in mind that English is read from left to right, and that text moves from the top of the page to the bottom. **Set a purpose** for reading, or decide why you will read the selection. You might want or need to adjust your purpose for reading as you read. Monitor your reading to check how well you understand and remember what you read.

How to Select and Use Prereading Strategies	
Title:	Surfing the Pipeline
Author:	Christina Rodriguez
Preview the Text (B)	• Look at the title: Surfing the Pipeline. • Look at the organization of the text, including any chapter titles, heads, and subheads. • Look at any photos and captions. • Think about what the selection is about.
Activate Prior Knowledge	• I know many people surf in the ocean on surfboards. • I've seen a film about people trying to surf on huge waves in California.
Ask Questions	• What is the pipeline? • Where is the pipeline? • Who surfs the pipeline? • Why do people try to surf the pipeline?
Set a Purpose for Reading	• I want to read to find out how people surf the pipeline.

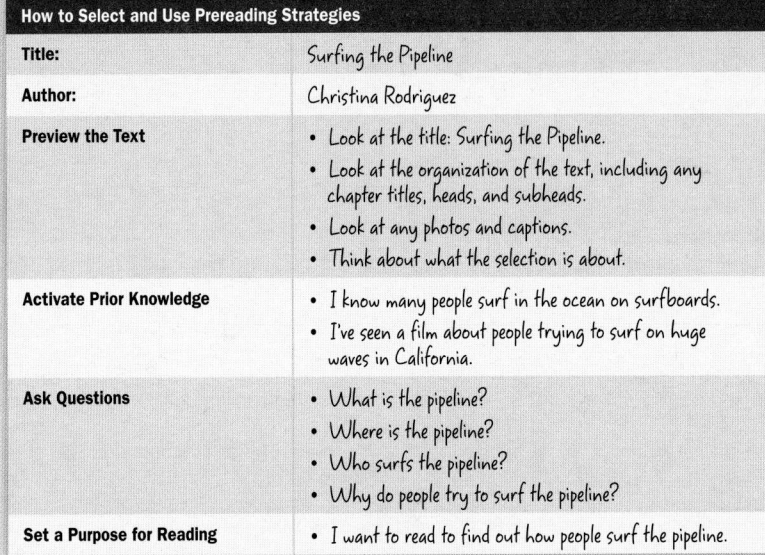

READING HANDBOOK

How to Make and Confirm Predictions

Making **predictions** about a selection will help you understand and remember what you read. As you preview a selection, **ask questions** and think about any **prior knowledge** you have about the subject. If you do not learn enough additional information from these steps, read the first few paragraphs of the selection.

Think about the events taking place, and then predict what will happen next. If you are reading fiction or drama, you can use what you know about common plot patterns to help you predict what may happen in the story. After you read each section, confirm your predictions, or see if they were correct. Sometimes you will need to revise your predictions for the next section based on what you read.

Preview to Anticipate Read the title. Think about what the selection will be about as you read the first few paragraphs. Look for clues about the selection's content.

Make and Confirm Predictions As you read, predict what will happen next in the selection based on text evidence or personal experience. Take notes while you are reading, and use a **Prediction Chart** to record your ideas. As you continue to read the selection, confirm your predictions. If a prediction is incorrect, revise it.

Surfing the Pipeline

There Uli was, standing on the white, sandy shores of Oahu, Hawaii. Right in front of her was the famous Banzai Pipeline—one of the most difficult and dangerous places to surf in the world. Uli looked out and saw twelve-foot waves crashing toward her.

Uli had been waiting for this day for a long time. She was ready.

Uli grabbed her surfboard and entered the water. The waves were fierce and strong that morning. It took all of Uli's energy to swim out to the surfing location. Uli could see rocks sticking up through the water. She finally found the perfect starting point and waited anxiously to begin surfing.

Prediction Chart

Prediction	Did It Happen?	Evidence
Uli is going to surf at the Banzai Pipeline.	Not yet, but she will soon.	She is at the starting point to begin surfing. (text evidence)
Surfing the Banzai Pipeline will be hard for Uli.	Not yet, but it will soon.	New activities are always hard when I try them for the first time. (personal experience)

Make and Confirm Predictions

Practice Present a nonfiction text that includes photographs, captions, and heads. Preview the text with students by displaying the visuals and reading aloud the title, captions, and heads. Ask:

- What do the photographs show you?
- What clues about the subject of the text can you get from the title and the heads?
- What do you learn from the captions?
- What do you think this text will be about?

Read aloud the first few paragraphs of the text. Have students use information from the preview, along with their own knowledge, to make a prediction about the content of the text. Record predictions on a prediction chart. Then read the entire text aloud. Have students confirm their predictions and revise them as needed.

ELL Rephrase Language Explain that a prediction is a good guess about something that will happen. To help students solidify the concept, have them predict what the weather will be like after school based on what the weather is like now, as well as a general knowledge of what after-school weather is like at this time of year.
RL.9-10.10

Extend Discuss common and archetypal plots, such as rags to riches, coming of age, quest, search for self, romance, and tragedy. Ask students to think of examples of each archetype. Explain to students that you can use these patterns to predict what may happen in films, television shows, novels, short stories, and plays.

CCSS Literacy.RL.9-10.10 By the end of grade 10, read and comprehend literature, including stories, dramas, and poems, at the high end of the grades 9–10 text complexity band independently and proficiently.

A Clarify Vocabulary

Expand Explain that students can use visual and contextual resources other than a dictionary or a thesaurus to clarify words and terms in a text. Point out the name *Oahu, Hawaii,* in "Surfing the Pipeline" on p. 735. Ask: What reference resources would give you information about Oahu? If needed, offer suggestions, such as maps, an atlas, an encyclopedia or the Internet. Have students find Oahu in one or more of the resources. Discuss how background knowledge of the location can help students better understand the text.

B Adjust Your Reading Rate

Practice Review with students the rules of English directionality. Offer the following examples and have students tell how and why they would adjust their reading rate for each:

- You are reading an entertaining story. The author includes a conversation with many difficult words.
- You are reading an adventure story that is not too difficult. The action gets more and more exciting.
- You are enjoying a nonfiction article. The author includes a paragraph with a lot of scientific information.

C Adjust Your Purpose for Reading

Reinforce Provide students with purposes for reading to help them with setting and adjusting a purpose: to be entertained, to learn something new, to visualize an experience, to compare to another text, etc.

How to Monitor Your Reading

When you **monitor your reading**, you are checking to make sure you understand the information you read. You can check your understanding by keeping track of your thinking while reading. Pause while reading to think about images you may be creating in your mind, connections you are making between words or topics within the text, or problems you are having with understanding the text. When you read something that doesn't make sense to you, use these monitoring strategies to help you.

Strategy	How to Use It	Example Text
Reread to Clarify Ideas	Reread silently the passage you do not understand. Then reread the passage aloud. Continue rereading until you feel more confident about your understanding of the passage.	I will silently reread the first paragraph. Then I will read it aloud. The paragraph is more understandable now.
Use Resources to Clarify Vocabulary (A)	Look up confusing words in a dictionary or thesaurus, or ask a classmate for help.	"... dangerous places to surf ..." I'm not sure what "surf" means. I'll look it up.
Read On and Use Context Clues to Clarify Ideas and Vocabulary	Read past the part of the text where you are confused. What does the rest of the information tell you? Are there nearby words or phrases, context clues or visuals that help you understand?	"... looked out and saw twelve-foot waves ..." Maybe "surf" means riding ocean waves.
Adjust Your Reading Rate (B)	Read slowly when something is confusing or difficult. Keep in mind that English is read from left to right and that text runs down the page from the top. If you are having a difficult time understanding what you're reading, first make sure that you're reading it in the right order.	"Right in front of her was the famous Banzai Pipeline ..." I've never heard of the Banzai Pipeline. I'll read slower to find out what it is.
Adjust Your Purpose for Reading (C)	Think of the purpose you set for reading before you started to read. Have you found a new purpose, or reason to read? If so, adjust your purpose and read on.	I originally wanted to read to find out how people surf the pipeline. Now I want to read to see if Uli actually does it.

How to Use Graphic Organizers

Before you read, you can use graphic organizers to prepare for better comprehension. For example, use a **KWL Chart** to record your prior knowledge about the topic.

KWL Chart

WHAT I KNOW	WHAT I WANT TO KNOW	WHAT I LEARNED

As you read, use a variety of graphic organizers such as diagrams and charts to help keep track of your thinking. Take notes about any ideas or vocabulary that confuse you. Writing down ideas keeps you actively involved in your reading. It also can help clear up any confusion you may have about information in a selection.

Use graphic organizers to capture your thoughts and to help you remember information based on how it was described in the text or based on the text structure. Here are some more examples of graphic organizers:

Sequence Chain

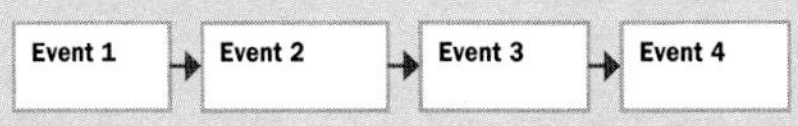

Cause and Effect

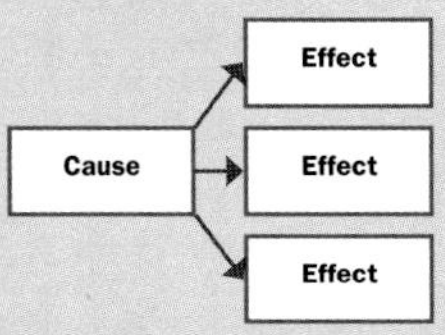

Problem and Solution

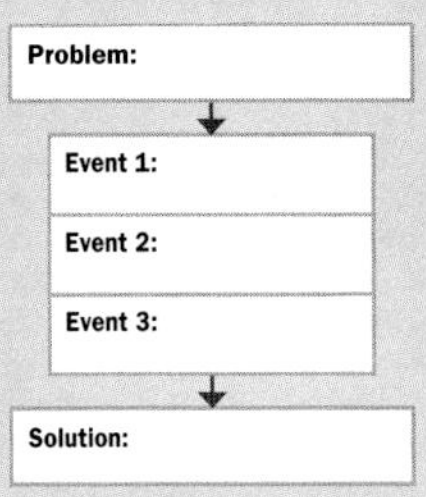

Main Idea

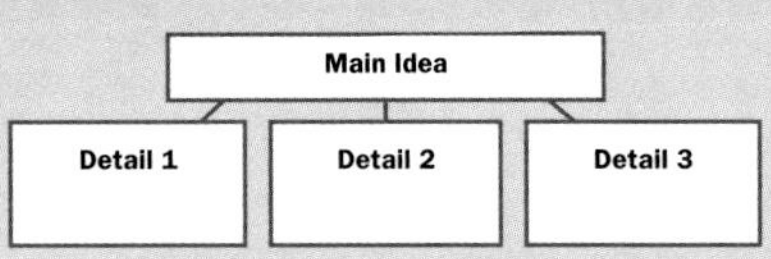

Definition Map

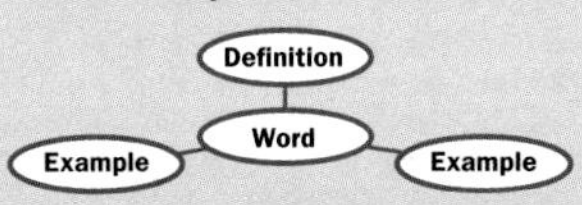

Time Line

For more graphic organizers, see the Index of Graphic Organizers on page 816.

Use Graphic Organizers

Expand Model how to create and interpret graphic organizers in conjunction with related texts. Have students help you fill in graphic organizers for texts that they have already read.

- **Nonfiction** Use a main idea chart to analyze and explain the structure and elements of one or more chapters in a nonfiction text.
- **Biography** Use a time line to record information about all or part of a subject's life.
- **Fiction** Use a problem-and-solution chart, sequence chain, or cause-and-effect chart to track events in all or part of a fiction story.
- **Other Texts** Use a sequence chain to record directions in a recipe or other how-to texts, or use a definition map to help define terms in an everyday text such as a job application, school form or a contract.

ELL **List Vocabulary** Before creating each graphic organizer, display a list of terms to be used, such as: *main idea, detail, problem, solution, event, sequence, cause, effect*. Explain or restate the terms, and have students create note cards for each that include the term, definition, and any synonyms that will enhance learning.

Summarize

Reinforce Model how to summarize "What's in a Name?" First read the entire passage aloud.

MODEL Say:

- *In order to summarize, I have to find the main idea and determine the importance of each detail. To do this, I will examine each sentence.*
- *The first sentence tells me the topic: sports team names.*
- *The next sentence doesn't seem to be the main idea. It is just a detail that supports the first statement.*
- *The next sentence seems important because it starts with "However." This shows me that a different idea is coming. "Should" indicates that the sentence is an opinion. I think this is the main idea: Team names should be unique.*
- *The rest of the sentences support the main idea. They give examples of unique names and make the claim that unique names make sports more interesting and fun.*
- *I can use the main idea and the important details to summarize: Team names should be unique because that makes them more interesting and fun.*

ELL Elaborate Show students a paragraph. Underline a sentence that reveals the topic. Ask: What is this paragraph about?

Underline an unimportant detail. Ask: Is this an important sentence? Why or why not? If students answer incorrectly, erase the sentence and ask: Can you still understand the paragraph without this sentence? Why?

Continue to examine each sentence, asking questions that help students determine which ones are important and which are not. Guide students to write a summary statement using the main idea and the important details.

Determine Importance

Determining importance is a reading strategy you can use to find the most important details or ideas in a selection. A good way to think about what is important in the selections you read is to **summarize**. When you summarize, you state the main idea and only the most important details in a selection, usually in a sentence or two. To summarize, identify the topic of a paragraph or selection, find the main idea and the most important details, and put them in your own words.

Stated Main Ideas

The main idea of a selection is the most important point a writer wants to relate to readers. Writers often state the main idea in a topic sentence near the beginning of a selection.

What's in a Name?

All college sports teams have special names. Many of these names are common, such as the Bears or the Tigers. However, more teams should have names that are unique and express the school's individuality. The University of Arkansas team names are Razorbacks and Lady Razorbacks. Virginia Tech athletes are called Hokies. Purdue has the Boilermakers. My favorite is the University of California at Santa Cruz's Banana Slugs and Lady Slugs. Slugs are unusual creatures. They have soft, slimy bodies and enjoy moist environments. These unique names make the college sports world a more interesting and fun place.

How to Identify Stated Main Ideas	
What is the paragraph about?	• names of college teams
Look for supporting details.	• Some teams have unique names like Razorbacks, Hokies, Boilermakers, and Lady Slugs. • The author feels these names make the college sports world more fun.
Eliminate unnecessary information or details.	• Slugs are slimy and enjoy moist environments.
Summarize the main idea.	• Unique sports team names are better and more fun than common names.

Implied Main Ideas

Sometimes a main idea is implied, or not directly stated. Readers have to figure out the main idea by studying all of the details in a selection.

The Future of Humankind

Many people agree that space exploration is important. However, when government spending is discussed, many people insist there are problems on Earth that need attention and money first. Don't they realize that the future of the human race depends on space exploration? Someday, the Earth's resources may run out. Paying for more exploration will allow us to learn more about space and how we can better care for our planet.

A

How to Identify Implied Main Ideas	
What is the paragraph about?	• space exploration
Find and list details.	• Many people feel other issues are more important than space exploration. • Our future depends on exploration.
What message is the author trying to convey?	• If we explore space now, we can better take care of ourselves and Earth.
Summarize the implied main idea.	• Space exploration should be paid for because it is just as important as any other issue. We could die without it.

Personal Relevance

An additional way to determine importance while reading a selection is to look for details that have personal relevance to you. These details may be important to you because they remind you of someone or something in your own life. For example, you might relate to "What's in a Name?" because you have a favorite sports team name. You might understand the main point that the writer is trying to make because you might agree that sports team names should be unique.

B

READING HANDBOOK

A Implied Main Idea

Practice Explain that an implied main idea is an idea that an author tries to convey, or give, to readers without writing it in words. An author does this by giving evidence, or details, that readers can use to figure out the main idea on their own. Ask: What is the author trying to persuade readers to think in "The Future of Humankind"?

Provide another persuasive text and have students use the questions in the chart to identify the main idea, as well as the evidence the author uses to support it.

ELL Use Visuals Show students an advertisement from a magazine. Prompt them to find the implied main idea by asking: How does this image make you feel about using or owning this product? What is the company *really* trying to tell you?
RI.9-10.1

B Personal Relevance

Reinforce Explain that students can find personal relevance in a text even if they don't know anything about the subject.

MODEL Say:

- *Even if I don't know anything about government spending, I can find personal relevance in "The Future of Humankind" because I am interested in how we can care for our planet.*

Practice Have students discuss stories they have read that they could personally relate to even though they were unfamiliar with the topic.

CCSS Literacy.RI.9-10.1 Cite strong and thorough textual evidence to support analysis of what the text says explicitly as well as inferences drawn from the text.

Make Connections

Reinforce Model questions that students can ask themselves when making text-to-self connections.

MODEL Say:

- *When I make text-to-self connections, I think about how the text reminds me of things in my own life.*
- *I ask questions such as: Have I ever done something like this? Have I ever felt this way? How are the people I am reading about like people I know?*
- *I use the answers to my questions to help me better understand what I am reading.*

Work with students to list questions they can ask when making text-to-text and text-to-world connections. For example:

- **Text to Text** What else have I read that reminds me of what I am reading now? How are the texts alike? What TV shows or movies remind me of what I am reading? How are people, places, and things the same or different?
- **Text to World** What is happening in the world right now that reminds me of this text? What do I know about other places or historical events that remind me of what I am reading?

ELL **Use a Graphic Organizer** Work with students through an example in the Make Connections Chart. Briefly summarize something the class has recently read. Encourage students to relate the text to their cultural backgrounds. Linking the text to their cultures will validate the English language learners' experiences and help them better relate to the topic.

Make Connections

Making connections is a reading strategy you can use to better understand or enjoy the information presented in a selection.

As you read, think about what the information reminds you of. Have you seen or heard something like this before? Have you read or experienced something like this? Thinking about what you already know helps you make a connection to the new information.

Type of Connection	Description	Example
Text to Self	A connection between the text you are reading and something that has happened in your own life. A text-to-self connection can also be a feeling, such as happiness or excitement, that you feel as you are reading.	This part of the story reminds me of the first time I drove a car. My dad showed me how to turn and stop. I remember how scared I was. Thinking about this memory helps me better understand how the character is feeling as he learns how to drive.
Text to Text	A connection between the text you are reading and another selection you have read, a film you have seen, or a song you have heard. Sometimes the text you are reading might have a similar theme, or message, to something you've read, seen, or heard before. A text may also belong to a genre, such as mystery or biography, that you are familiar with.	This part of the news article reminds me of a movie I saw about space. Astronauts were taking a trip to the moon, but their spaceship lost all power. I can think about the movie as I read about the most recent space shuttle mission.
Text to World	A connection between something you read in the text and something that is happening or has happened in the world. You might also make a connection with the time period or era that a selection takes place in, such as the Great Depression or the 1980s. The setting may also be familiar.	This part of the text reminds me of presidential elections. I remember candidates giving speeches to tell why they should be president. Thinking about this helps me understand why the characters in the selection give speeches.

Use a chart like the one below to help make and record text-to-self, text-to-text, or text-to-world connections as you read.

Make Connections Chart

The text says ...	This reminds me of ...	This helps me because ...

READING HANDBOOK

Make Inferences

Making inferences is a reading strategy in which you make educated guesses about the text's content based on experiences that you've had in everyday life or on facts or details that you read.

Sometimes people call making inferences "reading between the lines." This means looking at *how* the text was written along with what is being discussed. When you "read between the lines," you pay attention to the writer's tone, voice, use of punctuation, or emphasis on certain words. Writers can also use irony, dialogue, or descriptions to infer messages.

When you add your prior knowledge or personal experiences to what you are reading, you can make inferences by reading all the clues and making your best guesses.

How to Make Inferences Using Your Own Experience

Read the following paragraph and chart to learn how to make an inference using your own experiences.

The Waiting

Rain pounded against the windows as Sarah stomped up and down the stairs. She only stopped going up and down to check the time on the clock downstairs every five minutes. She had been dressed and ready to go for more than an hour! Sarah had spent weeks picking out her dress and shoes, and she had even paid $50 to have her hair styled. She threw the flower she had so excitedly bought yesterday in the corner beside the camera. Sarah wondered, "Where is he? Will I have to go alone tonight?"

Inferences Based on Your Own Experience

You read	Sarah had been dressed and ready to go somewhere for more than an hour. She spent a lot of time selecting her dress and shoes. She threw her flower in the corner by the camera.
You know	I know that people spend a lot of time choosing special outfits for events like dances, weddings, or parties. I know that my parents took a photo of me and my date for the prom last year. My date and I both had flowers for our outfits that night.
You infer	Sarah had a date to a special event that night. She was upset because she cared a lot about the event she was going to and didn't want to be late or go alone.

Make Inferences Using Experience

Reinforce Reread "The Waiting" and model an additional example of an inference that can be made using prior knowledge and experiences.

MODEL Say:

- *If I think about what I know and what I've experienced, I can make another inference about this paragraph. I know that even very considerate people are sometimes late for good reasons. I once waited an hour for a friend to pick me up for dinner. I thought she had forgotten me. It turned out that her dog was sick and she had to take it to an emergency veterinary clinic.*
- *Using my knowledge and experience, along with what the text tells me, I can infer that either Sarah's date is late for a good reason, or he is not a very considerate person.*
- *Sarah says, "Will I have to go alone tonight?" This sentence tells me Sarah is afraid of going to her event alone. I can infer that going alone will make Sarah sad or angry.*

Practice Invite students to discuss other inferences they can make about Sarah or her date based upon their own knowledge and experiences. Record the responses under the headings *You Know* and *You Infer.*
RL.9-10.1

CCSS Literacy.RL.9-10.1 Cite strong and thorough textual evidence to support analysis of what the text says explicitly as well as inferences drawn from the text.

Make Inferences Using Text Evidence

Practice Reread "The Waiting" aloud. Then write the following paragraph:

Suddenly the phone rang. Sarah ran to answer it. "Yes," she said. "Of course I understand! I'll have my dad drive me to the dance, and I'll meet you there. Try not to get too dirty changing the tire!"

Ask students to make an inference about events that have taken place based on evidence from the paragraph you added. Record responses under the headings *You Read* and *You Infer*.

ELL Sentence Frames Provide sentence frames to model language and support students in making inferences using text evidence:

- Sarah answered the phone and started talking to ______.
- The caller told Sarah that ______.
- Sarah said, "I'll meet you there" because ______.
- Sarah now feels ______ because ______.

RL.9-10.1

How to Make Inferences Using Text Evidence

Read the following paragraph and chart to learn how to make an inference by using clues that appear in the text.

The Waiting

Rain pounded against the windows as Sarah stomped up and down the stairs. She only stopped going up and down to check the time on the clock downstairs every five minutes. She had been dressed and ready to go for more than an hour! Sarah had spent weeks picking out her dress and shoes, and she had even paid $50 to have her hair styled. She threw the flower she had so excitedly bought yesterday in the corner beside the camera. Sarah wondered, "Where is he? Will I have to go alone tonight?"

Inferences Based on Text Evidence	
You read	Sarah had been dressed and ready to go somewhere for more than an hour. She spent a lot of time selecting her dress and shoes. She threw her flower in the corner by the camera.
You infer	Sarah had plans to go somewhere special that evening and was waiting for her date. She cared a lot about the event she was going to. Someone is late, and she is angry at him.

CCSS Literacy.RL.9-10.1 Cite strong and thorough textual evidence to support analysis of what the text says explicitly as well as inferences drawn from the text.

READING HANDBOOK

Ask Questions

You can **ask questions** to learn new information, to clarify, and to understand or figure out what is important in a selection. Asking questions of yourself and the author while reading can help you locate information you might otherwise miss.

How to Self-Question

Ask yourself questions to understand something that is confusing, keep track of what is happening, or think about what you know.

Ask and Write Questions Use a question word such as *Who, What, When, Where, Why,* or *How* to write your questions.

Examples: *How can I figure out what this word means? What are the characters doing? Why is this important? Do I agree with this?*

Answer the Questions and Follow Up Use the text, photographs, or other visuals to answer your questions. Write your answer next to the question. Include the page number where you found the answer.

A

How to Question the Author

Sometimes, you may have questions about what the author is trying to tell you in a selection. Write these types of questions, and then try to answer them by reading the text. The answers to these questions are known as "author and you" answers.

Questions to Ask the Author

- What is the author trying to say here?
- What is the author talking about?
- Does the author explain his or her ideas clearly?
- Does the author support his or her ideas or opinions with facts?

B

How to Find Question-Answer Relationships

Where you find the answers to your questions is very important. Sometimes the answers are located right in the text. Other times, your questions require you to use ideas and information that are not in the text. Some questions can be answered by using your background knowledge on a topic. Read the chart to learn about question-answer relationships.

Type of Answer	How to Find the Answers
"Right There"	Sometimes you can simply point to the text and say that an answer to one of your questions is "right there."
"Think and Search"	Look back at the selection. Find the information the question is asking about. Think about how the information fits together to answer the question.
"Author and You"	Use ideas and information that are not stated directly in the text. Think about what you have read, and create your own ideas or opinions based on what you know about the author.
"On Your Own"	Use your feelings, what you already know, and your own experiences to find these answers.

C

A Self-Question

Reinforce Model writing questions on a sheet of paper labeled *Questions and Answers.* As you read from a sample text, model how to use text, art, photos, and other visuals to find answers to your questions. Show students how to record answers and the page numbers on which they are found. Point out that doing this will help students keep track of information so that they can better understand what they read.

B Question the Author

Expand Review with students additional author-related questions:

- **Author's Purpose** Why did the author write this text: to entertain, to inform, or to persuade?
- **Author's Point of View** How does the author feel about this topic or situation? Is the author trying to convey a specific message?
- **Author's Bias** Does the author have personal feelings about a subject that is affecting his or her writing? Is the author using generalities or evidence?

C Question-Answer Relationships

Practice Provide a nonfiction text and have students record three or four questions and answers that are generated while reading. Have each student state their question, reading aloud portions of text as appropriate. Then have students state the answer to their question and describe how they determined the answer. Remind students to cite specific text evidence for Right There, Think and Search, and Author and You answers. RI.9-10.1

CCSS **Literacy.RI.9-10.1** Cite strong and thorough textual evidence to support analysis of what the text says explicitly as well as inferences drawn from the text.

Draw Conclusions

Reinforce Model how to draw conclusions about "Distracted Drivers." First, read aloud the paragraph.

MODEL Say:

- *To draw a conclusion, I first look for details in the paragraph. Here's a detail: "The more distracted drivers are, the more likely they are to be in an accident."*
- *Next, I think about what I know about the subject. I know from my own experience that some drivers who talk on cell phones have caused accidents.*
- *To draw a conclusion, I will combine what I learned with what I know to form a new understanding. I can conclude that talking on cell phones while driving is dangerous, and lawmakers should work on laws to stop drivers from being distracted.*

ELL **Sentence Frames** Have partners reread the paragraph and complete the following sentence frames:

- Two details from the paragraph are ______ and ______.
- I know that cell phones ______ and that drivers ______.
- When I combine the details with what I know about cell phones and driving, I understand ______.

Practice Have students reread "The Future of Humankind" on page 653. Then ask partners to discuss the conclusions they drew from the passage. Remind students to cite text evidence when describing conclusions.
RI.9-10.1

Synthesize

When you **synthesize**, you gather your thoughts about what you have read to draw conclusions, make generalizations, and compare the information to information you've read in other texts. You form new overall understandings by putting together ideas and events.

How to Draw Conclusions

Reading is like putting a puzzle together. There are many different parts that come together to make up the whole selection. Synthesizing is the process of putting the pieces together while we read. We combine new information with what we already know to create an original idea or to form new understandings.

Read this passage and the text that follows to help you understand how to synthesize what you read.

Distracted Drivers

Cell phone use in cars has steadily risen in the past decade. Studies from the Departments of Highway Safety show that the more distracted drivers are, the more likely they are to be in an accident. Lawmakers in some states have successfully passed laws requiring drivers to use hands-free accessories while a vehicle is moving. This means they may use an earpiece or a speaker-phone device but not hold the phone in their hands. Many people feel that talking on cell phones is not the only distracting activity that should be illegal for drivers.

Use text evidence from the selection and your own experience to draw conclusions as you read.

Drawing Conclusions	
Look for Details	The more distracted a driver is, the more likely he or she is to be involved in an accident. Cell phones are distracting.
Think About What You Know	I know people who have been in car accidents while talking on their cell phones.
Decide What You Believe	Lawmakers should continue to work on laws to stop drivers from being distracted.

CCSS Literacy.RI.9-10.1 Cite strong and thorough textual evidence to support analysis of what the text says explicitly as well as inferences drawn from the text.

READING HANDBOOK

How to Make Generalizations

Generalizations are broad statements that apply to a group of people, a set of ideas, or the way things happen. You can make generalizations as you read, using experience and text evidence from a selection to help you.

- **Take notes about the facts or opinions** Look for the overall theme or message of the selection.
- **Add examples** Think about what you know about the topic from your own knowledge and experience.
- **Construct a generalization** Write a statement that combines the author's statements and your own.

Example: *Using a cell phone while driving can make you have an accident.*

How to Compare Across Texts

Comparing two or more texts helps you combine ideas, develop judgments, and draw conclusions. Read the following paragraph, and think about how it connects to the paragraph on page 630.

Graduated Driver's License Programs

More and more states are creating graduated driver's license (GDL) laws. Studies show that these programs help teen driver accidents and deaths to decline. The programs differ from state to state, but most GDL programs require an adult with a valid driver's license to be present when a teen is driving, and a teen driver must enroll in a certified driver's education and training course. Each state has various restrictions for teen drivers and punishments for when those restrictions are ignored.

Think About Something You Have Already Read In "Distracted Drivers," you read that cell phones are distracting to drivers and that many people feel it should be illegal to use one while driving.

Think About What You Are Reading Right Now Many states have graduated driver's license programs. Accidents involving teen drivers have declined.

Compare Across Texts and Draw Conclusions Both articles are about laws related to driving. Lawmakers hope that all of the laws they pass related to driving will create safer driving conditions for everyone.

Comparing across texts can help you foster an argument or advance an opinion. Having multiple opinions and facts from different sources makes your argument or opinion more credible.

A Make Generalizations

Practice Read aloud a short article or a paragraph about the difficulties of getting into college (cost, competition, limited space, test scores, etc.) Have students discuss the facts and their opinions on getting into colleges and then form a generalization. *(Getting accepted into a college is hard.)*
RI.9-10.1

B Compare Across Texts

Reinforce Model how to draw a conclusion by comparing across texts. Read aloud "Graduated Driver's License Programs" and compare it to "Distracted Drivers" on p. 630.

MODEL Say:

- *When I compare two things, I think about how they are different or alike. "Distracted Drivers" and "Graduated Driver's License Programs" are alike because both are about laws related to driving.*
- *I'll draw a conclusion based on what I learned from both texts and what I already know.*
- *In "Distracted Drivers," I learned that driving can be dangerous. In "Graduated Driver's License Programs," I learned that new laws have been created to make driving safer. I know that lawmakers want to help people.*
- *I can conclude that lawmakers hope the driving laws they pass will create safer conditions for everyone.*

CCSS Literacy.RI.9-10.1 Cite strong and thorough textual evidence to support analysis of what the text says explicitly as well as inferences drawn from the text.

A Visualize Using Sketches

Reinforce Model how to use sketches to enhance visualizations. Read aloud "My Favorite Car Is a Truck." As you model, sketch for the students.

MODEL Say:

- *When I visualize, I picture in my mind what is happening in a text.*
- *Sketching what I picture in my mind helps me visualize the text.*
- *For this paragraph, I will draw the truck and the key. The drawing will help me better understand what the author is describing.*

Invite students to draw images based on the paragraph, too. Compare the pictures. Ask: Why are our pictures different (or alike)? What does this tell you about visualizing?

B Visualize Using Senses

Practice Read aloud "Surfing the Pipeline" on page 735. Then create a chart with the headings *I Smell*, *I Hear*, *I See*, and *I Feel*. Have students tell you how to fill in the chart with sensory information from the text. Invite students to make inferences as they visualize the scene. Ask: How does using your senses help you understand the character? The setting? The events?
RL.9-10.10

C Recognize Emotional Responses

Practice Have students name other texts they have read that made them feel emotions. Encourage them to tell how they felt and to recall words or phrases that generated those emotions.

ELL Practice Have students create a chart to trap key vocabulary from the text: *Nouns* (*car, dealership, pickup truck*), *Adjectives* (*red, gleaming, clean*), and *Verbs* (*working, pick out, found*). Then have them draw sketches based on the words they gathered.
RL.9-10.10

Visualize

When you **visualize**, you use your imagination to better understand what the author is describing. While reading, create an image or picture in your mind that represents what you are reading about. Look for words that tell how things look, sound, smell, taste, and feel.

My Favorite Car Is a Truck

My name is Stephen, and today was a magical day. I've been working hard and saving money all summer. I finally have enough money for a down payment on a new car. Today my father took me to a car dealership to pick out my car. I immediately found my favorite vehicle. It was a red, shiny pickup truck with gleaming wheels. I climbed inside and looked around. The brown seats were sparkling clean, and the truck still had that new car smell inside the cab. I put the key in the ignition and turned it on. The quiet hum of the engine made me so happy. After a long test-drive, my father and I agreed this was the truck for me.

A

How to Visualize Using Sketches

- **Read the Text** Look for words that help create pictures in your mind about the characters, setting, and events.
- **Picture the Information in Your Mind** Stop and focus on the descriptive words. Create pictures in your mind using these words.
- **Draw the Events** Sketch pictures to show what is happening. You could draw Stephen climbing inside the pickup truck.

B

How to Visualize Using Senses

- **Look for Words** Find adjectives and sensory words: smell, look, sound, taste, and feel. Stephen uses the words *red, shiny, with gleaming wheels*; *brown seats, sparkling clean*; *new car smell*; and *quiet hum of the engine* to talk about the truck.
- **Create a Picture in Your Mind of the Scene** What do you hear, feel, see, smell, and taste? Examine how these details improve your understanding.

I smell: new car smell **I hear:** engine humming
I see: red, shiny truck **I feel:** texture of the seats, the key

C

How to Recognize Emotional Responses

Do any of the words in the selection make you feel certain emotions? Asking yourself how you feel when you read can help you remember the information.

Example: I feel excited for the main character because I know what it's like to pick out something new.

CCSS Literacy.RL.9-10.10 By the end of grade 10, read and comprehend literature, including stories, dramas, and poems, at the high end of the grades 9-10 text complexity band independently and proficiently.

Reading Fluency

What Is Reading Fluency?

Reading fluency is the ability to read smoothly and expressively with clear understanding. Fluent readers are able to better understand and enjoy what they read. Use the strategies that follow to build your fluency in these four key areas:

- accuracy and rate
- phrasing
- intonation
- expression

How to Improve Accuracy and Rate

Accuracy is the correctness of your reading. Rate is the speed of your reading.

How to read accurately:

- Use correct pronunciation.
- Emphasize correct syllables.

How to read with proper rate:

- Match your reading speed to what you are reading. For example, if you are reading an exciting story, read slightly faster. If you are reading a sad story, read slightly slower.
- Recognize and use punctuation.

Test your accuracy and rate:

- Choose a text you are familiar with, and practice reading it aloud or silently multiple times.
- Ask a friend to use a watch or clock to time you while you read a passage.
- Ask a friend or family member to read a passage for you, so you know what it should sound like.

Use the formula below to measure a reader's accuracy and rate while reading aloud. For passages to practice with, see **Reading Fluency Practice**, pp. 751–771.

Accuracy and Rate Formula

______		______		______
words read in one minute	−	number of errors	=	words correct per minute (wcpm)

READING HANDBOOK

READING FLUENCY

The Reading Fluency section assists students with

- accuracy and rate
- intonation
- phrasing
- expression

Print copies of the fluency passages from myNGconnect.com to keep running records, record accuracy and rate formulas, and mark up as needed. Encourage students to use the online versions to make phrasing marks, keep track of difficult words, or to record their own periodic accuracy and rate improvements. The online versions provide specific line counts to ensure accuracy with the formulas.

Accuracy and Rate

Print a copy of a fluency passage from myNGconnect.com. Explain to students how the line counts work and how to mark the passage. Model marking for accuracy and rate as you read aloud the passage. Then have students practice using the accuracy and rate formulas with a partner.

ELL For accuracy, have students check that they are reading from left to right by marking where sentences begin and end.

For rate, build the passage one sentence at a time: read sentence 1, students repeat; read sentences 1 and 2, students repeat; and so on. Encourage students to rehearse reading the passage aloud several times, starting slowly and trying to speed up, before clocking the time and using the rate formula.

Intonation

Guide students through the bullet points and the chart. Model reading sentences aloud in a choppy way, a smooth way, and with proper rhythm and meter. Then have students write meaningful sentences about things they feel strongly about. Remind students to use a variety of methods to show emphasis such as using dashes, italics, and all capital letters. Have students practice reading the sentences aloud with partners.

ELL Discuss each type of visual cue and their meanings. Read aloud the "she is smart" samples from the chart, and have students repeat back to you while using the proper form of intonation.

Provide sentence frames for English learners to write meaningful sentences about things they feel strongly about:

1. I really love ______.
2. I feel sad when ______.
3. ______ makes me laugh!
4. How do I ______?

How to Improve Intonation

Intonation is the rise and fall in the tone of your voice as you read aloud. It means the highness or lowness of the sound.

How to read with proper intonation:

- Change the sound of your voice to match what you are reading.
- Make your voice flow, or sound smooth, while you read.
- Make sure you are pronouncing words correctly.
- Raise the sound of your voice for words that should be stressed, or emphasized.
- Use visual clues. (see box below)

Visual Clue and Meaning	Example	How to Read It
Italics: draw attention to a word to show special importance	She is *smart*.	Emphasize "smart."
Dash: shows a quick break in a sentence	She is—smart.	Pause before saying "smart."
Exclamation: can represent energy, excitement, or anger	She is smart!	Make your voice louder at the end of the sentence.
All capital letters: can represent strong emphasis, or yelling	SHE IS SMART.	Emphasize the whole sentence.
Bold facing: draws attention to a word to show importance	She is **smart**.	Emphasize "smart."
Question mark: shows curiosity or confusion	She is smart?	Raise the pitch of your voice slightly at the end of the sentence.

Use the rubric below to measure how well a reader uses intonation while reading aloud. For intonation passages, see **Reading Fluency Practice**, pp. 751–771.

Intonation Rubric

1	2	3
The reader's tone does not change. The reading all sounds the same.	The reader's tone changes sometimes to match what is being read.	The reader's tone always changes to match what is being read.

How to Improve Phrasing

Phrasing is how you use your voice to group words together.

How to read with proper phrasing:

- Don't read too quickly or too slowly.
- Pause for key words within the text.
- Make sure your sentences sound smooth, not choppy.
- Make sure you sound like you are reading a sentence instead of a list.
- Use punctuation to tell you when to stop, pause, or emphasize. (see box below)

Punctuation	How to Use It
. period	stop at the end of the sentence
, comma	pause within the sentence
! exclamation point	emphasize the sentence and pause at the end
? question mark	emphasize the end of the sentence and pause at the end
; semicolon	pause within the sentence between two related thoughts
: colon	pause within the sentence before giving an example or explanation

One way to practice phrasing is to copy a passage, then place a slash (/), or pause mark, within a sentence where there should be a pause. One slash (/) means a short pause. Two slashes (//) mean a longer pause, such as a pause at the end of a sentence.

Read aloud the passage below, pausing at each pause mark. Then try reading the passage again without any pauses. Compare how you sound each time.

There are many ways to get involved / in your school and community. // Joining a club / or trying out for a sports team / are a few of the options. // Volunteer work can also be very rewarding. // You can volunteer at community centers, / nursing homes, / or animal shelters. //

Use the rubric below to measure how well a reader uses phrasing while reading aloud. For phrasing passages, see **Reading Fluency Practice**, pp. 751–771.

Phrasing Rubric

1	2	3
Reading is choppy. There are few pauses for punctuation.	Reading is mostly smooth. There are some pauses for punctuation.	Reading is very smooth. Punctuation is being used properly.

Phrasing

Model reading a paragraph without pauses, running all of the words together. Then read the paragraph with proper pauses. Ask: What did I do differently in the two readings? Why is it important to group words together when reading? Have students discuss how your flow and meter affect their comprehension of the paragraph.

Print a copy of a fluency passage from myNGconnect.com. Model putting pause marks in the first few sentences, and then read them aloud. Have students mark the pauses for the rest of the passage. Encourage them to read aloud a few sentences at a time to find the right locations of the pause marks.

ELL Review the punctuation chart. Explain that a semicolon is used to separate two independent clauses, or to separate phrases or clauses that have commas. A colon is used to call attention to what follows, such as a second sentence that explains the first or a list that follows.

Display and read aloud the sentences below to show proper use of semicolons and colons.

- Herbs are a key ingredient for many cooks; they are used in recipes around the world.
- To make a good Italian meal, cooks use herbs such as basil, oregano, and rosemary; they choose only the freshest herbs; and they use olive oil.
- Cooks also use pasta in creative ways: they put tomatoes, meat, and cheese inside and on top of pasta.

Then erase the colons and semicolons and read aloud again. Have students explain the differences in your readings.

Expression

Guide students through the bullet points. Then show examples of different forms of writing: a sad poem, a serious newspaper article, a friendly short letter, etc. Model changing the sound of your voice to match what you are reading. Read the writings using incorrect and correct expression. Then ask students which style of expression is correct.

ELL Display and read aloud the following:

- Where do you think you are going?
- When you get there, you should wait for your parents.
- Hey, I want to come, too!

Model how to use gestures and facial expressions to enhance your reading style. Then read aloud again and have students repeat, using the same expression, gestures, and facial expressions.

How to Improve Expression

Expression in reading is how you use your voice to express feeling.

How to read with proper expression:

- Match the sound of your voice to what you are reading. For example, read louder and faster to show strong feeling. Read slower and quieter to show sadness or seriousness.
- Match the sound of your voice to the genre. For example, read a fun, fictional story using a fun, friendly voice. Read an informative, nonfiction article using an even tone and a more serious voice.
- Avoid speaking in monotone, or using only one tone in your voice.
- Pause for emphasis and exaggerate letter sounds to match the mood or theme of what you are reading.

Practice incorrect expression by reading this sentence without changing the tone of your voice: *I am so excited!* Now read the sentence again with proper expression: *I am so excited!* The way you use your voice while reading can help you to better understand what is happening in the text.

For additional practice, read the sentences below aloud with and without changing your expression. Compare how you sound each time.

- I am very sad.
- That was the most *boring* movie I have ever seen.
- We won the game!

Use the rubric below to measure how well a reader uses expression while reading aloud. For expression passages, see **Reading Fluency Practice**, pp. 751–771.

Expression Rubric

1	2	3
The reader sounds monotone. The reader's voice does not match the subject of what is being read.	The reader is making some tone changes. Sometimes, the reader's voice matches what is being read.	The reader is using proper tones and pauses. The reader's voice matches what is being read.

READING HANDBOOK

Reading Fluency Practice

Practice Expression: "The Good Samaritan"

Expression in reading is how you use your voice to express feeling. Use this passage to practice reading with proper expression. Print a copy of this passage from myNGconnect.com to help you monitor your progress. Practice independently and participate in shared reading to improve your expression. To use an Expression Rubric, see page 750.

A little later in the afternoon, Mr. Sánchez drove up in his truck, honking and honking at us. "Here they come. Maybe Orlando and Marty can play with us," someone said.

Pues, it was not to be. The truck had just come to a standstill when Mr. Sánchez shot out of the driver's side. He ran up to us, waving his hands in the air like a crazy man, first saying, then screaming, "What are you guys doing here? You all can't be here when I'm not here."

"But you told us we could come over anytime. And we knocked and knocked, and we were being very careful."

"It doesn't matter. You all shouldn't be here when I'm not home. What if you had broken something?" he said.

"But we didn't," I said.

"But if you had, then who would have been responsible for paying to replace it? I'm sure every one of you would have denied breaking anything."

"*Este vato!*" said Hernando.

"*Vato?* Is that what you called me? I'm no street punk, no hoodlum. I'll have you know, I've worked my whole life, and I won't be called a *vato*. It's Mr. Sánchez. Got that? And you boys know what—from now on, you are not allowed to come here whether I'm home or not! You all messed it up for yourselves. You've shown me so much disrespect today you don't deserve to play on my court. It was a privilege and not a right, and you messed it up. Now leave!"

From "The Good Samaritan," page 13

Expression Rubric

1	2	3
The reader sounds monotone. The reader's voice does not match the subject of what is being read.	The reader is making some tone changes. Sometimes, the reader's voice matches what is being read.	The reader is using proper tones and pauses. The reader's voice matches what is being read.

Accuracy and Rate Formula

______ words attempted in one minute	−	______ number of errors	=	______ words correct per minute (wcpm)

Expression

Print a copy of this passage and the accompanying rubrics from **myNGconnect.com**.

Teach/Model Assist students in using proper expression with "The Good Samaritan." For example:

- Explain that the words *pues* and *este vato* are italicized because they are Spanish, not because they need special emphasis. Remind students that most foreign language words will be italicized in printed writing, so they will have to pay special attention to context clues to find out how the word should be read aloud.
- Explain that the only clues about how to express the dialogue of the kids is the content of what they are saying. Model reading the dialogue aloud for the class, with and without proper expression.

Practice Have students use these daily fluency routines to develop expression:

1. **Listen While Reading** Students listen to the fluency model on the **Fluency Model CD** several times to internalize the reader's expression.
2. **Collaborative Reading** Partners read alternative sentences in the passage, listening for appropriate expression.
3. **Recorded Reading** Students record their readings and play them back, checking for their own expression.
4. **Student-Adult Reading** Students read the passage to an adult and receive feedback on their expression.
5. **Reading to Assess** Partners read aloud the passage and apply the checklist from p. 35.

Assess Have students read aloud the passage. Use the rubrics to assess expression, accuracy, and rate.
RL.9-10.10

myNGconnect.com

Fluency Practice

Comprehension Coach

CCSS Literacy.RL.9-10.10 By the end of grade 10, read and comprehend literature, including stories, dramas, and poems, at the high end of the grades 9–10 text complexity band independently and proficiently.

Phrasing

Print a copy of this passage and the accompanying rubrics from myNGconnect.com.

Teach/Model Assist students in using proper phrasing with "Thank You, M'am." For example:

- Have students read the first paragraph. Model reading the first few sentences aloud, first without and then with proper phrasing. Ask: How did my pauses help you understand what was happening?
- Explain that clues to proper phrasing can be small words, such as *and*, *in*, and *or*. Say: When you read aloud the sentence "The woman still had him by the neck in the middle of her room," you should pause after the word *neck*.

Practice Have students use these daily fluency routines to develop phrasing:

1. **Choral Reading** Mark an entire passage with pause marks. Students chorally read the passage, pausing only at the marks.
2. **Collaborative Reading** Partners read alternative sentences in the passage, listening for appropriate phrasing.
3. **Recorded Reading** Students record their readings and play them back, adding pause marks only where the recording indicates a pause.
4. **Reading and Marking** Working with a copy from myNGconnect.com, one student reads while the other records pause marks.
5. **Reading to Assess** Partners read aloud the passage and apply the checklist from p. 59.

Assess Have students read aloud the passage. Use the rubrics to assess phrasing, accuracy, and rate.
RL.9-10.10

myNGconnect.com

Fluency Practice

Comprehension Coach

Practice Phrasing: "Thank You, M'am"

Phrasing is how you use your voice to group words together. Use this passage to practice reading with proper phrasing. Print a copy of this passage from myNGconnect.com to help you monitor your progress. To use a Phrasing Rubric, see page 749.

Sweat popped out on the boy's face and he began to struggle. Mrs. Jones stopped, jerked him around in front of her, put a half nelson about his neck, and continued to drag him up the street. When she got to her door, she dragged the boy inside, down a hall, and into a large kitchenette-furnished room at the rear of the house. She switched on the light and left the door open. The boy could hear other roomers laughing and talking in the large house. Some of their doors were open, too, so he knew he and the woman were not alone. The woman still had him by the neck in the middle of her room.

She said, "What is your name?"

"Roger," answered the boy.

"Then, Roger, you go to that sink and wash your face," said the woman, whereupon she turned him loose—at last. Roger looked at the door—looked at the woman—looked at the door—*and went to the sink.*

From "Thank You, M'am," page 43

Phrasing Rubric

1	2	3
Reading is choppy. There are usually no pauses for punctuation.	Reading is mostly smooth. There are some pauses for punctuation.	Reading is very smooth. Punctuation is being used properly.

Accuracy and Rate Formula

______ words attempted in one minute	−	______ number of errors	=	______ words correct per minute (wcpm)

CCSS Literacy.RL.9-10.10 By the end of grade 10, read and comprehend literature, including stories, dramas, and poems, at the high end of the grades 9–10 text complexity band independently and proficiently.

READING HANDBOOK

Practice Intonation: "The Fashion Show"

Intonation is the rise and fall in the pitch or tone of your voice as you read aloud. Use this passage to practice reading with proper intonation. Print a copy of this passage from myNGconnect.com to help you monitor your progress. To use an Intonation Rubric, see page 748. When listening to a partner read, notice if you can understand the sound of each word. Then listen again to hear how your partner's intonation changes.

I felt torn and confused. I could not take part in the dance, of course, but should I be in the fashion show? I really wanted to do it. I had two beautiful Afghan outfits I could model. But I was also thinking, *My leg is damaged. What if I fall down?*

Finally, I said to myself, *Okay, next Wednesday I'll sit in on the practice session and see what it's like, and then I'll decide.*

That day the girl who always picked on me came to the practice session, because she was planning to be in the fashion show. The moment she saw me sitting there, she could tell I was thinking of entering the show, too. She didn't tell me to my face that I could not do it, but she immediately called out to the teacher. "Ms. Ascadam," she said, "when you model clothes at a fashion show, isn't this how you have to walk? Isn't this how models walk on a runway?"

Then she began to walk the way she thought a model should walk—with long strides, placing one foot in front of the other in a straight line that made her back end swing from side to side. "Is this the way you should walk?" she said. "If someone can't walk like this, should she be in the fashion show? She would just spoil the whole thing, wouldn't she?" And she kept walking back and forth, swinging from side to side.

From "The Fashion Show," page 81

Intonation Rubric

1	2	3
The reader's tone does not change. The reading all sounds the same.	The reader's tone changes sometimes to match what is being read.	The reader's tone always changes to match what is being read.

Accuracy and Rate Formula

words attempted in one minute − number of errors = words correct per minute (wcpm)

Intonation

Print a copy of this passage and the accompanying rubrics from myNGconnect.com.

Teach/Model Assist students in using proper intonation with "The Fashion Show." For example:

- Point to the question marks and italicized phrases in the first paragraph and explain that these are clues about the speaker's tone. Model reading the paragraph with proper intonation. Ask: When I read this with proper intonation, what do you understand about the narrator?
- Model reading the final paragraph aloud, making your voice smaller and sadder as the paragraph progresses. Ask: What effect does my tone of voice have on you?

Practice Have students use these daily fluency routines to develop intonation:

1. **Choral Reading** Underline parts of the passage that require special intonation. Students chorally read the passage, raising and lowering their voices as indicated.
2. **Collaborative Reading** Partners read alternative sentences in the passage, listening for appropriate intonation.
3. **Recorded Reading** Students record their readings and play them back, checking for proper intonation.
4. **Reading and Marking** Working with a copy from myNGconnect.com, one student reads while the other circles words and phrases that require special intonation.
5. **Reading to Assess** Partners read aloud the passage and apply the checklist from p. 87. While listening, students should focus on distinguishing the sounds and intonation patterns they hear.

Assess Have students read aloud the passage. Use the rubrics to assess intonation, accuracy, and rate.
RI.9-10.10

myNGconnect.com

Fluency Practice

Comprehension Coach

CCSS Literacy.RI.9-10.10 By the end of grade 10, read and comprehend literary nonfiction at the high end of the grades 9–10 text complexity band independently and proficiently.

Phrasing

Print a copy of this passage and the accompanying rubrics from myNGconnect.com.

Teach/Model Assist students in using proper phrasing with "The Hidden Secrets of the Creative Mind." For example:

- Remind students to pause briefly when they come to a comma or a dash. Tell students if the pause is too long, the listener may think they are finished.
- Model reading aloud the sentence that begins "In other experiments ...," with proper phrasing. Say: When I properly group these words together, the meaning of the sentence becomes clear.

Practice Have students use these daily fluency routines to develop phrasing:

1. **Choral Reading** Mark an entire passage with pause marks. Students chorally read the passage, pausing only at the marks.
2. **Collaborative Reading** Partners read alternative sentences in the passage, listening for appropriate phrasing.
3. **Recorded Reading** Students record their readings and play them back, adding pause marks only where the recording indicates a pause.
4. **Reading and Marking** Working with a copy from myNGconnect.com, one student reads while the other records pause marks.
5. **Reading to Assess** Partners read aloud the passage and apply the checklist from p. 133.

Assess Have students read aloud the passage. Use the rubrics to assess phrasing, accuracy, and rate.
RI.9-10.10

myNGconnect.com

Fluency Practice

Comprehension Coach

Reading Fluency

Reading Fluency Practice, continued

Practice Phrasing: "The Hidden Secrets of the Creative Mind"

Phrasing is how you use your voice to group words together. Use this passage to practice reading with proper phrasing. Print a copy of this passage from myNGconnect.com to help you monitor your progress. To use a Phrasing Rubric, see page 749.

Q: How have researchers studied this creative flash?

A: Some psychologists set up video cameras to watch creative people work, asking them to describe their thought processes out loud or interrupting them frequently to ask how close they were to a solution. In other experiments, subjects worked on problems that, when solved, tend to result in the sensation of sudden insight. In one experiment, they were asked to look at words that came up one at a time on a computer screen and to think of the one word that was associated with all of them. After each word they had to give their best guess. Although many swore they had no idea until a sudden burst of insight at about the twelfth word, their guesses got closer to the solution. Even when an idea seems sudden, our minds have actually been working on it all along.

From "The Hidden Secrets of the Creative Mind," page 129

Phrasing Rubric

1	2	3
Reading is choppy. There are usually no pauses for punctuation.	Reading is mostly smooth. There are some pauses for punctuation.	Reading is very smooth. Punctuation is being used properly.

Accuracy and Rate Formula

______ words attempted in one minute	–	______ number of errors	=	______ words correct per minute (wcpm)

CCSS Literacy.RI.9-10.10 By the end of grade 10, read and comprehend literary nonfiction at the high end of the grades 9–10 text complexity band independently and proficiently.

Practice Intonation: "Hip-Hop as Culture"

Intonation is the rise and fall in the pitch or tone of your voice as you read aloud. Use this passage to practice reading with proper intonation. Print a copy of this passage from myNGconnect.com to help you monitor your progress. Practice independently and participate in shared reading to improve your intonation. To use an Intonation Rubric, see page 748.

These innovators are the architects of culture. They started from the streets of the city and now influence suburban areas and even small rural towns. They took the hustle of the street and turned it into a Wall Street economy. It doesn't matter if you're in a city or suburb. It doesn't matter if you are Latino, Asian, or Irish. Hip-hop is influencing your situation.

Kids may not love hip-hop, but they're being influenced by it. If teens are wearing oversized jeans with the tops of their boxers showing, oversized athletic jerseys, or long chains around their necks, this is hip-hop. Girls on a bus braiding their hair in the style of an Ethiopian queen, that's hip-hop. There are things around you that daily scream at you, "long live hip-hop!" If you want to understand the culture teens live in today, it's important to understand hip-hop and understand it as culture, not just music.

From "Hip-Hop as Culture," page 141

Intonation Rubric

1	2	3
The reader's tone does not change. The reading all sounds the same.	The reader's tone changes sometimes to match what is being read.	The reader's tone always changes to match what is being read.

Accuracy and Rate Formula

______ words attempted in one minute	−	______ number of errors	=	______ words correct per minute (wcpm)

Intonation

Print a copy of this passage and the accompanying rubrics from **myNGconnect.com**.

Teach/Model Assist students in using proper intonation with "Hip-Hop as Culture." For example:

- Point out the words *suburban*, *even*, and *rural* in the second sentence. Explain that these words should be stressed, so that the reader's voice rises as the sentence continues. Model reading this sentence aloud, stressing these words.
- Read aloud the first sentence of the second paragraph with and without proper intonation. Ask students to tell you the difference.

Practice Have students use these daily fluency routines to develop intonation:

1. **Choral Reading** Underline parts of the passage that require special intonation. Students chorally read the passage, raising and lowering their voices as indicated.
2. **Collaborative Reading** Partners read alternative sentences in the passage, listening for appropriate intonation.
3. **Recorded Reading** Students record their readings and play them back, checking for proper intonation.
4. **Reading and Marking** Working with a copy from **myNGconnect.com**, one student reads while the other circles words and phrases that require special intonation.
5. **Reading to Assess** Partners read aloud the passage and apply the checklist from p. 155.

Assess Have students read aloud the passage. Use the rubrics to assess intonation, accuracy, and rate.
RI.9-10.10

myNGconnect.com

Fluency Practice

Comprehension Coach

CCSS Literacy.RI.9-10.10 By the end of grade 10, read and comprehend literary nonfiction at the high end of the grades 9–10 text complexity band independently and proficiently.

Expression

Print a copy of this passage and the accompanying rubrics from myNGconnect.com.

Teach/Model Assist students in using proper expression with "Slam: Performance Poetry Lives On." For example:

- Point out that the tone of the passage is conveyed through the context clues in the first paragraph. Read this paragraph aloud in a monotone. Then read it again with proper expression. Ask: What is the tone of this piece? How can you tell?
- Model reading the poetry aloud with proper expression. Explain that the feeling of the poem is different from the feeling of the passage.

Practice Have students use these daily fluency routines to develop expression:

1. **Listen While Reading** Students listen to the fluency model on the **Fluency Model CD** several times to internalize the reader's expression.
2. **Collaborative Reading** Partners read alternative sentences in the passage, listening for appropriate expression.
3. **Recorded Reading** Students record their readings and play them back, checking for their own expression.
4. **Student-Adult Reading** Students read the passage to an adult and receive feedback on their expression.
5. **Reading to Assess** Partners read aloud the passage and apply the checklist from p. 177.

Assess Have students read aloud the passage. Use the rubrics to assess expression, accuracy, and rate.
RI.9-10.10

myNGconnect.com

Fluency Practice

Comprehension Coach

Practice Expression: "Slam: Performance Poetry Lives On"

Expression in reading is how you use your voice to express feeling. Use this passage to practice reading with proper expression. Print a copy of this passage from myNGconnect.com to help you monitor your progress. To use an Expression Rubric, see page 750.

Poetry doesn't have to be the twelve lines on a page in a book that is sitting in the dustiest corner of the library. Poetry doesn't have to be something you don't understand. Poetry is moving, breathing, ever changing.

Want proof? Take a trip to the Urban Word Annual Teen Poetry Slam at the Nuyorican Poets Cafe in New York City.

Gathered in this tight space are hundreds of teens from every corner of the city. They've come together to compete for one of five top spots in Brave New Voices, the Eighth Annual National Youth Poetry Slam Festival.

Sitting in the cafe feels like being at a sporting event. A DJ revs up the crowd with upbeat music. Young people erupt into wild applause as one of their own hollers his latest creation of slam before the microphone.

Take a listen to this excerpt from "Elementary Invasion," by 16-year-old slam poet Kai Zhang:

squeeze
green putty oozing out of your hands
and hugging your fingers cold and rubbery
escaping
your silly efforts to contain
or hold . . .

From "Slam: Performance Poetry Lives On," page 163

Expression Rubric

1	2	3
The reader sounds monotone. The reader's voice does not match the subject of what is being read.	The reader is making some tone changes. Sometimes, the reader's voice matches what is being read.	The reader is using proper tones and pauses. The reader's voice matches what is being read.

Accuracy and Rate Formula

______ words attempted in one minute	–	______ number of errors	=	______ words correct per minute (wcpm)

CCSS Literacy.RI.9-10.10 By the end of grade 10, read and comprehend literary nonfiction at the high end of the grades 9–10 text complexity band independently and proficiently.

READING HANDBOOK

Practice Phrasing: "The Sword in the Stone"

Phrasing is how you use your voice to group words together. Use this passage to practice reading with proper phrasing. Print a copy of this passage from myNGconnect.com to help you monitor your progress. To use a Phrasing Rubric, see page 749.

Arthur went into the church and placed the sword on the high altar. The Archbishop took it up and touched Arthur on the shoulder with it to make him a knight. Then Arthur forgave the great nobles and knights for doubting him and swore an oath that he would be a just and true king for all his days.

He ordered the lords who held their land from the crown to fulfil the duties they owed him. Each one knelt before him in turn and promised to abide by the laws of the king. After this ceremony, Arthur said he would hear complaints about injustices and crimes committed in the land since the death of his father, Uther Pendragon. They told him of how lands and castles had been taken by force, and men murdered, and of how knights and ladies and common people were robbed and assaulted.

Arthur ordered that all lands and properties should be returned to their rightful owners and that everyone should respect the rights of others. When that was done, Arthur organized his government. Sir Kay was made High Steward of all Britain and the most trustworthy knights were appointed to high office. Merlin was confirmed as chief counsellor to the King.

From "The Sword in the Stone," page 211

Phrasing Rubric

1	2	3
Reading is choppy. There are usually no pauses for punctuation.	Reading is mostly smooth. There are some pauses for punctuation.	Reading is very smooth. Punctuation is being used properly.

Accuracy and Rate Formula

______ words attempted in one minute	–	______ number of errors	=	______ words correct per minute (wcpm)

Phrasing

Print a copy of this passage and the accompanying rubrics from **myNGconnect.com**.

Teach/Model Assist students in using proper phrasing with "The Sword in the Stone." For example:

- Explain that the word *and* has two possible uses in phrasing. When it appears between two phrases, there should be a pause just before it, as in "Arthur went into the church and placed the sword on the high altar." However, when it appears between two nouns, those words should be spoken together, as in "the great nobles and knights."

Practice Have students use these daily fluency routines to develop phrasing:

1. **Choral Reading** Mark an entire passage with pause marks. Students chorally read the passage, pausing only at the marks.
2. **Collaborative Reading** Partners read alternative sentences in the passage, listening for appropriate phrasing.
3. **Recorded Reading** Students record their readings and play them back, adding pause marks only where the recording indicates a pause.
4. **Reading and Marking** Working with a copy from **myNGconnect.com**, one student reads while the other records pause marks.
5. **Reading to Assess** Partners read aloud the passage and apply the checklist from p. 231.

Assess Have students read aloud the passage. Use the rubrics to assess phrasing, accuracy, and rate.
RL.9-10.10

myNGconnect.com

Fluency Practice

Comprehension Coach

CCSS Literacy.RL.9-10.10 By the end of grade 10, read and comprehend literature, including stories, dramas, and poems, at the high end of the grades 9–10 text complexity band independently and proficiently.

Expression

Print a copy of this passage and the accompanying rubrics from myNGconnect.com.

Teach/Model Assist students in using proper expression with "A Job for Valentín." For example:

- Explain how to emphasize the italicized word *children's*. Model reading this paragraph with proper expression. Then read it aloud in monotone and ask students to tell you the ways in which each reading has a different effect.

Practice Have students use these daily fluency routines to develop expression:

1. **Listen While Reading** Students listen to the fluency model on the **Fluency Model CD** several times to internalize the reader's expression.
2. **Collaborative Reading** Partners read alternative sentences in the passage, listening for appropriate expression.
3. **Recorded Reading** Students record their readings and play them back, checking for their own expression.
4. **Student-Adult Reading** Students read the passage to an adult and receive feedback on their expression.
5. **Reading to Assess** Partners read aloud the passage and apply the checklist from p. 257.

Assess Have students read aloud the passage. Use the rubrics to assess expression, accuracy, and rate.
RL.9-10.10

myNGconnect.com

Fluency Practice

Comprehension Coach

Practice Expression: "A Job for Valentín"

Expression in reading is how you use your voice to express feeling. Use this passage to practice reading with proper expression. Print a copy of this passage from myNGconnect.com to help you monitor your progress. To use an Expression Rubric, see page 750.

I can't swim very well, mainly because my eyesight is so bad. The minute I take off my glasses to get in the pool, everything becomes a blob of color and I freeze. But I managed to talk my way into a summer job at the city pool anyway. All I'll be doing is selling drinks and snacks, and I get to talk to everyone since the little concession stand faces the pool and the cute lifeguard, Bob Dylan Kalinowski. His mother named him after the old singer from the sixties.

It's a good first day. Mrs. O'Brien says I don't need any training. I can run a cash register, I can take inventory, and I am very friendly with customers. The only thing I don't really like is that Mrs. O'Brien expects to be told if I ever see Bob Dylan messing around on the job.

"People's lives, *children's* lives, are in that young man's hands," she says. "Keep an eye on him, Teresa, and use that phone to call me, if you need to."

I say, "Yes, ma'am," even though I feel funny about being asked to spy on Bob Dylan. He's a senior at my school and, yeah, a crazy man sometimes. But if they gave him the job as a lifeguard, they ought to trust him to do it right.

From "A Job for Valentín," page 239

Expression Rubric

1	2	3
The reader sounds monotone. The reader's voice does not match the subject of what is being read.	The reader is making some tone changes. Sometimes, the reader's voice matches what is being read.	The reader is using proper tones and pauses. The reader's voice matches what is being read.

Accuracy and Rate Formula

______ words attempted in one minute	–	______ number of errors	=	______ words correct per minute (wcpm)

CCSS Literacy.RL.9-10.10 By the end of grade 10, read and comprehend literature, including stories, dramas, and poems, at the high end of the grades 9–10 text complexity band independently and proficiently.

Practice Intonation: "The Woman in the Snow"

Intonation is the rise and fall in the pitch or tone of your voice as you read aloud. Use this passage to practice reading with proper intonation. Print a copy of this passage from myNGconnect.com to help you monitor your progress. To use an Intonation Rubric, see page 748.

Grady closed his eyes but couldn't keep them shut. She was still coming, but from where? The answer was too horrible to consider, so he chose to let his mind find a more reasonable explanation. From some dark corner of his childhood he heard his father's voice, slurred by alcohol, mocking him. *It ain't the same woman, dummy. You know how they all look alike!*

Grady remembered his father with bitterness and swore at the thought of him. This *was* the same woman, Grady argued with his father's memory, taking no comfort in being right. Grady watched the woman's movements breathlessly as she stepped out of the headlight beam and approached the door. She stood outside the door waiting ... waiting.

The gray coldness of Fear slipped into the driver's seat. Grady sucked air into his lungs in big gulps, feeling out of control. Fear moved his foot to the gas pedal, careening the bus out into oncoming traffic. Headlights. A truck. Fear made Grady hit the brakes. The back of the bus went into a sliding spin, slamming into a tree. Grady's stomach crushed against the steering wheel, rupturing his liver and spleen. *You've really done it now, lunkhead.* As he drifted into the final darkness, he heard a woman's sobs, a baby wailing—or was it just the wind?

From "The Woman in the Snow," page 265

READING HANDBOOK

Intonation Rubric

1	2	3
The reader's tone does not change. The reading all sounds the same.	The reader's tone changes sometimes to match what is being read.	The reader's tone always changes to match what is being read.

Accuracy and Rate Formula

______ words attempted in one minute	–	______ number of errors	=	______ words correct per minute (wcpm)

Intonation

Print a copy of this passage and the accompanying rubrics from myNGconnect.com.

Teach/Model Assist students in using proper intonation with "The Woman in the Snow." For example:

- Explain that proper intonation can help convey the mood of a passage. Read the first paragraph aloud using a cheerful tone. Ask students if your tone matches the words you read.
- Point out the clues to proper intonation for the italicized sentences at the end of the first paragraph: "slurred by alcohol, mocking him." Explain that these clues also apply to the italicized sentence in the final paragraph: "*You've really done it now, lunkhead.*"

Practice Have students use these daily fluency routines to develop intonation:

1. **Choral Reading** Underline parts of the passage that require special intonation. Students chorally read the passage, raising and lowering their voices as indicated.
2. **Collaborative Reading** Partners read alternative sentences in the passage, listening for appropriate intonation.
3. **Recorded Reading** Students record their readings and play them back, checking for proper intonation.
4. **Reading and Marking** Working with a copy from myNGconnect.com, one student reads while the other circles words and phrases that require special intonation.
5. **Reading to Assess** Partners read aloud the passage and apply the checklist from p. 285.

Assess Have students read aloud the passage. Use the rubrics to assess intonation, accuracy, and rate.
RL.9-10.10

myNGconnect.com

Fluency Practice

Comprehension Coach

CCSS Literacy.RL.9-10.10 By the end of grade 10, read and comprehend literature, including stories, dramas, and poems, at the high end of the grades 9–10 text complexity band independently and proficiently.

Phrasing

Print a copy of this passage and the accompanying rubrics from myNGconnect.com.

Teach/Model Assist students in using proper phrasing with "Curtis Aikens and the American Dream." For example:

- Tell students the series of commas in the first sentence indicate a quickness of speech. The narrator appears nervous. Explain that quick speech still needs proper phrasing. Read the sentence aloud with and without proper phrasing. Ask: What effect does the proper phrasing have on your understanding as a listener?

Practice Have students use these daily fluency routines to develop phrasing:

1. **Choral Reading** Mark an entire passage with pause marks. Students chorally read the passage, pausing only at the marks.
2. **Collaborative Reading** Partners read alternative sentences in the passage, listening for appropriate phrasing.
3. **Recorded Reading** Students record their readings and play them back, adding pause marks only where the recording indicates a pause.
4. **Reading and Marking** Working with a copy from myNGconnect.com, one student reads while the other records pause marks.
5. **Reading to Assess** Partners read aloud the passage and apply the checklist from p. 335.

Assess Have students read aloud the passage. Use the rubrics to assess phrasing, accuracy, and rate. RI.9-10.10

myNGconnect.com

Fluency Practice

Comprehension Coach

Practice Phrasing: "Curtis Aikens and the American Dream"

Phrasing is how you use your voice to group words together. Use this passage to practice reading with proper phrasing. Print a copy of this passage from myNGconnect.com to help you monitor your progress. To use a Phrasing Rubric, see page 749.

Curtis thought he had really screwed up, that no one would listen to him, that his television career was over, and that if the show had reached any illiterate adults, they would only be more convinced to hide their problem. But the opposite was true. Curtis's "screwup" had been one of those moments where television was at its best, where everything was real. The phone lines lit up, at the station and at literacy centers across the country. "It was a great day for literacy," Curtis concludes, without a hint of embarrassment or regret.

His story finished, the TV chef climbs up on his soapbox. The only reason he wanted to share all of this is because he has a cause: "Illiteracy is a problem that all of America can unite around. It doesn't know race, it doesn't know money, it doesn't know boundaries. This is one thing we can all get together on." That cause fully and completely contains Curtis's version of the American dream: "I don't get bored anymore, because I can read. I don't get lonely anymore, because I can read. I'm never out of friends anymore, because I can read. But I'm still trying to obtain the American dream, because I want to give everybody the ability to read. I know that sounds hokey, but there it is."

From "Curtis Aikens and the American Dream," page 317

Phrasing Rubric

1	2	3
Reading is choppy. There are usually no pauses for punctuation.	Reading is mostly smooth. There are some pauses for punctuation.	Reading is very smooth. Punctuation is being used properly.

Accuracy and Rate Formula

______ words attempted in one minute	–	______ number of errors	=	______ words correct per minute (wcpm)

CCSS Literacy.RI.9-10.10 By the end of grade 10, read and comprehend literary nonfiction at the high end of the grades 9-10 text complexity band independently and proficiently.

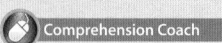

Practice Intonation: "It's Our Story, Too"

Intonation is the rise and fall in the pitch or tone of your voice as you read aloud. Use this passage to practice reading with proper intonation. Print a copy of this passage from myNGconnect.com to help you monitor your progress. To use an Intonation Rubric, see page 748.

On the first page, Esperanza explains how at school they say her name funny, "as if the syllables were made out of tin and hurt the roof of your mouth." I was hooked.

I knew nothing of the East Coast prep schools or the English shires of the books I had read before. But like Esperanza, I could remember how different my last name sounded when it was pronounced melodically by my parents but so haltingly by everyone else.

Cisneros's hometown of Chicago may have been hundreds of miles away from the palm-tree lined streets of Santa Barbara, California, where I grew up. But in her world I was no longer the minority.

That was a dozen years ago. Today, Latinos are the majority in cities like Santa Ana, California, where Cisneros spoke at Valley High School.

Today, these students can pick from bookstore shelves filled with authors such as Julia Álvarez, Victor Villaseñor, and Judith Ortiz Cofer. These are authors who go beyond census numbers to explain what U.S. Latino life is about.

Cisneros provided an hour of humorous storytelling that had the students busting with laughter. They crowded in line afterward, giddily waiting to get her autograph.

From "It's Our Story, Too," page 353

Intonation Rubric

1	2	3
The reader's tone does not change. The reading all sounds the same.	The reader's tone changes sometimes to match what is being read.	The reader's tone always changes to match what is being read.

Accuracy and Rate Formula

_____ words attempted in one minute − _____ number of errors = _____ words correct per minute (wcpm)

Intonation

Print a copy of this passage and the accompanying rubrics from **myNGconnect.com**.

Teach/Model Assist students in using proper intonation with "It's Our Story, Too." For example:

- Explain that the first clue about tone for this passage comes at the end of the first paragraph: "I was hooked." Read this paragraph aloud in a monotone, and then model reading it with proper intonation, raising the pitch of your voice excitedly as you progress through the paragraph. Ask students to tell you the difference.
- Point out these context clues: "bursting with laughter" and "giddily waiting." Say: These phrases tell you to use a happy, excited tone.

Practice Have students use these daily fluency routines to develop intonation:

1. **Choral Reading** Underline parts of the passage that require special intonation. Students chorally read the passage, raising and lowering their voices as indicated.
2. **Collaborative Reading** Partners read alternative sentences in the passage, listening for appropriate intonation.
3. **Recorded Reading** Students record their readings and play them back, checking for proper intonation.
4. **Reading and Marking** Working with a copy from **myNGconnect.com**, one student reads while the other circles words and phrases that require special intonation.
5. **Reading to Assess** Partners read aloud the passage and apply the checklist from p. 357.

Assess Have students read aloud the passage. Use the rubrics to assess intonation, accuracy, and rate.
RI.9-10.10

myNGconnect.com

Fluency Practice

Comprehension Coach

CCSS Literacy.RI.9-10.10 By the end of grade 10, read and comprehend literary nonfiction at the high end of the grades 9–10 text complexity band independently and proficiently.

Expression

Print a copy of this passage and the accompanying rubrics from myNGconnect.com.

Teach/Model Assist students in using proper expression with "The Fast and the Fuel-Efficient." For example:

- Explain that context clues alert the reader about how to express feelings. Have students define these phrases and words to find clues about expression: *disappointed, relieved, struggled with school, stay the course.*
- Model how to read the final paragraph with and without proper expression. Say: Notice how I emphasize the words *optimistic, actually pretty good,* and *simple.*

Practice Have students use these daily fluency routines to develop expression:

1. **Listen While Reading** Students listen to the fluency model on the **Fluency Model CD** several times to internalize the reader's expression.
2. **Collaborative Reading** Partners read alternative sentences in the passage, listening for appropriate expression.
3. **Recorded Reading** Students record their readings and play them back, checking for their own expression.
4. **Student-Adult Reading** Students read the passage to an adult and receive feedback on their expression.
5. **Reading to Assess** Partners read aloud the passage and apply the checklist from p. 381.

Assess Have students read aloud the passage. Use the rubrics to assess expression, accuracy, and rate.
RI.9-10.10

myNGconnect.com

Fluency Practice

Comprehension Coach

Practice Expression: "The Fast and the Fuel-Efficient"

Expression in reading is how you use your voice to express feeling. Use this passage to practice reading with proper expression. Print a copy of this passage from myNGconnect.com to help you monitor your progress. To use an Expression Rubric, see page 750.

A half-dozen team members pushed the car backwards, uphill to the school's garage, and gently rolled it onto a power car lift. The only thing to do now was saw off new axle halves from whole VW and Honda units, send them out to be welded ... and wait.

"We didn't expect it to break again," said a disappointed Joseph Pak, a lanky, earringed 10th grader with gel-spiked hair. Still, he said, he was relieved that it had happened well before the May competition.

For Pak and other team members who'd struggled with school, the car was an "in-your-face" affirmation of their talents and dreams. Pak, the team's only Asian member, admits he used to skip more school than he attended. "I was just hanging out." Now he gets straight As and wants to be an engineer.

"I've seen the extreme of not doing things when you should," Pak said. With the Attack, he said he's seen the extreme of what happens when you stay the course.

Hauger, though, was optimistic. "This is actually pretty good news," Hauger said. Their more complex engineering of the axle had held. This was a simple weld.

From "The Fast and the Fuel-Efficient," page 365

Expression Rubric

1	2	3
The reader sounds monotone. The reader's voice does not match the subject of what is being read.	The reader is making some tone changes. Sometimes, the reader's voice matches what is being read.	The reader is using proper tones and pauses. The reader's voice matches what is being read.

Accuracy and Rate Formula

_____ words attempted in one minute	–	_____ number of errors	=	_____ words correct per minute (wcpm)

CCSS Literacy.RI.9-10.10 By the end of grade 10, read and comprehend literary nonfiction at the high end of the grades 9–10 text complexity band independently and proficiently.

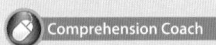

READING HANDBOOK

Practice Phrasing: "The Interlopers"

Phrasing is how you use your voice to group words together. Use this passage to practice reading with proper phrasing. Print a copy of this passage from myNGconnect.com to help you monitor your progress. Practice independently and participate in shared reading to improve your phrasing. To use a Phrasing Rubric, see page 749.

Ulrich von Gradwitz found himself stretched on the ground. One arm lay numb beneath him and the other was pinned helplessly in a tight tangle of forked branches. Both his legs were pinned beneath the fallen branches and it was obvious that he could not move without someone releasing him. The falling branches had slashed his face, and he had to wink away blood from his eyelashes before he could see the full disaster. At his side, near enough to touch, lay Georg Znaeym, who was alive and struggling, but obviously as helplessly pinned down as himself. All around them lay the thick wreckage of splintered branches and broken twigs.

Feeling a mixture of relief at being alive and exasperation at being trapped, Ulrich muttered a strange medley of thankful prayers and sharp curses. Georg, who was blinded by the blood in his eyes, stopped struggling for a moment to listen. Then he gave a short, snarling laugh.

"So you're not killed, as you ought to be, but you're caught, anyway," he cried. "Trapped. What a joke! Ulrich von Gradwitz trapped in his stolen forest. That's justice for you!"

And he laughed again, mockingly and savagely.

"I'm caught on my own land," retorted Ulrich. "When my men come to release us, you will wish you hadn't been caught poaching on a neighbor's land. Shame on you."

From "The Interlopers," page 415

Phrasing Rubric

1	2	3
Reading is choppy. There are usually no pauses for punctuation.	Reading is mostly smooth. There are some pauses for punctuation.	Reading is very smooth. Punctuation is being used properly.

Accuracy and Rate Formula

________ words attempted in one minute	–	________ number of errors	=	________ words correct per minute (wcpm)

Phrasing

Print a copy of this passage and the accompanying rubrics from myNGconnect.com.

Teach/Model Assist students in using proper phrasing with "The Interlopers." For example:

- Remind them to look for context clues, such as short words like *in* or *and*, in sentences without commas or semicolons. Model reading the sentence that begins "One arm lay numb ..." Ask: Did you notice that I grouped together the words "in a tight tangle of forked branches"? How would the sentence be different if I grouped the words incorrectly?

Practice Have students use these daily fluency routines to develop phrasing:

1. **Choral Reading** Mark an entire passage with pause marks. Students chorally read the passage, pausing only at the marks.
2. **Collaborative Reading** Partners read alternative sentences in the passage, listening for appropriate phrasing.
3. **Recorded Reading** Students record their readings and play them back, adding pause marks only where the recording indicates a pause.
4. **Reading and Marking** Working with a copy from myNGconnect.com, one student reads while the other records pause marks.
5. **Reading to Assess** Partners read aloud the passage and apply the checklist from p. 431.

Assess Have students read aloud the passage. Use the rubrics to assess phrasing, accuracy, and rate.
RL.9-10.10

myNGconnect.com

Fluency Practice

Comprehension Coach

CCSS Literacy.RL.9-10.10 By the end of grade 10, read and comprehend literature, including stories, dramas, and poems, at the high end of the grades 9–10 text complexity band independently and proficiently.

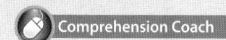

Expression

Print a copy of this passage and the accompanying rubrics from myNGconnect.com.

Teach/Model Assist students in using proper expression with "The Baby-Sitter." For example:

- Read the sentence "But what if something bad happened to *her*?" with and without emphasizing the italicized word. Ask students how this changes their comprehension of the sentence.

Practice Have students use these daily fluency routines to develop expression:

1. **Listen While Reading** Students listen to the fluency model on the **Fluency Model CD** several times to internalize the reader's expression.
2. **Collaborative Reading** Partners read alternative sentences in the passage, listening for appropriate expression.
3. **Recorded Reading** Students record their readings and play them back, checking for their own expression.
4. **Student-Adult Reading** Students read the passage to an adult and receive feedback on their expression.
5. **Reading to Assess** Partners read aloud the passage and apply the checklist from p. 457.

Assess Have students read aloud the passage. Use the rubrics to assess expression, accuracy, and rate.
RL.9-10.10

myNGconnect.com

Fluency Practice

Comprehension Coach

Practice Expression: "The Baby-Sitter"

Expression in reading is how you use your voice to express feeling. Use this passage to practice reading with proper expression. Print a copy of this passage from myNGconnect.com to help you monitor your progress. To use an Expression Rubric, see page 750.

Still puzzled, she went over to the plate of cookies, and as she got close, she stepped into something cold and wet. She looked down. There was a puddle on the floor, soaking into her right sock. An icy-cold puddle. Hilary looked out the kitchen window. It was raining.

Someone was in the house.

She didn't want to believe it, but there was no other explanation. Her whole body felt cold, and she could feel her heart stuttering in her chest. She thought about the twins sleeping upstairs, how she had told them she was hired to make sure nothing bad happened to them. But what if something bad happened to *her*? She shuddered and looked across the room. The telephone was hanging by the refrigerator. She could try and phone for help, or she could run outside and go to the nearest house. The Mitchells lived down a long driveway, and it was about a quarter mile to the next home. And dark. And wet. And she didn't know how many someones were in the house. Or outside. And maybe it was all her imagination.

But—and if her jaw trembled just the slightest she didn't think anyone could fault her—what if the someones wanted to hurt the twins? She was the only one home to protect them.

From "The Baby-Sitter," page 439

Expression Rubric

1	2	3
The reader sounds monotone. The reader's voice does not match the subject of what is being read.	The reader is making some tone changes. Sometimes, the reader's voice matches what is being read.	The reader is using proper tones and pauses. The reader's voice matches what is being read.

Accuracy and Rate Formula

________ words attempted in one minute	–	________ number of errors	=	________ words correct per minute (wcpm)

CCSS Literacy.RL.9-10.10 By the end of grade 10, read and comprehend literature, including stories, dramas, and poems, at the high end of the grades 9–10 text complexity band independently and proficiently.

Practice Intonation: "The Tell-Tale Heart"

Intonation is the rise and fall in the pitch or tone of your voice as you read aloud. Use this passage to practice reading with proper intonation. Print a copy of this passage from myNGconnect.com to help you monitor your progress. To use an Intonation Rubric, see page 748.

It was a low, dull, quick sound. It sounded like a watch wrapped in cotton. I gasped for breath. Still, the police officers did not hear it. I talked faster and louder, but the noise kept increasing. I stood up and moved around. I talked about things that were not important. I spoke in a high voice and I used violent gestures—but the noise kept getting louder.

Why *would* they not be gone? I walked back and forth on the floor with heavy steps, but the noise kept getting louder. Oh, God! What *could* I do? The noise grew louder—louder—*louder!* And still the men chatted pleasantly and smiled. Was it possible that they didn't hear the sound? Almighty God! No, no! They heard! They suspected! They knew! They were making fun of me! This is what I thought, and it is what I still think.

But anything was better than this agony! Anything was better than to let them go on making a fool of me! I could look at their smiles no longer! I felt that I must scream or die! And now, again, listen! The sound is louder! *Louder!*

"Villains!" I screamed. "Pretend no more! I admit the deed! Tear up the floor boards! Here, here! It is the beating of his hideous heart!"

From "The Tell-Tale Heart," page 465

Intonation

Print a copy of this passage and the accompanying rubrics from **myNGconnect.com**.

Teach/Model Assist students in using proper intonation with "The Tell-Tale Heart." For example:

- Point to the clues about proper intonation in the second paragraph: the italicized words, the exclamation points, and the dashes. Model reading the paragraph with proper intonation, letting the pitch of your voice convey the narrator's madness.
- Explain that the tension of the piece demands that the reader speak faster as he or she reads.

Practice Have students use these daily fluency routines to develop intonation:

1. **Choral Reading** Underline parts of the passage that require special intonation. Students chorally read the passage, raising and lowering their voices as indicated.
2. **Collaborative Reading** Partners read alternative sentences in the passage, listening for appropriate intonation.
3. **Recorded Reading** Students record their readings and play them back, checking for proper intonation.
4. **Reading and Marking** Working with a copy from **myNGconnect.com**, one student reads while the other circles words and phrases that require special intonation.
5. **Reading to Assess** Partners read aloud the passage and apply the checklist from p. 483.

Assess Have students read aloud the passage. Use the rubrics to assess intonation, accuracy, and rate.
RL.9-10.10

myNGconnect.com

Fluency Practice

Comprehension Coach

Intonation Rubric

1	2	3
The reader's tone does not change. The reading all sounds the same.	The reader's tone changes sometimes to match what is being read.	The reader's tone always changes to match what is being read.

Accuracy and Rate Formula

________ words attempted in one minute	–	________ number of errors	=	________ words correct per minute (wcpm)

CCSS Literacy.RL.9-10.10 By the end of grade 10, read and comprehend literature, including stories, dramas, and poems, at the high end of the grades 9–10 text complexity band independently and proficiently.

Expression

Print a copy of this passage and the accompanying rubrics from **myNGconnect.com**.

Teach/Model Assist students in using proper expression with "Ad Power." For example:

- Explain that starting the second paragraph with the short phrase "Me neither" clues readers in to the tone of the passage: irreverence and irritation. This should be expressed as students read it aloud.
- Read the third paragraph aloud, using proper expression. Ask: Did you notice how I emphasized the word *science*? How does this help to express the narrator's feeling that advertising is a form of trickery?

Practice Have students use these daily fluency routines to develop expression:

1. **Listen While Reading** Students listen to the fluency model on the **Fluency Model CD** several times to internalize the reader's expression.
2. **Collaborative Reading** Partners read alternative sentences in the passage, listening for appropriate expression.
3. **Recorded Reading** Students record their readings and play them back, checking for their own expression.
4. **Student-Adult Reading** Students read the passage to an adult and receive feedback on their expression.
5. **Reading to Assess** Partners read aloud the passage and apply the checklist from p. 537.

Assess Have students read aloud the passage. Use the rubrics to assess expression, accuracy, and rate.
RI.9-10.10

myNGconnect.com

Fluency Practice

Comprehension Coach

Practice Expression: "Ad Power"

Expression in reading is how you use your voice to express feeling. Use this passage to practice reading with proper expression. Print a copy of this passage from myNGconnect.com to help you monitor your progress. To use an Expression Rubric, see page 750.

Do you remember the day one of your parents sat you down to have a serious talk about advertising?

Me neither. And it's not something they ever test you on at school. That's too bad. Given how easy it is to remember jingles and slogans, an ad exam might be the one test all year you wouldn't have to study for.

Really, you've been "studying" the subject almost since the day you were born. Every time you got parked in front of the TV or carried past a billboard, you were absorbing the art—or some would say science—of persuasive communication.

Advertising is basically anything someone does to grab your attention and hold onto it long enough to tell you how cool, fast, cheap, tasty, fun, rockin', or rad whatever they're selling is. Some people have a different definition. They argue that advertising is trickery used to shut down your brain just long enough to convince you to open your wallet!

From "Ad Power," page 517

Expression Rubric

1	2	3
The reader sounds monotone. The reader's voice does not match the subject of what is being read.	The reader is making some tone changes. Sometimes, the reader's voice matches what is being read.	The reader is using proper tones and pauses. The reader's voice matches what is being read.

Accuracy and Rate Formula

______ words attempted in one minute	–	______ number of errors	=	______ words correct per minute (wcpm)

CCSS Literacy.RI.9-10.10 By the end of grade 10, read and comprehend literary nonfiction at the high end of the grades 9–10 text complexity band independently and proficiently.

READING HANDBOOK

Practice Intonation: "A Long Way to Go: Minorities and the Media"

Intonation is the rise and fall in the pitch or tone of your voice as you read aloud. Use this passage to practice reading with proper intonation. Print a copy of this passage from myNGconnect.com to help you monitor your progress. To use an Intonation Rubric, see page 748.

In one episode of *The $25,000 Pyramid*, a remarkable exchange occurred. In this TV game show, a word appears on a screen in front of one contestant. He then gives clues to try to get his partner to identify the correct word.

On that special day, the word "gangs" came up on the clue-giver's screen. Without hesitation, he fired out the first thing that came to his mind: "They have lots of these in East L.A." (a heavily Mexican American area of Los Angeles). His partner immediately answered, "gangs."

Under pressure, two strangers had linked "East L.A." with "gangs." Why? What force could have brought these two strangers to the same idea?

The answer is obvious—the mass media. The entertainment media have a fascination with Latino gangs. The news media also like to show them often. At the same time, the entertainment media rarely show other Latino characters. And the news media rarely show other Hispanic topics, except for such "problem" issues as immigration and language. The result has been a Latino public image—better yet, a stereotype—in which gangs are an important part.

From "A Long Way to Go: Minorities and the Media," page 545

Intonation

Print a copy of this passage and the accompanying rubrics from myNGconnect.com.

Teach/Model Assist students in using proper intonation with "A Long Way to Go: Minorities and the Media." For example:

- Point out the words that indicate the tone of the second paragraph. *Special day* and *fired out* are some examples. Model reading this paragraph aloud, emphasizing those phrases.
- Point out the words that are in quotation marks: *East L.A.*, *gangs*, *problem*. Explain that quotation marks are sometimes also used to indicate emphasis and tone. Read aloud the second and third paragraphs with and without proper intonation. Tell students to listen to hear the difference.

Practice Have students use these daily fluency routines to develop intonation:

1. **Choral Reading** Underline parts of the passage that require special intonation. Students chorally read the passage, raising and lowering their voices as indicated.
2. **Collaborative Reading** Partners read alternative sentences in the passage, listening for appropriate intonation.
3. **Recorded Reading** Students record their readings and play them back, checking for proper intonation.
4. **Reading and Marking** Working with a copy from **myNGconnect.com**, one student reads while the other circles words and phrases that require special intonation.
5. **Reading to Assess** Partners read aloud the passage and apply the checklist from p. 557.

Assess Have students read aloud the passage. Use the rubrics to assess intonation, accuracy, and rate.
RI.9-10.10

myNGconnect.com

Fluency Practice

Comprehension Coach

Intonation Rubric

1	2	3
The reader's tone does not change. The reading all sounds the same.	The reader's tone changes sometimes to match what is being read.	The reader's tone always changes to match what is being read.

Accuracy and Rate Formula

______ words attempted in one minute	–	______ number of errors	=	______ words correct per minute (wcpm)

CCSS Literacy.RI.9-10.10 By the end of grade 10, read and comprehend literary nonfiction at the high end of the grades 9–10 text complexity band independently and proficiently.

Phrasing

Print a copy of this passage and the accompanying rubrics from myNGconnect.com.

Teach/Model Assist students in using proper phrasing with "What Is News?." For example:

- Point to the phrasing clues in the first paragraph. Read the paragraph aloud without proper phrasing. Ask students how this affected their understanding of the passage.
- Tell students to pause longer for a period at the end of a paragraph when they read aloud. Model reading the second and third paragraphs, using an appropriate pause between the two paragraphs.

Practice Have students use these daily fluency routines to develop phrasing:

1. **Choral Reading** Mark an entire passage with pause marks. Students chorally read the passage, pausing only at the marks.
2. **Collaborative Reading** Partners read alternative sentences in the passage, listening for appropriate phrasing.
3. **Recorded Reading** Students record their readings and play them back, adding pause marks only where the recording indicates a pause.
4. **Reading and Marking** Working with a copy from myNGconnect.com, one student reads while the other records pause marks.
5. **Reading to Assess** Partners read aloud the passage and apply the checklist from p. 579.

Assess Have students read aloud the passage. Use the rubrics to assess phrasing, accuracy, and rate.
RI.9-10.10

myNGconnect.com

Fluency Practice

Comprehension Coach

Practice Phrasing: "What Is News?"

Phrasing is how you use your voice to group words together. Use this passage to practice reading with proper phrasing. Print a copy of this passage from myNGconnect.com to help you monitor your progress. To use a Phrasing Rubric, see page 749.

Research indicates that students get most of their political information from watching David Letterman, Jay Leno, *The Daily Show*, MTV, and from surfing the Web. As recent elections reveal, candidates gain appeal by reaching out to youth through the media. In 1994, former president Bill Clinton made his case to youth on MTV as part of their "Rock the Vote" campaign. And in 2003, California Governor Arnold Schwarzenegger announced his candidacy on Leno's show.

From online chats, instant messaging, blog writing, and market research, candidates know exactly how to find young people on the Internet who are engaged in news and current events activities.

Politicians and advertisers are using the media and "hipper" methods to attract young people. This bears close scrutiny of how youth react to the media messages they see and hear.

From "What Is News?," page 565

Phrasing Rubric

1	2	3
Reading is choppy. There are usually no pauses for punctuation.	Reading is mostly smooth. There are some pauses for punctuation.	Reading is very smooth. Punctuation is being used properly.

Accuracy and Rate Formula

________ words attempted in one minute	−	________ number of errors	=	________ words correct per minute (wcpm)

CCSS Literacy.RI.9-10.10 By the end of grade 10, read and comprehend literary nonfiction at the high end of the grades 9–10 text complexity band independently and proficiently.

Practice Phrasing: "My Mother Pieced Quilts"

Phrasing is how you use your voice to group words together. Use this passage to practice reading with proper phrasing. Print a copy of this passage from myNGconnect.com to help you monitor your progress. To use a Phrasing Rubric, see page 749.

they were just meant as covers
in winters
as weapons
against pounding january winds

but it was just that every morning I awoke to these
october ripened canvases
passed my hand across their cloth faces
and began to wonder how you pieced
all these together
these strips of gentle communion cotton and flannel nightgowns
wedding organdies
dime store velvets

how you shaped patterns square and oblong and round
positioned
balanced
then cemented them
with your thread
a steel needle
a thimble

From "My Mother Pieced Quilts," page 638

READING HANDBOOK

Phrasing Rubric

1	2	3
Reading is choppy. There are usually no pauses for punctuation.	Reading is mostly smooth. There are some pauses for punctuation.	Reading is very smooth. Punctuation is being used properly.

Accuracy and Rate Formula

_______ words attempted in one minute	–	_______ number of errors	=	_______ words correct per minute (wcpm)

Phrasing

Print a copy of this passage and the accompanying rubrics from myNGconnect.com.

Teach/Model Assist students in using proper phrasing with "My Mother Pieced Quilts." For example:

- Point out that the poem has no punctuation. Explain that when reading poems like this aloud, students must use context clues to know when to pause.
- Read the first stanza, pausing after the word "just." Then read it with correct phrasing. Ask: How does this affect the meaning?

Practice Have students use these daily fluency routines to develop phrasing:

1. **Choral Reading** Mark an entire passage with pause marks. Students chorally read the passage, pausing only at the marks.
2. **Collaborative Reading** Partners read alternative sentences in the passage, listening for appropriate phrasing.
3. **Recorded Reading** Students record their readings and play them back, adding pause marks only where the recording indicates a pause.
4. **Reading and Marking** Working with a copy from myNGconnect.com, one student reads while the other records pause marks.
5. **Reading to Assess** Partners read aloud the passage and apply the checklist from p. 641.

Assess Have students read aloud the passage. Use the rubrics to assess phrasing, accuracy, and rate.
RL.9-10.10

myNGconnect.com

Fluency Practice

Comprehension Coach

CCSS Literacy.RL.9-10.10 By the end of grade 10, read and comprehend literature, including stories, dramas, and poems, at the high end of the grades 9–10 text complexity band independently and proficiently.

Expression

Print a copy of this passage and the accompanying rubrics from myNGconnect.com.

Teach/Model Assist students in using proper expression with "Sonnet 30: A Modern Paraphrase." For example:

- Point out the words that indicate the tone of the poem: *regret, saddens, cry, died, heartbreaks*, etc.
- Point to the emotional turn in the poem: With the word *but* in the penultimate line, the tone of the poem shifts. Model reading the last four or five lines of the poem aloud, noting this shift with your voice. Tell students to listen carefully for this shift in expression.

Practice Have students use these daily fluency routines to develop expression:

1. **Listen While Reading** Students listen to the fluency model on the **Fluency Model CD** several times to internalize the reader's expression.
2. **Collaborative Reading** Partners read alternative sentences in the passage, listening for appropriate expression.
3. **Recorded Reading** Students record their readings and play them back, checking for their own expression.
4. **Student-Adult Reading** Students read the passage to an adult and receive feedback on their expression.
5. **Reading to Assess** Partners read aloud the passage and apply the checklist from p. 673.

Assess Have students read aloud the passage. Use the rubrics to assess expression, accuracy, and rate.
RL.9-10.10

myNGconnect.com

Fluency Practice

Comprehension Coach

Practice Expression: "Sonnet 30: A Modern Paraphrase"

Expression in reading is how you use your voice to express feeling. Use this passage to practice reading with proper expression. Print a copy of this passage from myNGconnect.com to help you monitor your progress. To use an Expression Rubric, see page 750.

When in moments of quiet thoughtfulness
I think about the past,
I regret that I did not achieve all that I wanted,
And it saddens me to think of the years that I wasted:
Then I cry, though I am not one who cries often,
For my good friends who have died,
And I cry again over heartbreaks that ended long ago,
And mourn the loss of many things that I have seen and loved:
Then I grieve again over past troubles,
And sadly I remind myself, one regret after another,
Of all the sorrows and disappointments in my life,
And they hurt me more than ever before.
But if I think of you at this time, dear friend,
I regain all that I have lost and my sadness ends.

From "Sonnet 30: A Modern Paraphrase," page 671

Expression Rubric

1	2	3
The reader sounds monotone. The reader's voice does not match the subject of what is being read.	The reader is making some tone changes. Sometimes, the reader's voice matches what is being read.	The reader is using proper tones and pauses. The reader's voice matches what is being read.

Accuracy and Rate Formula

______ words attempted in one minute	–	______ number of errors	=	______ words correct per minute (wcpm)

CCSS Literacy.RL.9-10.10 By the end of grade 10, read and comprehend literature, including stories, dramas, and poems, at the high end of the grades 9–10 text complexity band independently and proficiently.

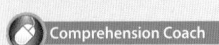

READING HANDBOOK

Practice Intonation: "I Hear America Singing"

Intonation is the rise and fall in the pitch or tone of your voice as you read aloud. Use this passage to practice reading with proper intonation. Print a copy of this passage from myNGconnect.com to help you monitor your progress. To use an Intonation Rubric, see page 748.

I hear America singing, the varied carols I hear,
Those of mechanics, each one singing his as it should be blithe and strong,
The carpenter singing his as he measures his plank or beam,
The mason singing his as he makes ready for work, or leaves off work,
The boatman singing what belongs to him in his boat, the deckhand singing on the steamboat deck,
The shoemaker singing as he sits on his bench, the hatter singing as he stands,
The wood-cutter's song, the ploughboy's on his way in the morning, or at noon intermission or at sundown,
The delicious singing of the mother, or of the young wife at work, or of the girl sewing or washing,
Each singing what belongs to him or her and to none else,
The day what belongs to the day—at night the party of young fellows, robust, friendly,
Singing with open mouths their strong melodious songs.

From "I Hear America Singing," page 682

Intonation Rubric

1	2	3
The reader's tone does not change. The reading all sounds the same.	The reader's tone changes sometimes to match what is being read.	The reader's tone always changes to match what is being read.

Accurracy and Rate Formula

_______ words attempted in one minute − _______ number of errors = _______ words correct per minute (wcpm)

Intonation

Print a copy of this passage and the accompanying rubrics from **myNGconnect.com**.

Teach/Model Assist students in using proper intonation with "I Hear America Singing." For example:

- Explain that a clue about intonation in this piece is the word *singing*. The reader's voice should have a song-like quality. Model this as you read aloud the first few lines of the poem.
- Point to the context clues that alert readers to the feelings and emotions of the passage: *blithe*, *delicious*, *friendly*, *strong*. Have students define these words to better understand the intonation of the text.

Practice Have students use these daily fluency routines to develop intonation:

1. **Choral Reading** Underline parts of the passage that require special intonation. Students chorally read the passage, raising and lowering their voices as indicated.
2. **Collaborative Reading** Partners read alternative sentences in the passage, listening for appropriate intonation.
3. **Recorded Reading** Students record their readings and play them back, checking for proper intonation.
4. **Reading and Marking** Working with a copy from **myNGconnect.com**, one student reads while the other circles words and phrases that require special intonation.
5. **Reading to Assess** Partners read aloud the passage and apply the checklist from p. 695.

Assess Have students read aloud the passage. Use the rubrics to assess intonation, accuracy, and rate. RL.9-10.10

myNGconnect.com

Fluency Practice

Comprehension Coach

CCSS Literacy.RL.9-10.10 By the end of grade 10, read and comprehend literature, including stories, dramas, and poems, at the high end of the grades 9–10 text complexity band independently and proficiently.

Ⓐ Create a Study Routine

Expand Explain that a routine is a pattern of behavior that a person does over and over again, and that having a routine can help make things easier to do. After reading through the tips for creating a study routine, invite volunteers to share the routine that works best for them.

Ⓑ Create a Study Environment

Expand Brainstorm with students a list of supplies and reference sources to be included in a study area. For example:

- **Supplies** pens, pencils, highlighters, paper, self-stick notes, calculator, ruler, stapler, scissors, note cards, erasers, paper clips, folders
- **Reference Sources** dictionary, thesaurus, atlas, almanac, encyclopedia, computer, style guide

Study Skills and Strategies

Before You Study

Studying can be difficult, especially when you are distracted or have many subjects you need to study all at the same time. There are several ways to prepare to study, including creating a routine and establishing a productive study environment. You can also make studying easier by studying subjects in a specific order and creating a schedule.

How to Create and Maintain a Study Routine

Before you begin studying, create a routine.

- Study at the same time and place for each session.
- Mark the study time in your calendar as an appointment, like going to the doctor. For example, *Tuesday: 3:30–4:30: Study English.*
- Set small, specific goals for each study session.
- Pay attention to what works best for you and repeat that method.
- Give yourself a small reward when you are finished. For example, call a friend or listen to your favorite music.

How to Create a Productive Study Environment

Setting up a study area will help you follow your routine. Find an area where you are comfortable that you can claim as your own.

Set Up Your Workplace
• Make sure your area is quiet or has background noise, depending on which you prefer.
• Make sure you have enough light—get an extra lamp if your area is too dark.
• Have everything you need for studying available beforehand.
• Designate certain places for each necessary item. Don't waste valuable time looking for books, notes, writing materials, self-stick notes, or information.
• After you have assembled the items you need, put them where you can easily access them.
• Keep a calendar and a watch or clock in your study area to help you stay focused on your available time and on your priorities.
• Keep your study area clean.

How to Create an Efficient Study Order

Creating priorities for study time will help you complete your tasks in an efficient order. Making a list of the things you need to do can help you organize your priorities. Look at the chart to understand how to create an efficient order for your study time.

Study Order Tips	
Label Your Assignments by Priority	• **Urgent** Must be done immediately • **Important** Must be done soon • **Upcoming** Must be done in the near future
Make a List	• List the things you have to do in order of importance. • Once you complete a task, cross it off your list.
Stay Organized	• Keep your list nearby to record new tasks or updates.

A

How to Complete Tasks on Schedule

A good schedule can help you stay focused and complete assignments on time. Create a schedule or purchase a day planner and record homework due dates, quizzes, and tests.

Think about events that might affect your schedule, such as appointments or extracurricular activities. You may need to postpone or cancel other plans to help you stay on schedule. If you are concerned about missing a date, circle the task.

Weekly Schedule

Subject	Monday	Tuesday	Wednesday	Thursday	Friday
Math	Chapter 6: Problems 1-10	None	Chapter 6: Problems 11-20	None	Chapter 7: Problems 1-15
Science	Study for Test	Review for Test	Test	Read Chapter 8	None
History	None	Read Chapter 11	Read Chapter 12	Study for Quiz	Quiz: Chapters 11 and 12
English	Read Chapter 3	Read Chapter 4 Study for Quiz	Quiz: Chapters 3 and 4	Read Chapter 5	None

B

READING HANDBOOK

A Create an Efficient Study Order

Expand Suggest that when students actually begin working, they might want to complete the most difficult assignment first and then move on to those that are less difficult. In this way, students can do the hardest work when they are most on task.

B Complete Tasks on Schedule

Practice Create a Weekly Schedule and have students help you fill it out for the week. Students can copy the schedule in their planners or on a separate sheet of paper.

A While You Study

Reinforce Point out that students should use a variety of study tools, both those that are familiar to them and new ones that they learn from teachers and classmates.

MODEL Say:

- *When I study, there are certain tools I always use because they work well for me.*
- *For example, I like to write notes about a subject on note cards and then summarize the information in an outline.*
- *I know that this works for me, but I'm always ready to learn new ways to study.*

B Review Effectively

Expand Have students create a weekly homework schedule, or review the schedule on page 773. Have students add review time to the lists of homework or tasks to show that daily reviewing is important.

While You Study

A There are many different ways to study. Talk with classmates and your teachers to learn new study techniques and strategies that might work for you, too. No matter which study strategies you use, you should use a variety, such as writing and using graphic organizers, until you figure out which strategies work best for you.

How to Use Writing as a Study Tool

Use writing as a tool to assist you:

- Write your own questions about the topic, and practice answering them.
- Condense your classroom notes onto note cards or into charts for easier reviewing.
- Create an outline from your notes, and then write a summary of the information.
- Write notes on self-stick notes as you read. Later, attach the self-stick notes in an organized manner to a sheet of notebook paper for at-a-glance study.

How to Use Graphic Organizers as a Study Tool

Graphic organizers are effective study tools. For example, a time line can be used to organize the events covered in a nonfiction selection. A word web can be used to learn new vocabulary words. See the Index of Graphic Organizers on page Index 1 for more examples of graphic organizers you can use as study tools.

How to Review

It is very important to review material. The best time to review is right after you have finished reading something for the first time. Reviewing gives you an opportunity to figure out anything you do not understand and to better remember information in the future.

B

Review Effectively
• When you read something new, review the information on the same day.
• Reread information to measure what you have learned.
• Go over notes in detail to clarify information you may have missed or don't understand. Combine your notes with any outlines or study guides that you have about the topic.
• Write down any new questions you may have.
• Plan a time to review each day. This will help you learn to review information regularly as part of your daily study schedule.

How to Use a Learning Log and Set Goals

You can use learning logs to record what you have learned, what you found interesting, and questions you have about the text. The purpose of a learning log is to think about your understanding of the material and to clarify your knowledge for further study. Use the **What parts am I struggling with?** and **What will I do next?** columns in the learning log to set future learning goals.

Learning Log

Title of Selection:

Dates and page numbers	What have I learned?	What parts am I struggling with?	What will I do next?

A

How to Seek Help

There will be times when you don't understand certain information, even after studying and careful note taking. You will need to seek help to understand the information. Make a list of the topics or problems that you don't understand. Include the page numbers where they are located in your textbooks. Make a chart that lists people and places you can seek help from. Then use these resources to help clarify confusing information.

Resources for Help
People: teachers, parents, siblings, classmates, librarians, tutors
Places: libraries, museums, study centers, school
Reference Sources: dictionaries, thesauruses, encyclopedias, atlases, newspapers, magazines, Web sites, television programs

B

READING HANDBOOK

A Use a Learning Log

Practice Explain how Learning Logs can be used as preparation for small-group or whole-class discussions. Have students create a learning log for material that they are currently studying. Then have students use learning logs in small group discussions. Partners can then share their learning logs and help each other set goals for further study. Have each student check off items they used for class discussion and reflect on how they can improve preparation for future discussions.

SL.9-10.1.a

B Seek Help

Practice Have students create their own personal chart listing resources they will use when they need help. Encourage students to name specific people, places, and reference sources. Invite students to work in groups or with partners to share their lists and gather more ideas. Remind students that information must be synthesized and carefully evaluated. Review how to evaluate information using page 723. Then have partners discuss the various sources and rate them on which might be more likely to include valid and reliable information.

> **ELL** **Elaborate** Display examples of a variety of reference sources that students might access, and review how to use each source. You might also take a trip to the school library or media center to point out where reference sources can be found. Encourage students to take advantage of any special resources for English language learners that you may have at your school.
>
> SL.9-10.2

CCSS **Literacy.SL.9-10.1.a** Come to discussions prepared, having read and researched material under study; explicitly draw on that preparation by referring to evidence from texts and other research on the topic or issue to stimulate a thoughtful, well-reasoned exchange of ideas. **Literacy.SL.9-10.2** Integrate multiple sources of information presented in diverse media or formats (e.g., visually, quantitatively, orally) evaluating the credibility and accuracy of each source.

How to Relate Words

Reinforce Provide examples of other activities that students can use to build vocabulary and relate new words to words or concepts they already know.

- **"What Is It?" Map** Create a semantic map with the heads *What Is It?, What Is It Like?,* and *Examples*, and complete the map for a new word.
- **Synonym/Antonym List** Make a list of words with meanings that are similar to and opposite of a new word.
- **Venn Diagram** Use a Venn diagram to explore how a new word is the same as and different from a familiar word.
- **Word Association** List familiar words that go with a new word and explain the association.
- **Personal Associations** Tell how a new word connects to one's own life.
- **Word Clues** Use prior knowledge to give clues about a new word and have a partner guess the word.

Model the activities with Key Vocabulary from the student book.

ELL Practice Help students create a word bank for the classroom to assist students in remembering correct spelling, relationships between words, and definitions of new words.
L.9-10.6

Vocabulary

How to Make Words Your Own Routine

When you cook, you follow the steps of a recipe. This helps you make the food correctly. When you read, there are also steps you can follow to learn new words. The following steps will help you practice the words in different ways and make the words your own.

Learning a Word

Follow these steps to add new words to your vocabulary.

1. **Pronounce the Word** Write and say the word one syllable at a time.
   - **realize**: re-a-lize
   - Think about what looks familiar in the word. For example, ***real*** is part of ***realize***.
2. **Study Examples** When you are given examples, read them carefully and think about how and why the word is being used.
   - **Example**: *Marietta did not* ***realize*** *that Lupe was so busy.* What does this sentence tell you about Marietta and Lupe?
   - Look for more examples to study in books or magazines.
3. **Elaborate** Create new sentences to check your understanding of the word.
   - Finish these sentence frames for practice:
   - I **realized** I was happy when ______.
   - Steve's mom **realized** he was growing up when ______.
   - How did your teacher **realize** that you ______?
4. **Practice the Words** Use the new word to write sentences.
   - Use the word in many different ways. This will help you remember the word and understand its meaning.

How to Relate Words

A good way to build your vocabulary is to **relate new words** to words or concepts you already know. Think about how the new word is similar to or different from words you are already familiar with. You can also create a **semantic map** to help you study the new word.

Semantic Map

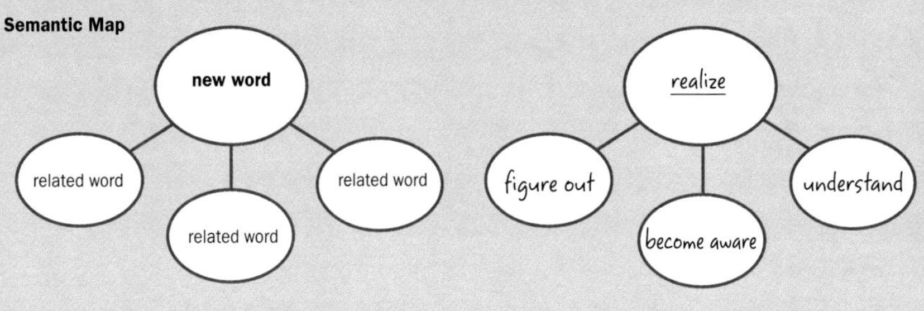

CCSS Literacy.L.9-10.6 Acquire and use accurately general academic and domain-specific words and phrases, sufficient for reading, writing, speaking, and listening at the college and career readiness level; demonstrate independence in gathering vocabulary knowledge when considering a word or phrase important to comprehension or expression.

How to Use Context to Understand Words

Context is the surrounding text near a word or phrase that helps explain the meaning of the word or phrase.

Unfamiliar Words

Context clues are hints in a sentence or paragraph that can help define unknown or unfamiliar words. Context clues can include synonyms, antonyms, explanations, definitions, examples, sensory images, or punctuation, such as commas and dashes.

- **Example**: *My fascination with* celestial bodies*—such as* ***stars, planets,*** *and* ***moons****—made me want to buy a* ***telescope.*** The words *stars*, *planets*, and *moons* are clues that tell me *celestial bodies* are objects in the universe. The word *telescope* tells me I can see these objects from Earth, probably at night.

A

Multiple-Meaning Words

Some words have different meanings depending on how they are used in a sentence. Check what context the words are used in to help determine which meaning is correct in the material you are reading. Substitute each meaning you know in the context of the sentence until you find the use that makes the best sense.

- **Example**: *Please sign your name before entering the museum.* The word *sign* has more than one meaning. Which meaning is correct in this sentence? *Sign* can mean "to write" or it can mean "something that hangs on a wall to provide information." The first meaning is correct.

B

Figurative Language

Figurative language is a tool that writers use to help you visualize or relate to what is happening in a selection. This type of language is nonliteral because it does not mean exactly what it looks like it says, or it is using a special meaning. Idioms, similes, and metaphors are common types of nonliteral, or figurative language. It is helpful to use mental images or context clues to better understand what you are reading.

Idioms

An **idiom** is a phrase or an expression that can only be understood as a complete sentence or phrase. The individual words have separate meanings and they will not make sense if they are thought of literally. Read the words before or after the idiom to figure out the meaning. Remember to think about an idiom as a group of words, not as individual words.

- **Example**: Don't *bite off more than you can chew* or you will never finish the job. This is an idiom used to advise people against agreeing to do more work than they are capable of doing. It is not a phrase about biting or chewing.

C

READING HANDBOOK

A Unfamiliar Words

Reinforce Explain that certain punctuation marks, such as commas and dashes, are helpful context clues for figuring out unfamiliar words. Dashes or commas may be used to set off a word or group of words that builds on an idea or explains the meaning of a certain term. In the example, the dashes give readers a clue that stars, planets, and moons are examples of celestial bodies. Students should look for key words that introduce explanations or descriptions of unfamiliar words, such as *in other words, like, for example,* and *such as.*

B Multiple-Meaning Words

Practice Remind students that they can use a dictionary, along with context clues, to check the correct meaning of a word. Display a list of multiple-meaning words: *kind*, *story*, *park*, *play*, *trip*, *light*, *check*, *band*.

Brainstorm with students multiple meanings for each word. Encourage students to use a dictionary if needed. Then have them use a word with one of the meanings in a sentence.

C Idioms

Expand Provide additional examples. Discuss how the literal meaning of the words is different from the meaning of the entire phrase:

- *food for thought*: things to think about
- *keep it under your hat*: keep it secret
- *piece of cake*: very easy to do
- *wet blanket*: someone who isn't fun

L.9-10.4

ELL **Elaborate** Help students make a connection to English idioms by asking them to cite examples from their home languages. Encourage students to use context to help them determine the meanings of idioms as they read. Help students create a chart of idioms and their meanings, and encourage students to ask others to elaborate when they hear an English phrase they do not understand.

CCSS **Literacy.L.9-10.4** Determine or clarify the meaning of unknown and multiple-meaning words and phrases based on grades 9–10 reading and content, choosing flexibly from a range of strategies.

A Figurative Language

Practice Have each student write a sentence using a simile or metaphor. Then have small groups exchange and evaluate sentences to select the best example of figurative language. Each group should then revise their choice. When groups have completed their revisions, have volunteers present the selected sentences aloud to the class. Have group members justify why the sentence they chose was the best example of figurative language.
L.9-10.5

B Technical and Specialized Language

Expand Discuss technical language that is used in professions:

- nautical terms (*all hands*, *boom*, *crow's nest*)
- military terms (*recruit*, *rank*, *brass*)
- medical terms (*stat*, *IV push*, *code blue*)

Have students brainstorm additional technical words. Model finding the meanings by using sample sentences and context clues. Encourage students to keep lists of technical or specialized vocabulary they encounter in everyday life.

C Denotation and Connotation

Practice Have students practice distinguishing between the denotations and connotations of words, both within sentences and also within whole passages, by writing sentences and short paragraphs to illustrate the concept. Have them exchange their samples and ask classmates to analyze and explain whether the text is explicit and exact (denotation) or if the text contains meanings that go beyond the literal meaning (connotation).

Be sure to point out that by using the context of the sentence or the context of a longer segment of text, readers can determine whether the writer intended the words to be taken literally or if there is a broader meaning that goes beyond the exact meaning of the words and text.
L.9-10.4.a, L.9-10.5

Similes and Metaphors

A

Similes use *like* or *as* to compare two things.

- **Example**: *The willow tree's branches are like silken thread.* This simile is comparing a tree's branches to silk thread. Think about the things that are being compared and what they each mean. Silk is very soft and smooth. The simile means the willow's branches are also very soft and smooth.

Metaphors compare two things without using *like* or *as*.

- **Example**: *The night sky is a black curtain.* This metaphor compares the night sky to a black curtain. A black curtain would block out light from coming in a window. This metaphor means the night sky is very dark.
- **Example**: *The company planned an advertising blitz to promote its new product.* The word *blitz* comes from the German word *blitzkrieg*, which refers to the bombing of London, England, by Germany during World War II. The term *advertising blitz*, therefore, is a metaphor that expresses the way advertisements will overwhelm the public.

You can also use sensory images to learn new words by asking yourself or others: What does it look like? Feel like? Sound like?

Technical and Specialized Language

B

Technical, or specialized, language provides important information about a topic. Many words in English have an everyday meaning and a special meaning in a career field. For example, the word *shift* can mean "to move something from one place to another." In the workplace, however, *shift* can mean "a time period for work."

Example: *Be sure to clean your mouse regularly to make the cursor move smoothly on the computer monitor.*

- Read the sentence to determine the specialized subject.
- Identify technical vocabulary: *mouse, cursor, computer monitor.*
- Use context clues to help you figure out the meaning of the technical language, or jargon.

Denotation and Connotation

C

Denotation is the actual meaning of a word that you would find in a dictionary. For example, if you looked up the word *snake* in the dictionary, you could find that one of its meanings is "a limbless scaled reptile with a long tapering body."

Connotation is the suggested meaning of the word in addition to its literal meaning. Connotations can be positive or negative. For example, the word *snake* can be used in a positive or negative way.

- **Example**: *Jenny was caught sneaking around Maria's locker. She wanted to steal Maria's homework and copy Maria's answers. Nobody could believe that Jenny would be such a snake.*

By using the context of the paragraph (*sneaking around*, *steal*), you can understand that the connotation of *snake* in this usage is negative.

CCSS **Literacy.L.9-10.4.a** Use context (e.g., the overall meaning of a sentence, paragraph, or text; a word's position or function in a sentence) as a clue to the meaning of a word or phrase. **Literacy.L.9-10.5** Demonstrate understanding of figurative language, word relationships, and nuances in word meanings.

Analogies

An **analogy** is a comparison. Think of analogies as word problems. To solve the analogy, figure out what the connection is. Use context to see how the word pairs are related.

- **Example**: *Hard* is to *rocks* as *soft* is to ______. *Hard* describes the feeling of *rocks*. Rocks are hard. What does *soft* describe the feeling of? *Hard* is to *rocks* as *soft* is to *blankets*.

Use the relationships between words in an analogy to infer the meaning of an unfamiliar word. For example, in the analogy "*sparse* is to *meager* as *quarrel* is to *argue*," you can infer that *sparse* and *meager* mean the same thing.

Allusions

An **allusion** is a reference to another text. If you know or can find out about the source that the writer is alluding to, you can better understand the word or phrase.

- **Example**: "It took a herculean effort, but she finally made it to graduation." *Herculean* refers to a character from Greek mythology named Hercules. He fought monsters and faced many dangers. So the character must have faced challenges too.

How to Analyze Word Parts

Each piece in a puzzle fits together to make a picture. Words have pieces that come together, too. Analyzing the parts, or structures, of words will help you learn the meaning of entire words. Use a print or electronic dictionary to confirm your word analysis.

Compound Words

Compound words are made when two separate words are combined to make a new word. To learn the meaning of a compound word, study its parts individually. For example, *doghouse* is one word made from two smaller words, *dog* and *house*. Since you know that *dog* is an animal and *house* is a structure where people live, you can figure out that *doghouse* means a house for a dog.

Greek and Latin Roots

Many words in the English language derived from, or came from, other languages, especially Greek and Latin. It is helpful to know the **origins**, or **roots**, of English words. You may be able to figure out the meaning of an unknown word if you know the meaning of its root. Roots can form many different words and can't be broken into smaller parts. The chart below has examples of roots.

Root Chart

Root	Meaning	English Example
crit (Greek)	to judge	*Criticize* means "to find fault." *Critique* means "an act of judgment."
mal (Latin)	bad	*Malady* means "an illness." *Malice* means "desire to harm another."

A Analogies

Expand An analogy is a way of explaining how a thing functions or describing something by comparing it to something that is familiar. Practice some analogies with students:

- *Club* is to *golfer* as *bat* is to ______. (hitter)
- *Steering wheel* is to *car* as *handlebars* are to ______. (cycle)
- *Food* is to *hunger* as *water* is to ______. (thirst)

Now have students work in pairs to produce two or three examples of each kind of analogy.

B Greek and Latin Roots

Expand Provide examples to expand the chart. Encourage students to suggest additional words and to use the words in sentences:

- *ast* (Greek): star
  astronomy: the study of the universe
  astronaut: a space traveler
  asterisk: a star-shaped symbol
- *dic* (Latin): say
  dictionary: a book of word meanings
  dictate: to speak words to be written
  predict: say what will happen
- *pod* (Greek): foot
  tripod: a three-legged frame
  podiatrist: a doctor who treats feet
  podium: a platform on which one stands
- *vac* (Latin): empty
  vacuum: an empty space
  evacuate: to clear out; to empty a place

Prefixes and Suffixes

Reinforce Model how to analyze the word *constellation.*

MODEL Say:

- *In order to figure out the meaning of the word* constellation, *I break it into parts*: con-, stella, -tion.
- *I know that* stella *is a Latin root meaning "star." I also know that the prefix* con- *means "together," and the suffix* -tion *means "the act of."*
- *When I put all I know together, I can figure out that a constellation is a group of stars.*

Practice Provide other examples and work with students to analyze the words:

- *midfielder*: one who is active in the middle of a playing area; prefix: *mid-* means "middle"; root: *field* means "playing area"; suffix: *-er* means "one who"
- *reusable*: can be put into action or service again; prefix: *re-* means "again"; root: *use* means "put into action or service"; suffix: *-able* means "can be"
- *counterclockwise*: in a direction opposite of the movement of a clock; prefix: *counter-* means "opposite"; root: *clock* means "device to tell time"; suffix: *-wise* means "direction"

L.9-10.4

Remind students that the best way to determine or confirm your word analysis is by using a print or an electronic dictionary.

Word Families Practice Use Vocabulary Routine 4 (PD30). Have students select a word from their Vocabulary Notebook and use it to demonstrate a word family. Have students copy Wordbench cards to display them for the class. Invite students to use self-stick notes to add words to the word bench cards.

L.9-10.4.b

Prefixes and Suffixes

If you know common roots, **prefixes**, and **suffixes**, you can figure out the meanings of many words. The chart below shows how to analyze the word *constellation*.

Word Part	Definition	Example
Root	The main part of a word	*stella* means "star"
Prefix	A word part placed in front of the root to create a new meaning	*con-* means "together"
Suffix	A word part placed after the root to create a new meaning	*-tion* means "the act of"
Example: A *constellation* is a group of stars.		

Inflected Forms

An **inflection** is a change in the form of a word to show its usage. You can learn new words by analyzing what type of inflection is being used.

Inflection	Meaning	Examples
-er	more	cold**er**, fast**er**
-ed	in the past	call**ed**, talk**ed**
-s	plural	pen**s**, dog**s**

Word Families

A word family is a group of words that all share the same root but have different forms. For example, look at the word family for *success*: *success**ful***, *success**fully***, ***un**success**ful***, ***un**success**fully***. If you know the meaning of the root word *success*, you can use what you know to help you understand the rest of the meanings in the word family.

Cognates and False Cognates

Cognates are words that come from two different languages but that are very similar because they share root origins. Cognates have similar spellings and meanings. For example, the English word *artist* and the Spanish word *artista* both mean "a person who creates art."

False cognates seem like they share a meaning but they do not. For example, the English word *rope* means "a cord to tie things with," but the Spanish word *ropa* means "clothing."

How to Use Cognates to Determine Word Meaning

- Think about what the word means in the language you are most familiar with.
- Substitute the meaning of the word with your language's definition.
- If your language's definition does not make sense, you may be using a false cognate. Try to learn the word using a different resource.

CCSS **Literacy.L.9-10.4** Determine or clarify the meaning of unknown and multiple-meaning words and phrases based on grades 9–10 reading and content, choosing flexibly from a range of strategies. **Literacy.L.9-10.4.b** Identify and correctly use patterns of word changes that indicate different meanings or parts of speech (e.g., analyze, analysis, analytical; advocate, advocacy).

Foreign Words in English

Some foreign words come directly into English, without changes in spelling. For example, the French phrase *avant-garde*, referring to a cutting-edge movement in art or music, is often used in English. Use a print or online dictionary to identify other foreign words in English.

How to Use a Reference

Dictionary

A dictionary lists words with correct spellings, pronunciations, meanings, and uses. It can be used to find the denotation, or exact meaning, of a word. Sometimes a dictionary definition may be helpful in determining the connotation, or feelings associated with a word.

- Read all the definitions of the new word to find the use and meaning you need. Use the dictionary's key to understand any abbreviations or symbols.
- Go back to the selection and reread the paragraph. Substitute the meaning you found for the original word. Check to make sure it is the correct use of the word.

A

fraud·u·lent
(frô' jə lənt), *adj.*: based on or done by fraud or trickery; deceitful. [ME *fraude* fr. L *fraud-*] –fraud' u · lent · ness, *n.* –fraud' u · lent · ly, *adv.*

Key	
ME	Middle English (an old version of English)
L	Latin
fr.	from
ô	pronounced like the *a* in *saw*
ə	pronounced like *uh*
'	accented syllable

Thesaurus

A thesaurus lists words with their synonyms and antonyms. Use a thesaurus to confirm word meanings.

- Try to identify a familiar word from the synonyms listed for the new word.
- Go back to the selection and reread the paragraph. Substitute the synonym you chose for the original word. Keep trying synonyms until the words make sense.

B

Glossary

A glossary is like a dictionary but only defines words found in a specific book.

- Check to see whether there is a glossary at the end of the book you are reading.
- Read the definition of the new word in the glossary.
- Reread the sentence and substitute the definition for the word.

Technology

The Internet links computers and information sites electronically.

Web Sites to Use for Vocabulary Support

- myNGConnect.com This Web site has links to reference sources.
- m-w.com The Merriam-Webster Dictionary Web site includes a dictionary, a thesaurus, Spanish-English translation, and word activities.

READING HANDBOOK

A Dictionary

Expand Display a dictionary and discuss how to use additional features:

- **Guide Words** Point out the guide words on a page. Explain that the guide word on the left indicates the first word on the page. The guide word on the right indicates the last word on the page. If a word comes alphabetically between the two words, it will be on that page.
- **Syllable Division and Pronunciation** Point out the syllable division of a word on the page and the pronunciation in brackets. Have students pronounce the word using these features.
- **Part of Speech Notations** Draw attention to the numbered definitions of a word and the notations that indicate part of speech. Explain that students can use the part of speech notations to help them choose the correct meaning of a multiple-meaning word.
- **Etymology Notes** Point out the etymology note for one or more words and discuss information about word origin.
- **Denotation/Connotation** Explain that the dictionary definition of a word is considered its denotation; however, the variety of meanings a word has may provide clues as to its connotation. Point out that connotation also depends on the context in which a word is used. Have students use a print or an online dictionary to explore the denotations and connotations of a few words, such as *brother, cool,* and *fighter.*

B Thesaurus

Reinforce Remind students to use a thesaurus (print or electronic) to determine the precise word to use.

Practice Display a list of words. Have each student select two words—one word they do not know and a second word that they know. Have students use a dictionary to determine the meaning of the unknown word and verify the meaning of the known word. Use the Vocabulary Notebook routine (see page PD28) to direct students. Ask students to include the pronunciation, meaning, part of speech, and etymology of the word in their notebook entry.
L.9-10.4.c, L.9-10.4.d

CCSS **Literacy.L.9-10.4.c** Consult general and specialized reference materials (e.g., dictionaries, glossaries, thesauruses), both print and digital, to find the pronunciation of a word or determine or clarify its precise meaning, its part of speech, or its etymology. **Literacy.L.9-10.4.d** Verify the preliminary determination of the meaning of a word or phrase (e.g., by checking the inferred meaning in context or in a dictionary).

Memorize and Review New Words

Reinforce Support students' understanding of why memorizing and reviewing new words are effective strategies for learning new words.

MODEL Say:

- *Writing and reading new words and their definitions help me remember the words and what they mean. When I write the words and definitions on index cards, I can use the cards like flashcards. I can also use the cards to start a file of all the new words I have learned. If I alphabetize the cards, I can go back to them at any time to quickly check their meaning.*
- *I also like to create mental images, or pictures, of the words. This gives me another way to think about the new words, and it helps me remember them.*
- *I can also use images around me to help me remember new words. I can describe my classroom or my school.*
- *When I review new words, I try to use them in sentences. Using the words in sentences helps me understand the meaning of the words, especially when the words have multiple meanings. It also helps me connect the new words to other words and ideas.*

ELL **Relate** Encourage students to create a list of new English words on the left side of a sheet of paper and a list of similar words or clues from their home languages on the right side. Then have students practice the words by covering up one of the lists.

Practice Your Vocabulary

When you are trying to learn something new, like a musical instrument, you practice. The more you practice, the better you become. Practicing vocabulary words is an important step in learning new words.

Memorize New Words

- Read the word and its definition silently and aloud.
- Cover the definition and try to restate the word's meaning.
- Write words on one side of index cards and their meanings on the opposite sides to make flashcards. Have someone show you the words, and try to recite their definitions from memory.
- Ask yourself questions using the definition and the word.
- Think of clues or mental images to associate with the new word to help you better remember its definition. You can also use real images to help you remember. For example, look around the classroom. Point to an object and say what it is. Use this to describe the entire classroom.

Review New Words

- Reread the definition of each word.
- Create sentences expressing the correct meaning of each word.
- Make lists of new words with their definitions in a notebook to periodically review.
- Study each word until you are confident you understand its meaning and how to use the word properly.

Word Awareness

It is important to choose the right words in order to clearly say what you mean. You need to be aware of different kinds of words and how they work. For example, remember that some words have multiple meanings. If you are not aware of this as you read, you might use the wrong meaning or misunderstand a sentence.

Synonyms and Antonyms

Synonyms are words that have the same or similar meanings.

- Think of a different word that has the same meaning of the word you want to use. For example, synonyms for the word *loud* include *noisy* and *roaring*.
- Use a thesaurus when trying to identify synonyms.

Antonyms are words that have opposite meanings.

- Think of words that are the exact opposite of the word you want to use. For example, antonyms for the word *break* include *fix* and *repair.*
- Remember that antonyms are usually listed at the end of an entry for a word in a thesaurus.

READING HANDBOOK

Homonyms and Homophones

Homonyms are words that are spelled the same but have different meanings.

- **Example**: *I rose out of my chair to pick the rose from the top of the bush*. In this sentence, *rose* has two meanings. One *rose* is a verb (past tense of *rise*), and the other *rose* is a noun (a type of flower). Using context clues, you can see that *out of my chair* signals that "the past tense of rise" comes at the beginning of the sentence. You can then conclude that "the flower" is the second *rose*.

Homophones are words that sound the same but have different meanings and spellings.

- **Example**: *The wind blew the clouds across the blue sky. Blew* and *blue* sound alike, but they are spelled differently. *Blew* is a verb (the past tense of *blow*), and *blue* is an adjective (a color). Using context clues, you can see that *the clouds* signals that "the past tense of blow" comes at the beginning of the sentence. You can then conclude that "a color" is the second *blue*.

When you hear a homonym or a homophone read aloud, it is easy to become confused. Visualizing the word can help you figure out its correct meaning and spelling.

Phrasal Verbs, or Two-Word Verbs

Phrasal verbs combine a particle such as *out*, *up*, or *on* with a verb. These phrases are often idiomatic because the two words on their own mean something different than the phrase.

- **Example**: *I* brought up *my fight with Leon during dinner. Brought* is the past tense of *bring*, and *up* is a direction. But when the words are combined in the context shown in the sample sentence, they mean "mentioned." *I mentioned my fight with Leon during dinner.*

You may be able to find some phrasal verbs in a dictionary. If you do not understand a certain phrase, ask for help or look for English usage resources in the library.

Slang

Slang is language that is informal and specific to certain groups.

- Slang words are created and used in place of standard terms. Popular culture and the media heavily impact slang words and usage.
- Learning when to use slang is important. Slang is OK for casual situations, but not for more formal ones, like school discussions, writing, or presentations.
- If you become familiar with common slang words and phrases, it may help you to better understand everyday conversations. Special dictionaries for slang can help you learn more terms.

Dialect and Regionalism

A **dialect** is a way people in a specific region or area use a language.

- People in different locations often have different ways to express or pronounce words from the same language.
- If you are unfamiliar with a dialect, try to find out more about the way local people use their language. You can use the Internet or library resources to study dialects.

Phrasal Verbs

Expand Provide additional examples of sentences with phrasal verbs. Have students use context clues to determine the meaning of each phrasal verb. For example:

- I *ran into* my teacher at the game. (*ran into*: met; encountered)
- Please *show up* for class on time. (*show up*: arrive, appear)
- I *dropped off* during the boring film. (*dropped off*: napped; slept)
- Did you *catch on* to the trick, or were you fooled by it? (*catch on:* understand, realize)

Practice Have students find additional examples of phrasal verbs in the materials they are currently reading. Then have students search for definitions of these phrasal verbs in the dictionary or using online resources.

ELL **Act Out** Guide students in using actions, gestures, and expressions to support the meaning of phrasal verbs. For example, students can act out "ran into," "show up," "dropped off," and "catch on."
L.9-10.4.c, L.9-10.4.d

CCSS **Literacy.L.9-10.4.c** Consult general and specialized reference materials (e.g., dictionaries, glossaries, thesauruses), both print and digital, to find the pronunciation of a word or determine or clarify its precise meaning, its part of speech, or its etymology. **Literacy.L.9-10.4.d** Verify the preliminary determination of the meaning of a word or phrase (e.g., by checking the inferred meaning in context or in a dictionary).

HANDBOOK

The **Writing Handbook** gives tips and information to help students improve their writing. It is divided into the following sections:

- **The Writing Process** Students learn the steps of the writing process, from developing an idea through producing a published piece.
- **Writing Traits** Students learn the characteristics of excellent writing and how to use rubrics to evaluate and improve their own writing. This section also includes strong and weak examples of student work.
- **Writing Purposes, Modes, and Forms** Students learn the purposes and modes of writing. This section also includes models of various writing forms.
- **Grammar, Usage, Mechanics, and Spelling** Students learn the parts of speech and rules of English usage as well as methods for improving mechanics and spelling to become a better writer.
- **Troubleshooting Guide** Students learn to recognize and correct common errors in grammar, mechanics, sentence structure and word usage.

The Writing Process

Writing Traits

Writing Purposes, Modes, and Forms

Grammar, Usage, Mechanics, and Spelling

Troubleshooting Guide

What Is the Writing Process?

Writing is like anything else—if you want to do it well, you have to work at it. This work doesn't happen all at once, though. Good writers often follow a series of steps called the Writing Process. This process helps the writer break the writing into manageable tasks.

Prewrite

Prewriting is what you do before you write. In this step, you gather ideas, choose your topic, make a plan, and gather details.

1 Gather Ideas

Great writing ideas are all around you. What interests do you have that other people might want to read about? Think about recent events or things you've read or seen. Brainstorm ideas with your classmates, teachers, and family. Then record your ideas in an "idea bank," such as a notebook, journal, or **word processing** file. Add to your idea bank regularly and draw from it whenever you are given a writing assignment.

2 Choose Your Topic

Your teacher may give you a topic to write about, or you may have to choose one for yourself. Find several suitable topics in your idea bank; then ask these questions:

- What do I know about this topic?
- Who might want to read about this topic and why?
- Which topic do I feel most strongly about?
- Which topic best fits the assignment?
- What important question can I ask about the topic?

Writing Ideas
visiting my family in Mexico
✔ my first job
teens and peer pressure

3 Make a Plan

Create a Writing Plan to focus and organize your ideas.

Writing Plan
Topic: What will I write about? my first job
Purpose: Why am I writing? to share a lesson with others
Audience: Who will read this? my teacher and classmates
Form: What form works best for my topic, audience, and purpose? autobiographical narrative
Controlling Idea: What is this mainly about? learning to do things for myself
Voice/Tone: What attitude and feeling do I want my writing to express? serious, with a little humor

B

4 Gather Details

A 5Ws and H chart will help you gather details for many kinds of writing assignments.

5Ws and H Chart	
Who?	my dad, my boss, and I
What?	first job
Where?	Garcia's Restaurant
When?	last summer to now
Why?	spending money, save for college
How?	fill out application, use bus to get to and from my job

A Gather Ideas

Expand Help students use their life experiences to develop writing ideas:

- Have them think about TV, movies, books, magazines, and newspapers. Ask: What is your favorite? Who is the best/scariest/most interesting character? Did you read about a real-life event that was unbelievable?
- Tell students to think about family and friends. Ask: Do you have unusual or funny stories? Has anyone ever given you really good advice? If so, what was it?
- Have students consider their physical surroundings, such as nature or the neighborhood. Ask: Is there a place you go to enjoy nature? What is happening in your neighborhood?

Give students time to write their own ideas. Allow volunteers to describe their favorite ideas. Tell students to listen carefully but also to write down any new ideas they think of while listening to their classmates.

B Develop Voice

Practice Remind students that voice and tone are not the same. *Voice* refers to the personality of the writer. *Tone* is the writer's attitude toward his or her subject. Use these questions to help students find their voice before they write:

- How do you approach solving a problem?
- Do you feel more comfortable in a group setting or sitting quietly by yourself?
- How do you want to sound in your writing? Serious? Funny? Helpful?

Have students write their own paragraphs about a first job.

Invite volunteers to read their paragraphs aloud, and challenge the class to identify the voice. Ask: How does voice affect the writing?
W.9-10.4

CCSS Literacy.W.9-10.4 Produce clear and coherent writing in which the development, organization, and style are appropriate to task, purpose, and audience.

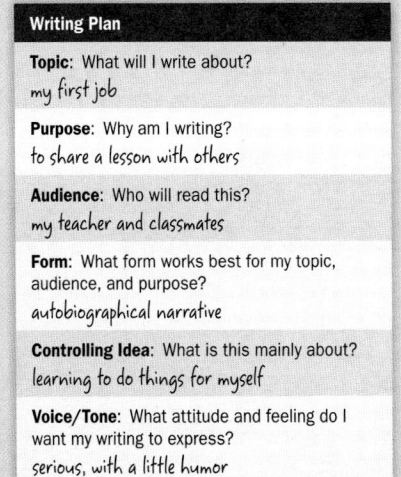

Controlling Idea

Expand Read the examples of topic sentences from the student page. Then explain each literary device:

- Position statement: This is a sentence that gives the writer's point of view or opinion.
- Question: The writer poses a question to the reader. The question may help set up the situation. Or it may ask the reader's opinion.
- Quotation: This will often be a famous quotation. Writers must use quotation marks and identify the speaker.
- Statistic: This is a factual statement. It can come from a research group or state department. This must have a verifiable source.

Remind students that statistics and quotations from well-known people must be properly cited.

Model how to make sure the literary device introduces the controlling idea.

Display these quotes by Mark Twain:

- "Courage is resistance to fear, not mastery of fear—not absence of fear."
- "Don't go around saying the world owes you a living. The world owes you nothing. It was here first."
- "A man cannot be comfortable without his own approval."

MODEL Say:

- *I want to use a quotation to introduce my essay about self-esteem. My controlling idea is: It is important for a person to believe in his or her own potential.*
- *I study these quotes to see if any of them will work with my controlling idea.*
- *The first one is about dealing with fear. This is not exactly the same as self-esteem.*
- *The second one is about working for what you want. I won't use this one.*
- *The third one seems to work fine. I could use it.*
- *None of these quotes is exactly right for my essay. I will search for other ones.*

❺ Research

Some writing forms and topics require research. Use these resources to find out more about your topic:

- **Internet** Develop a list of terms to enter into a search engine. Use sites that end in .edu or .gov for the most reliable information. For more on Internet research, see p. 608.
- **Library** Search the library's catalog and databases for books and articles about your topic. Ask a librarian for help.
- **Interview** You may want to interview a person who has knowledge about your topic. Prepare questions ahead of time and take notes on the responses.

❻ Get Organized

Review your details and choose a way to organize your writing. Use an appropriate graphic organizer such as a topic outline to show the main idea and details of your paragraphs in order. List your main ideas next to the roman numerals. List any supporting details underneath the main ideas, next to the capital letters.

Topic Outline

My First Job

I. Introduction: I joined the workforce.
 A. Many teens work.
 B. Work taught me responsibility.
II. Body: I looked for and got a job.
 A. I searched want ads.
 B. I applied for jobs.
 C. I interviewed.
III. Body: I learned the job.
 A. My first day was hard.
 B. I improved over time.
IV. Conclusion: I learned a lesson.
 A. I earned money for college.
 B. I learned responsibility.

For another sample outline, see **Language and Learning Handbook**, page 641.

Draft

The drafting stage is when you put your Writing Plan into action. Don't worry about making things perfect at this point. Drafts are meant to be changed. Instead, concentrate on writing out your ideas in complete sentences and paragraphs. The following ideas will help you organize your main idea and supporting details into a draft.

❶ Remember Purpose, Form, and Audience

Remember, you already made many important decisions about your work during the prewriting stage. Return to your Writing Plan often. Remind yourself of your purpose, form, and controlling idea as you organize your paragraphs. Think carefully about your audience, voice, and tone as you choose words and craft sentences.

❷ Introduce the Controlling Idea and Use Literary Devices

Your first paragraph should introduce your controlling idea and draw readers into your work. You can use any of the following literary devices to begin your paper in a clear and interesting way. Each device is an example of a **topic sentence**, which lets readers know what the text will be about.

- **Position Statement**: *Few things teach responsibility better than a part-time job.*
- **Question**: *Do you remember your first paycheck?*
- **Quotation**: *My dad always says, "If you really want something, you'll work for it."*
- **Statistic**: *In July 2006, almost 6 million teens in the United States held a job. I was one of them. It was my first job.*

The controlling idea is the main thing you are writing about, or the idea you want to express. It is more specific than the topic. The topic is the general area or subject of your writing. For example, if the topic of an article is baseball, the controlling idea could be learning how to hit home runs.

❸ Work Collaboratively

Involve other people in the writing of your draft early and often. Teachers, classmates, and family members can help you improve what you have written and determine what needs to be done. Listen carefully to what they have to say, and take notes on their suggestions.

❹ Use Technology to Draft

Continue writing until you have a complete draft. You can write your draft with a pen and paper or with a **word processor**. In either case, be sure to save a copy of your work.

Draft

My First Job

In July 2006, almost 22 million teens in the United States held a job (Bureau of Labor Statistics). I was one of them. It was my first job. That summer I learned lessons about responsibility that will last me the rest of my life.

The first thing I learned is that knowing how to find, apply for, and interview for a job is as important as knowing how to do the job itself. I searched the want ads in our local newspaper and on the Internet. In fact, I even filled out and submitted applications for several places online. I was sure to fill out each application as completely and honestly as possible. This work proved useful when two restaurants asked me to interview for busboy, or assistant server, positions. I dressed neatly and gave myself plenty of time to make it to the interviews on schedule. When I met the managers, I shook their hands, then listened closely to their questions before responding.

Revise

After you have written a draft, you need to revise it, or make changes. Revision is what takes your writing from good to great.

❶ Revise for Traits of Good Writing

Focus and Unity

- ☑ Do you have a clearly stated controlling idea or opinion?
- ☑ Is your controlling idea supported?
- ☑ Do your ideas and details flow logically?

Organization

- ☑ Do you have a title and an introductory paragraph?
- ☑ Do you transition between ideas?
- ☑ Are your ideas in a sensible order?
- ☑ Do you have a conclusion or ending?
- ☑ Does the organization match your purpose and audience?

B

Development of Ideas

- ☑ Are your ideas meaningful?
- ☑ Are your details vivid?
- ☑ Do your details answer questions that readers may have about the topic?
- ☑ Have you addressed purpose, audience, and genre to improve subtlety of meaning?

Voice and Style

- ☑ Is your writing unique and engaging?
- ☑ Are most of your sentences in active voice?
- ☑ Do the style and language used match your purpose and audience?
- ☑ Do you use figurative language to address purpose, audience, and genre?

Written Conventions

- ☑ Are your spelling, punctuation, capitalization, grammar, and usage correct?

See pages 706–715 for more information.

WRITING HANDBOOK

Ⓐ Drafts

Expand Remind students that they may not always be able to use a word processor, especially in a testing situation. Students should practice making their drafts legible. Here are some guidelines:

- Clearly cross out text that is not wanted. Reread the remaining text to be sure that it makes sense.
- Use neat handwriting with standard lettering. Do not use "fancy" letters. It is not appropriate for many types of writing, and might be hard for others to read.

Ⓑ Organization

Expand Read the questions under Organization on the student page. Discuss the last question.

Tell students that writing should be organized appropriately according to audience and purpose. If the purpose is to give important information or instructions, the writing must be organized so that the reader can find information easily. If the writer wants to entertain or tell a funny story, the writing might be simply organized in a way that keeps the reader's interest.

Ask students what would be the best way to organize the following types of writing:

- a letter requesting a donation from a business person
- an essay that responds to a poem
- a diary entry
- an entry for a magazine contest

Remind students that the genre one chooses to write in can affect meaning.

Peer Conference

Expand Tell students to make sure to tell the reviewer the occasion, purpose, and audience of their writing.

Present the different types of questions to help reviewers as they critique the writing:

- not "Do I like reading this?" but "Would this audience enjoy this writing?"
- not "Are the examples interesting or clear to me?" but "Are the examples appropriate for this purpose?"
- not "Do I like the way this is organized?" but "Is this the best way to organize a piece for this purpose and audience?"

Reviewers should also ask:

- What would this reader want to know?
- What is this reader most likely to already know about the topic?
- Is the format and language suited to the occasion and purpose?

Remind students that questions and suggestions from peers can help improve their writing. If the writing does not fit the purpose or occasion, for example, reviewers may suggest reorganizing content, or refining the style and word choice.

ELL **Rephrase Language** Display a birthday card and use it to explain the terms *occasion*, *purpose*, and *audience*:

The occasion is the overall reason. The occasion is the person's birthday.

The purpose is what the writer wants to do. People send birthday cards to show someone they care. The sender wants to make the person happy.

The audience is the person for whom the piece is written. The audience for the birthday card is the person whose birthday it is. Other people may read the card, but they are not the intended audience.

❷ Use Technology

The word processing software found on most computers will help you develop and make changes to your work quickly and easily. Here are some hints to help you get the most out of your computer:

- Save your work often. This will prevent the loss of your work in case of a computer malfunction.
- Create a "scrap file" of sentences and paragraphs you deleted as you revised. This deleted material may contain other ideas and details you can use in later writing.
- Think about how you will move your document from computer to computer. For example, if you e-mail yourself a copy, make sure the next computer you plan to use has Internet access.

❸ Hold a Peer Conference

Work with your classmates to improve each other's work.

Peer Review Guidelines

As Writer . . .

- Read your draft aloud or supply copies for each member of your group.
- Ask for help on specific points related to the traits of good writing.
- Listen carefully and take notes on your reviewers' comments.

As Reviewer . . .

- Read or listen to the complete writing. Take notes as you read or listen.
- Compliment the strong parts of the draft before you criticize weak points.
- Offer specific suggestions.

Edit and Proofread

After you have revised your draft for content, organization, and wording, it is time to check it for mistakes.

❶ Take Your Time

Successful editing and proofreading require attention to detail. The following hints will help you do your best work:

- Use a printed copy of your work. Text looks different on paper than on a computer screen. Many people catch more mistakes when they edit a printed version of their work.
- Set your work aside for a while. Your review may be more effective if you are rested.
- Read line by line. Use a ruler or piece of paper to cover the lines below the one you are reading. This will help you concentrate on the text in front of you.

❷ Check Your Sentences

Make sure your sentences are clear, complete, and correct. Ask yourself:

- Did I include a subject and a predicate in each sentence?
- Did I break up run-on sentences?
- Did I use a variety of sentence structures to keep my writing interesting?
- Did I combine short sentences, when possible, to create longer sentences?
- Did I use the active voice in most of my sentences?

❸ Check for Mistakes

Proofread to find errors in capitalization, punctuation, grammar, and spelling. Look especially for:

- capital letters, end marks, apostrophes, and quotation marks
- subject-verb agreement
- misspelled words

❹ Use Reference Tools

Reference tools are an important part of every writer's tool kit. Dictionaries, thesauruses, and electronic sources such as Web sites and the spell-checking features of most word processing programs are all reference tools available to the good writer. When in doubt, check different versions of several sources.

Use a **dictionary** to check the meaning and spelling of your words.

> I worked **diligently** that summer.
> *Is that spelled correctly?*

Use a **thesaurus** to find words that are livelier or more appropriate for your audience.

> I worked ~~diligently~~ **hard** that summer.
> *Maybe this word is clearer to my audience.*

Use a **grammar handbook** to fix sentences and punctuation errors.

> We ~~was~~ **were** cleaning the grill.
> *That's the correct verb.*

Use a **style guide** or **style manual**, which is a publication containing rules and suggestions about grammar, writing, and publishing, for help in **citing** your sources. When you use information and ideas from other authors, you need to give them credit for their work. **Plagiarism** is using someone's words or ideas without giving the person credit. When you reword another author's ideas, you still have to give the author credit for his or her ideas.

> In July 2006, almost 22 million teens in the United States held a job. (Bureau of Labor Statistics)
> *Now the statistic is properly cited, according to the method I found in the style guide.*

❺ Mark Your Changes

Use proofreader's marks to show changes on a printout of your draft. Then make changes to your word processed document.

> ¶ The first thing I learned is that knowing ~~how~~ how to find, apply for, and interview for a job is as important as knowing how to do the job itself. I ^searched the want ads in our local newspaper and on the Internet⊙ In fact, I even filled out and submitted applications for several places online. I was sure to fill out each application as completely and honestly as possible. I dressed neatly and gave myself plenty of time to make it to the interviews on schedule. This work proved useful when two restaurants asked me to interview for busboy, or assistant server, positions. when I met the ~~M~~anagers, I shook their hands, then listened closely to their questions before responding.

Proofreader's Marks

℘	Delete
∧	Add text
⊂→	Move to here
⊙	Add period
⁁	Add comma
≡	Capitalize
/	Make lowercase
¶	Start new paragraph

WRITING HANDBOOK

Ⓐ Reference Tools

Expand Point out that research involves looking at many different viewpoints and drawing a conclusion. Good research reports:

- provide supporting information from different sources. The writer shows that he or she used more than one source. There should be at least two sources with data to support the conclusion.
- present the opposing viewpoint. The writer gives the fact or idea and then explains why he or she disagrees.
- give proper credit for every source that is used.

Ⓑ Plagiarism

Reinforce Help students understand the full scope of plagiarism. Explain the following points:

- Plagiarism is a form of theft. One person says something or has an idea. Another person then claims those words or ideas are his or her own.
- If you use someone else's words or ideas in your writing and don't give credit, you are committing plagiarism.
- Plagiarism is a serious offense. Punishment for committing plagiarism varies. A student who plagiarizes could receive a failing grade on his or her paper or in the class. The student could be expelled, or removed, from school.

Ⓐ Visual Impact

Expand Talk about how pictures can make us feel or think a certain way. If possible, show several magazine ads of household items. Point to or identify different images in each ad. Ask: Why do you think the advertiser put this in? How do you think the advertiser hopes people will respond to this?

Explain that a written work can also have visual impact. A writer usually wants others to read what he or she has written. One way to get a potential reader to respond is to give the writing visual impact. Are there text features such as headings or italics to attract the reader's attention? If the writing is handwritten, does it appear legible and easy to understand?

Ⓑ Diagrams and Charts

Expand Ask: What are some common uses for charts and diagrams?

If possible, provide news and science magazines, textbooks, and newspapers for students to look through. Have individuals or groups describe the different ways these materials use diagrams, charts, and other graphics.

Encourage students to use graphics in their work. Students can use these questions to help them decide when to add a graphic:

- Am I explaining an idea or a step-by-step process that would be easier to understand with a picture?
- Do I give statistics or other numeric facts that could be shown in a graph?
- Would this information be easier to read in a chart than in a paragraph?

Publish and Evaluate

You've made it! You're now ready for the last step in the Writing Process. First, prepare your final document for your readers. Then, reflect back on what you've done well and what you could do better next time.

❶ Print Your Work

Ⓐ Ⓑ The final version of your work should be neat and easy to read. It should be visually appealing. You can increase the visual impact of the final version of your work by using different font types and sizes, headings, bullet points, or even diagrams and charts as a way to present data. Use the information below to format your document for final publication. Then print out and make copies of your work to share with others. Be sure to keep a copy for yourself.

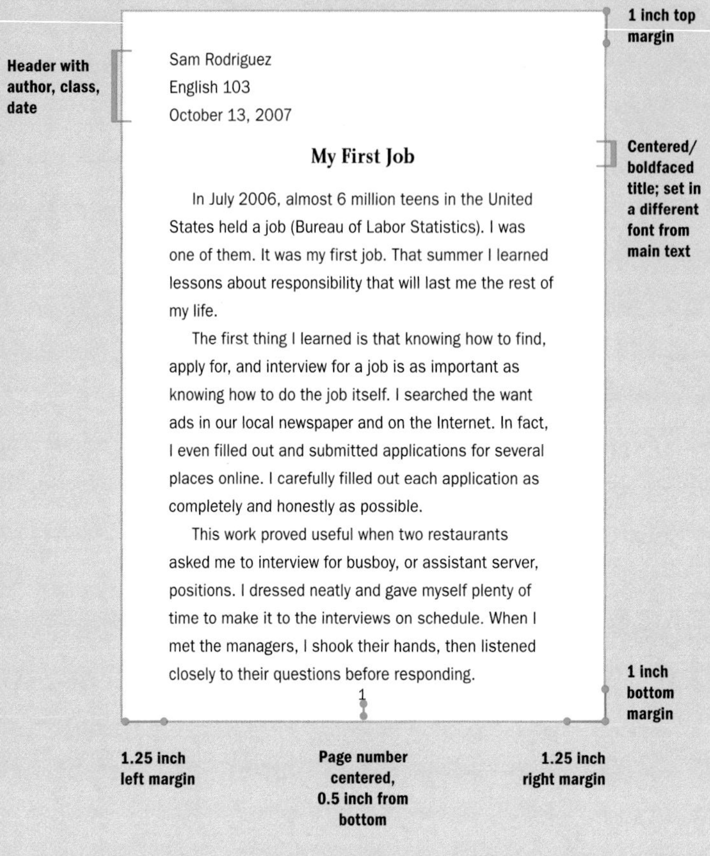

Sam Rodriguez
English 103
October 13, 2007

My First Job

In July 2006, almost 6 million teens in the United States held a job (Bureau of Labor Statistics). I was one of them. It was my first job. That summer I learned lessons about responsibility that will last me the rest of my life.

The first thing I learned is that knowing how to find, apply for, and interview for a job is as important as knowing how to do the job itself. I searched the want ads in our local newspaper and on the Internet. In fact, I even filled out and submitted applications for several places online. I carefully filled out each application as completely and honestly as possible.

This work proved useful when two restaurants asked me to interview for busboy, or assistant server, positions. I dressed neatly and gave myself plenty of time to make it to the interviews on schedule. When I met the managers, I shook their hands, then listened closely to their questions before responding.

1

❷ Publish Your Work

Take your work beyond the classroom and share it in new ways.

- Save examples of your writing in a portfolio. This will allow you to see the improvement in your writing over time. Organize your portfolio by date or form. Each time you add pieces to your portfolio, take some time to self-reflect and compare the new piece to your older work.

Portfolio Review

- ☑ How does this writing compare to other work I've done?
- ☑ What traits am I getting better at?
- ☑ What traits do I need to work on?
- ☑ What is my style? What kinds of sentences and words do I often use?
- ☑ What makes me a super writer?

- Expand your work by making it into a poster or other visual display, such as a video or a Web site. What images best express your ideas? How will the text appear?
- Many newspapers and Web sites publish teen writing. Ask a teacher or librarian for examples, or research them yourself. For writers, there are few things more satisfying than sharing their ideas with as wide an audience as possible.

❸ Evaluate Your Work

Now that you have completed your work, look to see what you can improve.

- Use rubrics to evaluate the quality and effectiveness of your writing. Rubrics contain criteria for evaluating your work. Review the rubrics on pages 706–715.
- Discuss your work with your teacher and classmates, then ask yourself:

What did I do well?

I added some description. My details were sequential and organized.

What are some weaknesses that I could improve on easily?

It lacks uniqueness. I need to vary my sentence structures.

How will I make sure I improve on those weaker areas?

I could pick topics that I feel strongly about. During revision I can check my sentence structure.

What are some weaknesses that may take time to improve?

Expanding my ideas, making my voice more mature.

- Set goals based on your evaluation. Make a list of goals; cross them out as you accomplish them. Then set new goals.

Goals to Improve My Writing

1. ~~I am going to use more descriptive sentences in my next narrative piece.~~
2. I am going to check all my sentence beginnings and make sure they are different.
3. I am going to add more "important" facts to my expository nonfiction pieces.

WRITING HANDBOOK

Publish

Expand Discuss different ways that students can use word processing programs to prepare their writing for submission or publication:

- Endnotes and footnotes. A word processor will automatically move a note when other text is added or deleted.
- Font sizes and formatting. Students can use larger fonts and boldface headings. They can easily italicize words in titles.
- Spell-check and grammar check. Students should be careful not to rely solely on these. Word processors do not always indicate words that are used incorrectly.

Explain that spell-check and grammar check programs will sometimes indicate an error in a word, phrase, or sentence that has been written for effect.

For example, a writer may use an unusual spelling of a word to make a point. Or the writer may use a sentence fragment, or an incomplete sentence, to make an impression in his or her writing.

Students should read carefully any potential errors in their writing indicated by spell-check and grammar check programs.

Practice Have each student choose a piece of writing from his or her journal. Have individuals use the unpublished work to practice using technology to display information. When they have completed the paper, have individuals create a brief cover sheet describing how the formats they chose meet their purpose, writing form, and audience. Have individuals place cover sheets and papers in a binder for other students to review.
W.9-10.6

CCSS Literacy.W.9-10.6 Use technology, including the Internet, to produce, publish, and update individual or shared writing products, taking advantage of technology's capacity to link to other information and to display information flexibly and dynamically.

Unity and Fluency

Reinforce Explain that unity means that sentences and ideas are connected and relate to the main topic or idea. Fluency refers to the flow of ideas.

To create unity, writers:

- add words and statements to show how ideas are related
- delete words, phrases, or sentences that do not relate to the main idea

To create fluency, writers:

- move sentences around
- use transition words and phrases

Read and display the paragraphs below. Discuss how the sentences in the first paragraph have unity but not fluency. Have students identify ways that the writer creates fluency in the second paragraph.

Paragraph 1: I really enjoyed reading this book. It was exciting, and the characters were very realistic. In the book, the youngest brother and oldest sister have a conflict. The reader comes to see that the siblings really do love each other, even if they show it in very different ways. The theme of the book was different ways that families show love. The writer presented this theme through the actions and words of the family members.

Paragraph 2: I really enjoyed reading this book. It was exciting, and the characters were very realistic. The theme of the book was different ways that families show love. The writer presented this theme through the actions and words of the people in one family. In the book, the youngest brother and oldest sister have a conflict. In the end, the reader comes to see that the siblings really do love each other, even if they show it in very different ways.

Writing Traits

What Are Writing Traits?

Writing traits are the characteristics of good writing. Use the traits and writing examples on the following pages to plan, evaluate, and improve your writing.

Focus and Unity

All the ideas in a piece of writing should be related, or go together well. **Focus** your writing by selecting a single central or **controlling idea**. Then give your work **unity** by relating each main idea and detail to that controlling idea. Use the rubric below to help maintain focus and unity in your writing.

Focus and Unity

	How clearly does the writing present a central idea or claim?	How well does everything go together?
4 Wow!	**The writing expresses a clear central idea or claim about the topic.**	**Everything in the writing goes together.** • The main idea of each paragraph goes with the central idea or claim of the paper. • The main idea and details within each paragraph are related. • The conclusion is about the central idea or claim.
3 Ahh.	**The writing expresses a generally clear central idea or claim about the topic.**	**Most parts of the writing go together.** • The main idea of most paragraphs goes with the central idea or claim of the paper. • In most paragraphs, the main idea and details are related. • Most of the conclusion is about the central idea or claim.
2 Hmm.	**The writing includes a topic, but the central idea or claim is not clear.**	**Some parts of the writing go together.** • The main idea of some paragraphs goes with the central idea or claim of the paper. • In some paragraphs, the main idea and details are related. • Some of the conclusion is about the central idea or claim.
1 Huh?	**The writing includes many topics and does not express one central idea or claim.**	**The parts of the writing do not go together.** • Few paragraphs have a main idea, or the main idea does not go with the central idea or claim of the paper. • Few paragraphs contain a main idea and related details • None of the conclusion is about the central idea or claim.

Focus and Unity: Strong Example, score of 3 or 4

"Mother to Son"—An Amazing Poem

Nobody writes poetry like Langston Hughes. In the poem "Mother to Son," he shows why he is such an amazing poet. He is a master of theme, rhythm, and figurative language.

The beginning states the controlling idea.

The theme of "Mother to Son" is about life's difficulties and the need to keep going. The voice in the poem is that of a mother. She talks about how her life has been such a struggle. The mother shares with her son that he is going to go through some tough times, too, but he has to stay strong and focused when life is hard.

The main idea of each paragraph is about the controlling idea.

Langston Hughes is also great at creating rhythm with words. His poems read like songs in your head, and "Mother to Son" is no different. He uses quick, short lines with repetitive beginnings to make the poem very rhythmic. Hughes also creates rhythm by adding just a couple of lines that rhyme.

Details support the main idea.

This poem is all about figurative language. The poem really is one big metaphor. The mother compares her life to a rough, worn-out staircase. The metaphor helps me to picture what the mother means about life being difficult sometimes. It also symbolizes that in order to get somewhere, you have to keep trying and working until you get to where you want to be.

Langston Hughes is an amazing poet. He is able to write poems that affect me by making them about something I can relate to and by making them rhythmic and creative.

The end connects to the beginning.

Focus and Unity: Weak Example, score of 1 or 2

An Amazing Poem

The narrator of the poem is that of a mother. She talks about how her life has been such a struggle. The mother shares with her son that he is going to go through some tough times, too, but he has to stay strong and focused when life is hard.

The controlling idea is unclear.

Langston Hughes is a great poet. His poems have theme, figurative language, and rhythm. This poem is all about figurative language. The poem really is one big metaphor. The mother compares her life to a rough, worn-out staircase. The metaphor helps me to picture what the mother means about life being difficult sometimes. It also symbolizes that in order to get somewhere you have to keep trying and working until you get to where you want to be.

The paragraphs have no clear main idea.

He uses quick, short lines with repetitive beginnings to make the poem very rhythmic. Hughes also creates rhythm by adding just a couple of lines that rhyme.

Langston Hughes is an amazing poet.

The conclusion is vague and abrupt.

WRITING HANDBOOK

Formal Writing

Expand Have students read the two examples on the student page. Point out that a literary analysis is one of the more formal types of writing. Ask: Who would be the typical audience for this type of writing?

Discuss how to determine tone and word choice for formal writing.

Tone:

- A formal piece should have a more serious tone.
- Serious tones can include humor, but this has to be done carefully.
- An informative piece must have a respectful tone. Do not insult or talk down to the reader.

Word Choice:

- A literary analysis should use academic words. Use exact language and correct terms, such as *metaphor* and *simile*.
- Formal writing uses more sophisticated words.
- Point out these sophisticated words in the Strong Example: *master, life's difficulties, focused, symbolizes.* Ask: How do these word choices make the writing better?

Remind students of the importance of using a mature tone in their writing, while maintaining their unique voice. If necessary, review the difference between voice and tone. Encourage students to use appropriate words they are familiar with and are comfortable saying.

Practice Have each student choose one piece of informational/expository writing from their portfolio. Allow them to select a shorter or longer piece of work—whichever example best illustrates a formal tone. Then have individuals highlight specific words, phrases, and sentences in their writing that demonstrate formal writing. Have partners share their examples and explain their choices for highlighting.
W.9-10.2.e

CCSS W.9-10.2.e Establish and maintain a formal style and objective tone while attending to the norms and conventions of the discipline in which they are writing.

A Organization

Expand Have students read the different patterns of organization listed on the student page. Give tips to help students determine the best organization pattern:

- A description of an event might use chronological order.
- A writer may compare and contrast viewpoints to show how one is better.
- Letters to the editor often use the problem-solution method.
- Order of importance ranks facts or ideas.

Practice Explain that writers can use subtitles to help the reader understand the topic. For each topic below, have volunteers choose an organization pattern and give a title and subtitle:

- a letter that asks the town council to pass a new law
- a news article about the different parks in town
- an essay that tells where to find the best deals
- a movie review
- a story about how two people became friends over the summer

W.9-10.4

B Transitions

Practice Talk about the importance of transition words and sentences. Point out that they:

- help the writer organize information
- help a reader follow the writing

Have students work with partners to make a list of transition words for each pattern of organization. For example, the transition words for chronological order could be *first*, *next*, *then*, *second*, *finally*, and *last*.
W.9-10.2.c

Organization

A

Having a clear central idea and supporting details is important, but in order for your audience to understand your ideas, make sure your writing is organized. Good **organization** helps readers move through your writing easily. In a well-organized work, all paragraphs work together to fulfill the author's purpose clearly and smoothly.

Organization

Scale	Does the writing have a clear and appropriate structure?	How smoothly do the ideas flow together?
4 Wow!	**The writing has a structure that is clear and appropriate for the writer's audience, purpose, and type of writing.**	**The ideas progress in a smooth and orderly way.** • The introduction is strong. • The ideas flow well from paragraph to paragraph. • The ideas in each paragraph flow well from one sentence to the next. • Effective transitions connect ideas. • The conclusion is strong.
3 Ahh.	**The writing has a structure that is generally clear and appropriate for the writer's audience, purpose, and type of writing.**	**Most of the ideas progress in a smooth and orderly way.** • The introduction is adequate. • Most of the ideas flow well from paragraph to paragraph. • Most ideas in each paragraph flow from one sentence to the next. • Effective transitions connect most of the ideas. • The conclusion is adequate.
2 Hmm.	**The structure of the writing is not clear or not appropriate for the writer's audience, purpose, and type of writing.**	**Some of the ideas progress in a smooth and orderly way.** • The introduction is weak. • Some of the ideas flow well from paragraph to paragraph. • Some ideas in each paragraph flow from one sentence to the next. • Transitions connect some ideas. • The conclusion is weak.
1 Huh?	**The writing is not clear or organized.**	**Few or none of the ideas progress in a smooth and orderly way.**

B

Common patterns of organization include:

- **chronological order**, in which details are told in time order
- **compare and contrast**, in which similarities and differences between two or more things are discussed
- **problem-solution**, in which a problem is discussed first and then one or more solutions are presented
- **order of importance**, in which the writer presents the strongest arguments first and last, and presents weaker arguments in the middle.

CCSS Literacy.W.9-10.2.c Use appropriate and varied transitions to link the major sections of the text, create cohesion, and clarify the relationships among complex ideas and concepts. Literacy.W.9-10.4 Produce clear and coherent writing in which the development, organization, and style are appropriate to task, purpose, and audience.

Organization: Strong Example, score of 3 or 4

Say No to Raising the Legal Driving Age

For teens in the United States, receiving a driver's license at age sixteen is an important part of growing up. However, some states are considering raising the legal driving age to eighteen years old. I believe that this idea would negatively affect teens and parents.

The beginning makes the purpose clear: to persuade.

One reason teens need to be able to drive at the age of sixteen is so they can get a job. Many teens need to get jobs to have money for food, clothes, and entertainment. Often, a teen who has a job must have a car and be able to drive it to work.

There are effective transitions between paragraphs.

Teens also want to be able to date and do other social activities on their own. Teens need the opportunity to be responsible and feel trusted. Being able to drive at sixteen helps teens earn this trust.

Details support the main idea.

Perhaps most importantly, teen students have to be able to drive to and from school. A lot of parents and guardians go to work before school starts and have to work until after school is out. The only way for some students to get to school or get to school events and practices is to drive. Without driver's licenses, students may end up missing a lot of school and school activities.

Each paragraph gives reasons that support the author's opinion.

While there may be some good reasons why the legal driving age should be raised, it is important to teens and parents that it stays the same. Sixteen-year-olds need to be able to drive to work, to social events, and to school functions.

Organization: Weak Example, score of 1 or 2

Teens and Driving

Can you imagine having your mom drive you to your high school graduation or to prom? How would you feel if you couldn't get a job? Many states want to make eighteen the legal driving age.

The purpose is not clear.

Many teens do not reach age eighteen until after they have been graduated from high school. It wouldn't be fun waiting until eighteen before you could drive. My friends and I drove once when we were fifteen. Many kids need to work to earn money. It would be difficult to get a job if the legal driving age was eighteen.

Paragraphs lack transitions.

Students need to be able to drive to school. If the driving age is eighteen, lots of kids will have to take the bus. My friends and I rode the bus for many years. There are thousands of students who have to ride the bus each year.

Can you imagine going on a date with your parents in the front seat? My mom drove me to a dance once, and I was so embarrassed. Students need to be able to go on dates.

The details here do not support the author's opinion.

The legal driving age needs to stay the same so teens can drive to school, work, and on dates.

Organization

Expand Remind students that transition words and conjunctions have a significant role. They tell the reader how two ideas are connected.

Have students read the first two sentences in the Strong Example. Point out *However* in the second sentence. Say: Suppose the writer used *Amazingly* or *Finally* instead of *However*. This would completely change the meaning of the sentence.

Explain that the word *however* usually shows that two events or ideas are in opposition. Say: These two sentences seem to show completely different viewpoints. The first one shows that teens might favor a legal driving age of 16. The second one shows that some states may favor a legal driving age of 18.

Practice Write these sentences:

- Perhaps most importantly, teen students have to be able to drive to and from school.
- Often, a teen who has a job must have a car and be able to drive it to work.
- Many kids work to earn money, but it is difficult to get a job without a driver's license.
- My job is not near a bus stop, so I could not get there without a car.

Work with the class to rewrite each sentence by replacing the underlined word or phrase. Talk about how the new transition word, phrase, or conjunction changes the entire meaning of the sentences.

If necessary, refer students to page 759 of the Grammar, Usage, Mechanics, and Spelling section in this handbook. Students can review the types and uses of conjunctions.
W.9-10.1.c

CCSS Literacy.W.9-10.1.c Use words, phrases, and clauses to link the major sections of the text, create cohesion, and clarify the relationships between claim(s) and reasons, between reasons and evidence, and between claim(s) and counterclaims.

Development of Ideas

Expand There are many different ways for writers to support their arguments. Explain these different types of supporting details:

- Describe real-life and fictional scenarios. Write about situations that support the argument. For example, in an essay about honesty, students can describe something that happened between friends or family members, as long as it helps demonstrate their point.
- Describe or respond to commonly held beliefs. The writer identifies the belief and then gives reasons he or she agrees or disagrees with it.
- Present a hypothesis. It can be the writer's own hypothesis or someone else's. The writer must give support for the hypothesis or explain why he or she agrees with someone else's.
- Use a definition. An essay about an idea like love or friendship will often include a definition of the term.

Development of Ideas

Good ideas are important, but so are the details that describe the ideas. Details develop your ideas, or help your reader to understand them. They also make your writing much more interesting to read. When you are writing, there may be many ideas to choose from, so consider which ideas are most important to your audience and support your purpose for writing.

Development of Ideas

Scale	How thoughtful and interesting is the writing?	How well are the ideas or claims explained and supported?
4 Wow!	**The writing engages the reader with meaningful ideas or claims and presents them in a way that is interesting and appropriate to the audience, purpose, and type of writing.**	**The ideas or claims are fully explained and supported.** • The ideas or claims are well developed with important details, evidence, and/or description. • The writing feels complete, and the reader is satisfied.
3 Ahh.	**<u>Most</u> of the writing engages the reader with meaningful ideas or claims and presents them in a way that is interesting and appropriate to the audience, purpose, and type of writing.**	**<u>Most</u> of the ideas or claims are explained and supported.** • Most of the ideas or claims are developed with important details, evidence, and/or description. • The writing feels mostly complete, but the reader still has some questions.
2 Hmm.	**<u>Some</u> of the writing engages the reader with meaningful ideas or claims and presents them in a way that is interesting and appropriate to the audience, purpose, and type of writing.**	**<u>Some</u> of the ideas or claims are explained and supported.** • Only some of the ideas or claims are developed. Details, evidence, and/or description are limited or not relevant. • The writing leaves the reader with many questions.
1 Huh?	**The writing does <u>not</u> engage the reader. It is not appropriate to the audience, purpose, and type of writing.**	**The ideas or claims are <u>not</u> explained or supported.** The ideas or claims lack details, evidence, and/or description, and the writing leaves the reader unsatisfied.

Development of Ideas: Strong Example, score of 3 or 4

Parent-for-a-Day

Have you ever wondered what it would be like if we could change places with our parents just for the day? I have, and there are a few things I would like to do.

No school! Making my parents go to school for me would be the first thing I would do as parent for the day. Oh, what fun to be the one to tell my parents to "wake up, eat your breakfast, get to school!" Off they would go to sit in classrooms while I headed to the park for a long game of soccer.

No chores! When my parents got home from school, they would take out the trash, they would do the dishes, and they would clean the house. Meanwhile, I would sit in front of the television and watch my favorite shows.

No bedtime! The last and best part of being a parent for the day is that there would be no bedtime. I would stay up until the wee hours of the morning watching television and finishing my favorite mystery novel.

I have my "parent-for-a-day" all planned out, but the hardest part remains. I still need to convince my parents it is a good idea.

The writer asks a question to engage the audience.

Each paragraph explains and supports the main idea.

The end returns to the topic in a new way.

Development of Ideas: Weak Example, score of 1 or 2

Parent-for-a-Day

Have you ever wondered what it would be like if we could change places with our parents just for the day?

No school! Making my parents go to school for me would be the first thing I would do as parent for the day.

No chores! When my parents got home from school, I would make them do all the chores.

No bedtime! The last and best part of being a parent for the day is that there would be no bedtime.

Now I just need to talk my parents into the idea.

Paragraphs offer little explanation or support.

The ending is abrupt.

WRITING HANDBOOK

Strong Conclusions

Reinforce Have students read and compare the last paragraph of each example on the student page. Point out that the paragraphs basically present the same idea. However, one ending is stronger than the other.

Give students these tips to help them write stronger endings to their essays:

- The ending should logically connect to the ideas just before it.
- The ending should present a conclusion based on the main idea of the essay.
- A strong conclusion can and should be brief. To be effective, however, the conclusion must still relate clearly to the beginning and sum up the main idea of the writing.

Practice Have each student review their portfolio and find an example of informational/expository writing. Ask them to review the conclusion of the paper and self-assess the conclusion using the points in the rubric. Invite students to draft alternative endings on self-stick notes and affix them to their original work.
W.9-10-2.f

CCSS Literacy.W.9-10.2.f Provide a concluding statement or section that follows from and supports the information or explanation presented (e.g., articulating implications or the significance of the topic).

Style and Audience

Expand Remind students that the audience and purpose will determine the level of formality in the piece. Formality can be reflected in word choice.

Point out that a piece that is written for a literary audience will use different types of words than one written for a peer. Sometimes it is acceptable to use slang and informal terms.

Help students understand the idea of formality in language:

- Write *formality*. Underline and point out the root *formal*.
- Describe different types of formal and informal restaurants, from fast-food to extremely fancy.
- Have students think of other things that are described as formal or informal. (Students may suggest a formal invitation, or even the noun usage of *formal*, which is a type of formal dance.)
- Discuss the difference between informal and formal things. Say: This is the same difference with formal and informal language in writing. One is more serious or structured. The other is more casual.

Voice and Style

Voice and **style** in writing contribute to communicating the meaning of writing. These qualities make each writer and piece of writing unique.

- **Voice** in writing is the quality that makes the words sound as if they are being spoken by someone. Voice communicates the author's or speaker's attitude.
- **Style** is the characteristic way a writer expresses his or her ideas. Part of that style is the author's **tone**, or attitude toward his or her subject as reflected in word choice. Tone, word choice, and sentence structure are all parts of a writer's style.

Matching Voice and Style to Audience

Because writing is intended to communicate, it is important to match voice and style to the audience. A serious subject may require a serious tone. The intended audience may also dictate whether you can use informal English. If the audience is your classmates, you might be able to use informal or casual English as you would in everyday conversation. If your audience is your teacher or other adults, use formal English in your writing. Whoever the audience, choose vivid words, and vary your sentence patterns.

Voice and Style

Scale	Does the writing have a clear voice and is it the best style for the type of writing?	Is the language interesting and are the words and sentences appropriate for the purpose, audience, and type of writing?
4 Wow!	**The writing fully engages the reader with its individual voice. The writing style is best for the type of writing.**	**The words and sentences are interesting and appropriate to the purpose and audience.** • The words are precise and engaging. • The sentences are varied and flow together smoothly.
3 Ahh.	**Most of the writing engages the reader with an individual voice. The writing style is mostly best for the type of writing**	**Most of the words and sentences are interesting and appropriate to the purpose and audience.** • Most words are precise and engaging. • Most sentences are varied and flow together.
2 Hmm.	**Some of the writing engages the reader, but it has no individual voice and the style is not best for the writing type.**	**Some of the words and sentences are interesting and appropriate to the purpose and audience.** • Some words are precise and engaging. • Some sentences are varied, but the flow could be smoother.
1 Huh?	**The writing does not engage the reader.**	**Few or none of the words and sentences are appropriate to the purpose and audience.** • The words are often vague and dull. • The sentences lack variety and do not flow together.

Voice and Style: Strong Example, score of 3 or 4

Dried Up

Some people are meant to make speeches, and others are meant to listen. I learned the hard way that I am definitely a listener.

I have always been comfortable speaking out in class, so when my friend Heather joined the speech team, I decided to give it a try. This kind of activity looks great on college applications, I figured. Moreover, how hard could it be?

I learned just how hard on the afternoon of the regional speech competition. Preparation certainly wasn't a problem. I had spent hours crafting my words. Each of us had rehearsed time and time again in front of our coach and each other. The rhythm and accents of my speech had been drilled into my mind and body.

When I stepped on stage, however, all that preparation dried up under the hot lights. My mouth felt as if it were filled with cotton, and I thought even the packed auditorium could hear my dry bones tremble. As I began to speak, my voice creaked like a rusty door.

I would like to say that I overcame that rough start, but I barely recall giving the rest of my speech. I slouched off stage and took my seat to the sound of weak applause, eager to take my place as the quietest, most intent listener in the room.

The voice is light-hearted and clear.

The sentence lengths are varied.

Vivid verbs and modifiers make the scene seem real and exciting.

Voice and Style: Weak Example, score of 1 or 2

A Bad Day

It was one of the worst days of my life. I tried to give a speech in front of a lot of people and ended up a failure.

This is what happened. My friend was part of the speech team. She talked me into trying out. I thought that it would be easy and it was, at least in front of my classmates.

At our first competition, I sat waiting until the judge called my name. I went on stage, and I could see a lot of people in the audience. I couldn't move, and then I almost passed out. The speech didn't go well at all.

It was an embarrassing moment, but I am glad I at least tried.

The voice is flat and lifeless.

Sentences have little variety.

Words are general and uninteresting.

Vivid Verbs and Modifiers

Expand Remind students that there are many ways to say the same thing. At the same time, words and phrases have different connotations. This is why word choice is so important. Good writers use precise language and pay careful attention to the subtlety of meaning.

Have students compare the descriptions of the auditorium:

- Strong Example: "hot lights"; "packed auditorium"
- Weak Example: "a lot of people in the audience"

Have students look for other precise language the Strong Example uses to describe what happened. ("mouth felt … filled with cotton"; "hear my dry bones tremble"; "voice creaked like a rusty door")

Discuss the subtlety of meaning for some of the descriptions, such as "dry bones tremble." Ask: What images do these words bring to mind?

Use the Weak Example to model how to use appropriate modifiers and choose sophisticated words. Read this part of the first sentence in the third paragraph: "I sat waiting until the judge called my name." Write your sentences as you think aloud.

MODEL Say:

- *How can I say this with more sophisticated words?*
- *I know. I'll start with a more vivid description: "I sat and listened to speaker after speaker. I was trying to listen to the other speakers, but all I could think about was my own speech that would be next."*
- *There's a better way to say that last sentence: "… all I could think about was my own upcoming speech."*

Cross out the old words and write the new phrase above it. Say:

- *Using the more sophisticated word made my sentence clearer. It added to the effectiveness of the writing.*

Practice Have pairs choose another sentence from the Weak Example and work together to revise it. Then have pairs combine into groups of four to compare revisions.
W-9-10.3.d

CCSS Literacy.W.9-10.3.d Use precise words and phrases, telling details, and sensory language to convey a vivid picture of the experiences, events, setting, and/or characters.

Ⓐ Grammar

Reinforce Have students read the introductory paragraph. Explain that grammar is about more than subject-verb agreement and tenses. It also includes syntax, or proper word order, and correct spelling.

Expand The best way to show how grammar deals with syntax is through poetry. Often poets use unusual or atypical word order. Choose one or two poets, such as William Wordsworth and Emily Dickinson. Examine one poem line by line, and show how the syntax would be different in prose or in an essay. Also, point out that the best way to achieve good syntax is to write it the way it would be said (with proper grammar, of course).

Ⓑ Text Features

Expand Explain that text features are different aspects of the text that help a reader follow the organization, such as the title, headings, subheadings, or a number sequence.

Practice Have student groups look through different textbooks or other materials to find examples of these text features.

Ask groups to report back to the class about the features they found. Ask: How did the features help you as a reader?
RI.9-10.10

Written Conventions

Ⓐ You want readers to focus on your ideas, but errors can make it hard to understand what you mean. Good writers pay attention to **written conventions**, that is, the accepted methods and rules for grammar, punctuation, spelling, and capitalization that are commonly used to write English.

Written Conventions Rubric

Scale	Grammar: Are the sentences grammatically correct?	Mechanics and Spelling: Are there errors in spelling, punctuation, or capitalization that affect understanding?
4 Wow!	**The writing contains grammatically correct sentences throughout.**	There are few or no mistakes in spelling, punctuation, or capitalization.
3 Looks Good.	**Most of the sentences contain proper grammar.**	There are mistakes in spelling, punctuation, or capitalization, but they do not affect understanding.
2 Hmm.	**Some of the sentences contain grammar errors.**	There are some mistakes in spelling, punctuation, and capitalization that affect understanding.
1 Huh?	**Many sentences contain grammar errors.**	There are many mistakes in spelling, punctuation, and capitalization that make the writing difficult to understand.

Ⓑ Written conventions also include using **complete sentences**, **organization**, and **text features** that people understand. Complete sentences have a subject and a predicate and express a complete thought. For more help with written conventions, see Grammar, Usage, Mechanics, and Spelling on page 738.

CCSS Literacy.RI.9-10.10 By the end of grade 10, read and comprehend literary nonfiction at the high end of the grades 9–10 text complexity band independently and proficiently.

Written Conventions: Strong Example, score of 3 or 4

> **A True Hispanic Hero**
>
> There are many Hispanic heroes, but my favorite is Miriam Colon Valle. With hard work and a strong belief in herself and her profession, she has become a role model for all.
>
> **Early Years**
>
> Miriam Colon Valle grew up in Puerto Rico in the 1940s. She participated in drama in high school, and her teacher saw that she had a lot of talent. Valle was then asked to take part in the drama program at the University of Puerto Rico. Her work at the university earned her scholarships that allowed her to attend the Lee Strasberg Acting Studio in the United States.
>
> **Rise to Stardom**
>
> In the United States, Valle worked hard. She played roles in more than thirty movies; one of her most famous was as the mother of Al Pacino in the movie *Scarface*. Valle was also on television shows, such as the soap opera *The Guiding Light*.
>
> Valle also loved the theater. In the 1950s she started her own theater group. She also acted in numerous Broadway productions. Her drive to help other Hispanic actors and to share theater with poor people inspired her to start the Puerto Rican Traveling Theater.
>
> Because of her love for acting and her love for Hispanic culture and theater, she was awarded a Lifetime Achievement Award in Theater. Miriam Colon Valle is an inspiration to Hispanics and people of all races.

Grammar is correct throughout.

Heads separate sections and give information.

Readers can easily understand the sequence of events.

Names and titles are properly formatted.

Punctuation occurs in the proper places throughout.

Written Conventions: Weak Example, score of 1 or 2

> **A true Hispanic Hero**
>
> There are many hispanic heroes. My favorite is Miriam Colon Valle. She is a role model for evrybody.
>
> Miriam Colon Valle grew up in puerto rico in the 1940s she participated in drama in high school. Valle then taken part in the drama program at the "university of puerto rico." Her work at the university lead her to The United States eventually.
>
> Valle also loved the theater. In the 1950s she started her own theater group. She also acted in a bunch of Broadway productions. She also started the Puerto Rican Traveling Theater. She was awarded a "Lifetime Achievement Award in Theater." Because of her love for acting and her love for hispanic culture and theater. Miriam Colon Valle is an inspiration to hispanics and people of all races.
>
> In The United States, Valle worked hard. She played roles in more than thirty movies. Valle was also on television shows. Including the soap opera The Guiding Light.

There are many misspellings.

Names and titles are not properly capitalized or formatted.

Poor organization and lack of heads make it difficult to follow information.

Sentences are incorrectly punctuated or too long.

WRITING HANDBOOK

Written Conventions

Reinforce Use the two examples to help students develop a proper understanding of English syntax.

Read the Strong Example. Discuss how the first paragraph demonstrates good syntax:

- In the first sentence the writer presents a fact and then clarifies it with another statement.
- The writer begins with a general statement about Hispanic heroes. Then the writer identifies the specific hero he or she will write about.
- In the second sentence the writer begins with an independent clause and then adds a dependent clause.
- The independent clause tells the reader more about Miriam Colon Valle. The dependent clause supports the independent clause. It tells the reader how Miriam Colon Valle became a role model for all.

Remind students to check the Grammar, Usage, Mechanics, and Spelling section for more about proper construction of sentences, and using dependent and independent clauses.

Expand Read this sentence from the Weak Example: Her work at the university lead her to the United States eventually. Discuss its syntax, or word order:

- The word *eventually* is an adverb of time. It tells when her work *led* her to the United States.
- Proper syntax would put the adverb with the verb it modifies, or tells more about.
- Rewrite the sentence to show this: Her work at the university eventually led her to the United States.

Practice Have pairs choose another example of a weak sentence from the Weak Example and work together to revise the sentence. Then have pairs combine into groups of four to share their revisions.
L.9-10.1

CCSS Literacy.L.9-10.1 Demonstrate command of the conventions of standard English grammar and usage when writing or speaking.

Writing Modes

Expand Display real-world examples of each writing mode. Have students examine the examples and discuss the unique features of each mode. Below are some possibilities. (You may find pieces that fit more than one mode.)

Descriptive Writing:
- a magazine advertisement for a food or household cleaner that uses descriptive language
- a short story that uses sensory images or figurative language that help the reader visualize what is described

Expository Writing:
- a magazine article that describes an environmental issue
- an organization newsletter article that details an organizational problem and how it was solved

Expressive Writing:
- personal journal or diary entries recording the events of a special trip or occasion
- a travel magazine article that gives the writer's observations about a destination

Narrative Writing
- a historical novel that tells the story of a fictional character
- an autobiography or memoir that describes the events of a person's life

Persuasive Writing
- a letter to the editor responding to an article that appeared in a newspaper or magazine
- a speech written to convince listeners to take a certain action

Writing Purposes, Modes, and Forms

There are many **forms** of writing, which appear in a number of **modes**, or types, based on the author's purpose and audience. Some writing is meant strictly to inform; other writing is meant to entertain. Other writing forms are intended to persuade or convince readers or listeners to act in certain ways or change their opinions or beliefs. Writing forms can often be categorized into more than one mode.

Writing Modes

A writing mode, or type, is defined by its purpose. Most of your writing tasks will occur in one of the modes described below.

Write to Inform or Explain

The purpose of **expository writing** is to present information or explanations about a topic. Many academic writing forms, such as research papers and literary response papers, are expository. Expository texts usually include a strong controlling idea or thesis in the first paragraph. Each of the body paragraphs presents a main idea and details related to the controlling idea. The final paragraph, or conclusion, restates, or sums up, the controlling idea.

Write Narratives

The purpose of **narrative writing** is to tell readers something they can follow in story form. Narratives can be fiction or nonfiction. They are often used for entertainment or to explain something that really happened. They offer a way of making sense of the world by ordering events into a clear beginning, middle, and end. Strong characters and interesting settings are usually key parts of narrative fiction. Most short stories are narratives, as are autobiographical and biographical essays.

Write Arguments

You can argue to defend your own ideas or opinions or you can try to influence the thinking or actions of other people. When you try to convince others, it's called **persuasive writing**. All arguments include a claim. A claim clearly states the writer's idea or opinion. Good arguments include evidence like facts, statistics, expert opinions, or personal experiences. Clear explanations, or reasons, connect evidence to claims. The reasons may appeal to the reader's emotions, ethics (sense of right and wrong), or to logic and understanding of facts. Persuasive texts should have an appropriate voice and tone for the intended audience, clear organization of ideas, and strong supporting details.

Common Academic Writing Forms

The following pages explain the most common writing forms you will use in school. You may be asked to write, read, evaluate, and respond to any of these forms while you are a student.

Cause-and-Effect Essay

A **cause-and-effect essay** traces the relationship between events. A cause is the reason something happens. An effect is the result of that cause.

Use a graphic organizer like the one below to develop your cause-and-effect essays.

Single Cause/Multiple Effects

Cause: Rhinoviruses are the main cause of colds.
→ **Effect:** tickly throat
→ **Effect:** runny or stuffy nose

Multiple Causes/Single Effect

Cause: you learn about colds →
Cause: you protect yourself →
Effect: you don't catch a cold

Check your essay for the following:

- A clear statement of the relationship that is being analyzed and discussed.
- A clear main idea for each paragraph.
- Appropriate supporting details.
- Signal words like *if/then* and *because.*

Causes and Effects of Colds

Cold season is almost here. It's a good time to review the causes and symptoms, or effects, of colds. The more you know, the better prepared you will be to protect yourself from catching a cold.

Most colds are caused by rhinoviruses. There are more than one hundred kinds of these tiny, disease-causing organisms. If a rhinovirus infects the lining of your nose or throat, then you have a cold.

The first effects of a cold are a tickling feeling in the throat and a runny or stuffy nose. Other symptoms include sneezing, headaches, and achiness.

A severe cold may cause further effects. For example, the cold sufferer may develop a low-grade temperature, or fever. If his or her chest becomes congested, then the person may also develop a cough.

College Entry Essay

If you apply to a college or university, you may be asked to submit an **entrance essay** as part of the application. A college entrance essay is a kind of **reflective essay**, in which a person tells stories about their experiences. Your essay should do more than introduce who you are to the college board. It should detail specific events in your life and how these events impacted you. Choose words that show your personality, point out your skills and talents, and outline your future plans. A good college entrance essay should explain how your unique talents and personality will make you a successful student.

A college may provide you with a topic to write about, or it may ask you to select your own topic.

College Entry Essay

Reinforce Have students read the description of a college entry essay. Point out that essays should:

- tell about personal experiences
- tell how life events have changed the writer or helped him or her grow
- reflect the writer's own voice
- identify the writer's skills and talents
- describe the writer's future goals

Model how to select a topic and begin writing a college entrance essay. Write notes and sentences as you talk.

MODEL Say:

- *I know I need to write about what I want to do with my life, what my skills are right now, and how I have grown. Let me start with a list.*

  Future: *I want to be an accountant.*
  Skills today: *I am good at math. I work well with people.*
  How I've grown: *I had a job last summer as a camp counselor. I learned how to lead people and how to earn their trust.*
- *I can first tell my future goal. "I plan to be an accountant."*
- *I continue writing, "I know that this means I need to go to college and study hard. I also know that a good accountant is someone who works well with numbers and people."*
- *Next, I need to show how my skills and experiences will help me achieve my goal.*
- *I write, "I am very good at math and feel confident I have the skills I need. Last spring, I won the math award in my high school."*

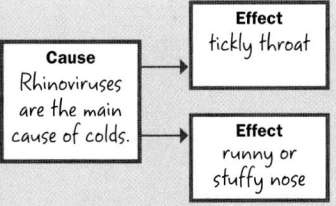

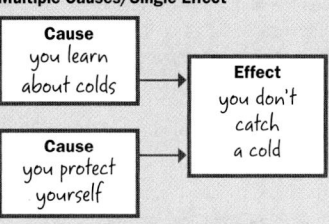

College Entry Essay Overview

Reinforce Use the model you created on the previous page. Now model how to develop the essay and make it more interesting.

MODEL Say:

- *Now that I have a first draft of an essay, I have to think about how to make it more interesting.*
- *I remember that I can use a literary device to help me start the essay. Maybe I will use a question or a quote.*
- *I can ask, "What do a camp counselor and an accountant have in common?"*
- *I can look for a quote from a famous person or a family member that relates to the topic.*
- *I think I will start with a different question: "How will my experience as a camp counselor make me a better student at State College?"*
- *Next, I will write about what I learned as a camp counselor. I will make sure to describe my skills and strengths.*
- *Then I will write about what I want to be—an accountant. I will relate my skills and my experiences to that goal.*
- *I will make sure to include interesting stories that relate to my main points: I will be a great addition to State College. I will be a good student and will bring my skills and talents to all aspects of college life.*

Use the graphic organizer below to develop your college entry essay.

College Entry Essay Overview

Beginning
Introduce yourself by writing in your own conversational tone. Get the reader interested with a good story or description. You might also present your controlling idea here.

Middle
Develop your main ideas with clearly organized supporting details. These details should help readers understand how your experiences have helped you grow as a person. Focus on how one or a few experiences helped you grow in one very important way.

End
Lead the reader back to the controlling idea. Leave a lasting, positive impression with a strong ending that tells who you are and why you should be accepted at the college.

Check your college entry essay for the following elements:

- clear focus on your own experience
- a personal voice and tone
- interesting details
- correct grammar, spelling, and punctuation

"Travel broadens the mind," my dad always says just before our summer road trip. Every June, he piles Mom, me, my sisters, and our dog into the car, and away we go. Though I used to dread our trips, I now realize how much I have gained from them. Our road trips have broadened my mind in many ways.

Comparison-Contrast Essay

A **comparison-contrast essay** tells how things are similar and different. Comparisons show how two or more things are alike. Contrasts show how they differ.

Use a Venn diagram to collect information for your comparison-contrast essay. List characteristics of each thing being described. Then, in the center, list the characteristics they share.

Venn Diagram

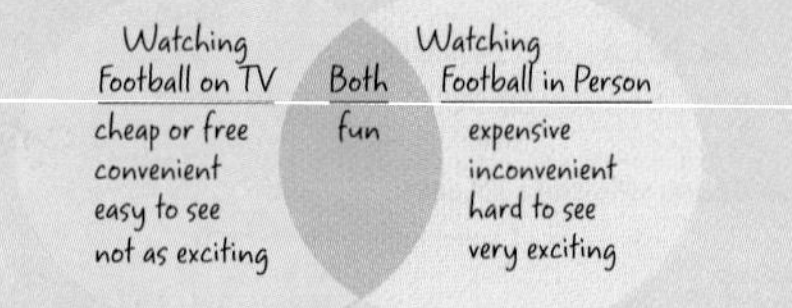

Check your essay for the following:

- A clear statement of what is being compared and contrasted
- A clear main idea for each paragraph
- Appropriate supporting details
- Signal words like *both/and*, *similar*, and *like* for comparisons; signal words like *but*, *however*, and *on the other hand* for contrasts

At Home or at the Stadium?

If you really like football, you probably watch it on TV every chance you get. You may even go to the stadium to see your home team play. Though both ways of watching football are fun, there are some important differences between the two.

The first big difference is cost. Watching a football game on TV costs little or nothing. If the game is on network TV, it's free. If the game is on cable, it may be included in the cable package. But a ticket to a professional football game is expensive. The average price for a ticket to an NFL game is $50.

Descriptive Essay

A **descriptive essay** provides the reader with a strong impression of a setting, event, person, animal, or object. The essay may contain many different sensory details, but all the details should work together to support the author's controlling idea.

Use a details web to gather and organize sensory details for your descriptive essay.

Details Web

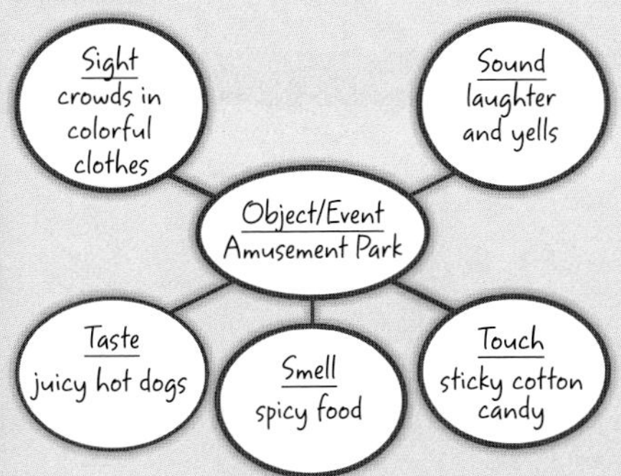

Check your descriptive essay for the following elements:

- a controlling idea that presents a single, strong impression that appeals to the five senses
- Information about how the subject affects more than one of the senses
- Vivid verbs, adjectives, and adverbs
- Clear organization of information, using a pattern such as spatial order (describing items from left to right, top to bottom, etc.)
- A unique style and appropriate tone for the audience

An Amusing Mixture

When summer vacation starts, I want to go to Alman's Amusement Park. Of course, I enjoy the thrilling rides there. But I enjoy the mixture of sights, sounds, smells, tastes, and feelings even more.

As I stroll past the Tilt-A-Whirl, I always see a blur of colors. People in bright summer clothes madly twirl, staining the sky with swirls of red, blue, green, and yellow. I hear the kids laughing and giggling, and I want to stop and watch. But I can't. The tempting scent of spicy food is in the air. I follow my nose to the Food Court for a juicy hot dog.

How-To Essay

A **how-to essay** explains a process. This kind of essay is also known as a process description or a technical document. A how-to essay describes the equipment, materials, and steps needed to complete a task. It answers any possible questions readers might have in order to make the process clear. The essay also often explains why the process is worth doing.

Use the chart below to collect information for your how-to essay.

How-To Planner

Task: Making a grilled cheese sandwich	
Materials:	Steps:
2 slices rye bread	First, butter one side of each piece of bread.
1 tablespoon butter	Next, place the cheese between the bread.
1, one ounce slice sharp cheddar cheese	Next, fry the sandwich until brown.
1 slice tomato	Then, add the tomato to the sandwich.
1 nonstick frying pan	Finally, serve the sandwich with chips.

How-To Essay

Expand Discuss the different features of the how-to essay and the technical document. Then point out the similarities in each type of writing:

How-To Essay:
- The how-to essay is typically written for a general audience.
- The writer uses informal or formal language, but not technical or special language.
- The writer can include his or her point of view or bias on the subject.

Technical Document:
- A technical document is typically written for professionals in highly specialized areas of study, like the sciences.
- The writer, usually a professional, uses technical or special language particular to that area of study.
- The writer will focus on the technical content, without giving his or her personal viewpoint.

How-To Essay and Technical Document:
- Both documents explain a process and include step-by-step instructions.
- The writer lists materials needed for the process.
- The writer can use the narrative or expository mode of writing.

Literary Response Essay

Reinforce Remind students that this type of essay should discuss the author's use of literary elements and stylistic devices. The essay should explain how well the author used those elements.

List these literary elements:

- rhythm, rhyme, repetition
- figurative language (including metaphor, simile, hyperbole)
- plot

Ask students to add other items to the list. Explain the elements as needed.

Tell students that stylistic devices can refer to the way an author uses word choice and sentence structure for effect. If necessary, review word choice and syntax.

Model how you could evaluate each of the literary elements listed by evaluating a fiction novel students have recently read or a movie the class has seen. Begin by writing the title of the work. Have students describe different aspects of the story, such as the plot or characters.

MODEL Say:

- *In order to make a good evaluation, I have to think about the plot and characters.*
- *Help me take notes about what happened. Did the writer tell the story as it happened? Or did the writer use flashbacks?*
- *What did the writer or film do best—that is, what part of the story was most powerful? I'll write that down. Then I can look back at it to decide what literary element the writer used.*
- *I can also take notes on the stylistic devices. Did the author's word choice and sentence structure affect meaning?*
- *After I take notes about the story and literary elements, I can use my notes to write my essay.*
- *It is important that I remember that my essay is a response to the literary elements. It should not just answer the question of whether or not I liked the piece.*

Check your **how-to essay** for the following elements:

- a clear statement of the process
- a complete list of materials and equipment needed to complete the process
- chronological organization of steps
- signal words such as *first*, *next*, and *then*
- complete description of the actions to take during each step
- benefits of performing the process

Deluxe Grilled Cheese Sandwich

A grilled cheese sandwich is delicious and easy to make. Try this simple but yummy recipe. All you need are two pieces of rye bread, a tablespoon of butter, a one-ounce slice of sharp cheddar cheese, a slice of tomato, and a nonstick frying pan.

First, spread half a tablespoon of butter on one side of each slice of bread. Be sure to spread the butter evenly, from corner to corner, so that the sandwich browns evenly when you fry it.

Next, place the unbuttered sides of the bread slices together. Put the piece of cheese inside the slices to form a sandwich. Make sure that the cheese slice is not larger than the bread. If it is, trim the cheese so that it fits inside the bread. Otherwise, when the cheese melts it will drip over the sides of the bread.

Literary Response Essay

In a **literary response essay**, you present your reactions to and analysis of a text. In an analysis, you look at elements that make up the text. For an analysis of fiction, for example, you might look at characters and conflict. For an analysis of nonfiction, you might look at word choice and meaning.

Use a graphic organizer like the one below to collect information and organize your literary response essay.

Literary Response Essay
Text Title: "Gettysburg Address"
Author: Abraham Lincoln
Date Written: November, 1863
Publishing Information: first published in newspapers
My Overall Impression of the Text: powerful speech!
Main Idea 1 about Text: nation founded on equality Supporting Detail: "soldiers gave their lives" for this Main Idea 2 about Text: other founding principles Supporting Detail: "of the people, by the people, for the people"
My Responses to Main Idea 1: Soldiers' sacrifices keep us free.
My Responses to Main Idea 2: I, too, have responsibilities to my country.

The text a writer responds to is called *a source text*. Read the source text below. Then note how the reader responded to it.

The Gettysburg Address
By Abraham Lincoln

Four score and seven years ago our fathers brought forth on this continent a new nation, conceived in liberty, and dedicated to the proposition that all men are created equal.

Now we are engaged in a great civil war, testing whether that nation, or any nation so conceived and so dedicated, can long endure. We are met on a great battle-field of that war. We have come to dedicate a portion of that field as a final resting place for those who here gave their lives that this nation might live. It is altogether fitting and proper that we should do this.

But, in a larger sense, we can not dedicate—we can not consecrate—we can not hallow—this ground. The brave men, living and dead, who struggled here, have consecrated it, far above our poor power to add or detract. . . . It is rather for us to be here dedicated to the great task remaining before us—that from these honored dead we take increased devotion to that cause for which they gave the last full measure of devotion—that we here highly resolve that these dead shall not have died in vain—that this nation, under God, shall have a new birth of freedom—and that government of the people, by the people, for the people, shall not perish from the earth.

The Message of Gettysburg

In 1863, President Abraham Lincoln traveled to Pennsylvania. The occasion was the dedication of a cemetery for the soldiers who had died at the Battle of Gettysburg. Lincoln's brief comments are today known as "The Gettysburg Address," and they present a new vision of the founding principles of the United States.

In the introductory paragraph,identify the author and date.

Lincoln begins his speech by noting that our nation was founded on the idea of equality just eighty-seven years prior to his speech. He then notes that the men buried at Gettysburg "gave their lives that this nation might live." This point makes me think of all the wars since then and the ways that soldiers' sacrifices allow me to enjoy the benefits of a democratic society.

State controlling idea of the text.

Include quotations from the text.

Describe reaction to a main idea.

Most powerfully, Lincoln ends his speech by restating the founding principles of the Declaration of Independence and the U.S. Constitution. Ours is a government "of the people, by the people, for the people." It was the brave sacrifice of those people and the ones who died at Gettysburg that Lincoln so beautifully honors in his speech. It reminds me that I have responsibilities to be a part of the government that so many have fought to keep alive.

Describe reaction to a main idea.

WRITING HANDBOOK

Literary Response Essay

Expand Model for students how to examine a writer's use of literary elements and stylistic devices. Have students read the Gettysburg Address.

MODEL Say:

- *First, I need to look for the literary elements and stylistic devices that are used.*
- *Lincoln uses poetic language to describe the year and set the tone.*
- *Lincoln ends the speech by restating the ideas that he described at the beginning.*
- *My essay needs to describe these techniques and tell how they make the speech effective.*

Write as you say:

- *Let me start the essay. "In the Gettysburg Address, Lincoln uses literary techniques and a poetic style to impress his listeners. When I read this speech, I am moved by the power of his words."*
- *Lincoln begins his speech in a poetic way. He could have simply said, "Eighty-seven years ago, people decided to start this country." But he did not. He used another way to express the number 87. He knew that a score is 20 years; so four score is the same as 80. Then he added the phrase, "and seven." He decided to use metaphor in his speech, by using the word fathers.*
- *Lincoln begins his speech in a more interesting way by saying "Four score and seven years ago…" His use of literary elements and stylistic devices help draw the listener in.*
- *My essay will continue to describe the techniques that Lincoln uses. It will also talk about the main ideas and how well Lincoln expresses them.*

A Autobiographical Narrative

Expand Tell students the difference between an autobiography and a memoir. The main focus of an autobiography is the author's own life. A memoir focuses more on the author's role in and interpretation of historical events.

B Short Story or Novel

Reinforce As students try their own hand at writing fiction, encourage them to use the plot diagram and checklist provided on p. 782. Ask students to work in pairs to create a very short story. Have them analyze their work based on the checklist and diagram, then exchange stories with other pairs of students to compare and provide feedback.

Expand Point out that descriptive elements include more than figurative language. Students should:

- try to appeal to all five senses
- describe characters' actions, gestures, and emotions. Help the reader "hear" the sound of the speaker's voice.

Also explain that the story's pace should match the mood. For example, if the scene is exciting, the language should be, too. If the scene is about a funeral, the language should have a slower pace with a more solemn tone.

C Plot Diagram

Expand Use "Cinderella" to demonstrate how to use a plot diagram for fiction. Keep the following in mind:

- Students from other countries or cultures may not know the story.
- Students may recall different versions.

Ask a volunteer to give a brief synopsis. Then make a plot diagram. For example:

Exposition: Cinderella lives with her stepsisters and stepmother. Both of her parents have died. Cinderella's stepmother and stepsisters dislike her. They treat Cinderella as their slave.

Narratives

Narratives can be either fiction or nonfiction. Fiction narratives tell stories featuring characters, settings, and plots. The forms of nonfiction narrative include:

- autobiographical essays/personal essays
- biographical essays
- diary or journal entries

Personal Essay or Autobiographical Narrative

In a personal essay, a writer describes events that he or she actually experienced. The purpose is often to entertain readers or to teach them.

Personal/Autobiographical Narrative Overview

Beginning
Introduce the people, setting, and situation. State why the event or experience was important.

Middle
Give details about what happened in the order that it happened. Share your thoughts and feelings. Use lively details and dialogue.

End
Explain how the action came to an end or the problem was solved. Summarize why the event or experience was important.

Personal Narrative Model

A Hard Lesson Learned

When Marie invited me to her birthday party, I was thrilled. She was the most popular girl in school. My best friend said, "Why do you want to go? Marie is not nice. She doesn't know how to be a friend." I wish I had listened, because my friend was right. The best I can say about my time with Marie is that it taught me a hard but valuable lesson about friendship.

Journal or Diary Entry

Journal entries are the least formal kind of nonfiction narrative. They are often used to record events from a person's life, but they can also be used as learning tools, such as when a person documents a research process or traces thoughts about something over time.

Journal Entry Model

January 4, 2007
I went to the library today to research my paper about hip-hop music. I was worried that I wouldn't find anything, but then I remembered a tip my teacher gave me: ask a librarian! So I did, and he was very helpful. We found three books, six magazine articles, and even a documentary film. I'm glad I thought to ask. It definitely made doing the assignment easier for me.

Short Story or Novel

Short stories and **novels** are common forms of narrative fiction. Novels are typically longer than short stories, with more developed characters and plots. Both of these forms usually include descriptive elements, such as figurative language and vivid word choice.

Plot Diagram for Fiction

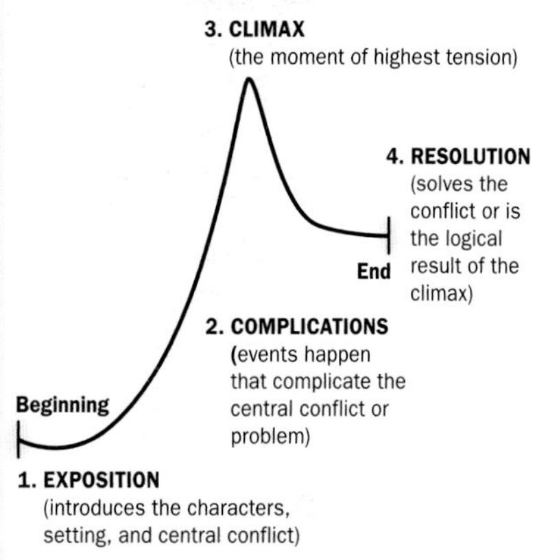

Using Persuasive Strategies

Good persuasive essays demonstrate effective use of persuasive strategies. Use persuasive strategies, such as appeals, to support your opinions. Note in the following examples how the writer's opinion statement changes depending on the appeal chosen.

Persuasive Essay

In a **persuasive essay**, you try to convince readers to agree with you or take a particular action. TV commercials, magazine ads, newspaper editorials, and campaign speeches are all kinds of persuasive media that begin as persuasive writing.

Persuasive Essay Planner

OPINION STATEMENT	I BELIEVE THAT WE SHOULD … KEEP OUR CATS INDOORS
Reason 1:	It's safe for the cat.
Evidence:	Many cats catch diseases outdoors.
Reason 2:	It's safer for wildlife.
Evidence:	Many animals are killed by outdoor cats each year.
Reason 3:	Cats lead happy lives indoors.
Evidence:	Experts say house cats are content.
Counter-argument	Cats like to be outside. However, they don't need to be.

Start a persuasive essay by stating an issue in a way that will make the audience care about it. Then state your opinion about the issue.

> **Keep Cats Indoors!**
>
> According to the American Bird Conservancy, pet cats kill thousands of birds each year. Now, I love cats. In fact, I own one. But I never let him go outdoors unless he is in his cat carrier. If you are a true animal lover, you will keep your cat indoors, too.

Support your opinion with reasons, evidence, and other appeals.

- An ethical appeal is directed at the reader's sense of right and wrong.

> It's just plain wrong to let your cat hunt and hurt other animals. Birds, rabbits, and other wildlife animals have the right to live just as your cat does.

- A logical appeal is directed at the reader's common sense.

> The fact is that it is dangerous for your cat to be outdoors. Your pet may be hit by a car. It may catch a serious disease from an infected animal. It may be chased by a dog or other larger animal.

- An emotional appeal is directed at the reader's feelings.

> Do you really want your cat to be lost? Picture how cold, lonely, scared, and hungry your pet might become while it is looking for your home.
>
> Now picture what it is like for a bird or a rabbit to be chased by a cat. Can you feel the terror of these little animals?

Additional things to remember:

- A personal anecdote, case study, or analogy validates your opinion.
- Think of questions or concerns your reader might have and address them.

Persuasive Strategies

Expand Discuss the difference between a position paper and a persuasive essay:

Position Paper:
- controlling idea is the writer's position on a topic or issue
- writer uses evidence and reasons to validate his or her position on the topic or issue
- conclusion should be a summary of the writer's position and evidence, and it should be memorable

Persuasive Essay:
- controlling idea is the writer's argument regarding a course of action or a topic or issue
- writer uses evidence and reasons to support his or her argument regarding a course of action or a topic or issue, as well as counter-arguments to opposing views from readers
- conclusion typically includes a call to action which the writer has tried to convince readers of in the body of the essay

Tell students that, often, an organization will have a formal position statement that outlines a position to which the organization is dedicated. The context in which the students present their essays also determines its organization.

Use Humor

Expand Tell students that one way to present their position and evidence in persuasive speech and writing is through humor. A persuasive speech in particular will benefit from humor:

- It can break the ice. Students may be nervous when they first start their speech. If they start with something funny, the audience will laugh. This may make the speaker feel more relaxed and confident.
- It can break the tension. Sometimes a speaker wants to convince the listener to take a drastic action or to radically change his or her viewpoint. Humor can lighten the listener's mood.

Practice Have students work in small groups to add humor to Play Your Way to Good Health on the student page. Allow students to share their examples with the class.
W.9-10.5

Position Paper

In a **position paper**, you state your opinion, or position, on an issue that has at least two sides to it. You also give reasons and evidence to support your position. The purpose of position papers is to persuade, or convince, your readers to agree with you.

Unlike a persuasive essay, a position paper does not necessarily include a call to action. A position paper also does not necessarily contain counter-arguments. The main purpose of a position paper is to state and support an opinion.

Position Paper Overview

Beginning
Introduce the issue. Show readers why they should care about it; then state your position, the controlling idea of the paper.

Middle
Support your position with reasons that will convince your audience. Organize the reasons strategically. Use transitions to help readers move smoothly from one reason to another.

End
Restate your position in a memorable way.

Check your position paper for the following elements:

- an attention-grabbing introduction with a clear statement of opinion
- supporting reasons with evidence for each reason
- clear organization and transition words, such as *first*, *next*, and *most important*

Play Your Way to Good Health

Recently, I joined the swim team. I had never been particularly interested in sports before. However, I have always been interested in having good health and making new friends. I received these benefits and many more from being on the swim team. Therefore, I think that all students should become involved in sports.

The first big benefit of becoming involved in a sport is that it will improve your health.

Persuasive Speech

A **persuasive speech** tries to convince the audience to take an action or believe something.

Persuasive Speech Overview

Beginning
Introduce the topic. Get listeners' attention. You might tell a story from your own experience or describe a case study of someone else's experience. Give necessary background information. End by stating your opinion. It is your controlling idea.

Middle
Support your position. Give reasons readers or listeners should agree with you. Also use ethical or emotional appeals when appropriate. Then state at least one possible objection, or counterargument, to your opinion and respond to it respectfully.

End
Sum up your reasons and give a call to action. Tell readers what action you want them to take or what belief you want them to have.

CCSS Literacy.W.9-10.5 Develop and strengthen writing as needed by planning, revising, editing, rewriting, or trying a new approach, focusing on addressing what is most significant for a specific purpose and audience.

Check your persuasive speech for the following elements:

- An attention-grabbing introduction with a clear statement of opinion.
- Paragraphs organized by reason.
- Strong appeals appropriate to the topic and audience.
- A counterargument with reasons and evidence against that argument.
- A summary of your opinion and a call to action.
- Respectful tone throughout.

Watch Educational Television

Can watching TV actually be good for you? Surprisingly, a recent university study suggests that it can. However, there's a catch. You have to watch educational TV, like nature shows and history programs. According to the study, watching shows like these can help improve your scores on standardized tests. Based on this study, I urge you to examine your TV habits and, if necessary, form a new habit: watching educational TV.

Though you may not at first believe it, watching educational TV shows can be fun. They can make a dry subject come alive for you. And when that happens, you learn and remember more. Let me give you an example. I had a hard time remembering anything I read about World War II. For me, the war happened so long ago that it did not seem real or interesting. When I watched a Public Broadcasting System series about the war, however, I began to feel differently. The subject became interesting to me when I watched and listened to interviews with people who lived through World War II. After watching the series, I reread my history book, and it made a lot more sense to me.

Problem-Solution Essay

A **problem-solution essay** informs readers about a problem and suggests one or more ways to solve it. A problem-solution essay has five main parts:

Problem-Solution Essay Planner

1. PROBLEM	Clearly state the problem. Where does it take place? When does it happen? Why does it matter?
2. CAUSES	Why does the problem happen? Who or what is to blame?
3. EFFECTS	Who is affected? How?
4. SOLUTIONS	Think about possible solutions. What has already been done? Has it helped? Think of new solutions. What are the benefits and risks of each idea?
5. CONCLUSION	Which solution is best? What makes it best? How could it be carried out? What do you want your reader or listener to understand? What do you want your reader or listener to do?

Reduce, Reuse, and Recycle

The United States is running out of land—land for landfills, that is. Landfills are where trash is taken and buried after workers collect it from homes or businesses and haul it away. Our landfill system is a good one. Or it would be, if we did not generate so much trash. Unfortunately, the average American throws away more than four pounds of paper, packaging, meal scraps, and other kinds of garbage each day. Multiply four pounds by the number of Americans, and you can see why we have a problem. Fortunately, there are simple solutions that anyone can put into effect. They are the "Three *Rs*": Reduce, Reuse, and Recycle.

Elements of Persuasive Speeches

Expand Have students read the list of elements to include in their speeches. Remind students to clarify and defend their positions with precise and relevant evidence. This should include:

- quotes and opinions from experts in the field
- explanations and responses to commonly held beliefs and ideas
- facts that support claims

Discuss ways in which students can properly respond to counter-arguments. Tell students to list and respond to:

- the reasons someone would disagree with their argument
- the types of biases that might prevent someone from sharing their opinion
- any expectations people have that might limit them from taking this action

Abstract

Reinforce Explain that an abstract is helpful because it identifies the main points of a report or essay. This can help a reader look for the details and evidence that support those main points.

Students can use an abstract to help them write a research report, too.

Model how to use an abstract to determine if a source is usable for research. Write and display these excerpts from sample abstracts:

Abstract

Air pollution has been linked to gas fumes from cars. This paper discusses the results of a study involving the use of electric cars in a small Midwestern town from 1990 to 1995. Data are included about effects on traffic, habits of drivers, and air quality in the town.

Abstract

Since 1970, the Environmental Protection Agency has helped to pass numerous laws to improve air and water quality. This study outlines the process of getting these laws passed—from the Clean Air Act to the Safe Drinking Water Act.

MODEL Say:

- *I have two journal articles that are possible sources for my research report. My controlling idea is: "Use of electric cars can help to improve air quality."*
- *The first abstract tells me the article is about the results of a study in which people used electric cars. This looks useful.*
- *The second abstract tells me the article is about laws passed to protect the environment. This might include some useful information.*
- *I think the first article will be more useful. I will read the article and take notes from it to support my research paper topic.*

Remind students that for the sources they use, they need to summarize or paraphrase information into their own words or use direct quotations in their research report. They then need to include the sources in their works cited list.

Summary or Abstract

A **summary** is a brief restatement of the main points of a text or visual medium, such as plays or books. An **abstract** is a summary of a research report that appears before the report. It tells the reader what your report is about. Begin a summary by giving information about the original work. Then present the main ideas and the most important supporting details. Use quotations and proper citation when necessary. (For sample citations, see the model research report on pp. 727–728.)

Summary Model

William Shakespeare wrote the tragic play *Hamlet* in about 1600. Since then, it has become one of the most famous plays in the English language.

As the play opens, Hamlet, the Prince of Denmark, is visited by the ghost of his father, the king. The king's ghost tells Hamlet that the king was murdered, and Hamlet decides to find out by whom. He suspects that his uncle Claudius, who has married his mother and taken over the role of king, is the murderer.

Hamlet's behavior grows stranger over the course of the play, as he is tormented by the idea of his father's murder and his mother's betrayal. He decides to create a play that he believes will show that Claudius is guilty. When Claudius does indeed show himself to be guilty, Hamlet's words and actions grow increasingly violent.

In the end, Hamlet, his mother, and Claudius are all killed during a duel. An invading army stumbles upon the bloody scene, and Hamlet is carried away to be buried.

Research Reports

A **research report** is a presentation of information about a topic. In a research report, you combine and organize facts from different sources of information. You put the information in your own words and let your readers know where you found the information you cite, or use, in your report.

Research reports are typically researched, written, and cited using either the Modern Language Association (MLA) style or the American Psychological Association (APA) style. The style is often determined by the subject matter.

To learn more about research, see the **Language and Learning Handbook**, pp. 639–644.

Analysis of an Issue

To write an **analysis of an issue**, research a controversial situation—one that has at least two sides to it. Then use the information to write a report that answers the question *How?* or *Why?* In an analysis, the writer's personal opinion does not need to be included. The purpose of the analysis is to inform and explain, not to persuade.

Use the following graphic organizer to organize your report.

Issue Analysis Overview

Beginning
Start with an interesting fact or idea about the issue. Make readers care about it. Give background if necessary. Then state your controlling idea.

Middle
Analyze the issue. Take it apart, and examine each part. Answer the question *How?* or *Why?*

End
Sum up the results of your analysis. You might state the importance, or significance, of what you discovered. Or you might restate your controlling idea in an interesting way.

Works Cited
List the sources of information you used.

The following pages show a Research Report with citations done in MLA style.

Smith 1

J. Smith
Mrs. Walker
English 100
January 10, 2013

> This section gives the name of the writer, the name of the writer's teacher, the name of the class, and the date.

An Analysis of the Global Warming Debate

The issue of global warming has divided the scientific community. Some scientists believe that carbon dioxide and other greenhouse gases are warming Earth, causing dangerous changes in the climate. Other scientists disagree. They believe that there is no proof of global warming or its effects on the climate. Is global warming real? And if it is, should we be worried about it?

> The introductory paragraph is clear and effective and states the controlling idea.
>
> The analysis focuses on these controlling ideas.

The theory of global warming is not new. It was first proposed in 1896 by Svante Arrhenius, a Swedish scientist. He said that people were unknowingly causing Earth's temperature to rise. The rise, he believed, was caused by people releasing carbon dioxide into the atmosphere when they burned coal and other carbon-based fuels. The carbon dioxide, he believed, raised Earth's temperature (Maslin 24).

> Parenthetical citations like this one tell readers where the student found information.

Over the years, other scientists further developed Arrhenius's theory, which has evolved into a scientific model called the "greenhouse effect." According to the effect, Earth's atmosphere is like the glass in a greenhouse. Glass lets sunlight in and re-reflects it, bouncing heat from sunrays back into the house and trapping it there. Similarly, carbon dioxide and other greenhouse gases re-reflect rays from the sun, trapping heat in the atmosphere around Earth.

> Background helps readers understand the issue.

The greenhouse effect is a natural process that protects us and our planet. Without the greenhouse effect, it would not be warm enough on Earth for plants and animals to live (Fridell 25). However, many scientists believe that problems occur when the level of greenhouse gases rises, causing the amount of heat energy trapped around Earth also to rise. This process, it is believed, may cause Earth to become warmer than it has ever been.

> The student uses a variety of sentence structures.

Most scientists believe that this temperature change has already happened. For example, scientists at the U.S. Environmental Protection Agency (EPA) say that over the past century Earth's surface temperature has increased about 1.4 degrees F ("Basic Information"). The EPA believes that the rise has been caused by carbon dioxide produced by the burning of gasoline, oil, and coal.

Does such a small rise in temperature really matter? Many scientists believe it does. They think that the higher surface temperature of Earth is causing dangerous changes to our planet. Temperature changes will result in changes in rainfall patterns like drought and flooding. As ice in the north and south poles melts, global sea levels will rise. People living near

> The student develops the analysis by explaining a main viewpoint on global warming.

WRITING HANDBOOK

Analysis of an Issue

Expand Have students look for the different data and facts in the analysis on the student page. Discuss how the data in this analysis support the research report topic. Have students read the highlighted sentences in the first paragraph. Ask: What details from this report support these controlling ideas?

Tell students to carefully evaluate the facts and details they want to use in their own research reports. They should use these criteria for the details and facts:

- They should support the main idea.
- They should come from a reputable source.
- They should be significant or meaningful.

Also tell students to try to use visual aids when they write research reports. Point out that technology can help them:

- Computer programs can help them put data into graphs and charts.
- They can print maps or diagrams from the Internet.

After students have completed their research reports, they should evaluate their overall quality. Emphasize that students should be prepared to revise their reports based on feedback from other students and the teacher.

Ⓐ Paraphrase

Practice Tell students that good research reports use some quotations, but only when the person's exact words are truly the best way to say something.

Remind students that they should paraphrase what they read as they take notes. This will make it easier to use their own words in the actual report.

Point out the quotations of different experts in this sample report. Have students work individually to paraphrase what the person said. Allow volunteers to share their paraphrases.

Ⓑ What Makes an Expert?

Expand Have students list the different experts quoted in this report. Discuss their professional titles or backgrounds. Ask: What makes someone a good expert? How can you be sure you support your argument with the right type of experts?

Smith 2

the ocean may lose land or experience more severe storms. People and animals will be impacted. ("Global Warming"). These changes will impact citizens across the globe, including people in the United States (Karl, J.M. et al).

Kerry Emanuel, a scientist at the Massachusetts Institute of Technology (MIT) is a strong believer in global warming. He thinks that global warming has caused hurricanes to be more powerful and destructive. After studying about 5,000 hurricanes, he found that storms increased in intensity during the same period that Earth's temperature began to rise. The number of big storms has increased since 1923 (Tollefson 2012). Emanuel believes that warmer ocean temperatures are to blame for the increase in storms' destructive power (Kluger 92).

Not all scientists agree that global warming is causing climate changes. Physicist S. Fred Singer is representative of this group. In an interview for the Public Broadcasting System (PBS), Singer said that "whether or not human beings can produce a global climate change is an important question [that] is not at all settled. It can only be settled by actual measurements, data. And the data are ambiguous.... Since 1979, our best measurements show that the climate has been cooling just slightly. Ⓐ Certainly, it has not been warming" ("What's up?"). Singer bases his conclusion on measurements from weather satellites, which he believes to Ⓑ be more accurate than measurements from ground-based thermometers.

The student develops the analysis by explaining a different main viewpoint on global warming.

Dr. Richard Lindzen, a scientist at MIT, shares Singer's doubts about global warming and climate change. According to Dr. Lindzen, rises in Earth's temperature and carbon dioxide levels "neither constitute support for alarm nor establish man's responsibility for the small amount of global warming that has occurred" (Lindzen). He believes that the computer models on which global warming forecasts have been made are flawed and incorrect.

Why, then, do so many scientists believe in global warming? Lindzen believes the answer has more to do with money than with science. He believes that government money is more often given to scientists whose work appears to predict and prevent disasters than to scientists whose work does not predict gloom and doom. Lindzen feels that because these kinds of projects tend to attract funding, some scientists have exaggerated the effects of global warming to get government grants (Lindzen).

The student answers the question Why?

And so the debate continues. Perhaps this is for the best. As James Hansen of the National Aeronautics and Space Administration (NASA) put it, "Science thrives on repeated challenges . . . and there is even special pleasure in trying to find something wrong with well-accepted theory. Such challenges eventually strengthen our understanding of the subject" (Hansen).

In the conclusion, the student effectively sums up the report.

Smith 3

Works Cited

"Basic Information." *Climate Change*. 14 Dec. 2006. U.S. Environmental Protection Agency. 5 Jan. 2007 <http://www.epa.gov/climatechange/basicinfo.html>.

Fridell, Ron. *Global Warming*. New York: Franklin Watts, 2002.

"Global Warming: A Way Forwrad: Facing Climate Change." National Geographic. Video and Audio. 30 Nov. 2012. <http://video.nationalgeographic.com/video/environment/global-warming-environment/way-forward-climate/>.

Hansen, James. "The Global Warming Debate." Education. Jan. 1999. NASA Goddard Institute for Space Studies. 7 Jan. 2007 <http://www.giss.nasa.gov/edu/gwdebate>.

Karl, T.R, Melillo, J.M, and Peterson T.C. *U.S. Global Change Research Program. 2009. Global climate change impacts in the United States*. Cambridge: Cambridge University Press, 2009.

Kluger, Jeffrey. "The Man Who Saw Katrina Coming." *Time* 8 May 2006: 92.

Lindzen, Richard. "Climate of Fear." Opinion Journal from the Wall Street Journal Editorial Page. 12 April 2006. WSJ.com. 2 Jan. 2007 <http://www.opinionjournal.com/extra/?id=110008220&mod=RSS_O>.

Maslin, Mark. *Global Warming: A Very Short Introduction*. Oxford: Oxford University Press, 2004.

Tollefson, J. "Hurricane Sandy Spins Up Climate Change Discussion." Nature. October 2012. <http://www.nature.com/news/hurricane-sandy-spins-up-climate-discussion-1.11706>. Accessed November 23, 2012.

"What's up with the Weather?" NOVA Frontline. 2000. WGBH/NOVA/FRONTLINE. 4 Jan. 2007 <http://www.pbs.org/wgbh/warming>.

The student lists all the sources of information cited in the research report.

Works Cited

Expand Students may be unsure about which sources to include in the list of works cited. Give them these guidelines:

- Include all sources from which data was recorded and used in the report.
- Include any graphic images, such as charts, tables, and maps.
- Include any interviews, letters, or e-mail messages used.
- Include any television and radio shows, movies, videos or other sound recordings.

Tell students that any facts they use in their reports that are not commonly known must be cited. If necessary, remind students to check style manuals if they are unsure of how to cite and list any of these or other sources.

Practice Provide access to printed or online style manuals. Have each student identify one printed source and one online source. Then have them use the style manual to practice creating citations.
L.9-10.3.a

CCSS Literacy.L.9-10.3.a Write and edit work so that it conforms to the guidelines in a style manual (e.g., *MLA Handbook*, Turabian's *Manual for Writers*) appropriate for the discipline and writing type.

Business Letter

Reinforce Tell students that a business letter should get to the point quickly.

Model how to highlight central ideas in an introductory letter. Have students volunteer information as you write a letter from a fictional teen. Write a business letter as you talk through the process.

MODEL Say:

- *I am going to write a business letter like the one shown here.*
- *Suppose our teen saw an ad for a camp counselor. One thing you would want to do is anticipate readers' questions. In this case, the reader would want to know why he or she should hire you instead of someone else. Let's think of the main ideas this letter should discuss. (work well with children, can handle a lot of responsibility, am creative and can solve problems on my own)*
- *I begin the letter with a short introduction. "To whom it may concern: I would like to respond to your ad for a camp counselor. I have included my résumé for your review."*
- *Now I need to get into the body of the letter.*
- *"I would be a great counselor at your camp. I work well with children. Last summer, I baby-sat two young children …"*
- *Now I need to close the letter.*
- *"I am available to work this summer after June 30. I can be reached on weekdays before 8 p.m. if there are any questions…"*

Career and Workplace Communication

In the world of work, there are expectations about the form and style of written communications. The following writing forms will help you at your workplace.

Business Letter

Business letters serve many purposes. You might write a business letter to make a request or to register a complaint with a business or other organization. The example below is a cover letter, a type of business letter in which the sender introduces himself or herself to an employer and states his or her qualifications for a job. Business letters should be typed on a computer or other word processor and should sound and look professional. Follow the business letter format below, and always check your letters carefully for grammatical or spelling errors.

Adam Russell
1297 Newport Ave.
Chicago, IL 79910
(555) 212-9402
May 18, 2013

Insert contact information for yourself followed by the person you are writing to.

Insert a space between the date and the contact information.

Ms. Carlita Ortiz
Ortiz Corner Grocery
2480 North Lincoln Ave.
Chicago, IL 79919

Dear Ms. Ortiz:

Use a formal greeting, addressing a specific person. Use formal titles and last names to show respect in business letters.

I recently read in the *Chicago Tribune* that you are taking applications for the position of full-time checkout clerk. I am very interested in interviewing for this position.

Do not indent paragraphs.

I worked for supermarkets for the previous two summers in similar positions, first at Green Grocers and then at The Grainery Foods. My managers always gave me good performance reviews, and I truly enjoy the work.

Use single-spaced paragraphs. Separate paragraphs with an extra space.

I currently attend Julius Jones High School, but I am available for work in the evenings and will be available in the summer after June 10, 2013. I can be reached after 4 p.m. on weekdays. I look forward to hearing from you about this opportunity and thank you for your consideration.

Always thank recipients for their attention.

Sincerely,

Adam Russell

Adam Russell

Include a traditional closing with a handwritten and typed signature.

Résumé

A résumé is a document that describes your qualifications for a job. A well-written résumé includes the kind of information a potential employer would like to know about you. Examples include previous work experience, skills, and achievements. It is very important that résumés be free of errors, so that the employer can see that you would take a job seriously and pay attention to detail. Use the format below to set apart your résumé from all the résumés of other applicants.

Adam Russell
1297 Newport Ave.
Chicago, IL 79910
(555) 212-9402

Objective
To obtain full-time, seasonal work in the food service industry.

Work History
2012, Grainery Foods
Full-time checkout and stock clerk at a busy supermarket

- Used a standard register and invoice-tracking equipment
- Trained new employees
- Met and exceeded cash handling accuracy reviews

2011, Green Grocers
Full-time retail assistant at a local outdoor market

- Set up and closed market stalls
- Supervised volunteer staff
- Assisted customers with pricing and selection

Education
Currently enrolled at Julius Jones High School.

Awards
Student of the Month, April 2013.

References
Available upon request.

Include your contact information clearly at the top of the page.

Use boldface type, italics, or underlining to make important information or headings stand out.

A

List your experience, starting with your most recent job.

Use bullet points to draw attention to specific skills or responsibilities.

Include information about your education and any information that would show what you have done well in the past.

Keep a list of 3 to 5 references available. Check with your references before you give their names out.

B

A Résumé

Reinforce Work with the class to create a résumé for a fictional student based on solicited responses from your students. Go over these parts of the résumé:

- name and address—Include your e-mail address, too.
- objective—This tells what type of job you hope to get.
- other experience—If you have done volunteer work or have been active in community or other organizations, you may list this on your résumé, too. Make sure the experience and activities you list are relevant to the skills you want to highlight.
- awards or certificates—List professional or academic awards, or any professional certificates (such as a CPR certificate). Include this head only if you have something to write here.

B References

Expand Give students these tips for developing a list of references:

- Check with each person to be sure it is OK if someone calls and asks about you.
- Choose people who will say positive things about you.
- References cannot be family members. You can ask a teacher, coach, or former employer.
- Be sure the address and phone number are up to date.

A Job Application

Expand Point out that students should come to a job interview prepared to fill out an application. This means they should bring:

- photo identification, such as a driver's license or student I.D.
- all information for each previous job—company name, contact (name of boss or manager), phone number, address, dates of employment
- information for references—name, address, phone number, how long they have known each person

Sometimes an employer will allow students to take the application with them and bring it back completed. Tell students to ask for two applications so that they can rewrite it neatly if they make a mistake.

B Business Memo

Reinforce Have students carefully review the sample memo on the student page. Point out that the memo does not have a greeting the way that formal letters do. However, the memo does anticipate the readers' question: "Why must I report to work one hour early on Sunday, July 1?" It answers this question in the first sentence: "as we will need help setting up the Independence Day Sale."

> **ELL** **Elaborate** Point to the line that says "Re: Independence Day Sale Hours." Explain that *Re* (or *RE*) is short for *regarding*. The writer of the memo tells the topic of the memo, or what it is about, here.

Students may also encounter the term when they call or visit a business person or doctor and the receptionist asks, "What is this regarding?" Tell them to respond by telling the person who asked the reason they are calling or visiting.

Job Application

Many jobs require you to fill out an **application**. Follow the instructions closely and write as neatly as possible or type the information. You will often need to provide reference information for your work ability or character. It is important to have personal identification with you when completing job applications. Ask a manager if you have any questions.

A

Please type or print neatly.

Today's Date: 5 / 1 / 13

First Name: Adam   Last Name: Russell

Address: 1297 Newport Ave.

City: Chicago   State: IL   Zip: 79910

Phone: (555) 212-9402   Birth date: 7 / 20 / 99

Sex: M ☑ F ☐

Follow instructions.

Education

High School Name: Currently attending Julius Jones High School.

Employment History (List each job, starting with most recent.)

1. Employer: The Grainery Foods   Phone: (555) 436-0090
   Dates: 5/2013 – 9/2013   Position: Full-time checkout and stock clerk
   Duties: Check out orders and stock inventory.

Provide complete and accurate information.

References

1. Name: Consuela Ybarra   Relationship: supervisor
   Company: The Grainery Foods
   Address: 123 Main Street, Chicago   Phone: (555) 436-0092
2. Name: Roman Hrbanski   Relationship: teacher/coach
   Company: Julius Jones High School
   Address: 321 N. Elm Street, Chicago   Phone: (555) 233-0765

Provide contact information for people who can tell the employer that you are a good and dependable worker.

Business Memo

B

A memo, or memorandum, provides employees with information concerning the business or organization.

Date: June 28, 2013
From: Carlita Ortiz, General Manager
To: All Full-Time and Part-Time Staff
Re: Independence Day Sale Hours

Please remember that all employees scheduled to work the morning of Sunday, July 1, should report at 7:00 A.M., one hour earlier than usual, as we will need special help setting up the Independence Day Sale.

Thank you for your attention.

Give information regarding date, sender, recipients, and the topic.

State the purpose of the memo and any supporting information.

Be short and specific.

Creative Writing

Your imagination is the most important tool in building the forms of creative writing. Some of these forms, such as plays and some kinds of poetry, have set structures. Others, such as parody, are defined by their purpose rather than their structure. Creative writing allows you to describe people, things, and events in new and interesting ways.

To learn more about these forms, see the **Literary Terms**.

Poetry

Poetry is a literary form in which special emphasis is given to ideas through the use of style and rhythm. In poetry, lines of text are called verses, and groups of verses are called stanzas. Rhyme and other sound effects within and among lines and words are popular elements of poetic style.

Some poems are written in conventional poetic forms. The number of lines, rhythm, and rhyme patterns are defined by the form. Other poems have a style all their own. These are called free verse:

Friendship

To never judge
To accept your true self
Through all your faults
Still loyal and caring.
That is the making,
An act of giving and taking,
of what we call a true friend.

Song Lyrics

A **song lyric** is text set to music and meant to be sung. Like lyric poetry, song lyrics often express personal feelings using rhythm and sound effects. These effects provide musical qualities similar to those often found in lyric poetry. In fact, the word *lyric* comes from the ancient Greek word for *lyre*, a musical instrument with strings.

Parody

A **parody** makes fun of, imitates, or exaggerates another creation or work. The parody can be sarcastic, and it is often used to make a point in a funny way. A parody can be in any form, from plays to essays to poems.

Twinkle, Twinkle?

Twinkle, twinkle unseen star,
Covered in our smog you are.
Up above our town once bright,
Now we cannot see your light.

Play/Skit

A **play** is a narrative that is meant to be performed before an audience. The text of a play consists of dialogue spoken by the characters and brief descriptions of sets, lighting, stage movements, and vocal tone. A **skit** is a very short play:

James. You mean I won? [*grabbing Paula's hands*]

Paula. Yes, you did. You won the Battle of the Singers competition!

James. [*shocked, then jumps, screaming and hooting*] I can't believe it!

Poster

A **poster** is used to get people's attention and give information in a visually appealing way. Posters should have the following:

- a purpose: What do you want people to know or think?
- attention-grabbing colors or pictures
- a large heading that tells people what the poster is about
- large print so people can read the poster from a distance
- just enough details to convey your message

Parody

Reinforce Have students read the explanation of a parody on the student page. Ask students to list parodies they have read in books or seen on TV or in movies. Remind students that many parodies poke fun at common social views.

Discuss the different parodies the class listed. Use questions such as these:

- How does this parody poke fun at a particular person, thing, event, or idea? How does it make fun of something about society in general?
- Is the parody trying to make a point? If so, what is it?
- Do you find the parody funny? Why or why not?

E-mail

Remind students when they write e-mail messages to include reader-friendly formatting techniques, such as the subject of the e-mail, as well as a greeting, a closing, and their name. Filling out the subject line anticipates readers' questions.

Explain that it is important for students to organize the information in their e-mail messages just as they would organize it in a letter. Remind them to use paragraphs so that readers can easily understand and follow their ideas.

Practice Have students draft an email message to you summarizing their learning goals for the year.

When students have finished writing an e-mail message, remind them to read over their message to make sure the message is complete and correct.
W.9-10.6

Blogs

Expand Explain that blogs and other online media include hyperlinks which a reader can click on to access other sources of information. Display and demonstrate how a link works using myNGconnect.com.

Explain that students will use a word processing program to add a link to a piece of writing. Display a word processing program. Type in the name of the school. Then use the tools menu of your software to model how to add a hyperlink to the school Web page using the tools menu.

Practice Have each student select a piece of expository or informative writing from their portfolio. Then have individuals search online for reliable information sources and select one source. Have students use a word processor and the source URL to add a hyperlink.
W.9-10.6

Electronic Communication

More and more, people are writing to each other using electronic forms of communication. Computers and portable devices, such as cell phones, offer a number of ways to research school assignments, conduct business, and keep in contact with friends and family. You need to protect your identity and stay safe online. Check your school's Acceptable Use Policy for guidance on how to protect your hardware and, more importantly, yourself.

E-mail

Electronic mail, or **e-mail**, allows users to exchange written messages and digital files over the Internet. Like traditional mail, e-mail requires an address to enable users to send and receive messages. This address is attached to an account that a user accesses through the Internet or through an e-mail software program. Keep the following rules in mind when writing e-mail:

- Carefully check the address of your recipient.
- Include the subject of the e-mail.
- Include a greeting.
- Be sure to supply enough background information to help the reader understand the topic and purpose of your e-mail.
- Unless you are writing to a peer, such as a friend or classmate, use a formal tone, proper punctuation, and grammar.
- Include a closing, and give your name.

From: student@studentweb.edu
To: n.patterson@njc.library.org
Subject: Library Books

Dear Ms. Patterson:

I have returned the books that you asked me about. I put the books in the return box. Please let me know if you don't receive them.

Thank you,
Jamie

Instant Messaging and Text Messaging

Instant messaging, or **IM**, allows two users to exchange messages instantly over the Internet. **Text messages** are sent over cell phone lines. Like e-mail, these messages require each user to have an account. Messaging is used most frequently by peers, so the writing style may be very casual. Abbreviations are often used to shorten the amount of time and space needed for the message.

Blogs

Web logs, or **blogs**, are Internet newsletters. Many individuals and organizations use blogs to communicate their ideas to a wide audience. Some blogs offer articles on a particular topic, much like a newspaper or magazine. Others are more like journals, with individuals documenting their interests or events from their lives. Most blogs are updated regularly.

Listserves

A **listserve** is an electronic forum in which users discuss and share information about a particular topic. Users sign up for the listserve, then post and respond to questions using their e-mail account. Many experts use listserves to exchange information with others in their field.

Message Boards

A **message board**, or **forum**, allows users to post thoughts and questions about a topic to a Web site and then see what others have to say about it. The site is usually organized by individual topics, called threads.

Social Media

There are many different kinds of tools and web sites that connect individuals to friends or groups. Individuals choose whether to subscribe, follow, or "like" an individual or group. This gives you access to that group. After you have access to a group, messages can be created or shared. You can join study groups, or connect with other readers or authors.

CCSS Literacy.W.9-10.6 Use technology, including the Internet, to produce, publish, and update individual or shared writing products, taking advantage of technology's capacity to link to other information and to display information flexibly and dynamically.

Media and Feature Writing

Many forms of **media and feature writing** are used in newspapers, magazines, radio, and television programs. Some of these forms are like narration because they tell a story. Other forms are types of persuasive writing. The most common forms are described below.

Advertisement

Advertisements, or **ads**, are meant to persuade readers to buy a product or service. Ad text should make an immediate impact on the reader and be easily remembered. Usually, advertisements appeal to people's emotions rather than to logic. Advertising messages are usually presented in visually interesting ways. Ads on TV may use visual techniques and background music to increase their effectiveness.

News Article and Feature Article

The purpose of a **news article** is to provide information. It should provide well-researched facts about a current event. It answers the questions: *Who? What? Where? When? Why?* and *How?* The first paragraph of a news article introduces the main facts, and the following paragraphs provide supporting details.

The purpose of a **feature article** is to provide information and points of view about something fun, entertaining, or important in people's daily lives. Feature articles are lively, fact-based discussions. Magazines contain many examples of feature writing, such as "Great Prom Ideas" or "The Year's Best Music." One characteristic of feature articles is a strong lead, or first paragraph, that draws readers into the piece.

Because they are based in fact, both news articles and feature articles can be considered narrative nonfiction.

Editorial/Letter to the Editor

Editorials are common features of most newspapers. These articles give newspaper staff writers the chance to voice their opinions on important issues. Many periodicals also publish letters to the editor, in which the public can voice opinions on a periodical's content or other topics of interest to its readers. When writing a letter to the editor, be sure to support your opinion with facts and evidence. Editorials and letters to the editor are usually persuasive in tone. **B**

Critique or Review

A **critique**, or **review**, presents the author's opinion of a book, movie, or other work. The review usually includes a brief plot summary or description of the work of art. A critique does more than just summarize the main ideas of a work, however. Details about performances or the author's opinion of the quality of the work supports the author's opinion. In an effective review, the author's opinions about the work are always supported by specific details. The purpose of critiques and reviews is to help readers decide whether to experience the work for themselves. **C**

Worth Seeing?

The Fellowship of the Ring is a movie version of the epic J. R. R. Tolkien novel about a mythical world threatened by the power of an evil ring. Director Peter Jackson uses beautiful computer graphics to show the struggle of a small group of adventurers who set out to destroy the ring. The rich characters, exciting action scenes, and incredible music make *The Fellowship of the Ring* a must-see for all fans of fantasy and adventure films.

A Advertisement

Reinforce Discuss with students the different types of emotions an advertisement might evoke, such as sympathy, hunger, fear, or the need to feel important.

Practice Have small groups create a list of their favorite advertisements and identify the emotion each one appeals to. Then have groups evaluate and draw conclusions about the credibility of the advertisements and then describe what details they use to evaluate credibility. Have each group share conclusions about appeal and credibility with the class.
SL.9-10.2

B Letter to the Editor

Practice Have students write a letter to the editor:

- Provide newspaper and magazine advertisements, a news article, and a feature article.
- If possible, also provide television or Internet commercial.
- Have students choose one item and write a letter to the editor in response to it.
- Display a copy of a letter to the editor for students to use as a model.

W.9-10.1

C Critique or Review

Reinforce Remind students that a critique is more than a summary, because it also expresses the writer's opinions and makes a claim. Point out the last sentence. Guide students to recognize that this is an unsubstantiated opinion, because the writer does not offer strong reasons and evidence.

Practice Have each student choose a book, movie, or other work. Ask them to write a critique for the work. Have partners exchange draft critiques and conduct a peer review. Have reviewers focus on evaluating whether every claim is supported by reasons and evidence. After peer review and revisions are complete, have partners reread both pieces of writing to discuss the differences between summaries and critiques.
W.9-10.1

CCSS **Literacy.W.9-10.1** Write arguments to support claims in an analysis of substantive topics or texts, using valid reasoning and relevant and sufficient evidence. **Literacy.SL.9-10.2** Integrate multiple sources of information presented in diverse media or formats (e.g., visually, quantitatively, orally) evaluating the credibility and accuracy of each source.

Ⓐ Plan a Speech

Expand Remind students of the following:

- The occasion of a speech is the setting where it will be given.
- The audience is the group of people who will listen to the speech.
- The purpose is what the speaker hopes to accomplish.

Practice Display the following lists:

Audiences:
- a school board
- a group of tennis team coaches
- a group of 6- and 7-year-old children
- classmates

Purposes:
- to entertain
- to inform about an issue
- to teach someone how to do something
- to convince listeners to take action

Have students describe speeches that are appropriate for each audience and purpose.
W.9-10.4

Ⓑ Speeches to Specific and General Audiences

Expand Remind students that a speech is a planned talk. As such, it should use proper English so that the audience will understand the message (unless the audience is one that expects dialect).

Offer these steps to help students use proper English in their speeches:

- Consider a controlling idea and identify evidence to support it.
- Write out the entire speech.
- Carefully read through the speech.
- Correct any grammatical errors. Highlight sentences and phrases that you corrected.
- Use the written-out speech to write an outline for the speech on note cards.
- Write out any sentences that you know may be difficult for you to say using proper grammar. (Use the highlighted sentences as a guide.)

Speech

A **speech** is a type of spoken message, often planned in advance and later delivered to a group of people. A speech can have many purposes:

Ⓐ
- **to inform or explain,** as when a community leader speaks to a group of news reporters about a new neighborhood program
- **to argue,** as when a political candidate makes a speech on TV to convince people to vote for him or her
- **to tell a story** and build relationships, as when a business leader makes a humorous after-dinner speech at a business convention, or tells their life story to inspire others to reach success.

Ⓑ Before planning a speech, identify the occasion for speaking, the audience, and your purpose. These three elements will help you select an appropriate tone, words, and details. For example, if you are planning a speech about computers for the members of a computer club, you will not need to define computer terms for your audience. If you were to give the same speech to a general audience, however, you might need to define the terms because some members of the audience may not know what the words mean.

Computer Speech for Computer Club

I am here to give you tips on creating Web pages. I will speak to you about the asynchronous qualities of Ajax and the advantages and disadvantages of pulling content with it.

Computer Speech for General Audience

I am here to give you tips on creating Web pages. I will speak to you about Ajax, which stands for "Asynchronous JavaScript and XML." Simply put, Ajax is a way to put content on a Web page by using codes that pull information from a server for you.

Script or Transcript

A **nonfiction script** is the prewritten text for a presentation or broadcast program. Like a news story, a nonfiction script contains the five *W*s, but no unnecessary details. A **transcript** is a written record of a live discussion or broadcast.

Scripts and transcripts usually follow the written conventions of plays. The names of the speakers are followed by their dialogue and brief descriptions of movement, visual material, and other information necessary to describe how the presentation should look when it happens or how it looked when it happened.

Transcript of WXQV TV Interview

MARCY RAY, INTERVIEWER: Coach, you must be very excited about the big win today. Can you describe your feelings for me and our viewers?

COACH: It's hard to put my feelings into words right now, Marcy. I guess what I'm feeling most is pride. The team worked so hard this year. Every one of those kids earned this win, and I'm very, very proud of the entire team.

[*Background cheers from team members*]

RAY: How will you and the team celebrate, Coach?

COACH: We won't be celebrating alone. This win belongs to the whole school. So there will be a celebration and ceremony in the school gym Monday morning at 9 a.m. Students, parents, faculty, staff—everyone in the school community—are invited.

CCSS Literacy.W.9-10.4 Produce clear and coherent writing in which the development, organization, and style are appropriate to task, purpose, and audience.

Social Communication

The forms of **social communication** help people establish and maintain relationships with friends and family. When you communicate socially, always think about the occasion for writing and how well you know the recipients. For example, if the occasion is informal and you know the recipients well, your tone and word choice can be informal. However, if the occasion is formal and you are not well acquainted with the recipients, a formal tone and formal language are more appropriate.

Friendly Letter

Before the development of electronic forms of communication, **friendly letters** were the most common way of exchanging ideas with friends and family. Today, the conventions of friendly letters are still used to write e-mail messages. The extra time and effort it takes to write and mail a letter show the recipient how much you care. Use the following rules to develop your friendly letters.

- Friendly letters can be handwritten or typed.
- Include the date.
- Include a salutation, or greeting, such as "Dear Joe."
- Indent the paragraphs.
- End the letter with a complimentary closing like "Sincerely," and your signature.
- Be sure to include the proper address and postage on the envelope.

> November 3, 2007
>
> Dear Grandfather,
>
> I want you to know how much we are all looking forward to your visit. It's been so long since we've seen you! Dad has already planned some special events for us, but I hope that we can go fishing.
>
> Yours truly,
> Carlos

Thank-You Letter

A **thank-you letter** is a brief, friendly letter in which the sender expresses appreciation for a gift or an act of kindness.

> September 4, 2007
>
> Dear Janita,
>
> Thank you so much for your help on the school newsletter. Your attention to detail and hard work were a big part of our success.
>
> Thanks again,
> Mr. Hahn

Invitation

An **invitation** gives the date, time, place, and purpose of a social event. An invitation often includes an RSVP. This is an abbreviation of *répondez, s'il vous plaît,* a French phrase for "please respond." Including an RSVP can help you plan for the number of people attending your event.

> **Come One, Come All!**
>
> Come celebrate Crystal's sixteenth birthday!
>
> Where: Elm Park
> 1900 Elm Street
>
> When: Friday, May 25
> 6:00–8:30 p.m.
>
> RSVP: Please let Crystal know by Wednesday, May 23, whether you can attend.

Civic Communication

Expand Discuss debates and petitions as forms of social communication. Tell students that living in a democratic society means we have the right and civic duty to communicate with leaders and share our views. Discuss debates and petitions as ways to do this. Explain the following:

Debate:

- A debate can be formal or informal. A formal debate follows strict procedures and rules.
- It is important to prepare for your debate by making notes, as if you were giving a speech.
- Carefully research and develop your viewpoint. Anticipate and prepare for responses to your viewpoint.
- Anticipate the viewpoint of the opponent.

Petition:

- A petition is a formal letter to a person or organization requesting a particular action.
- A petition is usually written to leaders, such as government officials. You must use formal language and appropriate word choice and organization.
- One person may have the idea and write the petition. Then the writer must convince others to sign the petition before it is submitted to the intended audience.
- When people sign a petition, it shows they support what is being requested.

Using the Section

Practice Ask students to take a few minutes and flip through the pages included in the Grammar, Usage, Mechanics, and Spelling section.

Point out how this portion of the **Writing Handbook** is organized and what is included in each section. Model for students how to locate specific information in each of the sections.

Create scenarios that could occur in class or at home while completing an assignment.

MODEL Say:

- *I am working on my research paper and want to include exact words from an article I read. I am not quite sure how to list the title of the article or the author's exact words. I think I need to use quotation marks.*
- *I can locate the section in the handbook on quotation marks. I see it says to use quotation marks to show the exact words quoted from a book. The handbook also says to use quotation marks to show the title of a magazine article.*
- *If I need help with other punctuation, I can look in this section.*

Use the scenarios to guide students to understand how to navigate the pages. Take this opportunity to emphasize the usefulness of the information in the handbook.
L.9-10.1.b

Grammar, Usage, Mechanics, and Spelling

Parts of Speech Overview

All the words in the English language can be put into one of eight groups. These groups are the eight **parts of speech**. You can tell a word's part of speech by looking at how it functions, or the way it is used, in a sentence. Knowing about the functions of words can help you become a better writer.

The Eight Parts of Speech	Examples
A **noun** names a person, place, thing, or idea.	**Erik Weihenmayer** climbed the highest **mountain** in the **world**. The **journey** up **Mount Everest** took **courage**.
A **pronoun** takes the place of a noun.	**He** made the journey even though **it** was dangerous.
An **adjective** describes a noun or a pronoun.	Erik is a **confident** climber. He is **strong**, too.
A **verb** can tell what the subject of a sentence does or has.	Erik also **skis** and **rides** a bike. He **has** many hobbies.
A **verb** can also link a noun or an adjective in the predicate to the subject.	Erik **is** an athlete. He **is** also blind.
An **adverb** describes a verb, an adjective, or another adverb.	Illness **slowly** took his eyesight, but it **never** affected his spirit. His accomplishments have made him **very** famous. He has been interviewed **so** often.
A **preposition** shows how two things or ideas are related. It introduces a prepositional phrase.	Erik speaks **to** people **around** the world. **In** his speeches, he talks **about** his life.
A **conjunction** connects words or groups of words.	Courage **and** skill have carried him far. He has one disability, **but** he has many abilities.
An **interjection** expresses strong feeling.	**Wow**! What an amazing person he is. **Hurray**! He reached the mountain top.

CCSS Literacy.L.9-10.1.b Use various types of phrases (noun, verb, adjectival, adverbial, participial, prepositional, absolute) and clauses (independent, dependent, noun, relative, adverbial) to convey specific meanings and add variety and interest to writing or presentations.

Grammar and Usage

Grammar and **usage** rules tell us how to correctly identify and use the parts of speech and types of sentences.

Nouns

A **noun** names a person, place, thing, or idea. There are different kinds of nouns.

Common and Proper Nouns	Examples
A **common noun** names a general person, place, thing, or idea.	A **teenager** sat by the **ocean** and read a **magazine**.
Capitalize a common noun only when it begins a sentence.	**Magazines** are the perfect thing to read at the beach.
A **proper noun** names a specific person, place, thing, or idea. Always capitalize a proper noun.	**Jessica** sat by the **Pacific Ocean** and read *Teen Talk Magazine*.

Count and Noncount Nouns	Examples
Count nouns name things that you can count. The singular form of a count noun names one thing. The plural form names more than one thing.	

Singular	Plural
one desk	two desks
one book	many books
one teacher	several teachers

(A)

You can count some food items by using a measurement word like **cup**, **slice**, or **glass** followed by the word **of**. To show the plural form, make the measurement word plural.

Jessica drank **a glass of water** after school.

Jessica drank **two glasses of water** while she was reading her book.

Noncount nouns name things that you cannot count. They can be divided into different categories.

Activities and Sports:	baseball, camping, dancing, golf, singing, soccer
Category Nouns:	clothing, equipment, furniture, machinery, mail
Food:	bread, cereal, cheese, lettuce, meat, milk, soup, tea
Ideas and Feelings:	democracy, enthusiasm, freedom, honesty, health
Materials:	air, fuel, gasoline, metal, paper, water, dust, soil
Weather:	fog, hail, heat, rain, smog, snow, humidity, sunshine

(B)

Some nouns can be either count or noncount nouns. It depends on how the nouns are used.

Jessica has read the book two **times**.

She is fascinated by the idea of traveling through **time**.

WRITING HANDBOOK

(A) Count Nouns

Reinforce Have students study the examples of the count nouns in the chart. Encourage students to name additional objects in the classroom they can count. Have students practice creating sentences for these objects using the singular and plural forms.

Then ask students to share their favorite type of pizza. Elicit from students that a piece of pizza is called a *slice*. Model creating the plural form of the word *slice*. Say: I ate one slice of pizza. My sister ate three slices of pizza. Repeat this activity using other food items and measurement words.

(B) Noncount Nouns

Reinforce Read the categories of noncount nouns together. Show students that some of the nouns can be count and noncount nouns depending on how they are used. Create example sentences such as: *Please get the **loaf of bread** out of the cabinet. My mother bought **two loaves of bread** at the grocery store.* Lead students to identify how *bread* becomes a count noun in the second sentence. Discuss other nouns on the chart that could be count and noncount nouns. Generate additional example sentences together using the nouns from the categories.

Forming Plurals of Count Nouns

Practice To assist students in forming plurals of irregular count nouns:

- Remind students that for some nouns, you cannot simply add an *-s* to make them plural.
- Make a list of singular irregular count nouns, such as *thief*, *wife*, *tooth*, *fish*, *life*, *self*, *ox*, *calf*, *goose*, *shelf*, *leaf*, and *mouse*.
- Work together to determine the plural forms of the words. Guide students in forming the plural form and write it next to the singular form on the list.

ELL **Elaborate** Display visuals for some of the singular and plural forms of the count nouns on the list. Write the singular and plural forms of the nouns on individual index cards. Remind students that the singular form names one person, place, or thing, and the plural form names more than one person, place, or thing.

Distribute the cards to the students. Have each student read aloud his or her word, one at a time. Then have students match the card to the visual. Ask them to identify if the noun is singular or plural.

L.9-10.1; L.9-10.2.c

Plural Nouns	Examples
Plural nouns name more than one person, place, thing, or idea. Add **-s** to most count nouns to make them plural.	My favorite **guitar** was made in Spain, but I also like my two American **guitars**.
Other count nouns follow simple rules to form the plural.	

Forming Noun Plurals

When a Noun Ends in:	Form the Plural by:	Examples
ch, **sh**, **s**, **x**, or **z**	adding **-es**	box—box**es** brush—brush**es**
a consonant + **y**	changing the **y** to **i** and adding **-es**	story—stor**ies**
a vowel + **y**	just adding **-s**	boy—boy**s**
f or **fe**	changing the **f** to **v** and adding **-es**, in most cases for some nouns that end in **f** or **fe**, just add **-s**	leaf—lea**ves** knife—kni**ves** cliff—cliff**s** safe—safe**s**
a vowel + **o**	adding **-s**	radio—radio**s** kangaroo—kangaroo**s**
a consonant + **o**	adding **-s**, in most cases; other times adding **-es** some nouns take either **-s** or **-es**	photo—photo**s** potato—potato**es** zero—zero**s**/zero**es**

A few count nouns are **irregular**. These nouns do not follow the rules to form the plural.

Forming Plurals of Irregular Count Nouns

For some irregular count nouns, change the spelling to form the plural.	one child many **children** one foot many **feet**	one man several **men** one ox ten **oxen**	one person a few **people** one woman most **women**
For other irregular count nouns, keep the same form for the singular and the plural.	one deer two **deer**	one fish many **fish**	one sheep twelve **sheep**

CCSS Literacy.L.9-10.1 Demonstrate command of the conventions of standard English grammar and usage when writing or speaking.
Literacy.L.9-10.2.c Spell correctly.

Possessive Nouns	Examples
Possessive nouns show ownership or relationship of persons, places, or things.	**Ted's** daughter made the guitar. The **guitar's** tone is beautiful.
Follow these rules to make a noun possessive:	
• Add **'s** to a singular noun or a plural noun that does not end in **s**.	When she plays the piano, it attracts **people's** attention.
• If the owner's name ends in **s**, form the possessive by adding **'s** or just an apostrophe. Either is correct.	**Louis's** music is playful and funny. **Louis'** music is playful and funny.
• Add an apostrophe after the final **s** in a plural noun that ends in **s**.	Three **musicians'** instruments were left on the bus.

A

Noun Phrases and Clauses	Examples
A **noun phrase** is made up of a noun and its modifiers. Modifiers are words that describe, such as adjectives.	**The flying frog** does not actually fly. It glides on **special skin flaps**. Thailand is **a frog-friendly habitat**.
A **noun clause** is a group of words that functions as a noun and has a subject and a verb. It may begin with *that*, *how*, or a *wh-* word such as *why*, *what*, or *when*.	**How any animal flies** is hard to understand. He explained **that it is called a flying frog**. Its name makes sense to **whoever sees it**.

B

Articles

An **article** is a word that helps identify a noun.

Articles	Examples	
A, **an**, and **the** are **articles**. An article often comes before a count noun. Do not use the articles **a** or **an** before a noncount noun.	It is **an** amazing event when **a** flying frog glides in **the** forest.	
A and **an** are **indefinite articles**. Use **a** or **an** before a noun that names a nonspecific thing.	**A flying frog** stretched its webbed feet. **An owl** watched from a nearby tree.	
• Use **a** before a word that starts with a consonant sound.	a **f**oot a **p**ool a **n**est	a **r**ainforest a **u**nion (*u* is pronounced like *y*, a consonant)
• Use **an** before a word that starts with a vowel sound.	an **e**gg an **a**dult an **o**cean	an **a**nimal an **a**mount an h**ou**r (The *h* is silent.)
The is a **definite article**. Use **the** before a noun that names a specific thing.	Leiopelmids are **the** oldest kind of frog in **the** world. They are survivors of **the** Jurassic period.	

A Possessive Nouns

Practice Emphasize that when the owner's name ends in *s*, they can add *'s* or just an apostrophe to form the possessive. Make sure they understand that either form is correct.

Help students generate a list of names that end with *s*. Write student responses on a chart. Have volunteers write the possessive form for the names listed on the chart.
L.9-10.2.c

B Noun Phrases and Clauses

Expand Review the definitions of phrases and clauses. Then explain that a noun phrase or clause can take the place of a noun anywhere in a sentence.

Use the examples to help students see how a phrase can be a subject, an object, or a predicate noun. Display each sentence and ask:

- What does not actually fly?
- On what does the frog glide?
- What is Thailand?

As students answer each question, underline the noun phrase and explain its function.

Demonstrate replacing each noun phrase with a noun. For example, *Peter does not actually fly.* It glides on *air. Thailand is a country.*

Use the same process to show how a clause can function as a noun. Ask:

- What is hard to understand?
- What did he explain?
- To whom does its name make sense?

As students answer each question, underline the noun clause and explain its function.

Practice Ask volunteers to replace the noun clause in each sentence with a noun. For example, *Biology is hard to understand. He explained evolution. Its name makes sense to Sarah.*
L.9-10.1.b

CCSS **Literacy.L.9-10.1.b** Use various types of phrases (noun, verb, adjectival, adverbial, participial, prepositional, absolute) and clauses (independent, dependent, noun, relative, adverbial) to convey specific meanings and add variety and interest to writing or presentations. **Literacy.L.9-10.2.c** Spell correctly.

Personal Pronouns

Expand Explain that personal pronouns can refer to the person or people speaking, being spoken to, or being spoken about. Point out that personal pronouns have distinct forms for each of these instances, as well as for the singular and plural. Make a chart for first-, second-, and third-person pronouns. Write the singular and plural forms of the pronouns for each person as you discuss these points:

- First-person pronouns refer to the person or people speaking. We use *I* and *me* in the singular form. We use *we* and *us* in the plural form. For example, *I want to go to the dance this weekend.* Have a volunteer identify the first-person pronoun used.
- Second-person pronouns refer to the person or people being spoken to. We use *you* for both the singular and plural forms. For example, *You will be getting your driver's license on Friday.* Invite a student to identify the second-person pronoun used.
- Third-person pronouns refer to the person or people being spoken about. We use *he*, *she*, and *it* in the singular form. We use *they* and *them* in the plural form. For example, *They got the CDs from Mr. Davidson.* Ask a volunteer to name the third-person pronoun used.

Practice Have pairs of students work together to use the personal pronouns listed on the chart to create sentences. Ask them to identify the pronoun used, identify the person, and tell if it is singular or plural.
L.9-10.1

Reciprocal Pronouns

Practice Point out that reciprocal pronouns act as object pronouns and can come after an action verb or a preposition. Remind students to use *each other* for two people and *one another* for more than two. Have students generate sample sentences using *each other* and *one another*.
L.9-10.1

Pronouns

A **pronoun** is a word that takes the place of a noun. **Case** refers to the form that a pronoun takes to show how it is used in a sentence.

Subjective Case Pronouns	Examples
Use a **subject pronoun** as the subject of a sentence.	**Antonio** is looking forward to the homecoming dance. **He** is trying to decide what to wear.
The pronoun **it** can be used as a **subject** to refer to a noun.	The **dance** starts at 7:00. **It** ends at 10:00.
But: The pronoun **it** can be the subject without referring to a specific noun.	**It** is important to arrive on time. **It** is fun to see your friends in formal clothes.

Subject Pronouns	
Singular	**Plural**
I	we
you	you
he, she, it	they

Objective Case Pronouns	Examples
Use an **object pronoun** after an **action verb**.	Tickets are on sale, so buy **them** now.
Use an **object pronoun** after a **preposition**.	Antonio invited Caryn. He ordered flowers for **her**.
Use **reciprocal pronouns** to show a two-way action between two or more people.	Mary and Juan tossed the ball to **each other**. Mary, Juan, and Lorenzo tested **one another** on the new math skills.

Object Pronouns	
Singular	**Plural**
me	us
you	you
him, her, it	them

CCSS Literacy.L.9-10.1 Demonstrate command of the conventions of standard English grammar and usage when writing or speaking.

Possessive Words	Examples
A **possessive pronoun** tells who or what owns something.	**His** photograph of a tree won an award.
Possessive pronouns take the place of a **possessive noun and the person**, **place**, **or thing it owns**. Possessive pronouns always stand alone.	Which camera is Aleina's? The expensive camera is **hers**. **Mine** is a single-use, disposable camera.
Some possessive words act as **adjectives**, so they are called **possessive adjectives**. Possessive adjectives always come before a noun.	Aleina's photographs are beautiful because of **her** eye for detail.

Possessive Pronouns	
Singular	**Plural**
mine	ours
yours	yours
his, hers	theirs

Possessive Adjectives	
Singular	**Plural**
my	our
your	your
his, her, its	their

A

Demonstrative Words	Examples
A **demonstrative pronoun** points out a specific person, place, or thing. It can point to something near or far away.	**That** is a good photo of my grandparents. **These** are good photos, too.
A demonstrative word can **act as an adjective**, answering the question *Which one*? or *Which ones*?	**This** photo album has pictures of my family. **These** photographs are of my grandparents.

Demonstrative Words		
	Singular	**Plural**
Near	this	these
Far	that	those

B

WRITING HANDBOOK

A Possessive Words

Practice Work together to create sentences using possessive pronouns and possessive adjectives. Have volunteers circle the possessive adjectives and identify if the singular or plural form is used.
L.9-10.1

B Demonstrative Words

Reinforce Explain that demonstrative words can function, or work, either as pronouns or adjectives. If a demonstrative word acts as an adjective, it points to a noun. If a noun is singular, you must use the singular form. If the noun is plural, you must use the plural form. The demonstrative adjective must agree with the noun.

Create example sentences using the demonstrative words in the chart both as pronouns and as adjectives. Help students describe how the demonstrative adjective points to the noun and answers the question "Which one?" or "Which ones?"

ELL **Elaborate** Display classroom objects and create several sentences about them containing demonstrative words. Use both singular and plural forms. Read each sentence aloud, point to the demonstrative word, and ask: Which one or ones is this word pointing to?

Help students identify the specific thing or things the demonstrative word is pointing to. Then lead them to create additional sentences for different classroom objects using a demonstrative adjective.

CCSS Literacy.L.9-10.1 Demonstrate command of the conventions of standard English grammar and usage when writing or speaking.

Relative Pronouns

Reinforce Discuss the relative pronouns listed in the chart. Make these points:

- You can use a relative pronoun to link one clause (either restrictive or nonrestrictive) to a main clause.
- Review which pronouns are used for people or things.
- Explain that some forms are acceptable to use when speaking but must be different in formal writing.

Write clauses such as *You may invite* and *you like to the party,* leaving a blank between the clauses. Help students identify if the clauses are referring to people or things. Ask a volunteer to choose the correct relative pronoun from the chart to connect the two clauses and write it on the line. Ask the class to read the completed sentence aloud. Work together to describe how the relative pronoun links the clause to a word in the sentence.

ELL **Elaborate** Explain to students that a relative clause provides important information that explains the main clause. The information is necessary to understand the sentence correctly.

Write sentences containing a relative pronoun and a relative clause. Help students identify the relative pronoun and relative clause. Lead them to understand the forms used for people and for things. Discuss how the relative pronoun connects the clause to a word in the sentence. Guide them to describe how the relative clause explains the main clause.

Tell students the word *that* is used to introduce a clause that helps identify a word that came earlier in the sentence (restrictive clause), while the word *which* introduces a clause that adds information that is not necessary, or non-essential, to the sentence (nonrestrictive clause).

Practice Have pairs take turns forming sentences with each relative pronoun in the list.
L.9-10.1.b; L.9-10.3

Indefinite Pronouns	Examples
Use an **indefinite pronoun** when you are not talking about a specific person, place, or thing.	**Someone** has to lose the game. **Nobody** knows who the winner will be.

Some Indefinite Pronouns

These **indefinite pronouns** are always singular and need a **singular verb**. another, either, nobody, someone anybody, everybody, no one, something anyone, everyone, nothing anything, everything, one each, neither, somebody	**Something is** happening on the playing field. We hope that **everything goes** well for our team.
These **indefinite pronouns** are always plural and need a **plural verb**. both, few, many, several	**Many** of us **are** hopeful.
These **indefinite pronouns** can be either singular or plural. all, any, most, none, some Look at the phrase that follows the indefinite pronoun. If the noun or pronoun in the phrase is plural, use a **plural verb**. If the noun or pronoun is singular, use a **singular verb**.	**Most** of the players **are** tired. **Most** of the game **is** over.

Relative Pronouns	Examples
A **relative pronoun** introduces **a relative clause**. It connects, or relates, the clause to a word in the sentence. Relative pronouns are used in restrictive and nonrestrictive clauses.	**Relative Pronouns** who, whoever, whosoever whom, whomever, whomsoever whose, which, whichever what, whatever, whatsoever
Use **who**, **whom**, or **whose** for people. The pronouns **whoever**, **whomever**, **whosoever**, and **whomsoever** also refer to people.	The student **who** was injured is Joe. We play **whomever** we are scheduled to play.
Use **which**, **whichever**, **what**, **whatever**, and **whatsoever** for things.	Joe's wrist, **which** is sprained, will heal.
Use **that** for people or things.	The trainer **that** examined Joe's wrist is sure. The injury **that** Joe received is minor.

Grammar Tip
In informal speech, it is acceptable to say "**Who** did you ask?" In formal writing, use the correct form, "**Whom** did you ask?"

CCSS **Literacy.L.9-10.1.b** Use various types of phrases (noun, verb, adjectival, adverbial, participial, prepositional, absolute) and clauses (independent, dependent, noun, relative, adverbial) to convey specific meanings and add variety and interest to writing or presentations. **Literacy.L.9-10.3** Apply knowledge of language to understand how language functions in different contexts, to make effective choices for meaning or style, and to comprehend more fully when reading or listening.

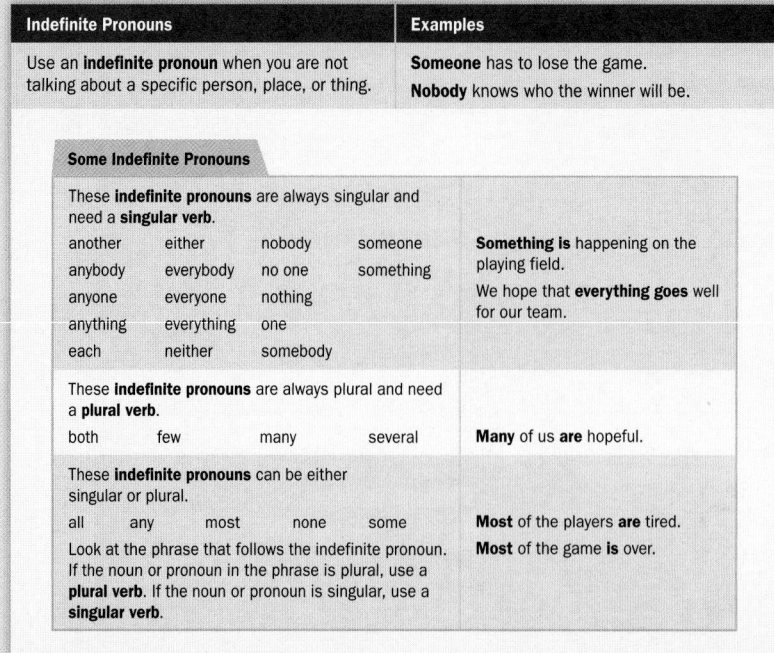

Reflexive and Intensive Pronouns	Examples
Reflexive and **intensive pronouns** refer to nouns or other pronouns in a sentence. These pronouns end with -**self** or -**selves**.	**I** will go to the store by **myself**.
Use a **reflexive pronoun** when the object **refers back to the subject**.	To surprise her technology teacher, **Kim** taught **herself** how to create a Web site on the computer.
Use an **intensive pronoun** when you want **to emphasize a noun or a pronoun** in a sentence.	The technology **teacher himself** learned some interesting techniques from Kim.

Reflexive and Intensive Pronouns	
Singular	**Plural**
myself	ourselves
yourself	yourselves
himself, herself, itself	themselves

A

Agreement and Reference	Examples
When nouns and pronouns **agree**, they both refer to the same person, place, or thing. The **noun** is the **antecedent**, and the **pronoun** refers to it.	**Rafael and Felicia** visited a local college. **They** toured the campus. *antecedent* *pronoun*
A pronoun must agree (match) in **number** with the noun it refers to. • **Singular pronouns** refer to one person. • **Plural pronouns** refer to more than one person.	**Rafael** plays violin. **He** enjoyed the music school. **The teenagers** were impressed. **They** liked this college.
Pronouns and adjectives must agree in **gender** with the nouns they refer to. Use **she**, **her**, and **hers** to refer to females. Use **he**, **him**, and **his** to refer to males.	Felicia told **her** uncle about the college visit. **Her** uncle told **her** that **he** received **his** graduate degree from that school.

B

Editing Tip

Find each pronoun in your paper. Find the noun it is replacing. Do they match?

A Intensive Pronouns

Expand Read aloud the intensive pronouns listed on the chart. Discuss the purpose of intensive pronouns. Point out that intensive pronouns are not used that often. Say:

- An intensive pronoun re-emphasizes a noun or pronoun by taking the place of the word that comes before it.
- Intensive pronouns are used to avoid repeating the same word.

Read aloud the example listed. Point out the intensive pronoun *himself*. Ask: What noun is *himself* re-emphasizing? Ask a volunteer to reread the sentence without saying the word *himself*. Guide students to discuss if the meaning of the sentence changed. Then lead them to understand that it is not necessary to use an intensive pronoun in this case. Generate additional examples using intensive pronouns to emphasize that they are not necessary in most cases, but are used for emphasis.

B Pronoun Agreement

Practice Remind students that pronouns must agree with the nouns they are representing. Write incorrect sentences such as: *Lori left the house early, but they forgot her purse. Jenny, Matt, and Pablo were happy he hadn't missed the beginning of the movie.* Help students edit the sentences for pronoun agreement.
L.9-10.1

CCSS Literacy.L.9-10.1 Demonstrate command of the conventions of standard English grammar and usage when writing or speaking.

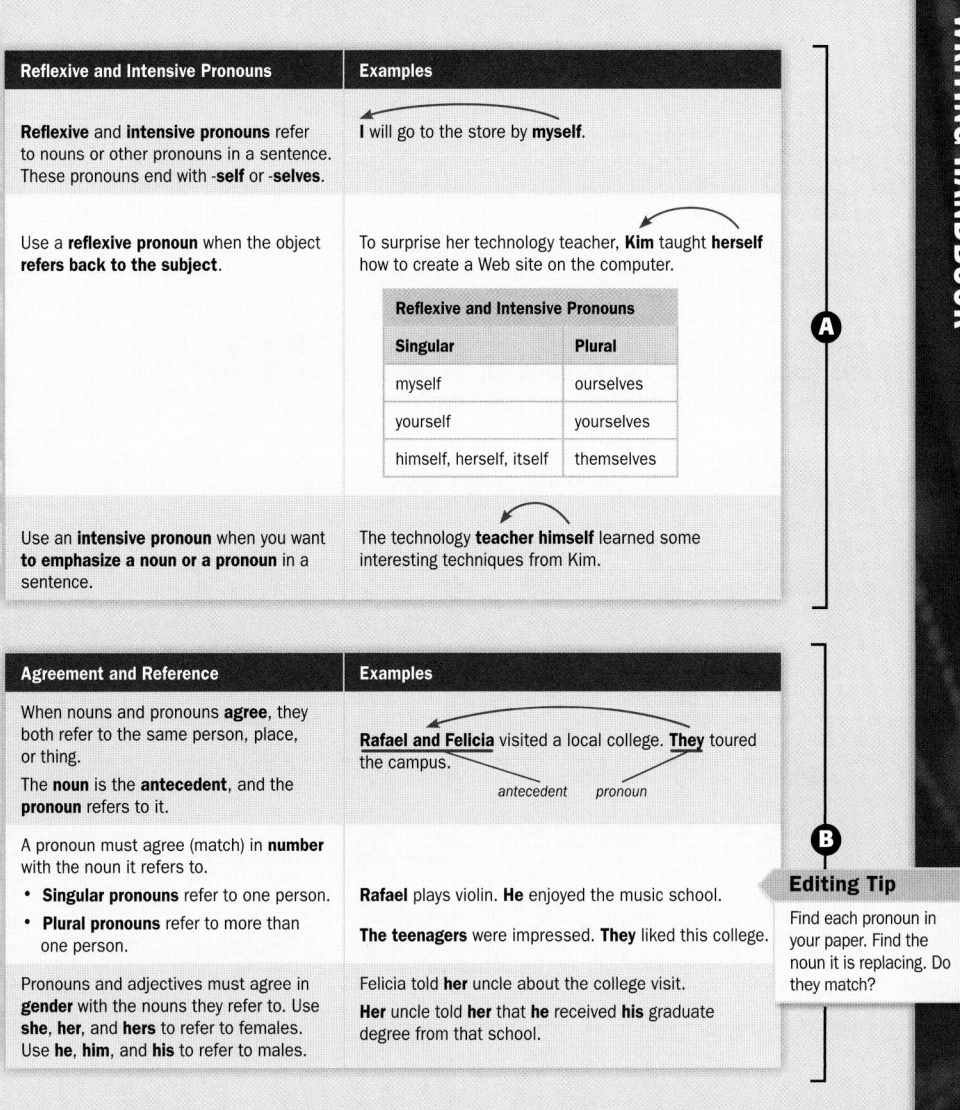

A Comparative Adjectives

Reinforce Point out to students that when we compare things, we see how they are the same or different. We can use adjectives to describe these differences.

Write these adjectives: *difficult, wonderful, expensive, comfortable, popular.* Point to, read aloud, and clap the syllables for each of the adjectives. Explain that each of these adjectives has three or more syllables. Tell students that the rule for all adjectives containing three or more syllables is to use *more* before the adjective when comparing.

Practice Have pairs of students work together to create sentences using *more* and comparative adjectives from the list. Ask them to share one of their sentences with the class.
L.9-10.1

B Adjective Phrases and Clauses

Expand Discuss the uses of adjective phrases and clauses using the definitions and examples on the chart. Then, display the following sentences:

- Plants that are in the family *Cactaceae* are called cacti.
- Cacti, which are native to the Americas, are best seen in the desert.
- Mexico, which has the greatest variety of cacti, has many colorful species.
- Cacti that do not bloom may not be getting enough sunshine.

Have partners discuss why some sentences have commas and others do not. Ask: *How would the meaning of the sentence change if the adjective clause was removed?* Guide students to understand that clauses that could be removed without changing the meaning require commas.

Practice Have pairs work together to write five sentences with adjective phrases. Have pairs exchange sentences. Challenge pairs to underline phrases and use arrows to indicate the phrase or clause and what is being modified.

L.9-10.1.b

Adjectives

An **adjective** describes, or modifies, a noun or a pronoun. It can tell what kind, which one, how many, or how much.

Adjectives	Examples
Adjectives provide more detailed information about a noun. Usually, an adjective comes before the noun it describes.	Deserts have a **dry** climate.
But an adjective can also come after the noun.	The climate is also **hot**.

A

Adjectives That Compare	Examples
Comparative adjectives help show the similarities or differences between two nouns.	Deserts are **more fun** to study than forests are.
To form the comparative of one-syllable adjectives and two-syllable adjectives that end in a consonant + **y**, add **-er**, and use **than**. Use **more** . . . **than** if the adjective has three or more syllables.	The Sechura Desert in South America is small**er** **than** the Kalahari Desert in Africa. Is that desert **more in·ter·est·ing than** this one?
Superlative adjectives help show how three or more nouns are alike or different.	Of the Sechura, Kalahari, and Sahara, which is the **largest**?
To form the superlative of one-syllable adjectives and two-syllable adjectives that end in a consonant + **y**, add **-est**.	Which of the three deserts is the **smallest**?
Use **most** if the adjective has three or more syllables.	I think the Sahara is the **most beau·ti·ful**.
Irregular adjectives form the comparative and superlative differently. good better best some more most bad worse worst little less least	I had the **best** time ever visiting the desert. But the desert heat is **worse** than city heat.
Some two-syllable adjectives form the comparative with either **-er** or **more** and superlative with either **-est** or **most**. **Do not form a double comparison by using both.**	Most desert animals are **more lively** at night than during the day. Most desert animals are **livelier** at night than during the day.

B

Adjective Phrases and Clauses	Examples
An **adjective phrase** is a group of words that work together to modify a noun or a pronoun. A phrase has no verb.	Plants **in the desert** have developed adaptations.
An **adjective clause** is also a group of words that work together to modify a noun or a pronoun. Unlike a phrase, however, a clause has both a subject and a verb.	Desert plants **that have long roots** tap into water deep in the earth.

CCSS Literacy.L.9-10.1 Demonstrate command of the conventions of standard English grammar and usage when writing or speaking. L.9-10.1.b Use various types of phrases (noun, verb, adjectival, adverbial, participial, prepositional, absolute) and clauses (independent, dependent, noun, relative, adverbial) to convey specific meanings and add variety and interest to writing or presentations.

Verbs

Every sentence has two parts: a subject and a predicate. The subject tells who or what the sentence is about. The predicate tells something about the subject. For example: The dancers / **performed** on stage.

The **verb** is the key word in the predicate because it tells what the subject does or has. Verbs can also link words.

Action Verbs	Examples
An **action verb** tells what the subject of a sentence does. Most verbs are action verbs.	Dancers **practice** for many hours. They **stretch** their muscles and **lift** weights.
Some **action verbs** tell about an action that you cannot see.	The dancers **recognize** the rewards that come from their hard work.

Linking Verbs	Examples
A **linking verb** connects, or links, the subject of a sentence to a word in the predicate.	**Linking Verbs** **Forms of the Verb *Be***: am, is, are, was, were **Other Linking Verbs**: appear, feel, look, seem, smell, become, taste
The word in the predicate can describe the subject.	Their feet **are** calloused.
Or the word in the predicate can rename the subject.	These dancers **are** athletes.

A

Conditional Verbs	Examples
Conditional verbs show, in the present, how one event depends on another event in the future.	Dancers **should** stretch to prevent injuries. An injury **might** prevent a dancer from performing.
Some Conditional Verbs can, could, might, must shall, should, will, would	
Sentences with conditional verbs often use **if** and **then** to show how two events are connected. Conditional verbs are sometimes called **modal verbs.**	**If** a principal dancer is unable to perform, **then** the understudy will perform the role.

B

WRITING HANDBOOK

A Linking Verbs

Reinforce Model how to determine if a verb is an action verb or a linking verb. Explain that if you can substitute *am*, *is*, or *are* for the verb and the sentence still makes sense, it is a linking verb. If, after the substitution, the sentence does not make sense, it is an action verb.

Say: Jonathan tasted the spicy enchilada casserole. Point out that *tasted* is the verb in this sentence. Try substituting *is* for *tasted*: Jonathan is the spicy enchilada casserole. Ask: Does this make sense? Lead students to identify that in this sentence, *tasted* is an action verb.

B Conditional Verbs

Practice Remind students that *if* and *then* are often used in sentences with conditional verbs to show how the two events are connected. For example, *If my brother were a foot taller, then he would be a great basketball player.*

Have partners work together to create sentences containing conditional verbs. Ask them to share their sentences with the class. Have the class identify the conditional verbs and explain how the two events are connected.
L.9-10.1.b, L.9-10.3

CCSS Literacy.L.9-10.1.b Use various types of phrases (noun, verb, adjectival, adverbial, participial, prepositional, absolute) and clauses (independent, dependent, noun, relative, adverbial) to convey specific meanings and add variety and interest to writing or presentations.
Literacy.L.9-10.3 Apply knowledge of language to understand how language functions in different contexts, to make effective choices for meaning or style, and to comprehend more fully when reading or listening.

Helping Verbs

Expand Explain to students that just like in any other language, the English language has rules that must be followed. These rules help our language make sense.

Write the words *ought to* and explain that this helping verb is used to express obligation or something you should do. Say: You ought to pick up your shoes more often. Discuss how the sentence would not flow as smoothly if *ought* was used alone.

Practice Have students take turns generating sentences using *ought to*.
L.9-10.1.b

Helping Verbs	Examples
Verb phrases have more than one verb: helping verbs and a main verb.	Ballet **is considered** a dramatic art form. (*is*: helping verb; *considered*: main verb)
The action word is called the **main verb**. It shows what the subject does, has, or is.	This dance form **has been evolving** over the years. (*has been*: helping verbs; *evolving*: main verb)
Any verbs that come before the main verb are the **helping verbs**.	Ballet **must have been** very different in the 1500s. (*must have*: helping verbs; *been*: main verb)
Helping verbs agree with the subject.	Baryshnikov **has performed** around the world. Many people **have praised** this famous dancer.
Adverbs can be in several places in a sentence. The adverb **not** always comes between the **helping verb** and the **main verb**.	If you **have** not **heard** of him, you can watch the film *Dancers* to see him perform. He sometimes **has danced** in films. Usually, he dances on stage.
In questions, the subject comes between the **helping verb** and the **main verb**.	**Have** you **heard** of Mikhail Baryshnikov?

Helping Verbs

Forms of the Verb *Be*		Forms of the Verb *Do*		Forms of the Verb *Have*	
am	was	do	did	have	had
is	were	does		has	
are					

Other Helping Verbs

To express ability: **can**, **could**	I **can** dance.
To express possibility: **may**, **might**, **could**	I **might** dance tonight.
To express necessity or desire: **must**, **would like**	I **must** dance more often. I **would like** to dance more often.
To express certainty: **will**, **shall**	I **will** dance more often.
To express obligation: **should**, **ought to**	I **should** practice more often. I **ought to** practice more often.

CCSS Literacy.L.9-10.1.b Use various types of phrases (noun, verb, adjectival, adverbial, participial, prepositional, absolute) and clauses (independent, dependent, noun, relative, adverbial) to convey specific meanings and add variety and interest to writing or presentations.

Verb Tense

The **tense** of a verb shows when an action happens.

Present Tense Verbs	Examples
The **present tense** of a verb tells about an action that happens now.	Greg **checks** his watch to see if it is time to leave. He **starts** work at 5:00 today.

Habitual Present Tense Verbs	Examples
The **habitual present tense** of a verb tells about an action that happens regularly or all the time.	Greg **works** at a pizza shop on Saturdays and Sundays. He **makes** pizzas and **washes** dishes.

Past Tense Verbs (Regular and Irregular)	Examples
The **past tense** of a verb tells about an action that happened earlier, or in the past.	Yesterday, Greg **worked** until the shop closed. He **made** 50 pizzas.
• The past tense form of **regular verbs** ends with **-ed**.	He **learned** how to make a stuffed-crust pizza. Then Greg **chopped** onions and peppers.
• **Irregular verbs** have **special forms** to show the past tense. For more irregular verbs, see the **Troubleshooting Guide**, page 773.	Greg **cut** the pizza. It **was** delicious. We **ate** all of it!

Some Irregular Verbs

Present Tense	Past Tense
cut	cut
is	was
eat	ate

Future Tense Verbs	Examples
The **future tense** of a verb tells about an action that will happen later, or in the future. To talk about the future, use:	Greg **will ride** the bus home after work tonight.
• the helping verb **will** plus a main verb.	Greg's mother **will drive** him to work tomorrow. On Friday, he **will get** his first paycheck.
• the phrase **am going to**, **is going to**, or **are going to** plus a **main verb**.	He **is going to take** a pizza home to his family. They **are going to eat** the pizza for dinner.

Verb Tense

Reinforce Display a time line and the words "past tense," "present tense," and "future tense" on the appropriate sections of the time line.

Discuss how the form changes between present, past, and future tense. Emphasize that the action verb must match the subject.

Practice Have students take turns describing things they have done in the past, in the present, or might do in the future. List their actions under the correct tense on the time line. Ask volunteers to create sentences using the action words on the time line. Encourage the class to identify the action verb and name the tense.

ELL **Elaborate** Write several example sentences using different verb tenses.

Guide students to identify and circle the action verb in each sentence. Help them look at the form used to determine the verb tense.
L.9-10.1.b

CCSS Literacy.L.9-10.1.b Use various types of phrases (noun, verb, adjectival, adverbial, participial, prepositional, absolute) and clauses (independent, dependent, noun, relative, adverbial) to convey specific meanings and add variety and interest to writing or presentations.

Perfect Tense Verbs

Practice Discuss the perfect tenses—past, present, and future—with students. Remind students that all verbs in the perfect tense have at least one helping verb and the past participle of the main verb. Point out the helping verbs used for each perfect tense. Explain:

- The present perfect tense uses the helping verbs *has* or *have*.
- The past perfect tense uses the helping verb *had*.
- The future perfect tense uses the helping verbs *will have*.

Guide volunteers to describe an action that began in the past and is still going on, an action that started at one point in the past and finished at another point, and an action that will end at a point in the future. Work together to create sentences using the actions described. Display the sentences on a chart. Have volunteers underline the helping verb or verbs and main verbs used. Lead students to identify and explain the perfect tense used in each sentence.

Practice Have partners generate additional sentences that model each verb tense. Then have partners exchange sentences with another pair and work together to identify the verb tense and describe when the action started and when or whether the action has been completed.
L.9-10.1.b; L.9-10.3

Perfect Tense Verbs

All verbs in the **perfect tenses—present**, **past**, and **future**—have a helping verb and a form of the main verb that is called the **past participle**.

Present Perfect Tense Verbs			Examples
For **regular verbs**, the past tense and the past participle end in **-ed**. To form the present perfect, use **has** or **have** with the past participle.			
	Present Tense	like	I **like** the Internet.
	Past Tense	liked	I **liked** the Internet.
	Present Perfect	has/have liked	I **have** always **liked** the Internet.
Irregular verbs have **special forms** for the past tense and past participle. Always use **has** or **have** with the past participle. See page 773.			
	Present Tense	know	I **know** a lot about the Internet.
	Past Tense	knew	I **knew** very little about the Internet last year.
	Present Perfect	has/have known	I **have known** about the Internet for a long time.
The **present perfect tense** of a verb can tell about an action that began in the past and is still going on.			The public **has used** the Internet since the 1980s. **Have** you **done** research on the Internet?

Past Perfect Tense Verbs	Examples
The **past perfect tense** of a verb tells about an action that was completed before some other action in the past. It uses the helping verb **had** and the past participle of the main verb.	Before the Internet became popular, people **had done** their research in the library.

Future Perfect Tense Verbs	Examples
The **future perfect tense** of a verb tells about an action that will be completed at a specific time in the future. It uses the helping verbs **will have** and the past participle of the main verb.	By the end of next year, 100,000 people **will have visited** our Web site.

Contractions

A **contraction** is a shortened form of a verb or verb and pronoun combination.

Contractions	Examples	
Use an **apostrophe** to show which letters have been left out of the contraction.	I ~~wou~~ld = I'd they ~~a~~re = they're	is n~~o~~t = isn't can ~~no~~t = can't
In contractions made up of a verb and the word **not**, the word **not** is usually shortened to **n't**.	I **can't** stop eating these cookies!	

CCSS Literacy.L.9-10.1.b Use various types of phrases (noun, verb, adjectival, adverbial, participial, prepositional, absolute) and clauses (independent, dependent, noun, relative, adverbial) to convey specific meanings and add variety and interest to writing or presentations. Literacy.L.9-10.3 Apply knowledge of language to understand how language functions in different contexts, to make effective choices for meaning or style, and to comprehend more fully when reading or listening.

Verb Forms

The **form** a verb takes changes depending on how it is used in a sentence, phrase, or clause.

Progressive Verbs	Examples
The **progressive verb** form tells about an action that occurs over a period of time.	
The **present progressive tense** of a verb tells about an action as it is happening. • It uses the helping verb **am**, **is**, or **are**. The main verb ends in **-ing**.	They **are expecting** a big crowd for the fireworks show this evening. **Are** you **expecting** the rain to end before the show starts?
The **past progressive tense** of a verb tells about an action that was happening over a period of time in the past. • It uses the helping verb **was** or **were** and a main verb. The main verb ends in **-ing**.	They **were thinking** of canceling the fireworks. A tornado **was heading** in this direction.
The **future progressive tense** of a verb tells about an action that will be happening over a period of time in the future. • It uses the helping verbs **will be** plus a main verb. The main verb ends in **-ing**.	The weather forecasters **will be watching** for the path of the tornado. I hope that they **will** not **be canceling** the show.

Transitive and Intransitive Verbs	Examples
Action verbs can be transitive or intransitive. A **transitive verb** needs an **object** to complete its meaning and to receive the action of the verb.	**Not complete**: Many cities **use** **Complete**: Many cities **use** fireworks.
The object can be a **direct object**. A direct object answers the question *Whom*? or *What*?	**Whom**: The noise **surprises** the audience. **What**: The people in the audience **cover** their ears.
An **intransitive verb** does not need an object to complete its meaning.	**Complete**: The people in our neighborhood **clap**. They **shout**. They **laugh**.
An **intransitive verb** may end the sentence, or it may be followed by other words that tell how, where, or when. These words are not objects since they do not receive the action of the verb.	The fireworks **glow** brightly. Then, slowly, they **disappear** in the sky. The show **ends** by midnight.

WRITING HANDBOOK

Transitive and Intransitive Verbs

Reinforce Explain to students that in order to determine if a verb is transitive or intransitive, they must ask, Does a noun receive the action of the verb? If it does, then the verb is transitive and the person or thing that receives its action is the direct object. If the noun does not receive the action, then the verb is intransitive.

Write example sentences, such as: *The doctor performs surgery everyday.* Guide volunteers as they underline the action verb and identify if the verb is transitive or intransitive.

ELL **Elaborate** Have students act out sentences such as: *Maria picks up the paper. Christopher claps loudly.*

Guide students to determine the action verb and identify if the action is being done to someone or something. Emphasize that transitive verbs require objects to complete the meaning of the sentence, while intransitive verbs do not.

Practice Display the following sentences. Have individuals underline the action verbs and identify whether the verb is transitive or intransitive.

- The librarian helps me find books when I need them.
- The counselor gives advice about careers or college.
- The school mascot jumps up and down.

L.9-10.1.b

CCSS Literacy.L.9-10.1.b Use various types of phrases (noun, verb, adjectival, adverbial, participial, prepositional, absolute) and clauses (independent, dependent, noun, relative, adverbial) to convey specific meanings and add variety and interest to writing or presentations.

Active and Passive Voice

Practice Explain that while it is usually best to write using the active voice, there are times when the passive voice is appropriate. Review the guidelines for when passive voice is appropriate and have students read the examples.

Point out that though the second example of passive voice could have been written in the active voice (*We held our celebration after the winds died down.*), the third would not have made sense. (*The U.S. made our fireworks.*)

Display sentences and invite students to discuss whether active or passive voice would be more appropriate in each and why. Tell students to consider the purpose or publication for which the sentence would be written. Allow for differences in opinion. For example:

- The fire was caused by unsupervised play with fireworks.
- The sparklers were donated by Anchor Plumbing.
- Black powder, the active ingredient in fireworks, was invented in China.
- During the finale, the national anthem was sung by Keisha Layne.
- At 8:47 p.m., a suspected arson was seen running from the fire.
- The firework display was enjoyed by everyone!

Point out that when a writer uses passive voice the writing sounds more formal and impersonal.

Guide students in rewriting sentences that would be better in active voice.
L.9-10.1.b; L.9-10.3

Active and Passive Voice	Examples
A verb is in **active voice** if the **subject** is doing the action.	Many cities **hold** fireworks displays for the Fourth of July.
A verb is in **passive voice** if the **subject** is not doing the action. A verb in passive voice always includes a form of the verb **be**, plus the past participle of the main verb.	Fireworks displays **are held** by many cities for the Fourth of July.
Use active voice to emphasize the subject. Use passive voice to put less emphasis on the subject, such as when:	
• the object, or receiver of the action, is more important than the doer	Our celebration **was held** after the winds died down.
• you don't know who the doer is	The fireworks **were made** in the U.S.
• you don't want to name the doer or place blame	The start time **is listed** incorrectly in the newspaper.

Two-Word Verbs

A **two-word verb** is a verb followed by a preposition. The meaning of the two-word verb is different from the meaning of the verb by itself.

Some Two-Word Verbs

Verb	Meaning	Example
break	to split into pieces	I didn't **break** the window with the ball.
break down	to stop working	Did the car **break down** again?
break up	to end	The party will **break up** before midnight.
	to come apart	The ice on the lake will **break up** in the spring.
bring	to carry something with you	**Bring** your book to class.
bring up	to suggest	She **brings up** good ideas at every meeting.
	to raise children	**Bring up** your children to be good citizens.
check	to make sure you are right	We can **check** our answers at the back of the book.
check in	to stay in touch with someone	I **check in** with my mom at work.
check up	to see if everything is okay	The nurse **checks up** on the patient every hour.
check off	to mark off a list	Look at your list and **check off** the girls' names.
check out	to look at something carefully	Hey, Marisa, **check out** my new bike!

CCSS **Literacy.L.9-10.1.b** Use various types of phrases (noun, verb, adjectival, adverbial, participial, prepositional, absolute) and clauses (independent, dependent, noun, relative, adverbial) to convey specific meanings and add variety and interest to writing or presentations. **Literacy.L.9-10.3** Apply knowledge of language to understand how language functions in different contexts, to make effective choices for meaning or style, and to comprehend more fully when reading or listening.

Two-Word Verbs, continued

Verb	Meaning	Example
fill	to place as much as can be held	**Fill** the pail with water.
fill in	to color or shade in a space	Please **fill in** the circle.
fill out	to complete	Marcos **fills out** a form to order a book.
get	to go after something	I'll **get** some milk at the store.
	to receive	I often **get** letters from my pen pal.
get ahead	to go beyond what is expected	She worked hard to **get ahead** in math class.
get along	to be on good terms with	Do you **get along** with your sister?
get out	to leave	Let's **get out** of the kitchen.
get over	to feel better	I hope you'll **get over** the flu soon.
get through	to finish	I can **get through** this book tonight.
give	to hand something to someone	We **give** presents to the children.
give out	to stop working	If she runs ten miles, her energy will **give out**.
give up	to quit	I'm going to **give up** eating candy.
go	to move from place to place	Did you **go** to the mall on Saturday?
go on	to continue	Why do the boys **go on** playing after the bell rings?
go out	to go someplace special	Let's **go out** to lunch on Saturday.
look	to see or watch	Don't **look** directly at the sun.
look over	to review	She **looks over** her test before finishing.
look up	to hunt for and find	We **look up** information on the Internet.
pick	to choose	I'd **pick** Lin for class president.
pick on	to bother or tease	My older brothers always **pick on** me.
pick up	to go faster	Business **picks up** in the summer.
	to gather or collect	**Pick up** your clothes!
run	to move quickly	Juan will **run** in a marathon.
run into	to see someone unexpectedly	Did you **run into** Chris at the store?
run out	to suddenly have nothing left	The cafeteria always **runs out** of nachos.
stand	to be on one's feet	I have to **stand** in line to buy tickets.
stand for	to represent	A heart **stands for** love.
stand out	to be easier to see	You'll **stand out** with that orange cap.
turn	to change direction	We **turn** right at the next corner.
turn up	to raise the volume	Please **turn up** the radio.
turn in	to give back	You didn't **turn in** the homework yesterday.
turn off	to make something stop	Please **turn off** the radio.

Two-Word Verbs

Expand Explain that a two-word verb is a verb plus another word that, when used together, have a different meaning from the one that the individual words have.

Discuss with students some of the examples of two-word verbs listed on the chart: *give out, pick up, turn off.* Have volunteers explain how the meaning of the two-word verb is different from that of the individual words.

Practice Ask groups of three or four students to work together to create sentences using the two-word verb listed on the chart. Encourage the groups to discuss the meaning of the two-word verb before generating a sentence. Have the groups share some of their best sentences. Challenge the class to identify the two-word verb and explain its meaning.

ELL **Elaborate** Write this sentence: *I will never get through all of this homework in one hour.* Read the sentence aloud and circle the idiom "get through." Show students how to use context clues to guess the meaning of the idiom. Emphasize that they must think about the meaning of the two words together rather than the words by themselves.
L.9-10.1.b; L.9-10.3

CCSS CCSS Literacy.L.9-10.1.b Use various types of phrases (noun, verb, adjectival, adverbial, participial, prepositional, absolute) and clauses (independent, dependent, noun, relative, adverbial) to convey specific meanings and add variety and interest to writing or presentations. Literacy.L.9-10.3 Apply knowledge of language to understand how language functions in different contexts, to make effective choices for meaning or style, and to comprehend more fully when reading or listening.

Irregular Verbs

Practice Organize the class into pairs and distribute index cards to each set of students. Have the pairs choose ten irregular verbs from the chart. Instruct them to create a sentence for each verb. Explain that on one side of the index card they will write the sentence, leaving a blank for the verb. They will then write the correct irregular verb on the back.

When all pairs have completed their sentences, ask them to trade cards with another group. Have the students practice completing the sentences correctly, checking the verb on the back.

Continue having pairs swap sets of cards as time permits.
L.9-10.1; L.9-10.2.c

Forms of Irregular Verbs

Irregular verbs form the past tense and the past participle in a different way than regular verbs. These verb forms have to be memorized.

Some Irregular Verbs

Irregular Verb	Past Tense	Past Participle	Irregular Verb	Past Tense	Past Participle
be: am, is be: are	was were	been been	eat	ate	eaten
beat	beat	beaten	fall (*intr.*)	fell	fallen
become	became	become	feed	fed	fed
begin	began	begun	feel	felt	felt
bend	bent	bent	fight	fought	fought
bind	bound	bound	find	found	found
bite	bit	bitten	fly	flew	flown
blow	blew	blown	forget	forgot	forgotten
break	broke	broken	forgive	forgave	forgiven
bring	brought	brought	freeze	froze	frozen
build	built	built	get	got	got, gotten
burst	burst	burst	give	gave	given
buy	bought	bought	go	went	gone
catch	caught	caught	grow	grew	grown
choose	chose	chosen	have	had	had
come	came	come	hear	heard	heard
cost	cost	cost	hide	hid	hidden
creep	crept	crept	hit	hit	hit
cut	cut	cut	hold	held	held
dig	dug	dug	hurt	hurt	hurt
do	did	done	keep	kept	kept
draw	drew	drawn	know	knew	known
dream	dreamed, dreamt	dreamed, dreamt	lay (*tr.*)	laid	laid
drink	drank	drunk	lead	led	led
drive	drove	driven	leave	left	left

CCSS Literacy.L.9-10.1 Demonstrate command of the conventions of standard English grammar and usage when writing or speaking. Literacy.L.9-10.2.c Spell correctly.

Forms of Irregular Verbs, continued

Irregular Verb	Past Tense	Past Participle
lend	lent	lent
lie (*intr.*)	lay	lain
let	let	let
light	lit	lit
lose	lost	lost
make	made	made
mean	meant	meant
meet	met	met
pay	paid	paid
prove	proved	proved, proven
put	put	put
quit	quit	quit
read	read	read
ride	rode	ridden
ring	rang	rung
rise (*intr.*)	rose	risen
run	ran	run
say	said	said
see	saw	seen
seek	sought	sought
sell	sold	sold
send	sent	sent
set	set	set
shake	shook	shaken
show	showed	shown
shrink	shrank	shrunk
shut	shut	shut

Irregular Verb	Past Tense	Past Participle
sing	sang	sung
sink	sank	sunk
sit	sat	sat
sleep (*intr.*)	slept	slept
slide	slid	slid
speak	spoke	spoken
spend	spent	spent
stand	stood	stood
steal	stole	stolen
stick	stuck	stuck
sting	stung	stung
strike	struck	struck
swear	swore	sworn
swim	swam	swum
swing	swung	swung
take	took	taken
teach	taught	taught
tear	tore	torn
tell	told	told
think	thought	thought
throw	threw	thrown
understand	understood	understood
wake	woke, waked	woken, waked
wear	wore	worn
weep	wept	wept
win	won	won
write	wrote	written

A Gerunds

Reinforce Explain that since a gerund is used as a noun, it will be found in a sentence where a noun ordinarily would be located. Use the chart to discuss the different functions of gerunds.

Practice Work together to generate more sentences that contain gerunds and list them. For example, *I like your cooking*. Have each student write the sentence, identify the gerund and label how it functions in the sentence. Point out the gerund is *cooking* and it is used as the object of the verb *like*.
L.9-10.1.b; L.9-10.3

B Infinitives

Reinforce Point out that an infinitive consists of the word *to* plus a verb and functions as a noun, adjective, or adverb. Display this sentence: *To see a shooting star is good luck*. Underline the infinitive, *to see*, and explain that it functions as the subject.

Practice Guide pairs of students to compose more involved sentences containing infinitives. Have them share their best sentence, identify the infinitive, and explain how it functions.
L.9-10.1.b; L.9-10.3

C Participles

Expand Point out that a participle functions as an adjective and points to a noun or pronoun. Use the chart to discuss how a participle is formed.

Practice Help students generate sentences to better understand the function and placement of participles and participial phrases. For example, *Flying high in the sky, the kites were beautiful.* Guide the class to name the participle, *flying*, and the noun it points to, *kites*.
L.9-10.1.b; L.9-10.3

Verbals

A **verbal** is a word made from a verb but used as another part of speech.

A

Gerunds	Examples
A **gerund** is a verb form that ends in **-ing** and that is used as a noun. Like all nouns, a gerund can be the subject of a sentence or an object.	**Cooking** is Mr. Jimenez's favorite hobby. (*subject*) Mr. Jimenez truly enjoys **cooking**. (*direct object*) Mr. Jimenez is very talented at **cooking**. (*object of preposition*)

B

Infinitives	Examples
An **infinitive** is a verb form that begins with **to**. It can be used as a noun, an adjective, or an adverb.	Mr. Jimenez likes **to cook**. (*noun*) Mr. Jimenez's beef tamales are a sight **to see**. (*adjective*) Mr. Jimenez cooks **to relax**. (*adverb*)

C

Participial Phrases	Examples
A **participle** is a verb form that is used as an adjective. For regular verbs, it ends in **-ing** or **-ed**. Irregular verbs take the past participle form.	His **sizzling** fajitas taste delicious. Mr. Jimenez also makes tasty **frozen** desserts.
A **participial phrase** begins with a participle. Place the phrase next to the noun it describes.	**Standing by the grill**, he cooked meat. **Not**: He cooked meat, standing by the grill.

Absolutes

An **absolute** is a sentence-like phrase. It is usually formed with a subject and a participle.

Absolutes	Examples
An **absolute** modifies all the remaining parts of the sentence.	**More guests having arrived,** Mr. Jimenez added burgers to the grill.
Use a comma to set off the **absolute** from the rest of the sentence.	Mr. Jimenez, **his plans for a good party accomplished**, smiled broadly.

A phrase that utilizes a gerund, an infinitive, a participle, or an absolute is known as a **verbal phrase**.

CCSS Literacy.L.9-10.1.b Use various types of phrases (noun, verb, adjectival, adverbial, participial, prepositional, absolute) and clauses (independent, dependent, noun, relative, adverbial) to convey specific meanings and add variety and interest to writing or presentations. Literacy.L.9-10.3 Apply knowledge of language to understand how language functions in different contexts, to make effective choices for meaning or style, and to comprehend more fully when reading or listening.

Adverbs

An **adverb** describes a verb, an adjective, or another adverb.

Adverbs	Examples
Adverbs answer one of the following questions:	
• How?	**Carefully** aim the ball.
• Where?	Kick the ball **here**.
• When?	Try again **later** to make a goal.
• How often?	Cathy **usually** scores.
Adverbs that tell how often usually come before the main verb or after a form of **be**. Other adverbs often come after the verb.	Our team **always wins**. The whole team **plays well**.
An adverb can strengthen the meaning of an **adjective** or another **adverb**.	Gina is **really good** at soccer. She plays **very well**.

Grammar Tip

Use an adjective, rather than an adverb, after a linking verb.

My teacher ***is*** *fair~~ly~~.*

Adverbs That Compare	Examples
Some **adverbs** compare actions.	Gina runs **fast**.
Add **-er** to compare the actions of two people.	Gina runs **faster** than Maria.
Add **-est** to compare the actions of three or more people.	Gina runs **the fastest** of all the players.
If the adverb ends in **-ly**, use **more** or **less** to compare two actions.	Gina aims **more carefully** than Jen. Jen aims **less carefully** than Gina.
Use **the most** or **the least** to compare three or more actions.	Gina aims **the most carefully** of all the players. Jen aims **the least carefully** of all the players.

Adverbial Phrases and Clauses	Examples
An **adverb phrase** is a prepositional phrase that modifies a verb, an adjective, or another adverb.	When Gina kicked the ball, it **went** <u>**into the net**</u>. The coach was **happy** <u>**about the score**</u>. Gina plays **best** <u>**under pressure**</u>.
An **adverb clause** has a subject and a verb. It modifies an independent main clause and cannot stand alone. Adverb clauses can tell when, why, or where.	<u>**After the team won**</u>, the coach praised the players. Everyone was muddy <u>**because it had rained**</u>. Soccer is popular <u>**wherever there are fields available**</u>.

WRITING HANDBOOK

A Adverbs That Compare

Reinforce Remind students that adverbs are used to describe how something is done and can be used to compare actions.

Create example sentences and have volunteers perform the actions. Use adverbs to compare the demonstrations. For example, have volunteers walk at varying speeds and describe their paces as *slow*, *slower*, or *slowest*. Discuss the rules and forms to follow when comparing two actions and when comparing three or more actions.

Practice Ask partners to work together to create sentences using adverbs to compare actions and share them with the class. Ask the class to confirm that the correct form has been used.

L.9-10.1

B Adverbial Clauses and Phrases

Expand Explain that clauses (with a subject and a verb) can work as adverbs. Point out that the most common types of adverbial clauses answer the question "Where?" "When?" "Why?" or "How?"

Write an example sentence containing an adverbial clause. (*I didn't go on the rollercoaster because I was scared.*) Underline the adverbial clause and have students identify the question the clause answers. Point to the word *because* and emphasize that most adverbial clauses can be recognized because they are introduced by a particular word. Common words used are *because*, *when*, *about*, *into*, *after*, or *before*.

Practice Form small groups and assign each group a word: *because*, *when*, *about*, *into*, *after* and *before*. Have each group form 3 sentences that include their assigned word as part of an adverbial clauses. Then have groups trade sentences and annotate the sentences with underlines and arrows to identify the clause and what the clause modifies.

L.9-10.1.b

CCSS **Literacy.L.9-10.1** Demonstrate command of the conventions of standard English grammar and usage when writing or speaking. **Literacy.L.9-10.1.b** Use various types of phrases (noun, verb, adjectival, adverbial, participial, prepositional, absolute) and clauses (independent, dependent, noun, relative, adverbial) to convey specific meanings and add variety and interest to writing or presentations.

Prepositional Phrases

Practice Review the uses of prepositions listed in the chart.

Have partners work together to create sentences that include prepositional phrases. Tell them to include prepositions that show location, time, or direction.

Ask partners to trade papers with another group. Have them underline the prepositional phrase and label if the preposition used shows location, time, or direction.

ELL **Elaborate** Model how to use a prepositional phrase to describe the location of a classroom object. For example, *The book is on the table*. Guide students to take turns using prepositional phrases to describe the location of additional classroom objects. Repeat this procedure and use prepositional phrases to show time and direction. For example, *The library is located down the hall from the main office.*
L.9-10.1.b

Prepositions

A **preposition** comes at the beginning of a prepositional phrase. **Prepositional phrases** add details to sentences.

Uses of Prepositions	Examples
Some prepositions show **location**.	The Chávez Community Center is **by my house**. The pool is **behind the building**.
Some prepositions show **time**.	The Teen Club's party will start **after lunch**.
Some prepositions show **direction**.	Go **through the building** and **around the fountain** to get **to the pool**. The snack bar is **down the hall**.
Some prepositions have **multiple uses**.	We might see Joshua **at the party**. Meet me **at my house**. Come **at noon**.

Prepositional Phrases	Examples
A **prepositional phrase** starts with a preposition and ends with a noun or a pronoun. It includes all the words in between. The noun or pronoun is the **object of the preposition**.	I live **near the Chávez Community Center**. (*object of preposition*: Chávez Community Center) Tom wants to walk there **with you and me**. (*objects of preposition*: you and me)
Prepositional phrases are often consecutive.	The Community Center is **up the street** and **on the right**.

Some Prepositions

Location		Time	Direction	Other Prepositions	
above	near	after	across	about	for
behind	next to	before	around	against	from
below	off	during	down	along	of
beside	on	till	into	among	to
between	out	until	out of	as	with
by	outside		through	at	without
in	over		toward	except	
inside	under		up		

CCSS Literacy.L.9-10.1.b Use various types of phrases (noun, verb, adjectival, adverbial, participial, prepositional, absolute) and clauses (independent, dependent, noun, relative, adverbial) to convey specific meanings and add variety and interest to writing or presentations.

Conjunctions and Interjections

A **conjunction** connects words or groups of words. An **interjection** expresses strong feeling or emotion.

Conjunctions	Examples
A **coordinating conjunction** connects words, phrases, or clauses.	
To show similarity: **and**	Irena **and** Irving are twins.
To show difference: **but**, **yet**	I know Irena, **but** I do not know Irving.
To show choice: **or**	They will celebrate their birthday Friday **or** Saturday night.
To show cause/effect: **so**, **for**	I have a cold, **so** I cannot go to the party.
To put negative ideas together: **nor**	My mother will not let me go, **nor** will my father.
Correlative conjunctions are used in pairs. The pair connects phrases or words.	**Some Correlative Conjunctions** both ... and; not only ... but also; either ... or; whether ... or; neither ... nor
A **subordinating conjunction** introduces a **dependent clause** in a complex sentence. It connects the **dependent clause** to the main clause.	**Some Subordinating Conjunctions** after, although, as, as if, as long as, because, before, if, in order that, since, so that, though, till, until, when, where, while
A **conjunctive adverb** joins two independent clauses. Use a semicolon before the conjunction and a comma after it.	**Some Conjunctive Adverbs** besides, consequently, however, meanwhile, moreover, nevertheless, then, therefore, thus

Grammar Tip

When you use paired words, make sure you use both words in the sentence. Don't leave one out!

Interjections	Examples
An **interjection** shows emotion. If an interjection stands alone, follow it with an exclamation point.	**Help!** **Oops!** **Oh boy!**
An interjection used in a sentence can be followed by a comma or an exclamation mark. Use a comma after a weak interjection. Use an exclamation mark after a strong interjection.	**Oh**, it's a baby panda! **Hooray**! The baby panda has survived!

Subordinating Conjunctions

Expand Show students that subordinating conjunctions can be used to show a cause-effect relationship between ideas. The words *because*, *as*, and *since* are commonly used in these types of sentences. Create an example sentence such as: *I will be late today because my car has broken down*. Lead students to understand the cause and effect stated in the example. Have volunteers take turns using *because*, *as*, or *since* to create sentences.

Point out that the words *although*, *where*, and *while* can be used to express differences between two things or ideas. Say: I didn't get wet although it was raining. Guide students to discuss the differences between the ideas presented in the sentence. Have them describe how the subordinating conjunction connects the clauses.

Practice Work together as a class to generate additional example sentences using subordinating conjunctions listed on the chart. Write the sentences. Have volunteers highlight the subordinating conjunction in each sentence and describe how it is used.
L.9-10.1.b

CCSS Literacy.L.9-10.1.b Use various types of phrases (noun, verb, adjectival, adverbial, participial, prepositional, absolute) and clauses (independent, dependent, noun, relative, adverbial) to convey specific meanings and add variety and interest to writing or presentations.

Sentence Types

Reinforce Discuss with students how to classify sentences using the chart. Emphasize how to make appropriate sentence choices based on audience, purpose, and form.

MODEL Say:

- *If I am writing a persuasive essay, I need to use declarative and imperative sentences to make my points. I might want to include exclamatory sentences to show strong opinions and questions to make the readers think.* Create a few examples with students that could be included in a persuasive essay.
- *When I am writing a research or technical report, I need to provide the reader clear details that explain the information. I most likely would use declarative and conditional sentences.* Have students create a few examples of declarative and conditional sentences for a research topic.

ELL **Elaborate** Sentence walls provide visual references of well-formed phrases and sentences. Guide students in creating sentence walls in order to better understand the different types of sentences.

- Think about the kinds of questions and statements students will have to make in the lesson. The sentences on the wall should be directly connected to the objectives of the lesson.
- Provide sentence frames to help the students generate questions and statements that describe, name, and explain the information.
- Guide students to complete the statements and answer the questions over the course of the lesson.

Sentences

A **sentence** is a group of words that expresses a complete thought. Every sentence has a subject (a main idea) and a predicate that describes what the main idea is, has, or does. Sentences can be classified according to their function and structure.

Sentence Types	Examples
A **declarative sentence** makes a statement. It ends with a period.	The football game was on Friday. The coach made an important announcement.
An **interrogative sentence** asks a question. It ends with a question mark.	Who heard the announcement? What did the coach say?
An **exclamatory sentence** shows surprise or strong emotion. It ends with an exclamation point.	That's fantastic news! I can't believe it!
An **imperative sentence** gives a command.	Give the team my congratulations.
• An imperative sentence usually begins with a verb and ends with a period.	**Be** on time.
• If an imperative sentence shows strong emotion, it ends with an exclamation point.	Beat the opponent!

Grammar Tip

Use **please** to make a command more polite: ***Please*** *call me if you have any questions.*

Negative Sentences	Examples
A **negative sentence** uses a **negative word** to say "no."	The game in Hawaii was **not** boring! **Nobody** in our town missed it on TV. Our team **never** played better.
Use only one negative word in a sentence. Using two negatives in one sentence is called a **double negative**. Two negatives cancel each other out. **I did not see no one**, means **I saw someone**.	The other team could not do ~~nothing~~ anything right. Their team never scored ~~no~~ any points.

Negative Words

no	none	no one	not
nowhere	never	nobody	nothing

Conditional Sentences	Examples
Conditional sentences tell how one action depends on another. These sentences often use conditional or modal verbs, such as **can**, **will**, **could**, **would**, or **might**.	**If** our team returns today, **then** we **will** have a party. **Unless** it rains, we **can** have the party outside.
Sometimes a conditional sentence tells about an imaginary condition and its imaginary result.	If my dog **could talk**, he **would tell** me his thoughts.

Sentence Structure

Phrases	Examples
A **phrase** is a group of related words that does not have both a subject and a verb. English can have noun phrases, verb phrases, adjective phrases, adverb phrases, prepositional phrases, and more.	The football team has won many games in overtime. (*noun phrase*, *verb phrase*, *noun phrase*, *prepositional phrase*)

Clauses	Examples
A **clause** is a group of words that has both a **subject** and a **predicate**. A clause can be a complete sentence.	California's population / grew during the 1840s. (*subject*, *predicate*)
An **independent clause** can stand alone as a complete sentence.	California's population / increased. (*subject*, *predicate*)
A **dependent clause** cannot stand alone as a complete sentence.	**because** gold / was found there during that time
An **adjective clause** gives more details about the noun or pronoun that it describes.	The news **that gold had been found** spread fast.
An **adverb clause** can tell when, where, or why.	**When someone found gold**, people celebrated.
A **noun clause** can function as a subject, a direct object, or an object of a preposition.	The reporter knew **why the miners were celebrating.**
A **nonrestrictive clause** is a clause that adds non-essential detail to your sentence. Set it off with commas.	The miners, **who were happy to hear the news,** leaped for joy.

Simple Sentences	Examples
A **simple sentence** is one independent clause with a subject and a predicate. It has no dependent clauses.	Supplies / were scarce. The miners / needed goods and services.

Compound Sentences	Examples
When you join two independent clauses, you make a **compound sentence**.	
Use a comma and a **coordinating conjunction** or a **semicolon** to join independent clauses.	People opened stores, **but** supplies were scarce.
Or use a **conjunctive adverb** with a semicolon before it and a comma after it.	People opened stores; supplies slowly arrived. Miners made money; **however**, merchants made more money.

Sentence Structure

Practice Review the correct placement of commas and semicolons with phrases and clauses. Then review the different sentence structures listed on the chart. Organize the class into groups of three students.

- Distribute strips of paper to each group. Guide groups in writing an example of a phrase, two different types of clauses, a simple sentence, and a compound sentence on individual strips.
- Once all groups have completed their examples, collect the strips and place them in a bag.
- Have volunteers reach into the bag and remove a strip. Ask them to read it aloud to the class and identify the type of sentence structure. If an incorrect answer is given, use the examples on the chart to guide students to identify the correct answer.
- Continue until all strips have been removed from the bag. L.9-10.1.b; L.9-10.2.a

CCSS Literacy.L.9-10.1.b Use various types of phrases (noun, verb, adjectival, adverbial, participial, prepositional, absolute) and clauses (independent, dependent, noun, relative, adverbial) to convey specific meanings and add variety and interest to writing or presentations. Literacy.L.9-10.2.a Use a semicolon (and perhaps a conjunctive adverb) to link two or more closely related independent clauses.

Modifiers

Practice Remind students that a modifier adds information to another part of the sentence. Point out that a misplaced modifier or dangling modifier makes the meaning of a sentence unclear. Make sure students understand the proper comma placements in nonrestrictive clauses and phrases, as well as compound sentences.

- Write example sentences that include a misplaced or dangling modifier. For example, *I was told I had been awarded the scholarship by my teacher.*
- Help students understand how to make the meaning of this sentence clear by repositioning the phrase: *I was told by my teacher that I had been awarded the scholarship.*
- Ask volunteers to identify the misplaced or dangling modifiers in the additional example sentences. Have them suggest how to revise the sentences. Discuss the suggestions with the class. Write the revised sentences.

ELL Elaborate Remind students that a modifier should be placed as close as possible to what it describes. Lead students through the steps to correctly placing modifiers in a sentence. Read this sentence aloud: *The girl was walking the dog in red boots.* Ask students to discuss how the meaning is unclear in this sentence. Ask: Does the dog wear red boots? Help students revise the misplaced modifier. Continue with other examples.
L.9-10.1.b; L.9-10.3

Complex Sentences	Examples
To make a **complex sentence**, join an independent clause with one or more dependent clauses.	Many writers visited camps **where miners worked**. (independent / dependent)
If the dependent clause comes first, put a **comma** after it.	**While the writers were there**, they wrote stories about the miners.
Use a comma or commas to separate the nonrestrictive clause from the rest of the sentence.	The writers, **who were from California**, lived in the same tents as the miners.

Compound-Complex Sentences	Examples
You can make a **compound-complex sentence** by joining two or more independent clauses and one or more dependent clauses.	Many miners never found gold, **but** they stayed in California **because they found other jobs there**. (dependent)

Properly Placed Modifiers and Clauses	Examples
Place **modifiers** as closely as possible to the word or words that they describe. The meaning of a clause may be unclear if a modifier is not placed properly.	Unclear: Some miners **only** found fool's gold. (Does *only* describe *found* or *fool's gold*?) Clear: Some miners found **only** fool's gold.
A **misplaced clause** may make a sentence unclear and accidentally funny.	Unclear: I read that miners traveled by mule **when I studied American history**. (Did the miners travel while you studied?)
When the clause is placed properly, it makes the meaning of the sentence clear.	Clear: **When I studied American history**, I read that miners traveled by mule.
A **misplaced modifier** is a phrase placed too far away from the word or words it describes.	Unclear: The stream rushed past the miners, **splashing wildly**. (Did the miners or the stream splash wildly?)
Correct a misplaced modifier by placing it closer to the word or words it describes.	Clear: **Splashing wildly**, the stream rushed past the miners.
A **dangling modifier** occurs when you accidentally forget to include the word being described.	**Standing in rushing streams**, the search for gold was dangerous. (Who stood in the streams?)
Correct a dangling modifier by adding the missing word being described, adding words to the modifier, or rewording the sentence.	The search for gold was dangerous for **miners** standing in rushing streams.

CCSS Literacy.L.9-10.1.b Use various types of phrases (noun, verb, adjectival, adverbial, participial, prepositional, absolute) and clauses (independent, dependent, noun, relative, adverbial) to convey specific meanings and add variety and interest to writing or presentations. Literacy.L.9-10.3 Apply knowledge of language to understand how language functions in different contexts, to make effective choices for meaning or style, and to comprehend more fully when reading or listening.

Parenthetical Phrases and Appositives	Examples
A **parenthetical phrase** adds nonessential information to a sentence.	Most miners did not, **in fact**, find gold.
You can leave out a nonessential phrase without changing the meaning of the sentence. Use commas to set off a nonessential phrase.	Gold, **every miner's dream**, lay deeply buried.
An **appositive phrase** renames the noun next to it. An appositive phrase usually comes after the noun or pronoun it refers to. Use commas to set off an appositive.	James Marshall, **a mill worker**, started the Gold Rush when he found gold nuggets in 1848.

Clauses with Missing Words	Examples
In an **elliptical clause**, a word or words are left out to shorten a sentence and avoid repetition. You can tell what word is missing by reading the rest of the sentence.	Henry found six nuggets; **James, eight**. (You can tell that the missing word is "found.")
You may also combine two or more sentences that are similar and include related information. Some words, usually any pronouns that refer back to the subject, can be left out of the combined sentence. This is called **structural omission**.	James counted his gold nuggets. He put them away. He counted them again later.
In this example, the three sentences are combined, using commas and the conjunction **and**. The pronoun *he* is omitted from the final two sentences. Do not use commas.	James counted his gold nuggets, put them away, **and** counted them again later.

Restrictive Relative Clauses	Examples
A **restrictive relative clause** is a clause that begins with a relative pronoun, such as **who**, **whom**, **which**, or **that**. You cannot remove the clause without changing its meaning. Do not use commas.	Only people **who have a ticket** can come in. The man **who found the dog** received a reward.

Coordination and Subordination	Examples
Use **coordination** to join clauses of equal weight, or importance.	Gold was often found next to streams, **and** it was also found deep beneath the earth.
Use **subordination** to join clauses of unequal weight, or importance.	The miners were called '49ers. (*main idea*)
Put the main idea in the main clause and the less important detail in the dependent clause.	Many miners arrived in 1849. (*less important detail*) The miners were called '49ers because many miners arrived in 1849.

Structural Omission

Practice Describe and discuss the writing technique of structural omission. Emphasize how combining sentences can make writing more effective.

Write several sets of example sentences. For example, *Sarah got out her bowl. She poured the cereal into the bowl. She added milk to the cereal. She sat down to eat breakfast.*

Lead the class to identify words that can be omitted to combine the sentences into one effective sentence. For example, *Sarah got out her bowl, poured the cereal, added the milk, and sat down to eat breakfast.*

Continue creating and combining sentences until students understand the technique of structural omission. L.9-10.1.b

CCSS Literacy.L.9-10.1.b Use various types of phrases (noun, verb, adjectival, adverbial, participial, prepositional, absolute) and clauses (independent, dependent, noun, relative, adverbial) to convey specific meanings and add variety and interest to writing or presentations.

Subjects

Practice Have students study the examples of subjects. Then discuss the components of each type.

Ask students to work in pairs to create additional example sentences containing different kinds of subjects. Circulate around the class as students work and provide support as necessary.

Have pairs share their completed sentences. Ask the class to identify the type of subject used in each sentence. Then have them name the word or words included in the subject.

ELL **Reinforce** Explain that an understood subject is one that does not appear in a sentence. It is not spoken or written, but the reader or writer can understand what the subject is. Point out that many commands have an understood subject. For example, say: Sit down, please. Explain that you gave them an instruction to sit down. Point out that the subject *you* is understood.
L.9-10.1.b

Subjects and Predicates

A **subject** tells who or what the sentence is about. A **predicate** tells something about the subject.

Complete and Simple Subjects	Examples
The **complete subject** includes all the words in the subject.	**Many people** visit our national parks. **My favorite parks** are in the West.
The **simple subject** is the most important word in the complete subject.	**Many people** visit our national parks. **My favorite parks** are in the West.

Understood Subject	Examples
When you give a command, you do not state the subject. The subject **you** is understood in an imperative sentence.	Watch the geysers erupt. Soak in the hot springs. See a petrified tree.

It as the Subject	Examples
As the subject of a sentence, the pronoun ***it*** may refer to a specific noun. Or ***it*** can be the subject without referring to a specific noun.	See that **stone structure**? **It** is a natural bridge. **It** is amazing to see the natural wonders in these parks.

Complete and Simple Predicate	Examples
The predicate of a sentence tells what the subject is, has, or does. The **complete predicate** includes all the words in the predicate.	People **explore caves in Yellowstone Park**. Many flowers **grow wild throughout the park**. Some people **climb the unusual rock formations**.
The **simple predicate** is the **verb**. It is the most important word in the predicate.	People **explore caves in Yellowstone Park**. Many flowers **grow wild throughout the park**. Some people **climb the unusual rock formations**.

Compound Subject	Examples
A **compound subject** is two or more simple subjects joined by **and** or **or**.	**Yosemite and Yellowstone** are both in the West. Either **spring or fall** is a good time to visit.

Compound Predicate	Examples
A **compound predicate** has two or more verbs joined by **and** or **or**.	At Yosemite, some people **fish and swim**. My family **hikes** to the river **or stays** in the cabin. I **have seen** the falls **and have ridden** the trails.

CCSS Literacy.L.9-10.1.b Use various types of phrases (noun, verb, adjectival, adverbial, participial, prepositional, absolute) and clauses (independent, dependent, noun, relative, adverbial) to convey specific meanings and add variety and interest to writing or presentations.

Complete Sentences and Fragments

A **complete sentence** has both a **subject** and a **predicate** and expresses a complete thought. A **fragment** is written like a sentence but is not a complete thought.

Sentences and Fragments	Examples
Begin a complete sentence with a capital letter, and end it with a period or other end mark.	These parks / have many tourist attractions. (subject / predicate)
A **fragment** is a sentence part that is incorrectly used as a complete sentence. For example, the fragment may be missing a subject. Add a subject to correct the problem.	**Incorrect:** Fun to visit because they have many attractions. **Correct:** Parks are fun to visit because they have many attractions.
Writers sometimes use fragments on purpose to emphasize an idea or for another effect.	I did not camp in bear country. **No way. Too dangerous.**

Subject-Verb Agreement

The number of a subject and the number of a verb must agree.

Subject-Verb Agreement	Examples
Use a **singular subject** with a **singular verb**.	Another popular **park is** the Grand Canyon.
Use a **plural subject** with a **plural verb**.	We **were amazed** by the colors of its cliffs.
If the simple subjects in a **compound subject** are connected by **and**, use a plural verb. If the compound subject is connected by **or**, look at the last simple subject. If it is singular, use a **singular verb**. If it is plural, use a **plural verb**.	A **mule** and a **guide are** available for a trip down the canyon. These **rafts or** this **boat is** the best way to go. This **boat or** these **rafts are** the best way to go.
The **subject** and **verb** must agree, even when other words come between them.	The **bikers** in the park **are looking** for animals.
The **subject** and **verb** must agree even if the subject comes after the verb.	There **are** other amazing **parks** in Arizona. Here **is** a **list** of them.

Editing Tip

Read your writing aloud to find mistakes in subject-verb agreement.

A

Grammar Tip

Subjects and verbs are not in prepositional phrases. Drop these phrases to find the subject and verb more easily.

Parallel Structure

A sentence is **parallel** when all of its parts have the same form.

Parallel Structure	Examples
The parts of a sentence must be **parallel**. Words, phrases, or clauses in a sentence that do the same job should have the same form.	They went hiking, rafting, and horseback riding. I know **that we must be** in shape to hike the Canyon, **that we have to carry** plenty of water, and **that we need to take and eat** salty snacks.

B

WRITING HANDBOOK

A Subject-Verb Agreement

Reinforce Discuss the rules to follow for subject-verb agreement. Help students identify the subject in each of the example sentences. Ask students to identify if the subject is singular or plural. Then have them locate the verb. Point out how the verb form matches the subject.

Write sentences and include two forms of the verb in parentheses. For example, *The man with all the cats (live, lives) on my street.*

Have volunteers choose the correct form of the verb.

ELL **Practice** Have students edit a recent piece of writing from their class binder for subject-verb agreement. Say: Mistakes in subject-verb agreement are often easier to find when you read aloud.

Expand Explain that verbs in the subjunctive mood, which express doubt, wishes, or possibility, may look like they disagree in number with the subject. For example, in past tense, the subjunctive mood of *be* is *were*, regardless of the subject: "If I were you," rather than "If I was you." Tell students that they should identify whether a statement is in the subjunctive mood before changing a verb. Point out that *if* and *that* can indicate a subjunctive mood. Provide the following examples:

- If it were summer, we could swim.
- I insist that we be ready early.

B Parallel Structure

Reinforce Model how to use parallel structure in lists. Write this example sentence: *The girls like to shop, to watch movies, and to play computer games.* Show students how all the parts of the sentence have the same form. Continue with another example using clauses such as: *The teacher told the students that they should get a lot of sleep, that they should eat a good breakfast, and that they should wear comfortable clothes on test day.*

Practice Guide students to create additional parallel sentences.
L.9-10.1.a; L.9-10.1.b;

CCSS Literacy.L.9-10.1.a Use parallel structure. Literacy.L.9-10.1.b Use various types of phrases (noun, verb, adjectival, adverbial, participial, prepositional, absolute) and clauses (independent, dependent, noun, relative, adverbial) to convey specific meanings and add variety and interest to writing or presentations.

Capitalization

Practice Lead the class to discuss the rules for capitalization.

Write a letter to the class stating the events that might happen that day. Do not capitalize any of the letters. Have volunteers take turns editing the letter. Ask them to write capital letters in the correct places. Have students explain why a capital letter is necessary.

After students have completed the revisions, discuss how proper use of capital letters made the writing more effective.

Ask students to write you a letter that tells what they would like to do in school. Emphasize they must use capital letters and correct punctuation.
L.9-10.2

Mechanics

Proper use of capital letters and correct punctuation is important to effective writing.

Capitalization

Knowing when to use capital letters is an important part of clear writing.

First Word in a Sentence	Examples
Capitalize the first word in a sentence.	**W**e are studying the Lewis and Clark Expedition.

In Direct Quotations	Examples
Capitalize the first word in a **direct quotation**.	Clark said, "**There is great joy in camp**." "**We are in view of the ocean**," he said. "**It's the Pacific Ocean**," he added.

In Letters	Examples
Capitalize the first word used in the **greeting** or in the **closing** of a letter.	**D**ear Kim, **Y**our friend,

In Titles of Works	Examples
All important words in a **title** begin with a capital letter. Articles (**a, an, the**), short conjunctions (**and, but, or, so**), and short prepositions (**at, for, from, in, of, with,** etc.) are not capitalized unless they are the first or last word in the title.	**book:** *The Longest Journey* **poem:** "Leaves of Grass" **magazine:** *Flora and Fauna of Arizona* **newspaper:** *The Denver Post* **song:** "Star-Spangled Banner" **game:** Exploration! **TV series:** "The Gilmore Girls" **movie:** *The Lion King*

Pronoun *I*	Examples
Capitalize the pronoun ***I*** no matter where it is located in a sentence.	**I** was amazed when **I** learned that Lewis and Clark's expedition was over 8,000 miles.

Proper Nouns and Adjectives	Examples
Common nouns name a general person, place, thing, or idea. Proper nouns name a particular person, place, thing, or idea. All the important words in a **proper noun** start with a capital letter.	**Common Noun**: team **Proper Noun**: **C**orps of **D**estiny

CCSS Literacy.L.9-10.2 Demonstrate command of the conventions of standard English capitalization, punctuation, and spelling when writing.

Proper Nouns and Adjectives, continued	Examples
Proper nouns include the following:	
• names of people and their titles	**S**tephanie **E**ddins **C**aptain **M**eriwether **L**ewis
Do not capitalize a title if it is used without a name.	The **captain's** co-leader on the expedition was William Clark.
• family titles like ***Mom*** and ***Dad*** when they are used as names.	"William Clark is one of our ancestors," **Mom** said. I asked my **mom** whose side of the family he was on, hers or my **dad's**.
• names of organizations	United Nations History Club Wildlife Society
• names of languages and religions	Spanish Christianity
• months, days, special days, and holidays	April Sunday Thanksgiving
Names of geographic places are proper nouns. Capitalize street, city, and state names in mailing addresses.	**Cities and States**: Dallas, Texas **Streets and Roads**: Main Avenue **Bodies of Water**: Pacific Ocean **Countries**: Ecuador **Landforms**: Sahara Desert **Continents**: North America **Public Spaces**: Muir Camp **Buildings, Ships, and Monuments**: *Titanic* **Planets and Heavenly Bodies**: Neptune
A **proper adjective** is formed from a **proper noun**. Capitalize proper adjectives.	Napoleon Bonaparte was from **Europe**. He was a **European** leader in the 1800s.

Grammar Tip

If the family title is preceded by a possessive pronoun, always use lower case.

A

Abbreviations of Proper Nouns

Abbreviations of geographic places are also capitalized.

Geographic Abbreviations

Words Used in Addresses				Some State Names Used in Mailing Addresses			
Avenue	Ave.	Highway	Hwy.	California	CA	Michigan	MI
Boulevard	Blvd.	Lane	Ln.	Florida	FL	Ohio	OH
Court	Ct.	Place	Pl.	Georgia	GA	Texas	TX
Drive	Dr.	Street	St.	Illinois	IL	Virginia	VA

B

WRITING HANDBOOK

A Proper Nouns

Practice Remind students that a proper noun is a noun that names a specific person, place, or thing. Point out that proper nouns are always capitalized. Review and discuss the different categories of proper nouns. Have volunteers generate additional examples.

Write example sentences such as: *The spanish club will meet at happy hamburger on central avenue.* Do not capitalize any of the proper nouns. Have volunteers take turns identifying the proper nouns and explain why they are considered proper nouns. Ask them to write capital letters in the correct places.
L.9-10.2

B Abbreviations of Proper Nouns

Practice Organize the class into pairs and distribute blank envelopes to each student. Have partners practice using abbreviations to address the envelope. Tell students to create addresses using abbreviations from the chart for the return address and mailing address. Ask partners to trade envelopes and check for correct capitalization and abbreviation.
L.9-10.2

CCSS Literacy.L.9-10.2 Demonstrate command of the conventions of standard English capitalization, punctuation, and spelling when writing.

Punctuation

Expand Explain that indirect questions are clauses that imply questions. Indirect questions always end with a period.

Write example sentences such as: *I wonder what will happen in the last chapter of the novel* and *Do you know what time the movie starts.* Do not place a punctuation mark at the end of the sentences. Have volunteers read aloud each of the examples listed. Lead the class to determine if the sentence is an indirect question or direct question. Ask students to place the appropriate punctuation mark at the end of each sentence. Help students generate additional examples of indirect questions.

Abbreviations of Personal Titles		
Capitalize abbreviations for a personal title. Follow the same rules for capitalizing a personal title.		
Mr. . . . . Mister	**Mrs.** . . . . . . Mistress	**Dr.** . . . . Doctor
Jr. . . . . Junior	**Capt.** . . . . . Captain	**Sen.** . . . . . . Senator

Punctuation

Punctuation marks are used to emphasize or clarify meanings.

Apostrophe	Examples
Use an **apostrophe** to punctuate a **possessive noun**.	
If there is one owner, add **'s** to the owner's name. If the owner's name ends in s, it is correct to add **'s** *or* just the apostrophe.	Mrs. Ramos**'s** sons live in New Mexico. Mrs. Ramos' sons live in New Mexico.
If there is more than one owner, add ' if the plural noun ends in **s**. Add **'s** if it does not end in **s**.	Her sons' birthdays are both in January. Her daughter**'s** birthday is in March.
Use an **apostrophe** to replace the letters left out of a contraction.	could ~~no~~t = couldn**'t** he ~~woul~~d = he**'d**

Grammar Tip

Never use an apostrophe to form a plural—only to show possession or contraction.

End Marks	Examples
Use a **period** at the end of a statement or a polite command.	Georgia read the paper to her mom**.** Tell me if there are any interesting articles**.**
Use a period after an indirect question. An indirect question tells about a question you asked.	She asked if there were any articles about the new restaurant on Stone Street near their house**.**
Use a **question mark** at the end of a question.	What kind of food do they serve**?**
Use a question mark after a tag question that comes at the end of a statement.	The food is good, isn't it**?**
Use an **exclamation point** after an interjection.	Wow**!**
Use an exclamation point at the end of a sentence to show you feel strongly about something.	The chicken parmesan is delicious**!**

Comma	Examples
Use a **comma**:	
• before the **coordinating conjunction** in a compound sentence	Soccer is a relatively new sport in the United States**, but** it has been popular in England for a long time.
• to set off words that interrupt a sentence, such as an **appositive phrase** or a **nonrestrictive clause** that is not needed to identify the word it describes	Mr. Okada**, the soccer coach,** had the team practice skills like passing**, for example,** for the first hour. Passing**, which is my favorite skill,** was fun.
• to separate three or more items in a **series**	Shooting**,** passing**,** and dribbling are important skills.
• between two or more adjectives that tell equally about the same noun	The midfielder's quick**,** unpredictable passes made him the team's star player.
• after an **introductory phrase or clause**	**In the last game,** he made several goals.
• to separate a **nonrestrictive phrase** or **clause**, or a **nonrestrictive relative clause.**	The cook**, who used to be a teacher,** made enough soup to feed all of us.
• before someone's exact words and after them if the sentence continues	Mr. Okada said**,** "Meet the ball after it bounces**,**" as we practiced our half-volleys.
• before and after a **nonrestrictive clause**	At the end of practice**, before anyone left,** Mr. Okada handed out revised game schedules.
• to set off a short phrase at the beginning of a sentence	**At last**, we could go home.
Use a comma in these places in a letter:	
• to separate contrasting phrases	I like to watch movies**,** not plays.
• between the city and the state	Milpas**,** AK
• between the date and the year	July 3**,** 2008
• after the greeting of a personal letter	Dear Mr. Okada**,**
• after the closing of a letter	Sincerely**,**

WRITING HANDBOOK

Commas

Practice Discuss with students the different uses of a comma. Point out the functions of a comma using the examples.

Display a business letter and discuss each section.

Have small groups of three or four students work together to write a business letter inviting a guest speaker from the community to the classroom.

Tell the groups to include the reasons why they would like this person to come and to in list in a series the materials they will provide the speaker. Instruct them to use phrases and clauses, including restrictive and nonrestrictive phrases and clauses, as well as nonrestrictive relative clauses that require commas (such as appositive phrases or nonrestrictive clauses), and to follow the examples. Circulate around the room as groups work and provide support as necessary to ensure comprehension.

Display the completed business letters. Have the groups share their letters, point out the places a comma was used, and explain why the comma is needed.
L.9-10.1.b; L.9-10.2

CCSS **Literacy.L.9-10.1.b** Use various types of phrases (noun, verb, adjectival, adverbial, participial, prepositional, absolute) and clauses (independent, dependent, noun, relative, adverbial) to convey specific meanings and add variety and interest to writing or presentations.
Literacy.L.9-10.2 Demonstrate command of the conventions of standard English capitalization, punctuation, and spelling when writing.

Ⓐ Dash

Expand Explain that a dash can be used to separate parenthetical information (information in the middle of the sentence), as well as emphasize other words, phrases, and clauses.

Ⓑ Ellipsis

Expand Remind students that an ellipsis consists of three evenly spaced dots to show that you have left out words or to show an idea that trails off.

Explain that if an entire sentence or paragraph is left out, the ellipsis will be placed after the period, making a total of four dots. Write this example: *Oh, those were the good old days.* . . .

Work together as a class to create additional sentences with an example of an ellipsis at the end.

Have volunteers explain the purpose of an ellipsis and the form to follow when it is used at the end of a sentence.

Dash	Examples
Ⓐ Use a **dash** to show a break in an idea or the tone in a sentence.	Water—a valuable resource—is often taken for granted.
Or use a dash to emphasize a word, a series of words, a phrase, or a clause.	It is easy to conserve water—wash full loads of laundry, use water-saving devices, fix leaky faucets.

Ellipsis	Examples
Ⓑ Use an **ellipsis** to show that you have left out words.	A recent survey documented **. . .** water usage.
Or use an ellipsis to show an idea that trails off.	The survey reported the amount of water wasted **. . .**

Hyphen	Examples
Use a **hyphen** to:	
• connect words in a number and in a fraction	**One-third** of the people wasted water every day.
• join some words to make a compound word	A **15-year-old boy** and his **great-grandmother** have started an awareness campaign.
• connect a letter to a word	They designed a **T-shirt** for their campaign.
• divide words at the end of a line. Always divide the word between two syllables.	Please join us in our awareness cam- paign.

Italics and Underlining	Examples
When you are using a computer, use **italics** for the names of:	
• magazines and newspapers	I like to read ***Time Magazine*** and the ***Daily News***.
• books	They help me understand our history book, ***The U.S. Story***.
• plays	Did you see the play ***Abraham Lincoln in Illinois***?
• movies	It was made into the movie ***Young Abe***.
• musicals	The musical ***Oklahoma!*** is about Southwest pioneers.
• music albums	***Greatest Hits from Musicals*** is my favorite album.
• TV series	Do you like the singers on the TV show ***American Idol***?
If you are using handwriting, underline.	

Parentheses	Examples
Use **parentheses** around extra information in a sentence.	The new story (in the evening paper) is very interesting.

Quotation Marks	Examples
Use **quotation marks** to show:	
• a speaker's exact words	"Listen to this!" Jim said.
• the exact words quoted from a book or other printed material	The announcement in the paper was: "The writer Josie Ramón will be at Milpas Library on Friday."
• the title of a song, poem, short story, magazine article, or newspaper article	Her famous poem "Speaking" appeared in the magazine article "How to Talk to Your Teen."
• the title of a chapter from a book	She'll be reading "Getting Along," a chapter from her new book.
• words used in a special way	We will be "all ears" at the reading.

Grammar Tip

Always put **periods** and **commas** inside quotation marks.

Semicolon	Examples
Use a **semicolon**:	
• to separate two simple sentences used together without a conjunction	A group of Jim's classmates plan to attend the reading; he hopes to join them.
• before a **conjunctive adverb** that joins two simple sentences. Use a comma after the adverb.	Jim wanted to finish reading Josie Ramón's book this evening**; however,** he forgot it at school.
• to separate a group of words in a series if the words in the series already have commas	After school, Jim has to study French, health, and math; walk, feed, and brush the dog; and eat dinner.

Colon	Examples
Use a **colon**:	
• after the greeting in a business letter	Dear Sir or Madam:
• to separate hours and minutes	The restaurant is open until 11:30 p.m.
• to start a list	If you decide to hold your banquet here, we can: 1. Provide a private room 2. Offer a special menu 3. Supply free coffee and lemonade.
• to set off a quotation	According to the review in *The Gazette:* El Gato Azul is *the* best place for tapas.
• to set off a list in running text	Among their best tapas are: fried goat cheese, caprece, and crab quesadilla.
• after a signal word like "the following" or "these"	Be sure to try these: black bean cakes, wontons con queso, and calamari frita.

WRITING HANDBOOK

A Quotation Marks

Practice Review the function of quotation marks.

Write example sentences such as: *I am preparing for my trip to Rome by reading an article titled A Guide to Italy. The best time of the year to visit Rome is in the spring, said Mr. Martin.* Do not place quotation marks in the examples. Read the sentences aloud. Have volunteers identify parts of the sentences that require quotation marks and explain why they are needed.
Literacy.L.9-10.2

B Using Semicolons

Practice Discuss the use of a semicolon using the examples listed on the chart.

On index cards write sentences that require semicolons. Organize the class into pairs and give each pair one or two cards. Have partners read their sentences, determine where a semicolon is needed, and add the semicolon. When all pairs are finished, have them take turns pointing out where they added a semicolon and explaining why it is needed.
L.9-10.1.b; L.9-10.2; L.9-10.2.a

C Using Colons

Practice Discuss the use of a colon using the examples listed on the chart.

Provide partners with the following prompt: *Your friend, a chef, has asked you to write to a famous restaurant critic about your meal at your friend's restaurant. Compose a business letter using a colon in each of the ways displayed on the chart.*

Display the completed letters. Have each pair point out where they used a colon and explain why it was needed.
L.9-10.2.b

CCSS **Literacy.L.9-10.1.b** Use various types of phrases (noun, verb, adjectival, adverbial, participial, prepositional, absolute) and clauses (independent, dependent, noun, relative, adverbial) to convey specific meanings and add variety and interest to writing or presentations.
Literacy.L.9-10.2 Demonstrate command of the conventions of standard English capitalization, punctuation, and spelling when writing.
Literacy.L.9-10.2.a Use a semicolon (and perhaps a conjunctive adverb) to link two or more closely related independent clauses.
Literacy. L.9-10.2.b Use a colon to introduce a list or quotation.

A Spelling Rules

Reinforce Remind students that correct spelling helps make writing clear. Emphasize that there are many rules they can learn to help improve their spelling. Point out and practice the following rule:

- Tell students if a word ends in *y*, they must change the *y* to *i* before adding *-est*. Make a list of words ending in *y*. (*funny, early, happy, silly, curly*) Have volunteers take turns changing the *y* to *i* and adding *-est*.

B Rules for Adding Endings

Expand Discuss and practice the spelling rules listed below:

- In words that end in a silent e, you must drop the e before you add a suffix. Write *hope*. Then write *hoping*. Point out that you dropped the silent e. Call out additional silent e words and have students write them on a piece of paper. Tell them to add specific endings to each word. Have volunteers write their answers.
- When adding a suffix to a word that ends with one vowel and consonant, you must double the final consonant before adding the ending. Write the word *begin*. Underline the *i* and the *n*. Then explain you must double the *n* before adding an ending. Write *beginner* and review the rule. Write additional examples. (*control, drop*) Have students take turns doubling the consonant before adding a suffix. (*controlled, dropping*)

Spelling

Correct spelling is important for clarity.

How to Be a Better Speller

To learn a new word:

- Study the word and look up its meaning.
- Say the word aloud. Listen as you repeat it.
- Picture how the word looks.
- Spell the word aloud several times.
- Write the word several times for practice.
- Use the word often in writing until you are sure of its spelling.
- Keep a notebook of words that are hard for you to spell.
- Use a dictionary to check your spelling.

Knowing spelling rules can help you when you get confused. Use the rules shown in the boxes to help improve your spelling.

Memorize Reliable Generalizations	Examples
Always put a **u** after a **q**.	The **quick** but **qu**iet **qu**arterback asked **qu**antities of **qu**estions. *Exceptions*: Iraq Iraqi
Use **i** before **e** except after **c**.	The f**ie**rce rec**ei**ver was ready to catch the ball. *Exceptions*: • **ei**ther, h**ei**ght, th**ei**r, w**ei**rd, s**ei**ze • w**ei**gh, n**ei**ghbor (and other words where **ei** has the long **a** sound)

Spell Correctly	Examples
If a word ends in a consonant plus **y**, change the **y** to **i** before you add -**es**, -**ed**, -**er**, or -**est**.	The coach was the happ**iest** when his players tried their best.
For words that end in a vowel plus **y**, just add -**s** or -**ed**.	For five days before the game, the team stay**ed** at practice an extra 30 minutes.
If you add -**ing** to a verb that ends in -**y**, do not change the **y** to **i**.	The players learned a lot from study**ing** the videos of their games.

A B

Troubleshooting Guide

In this section you will find helpful solutions to common problems with grammer, usage, and sentences. There is also an alphabetical list of words that are often misused in English. Use these to help improve your writing skills.

Grammar and Usage: Problems and Solutions

Use these solutions to fix grammar and usage problems.

Problems with Nouns

Problem: The sentence has the wrong plural form of an irregular noun. **Solution:** Rewrite the sentence using the correct plural form. (Check a dictionary.)	**Incorrect:** Many deers live there. **Correct:** Many deer live there.
Problem: The noun should be possessive, but it is not. **Solution:** Add an apostrophe to make the noun possessive.	**Incorrect:** The beginning should capture the readers interest. **Correct:** The beginning should capture the readers' interest.

Problems with Pronouns

Problem: The pronoun does not agree in number or gender with the noun it refers to. **Solution:** Match a pronoun's number and gender to the number and gender of the noun it is replacing.	**Incorrect:** Mary called Robert, but they did not answer him. **Correct:** Mary called Robert, but he did not answer her.
Problem: A pronoun does not agree in number with the indefinite pronoun it refers to. **Solution:** Make the pronoun and the word it refers to agree in number, so that both are singular or plural.	**Incorrect:** Everyone brought their book to class. **Correct:** Everyone brought his or her book to class. All the students brought their books to class.
Problem: A reciprocal pronoun does not agree with the number of nouns it refers to. **Solution:** Use *each other* when referring to two people, and use *one another* when referring to more than two people.	**Incorrect:** The three boys gave presents to each other. **Correct:** The three boys gave presents to one another.

WRITING HANDBOOK

Irregular Nouns

Expand Read the first problem and solution in Problems with Nouns with students. Point out that:

- some nouns always take the singular form; for example: *fish, moose, deer, money*
- some nouns take a plural form even though they are singular; for example: *politics, news, pants, scissors, (eye)glasses, headquarters*

Remind students to check a dictionary if they are unsure about how to form the plural of a particular noun.

Pronoun Rules

Reinforce Remind students to use *each other* for two people and *one another* for more than two people. Ask students to generate examples of when each phrase is appropriate.

ELL Use a Graphic Organizer Have students think of words in their native languages that follow unusual singular/plural patterns. Point out that these words may not follow those same rules in English.

Tell students to complete a chart like the one below for each word.

	My Language	English
Singular form		
Sentence with it as a singular		
Plural form		
Sentence with it as a plural		

Demonstrative Words

Reinforce Point out the example sentences in the third problem and solution box:

Write the four demonstrative words: *this, that, these, those*. Explain:

- These are the only demonstrative words.
- A demonstrative word helps to identify the specific person, place, thing, or idea you are talking about.

Model how to use a demonstrative adjective. Display three different pencils. Have a volunteer help you.

MODEL Say:

- *Use a complete sentence to tell me which one you would like.*
- The student should respond, "I would like that one." or "I would like this one."
- Write the student's response and underline the demonstrative adjective.
- If a student used the wrong word, explain how to use the list of demonstrative words to correct the mistake.

Troubleshooting Guide

Grammar and Usage: Problems and Solutions, continued

Problems with Pronouns, continued

Problem: It is hard to tell which noun in a compound subject is referred to or replaced. **Solution:** Replace the unclear pronoun with the noun it refers to.	**Incorrect:** Ana and Dawn own a car, but only she drives it. **Correct:** Ana and Dawn own a car, but only Dawn drives it.
Problem: It is unclear which antecedent a pronoun refers to. **Solution:** Rewrite the sentence to make it clearer.	**Incorrect:** The kitten's mother scratched its ear. **Correct:** The mother cat scratched her kitten's ear.
Problem: The object pronoun *them* is used as a demonstrative adjective. **Solution:** Replace *them* with the correct demonstrative adjectives.	**Incorrect:** Were any of them packages delivered? **Correct:** Were any of those packages delivered?
Problem: An object pronoun is used in a compound subject. *Remember that subjects do actions and objects receive actions.* **Solution:** Replace the object pronoun with a subject pronoun.	**Incorrect:** My brother and me rebuild car engines. **Correct:** My brother and I rebuild car engines.
Problem: A subject pronoun is used in a compound object. **Solution:** Replace the subject pronoun with an object pronoun.	**Incorrect:** Leticia asked my brother and I to fix her car. **Correct:** Leticia asked my brother and me to fix her car.
Problem: A subject pronoun is used as the object of a preposition. **Solution:** Replace the subject pronoun with an object pronoun.	**Incorrect:** Give your timesheet to Colin or I. **Correct:** Give your timesheet to Colin or me.
Problem: The subject pronoun *who* is used as an object. **Solution:** Replace *who* with the object pronoun *whom*.	**Incorrect:** Who am I speaking to? **Correct:** Whom am I speaking to?
Problem: The object pronoun *whom* is used as a subject. **Solution:** Replace *whom* with the subject pronoun *who*.	**Incorrect:** Whom shall I say is calling? **Correct:** Who shall I say is calling?

WRITING HANDBOOK

Problems with Verbs

Problem / Solution	Example
Problem: In a sentence with two verbs, the tense of the second verb doesn't match the first.	**Incorrect:** Yesterday, Alberto called me and says he has tickets for the game.
Solution: Keep the verb tense the same unless there is a change in time, such as from past to present.	**Correct:** Yesterday, Alberto called me and said he had tickets for the game.
Problem: The *-ed* ending is missing from a regular past-tense verb.	**Incorrect:** This morning, I ask my brother to go with us.
Solution: Add the *-ed* ending.	**Correct:** This morning, I asked my brother to go with us.
Problem: The wrong form of an irregular verb is used.	**Incorrect:** We brang our portable TV to the game.
Solution: Replace the wrong form with the correct one. (Check a dictionary.)	**Correct:** We brought our portable TV to the game.
Problem: The participle form is used when the past-tense form is required.	**Incorrect:** After the game, we run over to Marcia's house.
Solution: Replace the wrong form with the correct one. (Check a dictionary.)	**Correct:** After the game, we ran over to Marcia's house.
Problem: The passive voice is overused.	**Poor:** A new activity schedule will be created by the camp counselors. Several fun activities are being considered by the counselors.
Solution: Put the sentence in the active voice so that the subject does the action instead of receiving it.	**Better:** The camp counselors are creating a new activity schedule. The counselors are considering several fun activities.
Problem: The sentence has a split infinitive.	**Poor:** The boy wanted to slowly walk to school.
Solution: Rewrite the sentence to keep the infinitive as a single unit.	**Better:** The boy wanted to walk to school slowly.

A Compound Verbs

Practice Have students write two past tense sentences and two present tense sentences with compound verbs.

Tell students to exchange papers with a partner. The partner will rewrite the sentences by changing the past tense sentences to present tense and the present tense sentences to past tense.

Have partners switch papers again. Tell them to make the verbs in each sentence have the same tense. For example, if the sentence is in the past tense, both of its verbs should be in the past tense.
L.9-10.1

B Active and Passive Voice

Expand Remind students that changing the verb from active to passive voice changes the focus from the doer to the receiver of the action:

Active: *I wrote books.*

Passive: *Books were written.*

Passive: *Books were written by me.*

Point out the following:

- In a sentence written in the active voice, the doer of the action comes before the verb.
- In a sentence written in the passive voice, the doer of the action comes after the verb.

Practice Display the following sentences. Have individuals identify whether sentences are in active or passive voice. Then have pairs collaborate to rewrite passive sentences.

- Activity rules will be enforced by referees.
- Equipment and uniforms will be purchased by the camp director.
- Uniforms will be worn by all campers.

L.9-10.1; L.9-10.3

C Split Infinitives

Practice Ask students to write three sentences with split infinitives. Have them switch papers with a partner, and have the partner rewrite the sentences so they use infinitives correctly.
L.9-10.1

CCSS Literacy.L.9-10.1 Demonstrate command of the conventions of standard English grammar and usage when writing or speaking.
Literacy.L.9-10.3 Apply knowledge of language to understand how language functions in different contexts, to make effective choices for meaning or style, and to comprehend more fully when reading or listening.

Comparatives and Superlatives

Reinforce Remind students that comparatives are only used to compare two items. A superlative is only used for three or more items. For example:

- Suppose there are two children in a family.
- One brother is older. The other is younger.
- No one is the oldest or youngest.

Explain how to form regular comparatives and superlatives:

Comparative:
- Add *-er* to words with one or two syllables.
- Use the word *more* + the adjective for words with three or more syllables.

Superlative:
- Add *-est* to words with one or two syllables.
- Use the phrase *the most* + the adjective for words with three or more syllables.

Troubleshooting Guide

Grammar and Usage: Problems and Solutions, continued

Problems with Adjectives

Problem: The sentence contains a double comparison, using both an *-er* ending and the word *more*, for example. **Solution:** Delete the incorrect comparative form.	**Incorrect:** Joseph is more older than he looks. **Correct:** Joseph is older than he looks.
Problem: The wrong form of an irregular adjective appears in a sentence that makes a comparison. **Solution:** Replace the wrong form with the correct one. (Check a dictionary.)	**Incorrect:** Cal feels worser since he ran out of medicine. **Correct:** Cal feels worse since he ran out of medicine.
Problem: The wrong demonstrative adjective is used. **Solution:** Use *this* or the plural *these* for things that are near or "here." Use *that* or the plural *those* for things that are farther away or "there."	**Incorrect:** That car here is really fast. This car there is not as fast. **Correct:** This car here is really fast. That car there is not as fast.
Problem: The adjective *good* is used to modify a verb. **Solution:** Rewrite the sentence using the adverb *well*, or add a noun for the adjective to describe.	**Incorrect:** Julia did good on her test. **Correct:** Julia did well on her test. Julia did a good job on her test.

Problems with Adverbs

Problem: An adverb is used to modify a noun or pronoun after the linking verb *feel*. **Solution:** Rewrite the sentence using an adjective.	**Incorrect:** I feel badly about the mistake. **Correct:** I feel bad about the mistake.
Problem: An adverb is used but does not modify anything in the sentence. **Solution:** Rewrite the sentence changing the adverb to a verb.	**Incorrect:** Hopefully, I didn't make too many mistakes on the test. **Correct:** I hope I didn't make too many mistakes on the test.
Problem: Two negative words are used to express one idea. **Solution:** Change one negative word to a positive word.	**Incorrect:** We don't have no aspirin. **Correct:** We don't have any aspirin.

Sentences: Problems and Solutions

Some problems with sentences in English are the result of missing parts of speech or incorrect punctuation. Two common problems are sentence fragments and run on sentences.

Problems with Sentence Fragments

Problem: An infinitive phrase is punctuated as a complete sentence. **Solution:** Add a complete sentence to the phrase.	**Incorrect:** To show students alternative ways to learn. **Correct:** To show students alternative ways to learn, Mr. Harris organized the trip.
Problem: A clause starting with a relative pronoun is punctuated as a complete sentence. **Solution:** Add a subject and predicate to the sentence.	**Incorrect:** Who might be interested in going on the trip. **Correct:** Anyone who might be interested in going on the trip should see Mr. Harris.
Problem: A participial phrase is punctuated as a complete sentence. **Solution:** Add a sentence to the participial phrase.	**Incorrect:** When traveling overseas. **Correct:** When traveling overseas, always try to speak to people in their native language.

Problems with Run On Sentences

Problem: Two main clauses are separated by a comma. This is known as a comma splice. **Solution:** Add a semicolon between the clauses.	**Incorrect:** Many music students fail to practice regularly, this is frustrating for teachers. **Correct:** Many music students fail to practice regularly; this is frustrating for teachers.
Problem: Two or more main clauses are run together with no punctuation. This is known as a fused sentence. **Solution:** Change one of the clauses into a subordinate clause. Rewrite the sentence as two sentences.	**Incorrect:** I started playing guitar when I was twelve I thought I was great I knew very little. **Correct:** I thought I was great when I started playing guitar at age twelve. I knew very little!
Problem: Two or more main clauses are joined with a conjunction, but without a comma. **Solution:** Use a comma after the first main clause and before the conjunction.	**Incorrect:** I continued to take lessons and I realized that I had much to learn to become a good guitarist. **Correct:** I continued to take lessons, and I realized that I had much to learn to become a good guitarist.

Fragments

Expand Point out that students are most likely to write fragments when they are writing a paragraph. It can be hard to find the fragments because a person will read the fragment as part of the previous or next sentence.

Tell students to use this method to check their work:

- Read the last sentence of the paragraph aloud.
- Then read the next to last sentence aloud.
- Continue to work backward, and read each sentence aloud.
- If a sentence does not sound like it expresses a complete idea, it may be a fragment. Write it out separately. If it is a fragment, correct it.

Words Often Confused

Expand Discuss the word pairs on the student page. Use the tips below to help clarify some of the word pairs. Then have students practice writing sentences with the words.

a lot, allot: Say: Write "a lot" as two words unless it is the verb of the sentence.

all ready, already: Read the examples on the student page. Explain:

- In the phrase "all ready," *all* describes a group of people or things. *Ready* is an adjective that describes *all*.
- *Already* is an adverb. It shows that an action took place in the past and is completed.

ELL **Reinforce** Read the rule for *amount of* and *number of*.

Explain that some nouns cannot be counted. These are sometimes called mass nouns. Give students these examples: *blood, furniture, information, music*. Tell them to be careful not to add *s* to these nouns to form the plural.

Explain that this type of noun is often accompanied by a unit of measurement. For example, you may have a teaspoon of sugar or an ounce of water. To form plurals in this case, add *s* to the unit of measurement: two teaspoons of sugar.

Words Often Confused

This section will help you to choose between words that are often confused.

a lot, allot

A lot means "many" and is always written as two words, never as one word. *Allot* means "to assign."

I have **a lot** of friends who like to run.

We are **allotted** 30 minutes for lunch.

a while, awhile

The two-word form *a while* is a noun phrase and is often preceded by the prepositions *after, for,* or *in*. The one-word form *awhile* is an adverb and cannot be used with a preposition.

Let's stop here for **a while**.

Let's stop here **awhile**.

accept, except

Accept is a verb that means "to receive." *Except* can be a verb meaning "to leave out" or a preposition meaning "excluding."

I **accept** everything you say, **except** your point about music.

advice, advise

Advice is a noun that means "ideas about how to solve a problem." *Advise* is a verb and means "to give advice."

I will give you **advice** about your problem today, but do not ask me to **advise** you again tomorrow.

affect, effect

Affect is a verb. It means "to cause a change in" or "to influence." *Effect* as a verb means "to bring about." As a noun, *effect* means "a result."

The sunshine will **affect** my plants.

The governor is working to **effect** change.

The rain had no **effect** on our spirits.

aren't

Ain't is not used in formal English. Use the correct form of the verb *be* with the word *not*: *is not, isn't; are not,* or *aren't*.

We **are not going to sing** in front of you.

I **am not going to practice** today.

all ready, already

Use the two-word form, *all ready*, to mean "completely finished." Use the one-word form, *already*, to mean "before."

We waited an hour for dinner to be **all ready**.

It is a good thing I have **already** eaten today.

all right

The expression *all right* means "OK" and should be written as two words. The one-word form, *alright*, is not used in formal writing.

I hope it is **all right** that I am early.

all together, altogether

The two-word form, *all together*, means "in a group." The one-word form, *altogether*, means "completely."

It is **altogether** wrong that we will not be **all together** this holiday.

among, between

Use *among* when comparing more than two people or things. Use *between* when comparing a person or thing with one other person, thing, or group.

You are **among** friends.

We will split the money **between** Sal and Jess.

amount of, number of

Amount of is used with nouns that cannot be counted. *Number of* is used with nouns that can be counted.

The **amount of** pollution in the air is increasing.

A record **number of** people attended the game.

assure, ensure, insure

Assure means "to make feel better." *Ensure* means "to guarantee." *Insure* means "to cover financially."

I **assure** you that he is OK.

I will personally **ensure** his safety.

If the car is **insured,** the insurance company will pay to fix the damage.

being as, being that

Neither of these is used in formal English. Use *because* or *since* instead.

I went home early **because** I was sick.

beside, besides

Beside means "next to." *Besides* means "plus" or "in addition to."

Located **beside** the cafeteria is a vending machine.

Besides being the fastest runner, she is also the nicest team member.

bring, take

Bring means "to carry closer." *Take* means "to grasp." *Take* is often used with the preposition *away* to mean "carry away from."

Please **bring** the dictionary to me and **take** the thesaurus from my desk.

bust, busted

Neither of these is used in formal English. Use *broke* or *broken* instead.

I **broke** the vase by accident.

The **broken** vase cannot be fixed.

can't; hardly; scarcely

Do not use *can't* with *hardly* or *scarcely*. That would be a double negative. Use only *can't*, or use *can* plus a negative word.

I **can't** get my work done in time.

I **can scarcely** get my work done in time.

capital, capitol

A *capital* is a place where a government is located. A *capitol* is an actual government building.

The **capital** of the U.S. is Washington, D.C.

The senate met at the **capitol** to vote.

cite, site, sight

To *cite* means "to quote a source." A *site* is "a place." *Sight* can mean "the ability to see" or it can mean "something that can be seen."

Be sure to **cite** all your sources.

My brother works on a construction **site**.

Dan went to the eye doctor to have his **sight** checked.

The sunset last night was a beautiful **sight**.

complement, compliment

Complement means "something that completes" or "to complete." *Compliment* means "something nice someone says about another person" or "to praise."

The colors you picked really **complement** each other.

I would like to **compliment** you on your new shoes.

could have, should have, would have, might have

Be sure to use "have," not "of," with words like *could*, *should*, *would*, and *might*.

I **would have** gone, but I didn't feel well.

council, counsel

A *council* is a group that gives advice. To *counsel* is to give advice to someone.

The city **council** met to discuss traffic issues.

Mom, please **counsel** me on how to handle this situation.

coup d'état, coup de grâce

A *coup d'état* ("stroke of state") usually refers to the overthrow of a government. A coup de *grâce* ("stroke, or blow, or mercy") refers to a final action that brings victory.

different from, different than

Different from is preferred in formal English and is used when the comparison is between two persons or things. *Different than*, when used, is used with full clauses.

My interest in music is **different from** my friend's.

Movies today are **different than** they used to be in the 1950s.

each other, one another

Each other refers to two people. *One another* refers to more than two people.

Mika and I gave **each other** presents for Christmas.

Words Often Confused

Expand Read the word pairs for *being as*, *being that* and *bust*, *busted* on the student page. Remind students that these words and phrases should not be used in their writing. Point out the following words that people use but that are not really words in English. Tell students the correct word or phrase to use instead.

Incorrect	Use This Instead
ain't	(I) am not; (You) are not
anyways	anyway
anywheres	anywhere
hisself	himself
irregardless	regardless

Reinforce Explain that many words used to describe historical events are commonly used in English. The phrase *coup d'état*, often shortened in English to *coup*, is often used when speaking of a revolution in which people rise up and depose the existing government. Both *coup d'état* and *coup de grâce* are used figuratively as well, for example, to apply to business deals or sporting events.

Reinforce Restate the rules for reciprocal pronouns (each other, one another) and write some practice sentences.

Have students think of other words that might not be appropriate for use in formal writing. Ask volunteers to share their responses. Record the responses, and the correct forms, in a chart like the one above.

Words Often Confused

Expand Discuss the word pairs on the student page. Use the tips below to help clarify some of the word pairs. Then have students practice writing sentences with the words.

good, well: Caution students not to use *good* as an adverb. Say: Ask yourself if you are describing a verb or a noun.

it's, its: Point out that these are the only two spellings. *Its'* is incorrect. Explain how to decide which word to use:

- Try to replace the word with the phrase "it is."
- If the sentence still makes sense, use *it's*.
- If the sentence does not make sense, use *its*.

ELL **Reinforce** Use prefixes to figure out the meaning of words.

immigrate, emigrate: Read the sentences on the student page.

- Explain that *im-* means "in" and *em-* means "out."
- Point out that students may also see this pattern with *im-* and *ex-* word pairs, such as *import, export* and *implode, explode*.

- If necessary, refer students to **Reading Handbook**, page 694. Students can review using prefixes and suffixes to help them determine the meanings of words and choose the correct form to use in a sentence.

Troubleshooting Guide

Words Often Confused List, continued

The five of us looked out for **one another** on the field trip.

farther, further

Farther refers to a physical distance. *Further* refers to time or amount.

If you go down the road a little **farther**, you will see the sign.

We will discuss this **further** at lunch.

fewer, less

Fewer refers to things that can be counted individually. *Less* refers to things that cannot be counted individually.

The farm had **fewer** animals than the zoo, so it was **less** fun to visit.

good, well

The adjective *good* means "kind." The adjective *well* means "healthy." The adverb *well* means "ably."

She is a **good** person.

I am glad to see that you are **well** again after that illness.

You have performed **well**.

immigrate to, emigrate from

Immigrate to means "to move to a country." *Emigrate from* means "to leave a country."

I **immigrated to** America in 2001 from Panama.

I **emigrated from** El Salvador because of the war.

it's, its

It's is a contraction of *it is*. *Its* is a possessive word meaning "belonging to it."

It's going to be a hot day.

The dog drank all of **its** water already.

kind of, sort of

These words mean "a type of." In formal English, do not use them to mean "partly." Use *somewhat* or *rather* instead.

The peanut is actually a **kind of** bean.

I feel **rather** silly in this outfit.

lay, lie

Lay means "to put in a place." It is used to describe what people do with objects. *Lie* means "to recline." People can *lie* down, but they *lay* down objects. Do not confuse this use of *lie* with the noun that means "an untruth."

I will **lay** the book on this desk for you.

She **lay** the baby in his crib.

I'm tired and am going to **lie** on the couch.

If you **lie** in court, you will be punished.

learn, teach

To *learn* is "to receive information." To *teach* is "to give information."

If we want to **learn**, we have to listen.

She will **teach** us how to drive.

leave (alone), let

Leave alone means "not to disturb someone." *Let* means "to allow or permit."

Leave her **alone**, and she will be fine.

Let them go.

like, as

Like can be used either as a preposition or as a verb meaning "to care about something." *As* is a conjunction and should be used to introduce a subordinate clause.

She sometimes acts **like** a princess. But I still **like** her.

She acts **as** if she owns the school.

loose, lose

Loose can be used as an adverb or adjective meaning "free" or "not securely attached." The verb *lose* means "to misplace" or "not to win."

I let the dog **loose** and he is missing.

Did you **lose** your homework?

Did they **lose** the game by many points?

passed, past

Passed is a verb that means "moved ahead of" or "succeeded." *Past* is a noun that means "the time before the present."

The car **passed** us quickly.

I **passed** my English test.

Poor grades are in the **past** now.

precede, proceed

Precede means "to come before." *Proceed* means "to go forward."

Prewriting **precedes** drafting in the writing process.

Turn left; then **proceed** down the next street.

principal, principle

A *principal* is "a person of authority." Principal can also mean "main." A *principle* is "a general truth or belief."

The **principal** of our school makes an announcement every morning.

The **principal** ingredient in baking is flour.

The essay was based on the **principles** of effective persuasion.

raise, rise

The verb *raise* takes an object and means "to lift" or "to be brought up." The verb *rise* means "to lift oneself up." People can *rise*, but objects are *raised*.

Raise the curtain for the play.

She **raises** baby rabbits on her farm.

I **rise** from bed every morning at six.

real, really

Real means "actual." It is an adjective used to describe nouns. *Really* means "actually" or "truly." It is an adverb used to describe verbs, adjectives, or other adverbs.

The diamond was **real**.

The diamond was **really** beautiful.

set, sit

The verb *set* usually means "to put something down." The verb *sit* means "to go into a seated position."

I **set** the box on the ground.

Please **sit** while we talk.

than, then

Than is used to compare things. *Then* means "next" and is used to tell when something took place.

She likes fiction more **than** nonfiction.

First, we will go to town; **then** we will go home.

they're, their, there

They're is the contraction of *they are*. *Their* is the possessive form of the pronoun *they*. *There* is used to indicate location.

They're all on vacation this week.

I want to use **their** office.

The library is right over **there**.

There are several books I want to read.

this, these, that, those

This indicates something specific that is near someone. *These* is the plural form. *That* indicates something specific that is farther from someone. *Those* is the plural form of *that*.

This book in my hand belongs to me. **These** pens are also mine.

That book is his. **Those** notes are his, too.

where

Do not use *at* or *to* after *where*. Simply use *where*.

The restaurant is **where** I am right now.

Where is Ernesto?

who, whom

Who is a subject. *Whom* is an object.

Who is going to finish first?

My grandmother is a woman to **whom** I owe many thanks.

Grammar Tip

If you can replace *who* or *whom* with *he, she, they*, or *it*, use *who*. If you can replace the word with *him, her*, or *them*, use *whom*.

who's, whose

Who's is a contraction of *who is*. *Whose* is the possessive form of *who*.

Who's coming to our dinner party?

Whose car is parked in the garage?

you're, your

You're is a contraction of *you are*. *Your* is a possessive adjective meaning "belonging to you."

You're going to be late if you don't hurry.

Is that **your** backpack under the couch?

Words Often Confused

Expand Discuss the word pairs on the student page. Point out the following words that people use incorrectly. Offer students the following tips to determine correct usage of each word.

raise, rise:

- Tell students to remember the phrase "parents *raise* children."
- *Raise* is something done to someone or something else.

than, then:

- Tell students that people often pronounce these words the same.
- *Than* is used in comparisons. The words *comparison* and *than* both have an *a*.
- *Then* is used to show time order, and means "next." The words *next* and *then* both have an e.

who's, whose:

- Tell students to try to replace the word with *who is*.
- If the sentence still makes sense, use *who's*.
- If the sentence does not make sense, use *whose*.

Literary Terms

Literary Terms

A

Alliteration The repetition of the same sounds (usually consonants) at the beginning of words that are close together. *Example:* Molly makes magnificent mousse, though Pablo prefers pecan pie.
See also **Assonance; Consonance; Repetition**

Allusion A key form of literary language, in which one text makes the reader think about another text that was written before it. Allusion can also mean a reference to a person, place, thing, or event that is not specifically named. *Example:* When Hannah wrote in her short story that vanity was the talented main character's "Achilles heel," her teacher understood that Hannah was referring to a character in a Greek myth. So, she suspected that the vanity of the main character in Hannah's short story would prove to be the character's greatest weakness.
See also **Connotation; Literature; Poetry**

Analogy A way of illustrating a thing or an idea by comparing it with a more familiar thing or idea. *Example: Blogs* are to the *Internet* as *journals* are to *paper.*
See also **Illustration; Metaphor; Rhetorical device; Simile**

Antagonist A major character who opposes the main character, or protagonist, in a fictional narrative or a play. *Example:* In many fairy tales, a wolf is the antagonist.
See also **Protagonist**

Argument A type of writing or speaking that supports a position or attempts to convince the reader or listener. Arguments include a claim that is supported by reasons and evidence.
See also **Claim; Reason; Evidence**

Article A short piece of nonfiction writing on a specific topic. Articles usually appear in newspapers and magazines.
See also **Nonfiction; Topic**

Assonance The repetition of the same or similar vowel sounds between consonants in words that are close together. *Example:* The expression, "mad as a hatter."
See also **Alliteration; Consonance; Repetition**

Autobiography The story of a person's life, written by that person. *Example:* Mahatma Gandhi wrote an autobiography titled *Gandhi: An Autobiography: The Story of My Experiments With Truth.*
See also **Biography; Diary; Journal; Memoir; Narration; Personal narrative**

B

Biography The story of a person's life, written by another person.
See also **Autobiography; Narration**

Blank verse A form of unrhymed verse in which each line normally has 10 syllables divided into five pairs of one unstressed and one stressed syllable. Of all verse forms, blank verse comes closest to the natural rhythms of English speech. Consequently, it has been used more often, in more ways than any other verse form in English. *Example:* Today she darts from the room with delight./Bizarre she does seem, like a haughty queen./I long to make her hot cinnamon tea/ One day, she will love me as I do her./
See also **Meter; Rhyme; Stress; Verse**

C

Character A person, an animal, or an imaginary creature in a work of fiction.
See also **Characterization; Character traits; Fiction**

Characterization The way a writer creates and develops a character. Writers use a variety of ways to bring a character to life: through descriptions of the character's appearance, thoughts, feelings, and actions; through the character's words; and through the words or thoughts of other characters.
See also **Character; Character traits; Dynamic character; Motive; Point of view; Short story; Static character**

page 868

Character traits The special qualities of personality that writers give their characters.
See also **Character; Characterization**

Claim A statement that clearly identifies an author's ideas or opinion.
See also **Argument, Reason, Evidence**

Climax The turning point or most important event in a plot.
See also **Falling action; Plot; Rising action**

Comedy A play or a fictional story written mainly to amuse an audience. Most comedies end happily for the leading characters.
See also **Drama; Narration; Play**

Complication See **Rising action**

Conflict The main problem faced by the protagonist in a story or play. The protagonist may be involved in a struggle against nature, another character (usually the *antagonist*), or society. The struggle may also be between two elements in the protagonist's mind.
See also **Plot**

Connotation The feelings suggested by a word or phrase, apart from its dictionary meaning. *Example:* The terms "used car" and "previously owned vehicle" have different connotations. To most people, the phrase "previously owned vehicle" sounds better than "used car."
See also **Denotation; Poetry**

Consonance The repetition of the same or similar consonant sounds that come after different vowel sounds in words that are close together. *Example:* Sid did bid on a squid, he did.
See also **Alliteration; Assonance; Repetition**

D

Denotation The dictionary meaning of a word or phrase. Denotation is especially important in functional texts and other types of nonfiction used to communicate information precisely.
See also **Connotation; Functional text; Nonfiction**

Description Writing that creates a "picture" of a person, place, or thing—often using language that appeals to the five senses: sight, hearing, touch, smell, and taste. *Example:* The bright, hot sun beat down on Earth's surface. Where once a vibrant lake cooled the skin of hippos and zebras, only thin, dry cracks remained, reaching across the land like an old man's fingers, as far as the eye could see. The smell of herds was gone, and only silence filled the space.
See also **Imagery**

Dialect A form of a language commonly spoken in a certain place or by a certain group of people—especially a form that differs from the one most widely accepted. Dialect includes special words or phrases as well as particular pronunciations and grammar. Writers use dialect to help make their characters and settings lively and realistic. *Example:* While someone from the southern United States might say "ya'll" when referring to several friends, someone from the Northeast or Midwest might say "you guys."
See also **Diction; Jargon**

Dialogue What characters say to each other. Writers use dialogue to develop characters, move the plot forward, and add interest. In most writing, dialogue is set off by quotation marks; in play scripts, however, dialogue appears without quotation marks.

Diary A book written by a person about his or her own life as it is happening. Unlike an autobiography, a diary is not usually meant to be published. It is made up of entries that are written shortly after events occur. The person writing a diary often expresses feelings and opinions about what has happened.
See also **Autobiography; Journal**

Drama A kind of writing, in verse or prose, in which a plot unfolds in the words and actions of characters performed by actors. Two major genres of drama are comedy and tragedy.
See also **Comedy; Genre; Play; Plot; Tragedy**

LITERARY TERMS

page 869

Literary Terms

Dramatic conventions The usual ways of making drama seem real. Dramatic conventions include imagining that actors really are the characters they pretend to be and that a stage really is the place it represents.

Dynamic character A character who changes because of actions and experiences.
See also **Character; Static character**

E

Editorial An article in a newspaper or magazine that gives the opinions of the editors or publishers. *Example:* Rather than just reporting the facts, a newspaper editorial might argue that the city government should not clear preserved woodlands in order to build a shopping mall.

Electronic text Writing that a computer can store or display on a computer screen. Forms of electronic text include *Web sites* (groupings of World Wide Web pages that usually contain hyperlinks), *blogs* (Web logs—sites maintained by an individual or organization that contain various kinds of informal writing, such as diaries, opinion pieces, and stories), and *e-mail.*

Epic A long, fictional, narrative poem, written in a lofty style, that celebrates the great deeds of one or more heroes or heroines. *Example:* Homer's *The Odyssey* is a famous epic poem of over 12,000 lines. The hero, Odysseus, spends ten years overcoming various obstacles in order to return home to his wife and son after the end of the Trojan War.
See also **Fiction; Hero** or **Heroine; Poetry**

Essay A short piece of nonfiction, normally in prose, that discusses a single topic without claiming to do so thoroughly. Its purpose may be to inform, entertain, or persuade.
See also **Exposition; Nonfiction; Persuasion; Photo-essay; Review; Topic**

Evidence Information provided to support a claim. Facts, statistics, and quotes from experts are commonly used as evidence.
See also **Argument; Claim; Reasons**

Exposition The rising action of a story in which characters and the problems they face are introduced.
See also **Description; Functional text; Narration; Persuasion; Rising action**

F

Fable A brief fictional narrative that teaches a lesson about life. Many fables have animals instead of humans as characters. Fables often end with a short, witty statement of their lesson. *Example:* "The Tortoise and the Hare" is a famous fable in which a boastful, quick-moving hare challenges a slow-moving tortoise to a race. Because the overconfident hare takes a nap during the race, the tortoise wins. The moral of the fable is that slow and steady wins the race.
See also **Fiction; Folk tale; Narration**

Falling action The actions and events in a plot that happen after the climax. Usually, the major problem is solved in some way, so the remaining events serve to bring the story to an end.
See also **Climax; Conflict; Plot, Rising action**

Fantasy Fiction in which imaginary worlds differ from the "real" world outside the text. Fairy tales, science fiction, and fables are examples of fantasy.
See also **Fable; Fiction; Science fiction**

Fiction Narrative writing about imaginary people, places, things, or events.
See also **Fable; Fantasy; Folk tale; Historical fiction; Myth; Narration; Nonfiction; Novel; Realistic fiction; Science fiction; Short story; Tall tale**

Figurative language The use of a word or phrase to say one thing and mean another. Figurative language is especially important in literature and poetry because it gives writers a more effective way of expressing what they mean than using direct, literal language. *Example:* Upon receiving her monthly bills, Victoria complained that she was "drowning in debt."
See also **Hyperbole; Idiom; Imagery; Irony; Literature; Metaphor; Personification; Poetry; Simile; Symbol**

page 870

Flashback An interruption in the action of a narrative to tell about something that happened earlier. It is often used to give the reader background information about a character or situation.
See also **Character; Narration**

Folk literature The collection of a people's literary works shared mainly orally rather than in writing. Such works include spells, songs, ballads (songs that tell a story), jokes, riddles, proverbs, nursery rhymes, and folk tales.
See also **Folk tale; Folklore; Literature; Song lyrics**

Folk tale A short, fictional narrative shared orally rather than in writing, and thus partly changed through its retellings before being written down. Folk tales include myths, legends, fables, tall tales, ghost stories, and fairy tales.
See also **Fable; Folk literature; Myth; Tall tale**

Folklore The collection of a people's beliefs, customs, rituals, spells, songs, sayings, and stories as shared mainly orally rather than in writing.
See also **Folk literature; Folk tale**

Foreshadowing A hint that a writer gives about an event that will happen later in a story. *Example:* In a story about a teenage girl who starts getting into trouble, an early scene may show her friend stealing earrings from a jewelry store. Later the girl herself begins stealing. Based on the earlier scene, the reader might guess this is what the girl would do.

Free verse Writing that is free of meter, and thus not really verse at all. It is closer to rhythmic prose or speech. But like verse, and unlike prose or speech, it is arranged in lines, which divide the text into units of rhythm. Free verse may be rhymed or unrhymed.
See also **Meter; Prose; Rhyme; Rhythm; Verse**

Functional text Writing in which the main purpose is to communicate the information people need to accomplish tasks in everyday life. *Examples:* résumés, business letters, instruction manuals, and the help systems of word-processing programs.

G

Genre A type or class of literary works grouped according to form, style, and/or topic. Major genres include fictional narrative prose (such as short stories and most novels), nonfiction narrative prose (such as autobiographies, historical accounts, and memoirs), drama (such as comedies and tragedies), verse (such as lyrics and epics), and the essay.
See also **Essay; Fiction; Literature; Narration; Nonfiction; Prose; Style; Topic; Verse**

H

Haiku A form of short, unrhymed poetry that expresses a moment of sudden, intensely felt awareness. The words in haiku focus on what can be seen, smelled, tasted, touched, or heard. The haiku was invented in Japan, and it traditionally consists of 17 syllables in three lines of 5, 7, and 5 syllables. *Example:*

Gold, red leaves rustle
A baby cries somewhere near
Blue sky fades to gray.

See also **Imagery; Lyric; Poetry**

Hero or **Heroine** In myths and legends, a man or woman of great courage and strength who is celebrated for his or her daring feats; also, any protagonist, or main character.
See also **Myth; Protagonist**

Historical account A piece of nonfiction writing about something that happened in the past.
See also **Memoir; Nonfiction**

Historical fiction Fiction based on events that actually happened or on people who actually lived. It may be written from the point of view of a "real" or an imaginary character, and it usually includes invented dialogue.
See also **Fiction**

Humor A type of writing meant to be funny in a good-natured way. It often makes what characters look like, say, or do seem serious to them but ridiculous to the reader.
See also **Parody**

LITERARY TERMS

page 871

Literary Terms

Hyperbole Figurative language that exaggerates, often to the point of being funny, to emphasize something. *Example:* When his mother asked how long he had waited for the school bus that morning, Jeremy grinned and said, "Oh, not long. Only about a million years."
See also **Figurative language; Tall tale**

I

Idiom A phrase or expression that means something different from the word or words' dictionary meanings. Idioms cannot be translated word for word into another language because an idiom's meaning is not the same as that of the individual words that make it up. *Example:* "Mind your p's and q's" in English means to be careful, thoughtful, and behave properly.

Illustration Writing that uses examples to support a main idea. Illustration is often used to help the reader understand general, abstract, or complex ideas.

Imagery Figurative language that communicates sensory experience. Imagery can help the reader imagine how people, places, and things look, sound, taste, smell, and feel. It can also make the reader think about emotions and ideas that commonly go with certain sensations. Because imagery appeals to the senses, it is sometimes called *sensory language*.
See also **Description; Figurative language; Symbol**

Interview A discussion between two or more people in which questions are asked and answered so that the interviewer can get information. The record of such a discussion is also called an interview.

Irony A type of figurative language that takes three forms: (1) *verbal irony* means the opposite of what is said, or it means both what is said and the opposite of what is said, at once; (2) *dramatic irony* (a) contrasts what a speaker or character says with what the writer means or thinks, or (b) in a story, presents a speech or an action that means more to the audience than to the character who speaks or performs it, because the audience knows something the character does not; (3) *situational irony* (a) contrasts an actual situation with what would seem appropriate, or (b) contrasts what one expects with what actually happens.
Examples: 1. Verbal Irony: After having her car towed, getting drenched in a thunderstorm, and losing her wallet, Kate told her friend, "Let me tell you, today has been a real picnic."
2. Dramatic Irony: In the final scene of William Shakespeare's play *Romeo and Juliet*, Romeo finds Juliet drugged. While the audience knows that she is still alive, Romeo presumes that she is dead and decides to kill himself. Juliet shortly thereafter awakes and, upon finding Romeo dead, kills herself.
3. Situational Irony: In O. Henry's short story "The Gift of the Magi," a husband and wife each want to buy a Christmas present for the other. The wife buys her husband a chain for his watch; the husband buys the wife combs for her hair. To get enough money to buy these gifts, the wife cuts and sells her hair, and the husband sells his watch.
See also **Figurative language**

J

Jargon Specialized language used by people to describe things that are specific to their group or subject. *Example: Mouse* in a computer class means "part of a computer system," not "a rodent."
See also **Dialect; Diction**

Journal A personal record, similar to a diary. It may include accounts of actual events, stories, poems, sketches, thoughts, essays, a collection of interesting information, or just about anything the writer wishes to include.
See also **Diary**

L

Literature A body of written works in prose or verse.
See also **Functional text; Poetry; Prose; Verse**

Literary criticism The careful study and discussion of works of literature, mainly to understand them and judge their effectiveness.
See also **Literature**

page 872

Lyric One of the main types of poetry. Lyrics tend to be short and songlike, and express the state of mind—or the process of observing, thinking, and feeling—of a single "speaker."
See also **Haiku; Poetry; Song lyrics; Sonnet**

M

Memoir A written account of people the author has known and events he or she has witnessed. *Example:* Elie Wiesel's novel *Night* is a memoir. It documents his personal experiences in a concentration camp during World War II.
See also **Autobiography; Historical account**

Metaphor A type of figurative language that compares two unlike things by saying that one thing is the other thing. *Example:* Dhara says her grandfather can be a real mule when he doesn't get enough sleep.
See also **Figurative language; Simile; Symbol**

Meter The patterning of language into regularly repeating units of rhythm. Language patterned in this way is called *verse*. Most verse in English has been written in one of two main types of meter: (1) *accentual*, which depends on the number of stressed syllables in a line; (2) *accentual-syllabic*, which depends on the number of stressed and unstressed syllables in a line. By varying the rhythm within a meter, the writer can heighten the reader's attention to what is going on in the verse and reinforce meaning.
See also **Poetry; Rhythm; Stress; Verse**

Mood The overall feeling or atmosphere a writer creates in a piece of writing.
See also **Tone**

Motive The reason a character has for his or her thoughts, feelings, actions, or words. *Example:* Maria's motive for bringing cookies to her new neighbors was to learn what they were like.
See also **Characterization**

Myth A fictional narrative, often a folk tale, that tells of supernatural events as a way of explaining natural events and their relation to human life. Myths commonly involve gods, goddesses, monsters, and superhuman heroes or heroines.
See also **Folk tale; Hero** or **Heroine**

N

Narration The telling of events (a story), mostly through explanation and description, rather than through dialogue.
See also **Narrator; Point of view; Story**

Narrative Writing that gives an account of a set of real or imaginary events (the story), which the writer selects and arranges in a particular order (the plot). Narrative writing includes nonfiction works such as news articles, autobiographies, and historical accounts, as well as fictional works such as short stories, novels, and epics.
See also **Autobiography; Fiction; Historical account; Narrator; Nonfiction; Plot; Story**

Narrator Someone who gives an account of events. In fiction, the narrator is the teller of a story (as opposed to the real author, who invented the narrator as well as the story). Narrators differ in how much they participate in a story's events. In a first-person narrative, the narrator is the "I" telling the story. In a third-person narrative, the narrator is not directly involved in the events and refers to characters by name or as *he, she, it*, or *they*. Narrators also differ in how much they know and how much they can be trusted by the reader.
See also **Character; Narration; Point of view; Voice**

Nonfiction Written works about events or things that are not imaginary; writing other than fiction.
See also **Autobiography; Biography; Diary; Encyclopedia; Essay; Fiction; Historical account; Journal; Memoir; Personal narrative; Photo-essay; Report; Textbook**

Novel A long, fictional narrative, usually in prose. Its length enables it to have more characters, a more complicated plot, and a more fully developed setting than shorter works of fiction.
See also **Character; Fiction; Narration; Plot; Prose; Setting; Short story**

O

Onomatopoeia The use of words that imitate the sounds they refer to. *Examples: buzz, slam, hiss*

page 873

P

Paradox A statement or an expression that seems to contradict itself but may, when thought about further, begin to make sense and seem true. Paradox can shock the reader into attention, thus underscoring the truth of what is being said. *Example:* The Time Paradox: A man travels back in time and kills his grandfather. The paradox is that if he killed his grandfather, the man himself never would have been born.

Parody A piece of writing meant to amuse by imitating the style or features of another (usually serious) piece. It makes fun of the original by taking the elements it imitates to extreme or ridiculous lengths or by applying them to a lowly or comically inappropriate subject. *Example:* In 1729, Jonathan Swift wrote a pamphlet titled "A Modest Proposal." In it, he outrageously recommends that the poor sell their children as food to the wealthy in order to make money. "A Modest Proposal" is a parody of similar pamphlets distributed by the wealthy business class, whose practices, Swift believed, neglected human costs and made it difficult for the poor to overcome poverty.
See also **Genre; Humor; Style**

Personal narrative An account of a certain event or set of events in a person's life, written by that person.
See also **Autobiography; Narration**

Personification Figurative language that describes animals, things, or ideas as having human traits. *Examples:* in the movie *Babe* and in the book *Charlotte's Web*, the animals are all personified
See also **Figurative language**

Persuasion Writing that attempts to get someone to do or agree to something by appealing to logic or emotion. Persuasive writing is used in advertisements, editorials, sermons, and political speeches.
See also **Description; Editorial; Exposition; Narration; Rhetorical device**

Photo-essay A short nonfiction piece made up of photographs and captions. The photographs are as important as the words in giving information to the reader.
See also **Essay; Nonfiction**

Play A work of drama, especially one written to be performed on a stage. *Example:* Lorraine Hansberry's *A Raisin in the Sun*
See also **Drama**

Plot The pattern of events and situations in a story or play. Plot is usually divided into four main parts: *conflict* (or *problem*), *rising action* (or *exposition* or *complication*), *climax*, and *falling action* (or *resolution*).
See also **Climax; Conflict; Drama; Falling action; Fiction; Narration; Rising action; Story**

Poetry A form of literary expression that uses line breaks for emphasis. Poems often use connotation, imagery, metaphor, symbol, paradox, irony, allusion, repetition, and rhythm. Word patterns in poetry include rhythm or meter, and often rhyme and alliteration. The three main types of poetry are narrative, dramatic, and lyric.
See also **Alliteration; Connotation; Figurative language; Literature; Lyric; Meter; Narration; Repetition; Rhyme; Rhythm; Verse**

Point of view The position from which the events of a story seem to be observed and told. A first-person point of view tells the story through what the narrator knows, experiences, concludes, or can find out by talking to other characters. A third-person point of view may be *omniscient*, giving the narrator unlimited knowledge of things, events, and characters, including characters' hidden thoughts and feelings. Or it may be *limited* to what one or a few characters know and experience. *Example* of First-Person Point of View: I'm really hungry right now, and I can't wait to eat my lunch. *Example* of Third-Person Limited Point of View: Olivia is really hungry right now and she wants to eat her lunch. *Example* of Third-Person Omniscient Point of View: Olivia is really hungry right now and she wants to eat her lunch. The other students are thinking about their weekend plans. The teacher is wondering how she will finish the lesson before the bell rings.
See also **Character; Fiction; Narration; Narrator; Voice**

page 874

Prose A form of writing in which the rhythm is less regular than that of verse and more like that of ordinary speech.
See also **Rhythm; Verse**

Protagonist The main character in a fictional narrative or a play. He or she may be competing with an antagonist; sometimes called the hero or heroine. *Example:* Although the Tin Man, the Cowardly Lion, and the Scarecrow are important characters in *The Wizard of Oz*, Dorothy is the protagonist.
See also **Antagonist; Hero** or **Heroine**

Pun An expression, used for emphasis or humor, in which two distinct meanings are suggested by one word or by two similar-sounding words. *Example:* The following joke uses a pun on the way that the word "lettuce" sounds similar to "let us":
Q: Knock, knock. **A**: Who's there?
Q: Lettuce. **A**: Lettuce who?
Q: Lettuce in, it's cold out here!
See also **Humor**

R

Realistic fiction Fiction in which detailed handling of imaginary settings, characters, and events produces a lifelike illusion of a "real" world. *Example:* Although Upton Sinclair's *The Jungle* is a work of fiction, the author's graphic, detailed descriptions of the slaughterhouse workers' daily lives led to real changes in the meat packing industry.
See also **Fiction**

Reason A logical explanation that connects a piece of evidence to a writer or speaker's claim.
See also **Argument; Claim; Evidence**

Refrain A line, group of lines, or part of a line repeated (sometimes with slight changes) at various points in poetry or song.
See also **Poetry; Repetition; Song lyrics**

Repetition The repeating of individual vowels and consonants, syllables, words, phrases, lines, or groups of lines. Repetition can be used because it sounds pleasant, to emphasize the words in which it occurs, or to help tie the parts of a text into one structure. It is especially important in creating the musical quality of poetry, where it can take such forms as alliteration, assonance, consonance, rhyme, and refrain.
See also **Alliteration; Assonance; Consonance; Poetry; Refrain; Rhyme**

Report A usually short piece of nonfiction writing on a particular topic. It differs from an essay in that it normally states only facts and does not directly express the writer's opinions.
See also **Essay; Nonfiction; Topic**

Resolution See **Falling action**

Review An essay describing a work or performance and judging its effectiveness.
See also **Description; Essay**

Rhetorical device A use of language that differs from ordinary use in order to emphasize a point. It achieves its effects mainly by arranging words in a special way rather than by changing the meaning of the words themselves. Rhetorical devices include *analogy, antithesis* (placing words in contrast with one another), *anaphora* (repeating the same word or phrase in a series of lines, clauses, or sentences), the *rhetorical question* (asking a question not to request information, but to make a point more forcefully than simply stating it would do), and *apostrophe* (directly addressing an absent person, nonhuman, or an idea).
See also **Analogy; Figurative language**

Rhyme The repetition of ending sounds in different words. Rhymes usually come at the end of lines of verse, but they may also occur within a line. If rhymed sounds are exactly the same, they make a *perfect rhyme*. If the endings of rhyming words are spelled the same but sound different, they make an *eye rhyme*. And if the last stressed vowels of rhyming words are only similar but the rhyming consonants are the same (or nearly so), the words make a *partial rhyme* (also called *slant rhyme, near rhyme*, or *imperfect rhyme*). *Examples:* The words "look" and "brook" and "shook" are perfect rhymes. The words "slaughter" and "laughter" are an eye rhyme. The words "ought" and "fault" form a partial rhyme.
See also **Poetry; Repetition; Rhyme scheme; Stress; Verse**

page 875

Literary Terms

Rhyme scheme The pattern of rhymed line endings in a work of verse or a stanza. It can be represented by giving a certain letter of the alphabet to each line ending on the same rhyme. *Example:* Because the end word of every other line rhymes in the following poem, the rhyme scheme is *abab*:

Winter night falls quick (a)
The pink sky gone, blackness overhead (b)
Looks like the snow will stick (a)
Down the street and up the hill I tread (b)

See also **Rhyme; Stanza; Verse**

Rhythm The natural rise and fall, or "beat," of language. In English it involves a back-and-forth movement between stressed and unstressed syllables. Rhythm is present in all language, including ordinary speech and prose, but it is most obvious in verse.

See also **Meter; Prose; Stress; Verse**

Rising action The part of a plot that presents actions or events that lead to the climax.

See also **Climax; Conflict; Exposition; Falling action; Plot**

S

Science fiction A genre of fantasy writing based on real or imaginary scientific discoveries. It often takes place in the future.

See also **Fantasy; Fiction**

Script The text of a play, radio or television broadcast, or movie.

Setting The time and place in which the events of a story occur.

See also **Drama; Narration**

Short story A brief, fictional narrative in prose. Like the novel, it organizes the action, thought, and dialogue of its characters into a plot. But it tends to focus on fewer characters and to center on a single event, which reveals as much as possible about the protagonist's life and the traits that set him or her apart.

See also **Character; Fiction; Narration; Novel; Plot; Prose; Protagonist; Story**

Simile A type of figurative language that compares two unlike things by using a word or phrase such as *like, as, than, similar to, resembles,* or *seems. Examples:* The tall, slim man had arms as willowy as a tree's branches. The woman's temper is like an unpredictable volcano.

See also **Figurative language; Metaphor**

Song lyrics Words meant to be sung. Lyrics have been created for many types of songs, including love songs, religious songs, work songs, sea chanties, and children's game songs. Lyrics for many songs were shared orally for generations before being written down. Not all song lyrics are lyrical like poems; some are the words to songs that tell a story. Not all poems called songs were written to be sung.

See also **Folk literature; Lyric; Narration; Poetry; Refrain**

Sonnet A major form of poetry made up of 14 rhyming lines of equal length. Most sonnets in English take one of two basic patterns: (1) The Italian, or Petrarchan, sonnet consists of two parts: a group of eight lines rhyming *abbaabba*, followed by a group of six lines usually rhyming *cdecde*; (2) The English, or Shakespearean, sonnet is divided into three groups of four lines rhyming *abab cdcd efef* and a pair rhyming *gg*.

See also **Lyric; Meter; Rhyme; Rhyme scheme; Verse**

Speech A message on a specific topic, spoken before an audience; also, spoken (not written) language.

Stanza A group of lines that forms a section of a poem and has the same pattern (including line lengths, meter, and usually rhyme scheme) as other sections of the same poem. In printed poems, stanzas are separated from each other by a space.

See also **Meter; Rhyme scheme; Verse**

Static character A character who changes little, if at all. Things happen *to*, rather than *within*, him or her. *Example:* In Charles Dickens's novel *Great Expectations*, Joe Gargery is a static character. He is a poor, uneducated blacksmith who endures the cruelty of his wife and Pip, the main character. Throughout the novel, Joe remains humble, loyal, and supportive of those he loves.

See also **Character; Characterization; Dynamic character**

page 876

Story A series of events (actual or imaginary) that can be selected and arranged in a certain order to form a narrative or dramatic plot. It is the raw material from which the finished plot is built. Although there are technical differences, the word *story* is sometimes used in place of *narrative*.

See also **Drama; Narration; Plot**

Stress The force with which a syllable is spoken compared with neighboring syllables in a line of verse. A stressed syllable is spoken more forcefully than an unstressed one.

See also **Meter; Rhythm; Verse**

Style The way a writer uses language to express the feelings or thoughts he or she wants to convey. Just as no two people are alike, no two styles are exactly alike. A writer's style results from his or her choices of vocabulary, sentence structure and variety, imagery, figurative language, rhythm, repetition, and other resources.

See also **Diction; Figurative language; Genre; Imagery; Parody; Repetition; Rhythm; Voice**

Suspense A feeling of curiosity, tension, or excitement a narrative creates in the reader about what will happen next. Mystery novels, like horror movies, are often full of suspense.

See also **Narration**

Symbol A word or phrase that serves as an image of some person, place, thing, or action but that also calls to mind some other, usually broader, idea or range of ideas. *Example:* An author might describe doves flying high in the sky to symbolize a peaceful setting.

See also **Figurative language; Imagery**

T

Tall tale A kind of folk tale that wildly exaggerates a character's strength and ability, usually for comic effect. *Example:* Stories about Paul Bunyan, the enormous lumberjack whose footprints created Minnesota's 10,000 lakes, are considered tall tales.

See also **Hyperbole**

Textbook A book prepared for use in schools for the study of a subject.

Theme The underlying message or main idea of a piece of writing. It expresses a broader meaning than the topic of the piece.

See also **Topic**

Tone A writer's or speaker's attitude toward his or her topic or audience or toward him- or herself. A writer's tone may be positive, negative, or neutral. The words the writer chooses, the sentence structure, and the overall pattern of words convey the intended tone.

See also **Connotation; Figurative language; Literature; Mood; Rhythm; Topic**

Topic What or who is being discussed in a piece of writing; the subject of the piece.

See also **Theme**

Tragedy A play or a fictional narrative about the disastrous downfall of the protagonist, usually because of a flaw in his or her moral character. Though brought to ruin, the protagonist comes to understand the meaning of his or her actions and to accept the consequences. *Example:* William Shakespeare's play *Hamlet* is about the downfall and eventual death of the protagonist, Hamlet, so it is considered a tragedy.

See also **Drama; Narration; Protagonist**

V

Verse Language that differs from prose and ordinary speech by being arranged in regular units of rhythm called *meter*. The meter, in turn, occurs within a larger unit of rhythm and meaning: the *line*. In written verse, unlike written prose, the writer rather than the printer decides where one line ends and the next begins. Not all poetry is written in verse (poetry can even be written in prose), and not all verse is poetry (even skillfully written verse can be ineffective in communicating experience).

See also **Blank verse; Free verse; Meter; Poetry; Prose; Rhythm; Sonnet**

Voice The specific group of traits conveyed by the narrator or "speaker" in a literary work.

See also **Narrator**

page 877

Vocabulary Glossary

The definitions in this glossary are for words as they are used in the selections in this book. Use the Pronunciation Key below to help you use each word's pronunciation. Then read about the parts of an entry.

Pronunciation Key

Symbols for Consonant Sounds

b	box	**p**	pan
ch	chick	**r**	ring
d	dog	**s**	bus
f	fish	**sh**	fish
g	girl	**t**	hat
h	hat	**th**	earth
j	jar	**th**	father
k	cake	**v**	vase
ks	box	**w**	window
kw	queen	**wh**	whale
l	bell	**y**	yarn
m	mouse	**z**	zipper
n	pan	**zh**	treasure
ng	ring		

Symbols for Short Vowel Sounds

a	hat
e	bell
i	chick
o	box
u	bus

Symbols for Long Vowel Sounds

ā	cake
ē	key
ī	bike
ō	goat
yū	mule

Symbols for R-controlled Sounds

ar	barn
air	chair
ear	ear
īr	fire
or	corn
ur	girl

Symbols for Variant Vowel Sounds

ah	father
aw	ball
oi	boy
ow	mouse
oo	book
ü	fruit

Miscellaneous Symbols

shun	fraction
chun	question
zhun	division

Academic Vocabulary

Certain words in this glossary have a red dot indicating that they are academic vocabulary words. These are the words that are necessary for you to learn in order to understand the concepts being taught in school.

Parts of an Entry

The **entry** shows how the word is spelled and how it is broken into syllables.

The **pronunciation** shows you how to say the word.

part of speech
n. for noun
v. for verb
adj. for adjective
adv. for adverb.

The red dot signals that a word is an **academic vocabulary** word. Not all words have a red dot.

• **af • firm** (u-**furm**) *v.* showing, saying, or proving that something is true. *My decision to volunteer at the hospital was* ***affirmed*** *when I saw how happy the patients were because of my visit.*

The **definition** gives the meaning of the word.

The **sample sentence** uses the word in a way that shows its meaning.

VOCABULARY GLOSSARY

The **Vocabulary Glossary** provides for students an alphabetical listing of the Key Vocabulary words from the student book selections. Along with being able to easily access these words, the glossary:

- assists students with pronunciation of Key Vocabulary words
- highlights academic vocabulary from *The Academic Word List* (Coxhead, 2000)
- shows students how to read the parts of an entry
- shows students parts of speech, definitions, and sample sentences for each word

For ways to practice the vocabulary with students, see the Daily Vocabulary Routines in the front of this teacher's edition behind the second tab, Vocabulary & Fluency Routines.

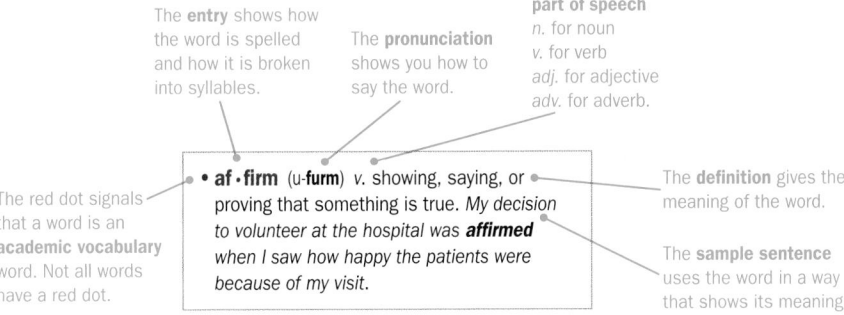

Vocabulary Glossary

VOCABULARY GLOSSARY

A

• **achieve** (u-**chēv**) *v.* to succeed or do well. *If you work hard, you can **achieve** your goals.*

advertising (**ad**-vur-tīz-ing) *n.* media that encourages people to buy, do, or use things. *The company uses **advertising** like TV commercials and Internet ads to sell its new product.*

• **affect** (u-**fekt**) *v.* to change something in some way. *You can **affect** the environment by using more or less water.*

affirm (u-**furm**) *v.* showing, saying, or proving that something is true. *My decision to volunteer at the hospital was **affirmed** when I saw how happy the patients were because of my visit.*

aggressive (u-**gre**-siv) *adj.* forceful, bold, and willing to take strong action. *She is an **aggressive** soccer player who scores lots of goals.*

alien (**ā**-lē-un) *adj.* a person who comes from another country. *When she moved to the U.S., she was an **alien** in a strange, new culture.*

• **alternative** (awl-**tur**-nu-tiv) *adj.* offering a choice that is different from what is usual or expected. *The **alternative** movie was created and filmed in a unique way.*

ambitious (am-**bi**-shus) *adj.* having big goals that you want to achieve. *The **ambitious** student studied day and night to win the science prize.*

anxiety (ang-**zī**-ut-ē) *n.* worry, concern. *I felt great **anxiety** before I started my new job.*

appeal (u-**pēl**) *v.* to ask for a good reaction. *That commercial **appeals** to my love of cars.*

arrogant (**ar**-u-gunt) *adj.* overly proud; thinking you are very smart or talented. *The **arrogant** girl acts like she is better than everyone else.*

ashamed (u-**shāmd**) *adj.* guilty or embarassed. *I felt **ashamed** about the way I had treated my friend when I was angry.*

• **assemble** (u-**sem**-bul) *v.* to put something together. ***Assemble** the model car out of the pieces in the box.*

• **assume** (u-**süm**) *v.* to think that something is true even if you do not know that it is. *He **assumes** that I am poor because my clothes are old.*

• **authority** (u-**thor**-u-tē) *n.* power over others. *Government leaders have the **authority** to make laws.*

B

• **bias** (**bī**-us) *n.* opinions that affect the way you see or present things. *He couldn't be partial because he is too **biased**.*

• **bond** (**bond**) *n.* a kind of connection between people or things. *My sister and I are held together by the strong **bonds** of family and love.*

boundary (**bown**-du-rē) *n.* a line that separates two places. *This fence marks the **boundary** between our yard and yours.*

boycott (**boi**-kot) *n.* a way to punish an organization by refusing to use its product or service. *We will hold a **boycott** of the company's products because we don't like the way it treats its workers.*

burden (**bur**-din) *n.* a heavy thing that you must carry or something difficult you have to do or know about. *Keeping my brother's secret was a great **burden** to me.*

C

• **capable** (**kā**-pu-bul) *adj.* able to do something. *We are all **capable** of doing good and bad things with our lives.*

career (ku-**rear**) *n.* the kind of work a person does. *The artist began her **career** by drawing comics in high school.*

cause (**kawz**) *n.* an idea you believe in and are willing to fight for. *I volunteer my time and money to the **cause** of helping the homeless.*

• **cease** (**cēs**) *v.* to stop. *The voices **ceased** when he entered the room, and it got completely quiet.*

circumstances (**sur**-kum-stans-uz) *n.* the situation a person is in. *There are many **circumstances** that cause people to make bad choices.*

page 879

Vocabulary Glossary

collaborate (ku-**lab**-u-rāt) *v.* to work together with one or more people on a specific task or project. *My friends and I **collaborate** on group projects for class.*

• **collapse** (ku-**laps**) *v.* to fall down suddenly. *The man **collapsed** to the floor when he heard the bad news about his son's accident.*

• **commit** (ku-**mit**) *v.* to perform, do, or carry out something, often a crime. *She **committed** the crime of robbery.*

• **commitment** (ku-**mit**-mint) *n.* something that you continue to work on even when it's difficult. *He shows his **commitment** to work by coming early every day.*

compassion (kum-**pash**-un) *n.* deep concern about other's suffering and troubles. *I felt **compassion** for the sad, lonely girl.*

compose (kum-**pōz**) *v.* to create something by writing it. *If you compose a poem, I'll **compose** music to go with it.*

confession (kun-**fe**-shun) *n.* something private or secret that you tell. *The boy made a **confession** to his mother, because he felt badly about what he had done.*

• **conflict** (**kahn**-flikt) *n.* disagreement, problem, or argument. *A story's **conflict** is the main problem.*

• **conquer** (**kon**-kur) *v.* to beat, to defeat. *The army **conquered** its enemy after a long battle.*

• **conscientiously** (**kon**-shē-en-shus-lē) *adv.* carefully and thoroughly. *Maribel **conscientiously** researched all the facts before writing her history essay.*

• **consequence** (**kon**-su-kwens) *n.* something that happens as the result of another action. *If you lie to a friend, you may have to face a **consequence**, like losing your friendship.*

• **constant** (**kon**-stunt) *adj.* stays the same; without any change. *No matter what changes, my love for my family will always stay **constant**.*

• **consumer** (kun-**sü**-mur) *n.* someone who buys or uses something. *Stores want **consumers** to buy their products.*

• **contact** (**kon**-takt) *n.* connection. *I am still in **contact** with my friends from first grade.*

• **contribute** (kun-**tri**-byūt) *v.* to give. *Students **contribute** ideas to a group discussion.*

• **convince** (kun-**vins**) *v.* to make someone believe something. *My friend tried to **convince** me to buy the expensive magazine.*

D

desperately (**des**-pur-it-lē) *adv.* a feeling of great need. *The doctors worked **desperately** to save the child's life.*

• **detect** (di-**tekt**) *v.* to discover or notice something that was not clear. *I **detected** uneasiness in her voice.*

• **device** (di-**vīs**) *n.* machine or tool that is used to do a particular job. *A cell phone is a **device** that makes it easy to communicate.*

devotion (di-**vō**-shun) *n.* love and dedication you feel toward someone or something. *Her poetry tells about the great **devotion** she feels for her family and friends.*

discourage (dis-**kur**-ej) *v.* to make someone not want to do something. *His laughter **discouraged** me from painting any more pictures.*

• **discrimination** (dis-kri-mu-**nā**-shun) *n.* unfair treatment to people in a particular group. *Racism is a form of **discrimination** that focuses on a person's ethnicity.*

disgusted (di-**skus**-tid) *adj.* to feel turned off or very upset. *I felt **disgusted** when I saw the rude way he treated others.*

disrespect (dis-ri-**spekt**) *n.* rudeness, lack of respect. *When children yell at their parents, they show **disrespect**.*

distracted (di-**strakt**-id) *adj.* unable to pay attention. *If you are **distracted** by too many activities after school, you may not have time for homework.*

page 880

• **diversity** (di-**vur**-si-tē) *n.* a variety of different people or things. *Having students from different countries creates **diversity** at our school.*

dread (**dred**) *n.* great fear. *The thought of death fills me with **dread**.*

E

efficient (i-**fi**-shunt) *adj.* working well without wasting energy. *My **efficient** car gets 35 miles per gallon of gas.*

empathy (**em**-pu-thē) *n.* understanding someone else's feelings or behavior. *I felt **empathy** for the lonely boy and could feel his sadness.*

endure (in-**dyūr**) *v.* to continue to exist for a long time. *Some old stories **endure** for centuries because people love to read and hear them.*

entreat (in-**trēt**) *v.* to ask, beg. *I **entreated** her to let me retake the test.*

• **environment** (in-**vī**-ru-munt) *n.* all of the things that surround you. *The race car driver's work **environment** is noisy and stressful.*

euphoria (ū-**for**-ē-u) *n.* great joy and happiness. *Our team was filled with **euphoria** after we won the art contest.*

• **evaluate** (i-**val**-ū-āt) *v.* to decide how good or valuable something is. *The teacher will **evaluate** your presentation and then give you a final grade.*

• **evidence** (**e**-vu-duns) *n.* information that helps prove something. *The detective looks for **evidence** that supports her ideas.*

• **expand** (ik-**spand**) *v.* to increase or grow larger. *Our group will **expand** if more members join.*

expectation (ek-spek-**tā**-shun) *n.* belief about how things will turn out. *If you have high **expectations**, you expect something to turn out well.*

• **expression** (eks-**pre**-shun) *n.* the ability to communicate in a creative way. *Poetry is one form of creative **expression**.*

F

fate (**fāt**) *n.* the future that is expected to happen. *Many people believe that you cannot change your **fate**, while others think that you can change it with hard work.*

• **feature** (**fē**-cher) *n.* the parts of your face. *His big, brown eyes are his best **feature**.*

feud (**fyūd**) *n.* an argument between two people, groups, families, or tribes. *The **feud** between our families lasted for years.*

G

• **generation** (je-nu-**rā**-shun) *n.* people who are about the same age. *We can learn a lot from our parents' **generation**.*

genuine (**jen**-yū-win) *adj.* real and not fake. *He thought that the statue was **genuine** gold, but it was really made of brass.*

• **grant** (**grant**) *v.* to give or allow. *My teacher **granted** us extra time to complete the project.*

grief (**grēf**) *n.* deep sadness or sorrow. *He felt great **grief** when his good friend died.*

• **guarantee** (gar-un-**tē**) *n.* a promise. *I'll make you a **guarantee** that you'll enjoy the movie.*

H

heritage (**her**-u-tij) *n.* background, race, or ethnic group you belong to. *Your **heritage** includes the traditions and beliefs given to you by your family, culture, and society.*

historian (hi-**stor**-ē-un) *n.* person who studies the events of the past and interprets them. *The **historian** wrote an article about World War II.*

humiliating (hyū-**mi**-lē-ā-ting) *adj.* very embarrassing. *A **humiliating** experience hurts your pride.*

I

identification (ī-den-tu-fu-**kā**-shun) *n.* a feeling that you understand a person or group of people. *I felt an **identification**, with the characters in the movie.*

imitation (im-u-**tā**-shun) *n.* something that looks or acts like something else. *I thought the painting was real, but it was just an **imitation**.*

VOCABULARY GLOSSARY

page 881

Vocabulary Glossary

• **impact** (**im**-pakt) *n.* to have an influence or effect. *Do movies and celebrities **impact** the things you choose to buy?*

• **impose** (im-**pōz**) *v.* to intrude. *After a few days with them, they felt he was beginning to **impose**.*

improvisation (im-prah-vi-**zā**-shun) *n.* something done without pre-planning. *When I forgot to prepare a speech for class, **improvisation** was my only option.*

influence (**in**-flū-uns) *v.* to affect a person in some way. *Some people believe that violence on TV can **influence** teens in harmful ways.*

• **inherent** (in-**hir**-unt) *adj.* something that you are born with. *She has always had an **inherent** sense of courage.*

• **inhibit** (in-**hib**-it) *v.* to stop or hold you back from doing something. *I want to swim, but my fear of water **inhibits** me.*

• **insight** (**in**-sīt) *n.* a new or special understanding about something. *The instruction sheet gave me **insight** into how to use the machine.*

• **inspire** (in-**spir**) *v.* to encourage someone to take action. *A movie about an Olympic athlete **inspired** me to start exercising.*

• **integrity** (in-**te**-gru-tē) *n.* honest and trustworthy. *I trust her because she shows **integrity** in everything she says and does.*

• **interpret** (in-**ter**-prut) *v.* to translate something from one language to another. *I often **interpret** letters and notices for my parents, who don't read English.*

• **invest** (in-**vest**) *v.* to provide time, money, or attention to help something grow. *I **invest** money in this business because I know it will earn more money later.*

• **investigation** (in-ves-ti-**gā**-shun) *n.* careful search or study that looks for facts. *We only found out the truth about the event after we conducted our own **investigation**.*

issue (**i**-shoo) *n.* an important topic or idea that people are concerned about. *How to stop school violence is an important **issue** that affects many teens.*

J

just (**just**) *adj.* guided by truth and fairness. *I admire leaders who make decisions that are reasonable, fair, and **just**.*

juvenile (**joo**-vu-nīl) *adj.* young. *The **juvenile** court is for people younger than eighteen.*

L

literacy (**li**-tu-ru-sē) *n.* ability to read and write. *Without **literacy**, it is difficult to complete a job application, use the Internet, or read a map.*

loyalty (**loi**-ul-tē) *n.* being faithful to someone or something. *The friends showed **loyalty** to each other by staying together no matter what happened.*

luxury (**luk**-shu-rē) *n.* expensive things that you do not really need. *Is it a **luxury** to have two pairs of dress shoes?*

M

• **major** (**mā**-jur) *adj.* great in size or importance. *We have a **major** problem that is too big for us to solve without help.*

majority (mu-**jar**-u-tē) *n.* a greater number of the whole. *Based on the results of the elections, you can tell the **majority** has spoken.*

• **manipulate** (mu-**ni**-pyu-lāt) *v.* to influence or control someone or something in a negative way. *That toy commercial uses popular cartoon characters to **manipulate** kids into wanting new toys.*

maturity (mu-**choor**-u-tē) *n.* the time when a person has all the abilities of an adult. *The girl's serious and responsible actions showed **maturity**.*

• **media** (**mē**-dē-u) *n.* different ways people use to communicate, inform, and entertain. *Newspapers, radio, and TV are **media** that provide news and entertainment to many people.*

melodious (me-**lō**-dē-us) *adj.* pleasant to hear, like music. *Whenever she sings, everyone enjoys her **melodious** songs.*

• **minor** (**mī**-nur) *adj.* small or unimportant. *My twin and I differ in **minor** ways, but we think alike and are interested in the same things.*

page 882

Vocabulary Glossary

VOCABULARY GLOSSARY

minority (mu-**nor**-u-tē) *n.; adj.* a group that has fewer members than most of the people. [*noun*] *Many **minority** groups feel they are treated unfairly by groups with more people.*

• **motivation** (mō-tu-**vā**-shun) *n.* reason for doing something or thinking a certain way. *My **motivation** for volunteering is to help my neighbors.*

N

neglect (ni-**glekt**) *n., v.* to ignore or disregard. *I saved the kittens from the **neglect** they suffered from the people who did not take care of them.*

O

• **objectivity** (ub-jek-**tiv**-u-tē) *n.* view or judgment that is not influenced by personal opinions. *We could trust his ideas because of his **objectivity**.*

obstacle (**ahb**-sti-kul) *n.* something that gets in the way or causes trouble. *The fallen tree was an **obstacle** on a road.*

• **obvious** (**ob**-vē-us) *adj.* easy to see or understand. *The answer to the riddle is **obvious** because everyone knows it.*

ominous (**ah**-mu-nus) *adj.* threatening. *The dark, cloudy sky looked **ominous**.*

• **option** (**op**-shun) *n.* a choice. *He had several **options** for lunch.*

P

• **perceive** (per-**sēv**) *v.* to see something in a certain way. *People with different points of view **perceive** things differently.*

• **persistent** (pur-**sis**-tunt) *adj.* continuing, unchanging. *The **persistent** woman kept asking for help even though everyone ignored her.*

persuasive (pur-**swā**-siv) *adj.* believable enough to make you do or believe something. *The **persuasive** man always gets people to help him.*

• **phenomenon** (fi-**nahm**-i-nahn) *n.* something different that people get really excited about. *The new music video is a real **phenomenon**; people everywhere are watching it.*

ponder (**pon**-dur) *v.* to think carefully about. *I **pondered** the meaning of the poem for hours.*

portrayal (por-**trā**-ul) *n.* a representation or picture. *The movie was a realistic **portrayal** of his life.*

poverty (**pov**-er-tē) *n.* the situation of being very poor. *People without enough money for food, shelter, or clothing live in **poverty**.*

• **precision** (pri-**si**-zhun) *n.* exactness and correctness. *A stopwatch keeps track of time with great **precision**.*

prejudiced (**prej**-u-dist) *adj.* to form negative opinions about others without thinking about the facts. *I try not to be **prejudiced** about people who are different than me.*

pretense (**prē**-tens) *n.* the act of pretending to do or be something. *Some people try to act tough, but my brother never shows any **pretense**.*

privilege (**pri**-vu-lij) *n.* something special that someone is allowed to have, be, or do. *The football team gets the **privilege** of leaving school early on game days.*

prodigy (**prah**-du-jē) *n.* young person who has unusual skills for his or her age. *They called the girl a **prodigy** because she could play the violin when she was four years old.*

• **profession** (pru-**fe**-shun) *n.* type of job that you need special training to do. *Because he chose the medical **profession**, he spent years studying to be a doctor.*

profit (**prah**-fut) *n.* the money you make when you sell something, after expenses are subtracted. *The bookstore increased its **profits** by selling more books and magazines this year.*

prophet (**pro**-fut) *n.* someone who can predict what will happen in the future. *The **prophet** warned us about the coming disaster.*

protest (**prō**-test) *v.* to say or show you are against something. *We **protest** the unfair way the students are being treated.*

page 883

provider (pru-**vī**-dur) *n.* someone who gives necessary things to someone else. *My mother is an excellent **provider**, because she gives us food, shelter, and love.*

provoke (pru-**vōk**) *v.* to force a person or thing to act. *We hope our protests against the unfair law will **provoke** the government to make a change.*

R

racism (**rā**-si-zum) *n.* belief that some races, or ethnic groups, are better than others. *The man shows **racism** when he judges others because of their ethnicity.*

recall (**rē**-kawl) *v.* to remember something from the past. *I **recall** many happy memories from my childhood.*

recitation (re-si-**tā**-shun) *n.* speaking a poem or other text aloud in front of other people. *For my class project, I will give a poetry **recitation**.*

reconciliation (re-kun-si-lē-**ā**-shun) *n.* agreement to make up after an arguement. *The men reached a **reconciliation** by talking about their problem.*

refuge (**re**-fyūj) *n.* a place of safety. *My bedroom is my **refuge** when I want to be alone.*

• **release** (rē-**lēs**) *v.* to let something go or set free. *Our teacher said he would **release** us from class as soon as the work was finished.*

• **relevance** (**re**-lu-vents) *n.* an idea that is important and connects to another thing. *The news story has **relevance** to my own life.*

• **rely** (ri-**lī**) *v.* to depend on. *Do you **rely** on your alarm clock to wake you up in the morning?*

reputation (re-pyu-**tā**-shun) *n.* the way people think about you. *He had a **reputation** as a shy person because he was always so quiet in class.*

resist (ri-**zist**) *v.* fight against. *I **resisted** the urge to scream during the scary movie.*

responsible (ri-**spon**-su-bul) *adj.* able to take care of. *If you borrow a pen, you are **responsible** for returning it when you are done.*

restore (ri-**stor**) *v.* to return something to the way it was before. *After we talked about our problems, our friendship was **restored** to the way it used to be.*

• **reveal** (ri-**vēl**) *v.* to show or display. *He would never **reveal** the secret of the magic trick.*

• **revolution** (re-vu-**lū**-shun) *n.* major or total change. *The American **Revolution** changed the government of our country.*

ritual (**ri**-chu-wul) *n.* set plan for or formal way of doing something. *Many cultures have **rituals** to protect children from danger.*

S

salvage (**sal**-vuj) *v.* to save or rescue. *I **salvaged** my friendship by telling my friend I was sorry.*

segregation (se-gri-**gā**-shun) *n.* separation of some people from others because of race. *In the past, **segregation** didn't allow black and white children to go to the same schools.*

self-esteem (**self** es-**tēm**) *n.* feeling that you are valuable; confidence in yourself. *The confident girl has high **self-esteem**.*

shame (**shām**) *n.* a painful feeling that is caused by embarrassment or guilt. *He felt **shame** about a mistake that he had made.*

• **significant** (sig-**ni**-fi-kint) *adj.* of great value or importance. *My friends and family are a **significant** part of my life.*

skeptic (**skep**-tik) *n.* someone who doubts beliefs that are generally accepted by others. *My friends believe in the legend, but I'm a **skeptic** who needs more proof.*

solution (su-**lū**-shun) *n.* the answer that solves or fixes a problem. *My team found a **solution** to our problem with the project.*

standard (**stan**-durd) *adj.* way people judge or measure things. *According to the teacher's high **standards**, Mary was a great student.*

stereotype (**ster**-ē-u-tīp) *n.* an idea people have about an entire group of people. *People say that all teens are lazy and rude, but that **stereotype** doesn't fit me.*

• **structure** (**struk**-chur) *n.* way something is set up or organized. *My poem has a **structure** that includes lots of rhyme.*

subside (sub-**sīd**) *v.* to become less strong. *When a storm **subsides** the wind and rain slow down.*

page 884

VOCABULARY GLOSSARY

successful (suk-**ses**-ful) *adj.* having done well. *The parents at the graduation were proud of their **successful** children.*

• **survivor** (sur-**vī**-vur) *n.* a person who overcomes some hardship or manages to live through a disaster. *The police rescued the **survivors** of the car accident.*

suspect (su-**spekt**) *v.* to believe that something may be different from what it seems. *I **suspect** that she is lying.*

• **symbol** (**sim**-bul) *n.* something that represents or stands for something else. *An eagle is a **symbol** of the* United States. A dove is a ***symbol*** of peace.

T

talent (**tal**-unt) *n.* special ability or skill. *She has a wonderful **talent** in music.*

technology (tek-**nah**-lu-jē) *n.* scientific knowledge as it is used in the world. *The car doesn't run on gas; it uses a battery-powered **technology**.*

territory (**ter**-u-tor-ē) *n.* a specific area of land that belongs to you. *A long fence marks the edges of our farm's **territory**.*

terror (**ter**-rur) *n.* feeling of great fear. *The actress in the horror movie had a look of **terror** on her face.*

token (**tō**-kun) *adj.* one person or thing that is included to supposedly represent a larger group. *A **token** female on the all-male team was supposed to show that the group included both sexes.*

• **trace** (**trās**) *n.* small sign that shows that someone or something has been in a place. *The police searched for fingerprints or any other **trace** of the man at the crime scene.*

tragedy (**tra**-ju-dē) *n.* a terrible event or disaster. *The earthquake **tragedy** left people homeless, and many children became orphans.*

transcend (tran-**send**) *v.* to rise above or go beyond. *Art is something that **transcends** the limits of language.*

• **transform** (trans-**form**) *v.* to change something in an important way. *I **transformed** my sketch into a painting.*

U

unite (yū-**nīt**) *v.* to bring together. *When neighbors **unite**, they can change their community.*

V

value (**val**-yū) *v.* to think something is important or useful. *I **value** friends more than money.*

variety (vu-**rī**-u-tē) *n.* representation of many different things. *The people in the group represent a **variety** of backgrounds from all over the world.*

vulnerable (**vul**-nu-ru-bul) *adj.* weak and easily hurt; helpless. *The small child was lost and **vulnerable** without his mother.*

page 885

Index of Graphic Organizers

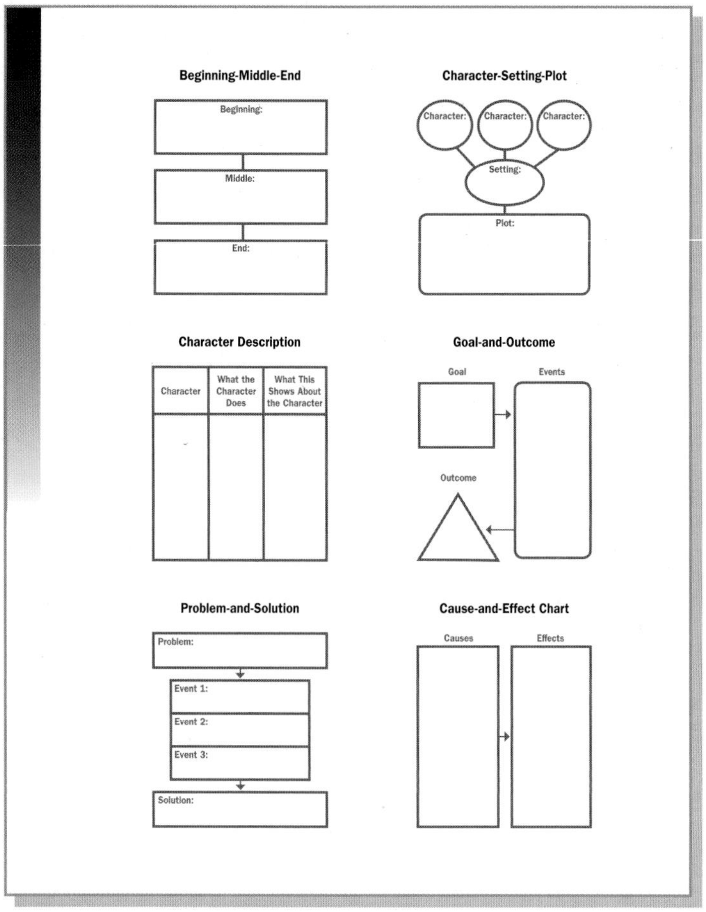

page 886

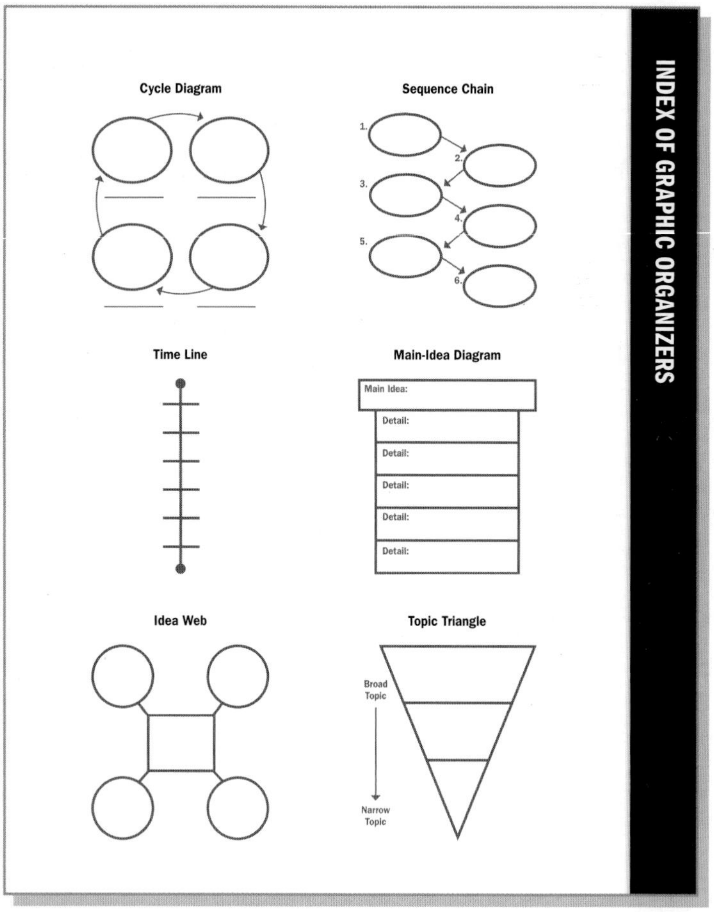

page 887

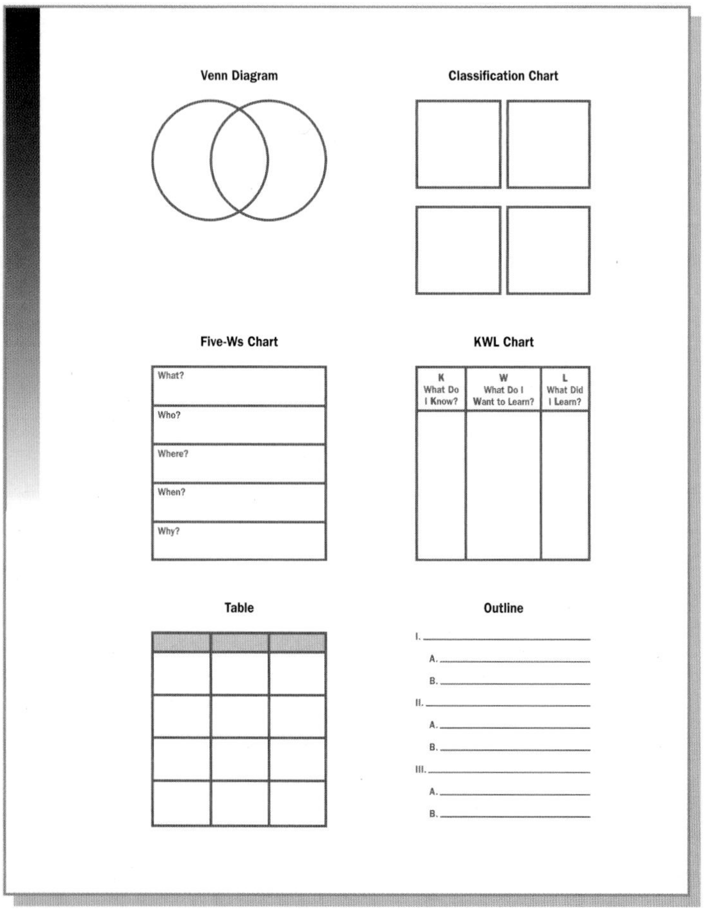

page 888

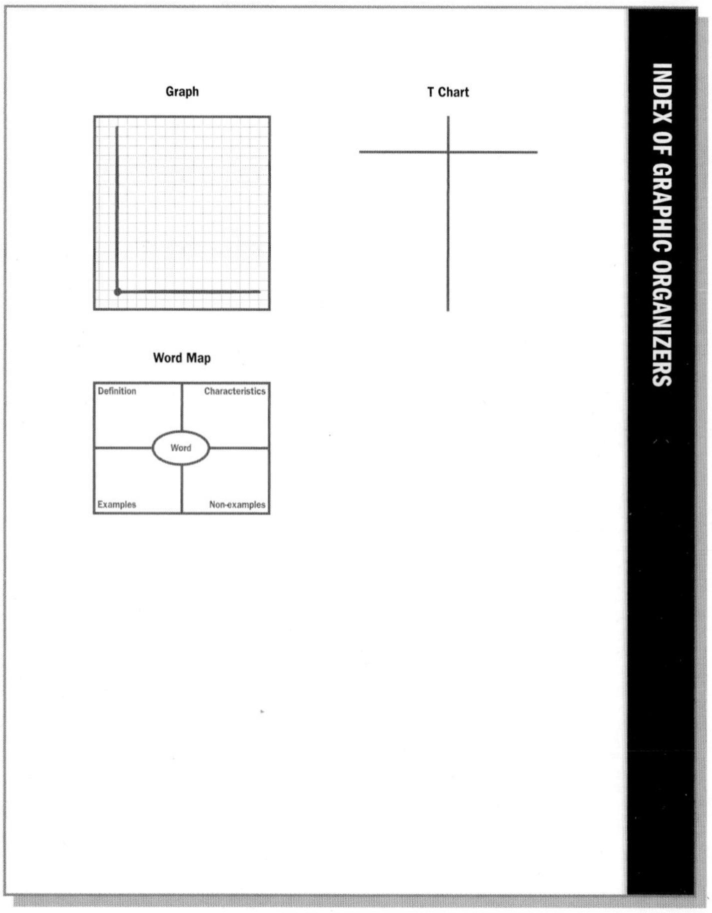

page 889

Common Core State Standards

myNGconnect.com

Search Lessons by Standard

my NG connect™

EDGE Teacher | NGL Sales Demo School C | Nat Geo Learning Sales Demo Room 23A | ▼ Help | Sign out

⌂ Home ▼ Global Search ✕

◄ 🔟 Planner Daily View

Simple Search **Standards Search**

The standards search allows you to find activities aligned to a standard.
1. Use the pull-down menus and keyword field to find your target standards.
2. Click a row in the standards table to find aligned activities.

Grade: 9-10 | ▼ Reading: Literature ▼

Keywords: [] Find Standards

9 Standards Found

Grade	Code	Strand	Standard
9-10	CC.RL.9-10.1	Reading: Literature	Cite several pieces of textual evidence to support analysis of what the text says explicitly as well as inferences drawn from the text.
9-10	CC.RL.9-10.2	Reading: Literature	Determine a theme or central idea of a text and analyze in detail its development over the course of the text, including how it emerges and is shaped and refined by specific details;provide an objective summary of the text.
9-10	CC.RL.9-10.3	Reading: Literature	Analyze how complex characters (e.g., those with multiple or conflicting motivations) develop over the course of a text, interact with other characters, and advance the plot or develop the theme.
9-10	CC.RL.9-10.4	Reading: L	
9-10	CC.RL.9-10.5	Reading: L	
9-10	CC.RL.9-10.6	Reading: L	
9-10	CC.RL.9-10.7	Reading: L	
9-10	CC.RL.9-10.9	Reading: L	
9-10	CC.RL.9-10.10	Reading: L	

NATIONAL GEOGRAPHIC LEARNING | CENGAGE Learning

my NG connect™ User Management Console (UMC) Jenny Morales Change Password Help Log out

Home Manage File Rostering Reports & Grading

Reports & Grading

Home → Period 2 Class → Standards Report → Life Science Standards Report

Edge Standards Report - Class
Reading: Literature

Level A | ▼ Reading Literature | ▼ Go

Teacher:	Morales, Jenny
Grade:	Level A
Class:	Period 2 Class
School:	Demo School
District:	Demo District

Student Performance by Standards

Student Name	Test Score	Standards Performance								
		CC.RL.9-10.1	CC.RL.9-10.2	CC.RL.9-10.3	CC.RL.9-10.4	CC.RL.9-10.5	CC.RL.9-10.6	CC.RL.9-10.7	CC.RL.9-10.8	CC.RL.9-10.9
Clayton, Lamar	50%	●	●	●	●	◐	◯	◐	●	●
Corah, Bailey	90%	●	●	●	◯	●	●	●	◐	●
Fuente, Manuel	50%	●	●	●	◐	◐	●	◐	●	●
Gomez, Alejandra	100%	●	●	●	●	●	◐	●	●	◯
Johnson, Shawn	80%	●	◐	●	◯	●	●	◐	●	◯
Class Average	**74%**	●	◐	●	◐	●	◐	●	●	●

● 0% - 49% ◐ 50% - 69% ◯ 70% - 79% ● 80% - 100%

NatGeoUI 1.1.6

NATIONAL GEOGRAPHIC LEARNING | CENGAGE Learning

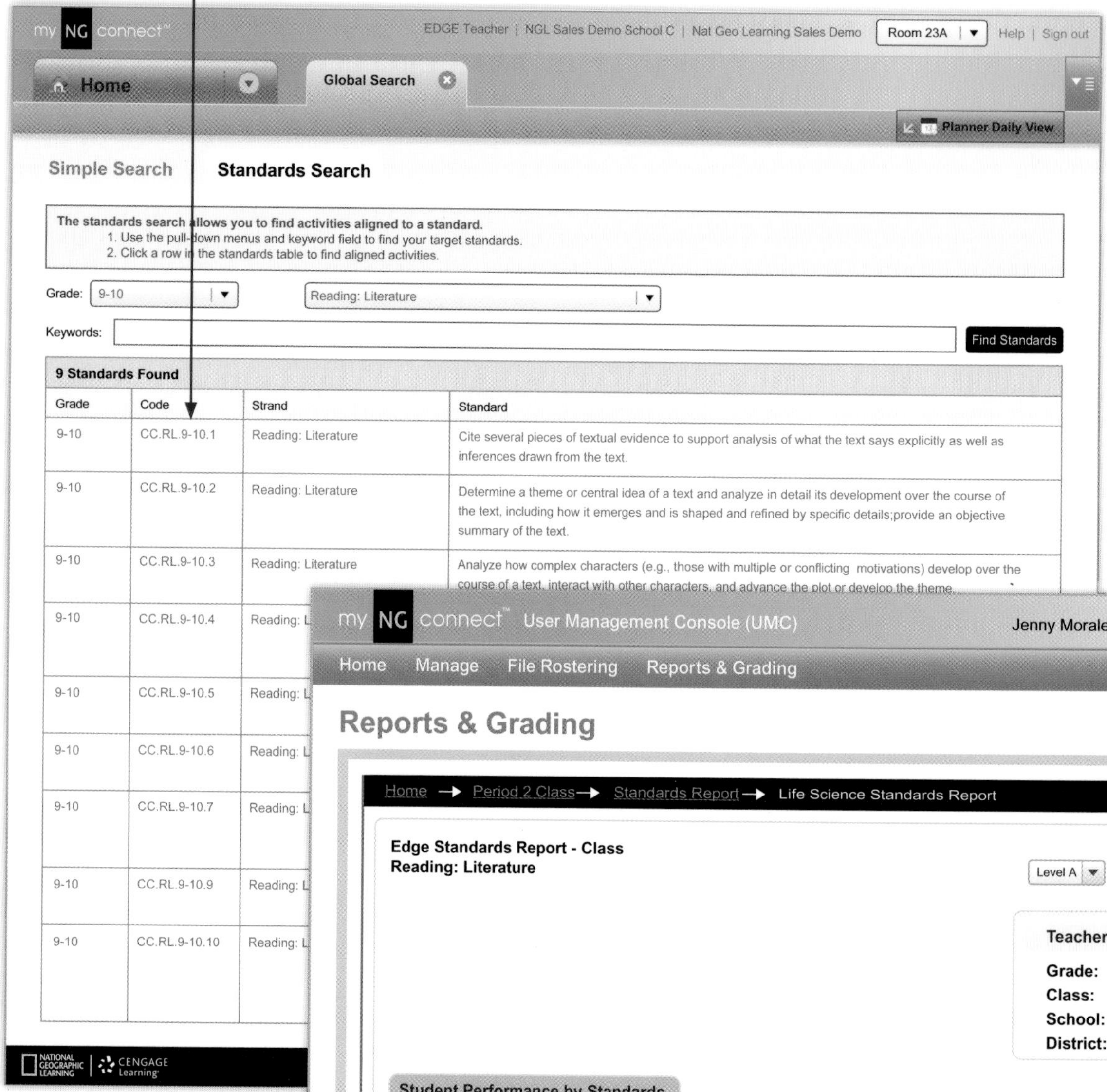

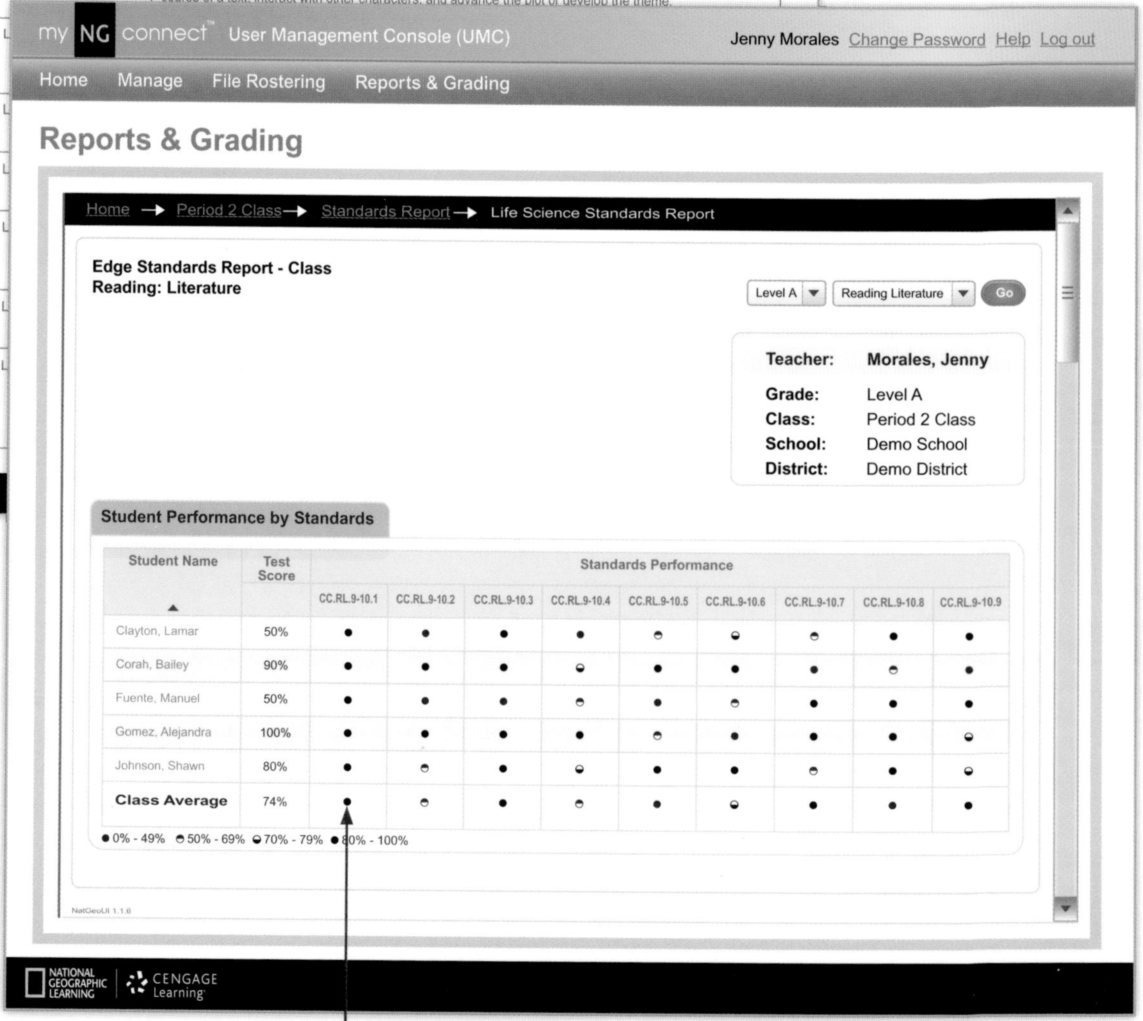

Monitor Progress

Contents

Framing Academic Language to Support English Language Learners

The Common Core State Standards (CCSS) present increased demands for all students, including English Language Learners (ELLs). ELLs must develop the same skills and strategies as their peers and also develop the language skills to understand English and express themselves in English. The CCSS require students to engage in rigorous activities that require academic language. They must describe their reasoning, share explanations, make conjectures, justify conclusions, argue from evidence, and negotiate meaning from complex texts. ELLs need instruction that enables them to comprehend abstract or unfamiliar ideas and concepts they encounter in both reading and listening. These are often called interpretative modes. In addition to constructing meaning from what they hear and read, ELLs need to express themselves through both speaking and writing using academic language. These are often called productive and collaborative modes. Without this language, ELLs cannot actively participate in these rigorous literacy activities.

A variety of point-of-use resources are integrated into this program to support ELLs' development of academic language. ***Edge, Reading, Writing, and Language*** incorporates Academic Language Frames, Multi-Level Strategies, language transfer supports, instruction in language functions, and other features to help meet the needs of ELLs. ***Edge*** also includes frequent and varied opportunities to engage in partner, small-group, and whole-class discussions. Research shows that when students engage in academic discussion, they build language proficiency. These discussions cover an array of instructional goals:

- **Language Development** Language lessons introduce language functions, grammar concepts, and provide meaningful, authentic opportunities to rehearse newly-acquired language skills.
- **Interpretive** As students encounter literature, media, and other resources in the program, they engage in critical evaluation central to meeting the rigorous goals of the CCSS. They analyze characters in literature, critique arguments in persuasive texts, evaluate word choice, and engage in other literacy activities that provide opportunities for oral language development.
- **Reading and Writing Process** Students use academic language as they engage in writing, plan presentations, conduct research, and participate in other expressive activities. This involves the collaborative of language.
- **Content** Students synthesize new ideas from reading and writing activities to engage discuss and debate Guiding Questions. Acquisition of content crosses all modes of language and includes dynamics that have unique challenges and needs.

To help ELLs express themselves as they work on lessons connected to the Common Core, this section includes oral language frames and strategies that can be general scaffolds for ELLs who have literacy or content knowledge and abilities but lack the English language skills to express what they are thinking or what they know. You will see that direct links are made for the reading and speaking and listening standards. For writing and language standards, we have focused on procedural language that supports students. This language includes frames for peer conferences that support the revising, editing, and proofreading steps in the writing process.

As you review these frames, notice we have organized them into B beginning I intermediate A advanced proficiency levels. In this way, all students at all proficiency levels can participate and express their knowledge and ideas. Note too that the frames are representative and do not capture the full universe for expressing ideas and sharing information.

Using the Language Frames

As you introduce or review skills and concepts, follow these steps for using the language frames.

1. **Model language**. Display the language frames and model the language you want your students to produce. If your classroom includes students at varying language proficiency levels, be sure to model expressions for all proficiencies to provide multiple access points. Consider posting the frames or having students add them to their notebooks or study guides for future student reference.

2. **Say the frame aloud**. Invite students to repeat the frames after you to rehearse pronunciation. This will help frontload the expressions so students can focus their attention on the new content and skills in the target lesson.

3. **Practice the frame with familiar content**. Give students opportunities to practice using language as they discuss familiar content—topics for which they have background knowledge or texts they have already read and enjoyed.

4. **Monitor and support students**. As students participate in the target activity, monitor and support students. Prompt self-correction and encourage the use of academic language.

Strategies for Supporting Language Frames

In addition to using this general routine, keep the following guidelines in mind:

Build a Supportive Classroom Culture Create a classroom culture where diverse students feel free to make mistakes, speak up, and express divergent opinions as they experiment with new language. Students from different home countries or family backgrounds will have varying experiences and comfort with practices common in U.S. classrooms. Remember too that adolescents from every language background pay more attention to peers than adults and adjust their behavior to navigate the social aspects of middle school. So, explicitly and frequently reiterate the importance of active participation in oral language activities and the importance of trying out new language.

Build Metalinguistic Awareness As students' language proficiency and knowledge increase, encourage students to think and discuss the structure of English. Support students as they think about parts of speech and how sentences are constructed. Foster word consciousness and encourage students to ask questions about vocabulary and syntax. Reward students for experimenting with language by recording alternative expressions to the list of frames displayed for the class.

Build linguistic awareness into self-monitoring and self-correction as well. When prompting self-correction, be explicit about how language functions, grammar, and usage rules apply in authentic contexts. By making the reason behind a particular correction explicit, students get authentic, contextualized reinforcement for previously-learned language functions and patterns.

Support Language-Learning Strategies New words and phrases are encountered every day and all students need to build strategies for learning new words and expressions. The following may be particularly useful to teach:

- **Circumlocution** – Students who struggle with new vocabulary or syntax to try expressing themselves in a different way.
- **Using Language Patterns** – Remind students to notice language patterns to more quickly acquire and use academic language. Students can listen for words that are often repeated and for patterns that are typical in expression.

Balance Scaffolds and Rigor Adjusting the level of scaffolding is critical to fostering learning and independence. Unfortunately, many students get "stuck" at intermediate or advanced proficiency levels and become long-term English language learners. To avoid this situation, adjust your use of scaffolds and expectations of rigor. Scaffolds must be deliberate and appropriate. When you display and model language frames, be sure to include all levels. Exposing students, even beginners, to more sophisticated language is important preparation for achieving longer-term success. As you monitor student participation in discussions and other oral-language activities, encourage students who are ready to elaborate or restate ideas using higher levels of language. By using the point-of-use scaffolds provided in ***Edge, Reading, Writing, and Language*** and incorporating the following Language Frames into instruction, you will help equip the ELLs in your classroom with the language and literacy skills essential for academic work in all subject-area classrooms and for later success in their college experiences and/or careers.

Language Proficiency Levels

Stages of Language Acquisition

The following descriptors and strategies should help you support your students at all stages of language proficiency. Keep in mind that the stages may vary by language domain. For example, some students may be beginning speakers and intermediate readers while others may be advanced speakers and beginning writers. Also recognize that proficiency will improve over time and that it is valuable to push students to use more advanced frames as they are able. The assessments provided in the program will help you measure and monitor language acquisition and adjust scaffolds, grouping, and challenges to support each individual student.

STAGES AND BEHAVIORS	TEACHING STRATEGIES
Beginning	
Newcomers & Beginners: • enter the program with little or survival vocabulary or language structures • respond non-verbally by pointing, gesturing, nodding, or drawing • participate in simple, face-to-face discussions • have little or no knowledge of foundational reading skills • lack the English vocabulary and English language structures necessary to address grade-appropriate writing tasks • begin to respond with yes/no or one- or two-word responses • read simple language that is familiar, patterned text; read language experience texts • comprehend familiar texts or topics presented in accessible ways • repeat and recite memorable language • use routine expressions independently • respond with phrases, fragments, and simple subject/verb-based structures • write patterned text, short captions; complete simple cloze sentences	**Newcomers & Beginners benefit when teachers:** • implement an intensive, individualized or small-group emergent literacy program, including instruction in the English alphabet • provide substantial language scaffolding for receptive and productive tasks including gestures, real objects, and other visuals to clarify concepts • provide ample age-appropriate oral-to-print and emergent literacy experiences • use visuals to teach key vocabulary and concepts for social, survival, and classroom settings • use visuals to teach key vocabulary and concepts necessary for academic discussion • use simple sentence structures and language patterns during instruction • provide abundant opportunities for active listening, utilizing props, visuals, and real objects • activate prior knowledge, build background, and use visuals before reading activities • provide opportunities to read literature in short "chunks" • support reading with direct phonics instruction • avoid forcing students to speak before they are ready but encourage them to try one or two words, choral speech, echoed responses, or patterned speech (including songs and chants) • model academic language • group students with more proficient learners • ask yes/no, either/or, and Who? What? Where? When? questions • have students label/manipulate pictures and real objects • provide short frames for students to complete with one- or two-word responses or word banks • use native language resources to build background of key concepts

STAGES AND BEHAVIORS	TEACHING STRATEGIES
Intermediate	
Intermediate students: • understand simple spoken English used in routine academic and social settings • have the ability to speak in a simple manner, using English commonly heard in routine academic and social settings • sustain connected discourse, using more extensive vocabulary • shows some independence in acquiring conceptual knowledge and related vocabulary • understand "chunks" or gist of language, when engaged in discussions or reading by using on picture clues, titles, and other cues • express comprehension and respond to literature with structured support • understand more details in spoken English • read resources independently following oral previews or experiences with print • use knowledge of English vocabulary, English language structures, and content to address grade-appropriate writing tasks with some scaffolding and pre-teaching • write from models for a variety of purposes, audiences, and tasks	**Intermediate students benefit when teachers:** • provide moderate language scaffolding • provide direct instruction in key vocabulary necessary for academic discussion • expose students to a variety of understandable texts • leverage scaffolds in texts including picture supports, vocabulary supports, and comprehension supports • use graphic organizers or storyboards for retelling or role-plays or note taking • structure and support group discussion to support application of language patterns • structure research projects and guide use of reference resources • ask open-ended questions; model, expand, restate, and enrich student language • provide language frames for students to complete with phrases and sentences • push students to elaborate their ideas orally and in writing, using models as appropriate • provide accessible content-area texts and multimedia resources, trade books, newspapers, magazines, etc., to promote conceptual development • respond genuinely to student writing and hold conferences that highlight student strengths and progress • teach vocabulary strategies such as using affixes, roots and cognates
ADVANCED	
Advanced students: • understand, with limited second language acquisition support, grade-appropriate spoken English used in academic and social settings • understand some non-literal, idiomatic, and academic language • respond with connected discourse, extensive vocabulary, and decreasing grammatical errors and some self-correction • initiate and sustain academic discussions using grade-appropriate English in academic and social settings with limited linguistic supports • understand and respond with increasing levels of accuracy, audience-appropriateness, and correctness • respond with longer phrases/sentences and increasing grammatical accuracy and may, with prompting and support, use more complex, grade-level language structures and patterns • independently read and comprehend increasingly complex texts, including texts with grade-level qualitative complexity and levels approaching grade-level quantitative complexity • recognize some language subtleties including an author's or speakers word choice • respond to literature by explaining, describing, comparing, analyzing, evaluating, and retelling • have English vocabulary and grasp of English language structures adequate to address grade-appropriate writing tasks with second language acquisition support • write connected narratives, informational texts, and arguments • use a repertoire of language-learning strategies to self-monitor, self-correct, and expand English language skills • read, write, and discuss content-area concepts in greater depth	**Advanced students benefit when teachers:** • provide light linguistic scaffolding and foster independence • provide opportunities to create oral and written narratives • focus on communication in meaningful contexts where students express themselves in speech and print for a wide range of purposes, tasks, and audiences • structure group discussions • recognize and encourage self-correction and the use of language-learning strategies • model and encourage use of more complex vocabulary and language patterns and structures • promote metalinguistic awareness and encourage the use of more sophisticated sentence structures, including the use of embedded clauses, in speaking and writing • guide use of reference resources for research • facilitate more advanced literature studies and provide access to increasingly complex texts • teach text features, genre distinctions, and guide students to attend to more subtle and abstract elements of texts including author's word choices • teach different types of writing and give practice opportunities for writing narratives, informational texts, and arguments.

Common Core Language Frames

Grades 9–10

Reading Literature

Key Ideas and Details

Code	Standard	Language Function/ Skill	Language Frames
RL.9-10.1	Cite strong and thorough textual evidence to support analysis of what the text says explicitly as well as inferences drawn from the text.	**Cite Text Evidence**	**B** **1.** I read ____. I think ____. **2.** Page ____ says ____. **3.** I read this. I think ____. **4.** This says ____. I think ____. **5.** The text says ____. That makes me think ____. **I** **1.** The [poem / paragraph / dialog / line / page] says ____. That makes me think [of] ____. **2.** The author writes/states ____. This means ____. **3.** The author uses the [word / phrase / image] ____. This tells me ____. **4.** I think ____ because the story/poem says ____. **A** **1.** The story/poem says ____, which makes me think [of] ____. **2.** Because the text/author says ____, I know ____. **3.** The ____ [word(s) / phrase(s) / image(s)] indicates ____. **4.** I think the author uses the [word / phrase / image] in order to ____.
		Make Inferences	**B** **1.** I read ____. I know ____. I think ____. **I** **1.** I read ____. I know ____ and so ____. **A** **1.** The text says ____. I know ____ so I can infer ____. **2.** The author does not say so explicitly, but he/she says ____, and I know ____, so ____. **3.** The author implies that ____, so ____.

Language Proficiency Level Key
B Beginner
I Intermediate
A Advanced

Reading Informational Text

Key Ideas and Details

Code	Standard	Language Function/ Skill	Language Frames
RI.9-10.1	Cite strong and thorough textual evidence to support analysis of what the text says explicitly as well as inferences drawn from the text.	**Cite Text Evidence**	**B** 1. I read ____. I think ____. 2. Page says ____. 3. I read this. I think ____. 4. This says ____. I think ____. 5. The text says ____. That makes me think ____. **I** 1. The [section / paragraph / quote / line] says ____. That makes me think [of] ____. 2. The author writes/says ____. This means ____. 3. The author uses [word / phrase / pictures] this tells me ____. 4. I think ____ because the text says ____. **A** 1. The ____ [section / paragraph / quote / line] says ____ which makes me think [of] ____. 2. Because the text author says ____, I know/think ____. 3. The ____ [word(s) / phrase(s) / image(s)] indicates ____. 4. I think the author uses the [word / phrase / image] in order to ____.
		Make Inferences	**B** 1. I read ____. I know ____. I think ____. **I** 1. I read ____. I know ____ and so ____. **A** 1. The text says ____. I know ____ so I can infer ____. 2. The author does not say so explicitly, but he/she says ____, and I know ____, so ____. 3. The author implies that ____, so ____.

Common Core Language Frames, continued

Grades 9–10

Code	Standard	Language Function/ Skill		Language Frames
Reading Literature, continued				
Key Ideas and Details, continued				
RL.9-10.2	Determine a theme or central idea of a text and analyze in detail its development over the course of the text, including how it emerges and is shaped and refined by specific details; provide an objective summary of the text.	**Determine Theme**	B	1. The theme / most important idea is ____. 2. The story is about ____. 3. The story mostly tells us/talks about ____.
			I	1. The theme of this text is ____. One clue is ____. 2. The characters / setting / symbols / plot support(s) the theme because ____.
			A	1. The theme of / most important idea in this text is ____, which is supported by details such as the ____. I know this because ____. 2. I think the author is trying to say ____ because ____. 3. Because ____, I can conclude ____.
		Summarize	B	1. The story is about ____ and ____. It happens in ____. 2. First ____. Next, / Then, ____. Last, / At the end, ____. 3. The author writes about ____ (and ____). This supports the theme/main idea.
			I	1. The text / story / article is about ____. 2. The first thing that happens is ____. The next event is ____. 3. The main character has to ____ because ____. As a result, he/she ____. Then ____. 4. The author explains the problem is that ____. One action taken is ____. Another possible solution is ____. The result is ____. 5. The author includes details such as ____ and ____ to support the theme/main idea.
			A	1. The story's is about ____; it takes place in ____. 2. The author begins by ____. He/She then ____, and concludes by ____. 3. In order to support the theme/main idea, the author includes details such as ____ and ____, which show ____.

Language Proficiency Level Key
B Beginner
I Intermediate
A Advanced

Reading Informational Text continued

Key Ideas and Details, continued

Code	Standard	Language Function/ Skill	Language Frames
RI.9-10.2	Determine a central idea of a text and analyze its development over the course of the text, including how it emerges and is shaped and refined by specific details; provide an objective summary of the text.	**Determine the Main Idea**	**B** 1. The central / main idea is ____. This detail shows the central idea. 2. The text is about ____. 3. The text mostly tells us/talks about ____. **I** 1. The main idea in this text is ____. I know that because ____. 2. The detail ____ support(s) the main idea because/by ____. **A** 1. The main idea is ____, which is supported by the details such as/like ____ and ____. 2. When I connect the details ____, ____, and ____ I can conclude that the main idea is ____. I think the author is trying to say ____ because ____. Because the ____[genre]____ says, I can conclude ____.
		Summarize	**B** 1. This is about ____. 2. First ____. Next, / Then, ____. Last, / At the end, ____. 3. The author writes about ____ (and ____). This supports the main idea. **I** 1. This ____[genre]____ is about____ and____. 2. First, the author writes____ and then____. Finally, he/she writes____. 3. The author includes details such as ____ and ____ to support the theme/main idea. **A** 1. The author begins by ____. He/She then ____, and concludes by ____. 2. To summarize, the ____[genre]____ explains / describes / argues / provides information about ____. 3. In order to support the theme/main idea, the author includes details such as ____ and ____, which show ____.

Common Core Language Frames, continued

Grades 9–10

Reading Literature, continued

Key Ideas and Details, continued

Code	Standard	Language Function/ Skill	Language Frames
RL.9-10.3	Analyze how complex characters (e.g., those with multiple or conflicting motivations) develop over the course of a text, interact with other characters, and advance the plot or develop the theme.	**Retell** **Analyze Plot**	**B** **1.** First ____. Next, ____. Last, ____. **2.** In the beginning, ____. Next, ____. Finally/at the end, ____. **I** **1.** First the ____ and then ____. Finally, ____. **2.** At the beginning, ____. As a result of / Since / Because ____, after that ____. Finally, ____. **3.** The conflict is that/between ____. One complication is ____. The climax is ____. In the resolution, ____. **A** **1.** The story conflict begins when ____. During the rising action, the complications are ____, ____, and ____. At the climax, ____. In the resolution, ____. **2.** When the story begins, ____. Consequently / Therefore, ____, after that ____. As the story ends, ____.
		Analyze Characters	**B** **1.** [Name] is / does ____. Then ____ happens. After that, [Name] is / does ____. **2.** [Event] happens. Then [Name] changes. First, he/she was ____. Then he/she was ____. **3.** [Name] wants (to) ____. He/She ____. **I** **1.** Because/Due to the fact that [event] happens, [Name] changes. He/She was ____. Then he/she was ____. **2.** At first, the character [Name] ____ because [event]. After [event] he/she _[Name] changes/responds by ____. **3.** Before [event] happens [Name] was ____. After [event] happens, he/she ____. **4.** Because [Name] wants (to) ____, he/she ____. As a result, ____. **A** **1.** The character [Name] begins by ____. He/She changes / responds / adjusts to ____ by ____. **2.** [Name] is motivated to ____ because ____.

Language Proficiency Level Key
B **Beginner**
I **Intermediate**
A **Advanced**

Reading Informational Text continued

Key Ideas and Details, continued

Code	Standard	Language Function/ Skill	Language Frames
RI.9-10.3	Analyze how the author unfolds an analysis or series of ideas or events, including the order in which the points are made, how they are introduced and developed, and the connections that are drawn between them.	**Analyze Interactions Among Ideas**	**B** 1. The author writes ____. It shows ____. 2. The author writes about ____. One example he/she gives is ____. Another example is ____. ____ is connected to ____. 3. First, the author writes ____. Next, ____. Last, ____. **I** 1. The author writes about ____[event]____. He/She tells about actions that led to the event, such as ____. He/She also describes the results of the event. One result was ____. 2. The author begins with ____. He/She then writes ____. Finally, he/she writes ____. **A** 1. The author | gives an example of / tells a story about | ____. to talk about ____ | (person) / (event) / (idea) |. 2. The author | gives an example of / tells a story | ____. In ____, he/she is showing the reader that | (person) / (event) / (idea) | ____. 3. The author first writes (about) ____, followed by ____. He/She concludes with/by ____.

Common Core Language Frames, continued

Grades 9–10

Reading Literature, continued

Craft and Structure, continued

Code	Standard	Language Function/ Skill	Language Frames
RL.9-10.4	Determine the meaning of words and phrases as they are used in the text, including figurative and connotative meanings; analyze the cumulative impact of specific word choices on meaning and tone (e.g., how the language evokes a sense of time and place; how it sets a formal or informal tone).	**Determine Word Meaning**	**B** 1. The writer says ____. 2. This word/phrase shows/means ____. **I** 1. The author used the word/phrase ____ to show ____. 2. The word/phrase ____ means ____. 3. The word/phrase means more than just ____. It means ____. **A** 1. The author used the word/phrase ____; its figurative/connotative meaning is ____, and it shows ____. 2. "____" is an example | of a simile / of a metaphor / of personification | . It compares ____ to ____. I think the author | means / wanted to say / wanted the reader to think | ____. 3. The author used the word/phrase ____; its figurative/connotative meaning is ____, and it shows ____. 4. Because the author used the | similar / metaphor / comparison | ____ I think he/she was trying to make the reader think/feel | ____ about ____. / that ____ was like ____. |
		Analyze Connotative Meanings	**I** 1. The word/phrase ____ means ____. It has a | positive / negative | connotation. It makes readers feel ____. 2. I think the author used the word/phrase ____ to make the reader feel ____. **A** 1. The word/phrase ____ makes the reader feel ____ about ____. 2. Because the author used the word ____, I think he/she wanted the reader to feel ____ about ____. 3. If the author had used the word ____ instead of ____ it would make the reader feel ____ instead of ____.
			This Language Function is not applicable to literature.

Language Proficiency Level Key
B Beginner
I Intermediate
A Advanced

Reading Informational Text

Craft and Structure, continued

Code	Standard	Language Function/ Skill	Language Frames
RI.9-10.4	Determine the meaning of words and phrases as they are used in a text, including figurative, connotative, and technical meanings; analyze the cumulative impact of specific word choices on meaning and tone (e.g., how the language of a court opinion differs from that of a newspaper).	**Determine Word Meaning**	**B** 1. The writer says ____. 2. This word/phrase shows/means ____. **I** 1. The author used the word/phrase ____ to show ____. 2. The word/phrase ____ means ____. 3. The word/phrase means more than just ____. It means ____. **A** 1. The author used the word/phrase ____; its figurative/connotative meaning is ____, and it shows ____. 2. "____" is an example | of a simile / of a metaphor / personification |. It compares ____ to ____. I think the author | means / wanted to say / wanted the reader to think | ____. 3. The author used the word/phrase ____; its figurative/connotative meaning is ____, and it shows ____. 4. Because the author used the | similar / metaphor / comparison | ____ I think he/she was trying to make the reader think/feel | ____ about ____. / that ____ was like ____. |
		Analyze Connotative Meanings	**I** 1. The word/phrase ____ means ____. It has a | positive / negative | connotation. It makes readers feel ____. 2. I think the author used the word/phrase ____ to make the reader feel ____. **A** 1. The word/phrase ____ makes the reader feel ____ about ____. 2. Because the author used the word ____, I think he/she wanted the reader to feel ____ about ____. 3. If the author had used the word ____ instead of ____, it would make the reader feel ____ instead of ____.
		Analyze Technical Meanings	**B** 1. The | word / phrase | ____ means ____. In | science, / math, / social studies, | it means ____. **I A** 1. | In everyday language, the | the | word / phrase | ____ means ____, but in | science, / math, / social studies, | it means ____.

Common Core Language Frames, continued

Grades 9–10

Code	Standard	Language Function/ Skill	Language Frames
Reading Literature, continued			
Craft and Structure, continued			
RL.9-10.4, continued	Determine the meaning of words and phrases as they are used in the text, including figurative and connotative meanings; analyze the cumulative impact of specific word choices on meaning and tone (e.g., how the language evokes a sense of time and place; how it sets a formal or informal tone).	**Analyze Author's Word Choice**	**B** 1. This word(s) makes me think/feel ____. **I** 1. I think the author chose the word because ____. 2. "____" is formal/informal. The author uses it to show ____. **A** 1. The author chose to use the word ____. He/She could have said ____. By saying ____, the author wanted the reader to think/feel ____. 2. The author used the word/phrase ____ instead of ____ because ____. 3. "____" is formal/informal language. The author uses it to set a ____ tone.
RL.9-10.5	Analyze how an author's choices concerning how to structure a text, order events within it (e.g., parallel plots), and manipulate time (e.g., pacing, flashbacks) create such effects as mystery, tension, or surprise.	**Analyze Author's Choices**	**B** 1. The author writes ____ because/to show ____. 2. This part goes back in time because/to show ____. **I** 1. The author uses the [sentence / paragraph / chapter / section] "____" [because / to show] it means ____. 2. The [sentence / paragraph / chapter / section] moves faster/goes back in time because/to show ____. **A** 1. The [sentence / paragraph / chapter / section] "____" builds the [story's / article's] ideas by ____. 2. The author manipulates time in this [paragraph / chapter / section] by using faster pacing/flashbacks in order to ____.

Language Proficiency Level Key
B **Beginner**
I **Intermediate**
A **Advanced**

Reading Informational Text

Craft and Structure, continued

Code	Standard	Language Function/ Skill	Language Frames
RI.9-10.4, continued	Determine the meaning of words and phrases as they are used in a text, including figurative, connotative, and technical meanings; analyze the cumulative impact of specific word choices on meaning and tone (e.g., how the language of a court opinion differs from that of a newspaper).	**Analyze Author's Word Choice**	B 1. This word(s) makes me think/feel ____. I 1. The author uses the word(s)/phrase ____ because ____. 2. I think the author chose the word because ____. 3. In a formal English, we say, ____. In a less formal English, we say ____. A 1. The author chose to use the word ____. He/She could have said ____. By saying ____, the author wanted the reader to think/feel ____. 2. The author used the word/phrase ____ instead of ____ because ____. 3. The reason the author used the word/phrase ____ instead of ____ is ____.
RI.9-10.5	Analyze in detail how an author's ideas or claims are developed and refined by particular sentences, paragraphs, or larger portions of a text (e.g., a section or chapter).	**Analyze Text Structure: Chronological Order**	B 1. The events are in order. 2. The text tells about events. First ____ happens / happened. Then/Next ____ happens / happened. Last ____ happens / happened. I A 1. The text tells what happened in the order it happened. 2. The text is in sequential/chronological order. 3 The text tells about a series of events. First ____________. Then ____________. After that, ____________. As a result of this / Finally, ____________
		Analyze Text Structure: Problem/ Solution	B 1. The author writes about a problem. The problem is ____. Then the author writes about a solution. The solution is ____. 2. __[Person]__ has a problem. It is ____________. [Person] thinks of a solution. It is ____________. I A 1. The author introduces the problem, which is ____________. He/She describes the issues: ____________ ____________, and ____. Then the author offers some possible solutions such as ____________ and ____________. Finally, the author explains the preferred option which is ____________. 2. The author writes about ____, which is a problem because ____. The author explains / describes / argues / notes ____. He/She advocates / suggests / presents / offers the solution ____, which solves the problem by ____.

Common Core Language Frames, continued

Grades 9–10

Code	Standard	Language Function/ Skill	Language Frames
Reading Literature, continued			
Craft and Structure, continued			
RL.9-10.5, continued	Analyze how an author's choices concerning how to structure a text, order events within it (e.g., parallel plots), and manipulate time (e.g., pacing, flashbacks) create such effects as mystery, tension, or surprise.	**Analyze Text Structure: Cause and Effect**	B I **1.** I read about how ____ cause(d) ____. **2.** As a result of __________, __________ happened. **3.** This part goes back in time because/to show ____. A **1.** First the author [describes / tells about] ____. Then the author [shows / describes] how ____ [results in / changes / causes] ____. **2.** The author writes about a character named ____. He/She [shows / suggests] that ____ because ____. **3.** I think that one reason that ____ in the story is because ____. As a result, ____.
		Analyze Text Structure: Compare and Contrast	B **1.** I read about ____ and ____. They are alike. They both ____. They are also different. One ____. The other ____. I **1.** The author compares ____ and ____. Both ____ and ____ have/are ____. ____ and ____ are different because. **2.** Although ________ and ________ are similar in some ways, such as ________ and ________, they are also different. One difference is ________. Another difference is ________. **3.** The [paragraph / chapter / section] moves faster/goes back in time because/to show ____. It shows how ____ and ____ are the same/different, because ____. A **1.** The author compares two things: ________ and ________. The author begins by telling how they are alike/different. For example, ________. Then the author explains their differences/similarities. One similarity is ________. A difference is ________. **2.** This text compares ____ and ____. Similarities include ____. Differences include ____. By comparing these things, the author shows ____. **3.** Some people think __[A]____ and ____[B]____ are the same. I disagree. ____[A]____ has/is ________ while ____[B]________ has/is __________.

Language Proficiency Level Key
B Beginner
I Intermediate
A Advanced

Reading Informational Text, continued

Craft and Structure, continued

Code	Standard	Language Function/ Skill	Level	Language Frames
RI.9-10.5, continued	Analyze in detail how an author's ideas or claims are developed and refined by particular sentences, paragraphs, or larger portions of a text (e.g., a section or chapter).	**Analyze Text Structure: Cause and Effect**	B	1. I read (in this paragraph/section/chapter) that ____ cause(s) ____. 2. ____ cause(d) ____. 3. First I read about ____. The effect of ____ is/was ____. 4. ____ happened. The result is/was ____________.
			I	1. First I read about ____. Then I learned how ____ cause(d) ____. 2. I read about ____ (in this paragraph/section/chapter). Then I read that ____ cause(d) ____. 3. I read about how ____ was/is caused by/causes ____. 4. The author tells about a cause and an effect. First he/she describes/tells about ____ (in this paragraph/section/chapter). Then he/she explains the solution ____. 5. As a result of ____________, ____________ happened.
			A	1. The author introduces the cause (in this paragraph/section/chapter), which is ____________. He/She describes the impact: ____________ ____________, and ____________. Then (in this paragraph/section/chapter) the author explains how ________ is a result of ________. 2. The author writes about ____. He/She shows / explains / describes / argues / notes the effects, which include ____ These effects clearly result from ____ because ____.
		Analyze Text Structure: Compare and Contrast	B	1. I read about ____ and ____. They are alike. They both ____. They are also different. One ____. The other ____.
			I	1. The author compares ____ and ____. Both ____ and ____ have/are ____. ____ and ____ are different because ____. 2. In this paragraph / section / chapter, the author shows how ____ and ____ are similar/different. Both ____ and ____ are/have. They are different because ____.
			A	1. The author compares two things: ________ and ________. The author begins by telling how they are alike/different. For example, ________. Then the author explains their differences/similarities. One similarity is ________. A difference is ________. 2. Some people think __[A]____ and ____[B]____ are the same. I disagree. ____[A]____ has/is ________ while ____[B]________ has/is ____________.

Common Core Language Frames, continued

Grades 9–10

Reading Literature, continued			
Craft and Structure, continued			
Code	**Standard**	**Language Function/ Skill**	**Language Frames**
RL.9-10.5, continued	Analyze in detail how an author's ideas or claims are developed and refined by particular sentences, paragraphs, or larger portions of a text (e.g., a section or chapter).	**Analyze Text Structure: Description**	B **1.** In this [paragraph / section / chapter], the author describes a ____. He/She says it has ____. I A **2.** The author describes (a) ____. He/She gives examples such as ____. **3.** The author describes (a) ____. It has several parts. One part is ____. Another part is ____.
RL.9-10.6	Analyze a particular point of view or cultural experience reflected in a work of literature from outside the United States, drawing on a wide reading of world literature.	**Explain Point of View / Analyze Viewpoint**	B **1.** The character says/thinks ____. It means ____. **2.** [Name] says/thinks ____. It means ____. **3.** [Name] is from ____. He/She feels ____. I **1.** The author writes ____. This shows the narrator's/speaker's point of view because ____. **2.** I know [Name] [is / thinks / believes] ____. We know this becasue the author writes ____. **3.** [Title] is a [legend / story / play / poem] from ____, so the narrator's/speaker's point of view is ____. A **1.** When the author writes that the narrator/speaker ____, it shows that he/she ____. **2.** [Name's] viewpoint is ____. We know this because the author writes____. **3.** Because [Title] is a [legend / story / play / poem] from ____, the narrator's/speaker's viewpoint is ____. In this way, the author shows ____.

Language Proficiency Level Key
B **Beginner**
I **Intermediate**
A **Advanced**

Reading Informational Text, continued

Craft and Structure, continued

Code	Standard	Language Function/ Skill	Language Frames
RI.9-10.6	Determine an author's point of view or purpose in a text and explain how it is conveyed in the text.	**Determine Point of View/ Purpose**	**B** 1. The author thinks ____. This is what he/she writes about it: "________." 2. I read/see ____. This shows the author is trying to [inform / explain / tell / argue] ____. 3. The author uses facts/feelings. He/She wants (to) ____. **I** 1. The author says ____ because [his / her] [point of view / purpose] is ____. 2. The author's purpose is ____ He/She [shows / explains / conveys] this by ____ 3. The author's viewpoint is ____. The reader understands this when the author writes ___________. 4. The author's viewpoint is ____. He/She uses facts/emotions to ____. **A** 1. When the author writes ____, it shows that [his / her] [point of view / purpose] is ____. 2. The words ____ show that the author thinks ____. 3. The author uses [logic / an emotional appeal / credibility] to show/convince readers (that) ____ .

Common Core Language Frames, continued

Grades 9–10

Reading Literature, continued			
Integration of Knowledge and Ideas			
Code	Standard	Language Function/ Skill	Language Frames
RL.9-10.7	Analyze the representation of a subject or a key scene in two different artistic mediums, including what is emphasized or absent in each treatment (e.g., Auden's "Musée des Beaux Arts" and Breughel's Landscape with the Fall of Icarus).	**Analyze Text Features/ Analyze Media**	**B** 1. The image / graph / video / sound shows ____. It is important becasue ____. 2. The image/graphic helps me understand because ____. 3. The story/poem has/doesn't have ____. The painting has/doesn't have ____. **I A** 1. The author included this illustration / diagram / chart / graph to show ____ (because ____). It is important because ____. 2. By adding the chart / graphic / photo, the author lets us see / shows us ____. This is important because ____. 3. The poem / story / painting emphasizes/omits ____ because the author/artist ____.
		Contrast Text and Media	**B** 1. I read ____. I felt / thought ____. I saw / heard ____. I felt/thought ____. **I** 1. When I read ____, I felt / thought / imagined ____. But when I saw / heard ____, I felt/thought ____. 2. The author / director / composer includes/leaves out ____ because ____. **A** 1. When I was reading ____, I imagined / pictured ____. Seeing / Hearing ____ was the same/different because ____. 2. When I read ____, I imagined / pictured ____. After seeing / hearing ____ however, I realized ____. 3. The author / director / composer emphasizes/omits ____ in order to ____.

Language Proficiency Level Key
B Beginner
I Intermediate
A Advanced

Reading Informational Text, continued

Integration of Knowledge and Ideas

Code	Standard	Language Function/ Skill	Language Frames
RI.9-10.7	Analyze various accounts of a subject told in different mediums (e.g., a person's life story in both print and multimedia), determining which details are emphasized in each account.	**Analyze Text Features/ Analyze Media**	B 1. The image / graph / video / sound shows ____. It is important becasue ____. 2. The image/graphic helps me understand because ____. I A 1. The author included this illustration / diagram / chart / graph to show ____ (because ____). It is important because ____. 2. By adding the chart / graphic / photo, the author lets us see / shows us ____. This is important because ____.
		Contrast Text and Media	B 1. I read ____. I felt / thought ____. I saw / heard ____. I felt/thought ____. I 1. When I read ____, I felt / thought / imagined ____. But when I saw / heard ____, I felt/thought ____. 2. The article/text says ____, but the movie/program says ____. It is different because ____. A 1. When I was reading ____, I imagined / pictured ____. Seeing / Hearing ____ was the same/different because ____. 2. When I read ____, I imagined / pictured ____. After seeing / hearing ____ however, I realized ____. 3. The author/director/composer emphasizes/omits ____ in order to ____.

Common Core Language Frames, continued

Grades 9–10

Reading Literature, continued			
Integration of Knowledge and Ideas, continued			
Code	**Standard**	**Language Function/ Skill**	**Language Frames**
RL.9-10.8	This Language Function is not applicable to literature.		

Language Proficiency Level Key
B **Beginner**
I **Intermediate**
A **Advanced**

Reading Informational Text, continued

Integration of Knowledge and Ideas, continued

Code	Standard	Language Function/ Skill	Language Frames
RI.9-10.8	Delineate and evaluate the argument and specific claims in a text, assessing whether the reasoning is valid and the evidence is relevant and sufficient; identify false statements and fallacious reasoning.	**Analyze Arguments**	**B** 1. The author says/believes ____. His/Her reason is ____. This reason supports/does not support his/her idea. 2. The author says ____. I think this is false/wrong because ____. **I** 1. The author claims/argues ____. The claim was supported/not supported by ____. 2. The author | claims / states / argues | ____. He/She | supports / does not support | the idea by/because ____ 3. The author | claims / states / argues | ____. The author includes evidence to support the claim. This evidence is ____. 4. The evidence ____ does not support the claim ____ because ________. 5. The claim ____ is not supported by clear evidence. 6. The author's statement ____ is false/incorrect because ____. **A** 1. I read the article ____. After evaluating it, the author did/did not do a good job supporting his/her claim. For example, ____. 2. The reason ____ helps the author connect the evidence ____ to the claim ____. 3. The author claims ____. He gives this/these reason(s) ____. It/They help(s) prove his point. 4. The evidence and reasons | are / are not | strong enough to support the claim ____. For example ____. 5. Although the author states/claims (that) ____, his/her reasoning is false/incorrect because ____.

Common Core Language Frames, continued

Grades 9–10

Reading Literature, continued			
Integration of Knowledge and Ideas, continued			
Code	**Standard**	**Language Function/ Skill**	**Language Frames**
RL.9-10.9	Analyze how an author draws on and transforms source material in a specific work (e.g., how Shakespeare treats a theme or topic from Ovid or the Bible or how a later author draws on a play by Shakespeare).	**Compare Genres**	**B** 1. Both stories are about ____. 2. The first one is/has ____. The second one is/has ____. 3. [Title] is/has ____. [Title] also is/has ____. 4. Both stories are about ____. [Title] is/has ____. But [Title] is/has ____. 5. [Title] is from ____ and [Title] is from ____. **I** 1. The stories' themes/topics are alike because they both ____. They are different because ____. 2. [Title] is a [form or genre]. And/But [Title] is a [form or genre]. They are both ____. 3. [Title] and [Title] are alike because ____. [Title] and [Title] are different because ____. 4. [Name] wrote [Title] in ____. [Name] developed the ideas in [Title], in ____. They are alike because ____. They are different because ____. **A** 1. The stories are alike because in the first text, the author approaches the theme/topic by ____. In the second, the author ____. They are different because ____. 2. [Title] is a [form or genre] so it has/is ____. And/But [Title] is a [form or genre] so it has/is ____. They are both ____. Although both are about ____, they take different approaches. In [Title 1], the author ____. In contrast, in [Title 2], the author ____. 3. [Title] was written by [Name] in ____. He/She develops/transforms the original idea by/because ____.

Language Proficiency Level Key
B Beginner
I Intermediate
A Advanced

Reading Informational Text, continued

Integration of Knowledge and Ideas, continued

Code	Standard	Language Function/ Skill	Language Frames
RI.9-10.9	Analyze seminal U.S. documents of historical and literary significance (e.g., Washington's Farewell Address, the Gettysburg Address, Roosevelt's Four Freedoms speech, King's "Letter from Birmingham Jail"), including how they address related themes and concepts.	**Compare Texts**	**B** 1. ____ is about ____. ____ is also about ____. Both tell/describe ________. 2. ____ is about ____. ____ is also about ____. They tell the story/event differently. [A] __________. [B] __________ **I** 1. The theme of both ____ and ____ is ____. 2. ____ and ____ are similar / different because ____. 3. ____ is ____. In contrast / However / On the other hand / Alternatively, ____ is ____. 4. ____ is ____. Similarly / Also, ____ is ____. 5. ____ is about ____. ____ is also about ____.____ and ____ are similar/ different because ____. **A** 1. While the theme of both ____ and ____ is ____, the first is a ____ and the second is a ____. They are similar/different because ________ 2. While the theme of both ____ and ____ is ____, the author of the first text ____ and the author of the second text ____. 3. ____ and ________ give different perspectives on ________ [story/event]. [A] does it by ________. [B], in contrast, ________.

Common Core Language Frames, continued

Grades 9–10

Reading Literature, continued			
Range of Reading and Level of Text Complexity			
Code	**Standard**	**Language Function/ Skill**	**Language Frames**
RL.9-10.10	By the end of grade 9, read and comprehend literature, including stories, dramas, and poems, in the grades 9-10 text complexity band proficiently, with scaffolding as needed at the high end of the range. By the end of grade 10, read and comprehend literature, including stories, dramas, and poems, at the high end of the grades 9-10 text complexity band independently and proficiently.	**Request Help**	**B** 1. Please help me [read / understand] this [word / sentence / section / verse / stanza / dialogue]. 2. What does ____ mean? **I A** 1. When I read ____, I needed some/no help. I need some help [reading / understanding] this [word / sentence / section / verse / stanza / dialogue]. 2. Can you tell me why [Name] thinks that ____?
		Reflect on Reading	**B** 1. I read ____, ____, and ____ [genres]. 2. I did not read any [genres]. **I A** 1. I didn't read any [genres]. 2. The hardest genre for me to understand is ____. The easiest genre for me to understand is ____.

Language Proficiency Level Key
B **Beginner**
I **Intermediate**
A **Advanced**

Reading Informational Text, continued

Range of Reading and Level of Text Complexity

Code	Standard	Language Function/ Skill	Language Frames
RI.9-10.10	By the end of grade 9, read and comprehend literacy nonfiction in the grades 9-10 text complexity band proficiently, with scaffolding as needed at the high end of the range. By the end of grade 10, read and comprehend literary nonfiction at the high end of the grades 9-10 text complexity band independently and proficiently.	**Request Help**	**B** 1. Please help me [read / understand] this [word / sentence / section / paragraph / chapter]. 2. What does ____ mean? **I A** 1. When I read ____, I needed some/no help. I need some help [reading / understanding] this [word / sentence / section / paragraph / chapter]. 2. Can you tell me why [Name] thinks that ____?
		Reflect on Reading	**B** 1. I read ____, ____, and ____ [genres]. 2. I did not read any [genres]. **I A** 1. I didn't read any [genres]. 2. The hardest genre for me to understand is ____. The easiest genre for me to understand is ____.

Common Core Language Frames, continued

Grades 9–10

A subset of writing standards are included in this section to reflect those skills and activities that involve more oral language.

Writing

Production and Distribution of Writing

Code	Standard	Language Function/ Skill	Language Frames
W.9-10.4	Produce clear and coherent writing in which the development, organization, and style are appropriate to task, purpose, and audience.	**Give Positive Feedback**	**B** **1.** This part / paragraph / section is good / clear / strong. **2.** I like this part because ____. **3.** I want to read more. **I** **1.** This section is very good / clear / interesting / entertaining / convincing because ____. **2.** This part / section / paragraph made me think/feel ____. **3.** This part is good. It reminds me of ____. **4.** This part / section / paragraph / scene has a strong voice / focus / development of ideas / organization. **5.** Your style works well for your audience because ____. **A** **1.** I like how you used the word(s) / phrase / example / detail ____ to show ____. It really makes the reader think / feel / understand ____. **2.** I think your readers will really feel / think / understand ____ because your ____ in this part / section / paragraph / scene is so ____. **3.** I noticed that you ____ in this part / section / paragraph / scene. That really made your writing ____.

Language Proficiency Level Key
B **Beginner**
I **Intermediate**
A **Advanced**

Writing continued

Production and Distribution of Writing continued

Code	Standard	Language Function/ Skill	Language Frames
W.9-10.5	Develop and strengthen writing as needed by planning, revising, editing, rewriting, or trying a new approach, focusing on addressing what is most significant for a specific purpose and audience.	**Request Clarification**	**B** 1. Can you make this [part / section / paragraph] more clear? 2. Why did you write this [word / sentence / paragraph / section]? **I A** 1. I'm not sure I understand this [part / section / paragraph]. 2. This [part / section / paragraph] is not [clear / complete]. 3. I'm a little confused because ____.
		Make Suggestions	**B** 1. You can make this [part / section / paragraph] ____. Try changing ____ to ____. 2. You should [add / take out / move] ____. That will make this [part / section / paragraph] better. 3. Try telling more about ____. **I A** 1. This [word / phrase / sentence / section] is/is not appropriate for your [task. / purpose. / audience.] 2. Remember, you are writing for [audience], so make the writing sound ____. 3. To make your writing more [interesting / clear / effective] you could [add / delete / move / change] ____. 4. I think this would be better if you added more [details / explanation / information / examples]. 5. I think this would be better if you [deleted / removed / shortened] ____ to this [part / section / paragraph]. 6. You could move/add ____. 7. To help the reader ____, you should revise your writing by ____.

Common Core Language Frames, continued

Grades 9–10

Writing continued			
Production and Distribution of Writing continued			
Code	Standard	Language Function/ Skill	Language Frames
W.9-10.5, continued	Develop and strengthen writing as needed by planning, revising, editing, rewriting, or trying a new approach, focusing on addressing what is most significant for a specific purpose and audience.		**8.** Because you are writing for ____, you should ____. **9.** Since your task / purpose / audience is ____, you should use (a) more ____ style / tone / words / phrases. **10.** If you ____, then your writing will be more / appropriate / better for your task / purpose / audience. **11.** You start each sentence the same way. Try ____. **12.** Your conclusion might be stronger if you ____. **13.** Look at the task again. I think you forgot to ____. So, ____.

Language Proficiency Level Key
B Beginner
I Intermediate
A Advanced

SPEAKING AND LISTENING

Comprehension and Collaboration

Code	Standard	Language Function/ Skill	Language Frames
SL.9-10.1	Initiate and participate effectively in a range of collaborative discussions (one-on-one, in groups, and teacher-led) with diverse partners on grades 9–10 topics, texts, and issues, building on others' ideas and expressing their own clearly and persuasively. a. Come to discussions prepared, having read and researched material under study; explicitly draw on that preparation by referring to evidence from texts and other research on the topic or issue to stimulate a thoughtful, well-reasoned exchange of ideas.	**Prepare for Discussions**	**B** 1. I [read / watched / studied] ____. It said ____. I think ____. 2. I am prepared. I [read / watched / studied] ____. 3. I read ____. It made me think (of) ____. **I** 1. I think/know ____ (about ____), because when I read/watched ____, it said ____. 2. To get ready for this discussion, I [read / watched / studied] ____. 3. [By reading / Because I read] ____, I learned more about ____. **A** 1. Before this discussion, I [read / watched / learned] (that) ____, so I think/know ____. 2. To prepare for this discussion, I [read / watched / learned] ____. 3. I knew we were going to discuss ____, so I ____.
	Initiate and participate effectively in a range of collaborative discussions (one-on-one, in groups, and teacher-led) with diverse partners on grades 9–10 topics, texts, and issues, building on others' ideas and expressing their own clearly and persuasively. b. Work with peers to set rules for collegial discussions and decision-making (e.g., informal consensus, taking votes on key issues, presentation of alternate views), clear goals and deadlines, and individual roles as needed.	**Engage in Discussion**	**B** 1. Please say that again. 2. I did not hear/understand you. 3. Please talk one at a time. 4. I want to ____. 5. My idea is different. I think ____. 6. May I interrupt? 7. Do you mean ____? 8. Excuse me. I'd like to say ____. **I A** 1. Can you say that again? I want to be sure I understand you. 2. I think you said ____. Is that right? 3. Please speak one at a time. 4. Did everyone get a chance to share their [ideas? / opinions? / thoughts?] 5. Can you connect what you said with the topic/text we are discussing? 6. I'd like to add on. My thought is ____. 7. That's not how I understood it. My interpretation is ____. 8. I agree with ____ and ____. 9. I disagree with ____. I think ____.

Common Core Language Frames, continued

Grades 9–10

SPEAKING AND LISTENING continued Comprehension and Collaboration continued			
Code	**Standard**	**Language Function/ Skill**	**Language Frames**
SL.9-10.1, continued	Initiate and participate effectively in a range of collaborative discussions (one-on-one, in groups, and teacher-led) with diverse partners on grades 9-10 topics, texts, and issues, building on others' ideas and expressing their own clearly and persuasively. b. Work with peers to set rules for collegial discussions and decision-making (e.g., informal consensus, taking votes on key issues, presentation of alternate views), clear goals and deadlines, and individual roles as needed.	**Set Goals and Deadlines**	**B** 1. We need to ____. 2. We must do this by ____. 3. It is due on ____. 4. When is this due? 5. What is the goal? 6. Our goal is to ____. **I A** 1. We need to ____ (and ____) by/before ____. 2. When is the deadline? 3. How much time do we have to ____? 4. Let's take a vote on ____. 5. By doing ____ by ____ we will be able to meet the goal.
		Define Roles	**B** 1. What is my/your role? 2. Can/May I do ____? **I A** 1. What are the jobs tasks responsibilities our roles ? 2. Who's going to ____ (and ____)? 3. I'd like to be responsible for ____. 4. I would be a good person to ____ because ____. 5. I can contribute participate add oversee complete manage ____.
	Initiate and participate effectively in a range of collaborative discussions (one-on-one, in groups, and teacher-led) with diverse partners on grades 9-10 topics, texts, and issues, building on others' ideas and expressing their own clearly and persuasively. c. Propel conversations by posing and responding to questions that relate the current discussion to broader themes or larger ideas; actively incorporate others into the discussion; and clarify, verify, or challenge ideas and conclusions.	**Ask Questions**	**B** 1. Who What When Where is are ____? 2. What do you think about ____? 3. I think ____. What do you think? **I A** 1. Who What When Where Why How is are ____? 2. My opinion (about ____) is ____. What do you think (about ____)? I wonder if ____. 3. How did you interpret ____? 4. Where can you find evidence in the text? 5. Why do you think that? 6. What about you, [Name]? What is your opinion on ____?

Language Proficiency Level Key
B Beginner
I Intermediate
A Advanced

SPEAKING AND LISTENING continued

Comprehension and Collaboration continued

Code	Standard	Language Function/ Skill	Language Frames
SL.9-10.1, continued	Initiate and participate effectively in a range of collaborative discussions (one-on-one, in groups, and teacher-led) with diverse partners on grades 9–10 topics, texts, and issues, building on others' ideas and expressing their own clearly and persuasively. c. Propel conversations by posing and responding to questions that relate the current discussion to broader themes or larger ideas; actively incorporate others into the discussion; and clarify, verify, or challenge ideas and conclusions.	**Respond to Questions** **Elaborate**	**B** 1. I disagree. / agree. I think ____. 2. My idea / thought / answer is ____ because ____ **I A** 1. I disagree / agree about ____. In addition, / Also, / Furthermore, ____. 2. You asked ____. I think ____ (because ____). 3. Not only do I think ____, but I also think ____. 4. Yes, / No, for example, / to illustrate, / for instance, ____. 5. In response to/Regarding ____, let me add ____. 6. In other words, ____. 7. My interpretation of ____ is ____ because ____. 8. After reading (about) ____ [something in the text], I presume/imagine ____ 9. Let me give you some other reasons. ____, ____ and ____. 10. To clarify, I think/conclude ____.
	Initiate and participate effectively in a range of collaborative discussions (one-on-one, in groups, and teacher-led) with diverse partners on grades 9–10 topics, texts, and issues, building on others' ideas and expressing their own clearly and persuasively. d. Respond thoughtfully to diverse perspectives, summarize points of agreement and disagreement, and, when warranted, qualify or justify their own views and understanding and make new connections in light of the evidence and reasoning presented	**Review Ideas**	**B I** 1. We read / talked about ____. 2. We shared several ideas. One was ____. Another was ____. 3. We agreed/didn't agree about ____. 4. I have a new idea about ____. I think ____. **A** 1. What we have talked about / decided / agreed is that ____. 2. You stated/pointed out (that) ____. 3. To summarize, / repeat, / conclude, ____. 4. Let's sum up. First we ____. Then we ____. Now we ____. 5. 5. I've rethought ____. Based on ____, I think ____.

Common Core Language Frames, continued

Grades 9–10

SPEAKING AND LISTENING continued			
Comprehension and Collaboration continued			
Code	**Standard**	**Language Function/ Skill**	**Language Frames**
SL.9-10.1, continued	Initiate and participate effectively in a range of collaborative discussions (one-on-one, in groups, and teacher-led) with diverse partners on grades 9–10 topics, texts, and issues, building on others' ideas and expressing their own clearly and persuasively. d. Respond thoughtfully to diverse perspectives, summarize points of agreement and disagreement, and, when warranted, qualify or justify their own views and understanding and make new connections in light of the evidence and reasoning presented	**Acknowledge Multiple Perspectives**	**B** **1.** You / He / She / [Name] | say(s) / think(s) | ____. **2.** I have a different | idea / thought / feeling | about that. **I** **1.** I think you said/meant ____. Did I get that right? **2.** I understand that you think ____ but I think ____ because ____. **3.** While some people think ____, other people think ____. **4.** I agree with what | you / he / she / [name] | says about ____ | but / and | I also think ____. Some of us thought ____. Others thought ____. We finally agreed on/that ____. I hadn't thought of that. It makes me think of ____. **A** **1.** While | you / he / she / [name] | think(s) / feel(s) | ____ about ____, | you / he / she / [name] | seem(s) to think/feel ____. **2.** I can appreciate that | you / he / she / [name] | think(s) / feel(s) | ____, but there are others who | think / feel | ____.

Language Proficiency Level Key
B Beginner
I Intermediate
A Advanced

SPEAKING AND LISTENING continued

Comprehension and Collaboration continued

Code	Standard	Language Function/ Skill	Language Frames
SL.9-10.2	Integrate multiple sources of information presented in diverse media or formats (e.g., visually, quantitatively, orally) evaluating the credibility and accuracy of each source.	**Interpret Media**	**B I** 1. The [picture / graph / chart / diagram] shows ____. 2. The [picture / chart / graph / image] shows (that) ____. 3. These [numbers / results] [show / prove / demonstrate] (that) ____ 4. The [picture / chart / graph / image] is/isn't credible/accurate because ____. **A** 1. When I looked at the data/graphic/photo, I realized/noticed ____. 2. I think the [picture / chart / graph / image] is/isn't credible/accurate because ____.
SL.9-10.3	Evaluate a speaker's point of view, reasoning, and use of evidence and rhetoric, identifying any fallacious reasoning or exaggerated or distorted evidence.	**Analyze Arguments**	**B** 1. The speaker says ____. 2. This fact supported/did not support it. **I** 1. The speaker claims ____. The claim was supported/not supported by ____. 2. The speaker includes the evidence ____ to support the claim ____. 3. The evidence ____ does not support the claim ____. 4. The claim ____ is not supported by clear evidence. 5. I think the speaker did/didn't exaggerate, because ____. **A** 1. The evidence and reasons are/ are not strong enough to support the claim ____. For example, ____. 2. I think the speaker exaggerated/distorted the evidence, because ____.

Common Core Language Frames, continued

Grades 9–10

SPEAKING AND LISTENING continued			
Comprehension and Collaboration continued			
Code	**Standard**	**Language Function/ Skill**	**Language Frames**
SL.9-10.4	Present information, findings, and supporting evidence clearly, concisely, and logically such that listeners can follow the line of reasoning and the organization, development, substance, and style are appropriate to purpose, audience, and task.	**Give Information**	**B** **1.** This is a ____. (It ____.) **2.** I think ____. **3.** I saw / observed / found ____. **4.** First, ____. Next, ____. Last, ____. This means ____. **I A** **1.** I think / believe / found / learned ____ (because) ____. **2.** I would argue that ____ because ____. My reasons are ____. **3.** First ____. Next ____. Then ____. Finally, ____. Therefore ____. **4.** When/After ____. **5.** Due to the fact that ____, I think / believe / found / learned ____.
		Support Ideas	**B** **1.** ____ is important. Here are some examples/details. **2.** This is a ____. It shows ____. **I A** **1.** To illustrate the fact that ____, ____. **2.** For example/For instance, ____. **3.** The ____ researcher / author / person looked at several things before drawing a conclusion, such as ____, ____, and ____. **4.** The ____ shows / supports / demonstrates ____ because ____.

Language Proficiency Level Key
B Beginner
I Intermediate
A Advanced

SPEAKING AND LISTENING continued

Comprehension and Collaboration continued

Code	Standard	Language Function/ Skill	Language Frames
SL.9-10.5	Make strategic use of digital media (e.g., textual, graphical, audio, visual, and interactive elements) in presentations to enhance understanding of findings, reasoning, and evidence and to add interest.	**Use Multimedia**	**B** 1. This shows ____. 2. My picture / music / sounds show(s)____. 3. I added this picture/music because ____. 4. This picture/music supports ____. **I** 1. I added a ____ to show ____. 2. I chose this/these video / music / image(s) / sounds because/to show ____. 3. Listen / Watch / Pay attention to this / these video / music / image(s) / sound(s) to ____. 4. I chose this image / music / effect to support ____ because ____. **A** 1. The images / graphics / sound effects clarify the meaning of ____ by ____. 2. In order to ____, I included this/these video / music / image(s) / sound(s). 3. This/These video / music / image(s) / sound(s) support ____ due to ____.
SL.9-10.6	Adapt speech to a variety of contexts and tasks, demonstrating command of formal English when indicated or appropriate.	**Adapt Language**	This standard does not lend itself to Academic Language Frames.

Common Core Language Frames, continued

Grades 9–10

LANGUAGE			
Conventions of Standard English			
Code	**Standard**	**Language Function/ Skill**	**Language Frames**
L.9-10.1	Demonstrate command of the conventions of standard English grammar and usage when writing or speaking.		This standard does not lend itself to language frames.
L.9-10.2	Demonstrate command of the conventions of standard English capitalization, punctuation, and spelling when writing.		This standard does not lend itself to language frames.
L.9-10.3	Apply knowledge of language to understand how language functions in different contexts, to make effective choices for meaning or style, and to comprehend more fully when reading or listening.		See related language frames in the Peer Editing section.

Language Proficiency Level Key
B Beginner
I Intermediate
A Advanced

LANGUAGE continued

Vocabulary Acquisition and Use continued

Code	Standard	Language Function/ Skill	Language Frames
L.9-10.4	Determine or clarify the meaning of unknown and multiple-meaning words and phrases based on grades 9–10 reading and content, choosing flexibly from a range of strategies. a. Use context (e.g., the overall meaning of a sentence, paragraph, or text; a word's position or function in a sentence) as a clue to the meaning of a word or phrase.	**Use context**	**B** 1. This word means ____. So I know the word ____ means ____. 2. This [sentence paragraph text] is about ____. I think the word means ____. **I** 1. I think this [word phrase] means ____, because the [word phrase sentence paragraph] ____ means ____. 2. The [word phrase sentence] ____ tells me that ____ means ____. 3. I think ____ means ____ because ____. 4. The word ____ can mean ____ or ____. I think it means ____ because ____. 5. The [story article poem], is about ____, so this word means ____. **A** 1. The context ____ is a clue that the word/phrase ____ means ____. 2. The word ____ is acting as a/an [noun verb adjective] so I know it means____. 3. It looks like the verb ____. As a noun, I think it means ____. 4. Because the subject of the [story article poem text] is ____, the word ____ means ____.

Common Core Language Frames, continued

Grades 9–10

LANGUAGE continued

Vocabulary Acquisition and Use continued

Code	Standard	Language Function/ Skill	Language Frames
L.9-10.4, continued	Determine or clarify the meaning of unknown and multiple-meaning words and phrases based on grades 9–10 reading and content, choosing flexibly from a range of strategies. b. Identify and correctly use patterns of word changes that indicate different meanings or parts of speech (e.g., analyze, analysis, analytical; advocate, advocacy).	**Use Affixes and Roots** **Use Word Patterns**	**B** 1. This part means ____. So that word means ____. 2. The word ____ is a/an noun / verb / adjective / adverb. It means ____. **I A** 1. ____ is a prefix / suffix / root. It means ____. So the word means ____. 2. One clue to the meaning of the word ____ is the prefix / suffix / root ____. 3. The prefix / suffix / root ____ means ____, so I think the word ____ probably means ____. 4. I know the prefix / suffix / root means ____, therefore I think the word means ____. 5. Words that end with the suffix ____ are nouns / verbs / adjectives / adverbs, so ____ is a ____.
	Determine or clarify the meaning of unknown and multiple-meaning words and phrases based on grades 9–10 reading and content, choosing flexibly from a range of strategies. c. Consult general and specialized reference materials (e.g., dictionaries, glossaries, thesauruses), both print and digital, to find the pronunciation of a word or determine or clarify its precise meaning, its part of speech, or its etymology.	**Use Reference Materials**	**B** 1. Please help me find the dictionary / glossary / thesaurus. 2. Please help me find ____ in the dictionary / thesaurus / glossary. 3. ____ means ____. 4. You say ____ like this: ____. 5. The word ____ comes from ____. **I** 1. ____ is a noun / pronoun / verb / adjective / adverb. I looked in the dictionary / glossary / thesaurus. 2. The word ____ comes from ____. It originally meant ____. **A** 1. I know that the meaning / pronunciation / part of speech of ____ is ____, because I looked in the dictionary / glossary / thesaurus. 2. The word ____'s origin is ____ and it had the meaning ____.

Language Proficiency Level Key
B **Beginner**
I **Intermediate**
A **Advanced**

LANGUAGE continued

Vocabulary Acquisition and Use continued

Code	Standard	Language Function/ Skill	Language Frames
L.9-10.4 continued	Determine or clarify the meaning of unknown and multiple-meaning words and phrases based on grades 9–10 reading and content, choosing flexibly from a range of strategies. d. Verify the preliminary determination of the meaning of a word or phrase (e.g., by checking the inferred meaning in context or in a dictionary).	**Verify Meaning**	**B** 1. I think ____ means ____. The dictionary says ____. 2. I think ____ means ____. I used the words/phrase ____ to check. **I** 1. I thought the word/phrase ____ meant ____. I looked in the dictionary, and it means ____. 2. I think the word ____ means ____ because ____. 3. I thought the word meant ____, but the dictionary says ____. 4. I thought the word meant ____ and I was right. The dictionary says ____. **A** 1. I thought that ____ is the meaning of the word/phrase ____. When I verified the definition in the dictionary, I found that it means ____. 2. I thought that the word/phrase ____ meant ____. When I read ____, I [found out / confirmed / verified / was sure] that it did/didn't have that meaning.
L.9-10.5	Demonstrate understanding of figurative language, word relationships, and nuances in word meanings.	**Relate Words**	**B** 1. The word ____ is like the word ____. Does the word ____ mean ____? 2. This word means ____. So I know the word ____ means ____. 3. This is about ____. I think the word means ____. **I A** 1. The word ____ shows cause/effect, so the word ____ means ____. 2. The word ____ is a part of ____, and it means ____. 3. The word ____ is an item/a category, so the word ____ means. 4. ____ is the opposite of/an antonym for ____. 5. ____ is the same as/is a synonym for ____. 6. ____ is like ____ but it means ____ is more/less ____.

Common Core Language Frames, continued

Grades 9–10

LANGUAGE continued

Vocabulary Acquisition and Use continued

Code	Standard	Language Function/ Skill	Language Frames
L.9-10.5, continued	Demonstrate understanding of figurative language, word relationships, and nuances in word meanings. a. Interpret figures of speech (e.g., euphemism, oxymoron) in context and analyze their role in the text.	**Interpret Figurative Language**	**B** 1. ____ is like ____. 2. ____ makes me feel (like) ____. 3. ____ and ____ are opposites. 4. ____ is a polite way to say ____. **I A** 1. In this sentence/paragraph, ____ describes ____ (as ____) because ____. 2. The author compared ____ to a ____ because ____. 3. The author uses this [metaphor / simile / personification] to show ____. 4. This [metaphor / simile / personification / relates / compares / connects] ____ and ____. That makes the [reader feel / think / imagine / understand] ____. 5. The word/phrase ____ is different than words/phrases like ____ and ____. I think the author chose that word in order to ____. 6. ____ is an oxymoron because ____. 7. ____ is a euphemism for ____.
	Demonstrate understanding of figurative language, word relationships, and nuances in word meanings. b. Analyze nuances in the meaning of words with similar denotations.	**Distinguish Connotations and Denotations**	**I** 1. ____ and ____ mean. ____ is [positive / negative / neutral / funny] and ____ is [positive / negative / neutral / funny]. 2. The literal meaning is ____ but the connotation is ____ **A** 1. The literal meaning of ____ and ____ is ____. 2. The connotation of ____ is [positive / negative / neutral / funny], but ____ is more [positive / negative / neutral / funny].

Language Proficiency Level Key
B **Beginner**
I **Intermediate**
A **Advanced**

LANGUAGE continued

Vocabulary Acquisition and Use continued

Code	Standard	Language Function/ Skill	Language Frames
L.9-10.6	Acquire and use accurately general academic and domain-specific words and phrases, sufficient for reading, writing, speaking, and listening at the college and career readiness level; demonstrate independence in gathering vocabulary knowledge when considering a word or phrase important to comprehension or expression.	**Learn and Use Words**	**B** 1. ____ means ____. I used / am using / will use it because ____. 2. The word is like the word ____. Does the word mean ____? 3. At work/In college, we say ____. **I** 1. The word ____ shows/means ____. 2. I used the word ____ to show/mean ____. 3. I can use this word to mean ____ or ____. 4. My readers/listeners are ____ so I should use words/phrases like ____. 5. If I use the word/phrase ____ then my audience will know/feel ____. 6. In my language, the word ____ means ____. Does ____ mean ____ in English? 7. At work/In college, it is better to say, ____. **A** 1. The word / phrase / expression ____ is/isn't appropriate for ____ (because ____). 2. I can use the word ____ for ____ (because ____). 3. My readers/listeners are ____ so I should use words/phrases like ____ that are ____. 4. I want my audience to know / understand / feel / imagine ____ so I will use the word/phrase ____ because it is ____. 5. ____ means ____ in [Language]____, so I think it means ____ in English. 6. It is more appropriate to say/use ____ in a college/work setting.

Common Core State Standards

Literacy Standards for Reading, Writing, Speaking and Listening, and Language

Standards for Reading: Literature			
Strand	**Code**	**Standards Text**	**Teacher's Edition Pages**
Key Ideas and Details	RL.9-10.1	Cite strong and thorough textual evidence to support analysis of what the text says explicitly as well as inferences drawn from the text.	**Unit 1**: T17, T35, T49, T51, T59, T78, T79, T87, **Unit 2**: T155, **Unit 3**: **T205**, **T209**, T213, T214, T215, T216, T218, T219, T221, T231, **T237**, T241, T242, T243, T244, T245, T246, T247, T248, T249, T250, T257, **T263**, T266, T267, T268, T269, T270, 272, T273, T275, T276, T277, T285, **Unit 4**: T352, T356, **Unit 5**: T421, T431, T450, T455, T456, T470, T471, T473, T479, T481, T483, T487, T489, **Unit 7**: **T607**, T639, T641, T662, T665, T673, T687, T694, T695, T699, **Handbook**: T741, T742
	RL.9-10.2	Determine a theme or central idea of a text and analyze in detail its development over the course of the text, including how it emerges and is shaped and refined by specific details; provide an objective summary of the text.	**Unit 1**: T17, T27, **T36**, **T41**, T46, T48, T50, T51, T73, T87, **T88**, T90, T93, **Unit 2**: **T150**, T151, T154, T155, **T174**, T176, T177, **Unit 3**: T241, T249, T251, **T258**, T285, **T286**, **Unit 5**: T431, T457, T486, T489, **Unit 6**: T527, T529, **Unit 7**: T616, T620, T640, T641, T672, T673, T687, T689, T694, T695, T698, T699
	RL.9-10.3	Analyze how complex characters (e.g., those with multiple or conflicting motivations) develop over the course of a text, interact with other characters, and advance the plot or develop the theme.	**Unit 1**: **T9**, T19, T21, T35, **T41**, T44, T46, T48, T50, T51, **T65**, T68, T69, T70, T71, T72, T76, T77, T79, T87, T91, T92, **Unit 3**: T221, **T232**, T247, T250, **Unit 5**: T448, T457, T467, **Unit 7**: T619, T620, T621, T631, T633, T641, **T647**, T650, T651, T652, T653, T654, T655, T656, T657, T659, T660, T661, T663, T664, T665
Craft and Structure	RL.9-10.4	Determine the meaning of words and phrases as they are used in the text, including figurative and connotative meanings; analyze the cumulative impact of specific word choices on meaning and tone (e.g., how the language evokes a sense of time and place; how it sets a formal or informal tone).	**Unit 1**: T10, T13, T15, T45, T49, T64, **T65**, T71, T73, T74, T75, T78, T79, **Unit 2**: T152, T153, **T156**, T175, **Unit 3**: T208, T212, T236, T240, T243, T271, **Unit 4**: **T358**, **Unit 5**: **T437**, T440, T441, T442, T443, T444, T447, T448, T450, T451, **T452**, T453, T455, T456, T457, **T474**, T475, T476, T477, T479, T480, T481, T483, **T484**, **Unit 6**: T528, T529, **Unit 7**: **T607**, T612, **T613**, T617, T621, T622, T623, T624, T625, T626, T627, T628, T629, T631, T632, T633, **T634**, T636, T637, T638, T639, T640, T645, **T647**, T658, T650, T651, T652, T654, T655, T656, T659, T660, T662, T664, T665, T669, T671, T672, **T679**, T682, T684, T686, T687, T688, T689, **T690**, T692, T693, T694
	RL.9-10.5	Analyze how an author's choices concerning how to structure a text, order events within it (e.g., parallel plots), and manipulate time (e.g., pacing, flashbacks) create such effects as mystery, tension, or surprise.	**Unit 1**: **T11**, T14, T16, T18, T20, T22, T23, T24, T25, T79, **Unit 2**: **T150**, T152, T153, T154, **T174**, T175, T176, T177, **Unit 4**: T352, **Unit 5**: **T413**, T416, T417, T419, T421, T422, T423, T431, **T432**, **T437**, T444, T447, T450, **T458**, **T463**, T466, T467, T468, T469, T471, T472, T473, T483, T487, T488, T489, **Unit 7**: **T666**, T668, T670, T672, **T690**, T692, T694
	RL.9-10.6	Analyze a particular point of view or cultural experience reflected in a work of literature from outside the United States, drawing on a wide reading of world literature.	**Unit 1**: T70, T77, T87, **T88**, **Unit 3**: **T205**, **T207**, **T209**, T212, T215, T217, T218, T221, **T237**, T240, T241, T243, T245, T246, T247, T248, T250, **T263**, T267, T268, T269, T272, T273, T274, T277, T285, **Unit 7**: T695

Standards for Reading: Literature, continued

Strand	Code	Standards Text	Teacher's Edition Pages
Integration of Knowledge and Ideas	RL.9-10.7	Analyze the representation of a subject or a key scene in two different artistic mediums, including what is emphasized or absent in each treatment (e.g., Auden's "Musée des Beaux Arts" and Breughel's Landscape with the Fall of Icarus).	**Unit 1:** T41, T43, T45, T47, T65, T67, T73, T74, T76, **Unit 3**: T201, T203, T210, T229, T233, T238, T255, T256, T258, T261, **Unit 4:** T340, T342, **Unit 5:** T401, T404, T433, T449, T451, T456, T462, T466, T472, T478 **Unit 7:** T609, T611, **T613,** T617, T618, T623, T626, T628, T632, T633, T643, T675, T699
	RL.9-10.8	(Not applicable to literature)	
	RL.9-10.9	Analyze how an author draws on and transforms source material in a specific work (e.g., how Shakespeare treats a theme or topic from Ovid or the Bible or how a later author draws on a play by Shakespeare).	**Unit 1:** T25, **Unit 7:** T696 *This standard is best suited for students at higher reading levels and language proficiency levels. See* ***Edge Level C*** *for thorough coverage of this skill.*
Range of Reading and Level of Text Complexity	RL.9-10.10	By the end of grade 9, read and comprehend literature, including stories, dramas, and poems, in the grades 9–10 text complexity band proficiently, with scaffolding as needed at the high end of the range. By the end of grade 10, read and comprehend literature, including stories, dramas, and poems, at the high end of the grades 9–10 text complexity band independently and proficiently	**Unit 1**: T1C, T3, **T7**, **T11**, T13, T14, T15, T17, T18, T20, T21, T23, T25, T35, T43, T44, T45, T48, T49, T67, T68, T69, T74, T75, T76, **Unit 2**: T109C, T113, T141, T175, T176, **Unit 3**: T203, **T205**, T211, T212, T213, T216, T219, T223, T231, T239, T240, T241, T242, T244, T245, T246, T247, T257, T265, T267, T270, T271, T272, T273, T285, **Unit 4**: T305C, T309, T375, **Unit 5**: T404C, T407, **T409**, **T413**, T415, T416, T417, T418, T420, T421, T423, T431, **T437**, T438, T439, T440, T441, T443, T444, T446, T447, T449, T450, **T452**, T453, T455, T456, T457, **T463**, T465, T466, T467, T468, T470, T471, T473, **T474**, T475, T476, T477, T479, T480, T481, T483, **Unit 6**: T505C, T509, T527, **Unit 7**: T605, T615, T616, T617, T618, T621, T622, T623, T624, T625, T628, T629, T630, T635, T641, **T642**, T650, T651, T657, T660, T661, T667, T669, T673, **T674**, T681, T682, T683, T691, T693, T695, **Handbook**: T735, T746, T751, T752, T757, T758, T759, T763, T764, T765, T769, T770, T771

Standards for Reading: Informational Text

Strand	Code	Standards Text	Teacher's Edition Pages
Key Ideas and Details	RI.9-10.1	Cite strong and thorough textual evidence to support analysis of what the text says explicitly as well as inferences drawn from the text.	**Unit 1**: T33, T58, T59, T85, T86, T87, **Unit 2**: T125, T127, T133, T143, T149, T155, T167, T168, T171, T173, **T178**, **Unit 3**: **T222**, T223, T226, T227, T229, T230, T231, **T252**, T255, T256, T257, **T278**, T280, T281, T283, T284, T285, T289, **Unit 4**: **T311**, **T315**, T319, T321, T322, T323, T325, T326, T328, T329, **T330**, T332, T333, T334, T335, T341, T344, T345, T346, T347, T348, T349, T350, T351, T354, T355, T356, T357, **T363**, T366, T369, T370, T371, T372, T373, T374, **T376**, T377, T378, T380, T381, T387, **Unit 5**: T430, **Unit 6**: T526, T536, T537, T551, T553, T557, T569, T572, T573, T577, T578, T579, T583, T585, **Handbook**: T739, T743, T744, T745
	RI.9-10.2	Determine a central idea of a text and analyze its development over the course of the text, including how it emerges and is shaped and refined by specific details; provide an objective summary of the text.	**Unit 1**: **T28**, T29, T31, T32, T34, **T52**, T53, T55, T56, T57, T58, T83, T87, **Unit 2**: **T115**, **T119**, T122, T123, T125, T126, T127, **T128**, T131, T132, **T139**, T143, T145, T146, T148, T149, T154, T155, **T161**, T166, T168, T169, T170, T171, T172, T173, T177, T180, **Unit 3**: T227, T229, T281, T284, T285, T288, **Unit 4**: T335, T367, T381, T384, **Unit 5**: T428, T429, T431, T482, **Unit 6**: T519, T521, T523, T533, T534, T535, T547, T557, T567, T578, T582, T585

Common Core State Standards, continued

Literacy Standards for Reading, Writing, Speaking and Listening, and Language

Strand	Code	Standards Text	Teacher's Edition Pages
Standards for Reading: Informational Text, continued			
Key Ideas and Details continued	RI.9-10.3	Analyze how the author unfolds an analysis or series of ideas or events, including the order in which the points are made, how they are introduced and developed, and the connections that are drawn between them.	**Unit 1**: **T52**, T54, T55, T56, T58, **Unit 2**: **T128**, T129, T130, T132, T182, **Unit 3**: **T278**, T280, T282, T284, **Unit 4**: T329, **T376**, T378, T379, T380, T385, T386, **Unit 5**: T429, **Unit 6**: T570, T571
Craft and Structure	RI.9-10.4	Determine the meaning of words and phrases as they are used in a text, including figurative, connotative, and technical meanings; analyze the cumulative impact of specific word choices on meaning and tone (e.g., how the language of a court opinion differs from that of a newspaper).	**Unit 1**: T40, T54, T57, **T80**, T82, T83, T84, T85, T86, **Unit 2**: T118, **T134**, T138, T144, **T156**, T160, T168, T182, **Unit 3**: T262, T272, **Unit 4**: T314, T332, T340, T348, T349, **T358**, T362, **Unit 5**: T412, **T424**, T425, T427, T429, T430, T436, T462, **Unit 6**: T514, **T530**, T531, T533, T536, T542, T547, T562, **T563**, T565, T566, T568, T569, T570, T572, T573, **Unit 7**: T646, T658, T678
	RI.9-10.5	Analyze in detail how an author's ideas or claims are developed and refined by particular sentences, paragraphs, or larger portions of a text (e.g., a section or chapter).	**Unit 1**: T29, **Unit 3**: **T222**, T223, T224, T225, T228, T230, **T252**, T253, T254, T256, **Unit 4**: **T313**, **T315**, T318, T320, T322, T324, T326, T327, T328, **T341**, T345, T346, T347, T349, **T350**, T353, T354, T356, **T363**, T366, T367, T368, T369, T371, T373, T374, T375, T385, T386, **Unit 6**: **T558**, **T574**, T575, T576, T578
	RI.9-10.6	Determine an author's point of view or purpose in a text and analyze how an author uses rhetoric to advance that point of view or purpose.	**Unit 1**: **T80**, T83, T85, T86, **Unit 2**: **T117**, **T119**, T122, T124, T126, T127, **T139**, T142, T144, T147, T149, **T161**, T164, T166, T167, T169, T170, T172, T173, T181, T182, **Unit 3**: T289, **Unit 4**: T353, **Unit 5**: T482, **Unit 6**: **T530**, T531, T533, T536, T537, **T538**, **T563**, T566, T567, T568, T569, T570, T571, T572, T573, T584, T585, **Unit 7**: T658
Integration of Knowledge and Ideas	RI.9-10.7	Analyze various accounts of a subject told in different mediums (e.g., a person's life story in both print and multimedia), determining which details are emphasized in each account.	**Unit 1**: **T28**, T30, T31, T32, T33, T34, T86, **Unit 3**: T254, **Unit 4**: **T330**, T333, T334, **Unit 6**: T564, T580, **Handbook**: T718
	RI.9-10.8	Delineate and evaluate the argument and specific claims in a text, assessing whether the reasoning is valid and the evidence is relevant and sufficient; identify false statements and fallacious reasoning.	**Unit 1**: T55, T56, T57, T58, **Unit 4**: T335, **Unit 6**: **T511**, **T513**, **T515**, T518, T519, T520, T521, T523, T526, **T530**, **T543**, T548, T549, T550, T551, **T552**, T554, T555, T556, T557, T567, T579, T580, T583, T584, T585
	RI.9-10.9	Analyze seminal U.S. documents of historical and literary significance (e.g., Washington's Farewell Address, the Gettysburg Address, Roosevelt's Four Freedoms speech, King's "Letter from Birmingham Jail"), including how they address related themes and concepts.	**Unit 3**: T289 *This standard is best suited for students at higher reading levels and language proficiency levels. See **Edge Level C** for thorough coverage of this skill.*
Range of Reading and Level of Text Complexity	RI.9-10.10	By the end of grade 9, read and comprehend literary nonfiction in the grades 9–10 text complexity band proficiently, with scaffolding as needed at the high end of the range. By the end of grade 10, read and comprehend literary nonfiction at the high end of the grades 9–10 text complexity band independently and proficiently	**Unit 1**: T1C, T3, **T5**, **T28**, T29, T30, T33, T34, T53, T59, T81, T87, **Unit 2**: T109C, T113, **T115**, T121, T123, T129, T131, T133, T141, T142, T143, T155, T163, T165, T177, **Unit 3**: T203, T253, T279, T281, **Unit 4**: T305C, T309, **T311**, T317, T318, T319, T321, T323, T325, T327, T331, T332, T335, T344, T345, T351, T357, T366, T367, T377, T378, T381, **Unit 5**: T404C, T407, **T424**, T425, T426, T427, T428, T430, **Unit 6**: T505C, T509, **T515**, T517, T518, T519, T521, T522, T524, T526, **T530**, T531, T532, T534, T535, T536, T537, **T543**, T545, T546, T547, T549, T551, **T552**, T553, T556, T557, T565, T566, T567, **T574**, T575, T576, T577, T578, T579, **Unit 7:** T605, **Handbook**: **T753**, T754, T755, T756, T760, T761, T762, T766, T767, T768, T800

Standards for Writing

Strand	Code	Standards Text	Teacher's Edition Pages
Text Types and Purposes	W.9-10.1	Write arguments to support claims in an analysis of substantive topics or texts, using valid reasoning and relevant and sufficient evidence.	**Unit 1:** T33, T35, T51, T59, T79, **Unit 2:** T133, **T135, T185, T192, T193, Unit 3:** T231, **T233, T287, Unit 4:** T349, T381, **T383, Unit 5:** T457, **T459, Unit 6:** T526, T536, **T539,** T551, T557, T559, T573, T578, T579, **T581,** T587, T592, **Unit 7:** T644, T675, **T697, Handbook:** T821 *See additional coverage below.*
	W.9-10.1.a	Introduce precise claim(s), distinguish the claim(s) from alternate or opposing claims, and create an organization that establishes clear relationships among claim(s), counterclaims, reasons, and evidence.	**Unit 1:** T35, T89, **Unit 2: T188, T190, T194, Unit 4: T383, Unit 5:** T459, **Unit 6:** T539, T551, T557, **T559, T590, T591, T596, Unit 7: T697**
	W.9-10.1.b	Develop claim(s) and counterclaims fairly, supplying evidence for each while pointing out the strengths and limitations of both in a manner that anticipates the audience's knowledge level and concerns.	**Unit 1:** T33, T35, T51, T59, T79, T89, **Unit 2: T188, T190, T194, Unit 3:** T256, **Unit 4: T383, Unit 5:** T459, **Unit 6:** T551, T556, **T559,** T579, T581, **T590, T596**
	W.9-10.1.c	Use words, phrases, and clauses to link the major sections of the text, create cohesion, and clarify the relationships between claim(s) and reasons, between reasons and evidence, and between claim(s) and counterclaims.	**Unit 2: T192, T194, Unit 3:** T287, **Unit 4: T383, Unit 5:** T459, **Unit 6:** T559, T581, **Handbook:** T795
	W.9-10.1.d	Establish and maintain a formal style and objective tone while attending to the norms and conventions of the discipline in which they are writing.	**Unit 2: T190, T194, T195, Unit 3:** T287, **Unit 4:** T383, **Unit 5:** T459, **Unit 6: T596, T597, Unit 7: T697**
	W.9-10.1.e	Provide a concluding statement or section that follows from and supports the argument presented.	**Unit 2:** T194, **Unit 3:** T287, **Unit 4:** T383, **Unit 5:** T459, **Unit 6:** T539, T579, T581, **T596**
	W.9-10.2	Write informative/explanatory texts to examine and convey complex ideas, concepts, and information clearly and accurately through the effective selection, organization, and analysis of content.	**Unit 1:** T25, **T37,** T58, **T61,** T87, **T89, Unit 2: T179, Unit 3:** T285, **T291, T296, Unit 4: T337,** T338, **T359,** T382, T388, **T389, T395, Unit 5:** T431, T434, T457, T483, **Unit 6:** T537, T557, T579, **Unit 7: T697** *See additional coverage below.*
	W.9-10.2.a	Introduce a topic; organize complex ideas, concepts, and information to make important connections and distinctions; include formatting (e.g., headings), graphics (e.g., figures, tables), and multimedia when useful to aiding comprehension.	**Unit 1:** T37, T61, **Unit 2: T179, Unit 3: T295, T296, T300, T305, Unit 4:** T382, **T393, T394, T398, T399, T403**
	W.9-10.2.b	Develop the topic with well-chosen, relevant, and sufficient facts, extended definitions, concrete details, quotations, or other information and examples appropriate to the audience's knowledge of the topic.	**Unit 1:** T25, T37, T61, T87, **Unit 2:** T127, **Unit 2: T179, Unit 3: T259,** T294, T300, T302, **Unit 4:** T382, T396, T398, **Unit 7: T697**
	W.9-10.2.c	Use appropriate and varied transitions to link the major sections of the text, create cohesion, and clarify the relationships among complex ideas and concepts.	**Unit 1:** T37, T61, **Unit 2: T179, Unit 3:** T296, **Unit 4: T394, T399, Unit 7: T697, Handbook:** T794
	W.9-10.2.d	Use precise language and domain-specific vocabulary to manage the complexity of the topic.	**Unit 3: T300, Unit 4: T398, Unit 5:** T431, T457, T483, **Unit 6:** T537, T557, T579
	W.9-10.2.e	Establish and maintain a formal style and objective tone while attending to the norms and conventions of the discipline in which they are writing.	**Unit 1:** T61, **Unit 3:** T259, **T287, Unit 4:** T382, **T398, T399, Unit 7:** T697, **Handbook:** T793
	W.9-10.2.f	Provide a concluding statement or section that follows from and supports the information or explanation presented (e.g., articulating implications or the significance of the topic).	**Unit 1:** T37, T61, **T67, Unit 2: T179, Unit 3:** T295, **T300, Unit 4: T397, Handbook:** T797
	W.9-10.3	Write narratives to develop real or imagined experiences or events using effective technique, well-chosen details, and well-structured event sequences.	**Unit 1:** T86, T87, **T95, T100, Unit 2:** T177, **Unit 4:** T356, T357, **Unit 5:** T431, **T433,** T640, T473, **T491, T496, Unit 7:** 665 *See additional coverage below.*
	W.9-10.3.a	Engage and orient the reader by setting out a problem, situation, or observation, establishing one or multiple point(s) of view, and introducing a narrator and/or characters; create a smooth progression of experiences or events.	**Unit 1:** T86, **T104, Unit 2:** T177, **Unit 4:** T356, T357, **Unit 5: T433,** T473, **T500, Unit 7:** 665
	W.9-10.3.b	Use narrative techniques, such as dialogue, pacing, description, reflection, and multiple plot lines, to develop experiences, events, and/or characters.	**Unit 1:** T86, **T104, Unit 2:** T177, **Unit 4:** T356, **Unit 5: T433, T496, T500, T501, Unit 7:** 665

Common Core State Standards, continued
Literacy Standards for Reading, Writing, Speaking and Listening, and Language

Standards for Writing, continued			
Strand	**Code**	**Standards Text**	**Teacher's Edition Pages**
Text Types and Purposes continued	W.9-10.3.c	Use a variety of techniques to sequence events so that they build on one another to create a coherent whole.	**Unit 1: T99, T104, Unit 2:** T177, **Unit 5: T495, T498, T500**
	W.9-10.3.d	Use precise words and phrases, telling details, and sensory language to convey a vivid picture of the experiences, events, setting, and/or characters.	**Unit 1: T100, T102, Unit 5: T433,** T473, **T496, T500, T503, Unit 7:** 640, 665, **Handbook:** T799
	W.9-10.3.e	Provide a conclusion that follows from and reflects on what is experienced, observed, or resolved over the course of the narrative.	**Unit 1:** T86, T99, T104, **T105, Unit 5:** T495, T496, **T500**
Production and Distribution of Writing	W.9-10.4	Produce clear and coherent writing in which the development, organization, and style are appropriate to task, purpose, and audience. (Grade-specific expectations for writing types are defined in standards 1–3 above.)	**Unit 1**: **T100, Unit 2: T190, Unit 3: T296, T299, Unit 4**: T338, **T383**, T388, **T394, T395, Unit 5**: T485, **T496, T503, Unit 6**: T540, **T592, Unit 7**: **T643, Handbook**: T785, T794, T822
	W.9-10.5	Develop and strengthen writing as needed by planning, revising, editing, rewriting, or trying a new approach, focusing on addressing what is most significant for a specific purpose and audience. (Editing for conventions should demonstrate command of Language standards 1–3 up to and including grades 9–10 on page 54.)	**Unit 1**: **T89, T98, T99, T102, T103, T105, Unit 2**: T157, **T188, T189, T192, T193, T195, Unit 3**: **T259, T287, 294, T295, T296, T300, T301, Unit 4**: **T337, T359, T392, T393, T397, T399, Unit 5**: **T433, T494, T495, T496, T499, T501, T504, Unit 6: T539, T559, T590, T591, T594, T595, T597, Unit 7**: **T675, T697**, **Handbook**: T810
	W.9-10.6	Use technology, including the Internet, to produce, publish, and update individual or shared writing products, taking advantage of technology's capacity to link to other information and to display information flexibly and dynamically.	**Unit 1**: T100, T107, **Unit 2**: T135, **T189,** T199, **Unit 3**: T295, T296, T305, **Unit 4**: T388, **T393,** T403, **Unit 5**: **T496,** T505, **Unit 6**: T535, 592, T601 **Handbook**: T721, T791, T820
Research to Build and Present Knowledge	W.9-10.7	Conduct short as well as more sustained research projects to answer a question (including a self-generated question) or solve a problem; narrow or broaden the inquiry when appropriate; synthesize multiple sources on the subject, demonstrating understanding of the subject under investigation.	**Unit 1**: T31, **T37**, T38, T73, T85, **T89**, T92, T93, **Unit 2**: T112, T131, **T135**, T136, T153, T156, T171, T183, **Unit 3**: T229, **T233**, T234, T245, T255, **T259**, T273, T283, T289, **Unit 4**: T327, T333, T336, T355, T360, T382, T386, **T392, T398, T399, Unit 5**: T422, T429, T434, T449, T455, T472, T479, T488, T489, **Unit 6**: T525, T540, T577, **T590, Unit 7**: T632, T665, T671, T693, **T697**, T699, **Handbook**: T725
	W.9-10.8	Gather relevant information from multiple authoritative print and digital sources, using advanced searches effectively; assess the usefulness of each source in answering the research question; integrate information into the text selectively to maintain the flow of ideas, avoiding plagiarism and following a standard format for citation.	**Unit 1**: T31, **T89**, **Unit 4**: **T392, T393, T394, Unit 5:** T422, **Unit 6**: T525, T590, **Unit 7:** T693, **T697, T700, Handbook**: T719, T726
	W.9-10.9	Draw evidence from literary or informational texts to support analysis, reflection, and research.	**Unit 1**: T51, T58, T79, **Unit 2**: T132, **Unit 3**: T291, T296, **Unit 5**: T457 *See additional coverage below.*
	W.9-10.9.a	Apply grades 9–10 Reading standards to literature (e.g., "Analyze how an author draws on and transforms source material in a specific work [e.g., how Shakespeare treats a theme or topic from Ovid or the Bible or how a later author draws on a play by Shakespeare]").	**Unit 1**: T25, **T61**, **Unit 2**: T154, T176, **Unit 3**: T221, T250, T257, T277, **Unit 4**: T356, T357, **Unit 5**: T423, T450, T456, T481, T483, **T484**, **Unit 7**: T633, T640, T641, **T643**, T663, T672, T673, T689, T694, T695, T699

Standards for Writing, continued

Strand	Code	Standards Text	Teacher's Edition Pages
Research to Build and Present Knowledge continued	W.9-10.9.b	Apply grades 9–10 Reading standards to literary nonfiction (e.g., "Delineate and evaluate the argument and specific claims in a text, assessing whether the reasoning is valid and the evidence is relevant and sufficient; identify false statements and fallacious reasoning").	**Unit 1**: T33, **Unit 2**: T149, T173, **Unit 3**: T230, **Unit 4**: T328, T334, T349, T357, T374, T381, T387, **Unit 5**: T430, **Unit 6**: T526, T536, T573, T585
Range of Writing	W.9-10.10	Write routinely over extended time frames (time for research, reflection, and revision) and shorter time frames (a single sitting or a day or two) for a range of tasks, purposes, and audiences.	**Unit 1**: T25, T79, T86, T93, **T95, Unit 2**: T127, T132, T136, T149, T154, T155, T173, T177, T183, **T185, Unit 3**: T221, T230, T250, T256, T277, T284, T289, **T291, Unit 4**: T328, T334, T335, T338, T349, T356, T374, T380, T387, **T389, Unit 5**: T423, T430, T434, T450, T456, T473, T481, T489, **T491, Unit 6**: T526, T536, T540, T551, T556, T573, T578, T585, **T587, Unit 7**: T633, T640, T644, T663, T665, T672, T689, T694, T699

Standards for Speaking and Listening

Strand	Code	Standards Text	Teacher's Edition Pages
Comprehension and Collaboration	SL.9-10.1	Initiate and participate effectively in a range of collaborative discussions (one-on-one, in groups, and teacher-led) with diverse partners on grades 9-10 topics, texts, and issues, building on others' ideas and expressing their own clearly and persuasively.	**Unit 1**: T0, T10, T26, T38, T40, T64, T103, T109, **Unit 2**: T110, T114, T118, T133, T136, T138, T155, T156, T160, T177, **Unit 3**: T200, T207, T208, T231, T236, T251, **T261**, T262, T285, T299, T305, **Unit 4**: T306, T313, T314, T340, T362, T403, **Unit 5**: T404, T412, T436, T458, T462, T480, **Unit 6**: T506, T514, T542, T558, T562, T595, **Unit 7**: T602, T612, T646, T665, T678, T687, **Handbook**: T713 *See additional coverage below.*
	SL.9-10.1.a	Come to discussions prepared, having read and researched material under study; explicitly draw on that preparation by referring to evidence from texts and other research on the topic or issue to stimulate a thoughtful, well-reasoned exchange of ideas.	**Unit 1**: T23, T24, T49, T60, T61, **T63**, T84, T93, **T94**, **Unit 2**: T183, **T184**, **Unit 3**: T204, T220, T225, T226, T232, T246, T257, T276, T282, T286, T289, **T290**, T301, **Unit 4**: T310, T324, T336, T359, T382, T387, **T388**, **Unit 5**: T408, T411, T427, T446, T477, T484, T488, T489, **T490**, **Unit 6**: T510, T524, T530, T533, T558, **T560**, **T561**, T571, T585, **T586**, T601, **Unit 7**: T606, T610, T620, T628, T636, T668, T687, T699, **T700**, **Handbook**: T775
	SL.9-10.1.b	Work with peers to set rules for collegial discussions and decision-making (e.g., informal consensus, taking votes on key issues, presentation of alternate views), clear goals and deadlines, and individual roles as needed.	**Unit 1**: T0, T3, T36, **Unit 2**: T110, T113, **Unit 3**: T200, T203, T258, **T261**, **Unit 4**: T306, T309, **Unit 5**: T404, T407, **Unit 6**: T506, T509, **T560**, **Unit 7**: T602, T665
	SL.9-10.1.c	Propel conversations by posing and responding to questions that relate the current discussion to broader themes or larger ideas; actively incorporate others into the discussion; and clarify, verify, or challenge ideas and conclusions.	**Unit 1**: **T94**, **Unit 3**: **T261**, **Unit 4**: T358, **Unit 6**: **T560**, **T561**, **Handbook**: T704, T708, T709, T714
	SL.9-10.1.d	Respond thoughtfully to diverse perspectives, summarize points of agreement and disagreement, and, when warranted, qualify or justify their own views and understanding and make new connections in light of the evidence and reasoning presented.	**Unit 1**: T105, **Unit 2**: T178, T195, **Unit 3**: **T261**, **Unit 3**: T301, **Unit 4**: T399, **Unit 5**: T499, T501, **Unit 6**: **T560**, **T561**, T597, T601, Unit 7: T642, **Handbook**: T714
	SL.9-10.2	Integrate multiple sources of information presented in diverse media or formats (e.g., visually, quantitatively, orally) evaluating the credibility and accuracy of each source.	**Unit 1:** T94, **Unit 2:** T184, **Unit 3:** T290, **Unit 4:** T361, T388, **Unit 5:** T490, **Unit 6:** T580, T586, **Unit 7:** T700, **Handbook:** T717, T720, T775, T821
	SL.9-10.3	Evaluate a speaker's point of view, reasoning, and use of evidence and rhetoric, identifying any fallacious reasoning or exaggerated or distorted evidence.	**Unit 1**: T0, **T63**, **Unit 2**: T110, **T159**, T199, **Unit 3**: T200, **T261**, **Unit 4**: T306, T336, **T361**, **Unit 5**: T404, T459, **Unit 6**: T506, T558, **T560**, **T561**, **T586**, T601, **Unit 7**: T602, **T677**, **Handbook**: T711

Common Core State Standards, continued

Literacy Standards for Reading, Writing, Speaking and Listening, and Language

Standards for Speaking and Listening, continued

Strand	Code	Standards Text	Teacher's Edition Pages
Presentation of Knowledge and Ideas	SL.9-10.4	Present information, findings, and supporting evidence clearly, concisely, and logically such that listeners can follow the line of reasoning and the organization, development, substance, and style are appropriate to purpose, audience, and task.	**Unit 1**: T2, T37, T61, **T63**, T88, **Unit 2**: T112, T134, T156, **T159**, **T184**, T199, **Unit 3**: T202, **Unit 4**: T308, T359, **T361**, T382, T403, **Unit 5**: T406, **T490**, **Unit 6**: T508, T538, **T560**, **T561**, T580, T581, **T586**, T601, **Unit 7**: T604, **T677**, **Handbook**: T711, T715
	SL.9-10.5	Make strategic use of digital media (e.g., textual, graphical, audio, visual, and interactive elements) in presentations to enhance understanding of findings, reasoning, and evidence and to add interest.	**Unit 2**: T135, **Unit 3**: **T290**, **Unit 4**: T403, **Unit 5**: **T490**, T505, **Unit 6**: T535, T581, **T586**, **Handbook**: T719, T724
	SL.9-10.6	Adapt speech to a variety of contexts and tasks, demonstrating command of formal English when indicated or appropriate.	**Unit 1**: **T94**, **Unit 2**: T178, T199, **Unit 3**: T257, T287, **Unit 4**: T382, T403, **Unit 5**: T432, T433, **T461**, T485, **T490**, T505, **Unit 7**: T643, T674, **T677**, T696, **Handbook**: T709, T712

Standards for Language

Strand	Code	Standards Text	Teacher's Edition Pages
Conventions of Standard English	L.9-10.1	Demonstrate command of the conventions of standard English grammar and usage when writing or speaking.	**Unit 1**: T16, T46, T48, T50, T56, T60, T70, T74, T76, T82, T88, T107, **Unit 2**: T124, T126, T130, T134, T144, T146, T148, T170, T197, **Unit 3**: T218, T224, T228, T242, T244, T268, T272, T274, T280, T286, T303, **Unit 4**: T326, T332, T368, T370, T378, T382, T401, **Unit 5**: T426, T468, T476, T503, **Unit 6**: T522, **Handbook**: T703, T707, T709, T710, T801, T826, T828, T829, T831, T832, T840, T843, T861 *See additional coverage below.*
	L.9-10.1.a	Use parallel structure.	**Unit 3**: T214, T232, T254, T258, **Unit 6**: T576, T599, **Handbook**: T716, T851
	L.9-10.1.b	Use various types of phrases (noun, verb, adjectival, adverbial, participial, prepositional, absolute) and clauses (independent, dependent; noun, relative, adverbial) to convey specific meanings and add variety and interest to writing or presentations.	**Unit 1**: T18, T22, T32, T36, T107, **Unit 2**: T128, T152, T156, T158, T166, T168, T172, T178, **Unit 3**: T248, T254, T258, T298, T299, T300, T301, **Unit 4**: T320, T322, T336, T346, T348, T352, T354, T358, T372, **Unit 5**: T418, T420, T428, T432, T442, T444, T448, T454, T458, T470, T478, T484, T500, T502, **Unit 6**: T520, T532, T534, T538, T548, T550, T551, T554, T558, T568, T570, T572, T576, T580, T595, T599, **Unit 7**: T618, T624, T630, T638, T642, T652, T656, T660, T670, T674, T684, T686, T688, T692, T696, **Handbook**: T824, T827, T830, T832, T833, T834, T835, T836, T837, T838, T839, T842, T843, T844, T845, T847, T848, T849, T850, T851, T855, T857 *See additional coverage below.*
	L.9-10.2	Demonstrate command of the conventions of standard English capitalization, punctuation, and spelling when writing.	**Unit 1**: T16, T106, T107, **Unit 2**: T148, T196, **Unit 3**: T302, **Unit 4**: T400, T502, **Unit 6**: T598, **Handbook**: T852, T853, T855, T857
	L.9-10.2.a	Use a semicolon (and perhaps a conjunctive adverb) to link two or more closely related independent clauses.	**Unit 6:** T598, T599 **Handbook**: T847, T857
	L.9-10.2.b	Use a colon to introduce a list or quotation.	**Unit 2**: T196, T197, **Handbook**: T857
	L.9-10.2.c	Spell correctly.	**Unit 1**: T46, T107, **Unit 2**: T148, T197, **Unit 3**: T218, T242, T244, **Unit 4**: T320, **Unit 5**: T442, T444, T470, **Unit 7**: T638, T642, **Handbook**: T826, T827, T840

Standards for Language, continued

Strand	Code	Standards Text	Teacher's Edition Pages
Knowledge of Language	L.9-10.3	Apply knowledge of language to understand how language functions in different contexts, to make effective choices for meaning or style, and to comprehend more fully when reading or listening.	**Unit 1**: T16, T63, T93, T107, **Unit 2**: T159, T183, T197, **Unit 3**: T289, T303, **Unit 4**: T361, T387, **Unit 5**: T461, T483, T489, **Unit 6**: T561, T585, T599, **Unit 7**: T677, T699, **Handbook**: T830, T833, T836, T838, T839, T842, T848, T861 *See additional coverage below.*
	L.9-10.3.a	Write and edit work so that it conforms to the guidelines in a style manual (e.g., *MLA Handbook*, Turabian's *Manual for Writers*) appropriate for the discipline and writing type.	**Unit 1**: T60, T106, T196, **Unit 3**: T302, **Unit 4**: T394, T398, T400, **Unit 5**: T502, **Unit 6**: T598, **Handbook**: T729, T815
Vocabulary Acquisition and Use	L.9-10.4	Determine or clarify the meaning of unknown and multiple-meaning words and phrases based on grades 9–10 reading and content, choosing flexibly from a range of strategies.	**Unit 1**: T26, **T39**, **Unit 4**: T319, T321, **T339**, **T359**, **Unit 6**: **T539**, **T541**, T547, **T559**, **Handbook**: T705, T777, T780 *See additional coverage below.*
	L.9-10.4.a	Use context (e.g., the overall meaning of a sentence, paragraph, or text; a word's position or function in a sentence) as a clue to the meaning of a word or phrase.	**Unit 1**: T65, T71, T73, T75, T78, T79, T80, T82, T83, T84, T85, T86, **Unit 2**: T130, **T135**, **T137**, T142, T147, **T157**, **T179**, T186, **Unit 3**: T214, T255, **Unit 4**: T368, T371, **Unit 5**: T427, T445, T492, **Unit 6**: T524, T534, **Unit 6**: T524, T534, **T562**, **Unit 7: T643**, **Handbook**: T785
	L.9-10.4.b	Identify and correctly use patterns of word changes that indicate different meanings or parts of speech (e.g., analyze, analysis, analytical; advocate, advocacy).	**Unit 1**: **T39**, **T89**, **Unit 3**: T214, **T233**, **T235**, T255, **T262**, **T287**, **Unit 4**: T371, **Unit 5**: T418, **Unit 7**: T670, **Handbook**: T780
	L.9-10.4.c	Consult general and specialized reference materials (e.g., dictionaries, glossaries, thesauruses), both print and digital, to find the pronunciation of a word or determine or clarify its precise meaning, its part of speech, or its etymology.	**Unit 1**: **T37**, **T39**, **T61**, **Unit 2**: **T118**, **T137**, T168, **Unit 3**: **T208**, T212, **T235**, **T259**, T292, **Unit 4**: **T337**, **T340**, **T359**, **T383**, **Unit 5**: T421, **T435**, T443, T445, T447, **T459**, **T462**, **Handbook**: T705, T781, T783
	L.9-10.4.d	Verify the preliminary determination of the meaning of a word or phrase (e.g., by checking the inferred meaning in context or in a dictionary).	**Unit 1**: **T39**, T96, T100, **Unit 2**: **T137**, **Unit 3**: **T233**, **T235**, **T287**, **Unit 4**: **T339**, T390, **Unit 5**: **T435**, T492, **Unit 6**: **T539**, **Handbook**: T781, T783
	L.9-10.5	Demonstrate understanding of figurative language, word relationships, and nuances in word meanings.	**Unit 1**: T27, **Unit 2**: T163, T194, **Unit 3**: T243, **Unit 5**: **T433**, **T435**, T480, **T485**, **Unit 7**: **T645**, T652, **T697**, **Handbook**: T716, T778 *See additional coverage below.*
	L.9-10.5.a	Interpret figures of speech (e.g., euphemism, oxymoron) in context and analyze their role in the text.	**Unit 1**: T74, **Unit 2**: **T157**, **T179**, **Unit 7**: T631, **T643**, **T645**, **Handbook**: T703
	L.9-10.5.b	Analyze nuances in the meaning of words with similar denotations.	**Unit 1**: T71, **Unit 2**: **T160**, T168, **Unit 5**: **T433**, T496, **Unit 6**: **T581**, T588, **Unit 7**: **T675**

Common Core State Standards, continued
Literacy Standards for Reading, Writing, Speaking and Listening, and Language

Standards for Language, continued			
Strand	**Code**	**Standards Text**	**Teacher's Edition Pages**
Vocabulary Acquisition and Use continued	L.9-10.6	Acquire and use accurately general academic and domain-specific words and phrases, sufficient for reading, writing, speaking, and listening at the college and career readiness level; demonstrate independence in gathering vocabulary knowledge when considering a word or phrase important to comprehension or expression.	**Unit 1**: T4, T7, **T10**, T13, T15, T19, T21, T25, T30, T33, T35, T38, **T40**, T45, T47, T51, T54, T58, T59, **T64**, T69, T71, T78, T79, T83, T86, T87, T90, T94, T96, **Unit 2**: T115, **T118**, T123, T125, T127, T132, T133, T136, **T138**, T143, T145, T147, T149, T154, T155, **T160**, T165, T167, T169, T173, T176, T177, T180, T182, T184, **Unit 3**: T205, **T208**, T213, T215, T216, T221, T227, T230, T231, T234, **T236**, T241, T243, T250, T256, T257, **T262**, T267, T270, T277, T281, T284, T285, T288, T290, T292, **Unit 4**: T311, **T314**, T319, T321, T323, T328, T334, T335, **T340**, T345, T347, T349, T353, T356, T357, **T362**, T367, T368, T369, T371, T373, T374, T380, T381, T384, T388, T390, **Unit 5**: T409, **T412**, T417, T419, T421, T423, T430, T431, **T436**, T441, T443, T445, T447, T450, T456, T457, **T462**, T467, T469, T473, T481, T483, T486, T490, **Unit 6**: T512, **T514**, T519, T521, T523, T526, T536, T537, **T542**, T547, T549, T551, T556, T557, **T562**, T565, T567, T569, T573, T578, T579, T582, T584, T586, T588, T599, **Unit 7**: T607, T611, **T612**, T617, T619, T622, T626, T633, T637, T640, T641, T644, **T646**, T651, T653, T654, T662, T665, T670, T671, T672, T673, **T678**, T683, T685, T689, T694, T695, T698, T700, **Handbook**: T703, T776

Common Core State Standards

Common Core State Standards

Student Handbooks

UNIT 1: Choices

SE Pages	Lesson	Code	Standards Text
0–1	Discuss the Essential Question	SL.9-10.1.b	Work with peers to set rules for collegial discussions and decision-making, clear goals and deadlines, and individual roles as needed.
		SL.9-10.3	Evaluate a speaker's point of view, reasoning, and use of evidence and rhetoric, identifying any fallacious reasoning or exaggerated or distorted evidence.
2	Analyze and Debate	SL.9-10.4	Present information, findings, and supporting evidence clearly, concisely, and logically such that listeners can follow the line of reasoning and the organization, development, substance, and style are appropriate to purpose, audience, and task.
3	Plan a Project	SL.9-10.1.b	Work with peers to set rules for collegial discussions and decision-making, clear goals and deadlines, and individual roles as needed.
3	Choose More to Read	RL.9-10.10	By the end of grade 10, read and comprehend literature, including stories, dramas, and poems, at the high end of the grades 9–10 text complexity band independently and proficiently.
		RI.9-10.10	By the end of grade 10, read and comprehend literary nonfiction at the high end of the grades 9–10 text complexity band independently and proficiently.
4–5	How to Read Using Reading Strategies	RI.9-10.10	By the end of grade 10, read and comprehend literary nonfiction at the high end of the grades 9–10 text complexity band independently and proficiently.
		L.9-10.6	Acquire and use accurately general academic and domain-specific words and phrases, sufficient for reading, writing, speaking, and listening at the college and career readiness level; demonstrate independence in gathering vocabulary knowledge when considering a word or phrase important to comprehension or expression.
6–9	How to Read Short Stories	RL.9-10.3	Analyze how complex characters develop over the course of a text, interact with other characters, and advance the plot or develop the theme.
		RL.9-10.10	By the end of grade 10, read and comprehend literature, including stories, dramas, and poems, at the high end of the grades 9–10 text complexity band independently and proficiently.
		L.9-10.6	Acquire and use accurately general academic and domain-specific words and phrases, sufficient for reading, writing, speaking, and listening at the college and career readiness level; demonstrate independence in gathering vocabulary knowledge when considering a word or phrase important to comprehension or expression.
Cluster 1			
10	Prepare to Read	RI.9-10.4	Determine the meaning of words and phrases as they are used in a text, including figurative, connotative, and technical meanings; analyze the cumulative impact of specific word choices on meaning and tone.
		SL.9-10.1	Initiate and participate effectively in a range of collaborative discussions (one-on-one, in groups, and teacher-led) with diverse partners on grades 9–10 topics, texts, and issues, building on others' ideas and expressing their own clearly and persuasively.
		L.9-10.6	Acquire and use accurately general academic and domain-specific words and phrases, sufficient for reading, writing, speaking, and listening at the college and career readiness level; demonstrate independence in gathering vocabulary knowledge when considering a word or phrase important to comprehension or expression.

page 890

Student Handbooks, continued

Cluster 1, continued

SE Pages	Lesson	Code	Standards Text
11	Before Reading: The Good Samaritan	RL.9-10.5	Analyze in detail how an author's ideas or claims are developed and refined by particular sentences, paragraphs, or larger portions of a text.
		RL.9-10.10	By the end of grade 10, read and comprehend literature, including stories, dramas, and poems, at the high end of the grades 9–10 text complexity band independently and proficiently.
12–25	Read The Good Samaritan	RL.9-10.1	Cite strong and thorough textual evidence to support analysis of what the text says explicitly as well as inferences drawn from the text.
		RL.9-10.2	Determine a theme or central idea of a text and analyze in detail its development over the course of the text, including how it emerges and is shaped and refined by specific details; provide an objective summary of the text.
		RL.9-10.3	Analyze how complex characters develop over the course of a text, interact with other characters, and advance the plot or develop the theme.
		RL.9-10.4	Determine the meaning of words and phrases as they are used in a text, including figurative, connotative, and technical meanings; analyze the cumulative impact of specific word choices on meaning and tone.
		RL.9-10.5	Analyze how an author's choices concerning how to structure a text, order events within it, and manipulate time create such effects as mystery, tension, or surprise.
		RL.9-10.10	By the end of grade 10, read and comprehend literature, including stories, dramas, and poems, at the high end of the grades 9–10 text complexity band independently and proficiently.
		W.9-10.9.a	Apply grades 9–10 Reading standards to literature.
		W.9-10.10	Write routinely over extended time frames (time for research, reflection, and revision) and shorter time frames (a single sitting or a day or two) for a range of tasks, purposes, and audiences.
		L.9-10.1.b	Use various types of phrases (noun, verb, adjectival, adverbial, participial, prepositional, absolute) and clauses (independent, dependent; noun, relative, adverbial) to convey specific meanings and add variety and interest to writing or presentations.
		L.9-10.2	Demonstrate command of the conventions of standard English capitalization, punctuation, and spelling when writing.
		L.9-10.3	Apply knowledge of language to understand how language functions in different contexts, to make effective choices for meaning or style, and to comprehend more fully when reading or listening.
		L.9-10.6	Acquire and use accurately general academic and domain-specific words and phrases, sufficient for reading, writing, speaking, and listening at the college and career readiness level; demonstrate independence in gathering vocabulary knowledge when considering a word or phrase important to comprehension or expression.
26–27	Postscript: Don't Go Gentle Into That Good Expressway	RL.9-10.2	Determine a theme or central idea of a text and analyze in detail its development over the course of the text, including how it emerges and is shaped and refined by specific details; provide an objective summary of the text.

page 891

Common Core State Standards, continued

Student Handbooks, continued

Cluster 1, continued

SE Pages	Lesson	Code	Standards Text
26–27	Postscript: Don't Go Gentle Into That Good Expressway continued	SL.9-10.1	Initiate and participate effectively in a range of collaborative discussions (one-on-one, in groups, and teacher-led) with diverse partners on grades 9–10 topics, texts, and issues, building on others' ideas and expressing their own clearly and persuasively.
		L.9-10.4	Determine or clarify the meaning of unknown and multiple-meaning words and phrases based on grades 9–10 reading and content, choosing flexibly from a range of strategies.
		L.9-10.5	Demonstrate understanding of figurative language, word relationships, and nuances in word meanings.
28	Before Reading: The World Is in Their Hands	RI.9-10.2	Determine a central idea of a text and analyze its development over the course of the text, including how it emerges and is shaped and refined by specific details; provide an objective summary of the text.
		RI.9-10.7	Analyze various accounts of a subject told in different mediums, determining which details are emphasized in each account.
		RI.9-10.10	By the end of grade 10, read and comprehend literary nonfiction at the high end of the grades 9–10 text complexity band independently and proficiently.
29–33	Read The World Is in Their Hands	RI.9-10.1	Cite strong and thorough textual evidence to support analysis of what the text says explicitly as well as inferences drawn from the text.
		RI.9-10.2	Determine a central idea of a text and analyze its development over the course of the text, including how it emerges and is shaped and refined by specific details; provide an objective summary of the text.
		RI.9-10.5	Analyze in detail how an author's ideas or claims are developed and refined by particular sentences, paragraphs, or larger portions of a text.
		RI.9-10.7	Analyze various accounts of a subject told in different mediums, determining which details are emphasized in each account.
		RI.9-10.10	By the end of grade 10, read and comprehend literary nonfiction at the high end of the grades 9–10 text complexity band independently and proficiently.
		W.9-10.9.b	Apply grades 9–10 Reading standards to literary nonfiction.
		L.9-10.1.b	Use various types of phrases (noun, verb, adjectival, adverbial, participial, prepositional, absolute) and clauses (independent, dependent; noun, relative, adverbial) to convey specific meanings and add variety and interest to writing or presentations.
		L.9-10.6	Acquire and use accurately general academic and domain-specific words and phrases, sufficient for reading, writing, speaking, and listening at the college and career readiness level; demonstrate independence in gathering vocabulary knowledge when considering a word or phrase important to comprehension or expression.
34	Postscript: Making a Difference	RI.9-10.2	Determine a central idea of a text and analyze its development over the course of the text, including how it emerges and is shaped and refined by specific details; provide an objective summary of the text.
		RI.9-10.7	Analyze various accounts of a subject told in different mediums, determining which details are emphasized in each account.

page 892

Student Handbooks, continued

Cluster 1, continued

SE Pages	Lesson	Code	Standards Text
34	Postscript: Making a Difference continued	RI.9-10.10	By the end of grade 10, read and comprehend literary nonfiction at the high end of the grades 9–10 text complexity band independently and proficiently.
35	Reflect and Assess Critical Thinking	RL.9-10.1	Cite strong and thorough textual evidence to support analysis of what the text says explicitly as well as inferences drawn from the text.
		RL.9-10.3	Analyze how complex characters develop over the course of a text, interact with other characters, and advance the plot or develop the theme.
	Write About Literature	W.9-10.1	Write arguments to support claims in an analysis of substantive topics or texts, using valid reasoning and relevant and sufficient evidence.
	Key Vocabulary Review	L.9-10.6	Acquire and use accurately general academic and domain-specific words and phrases, sufficient for reading, writing, speaking, and listening at the college and career readiness level; demonstrate independence in gathering vocabulary knowledge when considering a word or phrase important to comprehension or expression.
	Read with Ease: Expression	RL.9-10.10	By the end of grade 10, read and comprehend literature, including stories, dramas, and poems, at the high end of the grades 9–10 text complexity band independently and proficiently.
36	Grammar: Write Complete Sentences	L.9-10.1.b	Use various types of phrases (noun, verb, adjectival, adverbial, participial, prepositional, absolute) and clauses (independent, dependent; noun, relative, adverbial) to convey specific meanings and add variety and interest to writing or presentations.
36	Language Development: Ask and Answer Questions	SL.9-10.1.b	Work with peers to set rules for collegial discussions and decision-making, clear goals and deadlines, and individual roles as needed.
36	Literary Analysis: Analyze Theme	RL.9-10.2	Determine a theme or central idea of a text and analyze in detail its development over the course of the text, including how it emerges and is shaped and refined by specific details; provide an objective summary of the text.
36	Language Development: Give and Follow Instructions	SL.9-10.1.b	Work with peers to set rules for collegial discussions and decisions-making, clear goals and deadlines, and individual roles as needed.
37	Vocabulary Study: Prefixes	L.9-10.4.c	Consult general and specialized reference materials, both print and digital, to find the pronunciation of a word or determine or clarify its precise meaning, its part of speech, or its etymology.
37	Writing: Write a Definition Paragraph	W.9-10.2	Write informative/explanatory texts to examine and convey complex ideas, concepts, and information clearly and accurately through the effective selection, organization, and analysis of content.
37	Research/Speaking: Oral Report	W.9-10.7	Conduct short as well as more sustained research projects to answer a question (including a self-generated question) or solve a problem; narrow or broaden the inquiry when appropriate; synthesize multiple sources on the subject, demonstrating understanding of the subject under investigation.
		SL.9-10.4	Present information, findings, and supporting evidence clearly, concisely, and logically such that listeners can follow the line of reasoning and the organization, development, substance, and style are appropriate to purpose, audience, and task.

page 893

Common Core State Standards

Common Core State Standards, continued

SE Pages	Lesson	Code	Standards Text
Student Handbooks, continued			
Cluster 1, continued			
38	**Workplace Workshop: Inside a Law Office**	W.9-10.7	Conduct short as well as more sustained research projects to answer a question (including a self-generated question) or solve a problem; narrow or broaden the inquiry when appropriate; synthesize multiple sources on the subject, demonstrating understanding of the subject under investigation.
		SL.9-10.1	Initiate and participate effectively in a range of collaborative discussions (one-on-one, in groups, and teacher-led) with diverse partners on grades 9-10 topics, texts, and issues, building on others' ideas and expressing their own clearly and persuasively.
		L.9-10.6	Acquire and use accurately general academic and domain-specific words and phrases, sufficient for reading, writing, speaking, and listening at the college and career readiness level; demonstrate independence in gathering vocabulary knowledge when considering a word or phrase important to comprehension or expression.
39	**Vocabulary Workshop: Use Word Parts**	L.9-10.4.b	Identify and correctly use patterns of word changes that indicate different meanings or parts of speech.
		L.9-10.4.c	Consult general and specialized reference materials, both print and digital, to find the pronunciation of a word or determine or clarify its precise meaning, its part of speech, or its etymology.
		L.9-10.4.d	Verify the preliminary determination of the meaning of a word or phrase.
Cluster 2			
40	**Prepare to Read**	RI.9-10.4	Determine the meaning of words and phrases as they are used in a text, including figurative, connotative, and technical meanings; analyze the cumulative impact of specific word choices on meaning and tone.
		SL.9-10.1	Initiate and participate effectively in a range of collaborative discussions (one-on-one, in groups, and teacher-led) with diverse partners on grades 9-10 topics, texts, and issues, building on others' ideas and expressing their own clearly and persuasively.
		L.9-10.6	Acquire and use accurately general academic and domain-specific words and phrases, sufficient for reading, writing, speaking, and listening at the college and career readiness level; demonstrate independence in gathering vocabulary knowledge when considering a word or phrase important to comprehension or expression.
41	**Before Reading: Thank You, Ma'am**	RL.9-10.2	Determine a theme or central idea of a text and analyze in detail its development over the course of the text, including how it emerges and is shaped and refined by specific details; provide an objective summary of the text.
		RL.9-10.3	Analyze how complex characters develop over the course of a text, interact with other characters, and advance the plot or develop the theme.
42–51	**Read Thank You, Ma'am**	RL.9-10.1	Cite strong and thorough textual evidence to support analysis of what the text says explicitly as well as inferences drawn from the text.
		RL.9-10.2	Determine a theme or central idea of a text and analyze in detail its development over the course of the text, including how it emerges and is shaped and refined by specific details; provide an objective summary of the text.
		RL.9-10.3	Analyze how complex characters develop over the course of a text, interact with other characters, and advance the plot or develop the theme.

page 894

SE Pages	Lesson	Code	Standards Text
Student Handbooks, continued			
Cluster 2, continued			
42–51	**Read Thank You, Ma'am** continued	RL.9-10.4	Determine the meaning of words and phrases as they are used in a text, including figurative, connotative, and technical meanings; analyze the cumulative impact of specific word choices on meaning and tone.
		RL.9-10.7	Analyze the representation of a subject or a key scene in two different artistic mediums, including what is emphasized or absent in each treatment.
		RL.9-10.10	By the end of grade 10, read and comprehend literature, including stories, dramas, and poems, at the high end of the grades 9-10 text complexity band independently and proficiently.
		W.9-10.9	Draw evidence from literary or informational texts to support analysis, reflection, and research.
		L.9-10.1	Demonstrate command of the conventions of standard English grammar and usage when writing or speaking.
		L.9-10.2.c	Spell correctly.
		L.9-10.6	Acquire and use accurately general academic and domain-specific words and phrases, sufficient for reading, writing, speaking, and listening at the college and career readiness level; demonstrate independence in gathering vocabulary knowledge when considering a word or phrase important to comprehension or expression.
52	**Before Reading: Juvenile Justice**	RI.9-10.2	Determine a central idea of a text and analyze its development over the course of the text, including how it emerges and is shaped and refined by specific details; provide an objective summary of the text.
		RI.9-10.3	Analyze how the author unfolds an analysis or series of ideas or events, including the order in which the points are made, how they are introduced and developed, and the connections that are drawn between them.
53–58	**Read Juvenile Justice**	RI.9-10.1	Cite strong and thorough textual evidence to support analysis of what the text says explicitly as well as inferences drawn from the text.
		RI.9-10.2	Determine a central idea of a text and analyze its development over the course of the text, including how it emerges and is shaped and refined by specific details; provide an objective summary of the text.
		RI.9-10.3	Analyze how the author unfolds an analysis or series of ideas or events, including the order in which the points are made, how they are introduced and developed, and the connections that are drawn between them.
		RI.9-10.4	Determine the meaning of words and phrases as they are used in a text, including figurative, connotative, and technical meanings; analyze the cumulative impact of specific word choices on meaning and tone.
		RI.9-10.8	Delineate and evaluate the argument and specific claims in a text, assessing whether the reasoning is valid and the evidence is relevant and sufficient; identify false statements and fallacious reasoning.
		RI.9-10.10	By the end of grade 10, read and comprehend literary nonfiction at the high end of the grades 9-10 text complexity band independently and proficiently.

page 895

Common Core State Standards, continued

SE Pages	Lesson	Code	Standards Text
Student Handbooks, continued			
Cluster 2, continued			
53–58	**Read Juvenile Justice** continued	W.9-10.9	Draw evidence from literary or informational texts to support analysis, reflection, and research.
		L.9-10.1	Demonstrate command of the conventions of standard English grammar and usage when writing or speaking.
		L.9-10.6	Acquire and use accurately general academic and domain-specific words and phrases, sufficient for reading, writing, speaking, and listening at the college and career readiness level; demonstrate independence in gathering vocabulary knowledge when considering a word or phrase important to comprehension or expression.
59	**Reflect and Assess Critical Thinking**	RL.9-10.1	Cite strong and thorough textual evidence to support analysis of what the text says explicitly as well as inferences drawn from the text.
		RI.9-10.1	Cite strong and thorough textual evidence to support analysis of what the text says explicitly as well as inferences drawn from the text.
	Write About Literature	RI.9-10.1	Cite strong and thorough textual evidence to support analysis of what the text says explicitly as well as inferences drawn from the text.
	Key Vocabulary Review	W.9-10.1	Write arguments to support claims in an analysis of substantive topics or texts, using valid reasoning and relevant and sufficient evidence.
		L.9-10.6	Acquire and use accurately general academic and domain-specific words and phrases, sufficient for reading, writing, speaking, and listening at the college and career readiness level; demonstrate independence in gathering vocabulary knowledge when considering a word or phrase important to comprehension or expression.
	Read with Ease: Phrasing	RI.9-10.10	By the end of grade 10, read and comprehend literary nonfiction at the high end of the grades 9-10 text complexity band independently and proficiently.
60	**Grammar: Make Subjects and Verbs Agree**	RL.9-10.1	Cite strong and thorough textual evidence to support analysis of what the text says explicitly as well as inferences drawn from the text.
60	**Language Development: Express Ideas and Opinions**	SL.9-10.1.a	Come to discussions prepared, having read and researched material under study; explicitly draw on that preparation by referring to evidence from texts and other research on the topic or issue to stimulate a thoughtful, well-reasoned exchange of ideas.
60	**Literary Analysis: Analyze Dialogue**	L.9-10.3.a	Write and edit work so that it conforms to the guidelines in a style manual appropriate for the discipline and writing type.
61	**Vocabulary Study: Word Roots**	L.9-10.4.c	Consult general and specialized reference materials, both print and digital, to find the pronunciation of a word or determine or clarify its precise meaning, its part of speech, or its etymology.
61	**Writing on Demand: Write a Short Comparison Essay**	W.9-10.2	Write informative/explanatory texts to examine and convey complex ideas, concepts, and information clearly and accurately through the effective selection, organization, and analysis of content.
		W.9-10.9.a	Apply grades 9-10 Reading standards to literature.
61	**Listening/Speaking: Interview**	SL.9-10.4	Present information, findings, and supporting evidence clearly, concisely, and logically such that listeners can follow the line of reasoning and the organization, development, substance, and style are appropriate to purpose, audience, and task.

page 896

SE Pages	Lesson	Code	Standards Text
Student Handbooks, continued			
Cluster 2, continued			
62–63	**Listening and Speaking Workshop: Oral Response to Literature**	SL.9-10.1.a	Come to discussions prepared, having read and researched material under study; explicitly draw on that preparation by referring to evidence from texts and other research on the topic or issue to stimulate a thoughtful, well-reasoned exchange of ideas.
		SL.9-10.3	Evaluate a speaker's point of view, reasoning, and use of evidence and rhetoric, identifying any fallacious reasoning or exaggerated or distorted evidence.
		SL.9-10.4	Present information, findings, and supporting evidence clearly, concisely, and logically such that listeners can follow the line of reasoning and the organization, development, substance, and style are appropriate to purpose, audience, and task.
		L.9-10.3	Apply knowledge of language to understand how language functions in different contexts, to make effective choices for meaning or style, and to comprehend more fully when reading or listening.
Cluster 3			
64	**Prepare to Read**	RI.9-10.4	Determine the meaning of words and phrases as they are used in a text, including figurative, connotative, and technical meanings; analyze the cumulative impact of specific word choices on meaning and tone.
		SL.9-10.1	Initiate and participate effectively in a range of collaborative discussions (one-on-one, in groups, and teacher-led) with diverse partners on grades 9-10 topics, texts, and issues, building on others' ideas and expressing their own clearly and persuasively.
		L.9-10.6	Acquire and use accurately general academic and domain-specific words and phrases, sufficient for reading, writing, speaking, and listening at the college and career readiness level; demonstrate independence in gathering vocabulary knowledge when considering a word or phrase important to comprehension or expression.
65	**Before Reading: The Necklace**	RL.9-10.3	Analyze how complex characters develop over the course of a text, interact with other characters, and advance the plot or develop the theme.
		RL.9-10.4	Determine the meaning of words and phrases as they are used in a text, including figurative, connotative, and technical meanings; analyze the cumulative impact of specific word choices on meaning and tone.
		L.9-10.4.a	Use context as a clue to the meaning of a word or phrase.
66–79	**Read The Necklace**	RL.9-10.1	Cite strong and thorough textual evidence to support analysis of what the text says explicitly as well as inferences drawn from the text.
		RL.9-10.2	Determine a theme or central idea of a text and analyze in detail its development over the course of the text, including how it emerges and is shaped and refined by specific details; provide an objective summary of the text.
		RL.9-10.3	Analyze how complex characters develop over the course of a text, interact with other characters, and advance the plot or develop the theme.
		RL.9-10.4	Determine the meaning of words and phrases as they are used in a text, including figurative, connotative, and technical meanings; analyze the cumulative impact of specific word choices on meaning and tone.
		RL.9-10.5	Analyze how an author's choices concerning how to structure a text, order events within it, and manipulate time create such effects as mystery, tension, or surprise.

page 897

Common Core State Standards

Common Core State Standards, continued

Student Handbooks, continued

Cluster 3, continued

SE Pages	Lesson	Code	Standards Text
66–79	**Read The Necklace** continued	RL.9-10.6	Analyze the representation of a subject or a key scene in two different artistic mediums, including what is emphasized or absent in each treatment.
		RL.9-10.7	Analyze the representation of a subject or a key scene in two different artistic mediums, including what is emphasized or absent in each treatment.
		RL.9-10.10	By the end of grade 10, read and comprehend literature, including stories, dramas, and poems, at the high end of the grades 9–10 text complexity band independently and proficiently.
		W.9-10.9	Draw evidence from literary or informational texts to support analysis, reflection, and research.
		W.9-10.10	Write routinely over extended time frames (time for research, reflection, and revision) and shorter time frames (a single sitting or a day or two) for a range of tasks, purposes, and audiences.
		L.9-10.1	Demonstrate command of the conventions of standard English grammar and usage when writing or speaking.
		L.9-10.4.a	Use context as a clue to the meaning of a word or phrase.
		L.9-1-.5.a	Interpret figures of speech in context and analyze their role in the text.
		L.9-10.5.b	Analyze nuances in the meaning of words with similar denotations.
		L.9-10.6	Acquire and use accurately general academic and domain-specific words and phrases, sufficient for reading, writing, speaking, and listening at the college and career readiness level; demonstrate independence in gathering vocabulary knowledge when considering a word or phrase important to comprehension or expression.
80	**Before Reading: The Fashion Show**	RI.9-10.4	Determine the meaning of words and phrases as they are used in a text, including figurative, connotative, and technical meanings; analyze the cumulative impact of specific word choices on meaning and tone.
		RI.9-10.6	Determine an author's point of view or purpose in a text and analyze how an author uses rhetoric to advance that point of view or purpose.
		L.9-10.4.a	Use context as a clue to the meaning of a word or phrase.
81–86	**Read The Fashion Show**	RI.9-10.1	Cite strong and thorough textual evidence to support analysis of what the text says explicitly as well as inferences drawn from the text.
		RI.9-10.2	Determine a central idea of a text and analyze its development over the course of the text, including how it emerges and is shaped and refined by specific details; provide an objective summary of the text.
		RI.9-10.4	Determine the meaning of words and phrases as they are used in a text, including figurative, connotative, and technical meanings; analyze the cumulative impact of specific word choices on meaning and tone.
		RI.9-10.6	Determine an author's point of view or purpose in a text and analyze how an author uses rhetoric to advance that point of view or purpose.

page 898

Student Handbooks, continued

Cluster 3, continued

SE Pages	Lesson	Code	Standards Text
81–86	**Read The Fashion Show** continued	RI.9-10.7	Analyze various accounts of a subject told in different mediums, determining which details are emphasized in each account.
		RI.9-10.10	By the end of grade 10, read and comprehend literary nonfiction at the high end of the grades 9–10 text complexity band independently and proficiently.
		W.9-10.10	Write routinely over extended time frames (time for research, reflection, and revision) and shorter time frames (a single sitting or a day or two) for a range of tasks, purposes, and audiences.
		L.9-10.1	Demonstrate command of the conventions of standard English grammar and usage when writing or speaking.
		L.9-10.4.a	Use context as a clue to the meaning of a word or phrase.
		L.9-10.6	Acquire and use accurately general academic and domain-specific words and phrases, sufficient for reading, writing, speaking, and listening at the college and career readiness level; demonstrate independence in gathering vocabulary knowledge when considering a word or phrase important to comprehension or expression.
87	**Reflect and Assess Critical Thinking**	RL.9-10.1	Cite strong and thorough textual evidence to support analysis of what the text says explicitly as well as inferences drawn from the text.
		RI.9-10.1	Cite strong and thorough textual evidence to support analysis of what the text says explicitly as well as inferences drawn from the text.
		RL.9-10.2	Determine a theme or central idea of a text and analyze in detail its development over the course of the text, including how it emerges and is shaped and refined by specific details; provide an objective summary of the text.
		RI.9-10.2	Determine a central idea of a text and analyze its development over the course of the text, including how it emerges and is shaped and refined by specific details; provide an objective summary of the text.
		RL.9-10.3	Analyze how complex characters develop over the course of a text, interact with other characters, and advance the plot or develop the theme.
		RL.9-10.6	Analyze a particular point of view or cultural experience reflected in a work of literature from outside the United States, drawing on a wide reading of world literature.
	Write About Literature	W.9-10.3	Write narratives to develop real or imagined experiences or events using effective technique, well-chosen details, and well-structured event sequences.
	Key Vocabulary Review	L.9-10.6	Acquire and use accurately general academic and domain-specific words and phrases, sufficient for reading, writing, speaking, and listening at the college and career readiness level; demonstrate independence in gathering vocabulary knowledge when considering a word or phrase important to comprehension or expression.
	Read with Ease: Intonation	RI.9-10.10	By the end of grade 10, read and comprehend literary nonfiction at the high end of the grades 9–10 text complexity band independently and proficiently.

page 899

Common Core State Standards, continued

Student Handbooks, continued

Cluster 3, continued

SE Pages	Lesson	Code	Standards Text
88	**Grammar: Fix Sentence Fragments**	L.9-10.1	Demonstrate command of the conventions of standard English grammar and usage when writing or speaking.
88	**Language Development: Express Feelings and Intentions**	SL.9-10.4	Present information, findings, and supporting evidence clearly, concisely, and logically such that listeners can follow the line of reasoning and the organization, development, substance, and style are appropriate to purpose, audience, and task.
88	**Literary Analysis: Analyze Setting and Theme**	RL.9-10.2	Determine a theme or central idea of a text and analyze in detail its development over the course of the text, including how it emerges and is shaped and refined by specific details; provide an objective summary of the text.
		RL.9-10.6	Analyze a particular point of view or cultural experience reflected in a work of literature from outside the United States, drawing on a wide reading of world literature.
89	**Vocabulary Study: Suffixes**	L.9-10.4.b	Identify and correctly use patterns of word changes that indicate different meanings or parts of speech.
89	**Writing Trait: Focus and Unity: Thesis or Central Idea**	W.9-10.5	Develop and strengthen writing as needed by planning, revising, editing, rewriting, or trying a new approach, focusing on addressing what is most significant for a specific purpose and audience.
89	**Research/Writing: Research Report**	W.9-10.2	Write informative/explanatory texts to examine and convey complex ideas, concepts, and information clearly and accurately through the effective selection, organization, and analysis of content.
		W.9-10.7	Conduct short as well as more sustained research projects to answer a question (including a self-generated question) or solve a problem; narrow or broaden the inquiry when appropriate; synthesize multiple sources on the subject, demonstrating understanding of the subject under investigation.
		W.9-10.8	Gather relevant information from multiple authoritative print and digital sources, using advanced searches effectively; assess the usefulness of each source in answering the research question; integrate information into the text selectively to maintain the flow of ideas, avoiding plagiarism and following a standard format for citation.
Close Reading			
90–93	**Read The Grapes of Wrath**	RL.9-10.10	By the end of grade 10, read and comprehend literature, including stories, dramas, and poems, at the high end of the grades 9–10 text complexity band independently and proficiently.
Unit Wrap-Up			
94	**Present Your Project**	SL.9-10.1.c	Propel conversations by posing and responding to questions that relate the current discussion to broader themes or larger ideas; actively incorporate others into the discussion; and clarify, verify, or challenge ideas and conclusions.
		SL.9-10.6	Adapt speech to a variety of contexts and tasks, demonstrating command of formal English when indicated or appropriate.
	Reflect on Your Reading	SL.9-10.1.a	Come to discussions prepared, having read and researched material under study; explicitly draw on that preparation by referring to evidence from texts and other research on the topic or issue to stimulate a thoughtful, well-reasoned exchange of ideas.

page 900

Student Handbooks, continued

Unit Wrap-Up, continued

SE Pages	Lesson	Code	Standards Text
94	**Present Your Project** continued **Respond to the Essential Question**	SL.9-10.1.a	Come to discussions prepared, having read and researched material under study; explicitly draw on that preparation by referring to evidence from texts and other research on the topic or issue to stimulate a thoughtful, well-reasoned exchange of ideas.
Writing Project: Autobiographical Narratives			
95–99	**Study Autobiographical Narratives and Prewrite**	W.9-10.3.c	Use a variety of techniques to sequence events so that they build on one another to create a coherent whole.
		W.9-10.5	Develop and strengthen writing as needed by planning, revising, editing, rewriting, or trying a new approach, focusing on addressing what is most significant for a specific purpose and audience.
100–101	**Autobiographical Narrative: Draft**	W.9-10.3	Write narratives to develop real or imagined experiences or events using effective technique, well-chosen details, and well-structured event sequences.
		W.9-10.3.d	Use precise words and phrases, telling details, and sensory language to convey a vivid picture of the experiences, events, setting, and/or characters.
		W.9-10.4	Produce clear and coherent writing in which the development, organization, and style are appropriate to task, purpose, and audience.
		W.9-10.6	Use technology, including the Internet, to produce, publish, and update individual or shared writing products, taking advantage of technology's capacity to link to other information and to display information flexibly and dynamically.
102–105	**Autobiographical Narrative: Revise Trait: Focus and Unity**	W.9-10.3.a	Engage and orient the reader by setting out a problem, situation, or observation, establishing one or multiple point(s) of view, and introducing a narrator and/or characters; create a smooth progression of experiences or events.
		W.9-10.3.b	Use narrative techniques, such as dialogue, pacing, description, reflection, and multiple plot lines, to develop experiences, events, and/or characters.
		W.9-10.3.c	Use a variety of techniques to sequence events so that they build on one another to create a coherent whole.
		W.9-10.3.e	Provide a conclusion that follows from and reflects on what is experienced, observed, or resolved over the course of the narrative.
		W.9-10.5	Develop and strengthen writing as needed by planning, revising, editing, rewriting, or trying a new approach, focusing on addressing what is most significant for a specific purpose and audience.
		SL.9-10.1	Initiate and participate effectively in a range of collaborative discussions (one-on-one, in groups, and teacher-led) with diverse partners on grades 9–10 topics, texts, and issues, building on others' ideas and expressing their own clearly and persuasively.
		SL.9-10.1.d	Respond thoughtfully to diverse perspectives, summarize points of agreement and disagreement, and, when warranted, qualify or justify their own views and understanding and make new connections in light of the evidence and reasoning presented.

page 901

Common Core State Standards

Common Core State Standards, continued

Student Handbooks, continued

Writing Project: Autobiographical Narratives, continued

SE Pages	Lesson	Code	Standards Text
106–108	Autobiographical Narrative: Edit and Proofread Capitalization: Proper Nouns and Adjectives Punctuation: Quotations Spelling Complete Sentences	W.9-10.6	Use technology, including the Internet, to produce, publish, and update individual or shared writing products, taking advantage of technology's capacity to link to other information and to display information flexibly and dynamically.
		L.9-10.1	Demonstrate command of the conventions of standard English grammar and usage when writing or speaking.
		L.9-10.2	Demonstrate command of the conventions of standard English capitalization, punctuation, and spelling when writing.
		L.9-10.2.c	Spell correctly.
		L.9-10.3.a	Write and edit work so that it conforms to the guidelines in a style manual appropriate for the discipline and writing type.
109	Autobiographical Narrative: Publish and Present	W.9-10.6	Use technology, including the Internet, to produce, publish, and update individual or shared writing products, taking advantage of technology's capacity to link to other information and to display information flexibly and dynamically.
		SL.9-10.1	Initiate and participate effectively in a range of collaborative discussions (one-on-one, in groups, and teacher-led) with diverse partners on grades 9–10 topics, texts, and issues, building on others' ideas and expressing their own clearly and persuasively.
		SL.9-10.6	Adapt speech to a variety of contexts and tasks, demonstrating command of formal English when indicated or appropriate.
UNIT 2: The Art of Expression			
110–111	Discuss the Essential Question	SL.9-10.1.b	Work with peers to set rules for collegial discussions and decision-making (e.g., informal consensus, taking votes on key issues, presentation of alternate views), clear goals and deadlines, and individual roles as needed.
		SL.9-10.3	Evaluate a speaker's point of view, reasoning, and use of evidence and rhetoric, identifying any fallacious reasoning or exaggerated or distorted evidence.
112	Analyze and Debate	SL.9-10.4	Present information, findings, and supporting evidence clearly, concisely, and logically such that listeners can follow the line of reasoning and the organization, development, substance, and style are appropriate to purpose, audience, and task.
113	Plan a Project	SL.9-10.1.b	Work with peers to set rules for collegial discussions and decision-making (e.g., informal consensus, taking votes on key issues, presentation of alternate views), clear goals and deadlines, and individual roles as needed.
113	Choose More to Read	RL.9-10.10	By the end of grade 10, read and comprehend literature, including stories, dramas, and poems, at the high end of the grades 9–10 text complexity band independently and proficiently.
		RI.9-10.10	By the end of grade 10, read and comprehend literary nonfiction at the high end of the grades 9–10 text complexity band independently and proficiently.
114–117	How to Read Nonfiction	RI.9-10.2	Determine a central idea of a text and analyze its development over the course of the text, including how it emerges and is shaped and refined by specific details; provide an objective summary of the text.

page 902

Student Handbooks, continued

UNIT 2: The Art of Expression, continued

SE Pages	Lesson	Code	Standards Text
114–117	How to Read Nonfiction continued	RI.9-10.6	Determine an author's point of view or purpose in a text and analyze how an author uses rhetoric to advance that point of view or purpose.
		RI.9-10.10	By the end of grade 10, read and comprehend literary nonfiction at the high end of the grades 9–10 text complexity band independently and proficiently.
		L.9-10.6	Acquire and use accurately general academic and domain-specific words and phrases, sufficient for reading, writing, speaking, and listening at the college and career readiness level; demonstrate independence in gathering vocabulary knowledge when considering a word or phrase important to comprehension or expression.
Cluster 1			
118	Prepare to Read	RI.9-10.4	Determine the meaning of words and phrases as they are used in a text, including figurative, connotative, and technical meanings; analyze the cumulative impact of specific word choices on meaning and tone.
		SL.9-10.1	Initiate and participate effectively in a range of collaborative discussions (one-on-one, in groups, and teacher-led) with diverse partners on grades 9–10 topics, texts, and issues, building on others' ideas and expressing their own clearly and persuasively.
		L.9-10.4	Determine or clarify the meaning of unknown and multiple-meaning words and phrases based on grades 9–10 reading and content, choosing flexibly from a range of strategies.
		L.9-10.4.c	Consult general and specialized reference materials, both print and digital, to find the pronunciation of a word or determine or clarify its precise meaning, its part of speech, or its etymology.
		L.9-10.6	Acquire and use accurately general academic and domain-specific words and phrases, sufficient for reading, writing, speaking, and listening at the college and career readiness level; demonstrate independence in gathering vocabulary knowledge when considering a word or phrase important to comprehension or expression.
119	Before Reading: Creativity at Work	RI.9-10.2	Determine a central idea of a text and analyze its development over the course of the text, including how it emerges and is shaped and refined by specific details; provide an objective summary of the text.
		RI.9-10.6	Determine an author's point of view or purpose in a text and analyze how an author uses rhetoric to advance that point of view or purpose.
120–127	Read Creativity at Work	RI.9-10.1	Cite strong and thorough textual evidence to support analysis of what the text says explicitly as well as inferences drawn from the text.
		RI.9-10.2	Determine a central idea of a text and analyze its development over the course of the text, including how it emerges and is shaped and refined by specific details; provide an objective summary of the text.
		RI.9-10.6	Determine an author's point of view or purpose in a text and analyze how an author uses rhetoric to advance that point of view or purpose.
		RI.9-10.10	By the end of grade 10, read and comprehend literary nonfiction at the high end of the grades 9–10 text complexity band independently and proficiently.

page 903

Common Core State Standards, continued

Student Handbooks, continued

Cluster 1, continued

SE Pages	Lesson	Code	Standards Text
120–127	Read Creativity at Work continued	W.9-10.2.b	Develop the topic with well-chosen, relevant, and sufficient facts, extended definitions, concrete details, quotations, or other information and examples appropriate to the audience's knowledge of the topic.
		W.9-10.10	Write routinely over extended time frames (time for research, reflection, and revision) and shorter time frames (a single sitting or a day or two) for a range of tasks, purposes, and audiences.
		L.9-10.1	Demonstrate command of the conventions of standard English grammar and usage when writing or speaking.
		L.9-10.6	Acquire and use accurately general academic and domain-specific words and phrases, sufficient for reading, writing, speaking, and listening at the college and career readiness level; demonstrate independence in gathering vocabulary knowledge when considering a word or phrase important to comprehension or expression
128	Before Reading: Hidden Secrets of the Creative Mind	RI.9-10.2	Determine a central idea of a text and analyze its development over the course of the text, including how it emerges and is shaped and refined by specific details; provide an objective summary of the text.
		RI.9-10.3	Analyze how the author unfolds an analysis or series of ideas or events, including the order in which the points are made, how they are introduced and developed, and the connections that are drawn between them.
		L.9-10.1.b	Use various types of phrases (noun, verb, adjectival, adverbial, participial, prepositional, absolute) and clauses (independent, dependent; noun, relative, adverbial) to convey specific meanings and add variety and interest to writing or presentations.
129–132	Read Hidden Secrets of the Creative Mind	RI.9-10.2	Determine a central idea of a text and analyze its development over the course of the text, including how it emerges and is shaped and refined by specific details; provide an objective summary of the text.
		RI.9-10.3	Analyze how the author unfolds an analysis or series of ideas or events, including the order in which the points are made, how they are introduced and developed, and the connections that are drawn between them.
		RI.9-10.10	By the end of grade 10, read and comprehend literary nonfiction at the high end of the grades 9–10 text complexity band independently and proficiently.
		W.9-10.9	Draw evidence from literary or informational texts to support analysis, reflection, and research.
		W.9-10.10	Write routinely over extended time frames (time for research, reflection, and revision) and shorter time frames (a single sitting or a day or two) for a range of tasks, purposes, and audiences.
		L.9-10.1	Demonstrate command of the conventions of standard English grammar and usage when writing or speaking.
		L.9-10.4.a	Use context as a clue to the meaning of a word or phrase.

page 904

Student Handbooks, continued

Cluster 1, continued

SE Pages	Lesson	Code	Standards Text
129–132	Read Hidden Secrets of the Creative Mind continued	L.9-10.6	Acquire and use accurately general academic and domain-specific words and phrases, sufficient for reading, writing, speaking, and listening at the college and career readiness level; demonstrate independence in gathering vocabulary knowledge when considering a word or phrase important to comprehension or expression.
133	Reflect and Assess Critical Thinking	RI.9-10.1	Cite strong and thorough textual evidence to support analysis of what the text says explicitly as well as inferences drawn from the text.
		RI.9-10.10	By the end of grade 10, read and comprehend literary nonfiction at the high end of the grades 9–10 text complexity band independently and proficiently.
		SL.9-10.1	Initiate and participate effectively in a range of collaborative discussions (one-on-one, in groups, and teacher-led) with diverse partners on grades 9–10 topics, texts, and issues, building on others' ideas and expressing their own clearly and persuasively.
	Write About Literature	W.9-10.1	Write arguments to support claims in an analysis of substantive topics or texts, using valid reasoning and relevant and sufficient evidence.
	Key Vocabulary Review	L.9-10.6	Acquire and use accurately general academic and domain-specific words and phrases, sufficient for reading, writing, speaking, and listening at the college and career readiness level; demonstrate independence in gathering vocabulary knowledge when considering a word or phrase important to comprehension or expression.
	Read with Ease: Phrasing	RI.9-10.10	By the end of grade 9, read and comprehend literary nonfiction in the grades 9–10 text complexity band proficiently, with scaffolding as needed at the high end of the range. By the end of grade 10, read and comprehend literary nonfiction at the high end of the grades 9–10 text complexity band independently and proficiently.
134	Grammar: Use Subject Pronouns	L.9-10.1	Demonstrate command of the conventions of standard English grammar and usage when writing or speaking.
134	Language Development: Describe People, Places, and Things	SL.9-10.4	Present information, findings, and supporting evidence clearly, concisely, and logically such that listeners can follow the line of reasoning and the organization, development, substance, and style are appropriate to purpose, audience, and task.
134	Literary Analysis: Analyze Description	RI.9-10.4	Determine the meaning of words and phrases as they are used in a text, including figurative, connotative, and technical meanings; analyze the cumulative impact of specific word choices on meaning and tone.
134	Listening/ Speaking: Interview	SL.9-10.4	Present information, findings, and supporting evidence clearly, concisely, and logically such that listeners can follow the line of reasoning and the organization, development, substance, and style are appropriate to purpose, audience, and task.
135	Vocabulary Study: Context Clues	L.9-10.4.a	Use context as a clue to the meaning of a word or phrase.
135	Writing on Demand: Writing a Test Essay	W.9-10.1	Write arguments to support claims in an analysis of substantive topics or texts, using valid reasoning and relevant and sufficient evidence.

page 905

Common Core State Standards

Common Core State Standards, continued

Student Handbooks, continued

Cluster 1, continued

SE Pages	Lesson	Code	Standards Text
135	**Research/Speaking: Oral Presentation**	W.9-10.6	Use technology, including the Internet, to produce, publish, and update individual or shared writing products, taking advantage of technology's capacity to link to other information and to display information flexibly and dynamically.
		W.9-10.7	Conduct short as well as more sustained research projects to answer a question (including a self-generated question) or solve a problem; narrow or broaden the inquiry when appropriate; synthesize multiple sources on the subject, demonstrating understanding of the subject under investigation.
		SL.9-10.5	Make strategic use of digital media in presentations to enhance understanding of findings, reasoning, and evidence and to add interest.
136	**Workplace Workshop: Inside an Art Museum**	W.9-10.7	Conduct short as well as more sustained research projects to answer a question (including a self-generated question) or solve a problem; narrow or broaden the inquiry when appropriate; synthesize multiple sources on the subject, demonstrating understanding of the subject under investigation.
		W.9-10.10	Write routinely over extended time frames (time for research, reflection, and revision) and shorter time frames (a single sitting or a day or two) for a range of tasks, purposes, and audiences.
		SL.9-10.1	Initiate and participate effectively in a range of collaborative discussions (one-on-one, in groups, and teacher-led) with diverse partners on grades 9–10 topics, texts, and issues, building on others' ideas and expressing their own clearly and persuasively.
		L.9-10.6	Acquire and use accurately general academic and domain-specific words and phrases, sufficient for reading, writing, speaking, and listening at the college and career readiness level; demonstrate independence in gathering vocabulary knowledge when considering a word or phrase important to comprehension or expression.
137	**Vocabulary Workshop: Use Context Clues**	L.9-10.4.a	Use context as a clue to the meaning of a word or phrase.
		L.9-10.4.c	Consult general and specialized reference materials, both print and digital, to find the pronunciation of a word or determine or clarify its precise meaning, its part of speech, or its etymology.
		L.9-10.4.d	Verify the preliminary determination of the meaning of a word or phrase.
Cluster 2			
138	**Prepare to Read**	RI.9-10.4	Determine the meaning of words and phrases as they are used in a text, including figurative, connotative, and technical meanings; analyze the cumulative impact of specific word choices on meaning and tone.
		SL.9-10.1	Initiate and participate effectively in a range of collaborative discussions (one-on-one, in groups, and teacher-led) with diverse partners on grades 9–10 topics, texts, and issues, building on others' ideas and expressing their own clearly and persuasively.
		L.9-10.6	Acquire and use accurately general academic and domain-specific words and phrases, sufficient for reading, writing, speaking, and listening at the college and career readiness level; demonstrate independence in gathering vocabulary knowledge when considering a word or phrase important to comprehension or expression.

page 906

Student Handbooks, continued

Cluster 2, continued

SE Pages	Lesson	Code	Standards Text
139	**Before Reading: Hip-Hop as Culture**	RI.9-10.2	Determine a central idea of a text and analyze its development over the course of the text, including how it emerges and is shaped and refined by specific details; provide an objective summary of the text.
		RI.9-10.6	Determine an author's point of view or purpose in a text and analyze how an author uses rhetoric to advance that point of view or purpose.
140–149	**Read Hip-Hop as Culture**	RI.9-10.1	Cite strong and thorough textual evidence to support analysis of what the text says explicitly as well as inferences drawn from the text.
		RI.9-10.2	Determine a central idea of a text and analyze its development over the course of the text, including how it emerges and is shaped and refined by specific details; provide an objective summary of the text.
		RI.9-10.4	Determine the meaning of words and phrases as they are used in a text, including figurative, connotative, and technical meanings; analyze the cumulative impact of specific word choices on meaning and tone.
		RI.9-10.6	Determine an author's point of view or purpose in a text and analyze how an author uses rhetoric to advance that point of view or purpose.
		RI.9-10.10	By the end of grade 10, read and comprehend literary nonfiction at the high end of the grades 9–10 text complexity band independently and proficiently.
		W.9-10.9.b	Apply grades 9–10 Reading standards to literary nonfiction.
		W.9-10.10	Write routinely over extended time frames (time for research, reflection, and revision) and shorter time frames (a single sitting or a day or two) for a range of tasks, purposes, and audiences.
		L.9-10.1	Demonstrate command of the conventions of standard English grammar and usage when writing or speaking.
		L.9-10.2	Demonstrate command of the conventions of standard English capitalization, punctuation, and spelling when writing.
		L.9-10.2.c	Spell correctly.
		L.9-10.4.a	Use context as a clue to the meaning of a word or phrase.
		L.9-10.6	Acquire and use accurately general academic and domain-specific words and phrases, sufficient for reading, writing, speaking, and listening at the college and career readiness level; demonstrate independence in gathering vocabulary knowledge when considering a word or phrase important to comprehension or expression.
150	**Before Reading: I Am Somebody**	RL.9-10.2	Determine a theme or central idea of a text and analyze in detail its development over the course of the text, including how it emerges and is shaped and refined by specific details; provide an objective summary of the text.
		RL.9-10.5	Analyze how an author's choices concerning how to structure a text, order events within it, and manipulate time create such effects as mystery, tension, or surprise.

page 907

Common Core State Standards, continued

Student Handbooks, continued

Cluster 2, continued

SE Pages	Lesson	Code	Standards Text
151–154	**Read I Am Somebody**	RL.9-10.1	Cite strong and thorough textual evidence to support analysis of what the text says explicitly as well as inferences drawn from the text.
		RL.9-10.2	Determine a theme or central idea of a text and analyze in detail its development over the course of the text, including how it emerges and is shaped and refined by specific details; provide an objective summary of the text.
		RL.9-10.4	Determine the meaning of words and phrases as they are used in the text, including figurative and connotative meanings; analyze the cumulative impact of specific word choices on meaning and tone.
		RL.9-10.5	Analyze how an author's choices concerning how to structure a text, order events within it, and manipulate time create such effects as mystery, tension, or surprise.
		RL.9-10.10	By the end of grade 10, read and comprehend literature, including stories, dramas, and poems, at the high end of the grades 9–10 text complexity band independently and proficiently.
		RI.9-10.2	Determine a central idea of a text and analyze its development over the course of the text, including how it emerges and is shaped and refined by specific details; provide an objective summary of the text.
		W.9-10.9.a	Apply grades 9–10 Reading standards to literature.
		W.9-10.10	Write routinely over extended time frames (time for research, reflection, and revision) and shorter time frames (a single sitting or a day or two) for a range of tasks, purposes, and audiences.
		L.9-10.1.b	Use various types of phrases (noun, verb, adjectival, adverbial, participial, prepositional, absolute) and clauses (independent, dependent; noun, relative, adverbial) to convey specific meanings and add variety and interest to writing or presentations.
		L.9-10.6	Acquire and use accurately general academic and domain-specific words and phrases, sufficient for reading, writing, speaking, and listening at the college and career readiness level; demonstrate independence in gathering vocabulary knowledge when considering a word or phrase important to comprehension or expression.
155	**Reflect and Assess Critical Thinking**	RL.9-10.1	Cite strong and thorough textual evidence to support analysis of what the text says explicitly as well as inferences drawn from the text.
		RI.9-10.1	Cite strong and thorough textual evidence to support analysis of what the text says explicitly as well as inferences drawn from the text.
		SL.9-10.1	Initiate and participate effectively in a range of collaborative discussions (one-on-one, in groups, and teacher-led) with diverse partners on grades 9–10 topics, texts, and issues, building on others' ideas and expressing their own clearly and persuasively.
	Write About Literature	RL.9-10.2	Determine a theme or central idea of a text and analyze in detail its development over the course of the text, including how it emerges and is shaped and refined by specific details; provide an objective summary of the text.
		RI.9-10.2	Determine a central idea of a text and analyze its development over the course of the text, including how it emerges and is shaped and refined by specific details; provide an objective summary of the text.

page 908

Student Handbooks, continued

Cluster 2, continued

SE Pages	Lesson	Code	Standards Text
155	**Reflect and Assess** continued	W.9-10.10	Write routinely over extended time frames (time for research, reflection, and revision) and shorter time frames (a single sitting or a day or two) for a range of tasks, purposes, and audiences.
	Key Vocabulary Review	L.9-10.6	Acquire and use accurately general academic and domain-specific words and phrases, sufficient for reading, writing, speaking, and listening at the college and career readiness level; demonstrate independence in gathering vocabulary knowledge when considering a word or phrase important to comprehension or expression.
	Read with Ease: Intonation	RI.9-10.10	By the end of grade 10, read and comprehend literary nonfiction at the high end of the grades 9–10 text complexity band independently and proficiently.
156	**Grammar: Use Action Verbs in the Present**	L.9-10.1.b	Use various types of phrases (noun, verb, adjectival, adverbial, participial, prepositional, absolute) and clauses (independent, dependent; noun, relative, adverbial) to convey specific meanings and add variety and interest to writing or presentations.
156	**Language Development: Describe Experiences**	SL.9-10.1	Initiate and participate effectively in a range of collaborative discussions (one-on-one, in groups, and teacher-led) with diverse partners on grades 9–10 topics, texts, and issues, building on others' ideas and expressing their own clearly and persuasively.
156	**Literary Analysis: Analyze Style and Word Choice**	RL.9-10.4	Determine the meaning of words and phrases as they are used in the text, including figurative and connotative meanings; analyze the cumulative impact of specific word choices on meaning and tone.
		RI.9-10.4	Determine the meaning of words and phrases as they are used in a text, including figurative, connotative, and technical meanings; analyze the cumulative impact of specific word choices on meaning and tone.
156	**Research/Speaking: Oral Presentation**	W.9-10.7	Conduct short as well as more sustained research projects to answer a question (including a self-generated question) or solve a problem; narrow or broaden the inquiry when appropriate; synthesize multiple sources on the subject, demonstrating understanding of the subject under investigation.
		SL.9-10.4	Present information, findings, and supporting evidence clearly, concisely, and logically such that listeners can follow the line of reasoning and the organization, development, substance, and style are appropriate to purpose, audience, and task.
157	**Vocabulary Study: Context Clues for Idioms**	L.9-10.4.a	Use context as a clue to the meaning of a word or phrase.
		L.9-10.5.a	Interpret figures of speech in context and analyze their role in the text.
157	**Writing Trait: Focus and Unity**	W.9-10.5	Develop and strengthen writing as needed by planning, revising, editing, rewriting, or trying a new approach, focusing on addressing what is most significant for a specific purpose and audience.
158–159	**Listening and Speaking Workshop: Descriptive Presentation**	SL.9-10.3	Evaluate a speaker's point of view, reasoning, and use of evidence and rhetoric, identifying any fallacious reasoning or exaggerated or distorted evidence.
		SL.9-10.4	Present information, findings, and supporting evidence clearly, concisely, and logically such that listeners can follow the line of reasoning and the organization, development, substance, and style are appropriate to purpose, audience, and task.
		L.9-10.3	Apply knowledge of language to understand how language functions in different contexts, to make effective choices for meaning or style, and to comprehend more fully when reading or listening.

page 909

Common Core State Standards

Common Core State Standards, continued

Student Handbooks, continued

SE Pages	Lesson	Code	Standards Text
Cluster 3			
160	**Prepare to Read**	RI.9-10.4	Determine the meaning of words and phrases as they are used in a text, including figurative, connotative, and technical meanings; analyze the cumulative impact of specific word choices on meaning and tone.
		SL.9-10.1	Initiate and participate effectively in a range of collaborative discussions (one-on-one, in groups, and teacher-led) with diverse partners on grades 9–10 topics, texts, and issues, building on others' ideas and expressing their own clearly and persuasively.
		L.9-10.5.b	Analyze nuances in the meaning of words with similar denotations.
		L.9-10.6	Acquire and use accurately general academic and domain-specific words and phrases, sufficient for reading, writing, speaking, and listening at the college and career readiness level; demonstrate independence in gathering vocabulary knowledge when considering a word or phrase important to comprehension or expression.
161	**Before Reading: Slam: Performance Poetry Lives On**	RI.9-10.2	Determine a central idea of a text and analyze its development over the course of the text, including how it emerges and is shaped and refined by specific details; provide an objective summary of the text.
		RI.9-10.6	Determine an author's point of view or purpose in a text and analyze how an author uses rhetoric to advance that point of view or purpose.
162–173	**Read Slam: Performance Poetry Lives On**	RI.9-10.1	Cite strong and thorough textual evidence to support analysis of what the text says explicitly as well as inferences drawn from the text.
		RI.9-10.2	Determine a central idea of a text and analyze its development over the course of the text, including how it emerges and is shaped and refined by specific details; provide an objective summary of the text.
		RI.9-10.4	Determine the meaning of words and phrases as they are used in a text, including figurative, connotative, and technical meanings; analyze the cumulative impact of specific word choices on meaning and tone.
		RI.9-10.6	Determine an author's point of view or purpose in a text and analyze how an author uses rhetoric to advance that point of view or purpose.
		RI.9-10.10	By the end of grade 10, read and comprehend literary nonfiction at the high end of the grades 9–10 text complexity band independently and proficiently.
		W.9-10.9.b	Apply grades 9–10 Reading standards to literary nonfiction.
		W.9-10.10	Write routinely over extended time frames (time for research, reflection, and revision) and shorter time frames (a single sitting or a day or two) for a range of tasks, purposes, and audiences.
		L.9-10.1.b	Use various types of phrases (noun, verb, adjectival, adverbial, participial, prepositional, absolute) and clauses (independent, dependent; noun, relative, adverbial) to convey specific meanings and add variety and interest to writing or presentations.
		L.9-10.4.c	Consult general and specialized reference materials, both print and digital, to find the pronunciation of a word or determine or clarify its precise meaning, its part of speech, or its etymology.
		L.9-10.5.b	Analyze nuances in the meaning of words with similar denotations.

page 910

Student Handbooks, continued

SE Pages	Lesson	Code	Standards Text
Cluster 3, continued			
162–173	**Read Slam: Performance Poetry Lives On** continued	L.9-10.6	Acquire and use accurately general academic and domain-specific words and phrases, sufficient for reading, writing, speaking, and listening at the college and career readiness level; demonstrate independence in gathering vocabulary knowledge when considering a word or phrase important to comprehension or expression.
174	**Before Reading: Euphoria**	RL.9-10.2	Determine a theme or central idea of a text and analyze in detail its development over the course of the text, including how it emerges and is shaped and refined by specific details; provide an objective summary of the text.
		RL.9-10.5	Analyze how an author's choices concerning how to structure a text, order events within it, and manipulate time create such effects as mystery, tension, or surprise.
175–176	**Read Euphoria**	RL.9-10.2	Determine a theme or central idea of a text and analyze in detail its development over the course of the text, including how it emerges and is shaped and refined by specific details; provide an objective summary of the text.
		RL.9-10.4	Determine the meaning of words and phrases as they are used in the text, including figurative and connotative meanings; analyze the cumulative impact of specific word choices on meaning and tone.
		RL.9-10.5	Analyze how an author's choices concerning how to structure a text, order events within it, and manipulate time create such effects as mystery, tension, or surprise.
		RL.9-10.10	By the end of grade 10, read and comprehend literature, including stories, dramas, and poems, at the high end of the grades 9–10 text complexity band independently and proficiently.
		W.9-10.9.a	Apply grades 9–10 Reading standards to literature.
		L.9-10.6	Acquire and use accurately general academic and domain-specific words and phrases, sufficient for reading, writing, speaking, and listening at the college and career readiness level; demonstrate independence in gathering vocabulary knowledge when considering a word or phrase important to comprehension or expression.
177	**Reflect and Assess Critical Thinking**	RL.9-10.2	Determine a theme or central idea of a text and analyze in detail its development over the course of the text, including how it emerges and is shaped and refined by specific details; provide an objective summary of the text.
		RI.9-10.2	Determine a central idea of a text and analyze its development over the course of the text, including how it emerges and is shaped and refined by specific details; provide an objective summary of the text.
		RI.9-10.10	By the end of grade 10, read and comprehend literary nonfiction at the high end of the grades 9–10 text complexity band independently and proficiently.
		SL.9-10.1	Initiate and participate effectively in a range of collaborative discussions (one-on-one, in groups, and teacher-led) with diverse partners on grades 9–10 topics, texts, and issues, building on others' ideas and expressing their own clearly and persuasively.
	Write About Literature	RL.9-10.5	Analyze how an author's choices concerning how to structure a text, order events within it, and manipulate time create such effects as mystery, tension, or surprise.

page 911

Common Core State Standards, continued

Student Handbooks, continued

SE Pages	Lesson	Code	Standards Text
Cluster 3, continued			
177	**Reflect and Assess** continued	W.9-10.10	Write routinely over extended time frames (time for research, reflection, and revision) and shorter time frames (a single sitting or a day or two) for a range of tasks, purposes, and audiences.
	Key Vocabulary Review	L.9-10.6	Acquire and use accurately general academic and domain-specific words and phrases, sufficient for reading, writing, speaking, and listening at the college and career readiness level; demonstrate independence in gathering vocabulary knowledge when considering a word or phrase important to comprehension or expression.
	Read with Ease: Expression	RI.9-10.10	By the end of grade 10, read and comprehend literary nonfiction at the high end of the grades 9–10 text complexity band independently and proficiently.
178	**Grammar: Use Verbs to Talk About the Present**	L.9-10.1.b	Use various types of phrases (noun, verb, adjectival, adverbial, participial, prepositional, absolute) and clauses (independent, dependent; noun, relative, adverbial) to convey specific meanings and add variety and interest to writing or presentations.
178	**Language Development: Give and Follow Commands**	SL.9-10.6	Adapt speech to a variety of contexts and tasks, demonstrating command of formal English when indicated or appropriate.
178	**Literary Analysis: Literary Movements**	RI.9-10.1	Cite strong and thorough textual evidence to support analysis of what the text says explicitly as well as inferences drawn from the text.
178	**Media Study: Judging Panel**	SL.9-10.1.d	Respond thoughtfully to diverse perspectives, summarize points of agreement and disagreement, and, when warranted, qualify or justify their own views and understanding and make new connections in light of the evidence and reasoning presented.
179	**Vocabulary Study: Context Clues for Idioms**	L.9-10.4.a	Use context as a clue to the meaning of a word or phrase.
		L.9-10.5.a	Interpret figures of speech in context and analyze their role in the text.
179	**Writing: Write a How-To Paragraph**	W.9-10.2	Write informative/explanatory texts to examine and convey complex ideas, concepts, and information clearly and accurately through the effective selection, organization, and analysis of content.
Close Reading			
180–183	**Read The Creativity Crisis**	RI.9-10.10	By the end of grade 10, read and comprehend literary nonfiction at the high end of the grades 9–10 text complexity band independently and proficiently.
Unit Wrap-Up			
184	**Unit Wrap-Up Present Your Project**	SL.9-10.4	Present information, findings, and supporting evidence clearly, concisely, and logically such that listeners can follow the line of reasoning and the organization, development, substance, and style are appropriate to purpose, audience, and task.
	Reflect on Your Reading	SL.9-10.1.a	Come to discussions prepared, having read and researched material under study; explicitly draw on that preparation by referring to evidence from texts and other research on the topic or issue to stimulate a thoughtful, well-reasoned exchange of ideas.
	Respond to the Essential Question	SL.9-10.1.a	Come to discussions prepared, having read and researched material under study; explicitly draw on that preparation by referring to evidence from texts and other research on the topic or issue to stimulate a thoughtful, well-reasoned exchange of ideas.

page 912

Student Handbooks, continued

SE Pages	Lesson	Code	Standards Text
Writing Project: Position Paper			
185–189	**Study Position Papers and Prewrite**	W.9-10.1.a	Introduce precise claim(s), distinguish the claim(s) from alternate or opposing claims, and create an organization that establishes clear relationships among claim(s), counterclaims, reasons, and evidence.
		W.9-10.1.b	Develop claim(s) and counterclaims fairly, supplying evidence for each while pointing out the strengths and limitations of both in a manner that anticipates the audience's knowledge level and concerns.
190–191	**Position Paper: Draft**	W.9-10.1.a	Introduce precise claim(s), distinguish the claim(s) from alternate or opposing claims, and create an organization that establishes clear relationships among claim(s), counterclaims, reasons, and evidence.
		W.9-10.1.b	Develop claim(s) and counterclaims fairly, supplying evidence for each while pointing out the strengths and limitations of both in a manner that anticipates the audience's knowledge level and concerns.
		W.9-10.1.d	Establish and maintain a formal style and objective tone while attending to the norms and conventions of the discipline in which they are writing.
		W.9-10.4	Produce clear and coherent writing in which the development, organization, and style are appropriate to task, purpose, and audience.
192–195	**Position Paper: Revise Trait: Focus and Unity**	W.9-10.1	Write arguments to support claims in an analysis of substantive topics or texts, using valid reasoning and relevant and sufficient evidence.
		W.9-10.1.a	Introduce precise claim(s), distinguish the claim(s) from alternate or opposing claims, and create an organization that establishes clear relationships among claim(s), counterclaims, reasons, and evidence.
		W.9-10.1.b	Develop claim(s) and counterclaims fairly, supplying evidence for each while pointing out the strengths and limitations of both in a manner that anticipates the audience's knowledge level and concerns.
		W.9-10.1.c	Use words, phrases, and clauses to link the major sections of the text, create cohesion, and clarify the relationships between claim(s) and reasons, between reasons and evidence, and between claim(s) and counterclaims.
		W.9-10.1.d	Establish and maintain a formal style and objective tone while attending to the norms and conventions of the discipline in which they are writing.
		W.9-10.5	Develop and strengthen writing as needed by planning, revising, editing, rewriting, or trying a new approach, focusing on addressing what is most significant for a specific purpose and audience.
		SL.9-10.1	Initiate and participate effectively in a range of collaborative discussions (one-on-one, in groups, and teacher-led) with diverse partners on grades 9–10 topics, texts, and issues, building on others' ideas and expressing their own clearly and persuasively.
		SL.9-10.1.d	Respond thoughtfully to diverse perspectives, summarize points of agreement and disagreement, and, when warranted, qualify or justify their own views and understanding and make new connections in light of the evidence and reasoning presented.

page 913

Common Core State Standards

Common Core State Standards, continued

Student Handbooks, continued

Writing Project: Position Paper, continued

SE Pages	Lesson	Code	Standards Text
196–198	**Position Paper: Edit and Proofread** **Capitalization: Names of Groups** **Colons** **Spelling** **Present Tense Verbs**	L.9-10.1	Demonstrate command of the conventions of standard English grammar and usage when writing or speaking.
		L.9-10.2	Demonstrate command of the conventions of standard English capitalization, punctuation, and spelling when writing.
		L.9-10.2.b	Use a colon to introduce a list or quotation.
		L.9-10.2.c	Spell correctly.
		L.9-10.3.a	Write and edit work so that it conforms to the guidelines in a style manual appropriate for the discipline and writing type.
199	**Position Paper: Publish and Present**	W.9-10.6	Use technology, including the Internet, to produce, publish, and update individual or shared writing products, taking advantage of technology's capacity to link to other information and to display information flexibly and dynamically.
		SL.9-10.3	Evaluate a speaker's point of view, reasoning, and use of evidence and rhetoric, identifying any fallacious reasoning or exaggerated or distorted evidence.
		SL.9-10.4	Present information, findings, and supporting evidence clearly, concisely, and logically such that listeners can follow the line of reasoning and the organization, development, substance, and style are appropriate to purpose, audience, and task.
		SL.9-10.6	Adapt speech to a variety of contexts and tasks, demonstrating command of formal English when indicated or appropriate.
UNIT 3: The Hero Within			
200–201	**Discuss the Essential Question**	SL.9-10.1.b	Work with peers to set rules for collegial discussions and decision-making (e.g., informal consensus, taking votes on key issues, presentation of alternate views), clear goals and deadlines, and individual roles as needed.
		SL.9-10.3	Evaluate a speaker's point of view, reasoning, and use of evidence and rhetoric, identifying any fallacious reasoning or exaggerated or distorted evidence.
202	**Debate and Vote**	SL.9-10.4	Present information, findings, and supporting evidence clearly, concisely, and logically such that listeners can follow the line of reasoning and the organization, development, substance, and style are appropriate to purpose, audience, and task.
203	**Plan a Project**	SL.9-10.1.b	Work with peers to set rules for collegial discussions and decision-making (e.g., informal consensus, taking votes on key issues, presentation of alternate views), clear goals and deadlines, and individual roles as needed.
203	**Choose More to Read**	RL.9-10.10	By the end of grade 10, read and comprehend literature, including stories, dramas, and poems, at the high end of the grades 9–10 text complexity band independently and proficiently.
		RI.9-10.10	By the end of grade 10, read and comprehend literary nonfiction at the high end of the grades 9–10 text complexity band independently and proficiently.
204–207	**How to Read Short Stories**	RL.9-10.1	Cite strong and thorough textual evidence to support analysis of what the text says explicitly as well as inferences drawn from the text.
		RL.9-10.6	Analyze a particular point of view or cultural experience reflected in a work of literature from outside the United States, drawing on a wide reading of world literature.

page 914

Student Handbooks, continued

UNIT 3: The Hero Within, continued

SE Pages	Lesson	Code	Standards Text
204–207	**How to Read Short Stories** continued	RL.9-10.10	By the end of grade 10, read and comprehend literature, including stories, dramas, and poems, at the high end of the grades 9–10 text complexity band independently and proficiently.
		SL.9-10.1	Initiate and participate effectively in a range of collaborative discussions (one-on-one, in groups, and teacher-led) with diverse partners on grades 9–10 topics, texts, and issues, building on others' ideas and expressing their own clearly and persuasively.
		L.9-10.6	Acquire and use accurately general academic and domain-specific words and phrases, sufficient for reading, writing, speaking, and listening at the college and career readiness level; demonstrate independence in gathering vocabulary knowledge when considering a word or phrase important to comprehension or expression.
Cluster 1			
208	**Prepare to Read**	RL.9-10.4	Determine the meaning of words and phrases as they are used in the text, including figurative and connotative meanings; analyze the cumulative impact of specific word choices on meaning and tone.
		SL.9-10.1	Initiate and participate effectively in a range of collaborative discussions (one-on-one, in groups, and teacher-led) with diverse partners on grades 9–10 topics, texts, and issues, building on others' ideas and expressing their own clearly and persuasively.
		L.9-10.4.c	Consult general and specialized reference materials, both print and digital, to find the pronunciation of a word or determine or clarify its precise meaning, its part of speech, or its etymology.
		L.9-10.6	Acquire and use accurately general academic and domain-specific words and phrases, sufficient for reading, writing, speaking, and listening at the college and career readiness level; demonstrate independence in gathering vocabulary knowledge when considering a word or phrase important to comprehension or expression.
209	**Before Reading: The Sword in the Stone**	RL.9-10.1	Cite strong and thorough textual evidence to support analysis of what the text says explicitly as well as inferences drawn from the text.
		RL.9-10.6	Analyze a particular point of view or cultural experience reflected in a work of literature from outside the United States, drawing on a wide reading of world literature.
210–221	**Read The Sword in the Stone**	RL.9-10.1	Cite strong and thorough textual evidence to support analysis of what the text says explicitly as well as inferences drawn from the text.
		RL.9-10.3	Analyze how complex characters (e.g., those with multiple or conflicting motivations) develop over the course of a text, interact with other characters, and advance the plot or develop the theme.
		RL.9-10.4	Determine the meaning of words and phrases as they are used in the text, including figurative and connotative meanings; analyze the cumulative impact of specific word choices on meaning and tone.
		RL.9-10.6	Analyze a particular point of view or cultural experience reflected in a work of literature from outside the United States, drawing on a wide reading of world literature.
		RL.9-10.10	By the end of grade 10, read and comprehend literature, including stories, dramas, and poems, at the high end of the grades 9–10 text complexity band independently and proficiently.
		W.9-10.9.a	Apply grades 9–10 Reading standards to literature.

page 915

Common Core State Standards, continued

Student Handbooks, continued

Cluster 1, continued

SE Pages	Lesson	Code	Standards Text
210–221	**Read The Sword in the Stone** continued	W.9-10.10	Write routinely over extended time frames (time for research, reflection, and revision) and shorter time frames (a single sitting or a day or two) for a range of tasks, purposes, and audiences.
		L.9-10.1.a	Use parallel structure.
		L.9-10.2.c	Spell correctly.
		L.9-10.4.a	Use context as a clue to the meaning of a word or phrase.
		L.9-10.4.b	Identify and correctly use patterns of word changes that indicate different meanings or parts of speech.
		L.9-10.4.c	Consult general and specialized reference materials, both print and digital, to find the pronunciation of a word or determine or clarify its precise meaning, its part of speech, or its etymology.
		L.9-10.6	Acquire and use accurately general academic and domain-specific words and phrases, sufficient for reading, writing, speaking, and listening at the college and career readiness level; demonstrate independence in gathering vocabulary knowledge when considering a word or phrase important to comprehension or expression.
222	**Before Reading: Was There a Real King Arthur?**	RI.9-10.1	Cite strong and thorough textual evidence to support analysis of what the text says explicitly as well as inferences drawn from the text.
		RI.9-10.5	Analyze in detail how an author's ideas or claims are developed and refined by particular sentences, paragraphs, or larger portions of a text.
223–230	**Read Was There a Real King Arthur?**	RI.9-10.1	Cite strong and thorough textual evidence to support analysis of what the text says explicitly as well as inferences drawn from the text.
		RI.9-10.2	Determine a central idea of a text and analyze its development over the course of the text, including how it emerges and is shaped and refined by specific details; provide an objective summary of the text.
		RI.9-10.5	Analyze in detail how an author's ideas or claims are developed and refined by particular sentences, paragraphs, or larger portions of a text.
		RI.9-10.10	By the end of grade 10, read and comprehend literary nonfiction at the high end of the grades 9–10 text complexity band independently and proficiently.
		W.9-10.9.b	Apply grades 9–10 Reading standards to literary nonfiction.
		W.9-10.10	Write routinely over extended time frames (time for research, reflection, and revision) and shorter time frames (a single sitting or a day or two) for a range of tasks, purposes, and audiences.
		L.9-10.1	Demonstrate command of the conventions of standard English grammar and usage when writing or speaking.
		L.9-10.6	Acquire and use accurately general academic and domain-specific words and phrases, sufficient for reading, writing, speaking, and listening at the college and career readiness level; demonstrate independence in gathering vocabulary knowledge when considering a word or phrase important to comprehension or expression.

page 916

Student Handbooks, continued

Cluster 1, continued

SE Pages	Lesson	Code	Standards Text
231	**Reflect and Assess Critical Thinking**	RL.9-10.1	Cite strong and thorough textual evidence to support analysis of what the text says explicitly as well as inferences drawn from the text.
		RI.9-10.1	Cite strong and thorough textual evidence to support analysis of what the text says explicitly as well as inferences drawn from the text.
		SL.9-10.1	Initiate and participate effectively in a range of collaborative discussions (one-on-one, in groups, and teacher-led) with diverse partners on grades 9–10 topics, texts, and issues, building on others' ideas and expressing their own clearly and persuasively.
	Write About Literature	W.9-10.1	Write arguments to support claims in an analysis of substantive topics or texts, using valid reasoning and relevant and sufficient evidence.
	Key Vocabulary Review	L.9-10.6	Acquire and use accurately general academic and domain-specific words and phrases, sufficient for reading, writing, speaking, and listening at the college and career readiness level; demonstrate independence in gathering vocabulary knowledge when considering a word or phrase important to comprehension or expression.
	Read with Ease: Phrasing	RL.9-10.10	By the end of grade 10, read and comprehend literature, including stories, dramas, and poems, at the high end of the grades 9–10 text complexity band independently and proficiently.
232	**Grammar: Use Verb Tenses**	L.9-10.1.a	Use parallel structure.
232	**Language Development: Ask for and Give Information**	SL.9-10.1.a	Come to discussions prepared, having read and researched material under study; explicitly draw on that preparation by referring to evidence from texts and other research on the topic or issue to stimulate a thoughtful, well-reasoned exchange of ideas.
232	**Literary Analysis: Compare Character's Motives and Traits**	RL.9-10.3	Analyze how complex characters develop over the course of a text, interact with other characters, and advance the plot or develop the theme.
233	**Vocabulary Study: Word Families**	L.9-10.4.b	Identify and correctly use patterns of word changes that indicate different meanings or parts of speech.
		L.9-10.4.d	Verify the preliminary determination of the meaning of a word or phrase.
233	**Writing on Demand: Write a Test Essay**	W.9-10.1	Write arguments to support claims in an analysis of substantive topics or texts, using valid reasoning and relevant and sufficient evidence.
233	**Media Study: Compare Visuals**	W.9-10.7	Conduct short as well as more sustained research projects to answer a question (including a self-generated question) or solve a problem; narrow or broaden the inquiry when appropriate; synthesize multiple sources on the subject, demonstrating understanding of the subject under investigation.
234	**Workplace Workshop: Inside an Airport**	W.9-10.7	Conduct short as well as more sustained research projects to answer a question (including a self-generated question) or solve a problem; narrow or broaden the inquiry when appropriate; synthesize multiple sources on the subject, demonstrating understanding of the subject under investigation.
		L.9-10.6	Acquire and use accurately general academic and domain-specific words and phrases, sufficient for reading, writing, speaking, and listening at the college and career readiness level; demonstrate independence in gathering vocabulary knowledge when considering a word or phrase important to comprehension or expression.

page 917

Common Core State Standards

Common Core State Standards, continued

Student Handbooks, continued			
Cluster 1, continued			
SE Pages	**Lesson**	**Code**	**Standards Text**
235	Vocabulary Workshop: Find Familiar Words	L.9-10.4.b	Identify and correctly use patterns of word changes that indicate different meanings or parts of speech.
		L.9-10.4.c	Consult general and specialized reference materials, both print and digital, to find the pronunciation of a word or determine or clarify its precise meaning, its part of speech, or its etymology.
		L.9-10.4.d	Verify the preliminary determination of the meaning of a word or phrase.
Cluster 2			
236	Prepare to Read	RL.9-10.4	Determine the meaning of words and phrases as they are used in the text, including figurative and connotative meanings; analyze the cumulative impact of specific word choices on meaning and tone.
		SL.9-10.1	Initiate and participate effectively in a range of collaborative discussions (one-on-one, in groups, and teacher-led) with diverse partners on grades 9–10 topics, texts, and issues, building on others' ideas and expressing their own clearly and persuasively.
		L.9-10.6	Acquire and use accurately general academic and domain-specific words and phrases, sufficient for reading, writing, speaking, and listening at the college and career readiness level; demonstrate independence in gathering vocabulary knowledge when considering a word or phrase important to comprehension or expression.
237	Before Reading: A Job for Valentin	RL.9-10.1	Cite strong and thorough textual evidence to support analysis of what the text says explicitly as well as inferences drawn from the text.
		RL.9-10.6	Analyze a particular point of view or cultural experience reflected in a work of literature from outside the United States, drawing on a wide reading of world literature.
238–250	Read A Job or Valentin	RL.9-10.1	Cite strong and thorough textual evidence to support analysis of what the text says explicitly as well as inferences drawn from the text.
		RL.9-10.2	Determine a theme or central idea of a text and analyze in detail its development over the course of the text, including how it emerges and is shaped and refined by specific details; provide an objective summary of the text.
		RL.9-10.3	Analyze how complex characters develop over the course of a text, interact with other characters, and advance the plot or develop the theme.
		RL.9-10.4	Determine the meaning of words and phrases as they are used in the text, including figurative and connotative meanings; analyze the cumulative impact of specific word choices on meaning and tone.
		RL.9-10.6	Analyze a particular point of view or cultural experience reflected in a work of literature from outside the United States, drawing on a wide reading of world literature.
		RL.9-10.7	Analyze the representation of a subject or a key scene in two different artistic mediums, including what is emphasized or absent in each treatment.
		RL.9-10.10	By the end of grade 10, read and comprehend literature, including stories, dramas, and poems, at the high end of the grades 9–10 text complexity band independently and proficiently.
		W.9-10.9.a	Apply grades 9–10 Reading standards to literature.

page 918

Student Handbooks, continued			
Cluster 2, continued			
SE Pages	**Lesson**	**Code**	**Standards Text**
238–250	Read A Job or Valentin continued	W.9-10.10	Write routinely over extended time frames (time for research, reflection, and revision) and shorter time frames (a single sitting or a day or two) for a range of tasks, purposes, and audiences.
		L.9-10.1.b	Use various types of phrases (noun, verb, adjectival, adverbial, participial, prepositional, absolute) and clauses (independent, dependent; noun, relative, adverbial) to convey specific meanings and add variety and interest to writing or presentations.
		L.9-10.2.c	Spell correctly.
		L.9-10.5.a	Interpret figures of speech in context and analyze their role in the text.
		L.9-10.6	Acquire and use accurately general academic and domain-specific words and phrases, sufficient for reading, writing, speaking, and listening at the college and career readiness level; demonstrate independence in gathering vocabulary knowledge when considering a word or phrase important to comprehension or expression.
251	Postscript: Hero	RL.9-10.2	Determine a theme or central idea of a text and analyze in detail its development over the course of the text, including how it emerges and is shaped and refined by specific details; provide an objective summary of the text.
		SL.9-10.1	Initiate and participate effectively in a range of collaborative discussions (one-on-one, in groups, and teacher-led) with diverse partners on grades 9–10 topics, texts, and issues, building on others' ideas and expressing their own clearly and persuasively.
252	Before Reading: In the Heart of a Hero	RI.9-10.1	Cite strong and thorough textual evidence to support analysis of what the text says explicitly as well as inferences drawn from the text.
		RI.9-10.5	Analyze in detail how an author's ideas or claims are developed and refined by particular sentences, paragraphs, or larger portions of a text.
253–256	Read In the Heart of a Hero	RI.9-10.1	Cite strong and thorough textual evidence to support analysis of what the text says explicitly as well as inferences drawn from the text.
		RI.9-10.5	Analyze in detail how an author's ideas or claims are developed and refined by particular sentences, paragraphs, or larger portions of a text.
		RI.9-10.7	Analyze various accounts of a subject told in different mediums, determining which details are emphasized in each account.
		RI.9-10.10	By the end of grade 10, read and comprehend literary nonfiction at the high end of the grades 9–10 text complexity band independently and proficiently.
		W.9-10.1.b	Develop claim(s) and counterclaims fairly, supplying evidence for each while pointing out the strengths and limitations of both in a manner that anticipates the audience's knowledge level and concerns.
		W.9-10.10	Write routinely over extended time frames (time for research, reflection, and revision) and shorter time frames (a single sitting or a day or two) for a range of tasks, purposes, and audiences.
		L.9-10.1.a	Use parallel structure.
		L.9-10.1.b	Use various types of phrases (noun, verb, adjectival, adverbial, participial, prepositional, absolute) and clauses (independent, dependent; noun, relative, adverbial) to convey specific meanings and add variety and interest to writing or presentations.

page 919

Common Core State Standards, continued

Student Handbooks, continued			
Cluster 2, continued			
SE Pages	**Lesson**	**Code**	**Standards Text**
253–256	Read In the Heart of a Hero continued	L.9-10.4.a	Use context (e.g., the overall meaning of a sentence, paragraph, or text; a word's position or function in a sentence) as a clue to the meaning of a word or phrase.
		L.9-10.4.b	Identify and correctly use patterns of word changes that indicate different meanings or parts of speech.
		L.9-10.6	Acquire and use accurately general academic and domain-specific words and phrases, sufficient for reading, writing, speaking, and listening at the college and career readiness level; demonstrate independence in gathering vocabulary knowledge when considering a word or phrase important to comprehension or expression.
257	Reflect and Assess Critical Thinking	RL.9-10.1	Cite strong and thorough textual evidence to support analysis of what the text says explicitly as well as inferences drawn from the text.
		RI.9-10.1	Cite strong and thorough textual evidence to support analysis of what the text says explicitly as well as inferences drawn from the text.
		SL.9-10.1.a	Come to discussions prepared, having read and researched material under study; explicitly draw on that preparation by referring to evidence from texts and other research on the topic or issue to stimulate a thoughtful, well-reasoned exchange of ideas.
		SL.9-10.6	Adapt speech to a variety of contexts and tasks, demonstrating command of formal English when indicated or appropriate.
	Write About Literature	W.9-10.9.a	Apply grades 9–10 Reading standards to literature.
	Key Vocabulary Review	L.9-10.6	Acquire and use accurately general academic and domain-specific words and phrases, sufficient for reading, writing, speaking, and listening at the college and career readiness level; demonstrate independence in gathering vocabulary knowledge when considering a word or phrase important to comprehension or expression.
	Read with Ease: Expression	RL.9-10.10	By the end of grade 10, read and comprehend literature, including stories, dramas, and poems, at the high end of the grades 9–10 text complexity band independently and proficiently.
258	Grammar: Use Verb Tenses	L.9-10.1.a	Use parallel structure.
		L.9-10.1.b	Use various types of phrases (noun, verb, adjectival, adverbial, participial, prepositional, absolute) and clauses (independent, dependent; noun, relative, adverbial) to convey specific meanings and add variety and interest to writing or presentations.
258	Language Development: Engage in Discussion	SL.9-10.1.b	Work with peers to set rules for collegial discussions and decision-making (e.g., informal consensus, taking votes on key issues, presentation of alternate views), clear goals and deadlines, and individual roles as needed
258	Literary Analysis: Multiple Themes in Text	RL.9-10.2	Determine a theme or central idea of a text and analyze in detail its development over the course of the text, including how it emerges and is shaped and refined by specific details; provide an objective summary of the text.
259	Vocabulary Study: Borrowed Words	L.9-10.4.c	Consult general and specialized reference materials (e.g., dictionaries, glossaries, thesauruses), both print and digital, to find the pronunciation of a word or determine or clarify its precise meaning, its part of speech, or its etymology.

page 920

Student Handbooks, continued			
Cluster 2, continued			
SE Pages	**Lesson**	**Code**	**Standards Text**
259	Research/Writing: Profile	W.9-10.2.b	Develop the topic with well-chosen, relevant, and sufficient facts, extended definitions, concrete details, quotations, or other information and examples appropriate to the audience's knowledge of the topic.
		W.9-10.7	Conduct short as well as more sustained research projects to answer a question (including a self-generated question) or solve a problem; narrow or broaden the inquiry when appropriate; synthesize multiple sources on the subject, demonstrating understanding of the subject under investigation.
259	Writing Trait: Voice and Style	W.9-10.5	Develop and strengthen writing as needed by planning, revising, editing, rewriting, or trying a new approach, focusing on addressing what is most significant for a specific purpose and audience.
260–261	Listening and Speaking Workshop: Panel Discussion	SL.9-10.1.b	Work with peers to set rules for collegial discussions and decision-making (e.g., informal consensus, taking votes on key issues, presentation of alternate views), clear goals and deadlines, and individual roles as needed.
		SL.9-10.1.c	Propel conversations by posing and responding to questions that relate the current discussion to broader themes or larger ideas; actively incorporate others into the discussion; and clarify, verify, or challenge ideas and conclusions.
		SL.9-10.1.d	Respond thoughtfully to diverse perspectives, summarize points of agreement and disagreement, and, when warranted, qualify or justify their own views and understanding and make new connections in light of the evidence and reasoning presented.
		SL.9-10.3	Evaluate a speaker's point of view, reasoning, and use of evidence and rhetoric, identifying any fallacious reasoning or exaggerated or distorted evidence.
		L.9-10.3	Apply knowledge of language to understand how language functions in different contexts, to make effective choices for meaning or style, and to comprehend more fully when reading or listening.
Cluster 3			
262	Prepare to Read	RI.9-10.4	Determine the meaning of words and phrases as they are used in a text, including figurative, connotative, and technical meanings; analyze the cumulative impact of specific word choices on meaning and tone.
		SL.9-10.1	Initiate and participate effectively in a range of collaborative discussions (one-on-one, in groups, and teacher-led) with diverse partners on grades 9–10 topics, texts, and issues, building on others' ideas and expressing their own clearly and persuasively.
		L.9-10.4.b	Identify and correctly use patterns of word changes that indicate different meanings or parts of speech.
		L.9-10.6	Acquire and use accurately general academic and domain-specific words and phrases, sufficient for reading, writing, speaking, and listening at the college and career readiness level; demonstrate independence in gathering vocabulary knowledge when considering a word or phrase important to comprehension or expression.
263	Before Reading: The Woman in the Snow	RL.9-10.1	Cite strong and thorough textual evidence to support analysis of what the text says explicitly as well as inferences drawn from the text.
		RL.9-10.6	Analyze a particular point of view or cultural experience reflected in a work of literature from outside the United States, drawing on a wide reading of world literature.

page 921

Common Core State Standards

Common Core State Standards, continued

Student Handbooks, continued

Cluster 3, continued

SE Pages	Lesson	Code	Standards Text
264–277	**Read The Woman in the Snow**	RL.9-10.1	Cite strong and thorough textual evidence to support analysis of what the text says explicitly as well as inferences drawn from the text.
		RL.9-10.4	Determine the meaning of words and phrases as they are used in the text, including figurative and connotative meanings; analyze the cumulative impact of specific word choices on meaning and tone.
		RL.9-10.6	Analyze a particular point of view or cultural experience reflected in a work of literature from outside the United States, drawing on a wide reading of world literature.
		RL.9-10.7	Analyze the representation of a subject or a key scene in two different artistic mediums, including what is emphasized or absent in each treatment.
		RL.9-10.10	By the end of grade 10, read and comprehend literature, including stories, dramas, and poems, at the high end of the grades 9–10 text complexity band independently and proficiently.
		W.9-10.9.a	Apply grades 9–10 Reading standards to literature.
		W.9-10.10	Write routinely over extended time frames (time for research, reflection, and revision) and shorter time frames (a single sitting or a day or two) for a range of tasks, purposes, and audiences.
		L.9-10.1	Demonstrate command of the conventions of standard English grammar and usage when writing or speaking.
		L.9-10.6	Acquire and use accurately general academic and domain-specific words and phrases, sufficient for reading, writing, speaking, and listening at the college and career readiness level; demonstrate independence in gathering vocabulary knowledge when considering a word or phrase important to comprehension or expression.
278	**Before Reading: Rosa Parks**	RI.9-10.1	Cite strong and thorough textual evidence to support analysis of what the text says explicitly as well as inferences drawn from the text.
		RI.9-10.3	Analyze how the author unfolds an analysis or series of ideas or events, including the order in which the points are made, how they are introduced and developed, and the connections that are drawn between them.
279–284	**Read Rosa Parks**	RI.9-10.1	Cite strong and thorough textual evidence to support analysis of what the text says explicitly as well as inferences drawn from the text.
		RI.9-10.2	Determine a central idea of a text and analyze its development over the course of the text, including how it emerges and is shaped and refined by specific details; provide an objective summary of the text.
		RI.9-10.3	Analyze how the author unfolds an analysis or series of ideas or events, including the order in which the points are made, how they are introduced and developed, and the connections that are drawn between them.
		RI.9-10.10	By the end of grade 10, read and comprehend literary nonfiction at the high end of the grades 9–10 text complexity band independently and proficiently.
		W.9-10.10	Write routinely over extended time frames (time for research, reflection, and revision) and shorter time frames (a single sitting or a day or two) for a range of tasks, purposes, and audiences.
		L.9-10.1	Demonstrate command of the conventions of standard English grammar and usage when writing or speaking.

page 922

Student Handbooks, continued

Cluster 3, continued

SE Pages	Lesson	Code	Standards Text
279–284	**Read Rosa Parks** continued	L.9-10.6	Acquire and use accurately general academic and domain-specific words and phrases, sufficient for reading, writing, speaking, and listening at the college and career readiness level; demonstrate independence in gathering vocabulary knowledge when considering a word or phrase important to comprehension or expression.
285	**Reflect and Assess Critical Thinking**	RL.9-10.1	Cite strong and thorough textual evidence to support analysis of what the text says explicitly as well as inferences drawn from the text.
		RL.9-10.2	Determine a theme or central idea of a text and analyze in detail its development over the course of the text, including how it emerges and is shaped and refined by specific details; provide an objective summary of the text.
		RL.9-10.6	Analyze a particular point of view or cultural experience reflected in a work of literature from outside the United States, drawing on a wide reading of world literature.
		RL.9-10.10	By the end of grade 10, read and comprehend literature, including stories, dramas, and poems, at the high end of the grades 9–10 text complexity band independently and proficiently.
		RI.9-10.1	Cite strong and thorough textual evidence to support analysis of what the text says explicitly as well as inferences drawn from the text.
		RI.9-10.2	Determine a central idea of a text and analyze its development over the course of the text, including how it emerges and is shaped and refined by specific details; provide an objective summary of the text.
		SL.9-10.1	Initiate and participate effectively in a range of collaborative discussions (one-on-one, in groups, and teacher-led) with diverse partners on grades 9–10 topics, texts, and issues, building on others' ideas and expressing their own clearly and persuasively.
	Write About Literature	W.9-10.2	Write informative/explanatory texts to examine and convey complex ideas, concepts, and information clearly and accurately through the effective selection, organization, and analysis of content.
	Key Vocabulary Review	L.9-10.6	Acquire and use accurately general academic and domain-specific words and phrases, sufficient for reading, writing, speaking, and listening at the college and career readiness level; demonstrate independence in gathering vocabulary knowledge when considering a word or phrase important to comprehension or expression.
	Read with Ease: Intonation	RL.9-10.10	By the end of grade 10, read and comprehend literature, including stories, dramas, and poems, at the high end of the grades 9–10 text complexity band independently and proficiently.
286	**Grammar: Use Subject and Object Pronouns**	L.9-10.1	Demonstrate command of the conventions of standard English grammar and usage when writing or speaking.
286	**Language Development: Elaborate During a Discussion**	SL.9-10.1.a	Come to discussions prepared, having read and researched material under study; explicitly draw on that preparation by referring to evidence from texts and other research on the topic or issue to stimulate a thoughtful, well-reasoned exchange of ideas.
286	**Literary Analysis: Compare Themes**	RL.9-10.2	Determine a theme or central idea of a text and analyze in detail its development over the course of the text, including how it emerges and is shaped and refined by specific details; provide an objective summary of the text.
287	**Vocabulary Study: Word Families**	L.9-10.4.b	Identify and correctly use patterns of word changes that indicate different meanings or parts of speech.
		L.9-10.4.d	Verify the preliminary determination of the meaning of a word or phrase.

page 923

Common Core State Standards, continued

Student Handbooks, continued

Cluster 3, continued

SE Pages	Lesson	Code	Standards Text
287	**Writing: Write an Opinion Paragraph**	W.9-10.1	Write arguments to support claims in an analysis of substantive topics or texts, using valid reasoning and relevant and sufficient evidence.
		W.9-10.5	Develop and strengthen writing as needed by planning, revising, editing, rewriting, or trying a new approach, focusing on addressing what is most significant for a specific purpose and audience.
287	**Listening/Speaking: Oral Interpretation**	SL.9-10.6	Adapt speech to a variety of contexts and tasks, demonstrating command of formal English when indicated or appropriate.
Close Reading			
288–289	**Read The American Promise**	RI.9-10.10	By the end of grade 10, read and comprehend literary nonfiction at the high end of the grades 9–10 text complexity band independently and proficiently.
Unit Wrap-Up			
290	**Unit Wrap-Up Present Your Project**	SL.9-10.5	Make strategic use of digital media in presentations to enhance understanding of findings, reasoning, and evidence and to add interest.
	Reflect on Your Reading	SL.9-10.1.a	Come to discussions prepared, having read and researched material under study; explicitly draw on that preparation by referring to evidence from texts and other research on the topic or issue to stimulate a thoughtful, well-reasoned exchange of ideas.
	Respond to the Essential Question	SL.9-10.1.a	Come to discussions prepared, having read and researched material under study; explicitly draw on that preparation by referring to evidence from texts and other research on the topic or issue to stimulate a thoughtful, well-reasoned exchange of ideas.
Writing Project: Response to Literature			
291–295	**Study a Response to Literature and Prewrite**	W.9-10.2.a	Introduce a topic; organize complex ideas, concepts, and information to make important connections and distinctions; include formatting, graphics, and multimedia when useful to aiding comprehension.
		W.9-10.2.b	Develop the topic with well-chosen, relevant, and sufficient facts, extended definitions, concrete details, quotations, or other information and examples appropriate to the audience's knowledge of the topic.
		W.9-10.5	Develop and strengthen writing as needed by planning, revising, editing, rewriting, or trying a new approach, focusing on addressing what is most significant for a specific purpose and audience.
		W.9-10.6	Use technology, including the Internet, to produce, publish, and update individual or shared writing products, taking advantage of technology's capacity to link to other information and to display information flexibly and dynamically.
296–297	**Response to Literature: Draft**	W.9-10.2	Write informative/explanatory texts to examine and convey complex ideas, concepts, and information clearly and accurately through the effective selection, organization, and analysis of content.
		W.9-10.2.a	Introduce a topic; organize complex ideas, concepts, and information to make important connections and distinctions; include formatting, graphics, and multimedia when useful to aiding comprehension.
		W.9-10.4	Produce clear and coherent writing in which the development, organization, and style are appropriate to task, purpose, and audience.

page 924

Student Handbooks, continued

Writing Project: Response to Literature, continued

SE Pages	Lesson	Code	Standards Text
296–297	**Response to Literature: Draft** continued	W.9-10.6	Use technology, including the Internet, to produce, publish, and update individual or shared writing products, taking advantage of technology's capacity to link to other information and to display information flexibly and dynamically.
		W.9-10.9	Draw evidence from literary or informational texts to support analysis, reflection, and research.
298–301	**Response to Literature: Revise Trait: Voice and Style**	W.9-10.2.a	Introduce a topic; organize complex ideas, concepts, and information to make important co nnections and distinctions; include formatting, graphics, and multimedia when useful to aiding comprehension.
		W.9-10.2.b	Develop the topic with well-chosen, relevant, and sufficient facts, extended definitions, concrete details, quotations, or other information and examples appropriate to the audience's knowledge of the topic.
		W.9-10.2.d	Use precise language and domain-specific vocabulary to manage the complexity of the topic.
		W.9-10.2.f	Provide a concluding statement or section that follows from and supports the information or explanation presented.
		W.9-10.4	Produce clear and coherent writing in which the development, organization, and style are appropriate to task, purpose, and audience.
		W.9-10.5	Develop and strengthen writing as needed by planning, revising, editing, rewriting, or trying a new approach, focusing on addressing what is most significant for a specific purpose and audience.
		SL.9-10.1	Initiate and participate effectively in a range of collaborative discussions (one-on-one, in groups, and teacher-led) with diverse partners on grades 9–10 topics, texts, and issues, building on others' ideas and expressing their own clearly and persuasively.
		SL.9-10.1.d	Respond thoughtfully to diverse perspectives, summarize points of agreement and disagreement, and, when warranted, qualify or justify their own views and understanding and make new connections in light of the evidence and reasoning presented.
		L.9-10.1.b	Use various types of phrases (noun, verb, adjectival, adverbial, participial, prepositional, absolute) and clauses (independent, dependent; noun, relative, adverbial) to convey specific meanings and add variety and interest to writing or presentations.
302–304	**Response to Literature: Edit and Proofread Capitalization: Days of the Week and Months Punctuation: Appositives and Nouns of Direct Address Active Voice Verb Tense Consistency**	L.9-10.1	Demonstrate command of the conventions of standard English grammar and usage when writing or speaking.
		L.9-10.2	Demonstrate command of the conventions of standard English capitalization, punctuation, and spelling when writing.
		L.9-10.3.a	Write and edit work so that it conforms to the guidelines in a style manual appropriate for the discipline and writing type.

page 925

Common Core State Standards

Common Core State Standards, continued

Student Handbooks, continued

Writing Project: Response to Literature, continued

SE Pages	Lesson	Code	Standards Text
305	Response to Literature: Publish and Present	W.9-10.2.a	Introduce a topic; organize complex ideas, concepts, and information to make important connections and distinctions; include formatting, graphics, and multimedia when useful to aiding comprehension.
		W.9-10.6	Use technology, including the Internet, to produce, publish, and update individual or shared writing products, taking advantage of technology's capacity to link to other information and to display information flexibly and dynamically.
		SL.9-10.1	Initiate and participate effectively in a range of collaborative discussions (one-on-one, in groups, and teacher-led) with diverse partners on grades 9–10 topics, texts, and issues, building on others' ideas and expressing their own clearly and persuasively.
UNIT 4: Opening Doors			
306–307	Discuss the Essential Question	SL.9-10.1.b	Work with peers to set rules for collegial discussions and decision-making (e.g., informal consensus, taking votes on key issues, presentation of alternate views), clear goals and deadlines, and individual roles as needed.
		SL.9-10.3	Evaluate a speaker's point of view, reasoning, and use of evidence and rhetoric, identifying any fallacious reasoning or exaggerated or distorted evidence.
308	Analyze and Debate	SL.9-10.4	Present information, findings, and supporting evidence clearly, concisely, and logically such that listeners can follow the line of reasoning and the organization, development, substance, and style are appropriate to purpose, audience, and task.
309	Plan a Project	SL.9-10.1.b	Work with peers to set rules for collegial discussions and decision-making (e.g., informal consensus, taking votes on key issues, presentation of alternate views), clear goals and deadlines, and individual roles as needed.
309	Choose More to Read	RL.9-10.10	By the end of grade 10, read and comprehend literature, including stories, dramas, and poems, at the high end of the grades 9–10 text complexity band independently and proficiently.
		RI.9-10.10	By the end of grade 10, read and comprehend literary nonfiction at the high end of the grades 9–10 text complexity band independently and proficiently.
310–313	How to Read Nonfiction	RI.9-10.1	Cite strong and thorough textual evidence to support analysis of what the text says explicitly as well as inferences drawn from the text.
		RI.9-10.5	Analyze in detail how an author's ideas or claims are developed and refined by particular sentences, paragraphs, or larger portions of a text.
		RI.9-10.10	By the end of grade 10, read and comprehend literary nonfiction at the high end of the grades 9–10 text complexity band independently and proficiently.
		SL.9-10.1	Initiate and participate effectively in a range of collaborative discussions (one-on-one, in groups, and teacher-led) with diverse partners on grades 9–10 topics, texts, and issues, building on others' ideas and expressing their own clearly and persuasively.
		L.9-10.6	Acquire and use accurately general academic and domain-specific words and phrases, sufficient for reading, writing, speaking, and listening at the college and career readiness level; demonstrate independence in gathering vocabulary knowledge when considering a word or phrase important to comprehension or expression.

page 926

Student Handbooks, continued

Cluster 1

SE Pages	Lesson	Code	Standards Text
314	Prepare to Read	RI.9-10.4	Determine the meaning of words and phrases as they are used in a text, including figurative, connotative, and technical meanings; analyze the cumulative impact of specific word choices on meaning and tone.
		SL.9-10.1	Initiate and participate effectively in a range of collaborative discussions (one-on-one, in groups, and teacher-led) with diverse partners on grades 9–10 topics, texts, and issues, building on others' ideas and expressing their own clearly and persuasively.
		L.9-10.6	Acquire and use accurately general academic and domain-specific words and phrases, sufficient for reading, writing, speaking, and listening at the college and career readiness level; demonstrate independence in gathering vocabulary knowledge when considering a word or phrase important to comprehension or expression.
315	Before Reading: Curtis Aikens and the American Dream	RI.9-10.1	Cite strong and thorough textual evidence to support analysis of what the text says explicitly as well as inferences drawn from the text.
		RI.9-10.5	Analyze in detail how an author's ideas or claims are developed and refined by particular sentences, paragraphs, or larger portions of a text.
316–328	Read Curtis Aikens and the American Dream	RI.9-10.1	Cite strong and thorough textual evidence to support analysis of what the text says explicitly as well as inferences drawn from the text.
		RI.9-10.5	Analyze in detail how an author's ideas or claims are developed and refined by particular sentences, paragraphs, or larger portions of a text.
		RI.9-10.10	By the end of grade 10, read and comprehend literary nonfiction at the high end of the grades 9–10 text complexity band independently and proficiently.
		W.9-10.9.b	Apply grades 9–10 Reading standards to literary nonfiction.
		W.9-10.10	Write routinely over extended time frames (time for research, reflection, and revision) and shorter time frames (a single sitting or a day or two) for a range of tasks, purposes, and audiences.
		L.9-10.1.b	Use various types of phrases (noun, verb, adjectival, adverbial, participial, prepositional, absolute) and clauses (independent, dependent; noun, relative, adverbial) to convey specific meanings and add variety and interest to writing or presentations.
		L.9-10.2.c	Spell correctly.
		L.9-10.4	Determine or clarify the meaning of unknown and multiple-meaning words and phrases based on grades 9–10 reading and content, choosing flexibly from a range of strategies.
		L.9-10.6	Acquire and use accurately general academic and domain-specific words and phrases, sufficient for reading, writing, speaking, and listening at the college and career readiness level; demonstrate independence in gathering vocabulary knowledge when considering a word or phrase important to comprehension or expression.
329	Postscript: Think You Don't Need an Education?	RI.9-10.1	Cite strong and thorough textual evidence to support analysis of what the text says explicitly as well as inferences drawn from the text.
		RI.9-10.3	Analyze how the author unfolds an analysis or series of ideas or events, including the order in which the points are made, how they are introduced and developed, and the connections that are drawn between them.

page 927

Common Core State Standards, continued

Student Handbooks, continued

Cluster 1, continued

SE Pages	Lesson	Code	Standards Text
330	Before Reading: Go For It!	RI.9-10.1	Cite strong and thorough textual evidence to support analysis of what the text says explicitly as well as inferences drawn from the text.
		RI.9-10.7	Analyze various accounts of a subject told in different mediums, determining which details are emphasized in each account.
331–334	Read Go For It!	RI.9-10.1	Cite strong and thorough textual evidence to support analysis of what the text says explicitly as well as inferences drawn from the text.
		RI.9-10.4	Determine the meaning of words and phrases as they are used in a text, including figurative, connotative, and technical meanings; analyze the cumulative impact of specific word choices on meaning and tone.
		RI.9-10.7	Analyze various accounts of a subject told in different mediums, determining which details are emphasized in each account.
		RI.9-10.10	By the end of grade 10, read and comprehend literary nonfiction at the high end of the grades 9–10 text complexity band independently and proficiently.
		W.9-10.9.b	Apply grades 9–10 Reading standards to literary nonfiction.
		W.9-10.10	Write routinely over extended time frames (time for research, reflection, and revision) and shorter time frames (a single sitting or a day or two) for a range of tasks, purposes, and audiences.
		L.9-10.1	Demonstrate command of the conventions of standard English grammar and usage when writing or speaking.
		L.9-10.6	Acquire and use accurately general academic and domain-specific words and phrases, sufficient for reading, writing, speaking, and listening at the college and career readiness level; demonstrate independence in gathering vocabulary knowledge when considering a word or phrase important to comprehension or expression.
335	Reflect and Assess	RI.9-10.1	Cite strong and thorough textual evidence to support analysis of what the text says explicitly as well as inferences drawn from the text.
	Critical Thinking	RI.9-10.2	Determine a central idea of a text and analyze its development over the course of the text, including how it emerges and is shaped and refined by specific details; provide an objective summary of the text.
		RI.9-10.8	Delineate and evaluate the argument and specific claims in a text, assessing whether the reasoning is valid and the evidence is relevant and sufficient; identify false statements and fallacious reasoning.
		RI.9-10.10	By the end of grade 10, read and comprehend literary nonfiction at the high end of the grades 9–10 text complexity band independently and proficiently.
	Write About Literature	W.9-10.10	Write routinely over extended time frames (time for research, reflection, and revision) and shorter time frames (a single sitting or a day or two) for a range of tasks, purposes, and audiences.
	Key Vocabulary Review	L.9-10.6	Acquire and use accurately general academic and domain-specific words and phrases, sufficient for reading, writing, speaking, and listening at the college and career readiness level; demonstrate independence in gathering vocabulary knowledge when considering a word or phrase important to comprehension or expression.
	Read with Ease: Phrasing	RI.9-10.10	By the end of grade 10, read and comprehend literary nonfiction at the high end of the grades 9–10 text complexity band independently and proficiently.

page 928

Student Handbooks, continued

Cluster 1, continued

SE Pages	Lesson	Code	Standards Text
336	Grammar: Show Possession	L.9-10.1.b	Use various types of phrases (noun, verb, adjectival, adverbial, participial, prepositional, absolute) and clauses (independent, dependent; noun, relative, adverbial) to convey specific meanings and add variety and interest to writing or presentations.
336	Language Development: Define and Explain	SL.9-10.1.a	Come to discussions prepared, having read and researched material under study; explicitly draw on that preparation by referring to evidence from texts and other research on the topic or issue to stimulate a thoughtful, well-reasoned exchange of ideas.
336	Research/ Writing: Visual Presentation	W.9-10.7	Conduct short as well as more sustained research projects to answer a question (including a self-generated question) or solve a problem; narrow or broaden the inquiry when appropriate; synthesize multiple sources on the subject, demonstrating understanding of the subject under investigation.
336	Media Study: Evaluate Public Service Announcements	W.9-10.7	Conduct short as well as more sustained research projects to answer a question (including a self-generated question) or solve a problem; narrow or broaden the inquiry when appropriate; synthesize multiple sources on the subject, demonstrating understanding of the subject under investigation.
		SL.9-10.3	Evaluate a speaker's point of view, reasoning, and use of evidence and rhetoric, identifying any fallacious reasoning or exaggerated or distorted evidence.
337	Vocabulary Study: Dictionary and Jargon	L.9-10.4.c	Consult general and specialized reference materials, both print and digital, to find the pronunciation of a word or determine or clarify its precise meaning, its part of speech, or its etymology.
337	Writing Trait: Development of Ideas	W.9-10.2	Write informative/explanatory texts to examine and convey complex ideas, concepts, and information clearly and accurately through the effective selection, organization, and analysis of content.
		W.9-10.5	Develop and strengthen writing as needed by planning, revising, editing, rewriting, or trying a new approach, focusing on addressing what is most significant for a specific purpose and audience.
338	Workplace Workshop: Inside a Restaurant	W.9-10.2	Write informative/explanatory texts to examine and convey complex ideas, concepts, and information clearly and accurately through the effective selection, organization, and analysis of content.
		W.9-10.4	Produce clear and coherent writing in which the development, organization, and style are appropriate to task, purpose, and audience.
		W.9-10.10	Write routinely over extended time frames (time for research, reflection, and revision) and shorter time frames (a single sitting or a day or two) for a range of tasks, purposes, and audiences.
339	Vocabulary Workshop: Access Words During Reading	L.9-10.4.d	Verify the preliminary determination of the meaning of a word or phrase.
Cluster 2			
340	Prepare to Read	RI.9-10.4	Determine the meaning of words and phrases as they are used in a text, including figurative, connotative, and technical meanings; analyze the cumulative impact of specific word choices on meaning and tone.
		SL.9-10.1	Initiate and participate effectively in a range of collaborative discussions (one-on-one, in groups, and teacher-led) with diverse partners on grades 9–10 topics, texts, and issues, building on others' ideas and expressing their own clearly and persuasively.

page 929

Common Core State Standards

Common Core State Standards, continued

Student Handbooks, continued

Cluster 2, continued

SE Pages	Lesson	Code	Standards Text
340	**Prepare to Read** continued	L.9-10.4.c	Consult general and specialized reference materials, both print and digital, to find the pronunciation of a word or determine or clarify its precise meaning, its part of speech, or its etymology.
		L.9-10.6	Acquire and use accurately general academic and domain-specific words and phrases, sufficient for reading, writing, speaking, and listening at the college and career readiness level; demonstrate independence in gathering vocabulary knowledge when considering a word or phrase important to comprehension or expression.
341	**Before Reading: Superman and Me**	RI.9-10.1	Cite strong and thorough textual evidence to support analysis of what the text says explicitly as well as inferences drawn from the text.
		RI.9-10.5	Analyze in detail how an author's ideas or claims are developed and refined by particular sentences, paragraphs, or larger portions of a text.
342–349	**Read Superman and Me**	RI.9-10.1	Cite strong and thorough textual evidence to support analysis of what the text says explicitly as well as inferences drawn from the text.
		RI.9-10.4	Determine the meaning of words and phrases as they are used in a text, including figurative, connotative, and technical meanings; analyze the cumulative impact of specific word choices on meaning and tone.
		RI.9-10.5	Analyze in detail how an author's ideas or claims are developed and refined by particular sentences, paragraphs, or larger portions of a text.
		RI.9-10.10	By the end of grade 10, read and comprehend literary nonfiction at the high end of the grades 9–10 text complexity band independently and proficiently.
		W.9-10.1	Write arguments to support claims in an analysis of substantive topics or texts, using valid reasoning and relevant and sufficient evidence.
		W.9-10.9.b	Apply grades 9–10 Reading standards to literary nonfiction.
		W.9-10.10	Write routinely over extended time frames (time for research, reflection, and revision) and shorter time frames (a single sitting or a day or two) for a range of tasks, purposes, and audiences.
		L.9-10.1.b	Use various types of phrases (noun, verb, adjectival, adverbial, participial, prepositional, absolute) and clauses (independent, dependent; noun, relative, adverbial) to convey specific meanings and add variety and interest to writing or presentations.
		L.9-10.6	Acquire and use accurately general academic and domain-specific words and phrases, sufficient for reading, writing, speaking, and listening at the college and career readiness level; demonstrate independence in gathering vocabulary knowledge when considering a word or phrase important to comprehension or expression.
350	**Before Reading: A Smart Cookie/It's Our Story, Too**	RI.9-10.1	Cite strong and thorough textual evidence to support analysis of what the text says explicitly as well as inferences drawn from the text.
		RI.9-10.5	Analyze in detail how an author's ideas or claims are developed and refined by particular sentences, paragraphs, or larger portions of a text.
351–356	**Read A Smart Cookie/It's Our Story, Too**	RL.9-10.1	Cite strong and thorough textual evidence to support analysis of what the text says explicitly as well as inferences drawn from the text.
		RL.9-10.5	Analyze how an author's choices concerning how to structure a text, order events within it, and manipulate time create such effects as mystery, tension, or surprise.

page 930

Student Handbooks, continued

Cluster 2, continued

SE Pages	Lesson	Code	Standards Text
351–356	**Read A Smart Cookie/It's Our Story, Too** continued	RI.9-10.1	Cite strong and thorough textual evidence to support analysis of what the text says explicitly as well as inferences drawn from the text.
		RI.9-10.5	Analyze in detail how an author's ideas or claims are developed and refined by particular sentences, paragraphs, or larger portions of a text.
		RI.9-10.6	Determine an author's point of view or purpose in a text and analyze how an author uses rhetoric to advance that point of view or purpose.
		RI.9-10.10	By the end of grade 10, read and comprehend literary nonfiction at the high end of the grades 9–10 text complexity band independently and proficiently.
		W.9-10.9.a	Apply grades 9–10 Reading standards to literature.
		W.9-10.10	Write routinely over extended time frames (time for research, reflection, and revision) and shorter time frames (a single sitting or a day or two) for a range of tasks, purposes, and audiences.
		L.9-10.1.b	Use various types of phrases (noun, verb, adjectival, adverbial, participial, prepositional, absolute) and clauses (independent, dependent; noun, relative, adverbial) to convey specific meanings and add variety and interest to writing or presentations.
		L.9-10.6	Acquire and use accurately general academic and domain-specific words and phrases, sufficient for reading, writing, speaking, and listening at the college and career readiness level; demonstrate independence in gathering vocabulary knowledge when considering a word or phrase important to comprehension or expression.
357	**Reflect and Assess**	RI.9-10.1	Cite strong and thorough textual evidence to support analysis of what the text says explicitly as well as inferences drawn from the text.
	Critical Thinking	RI.9-10.10	By the end of grade 10, read and comprehend literary nonfiction at the high end of the grades 9–10 text complexity band independently and proficiently.
	Write About Literature	W.9-10.9.a	Apply grades 9–10 Reading standards to literature.
	Key Vocabulary Review	W.9-10.9.b	Apply grades 9–10 Reading standards to literary nonfiction.
		L.9-10.6	Acquire and use accurately general academic and domain-specific words and phrases, sufficient for reading, writing, speaking, and listening at the college and career readiness level; demonstrate independence in gathering vocabulary knowledge when considering a word or phrase important to comprehension or expression.
	Read with Ease: Intonation	RI.9-10.10	By the end of grade 10, read and comprehend literary nonfiction at the high end of the grades 9–10 text complexity band independently and proficiently.
358	**Grammar: Use Pronouns in Prepositional Phrases**	L.9-10.1.b	Use various types of phrases (noun, verb, adjectival, adverbial, participial, prepositional, absolute) and clauses (independent, dependent; noun, relative, adverbial) to convey specific meanings and add variety and interest to writing or presentations.
358	**Language Development: Clarify**	SL.9-10.1.c	Propel conversations by posing and responding to questions that relate the current discussion to broader themes or larger ideas; actively incorporate others into the discussion; and clarify, verify, or challenge ideas and conclusions.

page 931

Common Core State Standards, continued

Student Handbooks, continued

Cluster 2, continued

SE Pages	Lesson	Code	Standards Text
358	**Literary Analysis: Analyze Imagery**	RL.9-10.4	Determine the meaning of words and phrases as they are used in the text, including figurative and connotative meanings; analyze the cumulative impact of specific word choices on meaning and tone.
		RI.9-10.4	Determine the meaning of words and phrases as they are used in a text, including figurative, connotative, and technical meanings; analyze the cumulative impact of specific word choices on meaning and tone.
359	**Vocabulary Study: Multiple-Meaning Words**	L.9-10.4.c	Consult general and specialized reference materials, both print and digital, to find the pronunciation of a word or determine or clarify its precise meaning, its part of speech, or its etymology.
359	**Writing: Social Science: Write a Case Study**	W.9-10.2	Write informative/explanatory texts to examine and convey complex ideas, concepts, and information clearly and accurately through the effective selection, organization, and analysis of content.
		W.9-10.5	Develop and strengthen writing as needed by planning, revising, editing, rewriting, or trying a new approach, focusing on addressing what is most significant for a specific purpose and audience.
359	**Listening/Speaking: Oral Presentation**	SL.9-10.1.a	Come to discussions prepared, having read and researched material under study; explicitly draw on that preparation by referring to evidence from texts and other research on the topic or issue to stimulate a thoughtful, well-reasoned exchange of ideas.
		SL.9-10.4	Present information, findings, and supporting evidence clearly, concisely, and logically such that listeners can follow the line of reasoning and the organization, development, substance, and style are appropriate to purpose, audience, and task.
360–361	**Listening and Speaking Workshop: Oral Report**	W.9-10.7	Conduct short as well as more sustained research projects to answer a question (including a self-generated question) or solve a problem; narrow or broaden the inquiry when appropriate; synthesize multiple sources on the subject, demonstrating understanding of the subject under investigation.
		SL.9-10.2	Integrate multiple sources of information presented in diverse media or formats evaluating the credibility and accuracy of each source.
		SL.9-10.3	Evaluate a speaker's point of view, reasoning, and use of evidence and rhetoric, identifying any fallacious reasoning or exaggerated or distorted evidence.
		SL.9-10.4	Present information, findings, and supporting evidence clearly, concisely, and logically such that listeners can follow the line of reasoning and the organization, development, substance, and style are appropriate to purpose, audience, and task.
		L.9-10.3	Apply knowledge of language to understand how language functions in different contexts, to make effective choices for meaning or style, and to comprehend more fully when reading or listening.
Cluster 3			
362	**Prepare to Read**	RI.9-10.4	Determine the meaning of words and phrases as they are used in a text, including figurative, connotative, and technical meanings; analyze the cumulative impact of specific word choices on meaning and tone.
		SL.9-10.1	Initiate and participate effectively in a range of collaborative discussions (one-on-one, in groups, and teacher-led) with diverse partners on grades 9–10 topics, texts, and issues, building on others' ideas and expressing their own clearly and persuasively.

page 932

Student Handbooks, continued

Cluster 3, continued

SE Pages	Lesson	Code	Standards Text
	Prepare to Read continued	L.9-10.6	Acquire and use accurately general academic and domain-specific words and phrases, sufficient for reading, writing, speaking, and listening at the college and career readiness level; demonstrate independence in gathering vocabulary knowledge when considering a word or phrase important to comprehension or expression.
363	**Before Reading: The Fast and the Fuel-Efficient**	RI.9-10.1	Cite strong and thorough textual evidence to support analysis of what the text says explicitly as well as inferences drawn from the text.
		RI.9-10.5	Analyze in detail how an author's ideas or claims are developed and refined by particular sentences, paragraphs, or larger portions of a text.
364–374	**Read The Fast and the Fuel-Efficient**	RI.9-10.1	Cite strong and thorough textual evidence to support analysis of what the text says explicitly as well as inferences drawn from the text.
		RI.9-10.2	Determine a central idea of a text and analyze its development over the course of the text, including how it emerges and is shaped and refined by specific details; provide an objective summary of the text.
		RI.9-10.5	Analyze in detail how an author's ideas or claims are developed and refined by particular sentences, paragraphs, or larger portions of a text.
		RI.9-10.10	By the end of grade 10, read and comprehend literary nonfiction at the high end of the grades 9–10 text complexity band independently and proficiently.
		W.9-10.9.b	Apply grades 9–10 Reading standards to literary nonfiction.
		W.9-10.10	Write routinely over extended time frames (time for research, reflection, and revision) and shorter time frames (a single sitting or a day or two) for a range of tasks, purposes, and audiences.
		L.9-10.1.b	Use various types of phrases (noun, verb, adjectival, adverbial, participial, prepositional, absolute) and clauses (independent, dependent; noun, relative, adverbial) to convey specific meanings and add variety and interest to writing or presentations.
		L.9-10.4.a	Use context as a clue to the meaning of a word or phrase.
		L.9-10.4.b	Identify and correctly use patterns of word changes that indicate different meanings or parts of speech.
		L.9-10.6	Acquire and use accurately general academic and domain-specific words and phrases, sufficient for reading, writing, speaking, and listening at the college and career readiness level; demonstrate independence in gathering vocabulary knowledge when considering a word or phrase important to comprehension or expression.
375	**Postscript: Cartoon**	RL.9-10.10	By the end of grade 10, read and comprehend literature, including stories, dramas, and poems, at the high end of the grades 9–10 text complexity band independently and proficiently.
376	**Before Reading: Teens Open Doors**	RI.9-10.1	Cite strong and thorough textual evidence to support analysis of what the text says explicitly as well as inferences drawn from the text.
		RI.9-10.3	Analyze how the author unfolds an analysis or series of ideas or events, including the order in which the points are made, how they are introduced and developed, and the connections that are drawn between them.

page 933

Common Core State Standards

Common Core State Standards, continued

Student Handbooks, continued

Cluster 3, continued

SE Pages	Lesson	Code	Standards Text
377–380	Read Teens Open Doors	RI.9-10.1	Cite strong and thorough textual evidence to support analysis of what the text says explicitly as well as inferences drawn from the text.
		RI.9-10.3	Analyze how the author unfolds an analysis or series of ideas or events, including the order in which the points are made, how they are introduced and developed, and the connections that are drawn between them.
		RI.9-10.10	By the end of grade 10, read and comprehend literary nonfiction at the high end of the grades 9–10 text complexity band independently and proficiently.
		W.9-10.4	Produce clear and coherent writing in which the development, organization, and style are appropriate to task, purpose, and audience.
		W.9-10.10	Write routinely over extended time frames (time for research, reflection, and revision) and shorter time frames (a single sitting or a day or two) for a range of tasks, purposes, and audiences.
		L.9-10.1	Demonstrate command of the conventions of standard English grammar and usage when writing or speaking.
		L.9-10.6	Acquire and use accurately general academic and domain-specific words and phrases, sufficient for reading, writing, speaking, and listening at the college and career readiness level; demonstrate independence in gathering vocabulary knowledge when considering a word or phrase important to comprehension or expression.
381	Reflect and Assess	RI.9-10.1	Cite strong and thorough textual evidence to support analysis of what the text says explicitly as well as inferences drawn from the text.
	Critical Thinking	RI.9-10.2	Determine a central idea of a text and analyze its development over the course of the text, including how it emerges and is shaped and refined by specific details; provide an objective summary of the text.
		RI.9-10.10	By the end of grade 10, read and comprehend literary nonfiction at the high end of the grades 9–10 text complexity band independently and proficiently.
	Write About Literature	W.9-10.1	Write arguments to support claims in an analysis of substantive topics or texts, using valid reasoning and relevant and sufficient evidence.
		W.9-10.9.b	Apply grades 9–10 Reading standards to literary nonfiction.
	Key Vocabulary Review	L.9-10.6	Acquire and use accurately general academic and domain-specific words and phrases, sufficient for reading, writing, speaking, and listening at the college and career readiness level; demonstrate independence in gathering vocabulary knowledge when considering a word or phrase important to comprehension or expression.
	Read with Ease: Expression	RI.9-10.10	By the end of grade 10, read and comprehend literary nonfiction at the high end of the grades 9–10 text complexity band independently and proficiently.
382	Grammar: Use the Correct Pronoun	L.9-10.1	Demonstrate command of the conventions of standard English grammar and usage when writing or speaking.
382	Language Development: Verify or Confirm Information	SL.9-10.1.a	Come to discussions prepared, having read and researched material under study; explicitly draw on that preparation by referring to evidence from texts and other research on the topic or issue to stimulate a thoughtful, well-reasoned exchange of ideas.

page 934

Student Handbooks, continued

Cluster 3, continued

SE Pages	Lesson	Code	Standards Text
382	Research/Writing: Descriptive Diagram	W.9-10.2	Write informative/explanatory texts to examine and convey complex ideas, concepts, and information clearly and accurately through the effective selection, organization, and analysis of content.
		W.9-10.7	Conduct short as well as more sustained research projects to answer a question (including a self-generated question) or solve a problem; narrow or broaden the inquiry when appropriate; synthesize multiple sources on the subject, demonstrating understanding of the subject under investigation.
382	Listening/ Speaking: Speech	SL.9-10.4	Present information, findings, and supporting evidence clearly, concisely, and logically such that listeners can follow the line of reasoning and the organization, development, substance, and style are appropriate to purpose, audience, and task.
		SL.9-10.6	Adapt speech to a variety of contexts and tasks, demonstrating command of formal English when indicated or appropriate.
383	Vocabulary Study: Multiple-Meaning Words	L.9-10.4.c	Consult general and specialized reference materials, both print and digital, to find the pronunciation of a word or determine or clarify its precise meaning, its part of speech, or its etymology.
383	Writing on Demand: Write a Problem-Solution Essay	W.9-10.1	Write arguments to support claims in an analysis of substantive topics or texts, using valid reasoning and relevant and sufficient evidence.
		W.9-10.4	Produce clear and coherent writing in which the development, organization, and style are appropriate to task, purpose, and audience.
Close Reading			
384–387	Read The Sky Is Not the Limit	RI.9-10.10	By the end of grade 10, read and comprehend literary nonfiction at the high end of the grades 9–10 text complexity band independently and proficiently.
Unit Wrap-Up			
388	Unit Wrap-Up Present Your Project	W.9-10.2	Write informative/explanatory texts to examine and convey complex ideas, concepts, and information clearly and accurately through the effective selection, organization, and analysis of content.
		W.9-10.4	Produce clear and coherent writing in which the development, organization, and style are appropriate to task, purpose, and audience.
		W.9-10.6	Use technology, including the Internet, to produce, publish, and update individual or shared writing products, taking advantage of technology's capacity to link to other information and to display information flexibly and dynamically.
	Reflect on Your Reading	SL.9-10.1.a	Come to discussions prepared, having read and researched material under study; explicitly draw on that preparation by referring to evidence from texts and other research on the topic or issue to stimulate a thoughtful, well-reasoned exchange of ideas.
	Respond to the Essential Question	SL.9-10.1.a	Come to discussions prepared, having read and researched material under study; explicitly draw on that preparation by referring to evidence from texts and other research on the topic or issue to stimulate a thoughtful, well-reasoned exchange of ideas.

page 935

Common Core State Standards, continued

Student Handbooks, continued

Writing Project: Research Report

SE Pages	Lesson	Code	Standards Text
389–393	Study Research Reports and Prewrite	W.9-10.2.a	Introduce a topic; organize complex ideas, concepts, and information to make important connections and distinctions; include formatting, graphics, and multimedia when useful to aiding comprehension.
		W.9-10.5	Develop and strengthen writing as needed by planning, revising, editing, rewriting, or trying a new approach, focusing on addressing what is most significant for a specific purpose and audience.
		W.9-10.7	Conduct short as well as more sustained research projects to answer a question (including a self-generated question) or solve a problem; narrow or broaden the inquiry when appropriate; synthesize multiple sources on the subject, demonstrating understanding of the subject under investigation.
		W.9-10.8	Gather relevant information from multiple authoritative print and digital sources, using advanced searches effectively; assess the usefulness of each source in answering the research question; integrate information into the text selectively to maintain the flow of ideas, avoiding plagiarism and following a standard format for citation.
394–395	Research Report: Draft	W.9-10.2.a	Introduce a topic; organize complex ideas, concepts, and information to make important connections and distinctions; include formatting, graphics, and multimedia when useful to aiding comprehension.
		W.9-10.4	Produce clear and coherent writing in which the development, organization, and style are appropriate to task, purpose, and audience.
		W.9-10.8	Gather relevant information from multiple authoritative print and digital sources, using advanced searches effectively; assess the usefulness of each source in answering the research question; integrate information into the text selectively to maintain the flow of ideas, avoiding plagiarism and following a standard format for citation.
		L.9-10.3.a	Write and edit work so that it conforms to the guidelines in a style manual appropriate for the discipline and writing type.
396–399	Research Report: Revise Trait: Development of Ideas	W.9-10.2.a	Introduce a topic; organize complex ideas, concepts, and information to make important connections and distinctions; include formatting, graphics, and multimedia when useful to aiding comprehension.
		W.9-10.2.b	Develop the topic with well-chosen, relevant, and sufficient facts, extended definitions, concrete details, quotations, or other information and examples appropriate to the audience's knowledge of the topic.
		W.9-10.2.c	Use appropriate and varied transitions to link the major sections of the text, create cohesion, and clarify the relationships among complex ideas and concepts.
		W.9-10.2.d	Use precise language and domain-specific vocabulary to manage the complexity of the topic.
		W.9-10.2.e	Establish and maintain a formal style and objective tone while attending to the norms and conventions of the discipline in which they are writing.
		W.9-10.5	Develop and strengthen writing as needed by planning, revising, editing, rewriting, or trying a new approach, focusing on addressing what is most significant for a specific purpose and audience.
		W.9-10.7	Conduct short as well as more sustained research projects to answer a question (including a self-generated question) or solve a problem; narrow or broaden the inquiry when appropriate; synthesize multiple sources on the subject, demonstrating understanding of the subject under investigation.

page 936

Student Handbooks, continued

Writing Project: Research Report, continued

SE Pages	Lesson	Code	Standards Text
396–399	Research Report: Revise Trait: Development of Ideas continued	SL.9-10.1	Initiate and participate effectively in a range of collaborative discussions (one-on-one, in groups, and teacher-led) with diverse partners on grades 9–10 topics, texts, and issues, building on others' ideas and expressing their own clearly and persuasively.
		L.9-10.3.a	Write and edit work so that it conforms to the guidelines in a style manual appropriate for the discipline and writing type.
		L.9-10.2	Demonstrate command of the conventions of standard English capitalization, punctuation, and spelling when writing.
		L.9-10.3.a	Write and edit work so that it conforms to the guidelines in a style manual appropriate for the discipline and writing type.
400–402	Research Report: Edit and Proofread Capitalization: Titles of Publications Parentheses Verb Tense Consistency Pronoun-Antecedent Agreement	L.9-10.1	Demonstrate command of the conventions of standard English grammar and usage when writing or speaking.
		L.9-10.2	Demonstrate command of the conventions of standard English capitalization, punctuation, and spelling when writing.
		L.9-10.3.a	Write and edit work so that it conforms to the guidelines in a style manual appropriate for the discipline and writing type.
403	Research Report: Publish and Present	W.9-10.2.a	Introduce a topic; organize complex ideas, concepts, and information to make important connections and distinctions; include formatting, graphics, and multimedia when useful to aiding comprehension.
		W.9-10.6	Use technology, including the Internet, to produce, publish, and update individual or shared writing products, taking advantage of technology's capacity to link to other information and to display information flexibly and dynamically.
		SL.9-10.1	Initiate and participate effectively in a range of collaborative discussions (one-on-one, in groups, and teacher-led) with diverse partners on grades 9–10 topics, texts, and issues, building on others' ideas and expressing their own clearly and persuasively.
		SL.9-10.4	Present information, findings, and supporting evidence clearly, concisely, and logically such that listeners can follow the line of reasoning and the organization, development, substance, and style are appropriate to purpose, audience, and task.
UNIT 5: Fear This!			
404–405	Discuss the Essential Question	SL.9-10.1.b	Work with peers to set rules for collegial discussions and decision-making (e.g., informal consensus, taking votes on key issues, presentation of alternate views), clear goals and deadlines, and individual roles as needed.
		SL.9-10.3	Evaluate a speaker's point of view, reasoning, and use of evidence and rhetoric, identifying any fallacious reasoning or exaggerated or distorted evidence.
406	Analyze and Vote	SL.9-10.4	Present information, findings, and supporting evidence clearly, concisely, and logically such that listeners can follow the line of reasoning and the organization, development, substance, and style are appropriate to purpose, audience, and task.
407	Plan a Project	SL.9-10.1.b	Work with peers to set rules for collegial discussions and decision-making (e.g., informal consensus, taking votes on key issues, presentation of alternate views), clear goals and deadlines, and individual roles as needed.

page 937

Common Core State Standards

Common Core State Standards, continued

Student Handbooks, continued

UNIT 5: Fear This!, continued

SE Pages	Lesson	Code	Standards Text
407	**Choose More to Read**	RL.9-10.10	By the end of grade 10, read and comprehend literature, including stories, dramas, and poems, at the high end of the grades 9–10 text complexity band independently and proficiently.
		RI.9-10.10	By the end of grade 10, read and comprehend literary nonfiction at the high end of the grades 9–10 text complexity band independently and proficiently.
408–411	**How to Read Short Stories**	RL.9-10.10	By the end of grade 10, read and comprehend literature, including stories, dramas, and poems, at the high end of the grades 9–10 text complexity band independently and proficiently.
		SL.9-10.1.a	Come to discussions prepared, having read and researched material under study; explicitly draw on that preparation by referring to evidence from texts and other research on the topic or issue to stimulate a thoughtful, well-reasoned exchange of ideas.
		L.9-10.6	Acquire and use accurately general academic and domain-specific words and phrases, sufficient for reading, writing, speaking, and listening at the college and career readiness level; demonstrate independence in gathering vocabulary knowledge when considering a word or phrase important to comprehension or expression.
Cluster 1			
412	**Prepare to Read**	RI.9-10.4	Determine the meaning of words and phrases as they are used in a text, including figurative, connotative, and technical meanings; analyze the cumulative impact of specific word choices on meaning and tone.
		SL.9-10.1	Initiate and participate effectively in a range of collaborative discussions (one-on-one, in groups, and teacher-led) with diverse partners on grades 9–10 topics, texts, and issues, building on others' ideas and expressing their own clearly and persuasively.
		L.9-10.6	Acquire and use accurately general academic and domain-specific words and phrases, sufficient for reading, writing, speaking, and listening at the college and career readiness level; demonstrate independence in gathering vocabulary knowledge when considering a word or phrase important to comprehension or expression.
413	**Before Reading: The Interlopers**	RL.9-10.5	Analyze how an author's choices concerning how to structure a text, order events within it, and manipulate time create such effects as mystery, tension, or surprise.
		RL.9-10.10	By the end of grade 10, read and comprehend literature, including stories, dramas, and poems, at the high end of the grades 9–10 text complexity band independently and proficiently.
414–423	**Read The Interlopers**	RL.9-10.1	Cite strong and thorough textual evidence to support analysis of what the text says explicitly as well as inferences drawn from the text.
		RL.9-10.5	Analyze how an author's choices concerning how to structure a text, order events within it, and manipulate time create such effects as mystery, tension, or surprise.
		RL.9-10.10	By the end of grade 10, read and comprehend literature, including stories, dramas, and poems, at the high end of the grades 9–10 text complexity band independently and proficiently.
		W.9-10.9.a	Apply grades 9–10 Reading standards to literature.
		W.9-10.10	Write routinely over extended time frames (time for research, reflection, and revision) and shorter time frames (a single sitting or a day or two) for a range of tasks, purposes, and audiences.

page 938

Student Handbooks, continued

Cluster 1, continued

SE Pages	Lesson	Code	Standards Text
414–423	**Read The Interlopers** continued	L.9-10.1.b	Use various types of phrases (noun, verb, adjectival, adverbial, participial, prepositional, absolute) and clauses (independent, dependent; noun, relative, adverbial) to convey specific meanings and add variety and interest to writing or presentations.
		L.9-10.4.b	Identify and correctly use patterns of word changes that indicate different meanings or parts of speech.
		L.9-10.4.c	Consult general and specialized reference materials, both print and digital, to find the pronunciation of a word or determine or clarify its precise meaning, its part of speech, or its etymology.
		L.9-10.6	Acquire and use accurately general academic and domain-specific words and phrases, sufficient for reading, writing, speaking, and listening at the college and career readiness level; demonstrate independence in gathering vocabulary knowledge when considering a word or phrase important to comprehension or expression.
424	**Before Reading: An Interview with the King of Terror**	RI.9-10.4	Determine the meaning of words and phrases as they are used in a text, including figurative, connotative, and technical meanings; analyze the cumulative impact of specific word choices on meaning and tone.
		RI.9-10.10	By the end of grade 10, read and comprehend literary nonfiction at the high end of the grades 9–10 text complexity band independently and proficiently.
425–430	**Read An Interview with the King of Terror**	RI.9-10.1	Cite strong and thorough textual evidence to support analysis of what the text says explicitly as well as inferences drawn from the text.
		RI.9-10.2	Determine a central idea of a text and analyze its development over the course of the text, including how it emerges and is shaped and refined by specific details; provide an objective summary of the text.
		RI.9-10.3	Analyze how the author unfolds an analysis or series of ideas or events, including the order in which the points are made, how they are introduced and developed, and the connections that are drawn between them.
		RI.9-10.4	Determine the meaning of words and phrases as they are used in a text, including figurative, connotative, and technical meanings; analyze the cumulative impact of specific word choices on meaning and tone.
		RI.9-10.10	By the end of grade 10, read and comprehend literary nonfiction at the high end of the grades 9–10 text complexity band independently and proficiently.
		W.9-10.9.b	Apply grades 9–10 Reading standards to literary nonfiction.
		W.9-10.10	Write routinely over extended time frames (time for research, reflection, and revision) and shorter time frames (a single sitting or a day or two) for a range of tasks, purposes, and audiences.
		L.9-10.1.b	Use various types of phrases (noun, verb, adjectival, adverbial, participial, prepositional, absolute) and clauses (independent, dependent; noun, relative, adverbial) to convey specific meanings and add variety and interest to writing or presentations.
		L.9-10.4.a	Use context as a clue to the meaning of a word or phrase.
		L.9-10.6	Acquire and use accurately general academic and domain-specific words and phrases, sufficient for reading, writing, speaking, and listening at the college and career readiness level; demonstrate independence in gathering vocabulary knowledge when considering a word or phrase important to comprehension or expression.

page 939

Common Core State Standards

Student Handbooks, continued

Cluster 1, continued

SE Pages	Lesson	Code	Standards Text
431	**Reflect and Assess Critical Thinking**	RL.9-10.1	Cite strong and thorough textual evidence to support analysis of what the text says explicitly as well as inferences drawn from the text.
		RL.9-10.2	Determine a theme or central idea of a text and analyze in detail its development over the course of the text, including how it emerges and is shaped and refined by specific details; provide an objective summary of the text.
		RL.9-10.5	Analyze how an author's choices concerning how to structure a text, order events within it, and manipulate time create such effects as mystery, tension, or surprise.
		RL.9-10.10	By the end of grade 10, read and comprehend literature, including stories, dramas, and poems, at the high end of the grades 9–10 text complexity band independently and proficiently.
		RI.9-10.2	Determine a central idea of a text and analyze its development over the course of the text, including how it emerges and is shaped and refined by specific details; provide an objective summary of the text.
		L.9-10.6	Acquire and use accurately general academic and domain-specific words and phrases, sufficient for reading, writing, speaking, and listening at the college and career readiness level; demonstrate independence in gathering vocabulary knowledge when considering a word or phrase important to comprehension or expression.
	Write About Literature	W.9-10.3	Write narratives to develop real or imagined experiences or events using effective technique, well-chosen details, and well-structured event sequences.
	Key Vocabulary Review	L.9-10.6	Acquire and use accurately general academic and domain-specific words and phrases, sufficient for reading, writing, speaking, and listening at the college and career readiness level; demonstrate independence in gathering vocabulary knowledge when considering a word or phrase important to comprehension or expression.
	Read with Ease: Phrasing	RL.9-10.10	By the end of grade 10, read and comprehend literature, including stories, dramas, and poems, at the high end of the grades 9–10 text complexity band independently and proficiently.
432	**Grammar: Use Adjectives to Elaborate**	L.9-10.1.b	Use various types of phrases (noun, verb, adjectival, adverbial, participial, prepositional, absolute) and clauses (independent, dependent; noun, relative, adverbial) to convey specific meanings and add variety and interest to writing or presentations.
432	**Language Development: Tell a Story**	SL.9-10.6	Adapt speech to a variety of contexts and tasks, demonstrating command of formal English when indicated or appropriate.
432	**Literary Analysis: Analyze Irony**	RL.9-10.5	Analyze how an author's choices concerning how to structure a text, order events within it, and manipulate time create such effects as mystery, tension, or surprise.
433	**Vocabulary Study: Synonyms**	L.9-10.5.b	Analyze nuances in the meaning of words with similar denotations.
433	**Writing: Write a Character Sketch**	W.9-10.3	Write narratives to develop real or imagined experiences or events using effective technique, well-chosen details, and well-structured event sequences.
		W.9-10.5	Develop and strengthen writing as needed by planning, revising, editing, rewriting, or trying a new approach, focusing on addressing what is most significant for a specific purpose and audience.

page 940

Student Handbooks, continued

Cluster 1, continued

SE Pages	Lesson	Code	Standards Text
433	**Listening/ Speaking: Dramatization**	RL.9-10.7	Analyze the representation of a subject or a key scene in two different artistic mediums, including what is emphasized or absent in each treatment.
		SL.9-10.6	Adapt speech to a variety of contexts and tasks, demonstrating command of formal English when indicated or appropriate.
434	**Workplace Workshop: Inside a Newspaper Office**	W.9-10.2	Introduce a topic; organize complex ideas, concepts, and information to make important connections and distinctions; include formatting, graphics, and multimedia when useful to aiding comprehension.
		W.9-10.7	Conduct short as well as more sustained research projects to answer a question (including a self-generated question) or solve a problem; narrow or broaden the inquiry when appropriate; synthesize multiple sources on the subject, demonstrating understanding of the subject under investigation.
		W.9-10.10	Write routinely over extended time frames (time for research, reflection, and revision) and shorter time frames (a single sitting or a day or two) for a range of tasks, purposes, and audiences.
435	**Vocabulary Workshop: Make Word Connections**	L.9-10.4.c	Consult general and specialized reference materials, both print and digital, to find the pronunciation of a word or determine or clarify its precise meaning, its part of speech, or its etymology.
		L.9-10.4.d	Verify the preliminary determination of the meaning of a word or phrase.
		L.9-10.5	Demonstrate understanding of figurative language, word relationships, and nuances in word meanings.
Cluster 2			
436	**Prepare to Read**	RI.9-10.4	Determine the meaning of words and phrases as they are used in a text, including figurative, connotative, and technical meanings; analyze the cumulative impact of specific word choices on meaning and tone.
		SL.9-10.1	Initiate and participate effectively in a range of collaborative discussions (one-on-one, in groups, and teacher-led) with diverse partners on grades 9–10 topics, texts, and issues, building on others' ideas and expressing their own clearly and persuasively.
		L.9-10.6	Acquire and use accurately general academic and domain-specific words and phrases, sufficient for reading, writing, speaking, and listening at the college and career readiness level; demonstrate independence in gathering vocabulary knowledge when considering a word or phrase important to comprehension or expression.
437	**Before Reading: The Baby-Sitter**	RL.9-10.4	Determine the meaning of words and phrases as they are used in the text, including figurative and connotative meanings; analyze the cumulative impact of specific word choices on meaning and tone.
		RL.9-10.5	Analyze how an author's choices concerning how to structure a text, order events within it, and manipulate time create such effects as mystery, tension, or surprise.
		RL.9-10.10	By the end of grade 10, read and comprehend literature, including stories, dramas, and poems, at the high end of the grades 9–10 text complexity band independently and proficiently.

page 941

Common Core State Standards

Common Core State Standards, continued

Student Handbooks, continued

Cluster 2, continued

SE Pages	Lesson	Code	Standards Text
438–450	Read The Baby-Sitter	RL.9-10.1	Cite strong and thorough textual evidence to support analysis of what the text says explicitly as well as inferences drawn from the text.
		RL.9-10.3	Analyze how complex characters develop over the course of a text, interact with other characters, and advance the plot or develop the theme.
		RL.9-10.4	Determine the meaning of words and phrases as they are used in the text, including figurative and connotative meanings; analyze the cumulative impact of specific word choices on meaning and tone.
		RL.9-10.5	Analyze how an author's choices concerning how to structure a text, order events within it, and manipulate time create such effects as mystery, tension, or surprise.
		RL.9-10.7	Analyze the representation of a subject or a key scene in two different artistic mediums, including what is emphasized or absent in each treatment.
		RL.9-10.10	By the end of grade 10, read and comprehend literature, including stories, dramas, and poems, at the high end of the grades 9–10 text complexity band independently and proficiently.
		W.9-10.9.a	Apply grades 9–10 Reading standards to literature.
		W.9-10.10	Write routinely over extended time frames (time for research, reflection, and revision) and shorter time frames (a single sitting or a day or two) for a range of tasks, purposes, and audiences.
		L.9-10.1.b	Use various types of phrases (noun, verb, adjectival, adverbial, participial, prepositional, absolute) and clauses (independent, dependent; noun, relative, adverbial) to convey specific meanings and add variety and interest to writing or presentations.
		L.9-10.2.c	Spell correctly.
		L.9-10.4.a	Use context (e.g., the overall meaning of a sentence, paragraph, or text; a word's position or function in a sentence) as a clue to the meaning of a word or phrase.
		L.9-10.4.c	Consult general and specialized reference materials, both print and digital, to find the pronunciation of a word or determine or clarify its precise meaning, its part of speech, or its etymology.
		L.9-10.6	Acquire and use accurately general academic and domain-specific words and phrases, sufficient for reading, writing, speaking, and listening at the college and career readiness level; demonstrate independence in gathering vocabulary knowledge when considering a word or phrase important to comprehension or expression.
451	Postscript: Cartoon	RL.9-10.4	Determine the meaning of words and phrases as they are used in the text, including figurative and connotative meanings; analyze the cumulative impact of specific word choices on meaning and tone.
		RL.9-10.7	Analyze the representation of a subject or a key scene in two different artistic mediums, including what is emphasized or absent in each treatment.
452	Before Reading: Beware: Do Not Read This Poem	RL.9-10.4	Determine the meaning of words and phrases as they are used in the text, including figurative and connotative meanings; analyze the cumulative impact of specific word choices on meaning and tone.
		RL.9-10.10	By the end of grade 10, read and comprehend literature, including stories, dramas, and poems, at the high end of the grades 9–10 text complexity band independently and proficiently.

page 942

Student Handbooks, continued

Cluster 2, continued

SE Pages	Lesson	Code	Standards Text
453–456	Read Beware: Do Not Read This Poem	RL.9-10.1	Cite strong and thorough textual evidence to support analysis of what the text says explicitly as well as inferences drawn from the text.
		RL.9-10.4	Determine the meaning of words and phrases as they are used in the text, including figurative and connotative meanings; analyze the cumulative impact of specific word choices on meaning and tone.
		RL.9-10.10	By the end of grade 10, read and comprehend literature, including stories, dramas, and poems, at the high end of the grades 9–10 text complexity band independently and proficiently.
		W.9-10.9.a	Apply grades 9–10 Reading standards to literature.
		W.9-10.10	Write routinely over extended time frames (time for research, reflection, and revision) and shorter time frames (a single sitting or a day or two) for a range of tasks, purposes, and audiences.
		L.9-10.1.b	Use various types of phrases (noun, verb, adjectival, adverbial, participial, prepositional, absolute) and clauses (independent, dependent; noun, relative, adverbial) to convey specific meanings and add variety and interest to writing or presentations.
		L.9-10.6	Acquire and use accurately general academic and domain-specific words and phrases, sufficient for reading, writing, speaking, and listening at the college and career readiness level; demonstrate independence in gathering vocabulary knowledge when considering a word or phrase important to comprehension or expression.
457	Reflect and Assess Critical Thinking	RL.9-10.2	Determine a theme or central idea of a text and analyze in detail its development over the course of the text, including how it emerges and is shaped and refined by specific details; provide an objective summary of the text.
		RL.9-10.3	Analyze how complex characters develop over the course of a text, interact with other characters, and advance the plot or develop the theme.
		RL.9-10.4	Determine the meaning of words and phrases as they are used in the text, including figurative and connotative meanings; analyze the cumulative impact of specific word choices on meaning and tone.
		RL.9-10.10	By the end of grade 10, read and comprehend literature, including stories, dramas, and poems, at the high end of the grades 9–10 text complexity band independently and proficiently.
	Write About Literature	W.9-10.1	Write arguments to support claims in an analysis of substantive topics or texts, using valid reasoning and relevant and sufficient evidence.
		W.9-10.9	Draw evidence from literary or informational texts to support analysis, reflection, and research.
	Key Vocabulary Review	L.9-10.6	Acquire and use accurately general academic and domain-specific words and phrases, sufficient for reading, writing, speaking, and listening at the college and career readiness level; demonstrate independence in gathering vocabulary knowledge when considering a word or phrase important to comprehension or expression.
	Read with Ease: Expression	RL.9-10.10	By the end of grade 10, read and comprehend literature, including stories, dramas, and poems, at the high end of the grades 9–10 text complexity band independently and proficiently.

page 943

Common Core State Standards, continued

Student Handbooks, continued

Cluster 2, continued

SE Pages	Lesson	Code	Standards Text
458	Grammar: Compare Adjectives	L.9-10.1.b	Use various types of phrases (noun, verb, adjectival, adverbial, participial, prepositional, absolute) and clauses (independent, dependent; noun, relative, adverbial) to convey specific meanings and add variety and interest to writing or presentations.
458	Language Development: Make Comparisons	SL.9-10.1	Initiate and participate effectively in a range of collaborative discussions (one-on-one, in groups, and teacher-led) with diverse partners on grades 9–10 topics, texts, and issues, building on others' ideas and expressing their own clearly and persuasively.
458	Literary Analysis: Analyze Foreshadowing	RL.9-10.5	Analyze how an author's choices concerning how to structure a text, order events within it, and manipulate time create such effects as mystery, tension, or surprise.
459	Vocabulary Study: Thesaurus	L.9-10.4.c	Consult general and specialized reference materials (e.g., dictionaries, glossaries, thesauruses), both print and digital, to find the pronunciation of a word or determine or clarify its precise meaning, its part of speech, or its etymology.
459	Writing on Demand: Write a Literary Analysis	W.9-10.1	Write arguments to support claims in an analysis of substantive topics or texts, using valid reasoning and relevant and sufficient evidence.
459	Listening/Speaking: Storytelling	SI.9-10.3	Evaluate a speaker's point of view, reasoning, and use of evidence and rhetoric, identifying any fallacious reasoning or exaggerated or distorted evidence.
460–461	Listening and Speaking Workshop: Dramatic Reading	SL.9-10.6	Adapt speech to a variety of contexts and tasks, demonstrating command of formal English when indicated or appropriate.
Cluster 3			
462	Prepare to Read	RL.9-10.4	Determine the meaning of words and phrases as they are used in the text, including figurative and connotative meanings; analyze the cumulative impact of specific word choices on meaning and tone.
		SL.9-10.1	Initiate and participate effectively in a range of collaborative discussions (one-on-one, in groups, and teacher-led) with diverse partners on grades 9–10 topics, texts, and issues, building on others' ideas and expressing their own clearly and persuasively.
		L.9-10.4.c	Consult general and specialized reference materials, both print and digital, to find the pronunciation of a word or determine or clarify its precise meaning, its part of speech, or its etymology.
		L.9-10.6	Acquire and use accurately general academic and domain-specific words and phrases, sufficient for reading, writing, speaking, and listening at the college and career readiness level; demonstrate independence in gathering vocabulary knowledge when considering a word or phrase important to comprehension or expression.
463	Before Reading: The Tell-Tale Heart	RL.9-10.5	Analyze how an author's choices concerning how to structure a text, order events within it, and manipulate time (e.g., pacing, flashbacks) create such effects as mystery, tension, or surprise.
		RL.9-10.10	By the end of grade 10, read and comprehend literature, including stories, dramas, and poems, at the high end of the grades 9–10 text complexity band independently and proficiently.
464–473	Read The Tell-Tale Heart	RL.9-10.1	Cite strong and thorough textual evidence to support analysis of what the text says explicitly as well as inferences drawn from the text.
		RL.9-10.3	Analyze how complex characters develop over the course of a text, interact with other characters, and advance the plot or develop the theme.

page 944

Student Handbooks, continued

Cluster 3, continued

SE Pages	Lesson	Code	Standards Text
464–473	Read The Tell-Tale Heart continued	RL.9-10.5	Analyze how an author's choices concerning how to structure a text, order events within it, and manipulate time create such effects as mystery, tension, or surprise.
		RL.9-10.7	Analyze the representation of a subject or a key scene in two different artistic mediums, including what is emphasized or absent in each treatment.
		RL.9-10.10	By the end of grade 10, read and comprehend literature, including stories, dramas, and poems, at the high end of the grades 9–10 text complexity band independently and proficiently.
		W.9-10.3	Write narratives to develop real or imagined experiences or events using effective technique, well-chosen details, and well-structured event sequences.
		W.9-10.10	Write routinely over extended time frames (time for research, reflection, and revision) and shorter time frames (a single sitting or a day or two) for a range of tasks, purposes, and audiences.
		L.9-10.1.b	Use various types of phrases (noun, verb, adjectival, adverbial, participial, prepositional, absolute) and clauses (independent, dependent; noun, relative, adverbial) to convey specific meanings and add variety and interest to writing or presentations.
		L.9-10.2.c	Spell correctly.
		L.9-10.6	Acquire and use accurately general academic and domain-specific words and phrases, sufficient for reading, writing, speaking, and listening at the college and career readiness level; demonstrate independence in gathering vocabulary knowledge when considering a word or phrase important to comprehension or expression.
474	Before Reading: The Raven	RL.9-10.4	Determine the meaning of words and phrases as they are used in the text, including figurative and connotative meanings; analyze the cumulative impact of specific word choices on meaning and tone.
		RL.9-10.10	By the end of grade 10, read and comprehend literature, including stories, dramas, and poems, at the high end of the grades 9–10 text complexity band independently and proficiently.
475–481	Read The Raven	RL.9-10.1	Cite strong and thorough textual evidence to support analysis of what the text says explicitly as well as inferences drawn from the text.
		RL.9-10.4	Determine the meaning of words and phrases as they are used in the text, including figurative and connotative meanings; analyze the cumulative impact of specific word choices on meaning and tone.
		RL.9-10.10	By the end of grade 10, read and comprehend literature, including stories, dramas, and poems, at the high end of the grades 9–10 text complexity band independently and proficiently.
		W.9-10.9.a	Apply grades 9–10 Reading standards to literature.
		W.9-10.10	Write routinely over extended time frames (time for research, reflection, and revision) and shorter time frames (a single sitting or a day or two) for a range of tasks, purposes, and audiences.
		L.9-10.1.b	Use various types of phrases (noun, verb, adjectival, adverbial, participial, prepositional, absolute) and clauses (independent, dependent; noun, relative, adverbial) to convey specific meanings and add variety and interest to writing or presentations.

page 945

Common Core State Standards

Common Core State Standards, continued

Student Handbooks, continued

SE Pages	Lesson	Code	Standards Text
Cluster 3, continued			
475–481	Read The Raven continued	L.9-10.5	Demonstrate understanding of figurative language, word relationships, and nuances in word meanings.
		L.9-10.6	Acquire and use accurately general academic and domain-specific words and phrases, sufficient for reading, writing, speaking, and listening at the college and career readiness level; demonstrate independence in gathering vocabulary knowledge when considering a word or phrase important to comprehension or expression.
482	Postscript: The Mysterious Edgar Allan Poe	RI.9-10.2	Determine a central idea of a text and analyze its development over the course of the text, including how it emerges and is shaped and refined by specific details; provide an objective summary of the text.
		RI.9-10.6	Determine an author's point of view or purpose in a text and analyze how an author uses rhetoric to advance that point of view or purpose.
483	Reflect and Assess Critical Thinking	RL.9-10.1	Cite strong and thorough textual evidence to support analysis of what the text says explicitly as well as inferences drawn from the text.
		RL.9-10.4	Determine the meaning of words and phrases as they are used in the text, including figurative and connotative meanings; analyze the cumulative impact of specific word choices on meaning and tone.
		RL.9-10.5	Analyze how an author's choices concerning how to structure a text, order events within it, and manipulate time create such effects as mystery, tension, or surprise.
		RL.9-10.10	By the end of grade 10, read and comprehend literature, including stories, dramas, and poems, at the high end of the grades 9–10 text complexity band independently and proficiently.
	Write About Literature	W.9-10.9.a	Apply grades 9–10 Reading standards to literature.
	Key Vocabulary Review	L.9-10.6	Acquire and use accurately general academic and domain-specific words and phrases, sufficient for reading, writing, speaking, and listening at the college and career readiness level; demonstrate independence in gathering vocabulary knowledge when considering a word or phrase important to comprehension or expression.
	Read with Ease: Intonation	RL.9-10.10	By the end of grade 10, read and comprehend literature, including stories, dramas, and poems, at the high end of the grades 9–10 text complexity band independently and proficiently.
484	Grammar: Use Adverbs Correctly	L.9-10.1.b	Use various types of phrases (noun, verb, adjectival, adverbial, participial, prepositional, absolute) and clauses (independent, dependent; noun, relative, adverbial) to convey specific meanings and add variety and interest to writing or presentations.
484	Language Development: Compare and Contrast	W.9-10.9.a	Apply grades 9–10 Reading standards to literature.
		SL.9-10.1.a	Come to discussions prepared, having read and researched material under study; explicitly draw on that preparation by referring to evidence from texts and other research on the topic or issue to stimulate a thoughtful, well-reasoned exchange of ideas.
484	Literary Analysis: Analyze Mood and Tone	RL.9-10.4	Determine the meaning of words and phrases as they are used in the text, including figurative and connotative meanings; analyze the cumulative impact of specific word choices on meaning and tone.
484	Literary Analysis: Analyze Symbolism	RL.9-10.4	Determine the meaning of words and phrases as they are used in the text, including figurative and connotative meanings; analyze the cumulative impact of specific word choices on meaning and tone.

page 946

Student Handbooks, continued

SE Pages	Lesson	Code	Standards Text
Cluster 3, continued			
485	Vocabulary Study: Analogies	L.9-10.5	Demonstrate understanding of figurative language, word relationships, and nuances in word meanings.
485	Writing Trait: Organization	W.9-10.4	Produce clear and coherent writing in which the development, organization, and style are appropriate to task, purpose, and audience.
485	Listening/Speaking: Dramatization	SL.9-10.6	Adapt speech to a variety of contexts and tasks, demonstrating command of formal English when indicated or appropriate.
Close Reading			
486–489	Read Puddle	RL.9-10.10	By the end of grade 10, read and comprehend literature, including stories, dramas, and poems, at the high end of the grades 9-10 text complexity band independently and proficiently.
Unit Wrap-Up			
490	Unit Wrap-Up Present Your Project	SL.9-10.2	Integrate multiple sources of information presented in diverse media or formats evaluating the credibility and accuracy of each source.
		SL.9-10.4	Present information, findings, and supporting evidence clearly, concisely, and logically such that listeners can follow the line of reasoning and the organization, development, substance, and style are appropriate to purpose, audience, and task.
		SL.9-10.5	Make strategic use of digital media in presentations to enhance understanding of findings, reasoning, and evidence and to add interest.
		SL.9-10.6	Adapt speech to a variety of contexts and tasks, demonstrating command of formal English when indicated or appropriate.
	Reflect on Your Reading	SL.9-10.1.a	Come to discussions prepared, having read and researched material under study; explicitly draw on that preparation by referring to evidence from texts and other research on the topic or issue to stimulate a thoughtful, well-reasoned exchange of ideas.
	Respond to the Essential Question	SL.9-10.1.a	Come to discussions prepared, having read and researched material under study; explicitly draw on that preparation by referring to evidence from texts and other research on the topic or issue to stimulate a thoughtful, well-reasoned exchange of ideas.
Unit 5 Writing Project: Short Story			
491–495	Study Short Stories and Prewrite	W.9-10.3.c	Use a variety of techniques to sequence events so that they build on one another to create a coherent whole.
		W.9-10.5	Develop and strengthen writing as needed by planning, revising, editing, rewriting, or trying a new approach, focusing on addressing what is most significant for a specific purpose and audience.
496–497	Short Story: Draft	W.9-10.3.d	Use precise words and phrases, telling details, and sensory language to convey a vivid picture of the experiences, events, setting, and/or characters.
		W.9-10.4	Produce clear and coherent writing in which the development, organization, and style are appropriate to task, purpose, and audience.

page 947

Common Core State Standards, continued

Student Handbooks, continued

SE Pages	Lesson	Code	Standards Text
Unit 5 Writing Project: Short Story, continued			
498–501	Short Story: Revise Trait: Organization	W.9-10.3.a	Engage and orient the reader by setting out a problem, situation, or observation, establishing one or multiple point(s) of view, and introducing a narrator and/or characters; create a smooth progression of experiences or events.
		W.9-10.3.b	Use narrative techniques, such as dialogue, pacing, description, reflection, and multiple plot lines, to develop experiences, events, and/or characters.
		W.9-10.3.c	Use a variety of techniques to sequence events so that they build on one another to create a coherent whole.
		W.9-10.3.d	Use precise words and phrases, telling details, and sensory language to convey a vivid picture of the experiences, events, setting, and/or characters.
		W.9-10.3.e	Provide a conclusion that follows from and reflects on what is experienced, observed, or resolved over the course of the narrative.
		W.9-10.5	Develop and strengthen writing as needed by planning, revising, editing, rewriting, or trying a new approach, focusing on addressing what is most significant for a specific purpose and audience.
		SL.9-10.1.d	Respond thoughtfully to diverse perspectives, summarize points of agreement and disagreement, and, when warranted, qualify or justify their own views and understanding and make new connections in light of the evidence and reasoning presented.
502-504	Short Story: Edit and Proofread Capitalization: Quotations Punctuation Paragraph Structure Adjectives and Adverbs	L.9-10.1	Demonstrate command of the conventions of standard English grammar and usage when writing or speaking.
		L.9-10.1.b	Use a colon to introduce a list or quotation.
		L.9-10.2	Demonstrate command of the conventions of standard English capitalization, punctuation, and spelling when writing.
		L.9-10.3.a	Write and edit work so that it conforms to the guidelines in a style manual appropriate for the discipline and writing type.
505	Short Story: Publish and Present	W.9-10.6	Use technology, including the Internet, to produce, publish, and update individual or shared writing products, taking advantage of technology's capacity to link to other information and to display information flexibly and dynamically.
		SL.9-10.5	Make strategic use of digital media in presentations to enhance understanding of findings, reasoning, and evidence and to add interest.
		SL.9-10.6	Adapt speech to a variety of contexts and tasks, demonstrating command of formal English when indicated or appropriate.
UNIT 6: Are You Buying It?			
506–507	Discuss the Essential Question	SL.9-10.1.b	Work with peers to set rules for collegial discussions and decision-making, clear goals and deadlines, and individual roles as needed.
		SL.9-10.3	Evaluate a speaker's point of view, reasoning, and use of evidence and rhetoric, identifying any fallacious reasoning or exaggerated or distorted evidence.
508	Analyze and Debate	SL.9-10.4	Present information, findings, and supporting evidence clearly, concisely, and logically such that listeners can follow the line of reasoning and the organization, development, substance, and style are appropriate to purpose, audience, and task.

page 948

Student Handbooks, continued

SE Pages	Lesson	Code	Standards Text
UNIT 6: Are You Buying It?, continued			
509	Plan a Project	SL.9-10.1.b	Work with peers to set rules for collegial discussions and decision-making (e.g., informal consensus, taking votes on key issues, presentation of alternate views), clear goals and deadlines, and individual roles as needed.
509	Choose More to Read	RL.9-10.10	By the end of grade 10, read and comprehend literature, including stories, dramas, and poems, at the high end of the grades 9–10 text complexity band independently and proficiently.
		RI.9-10.10	By the end of grade 10, read and comprehend literary nonfiction at the high end of the grades 9–10 text complexity band independently and proficiently.
510–513	How to Read Nonfiction	RI.9-10.8	Delineate and evaluate the argument and specific claims in a text, assessing whether the reasoning is valid and the evidence is relevant and sufficient; identify false statements and fallacious reasoning.
		L.9-10.6	Acquire and use accurately general academic and domain-specific words and phrases, sufficient for reading, writing, speaking, and listening at the college and career readiness level; demonstrate independence in gathering vocabulary knowledge when considering a word or phrase important to comprehension or expression.
Cluster 1			
514	Prepare to Read	RI.9-10.4	Determine the meaning of words and phrases as they are used in a text, including figurative, connotative, and technical meanings; analyze the cumulative impact of specific word choices on meaning and tone.
		SL.9-10.1	Initiate and participate effectively in a range of collaborative discussions (one-on-one, in groups, and teacher-led) with diverse partners on grades 9–10 topics, texts, and issues, building on others' ideas and expressing their own clearly and persuasively.
		L.9-10.6	Acquire and use accurately general academic and domain-specific words and phrases, sufficient for reading, writing, speaking, and listening at the college and career readiness level; demonstrate independence in gathering vocabulary knowledge when considering a word or phrase important to comprehension or expression.
515	Before Reading: Ad Power	RI.9-10.8	Delineate and evaluate the argument and specific claims in a text, assessing whether the reasoning is valid and the evidence is relevant and sufficient; identify false statements and fallacious reasoning.
		RI.9-10.10	By the end of grade 10, read and comprehend literary nonfiction at the high end of the grades 9–10 text complexity band independently and proficiently.
516–526	Read Ad Power	RI.9-10.1	Cite strong and thorough textual evidence to support analysis of what the text says explicitly as well as inferences drawn from the text.
		RI.9-10.2	Determine a central idea of a text and analyze its development over the course of the text, including how it emerges and is shaped and refined by specific details; provide an objective summary of the text.
		RI.9-10.8	Delineate and evaluate the argument and specific claims in a text, assessing whether the reasoning is valid and the evidence is relevant and sufficient; identify false statements and fallacious reasoning.
		RI.9-10.10	By the end of grade 10, read and comprehend literary nonfiction at the high end of the grades 9–10 text complexity band independently and proficiently.
		W.9-10.1	Write arguments to support claims in an analysis of substantive topics or texts, using valid reasoning and relevant and sufficient evidence.

page 949

Common Core State Standards

Common Core State Standards, continued

Student Handbooks, continued

Cluster 1, continued

SE Pages	Lesson	Code	Standards Text
516–526	**Read Ad Power** continued	W.9-10.9.b	Apply grades 9–10 Reading standards to literary nonfiction.
		W.9-10.10	Write routinely over extended time frames (time for research, reflection, and revision) and shorter time frames (a single sitting or a day or two) for a range of tasks, purposes, and audiences.
		L.9-10.1.b	Use various types of phrases (noun, verb, adjectival, adverbial, participial, prepositional, absolute) and clauses (independent, dependent; noun, relative, adverbial) to convey specific meanings and add variety and interest to writing or presentations.
		L.9-10.4.a	Use context as a clue to the meaning of a word or phrase.
		L.9-10.6	Acquire and use accurately general academic and domain-specific words and phrases, sufficient for reading, writing, speaking, and listening at the college and career readiness level; demonstrate independence in gathering vocabulary knowledge when considering a word or phrase important to comprehension or expression.
527–529	**Postscript: Without Commercials**	RL.9-10.2	Determine a theme or central idea of a text and analyze in detail its development over the course of the text, including how it emerges and is shaped and refined by specific details; provide an objective summary of the text.
		RL.9-10.4	Determine the meaning of words and phrases as they are used in the text, including figurative and connotative meanings; analyze the cumulative impact of specific word choices on meaning and tone.
		RL.9-10.10	By the end of grade 10, read and comprehend literature, including stories, dramas, and poems, at the high end of the grades 9–10 text complexity band independently and proficiently.
530	**Before Reading: What's Wrong with Advertising?**	RI.9-10.4	Determine the meaning of words and phrases as they are used in a text, including figurative, connotative, and technical meanings; analyze the cumulative impact of specific word choices on meaning and tone.
		RI.9-10.6	Determine an author's point of view or purpose in a text and analyze how an author uses rhetoric to advance that point of view or purpose.
		RI.9-10.10	By the end of grade 10, read and comprehend literary nonfiction at the high end of the grades 9–10 text complexity band independently and proficiently.
531–536	**Read What's Wrong with Advertising?**	RI.9-10.1	Cite strong and thorough textual evidence to support analysis of what the text says explicitly as well as inferences drawn from the text.
		RI.9-10.2	Determine a central idea of a text and analyze its development over the course of the text, including how it emerges and is shaped and refined by specific details; provide an objective summary of the text.
		RI.9-10.4	Determine the meaning of words and phrases as they are used in a text, including figurative, connotative, and technical meanings; analyze the cumulative impact of specific word choices on meaning and tone.
		RI.9-10.6	Determine an author's point of view or purpose in a text and analyze how an author uses rhetoric to advance that point of view or purpose.
		RI.9-10.10	By the end of grade 10, read and comprehend literary nonfiction at the high end of the grades 9–10 text complexity band independently and proficiently.
		W.9-10.9.b	Apply grades 9–10 Reading standards to literary nonfiction.

page 950

Student Handbooks, continued

Cluster 1, continued

SE Pages	Lesson	Code	Standards Text
531–536	**Read What's Wrong with Advertising?** continued	W.9-10.10	Write routinely over extended time frames (time for research, reflection, and revision) and shorter time frames (a single sitting or a day or two) for a range of tasks, purposes, and audiences.
		L.9-10.1.b	Use various types of phrases (noun, verb, adjectival, adverbial, participial, prepositional, absolute) and clauses (independent, dependent; noun, relative, adverbial) to convey specific meanings and add variety and interest to writing or presentations.
		L.9-10.4.a	Use context as a clue to the meaning of a word or phrase.
		L.9-10.6	Acquire and use accurately general academic and domain-specific words and phrases, sufficient for reading, writing, speaking, and listening at the college and career readiness level; demonstrate independence in gathering vocabulary knowledge when considering a word or phrase important to comprehension or expression.
537	**Reflect and Assess Critical Thinking**	RI.9-10.1	Cite strong and thorough textual evidence to support analysis of what the text says explicitly as well as inferences drawn from the text.
		RI.9-10.6	Determine an author's point of view or purpose in a text and analyze how an author uses rhetoric to advance that point of view or purpose.
		RI.9-10.10	By the end of grade 10, read and comprehend literary nonfiction at the high end of the grades 9–10 text complexity band independently and proficiently.
	Write About Literature	W.9-10.2	Write informative/explanatory texts to examine and convey complex ideas, concepts, and information clearly and accurately through the effective selection, organization, and analysis of content.
	Key Vocabulary Review	L.9-10.6	Acquire and use accurately general academic and domain-specific words and phrases, sufficient for reading, writing, speaking, and listening at the college and career readiness level; demonstrate independence in gathering vocabulary knowledge when considering a word or phrase important to comprehension or expression.
	Read with Ease: Expression	RI.9-10.10	By the end of grade 10, read and comprehend literary nonfiction at the high end of the grades 9–10 text complexity band independently and proficiently.
538	**Grammar: Vary Your Sentences**	L.9-10.1.b	Use various types of phrases (noun, verb, adjectival, adverbial, participial, prepositional, absolute) and clauses (independent, dependent; noun, relative, adverbial) to convey specific meanings and add variety and interest to writing or presentations.
538	**Language Development: Persuade**	SL.9-10.4	Present information, findings, and supporting evidence clearly, concisely, and logically such that listeners can follow the line of reasoning and the organization, development, substance, and style are appropriate to purpose, audience, and task.
538	**Literary Analysis: Compare Authors' Purposes and Viewpoints**	RI.9-10.6	Determine an author's point of view or purpose in a text and analyze how an author uses rhetoric to advance that point of view or purpose.
539	**Vocabulary Study: Latin and Greek Roots**	L.9-10.4.d	Verify the preliminary determination of the meaning of a word or phrase (e.g., by checking the inferred meaning in context or in a dictionary).

page 951

Common Core State Standards, continued

Student Handbooks, continued

Cluster 1, continued

SE Pages	Lesson	Code	Standards Text
539	**Writing: Write a Letter to the Editor**	W.9-10.1	Write arguments to support claims in an analysis of substantive topics or texts, using valid reasoning and relevant and sufficient evidence.
		W.9-10.5	Develop and strengthen writing as needed by planning, revising, editing, rewriting, or trying a new approach, focusing on addressing what is most significant for a specific purpose and audience.
540	**Workplace Workshop: Inside a Department Store**	W.9-10.4	Produce clear and coherent writing in which the development, organization, and style are appropriate to task, purpose, and audience.
		W.9-10.7	Conduct short as well as more sustained research projects to answer a question (including a self-generated question) or solve a problem; narrow or broaden the inquiry when appropriate; synthesize multiple sources on the subject, demonstrating understanding of the subject under investigation.
		W.9-10.10	Write routinely over extended time frames (time for research, reflection, and revision) and shorter time frames (a single sitting or a day or two) for a range of tasks, purposes, and audiences.
541	**Vocabulary Workshop: Build Word Knowledge**	L.9-10.4	Determine or clarify the meaning of unknown and multiple-meaning words and phrases based on grades 9–10 reading and content, choosing flexibly from a range of strategies.
Cluster 2			
542	**Prepare to Read**	RI.9-10.4	Determine the meaning of words and phrases as they are used in a text, including figurative, connotative, and technical meanings; analyze the cumulative impact of specific word choices on meaning and tone.
		SL.9-10.1	Initiate and participate effectively in a range of collaborative discussions (one-on-one, in groups, and teacher-led) with diverse partners on grades 9–10 topics, texts, and issues, building on others' ideas and expressing their own clearly and persuasively.
		L.9-10.6	Acquire and use accurately general academic and domain-specific words and phrases, sufficient for reading, writing, speaking, and listening at the college and career readiness level; demonstrate independence in gathering vocabulary knowledge when considering a word or phrase important to comprehension or expression.
543	**Before Reading: A Long Way to Go: Minorities and the Media**	RI.9-10.8	Delineate and evaluate the argument and specific claims in a text, assessing whether the reasoning is valid and the evidence is relevant and sufficient; identify false statements and fallacious reasoning.
		RI.9-10.10	By the end of grade 10, read and comprehend literary nonfiction at the high end of the grades 9–10 text complexity band independently and proficiently.
544–551	**Read A Long Way to Go: Minorities and the Media**	RI.9-10.1	Cite strong and thorough textual evidence to support analysis of what the text says explicitly as well as inferences drawn from the text.
		RI.9-10.2	Determine a central idea of a text and analyze its development over the course of the text, including how it emerges and is shaped and refined by specific details; provide an objective summary of the text.
		RI.9-10.4	Determine the meaning of words and phrases as they are used in a text, including figurative, connotative, and technical meanings; analyze the cumulative impact of specific word choices on meaning and tone.
		RI.9-10.8	Delineate and evaluate the argument and specific claims in a text, assessing whether the reasoning is valid and the evidence is relevant and sufficient; identify false statements and fallacious reasoning.

page 952

Student Handbooks, continued

Cluster 2, continued

SE Pages	Lesson	Code	Standards Text
544–551	**Read A Long Way to Go: Minorities and the Media** continued	RI.9-10.10	By the end of grade 10, read and comprehend literary nonfiction at the high end of the grades 9–10 text complexity band independently and proficiently.
		W.9-10.1.b	Develop claim(s) and counterclaims fairly, supplying evidence for each while pointing out the strengths and limitations of both in a manner that anticipates the audience's knowledge level and concerns.
		W.9-10.10	Write routinely over extended time frames (time for research, reflection, and revision) and shorter time frames (a single sitting or a day or two) for a range of tasks, purposes, and audiences.
		L.9-10.1.b	Use various types of phrases (noun, verb, adjectival, adverbial, participial, prepositional, absolute) and clauses (independent, dependent; noun, relative, adverbial) to convey specific meanings and add variety and interest to writing or presentations.
		L.9-10.4	Determine or clarify the meaning of unknown and multiple-meaning words and phrases based on grades 9–10 reading and content, choosing flexibly from a range of strategies.
		L.9-10.6	Acquire and use accurately general academic and domain-specific words and phrases, sufficient for reading, writing, speaking, and listening at the college and career readiness level; demonstrate independence in gathering vocabulary knowledge when considering a word or phrase important to comprehension or expression.
552	**Before Reading: Reza: Warrior of Peace**	RI.9-10.8	Delineate and evaluate the argument and specific claims in a text, assessing whether the reasoning is valid and the evidence is relevant and sufficient; identify false statements and fallacious reasoning.
		RI.9-10.10	By the end of grade 10, read and comprehend literary nonfiction at the high end of the grades 9–10 text complexity band independently and proficiently.
553–556	**Read Reza: Warrior of Peace**	RI.9-10.8	Delineate and evaluate the argument and specific claims in a text, assessing whether the reasoning is valid and the evidence is relevant and sufficient; identify false statements and fallacious reasoning.
		RI.9-10.10	By the end of grade 10, read and comprehend literary nonfiction at the high end of the grades 9–10 text complexity band independently and proficiently.
		W.9-10.1.b	Develop claim(s) and counterclaims fairly, supplying evidence for each while pointing out the strengths and limitations of both in a manner that anticipates the audience's knowledge level and concerns.
		W.9-10.10	Write routinely over extended time frames (time for research, reflection, and revision) and shorter time frames (a single sitting or a day or two) for a range of tasks, purposes, and audiences.
		L.9-10.1.b	Use various types of phrases (noun, verb, adjectival, adverbial, participial, prepositional, absolute) and clauses (independent, dependent; noun, relative, adverbial) to convey specific meanings and add variety and interest to writing or presentations.
		L.9-10.6	Acquire and use accurately general academic and domain-specific words and phrases, sufficient for reading, writing, speaking, and listening at the college and career readiness level; demonstrate independence in gathering vocabulary knowledge when considering a word or phrase important to comprehension or expression.

page 953

Common Core State Standards

Common Core State Standards, continued

Student Handbooks, continued

Cluster 2, continued

SE Pages	Lesson	Code	Standards Text
557	Reflect and Assess Critical Thinking	RI.9-10.1	Cite strong and thorough textual evidence to support analysis of what the text says explicitly as well as inferences drawn from the text.
		RI.9-10.2	Determine a central idea of a text and analyze its development over the course of the text, including how it emerges and is shaped and refined by specific details; provide an objective summary of the text.
		RI.9-10.8	Delineate and evaluate the argument and specific claims in a text, assessing whether the reasoning is valid and the evidence is relevant and sufficient; identify false statements and fallacious reasoning.
		RI.9-10.10	By the end of grade 10, read and comprehend literary nonfiction at the high end of the grades 9–10 text complexity band independently and proficiently.
	Write About Literature	W.9-10.1	Write arguments to support claims in an analysis of substantive topics or texts, using valid reasoning and relevant and sufficient evidence.
		L.9-10.6	Acquire and use accurately general academic and domain-specific words and phrases, sufficient for reading, writing, speaking, and listening at the college and career readiness level; demonstrate independence in gathering vocabulary knowledge when considering a word or phrase important to comprehension or expression.
	Read with Ease: Intonation	RI.9-10.10	By the end of grade 10, read and comprehend literary nonfiction at the high end of the grades 9–10 text complexity band independently and proficiently.
558	Grammar: Use Compound Sentences	L.9-10.1.b	Use various types of phrases (noun, verb, adjectival, adverbial, participial, prepositional, absolute) and clauses (independent, dependent; noun, relative, adverbial) to convey specific meanings and add variety and interest to writing or presentations.
558	Language Development: Evaluate	SL.9-10.1.a	Come to discussions prepared, having read and researched material under study; explicitly draw on that preparation by referring to evidence from texts and other research on the topic or issue to stimulate a thoughtful, well-reasoned exchange of ideas.
558	Literary Analysis: Persuasive Text Structures	RI.9-10.5	Analyze in detail how an author's ideas or claims are developed and refined by particular sentences, paragraphs, or larger portions of a text.
558	Media Study: Report on Minorities and the Media	SL.9-10.1	Initiate and participate effectively in a range of collaborative discussions (one-on-one, in groups, and teacher-led) with diverse partners on grades 9–10 topics, texts, and issues, building on others' ideas and expressing their own clearly and persuasively.
		SL.9-10.3	Evaluate a speaker's point of view, reasoning, and use of evidence and rhetoric, identifying any fallacious reasoning or exaggerated or distorted evidence.
559	Vocabulary Study: Latin and Greek Roots	L.9-10.4	Determine or clarify the meaning of unknown and multiple-meaning words and phrases based on grades 9–10 reading and content, choosing flexibly from a range of strategies.
559	Writing Trait: Organization	W.9-10.5	Develop and strengthen writing as needed by planning, revising, editing, rewriting, or trying a new approach, focusing on addressing what is most significant for a specific purpose and audience.
560–561	Listening and Speaking Workshop: Debate	SL.9-10.1.a	Come to discussions prepared, having read and researched material under study; explicitly draw on that preparation by referring to evidence from texts and other research on the topic or issue to stimulate a thoughtful, well-reasoned exchange of ideas.

page 954

Student Handbooks, continued

Cluster 2, continued

SE Pages	Lesson	Code	Standards Text
560–561	Listening and Speaking Workshop: Debate continued	SL.9-10.1.b	Work with peers to set rules for collegial discussions and decision-making (e.g., informal consensus, taking votes on key issues, presentation of alternate views), clear goals and deadlines, and individual roles as needed.
		SL.9-10.1.c	Propel conversations by posing and responding to questions that relate the current discussion to broader themes or larger ideas; actively incorporate others into the discussion; and clarify, verify, or challenge ideas and conclusions.
		SL.9-10.1.d	Respond thoughtfully to diverse perspectives, summarize points of agreement and disagreement, and, when warranted, qualify or justify their own views and understanding and make new connections in light of the evidence and reasoning presented.
		SL.9-10.3	Evaluate a speaker's point of view, reasoning, and use of evidence and rhetoric, identifying any fallacious reasoning or exaggerated or distorted evidence.
		SL.9-10.4	Present information, findings, and supporting evidence clearly, concisely, and logically such that listeners can follow the line of reasoning and the organization, development, substance, and style are appropriate to purpose, audience, and task.
		L.9-10.3	Apply knowledge of language to understand how language functions in different contexts, to make effective choices for meaning or style, and to comprehend more fully when reading or listening.
Cluster 3			
562	Prepare to Read	RI.9-10.4	Determine the meaning of words and phrases as they are used in a text, including figurative, connotative, and technical meanings; analyze the cumulative impact of specific word choices on meaning and tone.
		SL.9-10.1	Initiate and participate effectively in a range of collaborative discussions (one-on-one, in groups, and teacher-led) with diverse partners on grades 9–10 topics, texts, and issues, building on others' ideas and expressing their own clearly and persuasively.
		L.9-10.4.c	Consult general and specialized reference materials, both print and digital, to find the pronunciation of a word or determine or clarify its precise meaning, its part of speech, or its etymology.
		L.9-10.6	Acquire and use accurately general academic and domain-specific words and phrases, sufficient for reading, writing, speaking, and listening at the college and career readiness level; demonstrate independence in gathering vocabulary knowledge when considering a word or phrase important to comprehension or expression.
563	Before Reading: What Is News?	RI.9-10.4	Determine the meaning of words and phrases as they are used in a text, including figurative, connotative, and technical meanings; analyze the cumulative impact of specific word choices on meaning and tone.
		RI.9-10.6	Determine an author's point of view or purpose in a text and analyze how an author uses rhetoric to advance that point of view or purpose.
564–573	Read What Is News?	RI.9-10.1	Cite strong and thorough textual evidence to support analysis of what the text says explicitly as well as inferences drawn from the text.
		RI.9-10.2	Determine a central idea of a text and analyze its development over the course of the text, including how it emerges and is shaped and refined by specific details; provide an objective summary of the text.

page 955

Common Core State Standards, continued

Student Handbooks, continued

Cluster 3, continued

SE Pages	Lesson	Code	Standards Text
564–573	Read What Is News? continued	RI.9-10.3	Analyze how the author unfolds an analysis or series of ideas or events, including the order in which the points are made, how they are introduced and developed, and the connections that are drawn between them.
		RI.9-10.4	Determine the meaning of words and phrases as they are used in a text, including figurative, connotative, and technical meanings; analyze the cumulative impact of specific word choices on meaning and tone.
		RI.9-10.6	Determine an author's point of view or purpose in a text and analyze how an author uses rhetoric to advance that point of view or purpose.
		RI.9-10.7	Analyze various accounts of a subject told in different mediums, determining which details are emphasized in each account.
		RI.9-10.8	Delineate and evaluate the argument and specific claims in a text, assessing whether the reasoning is valid and the evidence is relevant and sufficient; identify false statements and fallacious reasoning.
		RI.9-10.10	By the end of grade 10, read and comprehend literary nonfiction at the high end of the grades 9–10 text complexity band independently and proficiently.
		W.9-10.1	Write arguments to support claims in an analysis of substantive topics or texts, using valid reasoning and relevant and sufficient evidence.
		W.9-10.9.b	Apply grades 9–10 Reading standards to literary nonfiction.
		W.9-10.10	Write routinely over extended time frames (time for research, reflection, and revision) and shorter time frames (a single sitting or a day or two) for a range of tasks, purposes, and audiences.
		L.9-10.1.b	Use various types of phrases (noun, verb, adjectival, adverbial, participial, prepositional, absolute) and clauses (independent, dependent; noun, relative, adverbial) to convey specific meanings and add variety and interest to writing or presentations.
		L.9-10.6	Acquire and use accurately general academic and domain-specific words and phrases, sufficient for reading, writing, speaking, and listening at the college and career readiness level; demonstrate independence in gathering vocabulary knowledge when considering a word or phrase important to comprehension or expression.
574	Before Reading: How to Detect Bias in the News	RI.9-10.5	Analyze in detail how an author's ideas or claims are developed and refined by particular sentences, paragraphs, or larger portions of a text.
		RI.9-10.10	By the end of grade 10, read and comprehend literary nonfiction at the high end of the grades 9–10 text complexity band independently and proficiently.
575–578	Read How to Detect Bias in the News	RI.9-10.1	Cite strong and thorough textual evidence to support analysis of what the text says explicitly as well as inferences drawn from the text.
		RI.9-10.2	Determine a central idea of a text and analyze its development over the course of the text, including how it emerges and is shaped and refined by specific details; provide an objective summary of the text.
		RI.9-10.5	Analyze in detail how an author's ideas or claims are developed and refined by particular sentences, paragraphs, or larger portions of a text.
		RI.9-10.10	By the end of grade 10, read and comprehend literary nonfiction at the high end of the grades 9–10 text complexity band independently and proficiently.

page 956

Student Handbooks, continued

Cluster 3, continued

SE Pages	Lesson	Code	Standards Text
575–578	Read How to Detect Bias in the News continued	W.9-10.1	Write arguments to support claims in an analysis of substantive topics or texts, using valid reasoning and relevant and sufficient evidence.
		W.9-10.10	Write routinely over extended time frames (time for research, reflection, and revision) and shorter time frames (a single sitting or a day or two) for a range of tasks, purposes, and audiences.
		L.9-10.1.a	Use parallel structure.
		L.9-10.1.b	Use various types of phrases (noun, verb, adjectival, adverbial, participial, prepositional, absolute) and clauses (independent, dependent; noun, relative, adverbial) to convey specific meanings and add variety and interest to writing or presentations.
		L.9-10.6	Acquire and use accurately general academic and domain-specific words and phrases, sufficient for reading, writing, speaking, and listening at the college and career readiness level; demonstrate independence in gathering vocabulary knowledge when considering a word or phrase important to comprehension or expression.
579	Reflect and Assess Critical Thinking	RI.9-10.1	Cite strong and thorough textual evidence to support analysis of what the text says explicitly as well as inferences drawn from the text.
		RI.9-10.8	Delineate and evaluate the argument and specific claims in a text, assessing whether the reasoning is valid and the evidence is relevant and sufficient; identify false statements and fallacious reasoning.
		RI.9-10.10	By the end of grade 10, read and comprehend literary nonfiction at the high end of the grades 9–10 text complexity band independently and proficiently.
	Write About Literature	RI.9-10.1	Cite strong and thorough textual evidence to support analysis of what the text says explicitly as well as inferences drawn from the text.
		W.9-10.1	Write arguments to support claims in an analysis of substantive topics or texts, using valid reasoning and relevant and sufficient evidence.
	Key Vocabulary Review	L.9-10.6	Acquire and use accurately general academic and domain-specific words and phrases, sufficient for reading, writing, speaking, and listening at the college and career readiness level; demonstrate independence in gathering vocabulary knowledge when considering a word or phrase important to comprehension or expression.
	Read with Ease: Phrasing	RI.9-10.10	By the end of grade 10, read and comprehend literary nonfiction at the high end of the grades 9–10 text complexity band independently and proficiently.
580	Grammar: Use Complex Sentences	L.9-10.1.b	Use various types of phrases (noun, verb, adjectival, adverbial, participial, prepositional, absolute) and clauses (independent, dependent; noun, relative, adverbial) to convey specific meanings and add variety and interest to writing or presentations.
580	Language Development: Justify	RI.9-10.8	Delineate and evaluate the argument and specific claims in a text, assessing whether the reasoning is valid and the evidence is relevant and sufficient; identify false statements and fallacious reasoning.
		SL.9-10.4	Present information, findings, and supporting evidence clearly, concisely, and logically such that listeners can follow the line of reasoning and the organization, development, substance, and style are appropriate to purpose, audience, and task.

page 957

Common Core State Standards

Common Core State Standards, continued

SE Pages	Lesson	Code	Standards Text
Student Handbooks, continued			
Cluster 3, continued			
580	Media Study: Evaluate Bias in the Media	RI.9-10.7	Analyze various accounts of a subject told in different mediums (e.g., a person's life story in both print and multimedia), determining which details are emphasized in each account.
		SL.9-10.2	Integrate multiple sources of information presented in diverse media or formats (e.g., visually, quantitatively, orally) evaluating the credibility and accuracy of each source.
581	Vocabulary Study: Denotations and Connotations	L.9-10.5.b	Analyze nuances in the meaning of words with similar denotations.
581	Writing on Demand: Write a Response	W.9-10.1	Write arguments to support claims in an analysis of substantive topics or texts, using valid reasoning and relevant and sufficient evidence.
581	Listening/ Speaking: Oral Report	SL.9-10.4	Present information, findings, and supporting evidence clearly, concisely, and logically such that listeners can follow the line of reasoning and the organization, development, substance, and style are appropriate to purpose, audience, and task.
		SL.9-10.5	Make strategic use of digital media in presentations to enhance understanding of findings, reasoning, and evidence and to add interest.
Close Reading			
582–585	Read Is Google Making Us Stupid?	RI.9-10.10	By the end of grade 10, read and comprehend literary nonfiction at the high end of the grades 9-10 text complexity band independently and proficiently.
Unit Wrap-Up			
586	Unit Wrap-Up Present Your Project	SL.9-10.3	Evaluate a speaker's point of view, reasoning, and use of evidence and rhetoric, identifying any fallacious reasoning or exaggerated or distorted evidence.
		SL.9-10.4	Present information, findings, and supporting evidence clearly, concisely, and logically such that listeners can follow the line of reasoning and the organization, development, substance, and style are appropriate to purpose, audience, and task.
		SL.9-10.5	Make strategic use of digital media (e.g., textual, graphical, audio, visual, and interactive elements) in presentations to enhance understanding of findings, reasoning, and evidence and to add interest.
	Reflect on Your Reading	SL.9-10.1.a	Come to discussions prepared, having read and researched material under study; explicitly draw on that preparation by referring to evidence from texts and other research on the topic or issue to stimulate a thoughtful, well-reasoned exchange of ideas.
	Respond to the Essential Question	SL.9-10.1.a	Come to discussions prepared, having read and researched material under study; explicitly draw on that preparation by referring to evidence from texts and other research on the topic or issue to stimulate a thoughtful, well-reasoned exchange of ideas.
Unit 6 Writing Project: Persuasive Essay			
587–591	Study Persuasive Essays and Prewrite	W.9-10.1.a	Introduce precise claim(s), distinguish the claim(s) from alternate or opposing claims, and create an organization that establishes clear relationships among claim(s), counterclaims, reasons, and evidence.
		W.9-10.1.b	Develop claim(s) and counterclaims fairly, supplying evidence for each while pointing out the strengths and limitations of both in a manner that anticipates the audience's knowledge level and concerns.
		W.9-10.5	Develop and strengthen writing as needed by planning, revising, editing, rewriting, or trying a new approach, focusing on addressing what is most significant for a specific purpose and audience.

page 958

SE Pages	Lesson	Code	Standards Text
Student Handbooks, continued			
Unit 6 Writing Project: Persuasive Essay, continued			
587–591	Study Persuasive Essays and Prewrite continued	W.9-10.7	Conduct short as well as more sustained research projects to answer a question (including a self-generated question) or solve a problem; narrow or broaden the inquiry when appropriate; synthesize multiple sources on the subject, demonstrating understanding of the subject under investigation.
		W.9-10.8	Gather relevant information from multiple authoritative print and digital sources, using advanced searches effectively; assess the usefulness of each source in answering the research question; integrate information into the text selectively to maintain the flow of ideas, avoiding plagiarism and following a standard format for citation.
592–593	Persuasive Essay: Draft	W.9-10.1	Write arguments to support claims in an analysis of substantive topics or texts, using valid reasoning and relevant and sufficient evidence.
		W.9-10.4	Produce clear and coherent writing in which the development, organization, and style are appropriate to task, purpose, and audience.
		W.9-10.6	Use technology, including the Internet, to produce, publish, and update individual or shared writing products, taking advantage of technology's capacity to link to other information and to display information flexibly and dynamically.
594–597	Persuasive Essay: Revise Trait: Voice and Style	W.9-10.1.a	Introduce precise claim(s), distinguish the claim(s) from alternate or opposing claims, and create an organization that establishes clear relationships among claim(s), counterclaims, reasons, and evidence.
		W.9-10.1.b	Develop claim(s) and counterclaims fairly, supplying evidence for each while pointing out the strengths and limitations of both in a manner that anticipates the audience's knowledge level and concerns.
		W.9-10.1.d	Establish and maintain a formal style and objective tone while attending to the norms and conventions of the discipline in which they are writing.
		W.9-10.3.e	Provide a conclusion that follows from and reflects on what is experienced, observed, or resolved over the course of the narrative.
		W.9-10.5	Develop and strengthen writing as needed by planning, revising, editing, rewriting, or trying a new approach, focusing on addressing what is most significant for a specific purpose and audience.
		SL.9-10.1	Initiate and participate effectively in a range of collaborative discussions (one-on-one, in groups, and teacher-led) with diverse partners on grades 9–10 topics, texts, and issues, building on others' ideas and expressing their own clearly and persuasively.
		SL.9-10.1.d	Respond thoughtfully to diverse perspectives, summarize points of agreement and disagreement, and, when warranted, qualify or justify their own views and understanding and make new connections in light of the evidence and reasoning presented.

page 959

Common Core State Standards, continued

SE Pages	Lesson	Code	Standards Text
Student Handbooks, continued			
Unit 6 Writing Project: Persuasive Essay			
598–600	Persuasive Essay: Edit and Proofread Capitalization: Specific School Courses Semicolons and Commas Precise Language Effective Sentences	L.9-10.1.a	Use parallel structure.
		L.9-10.1.b	Use various types of phrases (noun, verb, adjective, adverbial, participial, prepositional, absolute) and clauses (independent, dependent; noun, relative, adverbial) to convey specific meanings and add variety and interest to writing or presentations.
		L.9-10.2	Demonstrate command of the conventions of standard English capitalization, punctuation, and spelling when writing.
		L.9-10.3.a	Write and edit work so that it conforms to the guidelines in a style manual appropriate for the discipline and writing type.
		L.9-10.6	Acquire and use accurately general academic and domain-specific words and phrases, sufficient for reading, writing, speaking, and listening at the college and career readiness level; demonstrate independence in gathering vocabulary knowledge when considering a word or phrase important to comprehension or expression.
601	Persuasive Essay: Publish and Present	W.9-10.6	Use technology, including the Internet, to produce, publish, and update individual or shared writing products, taking advantage of technology's capacity to link to other information and to display information flexibly and dynamically.
		SL.9-10.1.a	Come to discussions prepared, having read and researched material under study; explicitly draw on that preparation by referring to evidence from texts and other research on the topic or issue to stimulate a thoughtful, well-reasoned exchange of ideas.
		SL.9-10.3	Evaluate a speaker's point of view, reasoning, and use of evidence and rhetoric, identifying any fallacious reasoning or exaggerated or distorted evidence.
		SL.9-10.4	Present information, findings, and supporting evidence clearly, concisely, and logically such that listeners can follow the line of reasoning and the organization, development, substance, and style are appropriate to purpose, audience, and task.
UNIT 7: Where We Belong			
602–603	Discuss the Essential Question	SL.9-10.1.b	Work with peers to set rules for collegial discussions and decision-making (e.g., informal consensus, taking votes on key issues, presentation of alternate views), clear goals and deadlines, and individual roles as needed.
		SL.9-10.3	Evaluate a speaker's point of view, reasoning, and use of evidence and rhetoric, identifying any fallacious reasoning or exaggerated or distorted evidence.
604	Compare and Discuss	SL.9-10.4	Present information, findings, and supporting evidence clearly, concisely, and logically such that listeners can follow the line of reasoning and the organization, development, substance, and style are appropriate to purpose, audience, and task.
605	Plan a Project	SL.9-10.1.b	Work with peers to set rules for collegial discussions and decision-making (e.g., informal consensus, taking votes on key issues, presentation of alternate views), clear goals and deadlines, and individual roles as needed.
605	Choose More to Read	RL.9-10.10	By the end of grade 10, read and comprehend literature, including stories, dramas, and poems, at the high end of the grades 9-10 text complexity band independently and proficiently.
		RI.9-10.10	By the end of grade 10, read and comprehend literary nonfiction at the high end of the grades 9-10 text complexity band independently and proficiently.

page 960

SE Pages	Lesson	Code	Standards Text
Student Handbooks, continued			
UNIT 7: Where We Belong, continued			
606–609	How to Read Drama	RL.9-10.4	Determine the meaning of words and phrases as they are used in the text, including figurative and connotative meanings; analyze the cumulative impact of specific word choices on meaning and tone (e.g., how the language evokes a sense of time and place; how it sets a formal or informal tone).
		RL.9-10.10	By the end of grade 10, read and comprehend literature, including stories, dramas, and poems, at the high end of the grades 9-10 text complexity band independently and proficiently.
610–611	How to Read Poetry	RL.9-10.7	Analyze the representation of a subject or a key scene in two different artistic mediums, including what is emphasized or absent in each treatment.
		L.9-10.6	Acquire and use accurately general academic and domain-specific words and phrases, sufficient for reading, writing, speaking, and listening at the college and career readiness level; demonstrate independence in gathering vocabulary knowledge when considering a word or phrase important to comprehension or expression.
Cluster 1			
612	Prepare to Read	RL.9-10.4	Determine the meaning of words and phrases as they are used in the text, including figurative and connotative meanings; analyze the cumulative impact of specific word choices on meaning and tone.
		SL.9-10.1	Initiate and participate effectively in a range of collaborative discussions (one-on-one, in groups, and teacher-led) with diverse partners on grades 9–10 topics, texts, and issues, building on others' ideas and expressing their own clearly and persuasively.
		L.9-10.6	Acquire and use accurately general academic and domain-specific words and phrases, sufficient for reading, writing, speaking, and listening at the college and career readiness level; demonstrate independence in gathering vocabulary knowledge when considering a word or phrase important to comprehension or expression.
613	Before Reading: A Raisin in the Sun	RL.9-10.4	Determine the meaning of words and phrases as they are used in the text, including figurative and connotative meanings; analyze the cumulative impact of specific word choices on meaning and tone.
		RL.9-10.7	Analyze the representation of a subject or a key scene in two different artistic mediums, including what is emphasized or absent in each treatment.
614–633	Read A Raisin in the Sun	RL.9-10.1	Cite strong and thorough textual evidence to support analysis of what the text says explicitly as well as inferences drawn from the text.
		RL.9-10.2	Determine a theme or central idea of a text and analyze in detail its development over the course of the text, including how it emerges and is shaped and refined by specific details; provide an objective summary of the text.
		RL.9-10.3	Analyze how complex characters develop over the course of a text, interact with other characters, and advance the plot or develop the theme.
		RL.9-10.4	Determine the meaning of words and phrases as they are used in the text, including figurative and connotative meanings; analyze the cumulative impact of specific word choices on meaning and tone.
		RL.9-10.7	Analyze the representation of a subject or a key scene in two different artistic mediums, including what is emphasized or absent in each treatment.

page 961

Common Core State Standards

Common Core State Standards

Student Handbooks, continued

Cluster 1, continued

SE Pages	Lesson	Code	Standards Text
614–633	**Read A Raisin in the Sun** continued	RL.9-10.10	By the end of grade 10, read and comprehend literature, including stories, dramas, and poems, at the high end of the grades 9–10 text complexity band independently and proficiently.
		W.9-10.9.a	Apply grades 9–10 Reading standards to literature.
		W.9-10.10	Write routinely over extended time frames (time for research, reflection, and revision) and shorter time frames (a single sitting or a day or two) for a range of tasks, purposes, and audiences.
		L.9-10.1.b	Use various types of phrases (noun, verb, adjectival, adverbial, participial, prepositional, absolute) and clauses (independent, dependent; noun, relative, adverbial) to convey specific meanings and add variety and interest to writing or presentations.
		L.9-10.5.a	Interpret figures of speech in context and analyze their role in the text.
		L.9-10.6	Acquire and use accurately general academic and domain-specific words and phrases, sufficient for reading, writing, speaking, and listening at the college and career readiness level; demonstrate independence in gathering vocabulary knowledge when considering a word or phrase important to comprehension or expression.
634	**Before Reading: Family Bonds**	RL.9-10.4	Determine the meaning of words and phrases as they are used in the text, including figurative and connotative meanings; analyze the cumulative impact of specific word choices on meaning and tone.
635–640	**Read Family Bonds**	RL.9-10.1	Cite strong and thorough textual evidence to support analysis of what the text says explicitly as well as inferences drawn from the text.
		RL.9-10.2	Determine a theme or central idea of a text and analyze in detail its development over the course of the text, including how it emerges and is shaped and refined by specific details; provide an objective summary of the text.
		RL.9-10.4	Determine the meaning of words and phrases as they are used in the text, including figurative and connotative meanings; analyze the cumulative impact of specific word choices on meaning and tone.
		RL.9-10.10	By the end of grade 10, read and comprehend literature, including stories, dramas, and poems, at the high end of the grades 9–10 text complexity band independently and proficiently.
		W.9-10.9.a	Apply grades 9–10 Reading standards to literature.
		W.9-10.10	Write routinely over extended time frames (time for research, reflection, and revision) and shorter time frames (a single sitting or a day or two) for a range of tasks, purposes, and audiences.
		SL.9-10.1.a	Come to discussions prepared, having read and researched material under study; explicitly draw on that preparation by referring to evidence from texts and other research on the topic or issue to stimulate a thoughtful, well-reasoned exchange of ideas.
		L.9-10.1.b	Use various types of phrases (noun, verb, adjectival, adverbial, participial, prepositional, absolute) and clauses (independent, dependent; noun, relative, adverbial) to convey specific meanings and add variety and interest to writing or presentations.
		L.9-10.2.c	Spell correctly.

page 962

Student Handbooks, continued

Cluster 1, continued

SE Pages	Lesson	Code	Standards Text
635–640	**Read Family Bonds** continued	L.9-10.6	Acquire and use accurately general academic and domain-specific words and phrases, sufficient for reading, writing, speaking, and listening at the college and career readiness level; demonstrate independence in gathering vocabulary knowledge when considering a word or phrase important to comprehension or expression.
641	**Reflect and Assess Critical Thinking**	RL.9-10.1	Cite strong and thorough textual evidence to support analysis of what the text says explicitly as well as inferences drawn from the text.
		RL.9-10.2	Determine a theme or central idea of a text and analyze in detail its development over the course of the text, including how it emerges and is shaped and refined by specific details; provide an objective summary of the text.
		RL.9-10.3	Analyze how complex characters develop over the course of a text, interact with other characters, and advance the plot or develop the theme.
		RL.9-10.10	By the end of grade 10, read and comprehend literature, including stories, dramas, and poems, at the high end of the grades 9–10 text complexity band independently and proficiently.
	Write About Literature	W.9-10.9.a	Apply grades 9–10 Reading standards to literature.
	Key Vocabulary Review	L.9-10.6	Acquire and use accurately general academic and domain-specific words and phrases, sufficient for reading, writing, speaking, and listening at the college and career readiness level; demonstrate independence in gathering vocabulary knowledge when considering a word or phrase important to comprehension or expression.
	Read with Ease: Phrasing	RL.9-10.10	By the end of grade 10, read and comprehend literature, including stories, dramas, and poems, at the high end of the grades 9–10 text complexity band independently and proficiently.
642	**Grammar: Write in the Present Perfect Tense**	L.9-10.1.b	Use various types of phrases (noun, verb, adjectival, adverbial, participial, prepositional, absolute) and clauses (independent, dependent; noun, relative, adverbial) to convey specific meanings and add variety and interest to writing or presentations.
		L.9-10.2.c	Spell correctly.
642	**Language Development: Negotiate**	SL.9-10.1.d	Respond thoughtfully to diverse perspectives, summarize points of agreement and disagreement, and, when warranted, qualify or justify their own views and understanding and make new connections in light of the evidence and reasoning presented.
642	**Literary Analysis: Analyze and Compare Poetry**	RL.9-10.10	By the end of grade 10, read and comprehend literature, including stories, dramas, and poems, at the high end of the grades 9–10 text complexity band independently and proficiently.
643	**Vocabulary Study: Interpret Figurative Language**	L.9-10.4.a	Use context as a clue to the meaning of a word or phrase.
		L.9-10.5.a	Interpret figures of speech in context and analyze their role in the text.
643	**Writing on Demand: Write About Theme**	W.9-10.4	Produce clear and coherent writing in which the development, organization, and style are appropriate to task, purpose, and audience.
		W.9-10.9.a	Apply grades 9–10 Reading standards to literature.

page 963

Common Core State Standards, continued

Student Handbooks, continued

Cluster 1, continued

SE Pages	Lesson	Code	Standards Text
643	**Listening/ Speaking: Dramatization**	RL.9-10.7	Analyze various accounts of a subject told in different mediums, determining which details are emphasized in each account.
		SL.9-10.6	Adapt speech to a variety of contexts and tasks, demonstrating command of formal English when indicated or appropriate.
644	**Workplace Workshop: Inside a Real Estate Agency**	W.9-10.1	Write arguments to support claims in an analysis of substantive topics or texts, using valid reasoning and relevant and sufficient evidence.
		W.9-10.10	Write routinely over extended time frames (time for research, reflection, and revision) and shorter time frames (a single sitting or a day or two) for a range of tasks, purposes, and audiences.
645	**Vocabulary Workshop: Interpret Figurative Language**	RL.9-10.4	Determine the meaning of words and phrases as they are used in the text, including figurative and connotative meanings; analyze the cumulative impact of specific word choices on meaning and tone.
		L.9-10.5.a	Interpret figures of speech in context and analyze their role in the text.
Cluster 2			
646	**Prepare to Read**	RI.9-10.4	Determine the meaning of words and phrases as they are used in a text, including figurative, connotative, and technical meanings; analyze the cumulative impact of specific word choices on meaning and tone.
		SL.9-10.1	Initiate and participate effectively in a range of collaborative discussions (one-on-one, in groups, and teacher-led) with diverse partners on grades 9–10 topics, texts, and issues, building on others' ideas and expressing their own clearly and persuasively.
		L.9-10.6	Acquire and use accurately general academic and domain-specific words and phrases, sufficient for reading, writing, speaking, and listening at the college and career readiness level; demonstrate independence in gathering vocabulary knowledge when considering a word or phrase important to comprehension or expression.
647	**Before Reading: Pass It On**	RL.9-10.3	Analyze how complex characters develop over the course of a text, interact with other characters, and advance the plot or develop the theme.
		RL.9-10.4	Determine the meaning of words and phrases as they are used in the text, including figurative and connotative meanings; analyze the cumulative impact of specific word choices on meaning and tone.
648–665	**Read Pass It On**	RL.9-10.1	Cite strong and thorough textual evidence to support analysis of what the text says explicitly as well as inferences drawn from the text.
		RL.9-10.3	Analyze how complex characters develop over the course of a text, interact with other characters, and advance the plot or develop the theme.
		RL.9-10.4	Determine the meaning of words and phrases as they are used in the text, including figurative and connotative meanings; analyze the cumulative impact of specific word choices on meaning and tone.
		RL.9-10.10	By the end of grade 10, read and comprehend literature, including stories, dramas, and poems, at the high end of the grades 9–10 text complexity band independently and proficiently.
		RI.9-10.4	Determine the meaning of words and phrases as they are used in a text, including figurative, connotative, and technical meanings; analyze the cumulative impact of specific word choices on meaning and tone.

page 964

Student Handbooks, continued

Cluster 2, continued

SE Pages	Lesson	Code	Standards Text
648–665	**Read Pass It On** continued	RI.9-10.6	Determine an author's point of view or purpose in a text and analyze how an author uses rhetoric to advance that point of view or purpose.
		W.9-10.9.a	Apply grades 9–10 Reading standards to literature.
		W.9-10.10	Write routinely over extended time frames (time for research, reflection, and revision) and shorter time frames (a single sitting or a day or two) for a range of tasks, purposes, and audiences.
		L.9-10.1.b	Use various types of phrases (noun, verb, adjectival, adverbial, participial, prepositional, absolute) and clauses (independent, dependent; noun, relative, adverbial) to convey specific meanings and add variety and interest to writing or presentations.
		L.9-10.5	Demonstrate understanding of figurative language, word relationships, and nuances in word meanings.
		L.9-10.6	Acquire and use accurately general academic and domain-specific words and phrases, sufficient for reading, writing, speaking, and listening at the college and career readiness level; demonstrate independence in gathering vocabulary knowledge when considering a word or phrase important to comprehension or expression.
666	**Before Reading: Standing Together**	RL.9-10.4	Determine the meaning of words and phrases as they are used in the text, including figurative and connotative meanings; analyze the cumulative impact of specific word choices on meaning and tone.
		RL.9-10.5	Analyze how an author's choices concerning how to structure a text, order events within it, and manipulate time create such effects as mystery, tension, or surprise.
667–672	**Read Standing Together**	RL.9-10.2	Determine a theme or central idea of a text and analyze in detail its development over the course of the text, including how it emerges and is shaped and refined by specific details; provide an objective summary of the text.
		RL.9-10.4	Determine the meaning of words and phrases as they are used in the text, including figurative and connotative meanings; analyze the cumulative impact of specific word choices on meaning and tone.
		RL.9-10.5	Analyze how an author's choices concerning how to structure a text, order events within it, and manipulate time create such effects as mystery, tension, or surprise.
		RL.9-10.10	By the end of grade 10, read and comprehend literature, including stories, dramas, and poems, at the high end of the grades 9–10 text complexity band independently and proficiently.
		W.9-10.9.a	Apply grades 9–10 Reading standards to literature.
		W.9-10.10	Write routinely over extended time frames (time for research, reflection, and revision) and shorter time frames (a single sitting or a day or two) for a range of tasks, purposes, and audiences.
		L.9-10.1.b	Use various types of phrases (noun, verb, adjectival, adverbial, participial, prepositional, absolute) and clauses (independent, dependent; noun, relative, adverbial) to convey specific meanings and add variety and interest to writing or presentations.
		L.9-10.4.b	Determine or clarify the meaning of unknown and multiple-meaning words and Identify and correctly use patterns of word changes that indicate different meanings or parts of speech.

page 965

Common Core State Standards

Common Core State Standards, continued

SE Pages	Lesson	Code	Standards Text
Student Handbooks, continued			
Cluster 2, continued			
667–672	**Read Standing Together** continued	L.9-10.6	Acquire and use accurately general academic and domain-specific words and phrases, sufficient for reading, writing, speaking, and listening at the college and career readiness level; demonstrate independence in gathering vocabulary knowledge when considering a word or phrase important to comprehension or expression.
673	**Reflect and Assess Critical Thinking**	RL.9-10.1	Cite strong and thorough textual evidence to support analysis of what the text says explicitly as well as inferences drawn from the text.
		RL.9-10.2	Determine a theme or central idea of a text and analyze in detail its development over the course of the text, including how it emerges and is shaped and refined by specific details; provide an objective summary of the text.
		RL.9-10.10	By the end of grade 10, read and comprehend literature, including stories, dramas, and poems, at the high end of the grades 9–10 text complexity band independently and proficiently.
	Write About Literature	W.9-10.9.a	Apply grades 9–10 Reading standards to literature.
	Key Vocabulary Review	L.9-10.6	Acquire and use accurately general academic and domain-specific words and phrases, sufficient for reading, writing, speaking, and listening at the college and career readiness level; demonstrate independence in gathering vocabulary knowledge when considering a word or phrase important to comprehension or expression.
	Read with Ease: Expression	RL.9-10.10	By the end of grade 10, read and comprehend literature, including stories, dramas, and poems, at the high end of the grades 9–10 text complexity band independently and proficiently.
674	**Grammar: Write with the Perfect Tenses**	L.9-10.1.b	Use various types of phrases (noun, verb, adjectival, adverbial, participial, prepositional, absolute) and clauses (independent, dependent; noun, relative, adverbial) to convey specific meanings and add variety and interest to writing or presentations.
674	**Language Development: Use Appropriate Language**	SL.9-10.6	Adapt speech to a variety of contexts and tasks, demonstrating command of formal English when indicated or appropriate.
674	**Literary Analysis/ Research: Literary Criticism**	RL.9-10.10	By the end of grade 10, read and comprehend literature, including stories, dramas, and poems, at the high end of the grades 9–10 text complexity band independently and proficiently.
675	**Vocabulary Study: Denotation and Connotation**	L.9-10.5.b	Analyze nuances in the meaning of words with similar denotations.
675	**Writing: Write a Literary Critique**	W.9-10.1	Write arguments to support claims in an analysis of substantive topics or texts, using valid reasoning and relevant and sufficient evidence.
		W.9-10.5	Develop and strengthen writing as needed by planning, revising, editing, rewriting, or trying a new approach, focusing on addressing what is most significant for a specific purpose and audience.
675	**Listening/Speaking: Compare Media**	RL.9-10.7	Analyze the representation of a subject or a key scene in two different artistic mediums, including what is emphasized or absent in each treatment.
676–677	**Listening and Speaking Workshop: Narrative Presentation**	SL.9-10.3	Evaluate a speaker's point of view, reasoning, and use of evidence and rhetoric, identifying any fallacious reasoning or exaggerated or distorted evidence.
		SL.9-10.4	Present information, findings, and supporting evidence clearly, concisely, and logically such that listeners can follow the line of reasoning and the organization, development, substance, and style are appropriate to purpose, audience, and task.

page 966

SE Pages	Lesson	Code	Standards Text
Student Handbooks, continued			
Cluster 2, continued			
676–677	**Listening and Speaking Workshop: Narrative Presentation** continued	SL.9-10.6	Adapt speech to a variety of contexts and tasks, demonstrating command of formal English when indicated or appropriate.
		L.9-10.3	Apply knowledge of language to understand how language functions in different contexts, to make effective choices for meaning or style, and to comprehend more fully when reading or listening.
Cluster 3			
678	**Prepare to Read**	RI.9-10.4	Determine the meaning of words and phrases as they are used in a text, including figurative, connotative, and technical meanings; analyze the cumulative impact of specific word choices on meaning and tone.
		SL.9-10.1	Initiate and participate effectively in a range of collaborative discussions (one-on-one, in groups, and teacher-led) with diverse partners on grades 9–10 topics, texts, and issues, building on others' ideas and expressing their own clearly and persuasively.
		L.9-10.6	Acquire and use accurately general academic and domain-specific words and phrases, sufficient for reading, writing, speaking, and listening at the college and career readiness level; demonstrate independence in gathering vocabulary knowledge when considering a word or phrase important to comprehension or expression.
679	**Before Reading: Voices of America**	RL.9-10.4	Determine the meaning of words and phrases as they are used in the text, including figurative and connotative meanings; analyze the cumulative impact of specific word choices on meaning and tone.
680–689	**Read Voices of America**	RL.9-10.1	Cite strong and thorough textual evidence to support analysis of what the text says explicitly as well as inferences drawn from the text.
		RL.9-10.2	Determine a theme or central idea of a text and analyze in detail its development over the course of the text, including how it emerges and is shaped and refined by specific details; provide an objective summary of the text.
		RL.9-10.4	Determine the meaning of words and phrases as they are used in the text, including figurative and connotative meanings; analyze the cumulative impact of specific word choices on meaning and tone.
		RL.9-10.10	By the end of grade 10, read and comprehend literature, including stories, dramas, and poems, at the high end of the grades 9–10 text complexity band independently and proficiently.
		W.9-10.9.a	Apply grades 9–10 Reading standards to literature.
		W.9-10.10	Write routinely over extended time frames (time for research, reflection, and revision) and shorter time frames (a single sitting or a day or two) for a range of tasks, purposes, and audiences.
		SL.9-10.1	Initiate and participate effectively in a range of collaborative discussions (one-on-one, in groups, and teacher-led) with diverse partners on grades 9–10 topics, texts, and issues, building on others' ideas and expressing their own clearly and persuasively.
		L.9-10.1.b	Use various types of phrases (noun, verb, adjectival, adverbial, participial, prepositional, absolute) and clauses (independent, dependent; noun, relative, adverbial) to convey specific meanings and add variety and interest to writing or presentations.

page 967

Common Core State Standards, continued

SE Pages	Lesson	Code	Standards Text
Student Handbooks, continued			
Cluster 3, continued			
680–689	**Read Voices of America** continued	L.9-10.6	Acquire and use accurately general academic and domain-specific words and phrases, sufficient for reading, writing, speaking, and listening at the college and career readiness level; demonstrate independence in gathering vocabulary knowledge when considering a word or phrase important to comprehension or expression.
690	**Before Reading: Human Family**	RL.9-10.4	Determine the meaning of words and phrases as they are used in the text, including figurative and connotative meanings; analyze the cumulative impact of specific word choices on meaning and tone.
		RL.9-10.5	Analyze how an author's choices concerning how to structure a text, order events within it, and manipulate time create such effects as mystery, tension, or surprise.
691–694	**Read Human Family**	RL.9-10.1	Cite strong and thorough textual evidence to support analysis of what the text says explicitly as well as inferences drawn from the text.
		RL.9-10.2	Determine a theme or central idea of a text and analyze in detail its development over the course of the text, including how it emerges and is shaped and refined by specific details; provide an objective summary of the text.
		RL.9-10.4	Determine the meaning of words and phrases as they are used in the text, including figurative and connotative meanings; analyze the cumulative impact of specific word choices on meaning and tone.
		RL.9-10.5	Analyze how an author's choices concerning how to structure a text, order events within it, and manipulate time create such effects as mystery, tension, or surprise.
		RL.9-10.10	By the end of grade 10, read and comprehend literature, including stories, dramas, and poems, at the high end of the grades 9–10 text complexity band independently and proficiently.
		W.9-10.9.a	Apply grades 9–10 Reading standards to literature.
		W.9-10.10	Write routinely over extended time frames (time for research, reflection, and revision) and shorter time frames (a single sitting or a day or two) for a range of tasks, purposes, and audiences.
		L.9-10.1.b	Use various types of phrases (noun, verb, adjectival, adverbial, participial, prepositional, absolute) and clauses (independent, dependent; noun, relative, adverbial) to convey specific meanings and add variety and interest to writing or presentations.
		L.9-10.6	Acquire and use accurately general academic and domain-specific words and phrases, sufficient for reading, writing, speaking, and listening at the college and career readiness level; demonstrate independence in gathering vocabulary knowledge when considering a word or phrase important to comprehension or expression.
695	**Reflect and Assess Critical Thinking**	RL.9-10.1	Cite strong and thorough textual evidence to support analysis of what the text says explicitly as well as inferences drawn from the text.
		RL.9-10.2	Determine a theme or central idea of a text and analyze in detail its development over the course of the text, including how it emerges and is shaped and refined by specific details; provide an objective summary of the text.
		RL.9-10.6	Analyze a particular point of view or cultural experience reflected in a work of literature from outside the United States, drawing on a wide reading of world literature.
		RL.9-10.10	By the end of grade 10, read and comprehend literature, including stories, dramas, and poems, at the high end of the grades 9–10 text complexity band independently and proficiently.

page 968

SE Pages	Lesson	Code	Standards Text
Student Handbooks, continued			
Cluster 3, continued			
	Reflect and Assess continued **Write About Literature**	W.9-10.9.a	Apply grades 9–10 Reading standards to literature.
	Key Vocabulary Review	L.9-10.6	Acquire and use accurately general academic and domain-specific words and phrases, sufficient for reading, writing, speaking, and listening at the college and career readiness level; demonstrate independence in gathering vocabulary knowledge when considering a word or phrase important to comprehension or expression.
	Read with Ease: Intonation	RL.9-10.10	By the end of grade 10, read and comprehend literature, including stories, dramas, and poems, at the high end of the grades 9–10 text complexity band independently and proficiently.
696	**Grammar: Enrich Your Sentences**	L.9-10.1.b	Use various types of phrases (noun, verb, adjectival, adverbial, participial, prepositional, absolute) and clauses (independent, dependent; noun, relative, adverbial) to convey specific meanings and add variety and interest to writing or presentations.
696	**Literary Analysis: Allusions**	RL.9-10.9	Analyze how an author draws on and transforms source material in a specific work.
696	**Language Development: Use Appropriate Language**	SL.9-10.6	Adapt speech to a variety of contexts and tasks, demonstrating command of formal English when indicated or appropriate.
697	**Vocabulary Study: Figurative Language**	L.9-10.5	Demonstrate understanding of figurative language, word relationships, and nuances in word meanings.
697	**Writing Trait: Voice and Style**	W.9-10.5	Develop and strengthen writing as needed by planning, revising, editing, rewriting, or trying a new approach, focusing on addressing what is most significant for a specific purpose and audience.
697	**Research/Writing: Historical Figure Biography**	W.9-10.2	Write informative/explanatory texts to examine and convey complex ideas, concepts, and information clearly and accurately through the effective selection, organization, and analysis of content.
		W.9-10.7	Conduct short as well as more sustained research projects to answer a question (including a self-generated question) or solve a problem; narrow or broaden the inquiry when appropriate; synthesize multiple sources on the subject, demonstrating understanding of the subject under investigation.
		W.9-10.8	Gather relevant information from multiple authoritative print and digital sources, using advanced searches effectively; assess the usefulness of each source in answering the research question; integrate information into the text selectively to maintain the flow of ideas, avoiding plagiarism and following a standard format for citation.
Close Reading			
698–699	**Read Mending Wall**	RL.9-10.10	By the end of grade 10, read and comprehend literature, including stories, dramas, and poems, at the high end of the grades 9–10 text complexity band independently and proficiently.
Unit Wrap-Up			
700	**Unit Wrap-Up Present Your Project**	W.9-10.8	Gather relevant information from multiple authoritative print and digital sources, using advanced searches effectively; assess the usefulness of each source in answering the research question; integrate information into the text selectively to maintain the flow of ideas, avoiding plagiarism and following a standard format for citation.

page 969

Common Core State Standards

Common Core State Standards, continued

Student Handbooks, continued

Unit Wrap-Up, continued

SE Pages	Lesson	Code	Standards Text
700	**Unit Wrap-Up** continued **Reflect on Your Reading**	SL.9-10.1.a	Come to discussions prepared, having read and researched material under study; explicitly draw on that preparation by referring to evidence from texts and other research on the topic or issue to stimulate a thoughtful, well-reasoned exchange of ideas.
	Respond to the Essential Question	SL.9-10.1.a	Come to discussions prepared, having read and researched material under study; explicitly draw on that preparation by referring to evidence from texts and other research on the topic or issue to stimulate a thoughtful, well-reasoned exchange of ideas.
Language and Learning Handbook			
703–712	**Strategies for Learning and Developing Language**	SL.9-10.1.c	Propel conversations by posing and responding to questions that relate the current discussion to broader themes or larger ideas; actively incorporate others into the discussion; and clarify, verify, or challenge ideas and conclusions.
		SL.9-10.3	Evaluate a speaker's point of view, reasoning, and use of evidence and rhetoric, identifying any fallacious reasoning or exaggerated or distorted evidence.
		SL.9-10.4	Present information, findings, and supporting evidence clearly, concisely, and logically such that listeners can follow the line of reasoning and the organization, development, substance, and style are appropriate to purpose, audience, and task.
		SL.9-10.6	Adapt speech to a variety of contexts and tasks, demonstrating command of formal English when indicated or appropriate.
		L.9-10.1	Demonstrate command of the conventions of standard English grammar and usage when writing or speaking.
		L.9-10.4	Determine or clarify the meaning of unknown and multiple-meaning words and phrases based on grades 9–10 reading and content, choosing flexibly from a range of strategies.
		L.9-10.4.c	Consult general and specialized reference materials, both print and digital, to find the pronunciation of a word or determine or clarify its precise meaning, its part of speech, or its etymology.
		L.9-10.5.a	Consult general and specialized reference materials, both print and digital, to find the pronunciation of a word or determine or clarify its precise meaning, its part of speech, or its etymology.
		L.9-10.6	Acquire and use accurately general academic and domain-specific words and phrases, sufficient for reading, writing, speaking, and listening at the college and career readiness level; demonstrate independence in gathering vocabulary knowledge when considering a word or phrase important to comprehension or expression.
713–716	**Listening and Speaking**	SL.9-10.1	Initiate and participate effectively in a range of collaborative discussions (one-on-one, in groups, and teacher-led) with diverse partners on grades 9–10 topics, texts, and issues, building on others' ideas and expressing their own clearly and persuasively.
		SL.9-10.1.c	Propel conversations by posing and responding to questions that relate the current discussion to broader themes or larger ideas; actively incorporate others into the discussion; and clarify, verify, or challenge ideas and conclusions.
		SL.9-10.1.d	Respond thoughtfully to diverse perspectives, summarize points of agreement and disagreement, and, when warranted, qualify or justify their own views and understanding and make new connections in light of the evidence and reasoning presented.
		L.9-10.1.a	Use parallel structure.

page 970

Student Handbooks, continued

Language and Learning Handbook, continued

SE Pages	Lesson	Code	Standards Text
713–716	**Listening and Speaking** continued	L.9-10.5	Demonstrate understanding of figurative language, word relationships, and nuances in word meanings.
717–720	**Viewing and Representing**	RI.9-10.7	Analyze various accounts of a subject told in different mediums (e.g., a person's life story in both print and multimedia), determining which details are emphasized in each account.
		W.9-10.8	Gather relevant information from multiple authoritative print and digital sources, using advanced searches effectively; assess the usefulness of each source in answering the research question; integrate information into the text selectively to maintain the flow of ideas, avoiding plagiarism and following a standard format for citation.
		SL.9-10.2	Integrate multiple sources of information presented in diverse media or formats (e.g., visually, quantitatively, orally) evaluating the credibility and accuracy of each source.
		SL.9-10.5	Make strategic use of digital media in presentations to enhance understanding of findings, reasoning, and evidence and to add interest.
721–724	**Technology and Media**	W.9-10.6	Use technology, including the Internet, to produce, publish, and update individual or shared writing products, taking advantage of technology's capacity to link to other information and to display information flexibly and dynamically.
		SL.9-10.5	Make strategic use of digital media in presentations to enhance understanding of findings, reasoning, and evidence and to add interest.
725–730	**Research**	W.9-10.7	Conduct short as well as more sustained research projects to answer a question (including a self-generated question) or solve a problem; narrow or broaden the inquiry when appropriate; synthesize multiple sources on the subject, demonstrating understanding of the subject under investigation.
		W.9-10.8	Gather relevant information from multiple authoritative print and digital sources, using advanced searches effectively; assess the usefulness of each source in answering the research question; integrate information into the text selectively to maintain the flow of ideas, avoiding plagiarism and following a standard format for citation.
		L.9-10.3.a	Write and edit work so that it conforms to the guidelines in a style manual appropriate for the discipline and writing type.
Reading Handbook			
734–746	**Reading Strategies**	RL.9-10.1	Cite strong and thorough textual evidence to support analysis of what the text says explicitly as well as inferences drawn from the text.
		RI.9-10.1	Cite strong and thorough textual evidence to support analysis of what the text says explicitly as well as inferences drawn from the text.
747–771	**Reading Fluency**	RL.9-10.10	By the end of grade 10, read and comprehend literature, including stories, dramas, and poems, at the high end of the grades 9–10 text complexity band independently and proficiently.
		RI.9-10.10	By the end of grade 10, read and comprehend literary nonfiction at the high end of the grades 9–10 text complexity band independently and proficiently.

page 971

Common Core State Standards, continued

Student Handbooks, continued

Reading Handbook, continue

SE Pages	Lesson	Code	Standards Text
772–775	**Study Skills and Strategies**	SL.9-10.1.a	Come to discussions prepared, having read and researched material under study; explicitly draw on that preparation by referring to evidence from texts and other research on the topic or issue to stimulate a thoughtful, well-reasoned exchange of ideas.
		SL.9-10.2	Integrate multiple sources of information presented in diverse media or formats evaluating the credibility and accuracy of each source.
776–783	**Vocabulary**	L.9-10.4	Determine or clarify the meaning of unknown and multiple-meaning words and phrases based on grades 9–10 reading and content, choosing flexibly from a range of strategies.
		L.9-10.4.a	Use context as a clue to the meaning of a word or phrase.
		L.9-10.4.b	Identify and correctly use patterns of word changes that indicate different meanings or parts of speech.
		L.9-10.4.c	Consult general and specialized reference materials, both print and digital, to find the pronunciation of a word or determine or clarify its precise meaning, its part of speech, or its etymology.
		L.9-10.4.d	Verify the preliminary determination of the meaning of a word or phrase.
		L.9-10.5	Demonstrate understanding of figurative language, word relationships, and nuances in word meanings.
		L.9-10.6	Acquire and use accurately general academic and domain-specific words and phrases, sufficient for reading, writing, speaking, and listening at the college and career readiness level; demonstrate independence in gathering vocabulary knowledge when considering a word or phrase important to comprehension or expression.
Writing Handbook			
785–791	**The Writing Process**	W.9-10.4	Produce clear and coherent writing in which the development, organization, and style are appropriate to task, purpose, and audience.
		W.9-10.6	Use technology, including the Internet, to produce, publish, and update individual or shared writing products, taking advantage of technology's capacity to link to other information and to display information flexibly and dynamically.
792–801	**Writing Traits**	RI.9-10.10	By the end of grade 10, read and comprehend literary nonfiction at the high end of the grades 9–10 text complexity band independently and proficiently.
		W.9-10.1.c	Use words, phrases, and clauses to link the major sections of the text, create cohesion, and clarify the relationships between claim(s) and reasons, between reasons and evidence, and between claim(s) and counterclaims.
		W.9-10.2.c	Use appropriate and varied transitions to link the major sections of the text, create cohesion, and clarify the relationships among complex ideas and concepts.
		W.9-10.2.e	Establish and maintain a formal style and objective tone while attending to the norms and conventions of the discipline in which they are writing.
		W.9-10.2.f	Provide a concluding statement or section that follows from and supports the information or explanation presented.
		W.9-10.3.d	Use precise words and phrases, telling details, and sensory language to convey a vivid picture of the experiences, events, setting, and/or characters.

page 972

Student Handbooks, continued

Writing Handbook, continued

SE Pages	Lesson	Code	Standards Text
792–801	**Writing Traits** continued	W.9-10.4	Produce clear and coherent writing in which the development, organization, and style are appropriate to task, purpose, and audience.
		L.9-10.1	Demonstrate command of the conventions of standard English grammar and usage when writing or speaking.
802–823	**Writing Purposes, Modes, and Forms**	W.9-10.1	Write arguments to support claims in an analysis of substantive topics or texts, using valid reasoning and relevant and sufficient evidence.
		W.9-10.4	Produce clear and coherent writing in which the development, organization, and style are appropriate to task, purpose, and audience.
		W.9-10.5	Develop and strengthen writing as needed by planning, revising, editing, rewriting, or trying a new approach, focusing on addressing what is most significant for a specific purpose and audience.
		W.9-10.6	Use technology, including the Internet, to produce, publish, and update individual or shared writing products, taking advantage of technology's capacity to link to other information and to display information flexibly and dynamically.
		SL.9-10.2	Integrate multiple sources of information presented in diverse media or formats evaluating the credibility and accuracy of each source.
		L.9-10.3.a	Write and edit work so that it conforms to the guidelines in a style manual appropriate for the discipline and writing type.
824–858	**Grammar, Usage, Mechanics, and Spelling**	L.9-10.1	Demonstrate command of the conventions of standard English grammar and usage when writing or speaking.
		L.9-10.1.a	Use parallel structure.
		L.9-10.1.b	Use various types of phrases (noun, verb, adjectival, adverbial, participial, prepositional, absolute) and clauses (independent, dependent; noun, relative, adverbial) to convey specific meanings and add variety and interest to writing or presentations.
		L.9-10.2	Demonstrate command of the conventions of standard English capitalization, punctuation, and spelling when writing.
		L.9-10.2.a	Use a semicolon (and perhaps a conjunctive adverb) to link two or more closely related independent clauses.
		L.9-10.2.b	Use a colon to introduce a list or quotation.
		L.9-10.2.c	Spell correctly.
		L.9-10.3	Apply knowledge of language to understand how language functions in different contexts, to make effective choices for meaning or style, and to comprehend more fully when reading or listening.
859–867	**Troubleshooting Guide**	L.9-10.1	Demonstrate command of the conventions of standard English grammar and usage when writing or speaking.
		L.9-10.3	Apply knowledge of language to understand how language functions in different contexts, to make effective choices for meaning or style, and to comprehend more fully when reading or listening.

page 973

EDGE

Scope and Sequence

READING	Fundamentals/ Inside Phonics/ Inside the U.S.A.	Level A	Level B	Level C
LITERATURE				
Key Ideas and Details				
Use text evidence	●	●	●	●
Explicit evidence	●	●	●	●
Implicit evidence	●	●	●	●
Summarize, retell, or explain literature	●	●	●	●
Analyze elements of literature, poetry, and drama	●	●	●	●
Theme, main idea, or central idea	●	●	●	●
Character development, characterization (hero/heroine, protagonist/antagonist, static/dynamic, etc.)	●	●	●	●
Plot and conflict	●	●	●	●
Setting	●	●	●	●
Use reading strategies	●	●	●	●
Plan and monitor	●	●	●	●
Preview and set a purpose	●	●	●	●
Make and confirm predictions	●	●	●	●
Clarify ideas and vocabulary	●	●	●	●
Determine importance	●	●	●	●
Relate main ideas and details	●	●	●	●
Summarize	●	●	●	●
Ask questions	●	●	●	●
Make inferences	●	●	●	●
Make connections	●	●	●	●
Synthesize	●	●	●	●
Draw conclusions		●	●	●
Compare across texts	●	●	●	●
Form generalizations		●	●	●
Visualize	●	●	●	●
Craft and Structure				
Determine the meaning of words and phrases in a text	●	●	●	●
Unknown words	●	●	●	●
Multiple-meaning words	●	●	●	●
Figurative language (hyperbole, simile, metaphor, personification)	●	●	●	●
Connotative meaning		●	●	●
Determine the effect of words and phrases in a text	●	●	●	●
Analyze author's style and tone		●	●	●
Recognize and analyze literary devices and elements	●	●	●	●
Alliteration		●	●	●
Allusion			●	●
Analogy			●	●

READING, continued	Fundamentals/ Inside Phonics/ Inside the U.S.A.	Level A	Level B	Level C
Assonance and consonance		•	•	•
Description	•	•	•	•
Dialogue and dialect	•	•	•	•
Imagery/sensory language	•	•	•	•
Irony		•	•	•
Jargon			•	•
Narrator		•	•	•
Onomatopoeia			•	•
Paradox			•	•
Repetition	•	•	•	•
Symbolism		•	•	•
Analyze structure of literature	•	•	•	•
Climax		•	•	•
Flashback		•	•	•
Suspense, mystery, or surprise		•	•	•
Foreshadowing			•	•
Compare text structures	•	•	•	•
Recognize genres	•	•	•	•
Drama	•	•	•	•
Fantasy		•	•	•
Folk literature	•	•	•	•
Historical fiction	•	•	•	•
Novel		•	•	•
Parody			•	•
Poetry	•	•	•	•
Realistic fiction	•	•	•	•
Script	•	•	•	•
Short story	•	•	•	•
Song lyrics	•	•	•	•
Analyze elements of poetry	•	•	•	•
Rhyme and rhyme scheme	•	•	•	•
Rhythm and meter	•	•	•	•
Imagery	•	•	•	•
Analyze elements of drama (stage directions, dialogue)	•	•	•	•
Analyze author's purpose		•	•	•
Analyze point of view and viewpoint	•	•	•	•
Analyze cultural perspectives in literature	•	•	•	•
Integration of Knowledge and Ideas				
Compare	•	•	•	•
Compare texts	•	•	•	•
Compare text with oral or visual representations	•	•	•	•
Analyze multimedia features	•	•	•	•
Relate a piece of literature to its source				•

Scope and Sequence, continued

READING, continued	Fundamentals/ Inside Phonics/ Inside the U.S.A.	Level A	Level B	Level C
Range of Reading and Level of Text Complexity				
Read and comprehend literature	●	●	●	●
Instructional-level texts	●	●	●	●
Complex texts	●	●	●	●
Independent-level texts	●	●	●	●
Identify opportunities for reading improvement	●	●	●	●
Identify, assess, and apply effective reading strategies	●	●	●	●
Read collaboratively	●	●	●	●
Read for a variety of purposes	●	●	●	●
Read independently for sustained periods	●	●	●	●
Read widely	●	●	●	●
Apply literature to personal life	●	●	●	●
Respond to literature in a variety of ways	●	●	●	●
Defend interpretations of and responses to literature	●	●	●	●
Recognize that literature may elicit a variety of valid responses	●	●	●	●
INFORMATIONAL TEXT				
Key Ideas and Details				
Use text evidence	●	●	●	●
Explicit evidence	●	●	●	●
Implicit evidence	●	●	●	●
Identify and analyze main idea and details	●	●	●	●
Summarize, retell, or explain a text	●	●	●	●
Use reading strategies	●	●	●	●
Plan and monitor	●	●	●	●
Preview and set a purpose	●	●	●	●
Make and confirm predictions	●	●	●	●
Clarify ideas and vocabulary	●	●	●	●
Determine importance	●	●	●	●
Relate main ideas and details	●	●	●	●
Summarize	●	●	●	●
Ask questions	●	●	●	●
Make inferences	●	●	●	●
Make connections	●	●	●	●
Synthesize	●	●	●	●
Draw conclusions		●	●	●
Compare across texts	●	●	●	●
Form generalizations		●	●	●
Visualize	●	●	●	●
Analyze development of ideas		●	●	●
Relate ideas	●	●	●	●
Events in a sequence	●	●	●	●
Steps in a process		●	●	●
Cause and effect	●	●	●	●
Main idea to details	●	●	●	●
Conflict and resolution		●	●	●

READING, continued	Fundamentals/ Inside Phonics/ Inside the U.S.A.	Level A	Level B	Level C
Craft and Structure				
Determine the meaning of words and phrases in a text	•	•	•	•
Unknown words	•	•	•	•
Multiple-meaning words	•	•	•	•
Figurative language (hyperbole, simile, metaphor, personification)	•	•	•	•
Connotative meaning		•	•	•
Determine the effect of words and phrases in a text	•	•	•	•
Analyze author's style and tone		•	•	•
Analyze text structure	•	•	•	•
Chronology	•	•	•	•
Main idea and details	•	•	•	•
Cause and effect	•	•	•	•
Problem and solution	•	•	•	•
Logical order	•	•	•	•
Argument		•	•	•
Compare text structures	•	•	•	•
Analyze author's purpose		•	•	•
Analyze viewpoint		•	•	•
Analyze rhetorical devices		•	•	•
Recognize genres	•	•	•	•
Article	•	•	•	•
Autobiography	•	•	•	•
Biography	•	•	•	•
Diary/journal	•	•	•	•
Editorial	•	•	•	•
Electronic texts	•	•	•	•
Essay	•	•	•	•
Functional texts (business, consumer, everyday, technical)	•	•	•	•
Humor	•	•	•	•
Interview	•	•	•	•
Literary criticism			•	•
Memoir	•	•	•	•
Personal narrative	•	•	•	•
Report		•	•	•
Review	•	•	•	•
Speech	•	•	•	•
Textbook/encyclopedia	•	•	•	•
Integration of Knowledge and Ideas				
Analyze text features	•	•	•	•
Interpret visuals	•	•	•	•
Compare	•	•	•	•
Compare texts	•	•	•	•
Compare text with oral, media, or visual representations		•	•	•
Analyze arguments	•	•	•	•

Scope and Sequence, continued

READING, continued	Fundamentals/ Inside Phonics/ Inside the U.S.A.	Level A	Level B	Level C
Distinguish fact from opinion	●	●	●	●
Identify discrepancies and missing information		●	●	●
Evaluate reasons (valid or fallacious)		●	●	●
Evaluate evidence (relevant, sufficient)		●	●	●
Analyze counter-arguments		●	●	●
Analyze seminal documents		●	●	●
Range of Reading and Level of Text Complexity				
Read and comprehend text	●	●	●	●
Instructional-level texts	●	●	●	●
Complex texts	●	●	●	●
Independent-level texts	●	●	●	●
Identify opportunities for reading improvement	●	●	●	●
Identify, assess, and apply effective reading strategies	●	●	●	●
Read collaboratively	●	●	●	●
Read for a variety of purposes	●	●	●	●
Read independently for sustained periods	●	●	●	●
Read widely	●	●	●	●
Use texts to build knowledge	●	●	●	●
Use texts for research projects	●	●	●	●
Apply texts to personal life	●	●	●	●
Respond to texts in a variety of ways	●	●	●	●
Defend interpretations of and responses to texts	●	●	●	●
Recognize that texts may elicit a variety of valid responses	●	●	●	●
FOUNDATIONAL SKILLS				
Print Concepts				
Understand directionality of text	●			
Recognize the relationship of letters and words to speech	●			
Understand spaces between words	●			
Recognize and name alphabet letters	●			
Identify and distinguish uppercase and lowercase letters	●			
Recognize sentence punctuation	●			
Identify a sentence	●			

Use *Inside Phonics* to provide intervention for Foundational Reading Skills.

Phonological Awareness	Fundamentals/ Inside Phonics/ Inside the U.S.A.	Level A	Level B	Level C
Distinguish long and short vowel sounds	●			
Isolate words in a sentence	●			
Identify syllables	●			
Blend syllables to form a word	●			
Segment a word into syllables	●			
Identify rhyming words	●			
Generate rhyming words	●			
Match initial, medial, and final sounds	●			
Identify and isolate initial, medial, and final sounds	●			
Blend onset and rime	●			
Blend sounds to form a word	●			
Segment a word into sounds	●			
Manipulate sounds in words (add, delete, substitute)	●			

Use *Inside Phonics* to provide intervention for Foundational Reading Skills.

READING, continued	Fundamentals/ Inside Phonics/ Inside the U.S.A.	Level A	Level B	Level C
Phonics and Word Recognition				
Identify letter/sounds and read words	•			
Consonants	•			
Short vowels	•			
Long vowels	•			
Consonant blends and digraphs	•			
Vowel digraphs: *ai, ay, ee, ea, ie, igh, oa, ow, ui, ue*	•			
r-controlled vowels: *ar, or, er, ir, ur, air, eer, ear*	•			
Sounds for -*y*: /ē/, /ī/	•			
Diphthongs: *oi, oy, ou, ow*	•			
Variant vowels: *aw, au, al, all, oo, ew*	•			
Soft *c* and soft *g*	•			
Silent consonants *gn, kn, wr, dge, mb*	•			
Plurals -*s*, -*es*, -*ies*	•			
Read words with spelling patterns	•			
CVC*e* word patterns with *a, i, o, u, e*	•			
CV word patterns with *o, e*	•			
Short and long vowels in CVC and CVC*e* word patterns	•			
CVVC word patterns	•			
Read multisyllabic words	•			
VCCV syllable division (bas/ket, kit/ten)	•			
VCCCV syllable division (hun/dred)	•			
VCV syllable division (mu/sic, cab/in)	•			
Words with consonant + *le*	•			
Suffixes and prefixes	•			
Inflected forms	•			
Syllable types: *r*-controlled, consonant + *le*, vowel team, vowel + silent *e*	•			
Use decoding strategies	•			
Blend sounds to decode words	•			
Blend sounds to decode words	•			
Recognize word families and similarly spelled words	•			
Use structural clues	•			
Identify syllable types	•			
Recognize high frequency words	•			
Distinguish between similarly spelled words	•			
Read irregularly spelled words	•			
Fluency				
Read with purpose and understanding	•	•	•	•
Read with accuracy and appropriate rate	•	•	•	•
Use phrasing	•	•	•	•
Read with expression	•	•	•	•
Read with correct intonation	•	•	•	•
Read instructional-level materials fluently	•	•	•	•
Use context to support decoding	•	•	•	•

Use *Inside Phonics* to provide intervention for Foundational Reading Skills.

Scope and Sequence, continued

WRITING	Fundamentals/ Inside Phonics/ Inside the U.S.A.	Level A	Level B	Level C
Text Types and Purposes				
Write arguments	●	●	●	●
Present precise, well-defended claims	●	●	●	●
Provide valid reasons	●	●	●	●
Supply relevant and sufficient evidence	●	●	●	●
Develop counterclaims	●	●	●	●
Relate claim, counterclaim, reasons and evidence	●	●	●	●
Use words, phrases, and clauses to link the text and to clarify relationships	●	●	●	●
Establish and maintain a formal style	●	●	●	●
Provide a concluding statement	●	●	●	●
Write informative/explanatory texts	●	●	●	●
Introduce a topic	●	●	●	●
Organize ideas and information	●	●	●	●
Include text features		●	●	●
Include relevant and sufficient facts, details, or other information	●	●	●	●
Use transitions to link the text and to clarify the relationships	●	●	●	●
Use precise language and vocabulary	●	●	●	●
Establish and maintain a formal style	●	●	●	●
Provide a concluding statement	●	●	●	●
Write narratives	●	●	●	●
Introduce a problem, situation, or observation	●	●	●	●
Establish a point of view	●	●	●	●
Introduce a narrator and/or characters	●	●	●	●
Use narrative techniques (dialog, pacing, description, etc.)	●	●	●	●
Create a coherent sequence of events	●	●	●	●
Use precise words and phrases to convey a vivid picture	●	●	●	●
Provide a conclusion	●	●	●	●
Write to demonstrate comprehension	●	●	●	●
Write to respond to reading	●	●	●	●
Write as a way of learning	●	●	●	●
Write to sources	●	●	●	●
Write to summarize	●	●	●	●
Production and Distribution of Writing				
Write for a variety of audiences	●	●	●	●
Write for a variety of purposes	●	●	●	●
Write in a variety of forms	●	●	●	●
Description of a process		●	●	●
News article		●	●	●
Personal/autobiographical narrative	●	●	●	●
Persuasive essay/position paper	●	●	●	●
Problem-solution essay	●	●		
Research report/literary research report	●	●	●	●
Response to literature		●	●	●
Short story	●	●	●	●

WRITING, continued	Fundamentals/ Inside Phonics/ Inside the U.S.A.	Level A	Level B	Level C
Prewrite	●	●	●	●
Analyze a model	●	●	●	●
Determine the role, audience, form, and topic	●	●	●	●
Organize ideas	●	●	●	●
Draft	●	●	●	●
Use appropriate development and organization	●	●	●	●
Use technology to produce writing	●	●	●	●
Revise	●	●	●	●
Give and respond to peer suggestions	●	●	●	●
Add, combine, or delete details	●	●	●	●
Edit and proofread	●	●	●	●
Publish and present *See also* Speaking and Listening	●	●	●	●
Use visuals or multimedia to enhance meaning	●	●	●	●
Maintain a portfolio	●	●	●	●
Writing Traits	●	●	●	●
Development of ideas	●	●	●	●
Organization	●	●	●	●
Voice and style	●	●	●	●
Focus and unity	●	●	●	●
Written conventions	●	●	●	●
Research to Build and Present Knowledge				
Use the research process and the language of research	●	●	●	●
Conduct short research projects	●	●	●	●
Conduct more sustained research projects	●	●	●	●
Recall or gather information	●	●	●	●
Choose and focus a topic	●	●	●	●
Generate and develop research questions	●	●	●	●
Independent questions	●	●	●	●
Text-based questions	●	●	●	●
Locate and choose appropriate sources of information	●	●	●	●
Gather information	●	●	●	●
Analyze, evaluate, and use information		●	●	●
Integrate and synthesize information from multiple sources	●	●	●	●
Take and sort notes	●	●	●	●
Distinguish plagiarism from quoting or paraphrasing		●	●	●
Distinguish relevant from irrelevant information		●	●	●
Integrate quotations and citations		●	●	●
Convert data into graphic aids		●	●	●
Draw evidence from text to support analysis, reflection, and research	●	●	●	●
Provide a list of sources	●	●	●	●
Evaluate a research report and draw conclusions		●	●	●
Draw questions for further study from the conclusions		●	●	●

Scope and Sequence, continued

WRITING, continued	Fundamentals/ Inside Phonics/ Inside the U.S.A.	Level A	Level B	Level C
Range of Writing				
Write routinely over extended time frames	●	●	●	●
Write routinely over shorter time frames	●	●	●	●
SPEAKING AND LISTENING				
Comprehension and Collaboration				
Engage in collaborative discussions	●	●	●	●
Follow agreed-upon rules for discussion	●	●	●	●
Build on and connect others' ideas	●	●	●	●
Come to discussions prepared	●	●	●	●
Ask and answer questions for information, clarification, or understanding	●	●	●	●
Respond to questions with appropriate elaboration	●	●	●	●
Explain and review ideas and understanding	●	●	●	●
Express opinions, ideas, feelings, needs, and intentions	●	●	●	●
Restate ideas	●	●	●	●
Define and explain	●	●	●	●
Elaborate	●	●	●	●
Compare and contrast	●	●	●	●
Persuade		●	●	●
Negotiate			●	●
Verify or confirm information		●	●	●
Evaluate information presented in diverse media and formats	●	●	●	●
Analyze/evaluate a message		●	●	●
Integrate and evaluate media elements including visual, functional and auditory details	●	●	●	●
Evaluate a speaker's viewpoint	●	●	●	●
Evaluate a speaker's reasons and evidence	●	●	●	●
Listen actively	●	●	●	●
Listen for a purpose	●	●	●	●
Presentation of Knowledge and Ideas				
Present information	●	●	●	●
Describe a process		●	●	●
Describe people, places, and things, and actions	●	●	●	●
Describe with facts and details	●	●	●	●
Give and follow directions		●	●	●
Justify			●	●
Organize ideas	●	●	●	●
Persuade	●	●	●	●
Present ideas clearly, concisely, and logically	●	●	●	●
Provide supporting evidence	●	●	●	●
Engage in academic oral language activities	●	●	●	●
Ad campaign		●	●	
Choral reading and reader's theatre	●	●	●	
Conversation and classroom discussion	●	●	●	●
Debate		●	●	●
Demonstration	●	●	●	●

SPEAKING AND LISTENING, continued	Fundamentals/ Inside Phonics/ Inside the U.S.A.	Level A	Level B	Level C
Documentary		•	•	
Dramatization	•	•	•	•
Evaluation		•	•	•
Extemporaneous talk				•
Interview	•	•	•	•
Narrative presentation	•	•	•	•
Oral interpretation of literature		•	•	•
Oral report or presentation		•	•	•
Panel discussion		•	•	•
Persuasive speech		•		•
Political campaign		•		•
Press conference		•	•	•
Radio drama/podcast		•		
Reality TV show		•	•	•
Recommendation	•	•	•	•
Response to literature	•	•	•	•
Review		•	•	
Speech		•	•	•
Summary	•	•	•	•
TV talk show		•	•	
Use good presentation skills	•	•	•	•
Add visual, audio, or multimedia support	•	•	•	•
Adapt speech to the context and task	•	•	•	•
Produce complete sentences	•	•	•	•
Use appropriate language	•	•	•	•
Speak clearly, at an appropriate pace	•	•	•	•
LANGUAGE				
Conventions of Standard English				
Sentences	•	•	•	•
Statements, questions, exclamations, and commands	•	•	•	•
Negative sentences	•	•	•	•
Compound sentences	•	•	•	•
Complex sentences		•	•	•
Compound-complex sentences				•
Complete subject	•	•	•	•
Simple subject	•	•	•	•
Compound subject	•	•	•	•
Complete predicate	•	•	•	•
Simple Predicate	•	•	•	•
Compound predicate	•	•	•	•
Complete sentences	•	•	•	•
Fragment/dependent clause	•	•	•	•
Independent clause	•	•	•	•
Phrases	•	•	•	•
Run-on sentences		•	•	•

Scope and Sequence, continued

LANGUAGE, continued	Fundamentals/ Inside Phonics/ Inside the U.S.A.	Level A	Level B	Level C
Subject-verb agreement	●	●	●	●
Combining sentences		●	●	●
Parallel structure	●	●	●	●
Sentence variety		●	●	●
Parts of Speech	●	●	●	●
Nouns	●	●	●	●
Common and proper	●	●	●	●
Count and noncount	●	●	●	●
Plurals	●	●	●	●
Possessive	●	●	●	●
Articles/determiners	●	●	●	●
Pronouns	●	●	●	●
Subject	●	●	●	●
Object	●	●	●	●
Demonstrative	●	●	●	●
Indefinite		●	●	●
Reflexive		●	●	●
Relative			●	●
Possessive	●	●	●	●
Pronoun agreement	●	●	●	●
Adjectives	●	●	●	●
Comparative and superlative	●	●	●	●
Relative			●	●
Demonstrative		●	●	●
Predicate		●	●	●
Possessive	●	●	●	●
Indefinite		●	●	●
Proper		●	●	●
Order within sentences	●	●	●	●
Verbs	●	●	●	●
Action	●	●	●	●
Transitive/intransitive			●	●
Linking	●	●	●	●
Modals	●	●	●	●
Helping	●	●	●	●
Present tense	●	●	●	●
Past tense (regular and irregular)	●	●	●	●
Future tense	●	●	●	●
Present-perfect tense	●	●	●	●
Past-perfect tense	●		●	●
Future-perfect tense			●	●
Progressive forms	●	●	●	●
Verbals		●	●	●
Gerunds			●	●
Infinitives			●	●
Participles			●	●

LANGUAGE, continued	Fundamentals/ Inside Phonics/ Inside the U.S.A.	Level A	Level B	Level C
Contractions	•	•	•	•
Adverbs	•	•	•	•
Comparative and superlative		•	•	•
Adverbial clauses		•	•	•
Prepositions	•	•	•	•
Prepositional phrases	•	•	•	•
Conjunctions		•	•	•
Interjections		•	•	•
Mechanics	•	•	•	•
Capitalization	•	•	•	•
End Punctuation	•	•	•	•
Comma	•	•	•	•
Colon		•	•	•
Semicolon		•	•	•
Apostrophe	•	•	•	•
Quotation marks		•	•	•
Parentheses		•	•	•
Dash		•	•	•
Underlining or italics		•	•	•
Spelling	•	•	•	•
High frequency words	•			
Use phonetic knowledge to spell	•			
Consult reference materials to check spelling	•	•	•	•
Use spelling patterns	•	•	•	•
Homonyms		•	•	•
Prefixes and suffixes		•	•	•
Knowledge of Language				
Use social and academic language functions	•	•	•	•
Listen actively	•	•	•	•
Repeat spoken language	•			
Express social courtesies	•			
Ask and answer questions	•	•	•	•
Use a telephone	•			
Conduct a transaction	•			
Demonstrate nonverbal communication	•	•	•	•
Express likes and dislikes	•	•	•	•
Make and respond to requests and commands	•	•	•	•
Give and follow directions	•	•	•	•
Ask for and give information	•	•	•	•
Retell a story	•	•	•	•
Listen to a selection	•	•	•	•
Recite	•	•	•	•
Read a selection	•	•	•	•
Role-play	•	•	•	•
Interpret nonverbal communication	•	•	•	•

Scope and Sequence, continued

LANGUAGE, continued	Fundamentals/ Inside Phonics/ Inside the U.S.A.	Level A	Level B	Level C
Use social and academic language functions, *continued*	●	●	●	●
Tell an original story	●	●	●	●
Clarify information		●	●	●
Justify		●	●	●
Evaluate		●	●	●
Compare formal and informal uses of English	●	●	●	●
Recognize the difference between spoken and written English	●	●	●	●
Choose words and phrases for effect		●	●	●
Choose punctuation for effect	●	●	●	●
Maintain consistency in style and tone		●	●	●
Vary sentences for meaning, interest, and style	●	●	●	●
Identify and use language appropriate to the context	●	●	●	●
Vocabulary Acquisition and Use				
Determine meanings of unfamiliar and multiple-meaning words	●	●	●	●
Use inflections and affixes		●	●	●
Use context	●	●	●	●
Use root words	●	●	●	●
Use Latin, Greek, and Anglo-Saxon Roots		●	●	●
Use prefixes and suffixes	●	●	●	●
Use word families	●	●	●	●
Use multiple-meaning words	●	●	●	●
Identify jargon	●	●	●	●
Use a glossary, dictionary, and thesaurus	●	●	●	●
Specialized vocabulary	●	●	●	●
Explore word relationships	●	●	●	●
Categorize words	●	●	●	●
Identify antonyms	●	●	●	●
Identify synonyms	●	●	●	●
Identify connotation and denotation		●	●	●
Distinguish shades of meaning		●	●	●
Identify feeling words and sensory words	●	●	●	●
Distinguish literal from nonliteral meaning	●	●	●	●
Use analogies		●	●	●
Figurative and literary language	●	●	●	●
Explain similes	●	●	●	●
Explain metaphors	●	●	●	●
Identify personification		●	●	●
Interpret idioms, expressions, dialect, adages, proverbs, and sayings	●	●	●	●
Acquire and use academic vocabulary	●	●	●	●
Acquire and use domain-specific vocabulary	●	●	●	●

LANGUAGE, continued	Fundamentals/ Inside Phonics/ Inside the U.S.A.	Level A	Level B	Level C
Use learning strategies	●	●	●	●
Listen to and imitate others	●			
Reproduce teacher-modeled writing	●	●	●	●
Use gestures and mime to communicate ideas	●	●	●	●
Memorize	●	●	●	●
Incorporate language "chunks"	●	●	●	●
Practice new language	●	●	●	●
Use visuals to construct or clarify meaning	●	●	●	●
Semantic mapping	●	●	●	●
Use imagery	●	●	●	●
Review	●	●	●	●
Ask for help, feedback, and clarification	●	●	●	●
Take risks and explore alternative ways of saying things (circumlocution)	●	●	●	●
Identify and respond appropriately to nonverbal and verbal clues	●	●	●	●
Test hypothesis about language	●	●	●	●
Use prior knowledge	●	●	●	●
Make connections across content areas	●	●	●	●
Take notes about language	●	●	●	●
Compare elements of language and identify patterns	●	●	●	●
Compare written language conventions	●	●	●	●
Use reference aids	●	●	●	●
Self-monitor language use and self-assess	●	●	●	●
Use test-taking strategies	●	●	●	●
Use study skills and strategies	●	●	●	●
Acquire and maintain cultural perspectives	●	●	●	●
Multicultural awareness and appreciation	●	●	●	●
Appreciate, share, and compare aspects of the home, U.S., and world cultures	●	●	●	●
Analyze universal themes across texts		●	●	●
Analyze and compare discourse patterns across cultures		●	●	●
Demonstrate sensitivity to gender, age, social position, and culture	●	●	●	●

Index of Skills

D

E

F

G

H

T

U

V

Program Features and Resources Index

Indices of Authors and Titles & Art and Artists

Index of Authors and Titles

Author
Author biographical information
Fiction, poetry, and drama selections
Nonfiction selections

page 983

Index of Authors and Titles, continued

page 984

Index of Art and Artists

page 985

Acknowledgments

Acknowledgments, continued from page ii

Text

Teresa Palomo Acosta: "My Mother Pieced Quilts" by Teresa Palomo Acosta from *Festival de Flor y Canto*. Copyright © by Teresa Paloma Acosta. Used by permission of the author.

Alfred Publishing Co., Inc.: " I Am Somebody" words and music by Joseph Saddler, Nathaniel Glover, and Larry Dukes. Copyright © 1987 by WB Music Corp., E/A Music, Inc. and Grandmaster Flash Publishing, Inc. All rights administered by WB Music Corp. All rights reserved. Used by permission of Alfred Publishing Co., Inc.

Annick Press: "Ad Power" from *Made You Look* by Shari Graydon. Copyright © 2003 by Shari Graydon. Published by Annick Press. Reprinted with permission.

Arte Publico Press: "Legal Alien" from *Chants* by Pat Mora. Copyright © 1985 by Pat Mora. Recorded with permission from Arte Publico Press-University of Houston.

Susan Bergholz Literary Services: "A Smart Cookie" from *The House on Mango Street* by Sandra Cisneros. Copyright © 1984 by Sandra Cisneros. Published by Vintage Books, a division of Random House, Inc., New York, and in hardcover by Alfred A. Knopf in 1994. Reprinted by permission of Susan Bergholz Literary Services, New York. All rights reserved.

"My Father Is a Simple Man" by Luis Omar Salinas from *The Sadness of Days*. Copyright © 1987. Reprinted by permission of Susan Bergholz Literary Services, New York. All rights reserved.

Cartoonbank: "Guilt-Powered Car" by Mick Stevens. Copyright © 2001 Mick Stevens; "Shouldn't Willis be…" by Gahan Wilson. Copyright © 1999 Gahan Wilson. All cartoons copyright *The New Yorker* Collection from cartoonbank.com. All rights reserved. Reprinted with permission.

Center for Media Literacy: "A Long Way to Go: Minorities and the Media" by Carlos Cortes, from *Media 7 Values*, Issue 38, Winter, 1987. Copyright © 1987 by the Center for Media Literacy, www.medialit.org. Used by permission.

Curtis Brown: "The Baby-Sitter" by Jane Yolen from *Things That Go Bump in the Night*. Copyright © 1989 by Jane Yolen, published by HarperCollins. Reprinted by permission of Curtis Brown, Ltd.

Excerpt from *The Creativity Crisis* by Po Bronson and Ashley Merryman. Copyright © 2010 by Po Bronson and Ashley Merryman. Used by permission of Curtis Brown, Ltd.

Enslow Publishers: Adapted from *Advertising Information of Manipulation?* by Nancy Day. Copyright © 1999 by Nancy Day. Published by Enslow Publishers, Inc., Berkeley Heights, NJ. All rights reserved. Reprinted with permission.

Eric Feil: "The World Is in Their Hands" by Eric Feil from *Inspire Your World*. Used by permission of the author.

Farrar, Straus and Giroux: "Thank You, M'am" by Langston Hughes from *Short Stories*. Copyright © 1996 by Ramona Bass and Arnold Rampersad. Reprinted by permission of Hill and Wang, a division of Farrar, Starus and Giroux, LLC.

HarperCollins: "Curtis G. Aikens Sr." by Dan Rather from *The American Dream*. Copyright © 2001 by Dan Rather. Reprinted by permission of HarperCollins Publishers.

Joel Hoffmam: "Puddle" by Arthur Porges from *Alfred Hitchcock's Mystery Magazine*. Copyright © 1972 by Arthur Porges. Reprinted by permission of Joel Hoffman.

Henry Holt: "Nothing Gold Can Stay" by Robert Frost from the *Poetry of Robert Frost*, edited by Edward Connery Lathem. Copyright © 1987 by Henry Holt and Company By permission.

Houghton Mifflin Harcourt: "Without Commercials" by Alice Walker from *Horses Make a Landscape Look More Beautiful: Poems by Alice Walker*. Copyright © 1984 by Alice Walker, reprinted by permission of Houghton Mifflin Harcourt Publishing Corporation. All rights reserved.

Learning Seed: "How to Detect Bias in the News" by Jeffrey Schank/Learning Seed. Reprinted by permission of Learning Seed LLC.

Hal Leonard: "If There Be Pain" by Tupac Shakur. Copyright © 2000 Microhits Music Corp. Reprinted by permission of Hal Leonard.

"Hero," words and music by Walter Afanasieff and Mariah Carey. Copyright © 1993 WB Music Corp., Wallyworld Music, Songs of Universal, Inc., and Rye Songs. All rights on behalf of itself and Wallyworld Music administered by WB Music Corp. All rights for Rye Songs administered by Songs of Universal, Inc. All rights reserved. Used by permission.

Life: "In the Heart of a Hero" by Johnny Dwyer from *Life*, November 2005. Copyright © 2005 by Life Inc. Reprinted with permission. All rights reserved.

Lowe Worldwide: "Got Milk?" by permission of the National Fluid Milk Processor Promotion Board and Lowe Worldwide, Inc.

Lowenstein-Yost Associates: "Beware: Do Not Read This Poem" from *Ishmael Reed: New and Collected Poems,1964–2006*. Copyright © 1988 by Ishmael Reed. Permission granted by Lowenstein-Yost Associates, Inc.

Katy Murphy: "Never a Dull Friday Night" by Katy Murphy from the *Oakland Tribune*, March 27, 2006. Reprinted by permission.

McClatchy-Tribune Information Services: "Miami Pilot Dubbed 'Emerging Explorer' by National Geographic" from the *Miami Herald*, June 5, 2012, Copyright © 2012 the McClatchy Company. Used by permission of The McClatchy Company.

"Author Brings Back Memories of Not So Long Ago" by Yvette Cabrera from the *Orange County Register*, April 15, 2002. Copyright © 2002 by the McClatchy-Tribune Information Services. All rights reserved. Reprinted with permission.

National Geographic Society: "Was There a Real King Arthur?" by Robert Steward from *Mysteries of History*. Copyright © 2003 by the National Geographic Society. Reprinted with permission of the National Geographic Society.

Pearson Education, Inc.: "The Tell-Tale Heart" from *Great American Short Stories* retold by Emily Hutchinson. Copyright © 1994 by Pearson Education, Inc., publishing as AGS Globe. Used by permission.

Penguin Group (USA) Inc.: "Euphoria" by Lauren Brown. Copyright © 2000 by 17th Street Productions. by permission of Viking Penguin, A Division of Penguin Young Readers Group, A Member of Penguin Group (USA) Inc., 345 Hudson Street, New York, NY 10014. All rights reserved.

What Is Slam Poetry?" by Cecily Von Ziegesar, copyright © 2000, from *Slam*, edited by Cecily Von Ziegesar. Used by permission of Viking Penguin, a division of Penguin Group (USA) Inc.

Excerpt from *The Grapes of Wrath* by John Steinbeck. Copyright © 1939, renewed 1967 by John Steinbeck. Used by permission of Viking Penguin, a division of Penguin Group (USA) Inc.

"The Sword in the Stone," from *King Arthur and the Legends of Camelot* by Molly Perham. Copyright © 1993 by Molly Perham. Used by permission of Viking Penguin, A Division of Penguin Young Readers Group, A Member of Penguin Group (USA) Inc., 345 Hudson Street, New York, NY 10014. All rights reserved.

Philadelphia Inquirer: "The Fast and the Fuel Efficient" by Akweli Parker from the Philadelphia Inquirer, April 16, 2006. Copyright © 2006 by the *Philadelphia Inquirer*. Reprinted with permission of the Philadelphia Inquirer, all rights reserved.

Public Broadcasting Service: "What Is News?" from Greater Washington Educational Telecommunications Association, source: pbs.org.

Random House: "Human Family" from *I Shall Not Be Moved* by Maya Angelou Copyright © 1990 by Maya Angelou. Used by permission of Random House, Inc.

"The Good Samaritan" from *Finding Our Way* by René Saldaña, Jr. Copyright © 2003 by René Saldaña Jr. Used by permission of Random House Children's Books, a division of Random House, Inc.

"I, Too" by Langston Hughes from *The Collected Poems of Langston Hughes*. Copyright © 1994 by the Estate of Langston Hughes. Used by permission of Random House, Inc.

"A Message for Black Teenagers" from *Magic Johnson: My Life by Earvin "Magic" Johnson*. Copyright © 1992 by June Bug Enterprises. Used by permission of Random House, Inc.

Excerpt from *A Raisin in the Sun* by Lorraine Hansberry. Copyright © 1958 by Robert Nemiroff, as an unpublished work. Copyright © 1959, 1966, 1984 by Robert Nemiroff. Copyright renewed 1986, 1987 by Robert Nemiroff. Caution: Professionals and amateurs are hereby warned that A Raisin in the Sun, being fully protected under the Copyright Laws of the United States of America, the British Empire, including the Dominion of Canada, and all other countries of the Universal Copyright and Berne Conventions, is subject to royalty. All rights, including professional, amateur, motion picture, recitation, lecturing, public reading, radio and television broadcasting, and the rights of translation into foreign languages, are strictly reserved. Particular emphasis is laid on the question of readings, permission for which must be secured in writing. All inquiries should be addressed to the William Morris Agency, 1350 Avenue of the Americas, New York, NY 10019, authorized agents for the Estate of Lorraine Hansberry and for Robert Nemiroff, Executor. Used by permission of Random House, Inc.

"What's Wrong with Advertising" from *Ogilvy on Advertising* by David Ogilvy. Copyright ©1985 by David Ogilvy. Reprinted by permission of Carlton Publishing Group. Used by permission of Random House, Inc.

page 986

"The Woman in the Snow" from *The Dark Thirty* by Patricia C. McKissack. Copyright © 1992 by Patricia C. McKissack. Used by permission of Alfred A. Knopf, an imprint of Random House Children's Books, a division of Random House, Inc. Used by permission of Random House, Inc.

Scholastic: "A Job for Valentin" from *An Island Like You* by Judith Ortiz Cofer. Copyright © 1995 by Judith Ortiz Cofer. Reprinted by permission of Scholastic Inc.

"A Raisin in the Sun" by Lorraine Hansberry, adapted by Rachel Waugh, *Scholastic Scope*, September 20, 2004. Reprinted by permission of Scholastic Inc.

Interview excerpted from "Interview with Stephen King" by Byron Cahill, from *Writing*. Copyright © 2005 by Weekly Reader. Used by permission of Scholastic Inc.

"Slam: Performance Poetry Lives On" from *Writing*, April/May 2005. Copyright © 2005 by Weekly Reader. Special permission granted by Scholastic Inc. All rights reserved.

Simon & Schuster: "The Fashion Show" adapted from *The Other Side of the Sky* by Farah Ahmedi with Tamim Ansary. Text © 2005 Nestegg Productions LLC. Used with the permission of Simon Spotlight Entertainment, an imprint of Simon & Schuster Children's Publishing Division.

Efrem Smith: "Hip-Hop as Culture" by Reverend Efrem Smith. Reprinted by permission of the author.

Nancy Stauffer Associates: "Superman and Me" by Sherman Alexie from *The Most Wonderful Books: Writers on Discovering the Pleasures of Reading*, edited by Michael Dorris and Emilie Buchwald. Copyright © 1997 by Sherman Alexie. All rights reserved. Reprinted by permission.

Richard Thompson: "Teens Open Doors" by Richard Thompson from the *Boston Globe*, June 29, 2006. Copyright © 2006 by Richard Thompson. Reprinted by permission of the author.

Time: "The Hidden Secrets of the Creative Mind" by Francine Russo from *Time*, January 16, 2006. Copyright © 2006 by Time Inc. Reprinted by permission.

"Rosa Parks" by Rita Dove from "Time's 100 Most Important People of the Century" from *Time*, June 14, 1999. Copyright © 1999 Time Inc. Reprinted by permission.

Tribune Media Services: "Is Google Making Us Stupid?" by Nicholas Carr from *The Atlantic*, July 1, 2008. Copyright © 2008 by the Atlantic Media Co. Used by permission of Tribune Media Services. Reprinted by permission.

WGBH/Boston: "Juvenile Justice" from Frontline/WGBH Educational Foundation. Copyright © 2005 WGBH/Boston. Used by permission.

What Kids Can Do: "Creativity at Work" by Abe Louise Young, from the website "What Kids Can Do." Reprinted by permission of What Kids Can Do, Inc.

Nellie Wong: "Where Is My Country?" by Nellie Wong from *Chinese American Poetry: An Anthology*, edited by L. Ling-Chi Wang and Henry Yiheng Zhao. Copyright © 1987 by Nellie Wong. Reprinted by permission of the author.

Youth Philanthropy Worldwide: "Schools for Indigenous Children" from *Youth Philanthropy Worldwide*, April 2006. Reprinted by permission of Youth Philanthropy Worldwide.

Photo Credits

iv Rene Saldana. vii Magical Assortment, 2005 Peter Anton. Mixed media sculpture, private collection. **ix** Ethan Miller/Getty Images. **xi** The Life Line, 1864, Winslow Homer. Oil on canvas, Philadelphia Museum of Art/Superstock. **xiii** Trigal, 2004, Homero Aguilar. Oil on linen, private collection. **xv** George Tooker (1920-2011) Voice II, 1972 Tempera on panel National Academy Museum, New York, USA/The Bridgeman Art Library Courtesy of The Estate of George Tooker and DC Moore Gallery, New York. **xvii** John Eder/Getty Images. xix Dale Kennington/SuperStock. **xxiii** Lester Lefkowitz/CORBIS. 1 Magical Assortment, 2005 Peter Anton. Mixed media sculpture, private collection. **0-1** Amy Helene Johansson. **3** Sandpiper; Graphic Universe; Speak. **6** g215/Shutterstock. **7** Best View Stock/Shutterstock; David Katzenstein/CORBIS. 9 djem/Shutterstock. **10** Tetra Images/CORBIS; Ariel Skelley/CORBIS. **11** George Doyle/Getty Images. **12** Rene Saldana. **13** George Doyle/Getty Images. **14-15** Donald Gruener/Getty Images. **16** 2013/Polka Dot Images/Jupiterimages Corporation. **19** Emil Jacobsen/iStockphoto. 20 Stockbyte/Getty Images. **23** 2013 Fuse/CORBIS/Jupiterimages Corporation. **24** Donald Gruener/Getty Images. **26** William Whitehurst/CORBIS. **27** Damian Dovarganes/AP Images. **29** Tony Freeman/PhotoEdit, Inc. **31** Youth Service America 2007. **32** Michelle D. Bridwell/PhotoEdit, Inc. **34** XNR Productions; Shawn Henry; Youth Philanthropy Worldwide. **38** Jose Luis Pelaez, Inc./CORBIS; Bryan F. Peterson/CORBIS; RF/CORBIS. **40** Flying Colours Ltd; Rob Lewine/Getty Images. **41** 2013 The Jacob and Gwendolyn Lawrence Foundation, Seattle/Artists Rights Society (ARS), New York/Art Resource. **42** CORBIS. **43** 2013 The Jacob and Gwendolyn Lawrence Foundation, Seattle/Artists Rights Society (ARS), New York/Art Resource. **45** The City from Greenwich Village -John Sloan,1922 oil on canvas, National Gallery of Art, Washington D.C. **47** The Window, 1970, Bernard Safran. Oil on masonite, private collection; The Window, 1970, Bernard Safran. Oil on masonite, private collection. **49** Smithsonian American Art Museum, Washington, DC/Art Resource, NY; Liz Garza Williams. **52** From FRONTLINE Juvenile Justice website (http://www.pbs.org/wgbh/pages/frontline/shows/juvenile/bench/adulttime.html) 1995–2011 WGBH Educational Foundation; Ken Hurst/Shutterstock.com. **53** 2013 Comstock/JupiterImages Corporation. **54** Courtesy of FRONTLINE/WGBH Educational Foundation. Copyright 2005. WGBH/Boston/WGBH Media Library. **55** Courtesy of FRONTLINE/WGBH Educational Foundation. Copyright 2005. WGBH/Boston/WGBH Media Library. **56** Courtesy of FRONTLINE/WGBH Educational Foundation. Copyright 2005. WGBH/Boston/WGBH Media Library. **57** Courtesy of FRONTLINE/WGBH Educational Foundation. Copyright 2005. WGBH/Boston/WGBH Media Library. **58** From FRONTLINE Juvenile Justice website (http://www.pbs.org/wgbh/pages/frontline/shows/juvenile/bench/adulttime.html) 1995–2011 WGBH Educational Foundation. **60** Charles Barsotti/Cartoonbank. **63** Cleve Bryant/PhotoEdit, Inc. **64** Roger Tidman/CORBIS. **65** Karen Struthers/Shutterstock; Margherita Goldsmid, later Mrs Raphael (oil on canvas), Sargent, John Singer (1856-1925)/Private Collection/The Bridgeman Art Library. **66** Henry Guttmann/Getty Images. **67** Karen Struthers/Shutterstock.com; Margherita Goldsmid, later Mrs Raphael (oil on canvas), Sargent, John Singer (1856-1925)/Private Collection/The Bridgeman Art Library. **69** The Salon of Princess Mathilde (1820-1904) 1883 (oil on canvas), Nittis, Giuseppe or Joseph de (1846–84)/Pinacoteca Giuseppe de Nittis, Barletta, Italy/Alinari/The Bridgeman Art Library. **70** Alexander Mak/Shutterstock; Elio Ciol/CORBIS. **71** Elio Ciol/CORBIS; Elio Ciol/CORBIS. **73** 2013 Comstock/JupiterImages Corporation. **75** Scala/Art Resource, NY. **76** A Woman Ironing, 1873, Edgar Degas. Oil on canvas, The Metropolitan Museum of Art/Alamy. **77** Art Resource, NY. **81** Alyce Lytz. **82** Alyce Lytz. **84** Krisanne Johnson/White House via Getty Images. **86** Alyce Lytz. **90** John Vachon/Farm Security Administration/Office of War Information Photograph Collection/Library of Congress. **91, 92** Ralph Foster Archive, College of the Ozarks/VAGA. **93** Dorothea Lange/Farm Security Administration/Office of War Information Photograph Collection/Library of Congress. **94** Sandpiper; Graphic Universe; Speak. **95** Jeremy Walker/Getty Images; Christian Wheatley/iStockphoto; VisionsofAmerica/Joe Sohm/Getty Images. **101** Christian Wheatley/iStockphoto. **102-103** VisionsofAmerica/Joe Sohm/Getty Images. **110-111** REUTERS/Julie Adnam. **111** Ethan Miller/Getty Images. **112** Judie Long/Alamy. **113** Farrar, Straus and Giroux; Scholastic Paperbacks. **114** Digital Image The Museum of Modern Art/Licensed by SCALA/Art Resource, NY. 118 Maria Dryhout/Shutterstock. **119** Abe Louise Young/WKCD. **120** Ralph Freso/East Valley Tribune. **121** Abe Louise Young/WKCD. **122** Abe Louise Young/WKCD. **123** Abe Louise Young/WKCD; Abe Louise Young/WKCD; Abe Louise Young/WKCD. **124** Abe Louise Young/WKCD. **125** Abe Louise Young/WKCD; 2004 MJ Maloney. **126** Abe Louise Young/WKCD; Abe Louise Young/WKCD. **129** Ocean/CORBIS. **130** Matthias Kulka/zefa/CORBIS; Mark Harmel/Getty Images. **136** AP Photo/Plain Dealer, Lynn Ischay; Kelly-Mooney Photography/CORBIS; Alain Nogues/CORBIS. **138** Ocean/CORBIS; Ocean/CORBIS. **139** 2013 Thinkstock/JupiterImages Corporation. **140** 2013 Thinkstock/JupiterImages Corporation. **142** James Leynse/CORBIS; 2013 JupiterImages Corporation. **143** Wendell Metzen/Getty Images; 2013 Thinkstock/JupiterImages Corporation; GEMS/Redferns/MUSICPICTURES.COM; Reuters/CORBIS. **144** Ingram Publishing; Nicky J. Sims/Redferns/Getty Images; Wendell Metzen/Getty Images; Ebet Roberts. **145** Ebet Roberts; AP Photo/Lennox McLendon. **146** Robert Knight; Scott Gries/Getty Images. **147** Wendell Metzen/Getty Images; Tim Mosenfelder/Getty Images; AP Photo/Reed Saxon. **148** Wendell Metzen/Getty Images; David Bergman/CORBIS. **149** Carlo Allegri/Getty Images. **151** Frank Micelotta/I/Getty ImagesageDirect. **154** Alexis Maryon/Retna UK. **158** Hill Street Studios/Getty Images. **160** Lito C. Uyan/CORBIS. **161** 3RI. 163 3RI. **164** Courtesy of Kai Zhang. **165** 3RI; 3RI; 3RI; 3RI. **167** Joe McCary/Shakespeare Theatre Company. **168** Allen Ginsberg/CORBIS. **169** Guido Schiefer/Alamy. **170** James Lance/CORBIS. **171** Neville Elder/CORBIS. **172** Lawrence Lucier/Stringer/Getty Images. **173** Robyn Twomey. **174** 3RI. **175** Image Source/CORBIS. **176** Image Source/CORBIS. **180** John Hersey/theispot.com; Farrar, Straus and Giroux; Scholastic Paperbacks. **182** Iker Ayestaran/theispot.com. **183** Doggygraph/Shutterstock. **184** Penguin Group. **185** John Harper/CORBIS. **186** Jeff Greenberg/PhotoEdit, Inc. **191**

page 987

Acknowledgments, continued

Andy Sacks/Getty Images. **192** Andy Sacks/Getty Images. **200** The Life Line, 1864, Winslow Homer. Oil on canvas, Philadelphia Museum of Art/Superstock. **200-201** Ashley Cooper/CORBIS. **203** Graphic Universe; Candlewick; Harper Perennial. 204 Joe Cornish/Getty Images. **209** Pete Turner/Getty Images; Richard T. Nowitz/CORBIS. **211** Pete Turner/Getty Images; Richard T. Nowitz/CORBIS. **212** Pete Turner/Getty Images. **213** Mountain Dragon, 1992, Bob Eggleton. Acrylic on illustration board, private collection of Pat Wilshire, Pennsylvania. **217** Merlin and Arthur (bronze), John, Sir William Goscombe (1860-1952)/National Museum Wales/The Bridgeman Art Library ; Pete Turner/Getty Images. **219** The British Museum/Topham/The Image Works. **220** King Arthur, 1903 (oil on canvas), Butler, Charles Ernest (1864-c.1918)/Private Collection/ Christopher Wood Gallery, London, UK/The Bridgeman Art Library. **221** Pete Turner/Getty Images. **223** CORBIS; Scala/Art Resource, NY. **224** The Trustees of The British Museum; Roger Bamber/Alamy; Werner Forman/Art Resource, NY; Tokyo National Museum. **225** heraldryclipart.com; Ric Ergenbright/CORBIS; Alfred the Great (849-99), after a painting in the Bodleian Gallery (colour litho), English School, (19th century)/Private Collection/The Stapleton Collection/The Bridgeman Art Library ; Scala/Art Resource, NY. **228** Michael Jenner/Alamy. **229** Skyscan Photolibrary/Alamy; Roy Rainford/Getty Images. **234** Simon Marcus/CORBIS; Park Street/PhotoEdit, Inc. Inc.; AGStockUSA/Alamy. **236** Zave Smith/CORBIS. **237** Girl in Miami, 1999 (oil on panel) (see also 118567), Ferguson, Max/Private Collection/The Bridgeman Art Library. **238** Girl in Miami, 1999 (oil on panel) (see also 118567), Ferguson, Max/Private Collection/The Bridgeman Art Library ; University of Georgia, Peter Frey. **238–239** Verba/Shutterstock. **240** Verba/Shutterstock. **242** Verba/Shutterstock. **244** Verba/Shutterstock. **243** Trembling Hands, 2007, Andres Medrano Thompson, Ink on Paper, collection of the artist. **245** Elephant, 2006, Elephant rubber bands. Rubber bands and mixed media. **247** Verba/Shutterstock. **248** Reaching hands, 2007, Jerry Lindemann. Digital Illustration. **250** Verba/Shutterstock. **251** PhotoDisc/Getty Images. **253** AP Photo/Albany Times Union, Skip Dickstein, File; Colin Archer/Getty Images. **254** AP Photo/Mary Altaffer; AP Photo/The Post Star,T.J. Hooker. **258** Alan Schein/CORBIS. **260** Steve Skjold/Alamy. **263** Lonny Kalfus/Getty Images. **262** Benn Mitchell/Getty Images; Comstock/Thinkstock/JupiterImages. **264** JFK Presidential Library and Museum, Education Department. **265** Lonny Kalfus/Getty Images ; David Finn; Lonny Kalfus/Getty Images. **266** Pools of Defiance, 2001 (oil on canvas), Bootman, Colin (Contemporary Artist)/Private Collection/The Bridgeman Art Library. **267** John Ferrell, Farm Security Administration collection, Prints & Photographs Division, Library of Congress,LC-USF34-011465-D. **268** The Country Girl (oil on canvas), Ambrose, Lester J. (1879-1949)/Private Collection/Lawrence Steigrad Fine Arts, New York/The Bridgeman Art Library. **271** John Ferrell, Farm Security Administration collection, Prints & Photographs Division, Library of Congress,LC-USF34-011465-D; The Metropolitan Museum of Art. Image source: Art Resource, NY. **273** John Ferrell, Farm Security Administration collection, Prints & Photographs Division, Library of Congress,LC-USF34-011465-D. **279** AP Photo/Montgomery County Sheriff's office. **280** AP Photo/Horace Cort. **281** AP Photo/Gene Herrick. **283** Don Cravens//Time Life Pictures/Getty Images. **284** Fred Viebahn. **286** Bettmann/CORBIS. **288** Bruce Davidson/Magnum Photos. **289** Lori Ferber/Lori Ferber Collectibles. **290** Graphic Universe; Candlewick; Harper Perennial. **291** Jack Hollingsworth/PhotoDisc/Getty Images. **297** Rudi von Briel/PhotoEdit, Inc.; Frank Siteman/Getty Images. **306–307** Tino Soriano/National Geographic/Getty Images. **309** Yuri Arcurs/Shutterstock; Dover Publications; Rayo; Speak. **310** Photographer's Choice/Puncchstock. **311** Bud Endress; Felix Mizioznikov/iStockphoto. **314** Puncchstock. **315** Josh Westrich/CORBIS. **316** Josh Westrich/CORBIS. **319** Matthias Kulka/CORBIS. **322** Matthias Kulka/CORBIS. **321** dibrova/Shutterstock. **323** GeoffBlack/iStockphoto. **324** Lannis Waters/CORBIS. **326** Matthias Kulka/CORBIS. **327** William Morrow & Company. **330** The Enterprise Center. **331** Gregg Newton/CORBIS. **333** The Enterprise Center. **338** Michael Newman/PhotoEdit, Inc. **339** Digital Vision/Superstock. **340** The Andy Warhol Foundation for the Visual Arts/CORBIS; Courtesy Ronald Feldman Fine Arts, New York. **342** Ulf Andersen/Getty Images. **343** The Andy Warhol Foundation for the Visual Arts/CORBIS; Courtesy Ronald Feldman Fine Arts, New York. **351** Alicia Wagner Calzada/ZUMA. **352** The Dreamer, 2002, Patssi Valdez, Acryllic on canvas. Courtesy of Patricia Correia Gallery, Santa Monica, California. **353** Ray Laskowitz/Lonely Planet Images. **354** East on the 10, 2001. Frank Romero. Oil on wood, private collection.; Random House. **356** Ulf Andersen/Getty Images. **358** Ray Laskowitz/Lonely Planet Images. **360–361** Jonathon Nourok/PhotoEdit, Inc. **362** Roy McMahon/Stock Image/Getty Images; Louis DeLuca/Dallas Morning News/CORBIS. **363** Jose Luis Pelaez; Inc./CORBIS; Michael Perez/The Philadelphia Inquirer. **365** Michael Perez/The Philadelphia Inquirer. **366** Michael Perez/The Philadelphia Inquirer. **367** The Philadelphia Inquirer Graphics and Animation: Alan Baseden/Inquirer Staff Artist. **368** Gerald S. Williams/The Philadelphia Inquirer. **369** Michael Perez/The Philadelphia Inquirer. **371** Michael Perez/The Philadelphia Inquirer. **373** Michael Perez/The Philadelphia Inquirer. **375** Mick Stevens/The New Yorker Collection/www.cartoonbank.com. **376** 2013 Comstock Images/Jupiterimages Corporation; GINA GAYLE/INDEPENDENCE TECHNOLOGY/PRN/Newscom. 378 Feature Photo Service/Newscom. **379** Mark Wilson/The Boston Globe/Getty Images. **384–387** iStockphoto. **385** Jon Ross Photography. 386 Jon Ross Photography. **388** Dover Publications; Rayo; Speak. **389** Blend Images/Ariel Skelley/Getty Images. **396** Hemera Technologies/Getty Images. **404–405** Brian J. Skerry/National Geographic Stock. 406 Album/Art Resource, NY. **407** Dutton Juvenile; Harper; Graphia. **408** Judith Wagner/CORBIS. **413** Michael A. Keller/zefa/CORBIS. **413** Sherrie Nickol/CORBIS; Christoph Burki/Getty Images. **414** Time Life Pictures/Mansell/Time Life Pictures/Getty Images. **414–415** Christoph Burki/Getty Images. **416** Christie's Images/SuperStock. **420** Untitled, 1910, Emily Carr. Watercolor, graphite on paper, Collection of the Vancouver Art Gallery, Emily Carr Trust, VAG 42.3.87, Photo: Trevor Mills, Vancouver Art Gallery. **425** Amy Guip/CORBIS Outline. **426** Cat's Collection/CORBIS. **429** Simon & Schuster; Simon & Schuster; Arthur Tilley/Getty Images. **434** Elaine Thompson/ASSOCIATED PRESS; Ocean/CORBIS; Spencer Grant/PhotoEdit, Inc. **436** Adrianna Williams/CORBIS; Randy Faris/CORBIS; Jason Stemple Photographer. **437** Patricia McDonough/Getty Images; Digital Vision/Getty Images; W. EUGENE SMITH/Getty Images. **438** Patricia McDonough/Getty Images; Digital Vision/Getty Images. **439** W. EUGENE SMITH/Getty Images. **440** Bertrand Demée/Getty Images. **441** Amelie Sourget/Beateworks/CORBIS; John Slater/Getty Images; Per Gustafon/Getty Images. **442** Ryan McVay/Getty Images; Lena Sergeeva/Getty Images; Image Source/Thinkstock; Tim O'Leary/zefa/CORBIS; 2013 Image Source/Jupiterimages Corporation. **444** Bertrand Demée/Getty Images. **445** xyno/iStockphoto. **446** InnervisionArt/Shutterstock. **447** Bertrand Demée/Getty Images. **448** xyno/iStockphoto. **449** Donata Pizzi/Getty Images; Susanne Borges/A.B./CORBIS; Digital Vision/Getty Images. **451** Gahan Wilson/The New Yorker Collection/www.cartoonbank.com. **453** Julian Andrew Holtom/Getty Images; Peter Beavis/Getty Images; Vincent Besnault/Getty Images; Thomas Barwick/Getty Images; Digital Vision/Getty Images; Gandee Vasan/Getty Images; Gus Wedge/Getty Images; Olaf Tiedje/Getty Images; Christoph Wilhelm/Getty Images; Per Gustafon/Getty Images. **454** Nathan Griffith/CORBIS. **456** Christopher Felver/CORBIS. **458** Mick Stevens/The New Yorker Collection/www.cartoonbank.com. **460** Cleve Bryant/PhotoEdit, Inc. **462** Louis Moses/CORBIS; Owen Franken/CORBIS. **463** Mark Summers. **464** Time & Life Pictures/Getty Images ; Mark Summers. **466** Theodore Gericault (1791-1824) Dying, 1824 (oil on canvas), Correard, Alexandre (1788-1857)/Musee des Beaux-Arts, Rouen, France/Giraudon/The Bridgeman Art Library. **469** 2013 The Estate of Francis Bacon. All rights reserved./ARS, New York/DACS, London/Bridgeman Art Library. **471** George Marks/Retrofile/Getty Images. **472** Images.com/CORBIS. **475** Collier Campbell Lifeworks/CORBIS. **476** Collier Campbell Lifeworks/CORBIS. **478** Collier Campbell Lifeworks/CORBIS; Australian Raven, 2005, Kate Breakley. Handcolored silver gelatin photograph, Courtesy of Stephen Clark Gallery. **480** Collier Campbell Lifeworks/CORBIS. **482** Bettmann/CORBIS; Charles O'Rear/CORBIS. **486** Vetta/Getty Images. **486, 488, 489** Vittorio Bruno/Shutterstock. **489** Chase Jarvis. **490** Graphia; Judith Wagner/CORBIS. **491** Paul Mason/Getty Images. **492** Ryan McVay/Getty Images. **496–497** Todd Keith/Getty Images. **498** Vintage Image/Alamy. **497** James Strachan/Getty Images. **506–507** Stu Smucker/Lonely Planet Images/Getty Images. **507** John Eder/Getty Images. **509** Simon Pulse; University of Washington Press; Candlewick. **510** Hans Neleman/Getty Images. **511** PhotoDisc/Getty Images; PhotoDisc/Getty Images. **514** lightpoet/Shutterstock; CORBIS. **515** Alan Schein Photography/CORBIS. **516–517** Alan Schein Photography/CORBIS. **519** Harrison Eastwood/Getty Images; Harrison Eastwood/Getty Images; Harrison Eastwood/Getty Images; Karen Moskowitz/Getty Images. **520** CORBIS. **521** Liz Garza Williams; MacArt by Ray G; MacArt by 3RI; National Geographic. **522** The name and character of Smokey Bear are the property of the United States, as provided by 16 U.S.C. 580P-1 and 18 U.S.C 711, and are used with the permission of the Forest Service, U.S. Department of Agriculture. OR "16 U.S.A. 580P-1 and 18 U.S.C 711.". **523** AP Photo/Diane Bondareff. **525** Got Milk Ad. **529** Frank Capri/Hulton Archive/Getty Images. **531** 2013 John Lund/

page 988

JupiterImages Corporation. **532** 2013 Rubberball/Mike Kemp/JupiterImages Corporation. **533** 2013 Jack Hollingsworth/JupiterImages Corporation. **534** 2013 Brand X Pictures/JupiterImages Corporation. **535** Steve Nudson/Alamy; Steve Nudson/Alamy. **540** Jeff Greenberg/PhotoEdit, Inc.; Sarah Kastner/CORBIS; Bonnie Kamin/PhotoEdit. **542** Najlah Feanny/CORBIS; Allana Wesley White/CORBIS. **544–545** Douglas Schwartz/CORBIS. **546** Jeff Greenberg/PhotoEdit, Inc. **547** Mario Perez/ABC/Everett Collection. **549** Getty Images/Staff. **550** Bureau L.A. Collection/Sygma/CORBIS. **551** Alan Schein Photography/CORBIS. **553** Reza/National Geographic Stock; Reza Deghati/Webistan Photo Agency. **554** Reza/National Geographic Stock; Reza Deghati/Webistan Photo Agency. **555** AFP/Getty Images. **556** Reza Deghati/Webistan Photo Agency. **561** Frances Roberts/Alamy. **562** John Giustina/CORBIS. **563** Mike Hewitt/Getty Images. **564** Mike Hewitt/Getty Images. **566** Wides & Holl/Getty Images. **567** Peter Kramer/Getty Images; Bettmann/CORBIS. **569** Scott Nelson/Staff/Getty Images. **570** Michael Ainsworth/Dallas Morning News/CORBIS. **571** John A Rizzo/Getty Images; Jim Cummins/Getty Images. **572** David McNew/Getty Images; TIMOTHY A. CLARY/AFP/Getty Images; Frank Trapper/CORBIS; Mike Hewitt/Getty Images. **577** Evan Agostini/Getty Images; Evan Agostini/Getty Images. **584** Darren Hopes/CORBIS. **585** Gordon Studer/theispot.com. **586** Simon Pulse; University of Washington Press; Candlewick. **587** Mary Kate Denny/PhotoEdit, Inc. **588** Michael Newman/PhotoEdit, Inc. **572** Bob Daemmrich/PhotoEdit, Inc. **594** David-Young Wolfe/PhotoEdit. **602–603** Heather Liebensohn. **604** Sunday 10th, P.J. Crook, 2006. Acrylic on canvas, private collection. Bridgeman Art Library; 2013 Artists Rights Society (ARS), New York/Art Resource. **605** Gallery Books; Vintage Books; Simon Pulse. **606** Will & Deni McIntyre/CORBIS. **607** Rob Marmion/Shutterstock. **608** CORBIS; CORBIS/Punchstock. **610** Gypsy Maidens/Thomas Sully/Brooklyn Museum/CORBIS. **612** Paul Barton/CORBIS. **613** Joan Marcus Photography. **614** Bettmann/CORBIS. **615** Joan Marcus Photography; Jan Stromme/Getty Images. **617** Joan Marcus Photography. **619** Joan Marcus Photography. **623** Joan Marcus Photography. **627** Joan Marcus Photography. **628** Sara Krulwich/The New York Times Agency. **632** Joan Marcus Photography. **635** Randy Lincks/Masterfile. **636** Jacob van Hulsdonck/The Bridgeman Art Library/Getty Images. **637** Karen J. McClintock. **638** Blocks and Strips Quilt, 2003, Mary Lee Bendolph, Corduroy quilted fabric, collection of Tinwood Alliance, Atlanta Georgia. **640** Teresa Palomo Acosta. **642** Tom Prisk; Reproduction rights obtainable from www.cartoonstock.com. **644** Rolf Bruderer/Masterfile; Rolf Bruderer/Masterfile; Jerzyworks/Masterfile. **646** CORBIS; Don Thompson/Getty Images. **648** Photolibrary. **650** Photolibrary. **653** Josef Lindau/CORBIS. **657** Photolibrary. **658** Farrell Grehan/CORBIS. **661** Photolibrary. **665** Photolibrary. **667** Robert Holmes/CORBIS; Manny Hernandez/Getty Images. **669** Mitchell Gerber/CORBIS. **671** Bettmann/CORBIS. **672** Time Life Pictures/DMI/Time Life Pictures/Getty Images; Portrait of William Shakespeare (1564-1616) (colour litho), English School, (17th century) (after)/Private Collection/Ken Welsh/The Bridgeman Art Library. **677** Brand X Pictures/Punchstock. **678** Blasius Erlinger/Getty Images. **679** Danilo Calilung/CORBIS; Images.com/CORBIS. **681** Danilo Calilung/CORBIS; Images.com/CORBIS. **682** Mathew B. Brady Studio/CORBIS. **683** People of Colors, 2004, Elizabeth Rosen. Acrylic on board, private collection. **685** Morgan Lockamy; Robert W. Kelley//Time Life Pictures/Getty Images. **687** Asian Wind, 2004, Nicole Cardiff,. Colored pencil and watercolor, collection of the artist. **688** Bicultural Tablesetting. 1995, Rolando Briseno, Serigraph, private collection. **689** Cheron Bayna. **691** All Human Beings are Born Free and Equal in Dignity and Rights, 1998 (acrylic on board), Waddams, Ron (1920-2010)/Private Collection/The Bridgeman Art Library. **694** Chester Higgins Jr./Photo Researchers, Inc. **698–699** John Churchman/Getty Images. **700** Vintage Books; Simon Pulse; Will & Deni McIntyre/CORBIS. **704** Barna Tanko/Shutterstock; Jose Luis Pelaez, Inc./Blend Images/CORBIS. **708** Tim O'Hara/CORBIS. **709** Zero Creatives/Getty Images. **717** Steve Mason/Getty Images. **718** Jennifer Thermes/Getty Images; Christie's Images/The Bridgeman Art Library. **719** Terry Warner; Reproduction rights obtainable from www.Cartoonstock.com; Jeff Rotman/Getty Images; Darwin Wiggett/AllCanadaPhotos.com/CORBIS. **720** Skylines/Shutterstock; Flying Colours/Getty Images; Hiroshi Higuchi/Getty Images. **721** Maksim Kabadou/Shutterstock; Igor Klimov/Shutterstock; EDHAR/Shutterstock. **724** 2013 Microsoft; 2013 Microsoft; 2013 Microsoft. **879** Louis Moses/CORBIS; Roy McMahon/Stock Image/Getty Images. **880** lightpoet/Shutterstock. **883** Michael Prince/CORBIS. **885** Roger Tidman/CORBIS; David-Young Wolfe/PhotoEdit.

Illustration Credits

Annie Bissett: **p28** (teen volunteerism graphs), **p329** (education attained graph); XNR Productions: **p34** (Chiapas, Mexico map); National Geographic maps: **p226** (Europe in the Middle Ages map), **p344** (Washington state map).

page 989

Acknowledgments, continued

Photographs:

IFC ©VICTOR TRAYANOV/National Geographic Stock; vi ©JIMMY CHIN/National Geographic Stock; vii, x, xi, xvii, xvii, ix (laptop) ©Yuri Arcurs/Shutterstock; vii, xiv (MP3) ©trucic/Shutterstock; xxi ©Amy Helene Johansson; xxiii ©REUTERS/Julie Adnam; xxix ©BRIAN J. SKERRY/ National Geographic Stock; xxv ©Ashley Cooper/Corbis; xxvii ©TINO SORIANO/National Geographic Stock; xxxi ©Stu Smucker/Lonely Planet Images/Getty Images; xxxiii ©Heather Liebensohn; xxxvii ©Reza Deghati/Webistan Photo Agency; Tab 1 ©Ross Murphy; Tab 2 ©WANDY GAOTAMA/National Geographic Stock; Tab 3 ©ALEX COPPEL/National Geographic Stock; Tab 4 ©PAUL NICKLEN/National Geographic Stock; PD16 (c) ©Yuri Arcurs/Shutterstock, (b) ©Chris Schmidt/E+/Getty Images; PD32 ©Artville; PD39 ©Image Source/Getty Images; PD40 ©Getty Images; PD54 ©Corbis.

Fine Art:

xxxv Bicultural Tablesetting, 1998, Rolando Briseño. Serigraph, private collection.